Handbook of Research on Field-Based Teacher Education

Thomas E. Hodges
University of South Carolina, USA

Angela C. Baum
University of South Carolina, USA

A volume in the Advances in Higher Education and Professional Development (AHEPD) Book Series

Published in the United States of America by
    IGI Global
    Information Science Reference (an imprint of IGI Global)
    701 E. Chocolate Avenue
    Hershey PA, USA 17033
    Tel: 717-533-8845
    Fax: 717-533-8661
    E-mail: cust@igi-global.com
    Web site: http://www.igi-global.com

Library of Congress Cataloging-in-Publication Data

Names: Hodges, Thomas E., 1978- editor. | Baum, Angela C., 1971- editor.
Title: Handbook of research on field-based teacher education / Thomas E.
   Hodges and Angela C. Baum, editors.
Description: Hershey, PA : Information Science Reference, 2019. | Includes
   bibliographical references.
Identifiers: LCCN 2018005648| ISBN 9781522562498 (hardcover) | ISBN
   9781522562504 (ebook)
Subjects: LCSH: Student teaching. | Teachers--Training of.
Classification: LCC LB2157.A3 H335 2019 | DDC 370.71/1--dc23 LC record available at https://lccn.loc.gov/2018005648

This book is published in the IGI Global book series Advances in Higher Education and Professional Development (AHEPD) (ISSN: 2327-6983; eISSN: 2327-6991)

British Cataloguing in Publication Data
A Cataloguing in Publication record for this book is available from the British Library.

All work contributed to this book is new, previously-unpublished material. The views expressed in this book are those of the authors, but not necessarily of the publisher.

For electronic access to this publication, please contact: eresources@igi-global.com.

Advances in Higher Education and Professional Development (AHEPD) Book Series

Jared Keengwe
University of North Dakota, USA

ISSN:2327-6983
EISSN:2327-6991

MISSION

As world economies continue to shift and change in response to global financial situations, job markets have begun to demand a more highly-skilled workforce. In many industries a college degree is the minimum requirement and further educational development is expected to advance. With these current trends in mind, the **Advances in Higher Education & Professional Development (AHEPD) Book Series** provides an outlet for researchers and academics to publish their research in these areas and to distribute these works to practitioners and other researchers.

AHEPD encompasses all research dealing with higher education pedagogy, development, and curriculum design, as well as all areas of professional development, regardless of focus.

COVERAGE

- Adult Education
- Assessment in Higher Education
- Career Training
- Coaching and Mentoring
- Continuing Professional Development
- Governance in Higher Education
- Higher Education Policy
- Pedagogy of Teaching Higher Education
- Vocational Education

IGI Global is currently accepting manuscripts for publication within this series. To submit a proposal for a volume in this series, please contact our Acquisition Editors at Acquisitions@igi-global.com or visit: http://www.igi-global.com/publish/.

Titles in this Series

For a list of additional titles in this series, please visit: www.igi-global.com/book-series

Handbook of Research on Blended Learning Pedagogies and Professional Development in Higher Education
Jared Keengwe (University of North Dakota, USA)
Information Science Reference • copyright 2019 • 437pp • H/C (ISBN: 9781522555575) • US $225.00 (our price)

Handbook of Research on Promoting Higher-Order Skills and Global Competencies in Life and Work
Jared Keengwe (University of North Dakota, USA) and Robert Byamukama (Nkumba University, Uganda & Makerere University, Uganda)
Information Science Reference • copyright 2019 • 418pp • H/C (ISBN: 9781522563310) • US $225.00 (our price)

Handbook of Research on Media Literacy in Higher Education Environments
Jayne Cubbage (Bowie State University, USA)
Information Science Reference • copyright 2018 • 396pp • H/C (ISBN: 9781522540595) • US $255.00 (our price)

Changing Urban Landscapes Through Public Higher Education
Anika Spratley Burtin (University of the District of Columbia, USA) Jeffery S. Fleming (University of the District of Columbia, USA) and Pamela Hampton-Garland (University of the District of Columbia, USA)
Information Science Reference • copyright 2018 • 301pp • H/C (ISBN: 9781522534549) • US $175.00 (our price)

Preparing the Next Generation of Teachers for 21st Century Education
Siew Fun Tang (Curtin University, Malaysia) and Chee Leong Lim (Taylor's University, Malaysia)
Information Science Reference • copyright 2018 • 377pp • H/C (ISBN: 9781522540809) • US $210.00 (our price)

Promoting Ethnic Diversity and Multiculturalism in Higher Education
Barbara Blummer (Center for Computing Sciences, USA) Jeffrey M. Kenton (Towson University, USA) and Michael Wiatrowski (Independent Researcher, USA)
Information Science Reference • copyright 2018 • 309pp • H/C (ISBN: 9781522540977) • US $185.00 (our price)

Innovative Practices in Teacher Preparation and Graduate-Level Teacher Education Programs
Drew Polly (University of North Carolina - Charlotte, USA) Michael Putman (University of North Carolina - Charlotte, USA) Teresa M. Petty (University of North Carolina - Charlotte, USA) and Amy J. Good (University of North Carolina - Charlotte, USA)
Information Science Reference • copyright 2018 • 720pp • H/C (ISBN: 9781522530688) • US $275.00 (our price)

Critical Assessment and Strategies for Increased Student Retention
Ruth Claire Black (Imperial College London, UK)
Information Science Reference • copyright 2018 • 352pp • H/C (ISBN: 9781522529989) • US $195.00 (our price)

701 East Chocolate Avenue, Hershey, PA 17033, USA
Tel: 717-533-8845 x100 • Fax: 717-533-8661
E-Mail: cust@igi-global.com • www.igi-global.com

List of Contributors

Table of Contents

Section 2
Commitments to Equity, Social Justice, and Diversity

Section 3
Innovations in Pedagogical Design

Section 4
Systems of Feedback

Detailed Table of Contents

Section 1
Creating and Maintaining Systems of Partnership

Chapter 1

Ann Sebald, Colorado State University, USA
Heidi Frederiksen, Colorado State University, USA
Derek Decker, Colorado State University, USA
Jennifer Roth, Fort Collins High School, USA
Wendy Fothergill, Colorado State University, USA
Juliana Searle, Colorado State University, USA
Jody Drager, Colorado State University, USA
Jennifer Castor, Colorado State University, USA
Cerissa Stevenson, Colorado State University, USA
Angela Roybal Lewis, Colorado State University, USA
Andrea E. Weinberg, Arizona State University, USA

In this chapter, the authors discuss clinical practice as a key component to field-based teacher education. Clinical practice constructed within a professional development school (PDS) model is based upon the work of Dewey, Vygotsky, and Goodlad, and provide the basis for this work. Dewey's center of pedagogy and learning through direct experiences, connected with Vygotsky's socially constructed relational imitation experiences linked with common language, juxtaposed to Goodlad's simultaneous renewal of university and PK-12 partnerships all intersect in the work of clinical practice. The authors then present a logic model framework in which to design field-based educator preparation considering the theory and research discussed. The chapter concludes with highlighting practice-based solutions and recommendations through three case studies showcasing implementation of the logic model framework in action.

Marilyn Elaine Strutchens, Auburn University, USA
Ruthmae Sears, University of South Florida, USA
Jennifer Whitfield, Texas A&M University, USA
Stephanie Biagetti, California State University – Sacramento, USA
Patti Brosnan, The Ohio State University, USA
Jennifer Oloff-Lewis, California State University – Chico, USA
Pier Angeli Junor Clarke, Georgia State University, USA
Jamalee (Jami) Stone, SDBOR, USA
David R. Erickson, University of Montana, USA
Christopher Parrish, University of South Alabama, USA
Basil M. Conway IV, CSU, USA
Ruby L. Ellis, Auburn University, USA

A consortium of 24 universities and their school partners engaged in a networked improvement community design to develop clinical experience models designed to build candidates' facility with the effective mathematics teaching practices and other equitable teaching strategies to promote secondary school students' success in achieving college- and career-ready standards. The authors discuss mechanisms to aid in the implementation of two alternative models: 1) the paired placement model, in which two prospective teachers are paired with a single mentor teacher, allowing the mentor teacher to provide purposeful coaching and mentoring and the two pre-service teachers to offer each other feedback, mentoring, and support; and 2) co-planning and co-teaching, which has been found to help teacher candidates gain greater pedagogical content knowledge and knowledge of students through collaboration and communication between teacher candidates and mentor teachers who plan, implement, and assess instruction together.

Mary D. Burbank, University of Utah, USA
Andrea K. Rorrer, University of Utah, USA
Wynn Shooter, University of Utah, USA

Calls for recruitment and retention into teaching remain at all-time highs in math and science. Response initiatives may include alternative routes to licensure (ARL), streamlined curricula, financial incentives for participants, and intensive on-the-job training. While ARLs offer potential for innovation, challenges also exist when trying to maintain preparation quality and integrity. This project presents end-of-program findings from a five-year investigation into the factors that contribute to quality teacher preparation within an ARL framework. Summative outcomes document program dimensions where research-intensive preparation goals align with priorities for increasing the pool of future teachers. The roles of teacher mentors, curriculum impact, and classroom-based practica are highlighted.

Kristien Zenkov, George Mason University, USA
Seth A. Parsons, George Mason University, USA
Audra K. Parker, George Mason University, USA
Elizabeth Levine Brown, George Mason University, USA
Lois A. Groth, George Mason University, USA
Kristine E. Pytash, Kent State University, USA
Anthony Pellegrino, University of Tennessee – Knoxville, USA

Unprecedented and long-overdue attention has recently been given to the role of field-based clinical experiences in teacher preparation. Traditional models of university coursework disconnected from real world field-based clinical experiences serve neither prospective teachers nor PreK-12 students. This chapter presents a broader notion of field-based teacher preparation structures occurring in school-university partnership contexts and professional development schools, with the authors drawing from data of four field-based experiences, which fall along a continuum of partnership, from three teacher education programs at two universities. These partnerships illustrate a developmental framework for building mutually beneficial relationships that enhance the engagement of all stakeholders and acknowledge the need for differentiation in teacher education practice. A pathways orientation to school-university partnerships/PDSs and a project-based clinical approach offer chances to develop mutually beneficial learning opportunities for PreK-12 students and teacher candidates.

Danielle E. Dani, Ohio University, USA
Allyson Hallman-Thrasher, Ohio University, USA
Lisa M. Harrison, Ohio University, USA
Kristin Diki, Ohio University, USA
Mathew Felton-Koestler, Ohio University, USA
Michael Kopish, Ohio University, USA
Jodi Dunham, Shawnee State University, USA
Loretta W. Harvey, Shawnee State University, USA

One of the challenges of field-based teacher education is the perennial divide between university courses and field experiences. Collaborative mentoring is proposed as an approach to bridge this divide. The purpose of this chapter is to explore the affordances that a content-specific model of collaborative mentoring provides for achieving greater coherence within teacher education programs and nurturing stronger systems of partnerships between universities and schools. The chapter reports on research examining the benefits and challenges reported by teacher candidates, mentor teachers, and clinical educators who participated in the model.

Chapter 6

The Council for the Accreditation of Educator Preparation (CAEP) set forth a set of new standards that demand excellence to produce educators who raise P-12 student achievement. This pilot multi-case study describes perspectives and across-case themes of the lived experiences of national key stakeholders in educator preparation programs and their professional development school (PDS) partnership system. CAEP's five guiding principles of Standard 2: Clinical Partnerships and Practice as a priori codes describe experiences and perspectives of three key stakeholders of the university's clinical partnership. The three key stakeholders include (1) university-based teacher educators, (2) school-based teacher educators, and (3) teacher candidates. The researchers discuss results and implications for practice and offer avenues for future research.

Chapter 7

This chapter describes the author's work as a teacher educator to establish, sustain, and improve a methods course partnership with a local K-6 school using an integrated school-situated, practice-based model. The model was designed with an aim of improving the coherence of teacher candidates' experiences and learning to better prepare them for the complicated work of equitable teaching. Coherent field-based components in teacher education offer opportunities to mitigate divisions between 1) theory and practice and 2) coursework and fieldwork. The chapter begins with a definition of coherence, describes how this definition of coherence was used to design an elementary literacy/social studies methods course, shares data to evaluate the course from the perspective of the teacher candidates, and describes what candidates learned by participating in the course.

Chapter 8

In this chapter, two teacher educators share lessons learned when they adapted professional development structures for use with teacher candidates during the clinical practicum experience. Highlighted in this chapter are two field-based teacher education approaches that support the development of mutually beneficial partnerships. Teacher candidates and their cooperating teachers collaboratively used lesson study to examine mathematical discourse in an elementary setting, while teacher candidates used instructional rounds as a way for teacher candidates to observe more experienced teachers in secondary classrooms. Both structures attempted to bridge the persistent divide between university learning and clinical practice to the benefit of K-12 students, teachers, and teacher candidates. The chapter concludes with recommendations for increasing the number of teacher candidates and partnership schools involved in this field-based learning in ways beneficial to all those involved.

Chapter 9

Ann Schulte, California State University – Chico, USA

Rebecca Justeson, California State University – Chico, USA

The rural teacher residency (RTR) program at California State University – Chico was a program funded by a Teacher Quality Partnership (TQP) grant from 2010-2015. The RTR program prepared teachers through partnerships with four school districts in the rural region of northern California. This residency program was designed to provide targeted training and experience in co-teaching, action research, professional learning communities, and collaboration. In addition, RTR faculty hoped to impact the retention of teachers for hard-to-staff schools such as those with underserved students and/or in rural settings. The purpose of the chapter is to briefly overview the design features of the RTR program and to describe the qualitative data analysis of an evaluation of the program (i.e., focus groups, survey, observations/interviews) at the conclusion of the grant funding cycle.

Section 2
Commitments to Equity, Social Justice, and Diversity

Chapter 10

Eliza G. Braden, University of South Carolina, USA

Cathy Compton-Lilly, University of South Carolina, USA

Michele Myers, University of South Carolina, USA

Beth Lucas White, University of South Carolina, USA

Teachers with generative theories about teaching view themselves as capable and agential. They routinely engage in self-introspection as a means to dismantle problematic beliefs and biases. Generative teacher education is best developed in classrooms through embedded work with children. To explore generative teacher education, this chapter describes how one program sets the stage for the development of cultural competence through an initial course focused on culturally sustaining pedagogy. The authors then describe the significance of helping literacy teachers to notice and name children's emerging literacy abilities. The chapter ends with scenarios that illustrate the synergy that occurs when cultural competence is combined with embedded field experiences in literacy classrooms. The authors discuss both pedagogical possibilities and the importance of developing noticing practices and agential responses that are culturally and linguistically responsive.

Chapter 11

Laura Vernikoff, Teachers College, Columbia University, USA

Tom Schram, University of New Hampshire, USA

Emilie Mitescu Reagan, University of New Hampshire, USA

Colleen Horn, Teachers College, Columbia University, USA

A. Lin Goodwin, University of Hong Kong, Hong Kong

Leslie J. Couse, University of New Hampshire, USA

In this chapter, the authors describe two residency programs, an established urban teacher residency program, and a newly developed rural teacher residency program, and explain how the programs have expanded notions of field experiences to prepare teachers for specific schools, districts, and communities. The authors explore commonalities and connections across the programs, particularly in how each program conceptualizes the role of place in teacher education. In addition, this chapter considers differences in how each program enacts their theories of place in order to prepare teachers to learn from, with, and about the particular places they will teach within.

Chapter 12

Barbara A. Bradley, University of Kansas, USA
Andrea Miller Emerson, Western Oregon University, USA
Arsenio F. Silva, Clemson University, USA

The population of students in the United States is becoming increasingly diverse. At the same time, we live in highly interconnected global society with complex world problems. Thus, teachers need to prepare students to live and work collaboratively with people, locally and globally, from diverse background. Yet, how do in-service and preservice teachers support students if they have had limited experiences interacting with and understanding people from diverse backgrounds? This chapter describes a four-week summer study-abroad program in Italy, in which preservice teacher lived with a host family and observed and taught in an Italian school. It presents findings about what preservice teachers learned from (1) living with a host family, (2) observing in an Italian school, (3) becoming a culturally and linguistically diverse learner, and (4) teaching.

Chapter 13

Kamania Wynter-Hoyte, University of South Carolina, USA
Meir Muller, University of South Carolina, USA
Nathaniel Bryan, Miami University, USA
Gloria Swindler Boutte, University of South Carolina, USA
Susi Long, University of South Carolina, USA

This chapter provides a profile of an urban education collective that fosters relationships among preservice teachers, university faculty, and a local school district. The partnership supports preservice and in-service teachers serving marginalized communities using culturally relevant, humanizing, and decolonizing pedagogies. Drawing from decolonizing and humanizing theoretical and pedagogical frameworks, the collective highlights equity, asset-based, and anti-racist teachings. Insights gained from this initiative and recommendations for navigating challenges in equity work are presented. Implications for teacher education programs and future research goals are provided.

Section 3
Innovations in Pedagogical Design

Chapter 14

Rob Wieman, Rowan University, USA

Pre-service teachers (PSTs) often have to plan and teach a lesson in a practicum setting as part of their methods class. This assignment is designed to give PSTs a chance to enact ambitious instruction; however, they often encounter obstacles that prevent them from engaging students in core disciplinary practices. A structure, based on lesson study, provides opportunities for PSTs to experience and identify these obstacles, revise their plans to address them, and engage in ambitious instruction while re-teaching the revised lesson. This structure also recasts initial lessons as opportunities to learn and improve through collaborative reflection. Examples of this structure are described, including features that contribute to PST learning and lesson improvements. Obstacles to ambitious instruction as well as strategies to overcome those obstacles are identified and discussed. Parallels are drawn between ambitious mathematics teaching and ambitious teacher education.

Chapter 15

    Heidi L. Hallman, University of Kansas, USA

This chapter proposes the value of offering teacher candidates an opportunity to participate in community-based field experiences during their teacher education programs. Community-based field experiences, in contrast to traditional, classroom-based placements usually offered at this stage in prospective teachers' professional preparation, enable beginning teachers to conceptualize their own learning and the learning of their students in new ways. As part of teacher education programs, the community-based field experience serves a distinct purpose and place, and one that is often underexplored. This chapter describes the integration of community-based field experiences into teacher education programs and discusses the unique quality of community-based settings as potential sites for teachers' learning.

Chapter 16

    Timothy J. Murnen, Bowling Green State University, USA
    Jonathan Bostic, Bowling Green State University, USA
    Nancy Fordham, Bowling Green State University, USA
    Joanna Weaver, Bowling Green State University, USA

The goal of this chapter was to explore the impact of a field-centric, grade-band, and subject-area specific field experience model that is linked to corresponding coursework on novice teacher candidates' conceptions of what it means to be a teacher. Grounded in the work of scholars such as Dewey, Piaget, and Vygotsky, this study explores three questions: What aspects of the Adopt-an-Apprentice program do teacher candidates view as beneficial to their understanding of the profession and their development as teachers? What benefits, if any, do classroom teachers derive from hosting teacher candidates in the Adopt-an-Apprentice program? What is the impact of grade band/subject-area field experiences on teacher candidates' conceptions of being a teacher? Using quantitative and qualitative surveys, the study illustrates how coursework linked to authentic application in clinical settings empowered novice teacher candidates to understand and engage content, pedagogy, and standards.

Chapter 17

    Jan A. Yow, University of South Carolina, USA
    Patrice Waller, California State University – Fullerton, USA
    Belinda Edwards, Kennesaw State University, USA

This chapter shares the experience and preliminary findings from a national collaboration to improve secondary mathematics teacher preparation programs in the United States. Specifically, the chapter focuses on a research group tasked with strengthening field experiences into methods courses. Two modules are shared that a group of methods instructors have developed and are implementing in their courses. Findings from the first module are explained with implications for continued module development. These findings show the impact of the module on mentor teachers as well as the benefit the module has demonstrated in relation to the preservice teacher-mentor teacher relationship. Challenges and lessons learned from this national effort are also included.

Chapter 18

This chapter describes a model of integrating an elementary mathematics methods course with an afterschool club in order to support pre-service teachers' development of a teaching practice. The goal of the model was to help pre-service teachers integrate theory and practice as well as begin to notice particular elements of a classroom and lesson. Details of the model, the course, and how the partnership with the elementary school was formed are shared. In addition, results from analyzing pre-service teachers' journal responses indicate most teachers focused on classroom management initially; however, writing shifted to focus on students' mathematical ideas and the purpose of play. Learnings with respect to teacher education as well as ideas for future research are discussed.

Chapter 19

This chapter provides a description of three efforts to integrate practice-based approaches to preparing pre-service teachers to teach mathematics to elementary and middle grades learners. The vignettes include a university laboratory school focused on middle grades students, a tutoring program for elementary school students, and a small group teaching experience with elementary school learners. Within each vignette, the authors describe findings from examining how these experiences influenced pre-service teachers. Lastly, they close the chapter with implications and directions for future research.

Chapter 20

This chapter describes an innovative early field experience course for secondary teacher candidates that is held onsite at two local high schools. The chapter presents the course experience from the perspective of three stakeholders involved in the teaching and planning of the experiences: the university faculty instructor, a school administrator, and a practicum high school teacher. University candidate voices are also included through an analysis of survey data collected at the end of the most recent course offering. Each stakeholder describes both the tensions and benefits of the partnership and course experiences. By connecting theory and practice through interactions with all stakeholders during the course, the experience honors the expertise of all involved and builds a community of educators working together to improve secondary teacher education.

Section 4
Systems of Feedback

  Amy B. Palmeri, Vanderbilt University, USA
  Jeanne A. Peter, Vanderbilt University, USA

In disentangling the, often conflated, evaluative and educative functions of preservice teacher supervision, the authors reimagine supervisory practice within the specific context of the post-observation conference. Claiming the post-observation conference as a teaching space provided the impetus leading to the design of a theoretically grounded post-observation conference protocol foregrounding the educative function of supervision, leveraging the mediating role of the university supervisor in supporting preservice teacher learning, and reflecting the principles of effective feedback. A critical feature of the protocol is the intentional focusing of feedback on one of four superordinate elements of teaching that provides continuity and consistency across post-observation conferences allowing preservice teachers to connect knowledge and skill related to the development of complex practice.

  Melissa M. Goldsmith, University of Utah, USA
  Janice A. Dole, University of Utah, USA
  Mary D. Burbank, University of Utah, USA

Teacher candidates receive mentorship and evaluations from university supervisors and cooperating teachers, qualified educational professionals and stakeholders performing two different roles. The study examined to what extent university supervisors and cooperating teachers agreed and disagreed on effective teaching. University supervisors and cooperating teachers were asked to watch three videos of teaching episodes and rate them using a 20-question observation instrument. Follow-up focus groups were held to discuss reasons for the ratings. Results indicated that these groups generally agreed on many aspects of quality teaching, but substantive differences existed as well. Raters varied by role when rating facets of language development for language learners, instructional strategies and assessment. Differences in ratings between these groups were explained by the way they view their roles and responsibilities in the classroom as well as the way they interpreted the components of the observation instrument.

  David S. Allen, Kansas State University, USA
  A. Jill Wood, Kansas State University, USA
  Erica Sponberg, Kansas State University, USA
  Täna M. Arnold, Kansas State University, USA

This chapter focuses on the praxis behind the development of digitally mediated supervision and distance-based field experiences. The theoretical framework combines past principles of supervision with present technological models. The practical application lies in both a hybrid digitally mediated program at the undergraduate level and a fully functional model at the graduate level. The concerns addressed represent those facing higher education institutions across the United States, and the solutions presented are those initiated at a Mid-Western land-grant institution. The authors examine the hardware, firmware, and cloud technology used to deliver the program, and the reflective feedback model developed for online teacher preparation. Four types of feedback are defined: (1) self-reflection, (2) 10-minute walk-though, (3) focused feedback, and (4) formal evaluation.

Chapter 24

Sarah A. Nagro, George Mason University, USA
Laurie U. deBettencourt, Johns Hopkins University, USA

The purpose of this chapter is to explore the importance of reflection activities within clinical experiences that often are prescribed components of field-based teacher education. This chapter will include a review of documented attempts to understand the impact reflection activities have on teacher candidate growth. More specifically, this chapter will review what we know about the emphasis on reflective practice within teacher education and professional practice, what typical reflection activities within a field-based teacher education context are, and how reflective ability is measured within field-based clinical experiences. The chapter finishes with implications and recommendations for research and practice within teacher education.

Chapter 25

Gabrièle Abowd Damico, Indiana University, USA
Lawrence J. Ruich, Indiana University – Purdue University Columbus, USA
John M. Andrésen, Indiana University, USA
Gretchen Butera, Indiana University, USA

This chapter describes an approach to field experience that provides the opportunity for a long-term relationship between a teacher candidate and their supervising teacher in a teacher preparation program called Community of Teachers (CoT). CoT emphasizes the importance of this relationship in several ways. The program empowers teacher candidates and their mentors to choose one another. In addition, the length of the field experience provides an opportunity for teacher candidates to more deeply engage in the process of becoming a teacher within the context of a classroom and a school that they come to know well. A triadic relationship between the teacher candidate, supervising teacher, and university supervisor provides the opportunity for support as well as evaluative feedback for the teacher candidate. Benefits also accrue to the supervising teacher.

Chapter 26

Rajeev K. Virmani, Sonoma State University, USA

This chapter examines how three secondary mathematics preservice teachers and two teacher educators rehearse and enact the core teaching practice of leading a whole-class discussion in a math methods course and in student teaching placements. Findings indicate that there was substantial variation in the three preservice teachers' opportunities to practice key aspects of leading a whole-class discussion, the type of feedback they received from the teacher educators, and the authenticity of the rehearsal. The opportunity to approximate practice and receive feedback played a significant role in the generative nature of the preservice teachers' enactments of a whole-class discussion in their student teaching placements.

Chapter 27

Courtney K. Baker, George Mason University, USA
Laura E. Bitto, George Mason University, USA
Theresa Wills, George Mason University, USA
Terrie McLaughlin Galanti, George Mason University, USA
Cassandra Cook Eatmon, George Mason University, USA

Effective mathematics specialists require opportunities to apply knowledge from their advanced preparation programs to their practice. Just as pre-service teachers engage in field experiences to practice instructional strategies, in-service educators should engage in field experiences to apply leadership knowledge and skills while under the supervision of an experienced and highly-qualified teacher educator. This chapter describes the culminating self-study field experiences in a masters-level advanced certification program which prepares in-service teachers to be K-8 mathematics specialists. Through collaboration with critical friends, the mathematics specialist candidates connected research to practice in the design and implementation of a self-study project. Their work chronicled an important transformation from teachers to teacher leaders. The candidates also described their interest and their new capacity to conduct research beyond their certification programs for the purposes of impacting teacher and student learning within their organizations.

Preface

As administrators in a College of Education, we regularly talk with elected officials, business leaders and other stakeholders who express interest in improving public education. These individuals' priorities and associated legislation and policies often reflect a common narrative: *colleges of education are, at least in part, at fault for underwhelming student achievement and declining teacher supply.* As reflected in a series of policy shifts, accountability for student achievement is increasingly being moved from teacher, school and district, onto the universities that prepare them. Many states, in fact, track teacher performance, often using value-added measures, to look at the successes, or lack thereof, of teacher preparation programs. No one questions the need for accountability in teacher preparation; however, we must view our successes and opportunities for growth in public education as an intersection of local communities, higher education, and policy makers acting in concert with one another—and, most importantly, in the service of children. Promising approaches to improving teacher preparation – particularly designs that attract a highly competent and diverse workforce, create innovative pathways to teacher preparation, and bridge requisite knowledge and skills with in-the-classroom experiences – need to be highlighted and disseminated. In other words, there is another, more empowering, narrative to the work taking place in the field of teacher preparation -- a narrative that documents the powerful impact of schools, communities and university faculty engaging, as partners, in the education of future teachers.

We are often drawn to a quote from Stiger and Heibert's (1995) *The Teaching Gap*:

The star teachers of the twenty-first century will be those who work together to infuse the best ideas into standard practice. They will be teachers who collaborate to build a system that has the goal of improving students' learning in the "average" classroom, who work to gradually improve standard classroom practices. **In a true profession, the wisdom of the profession's members finds its way into the most common methods. The best that we know becomes the standard way of doing something**. *(pp. 178 – 179, emphasis added)*

While Sigler and Heibert's words were primarily focused on teaching in P-12 classrooms, the same can be said within the context of teacher preparation. We must engage in more collaborative efforts to build a teacher education system that leverages the "best of what we know" into our "standard way" of preparing educators. Our prior research highlights the importance of offering intentional and systematic opportunities for teacher candidates to make meaning of theories originating in the classroom (Hodges & Mills, 2014; Hodges, Mills, Blackwell, Scott, & Somerall, 2017), recognizing that this occurs most effectively within the context of strong partnerships between campus- and school-based teacher educators whose intent, purpose, and method are aligned (Baum & Korth, 2013; Baum, Powers-Costello, VanScoy,

Miller, & James, 2011; Hodges & Hodge, 2017). These sorts of "bridging activities" bring university faculty and P-12 educators together to design and deliver high quality teacher preparation programs. It is from this perspective that we saw a need for a volume of research activities focused on building, in teacher candidates, what Oonk, Verloop, and Graveneijer (2015) describe as *theory-enriched practical knowledge*. Born from teacher candidates' engagement in real classrooms with real children, the chapters in this handbook of research reflect a shared commitment to the education of future teachers and demonstrate innovative efforts taking place in a variety of institutions and institution types.

We have organized the chapters in this handbook into four sections, representing a chronological pathway for developing rich and robust teacher preparation programs. Section 1: Creating and Maintaining Systems of Partnership includes chapters focused on establishing meaningful and effective partnerships, between institutions of higher education and P-12 schools, between higher education institutions themselves, and in collaboration with state and local agencies. Systemic and intentional developments are critical to ensure that the cultivated relationships are flexible, sustainable and responsive to the needs of multiple constituencies. In the first chapter of this section, Sebald and colleagues describe ongoing efforts to ensure the sustainability of their professional development school partnership by integrating a logic model framework that guides decision-making and ensures supportive transitions from the university to the classroom. Strutchens and colleagues highlight a very different type of partnership – the Mathematics Teacher Education Partnership. This partnership engages over 90 colleges and universities utlizing network improvement communities via improvement science approaches (Bryk, Gomez, Grunlow, & LeMahieu, 2015) to systematize teacher candidate placements across a variety of institutions in the United States. Other chapters in this section provide significant insights into alternative preparation (Burbank, Rorrer, and Shooter) and the development of robust school-university partnerships consistent with the American Association of Colleges of Education's Clinical Practice 2018 Commission Report (Zenkov,Parsons, Parker, Brown, Groth, Pytash, and Pellegrino). Each chapter in this section provides compelling evidence of promising approaches to develop theory alongside practical knowledge and skills.

A commitment to equity and social justice undergirds strong teacher preparation programs. Teacher candidates must have opportunities to participate in field experiences that support the development of the knowledge, skills, and dispositions necessary to enact culturally responsive teaching. Section 2: Commitments to Equity, Social Justice, and Diversity reflects research focused on these principles. Opening this section is a chapter written by Compton-Lilly and colleagues which describes a *generative model of literacy teacher education* designed to support preservice teachers' development of cultural competence. Another chapter, written by Vernikoff and colleagues, is grounded in the notions of placed-based and place-conscious education and describes two residency programs that prepare preservice teachers to teach in urban and rural schools, districts, and communities, considering the unique characteristics of individual settings. The chapter written by Wynter-Hoyt and colleagues describes the development of an *Urban Education Collective* that focuses specifically on issues of equity in early childhood pedagogy, practice, and policy. Finally, the chapter written by Bradley and colleagues discusses the role that field experiences in international settings can play in preparing preservice teachers for working with children and families who are different from themselves. The chapters in this section will challenge teacher educators to critically examine their own coursework and programs and consider the extent to which they prepare preservice teachers engage in emancipatory teaching.

Pedagogical decision-making is at the core of teacher education practice. Section 3: Innovations in Pedagogical Designs takes up the role of field experiences in teacher education coursework and the ways in which they provide teacher candidates the opportunity to witness, act and reflect as they construct effective beliefs and practices. Muren and colleagues describe innovative early field experiences designed to support the development specific competencies in the company of P-12 students. Other chapters (e.g., Weiman; Yow, Waller, & Edwards; and Lotter, Smoak, Blakeney, & Plotner) showcase innovations in field experiences connected to methods coursework. The chapters from Hallman; Brown; and Polly and colleagues extend work with P-12 student to informal learning spaces, yet are designed to develop similar instructional competencies. In all, the chapters in this section illustrate pedagogical innovations taking place at in- and out-of-school contexts, enriching and complementing the knowledge gained in more traditional university settings.

The final section of chapters focuses on capstone and in-service feedback systems to improve teaching and learning. Section 4: Systems of Feedback provides innovative approaches to feedback and assessment of candidate and teacher learning whereby researchers advance our understandings of promising approaches to critically analyzing observations and artifacts connected to classroom practice. Palmeri and Peter; Goldsmith, Burbank and Dole; Allen and colleagues; and Virmani all bring into focus the nature and purpose of feedback on field experience performance. Each chapter, with its own lens, provides significant insights into the structure of feedback for novice teachers and how that feedback helps to elevate the instructional capacity of the teachers. Damico and colleagues provides a different focus to the structure of assessment in the creation of communities of practice around feedback systems for novice teachers. Finally, Baker illustrates how similar structures designed around self-study can help advance the instructional practices of in-service teachers of mathematics. We find this section to be an appropriate bookend to the handbook, both in terms of its chronological order in experiences, but also in its lasting impression on us as to the prominence of intentional structures and strategies for elevating constructive evaluations of teaching practices.

The diverse chapters, perspectives and foci presented in this handbook showcase a number of promising advancements in teacher preparation. In particular, the chapters provide compelling evidence of significant innovation in the design and sustainability of rich field experiences in teacher education. Furthermore, the chapters offer a strong counterargument to those who see teacher education as a stagnant enterprise. Rather, the projects highlighted here represent some of the best of what we know in developing synergistic activities among P-12 schools, higher education, and community stakeholders.

As editors, we thank the authors and reviewers who contributed to the final product showcased here. Their expertise and passion for high quality teacher preparation is ever-present in the chapters and has resulted in what we believe to be a rich publication useful for teacher education researchers and practitioners alike. We hope you'll agree.

REFERENCES

American Association of Colleges of Teacher Education. (2018). *A pivot towards clinical practice, its lexicon, and the renewal of educator preparation: A report of the AACTE Clinical Practice Commission.* Washington, DC: Author.

Baum, A. C., & Korth, B. B. (2013). Preparing classroom teachers to be cooperating teachers: A report of current efforts, beliefs, challenges, and associated recommendations. *Journal of Early Childhood Teacher Education*, *34*(2), 171–190. doi:10.1080/10901027.2013.787478

Baum, A. C., Powers-Costello, B., VanScoy, I., Miller, E., & James, U. (2011). We're all in this together: Collaborative professional development with student teaching supervisors. *Action in Teacher Education*, *33*(1), 38–46. doi:10.1080/01626620.2011.559429

Bryk, A. S., Gomez, L. M., Grunow, A., & LeMahieu, P. G. (2015). *Learning to Improve: How America's Schools Can Get Better at Getting Better*. Cambridge, MA: Harvard Education Press.

Hodges, T. E., & Hodge, L. L. (2017). Unpacking personal identities for teaching mathematics within the context of prospective teacher education. *Journal of Mathematics Teacher Education*, *20*(2), 101–118. doi:10.100710857-015-9339-2

Hodges, T. E., & Mills, H. (2014). Embedded field experiences as professional apprenticeships. In K. Karp (Ed.), *Annual Perspectives in Mathematics Education* (pp. 249–260). Reston, VA: National Council of Teachers of Mathematics.

Hodges, T. E., Mills, H. A., Blackwell, B., Scott, J., & Somerall, S. (2017). Learning to theorize from practice: The power of embedded field experiences. In D. Polly & C. Martin (Eds.), *Handbook of Research on Teacher Education and Professional Development*. Hershey, PA: IGI Global. doi:10.4018/978-1-5225-1067-3.ch002

Stigler, J. W., & Hiebert, J. (1999). *The teaching gap: Best ideas from the world's teachers for improving education in the classroom*. New York: Summit Books.

Section 1
Creating and Maintaining Systems of Partnership

Chapter 1
Preparing Educators for Sustainability:
One Center's Journey

Ann Sebald
Colorado State University, USA

Heidi Frederiksen
Colorado State University, USA

Derek Decker
Colorado State University, USA

Jennifer Roth
Fort Collins High School, USA

Wendy Fothergill
Colorado State University, USA

Juliana Searle
Colorado State University, USA

Jody Drager
Colorado State University, USA

Jennifer Castor
Colorado State University, USA

Cerissa Stevenson
Colorado State University, USA

Angela Roybal Lewis
Colorado State University, USA

Andrea E. Weinberg
Arizona State University, USA

ABSTRACT

In this chapter, the authors discuss clinical practice as a key component to field-based teacher education. Clinical practice constructed within a professional development school (PDS) model is based upon the work of Dewey, Vygotsky, and Goodlad, and provide the basis for this work. Dewey's center of pedagogy and learning through direct experiences, connected with Vygotsky's socially constructed relational imitation experiences linked with common language, juxtaposed to Goodlad's simultaneous renewal of university and PK-12 partnerships all intersect in the work of clinical practice. The authors then present a logic model framework in which to design field-based educator preparation considering the theory and research discussed. The chapter concludes with highlighting practice-based solutions and recommendations through three case studies showcasing implementation of the logic model framework in action.

DOI: 10.4018/978-1-5225-6249-8.ch001

INTRODUCTION

Since the Blue Ribbon Panel Report (2010), "the number of successful clinical practice programs and partnerships has increased, and clinical practice has advanced to a point of being nearly non-negotiable" (AACTE, 2018, p. 9). Dating back to when Dewey advocated for "centers of pedagogy" (Dewey, 1916), educators and education researchers have consistently recognized the need for clinical practice to be central to educator preparation programs in order for teacher candidates (TC) to move from theory to practice with authentic, hands-on experiences in exemplary schools (Ball & Forzani, 2009; Darling-Hammond, 2006; Goodlad, 1990, 1994; Zeichner, 2010; Zimpher & Howey, 2013). The *Clinical Practice Commission* (CPC), sanctioned by AACTE (2018) was a national charge for operationalizing clinical practice stating,

...to prepare effective teachers for 21ˢᵗ century classrooms, teacher education . . . must move to programs that are fully grounded in clinical practice and interwoven with academic content and professional courses (p. 5).

In order to add context to the clinical practice requisite in educator preparation, this chapter explores the development of clinical practice as the key element in educator preparation. Additionally, the need for establishing, maintaining, and growing intentional university and K-12 partnerships as one way to address the educator shortage through solid preparation will be addressed. Next, is a discussion of one exemplar of clinical practice at one institute of higher education where the development of a logic model framework is presented. The chapter concludes with highlighting solutions and recommendations within three case studies showcasing implementation of the logic model framework in action.

BACKGROUND

The key for improving teacher preparation lies on the importance of providing teacher candidates with field experience in a real world context. To achieve this goal, key stakeholders from PK-12 schools and key stakeholders from educator preparation programs (EPPs) must work together regardless of where they are along the developmental continuum toward a true clinical practice and partnership. Partnerships today between university faculty and K–12 teachers imply more than an instructional relationship based on a one-way flow of information from expert to his or her novice students (Tomanek, 2005). The construct of the term partnership implies direct benefits for all parties involved. Partnerships involve individuals with expertise or skills to contribute toward a common goal. The idea is that there is something to be gained by everyone (AACTE, 2018; Goodlad, Soder, & Sirotnik, 1990).

Although both PK-12 schools and teacher preparation focus on the development and education of students, often times the cultures of both entities are different and blending the two can prove to be challenging. Along with the challenges and barriers also comes a great opportunity for simultaneous renewal where every stakeholder can benefit mutually from the result of collectively working together. Whether stakeholders within a clinical partnership are collaborating on establishing, maintaining, or growing a program, there are certainly considerations at each stage to discuss and enact together as a unit.

Clinical Practice Is Key

Within the context of educator preparation, clinical practice is key. Clinical practice is the means by which teacher candidates begin to contextualize theoretical knowledge, interact with current educators and students, and develop requisite skills and knowledge to successfully navigate the current educational landscape. Most educator preparation programs have a clinical practice component that traditionally consists of a culminating internship commonly referred to as student teaching. These last anywhere from a few weeks for alternative programs like Teach for America to a semester-long or year-long experience commonly associated with university-based educator preparation programs.

Quality clinical practice is much more than a culminating experience prior to graduation. Clinical experiences embedded in every course at every level of educator preparation programs are crucial to quality clinical practice (AACTE, 2018). These experiences, whether simulated or within actual P-12 classrooms, are carefully scaffolded, developmentally appropriate, and intentionally designed to support the learning of teacher candidates through an iterative, spiraling process of the learning of theory and the application of theory. Within this framework, teacher candidates are afforded opportunity for feedback and guided reflection on learning.

Educator preparation programs with well-developed and embedded quality clinical practice and experiences such as Professional Development Schools (PDS) have demonstrated advantages and benefits for teacher candidates as compared to the more traditional semester-long student teaching experience (Boyd, Grossman, Lankford, Loeb & Wyckoff, 2009; Castle, Arends & Rockwood, 2008; Castle, Fox & Furman, 2009). These benefits include increased efficacy and confidence, more positive attitudes toward the teaching profession, better preparation for the realities of teaching, deeper content and pedagogical knowledge, better developed collaborative and leadership skills, and lower attrition rates (Sandholtz & Wasserman, 2001). Castle, Fox, and Fuhrman (2009) reported PDS teacher preparation produced:

beginning teachers who are more competent in some aspects of instruction, management, and assessment, and are more integrated and student-centered in their thinking about planning, assessment, instruction, management and reflection. (p. 78)

Teacher candidates trained with a PDS model were described as being better prepared and more marketable with the skills and dispositions of second or third-year teachers (Roth, 2017).

Clinical Partnerships Are Crucial

Sustaining quality clinical practice with its associated clinical experiences requires the framework of clinical partnership between a university's educator preparation program and local P-12 school districts. The key components of quality clinical partnerships are collaboration and positive impact on all stakeholders, defined by decision-making and shared accountability that is mutually beneficial, and practices that are sustaining and generative (CASPA, 2015). Quality partnerships break down the barriers between educator preparation programs and the P-12 school systems by bringing university-based teacher educators and teacher candidates into classrooms to work hand-in-hand with school-based teacher educators, thus, creating an interactive pathway for research to impact practice and practice to inform research (Coburn, Penuel, & Geil, 2013; Tseng, 2012; Yohalem & Tseng, 2015). All participants become researchers and practitioners. It is within these:

clinical field sites [that] school and university partners focus together on improving teacher education and the professional development of practicing teachers as well as increasing student achievement and conducting research. (Castle, Fox, & Souder, 2006, p. 65)

Establishing Clinical Partnerships and Practice

An initial meeting to determine mutual interest is usually the starting place in creating a clinical partnership and practice. At this meeting the goal should be to investigate the purpose for teacher preparation and PK-12 schools joining forces for the preparation of teacher candidates. Research from both sides should identify why teacher preparation in clinical settings is the most effective teacher training method. These vital discussions can create opportunities to build trust and a shared vision for what a successful partnership is from the perspective of each stakeholder. All stakeholders who are part of the initial establishment of the partnership assume boundary-spanning positions in which work as teacher educators takes place both on college or university campuses as well as in PK-12 school classrooms. This collaborative work is often highlighted in PDS models where university and PK-12 school interactions occur in a "third space," where practitioner and academic knowledge merges (Zeichner, 2010, p. 92).

Once the purpose for the partnership has been identified and stakeholders understand the importance of clinical partnership and practice, a bend toward understanding circumstantial variables of the community and specific contexts should be considered. The variables that could be discussed, for example, can include available resources, characteristics of each school within the partnership, school sites that could offer diverse experiences, school sites that highlight a variety of effective teaching practices, and perhaps even visitation of school sites to understand different building needs.

After a school site is selected and mutually agreed upon, the next logical step can focus on needs and expectations that account for program requirements and building needs. Examples of needs might include building space, curriculum that includes high-leverage teaching practices and approximations of practice, school-based teacher educators who will support the development of teacher candidates, and discussion on how resources will be distributed and shared. Equally important is a clear understanding of expectations for all stakeholders within the partnership. Many clinical partnerships establish a Memorandum of Understanding (MOU) to identify certain policies that govern the partnership. MOUs typically highlight the partnership's goals, mission, vision, financial stipends, and agreed upon pay for varying levels of instructor involvement. Additionally, MOUs can describe how partnerships will be compensated for space and resources needed from both University and PK-12 entities to run and operate the partnership.

Maintaining Clinical Partnerships and Practice

Once a strong relationship, common knowledge, and shared beliefs among school and university-based faculty have been established with a goal of transforming teaching, schooling, and teacher education, the partnership can then move toward maintenance discussions (Darling-Hammond, 2006). The task of maintaining clinical partnerships demands the full commitment and active involvement of both the EPP and PK-12 school districts (Darling-Hammond, 2014). While still accounting for the elements inherent in the establishing phase of a clinical partnership and practice, opportunities to discuss data for the purpose of programmatic change can now become a primary focus for the partnership.

Data are a vital element during the maintenance stage of a clinical partnership and practice. Though the maintenance stage represents that the partnership has moved beyond an established partnership, there are still many opportunities to improve the partnership. Data collection, for example, could include formalities like surveys sent to classroom teachers asking for feedback about their perceptions of teacher candidates' readiness and dispositions. Some partnerships provide a variety of trainings for PK-12 classroom teachers, university coaches, and faculty for professional development purposes, and surveys are sent to the participants to share what they viewed to be the successful elements of the training as well as what they would suggest to change. In that manner, everyone's voice is taken into consideration for future changes.

Additionally, a change to programmatic structure will certainly provide opportunity for faculty of EPPs to engage in conversation regarding tenure track and promotion. Often times research is perched at the pinnacle of the hierarchical ladder of a university. Clinical faculty members often believe the leaders their University and School of Education do not value teaching activities because promotion and tenure committees make decisions demonstrating that scholarship is much more esteemed than instruction and clinical partnership development (Evans-Andris, Kyle, Larson, Buecker, Haselton, Howell, . . . Weiland, 2014). Although service, as part of clinical faculties' load, is sometimes perceived as lesser value, the service portion is most important when it comes to clinical partnership and practice. Conversations regarding the value of service and clinical faculty should be highlighted and thoroughly discussed in the maintenance phase. It is time for clinical faculty as part of a clinical partnership and practice to sit on a level playing field with tenure-track and research faculty.

Growing Clinical Partnerships and Practice

The key to continual growth in clinical practice and the partnerships therein is to collectively celebrate successes, embrace and solve challenges, and find ways to recruit and retain diverse individuals in the teaching profession. Additionally, establishing consistent assessment reviews requires committing to evidence-based decision making and engaging all partners in the process. This type of communication and collaboration is recursive in action and is generally a non-linear process.

Regularly scheduled meetings should be expected as common practice between the EPP and PK-12 school district. In some clinical partnerships, EPP directors, deans, or chairs will meet on a monthly basis at school district administration meetings with the superintendent. A portion of the meeting minutes will be allocated to the growth and development of the partnerships. Some conversations may focus on policies and procedures outlined in an MOU, and other conversations may revolve around future curriculum and teaching ideas. Even though some meetings are scheduled on a formal basis, consistent face-time at the school partnership site will almost always lead to conversation that is current and directly applicable to either the PK-12 school or the EPP. The details of these informal conversations are often helping direct immediate and long-term decisions and goals.

It is a difficult task to effectively teach teacher candidates by asking them to imagine what they have never seen or suggesting they teach differently than what they have observed in the classroom. It is hard to measure the amount of coursework needed to counteract the powerful experiential lessons shaping what teachers actually do. Stakeholders from PK-12 and EPPs must work together to co-create experiences that benefit all who are involved in order to establish, maintain, and grow the partnership. Equally as important to key stakeholders within a clinical partnership and practice are the school sites and clinical educators from those sites that help provide the real contextual work and practices of teaching.

ADDRESSING THE EDUCATOR SHORTAGE THROUGH THE PDS MODEL

According to the latest research, there is national debate as to whether educator preparation programs are producing sufficient numbers of teachers to meet current and projected needs (Ingersoll & Strong, 2011; Sutcher, Darling-Hammond, & Carver-Thomas, 2016). In 2016, the Learning Policy Institute put forth resources to help understand the context of the teacher shortage in various states. Within the state of Colorado, there continues to be a dearth of graduates in all content areas with the teacher shortage critical in many rural areas of the state (Colorado Department of Higher Education, 2016, 2017). School district administrators and human resource directors are traveling out of state to recruit new teachers from other preparation programs to meet the demands of both urban and rural areas of the state (CASPA, 2015), with most recent data indicating up to 50% of Colorado's teachers are being recruited from outside the state (Colorado Department of Higher Education, 2017). In the 2015 school year, Denver Public Schools alone provided induction and mentoring supports to more than 2,000 new teachers (Bacon, Martinez, Mitchell, & Shaler, 2015). The state legislature passed HB 17-1003 requiring the departments of education and higher education to conduct a series of town hall meetings across the state, soliciting feedback from all stakeholders on how to address the educator shortage and develop a collaborative, strategic action plan whose results became public at the end of the year (Colorado Department of Education, 2017).

These realities, combined with a lack of retention among new teachers (Ingersoll & May, 2011; Ingersoll & Perda, 2010) and leaders (Drago-Severson, 2012; Gibbs, 2008), challenges educator preparation programs and PK-12 school districts to strategically work together to purposefully address the recruitment and retention of future teachers and leaders, along with purposeful engagement to support the profession of education as a whole (Wilhelm, 2016). Once prepared, teachers and leaders in today's schools are challenged with identifying differentiated and sustainable professional development, identifying and implementing research-based best practices, and are charged with implementing both of these positions toward the enhancement of student engagement. Again, education in the United States today has its fair share of challenges, but with challenges come opportunities.

Center for Educator Preparation: One PDS Exemplar

To help address the current challenges previously identified, the Center for Educator Preparation (CEP) at Colorado State University has designed and delivered teacher and principal licensure programming as a developmental progression of coursework and field experiences. The process carefully leads candidates through the initial process of learning to teach and culminates in final recommendation for licensure. Programs are delivered in four discrete phases of study and reinforced throughout by a consistent philosophical and programmatic core of learning based on standards (national, state, and institutional), by extensive and intensive partnerships between and within the university and local school communities, and by maximized experiential learning opportunities for candidates. This design is based upon the work of the National Council for Accreditation of Teacher Education (NCATE) Professional Development School (PDS) model (2001, 2014). As stated, PDSs are innovative institutions formed through intentional partnerships between professional education programs and school districts (NCATE, 2014). This model implements a four-fold mission of: (1) educator preparation; (2) faculty development; (3) inquiry directed at the improvement of practices, and; (4) enhanced student engagement. The overall intent is to create 21st Century *Centers of Pedagogy*. Centers of Pedagogy "are university-based hubs devoted entirely to supporting all practices and innovations, laboratory and clinical, necessary for creating high-quality teachers (and leaders). It is both a laboratory site and a satellite site for clinical classroom placements" (Zimpher & Howey, 2013, p. 409).

The PDS Clinical Practice model is grounded in John Goodlad's original work, *A Place Called School* (1984), in which he and colleagues conducted the first ever ethnographic study of public education across the United States to understand what, how, and when learning takes place. Findings indicated that the more teacher and principal training institutions and PK-12 schools can purposefully collaborate together, instilling a *simultaneous renewal* among all participants, the better schooling will be for children and youth, as well as the sustainability of the nation's public educational system. This seminal work resulted in the National Network for Educational Renewal (NNER), a network of educator preparation, Arts and Sciences faculty, and PK-12 school districts partnering to support and advance education in a democracy (NNER, 2016). This includes upholding a four pronged mission:

1. Providing access to knowledge for all children (equity and excellence);
2. Educating the young for thoughtful participation in a social and political democracy (enculturation);
3. Basing teaching on knowledge of the subjects taught, establishing principles of learning, and sensitivity to the unique potential of learners (nurturing pedagogy), and;
4. Taking responsibility for improving the conditions of learning in PK-12 schools, institutions of higher education and communities (stewardship).

As reported by Goodlad, Soder, and Sirotnik (1990), and others (Grossman, Compton, Igra, Ronfeldt, Shahan, & Williamson, 2009; Zimpher & Howey, 2013) faculty members in educator preparation have a responsibility to future teachers and leaders to not only transmit information, but to also model what their candidates are expected to do. In order to build appropriate competencies, the professional education faculty at Colorado State University is committed to teaching and modeling effective instructional practices that create an invitational environment that translates critical theory to classroom practice. Through experiencing and reflecting on these practices and environments, teacher and principal licensure students will better comprehend the role of the teacher and leader as facilitators of student success. Goodlad, et al. (1990) reminded educators:

faculty of the school must come together to plan the array of teaching methods to be demonstrated in the program, the kinds of faculty-student interactions to be modeled for and replicated by their students, and the ways in which students are to participate in evaluating the teaching they observe and the curriculum they experience. (p. 290)

This concept of effective modeling was similarly addressed in Vygotsky's (1986) concept of relational imitation and through John Dewey's (1938) notion of learning through direct experiences. In their endeavor to identify specific instructional features promoting meaningful growth in teacher candidates, Jensen and Winitzky (1999) examined over 43 studies on educational improvement. Thirty-two of these investigations reported meaningful learning in candidates when training programs emphasized course content used in context, repeated reflection, and modeling by faculty and other professional educators. As Goodlad et al. (1990) surmised:

We recommend, then, that the responsible faculty plan not just a sequence of courses and field experiences, but deliberate demonstration of pedagogical procedures their teacher and leader candidates will be expected to use in the practice part of their preparation programs. (p. 291)

The educator preparation programs at the CEP are developmental in their phase design, with courses and field experiences intended to address the progressive stages of learning to teach (or lead), and *take place in PK-12 schools*. Skills, knowledge and dispositions in each subsequent pre-service program phase are built upon those developed in earlier phases. The conceptual framework of these licensure programs supports the development of new teachers and leaders who understand how best to facilitate student learning based on their roles as learners, collaborators, and leaders. The components of this theme are grounded in a strong knowledge base developed from research and best practice.

Logic Model Development: Guiding Collaboration

Knowlton and Phillips (2013) identified two forms of logic models (theory of change and program), and they encouraged leaders to consider both as equally important to the overall success of the project or program. Theory of change logic models are constructed using backward design. Figure 1 shows how leaders are challenged to think about their intended results (Get), plan strategies leading them to their intended results (Do), define assumptions (Believe), support, and inform strategies, and understand the overall knowledge base upon which research, practice and theory are important to the unique work being informed.

Program logic models are more prevalent in use with project planning and include five components: resources, activities, outputs, outcomes, and impact. The first three aspects of program logic models are considered the planned work, and the outcomes and impact represent intended results of the project. Program logic models are often used in grant submissions as visual representations of a project's overall design, taking into consideration the planning, communication, and evaluation of the overall project.

Leaders of the CEP in collaboration with university faculty from various schools and departments developed a series of logic models designed to collectively communicate the current structure of the

Figure 1. Informing a Theory of Change
Figure 1 from The Logic Model Guidebook: Better Strategies for Great Results, by Wyatt-Knowlton & Phillips, 2013, p. 22. Copyright 2013 by Sage Publication. Used with permission.

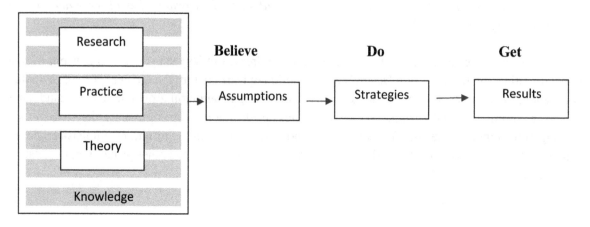

Center (Sebald & Frederiksen, 2017). These models are designed with a focus on future direction and program evaluation. When done effectively, logic models identify theories of change and establish overall program goals (Kellogg Foundation, 2004; Knowlton & Phillips, 2013).

As indicated earlier, the CEP has as its core the clinical practice PDS model as developed by NCATE (2001) and shown in Figure 2: (a) educator preparation; (b) faculty development; (c) inquiry designed for the improvement of practice, and; (d) student engagement. Given the interconnected nature of the Center throughout the Colorado State University system, it was important to identify current initiatives and areas of focus prior to considering future directions. At this institution, undergraduate students major in their content areas (e.g., science, mathematics, agriculture, business, speech) and take courses through the Center related to pedagogy and teacher licensure requirements. Faculty and staff, by design, are highly integrated throughout the university structure for the licensing of teachers. Undergraduate students interested in licensure must first complete content course requirements (e.g., science, art, mathematics, music, engineering, technology, social studies) prior to entering pedagogical training. This interconnectedness allows faculty and staff within the Center to collaborate among other university faculty who are content area experts.

Theory of Change

The first logic model developed is *theory of change*. Figure 3 shows this conceptual map that identifies the ultimate goal of the Center (Results), plans to obtain the Center's desired results (Do), challenges to identify and test assumptions and beliefs, and finally identifies the many frameworks supporting the work, including legislation like Every Student Exceeds Act (ESSA), Individuals with Disabilities Education Improvement Act (IDEA), and state legislation including Teacher Quality Standards (TQS) and Principal Quality Standards (PQS). The CEP theory of change logic model is static and is informing the development of the Center's four program logic models. Programmatic logic models are more detailed and guide how those in the Center plan to operate over the next five years.

Figure 2. CEP Logic Model Pillars

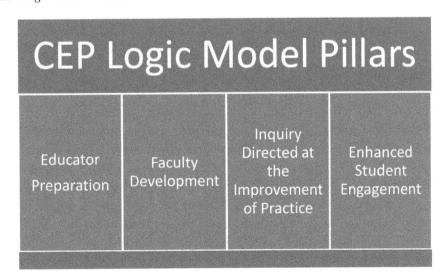

Figure 3. Excerpts from the CEP Theory of Change Logic Model

Result	Do	Assumptions/ Beliefs	Frameworks Informing Decisions (Research, Practice, Theory)
Exceptionally trained educators and leaders who remain in the field longer than 5 years who positively impact children and youth in all facets of learning	Curriculum intentionally connected to TQS & PQS Authentic experiences using the PDS model Faculty collaboration working toward the result Provide ongoing support for graduates and PDS partners	1. Our graduates have the knowledge, skills, and professional dispositions to meet the current demands of our constituents: PK-12 stakeholders. 2. Our graduates are experts in their content area and are well prepared to teach it. 5. Our graduates are diverse and well prepared to work with ELL and students with exceptional needs. 6. Our graduates remain in the field longer than the average, according to research (>5 years). 8. Faculty and staff want to continue using the PDS model. 9. All faculty and teaching partners in schools are well prepared and skilled at teaching pedagogy. 12. We believe that educator preparation in higher education is what is necessary to train educators and leaders to impact PK-12 students.	Educator preparation research (e.g., co-teaching) NNER Agenda for Democracy PDS model/ clinical practice High-Leverage Practices CAEP standards for accreditation Legislation (e.g., state, ESSA, IDEA, TQS, PQS)

Educator Preparation

CEP's first and primary role is the production of teachers and leaders for the field. Based upon the theory of change model, the Center's overall goal is more than increasing the number of educators entering the field. It encourages producing educators who are exceptionally trained, remain in the field longer than five years, [and] who positively impact children and youth in all facets of learning To do this effectively, faculty thoughtfully identified current resources and activities supporting the desired outputs, outcomes and overall impact. Because the CEP is striving to become a Center of Pedagogy using the PDS clinical practice model, stakeholders collaborate utilizing a variety of resources from the university, school districts, and overall education community. The university and clinical faculty work in collaboration to provide the necessary technical knowledge, skills, and dispositions for teacher and principal candidates, as identified through Goodlad's (1984) work. In reviewing the current five-year model for educator preparation, faculty are working with area school districts to:

- Analyze our teacher training curriculum to ensure it is intentionally connected to Colorado Teacher Quality Standards, Colorado Principal Quality Standards and teaching dispositions and make changes based upon findings ensuring all standards and dispositions are addressed and teacher candidates are engaged.
- Provide authentic PK-12 experiences using the PDS clinical practice model.
- Expand programming to include Early Childhood Special Education.
- Develop a recruitment plan for both teachers and principals.
- Meet regularly with district leaders to maintain partnerships and understand PK-12 stakeholder needs.
- Survey teacher candidates, university supervisors, cooperating teachers, administrators, and CEP instructors at the end of student teaching to understand perceptions of preparedness and make intentional changes to programs based upon feedback.
- Survey graduates and receiving school districts at the end of the first year of teaching to understand perceptions of preparedness and make intentional changes to programs based upon feedback.

Through specific focus on these activities using the current resources available, the output of these efforts will produce an increased number of graduates who are ready for the current challenges of working in schools and preparing PK-12 students for 21st Century Skills (P21, 2016). Additional outputs increase completion rates to better meet the teacher and leader needs of Colorado, maintain and expand our PDS clinical practice model for the improvement of educator preparation, and communicate the CEP and its goals to current stakeholders and potential grantors. These efforts will result in positively impacting the number of teachers needed within the state of Colorado, improve teacher retention among novice educators, and overall impact PK-12 student learning due to the increased numbers of teachers and leaders who remain in the field to develop their craft. This impact is critical to the PK-12 educational system considering up to 50% of teachers leave the classroom within their first five years of teaching (Ingersoll & May, 2011; Ingersoll & Perda, 2010). Research indicates experience matters in literacy and mathematics instruction (Harris & Sass, 2011; Papay & Kraft, 2014; Wiswall, 2013). Working with PK-12 schools promoting teacher longevity is necessary in positively impacting student growth.

Faculty Development

Faculty development is key to Goodlad's (1984) concept of *simultaneous renewal*. Done effectively, university and school district faculty work collaboratively in both settings to improve their practices with the goal of staying current in content and pedagogy. Faculty development within a PDS clinical practice model invites those from both university and school districts to work together for the improvement of practice for pre-service teachers and leaders with the ultimate goal of improved student learning. To that end, both research and clinical faculty at the Center have identified various resources designed to more purposefully work with both university and school district faculty, have identified specific personnel to support professional development around the PDS clinical practice model using Goodlad's (1984) foundational work, and have identified specific activities moving forward:

- University clinical and research faculty along with school district faculty provide workshops for current teacher candidates and district educators specific to the needs of classroom teachers.
- University clinical and research faculty along with school district faculty provide workshops for higher education faculty regarding the unique needs of teaching in today's classrooms.
- Using the concept of simultaneous renewal, meet with CEP, CSU's School of Education (SoE), and school district leaders to identify faculty development needs for both PK-12 and university that are both differentiated and sustainable for all parties.
- Develop a curriculum to educate all who train teachers and leaders at the CEP in the Agenda for a Democracy and the National Network for Educational Renewal.
- Work with SoE director to identify relevant and sustainable certificate programs for university and PK-12 school district teachers and leaders.

Again, it is through these activities where faculty from the Center will produce university and school district faculty who are well-trained in the preparation of teachers and leaders, produce university and PK-12 faculty who are well-versed in the Agenda for Democracy and the National Network for Educational Renewal, and encourage area school districts to maintain intentional partnerships with CSU to enhance teacher and principal effectiveness along with student learning. The overall outcomes and impact of intentional faculty development will improve university and PK-12 partnerships tied toward simultaneous renewal and the overall positive impact on enhanced student learning and engagement.

Inquiry Directed at the Improvement of Practice

While research is not new to faculty working at CSU and the Center, it is a new area of focus as it relates to the improvement of practice for those engaged in clinical practice within the Center. Resources available to those at the Center are the same as they are for all faculty working at CSU. Inquiry resources unique to teacher and principal preparation include the potential collaboration with national leadership organizations such as the Institute for Education Sciences (IES), the NNER–for which CSU is the state site–and the American Association for Colleges for Teacher Education (AACTE). Finally, the Center is regulated by the newest federal legislation Every Student Succeeds Act (ESSA) giving educational decision-making back to the states. How Colorado will interpret and implement this renewed locus of control has been submitted to the U.S. Department of Education. Faculty at the Center will continue to contribute to the conversation. To begin to understand how inquiry fits within the Center and its overall mission, this pillar communicates several activities for which faculty are currently involved:

- Identification of SoE faculty who are interested in partnering with CEP for inquiry directed at the improvement of practice.
- Identification of PK-12 teachers and leaders who are interested in partnering with CEP for inquiry directed at the improvement of practice.
- Researching co-teaching practices employed in educator preparation at CEP and nationally.
- Submitting for grants to support CEP initiatives, such as co-teaching during student teaching.
- Identification of areas of training for CEP faculty to support inquiry directed at the improvement of practice.

Since August of 2015, faculty at the Center have submitted fourteen internal and external grants designed to support current research initiatives. It is the goal of CEP leadership to increase the scholarship knowledge base among CEP core faculty, produce manuscripts for publication advancing the understanding of teacher and principal preparation and the improvement of practice, present at various conferences sharing the work of the Center and research findings, identify partners outside of the Center and CSU with which to collaborate on similar projects, and fund projects that are unique to CEP, advancing the PDS clinical practice model. These efforts will result in overall outcomes of the Center and CSU contributing to the voice of educator preparation research and the improvement of practice through the development of unified research areas of focus, thus, informing teacher and principal preparation programs at the state and national levels.

Enhanced Student Engagement

The work identified in the previous three models all lead to enhanced student engagement. Student engagement is defined as relevant to both the PK-12 perspective as well as the higher education perspective of teacher and principal candidates. Faculty engage with school partners exploring project-based learning; support PK-12 students through content area expertise in computer science, literacy, science and mathematics; collaborate with both PK-12 and university partners beyond educator preparation to work with children and youth throughout the partner schools; and provide career development opportunities for both teacher and leader candidates through collaborative and intentional connections among university, district, and community resources. Over the past two years, CEP faculty have supported Enhanced Student Engagement through a computer science outreach collaborative working with middle school "Girls Who Code" camp in an urban school district, supported elementary students during a summer Math Counts project, and have provided a panel discussion helping pre-service teachers learn from school district leaders how to cultivate community after tragedy.

In conclusion, the goal for those at CEP is to prepare *exceptionally trained teachers and leaders who remain in the field for longer than five years and who positively impact children and youth in all facets of learning*. Case studies incorporating all four logic model pillars will be described, highlighting the work as it connects with PDS clinical practice models of educator preparation with each leading to the overarching goal of increasing sustainability and longevity in the field.

PRACTICE-BASED SOLUTIONS AND RECOMMENDATIONS

The chapter began with discussion of theoretical components inherent to clinical practice, highlighting the intersection of the works of Dewey (1938), Vygotsky (1986) and Goodlad (1984). The authors then presented a logic model framework to discuss one field-based educator preparation design. What follows are practice-based solutions with recommendations presented in the form of three case studies providing exemplars of how faculty within CEP are working to bring to life the four pillar educational design of educator preparation, faculty development, inquiry directed at the improvement of practice, and enhanced student engagement. The three cases present initiatives taken by CEP faculty and include: a) development of a School Leadership Institute designed to support beginning educational leaders; b) co-teaching during student teaching and using the four pillars to support fidelity of implementation, and; c) program implementation exemplars highlighting the collaborative connection between theory and practice of the early childhood education program in connection with the university's on-site early child care center.

School Leadership Institute

The pressure is on leaders to perform at high levels in schools beginning their first day on the job. Support for newly practicing school leaders, however, is often nonexistent. If principals do not perceive a connection between newly learned information and problems they encounter in the workplace, they are less likely to retrieve and apply that knowledge spontaneously. Research suggests new leaders' abilities to exercise effective leadership is related to the purposeful quality of thought guiding administrative action (Wallace Foundation, 2016).

Emerging research on instructional leadership must address the thinking underlying the exercise of leadership, not simply describe discrete behaviors of effective leaders. Retaining consistent leadership is necessary to positively impact schools. Student growth is increasingly important and research has indicated it takes a minimum of three years for leadership to impact change (Fullan & Stiegelbauer, 1991; McAdams, 1997), and seven or more years before successful implementation of change is realized (Vanderhaar, Munoz, & Rodosky, 2006). Retention among school leaders is important for both rural and non-rural principals (Browne-Ferrigno & Allen, 2006), and retention can be challenging due to a lack of autonomy on the part of building principals (Beesley & Clark, 2015), demands of the position (Pollock, 2016), retaining strong teachers (Goldring, Taie, & Riddles, 2014), and pressures associated with student achievement (Akiba & Reichardt, 2004; Baker, Punswick, & Belt, 2010). Research has indicated high principal turnover can also lead to higher teacher turnover, and thus, negatively impact student achievement (Berrong, 2012; Miller, 2013; Robinson, Lloyd & Rowe, 2008).

High-quality leaders, therefore, are vital to the effectiveness of the nation's public schools, especially those serving the children with the fewest advantages in life. CSU's principal licensure program places many of the school leaders in our partner school districts, yet many graduates have requested additional support during the critical first years. Mentors in the CSU Principal Licensure Program report increased requests for support from recent graduates during their first years in leadership roles, yet a formalized system of ongoing support between recent graduates and university mentors did not exist. This School Leadership Institute is designed to provide for that need and improve the experience of graduates.

Initial Institute

The first CSU School Leadership Institute launched in fall, 2017. CSU principal licensure faculty contacted nine CSU principal graduates who were currently in their first few years in school leadership to take part in the initial institute. Participants intentionally recruited for the institute were practicing leaders from our partner schools. Practicing leaders from various regions across the state and country were also recruited to expand on experiential insights to further support the Professional Development School model. The first institute consisted of two three-day retreats (one in fall, 2017 and one in spring, 2018) taking place in a mountain setting. The setting was critical in allowing participants to concentrate on the goals of the project rather than the daily stressful demands of school leadership.

Overall goals of the first retreat included norm-setting and team building, reflection and professional development centered on the topics of focus and shared-leadership, and a series of three focus groups designed to inform adaptations to the current principal preparation program. This was to better understand the supports new practicing administrators need and the role CSU can play in providing stronger systems of support.

The current CSU principal preparation program is a cohort model in which strong, trusting relationships are formed through carefully crafted norm and team building activities sustaining the cohort throughout the program. This institute combined graduates from two different cohort years, so efforts were taken to re-establish a culture of trust, honesty and transparency. Throughout each day, team-building activities were planned to not only provide additional experience with the content being addressed but also to intentionally strengthen relationships amongst participants. Participants left the initial retreat with a final team-building responsibility designed to maintain supportive contact between participants outside of the retreats.

The professional development provided was delivered using two anchor texts. Participants were asked to read one text prior to the retreat and one was explored throughout the three-day retreat. Reflective activities guided participants through the content in the texts with a focus on defining their "why" for their current leadership role and identifying their current practices and gaps in meeting their "why."

A series of three focus groups were conducted over the course of the same weekend. The first focus group allowed participants to examine their principal preparation program and explore how it contributed to their current practices. The goal of the focus group was to gain authentic insight from practitioners in the field to guide necessary updates to the current principal preparation practices. During the first focus group, participants identified areas in which further preparation could have supported them in their current role. Data from this focus group will be analyzed and used to inform changes and additions to the current principal preparation program. The focus group work is directly tied to the first and third pillars of the Center for Educator Preparation logic model: educator preparation and inquiry directed at the improvement of practice.

Initial efforts already being implemented based on the analysis of data from this first focus group include conducting a series of webinars with community experts who can provide insight into the non-academic aspects of school leadership. In education, we have a habit of continuing to talk to other educators. However, when one leaves the classroom and moves into leadership positions, the skill set needed expands dramatically. Participants in the first focus group indicated a comfort in instructional leadership but a lack in preparation for the unexpected situations that occur in schools. To best meet this need, preparation programs must be expanded to include community members who can walk through some of these scenarios with principal candidates.

The second focus group allowed participants to reflect on their current states of being, both professional and personal. The questions were aimed at getting participants to identify current stressors and supports in their leadership positions as well as if and how their jobs impact their life outside of the workplace. Data from the second focus group will be analyzed and used to inform the second retreat of the initial institute and potential future institutes. This emphasis ties into the second pillar in the Center for Educator Preparation logic model: faculty development. Current leaders in our partner schools are engaging in this work both as participants and facilitators. Novice leaders, while at the institute, are participating in learning and reflecting during the institute as well as planning for future efforts once they return to their buildings. Additionally, expert school leaders in partner districts are engaging in this work by facilitating both focus groups and professional development while at the institute.

The final focus group provided participants the opportunity to begin to dream about how future supports may look. Questions asked participants to look at where they saw themselves in the future, both personal and professional, and what supports they would need in order to achieve professional goals. Data from this final focus group will be analyzed and used as a springboard to plan ongoing systems of support for future novice school leaders. CSU faculty plan to write a series of articles summarizing each data set with the hopes of further disseminating information so local partners, other preparation programs, and practicing school leaders can use the information to inform their own practices. This focus is dedicated to maintaining systems of support for CSU graduates as they enter into leadership positions within partner districts.

Future Efforts

In initial review of the data, one theme for new administrators is the need of scenario-based practices for community and crisis situations. This need spans from work related to investigation and interrogation, crisis response, counseling, and other first-responder situations. Faculty writing these articles plan to connect with experts in the community as references and practitioner-partners to enhance the principal preparation program. CSU faculty participants plan to write a series of articles summarizing each focus group data set obtained during the first institute retreat, further disseminating information so local partners, other preparation programs, and practicing school leaders can use the information to inform their own practices.

A second theme that is initially emerging in the data analysis, is the isolation experienced by people in new leadership roles. Participants from the initial institute will be writing essays chronicling their experiences in their first years in educational leadership. These essays will be compiled into an anthology of work to be published for use with future school leaders. Through this collection of stories, other new leaders can find solace in having a shared experience with others in similar positions. Through writing these essays, participants of the institute will continue to focus on the topics from the first retreat and be ready to use those as a springboard for future planning at the spring retreat.

In spring 2018, the initial group of nine participants will reconvene for a second retreat. The focus of this retreat will be planning for future sustainable systems of supports for new school leaders. In addition to writing their essays and connecting weekly with another Leadership Institute member, participants are reading a third anchor text to guide the spring work. These activities are crafted to steer participants toward a focus on the creation of meaningful experiences. At the spring retreat, the anchor text, peer essays, themes from focus group data, and reflection on participant experiences in their time away from the institute will be combined in a curriculum that leads participants through the design of future efforts to support new leaders. At the culmination of the spring retreat, each of the nine original participants will be "fellows" of the Leadership Institute. They will then take on an advisory and mentorship role as future plans are carried forward. Throughout this process, the Enhanced Student Engagement Logic Model pillar is embedded in the level of engagement on the part of the participants.

The idea of this institute was born in the concept of simultaneous renewal which is the foundation of the Faculty Development pillar in the Center for Educator Preparation logic model. Most partner districts have a formalized system of induction and mentorship for new school leaders. Often, the formal mentor assigned to a new leader is an expert at providing professional guidance and support. They can help the new leader navigate systems, processes and procedures, questions, and provide district-specific insights. However, our research has indicated a gap in the personal mentorship and support that new administrators need in acclimating to the job. New school leaders are often hesitant to share their vulnerabilities and stressors with a district assigned mentor, as they feel the need to prove themselves professionally in their new position. The long-term goal of this institute is to design systems of support for new administrators addressing this gap, thus increasing longevity and job satisfaction for leaders in partner districts. Simultaneously, by working closely with new leaders, CSU faculty will continue to glean insight into the ever-changing role and needs of educational leaders which can be applied to maintaining the high quality of the principal preparation program.

Evolution of Co-Teaching

As stated by the Colorado Department of Education (2017), Senate Bill 10-191 changes the way all educators (principals/assistant principals, teachers, and specialized service professionals) are evaluated in Colorado with the ultimate goal of continuously supporting educators' professional growth and, in turn, accelerating student results. Prior to SB-191's full implementation in 2013, CEP's teacher preparation program began to sense hesitancy from partner schools and districts to host teacher candidates based on the unknown changes coming in teacher evaluation for in-service educators. At that time CEP was utilizing a gradual release model of student teaching; whereby, mentor teachers were expected to fully give up their classrooms to a teacher candidate for a portion of the semester. Schools were voicing their concerns about allowing teacher candidates to fully take over in light of the potential impact to mentor teachers' evaluations. In response to the concerns from these partners, faculty began engaging in co-teaching professional development, and ultimately decided it was a model of student teaching they wanted to explore further. Upon initial training for the CEP faculty in 2013, a co-teaching model was offered as an option for student teaching placements within their educator preparation program.

Before delving into co-teaching implementation, it is important to clarify the term co-teaching from the perspective of the CEP faculty. *Co-teaching* is two or more teachers sharing physical space, planning, and implementation of lessons and assessment of student learning. With explicit explanations in these areas, teacher candidates and mentor teachers have a better understanding of how to authentically implement co-teaching within student teaching.

Advantages and Benefits of Co-Teaching

The Teacher Quality Enhancement Center at St. Cloud State University (2011) found in-service teachers who experienced co-teaching during student teaching had the following responses:

- Comfortable and capable of collaborating effectively
- Equipped to deal with classroom management issues
- Eager to receive feedback and sought opportunities to reflect
- Experienced more time teaching students
- Able to effectively differentiate instruction and had a deeper understanding of the curriculum
- Felt knowledgeable in ways to maximize the human resources available, including paraprofessionals, and volunteers

Mentor teachers participating in the co-teaching during student teaching model reported that they, too, benefited from this model in being able to better reach high need students, establish relationships with teacher candidates, experience professional growth through co-planning, and experience enhanced energy for teaching (Bacharach, Washut-Heck, & Dahlberg, 2010). Finally, PK-12 students reported while in co-taught classrooms they became more engaged by working in smaller groups; received more individual attention; got their questions answered faster; received papers, assignments and grades faster; and overall behaved better.

Co-Teaching Partnerships

Maintaining clinical practice through a Professional Development School model relies on the partnerships CEP intentionally cultivates and maintains with their partner schools and districts. Co-teaching is currently serving as an authentic bridge for these partnerships. Co-teaching has expanded extensively through student teaching and has become something their partner schools and districts are asking CEP to support through collaboration and professional development opportunities. This mutually beneficial endeavor provides simultaneous renewal that effectively scaffolds *educator preparation*, provides on-going support via *faculty professional development* of mentor/partner teachers and positively *enhances PK-12 student engagement* and growth through co-teaching and demonstrates CEP's commitment to the Professional Development School model and logic model outcomes.

Effective co-teaching does not occur on its own. Training, relationship building, co-planning, and time are all needed in order for co-teaching to be successful (Bacharach, Heck, & Dahlberg, 2008). CEP's faculty have all participated in co-teaching "Train the Trainer" workshops through the Academy of Co-Teaching and Collaboration at St. Cloud State University. As a faculty, CEP has taken the training and adapted it to the needs of the program teacher candidates and partner PK-12 students and mentor teachers. CEP plans and provides a co-teaching workshop prior to the beginning of each semester for all teacher candidates and mentor teacher teams. This professional development opportunity focuses on CEP's co-teaching philosophies and expectations within student teaching, and it provides an overview of the co-teaching models and relationship building activities aimed at helping teachers to get to know one another both on personal and professional levels. Since beginning the training in 2013, with an initial group of 22 participants, the co-teaching workshop has grown to more than 100 educators from multiple school districts.

Although co-teaching manifests differently for every team in every classroom, it is catching the attention of other teachers and administrators in the schools in which it is taking place. Subsequently, CEP is noticing an influx of requests from building principals who are interested in co-teaching training and support for their entire staff, including paraprofessionals. This speaks highly to the positive impacts educators and school leaders are observing in their classrooms.

The professional development school model and faculty collaboration offer authentic co-teaching experiences for PK-12 students, teacher candidates, mentor teachers, and faculty members. This model supports CEP's plan to obtain desired results within the theory of change conceptual map. This partnership work with schools is vital for the success of all stakeholders. CEP faculty members have supported school staff members in co-teaching professional development opportunities with their partner elementary, middle, and high schools based on each school's individual needs.

Researching this concept within a pilot study, findings indicated results to be similar to those of the St. Cloud State study (Sebald, Myers, Frederiksen, & Pike, in review). CEP faculty are now researching the fidelity of implementation of this model of student teaching through a longitudinal study. Preliminary results indicate the need to train university coaches in how best to support the co-teaching pairs in the model's continued implementation. Placing teacher candidates and mentor teachers together and providing an initial training is not sufficient to maximize the benefits that co-teaching during student teaching can have for all stakeholders.

In furthering this work, CEP and Colorado State University's Department of Biology collaborated with a local school district and were awarded a federal grant titled, The Mathematics and Science Partnerships (MSP) Program. The purpose of this grant is to recruit, support, and retain high quality teachers in science, technology, engineering, and mathematics (STEM). The district has a long history of partnering with CSU and is one of the field sites for the CEP's teacher preparation program. As part of the collaboration to enhance student engagement and learning, CEP faculty members are providing co-teaching professional development for in-service teachers, support staff, and long-term substitute teachers who have been hired to support classroom teaching and learning in designated district schools funded by the MSP grant. This work fully supports CEP's ultimate theory of change goal (Figure 3) of *exceptionally trained educators and leaders who remain in the field longer than five years, who positively impact children and youth in all facets of learning.*

Early Childhood Education

The Early Childhood Education (ECE) undergraduate program of study at Colorado State University espouses the four logic model pillars in CEPs mission to prepare educators to teach children birth through age eight. The ECE major is offered in collaboration with the accredited Center for Educator Preparation and Department of Human Development and Family Studies. It is a competitive entry program with 25-30 students accepted annually. Prior to the culminating student teaching experience, teacher candidates (TCs) complete four courses that are tightly aligned with the PDS model. To begin, the clinical practice portion of the program is divided equally across infant, toddler-preschool, and K-3 classrooms. Engaging in inquiry directed at the improvement of practice has produced findings that support TCs' development in their ability to bridge theory to praxis. Furthermore, findings have illuminated achievements CEP faculty have made to inform goals for the additional pillars of faculty development and enhanced student engagement.

TCs move through the two-year, four-phase program in a cohort model, ensuring an established professional network throughout the program and upon entering first year teaching positions. The cohort model also allows TCs to loop with professors providing deliberate demonstration of appropriate pedagogical practices that TCs are expected to employ (i.e., inquiry-focused learning grounded in research-based practices and accreditation standards). ECE majors achieve both core ECE program of study learning outcomes as well as all learning outcomes required by the state Department of Education, including knowledge of lifespan development processes, technical knowledge and skills aligning with high quality teaching, and foundational professional dispositions. Learning outcomes throughout the four-phase program are embedded in a PDS model that spans a collaborative network of early childhood education settings across Northern Colorado, representing a variety of curricula and instructional options. The focus of this section is a Reggio Emilia inspired infant, toddler, and preschool setting and a public K-3 setting.

To provide an opportunity to explore and develop major ECE learning outcomes, TCs engage in extensive clinical practice, completing anywhere between 2.5 to 10 hours weekly at PDS sites leading up to student teaching. Within the PDS clinical experiences, TCs are provided the opportunity to foster a deeper understanding of the teaching and learning process through the implementation of course related concepts into real time classroom activity; TCs grow their abilities through enhanced engagement and are better prepared for the realities of teaching. Clinical experiences have been developed with Grossman and colleagues (2009) *Pedagogies of Practice* framework in mind; therefore, the TCs clinical practice includes decomposition, representation, and approximation of practice. Clinical experiences are also meant to support the early childhood sites having opened their doors to CEP faculty with the goal of positively impacting young children, their families, and the profession.

The following vignettes are exemplars of the philosophical and clinical practice framework of two professional education courses required during Phase I and Phase II of the ECE program of study. Each vignette provides an overall view of the ECE PDS model and the varied approaches employed to enhance TC engagement and P-3 student learning. The first course, Literacy and the Learner, provides a foundation for the knowledge base TCs must have to support young children's (birth through age eight) inherent interest in communicating and encountering the world through literacy and mathematics. The second course, Diagnostic Teaching of Reading, supports teacher candidates' development of the knowledge base, skills, and strategies for teaching reading with a focus on implementation at the K-3 level. Together, these two courses highlight the careful scaffolding of TCs' knowledge and skills through a critical and constructivist pedagogy.

Vignette 1: Literacy and the Learner, Constructing the Lens of a Teacher

CEP faculty view the growth and development of literacy and mathematical skills as precursors to lifelong healthfulness and success. Towards these ends, Literacy and the Learner is designed to further define the aims and foundational knowledge of early childhood education and to help facilitate TCs exploration and understanding of concepts related to literacy and mathematical processes. The central themes for this course consist of: (a) provide authentic assessment through prolonged observations of young children's exploration and development of literacy and mathematical skills; (b) provide opportunities to build the lens of a teacher using a strength-based perspective, and; (c) provide a foundational understanding of how to develop inquiry-based instruction for young children that align with state performance-based standards and professional dispositions expectations.

PDS Site

The PDS for Literacy and the Learner is located in a building closely affiliated with the university. It is licensed by the Office of Early Childhood at the Colorado Department of Human Services and is accredited by the National Association for the Education of Young Children. The site is dedicated to the preparation of TCs for careers in early childhood education by offering high quality programming for young children. The building is a hybrid of original hardwood floors and state of the art observation technology. The site offers seven observable classrooms with children's ages ranging from 6 weeks through age five.

It is important to note that the site is Reggio Emilia inspired. Reggio Emilia is defined as constructivist in nature and is grounded in the philosophy of Loris Malaguzzi (Edwards, Forma, & Gandini, 1998). Reggio Emilia inspired learning centers on an image of the child as strong and competent, and Reggio Emilia inspired teachers view children as natural scientists who have their own hypotheses and theories about the world around them. Curriculum and instruction are emergent with a focus on natural materials and in-depth investigations.

Clinical Practice

During the first few weeks, teacher candidates begin to acquaint themselves with the general processes of early childhood classroom routines, get a feel for the expectations of their mentor teachers, and begin to develop relationships with the children through play. TCs spend a total of 2.5 hours per week for 16 weeks in the classroom: half of their clinical practice hours in varying infant, toddler, and preschool classrooms and the second half in observation booths equipped with audio and visual technologies.

Time spent together during face-to-face lecture is emergent and structured around TCs "ah-ha moments" and wonderings. Clinical practice experience is filtered through course content. A considerable amount of time is dedicated to the culture and climate of individual cohorts with the aim of cultivating a supportive professional network as well as provide space for the professor to model strategies for developing healthful, rigorous, and engaging learning environments. To these ends, democratic teaching strategies are attended to and provide opportunities to explore concepts related to inclusive practices and teaching for social justice.

Pedagogies of Practice

The approximation of practice emerges as TCs begin to identify young children's present levels of functioning across the literacy and mathematical domains of learning. The decomposition of practice is represented in the TCs growing understanding and use of authentic assessment. The representation of practice occurs through constant observations of teaching strategies employed that enhance and/or retain literacy and numeracy development.

Assessments

TCs demonstrate individual growth and development through a progression of authentic assessments that mirror the practice of authentic assessment in early childhood classrooms. Each assessment demonstrates the tight alignment of theory to praxis as well as the overarching goal of scaffolding essential observation and reflection skills required of early childhood professionals. Three of the four major assessments are co-taught in collaboration with the Educational Technology and Assessment course instructor as a means to integrate skills and teaching strategies across content and to demonstrate possible ways for TCs to communicate classroom activity and student learning to stakeholders in their future practice. All four assessments are facilitated through semi-structured writing prompts. The writing prompts serve as a medium for TCs to demonstrate their ability to name theoretical perspectives of learning in practice as it naturally unfolds.

Using thick description, TCs begin to match course content and early learning standards to young children's play, conversations, and spontaneous activity. TCs work at documenting and identify young children's emerging literacy and numeracy skills as well as take into consideration classroom demographics, emotional context of the classroom, materials and modalities of learning, and modifications to the general curriculum–all with the aim of developing the lens of a teacher. TCs are expected to think critically of their clinical practice experience and make meaning of dynamic ways literacy and numeracy affect the everyday lives of young children. Through continued engagement between course content and child observations, TCs begin to refine their observation and reflection skills of young children's growth and development, and in turn, document their own learning.

Alignment to the 4-Fold Mission

At mid-semester, TCs participate in an individual twenty-minute conference with the professor. Conferences are designed to provide space for TCs to reflect on their overall experience at the PDS site for Literacy and the Learner and highlight key connections they are making between theory and praxis. TCs also reflect on influential course readings and assessments and often provide suggestions to future TCs as a way to pay it forward. These conferences are essential to the TCs first attempt at identifying professional dispositions and goals for their program of study. These typically range from general professional dispositions, such as conveying professionalism at the PDS site to more complex dispositions related to cultural responsiveness. Mentor teachers at the PSD site also provide feedback of their experiences hosting TCs, including the benefits and challenges of navigating their role of mentor teacher and TC role model. Both allow for continuous reflection of practice on behalf of the professor and the overall program of study. Potential next steps for faculty development include faculty instructional rounds during face-to-face lectures conducted by fellow ECE faculty.

As TCs conclude their first courses of the ECE major, they begin to crystallize the type of education they hope to design and deliver to future students, and TCs work to consider the professional and moral dimensions of early childhood education. TCs are encouraged to keep Literacy and the Learner assessments as reference guides for the next phases of coursework: Integrated Methods and Diagnostic Teaching of Reading.

Vignette 2: Diagnostic Teaching of Reading and the Transition to Reflective Practitioner

The Diagnostic Teaching of Reading course is the first course TCs take at the K-3 level (spring semester, junior year). Literacy and the Learner introduces the concept of emergent literacy skills. The course is designed to help TCs learn how to develop instructional practices that make productive use of emerging literacy abilities to build a solid foundation for the acquisition of reading skills that students bring to the classroom. Aligned with the Colorado Teacher Quality Standards, teacher candidates learn how to design, implement, and guide reading instruction in kindergarten-third grade settings. By the end of this course, TCs gain experiences with fostering on-going assessment techniques for monitoring children's progress. The goal of Diagnostic Teaching of Reading is to assist Early Childhood Educators in developing the knowledge base, skills, and strategies for teaching reading within the diagnostic-prescriptive framework. They then apply their learning with emerging and developing readers. The course is held on campus for six weeks followed by ten weeks at an elementary school.

PDS Site

The PDS for Diagnostic Teaching of Reading is located in a public, k-5 elementary school. The school was established in 1963. Over the years enrollment has fluctuated; however, they currently serve 472 students. The school was named a winner of the Governor's Distinguished Improvement Award for the 2017-2018 school year. The award is given to schools that demonstrate exceptional student growth and "Exceeds Expectations" for longitudinal academic growth and "Meets or Exceeds Expectations" for academic growth gaps (J. Smith - pseudonym, personal communication, September 5, 2017). The school has consistently outperformed district and state testing scores. The site was officially established as a

PDS in 2014; although, several teachers had hosted teacher candidate internships since 2000. Nine K-2 classroom teachers and two literacy intervention teachers are actively involved in the PDS collaboration.

Clinical Practice

Teacher candidates spend time Monday-Wednesday-Friday for ten weeks at the site. Each two-hour block includes 30 minutes of lecture and modeling of the requirements, one hour working with K-2 students, and 30 minutes to debrief and reflect. TCs are incrementally introduced to components of guided reading instruction, adding a new component every two weeks. Table # outlines the timeline for implementation.

Pedagogies of Practice Framework

TCs approximate practice when they implement instruction with one K-2 student, rather than a small or large group of students. The divided parts of guided reading represent the decomposition of practice. The representation of practice occurs when the principal and literacy teachers model instruction.

Assessments

TCs are required to write and implement three lessons per week. TCs are paired with another student in the program, and they observe one another implement lessons. Then they support each other as they reflect and plan for subsequent lessons. Weekly reflection prompts guide TCs to connect their clinical experience to the content and theory initially introduced in the class. TCs also complete a midterm and final exam that are both designed to authentically assess their knowledge and skill acquired throughout the semester.

Alignment to the 4-Fold Mission

A mixed-methods study was designed to examine the PDS partnership and the impact on teacher educators, practitioners, and teacher candidates' knowledge to enhance TC and student learning. Findings suggest that both TC and student learning improved after implementation of the PDS (as evidenced by examining control and treatment group outcomes pre- and post- implementation of the PDS). Of particular note was the TCs' shift in their description of their experience. Prior to the establishment of the PDS model, TC reflections were often focused on self (e.g., expressed need for more time with students

Table 1. Guided Reading Implementation Timeline

Week 1	Week 3	Week 5	Week 7	Week 9
Get to know students	Read familiar books	Read familiar books	Read familiar book	Read familiar book
Read familiar books	Running record assessment	Running record assessment	Running record assessment	Running record assessment
		Word work	Word work	Word work
			Introduce new book	Introduce new book
				Guided writing

or a desire to practice a particular aspect of a lesson again). Following the implementation of the PDS, TCs' reflections were more focused on the students (e.g., identifying a student's specific needs and the subsequent focus of instruction).

Faculty development has been enhanced from the PDS as well. Lessons modeled for TCs are video recorded to be used for professional development for the teachers. Classroom teachers also completed a book study on the textbook that was then established for the course. This allowed for the continuation of professional development for the university instructor, the classroom teachers, and the teacher candidates.

Reflections of the Early Childhood Education-Professional Development School Model

When considering the vignettes offered from Phase I and Phase II of the ECE undergraduate program of study, the four pillars of NNER are reflected in the programs commitment to equity and excellence, enculturation of thoughtful participation in democracy, design and implementation of a nurturing pedagogy, and stewardship. The depth of TCs' learning and engagement connected to their clinical practice tightly aligns with the PDS model and is supported through consistent work with young children facilitated by the professional knowledge and expertise of practicing ECE teachers. Assessments across both courses highlight TCs' learning that is grounded in pedagogies of practices, particularly the processes of approximation, decomposition, and representation of theory and praxis. Most notable is the TCs' transition from building the lens of a teacher to working to become a reflective practitioner. Moreover, the inductive nature of TCs assessments and face-to-face lecture are couched in the logic model; whereas, inquiry designed to improve practice is reflected in the theory of change approach to faculty development and educator preparation.

FUTURE RESEARCH DIRECTIONS

In 2018, members of the Clinical Practice Commission published their work as it relates the lexicon and renewal of educator preparation through clinical practice. The commission put forth a conceptual model (p. 10) to guide high-quality teacher preparation focused and centered on clinical practice. In addition, members of the commission identified five proclamations central to supporting the pedagogical development of clinical practice within teacher preparation. Researchers engaged in the work of field-based educator preparation would do well to examine the effectiveness of these pedagogical concepts, working to explore first and second generation questions, are these models and proclamations effective in the preparation of future teachers; do these efforts lead to enhanced recruitment, support and retention of teachers; and if so, for whom do these work and under what conditions (Cole, Mills, Jenkins, & Dale, 2005).

Future research must also engage in purposefully addressing the teacher (and leader) shortage. As indicated, a teacher shortage is defined as the inability to staff vacancies at current wages with individuals qualified to teach in the fields needed (Sutcher, Darling-Hammond, & Carver-Thomas, 2016, p. 1). To what extent can and will clinical partnerships work to positively address the professionalization of teaching? The narrative regarding the teaching profession and how to best recruit, support and retain high-quality educators is necessary for the sustainability of our current educational system. Future researchers and policy makers need to have discussions addressing this narrative. Challenges related to working conditions, quality leadership and support, along with increased pay would do well in addressing the challenge of the teacher shortage.

Finally, more work needs to be done in exploring high quality university and PK-12 partnerships in the preparation of future teachers. Multiple examples (and non-examples) exist in how stakeholders developed, maintained and grew partnerships. Understanding the systems in place that support quality partnerships from both the university and PK-12 perspectives is critical. The public education system and national narrative have evolved since Goodlad's (1984) seminal work. Current technologies and data analytics allow us to critically examine systems in ways never before possible. Researchers must examine successful partnerships from a systems' perspective to help answer the second generation question.

CONCLUSION

The need for highly-qualified teachers has always been paramount in teacher (and leader) preparation programs. Given the current political and social climate, developing quality teachers who remain in the field to develop their craft is critical. Retention rates are of concern, given the speed at which novice teachers are leaving the classroom and profession, combined with the growing bubble of teachers eligible for retirement. Given that novice teachers and leaders need a minimum of three years to become proficient and perform at the level needed, maintaining high quality teachers is critical. If we cannot retain teachers, the likelihood of students having teachers with more than three to five years' experience will be low. The positive impact of having experienced teachers has been shown to be effective in the research for content areas such as literacy and mathematics. Universities and their receiving school district partners would do well to work collaboratively as a way to positively impact the teacher shortage through high-quality and supportive partnerships, providing authentic clinical experiences guised within the theoretical frameworks of Dewey (1938), Vygotsky (1986), and Goodlad (1984). It is only through researching field-based teacher (and leader) education program designs, can we continue to address the challenges facing the field of education.

REFERENCES

Akiba, M., & Reichardt, R. (2004). What predicts the mobility of elementary school leaders? An analysis of longitudinal data in Colorado. *Education Policy Analysis Archives*, *12*(18), n18. doi:10.14507/epaa. v12n18.2004

American Association of Colleges for Teacher Education (AACTE). (2018). *A pivot toward clinical practice, its lexicon, and the renewal of educator preparation: A report of the AACTE Clinical Practice Commission*. Retrieved from https://aacte.org/professional-development-and-events/clinical-practice-commission-press-conference

Bacharach, N., Heck, T. W., & Dahlberg, K. (2010). Changing the face of student teaching through co-teaching. *Action in Teacher Education*, *32*(1), 3–14. doi:10.1080/01626620.2010.10463538

Bacharach, N., Heck, T. W., & Dahlberg, K. (2011). What makes co-teaching work? Identifying the essential elements. *College Teaching Methods & Styles Journal, 4*(3), 43. doi:10.19030/ctms.v4i3.5534

Bacon, J., Martinez, K., Mitchell, R., & Shaler, L. (2015). *Teaching in Colorado: Who wants the job? Who stays? Who leaves?* Education Policy Networking Series: CU Boulder.

Baker, B. D., Punswick, E., & Belt, C. (2010). School leadership stability, principal moves, and departures: Evidence from Missouri. *Educational Administration Quarterly, 46*(4), 523–557. doi:10.1177/0013161X10383832

Ball, D., & Forzani, F. (2009). The work of teaching and the challenge for teacher education. *Journal of Teacher Education, 60*(5), 497–511. doi:10.1177/0022487109348479

Beesley, A., & Clark, T. (2015). How rural and nonrural principals differ in high plains U.S. states. *Peabody Journal of Education, 90*(2), 242–249. doi:10.1080/0161956X.2015.1022114

Berrong, D. A. (2012). *The relationship between principal turnover and student achievement un reading/ English language arts and math grades six through eight.* Lynchburg, VA: Liberty University.

Boyd, D., Grossman, P., Lankford, H., Loeb, S., & Wyckoff, J. (2009). Teacher preparation and student achievement. *Educational Evaluation and Policy Analysis, 31*(4), 416–440. doi:10.3102/0162373709353129

Browne-Ferrigno, T., & Allen, L. W. (2006). Preparing principals for high-need rural schools: A central office perspective about collaborative efforts to transform school leadership. *Journal of Research in Rural Education, 21*(1), 1–16.

Castle, S., Arends, R., & Rockwood, K. (2008). Student learning in a professional development school and a control school. *Professional Educator, 32*(1), 1–16.

Castle, S., Fox, R. K., & Fuhrman, C. (2009). Does professional development school preparation make a difference? A comparison of three teacher candidate studies. *School-University Partnerships, 3*(2), 58-68. Retrieved from https://eric.ed.gov/?id=EJ915871

Castle, S., Fox, R. K., & Souder, K. O. (2006). Do professional development schools (PDSs) make a difference? A comparative study of PDS and non-PDS teacher candidates. *Journal of Teacher Education, 58*(1), 65–80. doi:10.1177/0022487105284211

Coburn, C.E., Penuel, W.R., & Geil, K.E. (2013). *Research-practice partnerships: A strategy for leveraging research for educational improvement in school districts.* William T. Grant Foundation.

Cole, K. N., Mills, P. E., Jenkins, J. R., & Dale, P. S. (2005). Getting to the second generation questions. *Journal of Early Intervention, 27*(2), 92–93. doi:10.1177/105381510502700204

Colorado Association of School Personnel Administrators. (2015). *CASPA monthly meeting–Adams 12 five star schools.* Retrieved from https://co-case.site-ym.com/events/EventDetails.aspx?id=671493&h hSearchTerms=%22caspa%22

Colorado Department of Education. (2017). *Senate Bill 10-191.* Retrieved from https://www.cde.state. co.us/educatoreffectiveness/overviewofsb191

Colorado Department of Higher Education. (2016). *2016 legislative report: Educator preparation report AY2014-2015*. Retrieved from http://highered.colorado.gov/Publications/Reports/Legislative/ TED/201602_TED_toGGA.pdf

Darling-Hammond, L. (2006). *Powerful teacher education: Lessons from exemplary programs*. San Francisco, CA: Jossey-Bass.

Darling-Hammond, L. (2014). Strengthening clinical preparation: The holy grail of teacher education. *Peabody Journal of Education*, *89*(4), 547–561. doi:10.1080/0161956X.2014.939009

Dewey, J. (1916). *Democracy and education*. New York, NY: MacMillan Press.

Dewey, J. (1938). *Experience and education*. New York, NY: Macmillan Press.

Drago-Severson, E. (2012). The need for principal renewal: The promise of sustaining principals through principal-to-principal reflective practice. *Teachers College Record*, *114*(12), 1–56. Retrieved from http://www.tcrecord.org/ PMID:24013958

Edwards, C., Gandini, L., & Forman, G. (Eds.). (1998). *The hundred languages of children: The Reggio Emilia experience in transformation* (3rd ed.). Santa Barbra, CA: Praeger.

Evans-Andris, M., Kyle, D. W., Larson, A. E., Buecker, H., Haselton, W. B., Howell, P., ... Weiland, I. (2014). Clinical preparation of teachers in the context of a university-wide community engagement emphasis. *Peabody Journal of Education*, *89*(4), 466–481. doi:10.1080/0161956X.2014.942106

Fullan, M. G., & Stiegelbauer, S. (1991). *The new meaning of educational change*. New York, NY: Teachers College Press.

Gibbs, G. K. (2008). Tooting your own horn? *Management in Education*, *22*(1), 14–17. doi:10.1177/0892020607085625

Goldring, R., Taie, S., & Riddles, M. (2014). *Teacher attrition and mobility: Results from the 2012-2013 teacher follow-up survey* (NCES 2014-077). U.S. Department of Education. Washington, DC: National Center for Education Statistics. Retrieved September 19, 2014 from http://nces.ed.gov/pubs2014/2014077. pdf

Goodlad, J. (1984). *A place called school: Prospects for the future*. New York, NY: McGraw-Hill.

Goodlad, J. (1990). *Teachers for our nation's schools*. San Francisco, CA: Jossey-Bass.

Goodlad, J. (1994). *Educational renewal: Better teachers, better schools*. San Francisco, CA: Jossey-Bass.

Goodlad, J., Soder, R., & Sirotnik, K. A. (1990). *The moral dimensions of teaching*. San Francisco, CA: Jossey-Bass.

Grossman, P., Compton, C., Igra, D., Rongeldt, M., Shahan, E., & Williamson, P. (2009). Teaching practice: A cross-professional perspective. *Teachers College Record*, *111*(9), 2055–2100. Retrieved from http://www.tcrecord.org/

Harris, D., & Sass, T. (2011). Teacher training, teacher quality and student achievement. *Journal of Public Economics*, *95*(7-8), 798–812. doi:10.1016/j.jpubeco.2010.11.009

Ingersoll, R. M., & May, H. (2011). *Recruitment, retention and the minority teacher shortage* (CPRE Research Report # RR-69). Retrieved from Consortium for Policy Research in Education University of Pennsylvania and The Center for Educational Research in the Interest of Underserved Students, University of California, Santa Cruz website: http://www.cpre.org/sites/default/files/researchreport/1221_minori-tyteachershortagereportrr69septfinal.pdf

Ingersoll, R. M., & Perda, D. (2010). Is the supply of mathematics and science teachers sufficient? *American Educational Research Journal, 47*(3), 563–594. doi:10.3102/0002831210370711

Ingersoll, R. M., & Strong, M. (2011). The impact of induction and mentoring programs for beginning teachers: A critical review of the research. *Review of Educational Research, 81*(2), 201–233. doi:10.3102/0034654311403323

Jensen, J. W., & Winitzky, N. (1999, Feb.) *What works in teacher education?* Paper presented at the Annual meeting of the American Association of Colleges for Teacher Education, Washington, DC.

Kellogg Foundation. (2004). *W.K. Kellogg Foundation logic model development guide.* Retrieved from https://www.wkkf.org/resource-directory/resource/2006/02/wk-kellogg-foundation-logic-model-development-guide

Knowlton, L., & Phillips, C. (2013). *The logic model guidebook: Better strategies for great results.* Thousand Oaks, CA: Sage Publication.

Learning Policy Institute. (2016). *Understanding shortages: A state-by-state analysis of the factors influencing teacher supply, demand and equity.* Retrieved from https://learningpolicyinstitute.org/product/understanding-teacher-shortages-interactive

McAdams, R. P. (1997). A systems approach to school reform. *Phi Delta Kappan, 79*(2), 138–142.

Miller, A. (2013). Principal turnover and student achievement. *Economics of Education Review, 36,* 60–72. doi:10.1016/j.econedurev.2013.05.004

National Council for Accreditation for Teacher Education (NCATE). (2014). Professional development schools. Retrieved from http://www.ncate.org/ProfessionalDevelopmentSchools/tabid/497/Default.aspx

National Council for Accreditation for Teacher Education (NCATE), Report of the Blue Ribbon Panel on Clinical Preparation and Partnerships for Improved Student Learning. (2010). *Transforming teacher education through clinical practice: A national strategy to prepare effective teachers.* Retrieved from http://www.ncate.org/LinkClick.aspx?fileticket=zzeiB1OoqPk%3D&tabid=7

National Network for Educational Renewal. (2018). *Four pillars and twenty postulates.* Retrieved from https://nnerpartnerships.org/about-nner/four-pillars-twenty-postulates/

Papay, J., & Kraft, M. (2015). Productivity returns to experience in the teacher labor market: Methodological challenges and new evidence on long-term career improvement. *Journal of Public Economics, 130,* 105–119. doi:10.1016/j.jpubeco.2015.02.008

Partnership for 21st Century Learning (P21). (2016). *Framework for 21st century learning.* Retrieved from http://www.p21.org/our-work/p21-framework

Pollock, K. (2016). Principals' work in Ontario, Canada: Changing demographics, advancements in information communication technology and health and wellbeing. *International Studies in Educational Administration, 44*(3), 55–73.

Robinson, V. M., Lloyd, C. A., & Rowe, K. J. (2008). The impact of leadership on student outcomes: An analysis of the differential effects of leadership types. *Educational Administration Quarterly, 44*(5), 635–674. doi:10.1177/0013161X08321509

Roth, J. (2017). *Clinical partnerships in action: Renewal and innovation in educator preparation and research* (Doctoral dissertation). Retrieved from ProQuest Dissertations and Theses database.

Sandholtz, J., & Wasserman, K. (2001). Student and cooperating teachers: Contrasting experiences in teacher preparation programs. *Action in Teacher Education, 23*(3), 54–65. doi:10.1080/01626620.200 1.10463075

Sebald, A., & Frederiksen, H. (2017). Leading through logic modeling: Capturing the complexity. *Journal of Educational Leadership in Action, 4*(3). Retrieved from http://www.lindenwood.edu/academics/beyond-the-classroom/publications/journal-of-educational-leadership-in-action/all-issues/volume-5-issue-1/faculty-articles/sebald-frederiksen/

Sebald, A., Myers, A., Frederiksen, H., & Pike, E. (in review). Collaborative co-teaching during student teaching pilot project: What difference does context make? *Journal of Education.*

St. Cloud State University, Teacher Quality Enhancement Center. (2011). *Co-teaching in student teaching.* Retrieved from http://www.cehd.umn.edu/assets/docs/teaching/co-teaching-modules/SCSU-Facts-Sheet.pdf

Sutcher, L., Darling-Hammond, L., & Carver-Thomas, D. (2016). *A coming crisis in teaching? Teacher supply, demand, and shortages in the U.S.* Learning Policy Institute. Retrieved from https://learning-policyinstitute.org/product/coming-crisis-teaching

Tomanek, D. (2005). Building successful partnerships between k–12 and universities. *Cell Biology Education, 4*(1), 28–29. doi:10.1187/cbe.04-11-0051 PMID:15746977

Tseng, V. (2012). *Partnerships: Shifting the dynamics between research and practice.* New York, NY: William T. Grant Foundation.

Vanderhaar, J. E., Munoz, M. A., & Rodosky, R. J. (2006). Leadership as accountability for learning: The effects of school poverty, teacher experience, previous achievement, and principal preparation programs on student achievement. *Journal of Personnel Evaluation in Education, 19*(1-2), 17–33. doi:10.100711092-007-9033-8

Vygotsky, L. V. (1986). *Thought and language* (A. Kozulin, Ed.). Cambridge, MA: The MIT Press.

Wallace Foundation. (2016). *Improving university principal preparation programs: Five themes from the field.* Retrieved from http://www.wallacefoundation.org/knowledge-center/Documents/Improving-University-Principal-Preparation-Programs.pdf

Wilhelm, I. (2016). Owning the k-12 challenge. *The Chronicle of Higher Education.* Retrieved from http://chronicle.com/article/Video-Owning-the-K-12/236400

Wiswall, M. (2013). The dynamics of teacher quality. *Journal of Public Economics*, *100*, 61–78. doi:10.1016/j.jpubeco.2013.01.006

Yohalem, N., & Tseng, V. (2015). Commentary: Moving from practice to research, and back. *Applied Developmental Science*, *19*(2), 117–120. doi:10.1080/10888691.2014.983033

Zeichner, K. (2010). Rethinking the connections between campus courses and field based experience in college- and university- based teacher education. *Journal of Teacher Education*, *61*(1-2), 89–99. doi:10.1177/0022487109347671

Zimpher, N. L., & Howey, K. R. (2013). Creating 21st century centers of pedagogy: Explicating key laboratory and clinical elements of teacher preparation. *Education*, *133*(4), 409–421. Retrieved from https://eric.ed.gov/?id=EJ1032005

ADDITIONAL READING

American Association of Colleges for Teacher Education. (2018). *A pivot toward clinical practice, its lexicon, and the renewal of educator preparation: A report of the AACTE Clinical Practice Commission.* Retrieved from https://aacte.org/professional-development-and-events/clinical-practice-commission-press-conference

Bacharach, N., Heck, T., & Dahlberg, K. (2008). What makes co-teaching work: Identifying the essential elements. *College Teaching Methods and Styles Journal*, *4*(3), 43–48. doi:10.19030/ctms.v4i3.5534

Edward, C., Grandini, L., & Forman, G. (Eds.). (1998). *The hundred language of children: The Reggio Emilia experience in transformation* (3rd ed.). Santa Barbra, CA: Prager.

Heck, T., Bacharach, N., & Dahlberg, K. (2008). Co-teaching: Enhancing the student teaching experience. *Eighth Annual IBER & TLC Conference Proceedings 2008*. Retrieved from https://www.stcloudstate.edu/soe/coteaching/_files/documents/Clute_Oct_08.pdf

Institute of Medicine and National Research Council of the National Academies (2015). *Transforming the workforce for children birth through age 8: A unifying foundation.* doi: Retrieved from file:///C:/Users/asbld/Downloads/19401.pdf doi:10.17226/19401

Moomaw, S., & Heironymus, B. (2011). *Standards edition: More than counting: Preschool and Kindergarten.* St. Paul: Redleaf Press.

Otto, B. (2008). *Literacy development in early childhood.* Upper Saddle River, NJ: Pearson Merrill Prentice-Hall.

The Wallace Foundation. (2016). *Improving principal preparation programs. Five themes from the field.* Retrieved from http://www.wallacefoundation.org/knowledge-center/Documents/Improving-University-Principal-Preparation-Programs.pdf

KEY TERMS AND DEFINITIONS

Clinical Practice: Similar to the medical model of doctors learning to work in hospitals with patients, pre-service teachers learn to work within school buildings with students.

Co-Teaching During Student Teaching: A structured format consisting of seven strategies designed to intentionally utilize two or more teachers, including student teachers, working with children and youth in classroom settings.

Educator Preparation: Structured programs providing the technical knowledge, skills, and dispositions necessary to the pedagogy of teaching and leadership.

Enhanced Student Engagement: Student learning occurs when children and youth interact with the content. Enhancing the interaction of how this group interacts with content surrounds the essence of teaching and learning.

Faculty Development: Within a professional development school model, university and PK-12 teachers and leaders engage in professional development focused on enhancing the partnership to best prepare teachers and leaders.

Inquiry Directed at the Improvement of Practice: Research centered on the improvement of practice of teaching and leading within the classroom and schools.

Logic Model: A systematic approach to developing and evaluating projects or programs through theoretical and structured components.

Professional Development School Model: Partnership between universities and PK-12 schools and/or districts designed to support the training of teachers and leaders.

Chapter 2
Implementation of Paired Placement and Co–Planning/Co–Teaching Field Experience Models Across Multiple Contexts

Marilyn Elaine Strutchens
Auburn University, USA

Ruthmae Sears
University of South Florida, USA

Jennifer Whitfield
Texas A&M University, USA

Stephanie Biagetti
California State University – Sacramento, USA

Patti Brosnan
The Ohio State University, USA

Jennifer Oloff-Lewis
California State University – Chico, USA

Pier Angeli Junor Clarke
Georgia State University, USA

Jamalee (Jami) Stone
SDBOR, USA

David R. Erickson
University of Montana, USA

Christopher Parrish
University of South Alabama, USA

Basil M. Conway IV
CSU, USA

Ruby L. Ellis
Auburn University, USA

ABSTRACT

A consortium of 24 universities and their school partners engaged in a networked improvement community design to develop clinical experience models designed to build candidates' facility with the effective mathematics teaching practices and other equitable teaching strategies to promote secondary school students' success in achieving college- and career-ready standards. The authors discuss mechanisms to aid in the implementation of two alternative models: 1) the paired placement model, in which two prospective teachers are paired with a single mentor teacher, allowing the mentor teacher to provide

DOI: 10.4018/978-1-5225-6249-8.ch002

purposeful coaching and mentoring and the two pre-service teachers to offer each other feedback, mentoring, and support; and 2) co-planning and co-teaching, which has been found to help teacher candidates gain greater pedagogical content knowledge and knowledge of students through collaboration and communication between teacher candidates and mentor teachers who plan, implement, and assess instruction together.

INTRODUCTION

For nearly nine decades, student teaching and field experiences of teacher candidates have remained significantly unchanged (Guyton & McIntyre, 1990; King, 2006; Darling-Hammond, 2010). Historically, criticisms of teacher education have included the qualifications of teacher educators, the qualifications of teacher candidates, the structure of the institutions providing teacher education, the inconsistency of the curriculum in teacher education programs, and the gap between theory and practice (Darling-Hammond, 2010; Lanier & Little, 1986; Levine, 2006). However, since the early 2000s, there has been a global increase in research of reformed practices in teacher education programs and teacher candidate development (King, 2006; Capraro, Capraro, & Helfeldt, 2010; Tschida, Smith, & Forgarty, 2015; Lang, Neal, Karvouni, & Chandler, 2015). At the center of this reform has been an effort to connect theory to practice through well-designed field experiences (Darling-Hammond, 2010). According to the National Council for Accreditation of Teacher Education (NCATE) (2008), "field experiences and clinical practice are integral program components for the initial and advance preparation of teacher candidates" (p. 32). These experiences should allow teacher candidates to apply their acquired knowledge, skills, and dispositions in multiple settings relevant to their program of study (NCATE, 2008). Well designed and properly sequenced field experiences help teacher candidates to successfully develop the competencies necessary to begin careers as teachers (NCATE, 2008). Additionally, to align teacher candidates' pedagogical knowledge and teaching practices, collaboration among the teacher candidate, university instructor, and the mentor teacher must take place (NCATE, 2008, Putnam & Borko, 2000). The view of knowledge as socially-constructed clearly implies that an important part of learning to teach is becoming encultured into the teaching community (Putnam & Borko, 2000). It is clear that learning from practice is key to developing well-prepared teacher candidates (Duncan-Howell, 2010). To ensure field experiences provide teacher candidates with the opportunities to learn through practice, several aspects of the field experience must be considered.

First, the assigned field experiences and teacher candidates' education courses must be closely aligned and connected. In many cases, a disconnect exists between the university teacher-education courses and teacher candidates' assigned field experiences (Zeichner, 2010; Darling-Hammond, 2010). It is not uncommon for a mentor teacher to have little or no knowledge about the course, or objectives for the course, in which the assigned teacher candidate is currently enrolled. Similarly, the instructor of the university courses often has little knowledge of the teaching practices of the mentor teacher for which his or her teacher candidates have been assigned (Zeichner, 2010). This disconnect may often result from field placement assignments being outsourced to a central administrative office, with little or no consideration given from university faculty, mentor teacher, or school administration (Zeichner, 2010). The disconnect may be further compounded as many tenure track faculty are not assigned to student supervision within field placements, thus, placing further separation between the teacher candidates' courses and field placements (Ziechner, 2010).

Second, teacher candidates must be placed with quality and qualified mentor teachers (The National Council for Accreditation of Teacher Education [NCATE], 2010; Darling-Hammond, 2010). Darling-Hammond (2010) stated,

It is impossible to teach recruits how to teach powerfully by asking them to imagine what they have never seen or to suggest they 'do the opposite' of what they have observed in the classroom (p. 42).

No amount of education coursework can prepare students to be effective educators if they are only placed in settings that will further engrain ineffective teaching practices and beliefs (Darling-Hammond, 2010). Mentor teachers should–and must–be held to the highest of teaching standards; NCATE even recommended that multiple teacher education associations should collaborate in developing rigorous selection criteria to be used in selecting mentor teacher placements (NCATE, 2010).

In addition to mentor teachers being great teachers, mentor teachers must also have productive dispositions towards teacher education and mentoring (Darling-Hammond, 2010; NCATE, 2010; Zeichner, 2010). NCATE (2010) was specific in stating that those who serve as mentor teachers should have an understanding of how adults learn. Specific to mentoring, Zeichner and Bier (2015) stated,

Building the capacity of schools to host teacher candidates for their clinical experiences and developing the capacity of teachers to be high-quality mentors must be priorities if we are serious about making clinical experiences the central aspect of teacher education. (p. 25)

Furthermore, many states require mentor teachers to complete mentoring training prior to hosting teacher candidates (NCATE, 2010). Given the high demands and dual roles of mentor teachers–being both an effective teacher and teacher educator– mentor teachers should be compensated for their time and work (Darling-Hammond, 2010; NCATE, 2010; Zeichner, 2010).

The Clinical Experience Research Action Cluster (CERAC) of the Mathematics Teacher Education Partnership (MTE-P), a subsidiary of the Association of Public and Land Grant Universities, is one group that has taken on the challenge of transforming secondary mathematics teacher candidates' field/ clinical experiences MTE-P is a consortium of over 104 U.S. universities and colleges, along with partner school districts, focused on improving the initial preparation of secondary mathematics teachers. MTE-P uses a network improvement community (NIC) design that incorporates improvement cycles to develop adaptable interventions across contexts to support comprehensive program improvement (Martin & Gobstein, 2015). NICs, such as the MTE-P are defined by four main characteristics:

1. They are focused on a well-specified common aim;
2. They are guided by a deep understanding of the problem, the system that produces it, and a shared working theory of how to improve it;
3. Their work is disciplined by the rigor of improvement science, and;
4. They are coordinated to accelerate the development, testing, and refinement of interventions, their rapid diffusion out into the field, and their effective integration into varied educational contexts (Bryk, Gomez, Grunow, & LeMahieu, 2015; Russell, Bryk, Dolle, Gomez, Lemahieu, & Grunow, 2017, p. 3).

In summarizing the work of NICs, Russell et al. (2017) stated that "NICs are intended to situate practice improvement efforts in a supportive social architecture to accelerate a field's capacity to learn to improve (p. 3)." Rather than addressing a single dimension of a secondary mathematics program, MTE-P is undertaking parallel lines of research in multiple areas. Thus, the MTE-P is using improvement science as a mechanism to transform secondary mathematics education. Improvement Science is defined as "a disciplined approach to learning from practice, by deploying rapid tests of change to guide the development, revision and continued fine-tuning of new tools, work processes, roles and norms" (Russell, Bryk, Dolle, Gomez, Lemahieu, & Grunow, 2017, p. 17).

This chapter focuses on one of the MTE-P's lines of research related to clinical experiences. The CERAC consists of representatives of 24 university-led teams which have employed improvement science methods to developed resources that support improved models for both student teaching and early field experiences, as well as professional development for mentor teachers. Consistent with the calls for change in clinical experiences enumerated above and the NIC framework, the CERAC focuses on a problem that is two-fold:

1. There is an inadequate supply of quality mentor teachers to oversee clinical experiences. Too few teachers are well-versed in implementing the Common Core State Standards for Mathematics (CCSSM) and other college and career standards, and teachers are especially inexperienced with embedding the Standards for Mathematical Practice into their teaching of content standards. The Standards for Mathematical Practice are eight habits of mind that mathematics teachers should strive to develop in their students. They include: 1) Make sense of problems and persevere in solving them; 2) Reason abstractly and quantitatively; 3) Construct viable arguments and critique the reasoning of others; 4) Model with mathematics; 5) Use appropriate tools strategically; 6) Attend to precision; 7) Look for and make use of structure, and; 8) Look for and express regularity in repeated reasoning (National Governor Association [NGA] & the Council of Chief State School Officers, 2010.)
2. Bidirectional relationships between the teacher preparation programs and school partners in which clinical experiences take place are rare. Such relationships that reflect a common vision and shared commitment to the vision of CCSSM and other college and career standards, and other issues related to mathematics teaching and learning are critical to the development and mentoring of new teachers.

The CERAC began as a working group with MTE-P in 2012. CERAC held face-to-face meetings and conference calls to discuss problems of practice related to clinical experiences. The discussions held in the meetings directed CERAC to focus on the various approaches to clinical experiences and their outcomes, the development of mentor teachers as teacher educators, and the impact of field experiences. To expand the investigation, MTE-P also sent surveys to its higher education partners to identify areas in which they believed their programs needed improvement related to clinical experiences. Some specific survey question related to clinical experiences were:

1. How do you select mentor teachers to work with your teacher candidates?
2. What professional development do you provide for mentor teachers prior to them supervising interns?
3. Do you provide any continuing professional development for mentor teachers?

4.   What relationships exist between the program faculty and mentor teachers?
5.   Do you have the typical model for supervising interns? That is, you have one intern is assigned to one mentor teacher, with a university representative.
6.   Are mathematics content courses connected to the internship experience in any way?

To coalesce the data collected, CERAC wrote a white paper which included a review of existing literature related to clinical experiences, results of the MTE-P survey, and references to the MTE-P guiding principles (MTE-P, 2014); Guiding Principle 7, which focuses directly on clinical experiences, follows:

Guiding Principle 7: Clinical Experiences

The teacher preparation program provides clinical experiences to ensure that teacher candidates are able to demonstrate practices found to be effective in supporting student success in mathematics as defined in the CCSSM and other college- and career-ready standards.

Indicators of the guiding principle include:

1.   **7-A. Embedded, Early, Sequential, and Intensive Clinical Experiences:** The teacher preparation program provides teacher candidates with intentional and appropriate clinical experiences that begin early in their program and become increasingly intense as they progress through the program, focused on learning and demonstrating effective mathematical and educational knowledge.
2.   **7-B. Well-Supervised Clinical Experiences, Aligned with Program Goals:** The teacher preparation program provides supervision of clinical experiences based on a partnership between knowledgeable university faculty and master teachers of mathematics, who share a common vision of mathematics teaching and learning. (MTE-P, Revised 2014)

The Guiding Principles document contains other principles and indicators related to clinical experiences which focus on teacher candidates' content knowledge, disposition towards students, and awareness of equity issues. It is important to note that the Guiding Principles document served as one of the foundational documents for the writing of the *Standards for Preparing Teachers of Mathematics* (Association of Mathematics Teacher Educators, 2017).

The white paper provided a solid framework from which CERAC developed a fishbone diagram, "a tool that visually represents a group's casual systems analysis and is also known as a cause and effect diagram" (Bryk, Gomez, Grunow, & LeMahieu, 2015, p.198). The white paper also provided the initial driver diagram, which is a tool that visually represents a group's (NIC's) working theory of practice improvement, creates a common language, and coordinates the efforts among many different individuals joined together in solving a shared problem (Bryk, Gomez, Grunow, & LeMahieu, 2015, p.199). Table 1 contains the CERAC aim and driver diagram.

In the first column is the CERAC's aim, which focuses on teacher candidates' weekly implementation of the eight Mathematics Teaching Practices (MTPs) (National Council of Teachers of Mathematics [NCTM], 2014) during full-time student teaching field. NCTM's (2014) eight research-based Mathematics Teaching Practices (MTPs) delineate specific professional practices known to promote learning aligned with college and career ready content standards: 1) Establish mathematics goals to focus learning; 2) Implement tasks that promote reasoning and problem solving; 3) Use and connect mathematical representations; 4) Facilitate meaningful mathematical discourse; 5) Pose purposeful questions; 6) Build

Table 1. Components of the CERAC Driver Diagram

Aim	Primary Drivers (What)	Secondary Drivers (How)	Tertiary Drivers (Change Ideas)
During student teaching Teacher Candidates will use each of the eight Mathematics Teaching Practices (NCTM, 2014) at least once a week during full time teaching.	Transparent and coherent system of mentor selection and support	Increase the number of effective mentor teachers who are well versed in the CCSSM and MTPs.	The development of a professional development program related to mentoring mathematics teachers.
	Interdependency of methods course and early field experiences	Deliberate focus on connecting coursework of the methods course to the field experience of the candidates.	Provide ongoing professional development and course work related to the CCSSM and NCTM's MTPs.
	Student teaching as clinical training	Ensure self–assessment – feedback from TCs about student teaching experience.	
	Shared vision about teacher development	Establish collaborative meetings to negotiate conflicting beliefs and constraints relative to each partner.	Convene either face-to-face or online meetings to plan field experiences, articulate expectations, and reflect on norms and cultures within the class settings.
	Focus on access and equity	Develop infrastructures and clinical experiences that best meet the needs of the candidates.	

procedural fluency from conceptual understanding; 7) Support productive struggle in learning mathematics, and; 8) Elicit and use evidence of student thinking. Learning about the MTPs must be at the core of teacher preparation coursework and reflected in their clinical experiences. However, there are not enough mentor teachers at the secondary mathematics level prepared to foster the growth of teacher candidates, due to a lack of proficiency with this new approach to teaching, which is in alignment with the NCTM (1989, 1991, 1995, 2000, 2014) standards documents, particularly the eight MTPs. The quantity of potential mentor teachers who are well-versed in implementing the CCSSM and other college and career standards is limited, especially those regularly embedding the standards for mathematical practice into their teaching of content standards.

Even a cursory examination of the CCSSM and the MTPs reveals expectations for learning and teaching that are quite different from what is happening in many high school classrooms, and overwhelmingly so in the highest need schools, which remain more oriented toward shallow learning of formulas and algorithms (Flores, 2007; Strutchens, Quander, & Gutiérrez, 2011). While university coursework can provide knowledge about content and about teaching strategies, it is during clinical experiences that prospective teachers develop the craft of teaching—for instance, the ability to design lessons that involve important mathematical ideas, design or select tasks that will help students to access those ideas, and implement instructional strategies to successfully execute the lesson (Leatham & Peterson 2010a). Consequently, teacher candidates often find it difficult to learn to implement the MTPs advocated by NCTM (2014).

The primary drivers are in the second column of Table 1. Primary drivers represent the community's hypothesis about the main areas of influence necessary to advance the improvement aim (Bryk, Gomez, Grunow, & LeMahieu, 2015). The primary drivers in the diagram are as follows:

1. **Transparent and Coherent System of Mentor Selection and Support (Mentor Teachers and University Supervisors):** Organize mentor selection and support around deepening expertise with math content, math standards, MTPs, and mentoring strategies.
2. **Interdependency of Methods Course and Early Field Experiences:** Structure methods course assignments with a focus on MTPs and CCSSM such that they include engagement of mentor teachers.

3. **Student Teaching as Clinical Training:** Ensure that requirements for student teaching and feedback during student teaching emphasize the responsibility of teacher candidates to advance mathematics learning among secondary students through collaboration with more expert mentors in use of MTPs.
4. **Shared Vision about Teacher Development:** Ensure mutual agreement between district(s) and university about what quality teaching of secondary mathematics looks like and how to further skills of all teachers (including TCs) and see mentor teaching as part of a career ladder.
5. **Focus on Access and Equity:** Disrupt long-standing teaching practices that contribute to inequities in learning outcomes of students.

The secondary drivers are system components that are hypothesized to activate each primary driver change (Bryk, Gomez, Grunow, & LeMahieu, 2015). Table 1 shows the relationship between the primary drivers and the secondary drivers. Also included in Table 1 in the fourth column are tertiary drivers, change ideas that can help move the primary drivers forward. The tertiary drivers are action areas that the CERAC might address.

Organization of the CERAC

In order to meet their aim, the CERAC is made up of teams that contain representatives of the major stakeholders involved in clinical experiences. Each of the CERAC teams consists of at least one mathematics teacher educator, a mathematician, and a school partner. The CERAC is divided into three sub-RACs based on the three types of field experiences that CERAC is implementing to meet the goals that were set forth in their primary drivers and aim statement. The sub-RACs are: Methods, Paired Placement, and Co-Planning and Co-Teaching. In accordance with improvement science, each sub-RAC is implementing Plan-Do-Study-Act (PDSA) cycles based on goals and objectives. Below the components of the PDSA cycle are defined since this process is used as one of the most important tools for improving clinical experiences (Bryk, Gomez, Grunow, & LeMahieu, 2015, p. 122):

1. Plan
   a. Define the change.
   b. Make predictions about what will happen as a result.
   c. Design a way to test the change on an appropriate scale.
2. Do
   a. Carry out the change.
   b. Collect data and document how change was implemented.
3. Study
   a. Analyze the data.
   b. Compare what happened to predictions.
   c. Glean insights for next cycle.
4. Act
   a. Decide what to do next based on what you learned.
   b. Abandon the idea? Make adjustments? Expand the scale.

PDSA cycles help the CERAC to determine whether or not a change is actually an improvement and to move slowly in order to scale up more efficiently (Bryk, Gomez, Grunow, & LeMahieu, 2015). Moreover, PDSA cycles allow for opportunities to learn via practice, and is guided by three questions: "What is the group trying to accomplish? How will the group know that a change is an improvement? [and] What change can the group make that will result in an improvement?" (Lewis, 2015, p. 55). In addition to implementing PDSA cycles sub-RACs may create specific instruments to measure the effectiveness of the tools they develop and the particular field experience model they are studying. The assessments completed by teacher candidates across the sub-RACs include the Mathematics Teaching Practices Survey, the MTEP Completers Survey, and the MCOP2. Below is a description of each of the RAC instruments:

- **Mathematics Teaching Practices Survey (NCTM, 2014):** Is designed to monitor the extent to which teacher candidates have read, discussed, observed, planned, enacted, and received feedback on each MTP across the continuum. The teacher candidate will be asked to complete the survey multiple times throughout the continuum. The CERAC used a PDSA cycle to determine the correct format for the survey and to decide the best way to collect the data. The CERAC learned that the format for collecting the data was crucial in gathering usable data that could both inform institutions individually and collectively.
- **The Mathematics Classroom Observation Protocol for Practices (MCOP2):** Is a K-16 mathematics classroom instrument designed to measure the degree of alignment of the mathematics classroom with the standards for mathematical practice from the CCSSM (NGA & CCSSO, 2010); the NCTM (2000) process standards; and recommendations for undergraduate mathematics instruction. The instrument contains 17 items intended to measure three primary constructs (student engagement, lesson content, and classroom discourse) (Gleason & Cofer, 2014).
- **MTE-P Program Completer Survey:** Is designed for program completers to self-assess their success in developing the craft of teaching, based on the MTE-P Guiding Principles (MTE-P, 2014) and the mathematical teaching practices (NCTM, 2014). The survey also asks program completers to assess the success of their preparation program in alignment with the Guiding Principles, including their clinical experiences.

Teams work together via conference calls, email, and the Trellis (AAAS communication and collaborative platform). Dropbox and Trellis are used to share files and materials. CERAC has held several face-to-face meetings which included breakout meetings for sub-RACs. The sub-RACs have overlap areas that drive and focus the RAC, such as the emphasis on the effective Mathematics Teaching Practices (National Council of Teachers of Mathematics [NCTM], 2014), professional development for mentors related to the CCSSM and mentoring mathematics teacher candidates, and outcome measures. There are also specific goals to be attained within each of the sub-RACs. Each sub-RAC has developed its own specific research questions. The work of the CERAC is supported by NSF-IUSE collaborative grant entitled "Collaborative Research: Attaining Excellence in Secondary Mathematics Clinical Experiences with a Lens on Equity" (Project #1726362, #1726853, and #1726998). For the CERAC's purposes the concept of equity includes:

the fair distribution of material and human resources, intellectually challenging curricula, educational experiences that build on students' cultures, languages, home experiences, and identities; and pedago-

gies that prepare students to engage in critical thought and democratic participation in society. (Lipman, 2004, p. 3)

In this chapter, we report on the work of the Co-planning/Co-teaching and Paired Placement sub-RACs. The sub-RACs are designed to address issues with the traditional model for clinical teaching, also known as an apprentice-type model for clinical teaching. This model consists of a teacher candidate going into a mentor teacher's classroom for 8-15 weeks and gradually taking over the teaching responsibilities of the classroom. During this time, the teacher candidate receives feedback about his or her teaching practice from both the mentor teacher and the university supervisor. The success of the model depends upon many variables, one of which is the quality of the mentor teacher (Leatham & Peterson, 2010b). The teacher candidate depends on the mentor teacher to model effective instructional practices, to offer advice and helpful tips on facilitating student learning, to engage in reflection exercises, and to aid him or her in developing the craft of teaching. Nevertheless, finding sufficient numbers of quality mentor teachers, to ensure a meaningful clinical teaching experience for the teacher candidates, can be challenging. Limitations and challenges related to the traditional, apprentice-type model for clinical teaching highlight the need for researchers to explore other, non-traditional models for clinical teaching that may provide a more collaborative, reflective, and focused approach to providing a rich and meaningful culminating experience for teacher candidates. The paired placement model and the co-planning/co-teaching model are both approaches to student teaching that can lead to more progressive experiences for all stakeholders. Initially, the two sub-RACs worked parallel to each other and have shared ideas across sub-RACs during face-to-face meetings of the RAC as a whole. Each sub-RAC engaged in extensive literature reviews which informed their work separately. Thus, although there are some elements of the co-planning/co-teaching model that are shared with the paired placement model the groups have worked as separate but connected entities.

Co-Planning and Co-Teaching Sub-Research Action Cluster (Sub-RAC)

The CERAC's co-planning and co-teaching (CPCT) sub-research action cluster has made significant strides since the CERAC was formed in 2012. Being cognizant of differences that existed across programs (inclusive of differences in philosophical underpinning of school environment and university settings, challenges to recruit and retain teachers in schools which serve students from low income areas and have high mobility of teachers and students, limited professional development training provided to mentor teachers on new standard documents and curriculum materials, and minimal guidance provided of how to mentor teacher candidates) (Zeichner, 2010), the members of CERAC reviewed relevant literature across various disciplines to consider means to transform clinical experiences (Sears, Brosnan, Gainsburg, Oloff-Lewis, Stone, Spencer... Andreason, 2017). Co-teaching was deemed a promising change approach based on the success it facilitated in the field of special education (Bacharach, Heck, & Dahlberg, 2010). Based on the sub-RAC's use of improvement science, commitment to this work, and the results garnered thus far, they have found that CPCT is quite promising to transform the field of secondary mathematics.

As stated earlier the CPCT sub-RAC has employed an improvement science methodological approach to systematically scale up CPCT in secondary mathematics clinical experiences across multiple institutions, in different states. The CPCT sub-RAC goal was to increase the number of institutions that adopted CPCT into their mathematics education clinical experiences, in an effort to further promote effective mathematics teaching practices that provide each and every student with the opportunity to learn meaningful and useful mathematics. Therefore, the data garnered from the process and balancing measures provided insights into the extent the change idea of using CPCT during clinical experiences occurred. The change idea was considered to be an improvement for the educational system if the teacher candidates more readily demonstrated all of the NCTM (2014) effective teaching practices during their clinical experiences. Thus, to promote a change idea which resulted in improvement, members of the sub-RAC frequently reflected on variance within and across institutions in an effort to identify factors that can help or hinder the implementation of CPCT into mathematics education clinical experiences and revised our future PDSA cycles accordingly (Sears, Brosnan, Gainsburg, Oloff-Lewis, Stone, Spencer... Andreason, 2017).

Co-planning and co-teaching (CPCT) is a paradigm shift from traditional approaches to student teaching or as the sub-RAC refers to it in this paper as clinical experiences. The use of CPCT during enacted lessons can increase opportunities for both teacher candidates and mentor teachers' professional growth and job satisfaction, enhances teacher candidates' understanding of curriculum and instruction, and improves the academic performance of K-12 students with disabilities academic performance (Bacharach, Heck & Dahlberg, 2010; Dieker, 1998; Idol, 2006; Murawski & Dieker, 2003; Rea, McLaughlin & Walter-Thomas, 2002; Rice & Zigmond, 2000). Due to the benefits of CPCT, members of the CPCT sub-RAC, which is comprised of 11 institutions, infuse CPCT into clinical experiences for secondary mathematics teacher candidates. The goal of the CPCT sub-RAC is to enable mentor teachers and teacher candidates to carefully plan and subsequently use and focus on various co-teaching strategies throughout the clinical experiences. The sub-RAC focused on the following CPCT strategies: one teach, and one observe; one teach, and one assist; station teaching; parallel teaching; team teaching, and alternative teaching (Sears, Brosnan, Gainsburg, Oloff-Lewis, Stone, Spencer... Andreason, 2017). To promote CPCT as a viable model for the clinical experiences, members of the CPCT sub-RAC used an initial plan-do-study-act cycle (PDSA) that emphasized a need for professional development for the collaborative instructional pair (e.g., student teacher and mentor teacher) and university supervisors, measured the nature and extent of CPCT being implemented, and monitored the need for intervention support throughout the clinical experiences (Figure 1).

Moreover, the sub-RAC members have placed an emphasis on training and disseminating information about how to implement CPCT effectively. Initial findings indicate that even though the mentor teachers and teacher candidates perceived co-teaching to be beneficial because it increased opportunities for individualized instruction, they acknowledged a need for more subject-specific professional development (Sears, Brosnan, Oloff-Lewis, Gainsburg, Stone, Biagetti... Junor Clarke, 2017). Considering that there exists limited literature within the field of secondary mathematics education of how to employ CPCT during enacted lessons, the CPCT sub-RAC members have sought to provide practical instructional examples and insights into the complexities and challenges of implementing CPCT within the realm of secondary mathematics. Members of the sub-RAC are engaged in creating lesson plans and vignettes, and in writing articles for both research and practitioner audiences that illustrate how CPCT can be enacted within secondary mathematics settings. Additionally, the members have developed and facilitated CPCT professional development activities at their respective sites and assisted with data collection to provide insight into the nature of implementation of CPCT during clinical experiences.

In the subsequent paragraphs, an overview of literature pertinent to CPCT, a description of efforts to use CPCT within mathematics education clinical experiences, challenges that were encountered relative

Figure 1. Co-planning and co-teaching sub-research action cluster 2014 plan-do-study-act cycle

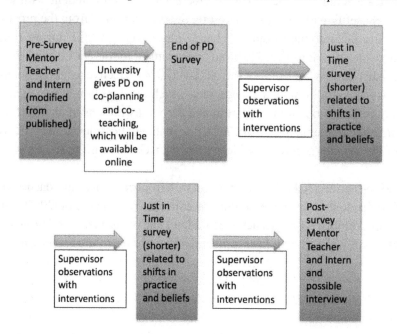

to the implementation of CPCT in secondary mathematics, and lessons learned thus far by the sub-RAC are provided.

Relevant Literature Pertaining to Co-Planning and Co-Teaching

There are various co-teaching strategies, inclusive of: one teach-one observe; station teaching; parallel teaching; alternative teaching; teaming; and one teach, one assist (Bacharach, Heck, & Dahlberg, 2010; Friend, & Cook, 2007; Sears, Brosnan, Gainsburg, Oloff-Lewis, Stone, Spencer... Andreason, 2017). During co-teaching, two teachers build a parity-based relationship by partnering together to facilitate the delivery and assessment of instruction to a diverse student population (Bacharach, Heck, & Dahlberg, 2010; Friend, Cook, Hurley-Chamberlain, & Shamberger, 2010; Kohler-Evans, 2006). Co-teachers share their instructional responsibilities, classroom spaces, and often engage in the negotiation of their roles to more readily use the expertise of all parties to promote students' academic success and closing achievement gaps that may exist (Friend, Cook, Hurley-Chamberlain, & Shamberger, 2010; Bacharach, Heck & Dahlberg, 2010). Thus, for the professional relationship between the teacher candidate and the mentor teacher to be perceived as co-teaching, the teacher candidate must be perceived and respected as a teacher in the classroom from the onset (Friend, Cook, Hurley-Chamberlain, & Shamberger, 2010). Administrative support (Scruggs, Mastropieri, & McDuffie, 2007), and professional development training is also needed to support teachers who seek to employ co-teaching (Cardullo & Forsythe, 2013). Cardullo and Forsythe (2013) noted that when co-teaching is adopted, professional development should be provided to inform mentor teachers and teacher candidates about their responsibilities, provide an opportunity to interact with each other, and address challenges that might be encountered (e.g., approaches to cultivate productive consultations) (Feiman –Nemser, 2001).

Co-teaching provides behavioral and academic support for students with and without disabilities (Scruggs, Mastropieri, & McDuffie, 2007), and has been proven effective in supporting English language learners (Pardini, 2006), and gifted students (Hughes & Murawski, 2001). According to Sileo and van Garderen (2010), co-teaching can benefit students with special needs because it enhances their confidence, self-esteem, academic performance, and relationship with their peers. Bacharach and Heck (2012) studied the impact of co-teaching on student achievement in an elementary mathematics and reading environment and found that the improvement in student performance was statistically significant.

Furthermore, co-teaching models can be beneficial to mentor teachers and teacher candidates (Sears, Brosnan, Gainsburg, Oloff-Lewis, Stone, Spencer... Andreason, 2017), because it encourages mutual support, sharing resources, and facilitates a partnership (Bacharach, & Heck, 2012). When co-teaching is employed it increases opportunities for personalized student instruction, promotes professional collaboration among teachers, fosters job satisfaction, and facilitates teachers overall professional growth (Sileo & Van Garderen, 2010). Teacher candidates value being introduced as teachers from the onset, being active in the classroom, and the professional bond that is established. Bacharach and Heck (2012) noted that:

students in a classroom that used the co-teaching model of student teaching statistically outperformed their peers in classrooms that were taught by either a single teacher or a mentor teacher and teacher candidate using a traditional model of student teaching in both reading and math. (Bacharach & Heck, 2012, p. 52)

The authors also reported that teacher candidates that engaged in co-teaching outperformed their peers on the state assessment measure for new teachers. Hence, co-teaching can be beneficial to students, mentor teachers, and teacher candidates.

Regardless of the co-teaching strategies that may be employed, it is essential that the instructional pair engages in careful planning of the lessons to identify the objectives that will be addressed, activities that will be used, and formative and summative strategies that will be employed (Scruggs, Mastropieri, & McDuffie, 2007). To better understand the fidelity of co-teaching, Bryant, Davis, Dieker, Pearl, and Kirkpatrick (2012) examined the nature of 755 co-teaching lesson plans and found that pairs planned together for 65% of the time, and one teach one assist was the most dominant approach employed. Although there are some challenges to effective co-planning (e.g., insufficient time), co-planning permits proactive discussions across the curriculum, use of varied instructional practices, utilization of various co-teaching models, and assessment of the CPCT models (which can be done by university supervisors and faculty members) (Murawski & Dieker, 2013).

Efforts to Advance Co-Planning and Co-Teaching in Secondary Mathematics Clinical Experiences

Since 2012, the CPCT sub-RAC has used improvement science to advance the goal of the NIC, and to increase the utilization of CPCT at multiple institutions. To measure the extent of our efforts we developed several instruments to measure the nature and implementation of CPCT during enacted lessons. Additionally, members of the sub-RAC participated in monthly virtual and annual face-to-face meetings, created modules and professional development training, and disseminated their work via multiple formats. In this section, activities in which the sub-RAC engaged to achieve their overarching goal are described.

Instrument Development to Measure CPCT

Weiss and Brigham (2000) suggested that there are problems with co-teaching research: Information about measures is omitted; only successful cases are reported; reports indicated that teacher personality was the critical variable in the success of the co-teaching; and subjective results are noted. Thus, "the future of co-teaching may be dependent on increasing the quantity and quality of research on it and placing co-teaching in the larger context of school reform and improvement" (Friend, Cook, Hurley-Chamberlain, & Shamberger, 2010, p. 10). Therefore, the CPCT sub-RAC sought to extend research related to co-teaching and address identified shortcoming of previous research by: (1) utilizing and sharing instruments used to measure the influence of co-teaching; (2) examining teacher candidates' experiences throughout their field-based preparation (i.e., practicum and internship), and; (3) examining the influence of professional development on the success of co-teaching. Thus, the CPCT sub-RAC created instruments to measure the nature of CPCT during clinical experiences, and the effectiveness of professional development that focused on CPCT. Particularly, members of the sub-RAC created the following instruments to obtain balancing and process measures relative to CPCT: Pre-survey, professional development survey, just-in-time survey, post-survey and mathematical practices survey. A brief description of the various instruments that were developed is described below:

- **Pre-Survey:** This survey asks respondents to rate the extent of their knowledge and ability to implement the Common Core Content Standards and the Standards for Mathematical Practice (CCSSO, 2010), strategies to teach diverse learners, perspectives about CPCT, and assessment practices using a Likert scale (Oloff-Lewis, Biagetti, Cayton, Grady, Stone, McCulloch, Edgington, & Sears, 2014a).
- **Professional Development Survey:** This survey asks respondents to describe the effectiveness of the training and their understanding of co-planning and co-teaching. Individuals are asked to rate their perceived knowledge about CPCT and the effectiveness of the professional development (Sutton, 2018).
- **Just-In-Time Survey:** This survey asks respondents to gauge their co-teaching experiences as the semester progresses using a Likert Scale. Individuals are asked to rate the quality of communication of the pair, the frequency of co-planning, benefits of co-teaching, and describe instructional norms. An additional comment section is included in the event individuals would like to elaborate on their experiences. There are two versions of the just-in-time survey, one for the mentor teachers, and the other for the teacher candidates (Sears, Maynor, Cayton, Grady, Stone, McCulloch, Edgington, & Oloff-Lewis, 2014).
- **Exit Survey:** This questionnaire includes open-ended questions to inquire about participants' experiences with co-teaching, interactions with collaborators, and the influence of the professional development (Oloff-Lewis, Biagetti, Cayton, Grady, Stone, McCulloch, Edgington, & Sears, 2014b).

Members of the CPCT sub-RAC have sought to garner data at their prospective sites and share observational findings during monthly and annual meetings, which are monitored longitudinally.

Accountability: Monthly Online Meetings and Annual Face-to-Face Meeting

In order to maintain momentum, and to promote a culture of accountability, holding frequent meetings of the members of the CPCT sub-RAC is vital (Darling-Hammond, 1989). Being cognizant that each faculty member has institutional and personal demands, in addition to the responsibilities required of them by the MTE-P, the sub-RAC members carefully plan meetings while being sensitive to time constraints. The sub-RAC members acknowledged that too many meetings could become burdensome, and too few meetings could potentially reduce the attention mathematics teacher educators placed on the implementation of CPCT during clinical experiences. Hence, a consensus was reached among sub-RAC members to hold a once a month, one hour, standing meeting, and that all parties would make a conscious effort to participate in a face-to-face annual meeting. During the monthly meetings, participants describe implementation challenges and complexities at their institution, reflect on data garnered, provide feedback to their peers, and identify factors that contribute to variances across the various sites. While at the annual meeting, the members of the sub-RAC reflect on the lessons learned across the year and create PDSA cycles to guide their efforts for the subsequent year.

Roles and responsibilities are assigned to all parties, and particularly a team leader has the responsibility to contribute to the sustainability of the efforts. For instance, members are assigned to be professional development facilitators, authors, data analysts, interviewers, and instrument developers. Giving each person a responsibility, empowered team members and increased opportunities for them to take ownership of the progress made.

Professional Development Training and Modules Development

To provide an overview of what CPCT is, and how it can be used to focus on students learning, members of the sub-RAC created three online training modules (Brosnan, 2014; Grady & Cayton, 2014; Grady & Cayton, 2016). These modules were disseminated among members of the sub-RAC and are currently accessible via Trellis, which allows for the sharing of multidisciplinary communications. Additionally, members of the sub-RAC facilitated a full-day professional development training at various sites for mentor teachers and teacher candidates. The instructional feedback on the professional development was rather positive. The data garnered from the pre-survey suggested preservice teachers perceived co-teaching to be quite promising. The preservice teachers noted,

I'll be able to learn how to influence more students in different ways, but finding which method works best for me will take some time. Preservice teacher 1, pre-survey - August 29, 2017

Benefits: More help and eyes in the classroom. Easier facilitation of ideas and activities with students and more support. Preservice teacher 2, pre-survey – August 29, 2017

Nevertheless, they also identified challenges of learning how to co-teach. Particularly they noted:

A challenge would be working with others. Preservice teacher 3, pre-survey – August 29, 2017

Learning how to work as a team and not having to remember every piece of information will be very beneficial. I also believe that it could help with teaching our strengths. Preservice teacher 3, pre-survey – August 29, 2017

The identified challenge of needing guidance as to how to enact co-teaching professional development was critical. Thus, the sub-RAC members sought to develop modules that can help individuals conceptualize how to co-teach. Highlights of the trainings were video recorded, and edited clips of the video recording will be accessible online. The creation of the modules and professional development training are needed to provide foundational insights for individuals seeking to adopt CPCT at their respective institutions, and to support instructional pairs who desire to diversify the CPCT strategies employed. As a result of the professional development, the following were perceived benefits:

I really enjoyed the training. I think that pairing pre-service and in-service teacher was incredibly helpful because it helped us see both perspectives. (Collaborating Teacher 1, Professional Development Survey – January 20, 2018)

Effective communication strategies to use with intern/mentor collaboration. (Collaborating Teacher 2 – Professional Development Survey – January 20, 2018)

I did learn some new information, and I like the presentation of strategies that I was not very familiar with and these can be implemented in the classroom.

I have FUSED in the past and unless it was a test day; both teachers were always up and moving. And this is a good strategy to share with the interning teachers from day one. (Collaborating Teacher 3, Professional Development Survey – January 20, 2018)

I enjoyed the activities that were provided for us to participate in throughout the day, and that we were able to learn multiple avenues to take with each strategy that we practiced together. (Preservice Teacher 4, Professional Development Survey – January 20, 2018)

Challenges

Even though the CPCT sub-RAC is a geographically dispersed team (GDT), the group does not face many of the same challenges that most GDTs face (Polzer, Crisp, Jarvenpaa & Kim, 2006; Gibson & Gibbs, 2006). For instance, a GDT might have poor communication, lack effective relationships, lack a common goal, and do not use technology. From the beginning, the CPCT sub-RAC faced two main challenges: 1) challenges within the sub-RAC relative to data collection and; 2) challenges in providing training at institutions across the sub-RAC.

Mathematics education is just one discipline among many subject-specific teacher education programs, which typically do not operate in a silo. Therefore, even if a faculty is willing to engage in our efforts, they may face resistance at their respective institution due to site-specific factors and norms, which may not easily be changed. Thus, in adopting change, it is important to reflect on the change idea in relation to the institutional norms that can potentially hinder or halt the idea from being implemented.

Challenges Within the CPCT Sub-RAC

The CPCT sub-RAC's primary challenge focuses mainly on the differences across the institutions, and how the members collect data and measure the impact of CPCT. Being cognizant that timelines for field experiences can vary across institutions, as well as institutions may use their own instruments, the CPCT sub-RAC was challenged to create and implement a common set of measures. The implementation of common measures requires the members of the sub-RAC to be flexible as to when the data is garnered, and how the data will be garnered. For instance, the survey questions may need to be added to a larger instrument used by a particular institution, and the timeline to collect data can vary across the fall and spring academic semesters.

Additionally, institutions have had uneven success in getting the instructional pairs to complete all survey instruments which makes capturing the fidelity of co-planning and co-teaching difficult. The instructional pairs acknowledged that too many instruments, and the time required to co-plan can be quite demanding. Hence, it is important that the end justifies the means, and the narrative used to market CPCT needs to be mindful of the amount of time required for an effective adoption.

Moreover, given that each institution was at a different stage of implementation of CPCT strategies, there existed variance in the nature of support needed at each institution. For example, while some institutions were piloting data collection with one teacher candidate, supervisor, and mentor teacher, other institutions had full implementation of CPCT. Hence, the CPCT sub-RAC readily reflected on the nature of the questions posed that guided their inquiry, and the systematic approach to collect data across the CPCT sub-RAC.

Institutional Challenges

Both teacher candidates and their mentors, need to be trained in the use of CPCT strategies. Each institution handles the professional development training of instructional pairs differently. As a result, the execution of CPCT varies tremendously across institutions. Furthermore, in order to accurately acquire data, all supervisors must be trained and calibrated using several instruments. Some states do not require that supervisors of secondary mathematics teacher candidates have a mathematics background, resulting in a smaller pool of qualified and trained supervisors who can collect data, which may lead to an overall reduction in the data.

Members of the CPCT sub-RAC also acknowledge that the cost to fund faculty to attend professional conferences to disseminate the work related to CPCT, and to attend the annual meeting can be expensive. Hence, we have frequently solicited grant funds to offset the cost, and hope that universities will support their faculty members as well.

Lessons Learned about the Use of Co-Planning and Co-Teaching During Clinical Experiences

Members of the sub-RAC found that CPCT can promote student learning and increase opportunities to engage in mathematical discourse between the instructional pairs. Nevertheless, there exists variance in the extent to which it is adopted across institutions. Despite differences across the sites, members of the CPCT sub-RAC have identified the need to provide professional development training to instructional pairs, and to support the use of CPCT throughout the clinical experience. Thus, the CPCT sub-RAC is now challenged to make resources readily available, via an online platform, to provide insights to the mathematics education community of how to unpack CPCT within the context of secondary mathematics clinical experiences.

Paired Placement Sub-RAC: Student Teaching Experience

To increase the quality of the student teaching experience and address the inadequate supply of quality mentor teachers to oversee the experiences, a sub-RAC was formed to focus on the paired placement student teaching model. In this model, a pair of student teachers work daily with an experienced mathematics mentor/coach who is devoted full time to helping the student teachers address the craft of teaching, plan lessons jointly, and teach those same lessons while actively observing, reflecting, and revising (Leatham & Peterson, 2010b). According to Leatham and Peterson (2010b), within this setting student teachers are slated to quickly realize not everyone learns the way they learn, and their focus shifts to the learning of their students rather than their own learning. For the past four years, the Paired Placement sub-RAC has been developing syllabi and workshop guides to help mathematics teacher education programs effectively implement the model across multiple contexts. The Paired Placement sub-RAC used PDSA cycles to refine the syllabi and workshop guides, and this process helped to refine and better guide the implementation of the paired placement model across multiple institutions. The different institutions within the sub-RAC are governed by individual state codes and other regulations related to clinical experiences, which forced the sub-RAC to develop syllabi, workshop guides, and other materials that could be adapted to different program contexts. Furthermore, the sub-RAC was challenged to both focused on the aim of the CERAC that "during student teaching Teacher Candidates (TCs) will use each of the eight Mathematics Teaching Practices (NCTM, 2014) at least once a week during full time teaching" and positive implementation of the paired placement model.

Selected Literature Related to the Paired Placement Model

Academic institutions in many countries have implemented a variety of field experience models for teacher candidates that are different form the traditional model. Paired field placements have seen an increase in England since the 90s (King, 2006). This field placement model requires teacher candidates to "work together in the same classroom, receiving joint mentoring, while sharing the timetable and collaborating on planning, teaching, and assessing" students' work (King, 2006, p. 371). Nokes, Bullough, Egan, Birrell and Hansen (2008) studied paired-placement internships of prospective secondary teachers, reporting that the student teachers learned through "tensions, dialog, and reflections" due to "being placed with a peer" (p. 2168). Results indicated students in these teachers' classrooms benefited from the collaboration of the teaching team. The push of the teachers to work through problems, along with the perturbation that comes from differences of opinion, led to better student understanding. In agreement, based on findings from a literature review focused on the paired placement model, Mau (2013) recommended placing pairs of student teachers with one mentor teacher and implementing a model of learning to teach that encourages collaboration, pedagogical risk taking, increased reflection, and better classroom management.

Even though this model has numerous benefits, Goodnough et al. (2008) identified pitfalls perceived by the teacher candidates, such as becoming dependent on each other in negative ways, not knowing who is in charge of managing the class, feeling a lack of individuality, and competing with each other.

Goodnough et al. (2008) also discussed perceived problems noted by mentor teachers, such as one of the teacher candidates becoming too dependent on the other one, the mentor teacher not feeling equally connected to both teacher candidates, the mentor teacher comparing the teacher candidates too much, and confusion as to which teacher in the room is in charge of managing the class. The authors claimed that the benefits far outweighed the possible pitfalls, which could be avoided if addressed from the onset of the experience.

More recently, academic institutions in Australia have also begun to implement field experience models that use paired placements. Australia's La Trobe University (LTU) Teaching School Model was developed from successful medical school models that have embedded clinical placements and Professional Development Schools in the United States (Lang, Neal, Karvouni, & Chandler, 2015). Additionally, principals from participating schools were heavily involved with the development of the model which resulted in a strong partnership between the university and the schools (Lang, Neal, Karvouni, & Chandler, 2015). The LTU Teaching School Model places pairs of teacher candidates in schools with one mentor teacher twice a week for one semester or one academic year. As a result, this model extends the number of professional field placement days for teacher candidates beyond the requirements set by the teaching regulation body (Lang, Neal, Karvouni, & Chandler, 2015). The benefits of the LTU Teaching School Model were bidirectional for teacher candidates and mentor teachers. Following their field placements, teacher candidates indicated that they had a greater appreciation of educational theory and greater knowledge of school workings (Lang, Neal, Karvouni, & Chandler, 2015). They also felt that they were better candidates for teaching positions and broadened their understanding of the role and requirements of the teacher in the school (Lang, Neal, Karvouni, & Chandler, 2015). Feedback provided from mentor teachers provided evidence that the Teaching School Model builds a community of educators. All of the mentor teachers indicated that they believed the extended placement and team-building approach allowed them increased opportunities to reflect on the teaching and learning that occurred in the classroom (Lang, Neal, Karvouni, & Chandler, 2015). Thus, the paired placement model has the potential to serve as a solution for several challenges for mathematics teacher education programs. Some of the challenges that could be addressed by using the paired placement model includes: decreasing the number of quality mentor teachers needed to support teacher candidates, improving the experience of student teaching for all stakeholders, and increasing the professional growth of all stakeholders.

Table 2. Pairs Implemented Per University for Fall and Spring Semesters 2013 – 2018

Semester	West University	Southeast	Central University
Fall 2013	1	0	0
Spring 2014	3	1	0
Fall 2014	0	0	0
Spring 2015	1	4	3
Fall 2015	0	0	0
Spring 2016	1	2	2
Fall 2016	0	0	0
Spring 2017	1	1	1
Fall 2017	1	1	0
Spring 2018	0	2	0

Efforts to Implement the Paired Placement Model in Secondary Mathematics Clinical Experiences

The paired placement sub-RAC is comprised of members representing five institutions. The sub-RAC focuses on the paired placement model for student teaching in which two prospective teachers are paired with a single mentor teacher. Teams are gradually implementing the model across the different universities. Below is a table showing the implementation of the pairs:

Members of the paired placement sub-RAC initially met through conference calls and Dropbox. Members of the sub-RAC discussed the pros and cons of the model and decided that it was worth trying out. Initially, the sub-RAC all agreed to try out the model with their strongest teacher candidates and mentor teachers. Sub-RAC members targeted mentor teachers with whom they had worked with extensively either through providing professional development, or they had gone through their graduate programs or both. The interns were selected based on their participation in classes, scholarly attributes, and work ethics. Sub-RAC members wanted to focus as much as possible on the execution of the model and not the differences in the participants. Sub-RAC members also thought carefully about the pairs of participants and their personalities. The West University team implemented the model fall 2013 and reported to the other teams about its findings. Spring 2014, other teams implemented the model. As teams implemented the model over the semesters listed in the chart they refined the syllabi, orientation materials and workshops to best meet the needs of the teams' contexts. Teams also worked with their participants to adjust the model within their context using PDSA cycles. Members of the teams monitored how well the three teachers worked together within the classroom, what timing and transitional issues needed to be addressed, and whether or not student learning was the primary focus of the three teachers within the paired placement setting. Now, teams monitor the process throughout the semesters. Teams meet via conference calls to discuss the results of the implementations and identify areas for change and improvement. Teacher candidates' journals; mentor teacher - university supervisor -and the pair debriefings which occur throughout the semesters; data from PDSA cycles; and teacher candidate observations and other university assessments are used to gather evidence of teacher candidates progress and the effectiveness of the model.

Paired placement sub-RAC workshop and orientation session protocols emphasize the major components of the model and the importance of the teacher candidates gradually implementing the eight mathematics teaching practices (NCTM, 2014). Below is a list of elements usually included in the sessions for both the mentor teachers and the teacher candidates:

1. Introductions (facilitators and participants)
2. Brief review of the Mathematics Teaching Practices (MTPs) (It is assumed that the students have learned about the practices throughout their program during their practicum courses.
   a. Read through the MTPs
   b. Watch a video to see how they are implemented in instruction
   c. Discuss the MTPs survey and the goals for the semester.
   d. Many of sub-RAC members also discuss the High Leverage Practices (HLPs)(http://www.teachingworks.org/work-of-teaching/high-leverage-practices) and ask the teacher candidates and mentor teachers to compare the two sets of practices. The HLPs include the MTPs and other practices that are essential to teaching and learning across disciplines.

3. Teams review the major elements of the paired placement model.
   a. There is always a lead teacher even though the three may plan together and assist students during the lesson.
   b. Pros and cons of the model, especially ways of preventing negative scenarios from happening, are discussed
   c. Benefits of the model, such as the opportunities to reflect on teaching, constant feedback, collaboration around student learning, and profession learning from other teachers in the room, are also discussed.
   d. Scheduling is another component of the model that is emphasized during the orientations and workshops:
      i. Need to meet state code requirements for teaching loads for both teacher candidates
      ii. Transition periods
      iii. Observations and other assessments
   e. Activities for the teacher candidates to do when they are not leading the lessons are also discussed:
      i. Assist the lead teacher
      ii. Purposeful observation tasks during a peer's lesson (The teacher candidate focuses on a certain aspect of teaching like discourse, student engagement, or questioning and reports findings during the debriefing of the lesson.)
      iii. Observe other mathematics teachers in the school.
   f. Purposeful times when the lead teacher (teacher candidate) has the opportunity to be in the classroom alone with the students to build management skills are also discussed.
4. Research related to the implementation of the model is also shared with the participants.
   a. PDSA Cycles
   b. Surveys
   c. Observations

Implementation of the Model Within Individual Universities

Three institutions have been actively implementing the model. The other institutions in the sub-RAC have participated in the development of the model but have not yet been able to implement it. A brief summary of the experiences at the three implementing institutions follows, followed by a summary of what was learned across the institutions.

West University

Efforts to revise the clinical experiences student teaching internship at West University began in March 2012. Representatives from two school districts and the university attended the initial MTE-P meeting in Atlanta and chose to focus upon providing future teachers with the opportunity to work with fewer more experienced mentor teachers by pairing the placements during the traditional student teaching 16-week semester. In-service sessions for the mentor teachers and university supervisors were provided in advance that allowed all to share questions and concerns about the model, which was a novel phenomenon to them. Co-planning lessons was essential, because for each lesson, there were three teachers in the room co-teaching the lesson–bouncing statements and questions off each other – in a classroom that was rearranged from rows to small groups of students with a focus on implementing the CCSSM's standards for mathematical practice in both theory and practice. One of the biggest obstacles was in overcoming the traditional model's hidden agenda that the teacher candidate should learn to survive on her or his own; and shifting to this new model's agenda of ensuring that each teacher candidate would learn to collaborate with others, to understand that the teacher does not know all, but works with her/his students to explain, to reason through problems together.

Team members at West University communicated that this craft of teaching was successful based on feedback received from teacher candidates, as exemplified in the following quotes from a teacher candidate:

I think the goal of the internship was to prepare my teaching partner and I to teach our own classes and collaborate with future colleagues. I also think the goal was to provide a better experience for the students, as they had access to multiple teachers and were able to get more one-on-one help. (Teacher Candidate, Spring 2014)

Another teacher candidate shared:

One time I took a risk when my mentor teacher suggested that I incorporate some type of group activity into my review lesson, so I developed a group activity that was a little more complex than I usually would have created. I created a lot more complex and meaningful tasks and activities that I possibly could not have come up with on my own. (Teacher Candidate, Spring 2014)

Central University

The paired placement model has been successfully implemented for three semesters at Central University. In spring 2015, they had three pairs, spring 2016 two pairs, and spring 2017 one pair. The decline in the number of pairs across the semesters was due to the number of teacher candidates and mentor teachers and nothing else. During each implementation, all pairs of teacher candidates were placed in the same mathematics department at the same school. No other models for student teaching were used at the selected school because program leaders believed that both the teacher candidates and the mentor teachers would be better supported if clinical teaching expectations and procedures were consistent within the school.

During each placement, the teacher candidates' level of teaching responsibility increased across a 14-week experience. The schedule started where collaboration as a trio (two teacher candidates and the mentor teacher) was emphasized, with the mentor teacher taking a lead role in all aspects of lesson planning, lesson implementation, and classroom management. During this time, the pair of teacher candidates took a secondary role. A few weeks into the experience, the role of the mentor teacher changed from a lead to a secondary role with an emphasis on facilitation of the pair of teacher candidates. During this time, the teacher candidates took the lead role working as a cohesive team by co-planning and co-teaching. They worked on lesson planning and implementation as a duo but relied on support from the mentor teacher to identify pitfalls and to strengthen weak aspects of their teaching. During the remaining weeks, the role of the mentor teacher remained the same, but the teacher candidates worked on formulating their individual teaching practices. They had to do so, however, in a uniform and syncretized manner to help ensure smooth orchestration of the classroom learning environment. During the last half of the 14-weeks, each teacher candidate took on full teaching responsibilities for five consecutive days. The other teacher candidate had focused assignments which included shadowing students, observing other mathematics teachers, interviewing students on their mathematical thought processes, and participating in a book study. The wide range of activities, increased level of responsibility, and multiple forms of support provided the teacher candidates a rich, complete, collaborative, and multi-focused clinical teaching experience that was very different from the traditional models. Below are quotes from participants which illustrate their experience and growth:

Ask for advice from each other, get input and encouragement from each other. This happened more at the beginning than at the end probably because we didn't see each other as much. Shared the grading, copying, covered each other's back. (Teacher Candidate, Spring 2015)

Toward the beginning we planned individually, but toward the end we started planning more together. We realized the importance of the two of us knowing how we each taught things and we had better ideas when we planned together. (Teacher Candidate, Spring 2015)

Collaboration was more intense at the beginning, but the option to comment on teaching remained throughout the whole experience. As the experience went on, we became more independent. We carpooled a lo,t and on the way back from school we could discuss the day. This helped us build community and reflect on previous days, ask each other questions and opinions. This helped us catch something that one didn't. (Teacher Candidate, Spring 2015)

Becoming professional teachers depends upon understanding that teachers model the behaviors they expect and demand from students and work in collaboration with partners across school districts and universities.

Southeast University

Team members at Southeast University had multiple constraints within their context, so they selected the teacher candidates and the mentor teachers carefully when they implemented the model. Thus, they use both the paired placement model and traditional model during the internship experience to meet the needs of their teacher candidates and to try an alternative model to student teaching. Mentor teachers who were selected to host paired teacher candidates either held advanced degrees from the program or had attended over 200 hours of professional development provided through projects directed by the secondary mathematics teacher education faculty at Southeast University. The program coordinator wanted to ensure that the mentor could assist the teacher candidates in developing the eight mathematics teaching practices. Team members provided two separate orientation workshops and sessions for teacher candidates using each model. During the paired placement workshop and orientation sessions, emphases are placed on the CCSSM (2010) Standards for Mathematical Practice and the NCTM (2014) Mathematics Teaching Practices, the craft of teaching as discussed by Leatham and Peterson (2010a), high leverage practices (Hill, Blunk, Charalambous, Lewis, Phelps, Sleep, & Ball, 2008), scheduling within the paired placement model, and pros and cons related to the paired placement model. Emphasis is also placed on the trio being cognizant of who will serve as the lead teacher for a given day. University required assessments and the assessments that are used across the CERAC are also discussed.

Student teaching at Southeast University lasts for 15 weeks in which the teacher candidate gradually takes on full responsibility for all of the mentor teacher's classes for twenty days, with ten of those days as consecutive days. This requirement of a full-teaching load is a state requirement. However, recently there has been more flexibility with the ten consecutive days being replaced with two sets of five consecutive days. Most of the pairs of student teachers have stated that planning their lead teaching schedule is the most difficult part of the experience due to the state regulations and the district holidays. Once the schedule for lead teaching and transitioning from teacher to each teacher candidate and from teacher candidate to teacher candidate is complete working with each other has gone well. Furthermore, coordinating the scheduling was one of the first improvements made as a result of implementing a PDSA cycle. Paired placement sub-RAC members learned that the pair of teacher candidates needed to be placed with the mentor teacher during their methods course prior to the internship experience so that the teacher candidates are familiar with the teacher and the school prior to the student teaching experience in order for the pair to be ready to take on teaching responsibilities quickly. Below is a schedule of rotation provided by one of the mentor teachers:

Week 1: Teacher candidates observe, help teach with homework, help with groups, etc.

Week 2: Teacher candidates co-teach with mentor teacher using mentor teacher's lessons

Week 3: Teacher candidates co-teach with co-planned lessons (transition week)

Week 4-Week 8: Teacher Candidate 1 takes main responsibility with Teacher Candidate 2 helping when needed or observing. Teacher Candidate 1's professional work sample (PWS) is completed during this time.

Week 9: Teacher Candidates co-teach with co-planned lessons (transition week)

Week 10-Week 14: Teacher Candidate 2 takes main responsibility with Teacher Candidate 1 helping when needed or observing. Teacher Candidate 2's PWS is completed during this time.

Week 15: Teacher Candidates co-teach with co-planned lessons (transition week)

Week 16: Teacher Candidates wrap-up, do more observations of other teachers, hand classes back to the mentor teacher. (The pairs usually begin one week earlier than the traditional model interns.)

The PWS that teacher candidates complete, is one of their assessments during student teaching. They are required to annotate their lesson plan, reflect on the lesson after a debriefing with their university supervisor, mentor teacher, and a peer who observed the same lesson, and discuss the students' understanding of the concepts taught. Quotes from teacher candidates participating in the model indicate that the model is affording the predicted opportunities for growth for the teacher candidates:

I am so glad that I got to have the experience of doing my internship alongside a peer. I truly believe that I learned more than I would have if I had been on my own. We constantly reflected with one another whether it was in the car to or from the school or in a more formal reflection time. (Teacher Candidate, Spring 2014)

We were continually talking to one another about our experiences.... After each class we talked about what worked and what didn't without realizing that we were reflecting on our teaching, which helped us improve. (Teacher Candidate, Spring 2014)

I also think this experience helped me to become a much more collaborative teacher. Before this semester I would have tended to simply work alone and not work with my fellow teachers. However, this semester I saw the importance of working with peers. It was so great when the three of us worked together with students' best interest as our priority. I saw first-hand that lessons ran more smoothly, and students benefitted the most when we all put input into how best to approach and teach a lesson. (Teacher Candidate, Spring 2014)

I think having the opportunity to collaborate and gain different perspectives and ideas from each other is the most beneficial part of paired internship. Not only having an experienced teacher is helpful, but also having another intern has been a major success for my learning during my internship. Mr. B. is full of wisdom about teaching and mathematics that I am so thankful to learn, but Jay has brought a unique perspective for me. Since he is also learning, he has been able to bring new ideas to the table and help me implement them. Through this we have been able to walk together through ideas that have failed and succeeded. I have truly enjoyed my paired internship and have been so thankful for this opportunity! (Teacher Candidate, Spring 2016)

Working together to better support the students has been great. One of the classes in particular needs more attention, and we are able to give it. It is also helpful to have two pairs of eyes watching me teach lessons during my first 10 days (from both a peer and a pro), as I feel like I am receiving genuine and helpful feedback from both. (Teacher Candidate, Spring 2018)

Additionally, there have been positive outcomes for the mentor teachers who have served as hosts for paired placements. Below are quotes from a mentor teacher:

Sought my colleagues' advice and tried to encourage collaboration in my department more after being a part of the experience.

Felt more accountable for holding teacher candidates to the mathematical teaching practices and mathematical practice standards and using them myself.

Encouraged the implementation of a social justice lesson.

Deep discussions: We constantly focused on lesson goals and standards, and discussions around assessment and proper measurements were a necessity. Little discussion was on classroom management.

1-1 vs. 2-1 placement: There was a sense of collaboration during discussions rather than a sense of critiquing or judgement. (Mentor Teacher, Spring 2015)

Overall, the paired placement model has gone well at Southeast University. Following are insights about the model from a university supervisor. This university supervisor was also a Ph.D. candidate in mathematics education and had previous experience teaching secondary mathematics. The supervisor had also recently completed a university supervisor apprenticeship with a mathematics teacher educator, which included supervising a teacher candidate individually and alongside the mathematics teacher educator. Although the apprenticeship was completed with a traditional internship model, the collaboration between the supervisor, mentor teacher, mathematics teacher educator, and teacher candidate provided the supervisor a perspective into collaboration and multiple perspectives also present within the paired-placement model. The following semester, the university supervisor was assigned one pair of student teachers; the assigned mentor teacher had previous experience implementing the paired-placement model. In order to meet the state requirement of 20-full time teaching days, a second mentor teacher was occasionally used. For example, while one teacher candidate completed her full-time teaching requirements within the primary mentor teacher's classroom, the other teacher candidate was able to teach approximately 2 to 3 class periods within the other mentor teacher's classroom. This provided the teacher candidate not completing her full-time requirements opportunities to teach mathematics and to still maintain a presence in the primary mentor teacher's classroom. Observations were planned in a manner that allowed the university supervisor to observe one of the candidates teach, while sitting alongside the second candidate. During the observation, the university supervisor and second teacher candidate often reflected and discussed possible improvements and strengths as related to the other teacher candidate's instruction. The university supervisor identified these unique observation opportunities as providing powerful learning opportunities. Following each observation, lesson debriefing included both interns, the mentor teacher, and the university supervisor. Given that all were provided equal opportunities to speak and reflect on the enacted lesson, a professional learning community of multiple perspectives developed. Lastly, the university supervisor observed an unspoken accountability between the interns to teaching using the Mathematics Teaching Practices. The university supervisor hypothesized that because both interns understood the teaching expectations, neither intern was willing to deviate from best practices due to the accountability of having their pair intern present.

Lessons Learned Across Universities

Through PDSA cycles and data collected from participants, the Paired Placement sub-RAC is learning much about the design, implementation, and monitoring of the model. As stated above, in one context state codes required that teacher candidates must teach full-time for 20 days during the internship and 10 of those days need to be consecutive. This individual constraint provided a good platform for discussion about maintaining flexibility of the model across institutions. The implementation of the model for consecutive years across institutions helped the sub-RAC reach numerous conclusions, some of which are: (a) placing teacher candidates with the mentor teacher for the clinical experience connected to the secondary methods course helps the teacher candidates to become familiar with the school environment, teacher's practices, and the students; (b) the peer-to-peer collaboration helps teacher candidates to assume teaching roles within the mentor teacher's classroom more rapidly; (c) the teacher candidates' anxieties regarding unfamiliar school contexts were eased largely because of the peer-to-peer support; (d) the teacher candidates needed to be clear to students who among the trio of teachers was the lead teacher, and; (e) to best support the students the teacher candidates need to be sure that their pedagogical approaches are aligned.

Another cross institutional finding is the importance of providing the non-lead teacher of the pair with targeted observation tasks. Various tasks across institutions were implemented and were adapted to meet the needs and constraints of the various programs. Some of the tasks focused on the lead teacher's orchestration of discourse including types of questions. Other tasks required the teacher candidates to investigate the students' mathematical thinking and problem-solving processes or identify techniques (like proximity) the lead teacher used for classroom management. Also included in the observation tasks were prompts for identifying particular students who were or were not participating in lesson activities and predicting reasons for lack of engagement. These focused observation assignments provided a better, and more focused, opportunity for each teacher candidate to be engaged in the teaching and learning process, and to analyze situations or contexts in which they may have previously not thought to observe.

Overall, the institutions involved in the Paired Placement sub-RAC agree the paired placement model has many advantages. Throughout their implementation of the model, the members of the sub-RAC have found that the paired placement model allows teacher candidates to better focus on student learning and the craft of teaching. The support of a peer who is exposed to similar experiences helps to bond the teacher candidates in ways that other models do not. Teacher candidates and mentor teachers who have experienced the paired placement model believe the model promotes both mentor teacher and teacher candidate growth in teaching as well as growth in the high school students' opportunity to learn and master mathematical content. Overwhelmingly, teacher candidates across all institutions stated that the paired placement model helped them to better understand the strengths of collaboration in teaching and has inspired them to be more collaborative in their own teaching practice. Across all universities, results indicate that the mentor teachers, teacher candidates, and students benefited from having three instructors in the classroom. The increased size of the teaching team allowed teacher candidates to focus more on how students learn mathematics and how students think about mathematics rather than classroom management and lesson planning.

Challenges of Implementing the Model

The challenges of implementation across the universities varied. Some of the challenges centered on individual state laws for clinical teaching, mentor teacher buy-in for the non-traditional model, and training university supervisors on the non-traditional model. At some institutions, the researchers have to play the role of university supervisors because the training for such supervisors had not yet been developed. Also, carefully pairing up the teacher candidates was cited as an attribute for successful implementation. Educating all stakeholders in the paired-placement model on possible situations that may arise and presenting possible solutions helps to better prepare all participants for challenges that might arise.

CONCLUSION

The CERAC is actively engaged in developing tools, testing clinical experience models, and analyzing the effectiveness of the tools and models on the development of teacher candidates' proficiency with the mathematics teaching practices. The sub-RACs have different foci and have accomplished different goals, however members of the sub-RACs have common interests in fostering effective field experiences for secondary mathematics teacher candidates. The work of CERAC has the potential to move the field forward. Team members have been pleased with the positive impact of the student focused and collaborative clinical experience models, co-planning and co-teaching and paired placement, that they have had the opportunity to explore in their programs. The CERAC members also see the work as scalable and transformative.

REFERENCES

Association of Mathematics Teacher Educators. (2017). *Standards for Preparing Teachers of Mathematics.* Available online at amte.net/standards

Bacharach, N., & Heck, T. W. (2012). Voices from the field: Multiple perspectives on a co-teaching in student teaching model. *Educational Renaissance, 1*(1).

Bacharach, N., Heck, T. W., & Dahlberg, K. (2010). Changing the face of student teaching through coteaching. *Action in Teacher Education, 32*(1), 3–14. doi:10.1080/01626620.2010.10463538

Brosnan, P. (2014) *Co-Planning/Co-Teaching Professional Development Module 1: Focus on Learning.* MTEP Meeting, Milwaukee, WI.

Bryant Davis, K. E., Dieker, L., Pearl, C., & Kirkpatrick, R. M. (2012). Planning in the middle: Co-planning between general and special education. *Journal of Educational & Psychological Consultation, 22*(3), 208–226. doi:10.1080/10474412.2012.706561

Bryk, A. S., Gomez, L. M., Grunow, A., & LeMahieu, P. G. (2015). *Learning to improve: How America's schools can get better at getting better.* Cambridge, MA: Harvard Education Press.

Capraro, M. M., Capraro, R. M., & Helfeldt, J. (2010). Do differing types of field experiences make a difference in teacher candidates' perceived level of competence? *Teacher Education Quarterly, 37*(1), 131–154.

Cardullo, V. M., & Forsythe, L. (2013). Co-teaching a new pedagogical practice for pre-service teachers. *School-University Partnerships, 6*(2), 90–96.

Darling-Hammond, L. (1989). Accountability for professional practice. *Teachers College Record, 91*(1), 59–80.

Darling-Hammond, L. (2010). Teacher education and the American future. *Journal of Teacher Education, 12*(1-2), 35–47. doi:10.1177/0022487109348024

Dieker, L. A. (1998). Rationale for co-teaching. *Social Studies Review, 37*(2), 62–65.

Duncan-Howell, J. A. (2010). Teachers making connections: Online communities as a source of professional learning. *British Journal of Educational Technology, 41*(2), 324–340. doi:10.1111/j.1467-8535.2009.00953.x

Feiman-Nemser, S. (2001). From preparation to practice: Designing a continuum to strengthen and sustain teaching. *Teachers College Record, 103*(6), 1013–1055. doi:10.1111/0161-4681.00141

Flores, A. (2007). Examining disparities in mathematics education: Achievement gap or opportunity gap? *High School Journal, 91*(1), 29–42. doi:10.1353/hsj.2007.0022

Friend, M., & Cook, L. (2007). *Co-teaching. In Interactions: Collaboration skills for professionals* (5th ed.). Boston, MA: Pearson.

Friend, M., Cook, L., Hurely-Chamberlin, D., & Shamberger, C. (2010). Co-teaching: An illustration of the complexity of collaboration in special education. *Journal of Educational & Psychological Consultation*, *20*(1), 9–27. doi:10.1080/10474410903535380

Gibson, C. B., & Gibbs, J. L. (2006). Unpacking the concept of virtuality: The effects of geographic dispersion, electronic dependence, dynamic structure, and national diversity on team innovation. *Administrative Science Quarterly*, *51*(3), 451–495. doi:10.2189/asqu.51.3.451

Gleason, J., & Cofer, L. D. (2014). Mathematics classroom observation protocol for practices results in undergraduate mathematics classrooms. *Proceedings of the Conference on Research on Undergraduate Mathematics Education*, *17*(1).

Goodnough, K., Osmond, P., Dibbon, D., Glassman, M., & Stevens, K. (2009). Exploring a tri model of student teaching: Teacher candidate and mentor teacher perceptions. *Teaching and Teacher Education*, *25*(2), 285–296. doi:10.1016/j.tate.2008.10.003

Grady, G., & Cayton, C. (2014). *Co-Planning/Co-Teaching Professional Development Module 2: Co-Teaching*. MTEP Meeting, Milwaukee, WI.

Grady, G., & Cayton, C. (2016). *Co-Planning/Co-Teaching Professional Development Module 3: Co-Planning*. MTEP Meeting, Atlanta, GA.

Guyton, E., & McIntyre, D. (1990). Student teaching and school experiences. In W. Houston (Ed.), *Handbook of research on teacher education* (pp. 514–534). New York: Macmillan.

Hill, H. C., Blunk, M. L., Charalambous, C. Y., Lewis, J. M., Phelps, G. C., Sleep, L., & Ball, D. L. (2008). Mathematical knowledge for teaching and the mathematical quality of instruction: An exploratory study. *Cognition and Instruction*, *26*(4), 430–511. doi:10.1080/07370000802177235

Hughes, C. E., & Murawski, W. A. (2001). Lessons from another field: Applying coteaching strategies to gifted education. *Gifted Child Quarterly*, *45*(3), 195–204. doi:10.1177/001698620104500304

Idol, L. (2006). Toward inclusion of special education students in general education: A program evaluation of eight schools. *Remedial and Special Education*, *27*(2), 77–94. doi:10.1177/07419325060270020601

King, S. (2006). Promoting paired placements in initial teacher education. *International Research in Geographical and Environmental Education*, *15*(4), 370–386. doi:10.2167/irg201.0

Kohler-Evans, P. A. (2006). Co-teaching: How to make this marriage work in front of the kids. *Education*, *127*(2), 260–264.

Lang, C., Neal, D., Karvouni, M., & Chandler, D. (2015). An embedded professional paired placement model: "I know I am not an expert, but I am at a point now where I could step into a classroom and be responsible for learning. *Asia-Pacific Journal of Teacher Education*, *43*(4), 338–354. doi:10.1080/1359866X.2015.1060296

Lanier, J., & Little, J. (1986). Research on teacher education. In M. Wittrock (Ed.), *Handbook of research on teaching* (pp. 527–569). New York, NY: Macmillan.

Leatham, K. R., & Peterson, B. E. (2010a). Purposefully designing student teaching to focus on students' mathematical thinking. In J. W. Lott & J. Luebeck (Eds.), *Mathematics teaching: Putting research into practice at all levels* (pp. 225–239). San Diego, CA: Association of Mathematics Teacher Education.

Leatham, K. R., & Peterson, B. E. (2010b). Secondary mathematics mentor teachers' perceptions of the purpose of student teaching. *Journal of Mathematics Teacher Education, 13*(2), 99–119. doi:10.100710857-009-9125-0

Levine, A. (2006). Will universities maintain control of teacher education? *Change, 38*(4), 36–43. doi:10.3200/CHNG.38.4.36-43

Lewis, C. (2015). What is improvement science? Do we need it in education? *Educational Researcher, 44*(1), 54–61. doi:10.3102/0013189X15570388

Lipman, P. (2004, April). *Regionalization of urban education: The political economy and racial politics of Chicago-metro region schools.* Paper presented at the Annual Meeting of the American Educational Research Association, San Diego, CA.

Martin, W. G., & Gobstein, H. (2015). Generating a networked improvement community to improve secondary mathematics teacher preparation: Network leadership, organization, and operation. *Journal of Teacher Education, 66*(5), 482–493. doi:10.1177/0022487115602312

Mathematics Teacher Education-Partnership (MTE-P). (2014). *Guiding Principles.* Retrieved on May 10, 2018 from http://www.aplu.org/projects-and-initiatives/stem-education/SMTI_Library/mte-partnership-guiding-principles-for-secondary-mathematics-teacher-preparation-programs/File

Mau, S. (2013). Letter from the editor: Better together? Considering paired-placements for student teaching. School Science and Mathematics, 113(2), 53–55.

Murawski, W. W., & Dieker, L. (2013). *Leading the co-teaching dance: Leadership strategies to enhance team outcomes.* Arlington, VA: Council for Exceptional Children.

National Council for Accreditation of Teacher Education (NCATE). (2008). *Professional standards for the accreditation of teacher preparation institutions.* Washington, DC: Author.

National Council for Accreditation of Teacher Education (NCATE). (2010). *Transforming teacher education through clinical practice: A national strategy to prepare effective teachers.* Washington, DC: Author.

National Council of Teachers of Mathematics. (1989). *Curriculum and evaluation standards for school mathematics.* Reston, VA: Author.

National Council of Teachers of Mathematics. (1991). *Professional standards for teaching mathematics.* Reston, VA: Author.

National Council of Teachers of Mathematics. (1995). *Assessment standards for school mathematics.* Reston, VA: Author.

National Council of Teachers of Mathematics. (2000). *Principles and standards for school mathematics.* Reston, VA: Author.

National Council of Teachers of Mathematics (NCTM). (2014). *Principles to actions: Ensuring mathematical success for all*. Reston, VA: Author.

National Governors Association Center for Best Practices & Council of Chief State School Officers. (2010). *Common core state standards for mathematics*. Author.

Nokes, J. D., Bullough, R. V. Jr, Egan, W. M., Birrell, J. R., & Hansen, J. M. (2008). The paired-placement of student teachers: An alternative to traditional placements in secondary schools. *Teaching and Teacher Education*, *24*(8), 2168–2177. doi:10.1016/j.tate.2008.05.001

Oloff-Lewis, J., Biagetti, S., Cayton, C., Grady, M., Stone, J., McCulloch, A., Edgington, C., Sears, R. (2014a). *Mentor Teacher Pre-Survey* [Survey instrument].

Oloff-Lewis, J., Biagetti, S., Cayton, C., Grady, M., Stone, J., McCulloch, A., Edgington, C., Sears, R. (2014b). *Mentee Exit Survey* [Survey instrument].

Pardini, P. (2006). In one voice: Mainstream and ELL teachers work side-by-side in the classroom teaching language through content. *Journal of Staff Development*, *27*(4), 20–25.

Polzer, J. T., Crisp, C. B., Jarvenpaa, S. L., & Kim, J. W. (2006). Extending the faultline model to geographically dispersed teams: How colocated subgroups can impair group functioning. *Academy of Management Journal*, *49*(4), 679–692. doi:10.5465/amj.2006.22083024

Putnam, R., & Borko, H. (2000). What do new views of knowledge and thinking have to say about research on teacher learning? *Educational Researcher*, *29*(1), 4–15. doi:10.3102/0013189X029001004

Rea, P. J., McLaughlin, V. L., & Walther-Thomas, C. (2002). Outcomes for students with learning disabilities in inclusive and pullout programs. *Exceptional Children*, *68*(2), 203–222. doi:10.1177/001440290206800204

Rice, D., & Zigmond, N. (2000). Co-teaching in secondary schools: Teacher reports of developments in Australian and American classrooms. *Learning Disabilities Research & Practice*, *15*(4), 190–197. doi:10.1207/SLDRP1504_3

Russell, J. L., Bryk, A. S., Dolle, J. R., Gomez, L. M., Lemahieu, P. G., & Grunow, A. (2017). A Framework for the Initiation of Networked Improvement Communities. Teachers College Record, 119(5).

Scruggs, T. E., Mastropieri, M. A., & McDuffie, K. A. (2007). Co-teaching in inclusive classrooms: A meta-synthesis of qualitative research. *Exceptional Children*, *73*(4), 392–416. doi:10.1177/001440290707300401

Sears, R., Brosnan, P., Gainsburg, J., Oloff-Lewis, J., Stone, J., Spencer, C., . . . Andreason, J. (2017). Using improvement science to transform clinical experiences with co-teaching strategies. In L. West and M. Boston (Eds.), Annual Perspectives of Mathematics Education (APME) (pp. 265–274). Reston, VA: National Council of Teachers of Mathematics.

Sears, R., Brosnan, P., Oloff-Lewis, J., Gainsburg, J., Stone, J., Biagetti, S., . . . Junor Clarke, P. (2017, January 3-7). *Co-Teaching Mathematics: A Shift in Paradigm to Promote Student Success*. Research report presentation at the Hawaii International Conference on Education, Honolulu, HI.

Sears, R., Maynor, J., Cayton, C., Grady, M., Stone, J., McCulloch, A., Edgington, C. & Oloff-Lewis, J. (2014). *Mentee Just in Time Survey* [Survey instrument].

Sileo, J. M., & van Garderen, D. (2010). Creating optimal opportunities to learn mathematics: Blending co-teaching structures with research-based practices. *Teaching Exceptional Children, 42*(3), 14–21. doi:10.1177/004005991004200302

Strutchens, M. E., Quander, J. R., & Gutierréz, R. (2011). Mathematics learning communities that foster reasoning and sense making for all high school students. In M. E. Strutchens & J. R. Quander (Eds.), *Focus in high school mathematics: Fostering reasoning and sense making for all students* (pp. 101–114). Reston, VA: National Council of Teachers of Mathematics.

Sutton, J. (2018). *Professional development survey* [Survey instrument].

Tschida, C., Smith, J., & Fogarty, E. (2015). "It just works better": Introducing the 2:1 model of co-teaching in teacher preparation. *Rural Educator, 36*(1), 11–26.

Weiss, M. P., & Brigham, F. J. (2000). Co-teaching and the model of shared responsibility: What does the research support? *Advances in Learning and Behavioral Disabilities, 14*, 217–246.

Zeichner, K. (2010). Rethinking the connections between campus courses and field experiences in college- and university-based teacher education. *Journal of Teacher Education, 61*(1-2), 89–99. doi:10.1177/0022487109347671

Zeichner, K., & Bier, M. (2015). Opportunities and pitfalls in the turn toward clinical experience in US teacher education. In E. R. Hollins (Ed.), *Rethinking clinical experience in teacher candidate education* (pp. 20–46). New York, NY: Routledge.

KEY TERMS AND DEFINITIONS

Co-Planning and Co-Teaching: Is an approach to clinical experiences where the teacher candidate and the mentor teacher co-share the responsibilities related to teaching and learning in a classroom.

Mathematics Teaching Practices: Teaching strategies espoused by the National Council of Teachers of Mathematics to support students' development of the standards for mathematical practice.

Mentor Teacher: Is a person who supports the growth and development of a teacher candidate during a clinical experience in the schools.

Network Improvement Community: Is a group of people with a common aim and who uses improvement science to solve a problem of practice.

Paired Placement: Is a clinical experience approach in which two teacher candidates are placed with one mentor teacher, and the candidates have the opportunity to learn from each other as well as receive support from their mentor teacher.

Research Action Cluster: A subgroup of a network improvement community focused on developing an understanding of a particular problem of practice through improvement science.

Secondary Mathematics Teacher Candidates: Are undergraduate or post-baccalaureate students preparing to teach in grades 6-12.

Student Teaching: Is the phase of teacher candidates' programs when the candidates spend 10 to 15 weeks in a school setting to learn about teaching at the grade level or course level they desire to teach upon completion of their program.

Chapter 3
Recruiting Teachers of Mathematics
Lessons From an Alternative Route to Licensure

Mary D. Burbank
University of Utah, USA

Andrea K. Rorrer
University of Utah, USA

Wynn Shooter
University of Utah, USA

ABSTRACT

Calls for recruitment and retention into teaching remain at all-time highs in math and science. Response initiatives may include alternative routes to licensure (ARL), streamlined curricula, financial incentives for participants, and intensive on-the-job training. While ARLs offer potential for innovation, challenges also exist when trying to maintain preparation quality and integrity. This project presents end-of-program findings from a five-year investigation into the factors that contribute to quality teacher preparation within an ARL framework. Summative outcomes document program dimensions where research-intensive preparation goals align with priorities for increasing the pool of future teachers. The roles of teacher mentors, curriculum impact, and classroom-based practica are highlighted.

INTRODUCTION

Calls for increased attention to the recruitment and retention of teachers remain persistent (Aragon, 2016; Ingersoll, 2011; Ingersoll & Perda, 2010; Papay, Bacher-Hicks, Page, & Marinell, 2017; Rich, 2015). While many recruiting efforts reside within the higher education settings, attached to a bachelor's or master's degree pathway, "alternative programs" have gained traction (e.g., Math for America, Teach for America, Utah State Board of Education, 2017). Programmatic characteristics often include

DOI: 10.4018/978-1-5225-6249-8.ch003

streamlined curricula, limited courses, financial incentives for participation, and intensive on-the-job training opportunities.

While recruitment and retention efforts are expanding, preparation must also ensure quality varied credentialing experience (Desimone & Long, 2010; Foote, Brantlinger, Haydar, Smith, & González, 2011; Heilig & Jez, 2010; Walsh & Jacobs, 2007). The goal of quality preparation is particularly important because many responses to teacher shortages such as Alternative Routes to Licensure (ARL) have had mixed results to date, including variance in program experiences, retention outcomes among graduates, and impact on diverse communities (Heilig & Jez, 2010; Laczko-Kerr & Berliner, 2002; Sass, 2013). Moreover, higher education settings recognize that adequate preparation of teachers, prior to entering the field, is necessary particularly because first-year teachers who arrive to the classroom underprepared are less effective and less likely to remain in the field, over time (Clotfelter, Ladd, & Vigdor, 2010; Goldrick, Osta, Barlin, & Burn, 2012).

This study highlights a summative analysis from a five-year investigation into the nuanced factors that contributed to teacher preparation in one university-based ARL program. Where Year 1 included program development and a streamlined pilot year, outcomes from Years 2-5 document components of an ARL program including both the merits and the limitations of efforts to recruit teachers. These finding are particularly critical within the context of climate, which forces efficiencies to increase and strengthening the pool of future teachers in science and math. Data include outcomes from years two through five of our work.

Project results suggest several programmatic strengths including overall curriculum adaptations, dedicated field experiences, mentoring and relationship building, and ongoing professional development. Findings also include several areas identified as in need of improvement (e.g. curriculum nuances, practicum experiences with diverse students, and opportunities for work with families and communities).

BACKGROUND

Debates regarding teacher quality and what counts as quality preparation have increased over the past two decades. In an attempt to resolve these debates, policy mandates, such as No Child Left Behind Act (2002) outlined the qualifications of those working in schools and the standards by which they are deemed qualified. Attention to the linkages between content knowledge and pedagogy became central to examinations of preparation and program quality (National Mathematics Advisory Panel, 2008) and have remained central within national conversations. Moreover, quality indicators have expanded to more comprehensive evaluations that include teacher preparation programs and their impact on teaching and learning (Dillon & Silva, 2011; Eaton, 2011; National Council on Teacher Quality, 2014; 2017).

Beginning with the premise that teacher quality is a significant predictor of student outcomes, research continues to address program attributes that produce the "best" teachers (Coggshall, Rasmussen, Colton, Milton, & Jacques, 2012; Rice, 2003). A review of research on teacher preparation suggests several characteristics of exemplary programs. For example, evidence suggests that programs must include deliberate preparation dimensions that equip teacher candidates with the skills to deliver content areas in ways that students understand, while simultaneously aligning with curriculum standards (Ball & Forzani, 2010; Ball, Themes, & Phelps, 2008; Ingersoll & Strong, 2011; Ma, 1999).

The need for quality curricula and dedicated attention to pedagogy are commonplace within education communities and are identified as essential for excellence in teaching. Further, beyond the nuances of content area preparation, effective programs must also include: A defined program vision that reflects broad-based goals related to teaching and learning, an understanding of learner differences, and strategies for teaching that link to these more global goals. Related to field experiences, the classrooms and schools in which training takes place must resemble the range of classrooms in which teachers are employed. Dedicated work with language learners and diverse student populations are specific areas that programs must consider in their development. Finally, an established curriculum with attention to critically reflective practices provides a foundation for teachers to consider the technical elements of their teaching practices, as well as more broad-based issues that situate P-12 education (Burbank, Ramirez, & Bates, 2016). While technical skill development in teacher preparation is essential (e.g., lesson planning and assessment), teachers must also be able to consider the unique needs of each learner, their backgrounds, and the impact of communities on their daily work.

Historically, quality focused primarily on the technical dimensions of teaching in areas, such as lesson planning, test construction, and basic classroom management. Today, educators must also consider how changing demographics, the role of standardized assessment, and data-based decision making are expected components of educators' work (Ball & Forzani, 2010; Boyd, Grossman, Lankford, Loeb, & Wyckoff, 2009; Darling-Hammond, 2006, 2010; Harris & Sass, 2011).

Tethered closely to programmatic components of educator preparation are the characteristics educators must possess to be effective in their work with students in P-12 classroom. Areas such as beliefs, attitudes, expectations, and skills, when working with all students, have a documented history regarding their impact on student learning. In fact, researchers have identified these areas as among the most important school-based predictors of student achievement (Holzberger, Phillipp, & Kunter, 2013; Klehm, 2014; Rice, 2003; Stipek, 2002; Wayne & Young, 2002).

The range of factors that impact preparation quality must remain central to recruiting and retention efforts. Unless these areas are made priorities, they have the potential to become an afterthought to the more urgent needs to fill vacant positions. This challenge may be particularly critical for alternative routes, where efficiencies and expediency in recruiting drive program development and implementation.

In light of current research, contemporary programs which are focused on recruitment and retention face numerous challenges, particularly in high need content areas, such as mathematics and science. First, those involved in teacher preparation must identify ways to make the teaching profession attractive to would-be candidates. Actions designed to reach this goal may require reforming the types and nature of the programs which are offered. Next, while it is important to expand the pool of candidates, program designs must maintain a robust content emphasis while ensuring that candidates demonstrate content competencies in response to all students and the environments in which they reside.

Alternative Routes to Licensure

A challenge facing traditional university preparation is to increase teaching candidates, while remaining steadfast in their commitments to research-based programs. The environment is further complicated when as market-based programs have entered the credentialing arena.

While an increase in the number of teacher preparation programs offer a practical solution to market demands, programs must also acknowledge their sometimes divergent agendas (Boyd, Goldhaber, Lankford, & Wyckoff, 2007; Walsh & Jacobs, 2007). For example, recruiting into math and science has often included a range of program options (e.g., Math for America, Teach for America). These nontraditional teacher education programs and others, which may be affiliated with state Math-Science Partnership and National Science Foundation projects, procure new pathways for teacher education (Robelen, 2011) have entered the preparation arena, in part, to increase the number of teachers. Yet, it is unclear whether their dimensions align with critical areas which are identified as highly effective components of quality teacher preparation (e.g., curricula, field experiences, and mentoring) (Darling-Hammond, Holtzman, Gatlin, & Heilig, 2010).

Research and practice underscore that teacher preparation must include course work and related experiences that prepare educators to work with a range of learners and their communities (e.g., English learners and children with disabilities). Recommendations for quality preparation often address pedagogical skill development, attention to lesson delivery, attitudes, and beliefs about teacher and student efficacy.

Alternative Routes to Licensure emerged in the early 1980s as a response to teacher shortages, particularly in math and science (Wayman, Foster, Mantle-Bromley, & Wilson, 2003). To date, 47 states have ARL sanctioned programs. Reportedly, up to one-third of teachers nationwide now enter the field through an alternative route (Grossman & McDonald, 2008; Kee, 2012; Alternative Teacher Certification Guide, 2018). The explosion of ARL programs has led to considerable program variation. While some practitioners, policymakers, and scholars alike have suggested that ARL programs are a valuable solution to getting teachers into schools, others have decisively criticized them.

Differences in program design and implementation are among the most frequently highlighted limitation of ARL programs (Boyd, Grossman, Lankford, Loeb, & Wyckoff, 2009). Specifically, empirical studies of ARL efforts report wide variation in requirements, implementation, and effectiveness (Darling-Hammond, Chung, & Frelow, 2002; Goldhaber & Brewer, 1999; Grossman & McDonald, 2008; Henry, Purtell, Bastian, Fortner, Thompson, Campbell, & Patterson, 2013; Kee, 2012; Qu & Becker, 2003; Sass, 2013; Scherer, 2012). Scholars cited dedicated preparation in pedagogy as among the least effective components of many programs with marked weaknesses within alternative programs (Wayman, Foster, Mantle-Bromley, & Wilson, 2003). Areas deemed essential include a teacher's ability to understand and respond to differences in learner ability, language, culture, and development.

The next section includes key end-of-program findings from a five-year initiative designed to increase the number of mathematics teachers. Project data illustrate the strengths and limitations of an alternative preparation program in alignment with research on effective teaching in secondary mathematics classrooms. Findings are presented in light of what research describes as critical components in teacher preparation (Boyd, Grossman, Lankford, Loeb, & Wyckoff, 2009; Darling-Hammond, 2006).

METHOD

Research Objectives

The primary research and evaluation objectives of the Recruiting into Math Teaching Initiative (RIMTI) were to: Identify program engagement and support received by participants, both as preservice teachers and during their early years as in-service teachers; understand the role of mentors; examine elements of professional cultures that contributed to the success of these beginning teachers; evaluate the impact of the RIMTI program on graduates' preparedness and effectiveness as secondary mathematics teachers. The Utah Education Policy Center (UEPC), a university-based research center at the University of

Utah, evaluated the program at various intervals. This research center served as an external evaluator of RIMTI where findings addressed the impact of the RIMTI program.

Program Overview

At the University of Utah, a 2010 a multitiered collaborative was initiated to increase the number of teachers in secondary level mathematics. Multiple project partners included a National Science Foundation (NSF) Robert Noyce Gant, private foundations, the Utah State Board of Education, and the University of Utah. Stakeholder resources provided support for the RIMTI which was linked to the Colleges of Education and Science and local school districts. The long-term goals of RIMTI were to: a) Increase the number of secondary level mathematics teachers, and; b) improve the quality of 6-12 mathematics education in schools.

Specific components of the RIMTI included a nontraditional licensure format that was adopted as university-state board of education ARL program. The course of study included an adapted curriculum, financial support for preservice teachers (i.e., Fellows), in-depth mentoring and professional development, and multiyear support for both Fellows and Mentors. Successful Fellow applicants met a series of admissions criteria (i.e., completed bachelor's degree, graduate school acceptance, demonstrated mathematics skills via Praxis performance on test numbers 5161 and 0063, written personal statement, letters of recommendation, and successful in-depth interviews and teaching demonstrations-i.e., individual and group interviews). Praxis test performance requirements aligned with Utah minimum scores.

The academic program into which Fellows were admitted is a Masters of Mathematics Education with secondary level teaching licensure. Fellows also made a five-year-teaching commitment in the state's secondary schools (i.e., grades 6 through 12), and were provided with scholarship and stipend support. Fellows were assigned a paid mentor who served in the position over multiple years at the preservice and in-service levels. Each Mentor also received a $5,000 stipend, for mentoring Fellows during student teaching experience, and an additional $2,500, during the RIMTI Fellows' second year, as employed full-time teachers.

Participants

The project participants included RIMTI Fellows, Mentors, and current principals. Thirty-four RIMTI Fellows were preservice teachers whose demographics included 31 White, two Latina/o, and one Asian student. Of the participants, 59% were female and 41% male. The Fellows' ages were in the range 25-45. Participating Mentors agreed to a five-year commitment to the program and to teach mathematics in a Utah State secondary school for four of those years. Year 1 included the preparation component of the RIMTI effort.

Twenty-seven Mentors worked with the Fellows in middle and high schools, and 29 principals rounded out the participant group. Mentors were selected based upon teaching experience, work with student teachers, and teaching within diverse communities. Among RIMTI Mentors, 90% taught between 6 and 11 years, with 8% having taught from between two and five years, and 4% who were not actively teaching. Ninety-six percent had worked with student teachers in the past at the middle or junior high or high school levels. Two-thirds of mentors were women and one-third, men.

As project participants, Mentors were required to meet regularly with their Fellow, formally observe lessons, and attend various meetings with their Fellow, over the first two years of the Fellow's experience. Principal participation in survey completion was voluntary.

In addition to the RIMTI mentoring support, a university supervisor conducted multiple classroom observations of all Fellows over the course of a year and completed a final student teaching equivalent following the Fellows' first year in the classroom.

Year 2: Program Implementation

During year two, Fellows completed course work as part of graduate degree in mathematics teaching through a traditional mathematics department, and licensure course work through a college of education. While the master's degree content course work may have been completed over multiple years, licensure course work was required during the first year. In addition to course work, Fellows also engaged in a supervised teaching experience under the direction of a Mentor for 12 hours a week, during which they observed and taught micro lessons within the context of their Mentor's classroom.

Year 2 professional development activities included monthly cohort meetings for both Mentors and Fellows. Topics included bi-yearly and summer workshops, as well as additional experiences which were focused on content and pedagogical instruction. Activity topics included collective math problem solving and pedagogical training. Mentors received tips designed to strengthen their advising and mentoring support. They were also provided with suggestions to develop a professional support network.

Curriculum

Curriculum during Year 2 included 21 hours of course work, where the content aligned with master's degree requirements in mathematics, with a specific focus on mathematics for classroom teachers. Specific mathematics courses included, but were not limited to, foundations of algebra, foundations of geometry, multivariate calculus, probability and statistics, history of mathematics, and differential equations.

Licensure course work included general state licensure courses addressing classroom management, technology for secondary classroom teaching, inclusion in secondary classrooms, multicultural education, and general pedagogy. As an alternative route, the RIMTI curriculum was deliberately streamlined from traditional program of the campus as a feature of efficiency. At the end of Year 2, Fellows were recommended for a state teaching license following the successful completion of student teaching and course requirements.

Years 3-5

During Year 3 Fellows were hired as full-time in-service teachers. Some individuals continued taking mathematics course work as a requirement of the master's degree. Fellows also received ongoing support from their Mentors. Years 3-5 included varied levels of support and network development, including meetings and layered professional development. During Year 4, formal Mentor support was no longer included, but networking was available for those who were interested in maintaining connections.

Data Analysis

Participants' perspectives on their experiences were evaluated through focus groups and surveys. Findings were used to determined program impact. The intent of this design was to gain insights into participant perceptions of Fellows' preparation and to elicit the observations of those familiar with the Fellows' teaching practices (i.e., Mentors).

Mentors were asked to report on the support they provided to Fellows. Fellows were asked to evaluate areas where they believed they were prepared and effective as early-career classroom teachers. The surveys were distributed at the end of Year 2 of program implementation to: 1) RIMTI preservice teachers; 2) RIMTI Mentor teachers, and; 3) school Principals where the RIMTI Fellows taught. Survey response rates were 88% among RIMTI Fellows, 81% among Mentors, and 14% among Principals.

Surveys

Survey questions for Fellows addressed views on multiple program areas, including the support provided by Mentors and peers, course work, readiness to teach, support provided at school sites, and usefulness of various professional development activities (e.g., a summer institute, workshops seminars, and monthly cohort meetings). Course work survey questions addressed the standard program of study at the University of Utah. The open-ended survey questions prompted participants to expand their responses and to elaborate on their feedback on specific survey questions. We analyzed quantitative survey data using descriptive statistics.

Survey focal areas also included comments on specific courses or course-related themes (e.g., working with language learners), class assignments (e.g., action research), classroom management, and overall perceptions of preparedness to work with a range of learners. Fellows identified the degree to which they were confident in their mastery of mathematics content and in their ability to translate that content to student learners.

During the third year of project implementation, we held focus groups with Mentors and Fellows (i.e., two groups with Fellows to accommodate group size, and one with Mentors). The goals of data collection were to determine program impact as well as the extent of professional relationships between the preservice and in-service teachers over time.

Focus Groups

In addition to the survey, a convenience sample was conducted with three focus groups. The focus groups took place at the end of the program to ascertain its progress, gather programmatic feedback, and document participant growth over time. Two of the focus groups were conducted with 16 Fellows and one with nine of their Mentors. For the Fellows, the questions prompted participants' reviews of elements of the RIMTI that impacted overall support and mentoring, structures within school contexts that enhanced Fellows' experiences, and perceptions of their effectiveness. For the Mentors, the focus group questions addressed the training they received to serve as Mentors, types of and adequacy of the support they received, goals and expectations for working with the Fellows, predictions of the Fellows' success, levels of participation in the RIMTI professional development, and how and in what ways their involvement in the RIMTI impacted the Mentors in their work.

We coded qualitative focus group data and open-ended survey responses first using constant comparative methods, which consist in an open coding process (Charmaz, 2006; Glaser & Strauss, 1967; Strauss & Corbin, 1998). During this phase of the analysis, we began with an initial round of descriptive and in vivo coding (Marshall & Rossman, 2016). These phrases represented the major data themes. Examples of these codes included preparedness and professional development. Next, using axial coding, we looked for subthemes. For example, mathematics content and general teaching content were situated within the larger theme of preparedness.

RESULTS

Teacher educators at the University of Utah developed RIMTI as an innovative alternative to both traditional teacher preparation programs and to other alternative routes. Specific goals included: Identifying the effectiveness of specific program components including the support preservice teacher participants received during preparation experiences and early years as in-service teachers; understanding the role of Mentors; examining elements of professional cultures that contributed to the success of these beginning teachers; evaluating the impact of the RIMTI on graduates' preparedness and effectiveness as secondary mathematics teachers.

Project findings highlight promising project dimensions as well as areas in need of further attention. Results are organized along key themes of programmatic curriculum, professional development and growth, school embedded experiences, and impact on Mentors. Findings present insights on alternative program components that impact overall quality.

Curriculum of the Recruiting Into Math Teaching Initiative and Fellow Preparedness

As part of the program degree requirements, the Fellows completed coursework for a Master's of Mathematics Teaching degree, including a teaching license. Mathematics content requirements were designed to prepare individuals to teach both general and advanced level mathematics in grades 6 through 12. As a result of the streamlined curricular focus of the RITMI, its participants completed fewer courses with dedicated attention to language learners, including limited opportunities for classroom-based work with children learning English under the direction of an experienced educator.

At the end of their preparation program, overall the Fellows reported feeling prepared to teach secondary mathematics with specific curricular references. The Mentors largely agreed with the Fellows' self-assessment. The results of the focus groups and surveys suggested that the Fellows had the most confidence in their preparedness around mathematics competency, mathematics teaching, and general classroom practices such as strategies for content delivery and technology integration. Many Fellows reported mastery of mathematics content as an important foundation for teaching. After one or more years of teaching, most Fellows agreed that the RIMTI contributed to their overall effectiveness as mathematics teachers. The Fellows also credited their preparedness to student teaching and working closely with their Mentors for a full year, before they took responsibility for their own classrooms, as beneficial.

Data from the surveys and focus groups also suggested potential gaps in coursework and preparedness, including the use of technology within the context of mathematics teaching, knowledge of applicable education laws, ability to successfully teach diverse students, and making community connections.

Fellows reported the greatest content disparity in their knowledge of education law and policy, and its impact on teaching and the ability to teach English learners. Interestingly, for these areas, the Mentors rated the Fellows as more prepared than the Fellows rated themselves.

Mathematics Content and Coursework

Regarding Fellows' preparedness in mathematics curriculum, the Mentors' knowledge of the Fellows' preparedness was limited to the content areas for which they had direct oversight within their classrooms (e.g., algebra). The Mentors indicated that the Fellows were very or extremely prepared in the Topics of Contemporary Math (i.e., mathematical research) and Linear Algebra (e.g., Euclidean space, linear systems, and determinants). In contrast to the Mentors' ratings, a few of the Fellows indicated that they were not very or extremely prepared in math topics outside of their assigned teaching experiences. Table 1 includes mathematics content areas where the Fellows felt very or extremely well prepared.

For all other areas of math preparedness items (i.e., Foundations of Analysis, Number Theory, Topics in Contemporary Mathematics, Advanced Topics in History of Mathematics, and Probability and Statistics), less than half of the Fellows reported feeling very or extremely prepared. One possible explanation may be the question prompt. Specifically, the prompt directed the Fellows to consider their current teaching experiences. Some content areas were simply not a part of their daily teaching.

As evidenced in reported concerns, some Fellows expressed limitations in the depth of their content preparation. However, some also believed they possessed a mastery of mathematics content that served as an important foundation for their teaching in specific areas in alignment with Utah state core standards.

In later recollections on their experiences as in-service teachers, the Fellows reported having a greater command of math content when compared with many of their peer teachers (i.e., graduates of other preparation programs). The Fellows linked their mastery of math content to their RIMTI participation and celebrated their success of gaining a strong foundation of math content knowledge.

I thought that class [capstone class] helped me to understand about the college algebra that I'm teaching in math three. We are teaching how to analyze cubics and quadratics, fifth order polynomials that stuff I didn't really realize until [my math professor] drove me through that this fall, and I'm like wow, and I feel so confident in that type of content now. (Fellow focus group)

I am one o –there's probably one other teacher at my school and we are probably the top as far as understanding mathematics. We might not be the best–I'm not the best at teaching obviously, but as far as understanding mathematics, I understand it really well, better than most other high school teachers because I [have] taken those classes. (Fellow focus group)

Table 1. Preparation in Mathematics

Areas of Mathematics Preparation	Very or Extremely Prepared
Methods	55%
Foundations of geometry	48%
Foundations of algebra	48%

Fellows believed their mathematics competencies were due to the focus of the RIMTI on graduate level coursework and the additional opportunities the Fellows experienced to further their understanding of mathematics. Activities such as cohort meetings and workshops often involved mathematical explorations that included solving math problems in groups. The programmatic emphasis on knowing and understanding math content was a salient aspect of the RIMTI program, and the Fellows communicated that in their comments.

General Teaching Content and Coursework

Program data highlighted RIMTI licensure coursework as aligning closely with state alternative route requirements which includes fewer courses and limited direct work with linguistically and culturally diverse students and families. Course work on general assessment (e.g., standardized assessment, criterion-referenced testing, and assessment for children with disabilities) was also absent in the RIMTI.

When we asked the RIMTI Fellows and Mentors to evaluate preparedness, similar to the math topics, both responded to a set of survey items on the general curricular program requirements. For the general topics, the Mentor reports of Fellows' preparedness were fairly well aligned with Fellows' views. The greatest disparity in Mentor and Fellow responses regarding preparedness in general topics included knowledge of law and policy (21% difference) and teaching English learners (16% difference). For both of these items, the Mentors rated the Fellows as more prepared than they rated themselves.

Within the category of general licensure topics, the Mentors viewed the Fellows' preparation as ranging from very or extremely well prepared to less-prepared along several areas. Table 2 illustrates these findings.

Additionally, the Mentors reported classroom management as an area where the Fellows were prepared either very well or extremely well, with a rating of 33%.

Fellows' reports of their preparedness to teach general areas linked to teaching (e.g., methods) reflected noticeable differences across curricular emphases. The highest was general instructional methodology, for which the Fellows reported 58% as very or extremely prepared, followed by 52% as very or extremely prepared in assessment of student learning.

Fellows identified their preparedness to work with varied student groups as a weakness. Where slightly more than half of the Fellows expressed agreement in their preparation to work with all types of learners, agreement changed when greater specificity was questioned for subgroups of students (e.g., children with disabilities). Table 3 includes these findings.

Table 2. General Preparation

Preparation in Licensure Areas	Very or Extremely Prepared
Assessment	63%
General instructional methodology	58%
Knowledge of law and policy	50%
Teaching English learners	29%
Understanding students with disabilities	17%

Table 3. Preparation for Work with Different Learners

Fellows Views of Preparation for Varied Groups	Very or Extremely Prepared
All types of learners	58%
English Language Learners	13%
Work with families	23%
Children with disabilities	29%

The Fellows' perceptions of the deficits in their preparation may have impacted them not only in their ability to work with one student group or another, but to differentiate instruction for a range of learners. These findings were furthered in reports once the Fellows started teaching in their own classrooms, where they found themselves underprepared to serve English learners.

I did not feel prepared to teach ELLs [English Language Learners] at all my first year. I was lucky because I didn't have any [students] in my first year. This year I have quite a few, and it's been a struggle for sure. So, I think that the courses are definitely available, but I was not pushed to take a SIOP [(a particular teaching model)] class, I don't think even [one] was. (Fellow focus group).

One program feature that may have impacted the Fellows' experiences with diverse learners was the RIMTI student teaching placements and the lack of more common practica experiences. Specific RIMTI classroom exposure did not allow for deliberate teaching, and related experiences linked to linguistically diverse learners.

As in other areas, the RIMTI Mentors were more confident about the Fellows' preparedness than were the Fellows themselves, and gave higher ratings on every item. Over half of the Mentors agreed or strongly agreed that the Fellows were prepared to work with all of the student groups, but considered them the least prepared to work with students with disabilities (54% agreed or strongly agreed) and to deal with disruptive students (58% agreed or strongly agreed).

Classroom Management

In an assessment of topics which were related to coursework and preparation necessary to be an effective math teacher, the Fellows evaluated a range of topics including: Variety instructional methods, content delivery, using technology and interpreting textbooks, responding to questions, planning, assessing student learning explaining concepts, and providing effective examples. Fellows cited Classroom management was a particular weakness, even though evidence showed dedicated course work on classroom management as part of their course of study. Some accounts reported that the RIMTI courses could have done more to prepare the Fellows to manage their classrooms effectively.

The Fellows and the Mentors, alike, suggested the need for additional preparation in classroom management. Both groups described the Fellows' struggles and lack of ability and sense of feeling inundated. Specifically, data comparisons between the Mentors and the Fellows reveal only 42% of the Fellows and 33% of the Mentors reported that the Fellows were very or extremely prepared in the area of classroom management. A Mentor explained their observation:

None of my Fellows have had questions about content or how should we teach. It [has] always been about these are the challenges I'm having with students, not the content, not the math, but the behavior type of things. (Mentor focus group)

A Fellow also noted:

If there is some way they can figure out how to teach new teachers behavior management skills, [it is needed]. Because that is one of the things that I feel is really lacking in my first year is I have no idea how to deal with some of these kids...I felt prepared math wise and I could explain this concept in these ways and this and I could tie all these things in together and the content was great, but managing my dear little knuckleheads, that was the part that kills me, made me want to quit, because I didn't know what to do with these–some of these kids. (Fellow focus group)

The Fellows' feedback illustrates that, while they struggled initially, they learned how to manage classrooms with experience.

You can learn how to deal with each student specifically, but some general overall management skills [would be helpful], I mean, it took me halfway through my first year before I realized [how to] make the kids ask to get up out of their seats. That seems like a really obvious thing now, I mean, but my first year, I'm like, why are you all running around in my classroom? (Fellow focus group)

While time spent in classrooms served the Fellows in their ability to manage classroom interactions and positively address student behaviors, frustrations and disappointments for the Fellows remained.

Professional Development and Growth for the Fellows

A central theme within the results was that the Fellows valued the relationships they built with their peers, with university faculty members, and with their Mentors. The Fellows reported that coursework, workshops, cohort meetings, and summer events provided shared experiences that offered emotional, academic, and professional support, as well as tangible ideas for practice. The Fellows reported they developed a sense of community through relationships that provided critical support during initial preparation as well as during the first year(s) of teaching. Most Fellows reported access to an experienced Mentor was essential in their success and reported various ways in which the Mentors helped them improve their teaching practices.

Networks for Fellows

Participation in the RIMTI created conditions where preservice teachers developed support networks, over time. For example, a RIMTI Fellow noted: "RIMTI has given me a network of people I can talk with to get ideas and support when I am struggling in my own classroom" (Fellow survey). As the Fellows worked together, a greater sense of community emerged. Community building was more than their participation in one activity over another. Instead, the collegiality allowed the participants to collectively engage in coursework, attend cohort meetings, solve problems together, and overcome challenges. "It's nice to know that there are other people in my same position that I can contact just for moral support, not even for a specific document but just like, are you tired, me too", said a RIMTI Fellow during a focus group. Another RIMTI Fellow explained:

I have people I can commiserate with and I also have people that are able to share their experiences and help me, because all the best teachers are actually thieves, so it helps me steal awesome things from other people to make my practice better. (Fellow focus group)

The Fellows shared common goals and experiences that provided additional depth and breadth to their preparation program. These shared opportunities resulted in a sense of community that provided emotional, academic, and professional support, as well as practical ideas that participants could use in their practice.

...There's a big support about us being in all different schools and different organizations, but feeling this interconnectedness because we took courses together and because we talked together and know each other...(Fellow focus group)

The Fellows indicated that the support they received and the network they developed with other participants served as a strong bond to be sustained in the early years of teaching practice. For instance, the Fellows continued to meet with their cohort during the first year of teaching. During a focus group, a Fellow shared:

Because of the cohort [meetings,]... you don't feel alone or frustrated that you're a failure. You see that everybody works through it so it gives you the energy boost in terms of being able to face your problems...I mean, so many people leave teaching in the first couple years I think because they don't have that. They can only look at people who have survived the experience. (Fellow focus group)

In addition to moral support and a sense of togetherness, the relationships the participants developed with their mentors were equally powerful. Though, following their student teaching year, some Fellows found it challenging to stay in close contact with the Mentors, particularly when there were geographical distances between them. While the Mentors' influence was often cited as significant, even at the end of the RIMTI some Fellows noted the lack of adequate preparation by their Mentor(s) and suggested additional needed training (e.g., lesson plan support). The Fellows and the Mentors reported that discussions increased their respective understandings of state teaching standards, assessment data, planning, and observational feedback. For the Mentors, participation in the RIMTI resulted in professional advancement and reflection on practice.

As colleagues, the Fellows learned to appreciate, rely upon, and value peers through their experience with the RIMTI. They recognized the need for a peer-support network to extend beyond the RIMTI. Overall, while some Fellows felt their schools lacked the support of a collaborative climate and specifically requested guidance in establishing a more collaborative atmosphere within their schools and departments, others celebrated their ongoing school-level peer collaborations. Despite this recognition, they had quite varied experiences once in the schools.

School-Embedded Experiences

Within the contexts of their student teaching placements, the Fellows had a range of school experiences. For example, most Fellows (85%) were observed by a school administrator at least once during the year or once a semester. However, Fellows described the observations as the least valuable component of their programs (52% agreed or strongly agreed as useful). Fellows reported that the most valuable areas in their work included collaboration with peer teachers to plan math lessons (58% cited at least once a month or more) and collaborating with peers to assess student learning (48% cited at least once a month or more). Most Fellows also reported that collaborations with peers were highly valued (91% and 81% agreed or strongly agreed, respectively). About half (48%) of the Fellows reported that a peer teacher observed them teaching, and 75% of the Fellows agreed or strongly agreed that those peer observations were valuable.

While Fellows viewed school administrators as part of their support networks, relatively few Fellows found observations or specific teaching feedback of school administrators particularly valuable. Instead, the Fellows consistently indicated that working with peers was important to them. Those who worked in collaborative settings found that rewarding and supportive.

From the survey choices, peer teachers (i.e., other Fellows) were the highest rated source of school support (90% agreed or strongly agreed). School administrators and a state required mentor were the second highest rated source of site-based support (60% and 59% agreed or strongly agreed, respectively). Less than half of the Fellows (43%) agreed or strongly agreed that district level content-based instructional coaches provided support.

In the surveys and in the focus groups the Fellows also noted that, despite the value of collaborations with peer teachers, building relationships takes time. They described experiences with their school peers that ranged from working fully independently to having close daily interactions. The Fellows specifically noted the influence of school leadership on collaboration and suggested that some school cultures embraced and promoted collaboration, while others did not.

The Fellows went on to explain that the extent to which they experienced collaboration within their schools was dependent upon the conditions in each unique school culture.

I had both sides of it. First two years at [school name] almost no collaboration in the level that came about was as I developed relationships with a couple of the teachers, especially one, her [sic] and I collaborated a lot . . . but as far as a department, it . . . kind of comes down from the department head, I mean what kind of culture are they trying to foster? And so there wasn't a lot, and then I went to [school name], and I'm having much more of this experience and I like it so much more. It is so much better. (Fellow focus group).

Weak collaboration might be difficult to overcome, but focus group data indicated the Fellows' willingness to assume leadership roles when collaboration was limited. One Fellow, who referenced a small number of math colleagues, valued the importance of taking a leadership role where peer collaboration was lacking.

Impact on Mentors

As key project stakeholders, RIMTI Mentors were chosen in the RIMTI were identified because of past experiences with the University of Utah, their willingness to collaborate in teacher preparation and to work with peers across schools. As key project stakeholders, the Mentors cited benefits and challenges in their roles. Positively, the Mentors found themselves with a new audience member who motivated them to attend more carefully to their teaching. Through conversations with the Fellows, the Mentors explored their own practices and targeted areas that could be improved. Of note was the degree to which the Mentors' experiences changed over time in ways that moved beyond the more technical support they provided to novices. By providing mentoring support for the Fellows, the Mentors had the opportunity to reflect on their own teaching. A mentor noted: "Any time I am observing and helping other teachers I find that I reflect on my own practices and often implement new ideas or procedures that benefit my own professional development" (Mentor Survey).

With the Fellows watching them closely and asking questions about their classroom teaching, the Mentors felt the need to look more deeply into their own teaching practices and be prepared to offer explanations and guidance. Another mentor shared:

It helped me focus on best practices. Being a good example forces you to do good things. It also allows for opportunities to talk about my own weaknesses/bad examples and try to fix them. (Mentor Survey)

The RIMTI Mentors noted that having the Fellows in their classrooms also prompted them to become more self-critical in ways they believed helped improve their own teaching practices. The confidence generated from the relationships with the Fellows, along with confidence in the Mentors' availability, served as support for both the Mentors and the Fellows. The following impressions highlight the impact of serving in the mentor role. The first-hand accounts of the Mentors illustrate benefits of participating in a community of math educators.

We get to talk and we get to see each other and I think that's one thing that the program has definitely created is that we are totally willing to collaborate and we're totally open minded with each other in that we are all friends…You know, if somebody moves to a different high school, boom, you have a friend, you have a connection, you have a network, and this is definitely creating a network. (Mentor focus group)

Working in professional teams provided the opportunity to connect with other math teachers who also appreciated the unique opportunity to share comradery and support.

I'm learning so much about what goes on in other districts and I'm learning about how to make our practice public. No longer—we don't want the teachers who go into their room, [close] their doors and say don't bother me. It is all about let me share what I'm doing in my classroom, let me share what I saw in somebody else's classroom, because it was so awesome. (Mentor focus group)

Together, the Mentors and the Fellows worked in concert and learned from one another through professional discussions that increased their collective understandings of state teaching standards, assessment data, planning, and observational feedback. Additionally, project participants formed long-term relationships as a result of their RIMTI engagement.

In addition to positive professional relationships formed among team members, there were also limitations. Some Fellows cited the need for increased Mentor interactions and support, including more frequent classroom visits. Mentors agreed with the critiques of the Fellows and cited constraints related to adequate time to commit to the role of mentor. During first year teaching for the Fellows, the Mentors noted that leaving their own classrooms to visit the classroom of a Fellow was not always possible due to time and distance. As such, more informal and impromptu conversations took place.

Additional areas that could be strengthened for the Mentors included better guidance on the feedback they provided to the Fellows. Mentors requested additional feedback on assessment and state standards as a part of their training. Finally, we noted barriers to consistent contacts by the Mentors during first year teaching may have limited the impact of the Mentors over time. As the Fellows entered full-time teaching, coaches and building peers were the more reliable source for support.

In summary, at the conclusion of the program, we found positive programmatic features of the RIMTI that contributed to professional growth for Fellows and the Mentors. Both groups cited the importance of contexts and an intensive mathematics curriculum. Areas in need of improvement include closer attention to a curriculum that addresses classroom management and a focus on the varied needs of learners including ability, language, and cultural differences. A fine-grained analysis of end-of-program data indicates the content specific needs of the Fellows' preparation. At the completion of their involvement in the RIMTI, the Fellows also cited the need for increased knowledge of families and communities. Of greater significance will be the long-term impact of this effort on classroom teaching and student learning in 6-12 grade classrooms.

SOLUTIONS AND RECOMMENDATIONS

While preservice preparation is critically important for teachers, the first few years of teaching can shape a new teacher's career dramatically. Induction is a critical time and first-year teachers are considered a vulnerable group (Goldrick, Osta, Barlin, & Burn, 2012; Wang, Odell, & Schwille, 2008). The role of the RIMTI Mentors was a critical element of support with daily work, and a vehicle for community building and professional camaraderie in ways that address both the needs of beginning teachers as well as those further advanced in their careers. The within and across-group dimensions of these professional partnerships are noteworthy findings of this effort.

For the Fellows, their experiences included expected growing pains typical of novices. However, the cohort model provided a platform for common goal setting, the unpacking of challenges and related experiences of beginning teachers, and performance informed discussions that included professional problem solving and long-term planning. Similarly, the Mentors experienced a venue, among peers, that allowed them the space to recharge through an acknowledgement of their expertise, informed by time in the classrooms and through critical examinations of mathematics content as part of the RIMTI discussions and professional development experiences.

Project findings highlight the importance of strong matches between the Mentors and the Fellows in ways that allowed for effective communication, explorations of curriculum, and familiarity with school contexts and local communities. Additional ways to strengthen the Fellow-Mentor relationship include alignment in communication styles and perspectives on teaching and learning. Future programs should attend to the degree to which the Mentors are trained to provide feedback, evaluate teaching, and facilitate environments within varied school contexts that allow beginning teachers to prosper.

Additional findings underscore that when preparation, in any format, addresses multiple components of teachers' work; teachers report a willingness to remain in the profession over time. Fellows cited the importance of school contexts and leadership as essential areas that contributed to their success and align with the findings of others (Goldhaber, Lavery, & Theobald, 2016; Johnson, Kraft, & Papay, 2012).

For the RIMTI Mentors, areas of improvement in support of their roles include: Dedicated training regarding their roles, explicit strategy preparation for providing feedback and evaluation, and formal opportunities for sustained contact with the Fellows, post licensure. An additional area that may be considered for the Mentors in their future professional development is defining how their influence and contributions could be formalized, over time, as part of preservice teacher preparation. As the traditional teacher education program hires practicing teachers for supervision and course instruction, the RIMTI Mentors may serve as a skilled and available pool of professionals for this work.

Finally, at program completion, 80% of graduates of the RIMTI planned to continue as educators, with less than 5% expressing plans to leave teaching. This outcome reveals significant potential for the long-term impact on a program committed to recruiting and retaining secondary teachers of mathematics. Of perhaps greater significance is the retention rate of the RIMTI graduates; indeed, 70% of graduates remained in the profession, for those in the program between 2010 and 2015.

FUTURE RESEARCH DIRECTIONS

Project findings from the RIMTI highlight both programmatic components necessary for ARL preparation as well as offer prompts for future areas of study. In addition to evaluations of program effectiveness, researchers are invited to consider how the ARL program may capitalize on the expertise of mentors for both supervisory support as well as a vehicle for professional development. Additional areas of study include critical conversations regarding the curriculum within ARL programs and how/whether these efforts adequately prepare 21st century educators. Changing demographics within contemporary classrooms and schools, the roles of families and communities, and innovation in areas such as technology integration and evaluations of performance for students and teachers must be considered.

Finally, innovation often comes at a cost. Researchers and practitioners are challenged to examine the ways in which both traditional and alternative programs may be developed and delivered in ways that support key stakeholders in teacher preparation.

Determining Effectiveness

The RIMTI project provides extensive information about the ways in which the RIMTI has been implemented to prepare secondary mathematics teachers. However, additional aspects of the program's impact were not addressed or considered in this study and should be researched in future work. Effectiveness data may be considered in two ways. First, the Fellows expressed a range of perspectives related to their perceptions of their students' performance outcomes. Among the Fellows who discussed yearly standardized tests as measures of effectiveness, one explained standardized test scores were not an accurate measure of student success, and another indicated that test results are a way to gauge teaching performance against colleagues. Additionally, some Fellows addressed more immediate outcomes as evidence of effectiveness, such as being present, investing in learning, and overcoming daily challenges.

Focus group data suggested the Fellows may not clearly understand what it means to be an effective teacher. Study findings indicated that "effectiveness" is manifest in multiple ways where the lack of clear and agreed-upon understandings of what constitutes effectiveness for teachers creates a situation where Fellows, Mentors, and program faculty held different perspectives (e.g., program satisfaction, grade 6-12 student performance as a result of the RIMTI teachers' work). While it is not uncommon for novices to hold narrow views of how student performance is measured, dedicated attention to this area should be considered as a natural component of teacher preparation.

Programmatic emphases of the RIMTI did not include in-depth analyses of program effectiveness as it relates to the Fellows' teaching competencies, over time. Specifically, we do not have adequate data that allow to explore the influence of the RIMTI Fellows on 6-12 grade level student achievement performance. While preliminary standardized assessment data show variance among the students of the RIMTI graduates following program completion, these data are limited to a narrow set of students in sixth through twelfth grade settings. As such, the degree to which the RIMTI Fellows are successful in supporting high levels of student achievement is a critical question to determine the viability of this and other programs.

The Expertise of Mentors

Regarding the role of the RIMTI Mentors, because they were hand-picked by program staff, this was a group of engaged math educators who were excited to learn from one another. In addition to working with the Fellows, the Mentors were inspired and encouraged by participating in a community of other Mentors who worked collectively to prepare preservice teachers. Beyond their roles in the RIMTI, the Mentors promoted the open sharing of ideas and provided ample opportunities to learn from experienced peers in ways that would impact their daily work. Not only did they discuss how to help their Fellows, but they shared experiences from their own teaching practices from a variety of different schools. In a sense, their participation elevated their roles and influence in ways that capitalized on their expertise, ability to engage with others, and in their growth as professionals. From a pedagogical perspective, the ripple effect of these opportunities is far reaching within the profession.

Costs

As with any specialized program that is designed to challenge traditional teacher preparation programs, the costs associated with a program may be prohibitive. For the RIMTI, the costs affiliated with intensive support for all stakeholders were considerable. Stipends toward graduate coursework and professional development, as well as costs affiliated with additional mentoring for both the Fellows and the Mentors were significant. Clearly, traditional teacher preparation programs are unable to offer the intensity of the mentoring, professional development, and long-term commitments for ongoing support affiliated with the RIMTI. A cost-benefit analysis would provide additional critical information about the viability of this program and could be used to inform teacher preparation programs based on the RIMTI findings about program implementation. We are confident that dimensions of the support provided could be nuanced in ways that keep viable the spirit of relationship building and professional development support.

Curriculum

Finally, further analyses of program features linked to curriculum, pedagogy, and supervisory support is also warranted beyond the scope of this study. The Fellows' reports of low preparedness to teach math topics are perplexing because they conflict with other data sources. In open-ended survey items and focus group discussions, the Fellows emphasized the focus of the program on math competency. Follow up on the nuances of these perceptions would allow for in-depth understandings of the Fellows' perceptions. Attention to the relationships between depths of content area preparation and impact within daily teaching are of particular interest to teacher education programs at this time.

In addition to content area preparation, the realities of contemporary classrooms and schools warrant greater attention to individual learners and their communities. Generic supervisory support, for example, is typically limited in scope and depth. Instead, the nuances of curriculum and supervisory support must be considered in ways that acknowledge specific dimension of language, culture, ability, and identities.

CONCLUSION

The demand for teachers in high need content areas persists over time (Ingersoll, 2011; Ingersoll & Perda, 2010; Papay, Bacher-Hicks, Page, & Marinell, 2017; Rich, 2015). Solutions to recruiting and retention run the gamut from traditional teacher preparation to alternative programs that may include streamlined curricula, perhaps a crash course in pedagogy, and "sink or swim" teaching experiences. Further, variations in teachers' expertise and impact on students requires differentiated support within the context of their careers (Papay, Bacher-Hicks, Page, & Marinell, 2017). Rather than debating the comparative effectiveness of ARLs to traditional preparation, researchers and practitioners are challenged to consider how to strengthen their collective work.

End-of-program findings from the RIMTI offer new perspectives for ARL preparation from the unique perspectives of preservice teachers and their mentors that align with research on best practices for curriculum, pedagogy, assessments and relationships with students and colleagues (e.g., Boyd, Grossman, Lankford, Loeb, & Wyckoff, 2009; Darling-Hammond, 2006; Darling-Hammond, 2010; Harris & Sass, 2011). The RIMTI model distinguishes itself from traditional ARL programs and past research, through a dedicated focus on content coverage as part of a master's degree with licensure, a student-teaching experience under the supervision of a high-quality pre and in-service mentor, and ongoing professional development that extends beyond the pre-service experience. The depth of this study highlights two stakeholder groups whose perspectives are based upon long-term engagement in the RIMTI.

Data gathered on RIMTI over a five-year period highlights the program's attention to many components of quality teacher preparation including content instruction within applied contexts, in-depth content preparation, and extended exposure in classrooms (Coggshall, Rasmussen, Colton, Milton, & Jacques, 2012; Darling-Hammond, 2010; Zeichner, 2010). A unique component of the program (i.e., the year-long component of guided student-teaching placement under the direction of an expert teacher) provided the preservice teachers with a critical dimension of preparation. Guided practice over time is consistent with recommendations for quality preparation.

Along with its strengths, summative data on RIMTI highlight the need for increased training for the RIMTI Mentors, increased coordination with the Mentors concerning the Fellows' needs, greater coherence between coursework and clinical experiences, and the intentional coordination among the

RIMTI Mentors and school-based personnel. Of greater concern is the degree to which the RIMTI fails to adequately prepare teachers to work with diverse student populations.

As an alternative program of study, the RIMTI was successful in increasing the number of mathematics teachers. Additionally, the program maintained many components necessary for quality teacher preparation (Desimone & Long, 2010; Sleeter, Neal, & Kumashiro, 2014).

Expected strengths and limitations of the RIMTI will also prompt continued attention to program curricula, attention to sustained and dedicated support for mentors, and increased opportunities for work within classrooms, beyond student teaching. Similar to many alternative licensure programs, the RIMTI is limited in its focus on curriculum and instruction designed to meet varied learner needs. Dedicated attention to curriculum and teaching contexts that resemble sites in which preservice teachers will eventually work are additional areas for program planning and essential components for 21st century teacher preparation.

Finally, it will be important for future research to evaluate the impact of RIMTI teachers on student performance. While the initial evaluation design included student achievement data, availability and access to complete data limited analyses in this area.

Alternative programs have the potential to impact positively teacher preparation. Informed by research, successful ARLs will embody many of the elements of quality including teacher-mentor community building, attention to curriculum, pedagogy, and knowledge of learners. Alternative programs that include research on best practice are, then, in the position to shape these cultures of teacher preparation in a critical time of need.

ACKNOWLEDGMENT

This project was supported by a Robert Noyce (0934894), National Science Foundation Grant and Dr. Hugo Rossi.

REFERENCES

Alternative Teacher Certification Guide. (2018). Retrieved from http://www.teachercertificationdegrees.com/become/#alt

Aragon, S. (2016). *Teacher shortages: What we know*. Denver, CO: Education Commission of the States. Retrieved from http://www.ecs.org/ec-content/uploads/Teacher-Shortages-What-We-Know.pdf

Ball, D., & Forzani, M. (2010). What does it take to make a teacher? *Teaching Education*, 92(2), 8–12.

Ball, D., Themes, M., & Phelps, G. (2008). Content knowledge for teaching: What makes it special? *Journal of Teacher Education*, 59(5), 389–407. doi:10.1177/0022487108324554

Boyd, D., Goldhaber, D., Lankford, H., & Wyckoff, J. (2007). The effect of certification and preparation on teacher quality. *The Future of Children*, 17(1), 45–68. doi:10.1353/foc.2007.0000 PMID:17407922

Boyd, D. J., Grossman, P. L., Lankford, H., Loeb, S., & Wyckoff, J. (2009). Teacher preparation and student achievement. *Educational Evaluation and Policy Analysis*, 31(4), 416–440. doi:10.3102/0162373709353129

Burbank, M. D., Ramirez, L., & Bates, A. (2016). The impact of critical reflective teaching: A rhetoric continuum. *Action in Teacher Education, 38*(2), 104–119. doi:10.1080/01626620.2016.1155095

Charmaz, K. (2006). *Constructing grounded theory: A practical guide through qualitative analysis.* London: Sage.

Clotfelter, C., Ladd, H., & Vigdor, J. (2010). Teacher-student matching and the assessment of teacher effectiveness. *The Journal of Human Resources, 41*(4), 778–782. doi:10.3368/jhr.XLI.4.778

Coggshall, J. G., Rasmussen, C., Colton, A., Milton, J., & Jacques, C. (2012). *Generating teaching effectiveness: The role of job-embedded professional learning in teacher evaluation.* Washington, DC: National Comprehensive Center for Teacher Quality. Retrieved from https://www.gtlcenter.org/sites/default/files/docs/GeneratingTeachingEffectiveness.pdf

Darling-Hammond, L. (2006). Constructing 21st-century teacher education. *Journal of Teacher Education, 57*(3), 300–314. doi:10.1177/0022487105285962

Darling-Hammond, L. (2010). Teacher education and the American future. *Journal of Teacher Education, 61*(1-2), 35–47. doi:10.1177/0022487109348024

Darling-Hammond, L., Chung, R., & Frelow, F. (2002). Variation in teacher preparation: How well do different pathways prepare teachers to teach? *Journal of Teacher Education, 53*(4), 286–302. doi:10.1177/0022487102053004002

Darling-Hammond, L., Holtzman, D., Gatlin, S., & Heilig, J. (2010). Does teacher preparation matter? Evidence about teacher certification, Teach for America, and teacher effectiveness. *Education Policy Analysis Archives, 13*(42), 1–28.

Desimone, L., & Long, D. (2010). Teacher effects and the achievement gap: Do teacher and teaching quality influence the achievement gap between Black and White and high-and low-SES students in the early grades? *Teachers College Record, 112*(12), 3024–3073.

Dillon, E., & Silva, E. (2011). Grading the teachers' teachers: Higher education comes under scrutiny. *Phi Delta Kappan, 93*(1), 54–58. doi:10.1177/003172171109300109

Eaton, C. (2011). Education Department's reform plan for teacher training gets mixed reviews. *The Chronicle of Higher Education.* Retrieved from https://www.chronicle.com/article/Education-Depts-Reform-Plan/129258

Foote, M., Brantlinger, A., Haydar, H., Smith, B., & Gonzalez, L. (2011). Are we supporting teacher success?: Insights from an alternative route mathematics teacher certification program for urban public schools. *Education and Urban Society, 43*(3), 396–425. doi:10.1177/0013124510380420

Glaser, B. G., & Strauss, A. L. (1967). *The discovery of grounded theory: Strategies for qualitative research.* Hawthorne, NY: Aldine.

Goldhaber, D., & Brewer, D. J. (1999). Teacher licensing and student achievement. In M. Kanstoroom & C. E. Finn, Jr. (Eds.), Better teacher, better schools (pp. 83-102). Washington, DC: The Thomas B. Fordham Foundation.

Goldhaber, D., Lavery, L., & Theobald, R. (2016). Inconvenient truth? Do collective bargaining agreements help explain the mobility of teachers within school districts? *Journal of Policy Analysis and Management, 35*(4), 848–880. doi:10.1002/pam.21914

Goldrick, L., Osta, D., Barlin, D., & Burn, J. (2012). *Review of state policies on teacher induction.* Santa Cruz, CA: New Teacher Center. Retrieved from https://newteachercenter.org/wp-content/uploads/brf-ntc-policy-state-teacher-induction.pdf

Grossman, P., & McDonald, M. (2008). Back to the future: Directions for research in teaching and teacher education. *American Educational Research Journal, 45*(1), 184–205. doi:10.3102/0002831207312906

Harris, D. N., & Sass, T. R. (2011). Teacher training, teacher quality, and student achievement. *Journal of Public Economics, 95*(7-8), 798–812. doi:10.1016/j.jpubeco.2010.11.009

Heilig, J. V., & Jez, S. J. (2010). *Teach For America: A Review of the Evidence.* Education and the Public Interest Center & Education Policy Research Unit. Retrieved from http://epicpolicy.org/publication/teach-for-america

Henry, G. T., Purtell, K. M., Bastian, K. C., Fortner, C. K., Thompson, C. L., Campbell, S. L., & Patterson, K. M. (2013). The effects of teacher entry portals on student achievement. *Journal of Teacher Education, 65*(1), 7–23. doi:10.1177/0022487113503871

Holzberger, D., Phillipp, A., & Kunter, M. (2013). How teachers' self-efficacy is related to instructional quality: A longitudinal analysis. *Journal of Educational Psychology, 105*(3), 774–786. doi:10.1037/a0032198

Ingersoll, R. (2011). Do we produce enough mathematics and science teachers? *Phi Delta Kappan, 92*(6), 37–41. doi:10.1177/003172171109200608

Ingersoll, R., & Strong, M. (2011). The impact of induction and mentoring programs for beginning teachers: A critical review of the research. *Review of Educational Research, 1*(2), 201–233. doi:10.3102/0034654311403323

Ingersoll, R. M., & Perda, D. (2010). Is the supply of mathematics and science teachers sufficient? *American Educational Research Journal, 43*(3), 563–594. doi:10.3102/0002831210370711

Johnson, S. M., Kraft, M. A., & Papay, J. P. (2012). How context matters in high-need schools: The effects of teachers' working conditions on their professional satisfaction and their students' achievement. *Teachers College Record, 114*(10), 1–39. PMID:24013958

Kee, A. N. (2012). Feelings of preparedness among alternatively certified teachers: What is the role of program features? *Journal of Teacher Education, 63*(1), 23–38. doi:10.1177/0022487111421933

Klehm, M. (2014). The effects of teacher beliefs on teaching practices and achievement of students with disabilities. *Teacher Education and Special Education, 37*(3), 216–240. doi:10.1177/0888406414525050

Laczko-Kerr, I., & Berliner, D. (2002). The effectiveness of "Teach for America" and other under-certified teachers on student academic achievement: A case of harmful public policy. *Education Policy Analysis Archives, 37*(10). Retrieved from https://epaa.asu.edu/ojs/article/view/316

Ma, L. (1999). *Knowing and teaching elementary mathematics*. Mahwah, NJ: Lawrence Earlbaum Associates.

Marshall, C., & Rossman, G. (2016). *Designing Qualitative Research, 6th Education*. Thousand Oaks, CA: Sage.

National Council on Teacher Quality. (2014). *State Teacher Policy Yearbook: National Summary*. Retrieved from https://files.eric.ed.gov/fulltext/ED556317.pdf

National Council on Teacher Quality. (2017). *2017 State Teacher Policy Yearbook*. Retrieved https://www.nctq.org/publications/2017-State-Teacher-Policy-Yearbook

National Mathematics Advisory Panel. (2008). *Foundations for success: The final report of the National Mathematics Advisory Panel*. Retrieved from https://www2.ed.gov/about/bdscomm/list/mathpanel/report/final-report.pdf

No Child Left Behind Act of 2001, P.L. 107-110, 20 U.S.C. § 6319 (2002).

Papay, J., Bacher-Hicks, A., Page, L., & Marinell, W. (2017). The challenge of teacher retention in urban schools: Evidence of variation from a cross-site analysis. *Educational Researcher*, *46*(8), 434–448. doi:10.3102/0013189X17735812

Preparing and Credentialing the Nation's Teachers: The Secretary's 10th Report on Teacher Quality. (2016). Retrieved from https://title2.ed.gov/Public/TitleIIReport16.pdf

Qu, Y., & Becker, B. J. (2003). *Does traditional teacher certification imply quality? A meta-analysis*. Paper presented at the Annual Meeting of the American Educational Research Association, Chicago, IL.

Rice, J. K. (2003). *Teacher quality: Understanding the effectiveness of teacher attributes*. Washington, DC: Economic Policy Institute.

Rich, M. (2015). Teacher shortages spur a nationwide hiring scramble (Credentials Optional). *New York Times*. Retrieved from http://www.nytimes.com/2015/08/10/us/teacher-shortages-spur-a-nationwide-hiring-scramble-credentials-optional.html

Robelen, E. (2011). Fellowship program works to beef up math teaching. *Education Week*, *9*(February). Retrieved from https://www.edweek.org/ew/articles/2011/02/09/20math_ep.h30.html

Sass, T. (2013). *Licensure and worker quality: A comparison of alternative routes to teaching*. Department of Economics W. J. Usery Workplace Research Group. Retrieved from http://aysps.gsu.edu/files/2016/01/13-09-Sass-Licensureandworkerquality.pdf

Scherer, M. (2012). The challenge of supporting new teachers: A conversation with Linda Darling Hammond. *Educational Leadership*, *69*(8). Retrieved from http://www.ascd.org/publications/educational-leadership/may12/vol69/num08/The-Challenges-of-Supporting-New-Teachers.aspx

Sleeter, C., Neal, L. V., & Kumashiro, K. (2014). *Addressing the demographic imperative: Recruiting, preparing, and retaining a diverse and highly effective teaching force*. New York: Routledge.

Stipek, D. (2002). *Motivation to learn* (4th ed.). Upper Saddle River, NJ: Pearson.

Strauss, A., & Corbin, J. (1998). *Basics of qualitative research: Techniques and procedures for developing grounded theory*. Thousand Oaks, CA: Sage.

Utah State Board of Education. (2017). *Academic Pathway to Teaching*. Retrieved from https://www.schools.utah.gov/curr/licensing/earning

Walsh, K., & Jacobs, S. (2007). *Alternative certification isn't alternative*. Washington, DC: National Council on Teacher Quality. Retrieved from https://files.eric.ed.gov/fulltext/ED498382.pdf

Wang, J., Odell, S., & Schwille, S. (2008). Effects of teacher induction on beginning teachers' teaching: A critical review of the literature. *Journal of Teacher Education, 59*(2), 132–152. doi:10.1177/0022487107314002

Wayman, J. C., Foster, A. M., Mantle-Bromley, C., & Wilson, C. A. (2003). A comparison of the professional concerns of traditionally prepared and alternatively licensed new teachers. *High School Journal, 3*(86), 35–40. doi:10.1353/hsj.2003.0005

Wayne, A., & Young, P. (2002). Teacher characteristics and student achievement gains: A review. *Review of Educational Research, 73*(1), 89–122. doi:10.3102/00346543073001089

Zeichner, K. (2010). Rethinking the connections between campus courses and field experiences in college-and university-based teacher education. *Journal of Teacher Education, 61*(1-2), 61–89. doi:10.1177/0022487109347671

ADDITIONAL READING

Berry, B. (2004). Recruiting and retaining "Highly Qualified Teacher" in hard-to-staff schools. *National Association of Secondary Schools Bulletin, 88*(638), 6–25.

Crowe, E. (2010). *Measuring what matters: A stronger accountability model for teacher education*. Washington, DC: Center for American Progress.

Gay, G. (2000). *Culturally responsive teaching: Theory, research, and practice*. New York: Teachers College Press.

Kuhn, D. (2015). Thinking together and alone. *Educational Researcher, 44*(1), 46–53. doi:10.3102/0013189X15569530

Ladson-Billings, G. J. (1995). Toward a theory of culturally relevant pedagogy. *American Educational Research Journal, 35*(3), 465–491. doi:10.3102/00028312032003465

Munoz, M., & Rodosky, R. (2015). School districts as partners in research efforts. *Phi Delta Kappan, 96*(5), 42–46. doi:10.1177/0031721715569469

Richmond, G. (2017). The power of community partnership in the preparation of teachers. *Journal of Teaching and Teacher Education, 68*(1), 6–8. doi:10.1177/0022487116679959

Ronfeldt, M. (2015). Field placement schools and instructional effectiveness. *Journal of Teacher Education, 66*(4), 304–320. doi:10.1177/0022487115592463

Sawchuck, S. (2011, March 8). Administration pushes teacher-prep accountability. *Education Week, 30*(23), 1.14.

Silin, J. G. (2008). Preface. In J. Snyder, M. Barry, S. Samuels, A. Sacks, & A. Ellenzweig (Eds.), *Alternative routes to teacher certification* (pp. 3–5). New York: Bank Street.

KEY TERMS AND DEFINITIONS

Collaboration: Individuals or groups working together to support mutual goals in ways that are mutually beneficial.

Curriculum: A course of study often identified by an oversight body.

Mentoring: A process of relationship building typically between a novice and an expert.

Performance Standards: In education, identified indicators referencing curricular performance, documented by measurable benchmarks.

Quality Teaching: An evaluation of instructional performance based upon indicators demonstrated in classroom settings.

Stakeholders: Individuals or groups committed to a common goal.

Teacher Preparation: A course of study for individuals working in classrooms and schools.

Chapter 4

From Collaborative Inquiry to Critical, Project–Based Clinical Experiences:
Strengthening Partnerships Through Field–Based Teacher Education

Kristien Zenkov
George Mason University, USA

Elizabeth Levine Brown
George Mason University, USA

Seth A. Parsons
George Mason University, USA

Lois A. Groth
George Mason University, USA

Audra K. Parker
George Mason University, USA

Kristine E. Pytash
Kent State University, USA

Anthony Pellegrino
University of Tennessee – Knoxville, USA

ABSTRACT

Unprecedented and long-overdue attention has recently been given to the role of field-based clinical experiences in teacher preparation. Traditional models of university coursework disconnected from real world field-based clinical experiences serve neither prospective teachers nor PreK-12 students. This chapter presents a broader notion of field-based teacher preparation structures occurring in school-university partnership contexts and professional development schools, with the authors drawing from data of four field-based experiences, which fall along a continuum of partnership, from three teacher education programs at two universities. These partnerships illustrate a developmental framework for building mutually beneficial relationships that enhance the engagement of all stakeholders and acknowledge the need for differentiation in teacher education practice. A pathways orientation to school-university partnerships/PDSs and a project-based clinical approach offer chances to develop mutually beneficial learning opportunities for PreK-12 students and teacher candidates.

DOI: 10.4018/978-1-5225-6249-8.ch004

INTRODUCTION

Policymakers, organizations, and teacher educators have recently given unprecedented and long-overdue attention to the role of clinical experiences in teacher preparation (AACTE, 2011, 2018; ATE, 2015). Yet current policy and practice cries for enhanced clinical practice are impacted by challenging financial and political realities for universities and PK-12 schools, as well as by the fact that field-based and partnership efforts operate across these distinct institutions, which have similar but not absolutely aligned missions (Dennis, Burns, Tricarico, Van Ingen, Jacobs, & Davis, 2017; Martin, Snow, & Franklin Torrez, 2011). Fortunately, the demands for earlier and more robust fieldwork alongside increasingly intentional and mutually beneficial collaborations with PK-12 sites seem to have been answered almost before they were made with the structures provided by school-university partnerships and professional development schools (PDSs) (Many, Fisher, Ogletree, & Taylor, 2012; Ipkeze, Broikou, Hildenbrand, & Gladstone-Brown, 2012).

Yet, if the promises of field-based teacher education efforts are going to be realized, those in the educator preparation field operating in school-university partnerships need not a single model of collaboration but multiple pathways to building and strengthening partnerships. The goal of this chapter is to share a broader notion of field-based teacher preparation structures occurring in school-university partnership contexts and PDSs, with the authors drawing from data of four field-based experiences—which fall along a continuum of partnership—from three teacher education programs at three universities. These illustrate frameworks for building and sustaining mutually beneficial relationships that enhance the engagement of all stakeholders and acknowledge the need for differentiation and flexibility in teacher education practice. This continuum provides a menu of means through which partnership-oriented, field-based teacher education efforts might be strengthened.

While the PDS model has existed as a lofty ideal since it was first formulated and enacted in the late 1980s and early 1990s, the authors of this chapter posit that this archetype has both inspired and deterred teacher education practitioners from engaging in authentic school-university partnership efforts and rich field-based teacher education efforts (Boyle-Baise & McIntyre, 2008). University-based teacher educators operating on the ground of educator preparation programs have long recognized the dramatic shift in university- and school-based teacher educator roles, the substantial financial resources, and the tremendous faculty time required to enact the PDS principles (Burns, Jacobs, & Yendol-Hoppey, 2016). To illustrate these PDS features, in this chapter the authors describe two structures: 1) "partner," "clinical practice, and "collaborative inquiry" examples implemented in an elementary education program, and; 2) a "critical, project-based" clinical experience occurring in three secondary education programs. The elementary education examples are detailed as cases to illustrate partnership practices, and the secondary education examples include more abbreviated information about these partnership practices but also integrate summary research analyses of these cases. Ultimately, the authors attempt to present a set of doors, rather than a single portal, through which others might strengthen these PDS- and school-university partnership-based structures and enhance teacher candidates' preparation (Note: We use the terms "teacher candidate," "preservice teacher," "future teacher," and "field hours student" interchangeably, to describe university students in educator preparation programs in semesters prior to the culminating student teaching internship).

BACKGROUND

Professional Associations and Policymakers

A number of professional association reports and policy proposals have recently highlighted the need for increased clinical experiences in preservice teacher education programs (AACTE, 2012, 2018; ATE, 2015). These calls were likely engendered by NCATE's (2010) *Blue Ribbon Panel Report* and have been echoed by the American Association of Colleges for Teacher Education (AACTE), the Council for the Accreditation of Educator Preparation (CAEP), and the Association of Teacher Educators (ATE). Educator preparation practitioners and scholars have articulated a need to "turn teacher preparation upside down" and put field-based clinical experiences at the center of these efforts (AACTE, 2010; Gatti, 2016; Levine, 2006; Gelfuso, Dennis, & Parker, 2015; NCATE, 2010).

The variety of these petitions for this turn toward field-based teacher education speaks to their significance. Numerous teacher education scholars have detailed how some of the most effective teacher preparation takes place in "practice-based" contexts (Lampert, 2010; Sleep, Boerst, & Ball, 2007; Zeichner & McDonald, 2011; Zeichner, 2013), "third spaces" (Ipkeze, Broikou, Hildenbrand, & Gladstone-Brown, 2012), or "hybrid spaces" (Zeichner, 2010), where practitioner and academic knowledge is blended and valued similarly. Likewise, the National Research Council (2010) identified clinical teacher education practice as one of three components of teacher education with the greatest potential to positively impact PK-12 learner outcomes. This emphasis also has a history in the recommendations of Teachers for a New Era (2001), a Carnegie Corporation-funded program focused on advancements in educator preparation, which listed clinical practice as one of its three essentials:

Education should be understood as an academically taught "clinical practice profession," requiring close cooperation between colleges of education and actual practicing schools; master teachers as clinical faculty in the college of education; and residencies for beginning teachers during a two-year period of induction. (p. 12)

In summary, "we know from research that good clinical experience is associated with effective teaching" (AACTE, 2010, p. 4).

Yet, as noted above, teacher education has too often seemed to consider the clinical elements of teacher candidates' programs as fringe features, rather than core components (Zeichner & Bier, 2015). Perhaps not surprisingly, educator preparation programs often face challenges securing quality placements for teacher candidates and establishing and maintaining school-university partnerships (Wimmer, 2008). Many teachers and administrators have reasonably grown wary of future teachers' presence, particularly as the professional stakes have grown higher for schools, with policy makers' increasing emphasis on standardized measures of PK-12 student achievement (Zeichner & Bier, 2015). The result is that preservice teachers are often viewed as distractions to students facing high-stakes assessments, while many teachers perceive a disconnect between the conceptual perspectives and pedagogies shared in university methods courses and the realities of their mentor teachers' classrooms (Smagorinsky, Rhym, & Moore, 2013; Smagorinsky, Shelton, & Moore, 2015).

Too often the result of this disconnect and these tenuous school-university relationships is a lack of intentionality in the design and implementation of the field-based structures, particularly with how teacher candidates and mentor teachers are matched (Thompson, Hagenah, Lohwasser, & Laxto, 2015). In the authors' own experiences over the past thirty years—as university faculty, doctoral students, mentor teachers, and teacher candidates across more than 15 universities—too many programs use what they have come to describe as the "cannon" method of making such placements (Ronfeldt, 2012). That is, a university staff member—typically not a faculty member engaged with preservice teachers on a day-to-day basis—launches candidates into a school district, hoping they will survive a sometimes-unannounced landing in a school and thrive with mentors usually selected through a request for volunteers and a principal's nod of an approval.

Unfortunately, these are not the only concerns with the traditional model of field-based experiences. Most candidates' clinical experiences—and particularly their early field experiences—are unintentionally designed and inadequately supervised (Darling-Hammond, 2009; Valencia, Martin, Place, & Grossman, 2009; Zeichner, 2010; Zeichner & Bier, 2015). Scholars have recently noted that current field-based teacher education models are often supervised by educators (e.g., graduate students or retired school administrators or teachers) with limited expertise in teacher preparation (Clift & Brady, 2005; Zeichner, 2012). As well, preservice teachers are provided insufficient opportunities to examine the dilemmas of teaching, with much of their learning in field-based experiences focused on the technical nature of schools and classrooms (Ball & Forzani, 2009; Caprano, Capraro, Capraro, & Helfeldt, 2010). An NCATE commentary offers a damning account of the state of field-based teacher preparation:

While new and experienced teachers repeatedly cite classroom-based experiences and student teaching as the most highly valued elements of their preparation, clinical practice remains the most ad hoc part of teacher preparation in many programs. (NCATE, 2010, p. 4)

School-University Partnerships

Teacher education programs offering quality, field-based clinical experiences exist, but these are too often "lighthouse" efforts, rather than the norm with structures that can be taken to scale in the wide-ranging contexts of educator preparation (Feurer, Floden, Chudowsky, & Ahn, 2013; Haj-Broussard, Husbands, Karge, McAalister, McCabe, Omelan, Payne, Person, Perterson, & Stephens, 2015). In response, numerous accrediting bodies, practitioners, and scholars have recognized the potential of strong school-university partnerships as foundational to such experiences (CAEP, 2015; NAPDS, 2008; Rust & Clift, 2015). In recognition of the potential of school-university partnerships for addressing these clinical experience needs CAEP's Standard 2, "Clinical Partnerships and Practice," highlights school-university partnerships as an answer this challenge.

While the professional development school (PDS) model embodies an emphasis on strong school-university partnerships, the field of teacher preparation has long debated the exact nature of PDSs. An early definition from the Carnegie Forum on Education and the Economy (1986) described a PDS as a clinical school comprised of chosen public schools and colleges of education and arts and sciences committed to preparing future teachers. Goodlad, Soder, and McDaniel (2008) named PDSs "schools of pedagogy," while Colburn (1993) called a PDS a "teaching hospital" (p. 9)—a concept that was extended by Anderson (1993), who argued that PDSs were induction schools for teacher candidates' completion of student teaching internships. Levine and Trachtman (1997) summarized a PDS as a symbiotic partnership between a college of teacher education and a public school. The Holmes Group (1986, 1990)—the key organization associated with developing and advocating for the PDS structure—determined that PDSs would be "a new kind of education institution" (p. ii).

The latest CAEP (2015) standards and the numerous national recommendations highlighted above align closely with the original PDS philosophy and tenets from the late 1980s, NCATE's (2001) original PDS standards, and NAPDS's (2008) "Nine Essentials"—particularly with regard to the nature of clinical preparation and its field-based elements. The field of educator preparation has witnessed a surge in PDS-related publications and scholarly materials in the past decade, with dozens of books and a research journal (*School-University Partnerships*) dedicated to examining the work of this model. Perhaps most importantly, an emerging body of research has scrutinized the impact of PDS and school-university structures on PK-12 student achievement, pre- and in-service teachers, and educator development (Boyle-Baise & McIntyre, 2008; Ipkeze, Broikou, Hildenbrand, & Gladstone-Brown, 2012; Wong & Glass, 2009).

One of the most significant benefits of PDS experiences—particularly related to teacher education experiences and as documented by recent research—is how PDSs champion collaboration within and across universities and schools and aid future teachers in integrating the theories they encounter in their university teacher education courses into their developing classroom pedagogies (Cochran-Smith, Ell, Grudnoff, Haigh, Hill, & Ludlow, 2016; Cozza, 2010; Henry, Tryjankowski, Dicamillo, & Bailey, 2010; Shroyer, Yahnke, Bennett, & Dunn, 2007). Additional studies have documented how experiences in PDS contexts during one's teacher education program are especially helpful in terms of new teacher induction and teacher hiring and retention in traditionally hard-to-staff schools (Fleener & Dahm, 2007; Flessner & Lecklider, 2017; Latham & Vogt, 2007). A growing number of studies have also documented how PDS- and school-university partnership-based teacher preparation is superior to teacher training that occurs in non-PDS contexts (Castle, Rockwood, & Tortorra, 2008; Grossman, 2010; Reynolds, Ross, & Rakow, 2002).

THE CHALLENGE

Based on this growing body of research and the authors' considerable experiences as teacher educators and in a variety of roles in teacher education programs, the PDS model seems to hold the greatest organizational promise for addressing these pressing field-based clinical practice needs. But, as noted in the introduction to this chapter, the authors hazard that the singular concept of PDS to which so many in the field of educator preparation have aspired for nearly 40 years is insufficient for this challenge. Rather, the authors propose a context-specific notion of PDS as a potential alternative to this grand, historical version of school-university partnerships. That is, this concept of partnership remains true to the NAPDS Nine Essentials and the NCATE PDS standards but is responsive to local needs.

As teacher educators, the authors of this chapter are committed to the most effective field-based clinical practice experiences for teacher candidates. They were all drawn to school-university partnership structures and particularly to the PDS model (Holmes Group, 1986, 1990) as the result of these frameworks' commitments to teacher education, in particular to addressing teacher candidates' needs for quality field-based clinical experiences. These school-university partnership structures and the PDS model offer all constituents—university-based teacher education faculty, veteran classroom teachers, future teachers, and, of course, Pre-K-12 students—a rich and overlapping set of advantages.

Yet, as veteran classroom teachers and seasoned partnership and PDS practitioners, the authors are conscious of the tensions between the current calls for enhanced field-based clinical experiences and the intensifying accountability measures now faced by classroom teachers and schools. The partnership and PDS structures detailed in this chapter are explicitly focused on addressing both the preparation of new teachers and the growth of PK-12 teachers. The authors' interpretation of the principles of PDS enables the novel structures that strengthen these partnerships, while highlighting impacts on teacher candidates.

This chapter's authors have welcomed the calls for enhanced and more effective clinical practice, which now includes the recent AACTE report *A Pivot Toward Clinical Practice, Its Lexicon, and the Renewal of Educator Preparation* (2018). They are also aware that preservice teachers' learning takes place in a host of settings, not all of which are formal educational arenas (Darling-Hammond, 2006a, 2006b, 2014; Grossman, Hammerness, & McDonald, 2009). These include community centers, college contexts, public and private school classrooms, and school extracurricular activities (Zeichner & McDonald, 2011). Yet, it is reasonable to assert that few experiences in teacher candidates' training are more significant than those occurring in school settings—from early field-based experiences that introduce them to their profession, to semester- and yearlong internships where they take on the more comprehensive set of teaching responsibilities (Heck & Bacharach, 2015; Wang, Spalding, Odell, Klecka, & Lin, 2010; Zeichner & Conklin, 2008).

Finally, the authors are conscious of the harsh realities facing many teacher education programs in the United States, with reduced enrollments and shrinking budgets. Nationally teacher education enrollment dropped by 31% between 2009 and 2013, a period during which overall post-secondary enrollment fell only 3% (USDOE, 2015). As a result, it is increasingly important that teacher educators "work smarter" and seek ways to enhance the partnership relationships and collaborative structures across our school-university contexts. The models of collaboration described in this chapter are offered as examples of these bolstered alliances.

Here the authors introduce a broader concept of school-university partnerships that relies on a continuum of collaborative practices and allows all constituents to engage in less demanding, lower stakes, and more abbreviated PDS-like structures. They describe two overarching partnership structures, one situated in an elementary education program and one utilized in three secondary programs—all being implemented in the authors' three home universities. Combined, these exemplify a context-specific framework for the mutually beneficial relationships that are at the core of the PDS paradigm and might strengthen others' partnership-oriented, field-based teacher education efforts.

First, the authors summarize George Mason University's elementary education program's pathways to partnership: "partner," "clinical practice," and "collaborative inquiry" PDS sites, providing examples of field-based teacher education efforts in each of these three PDS "pathways." They then describe efforts in three secondary education programs to employ a "project-based clinical experience" sub-model of PDS partnership. They support this portrayal with three summaries and initial studies of this form of field-based clinical experience from George Mason University, Kent State University, and the University of Tennessee, with unique applicability for schools and universities nationwide. Collectively, these two overarching models and the six examples represent enhancements to partnerships and PDSs, particularly as field-based clinical experience elements of teacher preparation and responsibility for improving teacher candidates' preparation experiences become more of a joint responsibility for university- and school-based teacher educators (Zenkov, Parker, Parsons, Pellegrino, & Pytash, 2017).

PARTNERSHIP STRUCTURE 1: PATHWAYS TO PARTNERSHIP IN THE ELEMENTARY EDUCATION PDS NETWORK AT GEORGE MASON UNIVERSITY

History and Contexts

Mason's elementary education program has been engaged in PDS work since 1991, a period during which the program has undergone four major revisions, each driven by input from stakeholders via its PDS advisory group (Parker, Parsons, Groth, & Levine-Brown, 2016; Parsons, Parker, Bruyning, & Daoud, 2016; Parsons, Groth, Parker, Brown, Sell & Sprague, 2017). A number of characteristics have remained foundational to the program across these iterations. These include a rigorous admissions process conducted by teams of program faculty—including authors Parsons, Parker, Brown, and Groth—and classroom teachers that includes an interview and a writing sample. Coursework facilitates the integration of theory and practice, field experiences occurs in partner sites, internships are guided by trained clinical faculty who complete online and face-to-face modules provided free-of-charge by the university, and university faculty and school-based personnel facilitating the PDS relationship.

Teacher candidates progress through the elementary education program in cohorts of approximately 20 via one of two program options. Each option includes a structured course sequence with field hour requirements, culminating in either a yearlong (following area school division calendars) or semester-long internship. A particularly unique feature of this program—and key evidence of the strength of its partnership—is the explicit and direct manner in which schools contribute tangible resources: Yearlong candidates receive small monthly stipends in exchange for their availability to substitute at their school sites for a specified number of days across the school year (Parker, Parsons, Groth, & Levine-Brown, 2016; Parsons, Parker, Brunying, & Daoud, 2016; Parsons, Groth, Parker, Brown, Sell, & Sprague, 2017).

Current Reforms

In the program reform initiated in 2013, several contextual challenges drove revisions—issues that Parsons, Parker, Brown, and Groth imagine will resonate with teacher preparation programs around the United States (Parker, Parsons, Groth, & Levine-Brown, 2016; Parsons, Parker, Brunying, & Daoud, 2016; Parsons, Groth, Parker, Brown, Sell, & Sprague, 2017). First, program faculty expressed concern that there were considerable differences in the level of and interest in collaborative engagement among the program's 17 elementary school PDS partners, which were all called by the same name and provided the same university faculty support and financial benefits. Some school sites had experienced dramatic administrative and staff turnover, which negatively impacted their abilities to fully engage in PDS work. Others partners had interest only in working with interns for either semester- or yearlong experiences, and inquiry projects conducted jointly by university faculty and classroom teachers held no appeal.

University faculty also faced a growing set of internal and external pressures. These included financial constraints in the college (related to changes in payment for internship supervision) and decreasing resources to support university faculty for their work in PDS sites. The ultimate consequence was that the program needed to be more consistent with matching a minimum number of interns in each PDS site and with university facilitators' supervision loads. As well, in response to CAEP Standard 2, the program needed to improve the quality of its early field experiences, including ensuring more diverse and rigorous experiences, which ultimately required an increase in the level of support provided to early field candidates.

As program faculty engaged with stakeholders regarding these issues, several non-negotiables emerged. While principals did not all have the resources or willingness to engage with all of the NAPDS's (2008) Nine Essentials, they wanted to be explicitly engaged in some form of PDS work and to be called a "PDS site." Second, the program's PDS partners overwhelmingly preferred to work with teacher candidates who were in the yearlong (rather than the semester-long) internship model, and they strongly advocated for an increase in the number of students in that particular program track. Third, the program's existing partnership structure mingled interns—student teachers in semester- and yearlong experiences—with field hours students—those teacher candidates completing early fieldwork—at the same school site. Partners consistently shared that this approach often confused mentor teachers, administrators, and even the program's own university facilitators, while diminishing schools' capacities for hosting candidates with high-quality mentor matches in both fieldwork and internship structures. The consequence was that field hours students felt they were relegated to second-class status and were often not placed with the most effective mentor teachers.

This intentional and extended series of program and partner conversations coincided with the elementary faculty member authors' planned open application process for their program's PDS network, another longstanding feature of the program. Every four to five years, schools engaged in the network were asked to review and renew their commitment to the program, and schools not already in the network but interested in collaboration were afforded an opportunity to apply for entry. These application and re-application processes were intended to both grow the network and to increase the diversity of the schools in which teacher candidates were able to work. Applying schools were required to provide student and community demographic information, as well as to demonstrate evidence of faculty buy-in and respond to questions related to teacher preparation, research goals, and professional development needs.

A Foundational Question and an Applicable Answer

Ultimately, these reform discussions caused elementary education faculty to question how to balance increasingly limited resources with their commitments to rich, sustained partnerships and the NAPDS Essentials (NAPDS, 2008), which these faculty believed was the best structure for preparing teacher candidates. The dilemma boiled down to foundational questions that the authors imagine many other university- and school-based teacher educators and teacher education programs are facing: How might we best use diminishing resources to support partner schools that are ready and willing to engage fully with the Nine Essentials and the most comprehensive version of PDS, while honoring the differentiated needs, capacities, and interests of all partners? Given the resource realities of schools and universities, how might we strengthen our partnerships to serve all of our constituents, with a primary focus on teacher candidates?

The remainder of this section details how these elementary program authors have answered these questions and explains their responses to these macro- and micro-level contextual issues. These responses triggered the development of differentiated routes—or pathways—to PDS participation (Gelfuso, Dennis, & Parker, 2015; Parker, Parsons, Groth, & Levine-Brown, 2016; Parsons, Parker, Brunying, & Daoud, 2016). These revised program structures have explicitly addressed the pressing need for earlier and more rigorous fieldwork in candidates' preparation sequences while simultaneously being attentive to the needs of school partners. As well, the resulting context-specific framework for establishing PDS relationships has enhanced the engagement of all stakeholders while it acknowledges the need for flexibility in PDS partnerships. In summary, these authors propose that such partnerships might be strengthened through the creation and implementation of differentiated collaborative structures. The examples detailed here are offered as illustrations of these pathways; while the authors have conducted research on the nature and impact of these structures, they do not share the results of these studies here, instead focusing on the details of these examples' implementation.

The elementary education authors of this chapter remain committed to all four of the original PDS objectives: (1) to enhance PK-12 student learning; (2) to promote professional development for all educators involved in PDS partnerships; (3) to support preservice teacher preparation endeavors, and; (4) to engage in collaborative inquiry. It was determined that the fourth element would be the primary point of differentiation among these pathways. Partner schools select the pathway that best fits their individual school context at a particular point in time. The three pathways—"partner" sites, "clinical practice" sites, and "collaborative inquiry" sites—allow for flexibility and movement within the PDS network, making room for unanticipated changes at PK-6 sites that may necessitate a shift in the degree of partnership engagement, but enabling sites to remain involved and not have to drop from the partnership work altogether. All elementary schools in the elementary education's PDS network are public schools from one of several school districts surrounding Mason, which is located in Fairfax, Virginia, twelve miles west of Washington, DC.

A number of features remain common across these three partnership options. For example, all schools in the network have a designated school-based point of contact that serves as the liaison between the school and the university. These "site facilitators" are instrumental in organizing placements, hosting orientations to the school, addressing the inevitable challenges that emerge in partnership work, and attending a range of constituent meetings across the academic year. All schools in the PDS network also have access to the college's mentor training or "clinical faculty" course, a three-credit graduate level class offered free-of-charge that prepares teachers for working with preservice teachers and for collaborating with the range of constituents of the elementary education program. All teachers hosting semester- or yearlong interns are encouraged to complete the clinical faculty course before or during their first year of serving as a mentor teacher. Finally, each site has some relationship with a university facilitator who is a university faculty member or adjunct that coordinates activities at each school. These university-based liaisons are points of contact based at the university, but in most cases are affiliated with one school site.

Elementary Example 1: Partner Site Pathway

Schools in the "partner" pathway host elementary teacher candidates in their early fieldwork. These field hours teacher candidates are given more attention and opportunities than is typical when they are at a site also populated with student teaching interns. As a result, they have more opportunities to interact with the school staff, and more high-quality mentors are available to work with them early and often. Given the program sequence and field hour requirements, this typically equates to about 30 hours of field work in a given semester. Teacher candidates complete these hours in 3-4 hour blocks of time across ten weeks of a given semester. Across their program sequence, candidates are required to complete field-based tasks that increase in intensity and teaching responsibility. All of these tasks are explicitly tied to coursework and represent opportunities for theory to practice connections. Each partner site has a dedicated site facilitator (a member of the school faculty or an administrator). This role is critical as it creates the infrastructure at the school site to support field hours students appropriately. A single university facilitator works with all of the partner sites, thus adding an additional layer of support.

School- and university-based teacher educators serving in these key capacities enable the program to establish effective communication channels throughout the semester.

While the value of the "partner site" pathway is clear from the details above, this option is also valuable to the PDS network as it provides a way for new school sites to engage with the elementary education program as well as for existing sites to decrease the intensity of their engagement. Given typical challenges in schools such as administrative turnover, changing state and school division mandates, and staff attrition, having an option to stay connected but change the level of engagement is significant. All teachers in partner schools have access to university-based staff development initiatives and trainings.

Field-Based Teacher Education in a Partner Site

Greer Elementary (a pseudonym) recently partnered with Mason's PDS Network to embrace one of the Nine Essentials, "collaboration," with key stakeholders to broaden the impact of the partnership on the education profession and the larger community. Specifically, for the past two years, Greer has partnered with chapter author Brown, a Mason faculty member with an expertise in Child Development, to host a university-based course onsite. The course is in the first block of work teacher candidates complete in the program, and therefore, the field requirements are typically observational in nature. Rather than follow the traditional model, the faculty member, an assistant principal, a site facilitator, and a handful of teachers eager to engage in teacher preparation collaboratively designed a site-based experience that integrated coursework and field hours in a blended model. Hallmarks of this experience have included: (a) university courses held at the school weekly with opportunities for candidate observation and in-service teacher and university faculty co-teaching; (b) candidate observation and participation in weekly collaborative learning team (CLT) meetings as well as other school-based activities (e.g., Back to School Night, Open House), and; (c) inclusion and attendance of candidates in school-based programs (e.g., Family Literacy, Special Education, Advanced Math).

These structures have allowed teacher candidates to move fluidly between coursework and observations, thus making what can be a theoretical topic (e.g., child development) more authentic. Support of a university-based teacher educator (the instructor), alongside school-based teacher educators (teachers), facilitated theory to practice connections and gave an important voice to both stakeholders. Also, stemming from this partnership, in-service teachers and school leaders have taken advantage of university resources (e.g., graduate classes, dissertation committee chairs, mentorship, conference presentations) to further their professional growth. The partner pathway allows Greer to play a unique, contextually appropriate and critical role in supporting early field hours students. Again, the partnership has been strengthened and the impact on teacher candidates and in-service teacher enhanced by the program's willingness to differentiate these PDS elements.

Elementary Example 2: Clinical Practice Sites

Schools may also elect to engage in the elementary PDS network as a "clinical practice" site. These sites host five or more student teaching interns. Clinical practice schools typically rotate between hosting semester-long and yearlong interns as a means of addressing PDS administrators' concerns that there should be an equitable distribution of yearlong teacher candidates among sites. Clinical practice sites differ from partner sites in that they must have a large cadre of teachers across grade levels who are able to mentor interns (a role that requires three years of teaching experience and a recommendation from an administrator) and who are willing to complete the advanced mentor training course. Each clinical practice site is served by a university-based teacher educator called a "university facilitator"— typically an adjunct faculty member but in some instances a full-time faculty member who is seeking to increase partnership efforts at a site. University facilitators spend one day each week at the school site.

Field-Based Teacher Education in a Clinical Practice Site

For the past three summers, two instructors (authors Parker and Groth) have integrated two courses and embedded their instruction and field work at a Title I clinical practice site. The courses have met daily for five weeks primarily at the site, thus maximizing the time at the end of the K-12 school year and the beginning of the May session semester at the university. Planning and preparation engaged both school-based teacher educators (site facilitators, administrators, mentor teachers) and university-based teacher educators (university faculty members and university facilitators). These shared conversations were key from a logistical standpoint but also revealed opportunities to engage school-based teacher educators such as literacy specialists and instructional coaches in ways that these authors had not considered.

Together, Parker and Groth created a field-based experience that placed teacher candidates in trios in the primary grades. The grade level placement served teacher candidates and the K/1 students well as it provided opportunities for additional support for early readers and real-world practice for teacher candidates. Logistically, it allowed teacher candidates to avoid interfering with the intermediate grades' testing schedule. Placing students in trios provided significant support for literacy instruction for a larger number of early readers in a given classroom. In addition, the trios created opportunities for teacher candidates to have shared observations and a collaborative orientation for working on their assignments.

Because of the intensity of the experience, the first few course meetings focused on content front-loading for both the "Literacy Methods" and "Differentiated Instruction" courses. At the end of the first week, the instructors (Parker and Groth) collaborated with the school site to host an orientation and tour and provided time for teacher candidates to do an initial visit into their mentor teacher's classroom. The day concluded with a session on working with language learners led by the school's English for Speakers of Other Languages (ESOL) teachers. Weeks two through four followed a pattern in which teacher candidates spent a portion of each day in their field experience classroom and a portion in their courses at the school site.

Because a key aspect of the integration of these two courses centered on understanding diverse learners and differentiating literacy instruction, the authors developed a number of field-based assignments that facilitated the transfer of course content into practice. These were particularly powerful as students moved fluidly between their coursework and K/1 placements each day. The field-based assignments included planning and implementing a structured read aloud, planning and implementing a differentiated extension for the read aloud, and planning and implementing a small guided reading group lesson. Prior to completing any of these tasks, the teacher candidate trios worked collaboratively to administer multiple forms of formative assessment to better understand their K/1 learners. In all lessons, teacher candidates used a video coding platform to provide feedback to each other and to critically reflect on their experiences.

Overall, the field-based courses created opportunities for candidates to make theory to practice connections, as well as collaborate with each other and mentor with planning, instruction, and reflection tasks. In this example, a clinical partner site—which also hosted interns—was able to engage in a site-based course experience that required more extensive mentorship and training. This was in part due to the presence of faculty members (course instructors) who were already present at the site weekly and beginning to build relationships with teams. This structure provided enhanced professional development and leadership opportunities for teachers who might not otherwise have been eligible to mentor interns. It is important to note that this site transitioned to the "collaborative inquiry" pathway following the first iteration of this experience and remains dedicated to supporting the work each summer.

Elementary Example 3: Collaborative Inquiry Sites

Collaborative inquiry sites represent the third pathway in the elementary education program PDS Network. Collaborative inquiry schools are exactly like clinical practice sites with two exceptions: collaborative inquiry sites have a full-time university faculty member onsite one day per week as the university facilitator and only host yearlong interns. The university facilitators at collaborative inquiry sites are responsible for internship supervision much like those faculty assigned to clinical practice sites. In addition, university facilitators in this pathway are available to support teachers' professional development, engage in collaborative inquiry project with teachers, and pursue grant opportunities. The consistent presence of a full-time university faculty member operating as a university facilitator creates opportunities for shared teaching and research endeavors, and collaborative inquiry sites are frequently tapped to experiment with program innovations.

Field-Based Teacher Education in a Collaborative Inquiry Site

A collaborative inquiry site recently served as an incubator for a university faculty/facilitator's (author Parsons) experimentation with a site-based literacy methods course. In addition to the responsibilities of internship supervision, the university facilitator maximized his relationships across the school to create an authentic experience. This included hosting a literacy methods course in the school's library and capitalizing on his knowledge of and relationship with literacy exemplars on the faculty and engaging classroom teachers as hosts for teacher candidates' observations of literacy instruction. In these observation cycles, classroom teachers attended the afternoon university class to reflect with candidates and the university facilitator on their instruction and address preservice teachers' questions. The opportunities presented here strengthened the partnership and provided additional opportunities to engage teacher candidates in practical ways with theoretical content. Our research demonstrated that teacher candidates' valued the site-based course and they learned much about literacy teaching and learning (Parsons, Groth, Parker, Brown, Sell, & Sprague, 2017).

Similarly, another university facilitator (author Groth) used an organic approach to grow the use of teacher inquiry at her newly minted collaborative inquiry site, which was using a Professional Learning Community (PLC) model. The site facilitator—who was the school-based literacy specialist—invited the university facilitator, an elementary literacy faculty member, to sit in on a kindergarten literacy PLC meeting. During the meeting, the kindergarten team (six teachers ranging in experience from 1-19 years, a special education teacher, an ESOL teacher, and an elementary intern) discussed the performance of their lowest achieving kindergartners. It was during that meeting that the possibility of research arose from the organic question of how to better help these learners.

The generation of a question led author Groth to share a typical action research model (Mills, 2017) with the kindergarten team—one that is used throughout the elementary education program and culminates in a capstone action research project during internship. In this instance, the university faculty/ facilitator guided the kindergarten team through the action research process: beginning with the question they were interested in and consultation with reading professional resources and academic research, transitioning to collecting data, and concluding with data analysis. Ultimately, the team presented their action research with the university facilitator at NAPDS's annual meeting and also made their work public by sharing it at a faculty meeting at the school site and at a school board meeting. Action research has now become a platform for several grade levels, which on the surface may appear to not directly impact teacher candidates. However, this site also hosts five teacher candidates in internship each year. These teacher candidates get to directly observe and experience the role of action research in their mentors' professional development.

Both collaborative inquiry site examples highlight how the presence of a faculty member strengthens the school-university partnership and ultimately impacts teacher candidate learning. The very nature of a collaborative inquiry site creates spaces in the PDS network for faculty and PK-12 educators to pursue inquiry and innovative practice. This is in part due to the relationships in place and shared dedication to mutually beneficial partnerships and inquiry. This directly impacts mentor teachers' and teacher candidates' professional learning.

PARTNERSHIP STRUCTURE 2: CRITICAL, PROJECT-BASED ESPERIENCES IN THE SECONDARY EDUCATION PROGRAMS AT GEORGE MASON UNIVERSITY, KENT STATE UNIVERSITY AND THE UNIVERSITY OF TENNESSEE

While the PDS model aligns well with elementary schools, secondary schools are departmentalized, which often reduces the number of potential mentor teachers for teacher candidates and shifts the nature of the partnerships faculty members can develop and implement. Yet, by considering a differentiated notion of collaboration, authors Zenkov, Pellegrino, and Pytash have discovered ways to strengthen their school-university partnerships and have a greater impact on teacher candidates. Specifically, these authors propose the "critical, project-based" clinical experiences model as one that is more responsive to secondary school settings, retains many of the impactful aspects of PDS (e.g., school-university partnership, authenticity, collaboration, reflective practice, etc.), but does not require full-school buy-in and engagement. None of the three universities whose educator preparation programs are considered in this chapter has a secondary education program that has been able to sustain the intensive school-wide partnership structures like those the elementary education program has established. The faculties at Mason, Kent, and Tennessee—all of which have relatively large secondary programs, averaging more than 200 teacher candidates each—have all experienced many fits and starts in their efforts to establish school-university partnerships to support their field-based teacher education efforts. Yet, like their Mason elementary education colleagues, Zenkov, Pellegrino, and Pytash have all recently been able to strengthen their partnerships through the implementation of a field-based innovation called "critical, project-based" clinical experiences.

Authors Zenkov, Pellegrino, and Pytash have now developed and implemented this new model of fieldwork practices across three university/school/community setting; this model is rooted in the primary objective of establishing partnership schools where preservice teachers might have meaningful field experiences. They believe this model holds the potential for extending their existing partnership efforts and establishing new partnerships, largely by connecting university-based teacher educators, teacher candidates, and school-based practitioners via collaborations on intervention-based instructional and research projects.

CPB clinical experiences provide short-term and intense opportunities for teacher candidates to engage with young people, with a particular focus on youths who have been marginalized in schools or who have been labeled as "struggling" learners. Such field-based experiences appeal to the notion that adolescents—whose perspectives are rarely considered in school structures and teachers' curricular and pedagogical decisions—might have central roles in teacher education reform and offer key input to future and veteran teachers about their pedagogies (Fine, Torre, Burns, & Payne, 2007; Lavadenz & Hollins, 2015). As such, CPB experiences intend to challenge some of the foundational assumptions of schools and society, engaging all of schools' and teacher education institutions' constituents with a critical orientation and social justice commitments (Zygmunt & Clark, 2016).

These short-term interventions rely on and promote traditional, multimodal, and civic literacies to consider authentic questions. CPB projects are oriented around questions that are at the core of a democratic society and enable teachers and teacher educators to integrate a focus on democratic education into instructional units, calling on young people and their teachers to answer questions like "What does it mean to be a citizen?" and "What does exceptional teaching look like?". These projects offer professional development opportunities for the broadest set of schools' and teacher education programs' participants, and result in outcomes and products with relevance for audiences in and beyond the school walls (Pellegrino, Zenkov, & Calamito, 2013; Pytash & Zenkov, 2018).

CPB clinical experiences meet preservice teachers' most pressing need—chances to engage with young people in teaching roles—while honoring veteran school-based teacher educators. They also simultaneously provide university-based teacher educators with new roles that make teacher education practices and education scholarship uniquely relevant to this fullest range of schools' constituents. These experiences call on preservice teachers to take an inquiry stance, with teacher candidates asking about who adolescents are, what they believe about grand topics, and how they best learn. Such a stance also repositions adolescents—again, typically viewed as the receivers of educational services—as co-teachers of educator preparation programs.

Perhaps most importantly to a consideration of field-based teacher education practices is the fact that CPB clinical experiences begin with classroom interventions that are of mutual interest to veteran teachers, preservice teachers, young people, and university-based teacher educators. Once a project focus has been identified—with input of classroom teachers—we consider the administrative structures of our partnering schools. Acknowledging the professional needs and pressures of the teachers involved is essential. With some projects, class meeting times might be an issue; with others, teachers require assessment components that meet accountability needs. All of these factors are taken into account before Zenkov, Pellegrino, and Pytash coordinate schedules with the participating teacher candidates. Across their three institutions and over the last five years these authors have worked with more than 100 teacher candidates, dozens of classroom teachers, and several hundred PK-12 students in our CPB projects (Pellegrino, Zenkov, Calamito, & Sells, 2014; Pytash & Zenkov, 2018; Zenkov, Bell, Lynch, Ewaida, Harmon, & Pellegrino, 2012; Zenkov, Pellegrino, Sell, Ewaida, Bell, Fell, Biernesser, & McManis, 2014). Many of these projects have been implemented with young people in juvenile justice facilities and "alternative" and traditional schools (Pytash, 2017; Zenkov & Pytash, in press), but each of these authors is increasingly integrating these experiences across their educator preparation programs and making them foundational features of the field-based elements of these programs.

Below Zenkov, Pellegrino, and Pytash provide summaries of three recent CPB projects they have facilitated in their Virginia, Ohio, and Tennessee contexts. They detail these projects in varying detail—offering a richer description of the Virginia project to best illustrate CPB efforts and where they fit in the context of the continuum of field-based teacher education efforts with which they are engaged. The authors then summarize their Ohio and Tennessee projects to illustrate the range of these projects in action and across contexts. With their explicit focus on partner teachers' curricula, these structures are strengthening these partnerships while providing teacher candidates with authentic teaching and learning opportunities. In the descriptions below the authors not only detail these CPB examples but offer summaries of their initial research on these partnership features.

Secondary Example 1: George Mason University's CPB Field Experiences With English Language Learners

In a recent CPB project, middle and high school youths were asked to share their perspectives on school via both images and writings. As a part of this project, the team of veteran and preservice teacher educators and teachers used "photovoice" methods to ask mostly English language learning (ELL) adolescents to take pictures that depicted what in their lives impacted their success in school (Streng, Rhodes, Ayala, Eng., Arceo, & Phipps, 2004; Zenkov, Pellegrino, Sell, Ewaida, Bell, Fell, Biernesser, & McManis, 2014). Utilizing the photographs they took in this project and supported by writing conferences with preservice teachers and author Zenkov and Pellegrino, these youths eventually described and illustrated a range of factors that resulted in what many often—mistakenly—perceive to be an indifference to school and writing. As a result of conducting this project with these diverse, mostly immigrant young people, teacher candidates were able to develop a deeper understanding of the methods through which middle and high school students are best able to engage with writing endeavors. This and other CPB projects have led Zenkov and Pellegrino and their colleagues to reconceptualize their program structure with field-based experiences as the foundation.

Authors Zenkov and Pellegrino are veteran university-based literacy and social studies teacher educators, and this CPB experience involved approximately 30 preservice teachers, several veteran middle and high school teachers, and approximately 90 young adults. This clinical experience effort was propelled, in part, by the question of what teachers and teacher educators could do to counter ELLs' school rejection. This profession- and education institution-spanning team recognized that these endeavors might be based not only in classroom and project activities, but, perhaps more importantly, these efforts might also be rooted in a field-based orientation, supporting attempts to help preservice teachers understand, approach, and teach these still new student populations. These teacher candidates were required to complete 15 hours of observations for their clinical experiences, but Zenkov and Pellegrino gave them the option of participating in this CPB project, letting them know that such an experience would give them almost daily opportunities to facilitate whole group, small group, and one-to-one instruction with diverse adolescents.

These inquiries rely on a "youths as experts" framework: the idea that adolescents can be participants in their own learning and determine and share insights into how teachers might help them navigate their academic experiences. Some researchers are considering students' points of view on our foundational educational institutions, in hopes of understanding youths' perspectives on school and to be able to better engage them in meaningful school activities (Easton & Condon, 2009; Yonezawa & Jones, 2009). Like this CPB project, many of these studies have used visually oriented media to understand factors related to the success and failure of these young people in these language arts and social studies classes (Cook-Sather, 2009; Pole, 2004; Zenkov, 2009; Zenkov & Harmon, 2009).

Teacher candidates co-facilitated this project, most often working in teams of two with one adolescent in each of two ex-urban settings and one urban school site, helping adolescents to complete digital photographic explorations and reflective writings based on the pictures youth took. Zenkov and Pellegrino called on young people to use photographs and related writings to illustrate and describe the purposes of school, the supports for their school achievement, and the impediments to their success. The authors shared examples of youths' images and writings from previous projects, then ensured that each team of a preservice teacher and a young person had a working smartphone camera. The teacher candidates then led young people on "photo walks" around their schools and their neighborhoods, the first real step in the photo elicitation process.

After participants took on average 100 images in response to the three project questions, the preservice teachers worked with students to examine, select, discuss, and write about photos they felt best represented the ideas they wanted to share. Zenkov and Pellegrino had previously modeled the series of writing elicitation conferences they employ to help young people write about both literal and abstract ideas in their pictures. These prospective teachers then dialogued with students to compose writings that elucidated the actions and concepts behind their images. The final step of the composition process involved teacher candidates transcribing youths' oral reactions to images and helping them edit their reflections on the photos that youth felt best answered the project questions.

In their post-session and post-project reflections the preservice teachers were surprised by how the chance to engage with students in one-on-one contexts revealed to them how they had to share something of themselves with young people if they were to be successful as teachers and if their young charges were going to find success as writers. This practice contradicted much of what they had been taught by other instructors in their licensure program, with Erin's quote among the most illustrative:

I was scared to screw up and from previous education classes they would always say do not mix your personal life with your teacher life. However…from the first day I found myself opening up to the students I worked with, which then led them to feel comfortable as well.

Another sentiment future teachers shared after engaging in this CPB experience related to adolescents' and their own comfort in teaching and learning situations. Erin spoke most articulately about this affective quality, reflecting that she learned "that it's important to make sure you're comfortable…or at least appear to be." She noted this comfort resulted from the "ability to bond with the student in a way that they felt comfortable talking." This notion of "comfort" was consistently linked with teachers' expressions of concern for their students, with Wilma commenting that she "never realized just how much it had an effect on students to know that their teachers really care."

Perhaps one of the most important lessons of these CPB writing instruction efforts that these teacher candidates noted was a contradiction to some of the insights about asking questions that had been gathered from earlier interventions. This CPB task was oriented around the questions of youths' impressions of school, and while Zenkov and Pellegrino most often pose these queries explicitly in the writing conferences they and the preservice teachers conduct, these authors have also generated a list of more than three dozen elicitation questions on which they rely. Teacher candidates noted that this elicitation process was as much an art as a science of asking set questions, based—again—on their own and their students' comfort.

Secondary Example 2: Kent State University's CPB's Experiences With Adjudicated Youths

Too often the reading and writing instruction preservice teachers observe in schools is focused on preparing students to take state standardized achievement tests (George, 2010). What they see in schools is frequently a scripted, skills-based approach to teaching reading and writing, particularly for those students labeled struggling readers and writers by their scores on those achievement tests. For a teacher educator such as Pytash, who led the project described in this section, the concern is that these types of early field experiences often lead preservice teachers to categorize success in school and literacy in narrow ways (Cervetti, Damico, & Pearson, 2006; Haddix & Sealey-Ruiz, 2012). As a result, each iteration of the CPB field experience that Pytash has implemented has been driven by the belief that there is a benefit to creating an opportunity in which preservice teachers have a personal experience getting to know the students who are most marginalized and disenfranchised—those students who are most often pushed out of schools.

Each semester, the CPB field experiences that Pytash leads differs, depending on the needs of the teachers and students at the detention center where these projects are conducted. Iterations of CPB field experiences have included participation from cohorts of Integrated Language Arts preservice teachers, two teachers at the detention center, and two university faculty members, as well as hundreds of youth who have been detained. However, guiding the work these teacher candidates are completing have been two broad questions: (1) Who are young adults as writers? And; (2) What does this mean for writing instruction?

These broad questions shape the pedagogical practices this team of novice and veteran teachers implement, with the preservice teachers working with small groups of young people, but with all pushing back against the narrowing definitions of writing and what counts as writing—which ultimately determine who counts as a writer. These guiding questions help everyone involved consider the rich writing practices that people engage in when sending tweets, or writing in poetry, short stories, persuasive speeches, or while uploading videos to YouTube channels. Ultimately, the object is to explore how "writing is embedded in complex social relationships and their appropriate languages" (NCTE, 2016).

CPB field experiences at the detention center—which are required as one of the early clinical experiences for Author's 6 cohort of future English teachers—are designed as writing workshops, which youth attend weekly. Workshops include lyric analysis, screenplay composing, flash fiction, micro-fiction, street photography, hypertext analysis, and concrete poetry. The goal is that through the instruction teacher candidates and students will engage in conversations about language and the broad ways human being communicate through written and visual texts—and often a merging of the two.

Typically, preservice teachers are placed in teaching groups of 3-4, serving as critical colleagues for each other, when planning and implementing instruction for a weekly writing workshop session. Their planning is supported by university faculty who assist by providing feedback during the process. During instruction, preservice teachers are also supported by a detention center teacher and a university faculty member, who also later provide feedback on instruction. Approximately 12-15 youth attend each weekly writing workshop.

One of the many insights these teacher candidates have garnered across these CPB projects is that too often in schools writing is assigned instead of taught. CPB field experiences provide preservice teachers the opportunity to conceptualize how they will teach writing and specific instructional approaches that they will implement. For example, Max, a future teacher who worked with a recent project, explained:

I never realized the importance of mentor texts in writing instruction. I've always thought that writing just kind of appears because of a combination of creativity and happenstance. I guess I've always just thought that teachers took a back seat in writing, when in reality teachers lay the foundation for written work.

Preservice teachers have also begun to consider how writing instruction is structured. For example, in written reflections, preservice teachers consistently mentioned giving students choice and freedom. Melanie explained:

I am well aware that with learning there is rarely one way that works for everyone. My experiences at the detention center this semester have reaffirmed that belief time and time again. My time working with students at the detention center has opened my eyes to the benefits of allowing degree of freedom and choice in the classroom. Teachers need to plan instruction that allow for various styles of expression and writing.

Preservice teachers' understandings about writing instruction seemed to stem from the relationships they developed with youth. Their initial stereotypes about detained youth were countered by their experiences from working closely with them. Preservice teachers often shared that before the experience they assumed youths would be "hostile" or that they might "act out" or "give us a hard time." Olivia admitted, "I had flashbacks of all of the 'bad kids in class' I grew up with."

Through course readings, debriefings, and, most importantly, these experiences with youths, preservice teachers began to explore the structures of schools and societies that might inhibit some youth from being successful in school. For example, Dom explained,

Our readings, this experience, made me think about how socioeconomic factors and race play a greater role in education and even contribute to the arbitrary labeling of students as lazy or uncaring.

Olivia went on to state,

I do not believe a person can be successfully taught by a person who has no faith in them or desire to see them succeed. For the rest of my career as an educator, I want to put my students' needs first and keep my personal reservations aside.

Ultimately this CPB example has resulted in teacher candidates' developing awareness of culturally relevant and culturally sustaining pedagogies. They are more conscious of the power they have as teachers and as adult in their interactions with young people, and they recognize that they need to take more of an "ask first" approach with young people. This model of field-based teacher preparation has provided these candidates with authentic teaching and learning opportunities, while extending our school-university partnerships to new contexts where the smaller teacher/student ratio is needed and results in benefits for all constituents.

Secondary Example 3: The University of Tennessee's Critical, Project-Based Clinical Experiences to Support Youths' Conceptual Learning

What is racism? The word has represented daily reality to millions of black people for centuries, yet it is rarely defined—perhaps just because that reality has been so commonplace - Carmichael and Hamilton, Black Power (1967, p. 3)

This quote from black civil rights activists, Stokely Carmichael and Charles Hamilton, written a half century ago, illustrates the enduring nature of racism and the challenges of eradicating it from U.S. society. Its message continues to resonate with many educators as a reminder of the complexity and ubiquity of racism then and now. Its message also was the driving force for a project a team led by chapter author Pellegrino undertook as a clinical partnership in their educator preparation program at the University of Tennessee. The project objectives were to help teacher candidates to work with young people in a high school U.S. history course think deeply about the nature and effects of racism, and in so doing, nurture the partnership between the program and a local high school where teacher candidates were often placed for clinical experience. The lessons, which drew upon tenets of historical thinking as well as principles of conceptual learning (NCSS, 2013; SHEG, 2015), were collaboratively designed and implemented by the clinical team that included author Pellegrino, a teacher educator; Caleb, a mentor teacher; and Steven, the teacher candidate. Through this project, this team strengthened their partnership and enacted a model of clinical experience that purposefully connected those involved in supporting teacher candidates through mentoring and high leverage instructional practices.

This CPB field experience took place within the context of the University of Tennessee's graduate-level social science program for prospective middle and high school social studies teachers. The central feature of this program is the yearlong internship that includes full-time work in a middle or high school with university coursework taken one evening per week. This model allows for simultaneous clinical and coursework experiences ideally designed to foster connections between theory and practice. Within the program, Pellegrino supervises interns each year, and in 2016-2017, worked with Steven and his mentor, Caleb.

Steven's placement was done through a collaboration between program faculty and the College Office of School-Based Experiences. Caleb, the mentor with whom Steven was paired, was voted "mentor of the year" by the University's College of Education, Health, and Human Sciences in the year prior to this project based on his extraordinary efforts to support teacher candidates and maintain a connection between candidates' coursework and clinical practice.

As a way to help Steven practice lesson planning and working collaboratively with colleagues, the team came to focus on the opportunity to help students in Caleb and Steven's U.S. history class build foundational and conceptual knowledge of race and racism. This was determined to be an area of the curriculum with which Caleb saw his students struggle to engage in previous years and one that is foundational to so many periods and events of U.S. history (Erickson, 2002; Grossman, Smagorinsky, & Valencia, 1999). For Steven, we anticipated that the project would help him become involved in planning lessons that supported conceptual understanding and see how students might be able to apply their conceptual learning in subsequent lessons and units (NCSS, 2013).

The project included lessons designed for six 90-minute class sessions, which were planned collaboratively by the team. The activities were developed to encourage students to think and dialogue about race and racism through a range of activities with differing degrees of learner/teacher interaction. Activities included concept map development, image analysis, and structured academic controversy (SHEG, 2015). Each activity was co-taught by the team and interspersed with whole class debriefing of the activity and discussion of the central concepts: race and racism. Each team member had the opportunity to lead and support classroom instruction.

Findings from the project suggested that the students broadened their conceptual understanding of race and racism. Students demonstrated progress toward learning about explicit and implicit expressions of racism and appropriating their knowledge into pre-existing schema (Grossman, Smagorinsky, & Valencia, 1999). While many students continued to struggle to apply the concept to their current lives, most demonstrated a deeper and more nuanced understanding beyond traditional curricular definitions and examples of racism.

The project also strengthened an existing school-university partnership by bringing together a university-based teacher educator with an experienced, school-based partner keen to find more meaningful ways to support teacher candidates in their clinical experiences. The result was that each member of this clinical team found a deeper appreciation for the possibility a robust clinical partnership and CPB experiences as one form of field-based structures can bring to teacher preparation.

CONCLUSION

Numerous scholars and national organizations such as CAEP, AACTE, and NAPDS have issued calls for teacher educators to turn educator preparation efforts "upside down" (NCATE, 2010, p. XX) in that they put clinical practice at the helm (Hollins, 2015; Liu, 2013; Nolan, 2015). The authors of this chapter have embraced these calls and have designed educator preparation that is not only field-based and clinically-rich but also innovative. The elementary education program at George Mason University designed "pathways to partnership" structures that allow partner schools different means of engaging with the program. Likewise, the secondary education programs at George Mason University, Kent State University, and the University of Tennessee have created three distinct "critical, project-based clinical experiences" that compel preservice teachers to reconsider how educators best meet secondary students' needs.

This chapter describes the outcomes of years of questioning the status quo of teacher education in part through efforts to enhance our school-university partnerships. While these pathways and projects we have described are distinct, they are united by their responsive nature; they are responsive to teacher candidates', veteran teachers', and youths' needs and interests. We acknowledge that the efforts to further promote teacher candidates' learning and PK-12 students' achievement is an ongoing endeavor. We invite other teacher educators to hear the clarion calls for reform and join us in reconceptualizing our practices as field-based teacher educators to construct clinical experiences that simultaneously serve future teachers and their students. We hope the structures and examples detailed in this chapter can inform others in their own reform efforts.

REFERENCES

American Association of Colleges for Teacher Education. (2011). *Transformations in educator preparation: Effectiveness and accountability*. Washington, DC: Author.

American Association of Colleges for Teacher Education. (2012). *Where We Stand: Clinical Preparation of Teachers*. Washington, DC: Author.

American Association of Colleges for Teacher Education (AACTE). (2010). *The clinical preparation of teachers: A policy brief*. Washington, DC: Author.

American Association of Colleges for Teacher Education (AACTE). (2018). *A Pivot Toward Clinical Practice, Its Lexicon, and the Renewal of Educator Preparation*. Washington, DC: Author.

Anderson, C. R. (Ed.). (1993). *Voices of change: A report of clinical schools project*. Washington, DC: American Association of Colleges for Teacher Education.

Association of Teacher Educators (2015). *Revised standards for field experience*. Author.

Ball, D. L., & Forzani, F. M. (2009). The work of teaching and the challenge for teacher education. *Journal of Teacher Education*, *60*(5), 497–511. doi:10.1177/0022487109348479

Boyle-Baise, M., & McIntyre, D. J. (2008). What kind of experience? Preparing teachers in PDS or community settings. In M. Cochran-Smith, S. Feiman-Nemser, D. J. McIntyre, & K. E. Demers (Eds.), Handbook of research on teacher education: Enduring questions in changing contexts (3rd ed.; pp. 307–329). New York, NY: Routledge.

Burns, R. W., Jacobs, J., & Yendol-Hoppey, D. (2016). The changing nature of the role of the university supervisor and the function of preservice teacher supervision in an era of clinically-rich practice. *Action in Teacher Education*, *38*(4), 410–425. doi:10.1080/01626620.2016.1226203

Caprano, R., Capraro, M., Capraro, R., & Helfeldt, J. (2010). Do differing types of field experiences make a difference in teacher candidates' perceived level of competence? *Teacher Education Quarterly*, *37*(1), 131–154.

Carmichael, S., & Hamilton, C. V. (1967). *Black Power: The Politics of Liberation in America*. New York: Vintage Books.

Carnegie Corporation of New York. (2001). *Teachers for a new era: A national initiative to improve the quality of teaching*. New York, NY: Author.

Carnegie Forum on Education and the Economy. (1986). *A nation prepared: Teachers for the 21st century: The report of the task force on teaching as a profession*. New York, NY: Author.

Castle, S., Rockwood, K. D., & Tortorra, M. (2008). Tracking professional development and student learning in a professional development school partnership. *School-University Partnerships*, *2*(1), 47–60.

Cervetti, G., Damico, J., & Pearson, P. (2006). Multiple literacies, New Literacies, and teacher education. *Theory into Practice*, *45*(4), 378–386. doi:10.120715430421tip4504_12

Clift, R., & Brady, P. (Eds.). (2005). Research on methods courses and field experiences. In M. Cochran-Smith & K. Zeichner (Eds.), Studying teacher education (pp. 309-424). New York, NY: Routledge.

Cochran-Smith, M., Ell, F., Grudnoff, L., Haigh, M., Hill, M., & Ludlow, L. (2016). Initial teacher education: What does it take to put equity at the center? *Teaching and Teacher Education*, *57*, 67–78. doi:10.1016/j.tate.2016.03.006

Colburn, A. (1993). *Creating professional development schools*. Bloomington, IN: Phi Delta Kappa.

Cook-Sather, A. (2009). *Learning from the student's perspective: A methods sourcebook for effective teaching*. Boulder, CO: Paradigm.

Council for the Accreditation of Educator Preparation (CAEP). (2015). *Standard 2: Clinical partnerships and practice*. Retrieved from http://caepnet.org/standards/standard-2

Cozza, B. (2010). Transforming teaching into a collaborative culture: An attempt to create a professional development school-university partnership. *The Educational Forum*, *74*(3), 227–241. doi:10.1080/00131725.2010.483906

Darling-Hammond, L. (2006a). *Powerful teacher education: Lessons from exemplary programs*. San Francisco, CA: Jossey-Bass.

Darling-Hammond, L. (2006b). Constructing 21st century teacher education. *Journal of Teacher Education*, *57*(3), 300–314. doi:10.1177/0022487105285962

Darling-Hammond, L. (2009, February). *Teacher education and the American future*. Charles W. Hunt Lecture presented at the annual meeting of the American Association of Colleges for Teacher Education, Chicago, IL.

Darling-Hammond, L. (2014). Strengthening clinical preparation: The holy grail of teacher education. *Peabody Journal of Education*, *89*(4), 547–561. doi:10.1080/0161956X.2014.939009

Dennis, D., Burns, R. W., Tricarico, K., Van Ingen, S., Jacobs, J., & Davis, J. (2017). Problematizing clinical education: What is our future? In. R. Flessner & D. Lecklider (Eds.), The Power of Clinical Preparation in Teacher Education. Lanham, MD: Rowman & Littlefield Education in association with the Association of Teacher Educators.

Easton, L., & Condon, D. (2009). A school-wide model for student voice in curriculum development and teacher preparation. In A. Cook-Sather (Ed.), *Learning from the student's perspective: A secondary methods sourcebook for effective teaching* (pp. 176–193). Boulder, CO: Paradigm Press.

Erickson, H. L. (2002). *Concept-based curriculum: Teaching beyond the facts*. Thousand Oaks, CA: Corwin Press.

Feuer, M., Floden, R., Chudowsky, N., & Ahn, J. (2013). *Evaluation of teacher preparation programs: Purposes, methods, and policy options*. Washington, DC: National Academy of Education. Retrieved from http://naeducation.org/NAED_080456.htm

Fine, M., Torre, M. E., Burns, A., & Payne, Y. (2007). Youth research/participatory methods for reform. In D. Thiessen & A. Cook-Sather (Eds.), *International handbook of student experience in elementary and secondary school* (pp. 805–828). Dordrecht, The Netherlands: Springer. doi:10.1007/1-4020-3367-2_32

Fleener, C., & Dahm, P. F. (2007). Elementary teacher attrition: A comparison of the effects of professional development schools and traditional campus-based programs. *Teacher Education and Practice*, *20*(3), 263–283.

Flessner, R., & Lecklider, D. R. (Eds.). (2017). The power of clinical preparation in teacher education. Rowman & Littlefield Education in association with the Association of Teacher Education.

Gatti, L. (2016). *Toward a framework of resources for learning to teach: Rethinking US teacher preparation*. New York: Palgrave Macmillan. doi:10.1057/978-1-137-50145-5

Gelfuso, A., Dennis, D. V., & Parker, A. K. (2015). Turning teacher education upside down: Enacting the inversion of teacher preparation through the symbiotic relationship of theory and practice. *Professional Educator*, *39*(2).

George, M. (2010). Chapter seven: Resisting mandated literacy curricula in urban middle schools. *Counterpoints*, *376*, 105–124.

Goodlad, J. I., Soder, R., & McDaniel, B. L. (2008). *Education and the making of a democratic people*. Boulder, CO: Paradigm Publishers.

Grossman, P. (2010). *Learning to practice: The design of clinical experience in teacher preparation*. Washington, DC: American Association of Colleges for Teacher Education.

Grossman, P., Hammerness, K., & McDonald, M. (2009). Redefining teaching, reimagining teacher education. *Teachers and Teaching*, *15*(2), 273–289. doi:10.1080/13540600902875340

Grossman, P. L., Smagorinsky, P., & Valencia, S. (1999). Appropriating tools for teaching English: A theoretical framework for research on learning to teach. *American Journal of Education*, *108*(1), 1–29. doi:10.1086/444230

Haddix, M., & Sealey-Ruiz, Y. (2012). Cultivating digital and popular literacies as empowering and emancipatory acts upon urban youth. *Journal of Adolescent & Adult Literacy*, *56*(3), 192–198. doi:10.1002/JAAL.00126

Haj-Broussard, M., Husbands, J. L., Karge, B. D., McAalister, K. W., McCabe, M., Omelan, J. A., ... Stephens, C. (2015). Clinical prototypes: Nontraditional teacher preparation programs. In E. R. Hollins (Ed.), *Rethinking field experiences in preservice teacher preparation: Meeting new challenges for accountability* (pp. 135–150). New York, NY: Routledge.

Heck, T., & Bacharach, N. (2015). A better model for student teaching. *Educational Leadership*, *73*(4), 24–28.

Henry, J. J., Tryjankowski, A. M., Dicamillo, L., & Bailey, N. (2010). How professional development schools can help to create friendly environments for teachers to integrate theory, research, and practice. *Childhood Education*, *86*(5), 327–331. doi:10.1080/00094056.2010.10521419

Hollins, E. R. (Ed.). (2015). *Rethinking field experiences in preservice teacher preparation: Meeting new challenges for accountability*. New York: Routledge.

Holmes Group. (1986). *Tomorrow's teachers: A report of the Holmes Group*. East Lansing, MI: Author.

Holmes Group. (1990). *Tomorrow's schools: Principles for the design of professional development schools*. East Lansing, MI: Author.

Ipkeze, C. H., Broikou, K. A., Hildenbrand, S., & Gladstone-Brown, W. (2012). PDS collaboration as Third Space: An analysis of the quality of learning experiences in a PDS partnership. *Studying Teacher Education, 8*(3), 275–288. doi:10.1080/17425964.2012.719125

Lampert, M. L. (2010). Learning teaching in, from and for practice: What do we mean? *Journal of Teacher Education, 61*(1-2), 21–34. doi:10.1177/0022487109347321

Latham, N. I., & Vogt, W. P. (2007, March). Do professional development schools reduce teacher attrition? Evidence from a longitudinal study of 1,000 graduates. *Journal of Teacher Education, 58*(2), 153–167. doi:10.1177/0022487106297840

Lavadenz, M., & Hollins, E. (2015). Urban schools as settings for learning teaching. In E. Hollins (Ed.), *Rethinking field experiences in preservice teacher education* (pp. 1–14). New York, NY: Routledge.

Levine, A. (2006). *Educating school teachers*. Washington, DC: Education Schools Project.

Levine, M., & Trachtman, R. (Eds.). (1997). *Making professional development schools work: Politics, practice and policy*. New York, NY: Teachers College Press.

Liu, M. (2013). Disrupting teacher education. *Education Next, 13*(3). Retrieved from http://education-next.org/disrupting-teacher-education

Many, J. E., Fisher, T. R., Ogletree, S., & Taylor, D. (2012). Crisscrossing the university and public school contexts as professional development school boundary spanners. *Issues in Teacher Education, 21*(2), 83–102.

Martin, S. D., Snow, J. L., & Franklin Torrez, C. A. (2011). Navigating the terrain of Third Space: Tensions with/in relationships in school-university partnerships. *Journal of Teacher Education, 62*(3), 299–311. doi:10.1177/0022487110396096

Mills, G. E. (2017). *Action research: A guide for the teacher researcher* (6th ed.). Boston, MA: Pearson.

National Association for Professional Development Schools. (2008). *What it means to be a professional development school*. Retrieved from http://napds.org/wp- content/uploads/2014/10/Nine-Essentials.pdf

National Council for Accreditation of Teacher Education (NCATE). (2001). *Standards for professional development schools*. Washington, DC: Author.

National Council for the Social Studies (NCSS), The College, Career, and Civic Life (C3). (2013). *Framework for Social Studies State Standards: Guidance for Enhancing the Rigor of K-12 Civics, Economics, Geography, and History*. Silver Spring, MD: Author.

National Council of Teachers of English. (2016). *Professional knowledge for the teaching of writing.* Retrieved from: http://www2.ncte.org/statement/teaching-writing/

National Research Council. (2010). *Preparing teachers: Building evidence for sound policy.* Washington, DC: Author.

NCATE. (2010). *Transforming teacher education through clinical practice: A national strategy to prepare effective teachers. Report of the Blue Ribbon Panel on Clinical Preparation and Partnerships for Improved Student Learning.* Washington, DC: Author.

Nolan, J. (2015) *Clinical Experiences as the Centerpiece of Excellent Teacher Preparation.* Invited Keynote Presentation at the Annual Spring Conference of the Pennsylvania Association of Colleges and Teacher Educators, State College, PA.

Parker, A. K., Parsons, S. A., Groth, L., & Levine-Brown, E. (2016). Pathways to partnership: A developmental framework for building PDS relationships. *School University Partnerships, 9*(3), 34-48.

Parsons, S. A., Groth, L. A., Parker, A. K., Brown, E. L., Sell, C., & Sprague, D. (2017). Elementary teacher preparation at George Mason University: Evolution of our program. In R. Flessner & D. Lecklider (Eds.), *Case studies of clinical preparation in teacher education.* Lanham, MD: Rowman & Littlefield.

Parsons, S. A., Parker, A. K., Brunying, A., & Daoud, N. (2016). Striving to enact the Professional Development School philosophy: George Mason University's Elementary Education program. *The Teacher Educators' Journal, 9.*

Pellegrino, A., Zenkov, K., & Calamito, N. (2013). "Pay attention and take some notes": Middle school youth, multimodal instruction, and notions of citizenship. *Journal of Social Studies Research, 37*(4), 221–238. doi:10.1016/j.jssr.2013.04.007

Pellegrino, A., Zenkov, K., & Calamito, N. (2013). "I just want to be heard": Developing civic identity through performance poetry. *Social Studies Research & Practice, 8*(1).

Pellegrino, A., Zenkov, K., Calamito, N., & Sells, C. (2014). Lifting as we climb: A citizenship project in a Professional Development School setting. *School-University Partnerships, 7*(1), 64–84.

Pole, C. (Ed.). (2004). *Seeing is believing? Approaches to visual research* (Vol. 7). New York, NY: Elsevier. doi:10.1016/S1042-3192(04)07001-6

Pytash, K. E. (2017). Preservice teachers' experiences facilitating writing instruction in a juvenile detention facility. *High School Journal, 100*(2), 109–129. doi:10.1353/hsj.2017.0002

Pytash, K. E., & Zenkov, K. (2018). Introduction to the guest-edited issue. *New Educator, 14*(3), 1–7. doi:10.1080/1547688X.2018.1486564

Reynolds, A., Ross, S. M., & Rakow, J. H. (2002). Teacher retention, teaching effectiveness, and professional preparation: A comparison of professional development school and non-professional development school graduates. *Teaching and Teacher Education, 18*(3), 289–303. doi:10.1016/S0742-051X(01)00070-1

Ronfeldt, M. (2012). Where should student teachers learn to teach? Effects of field placement school characteristics on teacher retention and effectiveness. *Educational Evaluation and Policy Analysis, 34*(1), 3–26. doi:10.3102/0162373711420865

Rust, F. O., & Clift, R. T. (2015). Moving from recommendations to action in preparing professional educators. In E. R. Hollins (Ed.), *Rethinking field experiences in preservice teacher preparation: Meeting new challenges for accountability* (pp. 47–69). New York, NY: Routledge.

Shroyer, G., Yahnke, S., Bennett, A., & Dunn, C. (2007). Simultaneous renewal through professional development school partnerships. *The Journal of Educational Research, 100*(4), 211–225. doi:10.3200/JOER.100.4.211-225

Sleep, L., Boerst, T., & Ball, D. (2007). *Learning to do the work of teaching in a practice-based methods course.* Atlanta, GA: NCTM Research Pre-session.

Smagorinsky, P., Rhym, D., & Moore, C. P. (2013, January). Competing centers of gravity: A beginning English teacher's socialization process within conflictual settings. *English Education, 45*(2), 147–183.

Smagorinsky, P., Shelton, S. A., & Moore, C. (2015). The role of reflection in developing eupraxis in learning to teach English. *Pedagogies, 10*(4), 285–308. doi:10.1080/1554480X.2015.1067146

Stanford History Education Group (SHEG). (2015). *Reading like a historian.* Retrieved from https://sheg.stanford.edu/

Streng, J. M., Rhodes, S. D., Ayala, G. X., Eng, E., Arceo, R., & Phipps, S. (2004). Realidad Latina: Latino adolescents, their school, and a university use photo voice to examine and address the influence of immigration. *Journal of Interprofessional Care, 18*(4), 403–415. doi:10.1080/13561820400011701 PMID:15801555

Thompson, J., Hagenah, S., Lohwasser, K., & Laxton, K. (2015). Problems without ceilings: How mentors and novices frame and work on problems-of-practice. *Journal of Teacher Education, 66*(4), 364–381. doi:10.1177/0022487115592462

U.S. Department of Education, Office of Postsecondary Education (2015). *Higher Education Act Title II Reporting System.* Author.

Valencia, S., Martin, S., Place, N., & Grossman, P. (2009). Complex interactions in student teaching: Lost opportunities for learning. *Journal of Teacher Education, 60*(3), 304–322. doi:10.1177/0022487109336543

Wang, J., Spalding, E., Odell, S. J., Klecka, C. L., & Lin, E. (2010). Bold ideas for improving teacher education and teaching. *Journal of Teacher Education, 61*(4), 2–15.

Wimmer, R. (2008). A multi-disciplinary study of field experiences: Possibilities for teacher education. *The Journal of Educational Thought (JET). Revue De La Pensée Éducative, 42*(3), 339–351. Retrieved from http://www.jstor.org/stable/23758502

Wong, P. L., & Glass, R. D. (Eds.). (2009). *Prioritizing urban children, teachers, and schools through professional development schools.* Albany, NY: State University of New York Press.

Yonezawa, S., & Jones, M. (2009). Student voices: Generating reform from the inside out. *Theory into Practice, 48*(3), 205–212. doi:10.1080/00405840902997386

Zeichner, K. (2010). Rethinking connections between campus courses and field experiences in college- and university-based teacher education. *Journal of Teacher Education, 61*(1-2), 89–99. doi:10.1177/0022487109347671

Zeichner, K. (2012). The turn once again toward practice-based teacher education. *Journal of Teacher Education, 63*(5), 376–382. doi:10.1177/0022487112445789

Zeichner, K., & Bier, M. (2015). Opportunities and pitfalls in the turn toward clinical experience in U.S. teacher education. In E. R. Hollins (Ed.), *Rethinking field experiences in preservice teacher preparation: Meeting new challenges for accountability*. New York, NY: Routledge.

Zeichner, K., & Conklin, H. G. (2008). Teacher education programs as sites for teacher preparation. In M. Cochran-Smith, S. Feiman-Nemser, & D. J. McIntyre (Eds.), Handbook on teacher education: Enduring questions in changing contexts (3rd ed.; pp. 269–289). Academic Press.

Zeichner, K., & McDonald, M. (2011). Practice-based teaching and community field experiences for prospective teachers. In A. Cohan & A. Honigsfeld (Eds.), *Breaking the mold of preservice and inservice teacher education: Innovative and successful practices for the 21st century* (pp. 45–54). Lanham, MD: Rowman & Littlefield Education.

Zenkov, K. (2009, Summer). The teachers and schools they deserve: *Seeing* the pedagogies, practices, and programs urban students want. *Theory into Practice, 48*(3), 168–175. doi:10.1080/00405840902997253

Zenkov, K., Bell, A., Lynch, M., Ewaida, M., Harmon, J., & Pellegrino, A. (2012). Youth as sources of educational equity: Using photographs to help adolescents make sense of school, injustice, and their lives. *Education in a Democracy, 4*, 79–98.

Zenkov, K., & Harmon, J. (2009). Picturing a writing process: Using photovoice to learn how to teach writing to urban youth. *Journal of Adolescent & Adult Literacy, 52*(7), 575–584. doi:10.1598/JAAL.52.7.3

Zenkov, K., Parker, A. K., Parsons, S., Pellegrino, A., & Pytash, K. (2017). From project-based clinical experiences to collaborative inquiries: Pathways to Professional Development Schools. In J. Ferrara, J. Nath, I. Guadarrama, & R. Beebe (Eds.), *Expanding opportunities to link research and clinical practice: A volume in Research in Professional Development Schools* (pp. 9–33). Charlotte, NC: Information Age Publishing.

Zenkov, K., Pellegrino, A. M., Sell, C., Ewaida, M., Bell, A., Fell, M., ... McManis, M. (2014). Picturing kids and "kids" as researchers: English language learners, preservice teachers and effective writing instruction. *New Educator, 10*, 306–330. doi:10.1080/1547688X.2014.965107

Zenkov, K., & Pytash, K. E. (in press). Critical, project-based clinical experiences: Their origins and their elements. In K. Zenkov & K. E. Pytash (Eds.), *Clinical experiences in teacher education: Critical, project-based interventions in diverse classrooms* (pp. 1–18). New York: Routledge.

Zygmunt, E., & Clark, P. (2016). *Transforming teacher education for social justice*. New York: Teachers College Press.

KEY TERMS AND DEFINITIONS

Field Experience: Placements that situate teacher candidates in "real world" contexts in order to facilitate theory to practice connections. In teacher preparation, these typically occur in PK-12 schools.

Professional Development Schools (PDS): A structure for building and maintaining partnerships between PK-12 schools and teacher preparation programs. The structure includes nine key tenets for guiding partnership development including mutually beneficial relationships, identification and formalization of stakeholder roles, and ongoing professional development for all participants.

School-University Partnerships: Mutually beneficial collaborations between institutes of higher education and PK-12 schools for the purpose of supporting teacher education, in-service teacher professional development and PK-12 student learning.

Student Teaching: The capstone experience in teacher preparation programs.

Supervisor: A mentor, coach, and/or evaluator for a teacher candidate during their field experiences or student teaching. Typically, supervisors are based at the university.

Teacher Candidate: A preservice teacher enrolled in a teacher preparation program.

Teacher Preparation: Coursework and field work designed to formally prepare preservice teachers for careers in PK-12 classrooms.

Chapter 5
Affordances of a Cyclical and Content–Specific Model of Collaborative Mentoring

Danielle E. Dani
Ohio University, USA

Allyson Hallman-Thrasher
Ohio University, USA

Lisa M. Harrison
Ohio University, USA

Kristin Diki
Ohio University, USA

Mathew Felton-Koestler
Ohio University, USA

Michael Kopish
Ohio University, USA

Jodi Dunham
Shawnee State University, USA

Loretta W. Harvey
Shawnee State University, USA

ABSTRACT

One of the challenges of field-based teacher education is the perennial divide between university courses and field experiences. Collaborative mentoring is proposed as an approach to bridge this divide. The purpose of this chapter is to explore the affordances that a content-specific model of collaborative mentoring provides for achieving greater coherence within teacher education programs and nurturing stronger systems of partnerships between universities and schools. The chapter reports on research examining the benefits and challenges reported by teacher candidates, mentor teachers, and clinical educators who participated in the model.

DOI: 10.4018/978-1-5225-6249-8.ch005

INTRODUCTION

In traditional teacher preparation programs, teacher candidates take a series of education courses, often with field experience components, which culminates with student teaching. This approach - a theory to practice model (Korthagen & Kessels, 1999) - is the prevailing paradigm in teacher preparation. This approach to teacher preparation is problematic because of the lack of connection between the university-based coursework and student teaching (Darling-Hammond, 2006a; Zeichner, 2010). Many institutions have embraced calls for increased clinical experiences (National Council for Accreditation of Teacher Education [NCATE], 2010) and adopted a practice-based approach to teacher education centering on the development of core teaching practices that are essential for successful classroom teaching and learning (Forzani, 2014; Zeichner, 2012). Yet, simply increasing teacher candidates' time in school without the necessary concomitant mentoring, support structure, and connections to university coursework limits teacher candidates' abilities to systematically learn from extended clinical experiences. Limited interactions and communications with mentors, university faculty, or clinical educators (also known as clinical supervisors) further constrain the mentoring process and teacher candidates' abilities to develop and enact core practices to promote student learning (Henning, Gut, & Beam, 2015).

Recently, the American Association for Colleges of Teacher Education (AACTE, 2018) emphasized the need for stronger partnerships between teacher preparation programs and the local school districts where candidates complete their field experiences. According to the National Association of Professional Development Schools (NAPDS), effective partnerships and high-quality clinical practice are central to the development of the knowledge, skills, and professional dispositions necessary for teacher candidates to demonstrate positive impact on P-12 student learning and development (NAPDS, 2008). Strong, effective partnerships are mutually beneficial: Partners share the responsibility for promoting teacher candidate learning through explicitly designed, complementary, and well-articulated experiences and expectations (Darling-Hammond, 2006b; NAPDS, 2008) and partnerships promote the professional growth of mentors in whose classrooms teacher candidates are placed. Effective partnerships necessitate the involvement of high-quality clinical educators, those who are responsible for observing and evaluating teacher candidates' practice in the mentors' classrooms, and clear communication between partners. Moreover, exemplary teacher preparation programs include clinical experiences that are carefully coordinated with coursework, involve expert clinical faculty in mentoring teacher candidates, and result in candidates who are more successful at managing the complex educational tasks of educating P-12 students (Zeichner & Conklin, 2005).

To maximize the impact of clinical experiences on teacher candidates' learning, a new content-specific model of mentoring was developed and implemented. Model features were explicitly designed to nurture stronger school-university partnerships. The purpose of this chapter is to describe the Cyclical and Content-specific Model of Collaborative Mentoring and share findings regarding the benefits and challenges that teacher candidates, mentor teachers, and clinical educators identified through their participation in the model.

BACKGROUND

A clinical model of teacher education is one that is "fully grounded in clinical practice and interwoven with academic content and professional courses" (NCATE, 2010, p.ii). Several key features characterize and define clinical practice and differentiate it from traditional field work in teacher education: Clinical practice engages teacher candidates in the pedagogical work of the profession of teaching, occurs in authentic educational settings, integrates closely with educator preparation coursework, and is supported by a formal school-university partnership (AACTE, 2018). In educator preparation programs, clinical internships (also known as student teaching) offer the culminating and most authentic clinical experience. Clinical internships vary in duration and are one semester long at minimum. Typically, all clinical internships require teacher candidates to assume full - and supervised - responsibility for teaching their mentors' classes (AACTE, 2018). Such supervision is usually the responsibility of mentor teachers and clinical educators.

Research in teacher education indicates clinical experiences are mainly the responsibility of mentor teachers (Feiman-Nemser, Parker, & Zeichner, 1990; Koemer, Rust, & Baumgartner, 2002). Mentor teachers take on a variety of roles, acting as instructional coach, providing emotional support, and socializing teacher candidates into the teaching profession (Butler & Cuenca, 2012). Not surprisingly, mentor teachers exert a large influence on teacher candidates' beliefs and the kinds of teaching practice that they adopt (Britzman, 2003; Darling-Hammond, 2006a). Mentors' influence can be problematic when they promote teaching practices and views of learning that support the traditional perspectives and practices about teaching that teacher candidates typically hold prior to entering programs of teacher education (Britzman, 2003). This problem is further complicated by the lack of clear expectations and communication about the role of mentor teachers, as well as the assumption that the process of mentoring is self-evident (Zeichner, 2005).

Clinical educators, or supervisors, also have significant impact on student teachers' learning and practice (Hammerness, Darling-Hammond, Grossman, Rust, & Shulman, 2005). Clinical educators can influence what teacher candidates do in the classroom (McNamara, 1995; Meijer, Korthagen, & Vasolos, 2009), enable them to plan for instruction (Urzúa & Vásquez, 2008), and nurture collaborations between universities and the schools in which teacher candidates complete their field experiences (Beck & Kosnik, 2002; Carroll, Featherstone, Featherstone, Feiman-Nemser, & Roosevelt, 2007). Typically, clinical educators are retired teachers, doctoral students, and lecturers or non-tenure track faculty (Beck & Kosnik, 2002; Grossman, Hammerness, McDonald, & Ronfeldt, 2008; Kosnik & Beck, 2008) and they receive limited preparation or on-the-job professional development to support their practice (Grossman, Hammerness, McDonald, & Ronfeldt, 2008; Kosnik & Beck, 2008; Valencia, Martin, Place, & Grossman, 2009). Absent a clear purpose and professional training, clinical educators use their experience as a supervisee to inform their supervisory practices, potentially undercutting the goals of the teacher education programs in which they work (Levine, 2011).

The challenges associated with mentoring and supervision widen the theory to practice divide and further contribute to the disconnect between university coursework and field experiences. Butler and Cuenca (2012) call for conversations between stakeholders (e.g., university-based teacher educators and classroom-based mentor teachers) as a first step towards "coherence" in teacher education programs (p. 305). Central to these conversations is a commitment to engage in "aspects of a shared practice" (e.g., debriefing discussions around videotapes of practice) as members of a community of practice (Levine, 2011, p. 939). When the work of the community of practice revolves around collaborative and inquiry-based approaches to learn from teaching, then professional learning results for all members of the community (Cajkler & Wood, 2016; Levine, 2011).

Situated Learning and Communities of Practice

Teacher candidate learning is highly influenced by the communities of practice within which learning takes place (Ball & Cohen, 1999; Darling-Hammond & Bransford, 2005; Korthagen, 2010; Zeichner & Conklin, 2005). In communities of practice, learning is situated (Lave, 1988; Lave & Wenger, 1991); it is embedded within authentic activity, context, and culture. The clinical internship is a community of practice that offers a collaborative social learning space which enables teacher candidates to co-construct and cultivate knowledge for the teaching profession with support from mentor teachers and clinical educators. As a community of practice, the clinical internship facilitates teacher candidate learning across three domains: knowledge-in-practice, knowledge-of-practice, and knowledge-for-practice (Cochran-Smith & Lytle, 1999). Knowledge-in-practice refers to teacher candidate learning that develops through authentic teaching experiences in schools during the clinical internship. Teacher candidates develop knowledge-of-practice by participating in ongoing reflection, mentoring, and seminars along with knowledge-for-practice through university methods and education coursework.

In a community of practice, novices—like teacher candidates—become members of a community by participating in authentic activities that are central to the functioning of the community. Candidates begin internships by participating in peripheral tasks, learning requisite vocabulary, becoming familiar with routines and organizing principles, and then gradually participate in additional tasks that are more central to the functioning of the classroom (Lave & Wenger, 1991). In doing so, they move from the periphery of teaching (*learning about*) to its center (*doing*) where they are more active and engaged in classroom practices. Furthermore, clinical internships provide opportunities for candidates to collaborate, as well as to engage in and shape community discourse (Wertsch, 1991).

Collaborative Mentoring

The view that learning to teach is situated and involves teacher candidates in communities of practice undergirds the development of strong partnerships to support clinical and practice-based teacher education. Partnerships typically involve collaborative mentoring from mentor teachers and university-based teacher educators who serve as clinical educators (AACTE, 2018). Collaborative mentoring involves teacher candidates in the examination of instructional processes through focused dialogue about practice (Graham, 2006), and participation in reflective opportunities to foster personal and professional growth (Kochan & Trimble, 2000). This form of mentoring involves teacher candidates in a facilitated exchange of expertise sharing (Schon, 1983). Collaborative mentoring also promotes reflective practice (Feiman-Nemser, 2001) that helps candidates make sense of classroom challenges, determine the nature of the problems they encounter, and develop potential solutions (Argyris & Schon, 1974). The mentor-mentee relationship promotes pedagogical thinking, the development of craft knowledge, and teaching of subject content (Lee & Feng, 2007).

Shulman (1987) conceptualized the knowledge of teaching of subject content as pedagogical content knowledge (PCK). He defined PCK as the "blending of content and pedagogy into an understanding of how particular topics, problems or issues are organized, represented, and adapted to the diverse interests and abilities of learners and presented for instruction" (Shulman, 1987, p. 8). PCK forms a critical component of teacher knowledge, exerts a strong influence on overall teaching performance (Ball, Thames, & Phelps, 2008; Brown & Borko, 1992; Darling-Hammond, 2006a), and develops over time as a repertoire of teacher pedagogical constructions that result from "repeated planning and teaching of, and reflection on the teaching of, the most regularly taught topics" (Hashweh, 2005, p. 277). Recent research highlights the importance of content-specific mentoring to the development of PCK (Barnett & Friedrichsen, 2015; Bradbury, 2010; Bradbury & Koballa, 2007).

Providing content-specific mentoring is particularly valuable because each discipline is characterized by its own structure and central modes of inquiry, including how knowledge is generated and what counts as evidence (Schwab, 1978). Beyond facing challenges that are common to all teachers, teachers of science, mathematics, and social studies face difficulties that are unique to their content area. For example, Luft, Roehrig, and Patterson (2003) described that beginning science teachers face the added complexity of "implementing inquiry lessons, planning and managing laboratory instruction, and fostering an understanding of the nature of science among students" (p. 79). Knowledge of content is necessary to represent discipline-specific ideas and practices to students (Bransford, Brown, & Cocking, 2000) and to notice and support student development (Bruner, 1966).

In practice, collaborative mentoring can take many forms but invariably consists of teacher candidates planning learning experiences for a specific group of students, implementing their plans, and evaluating outcomes through analysis of and reflection on practice that relies on theory, research, and student data (Burn & Mutton, 2015). This process is central to inquiry-based approaches to learning from practice. McNally (2016) describes observation cycles, a type of collaborative mentoring that provides structured opportunities for communication between teacher candidates, mentor teachers, and clinical supervisors. Observation cycles are similar in structure to Japanese lesson study, a form of professional development that engages teachers in examining student learning to support their enactment of effective teaching practices (Fernandez & Yoshida, 2004; Lewis, 2000; Lewis, Perry, & Murata, 2006; Stigler & Hiebert, 1999). A key feature of lesson study is a knowledgeable other who facilitates the process by asking questions, acting as a co-researcher, and adding new perspectives (Lewis & Hurd, 2011). Using lesson study and approaches like it have shown significant gains in preservice and in-service teachers' learning and critical reflection (Howell & Saye, 2016; McNally, 2016; Puchner & Taylor, 2006; Santagata, Zannoni, & Stigler, 2007).

Co-teaching, another example of collaborative mentoring, features active involvement of mentor teachers with teacher candidates' classroom instruction and a shared responsibility for student learning. Co-teaching involves mentor teachers and teacher candidates in cycles of collaborative lesson planning, lesson enactment, and lesson evaluation, which allows the mentor teacher to partner with the teacher candidate rather than simply handing over teaching responsibilities (Bacharach, Heck, & Dahlberg, 2010; Bacharach & Heck, 2012). Sharing responsibility for instruction and student learning enables mentor teachers to model and scaffold practical knowledge that is often tacit in teaching. Co-teaching promotes active learning, reflective thinking, and collaborative participation (Desimone, 2009). Modeling practices and sharing of knowledge between experienced teachers and teacher candidates help promote teacher learning (McDuffie, Mastropieri, & Scruggs, 2009).

CONTEXT

This project took place in the Middle Childhood Education (MCE) and Adolescent Young-Adult Education (AYA) educator preparation programs of two public universities located in the rural Midwest. MCE licensure in [state] spans grades 4-9, and candidates earn certification in two content areas. AYA licensure in [state] spans grades 7-12 and candidates earn certification in one content area. University

1 is a small (under 4,000) Baccalaureate-granting university, and University 2 is a large (over 27,000) doctoral-granting institution.

In response to recommendations from scholars investigating practice-based teacher education and the NCATE's Blue Ribbon Panel national reform agenda, both universities transformed their programs to address the shortcomings of traditional approaches to teacher preparation (Henning, Erb, Randles, Fults, & Webb, 2016). They designed a clinically-based model of teacher preparation that places practice at the center of teacher preparation (Ball & Forzani, 2009; Forzani, 2014; Grossman, Hammerness, & McDonald, 2009; Lampert, Franke, Kazemi, Ghousseini, Turrou, Beasley,...Crowe, 2013; McDonald, Kazemi, & Kavanaugh, 2013; NCATE, 2010; Zeichner, 2012). At the core of the clinical model at each institution is a focus on improving K-12 student learning through sustained and intensive field experiences that are integrated with coursework and incorporate co-teaching (mentor and teacher candidate). For this reason, the teacher education curriculum at each university was developed to scaffold teacher candidate activities in K-12 schools from the first field experiences through to the end of the year-long clinical internship of the senior year.

During their sophomore year, all MCE and AYA teacher candidates complete a 20 (University 1) or 40 (University 2) hour field experience in a diverse setting. During the junior year AYA candidates respectively complete 50 (University 1) and 80 (University 2) hours of a field experience coupled with general methods coursework. Because MCE candidates earn certification in two content areas, the MCE programs require teacher candidates to have field experiences in both content areas. At University 1, teacher candidates complete a field experience in two content areas (total of 50 hours) during the junior year. At University 2, teacher candidates spend a minimum of 160 hours in a field experience during the junior year that focuses on one of their licensure content areas. They focus on their second licensure content area during the year-long clinical internship.

Year-Long Clinical Internship

The culminating experience of both universities' clinical teacher education programs (for AYA and MCE candidates) is the year-long clinical internship that takes place during the senior year. The year-long internship far exceeds a typical semester-long student teaching experience and takes place in the same mentor classroom for the full academic year. In the fall semester, teacher candidates spend two full days each week (120-150 hours over the semester) in their mentor's classroom and complete university coursework including content-specific methods courses. In the spring semester teacher candidates spend 5 full days each week teaching in their mentors' classroom. Teacher candidates are afforded the opportunity to experience the development of a group of students in one classroom setting across an entire academic year. This extended time helps teacher candidates feel more comfortable and confident in their classroom management, see how a teacher establishes norms and routines at the beginning of the year and maintains them throughout the year, experience the academic and social development of students across a full year, gain familiarity with long term planning (a full year vs. just a unit or quarter), and see how students develop content understanding across an entire course.

To support their learning during the yearlong internship, teacher candidates are assigned a clinical educator. During the fall semester, the clinical educator meets with the mentor teacher and teacher candidate a minimum of three times: at the beginning of the semester to complete required paperwork, at the end of the semester to facilitate a general reflection on the experience, and a check on progress in between. In the spring semester, the clinical educator's responsibilities additionally include three supervisory visits that include observing teaching and completing an evaluation form that is shared with the teacher candidate, and a midterm and final meeting with the teacher candidate and mentor to assess teacher candidate performance. The clinical educator also facilitates 4 seminar meetings in which all the teacher candidates he or she supervises meet to discuss and reflect on issues of teaching and the challenges of transitioning to full-time teaching. At University 1, content specific methods instructors serve as clinical educators. At University 2, clinical educators are not content specialists.

THE CYCLICAL CONTENT-SPECIFIC MODEL OF MENTORING

The Cyclical and Content-specific Model of Mentoring (CCMM) was developed to maximize the impact of clinical experiences on teacher candidate learning and to strengthen the clinical practice component of the teacher preparation programs at both universities. The basis of CCMM is a collaborative triad-- teacher candidate, mentor teacher, and clinical educator-- who work towards developing the candidate's ability to enact effective teaching practices that support student learning of content. The clinical educator has expertise in the content area and grade band of the candidate's placement, and is the candidate's methods course instructor. This feature of the model was new to University 2, but not University 1.

In CCMM, the teacher candidate engages with both the clinical educator and mentor teacher in five teaching cycles of planning, enactment, and co-reflection that span the entire academic year (2 in Fall and 3 in Spring). For each cycle, the mentor teacher identifies particular topics or concepts for the candidates to teach. The clinical educator encourages the mentor to select topics or concepts that are typically challenging for students. The clinical educator and candidate meet to co-plan a lesson around the identified concept. The mentor reviews the plan before the candidate teaches it. When the candidate teaches the lesson, it is video recorded and both the mentor and clinical educator are present to observe the lesson. After teaching the lesson, the candidate watches the video and completes a reflection prompt. Then the candidate participates in a formal debrief meeting with both the mentor teacher and clinical educator. Feedback on one cycle then informs work on the subsequent cycle. Teaching cycles were new to both universities.

In addition to the teaching cycles, CCMM engages the triad in several meetings throughout the year to further support teacher candidates' learning. At the start of the year-long internship, the triad meets to share goals and discuss roles and expectations of one another. At the end of the first semester, they meet to reflect on the teacher candidate's growth and set goals for the next semester. The fall semester CCMM triad meetings and feedback were new to both universities. Similar to prior practice at both universities, CCMM spring semester requirements included at least three meetings of the triad: a goal-setting meeting at the start of the semester, a mid-semester feedback and collective evaluation session, and a final summative evaluation session.

A final, and new, feature of CCMM is its focus on the pedagogical practice of constructing and critiquing arguments, a common practice to the disciplines of mathematics, science, and social studies. Though the practice provides a unifying theme for working with teacher candidates in different schools and content areas throughout the academic year, it is important to note that the construction of arguments is operationalized differently within each content area. In social studies, students construct arguments by using primary vs. secondary sources. In mathematics, students use deductive reasoning to construct and critique arguments. In science, inductive reasoning is used to connect evidence to scientific principles.

METHODS

In this exploratory study, a qualitative research design (Bogdan & Biklen, 2007) was used to investigate the benefits and challenges of participating in the CCMM as identified by teacher candidates, mentor teachers, and clinical educators. A total of 28 triads engaged in the pilot implementation of CCMM at the two universities: teacher candidates completing their year-long clinical internship, mentor teachers who hosted the interns in their classrooms, and clinical educators who were university faculty. The data from two of the triads was excluded from the study because either the mentor teacher or teacher candidate withdrew from the study. Data from an additional triad was excluded because the teacher candidate withdrew from the teacher education program. Participants for this study were members of 25 of the 28 triads: 25 teacher candidates, 25 mentor teachers, and 6 clinical educators. Seven of the teacher candidates were in an AYA mathematics program, 5 in an MCE mathematics program, 4 in an AYA science program, 5 in an MCE science program, 2 in AYA social studies program, and 2 in an MCE social studies program. Mentor teachers were public school middle (grades 4-9) and secondary (grades 7-12) mathematics, science, and social studies teachers who had previous experience working with teacher candidates in the year-long clinical internship and could provide insight into the benefits of the model following its first-year implementation. Clinical educators were mathematics, science, and social studies teacher educators who were full-time faculty in the teacher preparation programs of each institution.

Data Collection

Data collection occurred over one academic year and was focused on participants' perceptions of CCMM. Data sources included audio recorded interviews with the teacher candidates and mentor teachers, as well as minutes from 16 clinical educator team meetings. Teacher candidates were interviewed at three points during the academic year: at the start (n=23), midpoint (n=22), and conclusion of the internship year (n=22). These interviews asked participants to reflect on their experiences within the support structure of the CCMM by discussing their teaching experience before and during the internship year, student learning, successes and struggles, perspectives on how they changed over the internship year, and perspectives of the structures that supported those changes. Individual interviews with mentor teachers were conducted at the beginning (n=22), middle (n=21), and end of the academic year (n=21). Mentor teacher interviews included questions about their perceptions of the CCMM.

Data Analysis

Data was analyzed through an open-coding process (Denzin & Lincoln, 2000) whereby the research team developed codes through cycles of reading and then discussing the data. First, transcripts of interviews were read and labels were created for chunks of the transcripts that described the meanings that researchers were seeing in the data (Denzin & Lincoln, 2000). The research team then shared their codes, and those codes common to all researchers became the basis for a coding scheme. To make coding of such a large data set more manageable, particular researchers coded subsets of data pertaining to a type of participant (e.g., mentor teacher interview transcripts). These researchers then generated categories based on relationships between codes. The team met as a whole to discuss the categories that emerged for each data set and identify emergent themes across data sets. The team then returned to the transcripts to look for exemplars of the identified themes and disconfirming evidence. When disconfirming evidence was found, the team revisited the transcripts and other data together to explore what might have led to the deviation.

FINDINGS

Five themes that were specific to the CCMM emerged across the data: (1) the value of a content-specific focus; (2) stronger field-methods connections; (3) the benefits of teaching cycles; (4) strong relationships among the triad, and; (5) logistical challenges.

Value of a Content-Specific Focus

Both teacher candidates and mentor teachers found value in the content-specific focus of the model. Teacher candidates found the content-specific feedback they received from their clinical educators to be helpful to their learning and different from the type of feedback they received from their mentor teachers. Teacher candidates identified the ways in which their clinical educators were able to provide content-specific support, as opposed to focusing on general pedagogical strategies. One teacher candidate described this attention to content:

My mentor teacher, while she can give me some help on the math, she does more of the general teaching tips and tricks. So [my clinical educator] was able to give me more feedback on the mathematical content and that aspect of the lessons and that was really helpful. (MCE Mathematics)

Teacher candidates described the university clinical educators' feedback as focused on the subject content that they were teaching from lesson ideas, to resources, to content elaborations. A social studies candidate described the extensive support and knowledge his clinical educator provided:

[My clinical educator is] an expert on everything there is to know about social studies. Brilliant man. So I never hesitated, "Hey, do you have any possible materials you could give me on how I could teach the judicial branch to the kids, or the powers of the presidency, powers of the legislative branch, what can Congress do and things like that?" He was always available to give me additional resources and he's always looking to put that local as well as global spin on it, too. (AYA Social Studies)

The content-specific feedback was perceived as especially valuable by middle childhood candidates who had limited prior experience teaching the content, as one described:

[The clinical educator's feedback] was beneficial. She had good insight because that one was a science lesson, a science lesson with three stations. I felt like it was good to get her insight on what she thought because I haven't taught a lot of science, so that was helpful. (MCE Science)

One candidate expressed her awareness of the importance of having a clinical educator who could provide content-specific feedback:

It's good having an actual math person be my clinical educator because having someone that isn't a math person be my clinical educator [would upset me]... It would be like me sitting in an English class [as a math teacher]. I'd be like, 'That was great.' That's all I could say about it. (AYA Mathematics)

Likewise, mentor teachers found value in the content-specific focus of the model. Mentor teachers stated that the CCMM had a positive impact on content-specific pedagogy, both the teacher candidates' and their own. First and foremost, mentor teachers recognized the positive influence of having clinical educators with content expertise on the teacher candidates' professional growth. As one teacher commented:

The level of support for my [teacher candidate] is more than I've ever seen...[H]aving somebody who's really tuned in to the teaching of science was fantastic. I felt like it really helped my [teacher candidate] reflect on her teaching in a different way. (AYA Science)

Clinical educators provided mentor teachers with resources that both they and the candidates could use in the classroom to accompany lessons, such as math manipulatives. Moreover, several mentor teachers expressed the benefit of having another content expert working with K-12 students in the classroom. They described the clinical educator as someone who assisted them and their students during classroom visits. A high school math teacher explained:

What I really like about [the clinical educator] is when he came to the classroom, he actually was a sort of an observer-participant because he's a math specialist, and so he was able to really almost be an extra person in the classroom. (AYA Math)

Finally, the mentor teachers indicated that having a clinical educator knowledgeable in their content area pushed them to reflect on their own pedagogical approaches. One mentor teacher stated, "Actually I learned some things from him just watching and observing him, how he was working with students as well" (AYA Mathematics). In addition, as we discuss next, the content specific focus of the model resulted in stronger connections between teacher candidates' field experiences and content-specific methods courses.

Stronger Connection Between Field and Methods

The fact that in CCMM methods instructors served as clinical educators allowed for connections across candidates' field experiences and their coursework. Candidates described how different features of the CCMM helped them connect their experiences in the field to university-based methods courses. One such feature, the methods instructor as clinical educator, helped clarify expectations for planning and teaching the content. For example:

Well, having my supervisor for last semester in Methods, I knew what we were wanting to do for student teaching. We talked about different ways of preparing information, so that whenever they would come in, I was prepared to discuss with them. We were on the same page. We knew what each other liked to do. It just made it a lot easier to talk one on one with him. (MCE Mathematics)

Another secondary mathematics candidate claimed his professional growth "all started in my methods classes. That's definitely where." He went on to describe how his content-specific methods taught by his clinical educator helped him gain a deeper understanding of content specific pedagogical issues:

I think I've kind of heard procedural/conceptual understanding, but I think in classes beforehand it was just kind of like extra material. In my methods class, we actually looked into it. She had us look it [activities related to conceptual understanding] up ourselves and stuff, so I think it stuck more. The fact that we were talking directly about math rather than just general stuff, I think it related to us more. It all started there [in content-specific methods course]. (AYA Mathematics)

A social studies teacher candidate indicated the benefit her methods course provided in helping develop her creativity in lesson planning. She highlighted her clinical educator's focus on the types of resources to implement in the classroom:

In [my] methods course, we learned to not use textbooks all the time, and I think that's really valuable. I mean there [are] so many other sources you can bring into the classroom. Primary, secondary, like video tapes, like audio recordings of people... (MCE Social Studies)

The teacher candidate further commented that in her meetings with her clinical educator, he was able to "relat[e] a lot of what [they] learned in [their] social studies methods to [her] classroom," which was helpful in her understanding of the global/local connection.

The process allowed mentor teachers to become aware of what was being taught in the methods courses. When mentor teachers and clinical educators met with teacher candidates together for the debrief conversation of the teaching cycles, mentor teachers were able to hear about the feedback and recommendations of clinical educators and observe how the content of courses supported teaching practice. For example, a mentor teacher for an MCE science teacher candidate stated:

I think, like with her science methods class, she got different methods and that was ... I didn't always know what she was doing in the methods class, so then when [the clinical educator] would come and say, "Well we did this in class and I'm not seeing that." Or, "I wish she would take that farther," then I knew, "Oh, she's gotten that skill." And now I know to help her get better at that skill of questioning and getting the kids to look outside, at their experiences and things.

The content expertise of the clinical educator also supported the candidates in developing awareness of, reflecting on, and negotiating disconnects between the university coursework and their placement classrooms. In some cases, both the clinical educator and teacher candidates highlighted the differences between the type of instructional strategies used in the classroom and the ones taught in the methods courses. Clinical educators noted the difficulties of creating opportunities for teacher candidates to observe, plan, and teach lessons that incorporated research-supported instructional strategies that integrated discipline-specific practices in classrooms where the dominant mode of instruction did not create space for such practices. For example, some practices that were observed in classrooms included reliance on textbooks and direct instruction that provided few opportunities for students to engage in inquiry-based and meaningful problem-based learning that candidates were learning about in their methods courses.

As an MCE science candidate described, "For this unit in particular, [teaching] has been a lot of out of the book. I know there's a lot of good information in there, but I don't know if that is the best method."

Recognizing this disconnect and the role that the clinical educator and teaching cycles can play in negotiating opportunities to use different instructional strategies, one candidate stated:

[Coursework] made me do the lessons and stuff, otherwise I might have just copied, or modeled is the better word, modeled what [the mentor teacher] did. I think it also pushed the mentor teachers to allow us to do that kind of stuff. (AYA Science)

Likewise, an AYA Social Studies candidate stated:

[My mentor teacher's] like, "Why are you trying that? It's stupid. It's not going to work." Stuff like that... Maybe [the clinical educators] putting more pressure on the mentor teachers to be receptive to changes, I think, is really important, because again, I make this sweet lesson for [my clinical educator] when he comes in, because I'm like, "Hey, I'm getting observed." Then [my mentor] he's receptive...

Clinical educators used different strategies in response to this challenge. For example, one of the science clinical educators engaged both the teacher candidate and mentor teacher in co-planning a lesson together. She also reached out to a science professor to get feedback on the lesson. Another approach that was used by one of the mathematics clinical educators was to teach a lesson in placement classrooms so that the teacher candidate and mentor could see an example of the instructional strategies from the methods courses enacted with actual high school students.

Benefits of Teaching Cycles

The teaching cycles were both a means of providing feedback to teacher candidates and of building relationships between candidates and clinical educators. In terms of feedback, teacher candidates pointed to the teaching cycles as a positive experience because "they made us focus in on how we can make what we're doing in the classroom better" (AYA Mathematics). Teacher candidates described the feedback they received during the teaching cycles as important because it validated their work and promoted growth in practice. An MCE science candidate stated, "I just remember feeling reassured that it was a decent lesson. She did give me some insight about the assessment portion of it, so that was helpful." Reflecting on the benefits of the process, another MCE science teacher candidate reported, "It's refreshing to hear her thoughts on it and get her opinions. Maybe you could try this next time or do this instead kind of thing."

The format of the feedback seemed especially useful; candidates appreciated the "one-on-one" opportunity to talk through a lesson plan or video of lesson with the clinical educator. One candidate declared, "The one on one stuff, that's just so awesome. I'm so happy that I got to do that." Likewise, the teacher candidate shared, "I think I learn best when I'm sitting down and talking with those people about what I did and what I can do better" (AYA Science).

In addition to the content focus that was described in the previous finding, teaching cycles created an opportunity for clinical educators to provide feedback and support about teaching and how to interact with students, as articulated by one candidate:

[My clinical educator] has been really instrumental in getting me on the right path, I think, to not just being a great educator but a good classroom [instructor and] manager... not just content and delivery. It's about how you interact with your students, and he's always shown me respect, and that's kind of what I'm coming at, coming from with my students. (AYA Social Studies)

In some cases, the teaching cycles also provided opportunities for candidates to get feedback from their peers, especially in the fall semester during their methods course:

Because when we did them in the fall, we all did the teaching cycles, whoever our clinical educator was, but we all went to that methods class, and we all talked with other math teachers [methods course peers] about them. I thought that was awesome. You could get input from them, because you could get other students to say that, "Oh, yeah, I tried this once and this worked, but I tried this and it didn't work," or something like that. I thought the teaching cycles in the fall semester were definitely the most effective as to actually analyzing your lesson. (AYA Mathematics)

In fact, the structured support the clinical educators provided in the field and in methods class was so well-received by the candidates that several candidates felt they could use more support of this kind, observations and feedback, from their clinical educators:

Maybe having one or two more lesson[s] observed like maybe one every month as opposed to just three times would have helped... Just so I can get more feedback, more formal lessons and more formal feed-back. (MCE Mathematics)

In addition to serving as a mechanism for providing feedback, the teaching cycles also provided a means of building relationships between teacher candidates, the clinical educators, and the mentor teachers. For instance, one candidate identified the value of having her clinical educator as her methods instructor in regard to the feedback she received after the teaching cycles:

It was really, really nice having my clinical educator be one of my professors from last semester. I've built a relationship with her. She's really easy to go to and everything. It's super nice. When we do all these teaching cycles and whatnot, we sit down in class, and she and I can [go] over them. She gives really good feedback and whatnot, and it's stuff that I have and can use for the teaching cycles I do now. (AYA Mathematics)

Mentor teachers also found the teaching cycles useful because they created a space for them and the clinical educator to collaboratively support teacher candidates' development as teachers. The process facilitated a "team" approach to providing feedback that allowed the mentor teacher and clinical educa-tor to highlight the strengths and weaknesses demonstrated by teacher candidates in one lesson and set goals for improvement. For example, a science teacher mentoring an MCE teacher candidate stated:

I think that [the teacher candidate] grew a lot and I think that it was a team effort because I do feel that we had to stay very positive with her so it was two people and one of us being like you haven't done this, but you have done this. So the two of us together made it easier to be able to show her where she was needing to do better, but then the other one always had something, "But you've done this well" or "This went well." Or she would say sometimes, "I taught you that in class and I saw you using that today in your lesson." So that was good. Or I would say, "I need you to do this more." And she'd go, "Remember, when we did that in class, I'm not seeing you do that part." And I'd go, "But, we did see this." So I felt like it was really, really a great relationship and I think it helped [the teacher candidate] grow a lot.

Teaching cycles provided teacher candidates with useful feedback to promote their professional growth and one means of strengthening relationships among the members of the triad, which we discuss in greater detail next.

Stronger Relationships Among Triad

Both teacher candidates and mentors cited the connection among the triad as a strength of the model. Teacher candidates found that because their contact with the clinical educator was more extensive during the yearlong [having him or her as an instructor prior to the clinical year and throughout the clinical], it strengthened their relationship. One candidate explained:

These last two years with [other instructor] and with [my clinical educator] have been just great, easily. I mean they're great professors. They really do care about the development of not only me, but every other student that they have under their wing. I got to give them credit. (AYA Social Studies)

Other candidates also noted their close relationships with their clinical educators and the way the latter supported their teaching and critically reflecting on their teaching. A teacher candidate shared:

I think working with [clinical educator] was really great. She has a lot to offer. I really wish that we would have been doing that kind of stuff before because I've learned so much from her. I think I was lucky because I don't think everyone gets to work as closely with her. I'm so thankful because she really did help. (AYA Science)

The creation of a supportive group of critical peers also supported teacher candidate growth:

In that methods class, I think we started, not only me, but the whole group, we all started connecting with [my clinical educator]. She'd ... we had a really good working relationship, our entire group, I felt like.

Another candidate pointed out how his experience being observed was a positive one considering his established relationship and familiarity with his clinical educator:

I feel like it's helped a lot [that my methods instructor is my clinical educator] because it's not scary...I already know what she has gone through because she was actually [a high school teacher], and I've learned what her experiences are. I know she knows what she's talking about...Having that knowledge helps me. I guess I'm more relaxed around her compared to somebody that I don't really know their background... (AYA Mathematics)

Mentor teachers also noted the strong connection of the triad. Mentors, many of whom had a history with the yearlong clinical experience that the candidates did not have, were able to compare the working relationship of the triad in the CCMM to their prior year-long mentoring experiences. Mentor teachers characterized the relationship as positive, reliable, and nurturing of trust. One of the science teachers articulated:

I've had [teacher candidates] before. I feel like this one was more of a team effort...I felt like I could email [the clinical educator] any time and she would help me out. Or I could tell her something in confidence and then we could meet...I felt like it was really a very positive relationship.

The mentor teachers also expressed that the increased presence of the clinical educators in the schools, along with added support, contributed to a stronger commitment of the triad to the success of the teacher candidate. They noted the benefit of having a clinical educator who had the teacher candidate in class as well.

There was a subset of mentor participants from one partnership school whose interpretations seemed to run counter to the other mentor teachers' experiences. This particular school previously had a teacher in the building who was responsible for facilitating the communication between the school and the university, serving as clinical educator for all candidates placed in that school. Their model of supervision changed due to administrative decisions in the district, which allowed for the CCMM to be implemented. In the prior model, the mentor teacher and clinical educator had an established relationship as colleagues working together in the same building, which allowed for easier communication and an in-house network of support that would not have been feasible otherwise.

Logistical Challenges

A challenge consistently described by all participants and noted by clinical educators was negotiating logistics. During the fall semester, coordinating observations and meetings proved to be difficult based on teacher candidates' full schedules. Fall semester is the last semester for teacher candidates to fulfill course requirements before entering the field; therefore many were enrolled in 15 or more credit hours (at least 5 courses) in addition to completing 150 hours at their field placements and substantial course assignments that needed to be completed in their field placements. This made it difficult to find time to engage in additional clinical supervision activities and requirements. One candidate explained:

Having an actual course load work on top of being a responsible plan for the days you were there was stressful. You had to balance between all. This is my teaching workload on top of my university workload and, if you were working, I know some students have to work in to be able to afford college in general on top of that. It can get hard. (MCE Science)

Spring semester provided a new set of logistical issues. Scheduling observations was difficult due to unpredictable weather and intensive state mandated testing that interfered with school schedules. These shifts in schedule became even more problematic for engaging in teaching cycles where the intent was to observe a lesson that was co-planned. Due to schedule changes, it was hard to predict when a lesson would be actually taught and therefore sometimes, to get in the required observations, clinical educators would opt to observe a lesson that they did not help to co-plan.

In some cases for the MCE teacher candidates, scheduling problems were further exacerbated by the nature of the placement. Some of the lower middle grades placements (e.g., 4th or 5th grade) presented additional difficulty for scheduling because in these grade levels, time is not equally parsed to the different content areas. For example, a candidate seeking licensure in MCE mathematics and science was placed with a mentor who taught both disciplines. According to the school schedule, science was only taught during the last twenty minutes of each day, with a slightly longer period on Fridays. Teacher candidates placed in such classrooms were not able to observe and teach both content areas equally. For example, an MCE science candidate articulated, "I didn't see a ton of science last semester." This meant that there was a small window of opportunity for the clinical educator to schedule observations. For these candidates, clinical educators completed observations on lessons that did not focus on their area of expertise. In these cases, candidates described a need for more communication:

I feel like it was good. I feel like ... professors are so busy that they just ... don't have enough time to do everything they could do? I feel like, I did get to speak with her and I did get to bounce a few things off of her but I feel like sometimes it was kind of hard to make plans because she's busy and we're busy and then ... So I felt like she was helpful, but of course, [my mentor teacher] was more helpful because I was with him every day.

While logistical details present a challenge for any supervision process, many of the tensions discussed above were exacerbated by the additional requirements of the CCMM.

DISCUSSION

Recall that the CCMM differed from past supervision of teacher candidates in several ways: (1) the use of content-specific clinical educators at University 2; (2) the use of teaching cycles; (3) giving more feedback on teaching, and; (4) a focus on discourse and argumentation across disciplines.

The findings of this study indicate that mentor teachers, teacher candidates, and clinical educators found the CCMM to be supportive of teacher candidates' learning to teach. The content-specific expertise of the university clinical educator and the content-specific nature of the feedback they provided emerged as especially valuable. As illustrated in this study, content-specific faculty supported teacher candidate learning in at least two ways: 1) helping them understand content in a deeper manner that is more conducive to transforming that content into engaging lessons that are accessible to students, and; 2) sharing research-supported content-specific strategies and resources to support the lesson planning process. As members of the mentoring triad, faculty members contributed to the development of teacher candidates' pedagogical content knowledge (Ball, Thames, & Phelps, 2008; Shulman, 1987). Moreover, a majority of teacher candidates acknowledged the importance of further developing the *knowledge for teaching* specific to their content area.

Involvement of content-specific faculty promoted articulation and alignment between the methods courses that they teach and the candidates' experiences in the field. One of the major challenges to the field of teacher education is bridging theory and practice (Darling-Hammond, 2006a; Korthagen & Kessels, 1999; Zeichner, 2010). As clinical educators, faculty members bridged this gap by creating opportunities for teacher candidates to teach the kinds of lessons that are advocated by the program and in the methods courses. These opportunities came about because the faculty members required that the lessons planned for each teaching cycle focus on constructing and critiquing arguments, supported the development of lessons with the same focus, and were present to support teacher candidates and K-12 students as they engaged in lesson activities. Such bridging opportunities were especially valuable in classrooms where the mentor teacher often relied on direct instruction as the primary pedagogical approach. In these classrooms, the faculty member's presence created a safe environment for the teacher candidates to plan and enact lessons that deviated from the teaching approach used by the mentor teacher.

Mentor teachers' description of clinical educators as "participant-observers" is significant because it signals a shift in the place and perception of the role of the clinical educator from the realm of observer to actor in the classroom. In this study, the clinical educators actively engaged in the K-12 classrooms using co-teaching. This form of engagement helped to give teacher candidates and mentor teachers real examples of different approaches to instruction, provided them with positive and successful experiences with these approaches to instruction, supported the development of a more robust image of teaching in the content areas, and may increase the likelihood of them adopting these practices themselves. Such a role is distinctly different from the supervisory and evaluative focus that is typical for clinical educators who sit in the back of the room taking notes. This new role paves the way for considering the collaborative mentoring space as a potential site for mentor teacher professional development. In such a space, the stakeholders involved - mentor teacher, clinical educator, and teacher candidate, engage in an inquiry-based approach to support professional learning. Cajkler and Wood's (2016) claim that lesson study, one such inquiry-based approach, provided professional development for mentors. The presence and active participation of the clinical educator, a content specialist, in the classroom additionally illustrates how a strong connection between the university and schools can positively impact student learning through the process of simultaneous renewal in which all stakeholders are "involved in the process to work together as a team with a shared mission" (Goodlad, Mantle-Bromley, & Goodlad, 2004, p. 23). The interaction between the university and schools creates an opportunity for mentor teachers to stay abreast of up-to-date pedagogical practices based on current research, as well as a chance for clinical educators to spend time in classrooms examining the relevance and feasibility of those research paradigms.

The teaching cycle created a second bridge to, and a new context for focusing on, the development of pedagogical content knowledge. During the teaching cycles, faculty helped teacher candidates consider the multiple, and sometimes inaccurate, perspectives that students might bring to a discussion of the content. They also co-planned and co-taught with candidates, thus changing the nature of the teaching cycle observation. The teaching cycles created a space for faculty to share examples of pedagogical content knowledge that was relevant for authentic contexts and real students, not a hypothetical group of students. Clinical educators engaged in in-depth co-teaching, meaning they interacted with students during the lessons; modeled formative assessment; co-planned lessons with teacher candidates (sometimes in collaboration with mentor teachers); in some cases teaching model lessons; and provided in-the-moment coaching, advice, and assistance while the teacher candidates taught. This approach to field supervision and co-teaching is different than past practices at both institutions and the typical approaches described in the literature (Bacharach, Heck, & Dahlberg, 2010; Bacharach & Heck, 2012; Desimone, 2009; McDuffie, Mastropieri, & Scruggs, 2009) where lesson planning and teaching is done between teacher candidate and mentor teacher.

Co-teaching in the field classroom, in the form of teaching model lessons and interacting directly with students, additionally allowed clinical educators to directly model the practices and pedagogical approaches that, as faculty members, they wanted teacher candidates to use. This represents a shift from more typical teacher education programs where the modeling of instructional practices is often only done in university classrooms and not the very settings and context where teacher candidates are teaching. The type of modeling and coaching afforded by the CCMM provides novice teachers with insights into the thought processes of an expert who is trained as a teacher educator (in a way that mentor teachers are not) and likely more adept at unpacking the thinking that informs a teacher's instructional decisions. As a result of this expertise sharing (Schon, 1983), teacher candidates develop *knowledge in action* (Cochran-Smith & Lytle, 1999). The teaching cycles additionally enriched the mentoring process by providing structured opportunities for teacher candidates to reflect on their own practice with input from a more experienced mentor. Reflection is central to the learning to teach process and results in the development of *knowledge of teaching* (Cochran-Smith & Lytle, 1999).

CCMM also nurtured a strong relationship between the members of the clinical community of practice. In other current models of supervision, the clinical educator does not typically have prior experience working with the candidate, and their interactions and communication tend to be limited (Henning, Gut, & Beam, 2015). The sustained nature of the CCMM collaboration between the mentor teacher and the clinical educator created a third bridge between university courses and field experiences. Teacher candidates, mentor teachers, and clinical educators shared a common knowledge-base and teaching experience (content and grade band). As they engaged in the shared activities of the CCMM - an introductory meeting, co-planning, co-teaching, and collaborative feedback sessions - throughout the year, members of the clinical triad developed a collective, coherent vision of long-term goals for supporting teacher candidate learning. In this manner, CCMM fostered the kinds of conversations advocated by Butler and Cuenca (2012) that result in more coherent teacher education programs. Critical to these conversations is a shared approach to inquiry that is central to the functioning of a community of practice (Lave, 1988; Lave & Wenger, 1991; Wenger, 1998).

SOLUTION AND RECOMMENDATIONS

Through the development and implementation of CCMM, the authors have learned much about building and maintaining systems of partnership with local schools and teachers that support teacher candidates' learning and adoption of research-supported instructional strategies. Preparing teachers is a collaborative process and therefore cannot occur in two separate silos, university courses and school-based clinical experiences. While school-university partnerships are recognized as essential for effective teacher preparation, the field of teacher education must additionally recognize that the mentoring of teacher candidates in the field cannot be the sole responsibility of mentor teachers and clinical university-based teacher educators. Teacher candidate mentoring is a joint responsibility of schools and universities and must involve university-based teacher educators. A collaborative mentoring model that involves university-based teacher educators can strengthen and maintain a system of partnership by involving stakeholders with varying roles and expertise in the mentoring process, fostering a space to promote critical conversations and inquiry into practice, and ultimately bridging the theory to practice divide.

A clear focus and a systematic process to examine practice are central features of an effective collaborative mentoring approach that nurtures the kinds of benefits described in this study. Coupling clinical practice with explicit models (e.g., teaching cycles) for facilitating teacher candidate reflection will advance the development of a practical knowledge (Cochran-Smith & Lytle, 1999) that is content-specific. A content-specific and cyclical focus to collaborative mentoring will further support teacher candidates' progression towards becoming more expert teachers (Hiebert, Morris, Berk, & Jansen, 2007).

The findings of this study highlight the benefits of engaging content-specific teacher educators in the role of clinical educator. The authors acknowledge that such engagement is not a novel practice. University faculty might engage in field mentoring in small teacher education programs but are typically less likely to be involved in this manner in larger programs. In rural areas and subject areas (e.g., mathematics and science) that report teacher shortages, the problem of finding highly-qualified clinical educators (with the requisite content expertise and teaching experience) is exacerbated. More typically, clinical educators are former classroom teachers who may or not may not have taught in the teacher's content area.

While the authors recommend that university-based and content-specific teacher educators engage in collaborative mentoring through models such as CCMM, the authors recognize the workload-related challenges such involvement might pose. For example, in the rural areas where this study took place, schools are small in size and interns cannot all be placed in the same building or district. Negotiating time to engage in CCMM activities was complicated by the variety in school schedules, geographic distance of placements, mentor teacher responsibilities, teacher candidate coursework, and faculty teaching, scholarship, and service responsibilities.

FUTURE RESEARCH DIRECTIONS

This chapter has described the features of a collaborative and content-specific model of mentoring to support the learning to teach process. The chapter additionally described the affordances that such a model provides to teacher education programs and the development of systems of school-university partnerships, according to teacher candidates, mentor teachers, and clinical educators. Future research should explore the ways in which such a model promotes teacher candidate learning (e.g., pedagogical content knowledge) and shifts in practice (e.g., lesson planning, facilitating students' ability to construct arguments). Future research should also explore the ways in which similar models can promote mentor teacher professional development. This study did not document the nature and content of the collaborative activities between the members of the clinical community of practice. Future research should use discourse analysis to examine how engagement in the shared activities creates opportunities for learning.

CONCLUSION

Using CCMM and collaborative models like it to support field-based teacher education is imperative. Both mentors and candidates described the model as beneficial to candidates' developing teaching practice. The content-specific nature of the model created a space for teacher candidates to attend to issues of pedagogical content knowledge, rather than more general teaching and classroom management strategies. It also helped to create space for candidates to apply research-supported teaching strategies. In this manner, the CCMM supported the candidates' active engagement in the classroom and also created more coherence and connections between university courses and school-based field experiences. The collaborative nature of the model further supported teacher candidates by nurturing a strong relationship among the triad members (teacher candidates, mentor teachers, and clinical educators) which allowed the candidates to receive better and more cohesive feedback. Because clinical educators acted as participant-observers (in co-planning and co-teaching), they were able to model best practices, support connections between the coursework and the field, and engage mentors in learning alongside the candidates. Using the CCMM over time and with a cadre of mentor teachers and school partners can mitigate some of the challenges identified by clinical educators in this study and result in stronger systems of school-university partnerships.

ACKNOWLEDGMENT

This research was supported through the [Organization Regional Research Grant].

REFERENCES

American Association of Colleges for Teacher Education. (2018). *A pivot toward clinical practice, its lexicon, and the renewal of educator preparation. A Report of the AACTE Clinical Practice Commission*. Washington, DC: AACTE.

Argyris, C., & Schon, D. (1974). *Theory in practice: Increasing professional effectiveness*. San Francisco: Jossey-Bass.

Bacharach, N., & Heck, T. W. (2012). Voices from the field: Multiple perspectives on a co-teaching in student teaching model. *Educational Renaissance*, *1*(1), 49–69.

Bacharach, N., Heck, T. W., & Dahlberg, K. (2010). Changing the face of student teaching through coteaching. *Action in Teacher Education*, *32*(1), 3–14. doi:10.1080/01626620.2010.10463538

Ball, D., & Cohen, D. (1999). Developing practitioners: Toward a practice-based theory of professional development. In G. Sykes & L. Darling-Hammond (Eds.), *Teaching as the learning profession: Handbook of policy and practice* (pp. 3–32). San Francisco, CA: Jossey-Bass.

Ball, D. L., & Forzani, F. M. (2009). The work of teaching and the challenge for teacher education. *Journal of Teacher Education*, *60*(5), 497–511. doi:10.1177/0022487109348479

Ball, D. L., Thames, M. H., & Phelps, G. (2008). Content knowledge for teaching: What makes it special? *Journal of Teacher Education*, *59*(5), 389–407. doi:10.1177/0022487108324554

Barnett, E., & Friedrichsen, P. J. (2015). Educative Mentoring: How a mentor supported a preservice biology teacher's pedagogical content knowledge development. *Journal of Science Teacher Education*, *26*(7), 647–668. doi:10.100710972-015-9442-3

Beck, C., & Kosnik, C. (2002). Professors in the practicum: Involvement of university faculty in preservice practicum supervision. *Journal of Teacher Education*, *5*(1), 6–19. doi:10.1177/0022487102053001002

Bogdan, R., & Biklen, S. (2007). *Qualitative research for education: An introduction to theory and practice* (5th ed.). New York: Pearson Education, Inc.

Bradbury, L. U. (2010). Educative mentoring: Promoting reform-based science teaching through mentoring relationships. *Science Teacher Education*, *94*, 1049–1071.

Bradbury, L. U., & Koballa, T. R. (2007). Mentor advice giving in an alternate certification program for secondary science teaching: Opportunities and roadblocks in developing a knowledge base for teaching. *Journal of Science Teacher Education*, *18*(6), 817–840. doi:10.100710972-007-9076-1

Bransford, J., Brown, A., & Cocking, R. (Eds.). (2000). Effective teaching: Examples in history, mathematics, and science. In How people learn: Brain, mind, experience, and school (pp. 155-189). Washington, DC: National Academy Press.

Britzman, D. P. (2003). *Practice makes practice: A critical study of teaming to teach* (Rev. ed.). Albany, NY: SUNY Press.

Bruner, J. (1966). *Toward a theory of instruction*. Cambridge, MA: Harvard University Press.

Burn, K., & Mutton, T. (2015). A review of 'research-informed clinical practice' in Initial Teacher Education. *Oxford Review of Education*, *41*(2), 217–233. doi:10.1080/03054985.2015.1020104

Butler, B. M., & Cuenca, A. (2012). Conceptualizing the role of mentor teachers during student teaching. *Action in Teacher Education*, *34*(4), 296–308. doi:10.1080/01626620.2012.717012

Cajkler, W., & Wood, P. (2016). Mentors and student-teachers' 'lesson studying' in initial teacher education. *International Journal of Lesson and Learning Studies*, *5*(2), 1–18. doi:10.1108/IJLLS-04-2015-0015

Carroll, D., Featherstone, H., Featherstone, J., Feiman-Nemser, S., & Roosevelt, D. (2007). *Transforming teacher education: Reflections from the field*. Cambridge, MA: Harvard University Press.

Cochran-Smith, M., & Lytle, S. L. (1999). Relationships of knowledge and practice: Teacher learning in communities. *Review of Research in Education*, *24*, 249–305.

Darling-Hammond, L. (2006a). Constructing 21st-century teacher education. *Journal of Teacher Education*, *57*(3), 300–314. doi:10.1177/0022487105285962

Darling-Hammond, L. (2006b). *Powerful teacher education: Lessons from exemplary programs*. San Francisco: Jossey-Bass.

Darling-Hammond, L., & Bransford, J. (Eds.). (2005). *Preparing teachers for a changing world: What teachers should learn and be able to do*. San Francisco: Jossey-Bass.

Denzin, N. K., & Lincoln, Y. S. (Eds.). (2000). *Handbook of qualitative research* (2nd ed.). Thousand Oaks, CA: Sage Publications.

Desimone, L. M. (2009). Improving impact studies of teachers' professional development: Toward better conceptualizations and measures. *Educational Researcher*, *38*(3), 181–200. doi:10.3102/0013189X08331140

Feiman-Nemser, S. (2001). From preparation to practice: Designing a continuum to strengthen and sustain teaching. *Teachers College Record*, *103*(6), 1013–1055. doi:10.1111/0161-4681.00141

Feiman-Nemser, S., Parker, M. B., & Zeichner, K. (1990, April). *Are mentor teachers teacher educators?* Paper presented at the annual meeting of the American Educational Research Association, Boston, MA.

Fernandez, C., & Yoshida, M. (2004). *Improving mathematics teaching and learning: The Japanese lesson study approach (Studies in Mathematical Thinking and Learning Series).* Mahwah, NJ: Lawrence Erlbaum Associates.

Forzani, F. M. (2014). Understanding "core practices" and "practice-based" teacher education: Learning from the past. *Journal of Teacher Education, 65*(4), 357–368. doi:10.1177/0022487114533800

Goodlad, J. I., Mantle-Bromley, C., & Goodlad, S. J. (2004). *Education for everyone: Agenda for education in a democracy.* San Francisco, CA: Jossey-Bass.

Graham, B. (2006). Conditions for successful field experiences: Perceptions of cooperating teachers. *Teaching and Teacher Education, 22*(8), 1118–1129. doi:10.1016/j.tate.2006.07.007

Grossman, P., Hammerness, K., & McDonald, M. (2009). Redefining teaching, reimagining teacher education. *Teachers and Teaching, 15*(2), 273–289. doi:10.1080/13540600902875340

Grossman, P., Hammerness, K. M., McDonald, M., & Ronfeldt, M. (2008). Constructing coherence: Structural predictors of perceptions of coherence in NYC teacher education programs. *Journal of Teacher Education, 59*(4), 273–287. doi:10.1177/0022487108322127

Hammerness, K., Darling-Hammond, L., Grossman, P., Rust, F., & Shulman, L. (2005). The design of teacher education programs. In L. Darling-Hammond & J. Bransford (Eds.), *Preparing teachers for a changing world: What teachers should learn and be able to do* (pp. 390–441). San Francisco: Jossey-Bass.

Hashweh, M. Z. (2005). Teacher pedagogical constructions: A reconfiguration of pedagogical content knowledge. *Teachers and Teaching, 11*(3), 273–292. doi:10.1080/13450600500105502

Henning, J. E., Erb, D. J., Randles, H. S., Fults, N., & Webb, K. (2016). Designing a curriculum for clinical experiences. *Issues in Teacher Education, 25*, 23–38.

Henning, J. E., Gut, D., & Beam, P. (2015). Designing and implementing a mentoring program to support clinically-based teacher education. *Teacher Educator, 50*(2), 145–162. doi:10.1080/08878730.20 15.1011046

Hiebert, J., Morris, A. K., Berk, B., & Jansen, A. (2007). Preparing teachers to learn from teaching. *Journal of Teacher Education, 58*(1), 47–61. doi:10.1177/0022487106295726

Howell, J., & Saye, W. J. (2015). Using lesson study to develop a shared professional teaching knowledge culture among 4th grade social studies teachers. *Journal of Social Studies Research, 40*(1), 25–37. doi:10.1016/j.jssr.2015.03.001

Kochan, F. K., & Trimble, S. B. (2000). From mentoring to co-mentoring: Establishing collaborative relationships. *Theory into Practice, 39*(1), 20–28. doi:10.120715430421tip3901_4

Koemer, M., Rust, F., & Baumgartner, F. (2002). Exploring roles in student teaching placements. *Teacher Education Quarterly, 29*, 35–58.

Korthagen, F., & Kessels, J. (1999). Linking theory and practice: Changing the pedagogy of teacher education. *Educational Researcher, 28*(4), 4–17. doi:10.3102/0013189X028004004

Korthagen, F. A. J. (2010). Situated learning theory and the pedagogy of teacher education: Towards an integrated view of teacher behavior and teacher learning. *Teaching and Teacher Education*, *26*(1), 98–106. doi:10.1016/j.tate.2009.05.001

Kosnik, C., & Beck, B. (2008). In the shadows: Non-tenure line instructors in preservice teacher education. *European Journal of Teacher Education*, *31*(2), 185–202. doi:10.1080/02619760802000214

Lampert, M., Franke, M. L., Kazemi, E., Ghousseini, H., Turrou, A. C., Beasley, H., ... Crowe, K. (2013). Keeping it complex: Using rehearsals to support novice teacher learning of ambitious teaching. *Journal of Teacher Education*, *64*(3), 226–243. doi:10.1177/0022487112473837

Lave, J. (1988). *Cognition in practice*. Cambridge, UK: Cambridge University Press. doi:10.1017/CBO9780511609268

Lave, J., & Wenger, E. (1991). *Situated learning: Legitimate peripheral participation*. Cambridge, UK: Cambridge University Press. doi:10.1017/CBO9780511815355

Lee, J. C., & Feng, S. (2007). Mentoring support and the professional development of beginning teachers: A Chinese perspective. *Mentoring & Tutoring*, *15*(3), 243–263. doi:10.1080/13611260701201760

Levine, H. (2011). Features and strategies of supervisor professional community as a means of improving the supervision of preservice teachers. *Teaching and Teacher Education*, *27*(5), 930–941. doi:10.1016/j.tate.2011.03.004

Lewis, C. (2002). What are the essential elements of lesson study? *The California Science Project Connection*, *2*(6), 1–4.

Lewis, C., & Hurd, J. (2011). *Lesson study step by step: How teacher learning communities improve instruction*. Portsmouth: Heinemann.

Lewis, C., Perry, R., & Murata, A. (2006). What is the role of the research in an emerging innovation? The case of lesson study. *Educational Researcher*, *35*(3), 3–14. doi:10.3102/0013189X035003003

Luft, J. A., Roehrig, G. H., & Patterson, N. C. (2003). Contrasting landscapes: A comparison of the impact of different induction programs on beginning secondary science teachers' practices, beliefs and experiences. *Journal of Research in Science Teaching*, *40*(1), 77–97. doi:10.1002/tea.10061

McDonald, M., Kazemi, E., & Kavanagh, S. S. (2013). Core practices and pedagogies of teacher education: A call for a common language and collective activity. *Journal of Teacher Education*, *64*(5), 378–386. doi:10.1177/0022487113493807

McDuffie, K. A., Mastropieri, M. A., & Scruggs, T. E. (2009). Differential effects of peer tutoring in co-taught and non-co-taught classes: Results for content learning and student-teacher interactions. *Exceptional Children*, *75*(4), 493–510. doi:10.1177/001440290907500406

McNally, J. C. (2016). Learning from one's own teaching: New science teachers analyzing their practice through classroom observation cycles. *Journal of Research in Science Teaching*, *53*(3), 473–501. doi:10.1002/tea.21253

McNamara, D. (1995). The influence of student teachers' tutors and mentors upon their classroom practice: An exploratory study. *Teaching and Teacher Education, 11*(1), 51–61. doi:10.1016/0742-051X(94)00014-W

Meijer, P. C., Korthagen, F. A. J., & Vasalos, A. (2009). Supporting presence in teacher education: The connection between the personal and professional aspects of teaching. *Teaching and Teacher Education, 21*(2), 297–308. doi:10.1016/j.tate.2008.09.013

National Association of Professional Development Schools (NAPDS). (2008). *What it means to be a professional development school?* Retrieved from http://www.napds.org/9%20Essentials/statement.pdf

National Council for Accreditation of Teacher Education. (2010). *Transforming teacher education through clinical practice: A national strategy to prepare effective teachers. Report of Blue Ribbon Panel on clinical preparation and partnerships for improved student landing.* Washington, DC: NCATE.

Puchner, L. P., & Taylor, A. R. (2006). Lesson study, collaboration and teacher efficacy: Stories from two school-based math lesson study groups. *Teaching and Teacher Education, 22*(7), 922–934. doi:10.1016/j.tate.2006.04.011

Santagata, R., Zannoni, C., & Stigler, J. W. (2007). The role of lesson analysis in pre-service teacher education: An empirical investigation of teacher learning from a virtual video-based field experience. *Journal of Mathematics Teacher Education, 10*(2), 123–140. doi:10.100710857-007-9029-9

Schon, D. (1983). *The reflective practitioner.* New York: Basic Books.

Schwab, J. (1978). Education and the structure of the disciplines. In J. Westbury & N. Wilkof (Eds.), *Science, curriculum, and liberal education.* Chicago: University of Chicago Press.

Shulman, L. S. (1987). Knowledge and teaching: Foundations of a new reform. *Harvard Educational Review, 57*(1), 1–21. doi:10.17763/haer.57.1.j463w79r56455411

Stigler, J. W., & Hiebert, J. (1999). *The teaching gap: Best ideas from the world's teachers for improving education in the classroom.* New York: The Free Press.

Urzúa, A., & Vásquez, C. (2008). Reflection and professional identity in teachers' future-oriented discourse. *Teaching and Teacher Education, 24*(7), 1935–1946. doi:10.1016/j.tate.2008.04.008

Valencia, S. W., Martin, S. D., Place, N. A., & Grossman, P. (2009). Complex interactions in student teaching. *Journal of Teacher Education, 60*(3), 304–322. doi:10.1177/0022487109336543

Wenger, E. (1998). *Communities of practice: Learning, meaning and Identity.* Cambridge, UK: Cambridge University Press. doi:10.1017/CBO9780511803932

Wertsch, J. (1991). *Voices of the mind: A Sociocultural approach to mediated action.* Cambridge, MA: Harvard University Press.

Zeichner, K. (2010). Rethinking the connections between campus courses and field experiences in college- and university-based teacher education. *Journal of Teacher Education, 61*(1/2), 89–99. doi:10.1177/0022487109347671

Zeichner, K. (2012). The turn once again toward practice-based teacher education. *Journal of Teacher Education, 63*(5), 376–382. doi:10.1177/0022487112445789

Zeichner, K. M. (2005). Becoming a teacher educator: A personal perspective. *Teaching and Teacher Education, 21*(2), 117–124. doi:10.1016/j.tate.2004.12.001

Zeichner, K. M., & Conklin, H. (2005). Teacher education programs. In M. Cochran Smith & K. M. Zeichner (Eds.), *Studying teacher education: The report of the AERA panel on research and teacher education* (pp. 645–735). Mahwah, NJ: Lawrence Erlbaum Associates.

KEY TERMS AND DEFINITIONS

Clinical Educator: A university-based teacher educator who coaches or supervises candidates in the field.

Clinical Model of Teacher Education: A practice-based model of teacher preparation that provides in-depth clinical experiences for teacher candidates that enable them to learn as they become part of school communities and share in the mission of positively impacting P-12 student learning.

Clinical Practice: A component of a clinical model of teacher education that engages teacher candidates in the pedagogical work of the profession of teaching, occurs in authentic educational settings, integrates closely with educator preparation coursework, and is supported by a formal school-university partnership.

Collaborative Mentoring: A process whereby mentor teachers and clinical educators work together to guide and support teacher candidates and nurture their personal and professional growth.

Community of Practice: A group of people who come together because they share a passion to learn and improve the practice of a shared profession.

Mentor Teacher: A school-based teacher educator who works directly with teacher candidates who are placed in his or her classroom, models teaching practices, provides ongoing support, and assesses the candidates' progress.

Pedagogical Content Knowledge: The blending of content knowledge and pedagogical knowledge into a specialized knowledge for teaching of specific subjects.

School-University Partnerships: A mutually beneficial collaboration between a university teacher preparation program and a local P-12 school or district.

Teaching Cycle: A three-phase sequence in which teacher candidates plan a lesson with the assistance of the clinical educator and mentor teacher, teach the lesson, then engage in an in-depth process of co-reflection as a team.

Chapter 6
Overcoming Barriers to Clinical Partnerships:
A National Taskforce Response

Derek Decker
Colorado State University, USA

Jennifer Roth
Fort Collins High School, USA

Donna Cooner
Colorado State University, USA

ABSTRACT

The Council for the Accreditation of Educator Preparation (CAEP) set forth a set of new standards that demand excellence to produce educators who raise P-12 student achievement. This pilot multi-case study describes perspectives and across-case themes of the lived experiences of national key stakeholders in educator preparation programs and their professional development school (PDS) partnership system. CAEP's five guiding principles of Standard 2: Clinical Partnerships and Practice as a priori codes describe experiences and perspectives of three key stakeholders of the university's clinical partnership. The three key stakeholders include (1) university-based teacher educators, (2) school-based teacher educators, and (3) teacher candidates. The researchers discuss results and implications for practice and offer avenues for future research.

INTRODUCTION

Nine years ago, *The Blue Ribbon Panel Report* (National Council for Accreditation for Teacher Education, 2010) set forth a comprehensive series of recommendations that would lead to necessary changes in policy, practice, and culture and norms of preparation programs and school districts. One of the recommendations of the report suggested the moral imperative to "remove barriers to preparation program/district collaboration and provide incentives for meeting district needs" (National Council for Accredita-

DOI: 10.4018/978-1-5225-6249-8.ch006

tion for Teacher Education, 2010, p. 22). The report was a call to action to all education stakeholders, yet the collaborations between P-12 schools, the universities that prepare teacher candidates, and the state/federal policy makers continue to be stifled with barriers that prevent the renewal of the education profession. Although many positive moves toward the renewal of teacher preparation have taken place in specific locations, the sheer number of barriers often limit the development of collaborative systems between the entities that play large roles in the development of future teachers. The result is a critical problem of practice.

SIGNIFICANCE

Increasingly, universities and school districts share responsibility for teacher and student learning. Sharing responsibility demands that both institutions work to develop closer relationships, yet many barriers arise from the complex work done in university-school partnerships. When two educational institutions work together to meet both state and federal demands, there are simultaneous efforts to maintain, reproduce, negotiate, and transcend institutional boundaries and barriers (Daniels, Edwards, Engeström, Gallagher, & Ludvigsen, 2010). Schools and universities challenge each other's expertise, practices, policies, and social arrangements that can create conflicts and tensions. Solutions and support for resolution of any barrier will have a far-reaching impact on partnership sites.

The purpose of this study is to describe barriers in teacher preparation programs that may slow, or halt, the renewal of teacher preparation. The researchers of this study, a unique team of school and university based educators who simultaneously work in both environments, assert that the renewal of teacher preparation begins by removing certain boundaries of governance between the higher-education system that prepares teachers and the P-12 system where teachers work so that teacher educators can respond to the needs in P-12 schools. All stakeholder groups represented in a typical teacher preparation clinical partnership as well as national groups associated with educator preparation participated in the focus groups for this study.

The following research questions guided the data analysis identified in the methods, findings, and discussion sections of this article:

Research Question One: How does current literature identify ways to help educator preparation programs turn barriers into opportunities for renewal?

Research Question Two: How do practitioners in educator preparation programs (EPPs) describe barriers in clinical partnerships and practice?

CONCEPTUAL FRAMEWORK

Professional Capital: An Answer to a Divided Profession

Hargreaves and Fullan (2012) described professional capital as made up of three other categories of capital: (a) human capital; (b) social capital, and; (c) decisional capital (p. 3). Human capital in teaching acquires and develops the required knowledge and skills. Hargreaves and Fullan explained:

[Human capital] is about knowing your subject and knowing how to teach it, knowing children and understanding how they learn, understanding the diverse cultural and family circumstances that your students come from, being familiar with and able to sift and sort the science of successful and innovative practice, and having the emotional capabilities to empathize with diverse groups of children and also adults in and around a school. (p. 89)

Research has shown that quality teaching matters to student learning. Teacher quality has been identified as the most important school-based factor in student achievement (McCaffrey, Lockwood, Koretz, & Hamilton, 2003; Rivkin, Hanushek, & Kain, 2000; Rowan, Correnti, & Miller, 2002; Wright, Horn, & Sanders, 1997). Teachers are the human capital of a school, and the more investment in this capital, the more teachers will improve their useful outputs over long periods of time. Although a focus on human capital is extremely important, improvement in human capital cannot increase in isolation. Teaching is not solely comprised of skills and knowledge of teaching pedagogy confined to the four walls of a classroom.

Building human capital is an individual endeavor undertaken by each teacher. Social capital, in comparison, is not a characteristic of the individual teacher but instead the relationships among teachers, among teachers and principals, and even among teachers, parents, and other key individuals in the community. Social capital refers to "how the quantity and quality of interactions and social relationship among people affects their access to knowledge and information" (Hargreaves & Fullan, 2012, p. 90). A study by Leana (2011) sampled 130 elementary schools in New York to determine mathematics achievement over the course of one year and found that schools with high social capital showed positive student achievement outcomes. Schools with strong social and human capital together did even better (Leana, 2011).

Even with strong human and social capital, a large decisional element exists that educators must develop and practice. Decisional capital is "the capital that professionals acquire and accumulate through structured and unstructured experience, practice, and reflection" (Hargreaves & Fullan, 2012, p. 93). This type of capital allows educators to make wise judgments in circumstances where there is no fixed rule or piece of evidence to guide them. Decisional capital is refined when operationalized through interaction with colleagues. Hargreaves and Fullan (2012) stated:

High-yield strategies become more precise and more embedded when they are developed and deployed in teams that are constantly refining and interpreting them. At the same time, poor judgements and ineffective practices get discarded along the way. And when clear evidence is lacking or conflicting, accumulated collective experience carries much more weight than idiosyncratic experience or little experience at all. (p. 124)

Human capital, social capital, and decisional capital emphasize the rationale for strong teacher preparation that develops the necessary knowledge and skills, collaboration pathways, and mindsets that the best decisions are made in collaboration with others. Professional capital, which encompasses human, social, and decisional capital, is a cornerstone that defines and brings together the critical elements of what it takes to create high quality and high performance in the education profession. Professional capital is "what you know and can do individually, with whom you know it and do it collectively, and how long you have known it and done it and deliberately gotten better at doing it over time" (Hargreaves & Fullan, 2012, p. 102).

The Complexities of Teaching: A Barrier in Disguise

Grossman, Hammerness, and McDonald (2009) stated that "teaching is complex work that looks deceptively simple" (p. 273). Education is not a straightforward process, and a lack of understanding the intricacies of becoming a skilled teacher can cause barriers between those who teach and those who do not. Those who do not teach may believe in the value of experienced teachers who have mastered their craft, yet they may think teaching is simply a matter of walking into a classroom and delivering a lesson to students. Hargreaves and Fullan (2012) stated:

If you want to change teaching, you have to understand it, and very often appreciate it. You have to understand the teachers who are responsible for the teaching–what motivates them and makes them tick. And you have to understand how to find not just a few young teachers for a few years, but how to keep the best of them until they reach their peak, how to circulate professional capital from one generation to the next, and how to recognize and re-energize the older teachers we already have. (p. 42)

Teaching is a complex cycle that takes place before, during, and after the lessons are delivered. Ball and Forzani (2009) defined the work of teaching as the core tasks that teachers must execute to help students learn, and they provided specific examples of the core tasks that include activities both in and beyond the classroom (p. 497):

leading a discussion of solutions to a mathematics problem, probing students' answers, reviewing material for a science test, listening to and assessing students' oral reading, explaining an interpretation of a poem, talking with parents, evaluating students' papers, planning, and creating and maintaining an orderly and supportive environment for learning. (p. 497)

Further, "teaching is one of the most common, and also one of the most complicated, human activities" (Ball & Forzani, 2010, p. 40), despite the prevailing view of teaching as "requiring little more than patience, basic content knowledge, and liking children" (Ball & Forzani, 2010, p. 40). Learning to use teaching practices in classrooms is intricate work requiring teacher education programs that are carefully designed in ways that help teacher candidates learn to skillfully utilize teaching practices. The skills involved in teaching do not come naturally (Jackson, 1986; Murray, 1989); however, effective teaching can be taught in teacher preparation programs.

Darling-Hammond (2006) mentioned that many prospective teachers come into the profession thinking little education and preparation is needed, but "most learn quickly that teaching is much more difficult than they thought, and they either desperately seek out additional training . . . or leave in despair" (p. 12). Clinically rich teacher preparation programs foster learning the practice of teaching and the intricacies of the vocation, and studies have consistently found:

With little knowledge of learning or child development to guide them, teachers who lack preparation rely more on rote methods of learning; are more autocratic in the ways they manage their classrooms; are less skilled at managing complex forms of instruction aimed at deeper understanding; are less capable of identifying children's learning styles and needs; and are less likely to see it as their job to do so, blaming students when their teaching is not successful. (Darling-Hammond, 2003, p. 17)

Clinically rich preparation bridges the gap to enable teachers to draw on a wide variety of methods and management systems, ultimately leading to better training, and therefore, more successful teachers.

How to Prepare Future Educators: A Barrier in Belief

The process of preparing effective teachers is changing. The college and university system of teacher preparation that has prepared most U.S. teachers for over the last fifty years has been declared a failure by many policymakers and mainstream media (Fraser, 2007). According to Zeichner, Payne, and Brayko (2014),

[Society is] on a course to dismantle the college and university system of teacher education and replace it with a host of entrepreneurial programs that will worsen rather than ameliorate the opportunity and learning gaps that continue to plague our public schools. (p. 122)

Boyd, Grossman, Lankford, Loeb, and Wyckoff (2006) declared that there are many ways to enter into the teaching field but few ways to evaluate the effectiveness of the variety of entry methods.

The Professional Development School Model

One traditional model of preparation successfully assuring quality field experiences and successfully blending theory with practice is the professional development school (PDS) model. The PDS model has gained traction due to "the position that interns at PDS schools achieve higher than do interns assigned to non-PDS schools" (Castle, Fox, & Souder, 2006; Darling-Hammond, 2007; Levine, 2002; Snyder, 1999). The PDS is a place where teacher candidates spend much of their time in a P-12 school, and the affiliation between a university and P-12 schools far outweighs preparation that is not based in the real world of schools (Wong & Glass, 2005). Castle et al. (2006) reported that a PDS produces:

beginning teachers who are more competent in some aspects of instruction, management, and assessment, and are more integrated and student-centered in their thinking about planning, assessment, instruction, management, and reflection. (p. 78)

METHODS

The researchers used a descriptive thematic analysis to frame their investigation of barriers to clinical partnerships and experiences in teacher preparation. The researchers collected data through a series of three focus group interviews. This method was selected as most advantageous due to the social nature of group conversation that provides an opportunity for collegial interactions among participants (Onwuegbuzie, Dickinson, Leech & Zoran, 2009).

Participants

All interviewees in the focus groups were members of American Association of Colleges for Teacher Education's (AACTE) Clinical Practice Commission (CPC) and active participants in clinical partnerships across the country. The range of CPC participants is reflected in Table 1. Several weeks in advance of the summit, the researchers sent an email to share the topics that would be addressed in the focus groups' conversations to the CPC members and to invite them to participate in the focus group.

Procedure

The researchers co-facilitated semi-structured 60 minute interviews either in person or on the phone. Prior to each focus group session, all participants signed a consent form and were provided access to the interview questions. After a brief introduction concerning the research project, the researchers prompted the participants to respond to the questions about clinical partnerships for the first 30 minutes of the session and the questions regarding clinical experiences during the second 30 minutes. The focus group participants' responses were audio-recorded with Microsoft Lifecam software and subsequently submitted to a transcription service that provided verbatim transcription of the focus group responses.

Analysis

Before conducting the focus group interviews, the researchers had identified *a priori* codes based on Council for the Accreditation of Education Programs' (CAEP; 2013) Standard 2 that defines required components of clinical partnerships and experiences; however, no codes had been identified to organize the participants' responses to the questions about barriers to clinical partnerships and experiences. After receiving the transcriptions, the researchers individually listened to the audio recordings and compared them to the transcriptions, making any necessary corrections and verifying the accuracy of the transcriptions. The researchers then met to devise a plan for the "preliminary exploratory analysis" (Creswell, 2008, p. 250) in order to gain a general understanding of the data and establish a broad organizational framework. To establish intercoder reliability, the researchers selected random samples from each focus group to code individually and then met to compare how the samples were coded.

To "make sense out of text data," because no prior coding framework existed, the researchers engaged in the following inductive coding process: "divide into text segments, label the segments with codes, examine codes for overlap and redundancy, and collapse these codes into broad themes" (Creswell, 2008, p. 251). The researchers' initial analysis resulted in 19 pages of text divided into 75 segments and labeled with 22 different codes. Through examinations and conversations of the data, the researchers reorganized the data into 17 codes. After several more iterations of the organizing scheme, the researchers succeeded in collapsing the codes into five overarching themes with associated codes and sub-codes. Table 2 illustrates the organizing themes with codes and sub-codes as well as the sources of specific data, (i.e., Focus Group 1, 2, or 3) and the number of times a code or sub-code was referenced.

FINDINGS

Upon completion of the coding process, five overarching themes emerged: *complexity of teacher education, policy barriers, logistical barriers, barriers within clinical partnerships*, and *barriers as impetus for renewal and improvement*. The number of times a theme was referenced varied greatly from a single reference for complexity of teacher education and barriers as impetus for renewal and change to 22 references for program design barriers and 24 references for barriers within clinical partnerships.

Three themes (policy barriers, logistical barriers, and barriers within clinical partnerships) were further dissected into sub-codes, reflecting the complexity of the identified barriers. The researchers did not attempt to attach a hierarchy of importance or relevance to the number of references, and instead, chose to analyze all themes that emerged from the focus group data. *In vivo* quotes (e.g., assigning a label to a section of data) of focus group participants were incorporated into the findings to bring to life the participants' voices as they described the barriers to effective teacher preparation and clinical partnerships they experienced in their own words.

Complexity of Teacher Education

The theme complexity of teacher education, though referenced only once, has been identified as a root cause for many of the challenges that have historically faced the profession of teaching and teacher education. Lampert (2010) highlighted the complexities of learning classroom teaching by stating that the:

multiple kinds of problems arise in establishing and maintaining relationships with students and subject matter, and the work that must be done to solve them is socially and intellectually complex. (p. 22)

One focus group participant identified learning teaching as a complex activity and spoke about the challenge of preparing a diverse pool of teacher candidates with a wide range of prior experiences and assumptions and the need to systematize their learning in order to produce effective educators in spite of all the variables:

The barriers of learning to teach: It's very individualized. So, every person comes to it differently and it's very contextualized. It has to do with your classroom. It's very hard to make a system that [will] prepare every single candidate to be at the top of their game. . . . I think that's the fundamental challenge for our professions. How do we?–and I think it's a really admirable goal, and I think the field is moving to every single person who comes through is going to be an effective educator from the get-go. But how do we do it given how variable all these experiences [are] . . . ? The individuals who come into the profession vary so much in their style and personalities, and the clinical educator that they're paired with, and their university supervisor.

Policy Barriers

The theme of policy barriers was referenced a total of 22 times by the three focus groups. Two sub-codes emerged from this theme: *teacher preparation program design barriers* and *tenure track and promotion policy barriers*. Policies are the principles and rules that organizations create or adopt to achieve long-term goals. Policies influence and guide decisions and actions of an organization and ensure that those decisions and actions translate into outcomes that are compatible with the goals of the governing body of the organization (Business Dictionary, n.d.). The profession of teaching and the endeavor of preparing teachers have been buffeted historically by policies emanating from an array of organizations whose governing bodies have opposing and contradictory goals. "Teachers have been embattled by politicians, philanthropists, intellectuals, business leaders, social scientists, activists on both the Right and Left, parents, and even one another" (Goldstein, 2014, p. 5). From federal to state and to local governments within public schools and across institutions of higher education, people with little understanding of the complexities of teaching are making decisions and implementing policies that impede the effective preparation of teachers and teaching profession, often without the input of the experts in the field. One participant explained:

I think another barrier is this sort of cultural paternalism and lack of professional agency at the individual level. And that resides in multiple places. I think it resides in the reform policies of late, but also it equally resides in collective bargaining. And so I think to get at a sense of professional responsibility for all the clinical educators involved with the partnerships is challenged by that pervasive paternalism throughout that educational system.

Teacher Preparation Program Design Barriers

The program design barriers sub-code was referenced 14 times by all three focus groups and reflected financial and other compensation barriers specific to implementing and maintaining a clinical partnership model.

Financial Barriers for Teacher Candidates

The financial burden on potential teacher candidates was discussed at length, and in particular, the impact of a year-long internship or residency program. While appreciating the advantages of a year-long internship, one participant acknowledged that his university also had to offer the more traditional semester-long student teaching:

The [teacher candidates] can do a year-long [internship] if they want to, or they can do the traditional route. We'd love to say you all have to do the year-long. But to ask someone to go without a job for a year, without being paid for what you're doing at interning, that's unreasonable.

In discussing the onerous financial burden for teacher candidates, another participant added, "In no other field do they go into an internship and not get paid. You're asked not to work, and don't get paid." In response, several teacher preparation programs that pay a stipend for internships were mentioned; however, one participant stated:

[The year-long internship] pays a stipend, but it's barely livable. It's not like they can survive on that money, so I think another area to work on is certainly that our students, in order to engage in high quality, clinically centered experiences, have to be able to have other supports in place or take out massive loans.

One participant expressed concern about how non-traditional students are able to engage in clinical experiences. The participant reflected on another program design barrier by explaining that adult students, known as non-traditional students, often have other limitations during the day, like a full-time job. The participant explained, "So they take the class at night. How are they getting their clinical experiences at a level that would be sufficient?"

In response, another participant suggested:

There almost needs to be modifications to a residency model that allow for even a day, a week or something, right? Where they can start to scaffold and build in that clinical experience. They can plan for the end one and hopefully– but the end one shouldn't necessarily be as long . . . if you're doing that buildup. But yeah, it's definitely a preventer, unless we can create paid internships, paid student teaching arrangements.

Compensation and Funding Barriers for Teacher Educators and Programs

Focus group participants identified the lack of adequate compensation for school-based teacher educators (SBTE), particularly in light of the language in CAEP Standard 2 that describes the expectation that clinical partnerships should be mutually beneficial (Council for the Accreditation of Education Programs, 2013). One participant described this barrier:

I think of the burden that we put on our classroom teachers. We talk about the great reciprocal benefits, and at the same time, we're really asking a lot of our classroom teachers to do this mentoring piece . . . without a whole lot of training or compensation.

Another participant described the lack of recognition for SBTEs who are stakeholders in a clinical partnership by comparing it to other professions:

You know in the profession [of education], it's just expected for you to donate your time and money out of the goodness of your heart. That never flies in the business world. It's something the businessmen and others outside of education can't fathom. Why would you do more work for no recognition, no extra pay? For decades, these teachers have been doing it.

Focus group participants acknowledged that clinical partnerships are expensive and identified numerous barriers associated with adequate and consistent funding to support and maintain the partnership model. One participant identified the reduction of financial resources for public and private institutions as a barrier by stating:

If there is a cut in resources, the partnership stuff will probably [get scaled back], if your institution's really threatened then you're going to scale back. Because you have to really be able to justify why you're working with these other folks, and why you're investing in that school and spending so much time with them.

Another participant identified the difficulty of funding a growing partnership with limited resources by stating, "As partnerships grow, how can we expect that to happen without an investment in time and money? We can't expect people to do it on their backs."

Tenure Track and Promotion Policy Barriers

Establishing and sustaining effective clinical partnerships as the centerpiece to teacher preparation demands the deconstruction of the traditional university and P-12 silos to promote cross-collaboration of all stakeholders and support hybrid teacher educators who bridge both worlds (Zeichner, 2010). By definition, the hybrid teacher educators' focus is the practice of teaching in order to support teacher candidates. Supporting the practice of teaching requires that these hybrid educators be in the field and on site in multiple P-12 settings. Zeichner (2010) explained:

[In fact,] a variety of different types of hybrid teacher educator positions exist today across the nation . . . . [These are] positions where clinical faculty work to build partnerships with local schools that focus on preservice teacher education . . . and positions where clinical faculty are based primarily in a [P-12] school where they make placements for teacher candidates and supervise their school experiences. (p. 94)

However, typical university policies that govern tenure and promotion prioritize research over practice, leading to the publish or perish mentality, marginalizing university-based teacher educators' (UBTEs) commitment to being practitioners in their field, and limiting UBTEs motivation to fully invest in a clinical partnership model.

The sub-code tenure track and promotion policy barriers was referenced eight times by two focus groups and addressed a range of concerns and unintended consequences stemming from university tenure and promotion policies. One participant, an associate professor, described the need to flatten the hierarchy often present in the relationship between university instructors and P-12 teachers, a hierarchy that manifests itself by valuing research and theory over practice and for which university professors are often criticized due to their lack of practical clinical experience. The participant said:

I tell my professors: Leave your PhD at the door. You're not any better than those teachers. They're out there on the front lines. You don't come in and start like a general, commanding them what to do. You're there to work with and learn. I've even said to my colleagues: Get up and go out and talk to teachers. How many of you have gone to see the school that you're getting [teacher candidates] ready to go into?

Some described the fear of going back out into the field because they had been isolated in the university silo for so many years. One participant, an associate professor in a vibrant clinical partnership, said:

Being in a large urban university, which I went to because of the vision of the partnerships, one of the greatest barriers revolves around fixed versus dynamic thinking. Our faculty, many of them sit and agree, but don't want to go to the field and/or are fearful of going to the field because they're so far removed.

Other professors described their frustration with the university's tenure and promotion policies that disadvantage the hybrid educator whose time in the field developing and sustaining strong clinical partnerships is not valued to the same extent as publishing and research. One participant stated:

Another [barrier] is faculty going into the [P-12] schools, but it's not looked at as a primary part of their tenure promotion. And so, unless they just have a love of it and they'll do it on their own, the faculty really might not be motivated to go out into the [P-12] schools. Why would they? It doesn't really help them.

The participants expressed an overwhelming desire to restructure university faculty load requirements to reward the fieldwork of hybrid educator roles essential to a true clinical partnership model.

Logistical Barriers

The *English Oxford Living Dictionaries* (2016) defines logistics as, "the detailed organization and implementation of a complex operation." As stated earlier, a clinical partnership is an expensive model; it is also a logistically complicated model with many moving parts, both human and resource-based. Council for the Accreditation of Education Programs (2013) Standard 2 defined an effective clinical partnership as "a co-constructed mutually beneficial P-12 school and community arrangement" (p. 14). The clinical partnership should "establish mutually agreeable expectations for candidate entry, preparation, and exit; ensure that theory and practice are linked; maintain coherence across clinical and academic components of preparation; and share accountability for the candidate" (CAEP, 2013, p. 14).

An effective partnership with high-quality clinical practice must provide teacher candidates with clinical experiences of "sufficient depth, breadth, diversity, coherence, and duration to ensure that candidates demonstrate their developing effectiveness and positive impact on all students' learning and development" in addition to university-based and school-based clinical educators who "demonstrate a positive impact on candidates' development and P-12 student learning and development" (Council for the Accreditation of Education Programs, 2013, p. 14). Negotiating the logistics of meeting the needs of all stakeholders to work across multiple systems is an endeavor that requires philosophical and financial commitment from both P-12 and university entities. This commitment involves a shared responsibility for decision-making, planning, and evaluating. The time required by all stakeholders to implement and sustain a clinical partnership was described as a "huge obstacle" by one participant. Another participant identified the logistical barrier of finding physical space for instruction in partnership schools.

Placement Barriers

Issues with teacher candidate placement in partnership schools emerged repeatedly and were referenced nine times during the focus group interviews. Three sub-codes made up the references in placement barriers and centered on the notion of quality: *quality teacher candidates*, *quality clinical educators*, and *sufficient quality placements*. Regarding quality teacher candidates, participants acknowledged that not all teacher candidates are equally ready to go into P-12 classrooms for their clinical experience, and in particular, the year-long internship or semester-long student teaching. Participants expressed concern about a sense of entitlement on the part of teacher candidates, and because they had already spent three years in an education program, their participation in an extended clinical experience was a given. Participants spoke of a need for strong leadership to keep less-than-quality teacher candidates out of the classroom and/or provide additional support for them prior to or throughout their extended clinical experience as a way to strengthen the education profession. One UBTE stated:

We're pushing [teacher candidates] along because there's a perception of entitlement. It requires strong leadership to say, "No, that's not okay." Because it's not ultimately good for the profession, [nor] the [P-12] pupils who are going to be on the receiving end of an under-prepared educator of this entire process.

Complementary to the need for quality teacher candidates is the need for quality clinical educators. Clinical educators include "all EPP- and P-12-school-based individuals, including classroom teachers, who assess, support, and develop a candidate's knowledge, skills, or professional dispositions at some stage in the clinical experiences" (Council for the Accreditation of Education Programs, 2013, p. 14).

Research has highlighted the crucial role that clinical educators, both UBTEs and SBTEs, play in the preparation of teacher candidates (Grossman, 2010; Ronfeldt, 2012). However, historically those assigned the role of clinical educator have struggled to bridge the disconnect between university and P-12-based teacher preparation due to a variety of reasons including a lack of preparation for school-based teachers to be an effective mentor and little incentives for university staff to engage in quality field supervision (Zeichner, 2010). Several focus group participants expressed concern regarding the quality of SBTEs. One participant stated, "Every practicing teacher isn't dispositionally ready to be a strong mentor of a preservice teacher." Another participant lamented the lack of training for P-12 teachers who mentor teacher candidates, stating:

The task of mentoring and coaching someone is something some of us have spent our entire [doctoral] programs learning to do. I just didn't grow up one day and know how to do this. I've worked really hard to learn the skills of helping to support teacher candidate development. That's a completely different skillset than I used as a classroom teacher. And where do people learn that? Where do people learn how to be good university or school-based teacher educators? And that is a whole piece that I think we pay so little attention to.

Another participant expressed concern about the lack of relevant, current experience on the part of the university educators who are often hired to provide field supervision for teacher candidates. The participant said:

We hire people who are either retired or adjuncts to go out and do [the supervision of teacher candidates]. Not our tenured, expert faculty; they just teach full-time. So there's that disconnect . . . some of them have 30 to 40 years experience, but they haven't been in the classroom in a long, long time.

Securing sufficient quality field placements for teacher candidates to engage in clinical experiences was also a topic of discussion among the focus group participants. Respondents expressed the challenge of the placement process to find the best mentor teachers to meet the individual needs of teacher candidates. At the same time, university-based preparation personnel need to find placements for all the candidates, and sometimes, with less than quality mentors. Other participants discussed the impact of legislative policies (i.e., increased standardized testing and teacher evaluation tied to student performance) on teachers' willingness to support and mentor teacher candidates. They expressed fear of a novice teacher in their classroom impacting student test scores, which could result in a negative evaluation and a deleterious effect on their tenure status. One participant, a field experience coordinator, stated:

There's been such a climative change in the last five years with standards and all of the national pieces that have been coming down, that we often find it difficult to have people volunteer to host teachers. They're not feeling comfortable . . . and so it's part of the partnership to work with them to help them understand that it's a learning process for everybody, and it's going to go through cycles, and it's okay.

Barriers Within Clinical Partnerships

Once established, a clinical partnership is sustained and expanded only through a significant investment of time and energy on the part of all stakeholders. Like any partnership in the public or private sector, expectations and common understandings must be revisited on a regular basis. External and internal changes in personnel, finances, and resources can impact the partnerships' ability to sustain and grow. Mechanisms must be in place to ensure that the partnerships' vision is shared among all stakeholders who are engaged in self-evaluation and reflective practices. American Association for Colleges of Teacher Education's (2016) Clinical Practice Commission confirmed:

It takes hard work to establish a clinical partnership, and equally hard work to sustain one. Existing relationships need to be nurtured, and roles clarified as new members are added. Communication chan-nels may need to expand as the partnership grows to include a wider array of stakeholders. Resources and goals may need to be revisited in light of changing policy contexts. Data will need to be collected and analyzed to inform continuous improvement. Without continued investment, partnerships cannot deepen and grow. (p. 42)

Focus group participants described a variety of barriers that can occur when even one of the part-nership cornerstones of communication, collaboration, and relationship-building among stakeholders is neglected. The theme of barriers within clinical partnerships was referenced 24 times by the three different focus groups and was further divided into five sub-codes: *lack of shared understanding, lack of shared values, lack of curriculum alignment, leadership barriers*, and *communication barriers*.

Lack of Shared Understanding

The lack of clarity among stakeholders around teacher preparation models can lead to a lack of shared understanding on the characteristics of a true clinical partnership. One focus group participant stated, "I think that one of the barriers is that lack of cohesion of what a good clinical model is. I think there's massive interpretations to that." A teacher preparation program with embedded field experiences does not automatically indicate a clinical partnership has been realized. A clinical relationship between a teacher preparation program and P-12 schools that provide placement opportunities for teacher candidates is often the starting point for the development of a true partnership that is defined by "co-constructed, mutually beneficial arrangements," "mutually agreeable expectations for teacher candidates," and "shared accountability for candidate outcomes" (Council for the Accreditation of Education Programs, 2013, p. 14). Failure to understand and implement these expectations with fidelity can impede the complete operationalization of a clinical partnership. As one participant stated, "If you don't take the time to build the relationship and figure those pieces out first, then it becomes a huge barrier to really getting to higher levels and deeper levels of a partnership."

Lack of Shared Values

Successful, sustainable clinical partnerships are built upon a foundation of shared values and common goals that are co-constructed by and mutually beneficial to all stakeholders. One focus group participant described this mutual benefit by saying:

There is a potentially productive space if all the interests can align . . . . If you have a researcher who's interested, [for example], in develop[ing] professional development modules on a long, ongoing, deep relationship sort of way to get that delivered, then the researcher's getting what he or she needs, the school's getting something that matters to them, and the relationship can really deepen from that, but it takes a long time to grope your way toward, "Where is the intersection for us in terms of skill sets and interest and needs?"

A lack of shared goals and values creates a barrier to the integrity of a partnership. One participant stated, "When the goals are not mutual, then it's not going to work for everybody, and the point is that it needs to work for everybody." Another participant warned that the lack of alignment in the value system between the P-12 and university environment "can impede the ability to find that sort of center of the Venn diagram that we're talking about here."

Lack of Curricular Alignment

CAEP's definition of a clinical partnership requires coherence between the theoretical and clinical components of teacher preparation (Council for the Accreditation of Education Programs, 2013); however, participants noted a frequent lack of curricular alignment among P-12 and university classrooms, university instructors in different academic units, and even different instructors within a school of education. One participant stated:

The disconnect between the accreditation person, the clinical person, and the faculty who are teaching the content and pedagogy could also be a barrier if they're not aligned or on the same page, which can create situations for the students.

This lack of curricular alignment was seen as having a detrimental impact of the success of teacher candidates and the health of the clinical partnership. One participant suggested an "on-going professional development that works together . . . so we're all on the same page" as a way to provide more curricular coherence among the courses and the clinical educators.

Leadership Barriers

Collaboration between a P-12 school system and a teacher preparation program relies heavily on the relationship of the leaders in those systems, namely school superintendents, school principals, directors of educator preparation programs, and deans of schools of education. Administrative leaders must understand the value of clinical partnership and be committed to supporting its tenets. Focus group participants expressed concern that often those in leadership positions were not committed to supporting and defending the vision of a clinical partnership. One participant, an assistant professor of elementary education, stated:

I think the big [barrier] is getting administration to understand the nature of PDS work in terms of things like load, and time, and getting recognition, and honoring that work both from a teaching perspective and a university faculty member perspective. I think it's a huge barrier.

Another participant added, "We need leaders who get what this work should look like. CAEP standards aren't enough."

Another barrier identified was the high turnover rates among school and university leaders whose roles are critical to successful clinical partnerships. The average tenure of a school superintendent in 2014 was between 3 and 4 years (Chingos, Whitehurst, & Lindquist, 2014; Will, 2014). Available data on school principal retention rates suggested that only approximately 50% of new principals remain in the same position after five years (Viadero, 2009). University deans in North America averaged five years in the same job (Bradshaw, 2015). Coburn, Penuel, and Geil (2013) discussed the difficulties partnerships face when leadership changes, citing the need to form new relationships and rebuild trust while maintaining focus on partnership work. Expressing concern about partnerships built more on people rather than a sustainable structure, one participant said:

[One barrier is] the whole sustainability piece when you have key personalities who are really leading this relationship move, be promoted, changed or, you know, turnover. Often times the structure is not there to keep going. It's like starting over every time you get a new dean or new clinical person.

Participants also communicated a frustration with district versus university leadership priorities that can impact the ability to implement innovations and policy changes in a timely fashion. This tension stems in part from the challenge to bridge the "different cultural worlds of researchers and practitioners" (Coburn, Penuel, & Geil, 2013, p. 14). Tasked with the responsibility of meeting current students' needs, district leaders demand implementation of immediate solutions; whereas, research driven by university leaders moves more slowly. One P-12 superintendent explained:

We want to get the program started now or within the school year, or at the start of the next school year; not do a feasibility study. And, when you have people that say, "Well, it went up and it's sitting at the vice chancellor's desk," it's tough.

Communication Barriers

Central to a successful partnership is the commitment to mutualism, or "sustained interaction" (Coburn, Penuel, & Geil, 2013, p. 3) that creates mutual benefits for all stakeholders. In order to assure a mutually beneficial relationship, all partners must have an equal voice. Focus group participants identified a lack of communication as a barrier within a partnership. One participant stated, "I think the lack of communication, or consistent communication within the partnership, can be a barrier just because needs change, elements change." Another participant expressed concern that not all voices in the profession carry the same weight due to perceived status or hierarchy. The participant said:

That is a key point of impediment in communicating across the profession, when a member of the profession has to wonder, "Is this a real role, or am I the token teacher?" [We must assure] that every voice is an active actor, has key responsibilities, and doesn't question their role in the work that's being done.

Though potentially time-consuming, consistent, open communication among stakeholders whose voices are equally respected and valued is essential to maintain meaningful, successful partnerships.

DISCUSSION

The researchers identified five overarching themes (i.e., complexity of teacher education, policy barriers, logistical barriers, barriers within clinical partnerships, and barriers as impetus for renewal and improvement) described by the focus group participants that subsumed the variety of complex and interconnected barriers impacting clinical partnerships and practice. A partnership that spans university and public-school systems has inherent complexities also impacted by local, state, and national policies and accreditation standards and legislation. Though challenging to unpack, these barriers fell into two categories: internal and external.

Internal Barriers

The themes of logistical barriers and barriers within clinical partnerships reflected internal barriers, namely, impediments to creating new partnerships and maintaining existing clinical partnerships. Focus group participants reported the following concerns: the quality of teacher candidates, UBTEs, and SBTEs; a lack of shared vision, values, and understanding among stakeholders, including those in leadership positions; the need for better curricular alignment; and the breakdowns in communication among stakeholders. It is interesting to note that many of the barriers identified by the focus group participants reflected gaps between a particular partnership's actual implementation and the ideal clinical partnership as described by CAEP Standard 2 (Council for the Accreditation of Education Programs, 2013). In accordance with CAEP Standard 2.1, a partnership is co-constructed by its stakeholders to be mutually beneficial to its stakeholders and ensures that "effective partnerships and high quality clinical practice are central to preparation" (Council for the Accreditation of Education Programs, 2013, p.14). Making sure all stakeholders' voices are represented equally in the co-construction of the partnership, and that the vision of all stakeholders aligns with the tenets of effective partnerships (Council for the Accreditation of Education Programs, 2013), the partnership can help overcome barriers such as a lack of shared vision, values, and understandings. Standard 2.1 requires partnerships to:

establish mutually agreeable expectations for candidate entry, preparation, and exit; ensure that theory and practice are linked; maintain coherence across clinical and academic components of preparation; and share accountability for candidate outcomes. (Council for the Accreditation of Education Programs, 2013, p.14)

A partnership implemented in accordance with these descriptors reduces concerns about candidate quality because the stakeholders have mutually agreed upon expectations and shared accountability for teacher candidates. The barrier, lack of curricular alignment, is also addressed through Standard 2.1 and outlines the expectation that theory and practice are intentionally linked through a curricular coherence between the clinical and academic components of the partnership.

Standard 2.2 addresses expectations for quality clinical educators (UBTEs and SBTEs) stating, "Partners co-select, prepare, evaluate, support, and retain high-quality clinical educators, both provider- and school-based" (Council for the Accreditation of Education Programs, 2013, p.14). This is likely the most challenging aspect of effective clinical partnerships because historically there has been little preparation specific to the supervision and mentoring of teacher candidates, little compensation financial or otherwise for clinical educators, and little value placed on their critical role in preparing teachers.

Often supervisors of teacher candidates and other UBTEs have been selected based on convenience and availability rather than the pedagogical skills and content knowledge necessary to effectively coach and develop new teachers within the context of the P-12 system. Likewise, SBTEs, including rarely evaluated mentor teachers, have received little to no pedagogical training on effective coaching or received nominal, if any, compensation and are often selected out of necessity to place a teacher candidate rather than for their ability to influence candidate growth. Steps need to be taken to actively address this gap. The American Association for Colleges of Teacher Education (2016) suggested:

[UBTEs and SBTEs] must understand the school and university curriculum as well as possess a supervision pedagogy that strengthens candidate learning in the field. When clinical experiences become central to candidate preparation, supervision will require universities and their school partners to rethink how supervision is resourced as well as how supervision is recognized as an important form of teaching. (p. 41)

Open, structured, and regular communication, effective collaboration, and healthy professional relationships among all stakeholders are paramount to overcome the barriers inherent in a complex, boundary-spanning system and realize the full benefits of a clinical partnership as envisioned by CAEP Standard 2 (Council for the Accreditation of Education Programs, 2013).

External Barriers

Focus group participants described the complexity of teacher education and policy barriers reflected in external barriers as beyond the sphere of influence held by partnership stakeholders, and therefore, more daunting to address and overcome. Focus group participants reported grave concerns about the design of teacher preparation programs that create financial barriers for teacher candidates and barriers to adequate compensation of SBTEs and UBTEs. Participants also identified outdated university tenure and promotion policies and a lack of commitment from districts, universities, and state policy makers to fund a clinical partnership as deterrents for UBTEs fully investing in a clinical partnership. These barriers are deeply ingrained in policy at the district, university, state, and national levels and will require stakeholders in clinical partnerships across many districts, universities, state, and national agencies to come together to create a groundswell of collective influence. Relying on arbitrary attempts to assert the level of influence needed for change and to renew the education profession with a cacophony of contradictory messages can no longer be relied upon. A common language is necessary to forge common understandings about clinical partnerships across multiple settings. "A unified professional structure with a shared understanding of clinical practice" (American Association for Colleges of Teacher Education, 2016, p. 4) will provide the framework to overcome many external barriers impacting the realization of clinical partnerships.

A clinical partnership, as defined by CAEP Standard 2 (Council for the Accreditation of Education Programs, 2013), represents what Wenger (2011) described as a community of practice composed of "groups of people who share a concern or a passion for something they do and learn how to do it better as they interact regularly" (p. 1). As stakeholders in a clinical partnership work collaboratively to improve the education profession, it is natural that barriers emerge and existing structures and policies need to be revisited and renegotiated. One focus group participant described the identified barriers as an impetus for improvement:

We need to see those barriers as opportunities for growth and change. Actually having the courageous conversations that we tend to shirk, or shrink away from, because we're afraid that it might upset the partnership itself or the experiences that our faculty and our students are having in both settings, and yet sometimes those barriers can force us to become a little bit more creative in how we think about clinical partnership because the concept in and of itself also needs its boundaries to be pushed a little bit more.

This iterative and dynamic process of evaluation, reflection, and adjustment can only take place in a community where the norms of communication, collaboration, and relationship-building have been established and where courageous and bold actions are celebrated. As referenced in the review of literature in this manuscript, professional capital with an investment in collaboration has a fundamental connection to transforming teaching.

The governance of teacher preparation cannot be isolated from the needs of the P-12 systems, nor isolated within institutions of higher education that may not be responsive to calls for renewal to public education. If institutions that prepare teachers work closely with institutions that will ultimately hire those teachers, everyone in the system will be better served; barriers that create roadblocks in the renewal of teacher preparation will diminish. The renewal of teacher preparation and the collective work it will take to get there rests solely in the hands of each key stakeholder within teacher preparation working together in shared accountability.

Historically, stakeholders have continued to operate in their respective silos: educational politics coupled with societal beliefs; universities which house teacher preparation programs; and P-12 public schools. The renewal of teacher preparation requires all key stakeholders to engage in collaboration to turn barriers into opportunities that strengthen clinical practice for educators and the students they teach. The power of professional capital is about collective responsibility, not individual autonomy (Hargreaves & Fullan, 2012), and leveraging that collective potential has the likelihood to strengthen the profession of teaching by placing clinical practice at the center of teacher preparation where it needs to be. Perhaps barriers can then become the impetus for a renewed education profession where all share in the accountability and renewal of the future of education.

REFERENCES

American Association for Colleges of Teacher Education. (2016). *The renewal of the teaching profession: A pivot toward clinical practice*. Unpublished manuscript.

Ball, D., & Forzani, F. (2009). The work of teaching and the challenge for teacher education. *Journal of Teacher Education*, *60*(5), 497–511. doi:10.1177/0022487109348479

Ball, D., & Forzani, F. (2010). Teaching skillful teaching. *Educational Leadership: The Effective Educator*, *68*(4), 40-45. Retrieved from http://www.highered.nysed.gov/Ballteaching.pdf

Boyd, D., Grossman, P., Lankford, H., Loeb, S., & Wyckoff, J. (2006). How changes in entry requirements alter the teacher workforce and affect student achievement. *Education Finance and Policy*, *1*(2), 176–216. doi:10.1162/edfp.2006.1.2.176

Bradshaw, D. (2015). Short tenure of deans signals a leadership void. *Financial Times*. Retrieved from https://www.ft.com/content/8af77ab4-e442-11e4-9039-00144feab7de

Business Dictionary. (n.d.). Policy. In *Business Dictionary*. Retrieved from http://www.businessdictionary.com/definition/policies-and-procedures.html

Castle, S., Fox, R., & Souder, K. (2006). Do professional development schools (PDS) make a difference? A comparative study of PDS and non-PDS teacher candidates. *Journal of Teacher Education, 58*(1), 65–80. doi:10.1177/0022487105284211

Chingos, M., Whitehurst, G., & Lindquist, K. (2014). *School superintendents: Vital or irrelevant*. Retrieved from https://www.brookings.edu/wp-content/uploads/2016/06/SuperintendentsBrown-Center9314.pdf

Coburn, C., Penuel, W., & Geil, K. (2013). *Research-practice partnerships: A strategy for leveraging research for educational improvement in school districts* (A white paper prepared for the William T. Grant Foundation). Retrieved from http://rpp.wtgrantfoundation.org/library/uploads/2016/01/R-P-Partnerships-White-Paper-Jan-2013-Coburn-Penuel-Geil.pdf

Council for the Accreditation of Education Programs, Council for the Accreditation of Education Programs Commission on Standards and Performance Reporting to the Council for the Accreditation of Education Programs Board of Directors. (2013). *CAEP accreditation standards and evidence: Aspirations for educator preparation*. Retrieved from http://docplayer.net/11050566-Caep-accreditation-standards-and-evidence-aspirations-for-educator-preparation.html

Creswell, J. (2008). *Educational research: Planning, conducting, and evaluating quantitative and qualitative research* (3rd ed.). Upper Saddle River, NJ: Pearson.

Daniels, H., Edwards, A., Engeström, Y., Gallagher, T., & Ludvigsen, S. (Eds.). (2010). *Activity theory in practice: Promoting learning across boundaries and agencies*. London: Routledge.

Darling-Hammond, L. (2003). Access to quality teaching: An analysis of inequality in California's public schools. *Santa Clara Law Review, 43*(4), 101–239. Retrieved from http://digitalcommons.law.scu.edu

Darling-Hammond, L. (2006). Securing the right to learn: Policy and practice for powerful teaching and learning. *Educational Researcher, 35*(7), 13–24. doi:10.3102/0013189X035007013

Darling-Hammond, L. (2007). The story of Gloria is a future vision of the new teacher. *Journal of Staff Development, 28*(3), 25–26. Retrieved from http://eric.ed.gov

English Oxford Living Dictionaries. (2016). Logistics. In *English Oxford Living Dictionaries*. Retrieved from https://en.oxforddictionaries.com/definition/logistics

Fraser, J. (2007). *Preparing America's teachers: A history*. New York, NY: Teachers College Press.

Goldstein, D. (2014). *The teacher wars*. New York, NY: Doubleday.

Grossman, P. (2010). *Learning to practice: The design of clinical experience in teacher preparation*. Washington, DC: American Association of Colleges for Teacher Education.

Grossmann, P., Hammerness, K., & McDonald, M. (2009). Redefining teaching, re-imagining teacher education. *Teachers and Teaching, 15*(2), 273–289. doi:10.1080/13540600902875340

Hargreaves, A., & Fullan, M. (2012). *Professional capital: Transforming teaching in every school*. New York, NY: Teachers College Press.

Jackson, P. (1986). *The practice of teaching*. New York, NY: Teachers College Press.

Lampert, M. (2010). Learning teaching in, from and for practice: What do we mean? *Journal of Teacher Education, 61*(1-2), 21–34. doi:10.1177/0022487109347321

Leana, C. (2011). *The missing link in school reform*. Retrieved from https://www2.ed.gov/programs/slcp/2011progdirmtg/mislinkinrfm.pdf

Levine, M. (2002). Why invest in professional development schools? *Educational Leadership, 59*(6), 65–70. Retrieved from https://eric.ed.gov

McCaffrey, J. R., Lockwood, D. F., Koretz, D. M., & Hamilton, L. S. (2003). *Evaluating value added models for teacher accountability*. Retrieved from http://www.rand.org/pubs/monographs/2004/RAND_MG158.pdf

Murray, F. (1989). Explanations in education. In M. Reynolds (Ed.), *Knowledge base for the beginning teacher* (pp. 1–12)., doi:10.1080/1047621910040129

National Council for Accreditation for Teacher Education, Report of the Blue Ribbon Panel on Clinical Preparation and Partnerships for Improved Student Learning. (2010). *Transforming teacher education through clinical practice: A national strategy to prepare effective teachers*. Retrieved from http://www.ncate.org/LinkClick.aspx?fileticket=zzeiB1OoqPk%3D&tabid=7

Onwuegbuzie, A. J., Dickinson, W. B., Leech, N. L., & Zoran, A. G. (2009). A qualitative framework for collecting and analyzing data in focus group research. *International Journal of Qualitative Methods, 8*(3), 1–21. doi:10.1177/160940690900800301

Rivkin, S. G., Hanushek, E. A., & Kain, J. F. (2005). Teachers, schools, and academic achievement. *Econometrics, 73*, 417-458. Retrieved from http://econ.ucsb.edu/~jon/Econ230C/HanushekRivkin.pdf

Ronfeldt, M. (2012). Where should student teachers learn to teach? Effects of field placement school characteristics on teacher retention and effectiveness. *Educational Evaluation and Policy Analysis, 34*(1), 3–26. doi:10.3102/0162373711420865

Rowan, B., Correnti, R., & Miller, R. (2002). What large-scale survey research tells us about teacher effects on student achievement: Insights from the prospects study of elementary schools. *Teachers College Record, 104*(8), 1525–1567. doi:10.1111/1467-9620.00212

Snyder, J. (1999). Professional development schools: Why? So what? Now what? *Peabody Journal of Education, 74*(3), 136–143. doi:10.120715327930pje7403&4_11

Viadero, D. (2009). *Turnover in principalship focus of research*. Retrieved from http://www.edweek.org/ew/articles/2009/10/28/09principal_ep.h29.html

Wenger, E. (2011). *Communities of practice: A brief introduction.* Retrieved from https://scholarsbank. uoregon.edu/xmlui/handle/1794/11736?show=full

Will, M. (2014). Average urban school superintendent tenure decreases, survey shows [blog]. Retrieved from http://blogs.edweek.org/edweek/District_Dossier/2014/11/urban_school_superintendent_te.html

Wong, P. L., & Glass, R. D. (2005). Assessing a professional development school approach to preparing teachers for urban schools serving low-income, culturally and linguistically diverse communities. *Teacher Education Quarterly, 32*(3), 63–77. Retrieved from http://files.eric.ed.gov/fulltext/EJ795321.pdf

Wright, S., Horn, S., & Sanders, W. (1997). Teachers and classroom context effects on student achievement: Implications for teacher evaluation. *Journal of Personnel Evaluation in Education, 11*(1), 57–67. doi:10.1023/A:1007999204543

Zeichner, K. (2002). Beyond traditional structures of student teaching. *Teacher Education Quarterly, 29*(2), 59–64. Retrieved from http://teqjournal.org/backvols/2002/29_2/sp02zeichner.pdf

Zeichner, K. (2010). Rethinking the connections between campus courses and field experience in college- and university-based teacher education. *Journal of Teacher Education, 61*(1-2), 89–99. doi:10.1177/0022487109347671

Zeichner, K., Payne, K., & Brayko, K. (2014). Democratizing teacher education. *Journal of Teacher Education, 66*(2), 122–135. doi:10.1177/0022487114560908

ADDITIONAL READING

American Association of Colleges for Teacher Education's Clinical Practice Commission. (2017). *A Pivot toward clinical practice, its lexicon, and the renewal of the profession of teaching.* Unpublished manuscript.

American Educational Research Association [AERA]. (2009). Studying teacher education: The report of the AERA panel on research and teacher education. In M. Cochran-Smith & K. M. Zeichner (Eds.), *Studying teacher education: The report of the AERA Panel on Research and Teacher Education* (pp. 309-424). Mahwah, NJ: Lawrence Erlbaum.

Clark, R. W., Foster, A. M., & Mantle-Bromley, C. (2006). Boundary spanners across the National Network for Educational Renewal. In K. R. Howey & N. L. Zimpher (Eds.), *Boundary spanners* (pp. 27–46). Washington, DC: American Association of State Colleges and Universities and the National Association of State Universities and Land Grant Colleges.

Commission on Standards and Performance Reporting to the CAEP Board of Directors. (2013). *CAEP accreditation standards and evidence: Aspirations for educator preparation* [report]. Retrieved from http://docplayer.net/11050566-Caep-accreditation-standards-and-evidence-aspirations-for-educator-preparation.html

Council for the Accreditation of Educator Preparation [CAEP], CAEP

Hasbun, T.C., & Rudolph, A. (2016). Navigating waters of accreditation: Best practice challenges, and lessons learned from one institution. *SAGE Open, 6*(2), 1 10.doi:10.1177/2158244016656719

National Council for Accreditation for Teacher Education [NCATE], Report of the Blue Ribbon Panel on Clinical Preparation and Partnerships for Improved Student Learning. (2010). *Transforming teacher education through clinical practice: A national strategy to prepare effective teachers.* Retrieved from http://www.ncate.org/LinkClick.aspx?fileticket=zzeiB1OoqPk%3D&tabid=7

KEY TERMS AND DEFINITIONS

Education Preparation Program (EPP): University-based program to prepare teacher candidates for the profession of education.

School-Based Teacher Educator (SBTE): Educator who works primarily with teacher candidates in a school or school district setting.

Teacher Candidate: Student admitted to an educator preparation program.

University-Based Teacher Educator (UBTE): Educator who works primarily with teacher candidates in a college or university setting.

APPENDIX

Table 1. CPC Key Stakeholders and Educator Agencies, Associations, Networks, or Departments Represented

Title, Agency, Association, Network, or Department
American Association of Colleges of Teacher Education (AACTE)
Assistant Professor of Elementary Education
Associate Dean of College of Education
Associate Director of Teacher Education
Associate Professor of Secondary Education
Association of Teacher Education (ATE)
Coordinator of Field Experiences
Dean, School of Education
Director of Clinical Partnerships and Practice
Executive Director, Center of Pedagogy
National Association for Professional Development Schools (NAPDS)
National Board for Professional Teaching Standards (NBPTS)
National Network for Educational Renewal (NNER)
P-12 Superintendent
P-12 Teacher

Table 2. Barriers Codes With Sources and Number of References

Theme	Focus Group (1, 2, 3)	No. of times referenced
1. Complexity of teacher education	2	Total code references: 1
2. Policy barriers	1, 2, 3	Total code references: 22
a. Program design barriers	1	1
1. Financial barriers for teacher candidates	1, 2, 3	6
2. Compensation barriers for SBTEs and UBTEs	1, 2, 3	8
b. Tenure track and promotion policy barriers		
1. Researcher vs. practitioner	1, 2	4
2. Fear	1, 2	2
3. Hierarchy	2	1
3. Logistical barriers	1, 2	Total code references: 11
a. Time	1	1
b. Physical space	1	1
c. Placement		
1. Teacher candidates	1, 2	3
2. Mentors for teacher candidates	1, 2	3
3. Sufficient quality placements	2	3
4. Barriers within clinical partnerships	1, 2, 3	Total code references: 24
a. Lack of shared understanding	1	2
b. Lack of shared values	1, 2	4
c. Lack of curriculum alignment	1, 2	3
d. Leadership barriers		
1. Sustainability	1	2
2. Supporting the vision of the partnership	2, 3	4
3. Bureaucracy and red tape	2	3
e. Communication barriers	1, 2	
1. Communication across the partnership	1, 2	2
2. Participation of all stakeholders		
a. Community and parent voice	1, 2	2
b. School-based educator voice	1	2
5. Barriers as impetus for renewal and improvement	1	Total code references: 1

Chapter 7

Improving Coherence in Teacher Education:
Features of a Field–Based Methods Course Partnership

Tracy L. Weston
Middlebury College, USA

ABSTRACT

This chapter describes the author's work as a teacher educator to establish, sustain, and improve a methods course partnership with a local K-6 school using an integrated school-situated, practice-based model. The model was designed with an aim of improving the coherence of teacher candidates' experiences and learning to better prepare them for the complicated work of equitable teaching. Coherent field-based components in teacher education offer opportunities to mitigate divisions between 1) theory and practice and 2) coursework and fieldwork. The chapter begins with a definition of coherence, describes how this definition of coherence was used to design an elementary literacy/social studies methods course, shares data to evaluate the course from the perspective of the teacher candidates, and describes what candidates learned by participating in the course.

INTRODUCTION

Coherent experiences are a necessary, yet often missing, characteristic of high quality teacher preparation (Weston & Henderson, 2015). Candidates' experiences in teacher education programs are often characterized as incoherent, fragmented, or haphazard (Bain & Moje, 2012; Hammerness, 2013; Hoban, 2005; Weston, 2018; Weston & Henderson, 2015), both between courses within the teacher preparation program, as well as between the activities and experiences implemented in campus-based and school-based classrooms. It is possible for candidates to experience significant learning from carefully designed and monitored field work (Florio Ruane & Lensmire, 1990; Grisham, Laguardia & Brink, 2000; Grossman, Valencia, Evans, Thompson, Martin, & Place, 2000; Lazar, 1998; Wilson, 1996), yet the problems associated with field work and the need for improved quality have been extensively documented for

DOI: 10.4018/978-1-5225-6249-8.ch007

quite some time (Clift, 1991; Eisenhart, Behm & Romagnano, 1991; Goodman, 1985; Griffin, 1989; Tabachnick, Popkewitz & Zeichner, 1981). Strengthening coherence within teacher education programs by improving theory/practice harmony of philosophies, ideas, and practices as well as campus/field convergence of experiences, activities, and assignments in both settings is one way to improve opportunities for candidates so that they more reliably develop the knowledge and skills required to effectively and equitably teach all learners (Ladson-Billings, 1995).

Building upon previous work to develop a school-situated approach to teacher preparation in literacy (Henderson, 2013) and a cross-disciplinary approach for mathematics and literacy teacher preparation (Weston & Henderson, 2015), in this work **coherence** indicates the relative quality of congruence across ideas, experiences, people, roles, components and settings and the relationship between theory and practice. Coherence is both a quality and a process, but it is not an "end" (Bateman, Taylor, Janik, & Logan, 2008; Canrinus, Klette, & Hammerness, 2017; Honig & Hatch, 2004; Nixon, 1991). Rather, it is a frame for dialogue and reflection, with an end goal of improving candidates' professional readiness for equitable, ambitious teaching (Lambert, 2001; Tatoo, 1996). In this chapter, coherence is conceptualized as having three necessary aspects:

1. Coherence requires a **shared vision** (Darling-Hammond, 2014; Fullan & Quinn, 2015; Grossman, Hammerness, McDonald, & Ronfeldt, 2008; Tatto, 1996) across people and roles (e.g., multiple faculty members, mentor teachers, supervisors).
2. Coherence requires **consistent, intentional experiences** (Buchmann & Floden, 1991; Canrinus, Klette, & Hammerness, 2017; Weston & Henderson, 2015) across settings (e.g., multiple courses, various field placements) that are designed to reflect and reinforce the shared vision (Grossman, Hammerness, McDonald, & Ronfeldt, 2008).
3. Coherence must be **evaluated from the perspective of the teacher candidates** (Broad, Stewart Rose, Lopez, & Baxan, 2013; Canrinus, Klette, & Hammerness, 2017).

The relationship between theory and practice, campus and field, from the point of view of candidates (Broad, Stewart Rose, Lopez, & Baxan, 2013; Canrinus, Klette & Hammerness, 2017), is a generative way to think about the interconnection between the constituent elements within a teacher education program, and can be used to design or evaluate a program or its more specific components, such as courses or assignments. In this chapter, the author describes how the aforementioned three aspects of coherence were used to design and evaluate a field-based methods course that was developed with the explicit aim of improving the coherence between theory and practice and course work and field work. The objective of this undertaking was to develop teacher candidates' capacities to teach interdisciplinary, concept-based literacy and social studies lessons that center content about identity, racism, and inequality. In this chapter, the author reviews previous research that informed the aforementioned definition of coherence, describes how this definition of coherence was used in the course design for an elementary literacy/social studies methods course, shares data to evaluate the course from the perspective of the teacher candidates, and describes what candidates learned by participating in the course.

RESEARCH QUESTIONS

This study examined the coherence of a field-based methods course through a situated case study design (Weston, 2011). The dual purpose was to understand candidates' perceptions of coherence and to investigate what candidates believed they learned in the course. The research questions for the study were as follows:

1. To what extent do candidates' experiences reflect and reinforce the shared vision used to design the course?
2. To what extent do candidates experience the course as coherent between theory/practice and campus/field?
3. What do candidates report they learned from participating in the course?

COHERENCE IN TECAHER EDUCATION

Defining Coherence

This section provides a review of previous teacher education research to justify the three aspects contained in the definition of coherence provided earlier in the chapter: shared vision, consistent experiences, and evaluation by candidates. As Feiman-Nemser (1990) stated, "Like any other normative concept, 'coherence' must be defined and justified as a desirable quality in a preservice program" (p.14). The language of coherence is used to build from Dewey's (1916/1985; 1938/1963) philosophy of educative experiences and incorporate current descriptions of the kind and quality of work needed to adequately prepare professionals for the complicated work of teaching (e.g., Ball & Forzani, 2009). Although all experiences have an impact, not all experiences are educational (Dewey, 1938/1963). The term *coherence* has been applied to preservice teacher education in a variety of ways to identify or emphasize different facets (Buchmann & Floden, 1993; Howey & Zimpher, Russell, 1989; McPherson & Martin, 2001), and generally indicates alignment of ideas and experiences among people, roles, components, and settings.

Shared Vision Across People and Roles

The first aspect of coherence is that it requires a shared vision (Darling-Hammond, 2014; Fullan & Quinn, 2015; Grossman, Hammerness, McDonald, & Ronfeldt, 2008; Tatto, 1996) across people and roles (e.g., multiple faculty members, mentor teachers, supervisors). Tatoo (1996) described coherence as "shared understandings" that exist across faculty, and Grossman et al. (2008) used the term "shared vision." Feiman-Nemser (1990) described the importance of considering the *conceptual* orientation within a teacher education program, and "includes a view of teaching and learning and a theory about learning to teach" (p. 20). Hammerness (2006) applied this idea for the term "conceptual coherence," which indicates a mutual professional vision held by those who work with candidates among and across settings (e.g., campus and field) (Hammerness, 2006).

Consistent, Intentional Experiences Across Settings

Secondly, coherence requires turning people's shared vision into consistent, intentional experiences across settings (e.g., multiple courses, various field placements) (Buchmann & Floden, 1991; Canrinus, Klette, & Hammerness, 2017; Weston & Henderson, 2015). In addition to considering conceptual orientation, Feiman-Nemser (1990) also described the importance of the *structural* orientation within teacher education, and Hammerness (2006) likewise applied this to describe *structural coherence*. Structural components within teacher education include the organization of a program, courses in the program of study, and the sequencing and relationships that exist between those courses (Feiman-Nemser, 1990) and relate to coherence through the assignments and experiences that happen both on campus and in the field (Hammerness, 2006). It is often structural aspects of a program or course that interfere with the possibility for candidates to experience consistent, intentional experiences across campus and field, or to experience a vibrant relationship between theory and practice. When describing coherence, Tatoo (1996) explained that "opportunities to learn have been arranged (organizationally, logistically)." Weston and Henderson (2015) defined coherent experiences as those that "build upon each other toward a consistent end and are intentional, continuous, unified, and clear" (p.323). Coherence requires not only a shared vision but also for that vision to be operationalized and organized so that there is continuity of experiences across settings and between theory and practice.

Evaluation by Teacher Candidates

The third aspect of coherence is that it must be evaluated from the perspective of the teacher candidates. This idea was also used by Grossman et al. (2008), who studied the relationship between features found in various types of teacher education programs and the impact they had on candidates' perceptions of coherence. Similarly, Canrinus et al. (2017) surveyed candidates across three institutions in three different countries to compare their perceptions of coherence to program features. They found variation in the perceived coherence by candidates, and that programs may have some elements that are experienced as coherent, while others are not (e.g., coherence between courses within the teacher preparation program versus coherence between courses and field placements). In both studies, candidates were asked directly about their perceptions of coherence, and their perspectives were used to study and improve coherence in teacher education.

Difficulties With Coherence

One area regarded as important, yet varying in degree of quality in teacher preparation is the consistency between course work and field work (Anderson & Stillman, 2013; Clift, 1991; Darling- Hammond, 2014; Goodman, 1985; Henderson & Weston, 2014; Hoban, 2005; Samaras, Frank, Williams, Christopher & Rodick, 2016). Studies have shown that candidates' field experiences can "wash out" the impact of course work (Zeichner & Tabachnik, 1981). Moreover, candidates often experience their teacher education program as fractured and inconsistent across courses, people, roles, and settings (Bain & Moje, 2012; Hammerness, 2013; Hoban, 2005; Weston & Henderson, 2015). Feiman-Nemser and Buchmann (1985) described the divide between the university and school settings as the "two-worlds pitfall." Although the need for coherence in teacher education seems absurd to argue against and is often stated as the "solution" to the theory-practice divide (Bamfield, 2014; Conway & Munthe, 2015; Darling-Hammond,

Burns, Campbell, Goodwin, Hammerness, Low... Zeichner, 2017; Grossman, Hammerness, McDonald & Ronfeldt, 2008; Moon, 2016), there remains relatively little direct or deep attention to this area in teacher education literature, and there are few empirical studies about programmatic components that increase the likelihood of coherence (see Grossman, Hammerness, McDonald, & Ronfeldt, 2008) or the impact undertakings to develop coherent programs have on their graduates (see Canrinus, Klette, & Hammerness, 2017; Hammerness, 2006).

Based on the previous experiences of the author, teaching methods courses that met entirely on campus quickly revealed the incoherence between theory/practice and campus/field. During such methods courses, candidates became better at activities including writing papers about teaching and analyzing classroom videos and student work samples, however many central concepts addressed throughout the semester did not translate into their actual teaching practices (Weston & Henderson, 2005). Field placements in which hours were logged outside of class sessions (even as many as two full days per week) did not remedy this problem, since candidates did not have the opportunity to do the kind of practice work envisioned in the methods course. Even if candidates were able to carry out field-based assignments and teaching activities, the methods course instructor did not observe them teach. These are typical problems that arise with methods courses that operate entirely on campus, and this structure interferes with coherence between theory/practice and campus/field.

Empirical studies about coherence identify needs for improvement in teacher education programs. Grossman et al. (2008) indicated that program revision, which often focuses on adjustments within and across campus courses, needs to pay more attention to clinical aspects. They also concluded that:

placing more attention on the links between field faculty and course faculty, coursework and fieldwork, could have important payoffs in terms of increasing the perceived coherence of student teachers' learning experiences. (p.282)

Similarly, Canrinus et al. (2017) concluded that:

to improve coherence in teacher education programs, teacher educators both at universities and in schools could improve their collaboration and their understanding of what is happening in each other's contexts, together constituting the teacher education program. (p.10)

Both studies also indicated that thoughtful links between campus and field settings are needed. As Grossman et al. (2008) stated:

What may matter most are not the number of hours but the extent to which those assignments that link coursework to fieldwork are thoughtful, purposeful, and well constructed. (p. 283)

Coherence and Clinical Practice in Teacher Education

Teacher education projects have focused attention on the development of high-leverage or core teaching practices (i.e., practices likely to lead to a relatively large amount of student learning) (Ball, Sleep, Boerst, & Bass, 2009; Kazemi, Franke, & Lampert, 2009; Lampert & Graziani, 2009) through practice-based work (Grossman, Compton, Igra, Ronfeldt, Shahan, & Williamson, 2009; McDonald, Kazemi & Kavanagh, 2013). Ball and Forzani (2009) stated that teacher preparation needs to be detailed and reliable, and that "teacher education should offer significantly more—and more deliberate—opportunities for novices to practice the interactive work of instruction" (Ball & Forzani, 2009, p.503). Canrinus et al. (2017) found that opportunities for practice-based work are related to coherence, and stated that "concurrent practice strengthens the linkage between theory and practice as well as program coherence" and:

assert(ed) that university courses and field experiences should be coherent with, for example, candidates trying out, during their fieldwork, teaching strategies they learned about at the university. (p.3)

Recently, the American Association of Colleges for Teacher Education's (AACTE, 2018) Clinical Practice Commission published a paper "grounded in the overarching belief that clinical practice is central to high-quality teacher preparation" (p.14). In it they state:

The process of learning to teach requires sustained and ongoing opportunities to engage in authentic performance within diverse learning environments, where course work complements and aligns with field experiences that grow in complexity and sophistication over time and enable candidates to develop the skills necessary to teach all learners. (p.14)

It is the assertion of the author that improving coherence in teacher education and improving clinical practice opportunities for candidates are part of the same project. That is, teacher educators can simultaneously attend to coherence and practice-based work, and improvements in one domain can improve the other. One way to improve the coherence of a course or program is to consider the nature, structure, and role of practice-based work (Grossman, Compton, Igra, Ronfeldt, Shahan, & Williamson, 2009; McDonald, Kazemi, & Kavanagh, 2013), or as AACTE stated, the way course work "complements and aligns with field experiences" (p.14). Providing candidates with the opportunity to bring theory and practice, course work and field work together, and unify them both conceptually and structurally, can result in improvements for clinical practice opportunities, candidate skill and knowledge development, and program coherence (Boyd, Grossman, Lankford, Loeb, & Wyckoff, 2009). The subsequent sections describe how coherence and clinical practice were simultaneously attended to in the process of designing a field-based methods course for elementary literacy/social studies instruction. Next, the context and the shared vision that were the starting point for designing a coherent field-based methods course are described.

FIELD-BASED METHODS COURSE

Context

In the summer of 2014, the author joined the Education Studies Program at Middlebury College and began working together with Principal Christina Johnston and teachers Catherine Canavan, Joy Dobson, Leigh Harder, Megan Sutton, and Christina Wadsworth at Weybridge Elementary School. Middlebury College is an undergraduate liberal arts college, and students enrolled in the Elementary Program in Teacher Licensure double major in education and a second major, complete a full semester of student teaching, and earn a Vermont teaching license upon successfully completing the program, state portfolio, and licensure exams. The mission of the program is to prepare teachers to "contribute to a more just, compassionate, and equitable society" (Affolter, Cooper, Miller-Lane & Weston, 2015), and there is a strong emphasis in introductory "foundations" courses on equity, inclusion, and cultural responsiveness. Weybridge Elementary School, one of nine schools in Addison Central School District, has approximately 50 students in grades K-6 across four classrooms (three of the four classrooms have two grades in the same classroom, e.g., K/1). The college and school are approximately 3.5 miles apart and set in rural Vermont. The elementary literacy/social studies methods course is candidates' first "methods" course, and they simultaneously complete a separate field placement in a local elementary classroom (one classroom per candidate), which they attend three hours per week on their own schedule.

Shared Vision

The first aspect of coherence is that there is a shared vision across people and roles. This meant a shared vision between the teacher educator, the principal, and the classroom teachers at WES, who created a shared vision for teacher education both in terms of structure and content. The shared vision for structure was largely based on the author's previous work (Weston & Henderson, 2015). The shared vision for content was collaboratively developed in planning sessions that identified contextual variables, resources, expertise, opportunities, and challenges in the school, district, and profession in order to create a "third space" for the partnership, which is the intersection of the teacher preparation program and the P-12 school that "resides in a zone not wholly controlled by any one party" (AACTE, 2018, p. 25). Our shared vision, which states three structural elements and three content elements, is as follows:

We believe teacher candidates develop knowledge and skills best when they experience regular opportunities to:

- Engage in consistent field-based practice through authentic work with students;
- Have their teaching observed by the methods teacher educator;
- Receive expert feedback on their teaching.

We believe teacher candidates need experiences in three critical areas:

- A move away from subject-specific silos towards more interdisciplinary teaching;
- A move away from instructional planning based on topics and themes towards concept-based teaching;
- A move away from silence towards developing teaching skills for difficult conversations about historical and current events pertaining to identity, racism, and inequality.

Consistent, Intentional Experiences

The second component of coherence is to operationalize the shared vision into consistent, intentional experiences that unify theory with practice and campus work with field work. The next section describes how each of the above components of the shared vision were operationalized in the course design, first reviewing the three structural aspects, then the three content-related aspects.

SHARED VISION: STRUCTURAL

Provide Regular Opportunities for Candidates to Engage in Field-Based Practice Through Authentic Work With Students

The course incorporates the author's research findings from a previous partnership, which included the importance of candidates practicing teaching elementary students, doing so while the methods teacher educator observed, and providing candidates with expert feedback (Weston & Henderson, 2015). In order to provide these experiences during class time, the central course component involves holding one (out of three) weekly class session (approximately 60 minutes) at Weybridge Elementary School (WES), where Middlebury College candidates observe and learn from WES teachers and work with a multi-grade group of third to sixth grade students. In the beginning of the semester, candidates are introduced to the school and systematically observe WES teachers model specific instructional practices within interactive read aloud that the candidates have read about and will soon attempt. Each candidate then begins working with a small group of five or six WES students. Their first session together is a book-sharing activity in which the candidates and WES students share an excerpt of a book that is important to them. After the first three visits observing and meeting students, the candidates write their own lesson plan (individually or in partners, depending on the numbers of candidates in the cohort) that they teach (or co-teach) to the same group of WES students weekly throughout the semester. After a few weeks, candidates also design and work on a culminating project as part of their weekly lessons, which is presented to all participants at the end of the semester.

The weekly practice is authentic work with students because every week candidates each plan a unique lesson, and over the course of the semester plan and teach a series of ten connected lessons, as well as a culminating project. Elements that contribute to coherence are that it is a regular opportunity (once each week and a total of ten lessons), a consistent setting (the same school), and consistent relationships (the same students) with whom candidates work for the semester. Working with the same students is a deliberate choice based on a commitment to coherence, as it provides consistency, a chance to build relationships, and an opportunity to follow the development of ideas among a particular group of students rather than having disjointed teaching episodes. As Dewey (1904/1964) explained, "the habit of making isolated and independent lesson plans for a few days' or weeks' instruction in a separate grade here or there...is likely to be distinctly detrimental" (p. 332).

Coherence is also attended to in the way that course readings and assignments are grounded through the integrated field-based work at WES. The focus of the weekly lesson plan in terms of pedagogy is based on the readings, discussions, and practice during the two on-campus sessions that week, and in turn, readings, discussions, and approximations are selected and sequenced with an eye towards candidates' emergent practices and knowledge. For example, at the beginning of the semester (which is the first formal lesson plan and teaching experience with elementary students in the program), the first area of focus is working to do book introductions and develop a lesson plan using a before/during/after reading format, which candidates read about early in the class (Fountas & Pinnell, 2006). Each week, the previous focal area is maintained and built on with a new target area that is read about as homework and discussed and workshopped on campus, and then layered into the next round of planning and teaching. The focal practice is the focus for teacher educator feedback on candidates' lesson plans and teaching, as well as candidates' individual reflections after the lesson. In this way, there is a direct and consistent relationship between what candidates read and do on campus and what they practice in their teaching groups at WES each week.

Provide Regular Opportunities for the Teacher Educator to Observe Candidates' Teaching

Since the weekly practice teaching happens during class time, it means the teacher educator is able to observe all candidates teach each week. During the candidates' weekly teaching sessions, the teacher educator (author) circulates and takes notes on what candidates and WES students are doing and saying. A synthesis of these notes is later typed and individual written feedback on the written lesson plan and instruction is provided in advance of the next teaching session. The opportunity to observe candidates teach each week reveals areas of growth and needed support, and informs the next class session(s), adjustments to course readings, in-class approximations, and reflection prompts. Thus, the field-based component offers a useful window into candidates' practices, which further informs the work of the teacher educator for the campus sessions.

Provide Candidates With Expert Feedback

In addition to written feedback provided by the teacher educator, expert feedback happens in three additional ways. First, there are times when it does not seem to make sense to "hold" feedback until the end of a lesson when student and candidate learning could be improved in real-time, so sometimes the teacher educator or WES faculty will briefly talk with the candidate or jump in the lesson with a question or brief comment. Candidates also receive expert feedback from WES faculty, who write comments, questions, and/or suggestions on post-it notes for candidates. The drive back to campus is also used for feedback, since all candidates ride together in a college van. If class sessions were longer or met only once per week, another way to provide expert feedback would be to stay at the school to debrief the lesson immediately after the teaching episode (Weston & Henderon, 2015).

Shared Vision: Content

Part of the shared vision that grounds this work was a desire to develop teacher candidates' readiness to teach interdisciplinary, concept-based literacy and social studies lessons that center content about identity, racism, and inequality. The shared vision of the teacher educator and school faculty is that there is a critical need to develop teacher candidates who have intentional experiences in these areas during teacher preparation. Again, coherence is not an end (Bateman, Taylor, Janik, & Logan, 2008; Canrinus, Klette, & Hammerness, 2017; Honig & Hatch, 2004; Nixon, 1991), meaning the "point" of developing a course is not to simply "be" coherent, but rather improve opportunities for teacher candidates to learn and develop the requisite knowledge and skills as a result of improved coherence, the extent to which would be unlikely in an incoherent arrangement. Having reviewed how the three structural aspects of the shared vision are operationalized through field-based work during class time, the three content-related aspects are explained next.

A Move Away From Subject-Specific Silos Towards More Interdisciplinary Teaching

The methods course is a combined literacy/social studies course in which candidates have experiences observing and teaching integrated, text-based lessons. In literacy, candidates teach Common Core State Standards, English Language Arts (ELA) (Council of Chief State Schools Officers, 2010) through interactive read-alouds (Fountas & Pinnell, 2006) that include explicit instruction about reading comprehension strategies (Almasi & Fullerton, 2012). Within the same lessons, candidates also integrate standards from the C3 framework (National Council for the Social Studies, 2013), as well as other information, including recent articles in *Social Studies and the Young Learner* (National Council for the Social Studies). For example, on the first page of the lesson plan template, candidates indicate a concept, central question, and a rationale for the question and relevant ELA and C3 standards. The example provided in Figure 1 is from Rachel's lesson that used the book *The People Shall Continue* by Simon Ortiz, and displays the integration of literacy and social studies content in the central question (left column: integrates storytelling, identity, and Native American peoples history and survival as explored in contemporary US society) and the rationale for this question (right column: reading comprehension strategy of comprehension monitoring, and social studies present-day Native Americans first-person perspectives about some of the topics in the book, including reservations).

The culminating project that each candidate developed also integrated literacy (reading, writing, speaking, and listening) and social studies learning and standards. For example, Emma focused on oral storytelling and Native American artifacts had students research a variety of artifacts, each select a different one, and then write their own folktale that included that particular artifact. For the final presentation, they shared their learning through oral storytelling. Emma's project, like the others, had students working on integrated literacy and social studies skills and allowed candidates to experience teaching and learning across literacy and social studies.

Figure 1. Candidate lesson plan excerpt showing the interdisciplinary nature of the central question and rationale

Procedures	Rationale
1. The central question you are working on today is: How does the story of one's identity relate to the importance of storytelling in regards to the history and survival of Native American peoples in today's society?	2. Specific rationale for your question and the relevant Standards: Rationale: 1. Students will use the reading strategy of comprehension monitoring to evaluate how the information in the text is presented in contrast to previous texts we have read. 2. Students will continue to gain a deeper understanding of the topic through use of videos of present-day Native Americans speaking about their associations with the themes present in the text.

A Move Away from Instructional Planning Based on Topics and Themes Towards Concept-Based Teaching

Given the small size of the partner school, all third through sixth grade elementary students participate in the field-based component of this course every year, which means the annual content of the lessons must be different. Therefore, over the summer the WES faculty set a school-wide concept that all grades (including K-2 students, outside of this course) will learn about. After the concept is set, the teacher educator adjusts course readings to match the school-selected concept. The candidates develop their own lessons and project underneath the concept, and have flexibility to develop an area of inquiry for their group. The concepts used in the course to date are as follows:

- **2014:** The Sun: Energy and story, patterns and cycles
- **2015:** Birds and Malala: Shelter and voice
- **2016:** African American Experiences Over Time: Identity, race and racism
- **2017:** Indigenous Peoples of North America: Traditions, storytelling, cultural assimilation, resistance – past and present

As a general introduction to concept-based teaching, candidates read two books early in the semester: *Creating Cultures of Thinking* (Ritchhart, 2015) and *Concept-based Curriculum and Instruction for the Thinking Classroom* (Erickson, Lanning & French, 2017). These books were identified collaboratively with WES teachers, who also read the books the first year they were used in the course, further improving coherence across people and roles. The first part of the lesson plan template asks candidates to identify "today's concept," so that they begin the planning process with this concept in mind. For example, the concept identified in Rachel's lesson plan before the section shown in Figure 1 was "storytelling is more than just about simply telling a story, it is connected to one's identity and the ways stories help build our identity."

A Move Away From Silence Towards Developing Teaching Skills for Difficult Conversations About Historical and Current Events Pertaining to Identity, Racism, and Inequality

When historical and contemporary issues are left undiscussed due to teachers' discomfort or unfamiliarity, schools are experienced as places where students, families, and groups of people are excluded instead of making schools places where people come together to talk about important aspects of their lives. In the third year, the teacher educator and school faculty selected a concept to focus teacher candidates' weekly teaching experiences on a semester-long study of racism, inclusion, access, and agency.

The main way conversations have been centered for candidates and scaffolded for elementary students is through the picture book collection that the school librarian and teacher educator compile related to that year's concept. For example, to learn about African American experiences over time in 2016, candidates began with some of the picture books by Jacqueline Woodson, and when studying Indigenous peoples in 2017, books recommended by the American Indian Library Association were used. Using literature in this way provides an entry point, language, and information to support student learning and candidates' capacity to facilitate text-based discussions about important topics. An additional strategy that emerged during the first year was to use a shared reading for all educators, candidates, and students to engage in conversations about identity, race, and racism. This was added to the course process after many candidates in the first cohort read *Wonder* (Palacio, 2012) because WES students were reading the book as part of a separate school-wide initiative. After seeing how the shared text could further improve coherence and also be a way to enter important conversations, it was added as an explicit part of the course in year two. The books that have been used each year are *Wonder* (Palacio, 2012), *I am Malala* (Yousafzai, 2015), *Brown Girl Dreaming* (Woodson, 2016), and *Birchbark House* (Erdrich, 2002). The themes, concepts, and events in the book are incorporated into course readings and discussions, and into candidates' weekly lessons at WES. The shared books are also available for families to borrow, and often there is a community night event to bring people together to discuss the book.

Evaluation

The third component of coherence is that it must be evaluated based on candidates' perspective. Therefore, the author collected data to evaluate and improve course coherence. Data related to the candidates is used to assess their growth, inform instruction, and inform subsequent iterations of the course. The methodology for this study is described in the subsequent section.

METHODOLOGY

The purpose of this study was to understand the extent to which candidates perceived their experiences as consistent with the shared vision used to design the course, coherent between theory/practice and campus/field, as well as what candidates learned through the field-based course. In this section, the study design, participants, data collection, and data analysis are described.

Data Collection

This study employed a situated case study design (Weston, 2011; see Figure 2), in which the three focal case studies were situated against a larger backdrop of data that was gathered from all candidates who participated in the course since its design in 2014 ($n = 36$ over four years). At the broadest level (Tier One), data analyzed for this particular study came from the 33 completed course evaluations to help answer research questions (RQs) one (the relationship of candidates' experiences to the shared vision used to design the course), two (the extent to which candidates experience the course as coherent between theory/practice and campus/field), and three (candidate-reported learning).

Participants

As indicated in the definition of coherence found earlier in this chapter, it is imperative to research candidate perceptions of their experiences to understand course or program coherence. For Tier Two data collection, three of the candidates from the Tier One group were selected to survey and interview using purposeful sampling from the fall 2017 course. The three candidates chosen, Emma, Rachel, and Sophie, were representative of recently updated programmatic requirements for course enrollment, including prior course work, major, and intent to student teach (the fourth candidate in the 2017 course did not meet these criteria). All three identify as female, and one identifies as middle eastern, one as multi-racial,

Figure 2. Situated case study design: Nested tiers of data collection

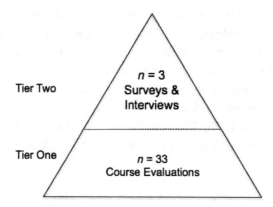

and one as white. They were all enrolled in the course the year before their fall 2018 student teaching. The three selected candidates, like all participants, completed course evaluations, as well as surveys and interviews, which are described in the next section.

Course Evaluations

Each year, the anonymous college-wide course evaluations were completed while the teacher educator (author) was out of the room during the final class session. The questions that were considered for this study include a question about course content and format (RQs 1 & 2), learning (RQs 2 & 3), and concluding remarks (RQs 1-3). The wording of each of these three questions is found below:

- **Course Content & Format:** How did the various components of the course contribute to your learning? Consider, as appropriate, lectures, readings, writing assignments, problem sets, films, labs, drills, studio work, debates, discussions, field work, or group work. Be specific.
- **Learning:** What have you learned from this course? Consider how the course deepened your critical or analytical abilities, factual knowledge, understanding of concepts, creativity, communication skills, and ability to pursue further work in the subject. Give concrete examples.
- **Concluding Remarks:** What comments would you make about maintaining or changing the course content and/or the instructor's methods of teaching? Comment on any aspects of the course, modes of teaching, or impact on your education that are not covered by the preceding questions.

Surveys

In order to answer the second research question about candidates' perceptions of coherence between theory/practice and campus/field, beginning in 2017 they were asked to provide anonymous, open-response written feedback through the following questions (RQs 1 & 2):

- How did working in a WES Group impact the coherence of your learning?
- How did working in a WES Group impact coherence between theory and practice?
- How did working in a WES Group impact coherence between campus work and field work?

Given that coherence is a quality and a process rather than the end goal (Canrinus, Klette, & Hammerness, 2017), candidates were also asked about what they learned (RQ 3):

- What did you learn during your WES Group?
- How did what you learn in your WES Group help you better understand the information you learned in the rest of the course (readings and class sessions)?

Interviews

The individual interviews helped answer the three research questions by providing data about the candidate's individual perceptions and learning at a greater depth than the surveys and course evaluations. The interviews included specific questions about coherence, opportunities, experiences, and learning. For example, candidates were asked how much opportunity they had to experience each of the six shared vision elements used to design the course (RQ 1), what experiences they had that reflected or reinforced the shared vision (RQ 1), their perceptions of coherence across theory/practice and campus/field (RQ 2), and learning they believed occurred through the course (RQ 3).

Data Analysis

Course Evaluations and Surveys

The author extracted and grouped all course evaluation and survey text that addressed each research question. To analyze RQ 1, *a priori* codes for statements about the six elements of the shared vision were used (1. practice work with students; 2. teacher educator observations; 3. expert feedback; 4. interdisciplinary teaching; 5. concept-based teaching, and; 6. teaching skills related to identity, racism, inequality). To analyze RQ 2, *a priori* codes of *theory/practice* and *campus/field* were used to indicate when these pairs of words were used by candidates in the same segment of text (e.g., if a candidate wrote about the role of theory but not practice, it was not coded as theory/practice).

For RQ 3 (candidate learning), the author wrote short memos focused on candidates' reports of learning during review of all course evaluations and surveys. These memos were used to generate codes for analysis, which were then grouped into broader themes through grounded theory (Glaser & Strauss, 2009). The three codes that emerged from this initial process were *teaching*, *planning*, and *theory or research*. These were considered present when candidates used any of these exact words to describe what they learned. Many of the candidates also included statements to identify more specific aspects of their learning in both the course evaluations and surveys, making sub-categories possible within the original three codes. For second-wave coding, each unique aspect candidates reported learning was listed and then grouped into broader themes. After an iterative process of refining and using the revised codes until the codes accounted for all statements beyond *teaching*, *planning*, and *theory or research*, and no further patterns could be found within the *other* category to generate a new code, the codes were: 1. *pedagogy* (knowledge of teaching); 2. *content* (knowledge of content); 3. *skills* (reflection, critical or analytic thinking, creativity); 4. *students* (knowledge of students), and; 5. *other* (all remaining statements of learning). After the five codes were defined, all course evaluations and surveys were reviewed and coded again. The text segments were then rearranged in a different order, coded again, and yielded the same results. The codes for *pedagogy* and *content* were further investigated in a third wave of coding to indicate whether those aspects of learning were described as *generic* (i.e., not content-specific), or whether the statement focused on *literacy* or *social studies* pedagogy or content learning.

Interviews

To analyze the interview data for the three focal candidates, their interviews were transcribed and then sections in which they spoke about the six shared vision elements, their perceptions of coherence, or their learning were extracted. The codes used were the same as those used to analyze the course evaluations and surveys, as indicated in the previous section.

RESULTS

First, the Tier One results from the course evaluations will be reported per each research question, then Emma's, Rachel's, and Sophie's perceptions of coherence and learning will be discussed in more detail. Given this study was based on qualitative data with small *n* values, descriptive statistics will be reported.

Research Question One: To What Extent Do Candidates' Experiences Reflect and Reinforce the Shared Vision Used to Design the Course?

The course evaluations indicated the frequency candidates reported the six elements of the shared vision through responses to open-ended questions about course features, their learning, and other comments (see Figure 2). In regards to the structural elements of the shared vision, of the 33 candidates who completed course evaluations, 30 (91%) indicated that the regular opportunities to work with students and practice teaching during class (shared vision element 1) contributed to their learning. None of the candidates included the teacher educator observing their teaching (shared vision element 2), however 18 candidates (55%) identified the written and in-class feedback from the teacher educator (shared vision element 3) as one of the aspects of "course content and format" that contributed to their learning. Although teacher educator observation was not specifically referred to, it would not be possible to have teacher educator feedback without the observations that roughly half of the candidates identified as helpful. In the past two years, 75% of the candidates included feedback in their answer to this question, and 73% of three of the four cohorts included feedback, meaning it was only in one of the four years that less than 73% of candidates included teacher educator feedback as contributing to their learning. It should be noted that "feedback" is not one of the 13 "various components of the course" listed as examples for students to consider (see questions in Figure 2), meaning the candidates who did include feedback did so unprompted. The three content elements of the shared vision (teaching that is interdisciplinary, concept-based, and justice-focused) were not frequently reported in course evaluations, which is not surprising given that the course evaluation questions are generic across campus, and may have contributed to candidates' tendency to write about teaching in broad terms. Therefore, the surveys and interviews of the three focal candidates are used to report on these areas in the next section.

Shared Vision: Structural

Emma's, Rachel's, and Sophie's perceptions about opportunities that reflected or reinforced the shared vision are discussed in this section. In regards to structural coherence, candidates reported that their opportunity to engage in authentic, field-based practice with students was "extensive." Both Rachel and Emma stated "we were (at WES) all the time," and all three candidates felt the time at WES was both authentic and substantial. When asked what experiences reflected or reinforced the shared vision, Emma again spoke about this element, and said that it was "the ability to go to school and actually having physical students—instead of doing a role play—that really allowed us to experience lessons, unlike in a pseudo-classroom. You don't get authenticity until you're really working with students in that age group."

Despite not appearing in course evaluations, when asked directly about the teacher educator observations all three focal candidates reported they had extensive opportunities for this, although Emma noted it was "not quite as extensive" because the teacher educator had to share time across groups that met in two different rooms. Rachel said the way the teacher educator "watched and took notes helped things solidify. So it wasn't just what we see, there was another observer to notice what we're not picking up on." They all also reported that it was helpful for the WES teachers to observe them teach. Rachel also explained having the methods professor present while candidates were teaching was helpful not only for observing and feedback,

but also for when we came back (to campus), to really debrief about exactly what happened, and dissecting all the different components of what was going on. I think (the methods professor had not observed), then perhaps it would have been 'we just did this lesson, and now we'll just think about the next one' and not really reflect and understand what was going on, what can be changed, or what can we think about in a different way, what did a student say that could actually motivate and help construct the rest of the lessons?

When asked about the opportunities to receive feedback, candidates again reported this as extensive and helpful, and in the interviews talked about receiving feedback from both the methods professor and the WES teachers. Rachel explained:

We definitely had a lot of feedback on teaching from different people, from teachers who actually knew the school and class dynamics, but also (the professor) that knew how to get what we needed out of it.

When asked later in the interview about experiences that added to coherence, Rachel again discussed the role of feedback, and how "we worked with teachers who actually wanted to help you become a better teacher. Their feedback was constructive to help me continue, so I really appreciated that." The three focal candidates reported that they had extensive opportunities to experience each of the three structural elements of the shared vision.

Shared Vision: Content

The first content-related aspect of the shared vision is experiencing interdisciplinary teaching, which in this course means between literacy and social studies. Emma stated this was extensive, and contrasted her experiences in her WES group with her past by saying, "when we were growing up, talking about

Native American cultures was very much thrown into social studies, we never thought about the literacy aspect." Sophie also reported that the attention on "the way literature could be worked with in social studies made me think more, and make links between the two areas." The three focal candidates also reported having opportunities to experience concept-based teaching, in Rachel's words, "all over the place." Emma explained, "we didn't just take Native American culture as a whole and as a theme, but we talked about very specific concepts within it." Sophie believed that "working with multiple texts to address a larger concept helped me both be grounded in those texts, but also work back and forth with the concept." She also described that within concept-based teaching, "trying to get to a big question, that was a real question, was a challenging and good process. (In the beginning,) I think I had concept-based questions that were like, 'I know the answer to this, but we can discuss it.' But being pushed to bring real questions, that were fully accessible to all the students, that was a theory/practice challenge that pushed me to develop better lessons.

The final shared vision element of developing teaching skills for difficult historical and contemporary events related to identity, race, and racism was also experienced extensively by candidates, and they believed they had regular opportunities to learn "how to actually go about" having important conversations with young people. Emma explained that she believed this was an area that:

I could have very easily ignored. I could have been like, 'these are things (Indigenous peoples) did in the past and everything was great and these were the beautiful stories they shared down the generations.' I think there was always the opportunity, but it's more so whether or not we wanted to take it, but there was extensive opportunity.

On this same topic, Rachel explained:

This was probably the most difficult task of all of the (shared vision elements). It takes so much experience working with younger minds, trying to craft lessons and consider what they're already thinking, and how to go about having these really hard conversations.

She credited working with WES teachers as helpful in this regard. Sophie stated that she had "a sense of urgency around teaching about social problems like racism and inequality" and that she learned to "design thoughtful lessons aimed at conceptual understanding in which I asked students real, tough questions...I can't imagine going into the classroom without this kind of experience." Emma also expressed the importance of this component of the course, and explained:

Pre-service teachers need to move beyond learning about the basics of teaching and learn how to address more discomforting topics that are guaranteed to come up when they enter student teaching and teaching as a whole. They must have actual experiences implementing culturally sustaining pedagogy—something that is developed through experience, not just by reading others' work.

Emma also stated that through this course she found "students are capable of engaging in difficult topics" in the following explanation:

Often, I think people shy away from having difficult conversations about identity in the classroom because it makes them uncomfortable or because they don't think it's something their students are capable of, but I think they are capable of engaging in difficult topics that lead to a more just, compassionate, equitable society and it's important to do so at a young age.

The three focal candidates reported extensive opportunities to engage in experiences that reflected and reinforced the shared vision elements used to design the course.

Research Question Two: To What Extent Do Candidates Experience the Course as Coherent Between Theory/Practice and Campus/Field?

Candidates wrote about opportunities to merge theory/practice ($n = 25$) or campus/field ($n = 4$) in 29 (88%) of the course evaluations. Emma, Rachel, and Sophie also reported coherence between these areas in their surveys and interviews. For example, Rachel reported in her survey:

Rather than feeling like this was an independent assignment that we go out and do each week, working with my group kept my educational values and goals as an educator at the forefront and helped me to continually reassess my role in my students' experience with learning each week.

Similarly, Emma reported:

By implementing teaching practices within the course, I was given an opportunity to apply and better comprehend course material that I would not have viewed the same way having only read about the theories and practices.

Likewise, Sophie reported, "Working with my group helped to consolidate the ideas and frameworks from the readings and class sessions we had before going out to WES each week." She also wrote:

The theory readings we did only became "real" to me through continuous, iterative practice enacting (or trying to enact) it at (WES). All of the messiness of working with students necessitated going back and forth between readings, discussions, lesson plans, reading groups, and personal and group reflection.

Rachel also experienced coherence between these areas and wrote that the course "was a great way to find a balance between theory/frameworks for teaching and actual implementation in the classroom. It helped me truly understand and improve on my pedagogy and strategies as a teacher." She also reported that the integrated practice work aligned with:

the way I learn best as a student, which is learning through practice and example. If I had just done the readings alone without critically thinking about and implementing the strategies into my lesson planning and time with my students, I do not think this semester would have been as successful as it was.

The three focal candidates described using the readings, theories, and ideas from campus in order to improve their teaching, and using regular teaching at WES to better understand the theories and ideas.

Research Question Three: What Do Candidates Report They Learned From Participating in the Course?

In the course evaluations, 88% of reporting candidates stated they learned about teaching, 73% about planning, and 64% about theory or research. Of the 73 specific learning statements that provided example(s) beyond these three areas, 32% were about pedagogy, 32% about skills, 12% about content, and 6% about students. Overall, the statements were 66% generic in nature (not content-specific), 18% were about social studies, and 16% were literacy-specific.

When asked what they learned through the course in surveys and interviews, Emma, Rachel, and Sophie each described lesson planning and teaching as two primary areas of learning. They each also identified a third area of learning, which were different from one another (Rachel: understanding of students, Emma: observing a classroom, Sophie: practicing discomfort). Similar to the course evaluation data, the first area the three focal candidates reported learning was lesson planning. Rachel stated she "really enjoyed the challenge" of lesson planning, and that at the beginning of the course she "focus(ed) on (her) growth as an educator" by asking questions during planning such as, "what activities will need the most scaffolding to work in a large group discussion?" She also described that the course "made it very clear that you have to plan so far ahead and really think about how the little bits and pieces actually fit together, and how difficult that actually is." Emma also reported similar learning, and stated, "During my WES Group, I really got an understanding of the level of difficulty in creating and executing lesson plans." She also said she learned how to backwards plan by first identifying what she wanted students "to get out of the lessons, and integrating that with standards" before planning her activities. Sophie reported she learned "to design thoughtful lessons aimed at conceptual understanding…to guide social inquiry using interdisciplinary materials through literature, videos, and photos."

In regards to learning about teaching, Emma explained that since this was the first methods course in the program, she learned to be comfortable teaching, talking with students, and "being able to direct a classroom." She also said that she learned to present information clearly, and improved "formatting my questions so they are good questions, and making sure, if someone wasn't able to answer, there was still some kind of entry way" for them to participate. She also reported learning how to make her questions "accessible to all the students at once." Emma further explained that being able to enact a lesson was helpful, stating that "It helped give me practice out in the field and figuring what actually does and doesn't work moving from lesson planning to the actual execution." Rachel explained that, in her teaching, she learned "different avenues for opening conversations and different types of teaching." She provided an example that in one lesson,

I found a video on-line about reservations, and what that word meant to Indigenous people, and I had the students write before watching that, and write out their connections to that word, and what they think it means, and that actually opened the conversation so much more. For me, learning how to do that and finding those different resources, actually was a shift in the way my group and I were working together. That interaction changed the whole course of the unit.

Each candidate reported a different third area of primary learning. Rachel reported, in both her survey and her interview, that a key area of learning for her was understanding her students. She described that her "biggest learning" was about "how students construct their learning" and improving her lessons so that there was "more of an inquiry-based interaction." She explained that she spent the first half of the semester focused on herself, her lesson plans, and her activities,

however, as the semester continued, my focus shifted towards understanding my students on a deeper level…focusing on understanding each of my students' mindsets, and as individuals and (their) interest(s). When I took into account my students as individual learners capable of reading, discussing, sharing, and evaluating on many levels, the shift in learning was phenomenal.

Rachel's shift from focusing on her behaviors to focusing on her students and viewing them as "capable learners" indicates professional growth during the course.

Emma's third area of reported learning was what she called "observing." She explained this in the following way:

I learned there's different ways of observing a classroom. Through (working at WES) we were able to focus on very specific things each time—how students were responding, or what materials were presented and how, or response to student ideas, or looking at materials they were given.

Emma seems to be describing growth in her perceived ability to attend to specific aspects of classroom interactions across a range of areas, including contingent areas of teaching, as well as the selection and use of instructional materials.

Sophie reported that a third key aspect of her learning was experiencing discomfort in trying to plan and enact what she referred to as "social justice-oriented lessons." She stated that "there's a sense of urgency in that for me, and a sense of importance." Sophie elaborated:

I think making mistakes or struggling, that's all scary and feels important and big, and I always go in wanting the lesson to land, and wanting for students to be engaged and we're all learning. But I think, especially with social justice-oriented content, making mistakes can feel scary in a particular kind of way, or having things not land, and I think you need to practice that discomfort. And that feels really important to me, that I've gotten the chance to practice that discomfort, and to reflect on it, and work to refine my teaching in response to it.

The opportunity to "practice discomfort" in a supported environment aligns with the shared vision element that teacher candidates need to have experiences developing teaching skills for difficult conversations.

DISCUSSION

The author's purpose in re-designing the methods courses to contain an integrated field-based component was to allow candidates the opportunity to continually practice and improve in ways that could not happen on campus or through field placements done independently outside of class. The design of this methods course is one response to the need for "significantly more—and more deliberate—opportunities for novices to practice the work of instruction" (Ball & Forzani, 2009, p.503). By including field-based practice during class, candidates practice teaching in a supported environment, develop relationships with students, and receive expert feedback. As a result of developing a methods course with an intentionally designed field-based component, the campus and field settings are no longer disconnected conceptually or structurally, and candidates now have guaranteed, regular opportunities to observe and practice what is read and discussed on campus (Canrinus, Klette, & Hammerness, 2017). Candidates integrated ideas and practices into their teaching, not just into their knowledge or beliefs. Practice work done under the view of the teacher educator further informed feedback and instruction. Ultimately, this course is successful due to the collaboration between educators at the school and college, and is a further example of improved coherence in a teacher education program resulting from improved collaboration across roles and settings (Canrinus, Klette, & Hammerness, 2017). As Rachel explained, "The combination of having the teachers at school, the professor observing, and everything happening in motion, it was a really good fit."

Through participating in a course with coherent opportunities for in-class practice teaching that was aligned with the shared vision, candidates learned about the connected relationship between theory and practice. In this way, the integrated practice teaching sessions and accompanying readings and discussions acted as a disruption to perceiving theory and practice as either disconnected or linear (i.e., theory-into-practice) (Skott, 2005). Instead, candidates described the relationship between theory and practice in a reciprocal manner that indicates the field-based practice necessitated candidates' return to theory in order to improve their next round of teaching. By participating in a course in which there was regular teaching practice with concurrent reading and learning about content and pedagogy, candidates saw the relevance and application from the readings and campus discussions to their weekly teaching. In their accounts, candidates seemed to describe the theory of teaching becoming "real and vital" to themselves as educator, which Dewey stated was needed in teacher education (1904/1964, p. 314).

Given the weekly assignment of both planning and teaching a lesson, it is not surprising that candidates identified as two primary areas of learning. Still, the way they often explained the importance of not just planning but also carrying out the lesson with elementary students is helpful for teacher educators to keep in mind regarding hypothetical lesson plan assignments or on-campus teaching with simulated students. An area for teacher educators to reflect on is when to use approximations of practice as stepping stones towards future authentic experiences and when to provide opportunities for authentic classroom experiences. It may also be helpful to consider when, in a course or program, candidates have the opportunity to plan and teach a series of lessons with the same students before student teaching, so that teaching is not perceived as only linear (planning-into-teaching) or as a context-free process, but rather that candidate teaching informs their subsequent planning and that both planning and instruction are based on knowledge of specific students and context.

The transition from candidates seeing themselves as the center of teaching toward focusing on "their" students who they see as "capable learners," which was stated by both Emma and Rachel, indicates an area of growth that is prerequisite to providing equitable teaching (Ladson-Billings, 2008). Perhaps engaging in earlier, coherent field-based practice work can provide opportunities to develop a student-focused stance earlier in their program of study and/or more reliably. Opportunities for candidates to practice discomfort over time in a supportive environment is another area for teacher educators to consider in terms of deliberate practice in teacher education. Future research could investigate the impact of coherent, field-based methods work on candidates' shifts in stance, disposition, beliefs, comfort, and perceptions.

Additional future research areas include determining the impact of these opportunities and experiences on candidates for the remainder of the program (e.g., during subsequent methods courses and during student teaching) as well as on program graduates. Some questions to consider include are candidates better prepared upon graduation (and in what ways?), and are they more likely to demonstrate practices that align with the shared vision in their future teaching? Such investigation could go "beyond describing teacher education from afar" and move to "the equally important work of talking about content and pedagogy of experiences, classes, and programs" (Wilson, 1990, p.2). Continuing to study the possible challenges or constraints associated with working towards coherence is also an ongoing need (Hammerness, 2006).

CONCLUSION

Teacher candidates have experiences across a range of courses, field placements, supervisors, mentor teachers, and professors. The complex coordination across people, settings, assignments, experiences, and semesters ought not be further fractured by a lack of coherence. It is the professional responsibility of teacher educators to reduce existing course and program divisions by attending to coherence. To this end, one area that merits more attention from teacher educators and researchers is attempts to develop coherent courses and programs by intentionally intertwining opportunities to merge theory and practice and campus and field experiences.

Innovative, coherent field-based methods courses can establish a vibrant relationship between theory and practice and course work and field work. The work done in this methods course between Middlebury College and WES is presented as one model of a methods course partnership with an integrated, school-situated, practice-based component. As indicated in the definition of coherence, the aim of coherence is not an end, but rather a process and a quality. Similarly, the vision and design elements of this course are offered as an example of leveraging a field-based component of teacher education not as an end, but rather a process to improve opportunities for candidates' development and readiness for equitable, ambitious teaching.

ACKNOWLEDGMENT

The author would like to thank Weybridge Elementary School principal, Christina Johnston, and teachers Catherine Canavan, Joy Dobson, Leigh Harder, Megan Sutton, and Christina Wadsworth for their expertise and investment in preservice teacher education, as well as the Weybridge and Middlebury College students with whom we have been fortunate to work.

This work was supported by an Academic Outreach Endowment Award from Community Engagement at Middlebury College [no grant number].

REFERENCES

Affolter, T., Cooper, C., Miller-Lane, J., & Weston, T. (2015). *Education Studies Program mission statement*. Retrieved from http://www.middlebury.edu/academics/edst/about

Almasi, J. F., & Fullerton, S. K. (2012). *Teaching strategic processes in reading*. New York: The Guilford Press.

Anderson, L. M., & Stillman, J. A. (2013). Student teaching's contribution to preservice teacher development: A review of research focused on the preparation of teachers for urban and high-needs contexts. *Review of Educational Research, 83*(1), 3–69. doi:10.3102/0034654312468619

Bain, R. B., & Moje, E. B. (2012). Mapping the teacher education terrain for novices. *Phi Delta Kappan, 93*(5), 62–65. doi:10.1177/003172171209300514

Ball, D. L., & Forzani, F. M. (2009). The work of teaching and the challenge for teacher education. *Journal of Teacher Education, 60*(5), 497–511. doi:10.1177/0022487109348479

Ball, D. L., Sleep, L., Boerst, T., & Bass, H. (2009). Combining the development of practice and the practice of development in teacher education. *The Elementary School Journal, 109*(5), 458–476. doi:10.1086/596996

Bamfield, L. (Ed.). (2014). *The role of research in teacher education: Reviewing the evidence: Interim report of the BERA-RSA inquiry*. London: British Educational Research.

Bateman, D., Taylor, S., Janik, E., & Logan, A. (2008). *Curriculum coherence and student access*. Saint-Lambert, Quebec, Canada: Champlain Saint Lambery Cegep.

Boyd, D. J., Grossman, P. L., Lankford, H., Loeb, S., & Wyckoff, J. (2009). Teacher preparation and student achievement. *Educational Evaluation and Policy Analysis, 31*(4), 416–440. doi:10.3102/0162373709353129

Broad, K., Stewart Rose, L., Lopez, A. E., & Baxan, V. (2013). Coherence as a verb: Reconceptualizing coherence in teacher education. In L. Thomas (Ed.), *What is Canadian about teacher education in Canada?* (pp. 234–258). San Fransisco, CA: Jossey Bass.

Buchmann, M., & Floden, R. E. (1991). Programme coherence in teacher education: A view from the USA. *Oxford Review of Education, 17*(1), 65–72. doi:10.1080/0305498910170105

Canrinus, E. T., Klette, K., & Hammerness, K. (2017). Diversity in coherence: Strengths and opportunities of three programs. *Journal of Teacher Education*, 1–14.

Clift, R. (1991). Learning to teach English-maybe: A study of knowledge development. *Journal of Teacher Education, 42*(5), 357–372. doi:10.1177/002248719104200505

Conway, P. F., & Munthe, E. (2015). The practice turn: Research-informed clinical teacher education in two countries. In J.-K. Smedby & M. Stephen (Eds.), *From vocational to professional education: Educating for social welfare* (pp. 146–163). London: Routledge.

Council of Chief State School Officers. (2010). *Common Core State Standards English Language Arts*. Washington, DC: National Governors Association Center for Best Practices, Council of Chief State School Officers.

Darling-Hammond, L. (2014). Strengthening clinical preparation: The holy grail of teacher education. *Peabody Journal of Education, 89*(4), 547–561. doi:10.1080/0161956X.2014.939009

Darling-Hammond, L., Burns, D., Campbell, C., Goodwin, A. L., Hammerness, K., Low, E. L., & Zeichner, K. (2017). *Empowered educators: How high-performing systems shape teaching quality around the world*. San Francisco, CA: Jossey-Bass.

Dewey, J. (1938/1963). *Experience and education.* New York, NY: Macmillan. (Original work published 1938)

Dewey, J. (1964). The relation of theory to practice in education. In R. D. Archambault (Ed.), *John Dewey on education: Selected writings* (pp. 313–338). Chicago, IL: University of Chicago Press. (Original work published 1904)

Eisenhart, M., Behm, L., & Romagnano, L. (1991). Learning to teach: Developing expertise or rite of passage? *Journal of Education for Teaching, 17*(1), 51–71. doi:10.1080/0260747910170106

Erdrich, L. (2002). *Birchbark House.* New York: First Hyperion.

Erickson, H. L., Lanning, L. A., & French, R. (2017). *Concept-based Curriculum and Instruction for the Thinking Classroom.* Thousand Oaks, CA: Corwin.

Feiman-Nemser, S. (1990). Teacher preparation: Structural and conceptual analysis. In W. R. Houston, M. Haberman, & J. Sikula (Eds.), *Handbook of research on teacher education* (pp. 212–233). New York, NY: Macmillan.

Feiman-Nemser, S., & Buchmann, M. (1985). Pitfalls of experience in teacher preparation. *Teachers College Record, 87,* 53–65.

Florio Ruane, S., & Lensmire, T. (1990). Transforming future teachers' ideas about writing instruction. *Journal of Curriculum Studies, 22*(3), 277–289. doi:10.1080/0022027900220305

Fountas, I., & Pinnell, G. S. (2006). *Teaching for comprehending and fluency: Thinking, talking, and writing about reading, K-8.* Portsmouth, NH: Heinemann.

Goodman, J. (1985). What students learn from early field experiences: A case study and critical analysis. *Journal of Teacher Education, 38*(6), 42–48. doi:10.1177/002248718503600607

Griffin, G. A. (1989). A descriptive study of student teaching. *The Elementary School Journal, 89*(3), 343–364. doi:10.1086/461579

Grisham, D. L., Laguardia, A., & Brink, B. (2000). Partners in professionalism: Creating a quality field experience for preservice teachers. *Action in Teacher Education, 21*(4), 27–40. doi:10.1080/01626620.2000.10462978

Grossman, P., Compton, C., Igra, D., Ronfeldt, M., Shahan, E., & Williamson, P. W. (2009). Teaching practice: A cross-professional perspective. *Teachers College Record, 111*(9), 2055–2100.

Grossman, P., Hammerness, K. M., McDonald, M., & Ronfeldt, M. (2008). Structural predictors of perceptions of coherence in NYC teacher education programs. *Journal of Teacher Education, 59*(4), 273–287. doi:10.1177/0022487108322127

Grossman, P. L., Valencia, S., Evans, K., Thompson, C., Martin, S., & Place, N. (2000). Transitions into teaching: Learning to teach writing in teacher education and beyond. *Journal of Literacy Research, 32*(4), 631–662. doi:10.1080/10862960009548098

Hammerness, K. (2006). From coherence in theory to coherence in practice. *Teachers College Record, 108*(7), 1241–1265. doi:10.1111/j.1467-9620.2006.00692.x

Hammerness, K. (2013). Examining features of teacher education in Norway. *Scandinavian Journal of Educational Research, 54*(4), 400–419. doi:10.1080/00313831.2012.656285

Henderson, S. C. (2013). *Iterative development of a literacy methods course inside a failing school.* Paper presented at the meeting of the American Educational Research Association, San Francisco, CA.

Henderson, S. C., & Weston, T. L. (2014). *Uncovering a problem of practice: Supervisors' field observations of preservice teachers' approximations of practice.* Paper presented at the meeting of the American Educational Research Association, Philadelphia, PA.

Hoban, G. F. (Ed.). (2005). *The missing links in teacher education design. Developing a multi-linked conceptual framework.* Dordrecht, The Netherlands: Springer. doi:10.1007/1-4020-3346-X

Honig, M. I., & Hatch, T. C. (2004). Crafting coherence: How schools strategically manage multiple, external demands. *Educational Researcher, 33*(8), 16–30. doi:10.3102/0013189X033008016

Howey, K., & Zimpher, N. (1989). *Profiles of preservice teacher education.* Albany, NY: State University of New York.

Kazemi, E., Franke, M., & Lampert, M. (2009). Developing pedagogies in teacher education to support novice teachers' ability to enact ambitious instruction. In R. Hunter & T. Burgess (Eds.), *Crossing divides: Proceedings of the 32nd annual conference of the Mathematics Research Group of Australia, 1.*

Ladson-Billings, G. (1995). But that's just good teaching! The case for culturally relevant pedagogy. *Theory into Practice, 34*(3), 159–165. doi:10.1080/00405849509543675

Ladson-Billings, G. (2008). I ain't writin' nuttin': Permissions to fail and demands to succeed. In L. Delpit & J. K. Dowdy (Eds.), *The Skin that We Speak: Thought on Language Culture in the Classroom* (pp. 109–120). New York: The New Press.

Lampert, M. (2001). *Teaching problems and the problems of teaching.* New Haven, CT: Yale University Press.

Lampert, M., & Graziani, F. (2009). Instructional activities as a tool for teachers' and teacher educators' learning in and for practice. *The Elementary School Journal, 109*(5), 491–509. doi:10.1086/596998

Lazar, A. M. (1998). Helping preservice teachers inquire about caregivers: A critical experience for field-based courses. *Action in Teacher Education, 19*(4), 14–28. doi:10.1080/01626620.1998.10462888

McDonald, M., Kazemi, E., & Kavanagh, S. S. (2013). Core practices and pedagogies in teacher education: A call for a common language and collective activity. *Journal of Teacher Education, 64*(5), 378–386. doi:10.1177/0022487113493807

Moon, B. (Ed.). (2016). *Do universities have a role in the education and training of teachers? An international analysis of policy and practice.* Cambridge, UK: Cambridge University Press.

National Council for the Social Studies (NCSS). (2013). *The College, Career, and Civic Life (C3) Framework for Social Studies State Standards: Guidance for Enhancing the Rigor of K-12 Civics, Economics, Geography, and History.* Silver Spring, MD: NCSS.

Nixon, J. (1991). Reclaiming coherence: Cross-curriculum provision and the National Curriculum. *Journal of Curriculum Studies*, *23*(2), 187–192. doi:10.1080/0022027910230209

Palacio, R. J. (2012). *Wonder*. New York: Random House.

Ritchhart, R. (2015). *Creating Cultures of Thinking*. San Francisco, CA: Jossey-Bass.

Samaras, A. P., Frank, T. J., Williams, M. A., Christopher, E., & Rodick, W. H. III. (2016). A collective self-study to improve program coherence of clinical experiences. *Studying Teacher Education*, *12*(2), 170–187. doi:10.1080/17425964.2016.1192033

Skott, J. (2005). The role of the practice of theorising practice. In M. Bosch, & ... (Eds.), *Proceedings of the 4th Conference of the European Society for Research in Mathematics Education* (pp. 1598-1608). Barcelona: FunEmi.

Tabachnick, B. R., & Zeichner, K. M. (1984). The impact of student teaching experience on the development of teachers' perspectives. *Journal of Teacher Education*, *35*(6), 28–36. doi:10.1177/002248718403500608

Tatto, M. (1996). Examining values and beliefs about teaching diverse students: Understanding the challenges for teacher education. *Educational Evaluation and Policy Analysis*, *18*(2), 155–180. doi:10.3102/01623737018002155

Weston, T. L. (2011). *Elementary preservice teachers' mathematical knowledge for teaching: Using situated case studies and educative experiences to examine and improve the development of MKT in teacher education* (Doctoral dissertation). Available from ProQuest Dissertations and Theses database. (UMI No. 3477561)

Weston, T. L. (2018). Using the Knowledge Quartet to support prospective teacher development during methods coursework. In S. E. Kastberg, A. M. Tyminski, A. E. Lischka, & W. B. Sanchez (Eds.), *Building Scholarly Practices in Mathematics Methods* (pp. 69–83). Charlotte, NC: Information Age Publishing.

Weston, T. L., & Henderson, S. C. (2015). Coherent experiences: The new missing paradigm in teacher education. *The Educational Forum*, *79*(3), 321–335. doi:10.1080/00131725.2015.1037514

Wilson, J. D. (1996). An evaluation of the field experiences of the innovative model for the preparation of elementary teachers for science, mathematics, and technology. *Journal of Teacher Education*, *47*(1), 53–59. doi:10.1177/0022487196047001009

Wilson, S. M. (1990). The secret garden of teacher education. *Phi Delta Kappan*, *72*(3), 204–209.

Woodson, J. (2016). *Brown Girl Dreaming*. New York: Puffin Books.

Yousafzai, M. (2015). I am Malala: How one girl stood up for education and changed the world (Young reader's edition). New York: Little, Brown and Company.

Zeichner, K., & Tabachnik, B. R. (1981). Are the effects of university teacher education "washed out" by school experience? *Journal of Teacher Education*, *32*(3), 7–11. doi:10.1177/002248718103200302

192

Chapter 8
Developing Mutually Beneficial Partnerships Through Purposeful Field–Based Experiences:
Lessons Learned From Professional Development

Maika J. Yeigh
Portland State University, USA

Nicole R. Rigelman
Portland State University, USA

ABSTRACT

In this chapter, two teacher educators share lessons learned when they adapted professional development structures for use with teacher candidates during the clinical practicum experience. Highlighted in this chapter are two field-based teacher education approaches that support the development of mutually beneficial partnerships. Teacher candidates and their cooperating teachers collaboratively used lesson study to examine mathematical discourse in an elementary setting, while teacher candidates used instructional rounds as a way for teacher candidates to observe more experienced teachers in secondary classrooms. Both structures attempted to bridge the persistent divide between university learning and clinical practice to the benefit of K-12 students, teachers, and teacher candidates. The chapter concludes with recommendations for increasing the number of teacher candidates and partnership schools involved in this field-based learning in ways beneficial to all those involved.

DOI: 10.4018/978-1-5225-6249-8.ch008

Copyright © 2019, IGI Global. Copying or distributing in print or electronic forms without written permission of IGI Global is prohibited.

INTRODUCTION

Genuine collaboration between K-12 schools and the university result in partnerships that provide benefits to both systems—not only in the immediate but also the long term. Mutually beneficial partnerships focus on the growth and goals of all participants and for this reason may draw upon practice-based professional development approaches (Ball & Cohen, 1999; Smith, 2001) to support both preservice and inservice teacher learning. The immediate benefits to both partners—and ultimately for K-12 students—come through the participation in professional development designs that focus on collaboration, inquiry, and reflective practice. The longer term benefit from the collaborative inquiry into practice is the shift from a view teaching as an isolating profession (Lortie, 1975) to a collaborative one (Little, 2003).

For teacher collaboration to make a difference in teacher and student learning, it must be centered on important work and be distinguished from mere collegiality (Hargreaves, 1994; Kelchtermans, 2006; Little, 2003). More specifically, collaborative planning is consistently a contributing factor for more skillful teaching and increased student achievement (Darling-Hammond, 2015). In response, more schools are structuring time for teachers to collaborate in professional learning communities (PLCs) that focus on instructional planning and analysis of student learning (Feimen-Nemser, 2012; Ronfeldt, Farmer, McQueen, & Grissom, 2015). Other benefits to structuring time and mindsets toward collaboration include increased teacher retention rates which can result in higher levels of student achievement (Goddard, Goddard, & Tschannen-Moran, 2007; Ronfeldt, Loeb, & Wyckoff, 2013). Finally, when K-12 school-university partnerships center on such professional collaboration, teacher candidates begin their careers seeing collaboration as a natural part of their teaching and become enculturated into collaborative professional learning as commonplace in schools (Hammerness, 2003; Lewis, Perry, & Hurd, 2004; Louis & Marks, 1998; Rigelman & Ruben, 2012).

The purpose of this chapter is to describe two field-based structures that have supported classroom teacher professional development alongside teacher candidate learning. It further delineates processes and structures for lesson study and instructional rounds and their connections to mutually beneficial partnerships; describes how these focused investigations of student thinking and classroom practice led to teacher and teacher candidate learning; and provides practical advice to those interested in replicating this work and/or revisioning approaches for linking coursework and clinical experiences on behalf of K-12 student learning.

BACKGROUND

The authors, as faculty members in a graduate-level teacher preparation program, recognized the need for more practical and structured field-experiences to complement the existing practicum structures. Portland State University's Graduate Teacher Education Program (GTEP) clinical structure is such that teacher candidates spend one year in a classroom with a cooperating mentor teacher while engaged in graduate level education coursework. GTEP coursework begins full time in the summer and then the number of courses decreases as the number of hours in the field placement increases across the academic year. By spring, teacher candidates are in their field placement full time using a combination of a traditional apprenticeship, *learn by observing and doing,* approach (Hansman, 2001) and a co-teaching, *learn through collaborative planning-teaching-debriefing practice,* approach (Bacharach, Heck, & Dahlberg, 2010; Kanold & Larson, 2012).

Through partnerships, GTEP seeks to better align teaching and learning approaches in our preparation program and our K-12 schools. These collaborative efforts attend to problems of practice that are both internal and external to the candidate experience. More specifically, candidates experience dissonance when they: (a) struggle to connect their course-based learning with their learning in clinical settings (internal), and; (b) cannot identify research-based practices being implemented in the placement classroom (external).

GTEP narrows the gap often lamented between theory and practice (Darling-Hammond, & Bransford, 2007; Korthagen & Kessels, 1999; Zeichner, 2009) by embedding field-based assignments and experiences in the university coursework. These assignments and experiences vary from one course to the next yet each involves the opportunity to implement course-based learning with support. Those assignments viewed most positively by the school and cooperating teachers are those that benefit their work in supporting K-12 student learning. Features may include the close examination of student thinking; implementation of instruction that involves modeling of an innovative instructional strategy and/or a communication-feedback loop; and collaboration between teacher candidates, cooperating teachers, and/or university faculty and supervisors. As these various stakeholders engage in this collaborative examination of teaching and learning, all become learners and the benefits of the partnership become more evident.

GTEP prioritizes partnerships with cooperating teachers who have a command of effective instruction and can articulate their instructional practices and routines while providing a rationale for their design and decision making. Employing both an apprenticeship and co-teaching model benefits teacher candidates when they are working with strong mentors but has limitations when research-based practices are not present in the placement classroom. Most beneficial are mentors open and willing to grow and learn from collaboration with the teacher candidates (Glenn, 2006; Killian & Wilkins, 2009).

As a result, these authors attended to the internal and external elements of purposeful course and field-based connections and strong mentor teachers within their mutually beneficial partnerships. Described in the next section are two field-based learning experiences that support teacher candidate learning while encouraging collaboration and "boundary crossing" (Zeichner, 2009) across the school and university.

PURPOSEFUL FIELD-BASED EXAMINATION OF TEACHING AND LEARNING

In this chapter, the authors highlight two field-based experiences—*lesson study* used in mathematics at the elementary level and *instructional rounds* used in English language arts at the secondary level. These projects are at different stages of partnership development with one involving both teachers and teacher candidates and the other involving teacher candidates and school instructional leadership. One project could be characterized as emerging from teacher enthusiasm for work that was happening in other schools in the district and the other from school-leadership team interest. The lesson study structure provides a space for preservice and inservice teacher learning through a cycle that includes collaborative planning, focused observation, and a debrief supported with coaching (Obara, 2010; West & Staub, 2003; Yopp, Burroughs, Luebeck, Heldema, Mitchell, & Sutton, 2011). Unlike traditional lesson study, the focus is on *tuning instructional practice* as opposed to *tuning a lesson* (Rigelman, 2017). Like the modified lesson study, instructional rounds have been an effective tool for increased focus on developing teaching practices (City, Elmore, Fiarman, & Teitel, 2009; Marzano, 2011). Regardless of the field-based structure, the careful set-up, focused observation of student learning, and collaborative debriefing process are critical in supporting teacher candidate's level of reflection and subsequent learning. Shown in Table 1 are the characteristics of the two structures used for examination of teaching and learning.

Teacher preparation programs use lesson study in different ways and have seen benefits to teacher candidates' development. When participating in lesson study teams, teacher candidates and cooperating teachers are more likely to have explicit discussions about content and pedagogy (Gurl, 2011; Kotelawala, 2012; Suh, King, & Weiss, 2014) as well as a more direct focus on the students' learning process (Sims & Walsh, 2009). Even working in lesson study teams in university classrooms and micro-teaching the lesson with other teacher candidates provides a rehearsal of key instructional practices (Ball & Forzani, 2011; McDonald, Kazemi, & Kavanagh, 2013); develops reflective practice skills; and reduces concerns about student teaching (Fernandez, 2010). Lesson study is a way of deepening teacher candidates' understanding and confidence with planning and instruction.

Instructional rounds models have been used as a professional development tool with promising results. Teaching teams visit other classrooms to observe teaching and learning; they follow an observational protocol and discuss what they learn after each observation (City, Elmore, Fiarman, & Teitel, 2009; Grose & Strachan, 2011). Instructional rounds are similar to the medical rounds model in which interns look at cases together under the guidance of a practicing doctor. This model, used by the first author, provides

Table 1. Characteristics of field-based examination of teaching and learning

	Modified Lesson Study	**Instructional Rounds**
Set-Up	Share protocol for the data-driven dialogue, establish the focus on facts and as opposed to inferences during the observation.	Share protocol for roles during the observation.
	Establish guidelines for observers.	Establish guidelines for observers.
Collaborative Planning	Plan routine or full lesson.	Not applicable.
Common Observation	Focus of observation is student mathematical discourse.	Focus of observation varies (e.g., teacher moves, student engagement) and shifts as teacher candidates progress through the program.
Role of Teacher Modeling the Lesson	Teacher makes decisions about how to make the collaboratively planned lesson their own just prior to implementation.	Teacher(s) welcome observers (teacher candidates) into classroom. *Most teachers also participate in the debrief session.*
Debrief	Discuss observations only (non-judgmental, data-based).	Teacher candidates discuss observations only (non-judgmental, data-based).
	Teacher is the first to talk during the debrief, talking-aloud about the lesson and decisions made during lesson implementation.	Teachers explain what candidates observed, providing context.
	Observers inquire into teacher decision-making.	Teacher candidates ask questions of the teacher(s) based on observations.
Reflection	All participants reflect individually about the lesson prior to any discussion of the data.	Teacher candidates reflect with peers in a group format, and individually through writing.
	Analyze student mathematical discourse levels, followed by review of student thinking (which may include written work or other classroom artifacts).	Teacher candidates reflect as a large group after teachers return to classrooms.
	After group and individual reflection, the discussion ends with participants each sharing ways they intend to adjust their teaching as a result of their observations and/or the dialogue.	

for the exchange of ideas within the context of professional practice and allows for a rich exchange of ideas about instructional practices. One of the most promising aspects of instructional rounds is that it brings the privacy of teaching into the open for study. Teachers rarely have the opportunity to leave their classrooms and observe other practitioners; instructional rounds is one way to provide an opportunity for critical observation focused on instruction methods. Teacher preparation programs can utilize the constructs of the instructional rounds model to the benefit of deepened learning for teacher candidates.

The immediate benefits of these field-based experiences are twofold: they support the development of the school-university partnership while also structuring the learning for the teacher candidates. Their purposeful nature leaves less to chance when compared to traditional clinical experiences in which the learning may be highly variable in the quality and nature. In the following two sections the authors describe how the use of lesson study and instructional rounds led to teacher and teacher candidate learning, followed by a section on illustrative findings focused on the examination of similarities and differences in the learning across these two models.

Lesson Study Supporting Learning Across the Professional Continuum

Taking advantage of the fact that elementary placements cluster teacher candidates in groups of four to six, the second author engaged cooperating teachers, teacher candidates, and university supervisors in common professional learning through monthly book studies and quarterly modified lesson studies. This structure is an example of a mutually beneficial partnership, given that: 1) the participants engaged as ongoing learners from their instructional practice; 2) the school welcomed teacher candidates into classrooms and teams that were willing to deprivatize and explore innovations in their instructional practice, and; 3) the building administrator viewed the collaborative work as so powerful for both teacher and teacher candidate learning that invitations and support (i.e., purchase of books, allocation of funds for substitute release time) were extended beyond the teacher candidates and cooperating teachers to the entire second through fourth grade teams to join the collaboration.

Through the lesson studies, teacher candidate/cooperating teacher teams engaged in common learning about mathematics, student thinking, and instructional practice with the added benefit of providing protocols and tools to support the team's ongoing collaborative planning and teaching cycles at both the classroom and PLC level. The quarterly lesson study cycles included four phases: pre-planning, collaborative planning, co-teaching/focused observing, and debriefing based on student data. A second component of the learning was monthly book studies and examination of student work during the PLC meetings. The PLC meetings supported teams with developing a shared vision for mathematics teaching and learning that focuses on eliciting and using student thinking to inform instruction and other examples of high-leverage teaching practices (Ball & Forzani, 2011; Ghousseini, 2009; Kazemi, Franke, & Lampert, 2009; McDonald, Kazemi, & Kavanagh, 2013). This learning aligned with the instructional practices introduced to teacher candidates in their methods course and provided a dedicated time and space to examine and carry out practices such as: implement tasks that promote reasoning and problem solving, facilitate meaningful mathematical discourse, and elicit and use evidence of student thinking (National Council of Teachers of Mathematics, 2014). The lesson and book studies also provided transparency regarding effective practices and established a community learning together, thus supporting cooperating teachers with specific ways to mentor their teacher candidates (Walkington, 2007). Taken together, the regular communication needed for the school-university-based project faculty to plan, facilitate, and debrief the professional learning resulted in deepening the relationships among the project faculty as well as quality and capacity of the partnership for ongoing and between cycle learning.

Lesson study is a "comprehensive and well-articulated process for examining practice" (Fernandez, Cannon, & Chokshi, 2003, p. 171) where teachers collaborate in developing a lesson. After collectively considering how the lesson fits within the learning goals and predicting students' responses based on their experience, current knowledge levels, and/or typical misconceptions, a teacher implements the collaboratively planned lesson. The other teachers in the group observe the lesson, focusing primarily on the students, with the intended purpose of observing and collecting data on student responses to the lesson. Following the lesson, the group meets to discuss and debrief the lesson, and to decide the extent to which the students met the learning goals. Based on this information, the teachers revise the lesson and another teacher teaches the lesson to a different group of students.

As noted above, the lesson study cycle described here is a modification of the traditional lesson study model in a few subtle ways. Once the group determined the focus for the lesson, the teacher candidate/ cooperating teacher team engaged in some initial planning of the lesson. This was not to diminish from gathering the input of others but rather to streamline the one day set aside for the cycle with the whole group. The teacher candidate/cooperating teacher team co-taught the planned lesson as a mechanism for also modeling various ways the teams might work collaboratively during the lesson. With a focus on meaningful mathematical discourse, observing teachers collected student mathematical discourse data along with other classroom artifacts (i.e., student work samples, images of collective representations, video recordings of students sharing their thinking) to support a data-based conversation about student understanding. Because the focus in this modified lesson study was on deepening understanding of student thinking and enhancing mathematical discourse, the debrief focused more on next steps for the students and take-aways for teachers regarding their practice.

This collaborative work, completed with five teacher candidate-cooperating teacher teams and their respective grade level PLCs (n=15) over the course of their yearlong field experience, not only benefited the students, but also the cooperating teachers and their teacher candidates, the members of the PLC, and grant leaders (i.e., district math specialist and faculty leading co-teaching and collaboration initiatives and supervisor professional learning). The classroom-based teams benefited because teachers learned ways to elicit and productively use student thinking in mathematical discussions that deepened student understanding and achievement. Similarly, their colleagues benefited from this careful examination of student thinking and classroom practice as well as broadened their views about ways teachers can collaborate. The district math specialist and building administrator benefited as teachers continued to study the improvement of their instructional practice. The faculty benefited through continued study and improvement of ways to develop mutually beneficial partnerships in schools. They were able to study this model and develop models/protocols that can be shared more broadly with partner schools, supervisors, and cohort leaders/faculty.

Instructional Rounds Supporting Candidate Learning

Instructional rounds models place observational focus on specific pedagogical practices (City, Elmore, Fiarman, & Teitel, 2009; Marzano, 2011). One common use of the rounds model is as a mechanism to study large educational systems, with teams of educators identifying an area on which to focus for improvement (Reagan, Roegman, & Goodwin, 2017). Participants in systemically-focused rounds can include stakeholders from within one system or from across multiple systems. Participants identify an area for improvement and study, make classroom observations, and take descriptive notes related to the area of focus. After visiting several classrooms, the team meets to discuss the observation, consider the evidence found to support a hypothesis, and determine next steps. This systematic approach encourages larger-scale organizational analysis.

A second commonly used instructional rounds structure focuses on practitioner-level examination (Del Prete, 2013; Ellis, Gower, Frederick, & Childs, 2015; Troen & Boles, 2014). Often referred to as *teacher rounds*, the focus of this structure is on individual teacher learning through collective observations and focused conversations. The focus can be on an instructional strategy, an area of improvement identified by the observed teacher, or a variety of other options. Small and varied groups of practicing teachers—in formats such as teaching teams, preservice and in service teachers together, and teachers alongside instructional leadership—observe one or more other teachers. The viewers take notes related to the identified purpose of the observation and include evidence of student learning. After the observations, the instructional rounds team and the observed teacher meet for a discussion.

Instructional rounds are one method that opens classrooms to be used as laboratories for the study of instructional practices and student learning. Whether analyzed at the system level or at the individual practitioner level, considering the interplay between instruction and learning ties the two together with evidence. The visibility of the instructional choices and the student learning provides the foundation for conversation and reflection.

In GTEP, teacher candidates focus on familiarizing themselves with the cooperating teacher and their students at the beginning of their practicum experience. During this initial period, candidates have limited time to observe other classrooms or participate in instruction-focused discussions with classroom teachers. As the school year progresses, teacher candidates take more ownership and responsibility for teaching in their placement classrooms, leaving even fewer opportunities to observe veteran teachers beyond their cooperating teacher. Using instructional rounds with teacher candidates from the beginning of their practicum provided structured observation opportunities focused on specific aspects of instruction. Over the course of six months, twenty-one teacher candidates participated in three days of instructional rounds, each at a different school location. All three schools have partnership agreements with GTEP and host several teacher candidates for their year-long clinical practicum experience. During each visit, teacher candidates followed a modified instructional rounds structure that matched the professional development model already in place at the school site. The participating school employed a "doors-open" policy; students and teachers were familiar with other adults conducting classroom observations. The instructional coach identified several classrooms in order for candidates to observe a variety of strategies and content areas; candidates observed at least four different classrooms during each school visit. Initially, the teacher candidate observations focused on lesson structure, which was appropriate for where candidates were in their professional learning and development (Henning, Erb, Randles, Fults, & Webb, 2016). Candidates analyzed opening routines, observable student engagement and understanding of the presented learning task, and classroom closure routines. After visiting several classrooms, candidates convened to debrief what they had noticed about how classroom teachers and their students interacted during the learning segment. In addition to teacher candidates discussing amongst themselves, the classroom teachers joined the candidates to share their reflections of the observed instructional segment, including background, decision-making, and their overall thoughts on the success of their instructional practices.

The instructional rounds project benefited both the teacher candidates and the participating classroom teachers, with potential positive impact for K-12 students. The teacher candidates benefited by participating in focused observations within a small group and reflecting with a team of more skilled teachers. While collaboration directly benefited both the new and experienced teacher, much of this collaboration is directly tied to the questions asked by novice teachers as they observe teachers teach and the reactions of the learners in the classroom. Teacher candidates have a multitude of questions; being able to interact with a veteran practitioner allows the novice to "see inside the brain" for a better understanding of the countless decisions made by teachers. Similarly, as practicing teachers explain their thinking to the novice teacher, they engage in reflective practice (Cochran-Smith, Barnatt, Friedman, & Pine, 2009). Reflective practice is a key for continuous learning, and continuous learning is important to improve teaching practices, and in turn, student achievement (Vescio, Ross, & Adams, 2007).

NATURE OF THE LEARNING FROM THESE FIELD-BASED MODELS

The examples illustrated in this chapter derive from two different professional development structures and vary based on the maturity and nature of each project as well as the learning needs of the participants. Both focus on routines—one on universal classroom routines and the other on routines to deepen content-specific learning. In this section, the authors contrast the approaches each project used to connect clinical practice with theoretical learning, the role that facilitation played in teacher candidate development, and how candidates used evidence gathered through observation to support context-specific decision-making.

Focus on Routines

Teacher preparation programs are relatively short; therefore, concentration on specific routines for management and instruction maximize the clinical experience for teacher candidates. The instructional rounds project began with a combination of candidate interests and perceived needs coupled with the knowledge of the facilitator on what is developmentally appropriate for teacher candidates. Candidates visited classrooms across multiple content-areas. Lesson study highlighted specific elements of instruction and classroom practice. Candidates focused on teacher instructional practices designed to deepen mathematical thinking and identified discourse as evidence of student learning.

Routines That Support Classroom Systems

City, Elmore, Fiarman, and Teitel (2009) use the term *problem of practice* to focus classroom walk-throughs on instructional issues supported by observable evidence. Educators predetermine the problem of practice to foster consistency in observations. Teacher candidates received support to determine instructional issues to observe since they have relatively little context on which to initiate their own instructional issues. The facilitator asked candidates to focus on specific aspects of the instructional segment during each observation and then focused the reflective conversation on aspects of that segment. By analyzing the classroom instructional period in smaller chunks, candidates began to understand that they could focus on strategies for a particular segment of class time. Initially, teacher candidates observed opening and closing routines that facilitated smooth classroom management. Besides noticing what the teacher was doing, the facilitator asked candidates to find evidence that the students in that classroom understood the routines. A common concern for teacher candidates is how they will "manage" classroom behavior. But even the term "classroom management" is unwieldy, encompassing so many aspects of the teaching segment. By isolating two parts of the instructional period where there are often management issues—the opening and closing of class—teacher candidates were able to identify the structures that supported student learning during those times. One candidate observed students following an opening routine projected onto a screen while the teacher took attendance and appeared to check in with a student who had been absent the day before. As the teacher began her instruction and made reference to the previous day, the student stood and helped themselves to a handout that was in a folder marked "Absent," without interrupting the teacher's instruction. The candidate noted this strategy for creating a smooth opening segment.

Routines That Support Learning About Instructional Practice

Kazemi, Franke, and Lampert (2009) use the term *instructional activity* to describe the nature of the tasks they use to support teacher candidates with developing effective mathematics teaching practices. These activities, when enacted in classrooms "structure the relationship between the teacher and the students around content in ways that consistently maintain high expectations of student learning" (p. 12). Similarly, the focus for the lesson study cycles was on instances of students sharing their mathematical thinking such as when debriefing their work on a cognitively demanding task or communicating their strategies on a computational task. The attention to this instructional routine provided opportunities for repeated, focused implementation and improvement for both the student and teacher as this can occur regularly in the classroom. Teachers and teacher candidates could then focus on the various structures that support such task implementation (i.e., task selection, launch strategies, questioning). In reflection, several candidates discussed the need to "take time and think through potential student thinking and representations before the lesson to make sure it will be effective and to be more responsive." Others described the need to support students with developing skills for "slowing down and making sense of a problem before you start work" and "convincing one another that they have found the correct answer" and helping them "act as skeptics, questioning the moves made by those explaining their thinking." Others requested the need to better understand the discourse levels and ways "to scaffold discourse for students to more effectively share ideas" and "move beyond explanations toward generalizations." These comments speak to what candidates attended to, what they realized they needed to learn, and what they want for their students' learning as they engage in the activity of "sharing."

Translating Across Theory and Practice

One challenge with clinical practice is connecting the theories presented in teacher education coursework with the practical clinical experiences (Darling-Hammond, 2009; Zeichner, 2009). The instructional rounds and lesson study projects each attempted to mitigate the potential disconnect between theory and practice but used different approaches, with one using clinical-to-theoretical connections and the other using theoretical-to-clinical. The instructional rounds project began with the clinical observations. Links were made back to theoretical principles during the debriefing process about the observed classroom practices. In contrast, the modified lesson study began with professional learning on mathematical practices that fostered mathematical discourse to deepen student learning. Teacher candidate/cooperating teacher teams designed instruction based on the theoretical learning of mathematical practices then observed and reflected on the results.

Connecting Practice and Theory

Structured instructional rounds support the identification of theoretical learning in classroom action. For example, candidates learn about growth mindset in their coursework (Dweck, 2006). Candidates observed a music teacher ask students to reflectively listen to themselves play a song segment. The teacher knew students were struggling with the fingering in some sections. Students identified a part that did not yet sound correct and then worked within their instrument sections to help each other with proper fingering. Students could hear improvements when they played it again, and candidates were able to see growth mindset in action. In another example of growth mindset in action, candidates observed a math classroom where students self-identified as either "experts" or "almost there" in their understanding of the homework assignment. The students who identified as experts went into the hallway to check their work against a teacher answer-key. Meanwhile, the teacher had the "almost there" students get into small groups who would each work with one of the experts when they returned to class. Candidates noticed two important elements in this example: Students were not afraid to identify with either label, knowing that the labels were flexible: on other assignment each student could be an "expert" or "almost there". In addition, one student who originally identified as an "expert" realized that she had misconceptions as she corrected her work. Not only did the student come to this realization herself, but with the established growth mindset climate in the classroom, she simply recategorized herself as "almost there" in her learning.

One important way the facilitator can connect theoretical learning with clinical experiences is to name the practices that students observe. After one observation, a candidate described the activity the class was doing to begin class.

The facilitator asked, "What do you think the teacher in that situation is trying to accomplish?"

The teacher candidate replied, "Checking in?"

"Yes," the facilitator responded, "Formative assessment right off the bat. So, she [the teacher] knew what they were doing right away."

With the reflective guidance of the facilitator, the candidate linked a concrete example of formative assessment to their theoretical coursework. Another candidate asked about an organizational strategy that he observed students using in one classroom. The candidate complimented the organizational scaffold provided to the students. The facilitator responded, "Yes, interactive notebooks are something that was are seeing more and more teachers using. Traditionally you think of interactive notebooks for science and math, but we are seeing them in English language arts and electives as a strategy for organizing work." The facilitator provided the candidate with a name for the strategy he had noticed and explained the purpose.

Connecting Theory and Practice

A second way that a facilitator purposefully brought course and field work together is through the use of research-based tools to focus the observation of student thinking and/or teacher moves that influence that thinking. In the lesson study, since the focus was on student mathematical discourse, we used the Student Discourse Observation Tool (Weaver, Dick, Higgins, Marrongelle, Foreman, & Rigelman, 2005, 2005) to frame the data collection and analysis when observing and debriefing the lesson. This tool prompted observers to collect only student-based data which included what they said and/or what they drew or modeled to convey their thinking. The debrief focused on both making sense of the students' thinking and categorizing their discourse along a continuum from *procedures and facts*, to *justifica-*

tion, and finally to *generalization*. Typical responses from participating teachers and teacher candidates included "I want to strive to get to more generalizations within my mathematical practice" and "Our students do a great job of explaining their processes and justifying, but how do I get them to generalize?" The later question served to shift toward further analysis of student thinking to determine what else would be needed for *generalization* or what teacher moves such as questions may prompt higher level thinking and discourse. Additional tools such as the *Task Analysis Guide* (Stein & Smith, 1998) and various questioning frameworks (Boaler & Brodie, 2004; Chapin, O'Connor, & Anderson, 2009) supported teachers in answering "How do I question for the generalization category?"

Context-Specific Decision-Making

Instructional decision-making is context specific; not only do teachers bring their own values and personalities into the classroom, they also make decisions based on the various needs, interests, and personalities of their students. The structure of the lesson study was such that candidates and teachers engaged in all parts of the process: planning, observing, and debriefing. Whereas, the structure of the instructional rounds was such that candidates engaged in observing and both candidates and teachers participated in debriefing. This difference meant candidates engaged with different aspects of the decision-making process. Providing teacher candidates with opportunities to understand how more experienced teachers use evidence of student learning and success to make professional judgements is an important part of their developmental process and supports the recognition that there is no one "right way to teach."

Not Just One Approach

Teachers make hundreds of decisions each day. Some teacher candidates want to know the "answer" to how to manage a class and plan curriculum and meet the needs of all of their students—and can feel dissatisfied to learn that a teacher's decisions are both complex and context-dependent. Listening to successful teachers talk through their decision-making processes illuminated for candidates that each individual teacher had their own approach. For example, one candidate asked, "When you have a student who is particularly chatty, what do you do?" Instead of giving a simple answer, the teacher replied, "It depends on the student. Why are they chatty? What they are chatting about? And, what is the classroom environment like today?" Instead of having a single response, the teacher demonstrated the need to consider context in decision-making. Additionally, candidates were able to hear teachers describe different approaches, reinforcing the idea that there is no one single approach for a successful classroom. One teacher candidate asked two teachers how they established classroom norms. The first teacher explained how she had her students use a brainstorming process to determine the classroom rules. The second teacher laughed and said, "I just give them my expectations, and tell them that they need to meet them. Neither way is better than the other—it has to do with your personality and your style." The candidates had observed both classrooms running smoothly, and through the subsequent conversation, candidates learned that each teacher had taken their own approach to reach a similar outcome.

In another observation, candidates looked for evidence to connect classroom environment with student engagement. Candidates noticed lighting (i.e., dim for silent reading, projector-only for focusing student attention on the board), seating arrangement choices (e.g., a U-shape for classroom discussion, desks pushed together for a group project), and a variety of seating options (i.e., low-to-the-ground tables on carpet, standing desks, wobble chairs). As the facilitator said:

different kinds of seating are becoming more popular here. Teachers who are not doing it have reasons. Some fear the lack of control. But teachers who use the alternative seating believe it increases engagement. We have a lot of students who need to move, so providing seating options without disrupting the flow of class can be very effective.

Teacher candidates voiced some surprise about the amount of choices—and decisions—teachers made to influence the classroom environment.

Decisions Based on Student Thinking

A component of the debriefing protocol in the lesson study included explicitly discussing student understanding and struggles based on evidence. This evidence may be drawn from the discourse data and/ or from students' written or documented work. The team considered where the student thinking may lead as well as how they might provide feedback to move the student thinking forward. The team used the Analyzing Trends in Student Thinking process (Burns, 2005) to support systematic consideration of next potential steps to take based on student thinking. This process began with an analysis of strategies as well as the nature of the thinking behind the strategy. Such a review supported planning for future lessons as well as provided focus for intervention with different students or groups of students. Teachers commented that "Analyzing student work was very valuable. I appreciate the opportunity to see multiple work samples" with teacher candidates specifically noting "This process could really help us with analyzing student work for the edTPA."

There can be advantages to using an observation protocol based on teacher-candidate identified interests and needs. Teacher candidates have immediate areas for concern as they take on more teaching responsibilities. Making observations that focus on how more experienced teachers tackle those areas for concern can facilitate learning that is relevant in-the-moment for the teacher candidates. However, novice teachers need guidance to design meaningful observations that connect theory, instructional practices, and evidence of student learning. Without a more structured observation protocol, observations can be less focused, and in turn, less useful. One of the foremost advantages of using a structured observation protocol is that the instructor can direct observations toward the specific instructional practices that connect with their goals, ensuring that instructional practice and educational theory are clearly linked for all participants. In addition, the collective analysis of instructional practices contributes to deeper learning for participants.

LEARNING ACROSS THE PROFESSIONAL CONTINUUM

As noted, these two field-based experiences are at various stages of development, with the lesson study approach described here having been used in teacher professional development and collaborative teacher candidate/cooperating teacher professional learning previously. As a result, this field-based learning opportunity had a number of protocols and tools that structured the collaborative learning. Because this collaboration positioned all participants as learners, our findings include insights into the learning that took place across the professional continuum from preservice teacher, to novice teacher, to expert teacher/teacher leader and to university faculty.

The cooperating teachers participating in the lesson study shared their enthusiasm for growth in their mathematics teaching practice. They commented "I will use strategies from today to increase engagement and deepen the quality of student discourse" and "I want to incorporate more partner sharing and more purposeful questioning skills targeted to the purpose of lesson." They noted appreciation for all parts of the lesson study day and in particular the discussion that followed the lesson observation.

The cooperating teachers also identified powerful aspects of the collaboration in general. Stating "This was useful, applicable and fostered connections between staff members, strengthening our PLC" and "I appreciate having the time to learn from colleagues in a safe environment and to see others in action. This was a very valuable experience." They noted that the learning was both meaningful and immediately applicable. One cooperating teacher also remarked on benefits to her co-teaching practice, "I appreciate how the lesson study includes co-teaching, helping me find better ways of collaborating with my teacher candidate."

Similarly, teacher candidates also reflected on growth in their view of what constitutes effective mathematics teaching. In particular, as seen in the following quotes, the candidates discussed the power of the Number Talks in drawing about students' mathematical thinking and reasoning as well as potentially an aspect they see as most transferable to their future classroom setting.

- "I am excited to continue to use Number Talks to encourage student discourse and improve mental math strategies."
- "Thinking about next year, I want to let the administrator know the benefits of the Number Talks and make sure that there is support for them in the building."

One teacher candidate stated "I feel like a teacher in this PLC; I know it will benefit me next year." This example connects to the fact that all participants were co-learners, from the cooperating teachers and their candidates in classrooms to the administrators and project leaders.

As with any professional learning, there were also challenges. Cooperating teachers identified challenges related to time—both instructional and planning—with others commenting on what it means to integrate their learning into their classroom practice. One stated, "I enjoy going more deeply with a few problems, I want to make sure I am covering enough content for my students, too." Another spoke of the challenge navigating fit with the district's curriculum:

I am trying to figure out how to follow the lesson plans and unit outlines of our curriculum but also incorporate the CGI ideas. I know that I want to emphasize fewer problems and deeper thinking, it is just taking me some time to figure out what that looks like on a daily basis. I would like to address through discussion and modeling how we use the curriculum we have and modify it to match best practices and the philosophy behind CGI.

The challenges identified by teacher candidates changed over time with comments early in the year related to their own opportunities to implement: "Just not a lot of time in the day to do it." and "I just haven't had the opportunities to really try to implement what I've learned. I think I will have many opportunities in the near future." Later in the year their comments shifted toward concerns that were similar to those of the cooperating teachers regarding implementation—asking the right questions at the right time and deepening student discourse. One candidate specifically commented on the need to make sure that plans for such discourse are incorporated into the lesson plans. Another teacher candidate remarked on the value of debrief and how those were lacking in their day-to-day collaboration.

The lesson study participants developed deeper understanding of purposefully structured student-led learning. They also developed their skills both with implementing such practice and reflecting upon the effect of that practice on student learning. The focus of the final lesson study lesson had an across-the-grades student misconception in mind. It attended to students' decomposition strategies when computing, yet built upon this strength to consider ways that this approach can be useful across subtraction problems. When reflecting on this process, teams commented on the value of the vertical conversations, the realization that it was not just one person's problem to fix, and the power of collaboratively taking risks and inquiring into their mathematics teaching practice. Sadly, based on changes in district-level leadership, the potential cooperating teacher leaders who could continue such collaboration in their grade level teams and with teacher candidates may have limited opportunities as they move away from the use of clustered placements.

In contrast to the lesson study model, the modified instructional rounds structure positioned classroom teachers as *expert* and teacher candidates as *learners*. The observation and questioning protocol placed an emphasis on inquiry, with teacher candidates' analysis connecting the new information to what was already individually known. While teacher candidates gained the most from the learning, the more experienced teachers who attended the debrief sessions together also engaged in reflective conversations about instructional practices. For example, one candidate asked a veteran teacher about an off-task group of students. The teacher acknowledged that the group was not working well when the observers were in the classroom. She encouraged the students to change course a number of times, but decided ultimately to let them fail with the assignment. She planned to meet with the group afterwards to see what the group could learn from the experience to be more successful with future group work. Another participating teacher disagreed with the practice of letting students fail. As a result, the two teachers had a hearty discussion about the pros and cons of the teacher's decision, to the benefit of the teacher candidates. Candidates questioned the classroom teachers in order to understand the decision-making process used by the more experienced practitioners. Interestingly, more than one classroom teacher lamented that the observed lesson needed improvements while teacher candidates thought the same lesson was successful. Teachers articulated their moves and the reasons for making those choices, while at the same time reflected on future changes. When more than one classroom teacher was present, they discussed strategies together.

IMPLICATIONS FOR FIELD-BASED EXPERIENCES AND PARTNERSHIPS

Field-based experiences like lesson study and instructional rounds facilitate more focused mentoring for the teacher candidate influenced by their common learning experience. They focused observations toward the varied influences on student engagement and learning as well as fostered reflective practice. They supported teacher candidates with identifying "problems of practice" and taking an active stance to study instructional practice as a means of improvement. These examples of field-based experiences illustrate how partnerships can be developed so that they are mutually beneficial to both the school and university--building on collaborative structures that improve teaching practice, supporting learning across the partnership, and invigorating teaching as a profession. The approaches also have the potential to improve teacher education as they better utilize and respect knowledge and expertise across the partnership than traditional models with separate course- and field-based learning.

These data reveal that while the collaborative partnership is highly valued, finding time for collaboration among cooperating teachers, teacher candidates, university supervisors and faculty is a challenge. Potential solutions lie in developing school-based capacity to continue this professional learning when university faculty and partners are not present. For example, the partnership can leverage collaboration time for the cooperating teacher and teacher candidate (e.g., planning, debriefing, analyzing student-based data) through the professional development structure itself. They can structure the teaching and meeting schedule to support collaboration. Finally, they can develop and use teacher leaders as facilitators of professional learning—recognizing their critical role in teacher education as they mentor and collaborate with teacher candidates.

FUTURE RESEARCH DIRECTIONS AND EMERGING TRENDS

Highlighted in this chapter are two field-based teacher education approaches that support the development of mutually beneficial partnerships. The authors provide examples of partnerships at various development stages but with shared commitment to innovative and reflective practice by all participants. High quality partnerships require ongoing dedication of the school and the university, both to maintain and be responsive to each partners' needs. The authors consider the evolving nature of partnerships and the need to develop school-based capacity to systematically support teacher education through purposeful field-based experiences. This may mean that some years are more high touch than others (e.g., when the partnership is new, where there are new initiatives for one partner or the other, when there is a need to develop leadership) while in the low touch years, faculty would be freed to build parallel experiences at other schools, in other subject areas, etc., with the hopes of taking the work to scale across the program. A critical finding is that there is a necessary investment of time if the partnership is to be truly mutually beneficial.

It is interesting to compare the structures of the two approaches. Both provided opportunity for candidate learning in ways that connected university learning with the clinical experience. However, the authors are left wondering how each approach could inform the other. The lesson study was highly structured leaving less room for participants to select an observational focus aligned to their professional learning needs. On the other hand, the instructional rounds project purposefully used observation questions that were personally relevant to individual teacher candidates, beginning with the field experience and linking back to the university instruction. Although the loose structure was intentional, could teacher candidate learning benefit from a more focused approach, as found in lesson study? One strength identified in lesson study was candidate teaching a specific aspect of mathematical thinking; candidates built their plans specifically around opportunities for their students to repeatedly practice and demonstrate understanding. A next step in future instructional rounds could be to provide candidates with the opportunity to observe specific content-area instruction and find evidence in student responses. In addition, candidates used collaborative planning during lesson study. Instructional rounds could be modified to provide candidates to talk with classroom teachers during the planning phase prior to the observation. This pre-lesson analysis would provide a different lens on instruction than that provided through the debrief sessions of the previous instructional rounds.

Because these examples of field-based teacher education connect to many aspects of teacher learning and instruction, future research could focus on ways that these approaches professionalize teaching, improve collaboration, and/or develop teacher leaders. Of interest may be an ongoing case study of a partner school to examine the evolution of a partnership across high and low touch years. Another possibility could be a follow-up study with teacher candidates to examine ways they take ownership of their own professional learning as early data reveal their capacity to identify "problems of practice" to study for improvement as well as their interest in exerting influence on their own professional learning (i.e., use of number talks in their school setting, learning together, observing one another's implementation).

CONCLUSION

Lesson study and instructional rounds both originated as professional development structures for inservice teachers. Each learning opportunity allowed practicing teachers to collectively focus on pedagogical approaches that improve instruction and support increased student learning through a shared community of practice (Lave & Wenger, 1991). Groups of practitioners determined an issue of importance and looked for evidence to inform their thinking on the issue through concentrated observations. The context-dependent, communal nature of the exploration enhanced the learning. Clinical practice for developing teachers can borrow from the body of research on professional development to create experiences that more closely align theoretical learning with practical classroom experiences. Modified versions of lesson study and instructional rounds structures can benefit teacher candidates during their clinical field experience, especially with the added support of partnerships between K-12 schools and the university personnel. By adopting professional development structures during the clinical experience, teacher educators have an opportunity to develop stronger field placement relationships, and in turn, can support the development of stronger cooperating teachers.

The ultimate goal of creating mutually beneficial partnerships, of course, is to benefit K-12 student learning. Student learning happens in a multitude of ways, but specifically designed teacher professional learning can amplify learning in ways that support growth of all participants. Lesson study was impactful because both cooperating teachers and teacher candidates engaged authentically in the learning process that focused on deepening students' thinking and discourse. The university facilitator focused the topic in a way that all participants were learners, even the experienced teachers - whether learning about deepened mathematics instruction or implementation of co-teaching approaches. As a result, participants all gained from the professional learning in ways that would not have happened independent of the lesson study process. Both mutually beneficial approaches to clinical practice promote new teachers' enculturation into the community of learning; all stakeholders benefit by having teachers who are more prepared to enter the profession using a reflective lens for continuous improvement of their work. The intentional boundary-crossing between the school-university partners allowed the team to leverage learning in a deepened and purposeful way. Tensions still exist, including the persistent question of how to structure learning opportunities so all stakeholders are truly learners, including the expert teacher and university faculty. Our lessons learned reveal that lesson study has made strides in this arena by engaging collaborative examination of both teaching and learning. Instructional rounds, as described in this chapter, are making headway in this direction, as well. The desired outcome with both is the transfer of professional learning into instructional practice to the benefit of K-12 students, which is the true benefit of the partnership.

ACKNOWLEDGMENT

This work was supported by the *Mutually Beneficial Partnership Grant* funding offered through Portland State University's Foundation. This funding is designed to support partnership innovations to improve the clinical experience while also informing programmatic change.

REFERENCES

Bacharach, N., Heck, T. W., & Dahlberg, K. (2010). Changing the face of student teaching through coteaching. *Action in Teacher Education*, *32*(1), 3–14. doi:10.1080/01626620.2010.10463538

Ball, D. L., & Cohen, D. K. (1999). Developing practice, developing practitioners: Toward a practice-based theory of professional education. In G. Sykes & L. Darling-Hammond (Eds.), *Teaching as the learning profession: Handbook of policy and practice* (pp. 3–32). San Francisco: Jossey Bass.

Ball, D. L., & Forzani, F. M. (2011). Building a common core for learning to teach: And connecting professional learning to practice. *American Educator*, *35*(2), 17.

Boaler, J., & Brodie, K. (2004, October). The importance, nature and impact of teacher questions. *Proceedings of the twenty-sixth annual meeting of the North American Chapter of the International Group for the Psychology of Mathematics Education*, 2, 774-782.

Burns, M. (2005). Looking at how students reason. *Educational Leadership*, *63*(3).

Chapin, S. H., O'Connor, M. C., & Anderson, N. C. (2009). *Classroom discussions: Using math talk to help students learn* (2nd ed.). Sausalito, CA: Math Solutions Publications.

City, E. A., Elmore, R. F., Fiarman, S. E., & Teitel, L. (2009). *Instructional rounds in education: A network approach to improving teaching and learning.* Cambridge, MA: Harvard Education Press.

Cochran-Smith, M., Barnatt, J., Friedman, A., & Pine, G. (2009). Inquiry on inquiry: Practitioner research and student learning. *Action in Teacher Education*, *31*(2), 17–32. doi:10.1080/01626620.2009.10463515

Darling-Hammond, D. (2009, February). *Teacher education and the American future.* Charles W. Hunt Lecture Presented at the annual meeting of the American Association of Colleges for Teacher Education, Chicago, IL.

Darling-Hammond, L. (2015). Want to close the achievement gap? Close the teaching gap. *American Educator*, *38*(4), 14–18.

Darling-Hammond, L., & Bransford, J. (2007). *Preparing teachers for a changing world: What teachers should learn and be able to do.* Hoboken, NJ: John Wiley & Sons.

Del Prete, T. (2013). *Teacher rounds: A guide to collaborative learning in and from practice.* Thousand Oaks, CA: Corwin Press. doi:10.4135/9781452268200

Dweck, C. S. (2006). *Mindset: The new psychology of success.* New York, NY: Ballantine Books.

Ellis, V., Gower, C., Frederick, K., & Childs, A. (2015). Formative interventions and practice-development: A methodological perspective on teacher rounds. *International Journal of Educational Research, 73*, 44–52. doi:10.1016/j.ijer.2015.06.002

Feimen-Nemser, S. (2012). Beyond solo teaching. *Educational Leadership, 69*(8), 10–16.

Fernandez, C., Cannon, J., & Chokshi, S. (2003). A U.S.-Japan lesson study collaboration reveals critical lenses for examining practice. *Teaching and Teacher Education, 19*(2), 171–185. doi:10.1016/S0742-051X(02)00102-6

Fernandez, M. L. (2010). Investigating how and what prospective teachers learn through microteaching Lesson Study. *Teaching and Teacher Education, 26*(2), 351–362. doi:10.1016/j.tate.2009.09.012

Ghousseini, H. (2009). Designing opportunities to learn to lead classroom mathematical discussions in pre-service teacher education: Focusing on enactment. In D. Mewborn & H. S. Lee (Eds.), Association of mathematics teacher educators monograph vi: Scholarly practices and inquiry in the preparation of mathematics teachers (pp. 137-152). San Diego, CA: Association of Mathematics Teacher Educators.

Glenn, W. J. (2006). Model versus mentor: Defining the necessary qualities of the effective cooperating teacher. *Teacher Education Quarterly, 33*(1), 85–95.

Goddard, Y. L., Goddard, R. D., & Tschannen-Moran, M. (2007). A theoretical and empirical investigation of teacher collaboration for school improvement and student achievement in public elementary schools. *Teachers College Record, 109*(4), 877–896.

Grose, K., & Strachan, J. (2011). In demonstration classrooms, it's show-and-tell every day. *Journal of Staff Development, 32*(5), 24–29.

Gurl, T. (2011). A model for incorporating lesson study into the student teaching placement: What worked and what did not? *Educational Studies, 37*(5), 523–528. doi:10.1080/03055698.2010.539777

Hammerness, K. (2003). Learning to hope, or hoping to learn? The role of vision in the early professional lives of teachers. *Journal of Teacher Education, 54*(1), 43–56. doi:10.1177/0022487102238657

Hansman, C. A. (2001). Context-based adult learning. In S. B. Merriam (Ed.), *New directions in adult and continuing education* (pp. 43–51). San Francisco, CA: Jossey-Bass.

Henning, J. E., Erb, D. J., Randles, H. S., Fults, N., & Webb, K. (2016). Designing a curriculum for clinical experiences. *Issues in Teacher Education, 25*(1), 23–38.

Kanold, T., & Larson, M. (2012). *Common Core Mathematics in a PLC at work™: Leader's guide.* Bloomington, IN: Solution Tree Press.

Kazemi, E., Franke, M., & Lampert, M. (2009). Developing pedagogies in teacher education to support teachers' ability to enact ambitious instruction. In R. Hunter, B. Bicknell & T. Burgess (Eds.), *Crossing divides: Proceedings of the 32nd annual conference of the Math Education Research Group of Australasia.* Palmerston North, NZ: MERGA.

Kelchtermans, G. (2006). Teacher collaboration and collegiality as workplace conditions. A review. *Zeitschrift fur Padagogik, 52*(2), 220.

Killian, J. E., & Wilkins, E. A. (2009). Characteristics of highly effective cooperating teachers: A study of their backgrounds and preparation. *Action in Teacher Education, 30*(4), 67–83. doi:10.1080/016266 20.2009.10734453

Korthagen, F., & Kessels, J. (1999). Linking theory and practice: Changing the pedagogy of teacher education. *Educational Researcher, 28*(3), 4–17. doi:10.3102/0013189X028004004

Kotelawala, U. (2012). Lesson study in a methods course: Connecting teacher education to the field. *Teacher Educator, 47*(1), 67–89. doi:10.1080/08878730.2012.633840

Lave, J., & Wenger, E. (1991). *Situated learning: Legitimate peripheral participation*. Cambridge, UK: Cambridge University Press. doi:10.1017/CBO9780511815355

Lewis, C., Perry, R., & Hurd, J. (2004). A deeper look at lesson study. *Educational Leadership, 61*(5), 18–22.

Little, J. W. (2003). Inside teacher community: Representations of classroom practice. *Teachers College Record, 105*(6), 913–945. doi:10.1111/1467-9620.00273

Lortie, D. (1975). *Schoolteacher: A sociological analysis*. Chicago, IL: University of Chicago Press.

Louis, K. S., & Marks, H. (1998). Does professional community affect the classroom? Teachers' work and student experiences in restructuring schools. *American Journal of Education, 106*(8), 532–575. doi:10.1086/444197

Marzano, R. J. (2011). Making the most of instructional rounds. *Educational Leadership, 68*(5), 80–81.

McDonald, M., Kazemi, E., & Kavanagh, S. S. (2013). Core practices and pedagogies of teacher education: A call for a common language and collective activity. *Journal of Teacher Education, 64*(5), 378–386. doi:10.1177/0022487113493807

National Council of Teachers of Mathematics. (2014). *Principles to actions: Ensuring mathematical success for all*. Reston, VA: Author.

Obara, S. (2010). Mathematics coaching: A new kind of professional development. *Teacher Development, 14*(2), 241–251. doi:10.1080/13664530.2010.494504

Reagan, E. M., Roegman, R., & Goodwin, A. L. (2017). Inquiry in the round? Education rounds in a teacher residency program. *Action in Teacher Education, 39*(3), 239–254. doi:10.1080/01626620.201 7.1317299

Rigelman, N. M. (2017). Learning in and from practice with others. In L. West & M. Boston (Eds.), *Annual perspectives in mathematics education: Reflective and collaborative processes to improve mathematics teaching* (pp. 65–76). Reston, VA: National Council of Teachers of Mathematics.

Rigelman, N. M., & Ruben, B. (2012). Creating foundations for collaboration in schools: Utilizing professional learning communities to support teacher candidate learning and visions of teaching. *Teaching and Teacher Education, 28*(7), 979–989. doi:10.1016/j.tate.2012.05.004

Ronfeldt, M., Farmer, S., McQueen, K., & Grissom, J. (2015). Teacher collaboration in instructional teams and student achievement. *American Educational Research Journal, 3*(52), 475–514. doi:10.3102/0002831215585562

Ronfeldt, M., Loeb, S., & Wyckoff, J. (2013). How teacher turnover harms student achievement. *American Educational Research Journal, 1*(50), 4–36. doi:10.3102/0002831212463813

Sims, L., & Walsh, D. (2009). Lesson study with pre-service teachers: Lessons from lessons. *Teaching and Teacher Education, 25*(5), 724–733. doi:10.1016/j.tate.2008.10.005

Smith, M. S. (2001). *Practice-based professional development for teachers of mathematics.* Reston, VA: National Council of Teachers of Mathematics.

Stein, M. K., & Smith, M. S. (1998). Mathematical tasks as a framework for reflection: From research to practice. *Mathematics Teaching in the Middle School, 3*(4), 268–275.

Suh, J. M., King, L. A., & Weiss, A. (2014). Co-development of professional practice at a professional development school through instructional rounds and lesson study. In D. Polly, T. Heafner, M. Chapman, & M. Spooner (Eds.), *Professional Development Schools and Transformative Partnerships* (pp. 176–182). Hershey, PA: IGI Global.

Troen, V., & Boles, K. C. (2014). Rounds process puts teachers in charge of learning. *Journal of Staff Development, 35*(2), 20–28.

Vescio, V., Ross, D., & Adams, A. (2007). A review of research on the impact of professional learning communities on teaching practice and student learning. *Teaching and Teacher Education, 24*(1), 80–91. doi:10.1016/j.tate.2007.01.004

Walkington, J. (2007). Improving partnerships between schools and universities: Professional learning with benefits beyond preservice teacher education. *Teacher Development, 11*(3), 277–294. doi:10.1080/13664530701644581

Weaver, D., Dick, T., Higgins, K., Marrongelle, K., Foreman, L., & Rigelman, N. M. (2005). *OMLI classroom observation protocol.* Portland, OR: RMC Research Corporation. Available at http://goo.gl/doQJ2p

West, L., & Staub, F. C. (2003). *Content-focused coaching: Transforming mathematics lessons.* Portsmouth, NH: Heinemann.

Yopp, D., Burroughs, E., Luebeck, J., Heldema, C., Mitchell, A., & Sutton, J. (2011). How to be a Wise Consumer of Coaching. *Journal of Staff Development, 32*(1), 50–53.

Zeichner, K. (2009). Rethinking the connections between campus courses and field experiences in college- and university-based teacher education. *Journal of Teacher Education, 61*(1-2), 89–99. doi:10.1177/0022487109347671

ADDITIONAL READING

Ball, D. L., & Cohen, D. K. (1999). Developing practice, developing practitioners: Toward a practice-based theory of professional education. In G. Sykes & L. Darling-Hammond (Eds.), *Teaching as the learning profession: Handbook of policy and practice* (pp. 3–32). San Francisco: Jossey Bass.

Del Prete, T. (2013). *Teacher rounds: A guide to collaborative learning in and from practice.* Thousand Oaks, CA: Corwin Press. doi:10.4135/9781452268200

Hurd, J., & Lewis, C. (2011). *Lesson study step-by-step: How teacher learning communities improve instruction.* Portsmouth, NH: Heinemann.

Loucks-Horsley, S., Stiles, K. E., Mundry, S., & Hewson, P. W. (Eds.). (2009). *Designing professional development for teachers of science and mathematics.* Corwin Press.

Rigelman, N. M. (under consideration). Eliciting mathematical discourse, supporting teacher learning.

Rigelman, N. M., Shrier, D., Crane, S., & Petrick, K. (in press). Synergizing mathematics teaching and learning. *The Learning Professional.*

Smith, M. S. (2001). *Practice-based professional development for teachers of mathematics.* Reston, VA: National Council of Teachers of Mathematics.

Stepanek, J., Appel, G., Leong, M., Mangan, M. T., & Mitchell, M. (2007). *Leading lesson study. A practical guide for teachers and educators.* Thousand Oaks, CA: Corwin.

Troen, V., & Boles, K. C. (2014). Rounds process puts teachers in charge of learning. *Journal of Staff Development, 35*(2), 20–28.

Chapter 9
Increasing Teacher Efficacy Through Rural Partnerships

Ann Schulte
California State University – Chico, USA

Rebecca Justeson
California State University – Chico, USA

ABSTRACT

The rural teacher residency (RTR) program at California State University – Chico was a program funded by a Teacher Quality Partnership (TQP) grant from 2010-2015. The RTR program prepared teachers through partnerships with four school districts in the rural region of northern California. This residency program was designed to provide targeted training and experience in co-teaching, action research, professional learning communities, and collaboration. In addition, RTR faculty hoped to impact the retention of teachers for hard-to-staff schools such as those with underserved students and/or in rural settings. The purpose of the chapter is to briefly overview the design features of the RTR program and to describe the qualitative data analysis of an evaluation of the program (i.e., focus groups, survey, observations/interviews) at the conclusion of the grant funding cycle.

INTRODUCTION

Teacher shortages are occurring throughout the United States, and these shortages may be especially felt in the rural areas of the country (Fong, Makkonen, & Jaquet, 2016). Many teacher preparation programs have concentrated on ways to address these impending teacher shortages, and some of these programs have focused on the importance of preparing teachers specifically for rural schools (e.g. Azano & Stewart, 2014). There are a plethora of teacher education programs to prepare urban teachers, but very few that address the needs of rural contexts specifically (Schafft, 2016).

In 2009 a group of faculty at California State University, Chico set out to create an innovative teacher education pathway built upon strong relationships and partnership with the schools in the rural region. The institution received a Teacher Quality Partnership (TQP) grant for 7.3 million dollars, funded by the federal Department of Education. The purpose of the grant was to improve student achievement by improving the quality of new teachers.

DOI: 10.4018/978-1-5225-6249-8.ch009

The program supports partnerships among universities, high-need school districts, and high-need schools to implement reforms in teacher preparation programs, especially those using a teacher residency program model. (Tuss & Wang, 2016, p. 1)

The funding for the RTR program lasted five years and produced 88 certified teachers in elementary or special education. School district partners included Cascade Union Elementary School District, Marysville Joint Unified School District, Orland Unified School District, and Palermo Union School District. The TQP grant also required business and community partners, which were established at the time of the grant application, but few of these partnerships emerged as strong connections throughout the course of the program.

California State University, Chico serves 12 counties in a 33,000 square mile region that is largely agricultural and mountainous. The School of Education typically partners with more than 50 school districts and annually prepares hundreds of teachers in the areas of elementary, secondary, special education, and bilingual education. The TQP grant enabled the School of Education to develop and implement an innovative new program of professional preparation for prospective teachers. The RTR program sought to establish partnerships with rural districts with hopes for more successful recruitment and retention of teachers in those districts and the surrounding areas. This grant project was comprised of two programs:

(1) a pre-baccalaureate blended program leading to a bachelor's degree in liberal studies with a minor in education and an elementary or special education credential, and; (2) the Rural Teacher Residency (RTR), an 18-month master's in education/elementary or special education credential program with a yearlong, full-time teaching residency. (Tuss & Wang, 2016, p. 1)

Together, the two programs were designed to provide highly qualified general and special education teachers for high-need schools. This chapter focuses specifically on the second program, a highly intensive blended credential and master's degree program, both because of the strong focus on partnership with regional school districts and because of the use of innovative methods for preparing teachers in the rural region.

In the twelve counties served by California State University, Chico, 32%, on average, of practicing teachers are predicted to retire between 2014 and 2024 (Fong, Makkonen, & Jaquet, 2016, p. A-2-A-3). Because the research (e.g. Reininger, 2012) suggests that teacher education graduates often choose to live near their hometown, the RTR program worked to recruit program participants from CSU, Chico's primarily rural region in order to help fill the predicted vacancies. In addition, there was some hope that RTR graduates who were not predisposed to teaching in rural contexts might choose to stay, as a result of their experience in the residency program. In order to incentivize graduates, the TQP grant funding provided students with a stipend which was forgivable if the graduates worked in a high need district (though not necessarily rural) for three years upon completion of the program. In urban residencies (e.g. Newark Montclair Urban Teacher Residency) it is common to guarantee graduates a job in the partner district. Although RTR graduates were highly sought after when partner districts were hiring (Principal C. Brown, personal communication, May 24, 2017), a guaranteed job is far more difficult in smaller rural districts where openings are more limited. To date, 20 (22%) of RTR graduates have been hired in one of the four partner districts, and 52 graduates (59%) have completed their service obligation in a high need school, most of which are also rural.

In the California State University, Chico region, it is very common for teachers to commute from Chico to teach in smaller communities. The RTR partner districts were located anywhere from 20 miles to 55 miles away from the university and the vast majority of residents did not reside in their placement district. Sharplin (2002) describes the binary discourse of preservice teachers with respect to expectations of teaching in rural areas. Her research found that pre-service teachers:

rely on narrow stereotypes of rural and remote teaching. They hold, sometimes simultaneously, images of rural and remote teaching as an idyllic retreat and outback hell. (Implications, para 7)

It is therefore necessary to address any preconceptions that preservice teachers have about rural places, even when they might have come from similar contexts. The federal TQP grant required that RTR partner with rural schools, therefore course readings and assignments addressed research and theories about rural education.

This chapter will briefly overview the development of the RTR program, will review the program design features, and will describe the qualitative data analysis from the program evaluation conducted at the conclusion of the grant funding cycle. This qualitative analysis included data from focus groups, a survey, and from graduate observations/interviews. Further, this chapter highlights and explores the themes of teacher efficacy and preparation for rural contexts, while emphasizing the value of university-school partnerships.

BACKGROUND

Development of Partnerships

As a first step in the development of the RTR program, faculty cultivated strong partnerships in the region with four rural school districts. These districts had high percentages of students on free and reduced lunch, as well as testing scores below the state average. These conditions satisfied the grant requirements for placing teachers in high-need schools. The university faculty members and K-12 teachers and administrators entered into this partnership willingly and with a shared vision of what graduates should know and be able to do.

To initially establish these partnerships, CSU, Chico faculty reached out to school district administrators, getting on the calendars of superintendents and principals to speak with them face-to-face about partnering to prepare teachers for their schools and our broader region. The university had a previous relationship with these districts as they had placed student teachers at these sites before, but this time the communication was more personal (and less transactional), and occurred in an intentional spirit of collaboration. Faculty wanted to be in partnership with districts, and knew that sharing ideas and responsibility for program success would be most effective. To this end, a planning board comprised of both university and K-12 school personnel was established early in the process, meetings were held to outline program goals and features, and to define the ways that professional relationships would be critical to the success of this project. Faculty sought the input of school district administrators on what they needed in a new teacher candidate, and included them in discussions about the research that informed the development of the RTR program design. Concrete efforts were also made to encourage a vision of shared investment in the preparation of teachers. For example, when establishing clinical supervision roles, the organizational chart reflected reciprocal roles on the university and district side. In other words, there was a university supervisor who went out to the site to evaluate and provide feedback to RTR program candidates, but there was also a district clinical coordinator who both supported the candidates placed in that district and who served as a liaison with a university counterpart. The grant did provide funds for this type of work, allowing a stipend to the district to fund the work of the district clinical coordinator.

Designated district staff were also responsible for participating in recruitment and selection of candidates to participate in the RTR program. In addition, typically all university faculty and district personnel, even beyond those working directly in the RTR program, were invited to participate in professional development opportunities thus extending the partnership beyond the residency program itself. Developing robust university-school partnerships is viewed as a method for creating a better learning experience for all involved (i.e., university teachers/researchers, teacher candidates, and the school staff and students) by facilitating more engagement and investment in the educational process and the community (Harkavy & Hartley, 2009).

Design Features of the RTR Program

Key components of the Rural Teacher Residency were:

1. Year-long placement in one classroom with a mentor teacher;
2. Supported co-planning and co-teaching strategies;
3. Participation in Professional Learning Communities (PLCs), and;
4. The practice of action research.

Berry, Montgomery, and Snyder (2008) have found that residency programs produce teachers who are more likely to remain in teaching, to have well-developed collaborative skills, and to be more likely to assume leadership positions in the profession. Co-teaching, while often discussed in the context of improving student achievement by virtue of having another adult in a classroom, also impacts one's ability to collaborate. The time spent planning and teaching with another professional initiates ways of being that include thinking together with others about how to meet student needs in the most effective ways (Friend, 2007). In addition, recent research by Perry (2016) demonstrated that co-teaching increases pre-service teachers' efficacy beliefs. High teacher efficacy results in a variety of positive outcomes, such as increased student learning, achievement and motivation (Bandura, 1997; Klassen, Tze, Betts, & Gordon, 2011).

Professional Learning Communities (PLCs) are a structure in which groups of teachers come together in teams to regularly examine student data and to discuss methods for improving achievement (DuFour, 2004). DuFour (2011) argues that collaboration is a critical aspect of what it means to be a *professional* educator and believes participation in collaboration meetings should be supported within the larger culture and systems of our schools. In addition, Rigelman and Ruben (2012) suggest that if collaboration is expected to become the norm in schools, direct experience with collaboration should begin at the pre-service level. Further, Cook and Friend (2010) contend that collaboration amongst professionals serving students with special needs is important if special needs students are to be successful in schools.

Darling-Hammond and Baratz-Snowden (2007) have found that action research develops stronger habits of reflection and analysis in teacher candidates. Action research:

is especially important for the success of beginning teachers. Early in their careers, teachers need to learn how to conduct their own inquiry project and delve into the research on their problem. (Diana, 2011, p. 173)

In addition, Hubbard and Power (2012) note that action research is more likely to encourage teachers to develop research communities, that is, groups of individuals who share their discoveries and reflections around the action research process. Both RTR residents and mentors were involved in learning about and supporting the process of action research (see Schulte, 2014).

RURAL TEACHER RESIDENCY PROGRAM EVALUATION

In late 2015 the California State University, Chico School of Education received a grant to evaluate the 2010-2015 implementation of the RTR program. The California State University Center for Teacher Quality (CTQ) served as evaluator of Project Co-STARS throughout the original grant period (see Tuss & Wang, 2016). California State University, Chico sought and secured additional funding from the U.S. Department of Education to extend the project evaluation for three additional years so that faculty might better understand which elements of the program were most effective in preparing teachers. The extended evaluation plan completed by Tuss and Wang (2016) included:

(1) an analysis of student achievement impacts attributable to the program; (2) an analysis of the relative efficacy of the Co-STARS program using data that are routinely collected to assess the overall effectiveness of California State University, Chico credential programs. (p. 1)

A third component of the evaluation included a qualitative study designed to inform faculty about which RTR program elements should be further adopted in the traditional credential programs.This qualitative research was conducted by the co-authors of this chapter.

The report by Tuss and Wang (2016) described the baseline data set to measure impacts of the program's graduates on student achievement outcomes using test data from the California Assessment of Student Performance and Progress (CAASPP) System. Some of the conclusions were that during the 2014-15 academic year, a total of 451 students in kindergarten through grade 8 were taught by 13 RTR multiple-subject graduates and 3 education specialist graduates in one of the four RTR partner districts. The 367 general education and 84 special education (451 total) students taught by RTR graduates were just 2 percent of the total population tested.

Students with valid test scores who were taught English or math in a self-contained classroom by a teacher who completed the Co-STARS residency program served as the treatment group for the baseline evaluation. Students with valid test scores who were taught English or math in a self-contained classroom by a teacher who did not complete the Co-STARS residency program served as the pool from which the matched comparison group will be selected. (Tuss & Wang, 2016, p. 3)

The number of teachers in the treatment group was quite small, "making it difficult to obtain sufficient statistical power to evaluate project impacts with confidence" (Tuss & Wang, 2016, p. 12). Although the data is very limited and focuses only on one point in time, analysis of the standardized tests scores reveal a "general pattern in which Co-STARS graduates teaching general education classes at the elementary grade levels (grades 3-5) appear to be more effective than teachers who did not participate in the Co-STARS residency", whereas, "Co-STARS graduates teaching special education classes in the middle school grades (grades 6-8) appear to be less effective" (Tuss & Wang, 2016, p. 8).

To complement Tuss and Wang's (2016) quantitative analysis, co-authors of this chapter used the additional program evaluation funding to conduct a qualitative analysis of the impact of program elements on graduates' teaching efficacy. The data collection included three phases. The first phase included conducting focus groups where 24 of the 88 total program graduates attended face-to-face sessions conducted by a facilitator with extensive experience with focus groups. Those who were located out of the area joined the group via video conferencing technology. Researchers transcribed (verbatim) focus group sessions and then conducted a content analysis. Themes were pulled from this analysis process and were used to inform the second phase of data collection. In the second phase, researchers designed a survey with an array of questions intended to probe the themes identified from the focus groups. There were 70 respondents (79%) to the survey. An analysis of the focus groups and survey items informed the third and final phase of data collection, which consisted of classroom observations and one-on-one interviews with a selected group of program graduates and their site administrators. In addition, data was collected through two additional focus groups that included some RTR mentor teachers, principals and former residents from two of the partner school districts.

Follow up observations were conducted at the program graduate's school and classroom. An observation protocol was used for these observations. CSU, Chico's School of Education recently adopted a new observation protocol, the California State University, Chico Observation Rubric for Educators (CORE), based on The New Teacher Project (TNTP) Core Teaching Rubric, an instrument piloted and adapted (with permission by TNTP) for local use (The New Teacher Project, 2014).

In addition to the CORE rubric assessment, the California Teaching Performance Expectations (TPEs) were also evaluated. Each graduate was observed over an extended period of time (no less than one hour, but often over the course of a day) and was scored on both the CORE rubric and the TPEs for a defined episode of teaching (i.e., a lesson). Extensive lesson observation notes were compiled as evidence and used to assign final rubric scores as per the School of Education's standard CORE rubric guidelines. Researchers talked with the graduate before and after the lesson observation and in most cases, interviewed the site administrator. Principals were asked questions such as:

What is your overall impression of this teacher? How might they compare to teachers from other credential programs? What are their skills in collaboration? Can you share other information about their development as a teacher?

Researchers used constant comparative analysis (Strauss & Corbin, 1998) to code the data looking for themes within and among the data sets. These themes were compared across sets of data and assembled around a common finding. The process to confirm data was iterative, in the sense that pieces of data were checked against other sources using both inductive and deductive processes. In some cases, the researchers' experience with the graduates was used to further inform understandings. The goal was to make meaning from the data and discover the relationships between the intentions of the RTR program and the outcomes in graduates' practice.

RURAL TEACHER RESIDENCY PROGRAM OUTCOMES

Theme One: Teacher Efficacy

The strongest theme that emerged from the data (i.e., focus groups, survey, interviews with graduates and their administrators, and systemwide exit survey data), was the notion that graduates of the Rural Teacher Residency program have a strong sense of teacher efficacy. Teacher efficacy is a relatively simple concept that has been powerfully linked to many meaningful educational outcomes, such as a teacher's persistence, enthusiasm for their practice, commitment to the profession, instructional behaviors, a preference for positive management strategies, as well as student outcomes, including achievement, motivation, and children's self efficacy beliefs (Tschannen-Moran, Hoy, & Hoy, 1998; Tschannen-Moran & Woolfolk Hoy, 2001). Teacher efficacy can be defined as a teacher's belief in, or confidence in, their ability to promote student learning (Hoy, 2000). Guskey and Passaro (1994) defined it as a "teachers' belief or conviction that they can influence how well students learn, even those who may be difficult or unmotivated" (p. 4). The concept of teacher efficacy grew out of Bandura's earlier work on self efficacy when he claimed that belief in one's ability was linked to how much effort one will put forth, how long one will persist in the face of obstacles, how resilient one is in dealing with failure, and how one copes emotionally during demanding situations (Bandura, 1997). A 1976 teaching study conducted by the RAND organization (Armor, Conroy-Oseguera, Cox, King, McDonnell, Pascal, Pauly, & Zellman, 1976) included items on teacher efficacy for the first time and found that the ways in which teachers think about their effectiveness in their professional role significantly impacts their performance in the profession. This landmark study launched teacher efficacy as a legitimate field of investigation and researchers have been rigorously studying the impacts of teachers' efficacy beliefs since that time.

Briefly, Bandura (1997) states that self-efficacy is developed primarily in four ways: though mastery experiences, through physiological and emotional arousal, through vicarious experiences, and through social persuasion. Graduates of the RTR program were given opportunities to development efficacy in the ways described by Bandura and others (Bandura, 1997; Tschannen-Moran, Hoy, & Hoy, 1998) through various program elements that contributed to these four aspects. For example, mastery experiences and physiological/emotional arousal in teaching occur when one engages in a real-life teaching episode and experiences success and the positive physiological and emotional signals one receives from successful execution of the managing, instructing, and evaluating of a classroom (Tschannen-Moran, Hoy & Hoy, 1998). Hoy and Spero (2005) state that "some of the most powerful influences on the development of teacher efficacy are mastery experiences during student teaching and the induction year" (p. 343). Vicarious experiences occurred as RTR candidates observed their mentor teachers in action, successfully and sometimes not successfully teaching their shared classroom, but refining their professional skills as a result of the experience. Verbal persuasion can contribute to self-efficacy within the RTR program through feedback from mentor teachers, clinical supervisors, peers, professional development workshops, etc.

In the RTR program evaluation data, 94% of survey respondents (N=70) either strongly agreed or agreed to feeling well-prepared to teach. Comments made during the focus groups, as well as on the qualitative portions of the survey, indicated strong feelings of preparedness and confidence. For example, graduates made general comments such as, "I felt very prepared. I felt confident in myself and my skills" and "I felt well-prepared on my first day of teaching on my own." However, graduates were able to shed light more specifically on how the program developed those feelings of efficaciousness as they described or commented on the various program elements and how those program elements developed their feelings of confidence in their abilities. On the survey, in the focus groups, and in interviews, graduates repeatedly referred to the residency, co-planning and co-teaching, the cohort, action research, and collaboration as being most significant in their feelings of preparedness.

Residency

RTR graduates describe the residency experience - that of being present on their school campus before the academic year begins, greeting their students on the first day of school, and being present as a fully-functioning member of the school staff until the last day of school - as critical to their success. They explained that, because they were fully present in the school culture and had an extended placement, they gained basic competence with the full range of experiences that a classroom teacher encounters. Graduates described this extended placement as enhancing their feelings of preparedness. For example, one graduate reported,

I feel like the rigor and demand of this program really sets you up for being a teacher and the expectation of what the reality is getting into the classroom, because you are in the same classroom all year. You get to see from the first day to the last day, and you see all that it encompasses. Being in the classroom for the entire year, everything is involved. Not just snippets, information here and there. Being in the same room all year made me feel well prepared to tackle my first teaching job. (focus group, May 31, 2016)

Another graduate described how the residency experience gave her a more complete picture of the school year. In the traditional credential programs, student teachers were placed for 10-15 weeks in two different placements and did not get the benefit of seeing student growth over nine months. She said, "You really get a start to end picture, which I think helped me be more confident creating a start to end picture when it was my own classroom" (focus group, October 27, 2016). Finally, another graduate summed it up this way,

I'm a residency apprenticeship evangelist. I'm hardcore evangelist on this. I have very strong feelings on the subject. I think it's vastly superior to all other models. I think it gives you confidence. It's more of a professional experience than a student-college experience. We talked about how we felt that we had mastery of our classroom upon entering the classroom. It's been spoken of more than once, on all the different pieces that you get to see in continuity and context as a professional on day one with your name on the door, and I think it's a rich professional experience that can't be beat. (focus group, October 27, 2016)

Co-Teaching

Graduates said that co-teaching, and the co-planning that accompanies it, with a highly qualified mentor contributed to their sense of teacher efficacy. Perry (2016) also found that co-teaching was an important source of teacher efficacy and, in her study, it accounted for 15 to 20% of the variance in teacher efficacy outcomes. Not only did RTR graduates identify co-planning and co-teaching as an important contributor to their feelings of effectiveness, they described that the best experiences were those with mentors with whom they had a strong relationship and good communication. Again, this information aligns with Perry

(2016) who identified relationship and communication as important elements in a co-teaching model, more relevant than even classroom knowledge base and applications within the participants' student teaching experiences.

Eighty-two percent of survey respondents reported that co-planning and co-teaching contributed to their feelings of preparedness. For example, one graduate attributed her confidence to her relationship with her co-teacher. "She was supportive and very skilled. She really gave me a good example of the dedication, love and professionalism it takes to be a great educator" (survey respondent). The graduates noted that having a strong mentor was critical to the success of the co-teaching partnership and noted that the experience would be less powerful if the mentor/candidate pairing didn't work. One graduate described co-teaching and co-planning with her mentor as "integral" to her learning, specifically in regards to learning how to organize.

Had my mentor teacher not been such a good match, I believe the RTR program would have been detrimental. I had a very good fit with my mentor and we still keep in touch through student pen-pal letters. (Survey Respondent)

The program researchers heard this type of comment repeatedly. Eighty-seven percent of the survey respondents reported having a good mentor relationship, but those who didn't had many ideas about the ways in which program faculty could be more diligent in the screening process. The feedback ranged from conducting *additional* compatibility assessments (program faculty did routinely conduct assessments to determine compatibility before matching resident and mentor), to ensuring that mentors were entering into the partnership for appropriate reasons and had the appropriate disposition to collaborate in the ways required in a co-teaching partnership. When the co-teaching relationships functioned well, which they did a majority of the time, graduates seemed to appreciate the support they received in reflecting on their teaching practice. One graduate reported, "... just an aspect of co-teaching that was nice, was having that person in the room to help you reflect" (focus group, October 27, 2016). Another agreed, saying,

There were times when she would let me struggle and do what I needed to do, but there were also times where she would step in when she needed to, and I would see right then immediately how something needed to be done, and then I could step back in and do something. I was able to get immediate feedback and an immediate model on what I could be doing. (focus group, October 27, 2016)

Graduates reported that being viewed as an equal in the classroom, by their co-teacher, by the students, and by the parents helped them to step into the full role of teacher and to act as an equal in the classroom. One said:

Even though we knew that we were still learning and we were the mentees in that mentoring relationship, the students weren't necessarily aware of that, and I think that made a big difference. (focus group, October 27, 2016)

Finally, another shared, "I was in parent conferences, I helped with Back-to-School Night, Open House. We were together and united, even to the parents" (focus group, October 27, 2016).

Cohort/Support

The RTR graduates explained that the cohort experience - having the majority of classes and sharing placement sites with the same group of peers - was one of the most transformative aspects of the program. While program faculty certainly intended to build support and opportunities for collaboration into the RTR program design, they were surprised by the extent of the impact of the cohort structure. Graduates described not feeling alone in their credential year and cited not only emotional support, but also relying on one another for ongoing reflection and as a resource for teaching knowledge or expertise. "The people in our cohort had different skills to offer, but I think the people in our cohort acted as a resource for us" (focus group, October 27, 2016). They reported that the cohort developed a "no-one will be left behind" quality, and described that being "in it together" mitigated the stress of an extremely intensive year. "We knew there was that safety net. There was just someone else that had your back and you just didn't feel alone" (focus group, October 27, 2016).

Graduates also mentioned the fact that the student cohort was served by a faculty cohort (the same group of professors and supervisors taught all classes in the program) and indicated that this provided additional levels of trust and support throughout the year. Candidates referred to the strong relationships between University faculty and school site faculty and said this enhanced their feelings of being supported in the program. In addition, they mentioned that being clustered in groups at their student teaching sites further facilitated the levels of support they needed and enhanced the importance of the cohort.

I think just being with the same cohort the entire year was so helpful because we all took the same classes, we were just in it together and we were able to ask each other questions and reflect together, and that was very helpful. We just didn't feel alone. (focus group, October 27, 2016)

Several graduates noted that having experienced a highly rigorous program with the support of others, gave them confidence and made them feel ready to endure the intensity of teaching in the future.

I find it very interesting that we're all talking the way we are about the cohort, in an age where I'm seeing so much press about teacher stress. I think the cohort obviously is a model for addressing teacher stress perhaps. (focus group, October 27, 2016)

Action Research

The RTR program provided myriad opportunities for reflection intended to prepare candidates to be able to learn from their own teaching and talk about teaching with other teachers. For example, 76% of the survey participants responded that they shared their knowledge of action research with other educators. All but one person in the survey felt prepared to ask for assistance that leads to professional growth, and all but two reported that they had been sought out by their colleagues for their perspectives on teaching. Some focus group participants also commented on how they were seen as having more expertise at their school site; one person commented, "My current school asked me to be on a pilot committee for doing action research into the impact on our students of doing no homework" (focus group, May 31, 2016). Another person shared the confidence they felt about their skills: "All my teachers at my site, they're all afraid of it [data analysis] and they don't know where to start and I'm like, okay, let's get to work" (focus group, October 27, 2016).

A major theme from both the focus group data and the survey was the level of confidence the graduates felt, and some of this was attributed to having done an action research study as part of the graduate level work. Many commented on their depth of experience and higher skill levels than many of the beginning teachers with whom they worked.

One of the main advantages that made RTR, in my opinion, so much better than a traditional credential program was that it was a significantly higher level of academic rigor. (focus group, October 27, 2016)

Many graduates commented on how the skills developed in the RTR program developed within them a disposition to consult data in decision making. One student reported,

I'm using the skills, maybe not as much as we did in the action research, but I'm using the skills, and anything that we're doing, any new adoption that we make, or whatever it is, we're trying things out, we're testing things, we're looking at the data from the literature; we're doing the same thing so I feel like I'm using the skills that I learned through the RTR program. (focus group, October 27, 2016)

Lytle and Cochran-Smith (1993) describe the benefits for teachers who look closely at classroom data in order to reflect on and make decisions about classroom practice. Additional research (e.g. Caro-Bruce & Zeichner, 1998; Kosnik & Beck, 2000, Levin & Rock, 2003; Mills Teacher Scholars, 2017) confirms that it increases both confidence and collaboration skills in teachers.

Collaboration

Program evaluation data indicated that RTR graduates had a marked desire to collaborate with other education professionals. Efforts to develop teachers with a collaborative mindset and skill set were infused into every part of the program as collaboration was a major goal of this program design. Graduates acknowledged the importance of this collaborative stance in their current professional lives. Over 97% of graduates responded that they work collaboratively with other professionals at their school site, 99% of graduates indicated that they ask for assistance from others that leads to their own professional growth, 92% stated that the co-planning/co-teaching aspect of the RTR program improved their collaboration ability with their current colleagues and 86% said that their experiences in RTR influenced them to engage collaboratively with current colleagues.

Both focus group and interview data provided more context for this propensity to collaborate. One graduate discussed how collaboration in the RTR program was good preparation for her job. "Getting that kind of practice has made it a lot easier to work with teachers of all different grades and concepts, just making it as perfect as possible" *(focus group, May 31, 2016)*. Another graduate discussed how the in-program collaboration prepared her to be independent in her current position.

The intense collaboration helped prepare me more for being independent because it gave me the experience of being in charge, of having a lot of responsibility, it was like gradual release of responsibility. So, when I got into my own classroom, I had supported experience in doing teaching...lesson pacing, time fillers, etc. etc. (C. Dale, personal communication, October 2, 2017)

In some cases, graduates are teaching in rural schools where they are the only teacher at their grade level and so they have reached out to teachers in other districts or networks to provide that opportunity for collaboration. One graduate noted,

...you get so used to collaboration and support from the RTR program; I don't have that support with my 5th grade team, we kind of butt heads against each other. So I've learned to seek it outside of my school. (focus group, October 27, 2016)

Respondents highlighted the implementation of co-teaching in the context of a residency field placement as contributing to their overall collaborative abilities. Graduates consistently mentioned co-teaching as a very important factor contributing to their desire to collaborate. They also consistently identified the cohort structure as a contributor to the development of their collaboration skills. Graduates did not identify their experiences with Professional Learning Communities (PLCs) at their school site to be as important as faculty had predicted. On the survey, for example, on an item asking respondents to select the top five program elements that contributed to their feelings of preparation, graduates only selected PLCs 50% of the time. The residency, co-teaching, the cohort model, action research, and a category related to working in areas of high student need all ranked higher in graduates' valuation. Another question asking graduates to identify the program aspects that prepared them for collaboration showed 55% of respondents selecting PLCs. Again, the residency, co-planning/co-teaching, and the cohort model were all selected as being more significant in contributing to their collaboration skills. Graduates reported that PLC quality varied by school (despite the attempts to control for this in school site selection), but they shared that a strong opportunity to collaborate, even if just within a grade level team outside of the formal PLC structure, was valuable in developing their collaboration skills. Graduates rarely mentioned the attempts to foster collaboration between general and special education candidates as an important factor, leading researchers to believe it was not highly impactful.

Leadership

Leadership is another topic that emerged frequently from the data. Originally, the authors were hesitant to identify leadership as a distinct theme, but came to believe that for respondents who reported greater opportunities for leadership, it is related to graduates leaving the program with high levels of teacher efficacy. Several RTR graduates described being viewed as leaders at their school sites, either by their peers or by the administration. One graduate had even been promoted to an administrative position shortly after being hired in his first job with the county office of education.

This leadership quality was sometimes described in the context of the graduate being selected for projects because their level of preparedness caused them to stand out when compared to their peers. Other times, the graduates were singled out as leaders for their ability to collaborate. For example, 97% of graduates indicated on the survey that they were sought out by others for their perspectives on teaching practice. Comments from the focus groups and interviews elaborate this notion. One respondent said, "I actually am now the lead of my team and have the most experience, which is weird, because I'm only now a fourth year teacher." She continued, "I just think my collaboration showed to my principal that I can handle that job" (focus group, October 27, 2016).

An RTR graduate's administrator had the following to say,

I've talked to her about her future because I see leadership abilities in her. She is a good listener, which is also an aspect of leadership, she incorporates other ideas she sees, which tells me that she listens and takes on new ideas that aren't her own. She doesn't want power, she just wants things to be successful. (Principal J. Eggers, personal communication, October 2, 2017)

Finally, another graduate reported that in only her second year, she was serving on four committees at the request of her principal. "Because you juggle so much in RTR, our principals have a great deal of confidence that we can hit the ground running and handle it like we are seasoned teachers" (focus group, May 31, 2016).

Trauma

Overall, RTR graduates reported feeling well prepared in most aspects of teaching. In the focus groups and the survey, several graduates reported that they felt under-prepared to respond to the trauma in the lives of many of their students. Educators often refer to these traumatic conditions as Adverse Childhood Experiences (ACE) (Center for Youth Wellness, 2013). One of the partner districts is in a county with the highest number of students with ACE scores in the state (Center for Youth Wellness, 2013).

I guess I wasn't prepared for the fact that because of the shortage of counselors and psychologists, that they've cut out of schools, it's really hard to teach when you have to cater to children who have moms and dads in rehab and in jail and they know it, and another child whose dad held up another store and is in jail and they go visit him on the weekends. (focus group, May 31, 2016)

In the survey, 76% of respondents reported that they did feel prepared by the RTR program to meet the needs of students living with trauma, but in both the focus group data and some of the follow up observations, a variety of community concerns surfaced.

It's definitely culture shock...but because there's no industry, the drugs have taken over and so unfortunately, I had to call on a parent, they were arrested. I never thought as a teacher I was going to be in the position to watch one of my student's parents get cuffed in front of carpool. You don't expect that. (focus group, October 27, 2016)

One focus group participant said "especially meth, in rural areas being more prevalent and that hugely affects your classroom because of the home lives and the baggage" (focus group, May 31, 2016).

Theme Two: Preparation for Rural Contexts

Walker-Gibbs, Ludecke, and Kline (2015) theorize that the preparation of teachers for rural schools is directly influenced by "an individual's conceptions and experiences of rurality" (p. 81). Teachers who are raised rural are more likely to live and teach in rural places (Reininger, 2012), and those who are not, are less likely to choose rural contexts (Boyd, Lankford, Loeb, & Wyckoff, 2005). "So for me I continue to work in the rural schools just because I grew up in it; it's basically all I know. I really like that experience" (focus group, October 27, 2016). Although 12 of the survey respondents who reported having grown up rural were not seeking jobs in rural places, it was true that the majority of respondents who had grown up rural reported that they had sought rural jobs at the completion of RTR.

Both survey respondents and focus group participants noted that they chose rural because that is what they knew or where they were currently living. Two teachers who had been recruited as paraprofessionals in one of the RTR partner districts described how they completed the program and sought jobs in their home district.

We both worked for our school district for several years before being teachers there. It was understanding the climate, the population, the clientele that we were dealing with. It was important to me. (focus group, May 31, 2016)

Corbett (2016) has noted one classic problem in rural education research has been an insensitivity to differences across contexts; "as the old saying goes, if you have seen one rural community, you have seen . . . well, one rural community" (p. 278). Even within the four partner districts, the culture and characteristics of the communities varied. The RTR graduate data also suggested that having grown up rural didn't necessarily prepare candidates for the rural communities in which they were placed.

I think I came very quickly to understand that there are different types of rural experiences. I grew up in a very small rural farming community. We didn't have a stoplight; everybody went and hung out at the store on the corner after school. My experiences are that nobody in my community struggled with money issues, we didn't have the poverty ...you're walking into that rural different perspective or different lens; it was eye opening. (focus group, May 31, 2016)

In the survey, nearly half (14/32) who said they did not have a rural upbringing also replied that they did not seek rural jobs. One graduate planned to move to Los Angeles and described Chico as small. "Where I'm from, Chico is rural in my perspective, so likely not" (focus group, May 31, 2016). Another focus group participant said,

Being totally honest, my interest wasn't in rural populations. I was really interested in being able to get my credential and my Masters in one year, and I was interested in working with disadvantaged, who come from disadvantaged backgrounds, not so much rural. (focus group, May 31, 2016)

During data collection, program researchers elicited information that might help determine whether or not their experience in the RTR program or with the teachers in the partner schools encouraged more graduates to seek out jobs in rural districts. Although the survey data is not comprehensive, this data could begin to point at how effective the RTR program was in encouraging teachers, who might not typically choose a rural school, to "go rural." Sixteen of the survey respondents reported that they: a) did not have a rural upbringing; b) agreed (10 *strongly agreed*) that they sought jobs in rural places and; c) were likely to stay rural. Although program candidates were not asked before they started the program if they were seeking to teach in rural places, the survey did ask what factors most influenced their decision to apply to RTR. Six of the 16 respondents in this group (those who did not grow up rural but were seeking rural jobs) said the fact that they would be placed in a rural context was in their top four reasons for choosing this program. This data may indicate that those six were in some way predisposed to the possibility of locating in a rural place, so of the remaining 10 who did not grow up rural, did not choose RTR for the rural context, but after graduating sought rural jobs, and wanted to stay rural - may have been influenced by the RTR program to teach rurally.

One example from this group of 10 is RTR graduate, Melissa (a pseudonym). Melissa grew up in an urban area of southern California and chose the RTR program because it enabled her to complete her credential and Masters in one year. When she was assigned to her rural school placement, she was not at all pleased about it. She had not heard good things about this place and even after conducting the community study in the summer RTR course, she did not feel very optimistic. However, with time she came to love the people and the school, and soon after completing RTR, she accepted a permanent teaching position in that partner district. When asked why she chose to work there, she replied, "This is home and always has been… since right after I got over being placed here." Melissa shared in her interview that collaboration and the collective ownership of the school and its students are how they are able to respond to the challenges. When a teacher or a student is struggling, all of the teachers rally to find ways to support them. Melissa said, "I've never felt alone in handling a student situation."

Theme Three: School Partnerships

Related to the theme of preparing teachers for rural contexts was the importance of university partnerships with the rural schools. Deep partnerships with districts allowed for an exponentially greater sense of community, higher levels of engagement, and a shared commitment to preparing new teachers. The RTR program worked with four partner districts, all of which provided qualified mentors and opportunities to participate in Professional Learning Communities (PLCs). The fact that there were cohorts of students placed in a district, and a university site supervisor to serve as a liaison with a district clinical coordinator, over the course of five years of the program meant that the connection between the university and school were significantly closer than typical. This connection benefited the district in that the teachers who worked with the residents received more professional development in teaching strategies such as common core standards and inclusion of students with special needs, which increased the chances that their elementary students would achieve at higher levels.

Much of the initial partnership work was done early in the program development process and, essentially, created a collaborative context in which the RTR program could exist. Likely because this relationship building occurred outside the awareness of RTR program candidates, graduates specifically referenced the importance of these partnerships less frequently in the survey and focus group data. However, there were allusions to the value of the partnerships, particularly within the cohort theme above. In the additional focus groups with partner school personnel, mentor teachers reported that they benefited from having the residents for a full year, where they operated nearly like a teacher of record, and some partner principals noted that the engagement with RTR, through opportunities of both attending trainings and presenting at national conferences, actually engendered leadership in a few of the mentor teachers. Because the program invited the partner mentors to present their expertise, they developed a passion for growing that expertise even after the program ended.

The university faculty also benefited from these partnerships. One of the most advantageous outcomes was the level of communication and camaraderie that grew out of more consistent contact across the organizational structures. This ease eliminated the mental barriers that might be involved in having frequent and authentic conversations about a candidate's progress or considering the best course of action for their growth or improvement. This more comfortable and frequent communication grew into more shared conversations about trends in the TK-12 public schools that were impacting teachers and likely influenced topics discussed in the university methods courses. Joint conversations around professional development desired by both district and university faculty led to shared professional development experiences funded by the grant. In these joint experiences, it was the program researchers' observation that some of the separation that can exist between schools and university-based teacher preparation programs began to dissipate and was replaced by a more reciprocal learning process. Mentor teachers were seen as colleagues rather than solely as clinicians who provided classroom placements for teacher candidates. Some district personnel became more interested in the research driving their practices and some university faculty became more interested in the practical classroom details.

FUTURE RESEARCH AND PROGRAM IMPROVEMENT

The RTR program, funded by the TQP grant, provided residents a stipend during the residency year, which was forgivable if the graduates worked in a high need district (but not necessarily rural) for three years upon completion of the program. If graduates intended to stay in the region, they chose rural schools primarily because there are few urban areas. Program directors expected that the forgivable loan would encourage graduates to work in rural schools long term, however the research literature has indicated these types of incentives have limited success (e.g. Hammer, Hughes, McClure, Reeves, & Salgado, 2005). Within these data sets, when asked why they chose to teach rural, very few of the graduates pointed to the forgivable loan as the reason for seeking rural jobs. One focus group participant who grew up urban noted that she did start out working in a rural school in order to meet her service obligation but stayed because she loved being a part of that community. In this case, this type of financial incentive was only successful because her sense of belonging further encouraged her to stay. This theme of connectedness and belonging has surfaced in some of the RTR graduates' data, but it is also appearing in program interviews with rural schools in the region where they have had success with retention of teachers. California State University, Chico faculty are pursuing further research to better understand how this type of school culture can be supported through partnerships between the rural school and the university. The careful attention to rural contexts has continued in the Residency in Secondary Education (RiSE) program (a second TQP funded program) and has also begun to spread to other teacher preparation pathways.

The TQP grant requirements included business and community partners and although these were established initially, few of these partnerships were sustained during the course of the grant. Research (e.g. Schafft, 2016) shows that community-school partnerships are key to the well-being of both rural schools and communities. These types of partnerships can begin to respond to the data in this study which points to graduates feeling under-prepared in meeting the needs of students with trauma. Efforts have been made to create more opportunities for training in trauma-informed practices as well as beginning to look at how to structure schools to support teachers in their own secondary trauma. It might also be that while trauma is a reality in the lives of students in underserved schools, it may also need to be acknowledged that the chronic stress present in these communities requires partnerships to create equitable and supportive institutions for students, their families, and their teachers. Future efforts for university programs and teacher preparation specifically should focus on strengthening ties to agencies that provide multi-tiered systems of support to rural school teachers, administrators, *and* children. Interdisciplinary partnerships across professional fields such as social work, public health, criminal justice, entrepreneurship and the arts support a comprehensive approach to rural school and community development.

One of the stated goals in the original TQP grant proposal was to foster high levels of collaboration between general education and special education teacher candidates. Each RTR cohort was comprised of roughly 20% special education candidates and the idea was that the cohort would function much like a school staff with the special education candidates sharing their perspectives with the broader group. The hope was that each type of teacher would gain a deeper knowledge of the practices of the other and feel very comfortable collaborating upon program completion to meet the needs of students with special needs. Although 87% of the survey respondents said they felt well-prepared to work with special needs students, there was no mention of the significance of this collaboration in the focus group data. It will be useful in the future to think intentionally about developing higher levels of collaboration between general education and special education teachers.

CONCLUSION

The Rural Teacher Residency (RTR) program, which existed for five years in the School of Education at California State University, Chico, prepared highly effective and collaborative teachers through partnerships with four rural school districts. The program elements of residency, co-teaching, cohort structure, action research, professional learning communities, and collaboration all contributed to graduates' high levels of teacher-efficacy and increased attention to the needs of rural schools.

The co-authors (and former program directors) conducted a qualitative study using data collected from focus groups, a survey, observations and interviews. The results of this qualitative investigation were shared in this chapter. A key finding of this study was that the program elements built into the RTR program worked together to develop a keen sense of teacher efficacy in graduates of the program. This sense of efficacy was expressed as graduates feeling very prepared to teach, citing a confidence in their preparedness and in their ability to be an effective teacher. The results confirmed much of the research literature indicating that both a residency model and co-teaching are effective as methods of developing highly prepared teachers. The residency was judged by graduates to be the most significant aspect of their preparation contributing to their feelings of efficacy, followed next by the use of the co-teaching model. Graduates cited being at the school from before the first day of school through to the last day of school as important. They also noted the importance of feeling a sense of belonging at their placement site, a sense of belonging that they perceive as deeper than a traditional credential program because of the additional investment of time (i.e., full year placement) and level of responsibility (i.e., co-teaching).

The use of a cohort structure was evaluated by program graduates as being a significant contributor to their feelings of preparedness. Graduates described that being able to rely on one another for both expertise and emotional support sustained them through a demanding program year and contributed to their collaborative skill sets. Program faculty were often concerned about the intensity of a highly-condensed program, but in general, graduates noted that the high stress levels actually better prepared them for the demands of teaching. Professional learning communities (PLCs) were evaluated by graduates as less significant than program researchers expected in developing graduates' collaborative abilities. Action research was credited with contributing to graduates' feelings of effectiveness, especially as it relates to fostering their reflective abilities and their comfort with and ability to use data to inform their teaching practice.

Program researchers learned that the RTR program could have done a better job in preparing program graduates to cope with the trauma experienced in high need communities. There may also be a need to be more intentional in the ways that program faculty foster collaboration between general education and special education teachers in cohorts.

Finally, the partnerships developed with the rural schools throughout the course of this project are what enabled the program to exist and to see the results observed across the five years of program implementation. Establishing deep relationships with the administrators and teachers in the partner districts led to sustaining relationships which were highly supportive to both the teacher candidates and those who instructed and mentored them. Continued attention to developing these relationships with other districts is warranted.

ACKNOWLEDGMENT

This research was supported by the US Department of Education, Office of Innovation and Improvement, Teacher Quality Partnership Program [U336S090119-13B].

REFERENCES

Armor, D., Conroy-Oseguera, P., Cox, M., King, N., McDonnell, L., Pascal, A., . . . Zellman, G. (1976). Analysis of the school preferred reading programs in selected Los Angeles minority schools (Rep. No. R-2007-LAUSD). Santa Monica, CA: RAND. (ERIC Document Reproduction Service No. 130 243)

Azano, A. P., & Stewart, T. T. (2015). Exploring place and practicing justice: Preparing Pre-service teachers for success in rural schools. *Journal of Research in Rural Education*, *30*(9), 1–12.

Bandura, A. (1997). *Self-efficacy: The exercise of control*. New York, NY: W.H. Freeman and Company.

Berry, B., Montgomery, D., & Snyder, J. (2008). *Urban teacher residency models and institutes of higher education: Implications for teacher preparation*. Center for Teacher Quality Report.

Boyd, D., Lankford, H., Loeb, S., & Wyckoff, J. (2005). The draw of home: How teachers' preferences for proximity disadvantage urban schools. *Journal of Policy Analysis and Management*, *24*(1), 113–132. doi:10.1002/pam.20072

Caro-Bruce, C. & Zeichner, K. (1998). *The nature and impact of an action research professional development program in one urban school district*. Final report to the Spencer Foundation.

Center for Youth Wellness. (2013, June). *A hidden crisis: Findings on adverse childhood experiences in California*. San Francisco, CA: Author. Retrieved from https://centerforyouthwellness.org/wp-content/themes/cyw/build/img/building-a-movement/hidden-crisis.pdf

Cook, L., & Friend, M. (2010). The state of the art of collaboration on behalf of students with disabilities. *Journal of Educational & Psychological Consultation*, *20*(1), 1–8. doi:10.1080/10474410903535398

Corbett, M. (2016). Rural futures: Development, aspirations, mobilities, place, and education. *Peabody Journal of Education*, *91*(2), 270–282. doi:10.1080/0161956X.2016.1151750

Darling-Hammond, L., & Baratz-Snowden, J. (2007). A good teacher in every classroom: Preparing the highly qualified teachers our children deserve. *Educational Horizons*, 111–132.

Diana, T. J. Jr. (2011). Becoming a teacher leader through action research. *Kappa Delta Pi Record*, *47*(4), 170–173. doi:10.1080/00228958.2011.10516586

DuFour, R. (2004). What is a "Professional Learning Community?" *Educational Leadership*, *61*(8), 6–11.

DuFour, R. (2011). Work together, but only if you want to. *Kappan*, *92*(5), 57–61. doi:10.1177/003172171109200513

Fong, A., Makkonen, R., & Jaquet, K. (2016). *Projection of California teaching retirements: A county and regional perspective*. Regional Educational Laboratory West. Retrieved from http://ies.ed.gov/ncee/edlabs/projects/project.asp?projectID=4551

Friend, M. (2007). *Co-Teach! A handbook for creating and sustaining effective classroom partnerships in inclusive schools*. Marilyn Friend.

Guskey, T. R., & Passaro, P. D. (1994). Teacher efficacy: A study of construct dimensions. *American Educational Research Journal*, *31*(3), 627–643. doi:10.3102/00028312031003627

Hammer, P. Hughes, G., McClure, C., Reeves, C., & Salgado, D. (2005, December). *Rural teacher recruitment and retention practices: A review of the research literature, national survey of rural super-intendents, and case studies of programs in Virginia*. Nashville, TN: Edvantia.

Harkavy, I., & Hartley, M. (2009). University-school-community partnerships for youth development and democratic renewal. *New Directions for Youth Development*, *122*(122), 7–18. doi:10.1002/yd.303 PMID:19593810

Hoy, A. W. (2000). *Changes in teacher efficacy during the early years of teaching*. Paper presented at the Annual Meeting of the American Educational Research Association, New Orleans, LA.

Hoy, A. W., & Spero, R. B. (2005). Changes in teacher efficacy during the early years of teaching: A comparison of four measures. *Teaching and Teacher Education: An International Journal of Research and Studies*, *21*(4), 343–356. doi:10.1016/j.tate.2005.01.007

Hubbard, R. S., & Power, B. M. (2012). *Living the questions: A guide for teacher-researchers*. Portland, ME: Stenhouse Publishers.

Klassen, R. M., Tze, V. M., Betts, S. M., & Gordon, K. A. (2011). Teacher efficacy research 1998-2009: Signs of progress or unfulfilled promise? *Educational Psychology Review*, *23*(1), 21–43. doi:10.100710648-010-9141-8

Kosnik, C., & Beck, C. (2000). The action research process as a means of helping student teachers understand and fulfill the complex role of the teacher. *Educational Action Research*, *8*(1), 115–136. doi:10.1080/09650790000200107

Levin, B. B., & Rock, T. C. (2003). The effects of collaborative action research on preservice and ex-perienced teacher partners in professional development schools. *Journal of Teacher Education*, *54*(2), 135–149. doi:10.1177/0022487102250287

Lytle, S. L., & Cochran-Smith, M. (1993). *Inside/Outside: Teacher research and knowledge*. New York: Teachers College Press.

Mills Teacher Scholars. (2017, June 13). The impact of teacher-led collaborative inquiry [Blog post]. Retrieved from http://millsscholars.org/the-impact-of-teacher-led-collaborative-inquiry/

Perry, R. K. (2016, Summer). Influences of co-teaching in student teaching on pre-service teachers' teacher efficacy. *Newsletter of the California Council on Teacher Education, 27*(2), 29–33.

Reininger, M. (2012). Hometown disadvantage? It depends on where you're from: Teachers' location preferences and the implications for staffing schools. *Educational Evaluation and Policy Analysis, 34*(2), 127–145. doi:10.3102/0162373711420864

Rigelman, N. M., & Ruben, B. (2012). Creating foundations for collaboration in schools: Utilizing professional learning communities to support teacher candidate learning and visions of teaching. *Teaching and Teacher Education, 28*(7), 979–989. doi:10.1016/j.tate.2012.05.004

Schafft, K. (2016). Rural education as rural development: Understanding the rural school-community well-being linkage in a 21st-century policy context. *Peabody Journal of Education, 91*(2), 137–154. doi:10.1080/0161956X.2016.1151734

Schulte, A. K. (2014). The preparation of mentors who support novice teacher researchers. *Networks: An Online Journal for Teacher Research, 16*(1), 1–11.

Sharplin, E. (2002). Rural retreat or outback hell: Expectations of rural and remote teaching. *Issues in Educational Research, 12*. Retrieved from http://www.iier.org.au/iier12/sharplin.html

Strauss, A., & Corbin, J. (1998). *Basics of qualitative research: Techniques and procedures for developing grounded theory*. Thousand Oaks, CA: Sage.

The New Teacher Project. (2014, February 18). *TNTP core teaching rubric: A tool for conducting common core-aligned classroom observations*. Brooklyn, NY: Author. Retrieved from https://tntp.org/publications/view/tntp-core-teaching-rubric-a-tool-for-conducting-classroom-observations

Tschannen-Moran, Hoy, & Hoy (1998). Teacher efficacy: its meaning and measure. *Review of Educational Research, 68*(2), 202-248. Retrieved from http://www.jstor.org/stable/1170754

Tschannen-Moran, M., & Hoy, A. W. (2001). Teacher efficacy: Capturing an elusive construct. *Teaching and Teacher Education, 17*(7), 783–805. doi:10.1016/S0742-051X(01)00036-1

Tuss, P., & Wang, Y. (2016, February 5). *Evaluation of the Co-STARS Rural Teacher Residency Program at California State University, Chico: First-Year Extended Evaluation Report on Baseline Student Achievement Results*. California State University Center for Teacher Quality.

US Department of Education. (n.d.). *Teacher Quality Partnership Grants*. Retrieved from https://www2.ed.gov/programs/tqpartnership/index.html

Villegas, A. M., & Lucas, T. (2002). *Educating culturally responsive teachers: A coherent approach*. Albany, NY: State University of New York Press.

Walker-Gibbs, B., Ludecke, M., & Kline, J. (2015). Pedagogy of the rural: Implications of size on conceptualisations of rural. *International Journal of Pedagogies and Learning*, *10*(1), 81–89. doi:10.1080 /22040552.2015.1086292

Zimpher, N. L., & Howey, K. R. (1992). *Policy and practice toward the improvement of teacher education: An analysis of issues from recruitment to continuing professional development with recommendations.* Oak Brook, IL: North Central Regional Educational Laboratory.

ADDITIONAL READING

Hong, C. E., & Lawrence, S. (2011). Action Research in teacher education: Classroom inquiry, reflection, and data-driven decision making. *Journal of Inquiry and Action in Education*, *4*(2), 1–17. Available at http://digitalcommons.buffalostate.edu/jiae/vol4/iss2/1

Justeson, R. (2013, Spring). Developing collaborative teachers. *Academic Exchange Quarterly*, *17*(1), 64–70.

Justeson, R. (2017, Winter). Developing well-prepared, collaborative teachers in the rural teacher residency program. *Academic Exchange Quarterly*, *21*(4), 386–398.

National Center for Teacher Residencies (NCTR). (2017, July). Recommendations for state support for effective teacher residencies. NCTR Report. Available at: https://nctresidencies.org/wp-content/ uploads/2017/06/Recommendations-for-State-Support-of-Effective-Teacher-Residencies.pdf

Roth, W. M., Masciotra, D., & Boyd, N. (1999). Becoming-in-the-classroom: A case study of teacher development through co-teaching. *Teaching and Teacher Education*, *15*(7), 771–784. doi:10.1016/ S0742-051X(99)00027-X

Schulte, A. K. (2017). The impacts of preservice action research in a rural teaching residency. *Journal of Inquiry and Action in Education*, *9*(1), 69–76. Available at http://digitalcommons.buffalostate.edu/ jiae/vol9/iss1/5

Schulte, A. K., & Klipfel, L. (2016). External influences on an internal process: Supporting preservice teacher research. *The Educational Forum*, *80*(4), 457–465. doi:10.1080/00131725.2016.1206158

Titus, N. E. (2013, Fall). A review of literature investigating co-teaching influences in teacher education programs. *Pennsylvania Teacher Educator*, *12*, 11–23.

KEY TERMS AND DEFINITIONS

Action Research: The process of systematically studying one's own practice using the tools of research.
Co-Teaching: Implementing a series of strategies with a colleague to provide instruction.
Cohort Model: A group of program participants engaging in all aspects of the program with the same group of peers and instructors.

Collaboration: Working cooperatively toward a shared purpose.

Education Specialist: Also known as a teacher of special education.

Residency: A full-year placement in one classroom.

Rural: Not metropolitan; generally smaller communities a distance from urban centers.

Teacher Efficacy: A teacher's belief in their ability to promote student learning.

Teacher Retention: Ability to reduce teacher mobility and provide more stable learning conditions in schools.

Trauma: Adverse experiences that significantly impact learning and life.

Section 2

Commitments to Equity, Social Justice, and Diversity

Chapter 10
Becoming Literacy Educators:
Embedded Field–Based Experiences and Embedding Social Justice Education

Eliza G. Braden
University of South Carolina, USA

Cathy Compton-Lilly
University of South Carolina, USA

Michele Myers
University of South Carolina, USA

Beth Lucas White
University of South Carolina, USA

ABSTRACT

Teachers with generative theories about teaching view themselves as capable and agential. They routinely engage in self-introspection as a means to dismantle problematic beliefs and biases. Generative teacher education is best developed in classrooms through embedded work with children. To explore generative teacher education, this chapter describes how one program sets the stage for the development of cultural competence through an initial course focused on culturally sustaining pedagogy. The authors then describe the significance of helping literacy teachers to notice and name children's emerging literacy abilities. The chapter ends with scenarios that illustrate the synergy that occurs when cultural competence is combined with embedded field experiences in literacy classrooms. The authors discuss both pedagogical possibilities and the importance of developing noticing practices and agential responses that are culturally and linguistically responsive.

DOI: 10.4018/978-1-5225-6249-8.ch010

INTRODUCTION

It is not to disparage teacher training that we remark upon the fact that teachers still learn to teach by teaching. The teacher gets something from experience which is not included in his [sic] "professional" courses, an elusive something which it is difficult to put between the covers of a book or work up into a lecture. (Waller, 1932/1961, p. 1)

Clearly, the idea that teachers learn to teach by teaching is not new. While we recognize that there are other ways for novice teachers to learn about teaching, our work with preservice teachers has convinced us of the power of mentored teaching experiences in the process of becoming culturally competent literacy teachers.

Teaching is complex work. In order to learn about teaching in all its facets and nuances, we believe that preservice teachers' experiences must be connected to children. Across two decades, literacy faculty at the University of South Carolina have worked to create embedded field experiences that entail carefully designed classroom experiences and close attention to children and pedagogical problem solving. These experiences promote and require agency and resourcefulness as novice teachers learn to negotiate challenges that accompany helping children learn to read and write. As we involve preservice teachers with children, we support them in crafting identities that treat teaching as fidelity to children rather than programs and position children and teachers as cultural and agential beings with unique passions, abilities, cultures, and lives.

To accomplish this, we must recognize how people – including children – are embedded in culture. As McNaughton (2002) argues, teaching literacy requires more than knowledge about reading and writing. Powerful teaching requires knowledge about how race, class, cultural differences, and privilege continuously translate into disparate opportunities for learning. Becoming a teacher entails content knowledge, social skills, patience, awareness of the diverse ways of being that students bring to classrooms, and a commitment to honoring and serving all children and their families.

Literacy learning is deeply connected to cultural and linguistic diversity. Differences in the cultures and languages that children and teachers bring to classrooms affect the texts they are exposed to and the literacy experiences they bring. Some children and teachers are exposed to print written in more than one language. Many children who bring linguistic differences to classrooms also bring experiences with transnational literacy practices, including exposure to folktales from their native countries, cartoons, and films in other languages, and using native languages to communicate with friends and relatives. Culture informs how stories are told and interpreted. Children who bring different language varieties to classrooms may sometimes apply home language features when they read affecting the miscues they make and the spelling variations that they produce. Because both literacy learning and culture entail language, both are affected by the linguistic and cultural experiences that teachers and children bring to classrooms.

In this chapter, we focus on how embedded field experiences not only address how to run classrooms, design lessons, and assess students, but also support preservice teachers as they move towards cultural competence. We refer to this as a generative model of literacy teacher education. The word generative, has been used by various scholars to describe educational experiences that generate new ways of thinking and knowing. Siegel (1995) defines generative processes as resulting in the production of new meanings. Freire (1986) argued for attention to the generative themes that students brought to learning. He maintained that a problem-posing and liberating education requires consideration of students' lived realities and the generative themes that defined their worlds. As he noted, "the generative theme cannot be found in men, divorced from reality; nor yet in reality, divorced from men. . . it can only be apprehended in the men-world relationship" (p. 97). Thus, educational practices that involve new understandings about children require critical consciousness and must connect to students and their relationship to literacy, learning, and schooling.

Learning to teach is a generative process. Assaf and López (2015) believe that "when teachers become generative learners, they create a habit of mind that sustains their learning throughout their teaching lives" (p. 324). Nieto (2000) refers to this as a "life-long journey of transformation" (p. 184) that entails facing and accepting ourselves as cultural beings, learning from our students, developing meaningful relationship with students, families, and communities, and learning to challenge racism and other biases. As preservice teachers develop generative theories about teaching, they transform from acting as passive individuals to becoming creative agents who see themselves as "capable of intervening in one's context to bring about change" (Wingeier, 1980, p. 563). Thus, Freire's definition of generativity calls to the forefront, relationships between the world and the word – including the ways children experience literacy and schooling.

More recently, Stephens and her colleagues (2012) describe the need for young readers to develop generative theories of reading and of themselves as readers. As they report, generative readers spontaneously and readily incorporate existing strategies to address novel reading challenges. Generative readers view themselves as capable and agential even when facing challenges with text. We agree that preservice teachers must develop a generative theory of literacy teaching and define a generative approach to literacy education as one that invites teachers to spontaneously and readily incorporate problem-solving stances towards challenges. Thus, novice teachers view themselves as capable and agential even in challenging instructional situations. When generative teachers encounter diverse ways of acting, being, and valuing, they do not judge or lament. Literacy teachers who bring generative theories routinely reflect on their engagements with children in ways that promote not only children's problem solving with text, but also entail self-reflection as means to dismantle problematic beliefs and biases. They readily seek and incorporate novel ways of thinking that are grounded in respect for all children and families. We argue for a generative teacher education model that honors and attends to equity, student diversity, and sociocultural competence, which is best developed through embedded work with children; it is only through direct work with children that the significance and limits of our own cultural experiences become clear as we listen, observe, and reflect on our teaching.

To explore what we refer to as generative teacher education, we first describe how we set the stage for the development of cultural competence through an initial course focused on culturally sustaining pedagogy. We then describe the significance of helping teachers to notice and name their teaching worlds. Teachers must notice when children understand text and when they do not. They must recognize children's attempts to problem solve and use these attempts as the basis for instruction. By noticing and naming the literacy work of children, teachers are prepared to engage in generative teaching; teaching that spontaneously and intentionally recognizes and engages children's emerging literacy abilities. The chapter ends with scenarios that illustrate the synergy that occurs when cultural competence is combined with embedded field experiences in literacy classrooms. We discuss both pedagogical possibilities, and the importance of developing noticing practices and agential responses that are culturally and linguistically responsive.

Lessons Learned About Learning to Teach

Before describing the Teacher Education Program at the University of South Carolina, we explore research that explores excellent teacher education models to identify potentially promising approaches that inform our work. Darling-Hammond (2006) maintained that the:

enterprise of teacher education must venture out further and further from the university and engage even more closely with schools in a mutual transformation agenda, with all of the struggle and messiness that implies. (p. 302)

Among the specific actions she recommends are extended clinical experiences that are interwoven with coursework, extensive use of performance assessments and case study methods, and explicit attention to the deep-seated assumptions and biases that preservice teachers often bring. Darling Hammond describes the critical importance of:

extensive and intensely supervised clinical work – tightly integrated with course work – that allows candidates to learn from expert practice in schools that serve diverse students. (p. 307)

This clinical work often involves candidates analyzing student work, viewing and discussing classroom video footage, and thoughtful scaffolding of connections among theory, readings, and practice.

Diversity is woven into this work. While recognizing the value of stand-alone multicultural education courses, Sleeter (2001) argues that attention to culturally sustaining practices across courses, especially courses offered in collaboration with schools that serve diverse children, present promising possibilities for teacher education. This model, she argues, would benefit from leadership from "strong culturally responsive teachers" (p. 101). Moore (2003) and Ziechner (2010) maintain that embedded experiences in schools provide preservice teachers with important opportunities for reflection on practice, which in turn supports the development of theoretical and personal knowledge bases. Moore notes the "need for preservice teachers, their supervisors, and their mentor teachers to examine and discuss the rationale behind pedagogical decisions" (p. 40), while Zeichner maintains that preservice teachers need "access to the thinking and decision-making of their experienced mentors" (p. 91).

In a critical analysis of research on reading teacher education, Risko, Roller, Cummins, Bean, Block, Anders, and Flood (2008) highlighted the importance of preservice teachers having opportunities to form relationships with students, experience carefully managed support from mentors, and receive feedback on their interpretations of teaching experiences. They noted that tutoring one student and the caring relationships that developed between tutors and students contributed to positive change in teaching and teachers. In short, they argue that the impact of a literacy education program is stronger when researchers report using a "learning and doing approach" (p. 276), in which mentors model teaching strategies and invite preservice students to enact those same strategies with students.

Together, a focus on extended classroom-based embedded teaching experiences, analysis of practice-based assessments, and attention to cultural competence has informed the teacher education program at the University of South Carolina.

The Teacher Education Program at the University of South Carolina

At the University of South Carolina, we believe that becoming literacy educators cannot be separated from the children and the diverse cultural, linguistic, and literacy experiences that they bring to classrooms. In addition to traditional practicum experiences, preservice teachers at the University of South Carolina partake in a series of embedded literacy, math, and science methods classes that are held in elementary schools. While taking these courses, preservice teachers have opportunities to visit classrooms, observe excellent teaching, and collaborate with in service teachers. In addition, we have crafted a unique model of embedded instruction. For one hour during each class, we work with an elementary teacher and his/her class. During this time, each preservice teacher is partnered with one child for the entire semester. We refer to the children as Small Teachers because they provide our preservice teachers - whom we refer to as Tall Teachers - with valuable lessons about teaching, kid watching, cultural competence, and building relationships. Because we intentionally choose schools with diverse student populations, we know that our Tall Teachers will encounter children who bring cultural, linguistic, and literacy differences. We believe that encountering this diversity is critical.

While we recognize the power of our embedded methods courses, we also recognize that our Tall Teaches need to be adequately prepared for these experiences – especially in terms of cultural competence. Thus, one of the very first courses in our program is a course focused on culturally sustaining pedagogy. This course is taught in schools and provides students with multiple opportunities to observe children, read and discuss ideas related to diversity, while reflecting on their own sociocultural experiences and practices.

Following this introductory course, our literacy program requires that our students take two embedded literacy courses. The first is a six-hour reading and writing methods course. The second is a three-hour literacy assessment course. Both of these courses feature the semester-long embedded experiences described above. During each class, the instructor or the classroom teacher models a reading or writing mini-lesson with the children. The Small Teachers and the Tall Teachers then partner-up and the work together to apply what was modeled to children's ongoing literacy projects. Both the course instructor and the classroom teacher circulate among the Small and Tall Teachers observing, talking notes, modeling, and providing feedback.

After working with the Small Teachers, the Tall Teachers journal about their experiences, analyze the children's work, and discuss their experiences and questions with the group. Sometimes writing samples or running reading records are collected and shared on a Smartboard. At other times, we view video to reflect on instructional possibilities. While literacy is ostensibly our focus, course instructors share a commitment to diversity. Because course instructors observe our Tall Teachers as they work with children, immediately after we can challenge our preservice teacher to consider linguistic and cultural differences that might affect how Small Teachers read and write their worlds. Specifically, we ask them to consider whether their Small Teachers might have experience with:

- Texts written in languages other than English,
- Transnational literacy practices,
- Folktales and texts from other countries (including cartoons or films),
- Using their native language to communicate in writing with friends or relatives,
- Different language structures that might affect their reading, and
- Language variations that might affect their spelling of particular words.

At the end of each semester, our preservice teachers produce a case study paper focused on their Small Teachers. Across these embedded experiences, our preservice teachers are required to attend to diversity, not only when it appears on our syllabus, but also when they encounter it in their work with Small Teachers. By participating in Tall Teacher/Small Teacher dyads and follow-up discussions that occur across all methods courses, our students are exposed to a rich range of student diversity and are invited to reflect on the significance of that diversity in collaboration with knowledgeable faculty members who have made a shared commitment to equity education.

Teacher Education and Cultural Competence

When I reflect on my education experiences, I have always had a voice, and my opinion and person were valued. I never had to fight against a stereotype of my race or carry the weight of someone's expectations of an entire social group. Skin color, race, and the way it impacts our lives in the United States of America is a powder keg of controversy. I must dig deep into my experience to prevent racist and dehumanizing behaviors.

These words were written by a preservice teacher who was taking the initial culturally sustaining pedagogy course. Her words shed light on how we help our preservice teachers begin to unpack the beliefs and unconscious biases that we all embody and confront those beliefs and biases on a conscious level. In doing so, we help preservice teachers begin systematic processes of self-introspection to dismantle beliefs and biases that oppress others. We all see the world through our cultural and social lived experiences. Those experiences are steeped in the families and the communities that have shaped us and continue to inform how we engage with others (Harro, 2000). Some beliefs are overt; others are invisible, but all beliefs guide our interactions. As educators working to nurture a generative stance, we have a unique responsibility to critically and continually examine how our beliefs and biases influence who we are, how we teach, and how we interact with others. The two embedded literacy courses that follow this course build on understandings related to diversity both in terms of literacy learners and the ways students learn to make sense of their interactions with children.

Our work with preservice teachers is informed by Ladson-Billings' (1995; 2014) three tenets of culturally relevant pedagogy—academic success, cultural competence, and sociopolitical consciousness. She writes:

By academic success I refer to the intellectual growth that students experience as a result of classroom instruction and learning experiences. Cultural competence refers to the ability to help students appreciate and celebrate their cultures of origin while gaining knowledge of and fluency in at least one other culture. Sociopolitical consciousness is the ability to take learning beyond the confines of the classroom using school knowledge and skills to identify, analyze, and solve real-world problems. (2014, p. 75)

While this culturally sustaining pedagogy class is not fully embedded, it is held in elementary schools and it requires preservice teachers to spend a significant amount of time in classrooms observing the work of carefully selected teachers who we believe employ culturally sustaining pedagogies. Prior to asking students to apply culturally sustaining pedagogies in their work with children, we have created a space in which preservice teachers are invited to engage in careful introspection of themselves, their teaching, and society (Souto-Manning, 2013). We believe this opportunity is critical for both self-transformation and transformative teaching.

In this section, we describe one of the assignments that our preservice teachers complete prior to taking their embedded literacy methods courses. The Critical School Memoir Project asks preservice teachers to consider who they are; how they are privileged and/or marginalized and/or oppressed, whose voices are heard or silenced, and how to avoid essentializing groups of people. We present excerpts from their final written reports and class discussions to illustrate their growing cultural competence. Next, we highlight two characteristics that we have observed in preservice teachers who are developing cultural competence: 1) an understanding of who they are, and; 2.) actively critiquing colorblind ideologies. We argue that these two competencies help to move our teachers beyond limited and superficial understandings of cultural competence (Ladson-Billings, 2014) and create a foundation for generative teaching for social justice.

The Critical School Memoir Assignment

The Critical School Memoir Project is designed to deepen our preservice teachers understanding of issues related to equity and privilege, and to reveal how teachers' decisions impact opportunities for children. This assignment, which takes about eight weeks to complete, requires our preservice teachers to critically narrate their schooling experiences in relation to a salient aspect of their own sociocultural identities (i.e., race, ethnicity, social class, gender, sexuality, religious preference, language, family structure, cognitive ability physical ability). With a critical and informed eye, preservice teachers reflect upon one salient identity dimension in relation to their own school experiences in elementary, middle, high school, and/or college. We ask them to focus on identity factors that push them beyond their comfort zones.

Preservice teachers are asked to analyze artifacts (i.e., photos, school flyers, school newspapers, yearbooks, award certificates) from their schooling years that will provoke detailed reflections on their own experiences. In order to dig deeper, we then ask them to interview at least two people whose identities differ from their own. For instance, if our preservice teacher identifies as Christian, he/she interviews at least two people whose religious affiliation is different (i.e. atheist, Muslim, Jewish). If the preservice teacher identifies as gay, he/she interviews at least two people whose sexual orientation differs (i.e., transgender, bi-sexual, heterosexual). We encourage our preservice teachers to adapt the following interview protocol as needed.

- What were the pivotal moments of your schooling experiences with regard to this identity factor both positively and negatively?
- Where did you feel affirmed or excluded by your teachers, school curricula, books and materials, classmates, or activities?
- Where, when, and how was this identity factor positively reinforced? Highly valued?
- Where, when and how was this identity factor silenced? Invisible? Demeaned or devalued? What did those experiences mean for you?
- What do you wish your school/teachers knew/understood about you? About your family? About the people and histories you represent?
- In what ways were the pedagogies used in your school congruent or incongruent with your cultural, linguistic, familial, or social identities?

- With regard to this identity factor, who in your family and/or community supported you as a student? How did he/she/they provide that support? What did they do or say? How was that support viewed by people at school?
- How do you believe members of your family, race, religion, sexual orientation, socioeconomic class were viewed by your teachers and peers? Why do you think that was the case?

Finally, to help preservice teachers extend their awareness and knowledge, we structure class sessions so that preservice teachers read, collect data, watch videos, and have conversations about these identity factors. Then we ask them to take weekly anecdotal notes as they work with a Small Teacher in classrooms. Their final product is a written report and oral presentation of their major findings. In the next section, we draw on data from Sally's and Kathleen's written reports, anecdotal notes, and class discussions to illuminate the emergence of cultural competence for two of our students – Shelly and Kathleen (pseudonyms are used for all participants).

Culturally Competent Teachers Know Who They Are

Sally is a preservice teacher who completed her Bachelors of Arts degree in elementary education several years after graduating from high school. Prior to taking the course, Sally was unaware of the many privileges that she was afforded simply because she was a White, middle class, Catholic woman. It was not until she engaged in critical self-introspection that she began to notice the many unearned affordances she had enjoyed and began to recognize that those affordances were not freely available to People of Color or those who brought economic and religious beliefs that challenged accepted societal norms. The following written reflection illustrates Sally's emerging cultural competence.

I am thirty-seven-years-old, married, mother of four, middle class, Catholic, and White. These social group markers affect how I view the world and how I will teach. If I do not look beyond my experience, I may not understand or be able to teach children of different backgrounds effectively. Worse, I may continue a cycle of oppression that reduces my students' potential to be fully human.

Sally names the social markers that she embodies and recognizes that her socialization could influence her interactions with her students if left unchecked. She recognizes that her lived experience is only one reality, and it is her responsibility to fully understand the sociocultural experiences of others if she really wants to educate them in humanizing ways.

Kathleen, a first-generation college student, is a White, middle class female who also admits that she never fully understood issues of power and privilege prior to the course. She admits to mistakenly thinking that hard work and determination were all people needed to succeed in the world. It was not until taking this course that she became critically aware of her privilege.

It wasn't until I was a kindergartener that I realized that to my parents I was the world, but to the [rest of] world I was a lower-middle class white female… I did not even begin to take into account how my being White privileged me. The word "White", while not explicitly stated in my upbringing, had granted me a number of privileges. I grew up thinking the things I was afforded were normal. That every other child or student would receive the same thing. It had become such a social norm that I convinced myself, when people were not afforded some of the simplest luxuries, that they were not trying as hard or that it was a fault that lied solely within them. I never questioned my place or even thought about privilege until college.

By understanding their own unnamed privileges and recognizing the challenges faced by others, Sally and Kathleen reveal how they were becoming increasingly culturally competent. In addition to naming privilege, Sally and Kathleen also began to reject a color-blind stance.

Culturally Competent Teachers Denounce Colorblind Ideologies

Well-intended people often, profess that they do not see color or that color does not matter. Silences around race and other forms of difference are deeply engrained in how many of us were raised. Norms of politeness often require that people do not mention race; however, these silences fail to consider how color affects available opportunities, perceptions, and resources. For most People of Color, seeing race does matter. When discussing colorblind ideologies in class, Kathleen reflected on what her mother had taught her.

She [My mother] preached that being colorblind was the way to go. She said that treating others the same and with respect, no matter their race, was important. My mom meant well. She wanted to raise a daughter who cared and respected all people, but the only way she knew to do this was to teach me to be colorblind. In doing this, she inadvertently diminished other's cultures and the issues of race. . .

In our course, we ask our preservice teachers to see color, and we provide spaces for them to discuss issues of race and racism in order to tackle colorblind ideologies. During one class discussion, Sally took a firm stand. She denounced colorblindness and recognized how colorblindness perpetuated stereotypical views while maintaining the status quo of Whiteness as the norm. She noted:

I will not teach just children who look like me but children from all walks and ways of life. To avoid silencing and dehumanizing my students, I must move beyond the empty rhetoric of colorblindness and see my students. I have to value their voices, represent their culture in the classroom, and appreciate their families. I must not fall into the trap of trying to homogenize my students to be more White because this reinforces a wrong notion of cultural imperialism that White makes right.

By declaring that teachers must see their students, Sally recognizes the need to utilize the funds of knowledge (Gonzalez, Moll, & Amanti, 2005) and sociocultural experiences of students. Sally maintains that if teachers intend to inspire students to strive toward their full potential, they must create environments in which all students are treated with dignity and respect (Nieto, 2009).

Kathleen and Sally are representative of the predominantly heterosexual, middle class, English speaking, White women who take our courses. Many of our preservice teachers have never experienced racial/cultural marginalization or oppression; yet, over the span of their careers, they will encounter students who have been marginalized, oppressed, and/or silenced based on race, ethnicity, language, physical or cognitive abilities, and/or sexual orientation. This is not an attack on our preservice teachers, but a cry for awareness and action. We emphasize the importance of developing culturally competent preservice teachers whose approach to teaching is not superficial (Ladson-Billings, 2014). Paris (2012) extends the work of Ladson-Billings by noting that educators must continuously to foster and perpetuate linguistic, literate, and cultural pluralism.

We hold firm that culturally competent teachers do more than add books with diverse characters to their class libraries or celebrate various traditions and festivals. Instead, we stress the importance of nurturing preservice teachers who can assume a generative stance as they build curricula with and for students. Our students learn what it means to be a culturally competent teacher while interacting with children and observing culturally competent teachers. Classroom provide spaces for reflection and strategizing while the rich diversity of children serves as a mandate for self-reflection. In the following section, we highlight how students learn to name and notice evidence of literacy learning alongside attention to the diversity of students.

Noticing and Naming Children's Literacy Learning

Immersing preservice teachers in schools and classrooms invites them to notice and name behaviors and propose theories about how their small teachers learn. It is through embedded experiences we can ask our students hard questions about literacy learning and the differences children bring to classrooms. When we sit beside a Tall Teacher who is sitting beside a Small Teacher and later collaboratively reflect and talk about that experience, we find that it is difficult for Tall Teachers to deny possibilities. As novice teachers and their instructors engage with children around literacy, the preservice teachers learn to consider, rethink, and address diverse experiences of students as they respond to children in the midst of moments.

Just as Routman (2004) argued that teaching skills in isolation does not foster writers, we believe that expecting preservice teachers to learn instructional strategies or attend to diversity without actually working with readers and writers robs them of opportunities to become thoughtful practitioners. As Schön (1995) explained, in real life, many "problems are messy and confusing and incapable of technical solution" (p. 27). He noted that these are the problems of greatest concern to individuals. Thus, the practitioner is faced with a dilemma:

Shall he remain on the high ground where he can solve relatively unimportant problems according to his standards of rigor, or shall he descend to the swamp of important problems where he cannot be rigorous in any way he knows how to describe? (p. 27)

The need to immerse preservice teachers in practical theorizing about both literacy development and diversity is clear. Generative literacy teaching is supported when preservice teachers engage in noticing and naming as data is collected, interpreted, questioned, revisited, and used to craft literacy lessons for a wide range readers and writers. In the following section, we describe activities designed to help students notice and name school culture and the reciprocity that often exists between children's reading and writing abilities.

Naming and Noticing School Culture

Embedded classes provide preservice teachers with opportunities to learn about the school communities. This begins the moment the preservice teachers step foot in schools. By noticing and naming as they walk through the halls, preservice teachers begin to make inferences about the beliefs of teachers and administrators based on hallway displays and interactions observed among teachers, support staff, parents, and the children. We invite our Tall Teachers to read the school with an eye toward literacy and diversity. Preservice teachers intentionally tour the school to gather data on students as readers and writers. The following questions (adapted from Routman, 2004) guide their noticing and naming:

- What do you notice about the amount of writing displayed?
- What do you notice about the content that was displayed? What languages are displayed?
- Do the hallways and classroom displays reflect all the children who attend the school? What holidays and cultural practices are reflected?
- What do you notice about the progression of the writing as you went from grade level to grade level?
- What do you notice about the amount of time allotted for literacy in schedules?
- What do you notice about reading instruction?
- What do you notice about books in the school? What cultural groups are represented?
- What do you notice about technology in the school?
- What and what is valued?

The preservice teachers then meet in small groups to share what they noticed. As examples are shared and collective group patterns named, they begin to generate inferences grounded in the data. The following response was written by John:

This past week as we walked the halls of Lima Elementary I noticed a school-wide appreciation for literacy. This school celebrates literacy; they want their students to write. As I made my way into the pre-school and kindergarten wing, I noticed typed writing hanging on the wall. From a distance the writing looked perfected, but as I moved closer I noticed misspellings in the typed writing. If I'm being completely honest, my first reaction was, "Yikes!!!" Thinking back upon this instance, I realized that I am so conditioned to believe that if something is typed or hanging in the hallway that it must be perfect. But what defines perfect? My initial reaction reminds me of what Cambourne (1984) stated, "With regard to the written mode of language, children are expected to display adult competence from the beginning" (p. 9). I am happy to see that Lima Elementary values their students' literacy skills, no matter their level, and celebrates their learning.

In this example, John is noticing what at first might have appeared to be conflicting messages. While, teachers and administrators at this school seemed to value and appreciate children's literacy learning, John was vexed when he noticed children's misspelling. Instead of judging the teachers, John considered this unfamiliar practice and revisited his understanding. He was able to move beyond his own assumptions to recognize connections between children's spelling approximations and the developmental theories he was reading about in class (i.e., Cambourne). John engaged in generative learning as he assumed novel ways of thinking that were grounded in questions raised through observation and noticing.

These school-based observations have effects that extend beyond this school. As preservice teachers enter other schools and eventually their own classrooms, they carry these observational experiences and lessons learned with them. Being in a classroom filled with diverse learners provides preservice teachers with opportunities to explore children's literacy practices and cultural ways of being. These reflections support Tall Teacher learning as they are invited to apply their emerging experiences, insights and theories to new situations (Johnston, 2004). They are encouraged to ask themselves, "How might I support the cultural and literacy practices of all my students?," "Do I honor the diversity of all students in my classroom?," "How might I contribute to the overall community of readers and writers at my school?", and "What might others infer about my beliefs about reading and writing?" As future teachers, the Tall Teachers collaboratively and continuously address these questions as they participate in embedded literacy courses, work with Small Teachers, and reflect on their teaching experiences in collaboration with their peers and course instructors.

Naming and Noticing Reciprocity Between Reading and Writing

While our primary goal is to support the learning of our Small and Tall Teachers, we are also learning lessons as we observe and interact with the children. In short, as course instructors, we are continuously refining our craft as we watch and reflect on the learning that is happening in the embedded classrooms. As part of this work, course instructors and classroom teachers often engage in shared investigations which not only support children as literacy learners but also inform our work with preservice teachers. At times these investigations focus on particular children and the challenges they face in becoming literate. In other cases, the investigations may focus on a particular aspects of literacy instruction – perhaps writing conferences, mini-lessons, or reading assessments – and the ways Tall and Small Teachers are negotiating these practices.

For example, while working in an embedded classroom, Beth sat beside Jasmine, an African American fifth grader, during independent reading time. As Jasmine read, Beth noted how often she spontaneously verbalized her thoughts as she read. At first, the course instructor assumed that Jasmine was merely verbalizing her enjoyment of the text. However, over several days, Beth realized that stopping to talk distracted Jasmine from engaging with the ideas in the text which affected her understanding of the text. When asked to talk about what she had read, Jasmine recalled random information and attempted to perform the comprehension strategies that she had been taught in class (i.e., making connections, questioning the text). However, she was unable to link these ideas together or assess the relative importance of various ideas. This noticing led Beth to wonder how this affected Jasmine's writing. As predicted Jasmine's writing revealed a wordiness that hindered her construction of a coherent message. Together Beth and the classroom teacher revisited Jasmine's work during reading and writing workshop and brainstormed instructional activities that would help Jasmine to focus on meaning construction. As professionals we find ourselves noticing and naming what we observe and using that to inform our work with children and with the preservice teachers.

In order to explore these insights about literacy and to model her own learning process with the preservice teachers, Beth invited Jasmine to visit the preservice teachers to model a reading conference which included her reading and retelling of a text excerpt. After Jasmine left, the preservice teachers turned and talked about what they had observed. The instructor then asked, "Now that you have observed Jasmine as a reader, what might you predict about her as a writer?" There was a lingering and poignant moment of silence. It was then that Beth realized that the preservice teachers were unaware of the reciprocity that often exists between reading and writing. This was an important lesson for Beth who then used this information to plan future lessons for her preservice teachers. The preservice teachers' observations of Jasmine and the ensuing discussion forced them into a generative stance of questioning, reconsidering, and rethinking instruction. One preservice teacher wrote the following in her journal:

Poor writers have good ideas but have difficulty with organization and structure" (Routman, 2004, p. 24). This reminds me of the (mock) reading conference that took place in class this past Tuesday. Not to say that the student who came to read is a poor writer because I don't know her pattern as a writer. However, after the student left the classroom, we talked about how we might foresee what her writing looks like given what we now know about her as a reader. Because she likes to thoroughly explain her thoughts and often loses track of what she was talking about, I wonder if this is what I would notice in her writing.

Through ensuing conversations, Tall Teachers were not only required to make sense of what they observed, but they also needed to consider the feedback they could provide to Jasmine or a small group of children exhibiting similar patterns in the midst of a teaching moment. Making meaning through noticing and naming is part of the fabric of embedded classrooms. It is modeled by instructors and classroom teachers, operating as an expectation for the preservice teachers. Vygotsky (1978) taught us that children grow into the intellectual lives around them. The same is true of preservice teachers if given the opportunity to participate in rich embedded courses that entail opportunities to develop literacy competence. Our role as teacher educators is to create and sustain these spaces by helping students to engage in noticing, naming, and agential teaching. In the following section, we bring literacy teaching and cultural competence together to illustrate the ways attention to literacy and culture is supported by embedded experiences.

Linking Literacy Learning With Cultural Competence

When our Tall Teachers are assigned to work with Small Teachers, the significance of cultural competence becomes indisputably real. As Tall Teachers worked with their Small Teachers and reflected on their efforts, who children are came to the forefront and issues of diversity which had previously inhabited course readings came alive.

Novice teachers often feel under-prepared to teach emergent bilingual students. Working through challenges at the intersection of literacy and diversity is best accomplished in embedded settings, where preservice teachers not only directly confront these challenges, but do so in situations where help and guidance are available. In one of our embedded literacy courses, one student admitted, "I honestly, don't feel like I know enough to work with English Learners." Statements like this, continuously remind us to reflect on how language, culture and literacy intersect and must be woven throughout our literacy methods courses.

Attention to diversity is an essential consideration for literacy educators. Connections between literacy and diversity include the role of texts written in languages other than English, the role of transnational literacy practices, children's knowledge of folktales and texts from other countries (including cartoons or films), their use of other languages or language variations to communicate in writing with friends or relatives, vernacular language structures that might affect reading, and pronunciation variations that might affect spelling. However, these differences are often invisible to preservice teacher who often do not bring extensive experiences with the communities served by local schools.

Our embedded work intentionally addresses intersections between literacy and student diversity in order to support cohorts of primarily White, middle-class, female preservice teachers in bringing students' home languages and cultures into literacy classrooms. During our weekly literacy classes, students read articles and engage in facilitated conversations about diversity resulting in an increased awareness of the diverse languages spoken by our students (i.e., African American Language, Southern Vernacular English, various forms of Spanish, Arabic). Through critical conversations, preservice teachers pose problems and ask questions that invite instructors to demonstrate the use of multimodalities (i.e., popular movies and music, children's literature, family stories, childhood media) that honor children's languages and cultures.

In the next two sections, we present two examples of how literacy and diversity converge in the experiences of preservice teachers as they work in embedded classrooms. First, we feature Rebecca, a Tall Teacher who worked alongside Araceli, an emergent bilingual Small Teacher. Next, we explore the experiences of Clare as she included issues of diversity in her thinking about her Small Teacher, James. We argue that embedded and supported instructional experiences that attend to both literacy learning and cultural competence are critical to developing generative approaches to children and teaching.

Bringing Cultural Competence, Language, and Literacy Together: The Case of Rebecca

Learning to teach literacy and growing as culturally competent educators are treated as symbiotic processes designed to foster generative theories about children and literacy learning. As preservice teachers, the Tall Teachers work with their Small Teachers to develop close relationships grounded on mutual trust and respect. The Tall Teachers pay attention to children's writing practices, their reading behaviors, and the books they choose to read. They attend to who children choose as reading and writing partners and begin to anticipate the types of challenges individual children face with literacy. However, this kid watching does not end with attention to children's reading and writing. We ask our Tall Teachers to attend to diversity including how language differences affect the ways children read and write. For example, some Tall Teachers might notice that some Spanish speaking children over-rely on phonetic decoding; children who speak Asian languages might substitute "da" for "the" in their writing, and some early readers who have been exposed to Arabic might demonstrate a tendency to track print from right to left. By requiring our Tall Teachers to look closely and listen intently, they begin to learn who children are as readers and writers. Equally as important, they learn about their Small Teachers as cultural beings who bring particular linguistic and literacy experiences and resources to reading and writing. In short, the Small Teachers teach the Tall Teachers and invite them to develop generative theories about children, learning, and themselves. This process occurs under the intentional guidance of knowledgeable classroom teachers and course instructors who scaffold Tall Teachers in translating observations, noticing, and naming into carefully considered instructional actions.

To humanize our students' embedded literacy experiences, we address the assets that culturally and linguistically diverse students bring to literacy learning. We highlight the bilingual abilities of children – recognizing bilingualism as an asset rather than a deficit. We address: (1) uncovering student's linguistic repertoires; (2) examining our assumptions about languages and language varieties; (3) understanding the power of contrastive analysis; (4) recognizing students' cultural and historical resources; (5) demonstrating the use of multimodal texts, including music, children's stories, families stories, and popular culture, and; (6) recognizing and acknowledging the hegemony of Eurocentric and monolingual messages conveyed through curriculum and traditional teaching. The decision to infuse these topics and participatory practices is the embodiment of generative practice as literacy learning is connected directly to culture and as preservice teachers interact with children and honor their cultural knowledge in classrooms. Without our embedded classroom experiences, the immediacy and passion that preservice teachers bring to literacy learning and the commitment they bring to teaching their Small Teachers would not exist. It is when preservice teachers face real children, in real classrooms, that lessons about literacy and diversity converge becoming meaningful and important.

Learning to Teach Araceli

In this section, we highlight Rebecca and her work alongside a Spanish-Speaking emergent bilingual, fourth-grader - Araceli. Rebecca is a White, female preservice teacher. Like many of our students, she was not accustomed to working with emergent bilingual students. Moreover, she had not considered how Small Teachers, including Araceli, experience school. Rebecca soon noticed that Araceli was sometimes embarrassed by being a native Spanish-Speaker in her English-only classroom. Rebecca wrote:

One of the most important things that I learned about Araceli when I first met her, was that her family speaks Spanish at home. This meant that English was her second language and so she often lacked confidence in her English speaking, reading, and writing abilities. This is what ultimately made Araceli such a shy student.

Although Rebecca recognized Araceli's language as an asset, she was surprised that Araceli avoided using Spanish or displaying her bilingual abilities during reading and writing activities. Recognizing Araceli's apparent shyness and trepidation led Rebecca to ask critical questions and explore instructional possibilities. As Rebecca debriefed with her course instructor after working with Araceli, Rebecca shared her dismay and wondered how to best support Araceli. They discussed the possibility of using children's literature selections to celebrate Araceli's culture and language. They predicted that Araceli might appreciate reading bilingual texts. Rebecca chose *Mango, Abuela, and Me* (Medina, 2015) because in the story the granddaughter supports her grandmother in learning English demonstrating the power of speaking two languages and the agency of a young girl. Soon after reading this book, Rebecca began to notice a change.

Before this semester, Araceli never saw the capability that her culture had to transform her writing into something special and unique. In fact, at one point in January, Araceli was too embarrassed to even tell me her cousin's names because they were Spanish [names]. From [that] moment, I encouraged Araceli to embrace her culture and notice how special it is. I began to show her that she could use that element of her life to aid in her writing. A few weeks later, Araceli had gained confidence in using Spanish words in her work and even expressed that she wanted to use more of them. As a result of this, Araceli was able to create her own piece of writing that not only used Spanish words, but made her feel special about her work as well.

During the following weeks, Rebecca continued to participate in writing conferences with Araceli and found multiple ways to draw upon Araceli's cultural and linguistic resources. Rebecca encouraged Araceli to write about her rich experiences of cooking with her mother. As she wrote about the time she spent in the kitchen, Rebecca encouraged her to write about the food they prepared and imagine what her mom might say in Spanish. She prompted Araceli to include details and dialogue that would tell her reader about these rich experiences. Rebecca noticed a growing ease in how Araceli approached writing and the quality of the stories she produced. Rebecca reported, that when she invited Araceli to use her full linguistic repertoire and rich cultural experiences, she realized that Araceli "was remembering more and making a better connection to her writing." Rebecca's work with Araceli demonstrates the power of invitations and honoring what children bring. Rebecca found ways to assure Araceli that her culture and language had a place in the classroom. As Laman writes (2013), "Multilingual children need to know that they do not have to give up who they are or the languages they speak in order to develop their literacies" (p. 11).

By working alongside her Small Teacher and her course instructor, Rebecca noticed and named what Araceli brought to her literacy classroom. Her work was generative in that she was able to use that knowledge to craft novel literacy experiences that were responsive to Araceli as a reader, writer, and as a person. We turn now to Clare and her Small Teacher, James to continue to explore the power of noticing and naming culture in embedded spaces.

Extending Noticing, Naming, and Cultural Competence to All Young Readers and Writers

Clare, a White Tall Teacher, wrote the following kidwatching notes about her small teacher, James, who is also White and in 2nd grade.

September 19: James stopped to lament that he had to stop writing his comic series because he no longer had a partner to write with him. When asked if he believed he could continue writing it on his own, he shook his head no and said, "I need someone for ideas, I don't know how to spell some words, and I'm best at sketching."

October 17: After a period of trying to avoid reading Stink, his book for independent reading, by asking me questions or telling me something about a game he played, James was asked by my instructor what grade he thought he had to be in to read this book. He responded, "Third grade." Later, when asked what he would do if he came to a word he did not know, he stated he would give up and get a different book.

After rereading these notes, Clare reflected:

These two collections of data hinted at a pattern I had begun to notice that James lacked agency in his reading and writing. From my first day with him, I would never have guessed that he would struggle with this issue. This data was an important reminder that collecting kidwatching data allows us to dig beyond the surface level of our students [overt behaviors] to find their areas of need. Without doing this, I may have never known to teach to this need.

Rather than viewing James as resistant or as simply a struggling reader, this reflective process led Clare to consider how James viewed literacy and how he approached literacy tasks. She asked questions about his behaviors with print and wondered how agency might be fostered for James. Perhaps surprisingly, given that James and Clare are both White and middle class, she connects James' dilemma to her own cultural competence:

1. How do we build a sense of agency in our students as readers/writers so that they know they are capable of persevering through obstacles and can succeed?

2.	How can we build such agency in our diverse students?

At first, I wondered how to respond to James' need to build agency within him as an individual. Then, I began to broaden this wondering to explore students as a whole. My internship site is diverse, including a 30% ELL population. This made me wonder further about how I could also take a cultural lens to this question.

This instance of noticing and naming is impressive because Clare is not just watching James; she is engaging in generative theory building about him as a reader, a writer, and a cultural being. While Clare could have dismissed James as a struggling reader or perhaps blamed his family for not providing him with the right literacy experiences at home, instead, Clare demonstrated thoughtfulness and a willingness to learn more about James and the resources he brought to the classroom. In short, Clare accepted the challenge to revisit her own practices and to explore possibilities for supporting James in becoming more agential and invested in his reading. This led her to consider culture. Next steps may have included exploring the texts and stories that James brought to the classroom, inviting James to share his online literacy practices, attending to how James told stories and seeking texts that echo those forms, listening to James' reading for evidence of linguistic differences that might affect his reading, and seeking texts that reflected James' home experiences. As Clare move through this process, her cultural competence developed in tandem with learning about James as a literacy learner. James was teaching Clare.

Becoming knowledgeable about meeting the needs of readers and writers is much like learning to read and write; it is a process. The process entails kidwatching, building a knowledge base about reading and writing, understanding children's cognitive processes, releasing responsibility to learners, recognizing the diverse experiences of learners, and being culturally responsive. To maximize learning, Tall Teachers work side by side with Small Teachers to implement and extend the theories they are learning in books.

CONCLUSION

In this chapter, we argue for generative teacher education experiences that engage preservice teachers in embedded teaching experiences that require them to spontaneously and intentionally incorporate problem-solving stances towards teaching. Our goal is for them to view themselves as capable and agential even in challenging situations. Through generative and embedded teaching experiences, we argue that preservice teachers learn to spontaneously and skillfully adjust their teaching to children. They routinely engage in self-introspection and readily incorporate novel ways of thinking about children as they teach. When Tall Teachers encounter diverse ways of acting and being, they seek solutions by questioning their own perspectives and practices, while striving to create opportunities for children to learn.

However, we have found that a stand-alone class dedicated to culturally sustaining pedagogy is not sufficient for fostering culturally competent novice teachers. Generative theory building is deeply connected to experiences with children. When teachers are immersed in schools, working with children, and provided with opportunities to talk and reflect on their experiences, discourses of possibility and agency are fostered. Students are not expected to independently make sense of cultural differences. Instead, Tall Teacher collaborate with their course instructors and classroom teachers, as they collaboratively notice, name, watch, and wonder. Working with actual children brings an urgency to conversations about equity that places children and learning opportunities at the center.

While we believe that cultural competence as an essential foundation for the development of generative teaching theories, noticing and naming of literacy learning is also critical for supporting learning for children from a range of backgrounds. Preservice teachers must notice and name what their Small Teachers do with text. As the case of Rebecca and Araceli reveals, cultural competence is explicitly linked to the teaching of reading and writing.

It is this immersion of self, culture, difference, children, curricula, and literacy that invites preservice teachers to negotiate learning in embedded classrooms. None of these dimensions operates independently, and cannot be learned independently. They are inseparable and must be learned in conjunction with each other. Embedded classes allow generative learning to happen. In short, our Small Teachers teach our Tall Teachers. When grappling with the learning of actual students alongside our own development as educators, we are forced to manage complexity – which can only be accomplished through active and agential efforts alongside careful self-examination that must occur in conversation with the magnificence of what all children bring to literacy learning.

REFERENCES

Assaf, L. C., & López, M. M. (2015). Generative Learning in a Service-Learning Project and Field-Base Teacher Education Program: Learning to Become Culturally Responsive Teachers. *Literacy Research: Theory, Method, and Practice*, *64*(1), 323–338.

Cambourne, B. (1984). *Towards a Reading-Writing Classroom*. Portsmouth, NH: Heinemann.

Darling-Hammond, L. (2006). Constructing 21st-century teacher education. *Journal of Teacher Education*, *57*(3), 300–314. doi:10.1177/0022487105285962

Freire, P. (1986). *Pedagogy of the oppressed*. New York: Continuum.

Goldring, R., Gray, L., & Bitterman, A. (2013). *Characteristics of Public and Private Elementary and Secondary School Teachers in the United States: Results from the 2011-12 Schools and Staffing Survey. First Look. NCES 2013-314*. National Center for Education Statistics.

González, N., Moll, L., & Amanti, C. (2005). *Funds of knowledge: Theorizing practices in households, communities, and classrooms*. Lawrence Erlbaum Associates, Publishers.

Harro, B. (2000). The cycle of socialization. *Readings for Diversity and Social Justice, 15,* 21.

Johnston, P. H. (2004). *Choice words: How our language affects children's learning.* Stenhouse Publishers.

Ladson-Billings, G. (1995). But that's just good teaching: The case for culturally relevant pedagogy. *Theory into Practice*, *34*(3), 159–165. doi:10.1080/00405849509543675

Ladson-Billings, G. (2014). Culturally relevant pedagogy 2.0: A.k.a. the remix. *Harvard Educational Review*, *84*(1), 74–84. doi:10.17763/haer.84.1.p2rj131485484751

McNaughton, S. (2002). *Meeting of the minds*. Wellington, NZ: Learning Media.

Medina, M. (2015). *Mango, Abuela, and me*. New York: Candlewick Press.

Moll, L. C., Amanti, C., Neff, D., & Gonzalez, N. (1992). Funds of knowledge for teaching: Using a qualitative approach to connect homes and classrooms. *Theory into Practice*, *31*(1), 132–141. doi:10.1080/00405849209543534

Moore, R. (2003). Reexamining the field experiences of preservice teachers. *Journal of Teacher Education*, *54*(1), 31–42. doi:10.1177/0022487102238656

Nieto, S. (2000). Placing equity front and center: Some thoughts on transforming teacher education for a new century. *Journal of Teacher Education*, *51*(3), 180–187. doi:10.1177/0022487100051003004

Nieto, S. (2009). *The light in their eyes: Creating multicultural learning communities*. New York: Teachers College Press.

Paris, D. (2012). Culturally sustaining pedagogy: A needed change in stance, terminology, and practice. *Educational Researcher*, *41*(3), 93–97. doi:10.3102/0013189X12441244

Risko, V. J., Roller, C. M., Cummins, C., Bean, R. M., Block, C. C., Anders, P. L., & Flood, J. (2008). A critical analysis of research on reading teacher education. *Reading Research Quarterly*, *43*(3), 252–288. doi:10.1598/RRQ.43.3.3

Rosenblatt, L. M. (1994). *The reader, the text, the poem: The transactional theory of the literary work*. Southern Illinois University Press.

Routman, R. (2004). *Writing essentials: Raising expectations and results while simplifying teaching*. Portsmouth, NH: Heinemann.

Schön, D. A. (1995). Knowing-in-action: The new scholarship requires a new epistemology. *Change: The Magazine of Higher Learning*, *27*(6), 27–34. doi:10.1080/00091383.1995.10544673

Siegel, M. (1995). More than words: The generative power of transmediation for learning. *Canadian Journal of Education/Revue canadienne de l'éducation*, 455-475.

Sleeter, C. E. (2001). Preparing teachers for culturally diverse schools: Research and the overwhelming presence of whiteness. *Journal of Teacher Education*, *52*(2), 94–106. doi:10.1177/0022487101052002002

Souto-Manning, M. (2013). *Multicultural teaching in the early childhood classroom: Approaches, strategies, and tools preschool-2ⁿᵈ grade*. New York: Teachers College Press.

Stephens, D., Cox, R., Downs, A., Goforth, J., Jaeger, L., Matheny, A., ... Thompson, T. (2012). "I Know There Ain't no Pigs with Wigs": Challenges of Tier 2 Intervention. *The Reading Teacher*, *66*(2), 93–103. doi:10.1002/TRTR.01094

Vygotsky, L. (1978). *Mind in society: The development of higher psychological processes*. Cambridge, MA: Harvard University Press.

Waller, W. (1932/1961). *The sociology of teaching*. Hoboken, NJ: John Wiley & Sons. doi:10.1037/11443-000

Wingeier, D. E. (1980). Generative words in six cultures. *Religious Education (Chicago, Ill.)*, *75*(5), 563–576. doi:10.1080/0034408800750508

Zeichner, K. (2010). Rethinking the connections between campus courses and field experiences in college-and university-based teacher education. *Journal of Teacher Education*, *61*(1-2), 89–99. doi:10.1177/0022487109347671

Chapter 11
Beyond Urban or Rural:
Field–Based Experiences for Teaching Residencies in Diverse Contexts

Laura Vernikoff
Teachers College, Columbia University, USA

Tom Schram
University of New Hampshire, USA

Emilie Mitescu Reagan
University of New Hampshire, USA

Colleen Horn
Teachers College, Columbia University, USA

A. Lin Goodwin
University of Hong Kong, Hong Kong

Leslie J. Couse
University of New Hampshire, USA

ABSTRACT

In this chapter, the authors describe two residency programs, an established urban teacher residency program, and a newly developed rural teacher residency program, and explain how the programs have expanded notions of field experiences to prepare teachers for specific schools, districts, and communities. The authors explore commonalities and connections across the programs, particularly in how each program conceptualizes the role of place in teacher education. In addition, this chapter considers differences in how each program enacts their theories of place in order to prepare teachers to learn from, with, and about the particular places they will teach within.

DOI: 10.4018/978-1-5225-6249-8.ch011

INTRODUCTION

Most teacher education programs offer generic, decontextualized preparation, intended to be applicable across a variety of schools and settings. As a result, scholars argue that many teachers are unprepared for *how* to learn in and from the communities they teach (White & Reid, 2008; Zeichner, Bowman, Guillen, & Napolitan, 2016). Teacher education programs must also prepare teachers to learn from and with the communities both inside and outside school walls.

Teacher residencies have been created with the understanding that teacher education should be place specific because urban and rural schools face distinct institutional challenges (Matsko & Hammerness, 2014; Williamson, Apedoe, & Thomas, 2016), and can provide unique avenues of support through community and social support networks (Gadsden & Dixon-Roman, 2017; Oakes, Franke, Quartz, & Rogers, 2002). Building on calls for prolonged and intensive field experiences at the core of teacher preparation (e.g., Guha, Hyler, & Darling-Hammond, 2017; NEW AACTE Clinical Practice Commission, 2018), teacher residency programs immerse teacher candidates (known as "residents") in PK-12 schools over the course of an entire school year under the guidance of a mentor teacher, often alongside coursework leading to a Master's degree. A key characteristic of the residency program model is the explicit partnerships with specific urban and rural districts to recruit, prepare and support teachers in hard to staff certification areas in under-resourced schools (Guha, Hyler, & Darling-Hammond, 2017).

In this chapter, the authors highlight two residency programs: an established urban teacher residency program in New York City (Teaching Residents at Teachers College, or TR@TC), and a newly developed rural teacher residency program in northern New Hampshire (University of New Hampshire Teacher Residency for Rural Education, or TRRE), then describe how the programs have expanded notions of school and community field experiences to prepare teachers for specific schools, districts, and communities. The authors represent faculty and staff who have occupied a variety of roles in the two programs including Program Director, Partnership Coordinator, Director of Pedagogy and Clinical Practice, and research assistant. One author worked at both residency programs, and drew upon her experience working with TR@TC to inform the development of the TRRE program. She also continues to work with the TR@TC research team, allowing for opportunities to collaborate and cross-pollinate across programs. These programs have many commonalities and connections, particularly in their commitments to preparing teachers who understand and draw upon the places they teach within and about. There are also significant differences between the programs as well (see Appendix).

Specifically, TR@TC is a federally funded (USDOE, 2009, 2014) Master's level program, which leads to certification in secondary Teaching English to Speakers of Other Languages (TESOL), Teaching Students with Disabilities (TSWD), and Science (added in 2014), in return for a commitment to teach in New York City (NYC) public schools after graduation. Across the program, from admissions, to coursework, to field placements, TR@TC residents are asked to engage with place explicitly and directly. The program has expanded from fourteen to eighteen months, giving residents an additional semester to fulfill requirements and to build a deeper understanding of NYC schools before beginning their residency. Throughout, residents each satisfy specific program/certification requirements while participating in residency-specific requirements that ground coursework in NYC schools. Residents take a sequence of four residency-specific courses, (one each in the spring, summer, fall, and spring semesters) parallel to field-based experiences, which help residents make sense of what they are learning in the context of NYC schools. In addition, residents complete a year-long residency, including four days of school placement a week at one school (all four days) or two schools (three days at one school, one at the other). Graduates are required to teach for three years in high-needs NYC schools. As of 2017, 84% of all program graduates were still teaching in NYC schools, including 79% of graduates who had remained in NYC schools after the fulfillment of their 3-year service agreement. Following graduation, residents receive formal induction support for two years, Many graduates have remained connected to the program after the formal induction period has ended, leading to the development of additional programming for more experienced teachers, such as curriculum planning or inquiry groups.

TRRE is a 15-month residency program that prepares elementary and secondary mathematics and science teachers for rural New Hampshire communities, located in the central and northern parts of New Hampshire. The program was funded by a grant from the US Department of Education in 2016, and launched its first cohort in May 2017. TRRE residents begin the program with a summer institute that involves three graduate level courses, school-based activities, interviews with key school personnel and community members, and an internship with a local community-based organization. During the academic year that follows, residents continue full-time graduate coursework and complete a residency placement in a partnership rural school for three days a week in the fall and four days a week in the spring, under the guidance of an experienced teaching mentor. In the second summer of the program, TRRE residents complete coursework leading toward a Master's degree and recommendation for initial teacher certification. Following completion of the Master's degree, TRRE graduates commit to teaching in a rural, high need partnership school for at least three years. During this time, graduates are offered mentoring and induction support from University faculty and staff. TRRE is currently in its second year, and will have its first graduating cohort of five residents in summer 2018.

The authors organize the remainder of this chapter as follows, describing: 1) research on urban and rural teacher preparation; 2) theories of place and teacher education; 3) the particular urban and rural communities and partnership schools; 4) field-based programmatic components of the two residency programs that draw upon the many assets in urban and rural places, and; 5) a synthesis of the common threads across programs that go beyond "urban" and "rural," and that offer implications for expanding notions of field experiences in the teacher education profession.

RELEVANT RESEARCH ON URBAN AND RURAL TEACHER PREPARATION

Existing research on "urban" and "rural" education in general, and on preparing teachers for urban and rural places in particular, suggests a lack of shared understanding about what, specifically, distinguishes urban and rural teaching from each other and from suburban teaching. Further, existing research on urban and rural education does not necessarily address diversity within particular urban or rural places. As a result, existing research does not always distinguish what, specifically, is important to attend to in urban or rural teaching. Instead, articles on urban or rural education might focus only on urban or rural students, and neglect other aspects of place (e.g., Milner, 2012).

The term "urban" is often used in education and teacher education as a synonym for students who are not White, or as a euphemism for deficit-based and often racialized characterizations of students, regardless of where they live or attend school (Frankenburg, Taylor, & Merseth, 2009; Watson, 2012). However, in this chapter the authors conceptualize urban, and cities, as referring to a high density and diversity not only of people, but also land use, businesses, cultural institutions, and other resources (Jacobs, 1992). As with all places, NYC has particular boundaries, physical forms, and diverse and complex meanings ascribed to it by its inhabitants and others (Gieryn, 2000). In addition, NYC's boundaries are porous, as people travel in and out for work and play, to visit or to stay. In this way, the local is always interacting with the global in NYC.

Urban teacher residencies aim to prepare teachers who may not be from urban areas themselves (Tindle, Freund, Belknap, Green, & Shotel, 2011), to develop the dispositions (Tindle, Freund, Belknap, Green, & Shotel, 2011) and skills (Hammerness & Craig, 2016; Williamson, Apedoe, & Thomas, 2016) specific to teaching in particular cities. Specifically, urban teacher residencies consider the context, or place of the residency to be content that must be taught along with pedagogical and content knowledges (Hammerness & Craig, 2016). In addition, urban teacher residencies are often designed to be directly and immediately beneficial to districts and current urban teachers through close partnerships that allow the residency to meet specific district needs and support mentor teachers (Hammerness, Williamson, & Kosnick, 2016; Solomon, 2009). Finally, urban teacher residencies aim to increase teacher retention in hard-to-staff urban districts through recruitment incentives, such as tuition exemptions, improved preparation, and induction support after graduation (e.g., Berry, Montgomery, & Snyder, 2008; Klein, Taylor, Onore, Strom, & Abrams, 2013; Solomon, 2009).

Characteristics commonly used to define rurality include low population density and isolation, school and community interdependence, a history of conflict regarding purposes of schooling, an "out-migration" of young talent, and a salient attachment to place (Biddle & Azano, 2016; Budge, 2006; Tieken, 2014). A general perception so often promulgated in the media and fiction is that small towns are a thing of the past, and thus must surely be declining (Wuthnow, 2013). In this chapter, the authors push against these definitions and conceptualize "rural," much like the notion of "community," as a concept that people construct and maintain through the ways they talk about it. As Kline and Walker-Gibbs (2015) suggest, "rurality" is defined as both "a quantitative measure of distance from an urban centre, and as a cultural construct concerned with community demographics and the interaction between residents" (pp. 68-69). Thus, its existence depends in part on the complex and overlapping considerations of geography, demography, and economy, but also in large part on the commonalities and norms of rurality that local inhabitants know, emphasize, and consider important, and that are constituted in everyday interactions and events. As Tieken (2014) further conveys:

This understanding, shared by many of the residents of rural communities, is tied to place; it provides a geography-dependent sense of belonging. Rural, in this conception, is not simply a matter of boundaries. It constitutes one's identity; it shapes perspectives and understandings; and it gives meaning to one's daily experiences. (p. 5)

While rural teacher residency programs are relatively new, rural teacher preparation programs have emphasized notions of place to effectively prepare teachers for rural and remote regions (Biddle & Azano, 2016). Research suggests that isolated experiences such as rural "field trips" (Richards, 2012; Trinidad, Sharplin, Ledger, & Broadly, 2014) are not enough to prepare teacher candidates to teach in rural communities. Rather, multiple field experiences that acknowledge the particularities of rural communities (White & Reid, 2008), along with reciprocal school-university-community partnerships may support the recruitment, preparation, and retention of teachers in rural schools and communities.

Many teacher residency programs are at least nominally urban or rural residencies, aiming to recruit, prepare, and retain teachers for urban and rural areas, which are considered hard to staff. Emerging research suggests that teacher residency programs have been successful in teacher recruitment, particularly in diversifying the teaching workforce and recruiting teachers for hard to staff fields such as science, math and special education (NCTR, 2016). Research also suggests that teacher residency program graduates tend to remain in teaching longer than their peers in the same districts (e.g., Berry, Montgomery, & Snyder, 2008), and that some elements of teacher residency programs, such as opportunities for residents to experience more practice teaching, observation of other classroom teaching, and feedback on their own teaching, may increase retention as well (Ingersoll, Merrill, & May, 2014).

FRAMING TEACHER EDUCATION WITHIN THEORIES OF PLACE

This chapter draws upon notions of place-based (Comber, Reid, & Nixon, 2007; Shamah & Tavish, 2009; Sobel, 2005) and place-conscious (Gruenewald, 2003) education. Although theories of place in education initially emerged from rural education (e.g., White & Reid, 2008), urban educators have also begun applying place-oriented lenses to both teaching and teacher education (e.g., Matsko & Hammerness, 2014). Theories of place within education consider the specific and unique ecological, structural, and human resources inherent to particular places, rather than aiming to provide a standardized learning experience intended to be applicable across all settings. Considering place within teacher education can help educators and teacher educators draw upon local resources in order to promote student learning.

The concept of "place-*based* pedagogies" (e.g. Sobel, 2004, 2005) has directed attention to developing teachers who appreciate and possess a context-specific sense of particular urban and rural places and people, their histories and complexity, their problems and their potential, and the particular issues of sustainability with which they are dealing. Toward this end, programmatic structures in both programs have aimed to ensure the relevance, responsiveness, and connectedness of curriculum and pedagogy to particular settings, while simultaneously equipping residents to find their own place as teachers and residents within the social and cultural geography of the local communities.

"Place-*conscious* pedagogies" (Greenwood, 2013; Gruenewald, 2003) more critically and comprehensively challenge us to consider how places "*teach* us about how the world works and how our lives fit into the spaces we occupy" (Gruenewald, 2003, p. 621), including how people shape places (Greenwood, 2013). A place-conscious approach has helped shed light, for instance, on one of the principle dilemmas for urban and rural schools and communities, namely, how local identities and the lived realities of those communities are reconciled against the backdrop of broader social, cultural, political, and economic changes. Programmatic structures can enhance awareness of community, never realized as entirely self-contained or fixed enclosures, even in the most dense or remote locales. Local inhabitants participate in the wider world, too, necessitating an outward-looking engagement with broader networks of influence and globalization (Wuthnow, 2013). This elicits responsibility on the part of both residency programs to come to understand each local community's relationships with other places.

Across both residency programs, the authors see place-based and place-conscious teacher preparation programs as opportunities for preservice teachers to learn about and engage with the communities and places in which they (will) teach in order to cultivate novice teachers as lifelong professional learners who are able to "understand how to work with others in the school and community to become leaders who can collaborate to change system constraints when they seem clearly less than ideal" (Hammerness, Darling-Hammond, & Bransford, 2005, p. 365).

In the following sections, the authors offer narratives of the cities and towns in which the residency programs are located, along with the partnership districts and schools with which the residency programs collaborate, and a description of field based experiences that prepare residents for these schools and communities. The authors aim to provide thick and rich descriptions that reveal "dynamic interaction among the different parts of the programs" (Hollins 2015, p. xii). In keeping with theories of place, the narratives take up the distinct voices of the authors and the places in which these programs are located.

URBAN TEACHER RESIDENCY

New York City and Its Schools

TR@TC was created to prepare teachers for NYC schools. New York City is a great city (Jacobs, 1992) with over 8 million residents, making it larger than 40 states. Cities, as Jacobs notes, are natural generators of diversity; as a result, it is difficult to describe and sum up NYC or its schools. New York City teachers must be aware of the great range of schools, neighborhoods, and communities within the borders of the five boroughs, and be equipped to learn from and draw upon that diversity. Even native New Yorkers who enroll in TR@TC may know only a small fraction of the city and its schools, and may hold stereotypes or misconceptions about other neighborhoods, their communities, and their students.

Although social science literature on NYC and its schools frequently focuses on the problems they face or embody, others celebrate NYC through music, novels, essays, poems, photographs, graffiti, sculptures, and a range of other texts that reveal the many different sides of the city, and concomitantly, the diversity and inclusive character of its schools. Students in NYC can see themselves represented in a wide range of books, tv series, movies, songs, and other texts, as long as their teachers know how to find and use these texts--but *can* does not always result in *do*. Still, local libraries offer these texts in a wide range of languages and modalities. For example, the Queens Library, serving just one of the five boroughs of NYC, has materials in over 60 languages, provides services for new immigrants, and offers a variety of free programs for children and young people including tutoring, board games, and coding classes (Queens Library, 2014).

New York is an international, global city. More than one third of city residents were born abroad, and more than half of city residents speak a language other than English at home, representing over 200 languages (NYC Department of City Planning, 2018). The NYC public school system, educating more than 1.1 million children, is the largest school system in the country. Over 175 languages are spoken in the public schools, and the district offers a variety of bilingual programs in languages such as Arabic, Bengali, Chinese, French, Haitian-Creole, Korean, Russian, Yiddish and Spanish (NYC Department of Education, 2018). However, individual schools range from highly segregated to "hyper-diverse" (Malsbary, 2016) contexts that encompass a range of languages, ethnicities, and socioeconomic statuses.

As with many aspects of living in a city, transportation is often public and communal. Less than half of NYC households own a car (NYC Economic Development Corporation, 2012). Even those who own cars do not necessarily use them on a regular basis. Instead, people walk or take public transportation--subways, buses, ferries, or a tram. New York City has the 7th largest annual subway ridership in the world (Metropolitan Transportation Authority, 2018), which means routinely, and on a daily basis, subways bring together New Yorkers, both native and adopted, from all walks of life, ethnicities, social positions, origins, professions, etc. into one space. However, access to public transit also varies quite a bit. The average commute time for high school students, who receive free MetroCards to get to school, was estimated to be 32 minutes in 2012, with approximately 20% of students commuting longer than 45 minutes each way, and almost 3% commuting more than 75 minutes each way (NYC Independent

Budget Office, 2014a). As a result, there may be many differences between students' home and school neighborhoods.

Neighborhoods across NYC vary tremendously. New York City has wide income disparities, ranging from a median income of $8,694 per household in one neighborhood in the Bronx, to over $200,000 per household in three neighborhoods in Manhattan. Affluent and low-income neighborhoods often sit side by side; for example, adjacent census tracts may have differences in median incomes of almost $150,000 (Venugopal, 2011). Neighborhoods in NYC also vary in density, languages spoken, and access to different types of services. For example, neighborhoods range in density from less than 25 people per acre to over 200 people per acre (NYC Department of City Planning, 2010). In different neighborhoods, store signs might be written in Spanish, Chinese, Arabic, Korean, Hindi, Yiddish, Hebrew, or a variety of other languages. Although the city as a whole is vast, within neighborhoods, there are communities of people who know each other and have relationships through sitting on stoops and talking, interactions at the local bodega or dog park, or taking the same bus at the same time each morning on the way to school or work.

Communities in NYC are not necessarily location-bound. Residents can use public transportation to travel across the city to participate in a variety of religious events at one of thousands of churches, or hundreds of houses of worship affiliated with other religions such as synagogues, mosques, temples, and shrines (Grimes, 2015). New Yorkers can also participate in games of pickup basketball or soccer, or join a Y, Jewish Community Center, or NYC Parks Department recreation center to play on youth and adult sport leagues. New Yorkers can also congregate in one of 205 public libraries, or 1,700 public parks across the city. At the same time, communities in NYC can be location-bound, with some residents rarely venturing outside their neighborhood or borough.

The NYC school system is similarly complex and vast, comprising over 1,800 schools. Over the last 17 years, there have been radical changes to the NYC school system related to a confluence of policy changes, particularly No Child Left Behind (2001) and Mayor Michael Bloomberg taking control of city schools, replacing the Board of Education with the Department of Education (NYCDOE) in 2002. Many large, zoned schools which had existed in neighborhoods for generations were closed down as they failed to make adequate yearly progress, and replaced with smaller schools that required applications to attend (NYCDOE, 2009); as of 2014, 54% of public secondary schools had been opened during or after 2001. Concurrently, racial segregation has increased in city schools, and a lawsuit filed by the Office of Civil Rights in 2007 argued that the new small schools frequently excluded young people receiving special education services (Jensen, 2012).

There are other layers of school systems within NYC including charter school networks and religious school systems. For example, one charter school network in NYC enrolls 15,500 students in 46 schools (Success Academy, 2018). The Islamic Schools Association supports a few thousand students. The Archdiocese of New York educates a religiously diverse student body of 85,000 in Catholic schools across the city. The Board of Jewish Education of New York's day schools enroll 100,000 students, which are more students than attend public school in Boston. The City University of New York (CUNY) and State University of New York (SUNY) run dozens of public institutions of higher education within NYC, but also run or partner with a few K-12 schools. For example, Hunter College Elementary and High Schools are public schools funded, operated, and staffed by CUNY rather than the NYCDOE. SUNY is responsible for several charter schools. Finally, independent private schools in NYC enroll approximately 40,000 students (NYC Independent Budget Office, 2014b); tuition at these schools can be as high as college tuition.

In addition, there is great disparity in both income and per pupil school funding between New York City neighborhoods and surrounding suburbs; for example, Westchester County, which borders the Bronx, has an average median household income of nearly a quarter million dollars; one district's averatge per pupil funding within Westchester was $29,215 in the 2015-16 school year (Newsday, 2014). On the other hand, the average per pupil funding in NYC was $8,255 in the 2013-2014 school year, not counting District 75 schools, which enroll only students with disabilities, but including special education programs and funding within community schools (NYC Independent Budget Office, 2015). In 1993, the Campaign for Fiscal Equity launched a lawsuit against New York State for inadequately funding NYC schools. After many appeals, the New York State Court of Appeals found that NYS had denied NYC students a "sound basic education" guaranteed in the State Constitution in 2006. However, much of the money that has been promised has not been delivered. Having such stark economic disparities in such close proximity can generate resentment (e.g., Kozol, 1991, 2005) and does not necessarily translate into opportunities for young people to attend schools across racial or socioeconomic lines.

Related to these initiatives, there have been many changes in the ways in which teachers and administrators have been recruited and compensated. Teacher salaries increased significantly under Mayor Bloomberg to become more competitive with other regional districts (NYC Office of the Mayor, 2006). However, more controversially, Bloomberg actively recruited chancellors and administrators from outside the field of education. Alternative certification programs such as New York City Teaching Fellows were also been developed to recruit more teachers into NYC schools; currently 12% of NYC teachers were recruited and prepared by the Fellows program (NYC Teaching Fellows, 2018).

Place-conscious educators and teacher educators can draw upon NYC's many resources, and must also be aware of the unequal and inequitable ways in which those resources are distributed across the city and made available to young people. Place-conscious educators and teacher educators must also navigate and work against pressures to standardize curricula rather than localize them, to pathologize minoritized urban youngsters, versus those of the majority, and to economize and reduce education spending in one of the richest cities on earth.

TR@TC Beginnings and Goals

TR@TC's mission is to prepare—and retain—excellent teachers for urban secondary schools in New York City who are ready and able to teach/reach all students with love, compassion and powerful pedagogy. The authors envision teachers as public intellectuals and social justice advocates, deliberative and reflective teacher-leaders who collaboratively work towards equitable education for all children, especially those neglected, marginalized and under-educated by schools. Teaching all students well figures prominently in education rhetoric, even while there is ample evidence that educators and schools are consistently better at teaching *some* students, not all. Rhetoric and good intentions notwithstanding, youth underserved by schools (and society) are invariably those who experience multiple vulnerabilities and are seen as less than because of their "differences"--race, poverty, language, gender, among other factors, diversities that are often construed as deficits. While space does not allow a comprehensive discussion of the reasons why this is the reality for too many youth, TR@TC strives to disturb this reality through the preparation of educators who can equitably and capably teach and advocate for the students they serve in high need, urban schools. The program's philosophy is that good teaching can and must be learned, that learning to teach is a developmental continuum, that teachers learn best in a community of peers, and that an inclusive, justice-focused disposition is inadequate in the absence of relevant knowledge and skill. The program's vision is also driven by societal and classroom realities, and thus its steadfast aim is to be responsive to the complexities of public schools, and to both prepare quality teachers, and enhance the learning of teachers already in place.

The program's vision is enacted concretely and deliberately through four instructional pillars: STEM Literacy and Enrichment; Instructional Technology and Assistive Technology; Universal Design for Learning (UDL) and Curriculum Development; and Co-Teaching and Co-Planning across Science, Special Education and ESL. Together, these four pillars undergird and frame the 18-month integrating seminar required of all residents, no matter their certification area. Each pillar is articulated so as to be directly relevant to educating diverse students in an unequal world, and thus is intended to support residents in developing the mindsets as well as the specific practices necessary for equalizing educational opportunity.

Still, as generative as the four pillars might be, they can easily become silos. TR@TC operates instead according to the axiom that teacher certification may be categorical, but children are not. Thus, the program defines social justice educators as intentionally prepared to cross disciplinary and specialization boundaries so as to confidently respond to the wide range of strengths and needs their (any) students will express, strengths and needs that are unlikely to be confined to the subject or area in which their teacher holds a license. The TR@TC core courses that together form the curricular backbone of the entire program ensure that residents, regardless of certification area, gain basic understandings of academic supports, strategies, rights, and resources related to students—and families—who will always present with a diversity of exceptional needs. Finally, the program unapologetically adopts a capacity-based versus deficit-based approach to teaching and learning.

TR@TC Place-Based and Place-Conscious Field Experiences

Over time, TR@TC has incorporated place more explicitly and purposefully in all aspects of the program, as the program has developed a broader understanding of what it means to educate for teachers for a particular place. Initially, TR@TC's curriculum focused primarily on preparing teachers for NYC's students, anchoring coursework in inclusive education, culturally relevant pedagogy. The program aimed to equip residents with foundational knowledge and skills to support diverse students, their needs, and their capacities. Program staff also designed events and activities throughout the program to unearth (unconscious) stereotypes about urban schools and youngsters as dysfunctional, pathological and broken (Noguera, 2003; Watson 2011), and to offer counter-narratives of possibility and capacity. The program carefully chose school partners and field placements to ensure that residents would experience schools that were designated as high need, but that evidenced strong leadership, expert teaching, and engaging curriculum. To accomplish this, program staff visited, observed, interviewed, and debated potential schools and mentor teachers, handpicking partners who could support our vision of place-based teacher preparation that would go beyond technical skills to engage residents in the social context of the school and the broader communities served by the school and district (Hollins, 2012; Weiner, 2006).

Over time, the program realized that the initial focus on students was too narrow, and that preparing teachers for NYC schools also meant helping them to navigate the particular bureaucratic and political structures of NYC; to draw upon the many resources found in NYC such as museums, community centers, and local businesses; and to understand the diversity within and across NYC schools (Vernikoff, Goodwin, Horn, & Akin, in press). The program learned that place was not simply a function of geography, nor an addendum to the curriculum or even an illustration of theory enacted, but 'the process of using the local community and environment as a starting point to teach concepts...[that]...this approach to education…helps students develop stronger ties to their community" (Sobel, 2004, p. 7). Once the program moved beyond place as a physical space, staff were able to recognize place-consciousness at the heart of place-based, and that the challenge lay in helping residents develop stronger ties to the communities in which they were/would be working, to come to embrace those communities as "theirs." Even residents from NYC who had attended its public schools as students might still be unfamiliar with the full range of communities and schools in the city, because "human beings are responsible for place making" (Gruenewald, 2003, p. 627), and place, is never just place.

One change the program made was in how it works with school partners who are so central to TR@ TC field based experiences. First, the program inverted typical notions of *field*-based so that field was not just out there, but in here. That is, the program deliberately invited those in place (e.g., mentor teachers) to play a formal role within the program as co-planners and co-teachers who could help deliberately scaffold residents' understanding of the many places labeled "NYC public school." In a similar vein, residents visit a variety of city schools through guided observations undertaken during the first semester of the program. These visits provide a space for residents, assisted by experienced guides, to contextualize what they observe. Supervisors, mentor teachers, and faculty, most of whom have experience teaching in local schools, help residents reflect on ways in which stereotypes about urban students, and assumptions about what urban students need, create barriers to authentic relationships with students and their families. Residents have expressed surprise that many of the schools they visit appear to be welcoming places, offering high-level instruction, and educating a more diverse group of students than the (exclusively Black and/or Latinx) students they expected to see.

Third, the configuration of placements was revised. In the first implementation of TR@TC, residents stayed in one placement throughout the year, but were required to have a second experience in a different school. By very definition, residencies are immersion experiences in one setting, so residents' second placement was therefore adjunct to the main placement, designed to provide them the opportunity to learn "urban school" from an alternate perspective. This second placement, although continuous, provided a truncated experience lasting first two weeks, and then a full month, which never afforded residents depth of understanding given their visitor status. In TR@TC's second implementation, each resident is now placed in two diverse placements from September to June, three days a week in one, and one day a week in another. Each placement serves a different purpose, but both allow residents to extend beyond learning *about* place, to become *of* place, and "provide opportunities for students to participate meaningfully in the process of place making, that is, in the process of shaping what our places will become" (Gruenewald, 2003, p. 627)

Finally, Community Walks are another example of an intentional place-based assignment or activity that has evolved with time. TR@TC uses community walks to provide a stronger role for schools and communities within the teacher education program (Zeichner, 2006), and as a source of place-based learning for residents (Matsko & Hammerness, 2014). Initially, community walks were completed during the Intensive Summer Institute. However, to better understand the complexities of place-based education in NYC, residents now engage the assignment multiple times throughout the program/residency, and in multiple spaces, and:

are encouraged to examine and respond to the needs of the(ir) communities, while gaining an understanding of how local institutions function and social relationships shape experiences of privileged and marginalized groups. (Flynn, Kemp, & Callejo-Perez, 2010, p. 138)

The community walks first acquaint residents with the physical form of the city as they move through different neighborhoods and consider where, how, why—and why not—things are located in relation to each other. The assignment is intended to interrupt deficit notions of place that residents might bring with them as they enter unfamiliar communities, to help them see with "fresh eyes" that "not all places are equal, and some places seem…to be more "fully" places than others" (McClay, 2014, p. 3). Here is where place-based and place-consciousness (e)merge, as residents critically examine how the world works differently—and unequally—for different communities, as issues of power, political will, economics and race, shape and decide opportunities for, resources in, and perceptions of neighborhoods.

In reflections and debriefs, residents consider ways in which locations are not neutral, but are mediated by and mediate social processes. Community walks show the diversity of people and places across the city, and help residents identify and draw upon nontraditional resources in teaching, such as local community-based organizations, local inhabitants, and local businesses. But, they also help residents to "see" how there are multiple worlds at play in any community, some of which are (and have historically been) deliberately structured to oppress certain communities and deny their basic and fundamental rights around health, nutrition, safety, employment, schooling, and housing, at the same time that communities, no matter how impoverished or empty they may appear—or are defined—are also resilient, rich with possibility, and filled with real people and families living full lives.

RURAL TEACHER RESIDENCY

North Country, New Hampshire and Its Schools

The Teacher Residency for Rural Education (TRRE) program has engaged teacher educators in a dialogue between the mutually informing conceptual frameworks of place-based and place-conscious pedagogy, that, on the one hand, foreground preparation of teachers for specific places, and, on the other hand, foster a consciousness of the importance of place beyond the immediate and local. The TRRE partnership communities highlighted in this chapter are located in northern New Hampshire (NH) in a geographically isolated region, known colloquially as the North Country. Driving from the University in the more heavily populated southern part of the state to the North Country entails a three hour car ride on two-lane roads, passing through some of the highest mountains in the Eastern United States. Upon passing through these mountains to the north, writes local author Rebecca Brown, "there is a palpable sense of arriving, of being in a different place from where you left" (2011, p. 369)—a jumbled geography of peaks, valleys, and ridges, more than ninety percent woods and water. It is a region that embraces its identity with the land as it concurrently grapples with the challenge of reinventing its economy and maintaining community vitality in the face of global pressures and trends. The demise of the industrial wood-based economy that had dominated the North Country for generations, while viewed by some as signaling the end of a strong heritage of independence, self-reliance, and local control, is increasingly perceived as an opportunity to foreground the region's equally strong traditions of adaptability, resilience, and nimbleness in the face of change. This latter perspective is captured in the assertion that the North Country's greatest strength remains in "elegant solutions predicated on the uniqueness of place" (Harris, 2011, p. 10).

In its broadest sense, the landscape is the common thread for those who live in the North Country, although maintaining an "integrity of place" (Brown, 2011, p. 371) has become increasingly daunting when set against such impactful realities as a persistent pattern of youth out-migration and the lack of access to affordable broadband service across significant parts of the region (Staunton & Jaffee, 2014). Although each community maintains a distinct identity and local history, the region as a whole reflects a pattern in rural America in which historically resource-dependent places experience decline in their traditional industries, even while natural amenities—foregrounding in this case the North Country's rugged and beautiful mountainous landscape—are widely perceived to offer potential advantage, not just for tourism and recreation but also lifestyle attractions that could draw other employers.

Recent research conducted in the state suggests that most people living in these North Country counties continue to be optimistic about their communities and their own situations (Hamilton, Fogg, & Grimm, 2017). The profound economic transformation of this previously extraction-based manufacturing dominated region over the past several decades, according to this research, has not shaken this confidence and optimism regarding quality of life. Some point, for example, to data that show while more than half of northern New Hampshire K-12 students plan to leave their communities sometime in the future, they also report feeling connected to their schools and have a strong attachment to the community (Staunton & Jaffee, 2014). More broadly, this reflects northern New Hampshire's strong history of support for community organizations, commitment to public education, and investment in local businesses beyond the paper and pulp mills (Duncan, 2014).

Broad agreement persists across communities that a lack of job opportunities, drug abuse, and population decline are problems that need to be addressed for optimism to continue (Hamilton, Fogg, & Grimm, 2017). Exacerbating these concerns are local perceptions, drawn from this same study, that local governments have limited power to deal with global competition and other large-scale or statewide forces affecting North Country life. The TRRE program is attentive to such challenges while remaining cognizant of opportunities afforded by its engagement with the geographically large and demographically diverse reality of the North Country, especially amidst ongoing efforts to reinvigorate local control and enhance community sustainability. In its work with school and community partners, the program is sensitive to how engagement around differing visions for educational and economic futures calls for an assets-based approach that deliberately promotes rural communities as strong, resilient, fluid, and dynamic, and that aims to reverse traditional power asymmetries between university, school, and community ways of knowing and learning.

The two Local Education Agencies (LEAs) with which TRRE established its first two cohorts of residents are part of a larger consortium of rural, high-needs LEAs in the state that committed to partnering with UNH to support the TRRE residency program. In New Hampshire, LEAs are organized as School Administrative Units (SAUs) that cluster districts under the leadership of one superintendent. Each SAU partnered with TRRE serves rural communities and is eligible either for the Rural Low-Income School Program (RLIS) or the Small Rural Schools Achievement Program (SRSA), or serves a population of more than 20% students in poverty (as indicated by 2014 census data). Given the challenge of attracting teachers to the districts, teacher turnover, and impending retirements across all the SAUs in the consortium, the superintendents projected 150 new teacher hires over the five-year period extending from 2016-2021, highlighting significant teacher need across the districts (UNH-TRRE LEA Partner Needs Assessment, 2016). Moreover, in 2014-2015, many districts within the SAUs had more than 5% of core classes taught by teachers who did not have appropriate qualifications or certification to meet highly qualified teacher status (NH State Department of Education, 2016).

SAU 3, commonly referred to as the Berlin school district and one of TRRE's two current SAU partners, is situated in the North Country's largest municipality with a population of approximately

9,500. Nestled along the banks of the Androscoggin River, Berlin was once the center of the pulp and papermaking industry and is noted as "the city that trees built." With the mill closures in recent decades and the resulting displacement of hundreds of employees, exacerbated in 2012 with two long-standing manufacturing businesses claiming bankruptcy, the schools and the hospital became the community's two biggest employers. The addition of a biomass electricity plant as well as two new prisons, one state and one federal, have maintained the community's blue-collar identity and helped to replace many of the lost mill jobs. However, the overall quality of the new jobs has decreased compared to the previously secure union jobs. Tourism, primarily serving All Terrain Vehicle (ATV) and snowmobile enthusiasts, many from out of state, has started to provide significant seasonal economic support.

The students served by SAU 3 are spread across a K-2 Title I elementary school, a 3-5 Title I elementary school, a 6-8 middle school, and a 9-12 high school that also houses a regional Career and Technical Center. The overall student population served by these schools is 91% White and 66% of the students are from low-income families. Despite an influx in recent years of low-income families on assistance, with children needing services, the SAU has continued to experience a long-term steady decline in enrollment across its 4 schools, from 1,666 students in 2001 to 1,154 in 2017. It is a "dependent SAU," meaning that its budget is set by the mayor and city council, though in recent years it has been actively exploring the advantages and disadvantages of becoming an independent administrative unit with control of its own budget and financial decisions.

SAU 36, the other of TRRE's two current SAU partners, is commonly referred to as the White Mountains Regional School District and serves an area of roughly 135 square miles spread across three townships. Although geographically the "neighboring" school district of SAU 3, SAU 36 is centered roughly 30 miles away from the Berlin schools. The students served by SAU 36 are spread across two PreK-8 Title I elementary schools, a 1-5 Title I elementary school (closing at the end of 2017-2018 school year due to decreased enrollments), and a 9-12 high school. The overall student population served by these schools is 94% White and 52% of the students are from low-income families. Similar to SAU 3, SAU 36 has continued to experience a long-term steady decline in enrollment across its 5 schools, from over 1,400 students in 2006 to roughly 1,100 in 2017.

Central to TRRE's work with its North Country school partners is understanding how each school, as the traditional heart of the rural community, is:

also situated at the focal point of external economic and social influences, as well as political requirements for change and renewal, and therefore functions as a barometer of community well-being. (White & Reid 2008, p. 2)

Especially relevant is the finding that the state's education funding formula has contributed to disadvantaging North Country communities (Norton & Bird, 2017). Under the current system for calculating state adequacy funding for public education, rural, property-poor communities, in both demographic and economic transitions, are those that are projected to experience the most significant reductions. The two school districts currently partnered with TRRE, SAU 3 and SAU 36, are among the six most negatively affected communities in the state. Current projections for these two districts indicate that they are likely to see a reduction of more than 10% in the aid they receive from the state between 2017 and 2022. Assuming nothing else changes, this means that these communities will have to increase their tax rates by as much as 10%—even before allowing for cost increases in other areas. In SAU 3, this translates into a cost impact of $219,824 annually over a 20-year period (Norton & Bird, 2017).

Both SAU 3 and SAU 36 have responded to such hard economic facts with community-level adaptability and resilience built upon a richness of social capital—longstanding investment in community organizations, a tradition of inclusive participation, and a demonstrated ability to forge responsive initiatives. These factors have not necessarily made change easy, but they have facilitated a "do-what-needs-to-be-done-to-survive" attitude around such hotly debated issues as school consolidation and regionalization of education. SAU 3, for example, was awarded a large grant by the Nellie Mae Education Foundation for calendar year 2018 to work with a neighboring district on a process to create a regional vision for educating their students at a time of declining state funding and declining student enrollment. Part of the process included "a robust community engagement process" designed to increase trust, improve communications, and strengthen relationships needed to implement whatever recommendations emerge from the process. Facing similar economic and demographic pressures, and following similar community stakeholder discussions, SAU 36 made the hard-fought decision to close one of its three elementary schools at the end of the 2017-2018 academic year, dividing the school's roughly 50 students in grades 1-5 between the two remaining elementary schools in separate towns.

Throughout both school districts' struggles and achievements over the years, local residents have sustained a deep commitment to public schools and an understanding of the value of education. As one local noted, "If you want to be anybody, you have to be educated" (Duncan, 2014, p. 223). In part, this sentiment reflects the broader effort among residents in both districts to hold on to the community identity and social fabric they knew—which includes acknowledging the deeply embedded virtue of a community anchored by its school—while seeking to reinvent themselves amidst a restructured economy and shifting demographics.

TRRE Program Vision and Aims

The creative tension of working through both place-based and place-conscious pedagogical frameworks has informed the program's responsiveness to the multiple ways in which place *matters*. This is manifested through the ways the program has integrated expanded notions of field experiences into programming for TRRE, including, more broadly, how the program has positioned the TRRE residents' fieldwork in both schools and the broader community as important contexts for meaningful inquiry (Cochran-Smith & Lytle, 2009) and deliberate, sustainable engagement (Zeichner, 2010; Zeichner, Bowman, Guillen, & Napolitan, 2016).

TRRE's mission is to increase access to quality public education in rural New Hampshire. Rural areas are well documented as having teacher shortages and lagging student academic performance compared with more populous and affluent communities (Institute of Education Sciences, 2013). Seeking to remove inequities in the distribution of resources among students in NH, particularly in rural schools, TRRE aims to attract, prepare, and retain high quality teachers for under-resourced rural schools.

Beyond addressing areas of teacher shortage, the TRRE program aims to enact an equity stance though shared power and decision-making with communities. Rather than seeing schools with a "high need" designation as ones shaped only by deficit, TRRE views communities as a source of strength (Hamilton, Fogg, & Grimm, 2017). In keeping with Moll, Amanti, Neff, and Gonzalez's notion of funds of knowledge (2005), the program operates from the belief that rural communities over time have accumulated bodies of knowledge and skills for household or individual living and well-being that is informed by their unique culture. Teachers need to learn about the rich cultural background of students they teach. Tapping into these funds of knowledge, as sources of curriculum, TRRE residents bring to bear the talents and interests of students, thereby making curriculum relevant.

These aims are actualized within TRRE's three curricular pillars that include content and pedagogy, clinical strength, and community and family competence. In particular, TRRE prioritizes teachers' clinical strength and community competence that "recognize[s] and value[s] the forms of social and symbolic capital that exists there [in the local community], rather than elsewhere" (Reid, Green, Cooper, Hastings, Lock, & White, 2010, p. 272), fostering the "interplay of knowledge from different sources" (Zeichner, 2010, p. 95), and promoting synergistic ways of knowing and learning between school and community (Longo, 2007). Clinical experience and community competence in TRRE are also predicated upon what it means to *come to know a place*, with each building upon an ethnographic, "go find out" ethos of community engagement on the part of teaching residents. Informed in part by Murrell's (2001) concept of the community teacher that directs attention to the importance of being able to draw on richly contextualized knowledge of culture, community, and identity in their professional work with children and families, program staff believe that the teaching residents must start with a "big picture" community focus (White & Reid, 2008) that strategically draws upon the expertise that exists in the broader community to educate them about how to be successful teachers in their communities. In this way, they also begin to see themselves not only as professionals who want to teach in rural schools but also as individuals who desire to build intentional and sustainable relationships with and within the local community.

Toward these ends, the teaching residents' ability to access the local communities varies according to whether they are so-called "home-grown" individuals (people who are already established in the local area, have families there, and are clearly committed to staying) and individuals from "away" (people who relocate to the area from other parts of the state or from other states). TRRE's first two cohorts represented a ratio of roughly 2:1 "home-grown" and "away." Community access also benefited from the North Country's strong history of support for community organizations and commitment to public education, as noted in the previous section. As a practical example, these factors facilitated the ways in which teaching residents from outside the region secured housing during the residency experience. In a region still characterized by a strong tradition of neighborliness and investment in the well-being of the school as a center of community activity, it was not unusual for an informal mention of housing needs to flow from a local school superintendent or teacher to a web of social contacts in the local community. A community college in the region also proactively shared contacts drawn from its long history of serving the housing needs of traveling nurses in the North Country.

All of these considerations reflect the TRRE program's twofold assumption that rural teacher education needs to produce teachers with certain forms of social capital (Reid, Green, Cooper, Hastings, Lock, & White, 2010) *and* put their learning as teachers in the context of long-term community-building and sustainability efforts (Longo, 2013). This is especially relevant as we consider how the historic centrality of schools in the rural community positions preservice and novice teachers to develop a consciousness of the significance of place and community for their teaching (Burton & Johnson, 2010; White & Reid, 2008).

TRRE Place-Based and Place-Conscious Field Experiences

Building on theories of place and the curricular aims and pillars of the TRRE program, the program conceptualized field experiences broadly to encompass where coursework occurs, the opportunities for residents to engage in and with the surrounding communities, as well as the school-based activities that are part of the residency program. Here, the authors highlight four of the field experiences that aim to bring together place-based and place-conscious pedagogies. While not exhaustive, these experiences are designed intentionally to position residents to come to know the place(s) in which they will teach and consider the communities in their work as teachers in and out of school settings.

First, throughout the entirety of the TRRE program, all TRRE courses are embedded within the local region (three hours north of the University) in local schools and professional development organizations in the communities where the residents are teaching. In making this physical move, the program strives to promote the reciprocal benefits of linking teacher education and the sustainability of rural communities (Kline, White, & Lock, 2013). The embedded nature of the program facilitates TRRE residents' ability to engage in deliberative dialogue with and about education in the community (Longo, 2013) and fosters their capacity to consider and act upon their work as connected to broader networks of people and organizations in supporting children, youth, and families (Cochran-Smith, 2010; McDonald, Bowman, & Brayko, 2013).

Second, TRRE's first summer institute prioritizes structured opportunities for teaching residents to interact with children and adolescents in non-school settings, seeing students in places—community and neighborhood centers, clubs, teams, family resource centers—where they are likely to be experiencing success in ways that are different from those afforded by school. These experiences are structured to both challenge and enhance teaching residents' understandings of how individual, family, community, school, and societal factors interact to create school success for some students and school failure for others. Residents are introduced to families and school personnel as part of course assignments, in symposia, and through informal networks. During this time, residents also complete a community-based internship, where they connect with students, families, and community members out of school settings such as local recreation centers and summer camps. Consequently, as teaching residents begin to recognize the underpinnings of their own beliefs, attitudes, and practices, they may become more attuned to the broader contextual and community influences that shape the learning and experiences of the students they will teach (Ladson-Billings, 2006), and, ultimately, better positioned to build on community strengths and develop greater community capacity (Zeichner, Bowman, Guillen, & Napolitan, 2016, p. 288).

Third, following the residency program model, residents complete their school-based residency placements over the course of an academic year in partnership schools in SAU 3 and 36. Through these experiences, residents learn to apply content and pedagogy from coursework and residency experiences from their teaching mentors, who take on roles as field-based teacher educators. Residents also are exposed to the central role of schools in the rural communities, as well as the complex relationships between schools and communities in terms of school resources, organization, and priorities, particularly in a state that prides itself on local control. To support residents' field experiences in schools, a UNH faculty member known as the "faculty in residence" (one of the authors on this chapter) relocates 4 days per week to the North Country to teach coursework, supervise the residents in their school-based residency placements, and meet regularly with school, district, and community partners.

Fourth, TRRE partners with a statewide civic engagement initiative, North Country Listens (2018), to train TRRE residents as group facilitators who can work directly with communities invested in proactive problem solving around local issues such as rural youth outmigration, school consolidation, and extended learning opportunities through regional apprenticeships. As part of this work, residents observe and participate in "conversations" with community members around local issues and learn skills to facilitate these conversations as part of a broader statewide initiative. They then apply the skills they develop through this training in periodic symposia with a range of community stakeholders to create space for reciprocal conversations that are grounded in real-world experiences then translate this experience into action in their classrooms, as well as in the broader surrounding communities. Together these and other field experiences in the TRRE program position the residents to consider the particularities and commonalities in and out of the schools in which they will teach.

DISCUSSION AND INSIGHTS

Place matters in teacher preparation. Over time, the authors have developed a more nuanced understanding of field experiences and of place. Place is not monolithic or static, and encompasses more than just the people who live, teach, and learn in that place's neighborhoods and schools. Breaking through fixed definitions of *urban* and *rural* that have been cemented in the collective psyche requires multiple opportunities to learn, re-learn, and unlearn place through immersion in authentic experiences over time. Residencies afford the opportunity to provide multiple and diverse experiences within and outside of schools, not simply more of a single experience, in order to disrupt deeply held beliefs and stereotypes, and to extend residents' understandings of the complexity and diversity found within particular urban or rural places and schools. Schools are located within particular places, but school communities may incorporate teachers and students with diverse relationships to those places, such as residents of or commuters to the neighborhoods where schools are located.

Ultimately then, the issue may not be *which* community our respective programs prepares its teaching residents for, but rather that our programs have equipped residents to learn from, live in, and work for a community, regardless of where that community might be (Corbett, 2007; Schafft, 2010). In other words, while each field experience should be specific and circumstantial, its relevance in the broader context should also be apparent. To illustrate, drawing on Tieken's (2014) framing of the nexus between the one and the many, *one* rural community's story of a hard-fought school closure decision is not the story of all rural communities, for its particulars are not the particulars of all rural communities. But *some* or *many* rural communities will share a few of those particulars—a revamped state funding formula, for example—while *all* might share a marginalized position in a metro-centric policy arena. In thus confronting the "complex specificness" (Geertz, 1973, p. 23) of a particular experience with a particular school or group of community stakeholders, a novice teacher can be presented with a means to think realistically and concretely about broader issues of equity, school-community relations, and economic sustainability.

An oft-occurring dilemma in teacher education has been posed as one of preparing novice teachers for rural schools versus urban schools or, more broadly, for *some*where versus *any*where—a dichotomy that arguably is a distraction from the real question, which is how teacher educators prepare teachers to think and work in ways that are both local and global, to "understand how the ways that lives are lived locally have *precisely* global, social, political, economic, and environmental implications" (Schafft, 2010, p. 286). Toward this end, the following questions can help frame each teaching resident's field experience:

- How might I regard this particular community and school to be *in certain respects* like *all* other communities and schools?
- How might I regard this particular community and school to be *in certain respects* like *some* other communities and schools?
- How might I regard this particular community and school to be *in certain respects* like *no* other communities and schools (Schram, 2006, p. 177; Wolcott, 2005, p. 164)?

Framed in this way, a field experience's attentiveness to particulars and its emphasis on broader contexts hold complementary positions as two sides of the same coin—they work off and depend on each other. Teacher educators' task then becomes one of articulating connections between the specific situation of a field experience and other situations to which teacher candidates might apply the learnings generated through that field experience. The authors look to a pedagogy of field experiences in teacher education that considers the dynamic notions of place and incorporates multiple, intentional opportunities for teacher candidates to learn teaching through experiences in PK-12 schools, communities, neighborhoods, towns, and cities.

REFERENCES

Berry, B., Montgomery, D., & Snyder, J. (2008). *Urban teacher residency models and institutes of higher education: Implications for Teacher Preparation*. Chapel Hill, NC: Center for Teaching Quality.

Biddle, C., & Azano, A. P. (2016). Constructing and reconstructing the "rural school problem": A century of rural education research. *Review of Research in Education*, *40*(1), 298–325. doi:10.3102/0091732X16667700

Brown, R. (2011). The rediscovery of the North Country. In J. R. Harris, K. Morgan, & M. Dickerman (Eds.), *Beyond the notches: Stories of place in New Hampshire's North Country* (pp. 367–374). Littleton, NH: Bondcliff Books.

Budge, K. (2006). Rural leaders, rural places: Problem, privilege, and possibility. *Journal of Research in Rural Education*, *21*(13), 1–10.

Cochran-Smith, M. (2010). Toward a theory of teacher education for social justice. In M. Fullan, A. Hargreaves, D. Hopkins, & A. Lieberman (Eds.), The International Handbook of Educational Change. Academic Press. doi:10.1007/978-90-481-2660-6_27

Comber, B., Reid, J., & Nixon, H. (2007). Environmental communications: Pedagogies of responsibility and place. In B. Comber, H. Nixon, & J. A. Reid (Eds.), *Literacies in place: Teaching environmental communications* (pp. 11–23). Newton, NSW: PETA.

Corbett, M. (2007). *Learning to leave: The irony of schooling in a coastal community*. Black Point, NS: Fernwood.

Duncan, C. M. (2014). *Worlds apart: Poverty and politics in rural America*. New Haven, CT: Yale University Press.

Eargle, J. C. (2013). "I'm Not a Bystander": Developing Teacher Leadership in a Rural School-University Collaboration. *Rural Educator*, *35*(1).

Flynn, J., Kemp, A. T., & Callejo-Perez, D. (2010). You can't teach where you don't know: Fusing place-based education and Whiteness studies for social justice. *Curriculum and Teaching Dialogue*, *12*(1-2), 137–151.

Frankenburg, E., Taylor, A., & Merseth, K. (2009). Walking the walk: Teacher candidates' professed commitment to urban teaching and their subsequent career decisions. *Urban Education*, 1–35.

Gadsden, V. L., & Dixon-Roman, E. J. (2017). "Urban" schooling and "urban" families: The role of context and place. *Urban Education, 52*(4), 431–459. doi:10.1177/0042085916652189

Geertz, C. (1973). *Toward an interpretive theory of culture.* New York: Basic Books.

Gieryn, T. F. (2000). A space for place in sociology. *Annual Review of Sociology, 26*(1), 463–496. doi:10.1146/annurev.soc.26.1.463

Greenwood, D. A. (2013). *A critical theory of place-conscious education.* New York: Routledge. doi:10.4324/9780203813331.ch9

Greunewald, D. A. (2003). Foundations of place: A multidisciplinary framework for place-conscious education. *American Educational Research Journal, 40*(3), 619–654. doi:10.3102/00028312040003619

Grimes, W. (2015). *Where New Yorkers worship: Finding God in a city of bustle.* Retrieved from: https://www.nytimes.com/2015/12/25/arts/where-new-yorkers-worship-finding-god-in-a-city-of-bustle.html

Guha, R., Hyler, M. E., & Darling-Hammond, L. (2017, Spring). The teacher residency: A practical path to recruitment and retention. *American Educator,* 31–44.

Hamilton, L. C., Fogg, L. M., & Grimm, C. (2017). *Challenge and hope in the North Country. (Issue Brief No. 130).* Durham, NH: Carsey School of Public Policy.

Hammerness, K., & Craig, E. (2016). "Context-specific" teacher preparation for New York City: An exploration of the content of context in Bard College's urban teacher residency program. *Urban Education, 51*(10), 1226–1258. doi:10.1177/0042085915618722

Hammerness, K., Williamson, P., & Kosnick, C. (2016). Introduction to the special issue on urban teacher residencies: The trouble with "generic" teacher education. *Urban Education, 51*(10), 1155–1169. doi:10.1177/0042085915618723

Harris, J. H. (2011). Introduction. In J. R. Harris, K. Morgan, & M. Dickerman (Eds.), *Beyond the notches: Stories of place in New Hampshire's North Country* (pp. 74–78). Littleton, NH: Bondcliff Books.

Hollins, E. (2012). *Learning to teach in urban schools: The transition from preparation to practice.* New York: Teachers College Press.

Hollins, E. (Ed.). (2015). *Rethinking field experiences in preservice teacher preparation: Meeting the challenges for accountability.* New York: Routledge.

Ingersoll, R., Merrill, L., & May, H. (2014). *What are the effects of teacher education and preparation on beginning teacher attrition?* CPRE Research Reports. Retrieved from https://repository.upenn.edu/cgi/viewcontent.cgi?article=1002&context=cpre_researchrep

Jacobs, J. (1992). *The death and life of great American cities.* New York: Vintage Books.

Jensen, S. B. (2012). Special education & school choice: The complex effects of small schools, school choice and public high school policy in New York City. *Educational Policy, 27*(3), 427–466. doi:10.1177/0895904812453997

Klein, E. J., Taylor, M., Onore, C., Strom, K., & Abrams, L. (2013). Finding a third space in teacher education: Creating an urban teacher residency. *Teaching Education, 24*(1), 27–57. doi:10.1080/1047 6210.2012.711305

Kline, J., & Walker-Gibbs, B. (2015). Graduate teacher preparation for rural schools in Victoria and Queensland. *Australian Journal of Teacher Education, 40*(3), 68–88.

Kline, J., White, S., & Lock, G. (2013). The rural practicum: Preparing a quality teacher workforce for rural and regional Australia. *Journal of Research in Rural Education, 28*(3), 1–13.

Kozol, J. (1991). *Savage inequalities*. New York: Crown Publishers.

Kozol, J. (2005). *Shame of a nation*. New York: Crown Publishers.

Ladson-Billings, G. (2006). It's not the culture of poverty, it's the poverty of culture: The problem with teacher education. *Anthropology & Education Quarterly, 37*(2), 104–109. doi:10.1525/aeq.2006.37.2.104

Longo, N. V. (2007). *Why community matters: Connecting education with civic life*. Albany, NY: SUNY Press.

Longo, N. V. (2013). Deliberative pedagogy in the community: Connecting deliberative dialogue, community engagement, and democratic education. *Journal of Public Deliberation, 9*(2), 1–18. Retrieved from http://publicdeliberation.net/jpd/vol9/iss2/art16

Malsbary, C. B. (2016). Youth and schools' practices in hyper-diverse contexts. *American Educational Research Journal, 53*(6), 1491–1521. doi:10.3102/0002831216676569

Matsko, K. K., & Hammerness, K. (2014). Unpacking the "urban" in urban teacher education: Making a case for context-specific preparation. *Journal of Teacher Education, 65*(2), 128–144. doi:10.1177/0022487113511645

McClay, W. M. (2014). Introduction: Why place matters. In W.M. McClay & T.V. McAllister (Eds.), Why place matters: Geography, identity, and civic life in modern America (pp. 1-3). New York: Encounter Books.

McDonald, M. A., Bowman, M., & Brayko, K. (2013). Learning to see students: Opportunities to develop relational practices of teaching through community-based placements in teacher education. *Teachers College Record, 115*(4). Retrieved from https://www.tcrecord.org/content.asp?contentid=16916

Metropolitan Transportation Authority. (2018). *Facts and figures: Subways*. Retrieved from: http://web.mta.info/nyct/facts/ffsubway.htm

Milner, H. R. IV. (2012). But what is urban education? *Urban Education, 47*(3), 556–561. doi:10.1177/0042085912447516

New York City Department of City Planning. (2010). *Population density by census tract New York City, 1950-2010*. Retrieved from: https://www1.nyc.gov/assets/planning/download/pdf/data-maps/nyc-population/historical-population/pop_density_1950_2010.pdf

New York City Department of City Planning. (2018). *New York City Population.* Retrieved from: https://www1.nyc.gov/site/planning/data-maps/nyc-population/population-facts.page)

New York City Department of Education. (2009). *Children First: A bold, common-sense plan to create great schools for all New York City children.* Retrieved from: http://schools.nyc.gov/NR/rdonlyres/51C61E8F-1AE9-4D37-8881-4D688D4F843A/0/cf_corenarrative.pdf

New York City Department of Education. (2018). *2017-2018 Anticipated bilingual education programs.* Retrieved from: http://schools.nyc.gov/NR/rdonlyres/9B8CC63A-85BD-4884-AB52-5A35CF72DC48/0/201718BilingualProgramListAugust2017.pdf

New York City Economic Development Corporation. (2012). *New Yorkers and cars.* Retrieved from: https://www.nycedc.com/blog-entry/new-yorkers-and-cars

New York City Independent Budget Office. (2014a). *How long is the commute for New York City high school students from their homes to their schools?* Retrieved from: https://ibo.nyc.ny.us/cgi-park2/2014/05/how-long-is-the-commute-for-new-york-city-high-school-students-from-their-homes-to-their-schools/

New York City Independent Budget Office. (2014b). *How many students attend nonpublic K-12 schools in New York City?* Retrieved from: https://ibo.nyc.ny.us/cgi-park2/2014/04/how-many-students-attend-nonpublic-k-12-schools-in-new-york-city/

New York City Independent Budget Office. (2015). *How much do public school budgets vary across the city's school districts and boroughs?* Retrieved from: https://ibo.nyc.ny.us/cgi-park2/2015/09/how-much-do-public-school-budgets-vary-across-the-citys-school-districts-and-boroughs/

New York City Office of the Mayor. (2006). *Mayor Bloomberg announces tentative agreement with the United Federation Of Teachers nearly one year before expiration of current contract.* Retrieved from: http://www1.nyc.gov/office-of-the-mayor/news/388-06/mayor-bloomberg-tentative-agreement-the-united-federation-teachers-nearly-one#/1

New York City Teaching Fellows. (2018). *Our history.* Retrieved from: https://nycteachingfellows.org/our-history

Newsday. (2014). *School spending data.* Retrieved from: http://data.newsday.com/long-island/data/education/school-spending/#o:c=;|

Noguera, P. (2003). *City schools and the American dream.* New York: Teachers College Press.

North Country Listens. (2018). *About us.* Retrieved from: https://www.northcountrylistens.org/about

Norton, S., & Bird, G. (2017). *Education finance in New Hampshire: Headed to a rural crisis?* Concord, NH: New Hampshire Center for Public policy. *Studies.*

Oakes, J., Franke, M. L., Quartz, K. H., & Rogers, J. (2002). Research for high-quality urban teaching: Defining it, developing it, assessing it. *Journal of Teacher Education, 53*(3), 228–234. doi:10.1177/0022487102053003006

Queens Library. (2014). *Queens library facts.* Retrieved from: http://www.queenslibrary.org/sites/default/files/about-us/Facts%20Sheet.pdf

Reagan, E. M., Coppens, A., Couse, L., Hambacher, E., Lord, D., McCurdy, K., & Silva Pimentel, D. (2018). Toward a framework for the design and implementation of the Teacher Residency for Rural Education. In M. Reardon & J. Leanord (Eds.), *Innovation and Implementation: School-University-Community Partnerships in Rural Communities* (pp. 81–106). Academic Press.

Reid, J.-A., Green, B., Cooper, M., Hastings, W., Lock, G., & White, S. (2010, November). Rural Social Space? Teacher Education for Rural—Regional Sustainability. *Australian Journal of Education, 54*(3), 262–276. doi:10.1177/000494411005400304

Richards, S. (2012). Coast to country: An initiative aimed at changing pre-service teachers' perceptions of teaching in rural and remote locations. *Australian and International Journal of Rural Education, 22*(2), 53.

Schafft, K. A. (2010). Economics, community, and rural education: Rethinking the nature of accountability in the twenty-first century. In K. A. Schafft & A. Y. Jackson (Eds.), *Rural education for the twenty-first century: Identity, place, and community in a globalizing world* (pp. 275–290). University Park, PA: Penn State Press.

Schram, T. (2006). *Conceptualizing and Proposing Qualitative Research.* Upper Saddle River, NJ: Merrill/Prentice Hall.

Shamah, D., & MacTavish, K. A. (2009). Purpose and perceptions of family social location among rural youth. *Youth & Society, 50*(1), 26–48. doi:10.1177/0044118X15583655

Sobel, D. (2004). *Place-based education: Connecting classrooms and communities* (2nd ed.). Great Barrington, MA: The Orion Society.

Sobel, D. (2005). *Place-based education: Reclaiming the heart in nature education.* Great Barrington, MA: The Orion Society and the Myrin Institute.

Solomon, J. (2009). The Boston teacher residency: District-based teacher education. *Journal of Teacher Education, 60*(5), 478–488. doi:10.1177/0022487109349915

Staunton, M. S., & Jaffee, E. M. (2014). *Key findings and recommendations from the Coos youth study: Research from the first half of the study (Issue Brief No. 41).* Durham, NH: Carsey School of Public Policy.

Success Academy. (2018). *Who we are.* Retrieved from: https://www.successacademies.org/about/#history

Tieken, M. C. (2014). *Why rural schools matter.* Chapel Hill, NC: University of North Carolina Press. doi:10.5149/northcarolina/9781469618487.001.0001

Tindle, K., Freund, M., Belknap, B., Green, C., & Shotel, J. (2011). The urban teacher residency program: A recursive process to develop professional dispositions, knowledge, and skills of candidates to teach diverse students. *Educational Considerations, 38*(2), 28–35. doi:10.4148/0146-9282.1132

Trinidad, S., Sharplin, E., Lock, G., Ledger, S., Boyd, D., & Terry, E. (2011). Developing strategies at the pre-service level to address critical teacher attraction and retention issues. *Australian and International Journal of Rural Education, 23*(2), 43-52.

Venugopal, A. (2011). *Census pinpoints city's wealthiest, poorest neighborhoods.* Retrieved from: https://www.wnyc.org/story/174508-blog-census-locates-citys-wealthiest-and-poorest-neighborhoods/

Vernikoff, L., Goodwin, A. L., Horn, C., & Akin, S. (in press). Urban residents' place-based funds of knowledge: An untapped resource in urban teacher residencies. *Urban Education.*

Watson, D. (2011). What do you mean when you say "urban"? Speaking honestly about race and students. *Rethinking Schools, 26*(1), 48–50.

Watson, D. (2012). Norming suburban: How teachers talk about race without using race words. *Urban Education, 47*(5), 983–1004. doi:10.1177/0042085912445642

Weiner, L. (2006). *Urban teaching: The essentials.* New York: Teachers College Press.

White, S., & Reid, J. (2008). Placing teachers? Sustaining rural teaching through place-consciousness in teacher education. *Journal of Research in Rural Education, 23*(7), 1–11.

Williamson, P., Apedoe, X., & Thomas, C. (2016). Context as Content in Urban Teacher Education: Learning to Teach in and for San Francisco. *Urban Education, 51*(10), 1170–1197. doi:10.1177/0042085915623342

Wolcott, H. F. (2005). *The art of fieldwork* (2nd ed.). Walnut Creek, CA: Sage.

Wuthnow, R. (2013). *Small-town America: Finding community, shaping the future.* Princeton, NJ: Princeton University Press. doi:10.1515/9781400846498

Zeichner, K. (2006). Reflections of a university-based teacher educator on the future of college-and university-based teacher education. *Journal of Teacher Education, 57*(3), 326–340. doi:10.1177/0022487105285893

Zeichner, K. (2010). Rethinking the connections between campus courses and field experiences in college- and university-based teacher education. *Journal of Teacher Education, 61*(1-2), 89–99. doi:10.1177/0022487109347671

Zeichner, K., Bowman, M., Guillen, L., & Napolitan, K. (2016). Engaging and working in solidarity with local communities in preparing the teachers of their children. *Journal of Teacher Education, 67*(4), 277–290. doi:10.1177/0022487116660623

APPENDIX

Table 1. Comparison of TR@TC and TRRE

	TR@TC – New York City	TRRE – North Country New Hampshire
Purpose and Funding	To prepare and retain highly effective teachers for high need schools through extended clinical one year residency, funded primarily through a federal Teacher Quality Partnership Grant from the US Department of Education.	
Place and District	· Diverse city of 8.3 million people · 304 square miles · 200+ languages spoken · 1.1 million public school students in 1800+ schools	· Rural mountainous region of 30,000+ people · 1800+ square miles (90% woods and water) · Primarily English speaking · Multiple towns and school districts
Program Trajectory	· Eighth cohort began January 2018 · 10-20 residents per year · 90 graduates	· Second cohort begins Summer 2018 · First cohort of 5 residents graduating Summer 2018
Conceptual Framework	· Curriculum · Inquiry · Social Justice	· Content and Pedagogy · Clinical Strength · Community and Family Competence
Program Characteristics	· M.A. + teacher certification · 18-month (3 semesters +1 summer) · 1 year residency co-teaching with a teaching mentor · 2 years induction mentoring and support post-graduation	· M.Ed. + teacher certification · 15-month (2 semesters + 2 summers) · 1 year residency co-teaching with a teaching mentor · 2 years induction mentoring and support post-graduation
Initial Teacher Certification Pathways	· Secondary Science (7-12) · English as a Second Language (K-12) · Special Education (7-12)	· Elementary Education (K-6) · Elementary Education with Middle School Science or Mathematics (K-8) · Secondary Mathematics (7-12) · Secondary Science (7-12)
Resident Support and Commitment	· $30,000 living stipend · 22 credit hours · 2 years of mentoring and support post-graduation · Commitment to teach for 3 years in NYC	· $28,000 living stipend · 50% tuition discount · Laptop · 2 years of mentoring and support post-graduation · Commitment to teach for 3 years in North Country
Place-Oriented Field Experiences	· Community Walks · Multiple Field Placements · Guided Observations	· Community-embedded Coursework · Integrated school and community field experiences · Facilitated Conversations with Community Stakeholders

Chapter 12
Enhancing Cultural and Linguistic Awareness Through an International Teaching Experience

Barbara A. Bradley
University of Kansas, USA

Andrea Miller Emerson
Western Oregon University, USA

Arsenio F. Silva
Clemson University, USA

ABSTRACT

The population of students in the United States is becoming increasingly diverse. At the same time, we live in highly interconnected global society with complex world problems. Thus, teachers need to prepare students to live and work collaboratively with people, locally and globally, from diverse background. Yet, how do in-service and preservice teachers support students if they have had limited experiences interacting with and understanding people from diverse backgrounds? This chapter describes a four-week summer study-abroad program in Italy, in which preservice teacher lived with a host family and observed and taught in an Italian school. It presents findings about what preservice teachers learned from (1) living with a host family, (2) observing in an Italian school, (3) becoming a culturally and linguistically diverse learner, and (4) teaching.

INTRODUCTION

The population of students in the United States (US) is becoming increasingly diverse (U.S. Department of Education, 2017). In addition, we live in a highly interconnected global society with complex world problems. Solving these problems will mean bringing together people from diverse cultural and linguistic backgrounds and working collaboratively toward creative solutions. For students to become

DOI: 10.4018/978-1-5225-6249-8.ch012

part of these solutions, we need teachers who can serve culturally and linguistically diverse (CLD) students (Howard, 2003) and who can help all students develop the ability to understand, learn from, and work collaboratively with people from cultures different from their own (Suárez-Orozco & Sattin, 2007; Wang, Lin, Spalding, Odell, & Klecka, 2011). How do teachers support CLD students if they, themselves, have had limited experiences interacting with, understanding, and collaborating with people from different backgrounds?

Teacher educators must fully commit to the important work of preparing preservice teachers to engage with students and families who are different from themselves. Teacher education programs typically include coursework related to language, culture, diversity, equity, and, as possible, they provide pre-service teachers with field experiences, internships, and/or student teaching in diverse settings. While these experiences are invaluable, intense first-hand experiences in a culture different from their own can provide pre-service teachers with additional insight into issues related to culture and language (Cushner, 2009). In fact, directly interacting with individuals in a foreign country creates opportunities for preser-vice teachers "to broaden their cultural knowledge, learn how others view the world from an insider's perspective, develop a global perspective, and increase their understanding of the value of multicultural education" (Cushner, 2009, p. 158). Further, intense personal experiences in an international setting can create opportunities for preservice teachers to gain perspective through experiencing unexpected and uncomfortable situations. Teacher educators can guidance preservice teachers as they make strong connections to their teacher preparation coursework and teaching experiences in the US and consider how they might use their experiences abroad in their future teaching.

Overview of the Field Experience in Italy

This chapter describes a 4-week study abroad program in which preservice teachers engaged in a field experience in a town in Northern Italy. The students accepted into this study abroad experience were enrolled in a teacher education program and had previous field experience in schools. Prior to departure, they attended several meetings and completed readings and assignments. Throughout the duration of the program, preservice teachers stayed with and became a part of an Italian host family. In addition, based on their career goals, preservice teachers were placed in classrooms to work alongside Italian teachers and students from preschool to high school. To the best of their abilities considering language differences, preservice teachers observed and participated in class activities and taught English to Italian students. During the program, preservice teachers attended weekly group meetings and several whole group ac-tivities (e.g., visiting schools or museums). Finally, preservice teachers reflected on their experiences living abroad and working in schools by completing a blog or journal.

Participants

In 2017, 27 preservice teachers from five universities located in the Midwest and Southeast portions of the US participated in the four-week study abroad program. This chapter highlights the experiences of 16 of these preservice teachers who gave consent to participate in this study. These participants came from three universities located in the Midwest and all were undergraduates. One participant was ma-joring in early childhood special education, 13 were majoring in elementary education, and two were majoring in middle/secondary education. Fifteen participants were female and one was male. Thirteen participants were European American and three participants were Hispanic, and two of these participants spoke Spanish. All participants had studied a foreign language in school but none had studied Italian. Therefore, all were Italian language learners in Italy.

Data

This chapter is based on the preservice teachers' blog and journal entries addressing guiding questions related to: (a) living with a host family; (b) participating in school activities; (c) becoming a culturally and linguistically diverse learner, and; (d) teaching Italian students. Using a qualitative approach (Gibbs, 2007), the researchers first read the blogs and journal data entries to determine potential coding categories. After comparing category notes, differences were reconciled through consensus and a codebook was created. The codebook was then used to code data and identify themes. Themes will be discussed in relation to the following categories: (a) understanding families; (b) experiencing a different educational system; (c) becoming culturally and linguistically diverse, and; (d) teaching.

Understanding Families

To provide meaningful instruction, teachers need to understand their students. This includes communicating, building relationships, and collaborating with students and their families, as well as understanding the communities in which their students live (Goe, Bell & Little, 2008). Teacher education programs include coursework related to developing a strong rapport with students and engaging families when teaching young children, students with special needs, and students from diverse backgrounds. While class readings and discussions during coursework provided preservice teachers with many insights, living with a host family in Italy and becoming immersed in their daily lives helped them develop a deeper understanding of how families were similar to or different from their own families. Many participants developed a strong relationship with their host family and some developed the confidence to have difficult discussions with family members. Three interrelated themes emerged from preservice teachers' experiences living with an Italian family: the importance of family, mealtimes, and the perspective of time.

Family

First, preservice teachers learned that family is important to Italians. They recognized that because immediate and extended family members often live near each other in Italy, family members interacted with each other more frequently and seemed to have stronger bonds with each other compared to many families living in the US. Preservice teachers also noted the many ways in which Italian family members supported each other. For example, since most children go home for lunch, some preservice teachers talked about grandparents picking up their grandchildren up after school and/or having lunch at their grandparents' home. This allowed preservice teachers to consider the value of multigenerational family interactions and how this helps children learn more about their family history and family values. Some preservice teachers also speculated that because grandparents are so central to family life, Italians might have different views about senior citizens and growing older. Lauren's (all names are pseudonyms) comments about her family exemplify what many preservice teachers wrote:

Family time in my host family was their number one priority. I loved it! Whether it was a bike ride, dinner, movies, tennis, etc. they loved doing things together. This is something I so dearly love about the Italian culture. Although family is important in America, it is common to see work being prioritized over family, technology consuming peoples' lives or divorce. While they do have these things in Italy, they didn't get in the way of family time. Something else that was special with my host family was that they had a house attached with my host mother's parents. It was so great to see how [my Italian brother] interacted with his grandparents. We had family dinners with them occasionally and afternoon coffee together was a must!

Mealtimes

As preservice teachers discussed the importance of family, they often talked about the different activities that families engaged in on a regular basis such as riding bikes, taking trips to the gelateria or watching movies together. However, they most often discussed mealtimes as demonstrating the importance of family, as well as food in the Italian culture. As Eva states:

Mealtimes bring Italians together and they really value spending time together, sharing their day or sharing stories during lunch and dinner. I've also noticed that the TV is not turned on when my Italian family has meals. At home, in the US, if or when we all sit down together to eat, there is usually a sports game or some television show on in the background. I've really enjoyed how much my family, and other Italians I've spent time with, values face-to-face conversations. I realize that spending time with family is something I value and want to be sure I do with own future family.

Mealtimes are about family but they are also about enjoying good food and food should be enjoyed at a leisurely pace. As Leigh noted:

I thought my first 5-course meal was in celebration of me arriving in Italy and starting the experience with my family. I quickly learned that having a 5-course lunch and dinner is normal for my family.

Likewise, Kimberly stated:

Lunch is important in Italy and students normally go home for lunch because schools dismiss around 1:00 pm. So lunch is a social time and a time to take a relaxing break. In my family, we had multiple courses and wine, so lunch could last up to 2 hours. Whereas in America, we chow down our Lunchables in under 20 minutes and get back to work.

Since food is important to Italians, preservice teachers talked about trying foods that they typically would not eat in the US. While some preservice teachers indicated that they were consciously using their experience abroad to move out of their comfort zone and try new thing, others simply did not want to be rude to their family. Regardless, it helped preservice teachers understand that being open-mined, flexible, and gracious helped them build relationships and grow as individuals. Further, they appreciated when Italians extended this courtesy to them. As Kara explains:

I chose to make beef tacos, sautéed Cajun spiced shrimp, Mexican rice, and guacamole with tortilla chips for my family. I don't think they loved it, but they were all super good sports and tried everything I made. I realized you don't have to like or agree with everything but it is important to be open-minded and at least try something different.

Time

How Italians view time was the third key point preservice teachers discussed and it intersected with the importance of family, relationships, and sharing meals. In her post, Danni wrote:

From the first day it was apparent that relationships and connections are very important to Italians. Their lifestyle allows for long lunches and dinners so that they can spend time with family, connect with friends, and have alone time, if needed, to reenergize. The Italian culture really highlights connections compared to our fast paced American culture where work responsibilities and scheduled activities sometimes get in the way of family time or free time with friends. For example, one day my host mother and I went to a café for breakfast before she dropped me off at school. I worried that we would be late to school but my host mother said, "School can wait. When it comes to mornings we like to take our time and enjoy ourselves with no rush." So we took our sweet time eating our croissants and sipping our coffee while talking with friends. While I enjoyed the time, it was also so confusing because I'm so used to coffee-to-go and rushing to work or school. When I arrived at school my host mother explained why I was late and no one seemed too concerned.

Ashlie stated:

One of the major differences I have observed is that time is not a thing that Italians worry or stress over the way that [Americans] do about school, work and life in general. At first this was hard for me to adapt to because I like having a schedule and knowing exactly when we are doing things but Italians like to do things at a more relaxed paced. I have learned that there was never a set time when dinner would be finished. There were plenty of nights where we would have dinner and stay at the table for hours talking. I actually really enjoyed sitting together and talking about our day. We really got to know one another and it was a time where we could relax after a long day.

Other Topics

Preservice teachers identified other cultural similarities and differences related to families. For example, they indicated that Italian families listened to popular American songs or watched American movies. Thus, they recognized how pop culture helped them to create a bond with their family and it might help them bond with their future students and their families. Preservice teachers also noted that the Italians were environmentally conscious and engaged in recycling, indicating that Italians were much more eco-friendly and pro-active compared to themselves or other Americans. Finally, preservice teachers recognized that Italians, like Americans, imposed stereotypes on others. For example, Sarah noted:

One of the most difficult things for me was, at first, accepting that my host families' stereotype of me as an American. They had hosted students before, so I am not sure if the stereotype came from those students or from the media, but it was definitely something I noticed. For example, they had the impression that as an American I would eat burgers or fast food multiple times a week, and that I would eat a lot of big meals. However, I am very health-conscious in my food choices and eat a balanced diet that includes primarily vegetables, fruits, and protein.

However, discussing stereotypes helped preservice teachers reflect on their own expectations as demonstrated by Eva:

Living with a host family was more difficult than I expected. I had gone into this trip thinking I was going to be surrounded by an Italian family who loved to cook and spend time together… but this was not my family, my host parents worked long hours. I learned to be flexible, eat many things I did not prefer to eat, and to be gracious toward my family…however, this served as an important reminder to me that no matter what the culture is, every family is unique. I think as an educator it's important not to stereotype or make assumptions about families because of their background or culture.

Summary

In sum, living with a host family provided preservice teachers an opportunity to see how another family lives and to understand their values in comparison to their own family's lifestyle and values. This context led to group discussions of cultural similarities and differences between Italians and Americans, and that some characteristics might be unique to a family rather than a culture. Further, preservice teachers considered their own identity and the identities of others, and reflected upon issues such as stereotypes and biases (Holmes, Bavieri, & Ganassin, 2015). Finally, living with a host family allowed preservice teachers to experience a new lifestyle, to participate in activities with a different perspective, and to be flexible, gracious, and appreciative. Thus, Niki's comment reflects many preservice teachers' thoughts:

Spending time with my host family was probably my favorite part of the entire experience. I looked forward to biking home with my host sister, seeing my host grandparents who spoke no English for lunch, and hanging out with the whole family in the evening. The stories my family told me of everyday life in Italy gave me a wonderful view of what it was like to live in this country and to be an Italian. My most valuable experiences came from just sitting with my family at dinner and hearing about their lives.

Experiencing a Different Educational System

Most preservice teachers who participated in this program had lived primarily in one location during their school years, so they had only experienced schooling in a particular part of the US. Further, many of their college classmates had similar school experiences, so it is difficult for them to imagine other ways of enacting school. This field experience created an opportunity for preservice teachers to compare and contrast two educational systems. For example, preservice teachers observed that preschools in this region of Italy are child-centered, play-based and teachers focus more on developing social-emotional skills compared with preschools in the US which tend to focus more on early academic skills. Preservice teachers observed that Italian elementary school teachers tend to engage in whole-class, teacher-led instruction and, because they are less schedule-driven, spend more time teaching students concepts to mastery compared to the US where instruction may consist of hands-on activities that occur in small groups. Preservice teachers placed in middle school learned that these students and their families must determine which type of high school they wish to attend and that this decision puts students on a college and career track. Further, like in the US, preservice teachers learned that there are high stakes tests in Italy. Italian students face the consequences of their performance, which can mean repeating an entire grade level if a team of teachers determines that a student did not do well on the tests. Finally, spending an extended period of time in one school, visiting other schools in the community, and discussing education with their host families helped preservice teachers reflect more deeply on and have meaningful discussions with their peers about the similarities and differences their own school experiences in the US (Colwell, Nielsen, Bradley, & Spearman, 2016).

In addition to these observations, themes identified in blogs and journals related to: (a) students' genuine interest and excitement; (b) teacher-student relationships; (c) meeting students' needs, and; (d) teachers' perspective and use of time.

Genuine Interest and Excitement

First, preservice teachers were surprised by the Italian students' genuine interest and excitement of having an American visitor in their class or school. Because this program is well established, some of this enthusiasm may be due to the fact that Italian teachers know what to expect and how to prepare their students for their American preservice teacher's arrival. Also, over the years, Italian teachers have learned how to better support visiting preservice teachers and help them grow as educators. Regardless, Leigh's comment reflects what many preservice teachers observed:

I was introduced to every staff member and the smile on everyone's faces was genuine and portrayed their excitement well. When I met the teacher I would be working with, she was walking her kids back from gym. She stopped them in the hallway to introduce me and explain who I was and why I was here. I was not exactly sure what she was saying in Italian, but I was able to watch the kids as their eyes widened and they smiled while whispering to each other. I adored this honest joy at meeting me - it was one of the coolest feelings I had. It reminded me of when I was in school in America and there was a foreign student who joined our class and an assistant teacher that would come to help us in our classroom, and no one seemed to care that much or was nearly as excited as these kids were to see me.

Situations like this, as well as in the community, helped preservice teachers reflect on their interactions with foreigners in the US. More often then not, they indicated that they had not been as welcoming to foreigners as Italians had been toward them and they would be changing their behaviors when they returned to the US.

Teacher-Student Relationships

Preservice teachers commented about the type of relationship teachers had with their students and the type of interactions or level of affection they displayed with each other. For example, Leigh noted:

Another cultural difference I found interesting is the way teachers are more personable with their students as well as their families. I found it very sweet that my teacher would go up to her first grade students when they were doing a good job and give them a big hug or a kiss them on the cheek. You don't see that in America because there are policies against physical closeness between teachers and students. The students were so adorable and I also wanted to show them affection and let them know how much I care about them.

Preservice teachers saw the value of hugging and how it demonstrated that teachers cared for students, so they easily understood Italian teachers' behaviors. They also understood why schools in the US had policies limiting physical contact between teachers and students. However, this situation clearly demonstrated how a behavior considered appropriate in one country might be considered inappropriate in another country, and that care needs to be taken so as not to impose one's beliefs, values or norms onto others or a situation.

Ashlyn described positive interactions but also interactions that would be considered inappropriate in the US, although they certainly occur in American classrooms.

I felt very welcomed and comfortable in my classroom. The students would come up to me daily and give me hugs and kisses. The teacher is also very nice so I was shocked when I heard her yell at students. When a student made a simple mistake she would raise her voice as if he did something terribly wrong. I looked around and saw that none of the other students seemed phased by it and the student that was being yelled at just nodded his head and the class moved on. If this happened in America, the student would have cried or the teacher would get in trouble. However, I also noticed that Italian students could do more things in the classroom such as walk around and talk with each other. Also, during their breaks, students can run around the classroom or in the hallways and teachers are completely okay with this. In America, students would get in trouble if they talked with peers or ran around in the school. After the first week of observing and working with this classroom I am shocked by how some things are very different and questioned why Italians do things a certain way, but I have also noticed that the class flows and their system works for them.

As preservice teachers explored the issue of teacher-student relationships and discipline, they tried to make sense of it. For example, they considered school structure (e.g., looping in Italian elementary school may have explained teacher-student relationships), policies (e.g., touching is permissible in Italian schools but generally not in schools in the US), school norms (e.g., Italians teachers get upset with students who do not do school/home work, American teachers get upset with disruptive behaviors), and cultural norms (e.g., Italians parents and teachers are less restrictive or more tolerant of children's behaviors compared to American parents and teachers). Preservice teachers, with faculty guidance, learned to ask, "Why do Italians do what they do?" and "Why do we do what we do?" Not surprisingly, this often led to discussions and reflections about what might be best for students and often ended with "it depends."

Meeting Students' Needs

Meeting student needs was the third theme raised by preservice teachers when comparing the Italian and American education system. In the following excerpt, this preservice teacher describes a field trip that led her to think about the experiences teachers create for students and why they do so.

I had the pleasure of attending a "gita" or field trip with my 1st grade class on Monday. My class and the other 1st and 2nd grade classes traveled to a nearby farm for what is the equivalent to a field day in the U.S. There was a petting farm with a rooster, a pony, bunnies, ducks, and other small animals... After visiting the petting zoo, the students made their own strawberry jam by crushing strawberries they had just picked from the farm...After washing up from the strawberry jam, the students moved to a large open field where the played outdoor games such as tug-of-war, three-legged races, and potato sack races. They had SO much fun. I found it really interesting many of the outdoor games in Italy and in the US were the same. After the games, we had a picnic together on the lawn...When I asked my host teachers why they decided to take this field trip, they said, "Many of our students are from newly immigrated families. Some students live with up to 10 family members in a small apartment and don't have the opportunity to explore. We wanted to give these students and all our students the opportunity to explore outside and foster a love of nature" Next year, I will be completing my student teaching...it will be interesting to see how teachers in the US give students important life-experiences through school activities.

As part of the program, preservice teachers visited several additional schools in the afternoons so that they could learn about the Italian education system in grades different from their primary classroom placement. During one of these visits, Kara said:

My favorite school visit this week was seeing a preschool. At the school, we were able to see how this preschool shapes the young minds of children by letting them control their own learning! Teachers choose topics that children are interested in and then they design a curriculum around those topics...One of my favorite rooms was the "safe room." The children use it to talk about serious topics with other kids and teachers that are bothering them. Then they draw how they are feeling on paper posted on the wall. The room is only supplied with black markers so that the kids can focus more on their drawing and their emotions rather than the colors or making pretty pictures.

School experiences like these allowed preservice teachers to consider how and why teachers make instructional decisions or what drives instruction in Italy and in the US. With respect to education in the US, preservice teachers talked about standards, high-stakes testing, the curriculum, and teacher choice. Preservice teachers reflected on their own schooling, as well as their experiences during school placements for their coursework. They discovered that there are more differences among schools in the US than they initially realized based on interconnected issues such as where a school is located, if it is a well-funded or not, and if it serves students from high or low-socioeconomic backgrounds. While there is no doubt that these discussions occurred in university classes, observing and working in a foreign school may have helped preservice teachers develop a stronger understanding of the differences in schools and provided a context for richer discussions. These discussions could also have been due, in part, to the fact that preservice teachers attended different universities, making differences in personal school experiences more tangible.

Perception and Use of Time

As noted with families, preservice teachers noticed how Italian teachers perceived and used time differently compared with teachers in the US, and they often talked about this observation in relation to student learning. For example, Ashlie said:

I also noticed time within the schools. The teachers didn't have set times on when they had to finish their activities. Students could work on activities until they were finished or the teacher would continue teaching until students understood the concepts. I think this is something the school systems back in the States should work on so that the class flows more smoothly and to make sure we are focusing on helping students learn material more thoroughly.

Eva wrote:

One of my biggest takeaways this week is the concept of "time" in the Italian culture. On a class gita (field trip), the students had the whole afternoon (3 hours!) to play with their friends in a field and there were NO organized activities. Kids were having fun but that seemed CRAZY to Sara and me! We kept fighting the urge to organize something and by hour 2 we were asking if we could start a game of Duck, Duck, Goose or Freeze Dance.... However, I also noticed this relaxed concept of time when I was asked [by my host teachers] about my time to teach students my English lessons. They said, "We always have time! How much time do you need?" This is a big contrast to field experiences in the US when I am always trying to get teachers to let me squeeze in one of my activities or lessons because it seems there is never enough time. Italian teachers are so flexible, schedules are so flexible and classes are so fluid that sometimes I can barely tell what subject they are teaching. Granted, this may because of my limited understanding of the Italian language, however, I think it is more than this! ...I really want to use this kind of flow and flexibility into my future classroom. I think this flexibility allows teachers to truly nurture students' learning and creativity which I really don't think is possible in our climate of pressuring kids to finish work in a set time.

While preservice teachers appreciated the relaxed view on time so that Italian teachers could ensure that students mastered a concept and so that they had more time to teach English to students, some preservice teachers still wanted to impose structures or limits, even when they recognized students were learning or having fun.

Summary

International field experiences provide preservice teachers with opportunities to develop intercultural understanding as they work with teachers and students. They also provide an opportunity to compare and contrast school systems, helping preservice teachers understand that there are different ways of structuring schools, interacting with students, providing instruction, meeting students' needs, and perceiving or utilizing time. While some differences may be confusing and uncomfortable based on preservice teachers' prior school experiences, international field experiences provide an important context for considering behaviors in terms of the host cultures' norms. Furthermore, they create opportunities for preservice teachers to reflect more deeply on their own beliefs, values and cultural norms, and to begin questioning educational practices in the US.

Becoming the Culturally and Linguistically Diverse Learner at Home and in School

Teachers who are sensitive to their students' culture, who are aware of cultural norms, and who are guided by multicultural pedagogical principles are more likely to create a classroom environment in which the social and academic needs of CLD learners can be addressed (Sleeter, 1995). That is, CLD learners are better served when their teachers believe that all students are capable learners who bring knowledge and strengths to the learning environment. However, teachers often have a deficit-based view of CLD students, which does not support student learning (Ladson-Billings, 1994). While teacher education programs engage preservice teachers in activities that help them to acquire the knowledge, skills, and dispositions to develop cultural awareness and implement culturally responsive teaching, preservice teachers can also benefit from opportunities that engage them in:

a cognitive and affective process or activity that: (1) requires active engagement on the part of the individual; (2) is triggered by an unusual or perplexing situation or experience; (3) involves examining one's responses, beliefs, and premises in light of the situation at hand, and; (4) results in integration of the new understanding into one's experience. (Rogers, 2001, p. 41)

This field experience, in a non-English speaking country, allowed preservice teachers to become the CLD learner in a family, school, and community, providing experiences that created the cognitive and emotional dissonance needed to examine their own beliefs and biases. This experience helped preservice teachers to better understand the challenges CLD learners encounter in the US, develop a more empathetic stance to CLD learners, and helped them to begin understanding how to apply practical strategies for welcoming and supporting CLD students into their future classrooms (Bradley & Emerson, 2017; Colwell, Nielsen, Bradley, & Spearman, 2016). The following section focuses on issues preservice teachers raised as CLD learners and more specifically, as language learners, at home and in school.

Language Learner at Home

Participants found living with their host family rewarding, but challenging, most often due to language differences. These challenges, however, provided an opportunity to engage in self-reflection, which sometimes led to painful realizations. For example, Eva described how her status as a monolingual English speaker made her feel inadequate:

I was very thankful for my host sister who is 15 years old and speaks English very well. Currently, she is in her first year of high school and has been studying three languages - English, German, and Spanish. My host sister has served as my translator to her parents (my host parents), to her grandparents, and pretty much every Italian I have contact with. It's comforting to have a conversation in English with an Italian without using big nonverbal gestures and movements and/or Google translate and my Italian-English dictionary. However, sometimes I felt very inadequate when I think of how little Spanish I know, even though after I studied it in high school, while my host sister is fluent in four languages.

Similarly, Leigh wrote:

It was such a blessing to be with my host family, but it was awkward not being able to communicate easily. It was very frustrating and so difficult and time consuming to use my Italian dictionary, I found myself not trying to communicate. I'm embarrassed that I didn't try harder to learn Italian and that I gave up so easily.

Of course, these challenges also led to positive self-realizations. As Angie notes:

Living with a host family who speaks a different language than you and living in a different culture creates many challenges, but also many learning experiences. I had a unique situation. My host parents and brother did not speak much English, but we learned to communicate through a lot of pointing, gesturing, and using a lot of simple words. Also, my host brother and I learned different ways to communicate by playing games such Wii, card games, sports, and making funny faces at each other. My 16-year-old sister knows English very well though, so she was my translator most of the time. Also, we could talk more easily about similarities and differences in our lives and about random topics. These interactions with my host family helped me learn that there are many ways of communicating, and I learned a lot about myself, but most importantly I learned to be respectful and patient.

Language Learners at School

Becoming the CLD learner in a class and school was an eye-opening experience for preservice teachers. They described learning a new language as exciting and rewarding, and also challenging and physically and emotionally exhausting. The stress and frustration most participants experienced helped them to appreciate the challenges English Language Learners (ELLs) encountered in the US, view ELLs in more positive terms, and consider practical ways they might support their future students. The following excerpt represents the sentiment of many preservice teachers:

One big takeaway for me is the importance of making English language learners (ELLs) feel welcome in a classroom. Through my experience as an Italian language learner, I know the isolation and discomfort of being the only person in a room who doesn't speak the primary language. Being a language learner in the classroom is very overwhelming and uncomfortable, and there is a sense of loss - much like the "deer in the headlights" feeling. I want my future ELLs to feel welcomed and safe in my classroom, and included – much like my Italian teachers made me feel from my first day.

Another preservice teacher wrote:

The most important thing I learned from this study abroad was how hard it is to be a language learner in a classroom. I did not understand the way these children felt growing up in America where English is the main language but not their first language. I can now sympathize with the children who come from different countries and speak foreign languages. I found myself dozing off in the classroom several times a day because the teacher who I worked with did not check on me personally to see if I was keeping up. While I understand that I was not her responsibility, I found I didn't want to try as hard to be involved because she was not trying to engage with me. This experience has helped me to realize I need to go above and beyond for my students who are learning English. I never want a child in my classroom to feel lonely or isolated the way I did in my Italian classroom. I want everyone to succeed and understand the content of what I am teaching. I am so grateful for this experience because now I understand a different perspective I had never even thought of prior to this trip.

While cognitively this preservice teacher recognized that she was not the teacher's primary responsibility, she still had a strong emotional reaction to her situation. Even when Italian teachers were open and welcoming, the language differences had a profound emotional effect on preservice teachers. Focusing on what was positive or emotionally rewarding, such as small gestures, were opportunities for growth.

This experience taught me the importance of valuing ELLs' culture and language. As a second language learner, I loved when people tried to speak to me in English (even if it was a simple hello or goodbye). I know most of those people didn't speak English but just trying and acknowledging me made me feel valuable. As a teacher, I know I will need to learn at least a few essential phrases to speak with my ELL students. Also, I can value my students' languages and culture by asking them to share words, songs, and games with the class like my Italian teachers did with their foreign students. It was amazing to see how my teachers positively positioned students in the classroom and valued their cultures and languages like the time they asked students to sing Happy Birthday to me in Russian, Chinese, Spanish, Romanian, and Bulgarian. It was truly amazing.

Prior to departure, preservice teachers were given a document describing five stages of language development: pre-production, early production, speech emergence, intermediate fluency and, advanced fluency (Jorgensen, 2008). In addition to describing student characteristics and behaviors of each stage, it provided sample teacher behaviors and questioning techniques to support language leaners. Prior to departure, preservice teachers identified themselves as being in the "pre-production stage" or leaners who are totally new to the language. Most believed that by the end of the four weeks, they would move up to a new stage, if not two or three stages and they would be able to have conversations in Italian. Preservice teachers quickly discovered that learning a new language, even when immersed in it, is difficult. Consequently, they often described strategies that they used to learn Italian and how that influenced their thinking about teaching and learning. For example, Leigh discussed the value of repetition:

My teacher was very helpful and translated many of the phrases used in the Italian classroom into English. I made sure to immediately write them down in my journal and practice every night before going to bed. Repetition, repetition, repetition! I quickly learned this is the most important aspect of learning a language.

Chris talked about how she could learn Italian by participating in instructional activities with her young students:

I was able to learn Italian today by doing the same work as my first grade students! It was fun because they were working on single and plural words and how articles change based upon whether a word is masculine or feminine. I had no idea about any of those things so it was a good lesson for me! I did the worksheet with my students and they corrected my work. They thought it was funny that I didn't always understand and I laughed with them, too.

Finally, Danni realized how attitude or emotional affect influenced language learning:

I came to Italy knowing only three words of Italian so I was the CLD learner for a month. I found it really hard to learn Italian because I was nervous and had a hard time pronouncing words correctly. I had to get over my embarrassment when pronouncing new words or reluctance to learn new words. Learning a new language is really hard! But, by the end of the program, I was able to say words and even a few sentences. Learning Italian has influenced my thinking as a teacher. I am now more aware of what my future English language learners will be feeling and that it will take them time and lots of practice to learn English. I can't rush them, I need to help them feel comfortable in my classroom so they will not be embarrassed to practice and take risks.

Summary

As previously mentioned, becoming a CLD learner in a home and school, and learning to navigate in these contexts when you do not speak the language, had a profound influence on preservice teachers' views about ELLs in the US and their future teaching. Despite their life experiences (e.g., studying a language in high school), university coursework (e.g., learning about length of time students need to learn academic and social language to support learning) and the preparation prior to departures (e.g., practicing words and phrases, and listening to storybooks read in Italian), preservice teachers repeatedly discussed the shock and challenges of not knowing the Italian language. They quickly discovered how physically and emotionally exhausting it is to be in an environment where you do not know the language and how difficult it is to learn a new language. This experience helped preservice teachers develop a strong empathetic stance towards ELLs and their families, and to begin understanding how they might apply practical strategies to support future students.

Teaching

Preservice teachers viewed different ways of teaching, considered how cultural norms influence what teachers and students do in a classroom, and thought about their future teaching during this international field experience. However, prior to departure, preservice teachers were told about some cultural norms and teaching differences so that they could think about "why Italian teachers do what they do" and "why American teachers do what they do" during their work in schools. By preparing preservice teachers, they were able to move more quickly through the "they're not doing it right" to thinking about the "how and why" of instruction. Ultimately, the goal was to help preservice teachers avoid viewing teaching as "good or bad" or "right or wrong" but to understand that instructional practices have strength and limitations. With this in mind, two themes emerged related to how the international field experience prepared them for future teaching.

Teaching Italian Students Better Prepares for Future Teaching

Preservice teachers were eager to teach English to their Italian students and they viewed their instruction as successful and positive for students. However, preservice teachers acknowledged the challenges of teaching a class of primarily non-English speaking students and described what they have learned from their experiences. Also, as in Eva's post, preservice teachers sometimes talked about how they had applied content learned in university coursework to their teaching:

This past week, I had the opportunity to teach my first English lesson! My teacher asked me to find an action song about something they were learning in English. My students are learning how to count to ten in English, so I created a lesson about counting to ten. I first reviewed the numbers with students in Italian and English. This meant I needed to learn the numbers myself and key vocabulary! Luckily, I had my host sister help me with this. I then taught them the song "5 Little Monkeys Swinging on a Tree." After the song, the students completed a drawing and labeled the numbers. In my Teaching English as a Second Language course (TESOL) this past year, I learned the importance of multiple modes of communication. While teaching students the song, I incorporated visuals, videos, and had the kids repeat back small sections of the song. However, teaching a lesson in English to a group of students who only speak only a little English was more difficult than I anticipated. What I thought was a small segment, was way to long for my first grade students to remember. And, from the blank stares of my students' faces, I quickly learned that I needed to slow down. Luckily, my teacher was there to help me translate some things into Italian. Overall, the lesson went well and I know the students enjoyed the song because each day, they ask to sing the monkey or "scimmia" song.

Teaching English to Italian students helped preservice teachers reflect on effective instructional practices such as giving multi-modal presentations, talking slowly, teaching bits of information, and engaging students in repetition. However, as Lauren noted, sometimes using multiple strategies or supports still was not sufficient:

From my time as a language learner and teaching, I realized how many resources I will need to use in my class in order for students to learn. I thought using simple English and giving students visuals would be enough, but I was wrong. For my lesson I printed pictures of flags and provided examples, and I had vocabulary words and phrases available for them to use. Even with all these supports, students struggled. As a teacher, I need to be prepared, flexible, understanding, and help students feel comfortable taking risks. Being able to teach English to a class of mainly Italian-speaking students was so amazing and I learned so much that will only make me a better teacher in the future.

Also, as Angie indicated, teachers need to be flexible with plans:

I read a book called "If You Give a Mouse a Cookie." When I did this lesson, I put the pages of the book on a PowerPoint so that it was easier for everyone to see and so that they could follow along reading the words to get more practice. I read the book all the way through once and then had 5 students come up to read the book again. They loved getting the chance to read so much that another 5 students raised their hands to read. I hadn't initially planned for more students to read aloud the book again, but they were so excited and engaged, so we did it again. I realized from this that students could be actively engaged and interested in a lesson if they get to interact with the material. I will keep this in mind when I am a teacher and will try to incorporate interactive lessons as much as possible. The way that these students' faces lit up when I said that they would get the chance to read aloud was amazing and I want to spark every student's interest like I did with these Italian students.

Finally, Chris touched on one aspect of teaching with which some preservice teachers struggled, at least initially. Specifically, they viewed teaching as presenting formal lessons, rather than informal interactions with others. However, in this excerpt, Chris clearly recognized she was teaching (and learning) during both formal and informal interaction and saw its value:

I had amazing experiences teaching English in Italy. I was able to teach around 10 formal lessons in my school, but that doesn't include random mini lessons scattered throughout each day. For example,

I was able to teach English words for animals on their field trip to the World Wildlife Foundation, and words that came up during their reading lessons. One time, I taught a student from my class who happened to be at the playground in my neighborhood. It was so much fun communicating with each other in English and Italian outside of the school. It's so awesome and important to teach language during all aspects of life and not just in school.

Being a CLD Learner Develops Empathy Toward and Strategies for Teaching ELLs

Being a CLD learner and teaching English to Italian students provided preservice teachers with a unique understanding of the challenges of learning a language while also negotiating different situations in a new culture. These challenges led to the cognitive and emotional dissonance necessary for preservice teachers to reflect on their knowledge, beliefs and biases, and to plan for future teaching. The following excerpts clearly show how this experience transformed one preservice teacher's thinking:

As a future educator, I have grown immensely on this trip as well. I think that having the opportunity to teach English as a second language while simultaneously being a second language learner myself is such a valuable experience. I now can empathize with second language learners because learning a second language can be difficult, isolating, and tiring. Further, it can be difficult to learn a new language while you are also trying to navigate a new culture. A big takeaway I have from this trip is the importance of making sure my second language learners feel welcome in my classroom. It is so important that they feel comfortable to make mistakes and ask questions. I want to build a supportive environment from day one in my classroom.

Finally, I learned how ELLs must feel in schools back in the US! At times I was just sitting in the class, listening to a language that I did not understand at all. I found myself zoning off because I had no idea of what was happening, which took away from my interest and made me tired. I learned that being an ELL is mentally and emotionally exhausting because you are trying to learn everything your classmates are learning (even something simple like addition), but you have to learn it in a language that you are not familiar with – so it's hard! I was just observing my classroom during these times, because I already understood the math equation, but I can only imagine how difficult it would be for me to learn a new math equation in a new language. This experience has made me sympathize for ELL students, and made me gain new approaches of working with them.

Although I was clueless while sitting in the Italian classroom, I learned so much about how I will teach in the future. I know how it feels to be in a new place and not know anyone or the language. I know how it feels to be lost and how difficult it is to follow something when you don't know what is going on. With this, I can empathize with my students who are coming into my class from a different culture and with a different language. I can better understand what they are going through as well as how to make them feel more comfortable. Personally, I would have liked to have a "buddy" who was with me to show me what they were doing or walk with me whenever we left the room. Often, I just followed what the kids were doing. For example, when they all got up to go somewhere, I had no clue where we were going unless Chiara told me. In situations like that, having a buddy would have been nice and would have given me a friendly face to rely on. Also, the skills I gained from this program can be used to work with families of new students who don't know the language. Making sure that the families are involved and have resources that are in their native language is important. If parents feel welcomed and involved in their students' education, chances are they will be more willing to work with the teacher or help their child when needed. Overall, I feel like the personal experience I had of being in a classroom that doesn't speak my language will help me tremendously in my future teaching, as well as being accommodating in other aspects of my life.

Chris further addressed what many preservice teachers learned about valuing students' home language and culture.

I have a whole new perspective and respect for the variety of families of my future students. I want to meet them where they are in life even if that means meeting with them at times that work best for them during parent-teacher conferences and during other times throughout the year. I want to give families various options to make them feel like they are apart of their child's learning even if it's something simple like taking the time to sign a Friday Folder and sending it back – simple, but meaningful. It's not that parents don't want to be involved; they just may not know how (I might need to explain what a Friday Folder is!) or they may struggle to find the time with everything they must do to provide for their family. I have a very new understanding and real appreciation for families who may not sign-up for every volunteer opportunity or come in to eat lunch with their student. It doesn't mean they don't care about their child. I want to take time to get to know my students' families for who they are as people. I don't want to make judgments about parents' thoughts and feelings toward their child and their child's education based on how much I see them do or don't do in the classroom. My host family has given me a first hand glimpse into daily life in another culture. I am forever thankful.

Summary

An international field experience allows preservice teachers to apply practices they have learned in their university coursework to unique situations, realizing that what they learned, or the ways in which they interpreted the content, does not always apply as easily as expected. Preservice teachers also learned that teaching is much more complex than they thought, and that they need to engage in critical reflection about the teaching context, students' needs, and instructional practices for teaching to be effective. By doing so, preservice teachers learned to modify their approach to teaching Italian students and, hopefully, will help them to better plan instruction that serves their future students.

LIMITATIONS

There are two obvious limitations to the findings presented in this chapter. The first limitation is that this field experience took place in a non-English speaking country. While this allowed preservice teachers to understand the challenges of being an Italian language learner and to relate their experiences to that of ELLs in the US, pre-service teachers may not have realized the high status they had as guests in homes, schools, and communities or as Americans teaching English, as contrasted with what ELLs and/or immigrants experience in the US. Further, because the preservice teachers did not speak Italian, there may have been limits to what they learned about the Italian culture and educational practices in Italy. A second limitation is that that the field experience took place in one European country. While the field experience in Italy allowed preservice teachers to think deeply about cultural issues, it is unclear if preservice teachers will be able to apply their new understandings of culture when teaching future students who will undoubtedly be from other countries. In short, additional research is needed to determine if future teachers can apply what they learned during an international field experience to better serve CLD students once begin their teaching careers in the US.

CONCLUSION

For teachers to effectively design and implement instruction that support diverse students, they need to develop an empathetic and caring stance towards all leaners; reflect on their beliefs about learners from cultures different from their own; reflect on their own cultural beliefs, values and perspectives; and become knowledgeable about other people and cultures (Rychly & Graves, 2012). Living with an Italian host family and being immersed in Italian schools and communities created meaningful interactions with people from the host community. By participating in an international field experience that placed them outside of their personal comfort zone and allowed them to view the world from a different perspective, preservice teachers were provided with important opportunities to reflect on their beliefs, values, biases, and actions, as well as consider new and different ways of interacting with others, including future students and families.

REFERENCES

Bradley, B. A., & Emerson, A. M. (2017). Learning about culture and teaching during an immersion study abroad program. In H. An (Ed.), *Efficacy and implementation of study abroad programs for P-12 teachers* (pp. 174–191). Hershey, PA: IGI Global Publications. doi:10.4018/978-1-5225-1057-4.ch010

Colwell, J., Nielsen, D. C., Bradley, B. A., & Spearman, M. (2016). Preservice teacher reflections about a short-term summer study abroad experience. In J. A. Rhodes & T. M. Milby (Eds.), *Advancing Teacher Education and Curriculum Development through Study Abroad Programs* (pp. 90–110). Hershey, PA: IGI Global Publications. doi:10.4018/978-1-4666-9672-3.ch006

Gibbs, G. (2007). *Analyzing qualitative data*. Los Angeles: Sage. doi:10.4135/9781849208574

Goe, L., Bell, C., & Little, O. (2008). *Approaches to evaluating teacher effectiveness: A research synthesis*. Washington, DC: National Comprehensive Center for Teacher Quality.

Holmes, P., Bavieri, L., & Ganassin, S. (2015). Developing intercultural understanding for study abroad: Students' and teachers' perspectives on pre-departure intercultural learning. *Intercultural Education*, *26*(1), 16–30. doi:10.1080/14675986.2015.993250

Jorgensen, K. (2008). Second Language Development Stages: Sample Behaviors in the Classroom [Class handout]. Lawrence, KS: University of Kansas, C&T 649.

Kehl, K., & Morris, J. (2007). Differences in global-mindedness between short-term and semester-long study abroad participants at selected private universities. *Frontiers: The Interdisciplinary Journal of Study Abroad*, *15*, 67–79.

Ladson-Billings, G. (1994). *The dreamkeepers: Successful teachers of African-American children*. San Francisco: Jossey-Bass.

McAllister, G., & Irvine, J. J. (2002). The role of empathy in teaching culturally diverse students: A qualitative study of teachers' beliefs. *Journal of Teacher Education*, *53*(5), 433–443. doi:10.1177/002248702237397

McGaha, J. M., & Linder, S. M. (2014). Determining candidates' attitudes toward global-mindedness. *Action in Teacher Education*, *36*(4), 305–321. doi:10.1080/01626620.2014.948225

Rogers, R. R. (2001). Reflection in higher education: A concept analysis. *Innovative Higher Education*, *26*(1), 37–57. doi:10.1023/A:1010986404527

Rogers, R. R. (2001). Reflection in higher education: A concept analysis. *Innovative Higher Education*, *26*(1), 37–57. doi:10.1023/A:1010986404527

Rychly, L., & Graves, E. (2012). Teacher characteristics for culturally responsive pedagogy. *Multicultural Perspectives*, *14*(1), 44–49. doi:10.1080/15210960.2012.646853

Salisbury, M., An, B., & Pascarella, E. (2013). The effect of study abroad on intercultural competence among undergraduate college students. *Journal of Student Affairs Research and Practice*, *50*(1), 1–20. doi:10.1515/jsarp-2013-0001

Sleeter, C. E. (1995). An analysis of the critiques of multicultural education. In J. A. Banks & C. A. McGee Banks (Eds.), *Handbook of research on multicultural education* (pp. 81–94). New York: Simon & Schuster Macmillan.

Suárez-Orozco, M., & Sattin, C. (2007). Wanted: Global citizens. *Educational Leadership*, *64*(7), 58–62.

U.S. Department of Education, Institute of Education Sciences, National Center for Education Statistics. (2017). *Racial/Ethnic Enrollment in Public Schools*. Retrieved from https://nces.ed.gov/programs/coe/indicator_cge.asp

Wang, J., Lin, E., Spalding, E., Odell, S., & Klecka, C. (2011). Understanding Teacher Education in an Era of Globalization. *Journal of Teacher Education*, *62*(2), 115–120. doi:10.1177/0022487110394334

KEY TERMS AND DEFINITIONS

Culturally and Linguistically Diverse Leaners: Students whose first language and culture is not the same as the dominant culture in which they live and attend school.

English Language Learners: Students who are learning to communicate in English and typically require modified instruction to learn English and the content.

Field Experience: Placement in a school setting so that preservice teacher can observe and teach in order to begin developing the knowledge, skills, and disposition to become an effective teacher.

Host Family Placement: The placement of preservice teachers with a family in the host country to promote cultural understanding and exchange of ideas.

Immersion: Living and possibly working or going to school in a country other than a person's own.

Preservice Teacher: A college student who is enrolled in a teacher preparation program in the United States in order to receive state licensure to teach specified grades and/or content areas.

Reflection: The act of looking back at one's words, actions, and beliefs to consider ways to make improvement to one's self.

School Placement: The placement of preservice teachers in a preschool, elementary, middle, or high school, based on their request, to observe and work to the best of their ability given the language differences, and to teach English to Italian students.

Chapter 13
Dismantling Eurocratic Practices in Teacher Education:
A Preservice Program Focused on Culturally Relevant, Humanizing, and Decolonizing Pedagogies

Kamania Wynter-Hoyte
University of South Carolina, USA

Meir Muller
University of South Carolina, USA

Nathaniel Bryan
Miami University, USA

Gloria Swindler Boutte
University of South Carolina, USA

Susi Long
University of South Carolina, USA

ABSTRACT

This chapter provides a profile of an urban education collective that fosters relationships among pre-service teachers, university faculty, and a local school district. The partnership supports preservice and in-service teachers serving marginalized communities using culturally relevant, humanizing, and decolonizing pedagogies. Drawing from decolonizing and humanizing theoretical and pedagogical frameworks, the collective highlights equity, asset-based, and anti-racist teachings. Insights gained from this initiative and recommendations for navigating challenges in equity work are presented. Implications for teacher education programs and future research goals are provided.

DOI: 10.4018/978-1-5225-6249-8.ch013

INTRODUCTION

Nationally, preservice teachers are entering the field of education with little to no awareness of issues of racism, xenophobia, heteronormativity, ableism, and gender bias (King, 2005; Sleeter, 2001; Swartz, 2005) that continue to dominate pedagogy, policy, and practice in educational institutions. In addition, they join a workforce that has had little opportunity (through their own teacher education programs or inservice professional development) to understand the ongoing effects of colonialism on curriculum, theory, and instruction (Asante, 2017; Au, Brown & Calderon, 2016). This means that Eurocratic (King & Swartz, 2016) curricula, policies, and practices continue to dominate in most educational settings rather than *normalizing* the community cultural wealth (Yosso, 2005) -- the strengths, accomplishments, values, and resources -- of cultural and racial communities that continue to be marginalized, misrepresented, or invisible in schools and in teacher education programs (Baines, Tisdale, & Long, 2018; Paris & Alim, 2017). Further, it is well documented that children of Color are consistently over-referred to special education (Codrington & Fairchild, 2013), under-referred to gifted programs (Ford, 2013), and inequitably disciplined (U.S. Department of Education Office of Civil Rights, 2014) and assessed (Rosner, 2002). As a result, preservice teachers, who may experience a class here or a professor there in their university programs focusing on equity issues or assets-based pedagogies, rarely have the knowledge, experience, confidence, or support necessary to sustain equity ideologies once they enter the teaching profession and we continue to lose students most marginalized in schools to an inequitable pedagogical status quo.

As university faculty, we brought these concerns to the development of an Urban Education Collective which encompasses five schools, their administrators and teachers; five university faculty; and a two-year Urban Education cohort of preservice teachers majoring in early childhood education. The work focuses on issues of equity in early childhood (grades PreK - Grade 3) pedagogy, practice, and policy. Through the work, teachers, preservice teachers, and university faculty engage together in investigating how Eurocratic practice not only disempowers communities and disenfranchises children who are marginalized, but how it communicates the centrality of Whiteness to every student (King & Swartz, 2016). We worked to develop a cohort experience for preservice teachers and a professional development experience for practicing teachers that would help both groups of educators learn realities of inequity as well as humanizing, decolonizing, and culturally relevant pedagogical strategies (Ladson-Billings, 2014, 2017) for change.

The school district in which the Collective takes place is an urban district of about 23,000 students. Seventy-three percent of the students are African American, 19% are European American, and 8% are listed by the school district as "other." A total of 72% of the students receive free/reduced-price lunch. The university's student demographics are approximately 69% European American, 15% African American, 4% Latinx, 3% two or more races, 2% Asian, and 4% of the students did not respond when asked by the university to self-identify according to the categories provided. Three of university professors involved in this collective are African American and two are European American. The 25 university students in the urban cohort involved in this work included five African American students, one Latina student and 19 European American students.

Within and across these contexts, the Urban Education Collective seeks to build a shared knowledge base and a collaborative network to support teachers and preservice teachers in better addressing the strengths and needs of young children. The authors of this chapter are the university faculty engaged in the work. We work toward sustainable pedagogical transformation and document our processes and practices to better understand how and if the development of a network of shared knowledge acts to encourage and sustain the abilities and convictions of student teachers and practicing teachers to dismantle and replace unjust practices. In this chapter, we describe the theoretical frame that guides us as we engage in the work of the Urban Education Collective and the Urban Education Cohort. The insights and implications reported in this chapter are preliminary and represent in process work and were gained through analysis of our first two years of operation.

Theoretical Framework

According to Bell (2007),

social justice involves social actors who have a sense of their own agency as well as a sense of social responsibility toward and with others, their society and the broader world in which we live. (p. 2.)

This chapter is theoretically and pedagogically grounded in a social justice framework, which examines how oppression and privilege perpetuate systems of power (Freire, 1970). The Urban Education Collective is situated in a school of thought that examines marginalized, mistreated, and mistaught early childhood education students through a humanizing and critical lens. Since, theory informs practice we use social justice as a framework to guide our data analysis and teaching practices in the urban cohort.

In order for students to strive towards a social responsibility for equitable teaching, our framework is dedicated to first disrupting years of distorted and incomplete teachings. Our pre-service teachers and the teachers with whom we work are inundated with Whiteness in their education about history, science, authors, mathematicians, explorers, inventors, and world leaders. The presentation of anything non-Eurocentric was often learned as an 'other', less than, or barbaric. Asante refers to this as *White esteem curriculum* (1992, p. 20). The process of disrupting this learning at times creates discomfort among our preservice teachers, the majority of whom are White, female, monolingual, and middle class. However, university faculty continues to support them in recovering historical content that "re-members" or re-connects knowledge of the past that has been silenced (King & Swartz, 2014). All coursework, social gatherings, and learning engagements are purposeful and used to deepen preservice teachers' insights and knowledge about equity pedagogies. The work is anchored in faculty convictions about social justice as directly linked to the concept of humanization (Kinloch & Dixon, 2018) recognizing that inequitable practices dehumanize students of color, students from low-income households, and LGBTQIA students. apply social justice as a theory to drive the process and as practice to propel us to the goal of building more equitable educational institutions.

Specifically, we anchor our work in pedagogies that are decolonizing (Battiste, 2013), humanizing (Freire, 1970), culturally relevant (Ladson-Billings, 1995) and culturally sustaining (Paris & Alim, 2017). Similar to Baines, Tisdale, and Long (2018) and Wynter-Hoyte, Braden, Rodriguez, and Thornton (2017), we seek to disrupt, dismantle, and replace deficit views that have been cultivated in colonized curriculum. We support teachers in acknowledging and appreciating the humanity of all students by building understandings that students' language (Boutte, 2016), literacies (Gregory, Long, & Volk, 2004), and funds of knowledge (Gonzalez, Moll & Amanti, 2005) are relevant (Ladson-Billings, 1995 and must be sustained (Paris & Alim, 2017) through equitable teachings.

The Urban Education Collective

From the first days of our thinking about an Urban Education Cohort, we (cohort faculty) knew that a part of the success of the model would depend on the schools where our students would be placed for practica and internships. In our program, students are engaged in schools from their sophomore year with longer internships in the senior year. Past experiences demonstrated that many of the insights about inequities and socially just teaching that our students took with them were often contradicted by teachers in their internship placements. This was not through the fault of the teachers. Most of them had not had opportunities for professional learning that focused on humanizing or culturally relevant pedagogies and had little understanding about ongoing presence of Eurocentric pedagogies or the need to decolonize practices. Their contradictions often came in the form of deficit language and dispositions about children and families of Color, those who are adding Standardized English to their linguistic repertoires, and children from households where income was low.

However, to paraphrase Maya Angelou, "when you know better you do better," so we began working with personnel in a local, urban school district to build relationships with a small group of schools which ultimately became known as the Urban Education Collective. Our agreement with the schools and the school system was that we would provide professional learning for teachers interested in serving as coaching/cooperating teachers for our student teachers. The goal was to create a collective across schools and with the university to build knowledge and impact practice together.

With five public school partners, five full time faculty members, and 25 undergraduates, the Urban Education Collective began to take shape. We designed a professional learning model to help educators address issues of individual, institutional, and pedagogical inequity by helping classroom teachers, administrators, and university students recognize and teach against those realities. We felt a strong commitment to supporting our undergraduates in teaching students most often marginalized and disenfranchised in schools as well as children representing dominant groups (White, middle class, Christian, heterosexual). We hoped that the Urban Collective would serve school children by deepening teacher and preservice teacher knowledge and ability to effectively teach students who have historically been underserved in schools as well as students from dominant cultural and linguistic groups who can easily develop inflated views of their place in the world (Baines, Tisdale, & Long, 2018; Nieto, 2010).

We worked to organize our goals around the school district's strategic plan which calls *for teaching that transforms lives, collaborates with an engaged community, and empowers all students to achieve their potential in safe, caring, academically challenging learning environments to develop productive citizens for a changing world*. By foregrounding the work in these goals all stakeholders (district personnel, university professors, and preservice teachers) are able to strongly align the goals of the schools and university. The overarching objectives for the Urban Collective schools were jointly constructed by district administrators, school-based educators and university professors include a commitment to:

- Children's academic growth resulting from deepened teacher/preservice teacher knowledge and ability to effectively teach in urban settings.
- Professional development tailored to each school's needs and conducted *in schools and regularly over time* as opposed to singular workshops or disconnected PD; facilitated by USC professors who consult nationally and internationally, but *who understand and are particularly committed to better educational outcomes in South Carolina.*

- Guidance to connect practices to district/state standards and teacher evaluation systems including *Read to Succeed* competencies, the *SC College and Career Readiness Standards*, and recently adopted *NIET* SC teacher evaluation system.
- A variety of delivery methods to meet the needs and schedules of teachers: after-school teacher study groups in individual schools, all-day PD sessions with all four schools together, and sessions in which all schools and the USC students come together for Urban Collective-wide conferences.
- Opportunities to address the curricular opportunity gap faced by children who have long been academically marginalized thereby creating local and national models of excellence.
- Opportunities for teachers to serve as coaching teachers for Urban Education students during their practicum and Internship experiences.
- Possibilities for graduate course work tailored to needs of teachers in the Collective.
- Opportunities for interactions with national collaboratives also committed to excellence in teaching in diverse communities and to highlight the schools at national conferences.

To reach these goals teachers are offered clear defined support from the faculty members. For each school, one professor serves as the school's university partner/consultant taking responsibility for ensuring that the professional learning for that school is regular and systematic, getting to know the school and its teachers, children, and community. Teachers also have opportunities to learn from the expertise of the other Urban Cohort professors through in-services that brings all four schools together. The tools being used to accomplish this ongoing, consistent, onsite scaffolding of teachers and preservice teachers include:

- Full and half-day in-service workshops (during the school year and in the summer)
- Biweekly professional study groups tailored to the needs of each school
- Onsite support for teachers in these classrooms
- Tailored sessions at local conferences

These components are developed in collaboration with each school's administrators and teachers, engaging them in learning about literacy, mathematics, science, and social studies depending on the needs of the school. Content is grounded in principles of culturally relevant, humanizing, and decolonizing pedagogies long documented as vital to the success of diverse learners. The content is typically delivered in 60-minute after school sessions (or their equivalent - on some occasions, this may be in the multi-hour sessions, in-class demonstrations and/or grade level sessions), three full day sessions (5 hours each, one per semester), and two-to-three full days in the summer. All of these professional development sessions provide continued education credit towards recertification and, in the state of South Carolina, part of the required *Read to Succeed* certification.

Joint sessions are offered when the four schools and pre-service teachers come together to share and deepen learning. Several of the preservice teachers' courses are taught on site at Urban Education Collective schools providing additional opportunities for inservice and preservice teachers to interact. An Urban Collective Facebook site provides a space where web links, instructional video clips, articles, questions and responses are posted by teachers, preservice teachers and instructors.

Each of these professional learning elements use a strong demonstration-and-engagement, theory-to-practice model meaning that the university faculty regularly present theoretical concepts (and research), provide examples of theory in practice, and engage and support teachers in generating, trying out, and evaluating the impact (and potential need for revision) of their work. Online support includes viewing videos of classroom practices and other national experts, responding to professional literature, sharing practices and receiving feedback.

The elements and competencies outlined above are simultaneously assessed through the following measures.

- **Lesson Plans:** Teachers develop, share, implement, and evaluate plans verbalizing how those plans support the major theories and research explored through the professional development sessions.
- **Documentation of Teaching:** Teachers collect data about the implementation of their lesson plans to share during professional development including: photos, children's work, video clips of children at work, interviews with children to assess engagement, and achievement data according to measures learned through professional development as well as those required by the district and in their schools.
- **Teacher Questionnaire:** Teachers respond to regular questionnaires and reflection queries prepared by university faculty to assess their understanding of key concepts as well as questions to assess further professional needs.
- **Classroom Collaboration:** University faculty spend time in classrooms collaboratively (with teachers) teaching together and assessing the implementation of new practices or revisions to existing practices. These collaborations also inform further professional development sessions in terms of teacher need.
- **Responses to Online Resources and Professional Reading:** Teachers regularly respond either online, as written reflection during professional development or verbally during class visits and grade level meetings, sharing specific take-aways or learning gained from their engagement with online resources and professional reading.
- **Using Learning to Plan:** During summer sessions teachers use the year's learning to develop plans for teaching as well as a classroom design (layout, culturally relevant and linguistically diverse and supportive texts and other materials)
- **Growth Reflections:** Teachers reflect regularly about their own growth particularly in terms of overturned deficit models, building belief in every child and family, and understanding how recognizing prior assumptions and biases impacts more equitable teaching.

The vision is to continue this collective as an ongoing program of professional learning and collaboration as we build long-term relationships with schools as new cohorts of Early Childhood students enter the program. In each successive year, the plan is for university faculty, preservice teachers, and teachers to engage family and community members in the collaboration as they continue to fine tune a model which includes more equitable, humanizing, and culturally relevant pedagogies.

The Urban Education Cohort

The Urban Education Cohort is typically made up of 25-28 undergraduate majors in early childhood education. During the students' sophomore orientation, faculty members explain that the purpose of the cohort is to focus on issues of educational equity in terms of issues such as race, class, language, ethnicity, sexual orientation, gender identification, and religion. We describe curricula that uncover educational inequities and strategies for taking part in pedagogical and institutional transformation. Soon after the sophomore orientation meeting, we call a special meeting for all students who have expressed interest in the Urban Education Cohort to orient them to the cohort and the courses within it. We explain fundamental elements of the cohort experience:

- The focus on humanizing, culturally relevant, and anti-colonial practices.
- Understanding how to teach literacy, mathematics, science, and social studies grounded in principles of culturally relevant pedagogy and why that matters.
- Courses in child development, play, classroom community and family involvement also grounded in identifying and countering exclusionary practices.
- Out-of-class experiences focused on issues of social justice such as films, speakers, and being involved in civil acts that challenge unjust conditions or events.

The courses taken by students in the Urban Education Cohort are the same as those taken by every other cohort. The difference is the intensity with which each course is undergirded by the issues and purposes at the forefront of the Urban Education Cohort purposes. The courses taught by Urban Education Cohort faculty typically include:

- Culturally Relevant Pedagogy
- Family Dynamics
- Community of Learners
- Linguistic Pluralism Across the Content Areas
- Child Development in the Primary Grades
- Teaching Reading in Early Childhood Education
- Teaching Writing in Early Childhood Education
- Teaching Social Studies in Early Childhood Education
- Internship Seminar

Some students in the Urban Education Cohort are also members REACH (Race, Equity, and Advocacy in Childhood Education) which is a student organization focusing on issues of race and racism in schooling and society. The organization meets evenings every other week where discussions emanate from local and national events, invited speakers, and video clips.

As professors who teach in the Urban Education Cohort, we bring a collective history of teaching, research, and publication in the fields of educational equity, culturally relevant teaching, critical race theory, and humanizing and decolonizing education. We are a collective within ourselves who regularly share readings, present together at conferences, and support each other in thinking through complex pedagogical and institutional issues. In addition, each faculty member serves within larger national and international networks of social justice educators bringing their experience to those bodies while learning from them and bringing new insights back to the collective.

Insights

Our examination of data from the first two-year Urban Education Collective and Cohort experience leads to insights that inform our ongoing work to build the program and that we offer for other teacher educators embarking on the same process. Below we discuss some of the insights that we have gained about successes and challenges.

Successes

The successes of the Urban Collective (which is now completing its second year) already seem impressive and exciting enough for us to persevere in deepening the impact and strengthening sites of challenge. We note successes among: (a) preservice teachers; (b) classroom teachers, and; (c) university faculty.

Preservice Teacher Growth

The growth of the preservice teachers who self-selected into the Urban Cohort has been exciting to watch. For example, one student's response when asked to name one experience that she remembered as influential captures the feelings of many. She explained, "I can't pick a course or experience that didn't make me feel brand new and special." In the sections below, we offer a range of responses to the UC experience as it impacted students personally and professionally in a variety of ways.

"It Has Changed My Life and Opened My Mind"

Repeatedly, students told us about how the Urban Education Cohort had changed their lives. The majority of our students come from towns and cities around the state, both rural and urban. Some of the students whose quotes are provided below describe their upbringing as segregated, others were not but the sentiments are similar:

The Urban Cohort has changed my life. I was brought up in a small, White community not knowing the impact and beauty of culture in our society. It has opened my heart in so many ways with each class and professor. I am able to go into my first classroom this fall and find inclusion through culture and the relevance of my students' backgrounds.

I have learned to grow through others and to be able to listen to them and reflect that in the early childhood classroom.

I feel as if I came into the college with a very narrow, blinded view of life. I was so oblivious to all the hurt but also the beauty that was around me. The Urban Cohort broadened my perspective and helped me see the rich culture that is all around me.

The Urban Cohort helped shape my views on race and racial issues.

Because of the training and learning that I received in the urban cohort, I have a new set of eyes. I can see systemic racism and its effect on the oppressed more clearly. Also, I can see the correlation between our education system and systemic racism.

These quotes highlight the impact on students' personal and professional growth as they critically self-reflect on their segregated living experiences and address issues of systematic racism, which is often challenging for pre-service teachers. Subsequently, students were able to juxtapose personal K-12 schooling experiences with institutional racism in education.

"I Learned About My Own Biases"

Over and over *and over* students told us about how their Urban Cohort experience not only broadened their worlds but helped them identify their own embedded biases, confront those biases, and work toward dismantling them. As one student expressed, essential to this was the "it's-okay-to-be-uncomfortable" environment we tried to create in each class. She wrote that, initially she felt challenged to open up and worried that she would say the wrong thing but, "the professors made it so that I could be myself, unjudged and so I blossomed daily." Students felt that they learned content knowledge and instructional strategies but that, beyond that and foundational to that, they learned about themselves and the biases they did not realize they held. A few of many testimonials about bias provide a glimpse into the impact of a focus on self-examination had on the cohort:

I have realized that I have biases and learned how to push those away to create an appreciative, supportive environment for all children who enter my classroom.

Personally, [the UC] has affected me being more open-minded. Coming from a small town . . . I had biases I didn't even know I had.

The Urban Cohort has taught me a lot about myself. I have learned about my personal bias and microaggressions and throughout the courses was able to reconstruct my ways of thinking.

The UC opened my eyes to a variety of different cultures that I had never had the experience of learning or talking about. I learned about biases and become (SIC) aware of my own biases.

Personally, I didn't realize the biases that I already carried with me when I entered the Urban Cohort . . . I've become more aware of my own microaggressions and have been more intent with my own words and actions.

The Urban Cohort Initiative provided a safe space for pre-service teachers to reflect and share how they were socialized in society and how this fostered the development of unconscious biases. This is another daunting process for pre-service teachers to engage in yet they acknowledged their discomfort and sustained through the difficult conversations and learning activities.

"I Gained Courage and Learned to Advocate for Children"

Perhaps one of the strongest outcomes was the development of the preservice teachers' ability, courage, and sense of purpose in advocating for students most often marginalized, misperceived, and oppressed in schools. They learned together about "awareness and ways to advocate for students." This was evidenced repeatedly in their outcome interviews with comments such as:

I now advocate for fellow students and women like myself to become strong and able to speak up.

The Urban Cohort has made me so strong.

I have found my voice through the Urban Cohort and I am much more comfortable talking about and advocating for children of Color.

When talking to other early childhood students, they are lost in the sense of inclusion and culturally relevant pedagogy. I was taught to be strong. Be bold. Be more than simply going into a classroom and teaching.

[My] internship stuck out to me because I feel like it showed me that there is a strong need for culturally relevant teachers who really care about their students. It is important that they not only care about them, but that they advocate for them.

The urban cohort gave me the tools that I needed to advocate for my students through the countless academic articles and textbooks that I have read. Therefore, I have documentation and research that I can use to support or disprove certain educational practices.

Most important, students learn how to take course content to inform and inspire advocacy. They accept the call to go beyond course learning engagements and become agents of change.

"I Loved Being With Like-Minded Peers"

For many of the students, being a part of a cohort that was together through most of their course work in their junior and senior years was an important and strong element of their undergraduate experience. They formed bonds that they feel they will carry into their professional life. As one student said, "I can't get over how tight we feel as a cohort." This closeness helped them deepen their knowledge and build courage. Another student explained the importance of being with peers who were developing the same dispositions: "Personally, the Urban Cohort linked me with a group of people who have the same mindset [so] we were able to learn together and grow together." Yet another student shared, "The Urban Cohort has given me a family of scholars with like ways of thinking."

It was crucial for students to have self-selected in the Urban Cohort with others who want to explore issues of racism and equity. This provided a non-combative space for students as well as instructors to stand in solidarity while engaging in anti-racist work.

"There Is Too Much Knowledge [for Me] to Describe"

Many elements of the Urban Education Cohort experience were shared by students as being particularly influential. Those elements often occurred when students connected university course learning with the Urban Cohort emphasis on self-reflection and experiences in early childhood classrooms. For example, one student drew on her class with Dr. Nathaniel Bryan and learning about the school-to-prison pipeline she recounted an experience in a PreK (four-year-olds) internship:

An experience I will always think about is when I realized the truth behind the school-to-prison pipeline. I had one student who was an African American male. Anything he did was called out and many times he was sent off the rug [away from class gathering time] for doing the exact same thing other students were doing. One day at recess, the student's turn on the bicycle was over so I asked him to give the next student a turn. He was very upset and I saw him go over to stand by the wall, breathing deeply. When I turned around, he was running at me and jumped on me and punched me in the throat. I brought him over to the wall and said 'I understand you're upset but you cannot hit me, that hurts me." By this time, the teacher walked over, grabbed his hand, and took him to the office for the third time that week. I never saw that four-year-old again because they suspended him for three days and his mother withdrew him from school. Suspend a four-year-old? My heart broke. I was so emotional and vowed never to feed into the awful school-to-prison pipeline. I can only hope that student finds a way to beat the systemic racism in schools.

Another student wrote about how her ability to take learning from Urban Cohort classes into the early childhood classroom allowed her to impact children typically marginalized in schools:

At my field placement, I tried my best to use the strategies that they Urban Cohort gave me to make my classroom inclusive and to make my students feel loved and cared about. At the end of the semester, one of my students wrote me a note that said, 'Thank you for letting me be my true self.' He affirmed that I had made some sort of impact on him and that he felt cared for.

These journal entries embody the Urban Cohort's strong impact on teaching. The first student was able to connect course content with the school-to-prison pipeline. She identified how teachers' disciplinary reactions and school suspensions are directly correlated with pushing students of color into penitentiaries. The second student described ethic of care with students and the importance of holistically valuing young learners. Both of these entries, exemplify how the knowledge gained empowered students and impacted their dispositions toward students of color.

"It Must Continue"

Students were adamant that the Urban Cohort should continue. They felt this not only from their course work but from experiences in public schools which helped them understand the need for a challenge to the Eurocratic status quo (King & Swartz, 2016). Their words about continuing the focus on anti-bias, anti-racist, decolonizing teaching using a cohort model came through loudly and clearly:

I hope this continues through USC's future . . . I cannot express my gratitude for the love and the experiences I have had. I want to relive your teachings in my classroom.

The Urban Cohort should live forever! I'd be happy to speak on behalf of our cohort and tell anyone why this NEEDS to be a part of the school of education for years to come.

While I have always had a heart for kids, I was still so far removed from the heart of teaching. It is so much more than the content and I feel much more prepared to embrace the beautifully diverse students who will walk into my classroom. I can't wait to be their home away from home.

The urban cohort should continue to ensure that future students get the education they truly deserve. The current education system is not made for all students' success. Right now, students of color or oppressed groups are being negatively impacted by our education system because it is not built for them. The urban cohort prepares future teachers with this reality. It teaches future teachers how to fight against this system in and outside of the classroom. Without the urban cohort, I would have never learned about culturally relevant practices to use in the classroom. I would not have faced my personal biases, and how they can potentially affect my students and my teaching. The urban cohort gave me the tools that I needed to be an effective teacher for all students. I cannot imagine future college of education students not receiving the knowledge, support from professors, and training that I received through the urban cohort.

These data points affirm the need for the Urban Cohort to maintain this work in social justice and equity. Students characterize their learning experiences as life changing by providing multiple ways to teach from a culturally relevant and sociocritical approach.

Classroom Teacher Growth

The growth in teacher knowledge and their excitement for pedagogical transformation is also exciting to see. The introduction of African American Language (AAL), for example, as a structured, historically-based, linguistically-recognized language (Boutte, 2016) was eye-opening for many teachers. In some cases, their attitudes toward languages altered significantly. They moved from "correcting" students' English use to teaching students that the language they brought from home was a legitimate language with structure and history. They taught lessons to children from kindergarten to third grade about the term bilingualism and West African roots of AAL. They taught the history of how languages change and grow and AAL as anchored in a past that reflects People who made foundational contributions to the world's knowledge. In this way, they began countering Eurocratic notions of history that typically marginalize, inaccurately portray, or suppress normalized inclusion of those contributions. They taught lessons in contrastive analysis using children's literature to demonstrate the literary use of AAL and taught each student how to translate from AAL to standardized English and back again. As a result, some of the teachers moved from thinking of AAL as bad or incorrect English to teaching students the art and skill of linguistic translation across languages. One teacher in particular reported that children who had rarely ventured to participate verbally in class became far more verbal once they recognized that they were not speaking poorly or incorrectly but they there were in fact bilingual and speaking a legitimate language.

After one professional development session on AAL with Dr. Gloria Boutte, a first-grade teacher commented, "So what I am learning is that it is not the students' language that is the problem, but how I have been seeing it." Several teachers also shared how they grew up speaking AAL and had been taught in schools that there was something wrong with their language.

In addition to language, teachers were able to acknowledge how they were indoctrinated through a colonial curriculum and replicated these same practices in their classrooms. During a professional learning session, teachers were instructed to Envision a Different World (Boutte, 2016, Box 2.1). This activity prompted teachers to fill in the blank with a list of nouns: What if all the _____ were African American? Some of the nouns included Presidents of the US, teachers, doctors, greeting cards, TV shows, colleges, faces on currency, members of the Senate, and police officers. One African-American female teacher confessed to the group that she was having difficulty with this activity, "I just can't picture it. This is hard and it makes me emotional that my mind won't let me do this. All my life I have been inundated with Whiteness." Her voice began to tremble. Another teacher, Ms. Brown, poised a series of powerful questions to the group, "If we can't imagine this as adults then what are our kids seeing? What kind of deficits do the kids see with their own race and culture?" As the facilitator of the session, I then asked, "When we start teaching African American history where do you start? Do you start with Blacks being enslaved or them being royalty before they were forced to the United States?" Another African-American female teacher responded, "That's not in our textbooks, that's why we don't teach it, right?" Ms. Brown challenged her colleagues to think about how different our viewpoints and teaching would be if Africans came to this country with all their culture, their languages were not stripped from them. Where would we be today? How would we see our students? And how would they see themselves?"

These types of engagements provide a space for teachers to confront their Eurocentric ideologies. Teachers critique their own deficit thinking on language and begin to explore how language is directly tied to identity; so, when they demand students to speak correct, they are sending internal messages to students that their way of being is wrong and incompetent. The second data point reveals how emotional yet important this process is. The teacher discovers how disheartening it is that she cannot imagine African Americans as the racial group which is empowered and dominant. This self-reflection led to other teachers evaluating the colonized curriculum and the effect this has on students of color. In essence, if this activity is difficult for adults to engage in imagine how young learners are overtly inundated by White and oppressive curriculum.

University Faculty Growth

The Urban Education Collective serves as a place of growth for university faculty as well as for teachers and preservice teachers. We continue to "up our game" as we are motivated to read further in the field of critical race, culturally sustaining, humanizing, and anti-colonial pedagogies. In conjunction with the larger group of Early Childhood faculty, we have been doing a book study of *Educating African American Students: And how are the children?* (Boutte, 2016). We continuously share readings among each other and post web links and video clips on our shared Urban Cohort faculty FB page.

Through our own networks of support within and beyond our university, we learn with colleagues across the country who are committed to the work of justice and equity in a racialized society. Each interaction with teachers and preservice teachers and the opportunity to spend time learning, planning, and teaching together with teachers and children in classrooms and teaching university courses onsite in schools deepens our learning and our commitment to seeking deeper knowledge. Through this learning, as we expect from teachers and preservice teachers, we commit to consistently examining our own embedded biases, particularly the White educators among us as we learn by listening and gain courage and confidence by continuing to commit to the work.

Deepening Understandings Through REACH

A powerful offshoot from the Urban Education Cohort is a student organization called REACH which stands for Race, Equity, and Advocacy in Childhood Education. The organization was envisioned by six university faculty members (most of whom are listed as authors of this chapter) and an initial group of students. While REACH is open to all students, it is important to note that most of its members are Urban Cohort students. REACH members meet bimonthly and together examine issues in a racialized society and educational system as well as their roles in affecting change within and beyond those systems.

National speakers are brought into meetings virtually such as Ronda Bullock who facilitates anti-racism summer programs for kindergartners and their families in Durham, North Carolina, Dr. Erin Miller, who shared her research about ways that White children learn White supremacy from an early age, and Dr. Jamila Lyiscott who shared the need for and forms of activism within and beyond educational spaces. Local guest speakers are also invited to REACH meetings including members of the local chapter of the #BlackLivesMatter movement who engaged the students in better understanding issues of racism locally and globally and strategies for engaged activism, and a university ad hoc student group organized to respond to racist actions in local student-patronized bars.

REACH faculty sponsors also present to the students: Dr. Nathaniel Bryan shared his work focusing on White privilege and microaggressions against Black male professors in the academy, Dr. Eliza Braden shared her research in bilingual education and diversity in children's literature, Dr. Kamania Wynter-Hoyte spoke about the importance of a focus on race, and Dr. Susi Long spoke about the colonization of society and curriculum. REACH members read texts such as Ta-Nehisi Coates' *Between the World and Me* and James Baldwin's *Fire Next Time*. Student and faculty representatives from the group presented their work at the 2016 National Council of Teachers of English national convention and at the "Let's Talk About Race" conference at North Carolina Central University in 2018. Continuing to build the network described in the introduction to this chapter, the intent is that REACH graduates will continue to meet with the incoming REACH members as they move into their first teaching positions. Through REACH students have gained confidence in their abilities to bring voice to their convictions and have done so by meeting with the Dean of the College of Education in addition to their professional presentations. During the meeting, they voiced concerns about micro- and macroaggressions in their college experience such as their peers sometimes negative treatment of Black professors in contrast to White professors teaching the same content; Black students being overlooked in class; and their feelings about the need for the REACH and Urban Education Cohort experiences for all students.

Issues and Challenges

While successes have been many we have also experienced challenges that we work together to negotiate. A few of those challenges including overextended teachers, sustaining professional development in schools, and issues surrounding the PRAXIS Core Academic Skills for Educators standardized test are described in the sections that follow.

Overextended Teachers

The local school district recognizes that teachers are often burdened by too many programs that they are required to address and they are working to streamline their approach to professional development by creating more choice for teachers in terms of the focus they want to follow. We recognized this as it was often a challenge for us as we worked to fit our professional development sessions into teachers' busy lives. In several ways, we worked to overcome this challenge: (a) by limiting after school sessions and extending time we spent working with teachers in classrooms; (b) by engaging in professional development during grade level meetings, (c) by conducting full day series of summer sessions; and (d) by focusing on pacing guides and standards that teachers were using.

Sustaining Professional Learning in Schools

Even in circumstances like the one we have described in which we had strong district-level support, engaged faculty, and highly motivated university students, we acknowledge that it is difficult to sustain professional development. One realistic consideration is the associated costs for professional development. In order to pay faculty to conduct bi-weekly professional development sessions over a two-year period (our commitment), the four schools had to commit some of their funds beyond the district's contribution to do so. While schools, districts, P-3 educators, and faculty are committed to increasing the academic and social success of students who have been marginalized, it can be difficult to find funding to do so. In our case, the district found ways to sustain the professional development, but many districts have competing priorities and will need support in thinking creatively about use of funding to make this kind of work possible.

Another challenge is incorporating sustained professional development in settings where teachers are committed to a wide range of obligations. They often feel pulled in many directions. One way we are working to negotiate this challenge is by working to frame our work with teachers as the groundwork in which every other aspect of their teaching is embedded. For example, teachers in our state are required to take the equivalent of four courses in the area of reading instruction. We developed a proposal that was approved by the state department of education to deliver content for one of those courses within our professional development.

PRAXIS (Core Academic Skills for Educators)

As is an issue in universities across the country, PRAXIS Core, the test approved by the Council for the Accreditation of Educator Preparation (CAEP) as a measure of academic proficiency (ETS, 2018) is a gatekeeper that puts up roadblocks for some of our students, particularly students of Color. Recognizing that standardized testing was intentionally developed to maintain a White elite (Singer, 2016), students must confront systemic issues (e.g., mandated passing score to be admitted into professional programs) as well as individual issues (e.g., test anxiety, irrelevant content, language discrimination, and financial difficulties). Because one of the goals of the Urban Education Cohort is to diversify the teaching force, we also do everything we can to ensure that students entering the program have every opportunity for support in passing gatekeepers like the PRAXIS Core. We know that, many students of Color have come from P-12 experiences where their community cultural wealth (Yosso, 2005) was rarely appreciated or activated, thus large segments of their knowledge base are invisiblized by curriculum, testing, and teacher disposition. This occurs when preservice teachers may not recognize ability and expertise beyond dominant cultural definitions. This means that many students of Color come to us having experienced P-12 schooling where expectations were low for them and teaching was consequently less effective than it was for their White peer (Gershenson, Hold, & Papageorge, 2016) and, therefore, less success on the already biased - Whitecentric - standardized tests.

Recognizing that these realities are one reason for the Whiteification of the teaching force and of our teacher education program, we have been working within our department to identify the most effective PRAXIS support programs/strategies and are currently piloting a model to provide systemic PRAXIS support for every preservice teacher in need of it. Hand-in-hand with finding this kind of support and institutionalizing it is working with staff and faculty to identify bias in areas such as student advisement and Praxis support policies to find real expertise in testing support. This means being alert to assumptions that may be made about students' potential and effort which only perpetuates the experiences many of them have had in P-12 education. As Urban Cohort faculty, we have intervened to ensure that students are supporting knowing that they are more than capable of being effective teachers.

Implications for Teacher Education Programs

We offer four implications for other teacher education programs that are interested in Advancing their equity emphasis: (1) ENSURE that equity is mission-critical to your Program; (2) Seek school administrators who will commit to a focus on equity; (3) engage internship supervisor, and; (4) recognize deflections to equity work and reject them. Each of these is discussed in the following sections.

Ensure That Equity Is Critical to Your Program

One of the reasons that we have experienced the level of success that we have thus far is because our work is also supported by a departmental mission which is focused on teaching issues of equity and preparing our students to be able to effectively teach students who are marginalized. While the mission statement is symbolic on some levels and implemented in uneven ways across the department, it is politically important to have support for doing work which focuses on equity since pushback is likely to occur sooner or later.

Seek School Administrators Who Will Commit to a Focus on Equity

As with universities and colleges, it is important for P-12 administrators to support work on equity. Hence, we suggest that teacher educators seek buy-in from administrators. Key to engaging administrators is to be able to emphasize that the goal is to increase the academic and social outcomes of students--particularly those who have often not fared well in school and testing (for a variety of reasons including those not inherent to the students and families).

Engage Internship Supervisors

In order to be successful, all aspects of the teacher education program should be considered. This includes strategic field placements (as previously discussed) as well as university supervisors (some of whom may be faculty members or adjuncts). Depending on the size of the program, this can be a demanding task. Yet, internship supervisors must be involved in ongoing professional development (like program faculty) in order to be on one accord regarding the focus on equity.

Recognize Deflections to Equity Work and Reject Them

Anyone who has engaged in equity work for any amount of time realizes that it goes against the grain in terms of conventions in P-12 schools and universities. Hence, deflections and push back should be anticipated as well as proactive ways of dealing with these. Common ones to expect during the early childhood school years are: (1) these issues are not 'developmentally appropriate' for young children; (2) we have to teach the standards and there is no time to do this--even though I think it is a good idea [the last part is often added for good measure], and; (3) we have to teach *all* children --or *I don't see color.*

While not doubting that these deflections are offered in the spirit of what some educators truly believe, they also (intentionally or not) can serve to deflect a focus on equity. Thus, teacher educators must be prepared to address these deflective attempts must. Our best advice is for teacher educators to be conversant with the extant literature on this topic as there are a multitude of works which counter these assertions. For example, *Rethinking Early Childhood Education* (Pelo, 2008) and *Anti-Bias education for young children and ourselves* (Derman-Sparks & Edwards, 2010) are a few of the many works which demonstrate rationales for why equity issues should be addressed in substantive ways early in life. (A sampling of others include Baines, Tisdale, & Long, 2018; Boutte, 2008; Boutte, 2016; Boutte and Strickland, 2008; Boutte, Lopez-Robertson and Costello, 2011; Cowhey, 2006; Delpit, 2007; Earick, 2009; Tenorio, 2007).

The deflection regarding the need to teach the standard should be probed. For more than five decades since 'standards-based' instruction has been on the scene, there are vast examples of evidence that the academic needs of culturally and linguistically diverse (CLD) students are not been met--as measured by current standardized test outcomes reported in yearly report cards and through data from the National Assessment of Education Progress. Hence, the standards *are not* and *have not* been successfully taught using conventional methods. On the other hand, there is evidence that instructional strategies such as culturally relevant pedagogy have been shown to be successful with CLD students (Boutte, 2016; Long, Hutchinson, & Neiderhiser, 2011).

Likewise, when educators pushback against focusing on students of color or students who have been minoritized in some other way (e.g., language, socioeconomic status) by explaining that the goal is to teach *all* students, it is important to recognize this as deflection and to interrupt it. Such assertions are often presented using colorblind ideologies which suggest that educators do not see color and should teach all students the same (Bonilla-Silva, 2006). It is important to call attention to the disproportionate percentage of students from minoritized groups are not faring well academically (as measured by test scores) and socially (as measured by disproportionality in special education, gifted classes, suspensions, expulsions, and dropout rates). Therefore, in order to enact effective instructional practices and school policies, it is necessary to identify and develop focused strategies for addressing these inequities.

FUTURE RESEARCH DIRECTIONS

A number of teacher education scholars have written about experiences working with preservice teachers around issues of equity (Boutte, 2012; Boutte, 2017; Powers-Costello, Lopez-Robertson, Boutte, Miller, Long, & Collins, 2012; Picower, 2009; Ukpokodu, 2007). Like this chapter, much of the research would benefit from also focusing on the influence and impact of equity pedagogies on P-12 student outcomes. In evaluating student outcomes, school systems typically value results from statistical or mixed methods. While we can see the need to gather such data, particularly because large-scale and localized quantitative studies tend to be the measures of choice for most school districts, we also see tremendous problems with depending on numerical data to understand the impact of culturally relevant and humanizing teaching.

We know that standardized tests typically used as quantitative measures of student achievement "are narrowly normed along White, middle class, monolingual measures of achievement" (Ladson-Billings, 2017, p. 143) and have a history in racist, classist, xenophobic attempts to create an elite, European-American class. This goes as far back as the creation of the first Scholastic Aptitude Tests (SAT) in the early part of this century for the purpose of further racializing schooling (Singer, 2016). Because the purpose of culturally relevant teaching is to dismantle norms that perpetuate inequities, it stands to reason that, a part of our work is to fight against such unfair measures of achievement. Thus, while there may be some usefulness for quasi-experimental and mixed methods studies to provide large-scale and demographically-bound data, we believe that: (a) series of longitudinal qualitative studies (case studies and educational ethnographies, for example) are essential to providing contexts for any numbers-based research; (b) any quasi-experimental or statistical studies need to be contextualized within the problems with such research mentioned above, and; (c) in cases where numbers-based studies are done, efforts must be made to tease out numerous factors that cannot be controlled including: variation among teachers in their implementation of the same content; levels of experience and effectiveness; classroom dynamics and relationships; and teacher, curricular, and policy biases. All this is to say that, politically, policymakers and educators who focus on equity issues often expect large scale results with little or no understanding of the complexities of the nature of equitable teaching and this needs to be pointed out emphatically in any future research focusing on student outcome.

Another area of research that is needed is research on the effectiveness of and support for preservice and inservice teachers of color. Considering that many teachers of color matriculate through teacher education programs, which have often neglected addressing issues of equity and diversity in its programs, they enter inservice teacher education programs unaware of the internalized biases they carry into classrooms. As a result, they too engage in culturally assaultive teaching and contribute to the school-to-prison pipeline, which disproportionately impacts the schooling experiences of children of color (Bryan, 2017). Thus, more research studies are needed focusing on preservice teachers of color in preservice teacher education programs as well as teachers engaged in professional learning and ways to support them, especially those who are members of similarly described Urban cohorts.

Finally, research is needed that looks at the backgrounds and knowledge base of teacher educators attempting to engage in culturally relevant and humanizing teachers at the university level. Much is claimed as "diversity-focused," "culturally relevant," and "equity based" which, in the words of Ladson-Billings (2017) actually constitutes corruptions of the intent of the work. Often this occurs when teacher educators themselves have not taken opportunities to engage deeply in their own ongoing professional grow. Questions undergirding this kind of research could look at teacher educators' knowledge base and the scholarship from which that is derived, the depth of time and study dedicated to ongoing knowledge building, relationships between knowledge building and programmatic planning, and impact on preservice and inservice teacher learning and curricular and dispositional change.

CONCLUSION

When we look at the Eurocractic nature of pedagogy and practice today's schools (King & Swartz, 2016) and, alongside that, the disenfranchisement of many students and families of Color and from other marginalized groups, we have no choice but to work toward change. Educational scholar, Molefi Kete Asante (2017), wrote that "our educational system does not need a tune-up . . . it needs an overhaul" (p. 90). As teacher educators, it seems clear that the buck stops with us. Teachers and preservice teachers cannot be held responsible for what they do not know. After all, the same system of miseducation (Woodson, 1933) has victimized all of us, a legacy of Eurocractic curriculum - developed intentionally to ensure White power, control, and wealth - instituted by colonizers and enslavers across the past five centuries. However, together, we can take responsibility for a better tomorrow. Thus, we can no longer espouse empty commitments to diversity and social justice in our institutions of higher education if we are not doing the work to overhaul our own practices. For us, one element in that work was the development of the Urban Education Collective as foundational to developing a broader network of social justice educators who, as one of the Urban Cohort undergraduates put it, "can look at everything through a critical lens . . . look[ing] out for whose voices are being heard and more important whose are not" and then taking action to change that status quo.

REFERENCES

Asante, M. K. (1992, December). Afrocentric curriculum. *Educational Leadership*, 28-31.

Asante, M. K. (2017). *Revolutionary pedagogy: Primer for teachers of Black children.* New York, NY: Universal Write Publications.

Au, W., Brown, A. L., & Calderón, D. (2016). *Reclaiming the multicultural roots of U.S. curriculum: Communities of color and official knowledge in education.* New York, NY: Teachers College press.

Baines, J., Tisdale, C., & Long, S. (2018). *"We've been doing it your way long enough": Choosing the culturally relevant classroom.* New York, NY: Teachers College Press.

Battiste, M. (2013). *Decolonizing education: Nourishing the learning spirit.* Saskatoom, Canada: Purich Publishing Limited.

Bell, L. A. (2007). Theoretical Foundations for social justice education. In M. Adams, L. A. Bell, & P. Griffin (Eds.), *Teachings for diversity and social justice* (2nd ed.; pp. 1–14). New York: Routledge.

Bonilla-Silva, E. (2006). *Racism without racists. Color-blind racism and the persistence of racial inequality in the United States.* Lanham, MD: Rowman and Littlefield.

Boutte, G. (2016). *Educating African American students: And how are the children?* New York, NY: Routledge.

Boutte, G. S. (2008). Beyond the illusion of diversity: How Early Childhood teachers can promote social justice. *Social Studies*, *99*(4), 165–173. doi:10.3200/TSSS.99.4.165-173

Boutte, G. S. (2012). Urban Schools: Challenges and Possibilities for Early Childhood and Elementary Education. *Urban Education*, *47*(2), 515–550. doi:10.1177/0042085911429583

Boutte, G. S. (2017). Teaching About Racial Equity Issues in Teacher Education. In T. Durden, S. Curenton, & I. Iruka (Eds.), *African American children in Early Childhood Education: Making the case for policy investments in families, schools, and communities* (pp. 247–266). Emerald. doi:10.1108/S2051-231720170000005011

Boutte, G. S., Lopez-Robertson, J., & Costello, E. (2011). Moving beyond colorblindness in early childhood classrooms. *Early Childhood Education Journal*, *39*(5), 335–342. doi:10.100710643-011-0457-x

Boutte, G. S., & Strickland, J. (2008). Making African American culture and history central to teaching and learning of young children. *The Journal of Negro Education*, *77*(2), 131–142.

Bryan, N. (2017). White teachers' role in sustaining the school-to-prison pipeline: Recommendations for Teacher Education. *The Urban Review*, *49*(2), 326–345. doi:10.100711256-017-0403-3

Codrington, J., & Fairchild, H. H. (2013). *Special education and the mis-education of African American children: A call to action*. Washington, DC: The Association of Black Psychologists.

Cowhey, M. (2006). *Black ants and Buddhists: Thinking critically and teaching differently in the primary grades*. Portland, ME: Sternhouse.

Delpit, L. (2007). Seeing color. In W. Au, B. Bigelow, & S. Karp (Eds.), *Rethinking our classrooms: Teaching for equity and justice* (2nd ed.; Vol. 1, pp. 158–160). Milwaukee, WI: Rethinking Schools.

Derman-Sparks, L., & Edwards, J. (2010). *Anti-Bias education for young children and ourselves*. Washington, DC: National Association for the Education of Young Children.

Earick, M. (2009). *Racially Equitable Teaching: Beyond the Whiteness of Professional Development For Early Childhood Teachers*. New York, NY: Peter Lang.

Ford, D. (2013). *Recruiting and retaining culturally different students in gifted education*. Waco, TX: Prufock Press, Inc.

Freire, P. (1970). *Pedagogy of the oppressed*. New York, NY: Continuum.

Gershenson, S., Hold, S. B., & Papageorge, N. W. (2016). Who believes me? The effect of student-teacher demographic match on teacher expectations. *Economics of Education Review*, *52*, 209–224. doi:10.1016/j.econedurev.2016.03.002

Gonzalez, N., Moll, L., & Amanti, A. (2005). *Funds of Knowledge: Theorizing Practices in Households, Communities, and Classrooms*. New York, NY: Routledge.

Gregory, E., Long, S., & Volk, D. (2004). *Many pathways to literacy*. London, UK: Routledge Falmer.

King, J. E. (2005). *Black Education: A Transformative Research & Action Agenda for the New Century*. Lawrence Erlbaum.

King, J. E., & Swartz, E. (2014). *"Re-membering" history in student and teacher learning: An Afrocentric culturally informed praxis*. New York, NY: Routledge.

King, J. E., & Swartz, E. E. (2016). *The Afrocentric praxis of teaching for freedom: Connecting culture to learning*. New York: Routledge.

Kinloch, V., & Dixon, K. (2017). Equity and justice for all: The politics of cultivating anti-racist practices in urban teacher education. *English Teaching*, *16*(3), 331–346. doi:10.1108/ETPC-05-2017-0074

Ladson-Billings, G. (1995). Toward a theory of culturally relevant pedagogy. *American Educational Research Journal*, *32*(3), 465–491. doi:10.3102/00028312032003465

Ladson-Billings, G. (2014). Culturally relevant pedagogy 2.0: A.k.a. the remix. *Harvard Educational Review*, *84*(1), 74–84. doi:10.17763/haer.84.1.p2rj131485484751

Ladson-Billings, G. (2017). The (r)evolution will not be standardized: Teacher education, hip hop pedagogy, and culturally relevant pedagogy 2.0. In D. Paris & S. Alim (Eds.), Culturally Sustaining Pedagogies: Teaching and Learning for Justice in a Changing World. Academic Press.

Long, S. (2011). Supporting students in the time of Common Core Standards, 4K Through Grade 2. Urbana, IL: National Council of Teachers of English.

Paris, D., & Alim, S. (2017). *Culturally sustaining pedagogies: Teaching and learning for justice in a changing world*. New York, NY: Teachers College Press.

Pelo, A. (2008). *Rethinking Early Childhood Education*. Milwaukee, WS. *Rethinking Schools*.

Picower, B. (2009). The unexamined Whiteness of teaching: How White teachers maintain and enact dominant racial ideologies. *Race, Ethnicity and Education, 12*(2), 197–215. doi:10.1080/13613320902995475

Powers-Costello, B., Lopez-Robertson, Boutte, G., Miller, E., Long, S., & Collins, S. (2012). Teaching for transformation: Responsive program planning and professional development aimed at justice and equity in urban settings. In A. Cohan & A. Honigsfeld (Eds.), Breaking the mold of education for culturally and linguistically diverse learners: Innovative and successful practices for the twenty-first century (Vol. 2, pp. 2330). Lanham, MD: Rowman & Littlefield Education.

Rosner, J. (2002). The SAT: Quantifying the unfairness behind the bubbles. In SAT Wars. 2012. Academic Press.

Singer, S. (2016). *Standardized tests have always been keeping people in their place*. Retrieved from: https://gadflyonthewallblog.wordpress.com/2016/04/05/standardized-tests-have-always-been-about-keeping-people-in-their-place/

Sleeter, C. (2001). Preparing teachers for culturally diverse schools: Research and the overwhelming presence of whiteness. *Journal of Teacher Education, 52*(2), 94–106. doi:10.1177/0022487101052002002

Swartz, P. C. (2005). It's elementary in Appalachia: Helping prospective teachers and their students understand sexuality and gender. In J. T. Sears (Ed.), *Gay, lesbian, and transgender issues in education: Programs, policies, and practices* (pp. 125–146). New York, NY: Harrington Park Press.

Tenorio, R. (2007). Race and respect among young children. In W. Au, B. Bigelow, & S. Karp (Eds.), *Rethinking our classrooms: Teaching for equity and justice* (2nd ed.; Vol. 1, pp. 20–24). Milwaukee, WI: Rethinking Schools.

Ukpokodu, N. O. (2007). Preparing socially conscious teachers: A social justice-oriented teacher education. *Multicultural Education, 15*(1), 8–22.

U.S. Department of Education Office for Civil Rights. (2014). Retrieved from https://www2.ed.gov/policy/gen/guid/school-discipline/index.html

Woodson, C. G. (1933). *The mis-education of the Negro*. Trenton, NJ: Africa World Press.

Wynter–Hoyte, K., Braden, E., Rodriguez, S., & Thornton, N. (2017). Disrupting the status quo: Exploring Culturally Relevant and Sustaining Pedagogies for Young Diverse Learners. *Race, Ethnicity and Education*, 1–20. doi:10.1080/13613324.2017.1382465

Section 3
Innovations in Pedagogical Design

Chapter 14
Scaffolding Ambitious Instruction:
Teaching and Re-Teaching in a Methods Practicum

Rob Wieman
Rowan University, USA

ABSTRACT

Pre-service teachers (PSTs) often have to plan and teach a lesson in a practicum setting as part of their methods class. This assignment is designed to give PSTs a chance to enact ambitious instruction; however, they often encounter obstacles that prevent them from engaging students in core disciplinary practices. A structure, based on lesson study, provides opportunities for PSTs to experience and identify these obstacles, revise their plans to address them, and engage in ambitious instruction while re-teaching the revised lesson. This structure also recasts initial lessons as opportunities to learn and improve through collaborative reflection. Examples of this structure are described, including features that contribute to PST learning and lesson improvements. Obstacles to ambitious instruction as well as strategies to overcome those obstacles are identified and discussed. Parallels are drawn between ambitious mathematics teaching and ambitious teacher education.

INTRODUCTION

This chapter is about a common assignment in a mathematics teaching methods course in which pre-service teachers (PSTs) plan and teach a single lesson in a practicum classroom. The author clarifies goals for that assignment, identifies common obstacles that PSTs experience, and describes an innovation that transforms those obstacles into valuable learning opportunities. The immediate goal of the innovation is to produce more effective opportunities for PSTs to develop and practice skills needed for ambitious teaching. Although the cases in this chapter occur in secondary mathematics, teacher educators can apply the innovation across grade levels and content domains. (For the sake of clarity throughout the chapter, "students" refers to students in K-12 classrooms. Teacher candidates will be referred to as pre-service teachers, or PSTs.)

DOI: 10.4018/978-1-5225-6249-8.ch014

Like any change in a complex system, this small innovation could have significant consequences. It is part of a growing movement within education to facilitate reform by utilizing design thinking and improvement science (Jenkins, 1997). In improvement science practitioners plan and enact small changes, collect data on their effectiveness and then make revisions to those changes based on analysis of that data. Through a gradual process of revision and refinement, these innovations are improved and adopted by a wider range of practitioners, who in turn revise and refine them for use in their particular contexts. Such small changes gradually result in overall systemic change that is created by, and responsive to those enacting the change (Bryk, Gomez, Grunow, & LeMahieu, 2015; Lewis, 2015). In addition, these changes provide an opportunity to build and sustain professional knowledge that is grounded in practice, with the potential to bridge the gap between the craft-based knowledge of practitioners and the more theoretical, scientific knowledge of researchers (Hiebert, Gallimore, & Stigler, 2002; Kennedy, 1999).

BACKGROUND

For decades, a wide variety of stakeholders have called for more rigorous and ambitious learning goals for students. In particular, they have advocated that students develop conceptual understanding of ideas and discipline-specific methods of inquiry, and that they use those ideas and methods to solve a range of problems inside and outside of school settings (Gardner, 1983; National Commission on Mathematics and Science Teaching for the 21st Century, 2000; National Council of Teachers of Mathematics, 2000, 2014). In response to these more ambitious learning goals, teacher educators expect PSTs to learn and practice *ambitious instruction*, instruction that supports students in making sense of fundamental ideas through enacting core disciplinary practices (Lampert, Franke, Kazemi, Ghousseini, Turrou, Beasley, . . . Crowe, 2013; Smith, Lee, & Newmann, 2001).

Ambitious mathematics teaching requires designing lessons that provide opportunities for students to solve difficult problems, reason about mathematical ideas, test conjectures, and make connections between different solution methods and representations. It aligns well with more rigorous content goals for school mathematics, and with instruction that requires students to engage in essential mathematical practices. For instance, the Common Core State Standards include "standards for mathematical practice." These include:

1. Make sense of problems and persevere in solving them
2. Reason abstractly and quantitatively
3. Construct viable arguments and critique the reasoning of others
4. Model with mathematics
5. Use appropriate tools strategically
6. Attend to precision
7. Look for and make use of structure
8. Look for and express regularity in repeated reasoning.

The authors of the Common Core standards for mathematical practice explicitly state hat these practices are not just important goals for students, but that students should consistently engage in these practices as a way to learn more specific content (CCSSI, 2010). As they write:

The Standards for Mathematical Practice describe ways in which developing student practitioners of the discipline of mathematics increasingly ought to engage with the subject matter as they grow in mathematical maturity and expertise throughout the elementary, middle and high school years.

PSTs often learn about ambitious instruction in methods courses paired with a practicum experience. A common assignment in such courses is to plan and teach a lesson that features elements of ambitious instruction. First, PSTs identify a learning goal that includes understanding a major concept. Then they plan a lesson in which students have opportunities to make sense of this concept by working with peers to solve a challenging problem using core disciplinary practices.

This is difficult and complex work, even for experienced mathematics teachers. Teachers struggle to maintain the cognitive demand of rich tasks while also providing support that gives all students access to essential prior mathematical knowledge, contextual information, and strategic thinking (Stein, Grover & Henningsen, 1996). When introducing the problem, effective teachers provide access to important mathematical ideas (Jackson, Garrison, Wilson, Gibbons & Shahan, 2013). However, even experienced teachers often reduce the demand of these tasks by simplifying problems, indicating specific solution strategies, or stressing correct answers rather than reasoning and justification (Stein, Grover & Henningsen, 1996; Warshauer, 2015). When teachers facilitate discussions about different solutions they must balance the need to provide essential information with the need to step back and allow students to evaluate others' arguments for themselves (Chazan & Ball, 1999). Even experienced teachers often lead discussions that are little more than a series of "show and tell" presentations in which students listen passively and fail to engage with each other's ideas (Stein & Lane, 1996).

Given these difficulties, it is not surprising that PSTs struggle to enact aspects of ambitious teaching when they teach lessons (Clift & Brady, 2005). A PST may present a demanding task in a way that that leaves students confused about what, exactly, they are supposed to accomplish, or the PST may suggest a specific method for solving the problem. As a result, students may not solve the problem, or may all solve it the same way. As a result, the PST is unable to enact a discussion in which students compare different strategies and representations or make and evaluate arguments. When they encounter these kinds of problems relatively early in the lesson, PSTs end up unable to practice planned elements of ambitious instruction.

How might this assignment be changed so that it provides PSTs with more opportunities to enact ambitious practices, and so that initial obstacles might be reframed as opportunities to learn? If the assignment were changed to support PSTs in experiencing, describing and then working through initial obstacles, PSTs might learn how to anticipate these obstacles. They might also learn how to improve their teaching and add to their professional knowledge by examining and revising their own practice. They might learn how to learn about teaching from collaborating with others to improve their own practice.

The revised assignment described in this chapter is modeled after Japanese lesson study (Lewis, Perry, & Hurd, 2004; Lewis, Perry, Hurd, & O'Connell, 2006; Stigler & Hiebert, 1999). In lesson study, teams of teachers participate in a cycle of planning, enactment, reflection and revision around one lesson. As part of this process, the teacher teams:

- Define clear learning goals.
- Carefully design activities and teacher moves that will support students in learning these goals.
- Observe and collect data while one of them enacts the lesson.
- Make revisions to the plan based on analysis of the data.

- Teach the lesson again, incorporating the revisions.
- Observe, collect data and analyze the data to see if the revisions resulted in improved learning.

Lesson study has taken a variety of forms in response to different contexts, goals and participants (Lewis, 2016). In its more extensive form, lesson study involves teams of teachers and outside experts planning in the context of a larger education inquiry (Huang, Gong & Han, 2015, or Lewis & Hurd, 2011). The team begins by choosing and extensively researching a lesson. They then use this research to inform their plan, which embodies specific learning goals, and hypotheses about how to most effectively support students in meeting the learning goal. One member of the planning team then teaches the lesson while the other members and invited guests observe. The team and observers then meet to discuss data collected during the lesson and suggest revisions to the plan based on analysis of the data. The team then plans revisions to the lesson and enacts the revised lesson. They, along with invited guests observe this second enactment and analyze data from the lesson to evaluate the effectiveness of the revisions.

Other forms of lesson study can be less extensive. For instance, Bieda, Cavanna and Ji (2015) describe "Mentor-guided lesson study" in the context of a PST's field experience. In this form, a mentor teacher and PST co-plan a lesson. The PST observes as the mentor-teacher enacts the plan. The mentor and co-teacher then analyze the first lesson and make revisions to the plan, which the PST then enacts with a second group of students. The overall process is similar to that described in the previous paragraph, but there is lesson connection to a set of shared educational questions, less extensive research on the lesson itself, and no large team of fellow teachers and outside experts.

Whatever its form, lesson study has the potential to support teacher learning about content, students and pedagogy (Lewis, 2016). This learning proves to be especially powerful because it is situated within actual problems of practice as defined by the teachers themselves. This is in marked contrast to research-generated knowledge that is divorced from teachers' contexts and whose applications to their own teaching may be difficult to discern (Hiebert, Gallimore, & Stigler, 2002). This has led some researchers to propose this model of planning, enacting, analyzing, revising and re-teaching as a structure for pre-service teachers in teacher education programs (Hiebert, Morris, & Glass, 2003).

This lesson cycle also holds the potential to address some of the obstacles that PSTs experience when they attempt to enact ambitious teaching in a practicum setting. If teacher candidates have more than one chance at teaching an ambitious lesson, initial lessons can serve as opportunities to identify and address obstacles to ambitious teaching. PSTs enacting revised and improved lessons would then have opportunities to enact ambitious teaching less encumbered by unforeseen obstacles.

This paper reports on a study of a middle school mathematics practicum assignment that was structured so that initial attempts at ambitious teaching could be improved through revision and re-teaching. PSTs in this study had increased opportunities to do three things. First, they had opportunities to notice and name common obstacles to ambitious teaching. Second, they were more likely to practice enacting ambitious teaching during revised lessons. Third, they had opportunities to see teaching as a learning profession, in which they gained knowledge through disciplined, collaborative inquiry into their own practice.

RESEARCH QUESTIONS

The following study was motivated by these research questions:

- What obstacles do PSTs experience when they try to enact ambitious teaching in middle school mathematics classrooms in the context of a methods practicum?
- Does collaboration based on a cycle of planning, enacting, reflecting/revising and re-teaching provide PSTs with opportunities to notice, name, and develop strategies for overcoming these obstacles?
- What aspects of the cycle of planning, enacting, reflecting/revising and re-teaching enable PSTs to notice, name, and develop strategies for overcoming these obstacles?

CONTEXT AND METHODS

These questions are addressed using four case studies which occurred during a secondary mathematics teaching methods course taught by the author. The overarching goal of the course was to prepare PSTs to engage in ambitious mathematics instruction. More specific goals that supported ambitious instruction included developing content knowledge for teaching, learning how to implement high leverage teaching moves, planning and enacting lessons, and anticipating and understanding student thinking. PSTs learned about enacting problem-based lessons using the launch-explore-summarize format (Lampert, 2001; Star, Herbel-Eisenman & Smith, 2000). In the first part of the lesson, the launch, the teacher introduces the task; she supports students in making sense of the context, activates students' prior knowledge, and sets clear expectations for how students are to work on the problem. During the explore, students work in small groups to solve the problem by explaining, justifying and representing their strategies. During the summary, the teacher facilitates a discussion in which she chooses particular students' strategies to share and asks questions to get students to make sense of each solution and notice important connections among the solutions (Stein, Engle, Smith & Hughes, 2008). By making sense of these connections, students develop an understanding of the underlying mathematical concepts. Launch-explore-summarize lessons also provide opportunities for students to develop habits of sense-making, perseverance, reasoning and communicating one's mathematical thinking.

PSTs learned about ambitious teaching in a variety of ways. First, they experienced ambitious teaching as mathematics students. The course instructor taught problem-based lessons using the launch-explore-summarize format. PSTs also read about important aspects of ambitious teaching such as how to facilitate a discussion, and the importance of maintaining the cognitive demand of tasks. They reflected on those readings, and how they were related to the teaching they experienced in their methods class and observed and practiced in their practicum placements.

As part of the methods course, PSTs engaged in a modified lesson study, in which two or three PSTs worked as partners to teach a launch-explore-summarize lesson to two different classes in a local middle school. Before the lesson took place, PSTs created written lesson plans with their partners, which they shared with their methods instructor and their cooperating teacher. PSTs were expected to use the launch-explore-summarize format for their lesson. On the day of the lesson, the instructor came to observe. One partner taught the lesson while the other partner and the instructor observed and took detailed notes describing what the teacher and the students said and did. These notes were usually taken on the plans themselves, which included a section for observers to write what actually happened next to each part of the plan. After the first enactment of the lesson, the PSTs and the instructor evaluated the effectiveness of the lesson based on evidence gathered from their notes and student work that they had collected. They then made revisions to the lesson plan based on this analysis. Then the other partner taught the revised lesson to a different group of students, while the partner who taught the first lesson and the instructor observed and collected data. All three then discussed the second lesson, specifically addressing whether the revisions to the plan resulted in the improvements that they intended. Finally, the partners wrote a reflection of the process and handed in their initial plan and reflection to the instructor. These reflections, the lesson plans, the observation notes and field memos written by the instructor comprise the data for the cases described below.

DESCRIPTION OF THE CASES

This study concerns four examples of PSTs working to enact and practice a launch-explore-summarize lesson. As with any descriptions of teaching, these cases foreground specific features of the lessons and the PSTs' experience, while leaving other aspects of the experience in the background. The descriptions highlight the cycle of planning, teaching/observing, revising and re-teaching, with a particular emphasis on how the initial lessons diverged from the intended plans. This illuminates common obstacles to ambitious teaching, and how the cycle allows teachers to address those obstacles. Certainly, each obstacle, and each lesson, is complex and multifaceted, and the descriptions below do not serve as exhaustive catalogs of all available interpretations. The author has worked to balance clarity with nuance, while staying true to the data and to the various interpretations of that data by the PSTs at the time.

Case 1: Heather and Cathy – Number Puzzles

One pair of teacher candidates, Heather and Cathy (all PST names are pseudonyms), had their students work to solve a series of number puzzles, in which letters stood for digits in simple addition and subtraction problems (see Figure 1).

Students were expected to figure out which letter stood for which digit and justify their answers using deductive arguments based on the structure of the base-ten number system. For example, for the second puzzle, students might begin by reasoning this way:

- SEE – AS = AS is the same as AS + AS = SEE.
- Since the greatest two-digit number is 99, and 99 + 99 = 198, the S cannot be greater than 1.
- The rules say that a number cannot start with a digit of zero, so S must stand for 1.

The mathematical content of this lesson was an understanding of addition and subtraction and place value. The lesson was designed to support students in developing persistence in the face of non-routine problems and in making logical arguments. These process goals align with ambitious teaching and the

Figure 1. Sideways math problems (adapted from Sachar, 1989)

$$
\begin{array}{cc}
\begin{array}{r}
\text{STAYS} \\
+ \text{ SAY} \\
\hline
\text{TRUST}
\end{array}
&
\begin{array}{r}
\text{SEE} \\
-\text{AS} \\
\hline
\text{AS}
\end{array}
\end{array}
$$

first and third standards for mathematical practice in the CCSSM, make sense of problems and persevere in solving them (SMP1), and construct viable arguments and critique the reasoning of others (SMP3).

Heather was the first PST to enact the *Number Puzzles* lesson. After introducing the problem and letting students work on it for a few minutes, she noticed that one student had solved the puzzle correctly. She asked that student to come to the board and explain how she solved the puzzle. At this point, other students copied down the first student's solution. Heather then gave the second number puzzle, and soon noticed a student that had a solution and asked her to share. Again, other students stopped working on the problem and listened and copied down the first student's solution. However, in the middle of her explanation, the student realized that she may have made a mistake. She stopped explaining and stood at the board, thinking. Heather, along with the rest of the class, worked to make sense of the student's solution and re-engaged with the problem. While this was happening, the methods instructor asked Heather to notice what the students were doing, and Heather decided to not interject or make corrections. This led to a long period in which students worked on the puzzle, often arguing about why a certain letter could, or could not, be a specific digit. Heather monitored their conversations, and then led a short discussion where different groups shared their reasoning about their solutions.

When Heather, Cathy and the instructor reflected and revised the lesson, they began by reminding themselves of the ambitious teaching goal, to have students persevere in the face of difficult problems, and develop arguments using logic to defend their answers. They then compared the student behavior and engagement during the first explanation and the second explanation. They noted how much more engaged the students were, and how much more they persevered, reasoned, and justified their solutions when the teacher was not sure of the answer. The instructor and PSTs hypothesized that the teacher had originally given the answer too early, while many students were still working to solve the problem and had not yet had a chance to reason about various partial solutions and first steps. This diminished opportunities for perseverance and reasoning, making it difficult for students to understand their peers' thinking.

For the second enactment of the lesson, the instructor and PSTs planned to refrain from sharing answers until much later in the lesson, allowing students more time to work and discuss with partners. As predicted, during the second lesson, students worked on the problems for much longer, with some moving more quickly to the second problem while others took much longer on the first. In addition, students moved around the room arguing and discussing their various solutions. Students were able to persevere in working on a difficult problem for an extended period of time, to develop arguments, and to critique those of others. During the final discussion, there was much less talking by one person, and more contributions from a range of students.

Case 2: Corey and Wendy – Understanding and Generalizing Inverse Relationships

Corey and Wendy taught a lesson designed to support students in understanding inverse relationships and how they might use and represent those relationships to solve equations algebraically. The lesson featured a problem about a school trip that cost \$750. They wanted students to create a rule for the relationship between the number of students and the cost of the trip per student (i.e. $C = 750 \div S$). They hoped that by working on this task students would see how inverse relationships "undo" each other, and how they underlay the algebraic techniques the students were learning. In particular, they wanted students to see the relationship between the equations 1 and 2 in Figure 2, and how one could move between the two by dividing or multiplying both sides of the equation by the same number. This problem provides students

Figure 2. Inverse Relationships

<u>**Equation 1**</u>　　　　　　　<u>**Equation 2**</u>

C x S = 750　　　　　　$C = \dfrac{750}{S}$

Moving from equation 1 to equation 2: "Undoing" multiplication by dividing

Equation 1:　　C x S = 750

Divide both sides by S:　　$\dfrac{C \times S}{S} = \dfrac{750}{S}$

Simplify to get equation 2:　　$C = \dfrac{750}{S}$

Moving from equation 2 to equation 1: "Undoing" division by multiplying

Equation 2:　　$C = \dfrac{750}{S}$

Multiply both sides by S:　　$C \times S = \dfrac{750}{S} \times S$

Simplify to get equation 1:　　C x S = 750

opportunities to engage in several of the mathematical practices, in particular, modeling with mathematics (SMP4) and making sense of problems and persevering in solving them (SMP1).

During the first enactment of this lesson, Corey explained that the school was sponsoring a trip. The total cost of the trip would be shared by all the students who went on that trip. Corey then introduced the equation S x C = 750 to describe this situation and asked the students to create an equation that would relate the cost per student to the number of students. At this point, students did not respond, and after asking several questions, Corey derived the equation he was looking for, $C = \dfrac{750}{S}$, on the board himself, explaining how the equation showed the relationship between the cost of a single ticket and the number of students who went on the trip. Corey then asked students to use that equation to figure out how much a ticket would cost if 10, 20 or 50 students went on the trip. Again, students did not respond, and he ended up solving those problems himself on the board.

In the reflection/revision discussion, Corey, Wendy and the instructor hypothesized that the introduction of the abstract symbols may have been difficult for students, so for the second enactment they planned to have students solve specific problems first, before creating an equation with variables (i.e. How much would it cost for each student if 10 students went? 20? 50?) When Wendy taught the lesson, students were able to solve the problems with specific numbers quite quickly. Then, she asked them the same question that Corey had asked ("What is your rule for finding the cost of a ticket if you know the number of students?"). This time students came up with a variety of responses, from a description using words ("I just do 750 divided by the number of students") to an equation without variables (cost per student = 750 ÷ number of students) to an equation using variables ($C = \dfrac{750}{S}$). Wendy was able to ask students to explain of these three solutions, and then ask them how they were connected. Students, in turn, were able to explain those connections, and to give meaning to the variables in the equations.

Case 3: Gail, Petra and Maria – Getting Close

Three PSTs. Gail, Petra and Maria, planned to have their students play *Getting Close*. In this game, players choose two cards from a deck of fractions and decimals, and then choose which whole number (0, 1, 2, or 3) is closest to the sum of the two cards. This game is designed to support students in using benchmarks to develop an understanding of the magnitude of fractions and decimals. (For instance, if the two cards are 11/12 and ¼, students could reason that 11/12 is almost 1, and that ¼ is less than a half, so their sum is more than one, but less than 1½, so the closest whole number is 1.) The PSTs planned for the students to play in groups of four, with two teams of two playing against each other, so partners could discuss the reasoning behind their moves. Ideally, these discussions would provide opportunities for students to persevere in solving problems (SMP1), reason quantitatively about fractions and decimals (SMP2), and to construct viable arguments and critique the arguments of others SMP3).

During the first iteration of the *Getting Close*, Gail described the rules of the game and showed written directions, and then told the students to play. Almost immediately groups had questions and she found herself re-explaining the rules to each group, one at a time. This took much of the lesson, and many groups had little to do while waiting as Gail explained the rules to another group. As a result, students developed few strategies, and there was little time to discuss strategies at the end of class.

While reflecting on the first enactment of the lesson, the planning team hypothesized that students needed to be more deeply immersed in the game to understand it. They planned to have the teacher play the game in front of the class with a student, in addition to giving written instructions. During the second enactment of the lesson, students learned from watching the teacher model the game, and groups were able to play immediately after that. With more time to play, students created and discussed a wider variety of strategies, both in small groups and with the whole class.

Case 4: Kate, Becky, Lee and Natasha – Tracing and Similarity

Kate, Becky, Lee and Natasha were placed in two different seventh grade classrooms and both pairs of PSTs decided to teach the same lesson on similarity. The lesson was designed to give students the opportunity to develop language around corresponding shapes and multiplicative comparisons (i.e. twice as big, half as big), and to look for and identify relationships between similar figures (i.e. congruent angles, constant scale factor between corresponding sides of similar figures). Developing this language supports students in attending to precision (SMP6).

The lesson involves using two rubber bands to trace a given figure (see Figure 3). (See Wieman, 2018, for another description of this case in a different research context.) After students create traced drawings, they answer a series of questions about how the originals and traced images are related. Because Kate and Becky taught this lesson first, and then shared their results with Lee and Natasha prior to Lee and Natasha teaching, these four PSTs were able to enact four versions of this lesson.

Figure 3. Tracing using knotted rubber bands

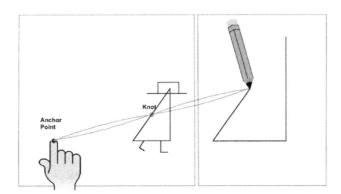

- Knot two rubber bands together, hold one end stationary at the anchor point
- Place a pencil in the end that is not on the anchor point.
- Draw with the pencil so that the knot traces along the original figure.
  (Lappan, Fey, Fitzgerald, Friel, & Phillips, 2006)

In planning the *Tracing Lesson*, Kate and Becky spent time thinking about directions. Kate taught the first lesson, giving students written directions and demonstrating tracing herself. Some students produced accurate tracings (see Figure 4).

However, a number of students made tracing mistakes (see Figure 5) which prevented them from using their figures as examples of similar figures. As a result, these students were unable to engage in substantive discussions about how different elements of the traced and original figures compared to each other.

During their revision discussion, Kate and Becky planned to model specific tracing mistakes that they had observed and to ask students to correct the teacher. For instance, Becky began by placing the stationary end of the rubber band somewhere other than the "anchor point." After students corrected

Figure 4. Successful tracing

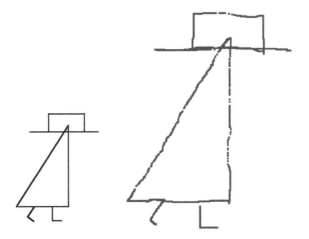

Figure 5. Unsuccessful tracing

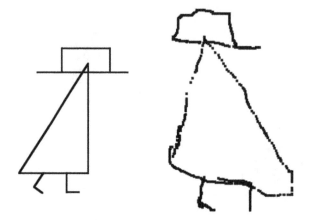

her by instructing her to put one end on the anchor point, she then placed her pencil so that the knot was not on the outline of the original figure. During the second lesson, after receiving both directions and an opportunity to evaluate Becky's "improper" tracing, many more students were able to produce accurate drawings, and Becky was able to involve more students in a discussion about similarity. However, both Becky and Kate concluded that the discussion did not achieve their goals. Some of the ideas came out, but students did not deeply engage with the ideas or think about them critically. Individual students mentioned some comparisons between different parts of the different triangles, but key ideas about additive and multiplicative relationships did not emerge.

Lee and Natasha taught the same lesson later, and incorporated Kate and Becky's planning ideas about tracing. They also planned more thoroughly for the discussion by identifying the specific relationships that they wanted students to think about and articulate and the important vocabulary connected to those ideas. As a result, Lee was able to lead a discussion about similarity, in which he introduced important vocabulary, and differentiated between additive comparisons and multiplicative comparisons (i.e. 3 inches longer vs. three times as long). However, Lee made many of the important mathematical points himself, rather than the students.

In the final revision/reflection session Lee, Natasha and the instructor concentrated on identifying common ways that students compared the figures (based on written student work from Lee's enactment) and used the students' thinking to plan in greater detail *how* Natasha would facilitate group work and the whole class discussion. Moving beyond the *content* of the discussion, they planned specific questions for her to ask, specific descriptions for her to share, and when she would introduce specific vocabulary. The last lesson is described in more detail in the results section.

RESULTS

In each of the cases described above, PSTs initially had difficulty enacting instruction that supported their ambitious goals for students. The PSTs and the supervisor shared data that they had collected from their observations of the first lesson. Based on this data, they worked to explain when, and why, the lesson did not work as planned, and how the lesson might be changed to more effectively support students. Although each specific case was different, in looking back over the cases as a whole, two themes emerged. First, students did not understand the task well enough to access the important mathematics. Second, PSTs took over the mathematics and lowered the cognitive demand. In answering the first research question, we will examine these difficulties in more detail. In answering the second and third research questions, we will see how the cycle of planning, teaching/observing, analyzing/revising, re-teaching/observing, re-analyzing enabled PSTs to turn these initial obstacles into valuable learning opportunities.

What Obstacles Do PSTs Experience When They Try to Enact Ambitious Teaching in Middle School Math Classrooms in the Context of a Methods Practicum?

Obstacles to Student Access

When learning from demanding tasks, students need to understand the problem they are trying to solve. One challenge teachers face in using demanding tasks is helping students understand those tasks without lowering the cognitive demand (Jackson, Garrison, Wilson, Gibbons, & Shahan, 2013). If students do not understand the task, they may end up engaging in off-task behavior, or unsystematic exploration that is not connected to the mathematical goal of the lesson (Hiebert, Carpenter, Fennema, Fuson, Wearne, Murray,. . . Human, 1997; Stein, Grover & Henningsen, 1996). However, if teachers provide access to the task by making the problem itself less ambiguous or if they describe or indicate a specific solution strategy, they reduce opportunities for students to engage in many of the mathematical practices that develop conceptual understanding, such as making sense of problems, reasoning, modeling and critiquing arguments (Stein, Grover & Henningsen, 1996).

In three cases, during the first enactment many students did not understand the task well enough to engage in the above practices. In two of these cases, students were initially unable to make sense of PST directions. During the first iteration of the *Getting Close* (case 3), Gail described the rules of the game, as well as showing written directions, and then told the students to play. Almost immediately she found herself re-explaining the rules to each group, one at a time. This substantially reduced the amount of time students played the game, so they had less time to develop strategies. It also prevented Gail from assessing student strategies, since she was actively re-explaining the rules. In addition, while they were waiting for Gail's help, many students engaged in off-task behavior, which made it even more difficult for Gail to attend to student strategies and explain directions. At the end of the lesson, Gail found herself with less time to discuss strategies, few strategies to discuss, and little awareness of the strategies that students had used.

In the *Tracing Lesson*, Kate and Becky worked hard to provide written directions and demonstrated tracing themselves. Kate taught the first lesson, and a number of students made tracing mistakes (see Figure 5). As a result, they could not use their tracings to think about and describe relationships between similar figures. Students were unable to have the conversation Becky and Kate had planned, thus foreclosing opportunities for sense-making and developing precise language.

In both *Getting Close* and the *Tracing Lesson*, PSTs planned to engage students in an activity that would provide experiences that students would then analyze. Because students initially struggled with the directions for the activity, they failed to have the requisite experiences. They could not engage in a rich mathematical discussion because they did not have enough to talk about. In *Understanding and Generalizing Inverse Relationships* (case 2), Corey and Wendy also wanted to build on student experiences. They hoped a real-world context would support students in making meaning of algebraic manipulations and inverse functions. They started with a familiar situation - a school trip that cost 750 dollars in total. However, they immediately introduced the equation S x C = 750 to describe this situation and asked the students to create an equation that would relate the cost per student to the number of students (specifically, the equation $C = \dfrac{750}{S}$). By couching the task in symbols right from the beginning, Corey and Wendy moved the problem from math that students had experience with (figuring out a specific cost per ticket given a specific number of students) to math they did not have experience with (manipulating variable expressions). Corey and Wendy unwittingly asked students to generalize using an unfamiliar mathematical language before they had had a chance to solve a number of specific cases. At this point, students appeared stymied, without a way to begin.

PST Assistance That Reduced the Cognitive Demand

A second group of obstacles to ambitious teaching occurred when PSTs responded to student struggle by offering assistance or providing explanations that reduced the cognitive demand of the task. This denied students opportunities to engage in core mathematical practices such as making sense of problems, making and critiquing arguments and attending to precision. PSTs reduced the cognitive load in a number of ways. First, they provided clear definitions, descriptions and explanations before students had a chance to develop clear and concise language themselves. Second, they identified answers as correct before students had a chance to evaluate arguments.

During the third iteration of the tracing lesson, Lee engaged students in a discussion about the relationships between the traced figure and the original. One of the goals of the discussion was to support students in developing precise language to describe similarity and multiplicative relationships. However, when Lee, Natasha, and their instructor looked at their records of the discussion, they noticed that Lee had made many of the important mathematical points himself – he had introduced important vocabulary and differentiated between additive comparisons and multiplicative comparisons (i.e. 3 inches longer vs. three times as long). Students had had relatively few chances to practice using precise mathematical language themselves; consequently, it was not clear exactly how much they understood.

The *Number Puzzles Lesson* (case 1) provides another example of teachers reducing the cognitive demand of the task. As soon as Heather saw a student that had solved the puzzle correctly, she asked that student to show their work. As a result, most students did not have a chance to solve the problem; they spent much of their time copying down what the demonstrating student did or staring into space. Interestingly, Heather did not take over the mathematics by explaining the solution directly. However, by identifying one answer as correct early in the lesson, she precluded students from evaluating solutions and justifying arguments themselves. In addition, by choosing to have students stop and attend to another student's explanation, Heather also stopped students who were in the active process of creating, testing and justifying hypothetical solutions to the problem.

Obstacles Connected: Lack of Access Leads to
PSTs Reducing the Cognitive Demand

Sometimes both types of obstacles reinforced each other, as in the *Understanding and Generalizing Inverse Relationships Lesson* (case 2). The first enactment of this lesson began with an abstract task that was inaccessible to the students – they struggled to create an equation for finding the cost per ticket when given the initial equation S x C = 750. Corey tried to prompt student thinking through questioning. He asked them what the S and the C stood for, and what they might do to get C by itself. When students were unable to answer his second question, he did the problem himself on the board, dividing both sides of the equation S x C = 750 by S to get the new equation $C = \dfrac{750}{S}$. He explained that dividing both sides by S would get C alone, and that this new equation showed the relationship between the cost of a single ticket and the number of students going on the trip. He then asked students to use this equation to find the cost per student if there were 10 students, or 20, or 50. Again, when students were unable to start, he did the problem himself on the board. When students did not have access to a task, Corey took over the problem and solved it himself; it was not clear to him what else he could do.

Does Collaboration Based on a Cycle of Planning, Enacting, Reflecting/Revising and Re-Teaching Enable PSTs to Notice, Name and Develop Strategies for Overcoming These Obstacles?

In each of the four cases PSTs were able to identify and develop ways to avoid initial obstacles to ambitious instruction. When meeting to discuss the first enactment of the lesson, they were able to use what they had observed to identify that their goals had not been satisfactorily met and were able to identify specific aspects of their plan that could be improved. Each team was also able to make improvements to the plan that resulted in more effective lessons. In so doing, they developed strategies for planning and teaching that would be helpful in other future lessons.

Overcoming Obstacles to Access

In both the *Tracing Lesson* (case 4) and in *Getting Close* (case 3), PSTs quickly identified that struggles with directions prevented students from accessing a set of shared experiences that would, in turn, allow them to engage in the mathematical thinking that was the focus of the lesson. For each of these groups, the key to overcoming this obstacle was revising the directions. Specifically, they enacted a preview of the activity that would support students in actively envisioning how the activity would unfold and provided them with opportunities to encounter and overcome potential difficulties.

When Kate and Becky and their instructor met to discuss the first enactment of the tracing lesson, they observed that some students had made tracings that did not sufficiently mimic the shape of the original, and this had prevented these students from thinking about the important mathematics of the lesson (see Figures 4 and 5). Kate and Becky discussed the tracing mistakes, describing them in detail based on their observations and student work. For their revised lesson, Becky demonstrated these particular mistakes and asked students to identify and correct them before she dismissed them to make their own tracings. As a result, the second class, even though it had a higher percentage of students with special needs, did a better job of tracing. Therefore, more students in the second class were able to use their drawings to notice and describe relationships between similar shapes. Kate and Becky had moved the lesson from one focused on tracing, to one focused on discussing the relationship between the tracing and the original.

During the revision of *Getting Close* the planning team first wondered why students needed the game re-explained. They hypothesized that verbal directions were not enough, and that students needed to be more deeply immersed in the game before playing on their own. They decided to have the teacher play some rounds of the game with a volunteer student in front of the class as part of the directions. During the second lesson, after enacting this change, every group was able to play the game without further instruction. This resulted in more time for students to create and discuss strategies for estimating the sum of fractions and decimals, and more time for a whole group discussion at the end of class in which they shared those strategies.

In talking through *Understanding and Generalizing Inverse Relationships* (case 2), Corey and Wendy realized that students had failed to engaged in problem solving, but not because of ineffective directions. For the PSTs, the meaning of the symbols and their connection to the context were obvious. They began to see that for students, who were still learning about algebraic symbols, this was not yet the case. Corey, Wendy and their instructor hypothesized that introducing equations so quickly had introduced a level of abstraction that made it difficult for students to think about the context and bring their previous knowledge to bear. They predicted that if the PSTs did not introduce the equation, students would be able reason about the situation and quantities involved and then use this reasoning to generate their own equations later in the lesson.

In the revised lesson, Wendy did not present one algebraic equation and ask for a second one. Instead, she explained that a school trip cost $750 and asked how much the trip would cost per student if 10 students went on the trip, and then if 20 went, and if 50 went. Wendy then asked students to create a rule that would help them find the cost per student if they knew the number of students. Wendy then, according to the revised plan, shared the rules, and discuss them, beginning with narrative rules (i.e. "I divided 750 by the number of students") and ending with the equation $C = \dfrac{750}{S}$. Finally, Wendy asked students about the equation S x C = 750, and how it was related to the rule $C = \dfrac{750}{S}$.

The second lesson was considerably different from the first. Students were quickly able to find the cost per student for 10, 20 and 50 students. This, in turn, enabled Wendy to lead a discussion, in which students were able to generalize, connect their generalization to the equation $C = \dfrac{750}{S}$, and connect that equation to the equation S x C = 750. Because students had a chance to solve a variety of examples of a similar type of problem, they were able to begin to generalize, and then were able to tie this generalization to a rule, and to the abstract variable notation. Seeing the connection between a generalization that they had already made to an abstract representation of that generalization turned out to be a different, and more meaningful, task than trying to make sense of an abstract equation in the absence of a previous generalization.

Overcoming Assistance That Reduced the Cognitive Demand

In three cases the teacher took over the mathematics in ways that reduced the cognitive demand of the task. In each of these cases, PSTs were able to identify this as an obstacle to student learning and made revisions to the lesson so that during re-teaching they were able to provide more opportunities for students to engage in reasoning and problem-solving.

In case 2 (*Understanding and Generalizing Inverse Relationships*) Corey and Wendy accomplished this through revising the task. During the first lesson, students were presented with an equation and then told to create a different equation. When students struggled with this task, Corey ended up doing the task for them and having them replicate his work. When Corey and Wendy changed the task by having students solve a series of concrete problems before creating a general rule and then connecting their rule to al algebraic representation, there was no need for Wendy to solve the task herself. A critical mass of students solved the problems and made a general rule. As a result, all students were able to engage in a conversation that provided opportunities to reason and make sense of the important mathematics.

In the *Tracing Lesson* (case 4) Lee was able to lead a discussion about important relationships, but he made many of the important mathematical points himself. In discussing the lesson, it became clear that Lee and Natasha had planned what they wanted the discussion to be about, but they had not anticipated what students might say and think in sufficient detail. Without clearly anticipating student thinking and planning how to use that thinking during a discussion, it was quite difficult for Lee to facilitate a discussion in which students did most of the talking, while continuing to maintain a focus on the goals of the lesson. When revising the lesson, Lee, Natasha and the instructor read students' written answers to questions about how the original and traced figures were related. They sorted the responses from Lee's lesson into piles according to the way students described these relationships. They predicted that other students would display the same range of responses and planned which responses Natasha would share, and in what order. Then they planned questions that Natasha would ask about those responses that would require students to make important connections. For instance, they planned to share student responses like:

- The image is twice as big as the original.
- The traced one is double the original.
- The "real" one is half as big as the one I drew.
- The traced one is three centimeters longer than the one we started with.

They also planned to ask if these comments were all the same. They assumed that students would, ultimately, agree that the first three were equivalent, but that they were different than the third. This would surface the difference between multiplicative (A is twice as big as B, F is 5 times larger than G, etc.) and additive reasoning (A is three cm longer than B, F is 5 less than G, etc.). This discussion would also give students experience with different ways to express multiplicative reasoning (half as big, twice as big, two times the size, double the length, etc.). They also planned specific talk moves Natasha would make to support students in these discussions. For instance, she would ask them to turn and talk with a partner about certain question before talking about it with the whole class. They reasoned that having students explain the same idea in a variety of ways would help them make sense of the ideas and develop precise language around similarity. It would also give Lee and Natasha more evidence of what students actually understood about proportional relationships.

When Natasha taught the lesson the overwhelming majority of students quickly made serviceable drawings. During students' group work, they shared specific observations about how their figures were related, using much of the language that Natasha and Lee had predicted. When students struggled to describe those relationships, Natasha used the planned moves to support their reasoning and discourse. As planned, she kept track of important comments students made. Later when she led a full group discussion, she used the specific student responses she had recorded. She pushed for students to differentiate between additive and multiplicative reasoning. She crafted a discussion of angles that demonstrated the necessity of precise language and introduced the term "corresponding angles." This discussion supported students in developing a variety of ways of precisely expressing geometric relationships.

Throughout the lesson, Natasha used sophisticated teacher moves to great effect. For instance, when students asked her questions, she redirected them to their peers, facilitating student reasoning and communication. She asked students to turn and talk to a partner during key moments. This helped them make sense of important ideas and gave Natasha a chance to assess their thinking. All of this was the result of a greatly improved plan, made possible by the three previous enactments of the lesson along with the detailed analysis of what had, and had not worked.

In case 1 (*Number Puzzles*) Heather and Cathy were able to revise the lesson so that students spent the majority of the class period actively solving problems and using reasoning to justify their methods and solutions. Interestingly, this began to happen serendipitously during the first iteration of the lesson. Heather had interrupted the class to have a student with a correct solution come to the front of the room to share. However, partway through her explanation, the student got confused. During this moment of confusion, the other students quickly became much more engaged, actively working to solve the puzzle and arguing among themselves about possible solutions. Ironically, it was a student mistake that provided the opportunity for students to persist in solving a difficult problem and to create and critique logical arguments.

During the revision, the team noticed how engaged the students had become during that moment of confusion. They hypothesized that leaving the question open was motivating for students, and that sharing the answers too quickly took away the opportunity to think about the problem. They revised the lesson so that Cathy would avoid discussing the answers until much later, allowing more students to engage in solving the problem and prompting them to reason with each other in the absence of a teacher-sanctioned response. During the second lesson, student engagement improved markedly. Students were able to solve the problems on their own and explain their reasoning, both with partners and with the class as a whole. Their cooperating teacher even pointed out that a group of boys that generally had great difficulty staying on task were highly engaged and motivated, actively sharing their reasoning with other students, listening intently to their peers' solutions, and using reasoning to critique solutions with which they disagreed.

What Aspects of the Cycle of Planning, Enacting, Reflecting/ Revising and Re-Teaching Enable PSTs to Notice, Name and Develop Strategies for Overcoming These Obstacles?

Each team of PSTs planned to engage in ambitious teaching that supported students in developing important mathematical ideas and practices through problem solving, reasoning and justifying. In each case, PSTs were unable to enact the lesson as envisioned, but after analyzing the lesson they were able to identify obstacles to their original plans, and make revisions that enabled them to engage in ambitious teaching when they retaught the plan. Certainly, improvement is a complex process, but in analyzing the four cases, three aspects of the teaching cycle were especially important in creating opportunities for PSTS to identify and overcome initial obstacles to ambitious teaching, observation, reflection/revision, and re-teaching.

Observation

The chance to observe lessons allowed PSTs to notice and name obstacles to ambitious instruction without being distracted by the in-the-moment challenges of teaching. Novice teachers often struggle to notice important aspects of a lesson because they are simply overwhelmed with all the information they are receiving and have to make sense of it and decide how to act (Berliner, 1994, cited in Jacobs, Lamb & Philipp, 2010). The opportunity to observe freed one PST partner from having to act in response to students, and this partner could focus more closely on what was happening. When Kate taught the first iteration of *Tracing and Similarity* she had difficulty cataloging all of the problems students had tracing. She noticed that many of the traced figures did not look like enlarged versions of the original and worked to show students how to trace correctly. Because she was occupied with individual students, as well as monitoring conversations and whether students were on task, she was unable to observe all of the mistakes. Becky, unencumbered by having to monitor behavior and support students in the moment, was able to observe and describe the exact mistakes students made. She was then able to share those with Kate during the reflection and revision.

This chance to observe was also supported by the presence of the instructor, who had more experience noticing important aspects of lessons and could focus the attention of both the observing and the teaching PSTs. For instance, when the student in the class that Heather was teaching (*Number Puzzles*) made a mistake, Heather immediately focused on the mathematics. The instructor was able to quietly direct Heather's attention to the students, asking Heather what she noticed about what the students were doing. With the help of the instructor, Heather was able to notice that this "mistake" had resulted in furthering her instructional goal of having students engage in problem solving and reasoning. Observation allowed participants to collect data that was essential to the reflection and revision described below. This data, in turn, grounded the reflection and revisions in corroborated evidence, rather than vague impressions or inexact memories.

Reflection/Revision

With the help of their instructor, PSTs were able to reflect on what they observed and identify where the lesson enactment had hit obstacles. Then they revised plans to more effectively support students in achieving the learning goal. The team (the PSTs and the instructor) followed a general protocol that involved:

- Restating the purpose of the teaching assignment (to learn about teaching by testing and improving a lesson plan).
- Restating the original learning goals of the lesson.
- Using data (observation notes and student work) to identify where the lesson did (and did not) go according to plan and to understand students' thinking.
- Identifying possible cause and effect relationships connecting planned teacher actions and student learning and behavior.
- Revising or refining the learning goals based on observed student thinking.
- Making revisions to the plan based on hypotheses about what students might do if teachers did something differently.

The revision began with a reminder that the point of the assignment was to create a plan, try it, and then improve it based on data collected during the first enactment. The instructor then reviewed the goals of the lesson, as well as restating questions the PSTs had about the plan before the first enactment. Then team members reviewed their notes and wrote down initial impressions. Next, the team discussed the plan, describing specific moments when the plan worked as predicted, and when it did not. The team then looked at student work together, assessing student learning and identifying specific difficulties students were having.

Once the team had identified important student thinking and points in the lesson that did not go as anticipated, the team selected specific parts of the lesson that might need revision. They worked to create hypotheses for why students did not act as anticipated, and then worked together to change the plan, continually returning to their hypotheses and their understanding of the mathematical goal and how it related to current student thinking to drive the design of the changes. The revision meeting ended with a specific summary of the critique of the plan, a description of the specific revisions, and a prediction about how students would react to the changes.

Several features of the cycle were essential to this reflection and revision. First, PSTs had a working plan with clear learning goals and hypotheses about how teaching might support those learning goals. Second, PSTs and their instructor collected observations and student work, and followed a clear discussion protocol when talking about the lesson. Revising the plan provided a clear purpose for the discussion, and the data focused revision discussions on evidence of student learning. By looking at the results of specific planned moves, and then at data of how students responded to those moves, all in the context of the learning goal, PSTs were able to decide if those moves were effective. They could then decide to plan to include them, or plan to change them.

Another set of features that were essential to the success of this assignment were more mundane, but no less important. PSTs and the instructor needed two different sections of students to teach, a period of time between those two sections, and a place to meet free from distractions and with enough space to look at student work. Given the scheduling and space constraints of many schools, this can be a challenge.

Re-Teaching

Re-teaching the revised lesson provided opportunities for PSTs to enact more ambitious instruction. By revising plans in ways that removed obstacles to productive student engagement PSTs had opportunities to try out sophisticated teaching moves. By opening up the task in *Generalizing Inverse Relationships*, Wendy was able to facilitate a discussion in which students built on their own initial thinking to construct and make sense of the generalized algebraic representation, a discussion that had not happened when Corey taught the lesson. Similarly, in the *Number Puzzles* lesson Cathy was able to facilitate small group work, in which students actively disagreed with each other, and worked to justify their thinking. She was also able to facilitate a whole class discussion in which students compared different ways of solving the puzzle. Similarly, Natasha was able to support students in creating accurate tracings, assess students during group work, identify important student ideas to share, highlight them during a discussion and use specific talk moves, all because of a revised plan that supported students in engaging with the task in a more meaningful way.

Clearly, PSTs that teach first are more likely to experience obstacles and are less likely to practice facilitating rich discussions or engaged group work. This may be remedied by engaging in this cycle more than once and rotating who teaches first. Even if this is not possible, the benefits of engaging in this cycle, seeing what obstacles exist, and how they might be overcome far outweigh the alternative to simply experiencing the obstacles without any opportunity to make improvements.

DISCUSSION

PSTs are often asked to practice ambitious teaching by planning and enacting a lesson in the practicum part of their methods course. As described above, this assignment may result in lessons that do not go as planned, leaving PSTs without an opportunity to practice the kind of ambitious teaching they are learning about. A revised lesson study, in which PSTs worked with partners and a supervisor to plan, teach/observe, analyze/revise, reteach/observe and reflect enabled PSTs to learn from their first enactment, and to create improved plans that helped them enact and observe ambitious teaching. The case studies in this chapter identified obstacles novices may frequently experience when attempting ambitious teaching. They demonstrate how experiencing these obstacles can provide valuable learning opportunities for PSTs. These cases also provide a model for how teacher educators might support the kind of cultural change in teacher education called for by a wide range of researchers.

One obstacle was that students had difficulty accessing the task because they were confused about the directions. In these cases, PSTs found that demonstrating the activity, including demonstrating common mistakes and inviting students to correct the demonstrator provided access to the activity without lowering the mathematical demand of the task itself. In other situations, PSTs learned that starting with specific problems and examples, and then asking students to generalize provided many more opportunities for students to build on their own knowledge and make their own generalizations. A second obstacle was PSTs taking over the mathematical thinking. PSTs learned to give students time to complete the task before asking students to share. They also learned to not identify a solution as correct, and to predict and plan to use student thinking during a discussion.

These collaborations supported PSTs in ways that are consistent with past accounts of lesson study. Specifically, PSTs were able to observe their plan in action, analyze the plan with respect to student learning, revise the lesson based on that analysis, and then re-teach the lesson based on the revised plan. This led to larger learning that often accompanies lesson study, increased teacher content knowledge, increased knowledge of pedagogy, and increased ability to observe students (Lewis, 2002, 2016).

One possible outcome of this study is that teacher educators may be able to support PSTs in planning for predictable difficulties more effectively. This may make it more likely that PSTs will have opportunities to practice ambitious teaching and improve learning opportunities for the K-12 students in a single practicum lesson. Although this is most certainly true, creating perfect lessons and enacting them flawlessly is unrealistic and does not align with the goal of preparing novices to enact ambitious instruction. Indeed, struggling with initial attempts at teaching, and learning to identify difficulties and learn from them is an important experience for novice teachers.

There are clear parallels between preparing novice teachers and ambitious instruction in mathematics itself. American classrooms have been marked by an overemphasis on procedures, disconnected from applications and larger concepts (Fey, 1978; Hiebert, Stigler, Jacobs, Givvin, Garnier, Smith, ... Gallimore, 2005). The movement towards ambitious teaching described in the introduction to this chapter is an attempt to support students in developing more robust and flexible mathematical knowledge. Teaching mathematics for these more ambitious goals turns out to be much more complex than teaching for procedural fluency alone (Lampert, Beasley, Ghousseini, Kazemi, & Franke, 2010). It involves providing students with opportunities to struggle with important mathematical ideas in the context of solving non-routine problems (Hiebert & Grouws, 2007). Although it is tempting, in the face of student struggles, to simply tell them how to solve mathematical problems, research has shown that such "assistance" actually deprives students of the opportunity to learn by prematurely shutting down the very cognitive struggle that leads to deep learning (Stein & Lane, 1996). Supporting students in developing deep understanding through solving problems requires that teachers make sophisticated moves in response to variable student responses and contextual conditions. Although researchers and practitioners have developed pedagogical routines and structures to manage this complexity (see, Lampert, Beasley, Ghousseini, Kazemi, & Franke, 2010 and Stein, Engle, Smith & Hughes, 2008 for especially influential examples), it is impossible to eliminate it completely.

Just as supporting *students* in learning powerful *mathematical understanding* requires more complex mathematics teaching, supporting *novice teachers* in developing *ambitious instruction* requires more complex teacher education. Because teaching, similar to mathematics, involves applying foundational ideas in the service of solving problems (Lampert, 2001), simply telling novices how to teach will not, by itself, help them develop the deep knowledge that they need to teach ambitiously. Because ambitious teaching requires teachers to consistently apply foundational ideas and teaching moves in response to novel situations, novices need opportunities to identify, reflect on, and solve problems of practice. In addition, because of the complexity and highly contextual nature of teaching, it is impossible to equip novices with all of the knowledge they would need to be expert teachers before they begin (Hiebert, Morris & Glass, 2003). Instead of working to teach novices all they need to know, teacher educators would do better to support PSTs in learning how to learn from analyzing their practice. The cases described above are powerful examples of what this learning might look like.

However, learning how to analyze practice is not enough. Teaching also involves performance, and novices need opportunities to enact specific teaching moves and practices while making sense of student thinking and managing student discourse (Grossman, Compton, Igra, Ronfeldt, Shahan, & Williamson, 2009; Lampert, Beasley, Ghousseini, Kazemi, & Franke, 2010). Like many other professions, learning how to teach requires a balance of analyzing and practicing performance. The modified lesson study described in this chapter provides novice teachers with a scaffolded opportunity to engage in both performance practice and analysis of teaching.

RECOMMENDATIONS

The study described in this chapter suggests that a typical assignment in a university-based methods class, in which pre-service teachers are asked to plan and teach an ambitious mathematics lesson is unlikely to lead to enactment of ambitious teaching on the first try. These cases point to the power of using a cycle of planning, teaching/observing, reflecting/revising, and re-teaching/observing in the context of an initial practicum teaching assignment in methods classes. Having PSTs collaborate with partners in this cycle with the support of an expert allows them to experience and overcome common obstacles to ambitious teaching, and allows them to see initial, imperfect lessons as opportunities for professional learning.

This adjustment to a common methods assignment does require some important pre-conditions in order for it to work as envisioned. PSTs need to plan collaboratively with a partner and have the opportunity to teach the same lesson to two different groups of somewhat similar students. In middle and high school, where teachers often teach more than one section of the same class, placing two PSTs as partners with the same teacher would allow them to plan together and observe each other. With elementary PSTs who are placed in self-contained classrooms, it might be beneficial to have two PSTs placed in the same grade collaborate on a lesson, and then arrange to observe each other teach it in each other's classroom.

No matter what the context, PST will need time and space to debrief the first lesson and make revisions to it based on their analysis.

A second key element of this assignment is the presence of a knowledgeable facilitator who can help the PSTs observe, analyze and make revisions. This kind of collaboration requires that universities provide their staff with time to work with PSTs at their field placements. If cooperating teachers were to take on the role of facilitator, then they would ideally share fundamental ideas about mathematics teaching and PST learning. Creating alignment between university teacher educators, education researchers and classroom teachers lies beyond the scope of this paper; but needless to say, it is not an easy problem to solve.

Finally, the criteria for evaluating PSTs on this assignment may have to change if teacher educators expect initial difficulties and value the goal of learning from practice. Instead of evaluating PSTs on their individual performance of ambitious teaching during the lesson, teacher educators should clarify a different set of learning goals for teams of PSTs, goals that reflect the reality of common obstacles to ambitious teaching, and the importance of using evidence to analyze and address those obstacles through collaborative reflecting and re-teaching. Evaluations should reflect the nature of true collaboration, in which success and failure is shared. They also need to provide assessment and feedback on how well PSTs identify and work to address initial problems with plans, and how well they work together to support each other in getting smarter about teaching and learning. Certainly, PSTs need to continue to demonstrate their individual skill and knowledge. But having them engage in collaborative cycles of teaching, revising, and re-teaching would give them an opportunity to engage in, and be evaluated for, something even more important to their own future success and that of their students, their ability to work with others to learn from their practice.

FUTURE RESEARCH DIRECTIONS

This study is just a beginning foray into researching how relatively small changes to a common assignment might create improved learning opportunities for PSTs. It also serves as a proof of concept for the idea that practicum students could collaborate in ways that enable them to overcome initial difficulties and turn them into examples of how one might learn from practice. Future research could expand on this study in several ways.

First, researchers could further investigate common obstacles methods students experience when trying to teach ambitiously for the first time. The obstacles described in this chapter occurred in middle school mathematics classrooms. Other studies could examine obstacles in middle school mathematics in greater detail. Research could also begin to examine what kinds of obstacles exist in other contexts, with different age students, for example, or in different content domains. Larger studies could look for patterns both within age groups and content domains, and between them, identify obstacles specific to age groups or content areas, and obstacles that are more general in nature.

Second, researchers could investigate how the cycle of planning, teaching/observing, revising, re-teaching/observing works. This chapter gives some sense of important elements of the cycle that might lead to its success, but further research could describe, in more detail the nature of the collaboration, and the how different actors contribute to improved learning opportunities. Of particular interest might be the role of teacher educators, cooperating teachers, and the relationship between them in enacting this cycle effectively.

CONCLUSION

All experienced teachers will tell you that much of what they know about teaching they learned on the job. Their first years of teaching were marked by tremendous professional learning that was fueled, to a great extent, by lessons that did not go as planned. Even the most experienced teachers continue to revise their lessons based on what they learn from looking at students and student work. By identifying common obstacles to initial attempts at ambitious instruction and embedding initial teaching experiences in a cycle of collaborative planning, teaching and observing, revising, and re-teaching, teacher educators may give PSTs a much greater chance to practice ambitious teaching strategies, and provide them with a model of what it looks like to work with others to improve one's own practice.

ACKNOWLEDGMENT

The author would like to thank Ronald Gallimore and Sarah Ryan for their assistance and feedback on this chapter.

REFERENCES

Berliner, D. C. (1994). Expertise, The wonder of exemplary performances. In J. N. Mangieri & C. C. Block (Eds.), *Creating powerful thinking in teachers and students: Diverse perspectives* (pp. 161–186). Fort Worth, TX: Harcourt Brace.

Bieda, K. N., Cavanna, J., & Ji, X. (2015). Mentor-guided lesson study as a tool to support learning in field experiences. *Mathematics Teacher Educator, 4*(1), 20–31. doi:10.5951/mathteaceduc.4.1.0020

Bryk, A. S., Gomez, L. M., Grunow, A., & LeMahieu, P. G. (2015). *Learning to improve: How America's schools can get better at getting better.* Cambridge, MA: Harvard Education Press.

CCSSI (Common Core State Standards Initiative). (2010). *Common Core State Standards for Mathematics.* Retrieved from http://www.corestandards.org/the-standards/mathematics

Chazan, D., & Ball, D. L. (1999). Beyond being told not to tell. *For the Learning of Mathematics, 19*(2), 2–10.

Clift, R. T., & Brady, P. (2005). Research on methods courses and field experiences. In M. Cochran-Smith & K. M. Zeichner (Eds.), *Studying teacher education: The report of the AERA panel on research and teacher education* (pp. 309–424). Mahwah, NJ: Erlbaum.

Fey, J. T. (1978). Mathematics teaching today: Perspectives from three national surveys. *Mathematics Teacher, 72*(7), 490–504.

Gardner, D. P. (1983). A nation at risk. Washington, DC: The National Commission on Excellence in Education, US Department of Education.

Grossman, P., Compton, C., Igra, D., Ronfeldt, M., Shahan, E., & Williamson, P. (2009). Teaching practice: A cross-professional perspective. *Teachers College Record, 111*(9), 2055–2100.

Hiebert, J., Carpenter, T. P., Fennema, E., Fuson, K. C., Wearne, D., Murray, H., & Human, P. (1997). *Making sense: Teaching and learning mathematics with understanding*. Portsmouth, NH: Heinemann.

Hiebert, J., Gallimore, R., & Stigler, J. W. (2002). A knowledge base for the teaching profession: What would it look like and how can we get one? *Educational Researcher*, *31*(5), 3–15. doi:10.3102/0013189X031005003

Hiebert, J., & Grouws, D. A. (2007). The effects of classroom mathematics teaching on students' learning. In F. K. Lester (Ed.), *Second handbook of research on mathematics teaching and learning*. Charlotte, NC: Information Age Publishing.

Hiebert, J., Morris, A. K., & Glass, B. (2003). Learning to learn to teach: An "experiment" model for teaching and teacher preparation in mathematics. *Journal of Mathematics Teacher Education*, *6*, 201–222. doi:10.1023/A:1025162108648

Hiebert, J., Stigler, J. W., Jacobs, J. K., Givvin, K. B., Garnier, H., Smith, M., ... Gallimore, R. (2005). Mathematics teaching in the United States today (and tomorrow): Results from the TIMSS 1999 video study. *Educational Evaluation and Policy Analysis*, *27*(2), 111–132. doi:10.3102/01623737027002111

Huang, R., Gong, Z., & Han, X. (2015). Implementing mathematics teaching that promotes students' understanding through theory-driven lesson study. *ZDM*, 1-15.

Jackson, K., Garrison, A., Wilson, J., Gibbons, L., & Shahan, E. (2013). Exploring relationships between setting up complex tasks and opportunities to learn in concluding while-class discussions in middle-grades mathematics instruction. *Journal for Research in Mathematics Education*, *44*(4), 646–682. doi:10.5951/jresematheduc.44.4.0646

Jacobs, V. R., Lamb, L. L. C., & Philipp, R. A. (2010). Professional noticing of children's mathematical thinking. *Journal for Research in Mathematics Education*, *41*(2), 169–202.

Jenkins, L. (1997). *Improving student learning: Applying Deming's quality principles in classrooms*. Milwaukee, WI: ASQC Quality Press.

Kennedy, M. M. (1999). Ed schools and the problem of knowledge. In J. D. Raths & A. C. McAninch (Eds.), What counts as knowledge in teacher education. Stamford, CT: Ablex.

Lampert, M. (2001). *Teaching problems and the problems of teaching*. New Haven, CT: Yale University Press.

Lampert, M., Beasley, H., Ghousseini, H., Kazemi, E., & Franke, M. (2010). Using designed instructional activities to enable novices to manage ambitious mathematics teaching. In M. K. Stein & L. Kucan (Eds.), *Instructional explanations in the disciplines* (pp. 129–141). New York: Springer. doi:10.1007/978-1-4419-0594-9_9

Lampert, M., Franke, M. L., Kazemi, E., Ghousseini, H., Turrou, A. C., Beasley, H., ... Crowe, K. (2013). Keeping it complex: Using rehearsals to support novice teacher learning of ambitious teaching. *Journal of Teacher Education*, *64*(3), 226–243. doi:10.1177/0022487112473837

Lappan, G., Fey, J. T., Fitzgerald, W. M., Friel, S. N., & Phillips, E. D. (2006). *Stretching and shrinking: Understanding similarity (Connected Mathematics 2, Grade 7)*. Boston: Pearson/Prentice Hall.

Lewis, C. (2002). *Lesson study: A handbook of teacher-led instructional change*. Philadelphia: Research for Better Schools.

Lewis, C. (2015). What is improvement sciences? Do we need it in education? *Educational Researcher, 44*(1), 54–61. doi:10.3102/0013189X15570388

Lewis, C. (2016). How does lesson study improve mathematics instruction? *ZDM, 48*(4), 571–580. doi:10.100711858-016-0792-x

Lewis, C., & Hurd, J. (2011). *Lesson study step by step: How teacher learning communities improve instruction*. Portsmouth, NH: Heinemann.

Lewis, C., Perry, R., & Hurd, J. (2004). A deeper look at lesson study. *Educational Leadership, 61*(5).

Lewis, C., Perry, R., Hurd, J., & O'Connell, M. P. (2006). Lesson study comes of age in North America. *Phi Delta Kappan, 88*(4), 273–281. doi:10.1177/003172170608800406

National Commission on Mathematics and Science Teaching for the 21st Century (US), & Chair Glenn. (2000). *Before it's too late: A report to the nation from the National Commission on Mathematics and Science Teaching for the 21st Century*. United States. Department of Education.

National Council of Teachers of Mathematics (Ed.). (2000). *Principles and standards for school mathematics* (Vol. 1). Reston, VA: NCTM.

National Council of Teachers of Mathematics. (2014). *Principles to actions: Ensuring mathematical success for all*. Reston, VA: NCTM.

Sachar, L. (1989). *Sideways arithmetic from the Wayside School*. New York: Scholastic.

Smith, J. B., Lee, V. E., & Newmann, F. M. (2001). *Instruction and achievement in Chicago elementary schools*. Chicago, IL: Consortium on Chicago School Research.

Star, J. R., Herbel-Eisenmann, B., & Smith, J. P. (2000). Algebraic concepts: What's really new in new curricula? *Mathematics Teaching in the Middle School, 5*(7), 446–451.

Stein, M. K., Engle, R. A., Smith, M. S., & Hughes, E. K. (2008). Orchestrating productive mathematical discussions: Five practices for helping teachers move beyond show and tell. *Mathematical Thinking and Learning, 10*(4), 313–340. doi:10.1080/10986060802229675

Stein, M. K., Grover, B. W., & Henningsen, M. (1996). Building student capacity for mathematical thinking and reasoning: An analysis of mathematical tasks used in reform classrooms. *American Educational Research Journal, 33*(2), 455–488. doi:10.3102/00028312033002455

Stein, M. K., & Lane, S. (1996). Instructional tasks and the development of student capacity to think and reason: An analysis of the relationship between teaching and learning in a reform mathematics project. *Educational Research and Evaluation, 2*(1), 50–80. doi:10.1080/1380361960020103

Stigler, J. W., & Hiebert, J. (1999). *The teaching gap: Best ideas from the world's teachers for improving education in the classroom*. New York: Free Press.

Warshauer, H. K. (2015). Productive struggle in middle school mathematics classrooms. *Journal of Mathematics Teacher Education, 18*(4), 375–400. doi:10.100710857-014-9286-3

Wieman, R. (2018). Data do not drive themselves. *Mathematics Teacher, 111*(7), 535–539. doi:10.5951/mathteacher.111.7.0535

ADDITIONAL READING

Bryk, A. S., Gomez, L. M., Grunow, A., & LeMahieu, P. G. (2015). *Learning to improve: How America's schools can get better at getting better.* Cambridge, MA: Harvard Education Press.

Hiebert, J., Gallimore, R., & Stigler, J. W. (2002). A knowledge base for the teaching profession: What would it look like and how can we get one? *Educational Researcher, 31*(5), 3–15. doi:10.3102/0013189X031005003

Hiebert, J., Morris, A. K., & Glass, B. (2003). Learning to learn to teach: An "experiment" model for teaching and teacher preparation in mathematics. *Journal of Mathematics Teacher Education, 6*, 201–222. doi:10.1023/A:1025162108648

Jenkins, L. (1997). *Improving student learning: Applying Deming's quality principles in classrooms.* Milwaukee: ASQC Quality Press.

Lampert, M. (2001). *Teaching problems and the problems of teaching.* New Haven: Yale University Press.

Lampert, M., Franke, M. L., Kazemi, E., Ghousseini, H., Turrou, A. C., Beasley, H., ... Crowe, K. (2013). Keeping it complex: Using rehearsals to support novice teacher learning of ambitious teaching. *Journal of Teacher Education, 64*(3), 226–243. doi:10.1177/0022487112473837

Lewis, C. (2002). *Lesson study: A handbook of teacher-led instructional change.* Philadelphia: Research for Better Schools.

National Council of Teachers of Mathematics. (2000). *Principles and standards for school mathematics.* Reston, VA: Author.

Stein, M. K., & Lane, S. (1996). Instructional tasks and the development of student capacity to think and reason: An analysis of the relationship between teaching and learning in a reform mathematics project. *Educational Research and Evaluation, 2*(1), 50–80. doi:10.1080/1380361960020103

Chapter 15

Community–Based Field Experiences in Teacher Education:
Theory and Method

Heidi L. Hallman
University of Kansas, USA

ABSTRACT

This chapter proposes the value of offering teacher candidates an opportunity to participate in community-based field experiences during their teacher education programs. Community-based field experiences, in contrast to traditional, classroom-based placements usually offered at this stage in prospective teachers' professional preparation, enable beginning teachers to conceptualize their own learning and the learning of their students in new ways. As part of teacher education programs, the community-based field experience serves a distinct purpose and place, and one that is often underexplored. This chapter describes the integration of community-based field experiences into teacher education programs and discusses the unique quality of community-based settings as potential sites for teachers' learning.

COMMUNITY-BASED FIELD EXPERIENCES AS POTENTIAL SITES FOR TEACHERS' LEARNING

Early and diverse field experiences have been discussed as one of the keys to successful teacher education programs (Darling-Hammond, 2006; Feiman-Nemser & Buchman, 1987; Sleeter, 2008; Zeichner, 2010). Early field experiences exist to promote teacher candidates' understanding and practice of culturally relevant pedagogy (Ladson-Billings, 2001), and in teacher education, field experiences, as a whole, bridge beginning teachers' reflection on the constructs of theory and practice present in the teaching act (Shulman, 2005). As field experiences in teacher education continue to be re-framed as important sites for teacher learning rather than merely spaces for prospective teachers to "try out," demonstrate, or apply things they have learned about (Zeichner, 1996), they move toward being conceptualized as

DOI: 10.4018/978-1-5225-6249-8.ch015

sites for teacher learning. Cochran-Smith and Lytle's (2009) articulation that one's teaching practice is a site for inquiry reiterates that field experiences are, indeed, critical experiences for teacher growth.

Coffey (2010) suggests that community-based field experiences have the power to transform the ways that beginning teachers think about the effects of schooling in their students' lives, as well as the extent to which social factors influence students' success in school. Community-based field sites, often contrasted with traditional 'apprenticeship of observation' models of fieldwork (Lortie, 1975) within classrooms and schools, work toward the goals of broadening beginning teachers' conceptions of where student learning takes place as well as support the idea that teachers are not only part of a school but part of a larger community. These goals are accomplished through the ways in which such experiences encourage "beginning teachers to contextualize students' lives as part of the fabric of the larger community" as they "emphasize that familiarity with students' communities is important to the work of teaching" (Hallman, 2012, p. 243). Further, in the context of the broader community, students' school-based and personal identities often co-exist and prospective teachers are able to learn who students are beyond the school-based identity that they project in the classroom/ school.

Community service, more broadly, has been embraced by the academy in the form of service-learning and civic responsibility. Community service, as Flower (2008) notes, brings:

idealism and social consciousness into the academy; it brings a human face and complex lives into discussion of ideas and issues. But, it can also plunge teachers and students into its own set of contradictory and sometimes profoundly conflicted social and literate practices. (p. 153)

As Moore (2014) states, the concept of service-learning is often still fraught with 'mixed messages' (p. 109), and in common parlance is sometimes referred to as volunteerism. Service-learning's relationship with concepts of *server* and *served* demands a more complex and nuanced understanding of the goals of working with others in the community outside/ surrounding the academy. In teacher education, there is certainly a danger of pre-service teachers seeing themselves in the role of 'server' while seeing those they work with in the role of 'served.' Scholars in teacher education, including Wade (2000, 2001) have stressed the importance community service-learning, arguing that service is not just about meeting individual needs, it is about working toward the ideal of society that upholds the worth and potential of all its member (Wade, 2000). Similarly, Epstein (2010) describes social action literacy projects, projects that allow both teachers and students to advocate for civic action within their communities. In both of these examples, the community's needs are highlighted and the role of 'server' and 'served' is again problematized.

This chapter views community-based field experiences as drawing from service-learning's conception; yet, it also sees community field experiences as specific to teacher education in that field experiences promote an understanding of the processes of teaching and learning. Community-based field experiences, like service-learning, resonate with the notions of both 'service' and 'inquiry,' (e.g., Flower, 2002, 2008; Schutz & Gere, 1998) and aim to accomplish the goal of finding a balance between the two.

This so-called balance between service and inquiry is not always straightforward. Scholars in Composition Studies, such as Flower (1997, 2002, 2008) have problematized the server-served dichotomy within service-learning. Flower has worked toward service-learning's redefinition, articulating a more complex picture of the potential role reversals present in the act of service-learning, and her work (1997, 2002, 2008) features *reciprocity*—a concept that refers to both the interchange in roles between teacher and student as well as the interchange between university and community partnerships. Reciprocity is central to service-learning's definition, and is central to community-based field experiences in teacher education as it seeks to reverse the long-standing practice of the academy using the community for the academy's own ends (Zlotkowski, 1996). Reciprocity is a key concept for thinking about how the college-aged prospective teachers involved in a community-based field experience evolve in their understanding of the role of such experiences within teacher education programs. Prospective teachers were challenged to think conceptually about their work with youth in the community and the concepts of *teacher identity* and *role* were reconfigured as prospective teachers embarked on this work.

Teacher Identity and Role

Community-based field experiences demand that prospective teachers reconsider the role of *teacher*. Oakes, Franke, Hunter Quartz, and Rogers' (2006) assert that community-based field placements possess the potential for teachers to draw on local knowledge that extends outside of the school. The notion of 'expert,' then, becomes not only a role for teachers or teacher educators, but rather a role that can be assumed by others in the community. As Portes and Smagorinsky (2010) state, beginning teachers are socialized into a dominant model of classroom teaching—one that adheres to a model of 'teacher as authority.' Thonus (2001), who writes about writing center tutors, also reflects that there is a dominant model for socializing *tutors* (the label sometimes applied to teacher candidates who work within community-based field experiences). The dominant model is one that differentiates *tutor* and *teacher*, with a tutor's role being distinct and different from a teacher's. Yet, Thonus notes that this is a tutoring mythology—a mythology that constrains the tutor's role, limiting it to "issues of personality and strategies of interpersonal interaction" (p. 61). As there is exists a tutoring mythology, there also exists a teaching mythology, one that bolsters the model of teacher as authority. Teacher as authority remains a dominant force in beginning teachers' conceptualizations of themselves as future teachers. Through work in community-based settings, prospective teachers begin to challenge this model. In being witness to prospective teachers' understandings of their process of becoming teachers, this chapter considers the ways teacher candidates narrate their understandings of their growth as teachers.

Central to these narratives are the ways in which future teachers consider themselves as "*particular types of professionals*" (Zembylas, 2008, p. 124, italics in the original) and take up their teacher identity as a project of continuous "becoming" (Gomez, Black, & Allen, 2007) over time. Furthermore, teachers mediate their stories of who they are as educators with the cultural and institutional expectations of what it means to be a teacher. *Identity* is viewed as constructed through interactions between people and *identity work* is accomplished by individuals staking claims about who they are in relationship to others. Identity is intimately tied to literacy, as literacy is positioned as a vehicle by which individuals can make such claims. Further, one's identity is always connected with one's use of *Discourses* (Gee, 1999), which act as "'identity kits' and come complete with the appropriate costume and instructions on how to act, talk, and often write, so as to take on a particular role that others will recognize" (Gee, 2001, p. 526). *Discourses* become conceptual forums from which individuals assert their affiliations and undertake identity work. Through such a view, one's "self," or identity, doesn't exist as an individually created entity, but rather is formed within a nexus of social relationships and affiliations. Moreover, one's identity, because of being situated within a social context, is subject to change over time. As contexts and affiliations change, so does one's identity. *Identity*, as Hall (2000) asserts, is something which is "not already 'there'; [but] rather, ... a production, emergent in process. It [identity] is situational—it shifts from context to context" (p. xi). As a consequence, identity work is undertaken as a fluid process—one is never finished with constructing his or her identity.

This understanding of identity creates the possibility for teachers' identities to become "texts" and and others are positioned as "readers" of these texts. Identity, inhabited by Discourses, becomes a performance and also becomes visible, therefore giving rise to the possibility for multiple interpretations by readers. In crafting identity as "text," teachers create a portrait of themselves as teachers. This portrait is created through a variety of means, including teachers' actions, teachers' interactions with others, and teachers' writing. This chapter now moves toward describing the context of a community-based field experience within a teacher education program and then illuminating the stories, or narratives, that beginning teachers tell about their experiences working in community-based field sites.

Context of the Community-Based Field Experience

Prospective teachers featured in this chapter worked with youth from Family Partnership, a community organization for homeless families, over the course of one semester; the larger project of including community-based field experiences in teacher education has been occurring at Green State University (GSU), a public university in the Midwest[1], over the past eight academic years. At GSU, prospective teachers' work at Family Partnership was premised on the idea that preservice teachers' work with youth would expand beyond the traditional role of *teacher*. In this field experience, cohorts of teacher candidates worked with homeless youth through a partnership with the Family Partnership organization. Family Partnership, a national, nonprofit organization, was founded with the goal of helping low-income families achieve lasting independence. This model is oftentimes contrasted with a "shelter model" of assisting homeless individuals and families, as the program is founded an integrated approach to addressing issues of homelessness. The organization works with a small group of families over the course of a period of three to four months with the intention of fostering families' independence. In the community, Family Partnership is one of several programs serving homeless individuals, and working with Family Partnership was purposeful, as the directors at Family Partnership had sought connections with GSU, intending to initiate an after-school initiative for the youth who were part of the Family Partnership program.

A focus on a community-based field site that serves homeless families and youth is significant. An emphasis on this demographic of students acknowledges that the education of homeless youth has been continually represented in scant ways in the research literature. It is now estimated that approximately 36,900 unaccompanied youth or minors in the United States are homeless for six months or longer (National Alliance to End Homelessness, 2017). The National Alliance for Homelessness recognizes this number is likely inaccurate as youth are a particularly difficult population to account for as they often reside in different places than homeless adults reside. This number also does not include homeless families, of which youth comprise a significant proportion. Chronically homeless families represent 2% of the homeless population (approximately 13,105 people). Most typically, the homeless youth population has been represented as residing in the inner-city with single-parent (female)-headed families.

Since 2014, the national trend for numbers of homeless individuals and families has continued to decline (National Alliance to End Homelessness, 2017). Yet, many people experiencing homelessness experience "unsheltered" homelessness, meaning that they are in a place unfit for human habitation, such as the street or in a car. The "face" of homelessness also continues to change; it is now estimated that 14 out of every 10,000 people are "rural" or "suburban" homeless (as compared to 29 out of every 10,000 people who are "urban" homeless) (National Alliance to End Homelessness, 2017).

Cedar Creek, a community of approximately 90,000 people, is classified as a suburban community. The suburban nature of the community, as well as the presence of Green State University in the community of Cedar Creek, challenges the idea that homeless individuals and families can exist in such communities. However, this may make it more imperative that prospective teachers enrolled at Green State University become aware of and acquainted with the diversity within their local community.

Community-Based Field Experience Within Teacher Education Programs

Logistical challenges have been documented in much of the research literature surrounding the integration of service-learning and community-based field experiences into university classes, such as freshman composition (e.g., Mintz & Hesser, 1996). Mikolchak (2014) notes that her first service-learning teaching endeavor was difficult due to the specifics and logistics of the project. Although she found an ideal site for the service-learning experience that was part of her composition course, a shelter for battered women, she notes that it was also a place with limited access to the public, "with a strict security system and a number of other regulations that are necessitated by the very sensitive nature of the site" (p. 214). Mikolchak writes that challenges included "time management, transportation, work supervision, providing lunch, and other such details" (p. 215). In integrating community-based field experiences with teacher education programs at GSU, I also recognized that specific locales offered different opportunities for students to engage in the community.

Considering the integration of community-based field experiences into teacher education resonates with many of these challenges. Over time, because the community-based field experience initiative has been ongoing at GSU, some of these obstacles turned into routines that became cemented in the course structure. In this section, I describe how the integration of community-based field experiences aimed to work within the confines of the university, yet provide meaningful service to people in the broader community. I describe how the project and research emerged and how, in some ways, the university structure has helped it be sustained for multiple years. Through this detail, I hope to provide others who teach within teacher education programs ideas for integrating community field experiences into programs.

In the context of this chapter, the prospective teachers who are portrayed have already determined that they want to work in education. They want to be teachers. The community-based field experience encourages them to learn through their interactions with the community, as well as through their writing about the community, what it will mean to be a teacher. The students involved in the initiative are developing, through their writing and reflection, what their teacher identity will be and are learning how to work closely with individual students and see these students in a different light before being in their own classroom.

Within the context of a larger teacher education program, the community-based field experience occurred as a component of a content-area methods course, *Curriculum and Instruction in Middle/ Secondary English Language Arts Classrooms*. Students typically enrolled in this course during their junior year of college, and during their third semester as students in the GSU School of Education. The teacher education program at GSU that is designed to educate pre-service teachers to understand the context of schooling in the United States; the relationships between schools, society, and families; knowledge about curriculum and pedagogy within the field of English language arts; and knowledge about oneself as a teacher. It is a 4-year program that culminates with a student teaching experience, a full-time semester in a K-12 classroom.

Placing a community-based field experience mid-way through the teacher education program had defined benefits to prospective teachers as it urged them to connect their work to the content-area domain of English/ literacy. Because of the nature of literacy itself, prospective teachers could imagine the ways in which literacy was part of students' lives outside of the school day. For example, reading and writing with students was a primary way that the community-based field experience was able to be connected to the content domain. Still, the bridge between in-and-out of school literacies is still something that prospective teachers question, as they often see out-of-school literacies as peripheral to school-based literacies. Despite a plethora of research in this area (e.g., Hull & Schultz, 2002), beginning teachers need guidance in recognizing these connections.

Placement of a Community-Based Field Experience Within a Content-Area Methods Course

As previously mentioned, the community-based field experience described in this chapter was part of the course *Curriculum and Instruction in Middle/ Secondary English Language Arts Classrooms,* a secondary English language arts methods class that resided in a School of Education.

During the first semester that a community-based field experience was included as a component of the course, the community-based field experience had several options. Family Partnership, the program for homeless families, was just one option in year one. However, Family Partnership became the sole community field partner for the methods course at GSU. Over the years, multiple cohorts of students, all consisting of 7-10 students, were involved in the experience. These cohorts were comprised of a sub-set of the students enrolled in the methods class. For example, oftentimes half of the students in the methods course elected to participate in the community-based field experience while the other half elected to complete their field experience in a 'traditional' classroom placement. From the beginning of the project, the community-based field experience has been posed as a contrast to the option of a traditional, classroom field placement. Therefore, in some years, more students wished to participate in a 'traditional' field placement in an English classroom while a smaller portion of the students participated in a community-based field experience. The students featured in this chapter had elected to participate in the community-based field experience.

In making a choice to contrast community-based field experiences with 'traditional' classroom place-ments, it may be that an automatic binary between community-based field experiences and traditional classroom placements was set up. In some ways, this goes against the aim to move beginning teachers into thinking about the value of community-based sites as contributing to knowledge about teaching rather than contributing a contrasting knowledge about teaching to that gained within a classroom. In building a community-based field site within a teacher education course, it is important to stress, to prospective teachers, how working within a community-based field site reflects a commitment that prospective teach-ers must have to teaching children alongside their emerging awareness of the importance of relationship building within the teaching act. As I continue to move forward with the project in current and future years, I have considered having all students enrolled in the methods course participate in both experi-ences: a community-based field experience and 'traditional' field experience in an English classroom.

The next section details these key reflective assignments in an effort to assist other teacher educa-tion programs in the creation of similar reflective assignments that accompany community-based field experiences. I then move to present portraits of the four prospective teachers and how they used both the assignments and the experience to think further about their role as a teacher, their students' learning, and the value of the community-based field experience.

REFLECTIVE ASSIGNMENTS THAT ACCOMPANY COMMUNITY-BASED FIELD EXPERIENCES

The key reflective assignments that accompany the community-based field experience include the following: fieldnotes, guided journaling, instructional planning, and life graphs. Each of the assignments aims at a distinct goal, described in detail below.

Fieldnotes

An assignment linked with participation in community-based field experiences was the writing of fieldnotes. Fieldnotes, for the prospective teachers working at Family Partnership, served as the link between describing what was happening, in a literal sense, to how these events that connected to larger concepts about students' learning. In the Family Partnership experience, prospective teachers were asked to write fieldnotes after each session spent with youth at the day center. Then, bringing these fieldnotes to the content-area methods class, discussion ensued with their peers about how to translate the meaning of such events into tangible action with the children at Family Partnership. Through discussions with their peers who were also working with youth at Family Partnership, beginning teachers began to see how their perceptions of homeless youth affected their representations of these youth in their fieldnotes. The fieldnotes, themselves, become a text to question, and prospective teachers began to embrace how their observations could translate to practice. Fieldnotes were taken every time the prospective teachers worked with youth at Family Partnership and were discussed every other week in the content-area methods class.

Guided Journaling

In the Family Partnership experience, prospective teachers were asked to move from writing fieldnotes to writing guided journal entries. Guided journaling was meant to incorporate both aspects of fieldnote writing and instructional planning, yet remain removed from designing concrete plans for action with youth. Beginning teachers felt that guided journaling was an assignment that asked them to move a step closer to 'action' with working with students. Yet, the guided journal entries were often where beginning teachers expressed their struggles. Many of the narratives featured in this chapter are drawn from prospective teachers' guided journals.

The 'guided' part of the journaling experience meant that prospective teachers responded to a prompt that I presented to them when we discussed the field experience in the methods course. Some of the prompts included:

- What themes that were pertinent in the volunteer training are arising in your work at Family Partnership? How have these themes impacted your awareness of the issues you are seeing?
- Describe the youth who you are working with at Family Partnership. What do you see as their strengths? In what ways are you working with them on activities related to literacy learning?

Prospective teachers appreciated being given a direction for their journaling (as opposed to freewriting) and guided journaling also assisted me in highlighting connections between the themes we were discussing in class and the themes that prospective teachers were seeing in action for the first time.

Instructional Planning

Through discussions with their peers who were also working with youth at Family Partnership, beginning teachers were able to collaborate with each other and design instructional plans for youth. These instructional plans were intended to be used with one child at Family Partnership with whom the prospective teacher had worked with consistently for a number of weeks. Mid-point in the semester, prospective teachers were able to assess many aspects of the literacy learning of the youth at Family Partnership; these included motivational aspects as well as cognitive aspects. In the content-area methods class, prospective teachers had studied the use of reading strategy work with youth, and often the instructional plans they created included concrete actions that would assist youth with learning literacy and reading. Being passionate about designing reading and writing activities for youth at Family Partnership, prospective teachers were eager to incorporate the knowledge they had gained about both the lives and literacies of the students at Family Partnership into concrete instructional plans for students.

Many prospective teachers designed a reading plan for students at Family Partnership. This consisted of designing activities that the youth could do alongside reading a book with prospective teachers. Often teachers also found additional books that would appeal to the youth and were able to find copies of these books to share. In the methods class, I stressed that out-of-school reading had different goals than in-school reading; for example, I did not want to see prospective teachers administering tests about the reading material in the out-of-school space; this would be inappropriate and could defeat the enjoyment of the activity. Instead, I urged prospective teachers to think of enjoyable activities—such as writing a chapter that could continue the book or writing a screenplay. Such activities were much more engaging for youth than question and answer activities.

Life Graphs

As a culminating assignment for the semester, prospective teachers were asked to write *life graphs* (Burke, 2007), a visual timeline of events that detailed their perceptions of the Family Partnership experience over the course of the semester. Life graphs purposely integrated the experiences that teachers had in the field site with other events that occurred alongside of the work in the field site. What was interesting about the life graphs was that they urged prospective teachers to think about the community-based field experience in a holistic way—and in a way that integrated it with their learning in other courses. Experiences from the semester were included so helped prospective teachers focus on their growth over a one-semester time period.

Prospective Teacher Participants Featured

The remainder of this chapter details the experiences of four particular prospective teachers, Michele Christenot, Bryce Adam, Aurora Brown, and Henry Taylor, who worked with students from Family Partnership over the course of a semester. The portraits highlight the ways in which the reflective assignments presented in the methods course intersected with the prospective teachers' learning. Though I draw specifically on these teachers' experiences within this chapter, a cohort of ten prospective teachers worked in this community-based field site over the course of the semester. Though prospective teachers who were part of the community-based field experience needed to complete at least twenty hours of tutoring/mentoring with young people, aged birth-17, at Family Partnership's after-school initiative for homeless youth, the teachers featured in this chapter went above and beyond the required twenty hours. The four teachers featured in this chapter completed between 30-35 hours of work at the community-based site.

Throughout the semester, prospective teachers completed key assignments in the content-area methods course that connected the work they were doing in the field site to the teacher education program. Participation with Family Partnership immediately asked beginning teachers to question what the role of 'teacher' entailed. In fact, many times taking the role of 'observer' was unsatisfactory to beginning teachers as they continuously questioned how the knowledge they were gaining directly translated into the act of teaching. In other words, they were eager to have an active role working with youth.

Throughout the duration of the experience at Family Partnership, I found that the narratives that prospective teachers told about their experiences were important windows into understanding how they negotiated their role as 'teacher.' Mishler (1999) notes that the stories we, as people, tell about our lives are the ways we "express, display, [and] make claims for who we are—in the stories we tell and how we tell them" (pp. 19-20).

PORTRAITS OF PROSPECTIVE TEACHERS' WORK IN COMMUNITY-BASED FIELD EXPERIENCES

Michele Christenot

Michele, a white prospective teacher in her early 20s, grew up in the community of Cedar Creek. Michele expressed resonance with the kind of diversity she viewed as present within the community. Though she described it as mainly 'economic diversity,' she noted that she was not surprised that homeless families resided in Cedar Creek, but noted that the families were likely more 'hidden' in a college town than they might be in other communities. Michele had attended one of the city's two local high schools before beginning at GSU, and expressed comfort and awareness with the resources available in the community. For example, Michele was aware that Cedar Creek had a homeless shelter and a women's shelter in addition to the Family Partnership program. Particularly, she noted that because Cedar Creek was a mid-sized college town, most people in the state had always perceived the community as more expensive, more educated, and more competitive in terms of job prospects than other towns throughout the state. This, in turn, had perpetuated a notion that issues such as homelessness were not present or critical in Cedar Creek.

Despite living in the community for her entire life, Michele stated that she began her experience at Family Partnership with fear and apprehension. As she noted in her life graph, completed at the close of the semester, fear dominated her feelings in the early part of the semester. Michele also noted how feelings of chaos, apprehension, fear, and, eventually, 'breakthroughs' characterized her experience at Family Partnership.

Though Michele characterized Cedar Creek as a comfortable and familiar place for herself, she began to see that the community had different meaning for the students she worked with at Family Partnership. In April, on her life graph, Michele noted that there was "little communication...between the schools and the organization itself." She said, "These kids received no counseling, little structure, and are perceived as normal students in class." Michele's awareness of the issues of homelessness and the available resources led her to make the conjecture that it is, indeed, easy for some kids, such as the kids who are part of the Family Partnership program, to "fall through the cracks."

At times, prospective teachers like Michele began to question the links between the school and students' home life. Michele told a story of one youth, Dylan, at Family Partnership who was given detentions every day because he was late. Dylan was late to school because the family needed to drop off a young sibling at another school before dropping off him. Resistant to discussing his family's homelessness, Dylan often served the detentions without explaining any of the circumstances to the school's administrators. Michele was astounded that the student did not advocate for himself but was also in shock that there was no formal mechanism in the school to recognize students who were homeless or in programs, such as Family Partnership, that serve homeless families.

Michele also referred to 'breakthroughs' in her life graph. She claimed that, despite the chaos and frustration she experienced at times throughout the semester, breakthroughs were what propelled her to seek a commitment to the community-based field experience. Michele's ability to focus on these breakthroughs, or recognitions of how the theoretical issues connected to the actual issues in the community-based site, confirmed her pursuit of a career as a teacher. She was able to observe the tangible difference she believed she was making for the students she worked with and this affirmed her work as a future teacher. Her comments reinforced this affirmation:

This experience [at Family Partnership program for homeless families] took me outside of the classroom and into the everyday life of a student with an alternative home life. Knowledge and experiences like this are critical, in my opinion. While it wasn't what I expected, it was definitely worth the work.

The comment, "it wasn't what I expected" is an interesting one and one expressed often by prospective teachers. In the content-area methods class, we explored the idea of 'expectation' and related it to the profession of teaching. Just as most students endorsed a 'teacher as authority' model, they also endorsed a model of teacher education that would put them and their needs at the center of all experiences within the program. This became challenging for some students, and students like Michele made the following comment that reiterated the sentiment of being displaced from the center:

When I worked with the kids this semester, I really recognized that teaching is a relationship between teacher and student. So far in the program, I had been so concerned about me as the teacher: what would my lesson plans look like? Am I grading the right way? But this experience has shifted my sense of what's at the center because it is really the student and their learning.

One challenging aspect of the recognition that it is teacher educators' job to balance the importance of teacher identity while, at the same time, urging prospective teachers to always value the relational aspect of teaching. The development of oneself as a teacher is important to prospective teachers yet can run the risk of overemphasizing the role of teacher to the exclusion of the relational piece of teaching. The community-based field experience at Family Partnership complemented Michele's discovery of self with an emphasis on the youth as they reside within their out-of-school context. In contrast to the official space of the classroom, work in community-based spaces emphasizes context, community, and relationships—often the components of youth's lives that must be made visible to prospective teachers.

Bryce Adam

Bryce Adam, a white prospective teacher in his early 20s, attended a predominantly African American high school in the state's metropolitan center. Because of this experience, Bryce frequently discussed his comfort with working with diverse students. Unlike his peers, Bryce understood that Family Partnership, as a non-profit organization, did not have unlimited funds to supplement the programs they had in place. Instead, Bryce was fully aware that the organization relied heavily on volunteers. Throughout the semester, Bryce affiliated with the concept of 'volunteer' and was one of the few in his cohort to join Family Partnership families during their dinner hour at a local congregation several times during the semester.

Bryce's adoption of the volunteer role opened doors for expanding his relationship with the youth at Family Partnership. Instead of working on homework and academic tasks, Bryce was most proud of the relationship he developed over the semester with one 9-year old, Dominic. Dominic had a love for fishing, and would often relate stories of fishing with family and friends to Bryce. Because this was such a topic of interest to Dominic, Bryce encouraged him to draw pictures of himself fishing. After Dominic completed one of the pictures, he gave it to Bryce.

After this, drawing became something that Bryce and Dominic did together in their hours at Family Partnership. One day, Bryce taught Dominic how to do "perspective drawing." He taught Dominic new drawing techniques and Bryce conveyed to peers that Dominic was very excited about learning this new technique and went on to create several perspective drawings.

In his journal entries, Bryce wrote that sharing an experience drawing with 9-year old Dominic helped Dominic "open up to him and create a more personal relationship." Yet, despite having this success, Bryce also wrote that there were difficult times working with the children at Family Partnership. He noted:

The shear resistance I got from a couple of the children reinforced my apprehensions about certain behaviors that aren't always the easiest to assuage and alleviate. Namely, it is the apathy and refusal to perform that shakes me…I will not make them fearful with empty discipline threats, so at least working with them becomes less tense, in that regard, and allows for reciprocity.

In the out-of-school environment of the Family Partnership day center, Bryce saw apathy and disengagement in ways that could be similar to what one might sometimes witness within a traditional classroom. Because the prospective teachers did not work in a traditional school space, they sometimes encountered youth who resisted their efforts to engage them in reading and writing. In the after-school hours at Family Partnership day center, sometimes youth would claim that they were done with the school day and ready to take a break. In these cases, prospective teachers wondered what it might take to change students' attitudes, some which may have been ingrained for many years, yet also understand the youths' position.

Above, Bryce's commentary about difficulty in working with disengaged youth urges us to think about how to help prospective teachers recognize the positive work they do with students and also the work that remains troubling. Bryce specifically points out that working with apathetic students is challenging and sharing this with his peers upon reflection in the methods class, peers were able to present some possible options for working with such students. Through this collaboration, prospective teachers began to consider the power of gaining multiple perspectives on working with youth. Such perspectives could be a door to new possibilities for practice. In a discussion in the methods class, Bryce brought this conundrum to bear. The following conversation highlights the importance of peer interaction and discussion in the methods course in support of community-based field experiences. Lindsey was a peer in Bryce's content-area methods class and they discussed Bryce's frustration.

Bryce: *So, I am working with this kid who is about 11. His name is Michael. When I suggest that we read or write and that we can do those things together, he just shakes his head or shrugs. He doesn't seem interested and would rather literally do nothing than work with me.*

Lindsey: *He has a certain book he's reading?*

Bryce: *I've tried to use the work from school—the homework he has in his bag—and do that together.*

Lindsey: *Maybe starting with something else…something he chooses and then let him see that reading and writing doesn't just have to be his homework? Would Michael pick something out for you and he to read together?*

Bryce: *He might. He'd probably be more open to that. I just assumed he would want me to help him with his homework since he has to get it done anyway. I just feel reluctant to keep pressuring him.*

Lindsey: *You might see it as pressuring him but I'd try just opening it up to his choosing. It's ok if you don't feel like you are getting all the homework done. I think building the relationship is the most important thing.*

Bryce and Lindsey were able to talk through what working with an individual student might look like—and that it might not always accomplish homework tasks at hand or the reading and writing activities that prospective teachers had designed. Though Bryce was open to the experience, he still benefitted from thinking through different possibilities.

Late in the semester, when Bryce talked about Michael to a group of peers in methods class, he was able to reflect on this:

I thought giving Michael a choice of what to read would not work at all. But, he did then show me a graphic novel that he was willing to read with me. He had the book and started telling me about the characters. I was able to use this and I eventually found that there was an entire series…Big Nate, the series is called. It's by an author Lincoln Peirce. It became ok not to work on his assigned reading for school. Honestly, he didn't really ever tell me if he was completing that or not. But, he always gave me the Big Nate update.

Through this experience, Bryce had engaged with instructional planning around literacy. He took the steps necessary to decide how to assist Michael in selecting a book that was of interest to him and then worked with Michael to continue the relationship with this book series.

Aurora Brown

Aurora Brown, a prospective teacher in her early 20s, could be considered representative of the majority of Green State University's pre-service teachers in several ways. Aurora was white, and well prepared in her content area, English. Her plans for post-graduation from the teacher education program included residing within a one-hour driving proximity to both Green State University and the Marshall City metropolitan area. She also intended to continue pursuing graduate coursework that would lead to the completion of her master's degree while beginning her first English teaching position the year following her student teaching year.

Aurora struggled with what she viewed as occurring during the time designated for tutoring at Family Partnership. She wrote:

Tonight at tutoring, I helped one of the students with her math homework and based on her worksheet, she was not struggling with the multiplication tables. When we were working together, the student got very distorted by the other activities going on in the room. I think this was troublesome for her concentration because she felt like, "They aren't doing anything, why should I be productive?". I do not blame her for feeling like that and I wish the organization would set up a separate room for tutoring and education. As for now, the tutors work with students in the same space as they eat dinner, socialize, play games, etc. To most benefit the student's learning and success in school while in the program, I think the organization should focus more on these details and organize how they can best fit the needs of their students.

Aurora seemed to have many suggestions for Family Partnership and how the organization could change things in order to better benefit students. Though she was at the day center for only two hours each week, Aurora felt that her viewpoint was sufficient to recommend such changes. Aurora began to shift her focus to herself and her role at Family Partnership, yet struggled with how to maintain this focus on self. She certainly questioned her identity as a tutor, mentor, and teacher. In her final journal entry, Aurora wrote:

Upon leaving tutoring, I begin to think about how my thinking has shifted from participating in this experience. At the beginning, I thought I was going to tutor students and possibly even be assigned a particular student to help for the entire semester. However, after the first meeting, I realized that the structure for tutoring was not really set up. This was very frustrating because I felt like my time was being wasted if I was not going to help the students with schoolwork. But then I began to get to know the students, about their situation and realized that I needed to shift my thinking in terms of what I am providing for these students and what I am gaining from this experience. I think that the organization should set expectations with everyone involved, including us as tutors. If this happened, I think we could utilize our time with the students much more than what is currently happening, even if the expectations are just that we should mentor the student and play games with them.

For Aurora, expectations and goal-setting appear to be a positive solution to what she perceives of as the difficulties she experiences. Expectations, in her mind, will lead to better outcomes for all. Yet, in Aurora's journal entries, there is never a mention of the life circumstances of children at Family Promise. Because, as she says, "the tutors work with students in the same space as they eat dinner, socialize, play games, etc.," the experience lack of structure and the possibility of being 'successful.' To Aurora, the life circumstances of the children appeared to influence their learning in ways that could be easily identified and remedied.

Aurora was a critic for most of the semester. Yet, her criticisms began to shift as the semester came to a close. Instead of proposing only changes for the organization, and as she calls her life graph, "internal interviews or 360-degree reviews," Aurora began to recognize that she could also implement change in the context of her working relationships with youth. She also had a broader understanding of the youth within her community, writing:

Previously, I had thought that there were only a few families in [Cedar Creek] that were in a homeless situation, however the organization shifted my belief and clued me in on the reality in [Cedar Creek]. The students are doing poorly in school and the parents are searching for jobs, which creates a steady flow of stress in the program. Thus, as a teacher I am going to be more understanding and accommodating of student's life situations.

In many ways, Aurora's perspective shifted over the course of the experience to one that included recognition of the context and its challenges, a key to teachers' ability to work with diverse student populations.

Henry Taylor

Like others in his cohort of beginning teachers, Henry Taylor struggled to view the work at Family Partnership as teaching work. Henry was also a white prospective teacher who was in his 20s. Unlike most of the other prospective teachers, Henry was unsure whether he wanted to teach at the elementary or secondary level and grappled with this throughout the semester's experience at Family Partnership.

Henry recognized that the work at Family Partnership was often different than that of a secondary English teacher in that there were varied ages of children in one setting; interactions were not focused through a traditional school time schedule; learning was not organized through teacher-driven curriculum; and the interactions took place in a residential space. Since the context was different than in a traditional school setting, the work and interactions that the prospective teachers encountered were different as well. Though this had been emphasized within discussions and assignments in the methods course, several prospective teachers reiterated this. But, because of this, teacher identity was no longer defined or cemented in the way it was manifested within schools.

In his journal, Henry described continued conflicts about whether or not he should go into teaching. He said he wanted to be a teacher, and if he could not embody his first choice, an elementary school teacher, he seemed settled on becoming a secondary English teacher. He still had doubts, though, about becoming a teacher as he saw how society viewed teachers, with the expectation that they embody the lofty goal of role model and degrading role of babysitter all at once.

Henry wrote in his journal regarding the ways he saw gender limiting his identity as an English teacher:

…we carry these things in our heads. The majority of my male peers seem to fall into one of two categories – we all think we're going to be laid-back football coaches or self-important trouble makers. It's a silly sort of vanity either way, but I think it demonstrates an honest reflection of our values…

Henry, though he described it as "an honest reflection of our values," was also interpreted by society as expectations of one's masculinity. As an English teacher, Henry saw two possible identities: a coach or a trouble-maker. Both of these are traditional, masculine roles, and by stepping outside the school-defined context of teaching, Henry was able to identify such roles and see them as contrasting with the one he enacted at Family Partnership. The conflicts of identity came to bear with Henry's imaginings of his role within society at large. He considered what it meant to be an elementary teacher in society.

What did it mean to be a man who works with young children and what assumptions will be made about a male's identity if he takes on this job? Although Henry was negotiating what he believed to be a less problematic role, as a secondary English teacher, he still acknowledged social identity markers that he may not want to embody.

Within the semester, there was an event that spurred Henry to really consider what the role of teacher meant. The event occurred about four weeks into the semester. Henry was working at Family Partnership one afternoon by himself with five children ages 4-14. He described being worried that he was on his own with all the children, but also said the kids were well-behaved and no problems arose. At one point during the afternoon, however, the telephone rang, and 11-year-old Annie answered it. The caller wanted to donate a mattress and was calling to contact someone at Family Partnership to make arrangements to do so. Since there were no Family Partnership employees present, Annie decided Henry was the person who should handle the call. Henry described Annie's decision as a very significant moment in which he felt he was defined in an unexpected way:

Annie picked up the phone, listened for a few minutes, said 'let me hand you to a grown-up' and in one of the more surreal experiences in my life, handed the phone to me . . . It took me a few moments to register that by 'grown-up' she meant me, and I had to fight this unsettling realization . . .

Henry took the caller's contact information and was abruptly set off balance. He wrote: ". . . after I hung up I was strangely aware of something the kids had taken for granted – *I* was The Grown-up." Henry described that "suddenly and without warning" he was forced to acknowledge a role he had never embraced before – a role that would be assumed without question if he were the teacher within a classroom. Legally, society saw him as a grown-up, a person who was no longer a minor, someone who was able to vote, drink and otherwise take on adult legal responsibilities. Situated as he was within the space of Family Partnership, Henry was also a grown-up, an authority figure to the children who were under his direction. Annie saw he was the authority figure in the room, and the caller also accepted his authority as someone with whom he could share grown-up information. Socially, Henry was made into a grown-up before he was willing to accept this role. He wrote in his journal about being somewhat shocked that he had been made into an authority figure without his conscious choice of that becoming:

I hadn't learned anything or done anything – all it took to become The Grown-up was to remain in the room after everyone I thought was The Grown-up had left. The kids took this for granted, as I've always taken it for granted when identifying The Grown-ups in my life . . . it correlates more with accountability . . . Maturity is something you grow into – something you seek and make a part of yourself. You become a Mature, but it seems like being The Grown-up just happens to you, oftentimes suddenly and without warning.

Henry said he had "always taken it for granted" when identifying the grown-ups in his life, and in saying this, he also acknowledged that the children at Family Partnership have likely "taken it for granted" that he was the authority figure. This defining moment, for Henry, was recounted within the methods class and several of his peers acknowledged their coming-of-age as both teacher and grown-up.

Implications of Implementing Community-Based Field Experiences in Teacher Education Programs

What do the experiences of Michele, Bryce, Aurora, and Henry tell teacher educators about the value of prospective teachers' work in community-based settings? First, despite viewing this experience working with homeless youth as a unique opportunity within their teacher education program, prospective teachers continued, throughout the experience, to compare the work they undertook in the community setting to the work they viewed as "teaching." The questions and situations that arose for each of them elicited unique themes as related to their teaching. For Michele Christenot, the connections (or lack thereof) between schools and communities was a pivotal facet of her growth throughout the semester. Bryce Adam, already understanding of the complexities between schools, communities, and youth, sometimes struggled to work at the individual level with students. Throughout the semester, his peers assisted him in taking his deep theoretical knowledge of community to the individual work he did with students, especially with one particular student, Michael. Out of the four prospective teachers featured in this chapter, Aurora Brown perhaps made the most overall movement in terms of how she recognized the influence of life circumstances on students' academic lives. Finally, Henry Taylor grappled with questions surrounding gender roles and maturity.

Bryce and Aurora, in particular, became somewhat disenchanted at the end of the semester as they articulated hopes that more might have been accomplished during the semester. Bryce, in a final journal entry, said that if the project were to continue in future semesters, prospective teachers should be aware that the experience would be, as he wrote, "a mentoring experience versus a tutoring experience." These differences, even at the end of the experience, stood as binaries for Bryce and Aurora, and each was determined to reconcile what their experience in the community-setting meant to their work as future teachers. In many ways, this strict adherence to presumed teacher roles is not surprising, as it has been shown that beginning teachers' adherence to an "apprenticeship of observation" (Lortie, 1975) is one of the salient traits that runs throughout research on field experiences in teacher education (see Zeichner, 2010).

Michele and Henry, on the other hand, experienced events that could be seen as 'breakthroughs,' using Michele's words. The breakthroughs, in some ways, occurred because their taken-for-granted assumptions about their role in and out of the classroom was questioned and reconfigured. It was important that these breakthroughs be acknowledged and that there was a space to discuss them alongside the day-to-day occurrences of the experience itself. Prospective teachers who worked with homeless youth were purposefully urged to re-negotiate the relationship between teacher and student and contemplate what benefits such a re-negotiation might have to their future position as a classroom teacher. Such a contemplation is rarely undertaken early in prospective teachers' programs, as traditional field experiences provide a clear model for what constitutes the role of teacher. Despite this clear model, beginning teachers are often directed to assume this model rather than question it. Through critical questioning early in their teaching careers, beginning teachers are encouraged to be more cognizant of the roles and relationships involved in a teaching career.

Within teacher education programs, community-based field experiences offer an opportunity for beginning teachers to not just question reconfigured roles, but actually see these new roles in action.

Whether it be teacher, tutor, mentor, or grown-up, teacher education must explicitly provide opportunities that will allow prospective teachers to engage in authentic learning experiences that allow them to work authentically with youth in communities. Embedding community-based field experiences in teacher education is one significant method of promoting such opportunities.

REFERENCES

Alsup, J. (2006). *Teacher identity discourses: Negotiating personal and professional discourses*. Mahwah, NJ: Lawrence Erlbaum.

Burke, J. (2007). *The English teacher's companion* (3rd ed.). Portsmouth, NH: Heinemann.

Cochran-Smith, M., & Lytle, S. (2009). *Inquiry as Stance: Practitioner research in the next generation*. New York: Teachers College Press.

Coffey, H. (2010). *"They* taught *me"*: The benefits of early community-based field experiences in teacher education. *Teaching and Teacher Education, 26*(2), 335–342. doi:10.1016/j.tate.2009.09.014

Darling-Hammond, L. (2006). *Powerful teacher education*. San Francisco: Jossey-Bass.

Epstein, S. (2010). Activists and Writers: Student expression in a social action literacy project. *Language Arts, 87*(5), 363–372.

Feiman-Nemser, S., & Buchman, M. (1987). When is student teaching teacher education? *Teaching and Teacher Education, 3*(4), 255–273. doi:10.1016/0742-051X(87)90019-9

Flower, L. (1997). Partners in inquiry: A logic for community outreach. In L. Adler-Kassner, R. Crooks, & A. Watters (Eds.), *Writing the community: Concepts and models for service learning in composition* (pp. 95–117). Washington, DC: American Association for Higher Education Press.

Flower, L. (2002). Intercultural inquiry and the transformation of service. *College English, 65*(2), 181–201. doi:10.2307/3250762

Flower, L. (2008). *Community literacy and the rhetoric of public engagement*. Carbondale, IL: Southern Illinois Press.

Flower, L., Long, E., & Higgins, L. (2000). *Learning to rival: A literate practice for intercultural inquiry*. Mayhew, NJ: Lawrence Erlbaum.

Gee, J. P. (1999). *An introduction to discourse analysis: theory and method*. New York: Routledge.

Gee, J. P. (2001). Literacy, discourse, and linguistics: Introduction. In E. Cushman, M. Rose, B. Kroll, & E. R. Kintgen (Eds.), *Literacy: A critical sourcebook* (pp. 525–544). Boston: Bedford/ St. Martin's.

Gomez, M. L., Black, R. W., & Allen, A. (2007). "Becoming" a teacher. *Teachers College Record, 109*(9), 2107–2135.

Hall, S. (2000). Foreword. In D. A. Yon (Ed.), *Elusive culture: Schooling, race, and identity in Global times* (pp. ix–xii). Albany, NY: SUNY Press.

Hallman, H. L. (2012). Community-based field experiences in teacher education: Possibilities for a pedagogical third space. *Teaching Education, 23*(3), 241–263. doi:10.1080/10476210.2011.641528

Hallman, H. L., & Burdick, M. N. (2011). Service learning and the preparation of English teachers. *English Education, 43*(4), 341–368.

Hallman, H. L., & Burdick, M. N. (2015). *Community Fieldwork in Teacher Education: Theory and Practice*. New York: Routledge.

Hull, G., & Schultz, K. (2002). *School's Out! Bridging out-of-school literacies with classroom practice*. New York: Teachers College Press.

Ladson-Billings, G. (2001). *Crossing over to Canaan: The journey of new teachers in diverse classrooms*. San Francisco: Jossey-Bass.

Lortie, D. (1975). *Schoolteacher: A sociological study*. Chicago: University of Chicago Press.

Mikolchak, M. (2014). Service-learning in English comp. In V. Kinloch & P. Smagorinsky (Eds.), *Service-learning in literacy education: Possibilities for teaching and learning* (pp. 211–224). Charlotte, NC: Information Age Publishing.

Mintz, S. & Hesser, G. (1996). Principles of good practice in service-learning. *Service-learning in higher education*, 26-52.

Mishler, E. (1999). *Storylines: Craftartists' narratives of identity*. Cambridge, MA: Harvard University Press.

Moore, M. (2014). Service-learning and the fields-based literacy methods course. In V. Kinloch & P. Smagorinsky (Eds.), *Service-learning in literacy education: Possibilities for teaching and learning* (pp. 105–115). Charlotte, NC: Information Age Publishing.

National Alliance to End Homelessness. (2017). Retrieved December 1, 2017 from http://www.end-homelessness.org/

Oakes, J., Franke, M. L., Hunter Quartz, K., & Rogers, J. (2006). Research for high quality urban teaching: Defining it, developing it, assessing it. *Journal of Teacher Education, 53*(3), 228–235. doi:10.1177/0022487102053003006

Portes & Smagorinsky, P. (2010). Static structures, changing demographics: Educating teachers for shifting populations in stable schools. *English Education, 42*(3), 236–247.

Schutz, A., & Gere, A. R. (1998). Service learning and English studies: Rethinking "public" service. *College English, 60*(2), 129–149. doi:10.2307/378323

Shulman, L. (2005). Pedagogies. *Liberal Education, 91*(2), 18–25.

Sleeter, C. (2008). Equity, democracy, and neoliberal assaults on teacher education. *Teaching and Teacher Education, 24*(8), 1947–1957. doi:10.1016/j.tate.2008.04.003

Thonus, T. (2001). Triangulation in the writing center: Tutor, tutee, and instructor's perception of the tutor's role. *Writing Center Journal, 22*(1), 59–82.

Wade, R. C. (2000). Beyond Charity: Service learning for social justice. *Social Studies and the Young Learner, 12*(4), 6–9.

Wade, R. C. (2001). Social Action in the Social Studies: From the ideal to the real. *Theory into Practice, 40*(1), 23–28. doi:10.120715430421tip4001_4

Zeichner, K. (1996). Designing education practicum experiences for prospective teachers. In K. Zeichner, S. Melnick, & M. L. Gomez (Eds.), *Currents of reform in preservice teacher education* (pp. 215–234). New York: Teachers College Press.

Zeichner, K. (2010). Rethinking the connections between campus courses and field experiences in college-and University-based teacher education. *Journal of Teacher Education, 61*(1-2), 89–99. doi:10.1177/0022487109347671

Zembylas, M. (2008). Interrogating 'Teacher identity': Emotion, resistance, and self- formation. *Educational Theory, 58*(1), 107–127. doi:10.1111/j.1741-5446.2003.00107.x

Zlotkowski, E. (1996). A new voice at the table? Linking service-learning and the academy. *Change, 28*(1), 21-27. doi:10.1080/00091383.1996.1054425

ENDNOTE

[1] The community-based field experience initiative within GSU's English education program has been ongoing for eight academic years. Each spring semester, as part of the English language arts methods course, a new group of prospective teachers is introduced to a community-based field experience. Several community-based sites, including a tutoring program for English language learners and a creative writing program for high school aged foster youth, have been partnered with over this eight-year time period. This chapter, however, specifically draws on the experience with one site, Family Partnership, a program for homeless families in the local community.

Chapter 16
Adopt-an-Apprentice Teacher:
Re-Inventing Early Field Experiences

Timothy J. Murnen
Bowling Green State University, USA

Jonathan Bostic
Bowling Green State University, USA

Nancy Fordham
Bowling Green State University, USA

Joanna Weaver
Bowling Green State University, USA

ABSTRACT

The goal of this chapter was to explore the impact of a field-centric, grade-band, and subject-area specific field experience model that is linked to corresponding coursework on novice teacher candidates' conceptions of what it means to be a teacher. Grounded in the work of scholars such as Dewey, Piaget, and Vygotsky, this study explores three questions: What aspects of the Adopt-an-Apprentice program do teacher candidates view as beneficial to their understanding of the profession and their development as teachers? What benefits, if any, do classroom teachers derive from hosting teacher candidates in the Adopt-an-Apprentice program? What is the impact of grade band/subject-area field experiences on teacher candidates' conceptions of being a teacher? Using quantitative and qualitative surveys, the study illustrates how coursework linked to authentic application in clinical settings empowered novice teacher candidates to understand and engage content, pedagogy, and standards.

INTRODUCTION

Teacher education has evolved in the past twenty years to attempt to better address the complexities of contemporary classrooms by finding better ways to prepare teacher candidates to meet the needs of PK-12 students. Ball (2000) contended that fragmentation between theory and practice existed in teacher preparation and called for the integration of knowledge and practice to help candidates develop as ef-

DOI: 10.4018/978-1-5225-6249-8.ch016

fective teachers. Effective teacher education programs will need to continue to connect the ideas and strategies taught in college classrooms with the real-world context of PK-12 classrooms. The goal of this study was to explore the impact of a field-centric, grade-band and subject-area specific field experience model—linked to corresponding coursework—on novice teacher candidates' conceptions of what it means to be a teacher. To address varying definitions such as *clinical experiences, internships,* and *field experiences,* in this chapter "field experiences" or "early field experiences" refer to experiences occurring in school settings *prior to* the now-common methods semester that typically precedes student teaching.

BACKGROUND

The means by which teacher candidates learn to teach has been the subject of exploration by numerous researchers in the past three decades. While research from the 1980s and 1990s demonstrated that teacher candidates spent most of their time in campus classrooms absorbing knowledge *about* teaching, with a single, final semester of *applied* teaching (Huling, 1998), research by the late 1990s spotlighted successful programs that featured systematic, long-term collaboration (Wideen, Mayer-Smith, & Moon, 1998).

Since then, calls for improved teacher preparation through early, frequent, varied, and purposeful field experiences in authentic school settings have multiplied (Boyd, Grossman, Lankford, Loeb, & Wyckoff, 2009; Cochran-Smith & Zeichner, 2005; Coffey, 2010; Zeichner, 2010). Darling-Hammond (2010) has long argued that the clinical side of teacher education is frequently "haphazard" and "dependent on the idiosyncrasies of loosely selected placements with little guidance about what happens in them and little connection to university work" (p. 40). In addition, Zeichner (2010) argued that the lack of meaningful partnership between colleges of education and K-12 schools signified the core problem in teacher education.

Studies have explored various models of candidate learning and teaching during student teaching internships, from advocating smaller changes such as co-teaching (Baeton & Simons, 2016; Heck, 2010), to more explicit work in collaboration (Weiss, Pellegrino, & Brigham, 2017), to a total re-configuration of educator preparation with a focus on the critical role of field experiences (Boyd, Grossman, Lankford, Loeb, & Wyckoff, 2009; Darling-Hammond, 2006; Meyer, 2016). In particular, a Standard authored by the Council for the Accreditation of Educator Preparation (CAEP) advocates the shared, reciprocal role of clinical partnerships, where:

The provider works with partners to design clinical experiences of sufficient depth, breadth, diversity, coherence, and duration to ensure that candidates demonstrate their developing effectiveness and positive impact on all students' learning and development. (Council for the Accreditation of Educator Preparation, 2013, 2.3)

In short, research consistently cites strong partnerships between universities and schools, along with coursework examining teacher practice, as a hallmark of quality education programs (Ball & Forzani, 2011; Cochran-Smith, Villegas, Abrams, Chavez-Moreno, Mills & Stern, 2015; Coffey, 2010; Darling-Hammond, Chung, & Farlow, 2002; Wilson, Floden, & Ferrini-Mundy, 2001).

With these calls for earlier and more frequent field experiences, Wideen et al. (1998) contended that transforming the beliefs of novice teacher candidates is one of the goals of early and extensive field experiences. Researchers argue that student beliefs are well-established (Britzman, 1998; Weinstein, 1990; Wideen, Mayer-Smith, & Moon, 1998) and overly-simplistic (Darling-Hammond, 2006), but amenable to change (Richardson & Kile, 1992) by factors such as coursework and field experiences (Cochran-Smith & Zeichner, 2005). Other literature asserts that teacher candidates' conceptions of teaching and learning can be transformed through observation, interaction, and analysis in field settings (Wilson, Floden, & Ferrini-Mundy, 2001).

Responding to all of this research, the National Council of Accreditation for Teacher Education (NCATE) Blue Ribbon Panel (2010) called on teacher education programs to be "turned upside down" by shifting away from "course work loosely linked to school-based experiences" toward programs "fully grounded in clinical practice and interwoven with academic content and professional courses" (National Council for the Accreditation of Teacher Education, 2010, p. ii). However, while the 2010 report focused on strengthening capstone field experiences such as methods and student teaching, little research has focused on models to strengthen early field experiences.

Faculty surmised that turning a teacher education program upside down needed to begin with re-envisioning early field experiences that, until recently, were loosely tied to individual courses—but not structured to produce a coherent framework of clinical practice. Grounded in the panel's "Ten Design Principles" (NCATE, 2010, pp. 5-6), researchers created the *Adopt-An-Apprentice Teacher* Program to provide an early field model integrated into coursework. In particular, this project focused on the first six of the Blue Ribbon Principles (NCATE, 2010), reframed here as action statements:

1. Teacher candidates should be of service to the classroom teacher and their students.
2. Content and clinical practice need to be woven together to prepare preservice teachers to be of service.
3. An assessment system to collect and analyze data about our candidates is needed to strengthen the program.
4. Classroom mentor teachers should mentor candidates in ways that encouraged candidates to be innovators, collaborators, and problem solvers.
5. Candidates, faculty, and classroom mentor teachers should develop an interactive professional community.
6. Building systematic partnerships (Jones, Hobbs, Kenny, Campbell, Chittleborough, Gilbert, Herbert, & Redman, 2016; Sharp & Turner, 2008) with schools that have a shared vision and implementation plan for our teacher education program are central for developing candidates. Since the creation of this early field model, the recent publication of the American Association of Colleges for Teacher Education's report (American Association of Colleges for Teacher Education, 2018) calls for the development of more robust early field experiences, thus validating the general trajectory of this model.

To evaluate the merits of this program, we set out to answer three questions: What aspects of the *Adopt-An-Apprentice* program do teacher candidates view as beneficial to their understanding of the profession and their development as teachers? What benefits, if any, do classroom teachers derive from hosting teacher candidates in the *Adopt-An-Apprentice* program? What is the impact of grade band/subject-area field experiences on teacher candidates' conceptions of being a teacher?

THEORETICAL FRAMEWORK

Teacher candidate field experiences, dovetailed into campus coursework, are grounded in the work of educational scholars such as Dewey, Piaget, and Vygotsky. In his experiential learning theory, Dewey (1938) argued that learning occurs through experience. The learner adapts and learns by interacting with real concepts, problems, and world issues—by abstracting principles from lived experience. Piaget broke this idea down even further, exploring how learners construct meaning by juxtaposing new knowledge against prior knowledge through assimilation and accommodation (Piaget, 1954). Piaget explained how schematic maps, or schema, are constructed by organizing knowledge into a coherent framework. Through assimilation, the learner fits new concepts into existing schema. Accommodation occurs when new knowledge doesn't fit nicely into the existing schema, so the learner needs to stretch, reshape, or reframe the existing schema. Similarly, in Vygotsky's theory (1978), the learner learns not by remaining within his or her current developmental zone, but by being challenged or stretched beyond the current developmental zone across a zone of proximal development. Vygotsky understood that learning takes place by leaving this comfort zone, with support (i.e., scaffolding) from a mentor or more learned peer. All of these theories suggest that learning is not passive but active, not the absorption of information, but the active construction of meaning through interaction with the world. Real-world contexts give shape and meaning to the new concepts being learned, suggesting that classroom learning alone without a real-world context for application is insufficient.

IMPLEMENTING THE *ADOPT-AN-APPRENTICE* PROGRAM

Building Systematic Partnerships by Reframing the Discourse

At the beginning of this program, state-mandated testing associated teachers' performance and students' outcomes in ways that might lead to pay differences or removal from their positions; teachers feared losing their jobs if their students did not perform well. Some district partners considered rejecting student teachers because the burden of training them in 15 weeks, with testing outcomes on the line, was too great a risk. Simultaneously, program designers were about to ask districts to take on nearly 500 more first-year teacher candidates in new early field placements.

To help administrators and teachers re-envision the roles of first-year teacher candidates in the classroom, researchers reframed the discourse about the role of teacher candidates, focusing on how they might assist in classrooms. Doing so engaged NCATE principle six, building systematic partnerships (NCATE, 2010). Rather than ask districts to take on our first-year teacher candidates—language that suggests a burden—program designers communicated, "We have a large team of students who can be of service to you and want to learn. Would you like an apprentice teacher for the semester?" When the question was reframed, and the goals of the early field placements restructured, teachers began requesting first-year teacher candidates.

Method

This study examined the results of the newly created *Adopt-An-Apprentice Teacher* program, which merged introductory classes with field experiences early in teacher candidates' academic careers. The investigation occurred in a midwestern public university's large undergraduate teacher education program over a two-year academic period, 2015-2017. Candidates in the study represented two teacher preparation programs: those seeking licensure in Adolescence-to-Young Adult Education (AYA), grades 7-12, and Middle Childhood Education (MCE), grades 4-9.

Participants

This study focused on participants in two sizeable teacher education programs and included a total of 468 candidates from both. Students in the Adolescent to Young (AYA) Education comprised majors in all four core disciplines: English language arts, math, science, and social studies. Candidates in the Middle Childhood Education (MCE) program, by state law, chose any combination of two concentration areas from among the same four subject areas. Commonly, candidates select either Language Arts and Social Studies, or Math and Science, as concentration areas, though any blend is permitted. All teacher candidates were enrolled in required, newly designed introductory freshman-level courses, for example, *Introduction to Teaching Secondary Mathematics* or *Introduction to Teaching Middle Grades Science*.

Also participating in the study were 85 teachers in 16 districts and 43 schools. Initial meetings with district superintendents led to the recruitment of teachers in grades 4-12. Education faculty sought suggestions from teachers about tasks novice teacher candidates might ably perform in their classrooms, and these were compiled into a list of task/activity recommendations distributed to both mentor teachers and candidates (See *Apprentice Activities Checklist* in Appendix). This initial collaboration, along with personal visits to school administrators and teachers, helped us begin to address NCATE principle five: "Candidates, faculty, and classroom mentor teachers should develop an interactive professional community."

Field Experiences

Teacher candidates enrolled in the newly created introductory courses were assigned to interested teachers in school classrooms correlating with candidates' grade bands and subject area specialties. Field visits occurred one morning per week, with busing to schools provided. Before placement visitation commenced, candidates participated in an orientation session outlining professional expectations, bus schedules, confidentiality, and other relevant issues. Keeping in mind NCATE statement 1, faculty stressed to candidates that their job was, first and foremost, to be of service to classroom teachers and students. Candidates were told they would be able to evaluate the *Apprentice* program and their field experiences at semester's end. Additionally, they were advised that classroom teachers would assess candidates' performance, as well.

Introductory Courses

Instructors in corresponding introductory courses offered both spring and fall semesters familiarized candidates with curriculum standards, inquiry-based pedagogical strategies, lesson planning fundamentals, and usually, an introduction to classroom management. Instructors linked field-based observations and activities with reflective assignments and follow-up discussions, in addition to course tasks associated with the discipline, making connections with students' experiences in field classrooms. Commonly, these links were fostered via required written reflections on candidates' perceptions gleaned from their experiences in the field. These observations led to campus discussions about teacher duties, workload, and demeanor; teaching strategies; student abilities, motivation, and behavior; and classroom management, aligning with our interpretation of NCATE statement two: "Content and clinical practice need to be woven together to prepare preservice teachers to be of service."

Placements

As anticipated, the most challenging undertaking of the *Adopt-An-Apprentice-Teacher* program was securing placements for the approximately 468 teacher candidates in our middle childhood education (MCE) and secondary education (AYA) programs each year. We utilized existing school sites where student teachers were placed in previous years and added new potential sites received via responses on a survey sent to teachers. Our next step was to match candidates with field sites in their majors and grade bands. Initially, just five school districts accepted our MCE and AYA apprentices. Fortunately, some larger school district partners hosted as many as 40 teacher candidates per week, so eventually, all candidates received placements.

Evaluation

To facilitate the program evaluation process, teacher candidates were surveyed at the end of the semester to determine the value of the field experience in their overall learning (See *Apprentice Candidate Survey* in Appendix). As well, classroom mentor teachers (CMTs) were surveyed at the end of the semester to ascertain how they perceived the efforts of the teacher candidates placed in their classrooms (See *Apprentice CMT Survey* in Appendix). This was one step in responding to NCATE statement three—constructing an assessment system to collect and analyze data about our candidates to strengthen the program.

TWO CONTENT-SPECIFIC COMPONENTS OF *ADOPT-AN-APPRENTICE*

Within this larger framework of the *Apprentice* project, we spotlight two case studies that illustrate the rich impact such a field-based program can have on how candidates prepare to become teachers. The first project illustrates how an introductory mathematics education course focused on mathematical standards, and linked to authentic application in clinical settings, empowered secondary mathematics students to understand and engage mathematical standards. The second project illustrates how providing focused training in IRIs (Informal Reading Inventories) and text readability formulas enabled teacher candidates to assist with assessment and intervention of struggling readers in high school and middle school settings—thus having immediate positive impact on classrooms.

EXPLORING MATHEMATICAL STANDARDS IN REAL CONTEXTS

Programmatic Expectation for Secondary Mathematics Teacher Preparation

The Mathematical Education of Teacher [MET] II (American Mathematical Society, 2012) document provides clear guidelines about the expectations of mathematics teacher educator programs. It suggests that future mathematics teachers should have multiple mathematics education courses alongside appropriate mathematics content courses (American Mathematical Society, 2012). Similarly, the Standards for Preparing Teachers of Mathematics (Association of Mathematics Teacher Educators, 2017) are:

intended as a national guide that articulates a vision for mathematics teacher preparation and supports the continuous improvement of teacher preparation programs. (p. 2)

The Council for the Accreditation of Educator Preparation (CAEP, 2016) also has standards for teacher preparation. All of these documents highlight the need for embedded field experiences that link university instruction with future classroom practices.

In this section, we illustrate how the *Adopt-An-Apprentice* model, particularly the early courses designed for first-year candidates, better link BGSU's middle grades and secondary mathematics teacher education program with guidelines and provides new opportunities for candidates to demonstrate competency. In particular, we focus on the second and fourth action statements.

Secondary Mathematics Education Coursework

BGSU coursework provides a pathway for candidates desiring to become secondary (grades 7-12) mathematics teachers. Prior to *Adopt-An-Apprentice*, students completed a course titled "Introduction to Secondary Mathematics Education" during their second year. This introductory course aimed to introduce candidates to ideas about the daily work of mathematics teachers, some content found in the secondary curriculum that is often difficult to teach, and a brief 10-hour field component. Where they spent those 10 hours was largely outsourced to faculty teaching the course, drawing on connections with teachers in the area. This posed an enormous burden on faculty and cooperating teachers and there were not systematized means for field placements.

During their third year, candidates completed a pre-methods course, which did not include a field component. During fall semester of the fourth year, candidates took a mathematics methods course. This methods course included a significant (120+ hour) field component, in which they became familiar with their students, their teacher, and the learning environment. They also taught a unit of instruction and become acquainted with school policies and expectations.

Spring semester of the fourth year included a student teaching internship, during which candidates worked alongside their cooperating mentor teachers for a full semester, teaching or co-teaching a minimum of twelve weeks. When BGSU initiated the *Adopt-An-Apprentice* model, it created a trickle-up effect such that faculty coordinated with school districts to move courses around during students' program, better integrate field work into current courses, and create new courses to meet students' needs.

Program revisions included moving the introductory course to the first year and leveraging the fieldwork for furthering candidates' thinking about mathematics teachers' roles and responsibilities. The fieldwork component changed from an unscheduled arrangement of 10 hours with two or three teachers to a series of scheduled weekly site visits for approximately 30 hours of apprenticing with one mathematics teacher. Two new mathematics content courses were developed for the second year of the program, which partnered with other education courses that allowed the *Adopt-An-Apprentice* model to be incorporated. We expected candidates to be better prepared for the teaching profession as a result of these changes, which we discuss in the next section. For this mathematics case study, our research question is: *How has candidates' knowledge of the SMPs and SMCs developed through the Adopt-An-Apprentice model?*

Standards and Their Applications in Mathematics Instruction

Prior to the *Adopt-An-Apprentice* model, candidates were not introduced to standards in a meaningful way until their third year. Under the *Adopt-An-Apprentice* model, they completed an in-depth exploration into both content (*Standards of Mathematics Content*; SMCs) and practice (*Standards for Mathematical Practice*; SMPs). The SMCs describe what students should know and guides discussions about content that should be taught in each grade level or course (Council of Chief State School Officers, 2010). The SMPs characterize behaviors and habits that students and teachers should exemplify during mathematics teaching and learning (Bostic, Matney, & Sondergeld, 2017; Council of Chief State School Officers, 2010). Teachers are expected to know their standards and develop coherent lessons, using standards as a foundation (National Council of Teachers of Mathematics [NCTM], 2014, 2000).

DATA SOURCES AND ANALYSIS

Instrumentation

The data for this section come from two sources. First, there was a set of assignments in which candidates were required to select two questions about the secondary mathematics classroom and explore them. These questions were aligned with various NCTM standards (2014, 2007, 2000). Questions focused on topics including, but not limited to, learning environment, mathematical discourse, rich tasks, lesson planning and task enactment, use of technology, and equity. The second source was a final exam, which asked candidates to: (a) locate and describe evidence of the SMPs and SMCs in a case study and; (b) express two notions they learned as a result of experiences in the course. A common thread across these two sources was knowledge of SMCs and SMPs. Thus, this section answers the question: *How has candidates' knowledge of the SMPs and SMCs developed through the Adopt-An-Apprentice model?* Effective responses for both data sources included claims, evidence from their fieldwork, and justification of their evidence using readings, class discussions, and other resources.

Participants and Context

To answer the research question, five semesters (i.e., two-and-a-half years) of candidates' responses to these questions were analyzed using inductive analysis (Hatch, 2002). In total, responses from 101 secondary teacher candidates who completed the first-year introductory mathematics course were analyzed, with the average class size being 20 candidates per semester. BGSU has a rich history in secondary mathematics teacher preparation; it is the 13th largest secondary mathematics teacher preparation program in the country and is unusually large compared to its overall institutional size (Fennell, 2015).

Analysis

A goal of inductive analysis is to draw out a theme (Hatch, 2002). After generating a series through analysis of initial candidates' ideas that broadly answered the question, responses were read a third time to discern whether there was sufficient evidence for them and/or counter evidence. Finally, topics that had a plethora of evidence and paucity of counter evidence became themes. Those ideas that became themes are shared here. All uses of names are pseudonyms.

Results

A single theme was broadly supported: Candidates linked university and field-based work in ways that demonstrate rich understanding of the SMPs and SMCs. Results suggested that the majority of secondary math candidates were able to correctly identify teachers' enactment of SMPs and SMCs, as well as students' engagement in them. Moreover, they frequently reported that their ideas about teaching and preparation for teaching changed dramatically, usually focusing on the uses of standards during lesson planning and implementation. Maria articulated how drawing on fieldwork through the *Apprentice* program supported her understanding of coursework:

Before this class and going into the field, I knew nothing about lesson planning, differentiation....I now have a much deeper meaning of what it means to be a teacher. My change in thinking started in the field.

After her experiences in the field site classroom, Megan articulated a more nuanced understanding of the methodologies she was being taught in her course: *I realize that there are ways in which to teach mathematical content so that students can understand mathematics more efficiently and be successful.*

Finally, Kaylie connected the importance of knowing the standards early in her program with her fieldwork:

SMPs were hard for me to grasp at first [in university coursework] and it was hard for me to be able to apply them in a classroom situation, but by seeing someone apply them in her classroom situation, it helped me deeply understand the SMPs....Because I was fortunate to see first-hand how she does this and talk with her about them, I was better able to understand the SMPs in our university classroom. Because the SMPs are very important, it is good that I got a better understanding of them so soon in my program.

From analysis of these comments and other similar candidate observations, we concluded that the *Adopt-An-Apprentice* model offered a unique opportunity to first-year students and sufficiently prepares them for further coursework and teacher preparation experiences.

Discussion: Connections to Programmatic Standards

As a result of the new first-year course and the *Apprentice* model, candidates were involved in weekly fieldwork within mathematics teaching contexts in appropriate grade-level settings. The connection between courses and fieldwork starting from the first year allows unique discussions to occur in the university setting, thus addressing CAEP's push for meaningful examinations of clinical partnerships and practice and programmatic impact. During the first year, teacher candidates deeply explore how mathematics content and standards are planned and enacted in their field placement. They use field notes as evidence of what they observed for field-based assignments, and draw upon foundational texts (e.g., CCSSO, 2010; NCTM, 2014) to substantiate how their observations align with evidence that address classroom standards explored in class. Thus, their ideas are keenly grounded in the fieldwork through the *Adopt-An-Apprentice* model. Previously, such discussions about standards and classroom practice did not occur until teacher candidates' third year. Moreover, ten hours of fieldwork was not sufficient for students to gather meaningful data about teaching. Anecdotally, the discussion about SMPs and SMCs was superficial at best under the earlier teacher preparation program. Students rarely connected their ideas to fieldwork and, furthermore, could not effectively communicate the meaning of the SMPs and SMCs beyond reading the title. On the other hand, secondary mathematics teacher candidates in the new *Adopt-An-Apprentice* program are more effectively prepared to apply their knowledge and analyze instruction using enactment of the SMPs and SMCs as a lens. Drawing on a programmatic perspective, faculty recognize that meaningful field experiences working alongside teachers early in their teacher education program allow for deep explorations that could not have occurred under the old model.

It can be concluded that through the *Adopt-An-Apprentice* model, students learned about the standards they might teach and more importantly, what it means to engage 7th-12th graders in those practice and content standards. In sum, the apprentice model builds new avenues for teacher candidates' learning and connects their learning with authentic classroom experiences.

TRAINING PRE-SERVICE TEACHERS TO TEACH STRUGGLING READERS

The *Adopt-An-Apprentice* program is further strengthened in the introductory courses by providing cross-curricular training sessions during the initial weeks of the program. These sessions focus on working with struggling readers in the classroom. Research studies support the need for teacher preparation that helps build self-efficacy by providing reading strategies teachers can use in classroom contexts (Bandura, 1977; Massey & Lewis, 2011; Ness, 2008; Plucker, 2010).

Training sessions helped transform introductory candidates' beliefs in the simplicity of teaching, and opened their eyes to the scope of skills they need to be effective teachers who reach all learners (Darling-Hammond, 2006). Key skills such as assessing the readability of texts, assessing the reading level of students, and matching texts to students are often overlooked across content areas, or are often not taught until the third or fourth year of an undergraduate literacy program. Providing these skills earlier not only helps teacher candidates focus on the importance of reaching every learner, but also it allows them to be actively involved their early field placements during *Adopt-An-Apprentice*.

The goal for these sessions was to provide candidates with a skill set they could use within their *Adopt-An-Apprentice* field placement. If the classroom mentor teacher (CMT) had struggling students, our candidates would be equipped to work with them, and this would benefit the CMT, the struggling student, and our teacher candidates. With the skill set acquired during the training sessions, candidates would be able to measure readability levels of text and provide comprehension strategies that would strengthen the struggling students' understanding of content.

This case study focused on these research questions were: How did the struggling reader workshop change candidates' thinking about the importance of reading in their content areas? What assessment and intervention strategies did teacher candidates use in their *Adopt-An-Apprentice* field placement as a result of the professional develop workshop?

The Struggling Reader Workshop

The struggling reader workshop included two sessions. The first session explored an understanding of struggling readers in content areas and included the Informal Reading Inventory (IRI) training (Roe & Burns, 2011). The second session included training using readability formulas, including the Fry Readability Formula. In addition, candidates practiced vocabulary and comprehension strategies.

The First Session

The first session of training consisted of modeling and practicing the IRI. The IRI is a diagnostic assessment that evaluates key components of a student's reading ability, and is considered valid and reliable for matching students' reading abilities with the difficulty level of texts (Spector, 2005). The IRI consists of two components: lists of words in isolation and reading passages, both coded by grade level. Students' comprehension of the words in the lists helps establish a baseline reading level to begin assessing their comprehension of the leveled passages. After reading passages, students respond to follow-up questions that assess comprehension. Using scores from both components of the assessment, teachers arrive at a student's reading level. From here, teachers come to understand "the levels of reading material pupils can read both with and without teacher assistance" (Roe & Burns, 2011, p. 1),

The Second Session

The second session began with an exploration of the need to match texts to students reading levels using the Fry readability formula (Fry, 1977) and specific vocabulary and comprehension strategies. Using samples provided, candidates assessed the readability of a content area textbook. In addition, they explored the potential disconnects between their prospective students' reading levels (learned in session 1), and the readability levels of the texts they may be using in their classrooms.

Candidates then worked with various vocabulary and comprehension strategies that would provide students with background knowledge before working in the content, comprehension strategies that would monitor understanding during the process, and strategies that would measure comprehension and vocabulary acquisition following the lesson. These strategies included various graphic organizers, including the Frayer Model and LINCS for vocabulary, and various graphic organizers to organize student thinking around main ideas, details, sequencing, cause-and-effect, reasoning and problem- solving skills. These strategies would help to close the gap between text readability levels and struggling students' reading levels. The strategies and skills candidates practiced during both sessions could be utilized in their *Adopt-An-Apprentice* field placement.

DATA SOURCES AND ANALYSIS

Instrumentation

The data for this section came from pre- and post-surveys. The pre-workshop surveys were administered at the beginning of the workshop. Survey questions were open-ended and focused on participants' prior experiences using the IRI, the Fry readability formula, interest surveys, experience working with struggling readers, and personal experiences as readers. The post-surveys were collected from candidates at the end of the semester at the conclusion to *Adopt-An-Apprentice*. Several were then interviewed at the end of the semesters to discover how they used the skills learned during training.

Participants and Context

In the spring of 2016, 39 AYA Integrated Language Arts (ILA) majors attended the struggling reader workshop. In fall of 2016, this expanded to 50 teacher candidates, including integrated social studies (ISS) students and ILA students. Since 2016, the program has grown further to include two semesters of training in all content areas. Starting fall 2017, training 125 candidates were trained. In spring 2018, an additional 100 teacher candidates were added across content areas each semester.

Analysis

To answer the research questions, qualitative data from pre-workshop surveys were analyzed using inductive analysis (Hatch, 2002) to understand candidates' prior assumptions about the relative importance of reading in content courses. Post-tutoring surveys and interview results were also analyzed using inductive analysis to develop key themes, and to focus on particular observations of interviewees. Finally, other data were gathered from the general end-of-semester survey administered to all *Apprentice* candidates. All uses of names are pseudonyms.

Results

Prior to the workshop, 84% of participants, outside of the language arts candidates, initially believed that teaching reading strategies belonged only in the language arts classroom or taught at the middle school level. While they had never considered having to teach reading strategies in their content area classrooms, during the training they became more aware of the complex needs of all learners and the strategies they might use to instruct them. They all (100%) agreed that reading does take place in their discipline and that they need to know the teaching and assessment strategies to work with struggling readers. Among several questions on post-tutoring surveys, candidates were asked: *Across the content areas, where does reading instruction belong, and who is responsible for teaching the reading strategies?* While roughly half (46%) the candidates said that the English or reading teacher is responsible, just over half (54%) felt that reading was important across the content areas. Several gave somewhat nuanced responses, characterized by this statement: "I think reading should be across the content areas, but reading specialists should teach strategies." This student's other responses suggested that her thinking about reading had shifted, but her experience doing the IRI, the Fry readability, and her experience in *Adopt-An-Apprentice* brought her around to understand how complex and important it was to perform assessment and intervention correctly.

After the *Adopt-An-Apprentice* semester was complete, we collected interview feedback from candidates, in response to three questions: (1) Was the Struggling Reader Workshop helpful in *Adopt-An-Apprentice*? How so? What specific skills did you get from the workshop, and what specific strategies are you applying in your field placement?

CONCLUSION

Two key reciprocal features of the struggling reader workshop illustrate its strengths. Candidates learned concepts and strategies in the workshop that enabled them to be more useful in the classroom. In addition, candidates' real-world hands-on classroom experiences helped them understand the core concepts taught in the workshop. Anna, for instance, learned specific assessment and intervention strategies that she applied to her *Adopt-An-Apprentice* experience:

I found the Struggling Reader Workshop to be incredibly helpful, as I had no prior experience before that. One aspect of the workshop I particularly liked was learning about the Fry Readability formula. This was crucial throughout my experience. Additionally, practicing the IRI with a partner during the workshop was beneficial because I felt more confident when it came time for me to facilitate it.

A second candidate, Kenzie, captured the level of insight she developed as a result of the workshop:

The workshop was incredibly helpful for me. I learned how to use the IRI and find the Fry Readability of different passages. Through the course of the semester and multiple 'retestings' of the IRI, I found out that one of my students was not at an 8th grade reading level as originally reported by her teacher. She was actually at grade 11 which was right where she should be for her grade, and the only thing holding her back was her confidence in reading. I was able to apply the IRI training that we had received to this exact situation and was able to more accurately understand what was going on in my student's life.

These training sessions provided early-career university students with their own hands-on, purposeful learning and developmental experience as they practiced administering and assessing reading levels and strategies during their *Adopt-an-Apprentice* field placement. The skills learned during the sessions were utilized during the *Apprentice* program as teacher candidates assisted classroom teachers.

EVALUATION OF THE ADOPT-AN-APPRENTICE PROGRAM

Evaluation Approach

This section offers an overview of the data generated through the *Adopt-An-Apprentice* program. This perspective may guide other programs considering structured changes to their teacher preparation program. The purpose of the semester evaluations were to explore the success of the program for MCE (grades 4-9) and AYA (grades 7-12) teacher candidates, with respect to these questions: What aspects of the *Adopt-An-Apprentice* program do teacher candidates view as beneficial to their understanding of the profession and their development as teachers? What benefits, if any, do classroom teachers derive from hosting teacher candidates in the *Adopt-An-Apprentice* program? What is the impact of grade band/subject-area field experiences on teacher candidates' conceptions of being a teacher? Researchers utilized a context, input, process, product approach (aka CIPP), which focuses on analysis of program improvement (Stufflebeam, 2003), rather than proving that the program works. This aligns with CAEP's Standards (2015), which are intended to foster program improvements. Our methodological frame for evaluation was a mixed-methods explanatory approach (Cresswell, 2012). The explanatory approach provides users the ability to explain quantitative findings using qualitative data.

Data Sources

Instrumentation

Teacher candidates completed a survey at the end of each semester of their introduction to teaching the content courses. AYA majors took one introductory course during the freshman year, and MCE majors took two, corresponding to their two chosen areas of concentration, per state licensure requirements. The purpose of the survey was to gather perceptions about their apprentice experiences for program improvement. Survey questions were both quantitative and qualitative in nature.

Classroom mentor teachers (CMTs) completed a separate survey at the end of each semester, grounded in Danielson's Framework for Evaluating Teachers (2013) and INTASC Standards (CCSSO, 2011), focusing on candidate dispositions in four domains: (1) Planning and Preparation (for any tasks the teacher might assign); (2) Classroom Environment (i.e., demonstrating positivity, respect, and engagement with students, faculty, and staff); (3) Instruction (if presented the opportunity): individual, small group, and/or whole class, and; (4) Professional Responsibilities. CMTs were also invited to meet with programmatic faculty working in the *Adopt-An-Apprentice* program at the end of the academic year. These small-group interviews added further details about teachers' perceptions of the program. All names are pseudonyms.

Participants

Data were collected across the initial two years of the *Adopt-An-Apprentice* program. These data came from 468 first-year teacher candidates and their cooperating mentor teachers. Of the MCE and AYA apprentices, 72.5% (n=340) responded to the survey. Teacher candidates were placed in urban, suburban, and rural schools. Depending on the variety of candidates and teacher interest, students may be placed in public, charter, private, vocational, or religiously-affiliated schools. Eighty-five unique teachers hosted middle and secondary students over two years. Teachers often hosted one or two students each semester related to a particular subject area. It was typical for teachers who hosted students one semester to adopt an apprentice subsequent semesters.

Analysis

Quantitative data were analyzed using descriptive statistics. Qualitative data were analyzed using inductive analysis (Hatch, 2002). The process for creating a theme followed the same procedure as that done in an earlier section focusing on students' outcomes from the first-year mathematics program.

RESULTS

Quantitative Survey Results: Teacher Candidates

In this section, we highlight candidates' qualitative and quantitative evaluation data, followed by classroom teachers' evaluations. These results help to answer two questions: What aspects of the *Adopt-An-Apprentice* program do teacher candidates view as beneficial to their understanding of the profession and their development as teachers? What is the impact of grade band/subject-area field experiences on teacher candidates' conceptions of being a teacher?

Types of Teacher Activity

Eighty-three percent (n = 282) of respondents reported they were actively engaged in three key types of teacher activity: (1) interacting with students or instruction; (2) preparation or lesson planning, and; (3) clerical (Table 1). Examples related to those three key types are shown below.

Of the respondents, 17% (n=58) reported non-interactive tasks such as observation or clerical-only tasks that did not include any interaction with students. Observational experiences ranged from simple classroom observations to more focused IEP observations. Clerical tasks included grading, setting up bulletin boards, sorting material in filing cabinets, finding online resources, displaying projects, entering grades, and watching the teacher lecture.

Benefits of The Apprentice Program Field Experience

Both quantitative and qualitative survey data revealed the benefits of the *Adopt-An-Apprentice* program. Quantitative survey results indicated that approximately 95% (n=323) of students reported positive

Table 1. Activities completed by teacher candidates

Interacting with Students or Instruction	Lesson Planning	Clerical
Working one-on-one with students or leading stations as part of co-teaching	Preparing mini-lessons to teach on their own	Grading
Assisting with technology/inquiry lessons that require hands-on activity and writing	Helping the teacher revise/ develop lesson plans	Finding supplemental materials to scaffold comprehension
Administering small formative assessments and reviewing content before unit test with students	Setting up science labs	Creating/setting up bulletin boards
Re-teaching (e.g., preparing students for state assessments) and engaging in close reading of texts/math problems		Sorting cabinets
Assisting with math concept formation		Finding online sources
Co-teaching small groups with teacher including leading warm-up activities		Finding supplemental materials to scaffold comprehension
Assisting with technology, inquiry lessons that require hands-on activity, and writing		

experiences in their field placements, with only 5% (n=17) indicating neutral or negative sentiments. Qualitative results indicated ten key factors that made the *Adopt-An-Apprentice* program a beneficial experience (Table 2).

Many candidates shared how beneficial it was to experience classroom management strategies in a real classroom setting. Others were excited to develop their rapport with students as they learned to be perceived as a knowledgeable adult figure in the classroom. Still others felt the opportunity to get hands-on experience was beneficial to the extent that it led to improving their skills as teachers. Other candidates reflected that the field experience helped them gain new perspectives on teaching; it opened their eyes to the benefits and challenges of new school settings, such as urban schools. Some of them shifted their teaching focus, recognizing that they would be happier in a different grade band or content area. Others noted a growth in their own dispositions; they learned patience and a deeper understanding of diversity. Still others reported that learning about classroom assessments, and state-mandated assessment, led them to see the rigor and complexity of the teaching profession. In addition, while some candidates noted that the field experience made them feel more comfortable in the classroom, others argued that it pulled them out of their comfort zone—something they saw in a positive light. Finally, one of the largest set of responses clustered around the benefits of working with really strong or excellent teachers; they felt mentored by someone they aspired to be like.

The 5% (n=17) of candidates who reported few-to-no benefits after the *Adopt-An-Apprentice* field experience indicated they had not been permitted to actively participate in their classrooms and had simply sat and observed. Four candidates reported they had been placed with negative or ineffective teachers. The only benefit two described deriving from their placements was learning what kind of teachers they did *not* want to become: *"I learned what not to do and how a teacher's work ethic and enthusiasm impact a classroom." "I got to experience a kind of teaching that I never want to experience again. I now know what kind of teacher I want to be and how I want to teach."*

Qualitative Survey Results: Teacher Candidates

This project explored the question: What aspects of the *Adopt-An-Apprentice* program do teacher candidates view as beneficial to their understanding of the profession and their development as teachers? Beyond the statistical analysis, the qualitative results allowed us to unpack richer answers to those questions. Several candidates' comments illustrate a key feature of the program: *Adopt-An-Apprentice* uniquely positioned candidates with classroom mentor teachers in ways that leveraged opportunities for professional growth. For example, one candidate, Matthew, wrote:

Table 2. Key factors of benefits of Adopt-An-Apprentice program

(1) Classroom management experience	(6) New teaching focus
(2) Developing rapport with students	(7) Shift in dispositions
(3) Improved skills	(8) Learning about assessment
(4) New perspectives	(9) Expanding one's comfort zone
(5) New school settings	(10) Opportunity to work with a strong teacher

Note: Factors are ordered in most frequently cited to least.

I was able to see the many different aspects that go into teaching, such as lesson planning and prepping for classes. I was able to see when lessons go smoothly and as planned or when they do not go as planned. I was able to work with small groups and figure out how they can best be helped with the activity they were working on.

Another candidate, Josephine, added:

I was involved in team planning, making lesson plans, co-teaching, and many other things. I got the opportunity to be part of an inclusive classroom. It has sparked my new passion for co-teaching and inclusion. I learned a lot, and to have early experience in the classroom helps tremendously.

Similarly, Jackson reported: *I feel so much more confident in a classroom. My cooperating teacher told me she could really see me grow this past semester.* Candidates' saw their growth arise not only from being able to observe strong teaching, but from being invited to participate in the design and implementation of the lesson, and from close interaction with students.

Quantitative Results: Classroom Teacher

Results from classroom teachers helped to address one of our questions: What is the impact of grade band/ subject-area field experiences on teacher candidates' conceptions of being "a teacher"? Teachers ranked and commented on candidates' performance in each of the four Danielson (2013) domains—Planning and Preparation, Classroom Environment, Instruction (where applicable), and an overall evaluation of candidate Professionalism (Table 3).

Table 3. Candidates' performance as rated by teacher

Question	Always	Some times	Rarely/ Never	N/A
The teacher candidate prepares and completes tasks, as assigned by the classroom teacher, in a timely and high-quality fashion **(Planning and Preparation)**	92%	7%	1%	0%
The teacher candidate demonstrates positivity and appropriate respect in all interactions with school students and staff, regardless of race, language, ability, physical characteristics, etc., actively engages with the classroom teacher, actively engages with students, and seeks to assist and provide service in whatever ways needed **(Classroom Environment)**	84%	12%	4%	0%
The teacher candidate, if instructing individuals, small groups, or the whole class, is knowledgeable and engages appropriately with students, and demonstrates initial understanding of students' developmental needs **(Instruction)**	49%	13%	1%	36%
The teacher candidate attends regularly and punctually, as required, communicates clearly, promptly, and accurately in reporting absences, schedule changes, etc., dresses appropriately for the school setting, and exhibits suitable and respectful written and oral communication **(Professionalism)**	90%	7%	3%	0%

Note: n (teachers) = 85.

There was strong agreement that candidates were active and responsive to classroom teachers' needs, and that teachers felt candidates were positive, respectful, and engaged. However, while there was strong agreement across that teachers felt candidates demonstrated an understanding of students' developmental needs, data suggest that some teacher candidates did not get an opportunity to interact with students on a level that addressed students' developmental needs. Overall, there was strong agreement across our sample suggesting that teachers felt candidates were professional.

Regarding overall professionalism and CMTs' desire to have the candidates return, 95% (n=81) of CMTs responded positively (Table 4).

Qualitative Results: Classroom Teachers

Results related to classroom teachers helped to answer the following question: What benefits, if any, do classroom teachers derive from hosting teacher candidates in the *Adopt-An-Apprentice* program? Teachers' comments illustrate several salient features of the program: Developing strong teacher candidates happens over time through supportive professional mentoring, but the payoff is enthusiastic students who are engaged and supported in their learning process. Mr. Kruser described the evolution of his teacher candidate:

He was very engaged with students. They absolutely loved working with Davis. He was very hands-on with students any time I needed. By mid-semester, I felt comfortable providing him with instruction and trusted him to assist students as I hoped.

Ms. Schlossing's description reveals a thoughtful, knowledgeable teacher candidate who was building connections between course content and the pedagogy of the classroom:

Brooke was reflective about the things that she saw in the classroom and how they related to what she was learning in her university classes. We were able to have conversations about the mathematics being taught by the student teacher. Brooke seems strong in her math knowledge for a first-year candidate and is eager to learn methods for effective instruction.

A third comment from Mr. Folgers captured the engagement a motivated candidate can bring to a classroom:

She [Elizabeth] was always engaged with the students. Even though a lot of her initial work was observation, when I was working on things with students – she jumped right in and helped. The students loved it when she was in the room!

Table 4. Results from CMTs' responses to survey

Professionalism	Extremely	Moderately	Neutral/Negative
CMT Response	75%	18%	5%
Would you want the candidate to return?	**Yes**	**Possibly**	**No**
CMT Response	81%	14%	4%

Note: n (teachers) = 85.

It was clear that it took time for teachers to build trust with their teacher candidates, but after forging that relationship, teachers were prepared to offer candidates more teaching responsibilities, and perceived candidates as both reflective practitioners and welcome additions to their classrooms.

Further Qualitative Results

Results helped to illuminate the phenomenon related to the question: What is the impact of grade band/subject-area field experiences on teacher candidates' conceptions of being a teacher? Candidates' and teachers' comments reveal the interactive learning that happens even in the less-than-glamorous tasks associated with teaching. Candidates reported that they learned about life as a teacher and had more data with which to make career choices. Chloe articulated a fundamental discovery about the importance of grading.

I found out the time it takes to grade everything! My teacher had me grade stuff every time I visited. While grading takes time, I know how important it is for my future students to get feedback about what their [sic] learning.

Teachers such as Mr. Spearing captured the value in having candidates face the realities of teaching early in their careers.

This program forces candidates to confront whether this is truly the profession for them, which is a great way to help young college students carve out a career path.

It was evident that both candidates and teachers perceived knowing the profession as an apprentice leveraged new knowledge that was not previously available without substantial fieldwork integrated into university courses. While the survey data and end-of-semester course feedback confirm that the *Adopt-An-Apprentice* field experience is widely viewed by candidates and classroom teachers as a value-added component to our introductory content classes, this study gives us a lens through which to assess our progress toward our overall conceptual goals, and address the ongoing logistical challenges and conceptual issues that require our attention for improvement.

IMPLICATIONS AND RECOMMENDATIONS

There are many aspects of the *Adopt-An-Apprentice Program* that need to be improved, but there are clearly two overarching aspects: logistical applications and CAEP core principle implementation.

Logistical Issues

Candidates' suggestions for program improvement clustered around seven issues: transportation, placement issues, more teaching opportunities, stronger mentoring, clearer orientation, more time in the classroom, and no improvement needed—although transportation was by far students' biggest concern. This is likely because busing problems detracted from quality time in classrooms getting opportunities to teach, co-teach, or interact with students.

Despite the massive conceptual and logistical reconfiguration that has led to the success of the *Adopt-An-Apprentice* program, there are still many challenges to be worked out regarding the suitable placement, transportation, communication procedures and site monitoring, and assessment of so many students and their field site CMTs. These logistical problem will need to be explored more systematically beyond the scope of this study. However, they hint at a deeper conceptual challenge: While these teachers are integral in establishing a shared vision, that shared vision does not yet exist. Ironing these things out will take stronger collaboration with school partners.

Engaging the CAEP Core Principles

Despite the researchers efforts to engage CAEP principles, three of the core action statements remain under-realized, and thus serve as a compass to guide next efforts: (1) Classroom mentor teachers should mentor candidates in ways that encourage candidates to be innovators, collaborators, and problem solvers; (2) Candidates, faculty, and classroom mentor teachers should develop an interactive professional community, and; (3) Building systematic partnerships with schools that have a shared vision and implementation plan for our teacher education program are central for developing candidates. While this program has begun to move novice teacher candidates in the direction of being innovators, collaborators, and problem solvers, we do not yet have a systematic or comprehensive approach across the *Adopt-An-Apprentice* program. In individual cases, candidates engage opportunities to use their research skills to assist the CMT in planning a future unit or lesson, or developing a more innovative approach to a topic. In some cases, our candidates have opportunities to collaborate with their CMTs by taking over small group interactions within the larger class dynamic. In the case of the literacy workshop, some candidates are being given the opportunity to be problem solvers, by applying their newly-honed skills of IRI pre-assessment and text analysis as they work with struggling readers, while others are not.

However, the systematic partnerships with schools, and the shared vision and implementation plans, have not been fully realized. We are moving in this direction. Recent planning retreats have paired campus faculty with some of our strongest lead teachers to frame the next steps in the shared vision and implementation of our teacher education program. So far, it has been driven predominantly by campus faculty. This shared vision will need to happen when we tackle the field component for the second year of the teacher education program.

NEXT STEPS FOR THE *ADOPT-AN-APPRENTICE* PROGRAM

There are several components necessary to the achievement of our CAEP goals. First, we need to strengthen existing school partnerships to better implement the *Adopt-An-Apprentice* first year field experience. Similar successful projects are built on "third space" models where university-based needs and school-based needs are met and balanced by developing a third space—shared design components to achieve shared goals (AACTE, 2018; Reischl, Khasnabis, & Karr, 2017). Second, we need to extend and adapt the clinical partnership model in the second and third years of candidates' coursework and field experiences. Program designers are currently in the process of framing goals for the second-year experience.

One way that we are making revisions is using the struggling reader workshop model to further train candidates to work more closely with individuals and small groups of students. This framework is evolving in response to calls from administrators asking for tutors. Third, involvement of campus faculty needs to be strengthened. The *Adopt-An-Apprentice* program was developed and piloted by a small dedicated team. Sustaining it will require a wider involvement in the day-to-day management of the project, in the regular classroom visits, and in the shared partnership model described above. Finally, while the program has already engaged in assessment, advisement, and intervention of these novice candidates—especially those struggling in field experiences—these elements will need to be integrated into the more comprehensive candidate support and intervention model used with our fourth-year methods and student teachers. And beyond intervention of candidates struggling in their field experiences, a stronger system for the recognition of outstanding teacher candidates needs to be developed.

CONCLUSION

Two key reciprocal features of the *Adopt-An-Apprentice* program illustrate its greatest strengths: (1) Students learned concepts and strategies in coursework and workshops that enabled them to be more useful in the classroom, and; (2) Students' real-world hands-on classroom experiences helped them understand the core concepts taught in their intro courses and workshops. Both the literacy and mathematics case studies illustrate the reciprocal nature of this partnership between university teacher education programs and field site schools. Candidates from both projects also captured the more interesting aspect of *Adopt-An-Apprentice*—that the experiences they brought back from the field deepened their understanding of course concepts.

It is important to note that the mathematics and literacy projects were built on two very different models—in-class exploration of mathematics SMCs and SMPs, and workshops in reading assessment. *Adopt-An-Apprentice* is not a one-size-fits-all approach, but a framework in which university faculty were empowered to follow their lines of research and expertise and deliver content and pedagogical tools to candidates that will serve the needs of teachers and students in their partner schools.

Adopt-An-Apprentice was developed within an experiential learning framework (Dewey, 1938) where learners construct deeper understandings of concepts through real-world scenarios guided by a mentor or more learned peer (Vygotsky, 1978). The program was also developed in part to address the NCATE Blue Ribbon Panel's *Ten Design Principles* (NCATE, 2010) and AACTE's new *pivot* challenge (AACTE, 2018). Program designers set out to have teacher candidates be of service to classroom teachers within a framework that allowed them to collect and analyze data for program improvement. These components are firmly in place and can evolve as program needs, goals, and vision evolve. Program designers also set out to foster candidates alongside their classroom mentor teachers to be innovators, collaborators, and problem solvers. Another goal was to build systematic partnerships with schools that engage a shared vision and implementation plan. These last two components of our teacher education program will become the focus of the next steps in program development.

ACKNOWLEDGMENT

We are deeply thankful to Lance Kruse for his work on developing the surveys, and to all of our teachers and administrators in our partner districts. This research received no specific grant from any funding agency in the public, commercial, or not-for-profit sectors.

REFERENCES

American Association of Colleges for Teacher Education. (2018). *A pivot toward clinical practice, its lexicon, and the renewal of educator preparation: A report of the AACTE clinical practice commission.* Washington, DC: AACTE.

American Mathematical Society. (2012). *The mathematical education of teachers II.* Retrieved from http://www.cbmsweb.org/archive/MET2/met2.pdf

Association of Mathematics Teacher Educators. (2017). *Standards for preparing teachers of mathematics: Executive summary.* Retrieved from https://amte.net/sites/default/files/SPTM_ExecSummary.pdf

Baeton, M., & Simons, M. (2016). Innovative Field Experiences in Teacher Education: Student-Teachers and Mentors as Partners in Teaching. *International Journal on Teaching and Learning in Higher Education*, *28*(1), 38–51.

Ball, D. L. (2000). Bridging practices: Intertwining content and pedagogy in teaching and learning to teach. *Journal of Teacher Education*, *51*(3), 241–247. doi:10.1177/0022487100051003013

Ball, D. L., & Forzani, F. M. (2011). Building a common core for learning to teach, and connecting professional learning to practice. *American Educator*, *35*(2), 17–21, 38–39.

Bandura, A. (1997). *Self-efficacy: The exercise of control.* New York: W. H. Freeman and Company.

Bostic, J., Matney, G., & Sondergeld, T. (in press). A lens on teachers' promotion of the Standards for Mathematical Practice. *Investigations in Mathematics Learning.* doi:10.1080/19477503.2017.1379894

Boyd, D. J., Grossman, P. L., Lankford, H., Loeb, S., & Wyckoff, J. (2009). Teacher preparation and student achievement. *Educational Evaluation and Policy Analysis*, *31*(4), 416–440. doi:10.3102/0162373709353129

Britzman, D. (2000). Teacher education in the confusion of our times. *Journal of Teacher Education*, *51*(3), 200–205. doi:10.1177/0022487100051003007

Cochran-Smith, M., Villegas, A. M., Abrams, L., Chavez-Moreno, L., Mills, T., & Stern, R. (2015). Critiquing Teacher Preparation Research: An Overview of the Field, Part II. *Journal of Teacher Education*, *66*(2), 109–121. doi:10.1177/0022487114558268

Cochran-Smith, M., & Zeichner, K. (Eds.). (2005). *Studying teacher education: The Report of the AERA Panel on Research and Teacher Education.* Washington, DC: American Educational Research Association.

Coffey, H. (2010). *"They* taught *me"*: The benefits of early community-based field experiences in teacher education. *Teaching and Teacher Education*, *26*(2), 335–342. doi:10.1016/j.tate.2009.09.014

Council for the Accreditation of Educator Preparation. (2013, June). *The CAEP Standards.* Retrieved from http://caepnet.org/standards/

Council of Chief State School Officers. (2010). *Common core state standards initiative: Common core state standards for mathematics.* Washington, DC: National Governors Association Center for Best Practices and Council of Chief State School Officers. Retrieved from http://www.corestandards.org

Council of Chief State School Officers. (2011). *Interstate Teacher Assessment and Support Consortium (InTASC) Model Core Teaching Standards: A Resource for State Dialogue.* Washington, DC: Author.

Cresswell, J. (2012). *Educational research: Planning, conducting, and evaluating quantitative and qualitative research* (4th ed.). Boston: Pearson.

Danielson, C. (2013). *The framework for teaching evaluation instrument.* The Danielson Group.

Darling-Hammond, L. (2006). Constructing 21st-century teacher education. *Journal of Teacher Education, 57*(3), 300–314. doi:10.1177/0022487105285962

Darling-Hammond, L. (2010). Teacher education and the American future. *Journal of Teacher Education, 61*(1-2), 35–47. doi:10.1177/0022487109348024

Darling-Hammond, L., Chung, R., & Farlow, F. (2002). Variation in Teacher Preparation: How Well Do Different Pathways Prepare Teachers to Teach? *Journal of Teacher Education, 53*(4), 286–302. doi:10.1177/0022487102053004002

Dewey, T. (1938). *Experience and education.* Collier Books.

Fennell, F. (2015, February). *Mathematics teacher education: Normal schools to now.* Paper presented at the meeting of the Association of Mathematics Teacher Educators conference, Orlando, FL.

Fry, E. (1977). Fry's readability graph: Clarifications, validity, and extensions to level 17. *Journal of Reading, 21*(3), 242–252.

Hatch, A. (2002). *Doing qualitative research in education settings.* Albany, NY: State University of New York Press.

Heck, T. W. (2013, Nov. 1). *A new student teaching model for pairing interns with clinical teachers.* Retrieved from https://www.edutopia.org/blog/co-teaching-internship-model-teresa-heck

Huling, L. (1998). *Early field experiences in Teacher Education.* Washington, DC: ERIC Clearinghouse on Teacher Education.

Jones, M., Hobbs, L., Kenny, J., Campbell, C., Chittleborough, G., Gilbert, A., ... Redman, C. (2016). Successful university-school partnerships: An interpretive framework to inform partnership practice. *Teaching and Teacher Education, 60*, 108–120. doi:10.1016/j.tate.2016.08.006

Massey, D. D., & Lewis, J. (2011). Learning from the "Little Guys": What do middle and high school preservice teachers learn from tutoring elementary students? *Literacy Research and Instruction, 50*(2), 120–132. doi:10.1080/19388071003725705

Meyer, S. J. (2016). *Understanding field experiences in traditional teacher preparation programs in Missouri (REL 2016–145).* Washington, DC: U.S. Department of Education, Institute of Education Sciences, National Center for Education Evaluation and Regional Assistance, Regional Educational Laboratory Central. Retrieved from http://ies.ed.gov/ncee/edlabs

National Council for Accreditation of Teacher Education. (2010). *Transforming teacher education through clinical practice: A national strategy to prepare effective teachers. Report of the blue ribbon panel on clinical preparation and partnerships for improved student learning*. Washington, DC: National Council for Accreditation of Teacher Education.

National Council of Teachers of Mathematics. (2000). *Principles and standards for school mathematics*. Reston, VA: Author.

National Council of Teachers of Mathematics. (2007). Mathematics teaching today: Improving practice. In T. Martin (Ed.), *Improving student learning* (2nd ed.). Reston, VA: National Council of Teachers of Mathematics.

National Council of Teachers of Mathematics. (2014). *Principles to action: Ensuring mathematical success for all*. Reston, VA: Author.

Ness, M. K. (2008). Supporting secondary readers: When teachers provide the "What," not the "How.". *American Secondary Education, 37*(1), 80–95.

Piaget, J. (1954). *The construction of reality in the child*. Basic Books. doi:10.1037/11168-000

Plucker, J. M. (2010). Baiting the reading hook. *Educational Leadership, 68*(2), 58–63.

Reischl, C., Khasnabis, D., & Karr, K. (2017, May). Cultivating a school-university partnership for teacher learning. *Phi Delta Kappan*, 48-53.

Richardson, V., & Kile, R. S. (1999). The use of videocases in teacher education. In M.L. Lundberg, B. Levin, & H. Herrington (Eds.), Who Learns from Cases and How? The Research Base for Teaching With Cases. Jossey Bass.

Roe, B., & Burns, P. (2011). *Informal Reading Inventory: Preprimer to twelfth grade* (8th ed.). Belmont, CA: Wadsworth.

Sharp, S., & Turner, W. (2008). Sustaining relationships in teacher education partnerships: The possibilities, practices and challenges of a school-university partnership, preparing teachers for the future. *International Journal of Learning, 15*(5), 9–14. doi:10.18848/1447-9494/CGP/v15i05/45772

Spector, J. (2005). How reliable are informal reading inventories? *Psychology in the Schools, 42*(6), 593–603. doi:10.1002/pits.20104

Stufflebeam, D. L. (2003). The CIPP Model for Evaluation. In T. Kellaghan & D. Stufflebeam (Eds.), *International Handbook of Educational Evaluation*. Dordrecht, Netherlands: Springer. doi:10.1007/978-94-010-0309-4_4

Vygotsky, L. (1978). *Mind in society*. Boston, MA: Harvard University Press.

Weinstein, C. S. (1990). Prospective elementary teachers' beliefs about teaching: Implications for teacher education. *Teaching and Teacher Education, 6*(3), 279–290. doi:10.1016/0742-051X(90)90019-2

Weiss, M., Pellegrino, A., & Brigham, F. (2017). Practicing collaboration in teacher preparation: Effects of learning by doing together. *Teacher Education and Special Education, 40*(1), 65–76. doi:10.1177/0888406416655457

Wideen, M., Mayer-Smith, J., & Moon, B. (1998). A critical analysis of the research on learning to teach: Making the case for an ecological perspective on inquiry. *Review of Educational Research*, *68*(2), 130–178. doi:10.3102/00346543068002130

Wilson, S. R., Floden, R. E., & Ferrini-Mundy, J. (2001). *Teacher preparation research: Current knowledge, gaps, and recommendations*. Center for the Study of Teaching and Policy, University of Washington.

Zeichner, K. (2010). Rethinking the connections between campus courses and field experiences in college and university-based teacher education. *Journal of Teacher Education*, *61*(1-2), 89–99. doi:10.1177/0022487109347671

APPENDIX

Apprentice Activities Checklist: Learning Activities for BGSU Apprentice Teachers in School Sites (Suggested by Classroom Teachers!)

BGSU Apprentice: _____

Classroom Teacher: _____

Teachers: Our apprentice teachers learn the most when they are actively involved, assisting you and your students! Please mark and share with your apprentice the following list of tasks you would like him or her to be responsible for during his/her time in your school and classroom. Thank you!!

_____ Read over a lesson to be taught in the near future. List or describe possible obstacles the students might encounter during the lesson. How might these obstacles be addressed/overcome?

_____ Grade and record papers/tally most missed questions.

_____ Work with a small group of students to help them better understand ideas from a homework assignment.

_____ Look online for a lesson through ohiorc.org that is on the same topic the teacher is teaching.

_____ Take notes for absent student/take responsibility for collecting and getting missed material to absent students/work with absent student to help with missed content while gone.

_____ Shadow one particular student through entire day; record similarities and differences from class to class.

_____ Observe 2 or more teachers teaching the same topic and record similarities and differences.

_____ Pass out, collect, organize, and/or review student papers.

_____ Design a new seating arrangement after becoming familiar with the students / design different grouping structures for different purposes

_____ Select one student and record their behavior once every 60 seconds; attend to and describe the level of engagement at each interval

_____ If the teacher desires, chart his/her interaction with students. Tally interaction between males verses females, etc. Look for patterns.

_____ Similarly, with teacher approval, tally who is speaking every 60 seconds: teacher or student?

_____ Identify and tally type of teacher talk: directive, reinforcement, question, praise, etc.

_____ Read one of the Teachers SLO's and write recommendations on how students might achieve it.

_____ Complete an OTES walk-through check sheet for one or more teachers.

_____ Using an OTES rubric, highlight each piece of evidence for a complete lesson.

_____ Create alternate form of a quiz or test / create alternative assessment with modifications for a specific IEP.

_____ Draw the room layout including student desks, teacher desks, windows, shelves, white/blackboards, storage areas, etc. Consider and comment on changes that might improve the learning environment.

_____ Choose a material to create or improve for the teacher, such as poster, game, handout, display power point, flash cards, adaptive material, sample project, interactive white board activity.

_____ Create a bulletin board.

_____ Walk around the room, observe students working, and write down the names of students whose work should be shared with the whole class.

_____ Create an exit or entrance ticket for a lesson. Analyze the data and make a recommendation.

_____ Analyze test data for the classroom teacher.

_____ Research an upcoming lesson topic for the classroom teacher.

_____ Create a PowerPoint or Smart Board presentation on a topic requested by the classroom teacher.

_____ Lead a class discussion, plan a brief learning activity, or co-plan and teach with the classroom teacher.

_____ Other:_____

Apprentice Candidate Survey

Please answer this brief survey regarding the field experience(s) associated with your Introduction to Math, Science, Social Studies, and/or Language Arts courses as well as the Introduction to Education course.

1. In what program area are you enrolled? (i.e. Inclusive Early Childhood, Middle Childhood, Adolescent and Young Adult, etc.)
2. What is you major or concentration areas. (i.e. Early Childhood, Integrated Language Arts, Math, Science, Social Studies, etc.)
3. Which introductory class(es) did you take (please check all)?
4. When did your field experience begin?
5. In what school where were you placed?
6. Were you able to observe teaching in your field experience?
7. Were you able to participate in teaching-type activities?(i.e. .....)
8. Please identify the types of teaching activities in which you were engaged.
9. If you were not participating in teaching-type activities, what activities were you performing in your field placement?
10. What benefits did you derive from the field experience?
11. What suggestions do you have for improving the field experience(s) associated with these classes? (Please be specific to which course you are referring to.)

Apprentice Classroom Mentor Teacher (CMT) Survey

BGSU teacher candidates at all levels are expected to demonstrate professionalism in the following domains, which are aligned with InTASC Core Teaching Standards (April 2013), as well as Charlotte Danielson's (2013) Framework for Teaching:

- Planning and professionalism
- Maintaining a positive classroom presence/environment
- Instruction (where possible)
- Professional responsibilities

We encourage you to provide feedback on the BGSU teacher candidate(s) working in your classroom, so we can offer appropriate guidance to these young students. We value your input!!

1. Candidate Name
2. Teacher Name
3. School
4. Semester/Term
5. Subject and Grade Level
6. Domain I. Planning and Preparation. The teacher candidate prepares and completes tasks, as assigned by the classroom teacher, in a timely and high-quality fashion.
7. Domain II. The Classroom Environment. The teacher candidate demonstrates positivity and appropriate respect in all interactions with school students and staff, regardless of race, language, ability, physical characteristics, etc., and actively engages with the classroom teacher, actively engages with students, seeks to assist and provide service in whatever ways needed.
8. Domain III. Instruction. (May not be applicable for Year 1 and Year 2 students). The teacher candidate (if instructing individuals, small groups, or the whole class) is knowledgeable and engages appropriately with students and demonstrates initial understanding of students' developmental levels.
9. Domain IV. Professional Responsibilities. The teacher candidate attends regularly and punctually, as required, communicates clearly, promptly, and accurately in reporting absences, schedule changes, etc., dresses appropriately for the school setting, and exhibits suitable and respectful written and oral communication.
10. The teacher candidate uses appropriate language and gestures, displays receptiveness to feedback on performance, seeks to implement suggestions, demonstrates ethical and legal use of technology and social media, safeguards confidential information regarding students, families, faculty, and staff, displays integrity and ethical conduct, and complies with school and district regulations.
11. Overall rating of candidate's professionalism/Comments:
12. Has this teacher candidate's performance been such that you would welcome him/her back into your classroom at some point in the future?
13. Comments on candidate's professionalism:
14. Comments or suggestions for program improvement:

Chapter 17
A National Effort to Integrate Field Experiences Into Secondary Mathematics Methods Courses

Jan A. Yow
University of South Carolina, USA

Patrice Waller
California State University – Fullerton, USA

Belinda Edwards
Kennesaw State University, USA

ABSTRACT

This chapter shares the experience and preliminary findings from a national collaboration to improve secondary mathematics teacher preparation programs in the United States. Specifically, the chapter focuses on a research group tasked with strengthening field experiences into methods courses. Two modules are shared that a group of methods instructors have developed and are implementing in their courses. Findings from the first module are explained with implications for continued module development. These findings show the impact of the module on mentor teachers as well as the benefit the module has demonstrated in relation to the preservice teacher-mentor teacher relationship. Challenges and lessons learned from this national effort are also included.

MATHEMATICS TEACHER EDUCATION PARTNERSHIP AND THE NETWORKED IMPROVEMENT COMMUNITY MODEL

United States (US) public school districts often face a shortage of highly qualified mathematics teachers who are proficient in both the content and practice standards of the Common Core State Standards for Mathematics (CCSS-M) (National Governors Association Center for Best Practices & Council of Chief State School Officers, 2010). The Mathematics Teacher Education Partnership (MTE-Partnership) was

DOI: 10.4018/978-1-5225-6249-8.ch017

formed to address the significant national shortage of well-prepared secondary mathematics teachers who can support their students in learning mathematics and achieving the state and national standards for mathematics. Organized using the Networked Improvement Committee (NIC) model, the MTE-Partnership consists of institutions of higher education, k-12 schools, school districts, and other stakeholder organizations with an aim to build a national dialogue around guiding principles for the preparation of secondary mathematics teachers through coordinated research, development, and implementation efforts to promote best practices in mathematics teaching and learning (Martin & Gobstein, 2015).

NIC is an "intentionally designed social organization" that focuses on a specific educational issue, the system that produced the issue, and a network of members (Bryk, Gomez, & Grunow, 2011, p. 10) who work collaboratively to address the educational issue or idea. NIC is especially powerful because it is organized around improvement science principles that include: 1) focusing on a well specified common aim; 2) understanding and specifying the problem or issue that needs to be addressed, the system that produces it, and a shared theory of practice improvement; 3) being disciplined by the rigor of improvement science and measuring for accountability and scale, and; 4) networking/coordinating to accelerate the development of interventions and carefully examining variation in educational contexts. Each member in the NIC actively contributes to improving an educational issue.

A major focus for the MTE-Partnership is the work of Research Action Clusters (RACs), smaller sub-groups focused on specific areas of research concern. Institutions within each RAC are developing, implementing, and revising interventions or modules that are created using a Plan-Do-Study-Act (PDSA) model. At the heart of the iterative PDSA model is data. For example, after identifying an appropriate plan of intervention and carrying out the plan, NIC members study the data to assess progress to determine if changes to the intervention should be made. Each cycle is essentially a mini-experiment where observed outcomes are compared to prediction, as discrepancies between the observation and the prediction become a major source of learning. As the interventions are shown to be successful, they are made available to other teams for implementation and adaptations that are needed in a local context. The overall process of change is data driven, intentional and coordinated, which leads to accelerated propagation of the intervention, module, or educational improvement (Bryk, Gomez, Grunow, 2011; Martin & Gobstein, 2015).

This chapter focuses on the work of the RAC focused on enhancing field experiences in secondary mathematics methods courses. The authors begin by sharing existing literature related to field experiences, methods courses and mentor teachers. Then, a description of the journey to improve field experiences for methods course students follows. The authors include examples of learning modules with key foci on field experience components and close by sharing next steps in this journey.

FIELD EXPERIENCES, METHODS COURSES, AND MENTOR TEACHERS

Methods coursework is the hallmark of effective secondary mathematics teacher education programs. It provides preservice teachers with the opportunity to develop pedagogical strategies to facilitate mathematics learning, and reflect on the role of a mathematics teacher in helping students learn (Grossman, Hammerness, & McDonald, 2009). However, there is great variation in structure, instructional methods, assignments, and activities covered within methods courses (Kidd, 2008; Taylor & Ronau, 2006; Yee, Otten, & Taylor, 2017). There is no common professional curriculum for teacher education; and while this is not entirely problematic, variation in teacher preparation curriculum makes it potentially difficult to evaluate the effects of teacher preparation on beginning teachers' practice. Though there is a considerable amount of variation in structure and philosophy within teacher education programs across the United States (US), they all tend to emphasize the importance of pedagogical content knowledge and field experiences (Youngs & Hong, 2013).

There is common agreement among mathematics teacher educators on the importance of providing opportunities for preservice teachers to learn pedagogy that are grounded in teaching practice within a field experience (Forzani, 2014; Ball, Sleep, Boerst, Bass, 2009). Such an experience would be a critical component of teacher preparation in developing effective teachers if the clinical field experiences are interwoven with and supports methods coursework (Darling-Hammond, 2014). Multiple studies (e.g., Evertson, Hawley, & Zlotnick, 1985; Wilson, Floden, and Ferrini-Mundy, 2001; Zeichner, 2010) have linked clinical field experiences with successful classroom practice and student achievement. To prepare effective teachers for 21st century classrooms, the National Council for Accreditation of Teacher Education [NCATE[1]] (2010) recommends a "clinically based preparation for prospective teachers, which fully integrates content, pedagogy, and professional coursework around a core of clinical experiences" (p. 8). However, in many teacher education programs across the US, the clinical field experience and methods course is taught in isolation.

Curriculum in secondary math methods courses and coursework has long been seen as diverse. Ball and colleagues (2009) argued that the lack of a shared professional curriculum for teacher preparation means that "student teachers' learning opportunities reflect the orientations and expertise of their instructors and cooperating teacher" rather than "common agreements about the preparation required for initial practice" (p. 459). In an effort to create these common agreements and streamline secondary mathematics methods courses, scholars have created secondary methods textbooks (Goos, Vale, & Stillman, 2017; Posamentier & Smith, 2009) and examined topics within courses that are common across syllabi. Kidd (2008) conducted an analysis of syllabi of methods courses across the California State University and University of California systems and found that the foci of these courses vary broadly. However, some of the common elements included lesson and unit planning, readings, research, reflections, technology, manipulatives, and mini-lesson microteaching among others. Otten et al. (2015) surveyed 116 methods instructors and found that secondary methods instructors around the US valued key specific "touchstone" topics and activities (p. 773) similar to those referenced in Kidd's syllabi analysis. Ultimately, these studies reveal that the structure and content being taught in secondary methods courses appears to vary widely.

While research has shown that clinical field experiences are most effective when interwoven with coursework, little is known about the impact integrating secondary mathematics methods coursework with a clinical field experience has on pre-service teacher (PSTs) learning to teach mathematics in the context of enacting the standards for mathematical practice and mathematics teaching practices. In her literature review related to clinical field experiences connected to methods courses, Strutchens (2017) found evidence to suggest that the clinical experience plays an important role in enabling PSTs' to improve their lesson planning and teaching strategies through reflection (Nguyen, Dekker, & Goedhart, 2008) and growth in understanding mathematics for teaching (Cavey & Berenson, 2005). Though these studies occurred in the context of a methods course, the PSTs did not enact their lessons or interact with K-12 students during the field experience. Further, the focus of these studies were limited to one program and not enacted across multiple programs over multiple iterations, which is a focus of our work.

Clift and Brady (2005) shared findings about additional research related to connecting mathematics methods courses and field experiences. Clift and Brady (2005) found that "enacting a desirable practice is more likely when there is coherence between the methods courses and the fieldwork" (p. 319). Such coherence should include understanding how PSTs' mathematics teaching and learning develops when interacting with students in the classroom. Though there exists some research in the area of elementary mathematics methods involving embedded field experiences (Downey & Cobbs, 2007), less is known about the field experiences of PSTs' practice at the secondary level. Thus, this work seeks to fill the gap in the knowledge base around integrating field experiences into the secondary mathematics methods coursework across multiple teacher education programs.

Improving the clinical practice experience is a key component for improving teaching, learning, and academic achievement in P-12 schools (National Research Council [NRC], 2010). As such, many teacher preparation programs across the US are focused on strengthening and improving their programs by partnering with local schools and school districts to integrate mathematics coursework, methods coursework, and practitioner knowledge. Establishing strategic partnerships with local schools provides opportunities for PSTs to enact the mathematics teaching practices and facilitate learning using the standards for mathematics practice within an authentic educational setting with the support of their mentor teacher (Loughran, 2002). Zeichner (2010) speaks to the hopeful transitions of many university-based teacher education programs exploring better ways to partner with communities, schools, and mentor teachers (MTs) in which their PSTs will spend time at school sites learning the methods of teaching.

An additional layer of consideration when examining field experiences in method courses is the MTs with whom PSTs work. There has been a recent call for teacher preparation programs to be more involved and intentional in the preparation of MTs (Gareis & Grant, 2015; Hoffman, Wetzel, Maloch, Greeter, Taylor, DeJulio, & Vlach, 2015). MTs own perspectives of effective teaching greatly impact the ways in which they work and critique interns (Goodwin, Roegman, & Reagan, 2016). PST identities are influenced by the nature of the relationship they form with their MTs. PST confidence in teaching styles and teaching abilities can be both positively and negatively affected by their MTs (Izadinia, 2015). Therefore, creating spaces and structure for ways that MTs and PSTs talk about teaching can be helpful (Lawley, Moore, & Smajic, 2014). Tasks where MTs and PSTs can participate together as learners support co-understanding of research-based practices such as inquiry learning (Gunckel& Wood, 2015). Methods courses also provide a potential space for these co-learning activities to occur (Wood & Turner, 2014).

While efforts to explore math methods coursework have provided a general idea of what is taking place in methods courses, they have failed to provide a common practice lens for secondary methods curricula nationally. Through the MTE-Partnership clinical experiences RAC, methods instructors from colleges and universities across the country have come together to share resources and create research based modules that help to better define topics and design common activities that model high leverage practices in the secondary math classroom. In this work, the authors will draw upon the most highly valued methods activities, related to the process standards and mathematics teaching practices (NCTM, 2000) and standards for mathematics practice (Common Core State Standards for Mathematics [CCSS-M], 2010) in an examination of the influence of implementing common field-based methods tasks across multiple teacher preparation sites. Research has shown that there is a need to develop a more systematic preparation of teachers in the development of common assignments/modules that all PSTs experience as practice becomes a major component of teacher preparation (Ball, Sleep, Boerst, & Bass, 2009; Grossman, Hammerness, & McDonald, 2009). The MTE-Partnership group has developed a set of modules around the standards for mathematical practice. These modules are defined as a set of practices that focus on the mathematical teaching practices that are fundamental to supporting student learning. While there will be some variation in the implementation of modules within RAC members across the country, application of the NIC model will enable testing, comparison, and refinement of module activities before sharing with the broader teacher education audience (Martin & Gobstein, 2015).

BEGINNINGS

As mentioned earlier, as part of the larger MTE-Partnership initiative, the authors are a part of a RAC on Clinical Experiences. The sub-RAC's focus is to strengthen field-based experiences in connection with secondary mathematics methods courses. Central to the MTE-Partnership mission is the importance of the inclusion of school-based partners in the preparation of teachers. To be a part of the initial MTE-Partnership, each local "partnership team" had to "include a lead institution that is a member of APLU; at least one K-12 school partner; and other partners, which in many cases include additional colleges and universities from their region" (Martin & Gobstein, 2015). Some partnerships include multiple institutions of higher education as well as multiple school districts as part of their local partnership team. In some cases, additional partners include local teacher professional organizations, technical or community colleges.

For example, the University of South Carolina Midlands Mathematics Teacher Education Partnership (USC – Midlands MTE-Partnership) included the University of South Carolina, Midlands Technical College, Richland County School District One, and Richland County School District Two. As the USC – Midlands MTE-Partnership developed, each secondary mathematics district coordinator from the two partner districts was invited to join weekly methods course meetings. They joined in on discussions about readings and offered invaluable practical insight to apply topics being discussed in the course into their everyday work with mathematics teachers in schools.

As partnerships developed and more focused work began, the initial group began with four methods instructors from four institutions. The sub-RAC has grown to include thirteen methods instructors across ten institutions. The group also has methods instructors from other MTE-Partnerships who are not a part of the core planning group learning from and implementing the work, which will be explained later in the chapter.

The charge as part of the NIC model was to collectively develop small, doable changes in methods courses to better incorporate field based partners. The group began by discussing how current methods courses worked: foundational readings, salient tasks, and current field experiences already embedded within the courses. The group soon realized that a common challenge all faced was the implementation of the Common Core State Standards in Mathematics (National Governors Association Center for Best Practices & Council of Chief State School Officers, 2010). The goal was to improve methods courses by better engaging clinical partners, but soon realized several challenges.

CHALLENGES

As a group of diverse colleagues from across the nation, the group quickly learned the challenges of trying to talk across enacted methods courses. The differences in individual state and programmatic requirements initially seemed daunting, but the group worked to focus on the similarities across the methods courses. As the group discussed their respective courses, they outlined:

1. Who took these courses? Some programs were undergraduate while others were graduate programs. In undergraduate programs, some students were underclassmen while others were upperclassmen. Some programs have a methods course that serves both middle and high school mathematics PSTs while others have methods courses that solely serve each group – one methods course for middle school mathematics PSTs and one methods courses for high school mathematics PSTs. Some states have grades 7-12 licensure only while other states have grades 6-8 and grades 9-12 licensure.
2. Where are these courses placed in the program? Some methods courses represented in our group were placed early and as initial courses in programs while others were placed later and situated as advanced education courses.
3. What Standards each state was using? When this work began, CCSS-M was just being implemented and several state governments were in the process of deciding if and to what extent they would implement CCSS-M. Some states had decided to decline the CCSS-M and develop their own Standards. Since most of the initial participating partner states were using CCSS-M, it was decided to focus on this set of Standards.
4. What field experiences were already embedded? The methods courses included in the initial group of participants ranged from having no integrated field experiences associated with the course to having substantial integration of field-based experiences embedded in the coursework.

Much of the initial group meetings were spent simply trying to better understand one another's methods courses so as to determine how best to work collectively to implement or improve the field experiences within the courses. As CCSS-M was a new set of standards in which this group, students, and MTs were having to engage and understand, it was decided the first charge was to develop tasks that enable this collective group to collaboratively engage in unpacking the CCSS-M.

Just as the group had learned from initial meetings, the group learned the challenges associated with developing a common task emphasizing field experiences across courses, states, and evolving Standards. The decision was made there was a need for methods students to be systematically immersed in the CCSS-M *before* enacting a task within their field experience, along with the need to develop common measures with which to judge the effectiveness of the task. Finally, there was a need to find a common location to house measures such that both the whole group and individual campuses could use the data.

A final challenge, which is also seen as a strength, is the continuing evolution of the RAC partners. As mentioned earlier, the work began with a smaller group and the sub-RAC has now tripled in size. This work began as a group of four methods instructors across four institutions that initially piloted and revised the initial task (Module 1 further described in the subsequent section). The growth from four to thirteen instructors (with additional methods instructors not a part of the core RAC planning group also implementing the tasks) has forced the need to think about how to keep the momentum of the initial group moving while also capitalizing on the knowledge and expertise added to the group as membership grows. The challenges of how best to disseminate task implementations and learn from a growing group of users continue to be addressed. The strength of having a larger number of implementers as well as a broader group from which to learn is invaluable. As more members join the sub-RAC, additional Modules continue to be developed and available for use.

FIELD-BASED MODULE EXAMPLES

Two modules are presented below. They are not designed to be used consecutively but could be used as such. The goal of Module 1 (Unpacking CCSS-M in the Field) is to deeply familiarize PSTs and MTs with the CCSS-M Standards for Mathematical Practices (SMPs), eight areas of expertise all mathematics students should develop (National Governors Association Center for Best Practices & Council of Chief State School Officers, 2010). The goal of Module 2 (Lesson Implementation in the Field) is to develop and implement a lesson plan based on a research-based teaching protocol.

Module 1: Unpacking CCSS-M in the Field

The first module has been implemented at eight locations across the nation and consists of three parts. The authors will focus heavily on Part 3 since that is the part deeply connected to field experiences, but will briefly describe Parts 1 and 2 so readers get a sense of the scaffolding that occurs before PSTs take the task into the field. Part 1 asks students to identify habits mathematics students have formed by the 10th grade. These habits tend to be negative habits such as *a lack of persistence when engaging in problem solving*. PSTs then spend time unpacking the SMPs. By revisiting the initial habits list and comparing it to the SMPs, PSTs realize the disconnect between observed students' habits and the habits the SMPs demand. Figures 1 and 2 depict two digital posters created by students around the SMPs.

Students provided profound reflections while unpacking the SMPs. Students were asked "What new habits will students develop if they are to become proficient in these practices?" One student stated:

Figure 1. Digital Poster of Students' interpretation of SMP 2

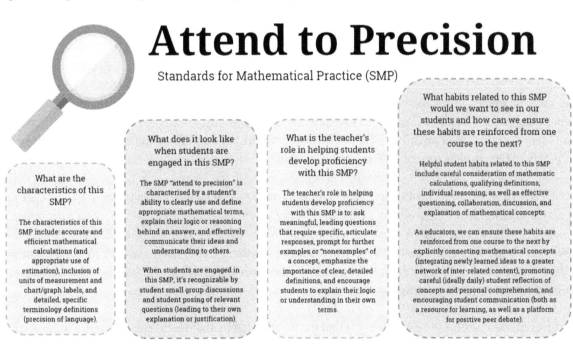

Figure 2. Digital Poster of Students' interpretation of SMP 4

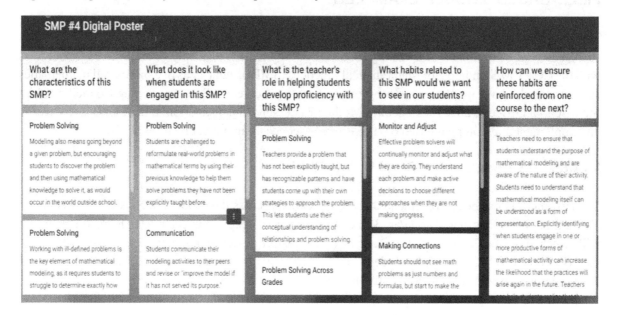

As you work your way through the SMPs you begin to see how they interact, overlay and intertwine some of their characteristics, skill expectations and math productivity. In a sense, this is what students need to also develop as a mathematical learner. The days of rigid, rule based, algorithmic processing are over. Does that mean the old learning is wiped away; No! Instead, with CCSS, math is to be presented as fluid, evolving, and dynamic. As a result, students need to be open to exploring ideas, concepts, and patterns in which there will be successes and mishaps that help to shape, contour and define conceptual understanding of mathematics. Additionally, as students explore mathematics they begin to develop connections to traditional and alternate ways of thinking and global concepts.

During these reflections PSTs also expressed the challenges that they might face when implementing these practices. Moving away from the traditional teacher facilitated classroom to a more student centered approach was emphasized. PSTs expressed their familiarity with the teacher centered approach and identified that other practices were out of their comfort zone and for some even beyond their scope of practice. One middle school PST reflected:

I think one aspect of these proficiencies that will be hard for me personally to implement will be allowing students to struggle with a problem. I currently work as a private tutor, and since parents are paying by the hour, our lessons tend to be mostly direct instruction—I tell the student how to do a problem, and we practice it until the student has mastered the concept. We don't really leave time for the student to find a strategy on his/her own. So I think it's going to be a bit of a paradigm shift, letting students stumble around until they find an answer on their own.

Overall, there seems to be a consensus that the positive habits that math teachers desire to see in their classrooms were evident in multiple ways in the SMPs. A student summarized:

I am noticing that a lot of the habits and practices we would hope to see in students and teachers overlap across several SMP's. This is encouraging and helpful to see how all of these ideas are interconnected and build upon on another.

Part 2 of Module 1 involves students completing an inquiry-based lesson that emphasizes select SMPs. The methods instructor plays the role of "teacher" as the PSTs complete the inquiry activity as "students." The group then discusses what the teacher did during the lesson to encourage student develop of the SMPs. The next step is to watch select video clips from the same inquiry-based lesson enacted with high school students (Inside Mathematics, 2017) for additional evidence of how a teacher uses instruction to facilitate the SMPs.

In Part 3, PSTs take a common video excerpt from the *Inside Mathematics* lesson and watch that video lesson with their MTs in their field placements, which vary across sites. One site, for example, has a field placement co-requisite course alongside the methods course, where PSTs spend at least 10 hours a week in the field implementing lesson plans and tasks from the methods course with an additional 20% of the methods course spent in classrooms. PSTs and their MTs use the *Engaging in the Mathematical Practices Look Fors* rubric (Elementary Mathematics Specialists & Teacher Leader Project, 2012), in addition to discussion prompts below to serve as a lens while watching the clip and a guide for their subsequent discussion:

1. What were the students doing? What content were they discussing? How would you describe their level of engagement?
2. Using the "Students" column of the Mathematical Practices Look-Fors, read through the Indicators for each of the SMPs and discuss whether these characterize any of the interactions from the video. Provide specific evidence from the video to support your claims (Note: some SMPs may not be demonstrated in this video clip)
3. What can you take-away from this clip that could impact your own instruction?

At one site, PSTs complete this exercise twice as they are in two different placements during the semester. The group then returns as a whole group to discuss the outcomes of the discussions with their mentor teachers and how the overall module will impact their own implementation of the SMPs.

PST Responses Based on the Field Work

PSTs provided a variety of responses for the aforementioned questions and their responses are described below.

1. What were the students doing? What content were they discussing? How would you describe their level of engagement?

PST responses to this prompt offered explanations of the students and the content in the video. PSTs wrote, for example,

students are attempting to find ways to make different quadrilaterals by experimenting with the diagonals. When the diagonals are in specific positions it creates specific characteristics in the quadrilaterals.

PSTs also noted that students in the video were "highly engaged with the material. We know this because they were challenging what they knew and forming new ideas about the material while learning from their peers." Field Work write-ups also demonstrated that PSTs and MTs talked about how they may try to emulate similar levels of engagement in their own classrooms. Specifically, they spoke to the need to "practice students' engagement with the material and motivation to learn new content" to help prepare their own students for similar high level engagement in content.

2.   Using the "Students" column of the Mathematical Practices Look-Fors, read through the Indicators for each of the SMPs and discuss whether these characterize any of the interactions from the video. Provide specific evidence from the video to support your claims (Note: some SMPs may not be demonstrated in this video clip)

PST responses to this prompt indicated discussion around multiple SMPs with their MTs. PSTs and MTs "looked at making sense of problems and persevere in solving them" and agreed there were "multiple entry points in the activity, as exemplified by the students opening the conversation to all members of the group by asking things like, 'Which quadrilaterals did you find?'". They also discussed the SMPs involving "making conjectures and planning a solution pathway" and "their attention to precision: we saw the students communicating precisely using definitions to describe the rhombus, parallelogram, and other quadrilaterals." Other PST and MTs spoke to additional SMPs such as the student's ability to "reason abstractly and quantitatively" and to "model with mathematics." Additional comments included that students in the video:

constructed viable arguments and critiqued the reasoning of others by making conjectures and counterexamples to build a logical progression of statements to explore and support ideas, like when the students ask how to form a trapezoid and whether the diagonals would cross at the midpoints. The other students had to listen to one student's explanation of why the trapezoid needed the midpoint of diagonals to cross. That student defended her mathematical reasoning using her diagram.

Through this prompt, PSTs and MTs were able to explore multiple SMPs and provide support for how and why they were seeing these SMPs in the lesson.

3.   What can you take-away from this clip that could impact your own instruction?

PSTs wrote about multiple "take-aways" for both themselves and their MTs from this viewing For example, PSTs noted the importance of the group unit in the video and the need for each group member to know their role and responsibility as it gave ownership to the learning groups. Another PST/MT pair emphasized the teacher's role in the clip, "One of the most obvious things my master teacher and I noted were how absent the instructor is from all these conversations. She is nearly invisible and does very little to redirect or even trigger discussions." This pair continued to explain how the actions of the teacher allowed "students to lead and organize their own conversations as they collaborate and share." Another PST/MT pair also spoke to the ease of the assignment in that they "didn't even have to leave our classroom [or give] too much extra time outside of our routine schedules" which also was a benefit and increased the viability of the task.

MODULE 1: IMPLEMENTATION RESULTS

Module 1 is in the fifth year of implementation. As noted earlier, implementation has grown from four institutions to ten institutions and continues to grow. These findings come from the first four years of implementation and data collected from five institutions (MT data was collected from three institutions of those institutions and PST data was collected from all five institutions). Though the previous experiences of the PSTs varied across institutions, PSTs were typically in their first methods course when this data was collected so may have had some experience in field placements prior to this experience. This field placement experience, however, was focused in a secondary mathematics classroom and PSTs spent much more time (for example, ten hours a week) in this field placement than in previous placements (where they may have only spent one to two hours). MT experience also varied across implementation sites but typically MTs had taught for at least three years before serving as MTs. Some had hosted PSTs before while others had not. The mathematics courses taught by the MTs also varied but ranged from pre-algebra to AP Calculus. Given that the focus of this chapter is on the field experience associated with the methods course, the authors chose to only focus on the three areas of data collection directly tied to Part 3 of Module 1, which included a pre-post survey, MT video discussion reflections, and exit slips.

Pre-Post Survey

PSTs and MTs complete a pre- and post-survey at the beginning and end of the Module to help better understand what PSTs and MTs are thinking before and after the group engages deeply with the CCSS-M Mathematical Practices. Most questions are likert related to the SMPs. Some sample questions include:

1. To what extent do you agree or disagree with the following statements:
   a. Drill and practice are essential for developing mathematical understanding,
   b. Understanding concepts should precede fluency with computations?
2. In your mathematics lessons, how often do you (or have/would) you ask students to do the following:
   a. Explain the reasoning behind an idea,
   b. Practice computational skills,
   c. Form and explain mathematical conjectures,
   d. Work on problems for which there is no immediately obvious method of solution?
3. In mathematics lessons you teach (have/will teach), how often do students:
   a. Work individually without assistance from the teacher,
   b. Work together as a class with the teacher teaching the whole class,
   c. Work together as a class with students responding to one another,
   d. Work in pairs or small groups without assistance from the teacher?

Only the MT responses were analyzed for this study so as to highlight the impact that Module 1 has on MT responses to the survey.

MT Video Discussion Reflection

PSTs complete a MT Video Discussion Reflection upon completion of watching and discussion the lesson video with their MTs. The video clip lasted approximately ten minutes. PSTs are given the following guidelines:

1. Write up a detailed narrative of the discussion of Prompt #1 with their mentor teacher.
2. Write a detailed explanation of the SMPs you and your mentor teacher observed the students engaging in and the extent (based on Mathematical Practices Look-Fors) students engaged in those practices. In what ways did the design of the activity support students as they engaged in the SMPs? You must provide evidence from the video and our work with the SMPs to support any claims or conclusions.
3. Based on the conversation you had with your mentor teacher about the quadrilaterals task and video clips, share 2-3 reflections you have about the skills you will need to develop as an instructor (think about planning, implementation, and assessment) to support students' engagement in the SMPs.

Exit Slips

PSTs also complete Exit Slips after each Part of the Module. After Part 3 where PSTs have engaged their MTs in a discussion about the SMPs, the Exit Slip asks two questions: (1) What was challenging about the discussion of the video clip with your mentor teacher? Give specific examples and/or references to the video and the SMPs, and; (2) How was your discussion with your mentor teacher similar to and different than our discussion of the video in class?

Analysis

Each of the three points of data collection was analyzed. The pre-and post-survey reports quantitative data that highlights changes in MT responses from before they participated in Module 1 Part 3 (pre-) and after they participated in Module 1 Part 3 (post-). Sixteen MTs completed the pre-survey and seven MTs completed the post-survey. Responses from the MT Video Discussion Reflection and Exit Slips data points were analyzed using a qualitative approach. Forty-three PSTs completed the MT Video Discussion Reflection and Exit Slips. Responses were read multiple times to analyze for common themes that emerged. These themes were triangulated (O'Donoghue & Punch, 2003) across the three data points utilizing the constant comparative method (Bogdan & Biklen, 1998). Salient quotes that highlight each theme were determined and shared below. For example, qualitative analysis of the MT Video Discussion Reflection and Exit Slips began to reveal codes such as "time to talk with MTs" and "logistics and realism." These codes indicated Finding 2 below of "Collegial Conversations" as the data suggested Module 1 offered time and space for MTs and PSTs to have conversations as colleagues around teaching.

Findings

Initial findings from analysis of these first four years of implementation indicate that MTs are showing growth in their thinking, willingness, and implementation of some of the SMPs highlighted in the video lesson and discussed with the PSTs. It is important to note that the pre-post survey data are self-reported.

However, further non-self-reported data can be drawn from MT Video Discussion Reflections and Exit Slips. Findings are also showing the benefits of having PSTs and MTs systematically and intentionally view and think through a video lesson.

Finding 1: MT Growth

Based on quantitative data analysis, MT responses indicate that after hosting PSTs and engaging in the video lesson dialogue with the PST, their beliefs and practices changed. Table 1 lists the percentage of MTs responding the questions listed in the pre-survey, the percentage of MTs responding to the same questions in the post-survey, with the change (increase or decrease) listed in the final column. The items were selected to include in the table because they showed the more dramatic changes that occurred in the pre- and post-survey questions.

Table 1. MT Pre- Post-Survey Response Results

1. To what extent do you agree or disagree with the following statements:			
	Strongly Agreed (%-n)		
	Pre (N=16)	**Post (N=7)**	**Change**
(a) Hands-on activities are important for learning	50-8	86-6	+ 36
(b) Understanding concepts should precede fluency with computations	50-8	75-5	+25
(c) More than one representation (picture, concrete, material, symbol, set, etc.) should be used in teaching a mathematics topic	75-12	86-6	+11
(d) Some students have a natural talent for mathematics and others do not	25-4	0-0	-25
2. In your mathematics lessons, how often do (or have/would) you ask students to do the following?			
	Most/Every Lesson (%-n)		
	Pre	**Post**	**Change**
(a) Explain reasoning behind an idea	89-13	100-7	+11
(b) Represent and analyze relationships using tables, charts, or graphs	56-9	86-6	+30
(c) Write equations to represent relationships OR articulate connections between algebraic procedures and contextual meaning	44-7	100-7	+56
(d) Form and explain mathematical conjectures	50-8	100-7	+50
(e) Justify their choice of variables and procedures and evaluate the appropriateness of a model	50-8	100-7	+50
(f) Connects concepts to prior and future concepts to develop an understanding of procedural shortcuts	69-11	100-7	+31
3. In mathematics lessons you teach (have/will teach), how often do students...			
	Most/Every Lesson (%-n)		
	Pre	**Post**	**Change**
(a) Work individually without assistance from the teacher	43-7	14-1	-29
(b) Work in pairs or small groups without assistance from the teacher	50-8	58-4	+8
(c) Work in pairs or small groups with assistance from the teacher	69-11	58-4	-11

In the first set of questions in Table 1, MT responses indicated an increased understanding of the importance of the SMPs discussed in Module 1. For example, a 36% increase in MTs who Strongly Agreed with statement 1a (Hands-on activities are important for learning) suggests an increased awareness and need to attend to SMP 4 which calls for students to be able to model with mathematics (National Governors Association Center for Best Practices & Council of Chief State School Officers, 2010). Part of SMP 4 requires students to be able to apply learning to everyday situations. The increase also suggests an increased awareness to SMP 5 that focuses on the need to use appropriate tools strategically (National Governors Association Center for Best Practices & Council of Chief State School Officers, 2010). This SMP speaks to the need for students to be able to use manipulatives and select appropriate tools (such as graphing paper or a dynamic geometry software) to be able to solve a mathematical problem. Items 1b and 1c also indicate an increased awareness among MTs for conceptual understanding and the need for students to be able to provide multiple representations to deepen and demonstrate understanding. Item 1d was also encouraging as the 25% decrease suggests that MTs were beginning to think more broadly about who could do mathematics after participating in the module.

Similarly, the increase in Item 2 indicate that following participation in the module, MTs had improved their implementation of some of the core habits espoused in the SMPs, particularly 1b, 1c, and 1d, all of which saw growth of 50% or higher. For example, 1c and 1d (form and explain mathematical conjectures; justify their choice of variables and procedures and evaluate the appropriateness of a model) both saw growth of 50%. Among other SMPs, these two address SMP 3 that requires students to "construct viable arguments" (National Governors Association Center for Best Practices & Council of Chief State School Officers, 2010).

Finally, Item 3 indicates MTs thinking more deliberately about how they facilitate student learning in their classrooms. The 29% decrease in item 3a (work individually without assistance from the teacher) and the 11% decrease in item 3c (work in pairs or small groups with assistance from the teacher) coupled with the slight increase in item 3b (work in pairs or small groups without assistance from the teacher) suggest that MTs are realizing the importance of students working together to discuss ideas and may help in addressing the second part of SMP 3 which asks students to "critique the reasoning of others" (National Governors Association Center for Best Practices & Council of Chief State School Officers, 2010). Of course, these items do not indicate the quality of the work or discussions taking place as students rely more on others but it does indicate increased opportunities for such conversations to occur. Given these areas of growth were less dramatic, this data also offers an area of improvement for this part of the Module – the need to more explicitly talk and see teacher and student roles during a lesson. In addition to the survey results, one PST shared that her MT teacher did not incorporate group work but then after viewing the video, decided to try it:

My coaching teacher uses instruction that does not allow for group work. The video that we watched together shows the impact group work can have on engaging students. The task also allowed students to investigate and discover the relationships between quadrilaterals on their own. The teacher gave a handout that had the definitions of various quadrilaterals, but the relationships were left to be discovered by the students. We both discussed how we were pleasantly surprised by how the students were able to identify the similarities between definitions which seemingly no help from the instructor. After the video my teacher decided she wanted to incorporate more group work into her curriculum.

Another PST noted that her MT shared at the end of the activity that her "biggest take away is that if given the opportunity, time, and appropriate tasks students can learn a great deal from each other." Not all MTs, though, were as moved by the video. One PSTs noted that her MT "thought it would be a waste of time to include this in her class because she did not see how this activity created a deeper understanding when compared to a typical lesson she does" and that they "were not sure that this type of activity would work in every classroom." This same PST, however, did comment that even though her MT was not as impressed with the video, she herself would like to try to create similar tasks that so effectively addressed multiple SMPs.

Finding 2: Collegial Conversations

Data from the MT Video Discussion Reflections and Exit Slips portrayed PSTs and MTs engaged in collegial conversations about teaching mathematics. Whereas often times the MT is seen as the expert, an rightfully so, and the PST as seen as the learner, this shared experience gave the pair the chance to talk about a "safe" lesson (meaning a lesson that was taught by a third party that neither of them knew so they could feel more safe to freely discuss it) as colleagues rather than a supervisor-supervisee. PSTs wrote in the exit slips that this gave them the chance to talk about how they may better implement some of the practices seen in the video lesson into their classroom. PSTs also said the activity made their MTs more "real" – often times the MTs merely tell PSTs what to teach and the PSTs teach it, with little time available to talk about the lesson. This task forced time to explicitly reflect on a lesson with PSTs said they felt they typically had little time to do with MTs, given the fast pace of a school day.

Similarly, PSTs were excited that the video encouraged conversations about mathematics with their MTs and conjecture about future lessons. One PST wrote:

Lastly, Ms. Baker and I got into the discussion of trapezoid and what the real definition of it is. Would it be a quadrilateral with only ONE pair of parallel lines or a quadrilateral with AT LEAST one pair of parallel lines? It's definitions like these that lead to a lot of misconceptions with students and how they prove geometric problems.

Another PST shared how this lesson fostered pondering with her MT about future lessons:

After watching this video, we both wondered about what comes next? After this activity, what does the teacher do? Does the teacher become more abstract with constructions, or does the teacher continue on using the manipulatives throughout the remainder of the unit of quadrilaterals?

Another component of these collegial conversations were that MTs and PSTs were able to co-create a list of SMPs addressed in the video. PSTs noted that sometimes they would miss, or their MTs would miss, an enacted SMP so they could create a more comprehensive list, and therefore understanding, of more SMPs. Watching the videos together also allowed the PSTs and MTs to focus on poignant excerpts from the lesson that interested them. The guiding questions did offer some direction, but PSTs noted that there was still room for the pair to decide what was of most interest to them. In addition, PSTs were able to see their MTs reflect verbally on a lesson. For example, one PST was struck when she asked her MT to talk about her take-away from the lesson. She was able to hear what most of the time teachers do in their head but not verbally with PSTs. Furthermore, the MTs were able to "give logistics and realism" to the implementation of the video lesson in their classroom. The PSTs valued that the MT were able to communicate a "realistic time frame" to doing this activity in their classroom as well as help the PSTs think through the ever existing challenge for teachers of deciding how much time to spend on what tasks during a class period.

Finally, a few PSTs did still note that they felt less vocal when discussing the video with their MTs than they did when the lesson is discussed in class. In class, "we are all novice teachers" so they felt more comfortable talking openly whereas with their MTs, "the MT has more experience so I listened more to them and they dominated the conversation." This last consideration does indicate the power dynamic that still exists between PST and MT and further thinking on how to make both parties more comfortable in the conversation is warranted.

Finding 3: Value in Multiple Viewings, but Not Too Many

Depending on the structure of methods courses and companion field experiences at teach site, some PSTs watch the video with two different MTs. PSTs that were able to watch the video twice with two different MTs noted the value in multiple viewings. One PST wrote, "Watching the video with Ms. Grand provided me an opportunity to take a second look at several things." Similarly, another PST noted, "I really enjoyed getting to watch this video with Coach Cane. I realized even more about this video than I had the last two times and identified more examples of the SMPs throughout the video." Being able to view the video with multiple MTs also allowed PSTs to hear different perspectives on the lesson:

Seeing the video a second time with my second mentor teacher was a very different experience for me.... After watching this video a second time with my second mentor teacher I find it very interesting the different points of view of my two mentor teachers, and the similarities they share. Reflecting on what my two mentor teacher told me about the video I must say that I can changed my overall view of the project. I can see that planning does make a difference. It may not be perfect the first or second time you do a project, but making sure it gets better each time for the students. The need to make sure the project you are going to give the students need to have an overall objective and not be some just for the students to do. I feel that if you plan something for students just to be busy. The students may begin to feel it is a waste of time without any meaning to the work they are doing. Having clear objectives and expectations will keep students on task. Overall my mentor teacher liked the video and the many possibilities that something like this could be done.

Some PSTs also noted the challenge of only watching a short clip of a much longer lesson. Because the PSTs had completed the task as a class as well as watched more of the lesson, they felt they had an unfair advantage of contextual knowledge than did their MTs when viewing the video. One PST/MT pair decided to watch the entire lesson on their own so as to have a better complete picture of the lesson when they discussed it. Assigning only a short clip of the video was intentional so as not to over burden an already overworked-under(no)paid MT, but this does impact the ability for the viewers to have a more holistic view of the lesson and therefore, most likely, a richer discussion. In addition, this clip was deliberately chosen because it focuses on student group work and student thinking. It does not, however, show the teacher much in the clip – other than brief exchanges with students as they work in groups – so possibly including a longer clip, or additional clip, that better focuses on the teacher would also be beneficial. Lastly, some PSTs did share that they felt that they were asked to watch the same video too many times. They found it interesting, but watching it several times also made them "zone out" on the later viewings. Suggestions were made to possibly include a variety of clips from the lesson with multiple viewings as opposed to the same clip each time.

Summary

Given that Module 1 is the most developed of the modules to date, the reader will note there is much more data on Module 1 than on Module 2 that follows. Module 2 is in the early stages of development but the authors do feel it is important to include so the reader can see the evolution of Modules as the RAC grows and develops as well. The findings from the data analysis of Module 1 is promising. They show that the field-based experience connected with Module 1 seems to be having an impact on school partners as well as PSTs. The sub-RAC is seeing growth in MTs. The research is showing MTs and PSTs participate in collegial conversations that foster relationships where colleagues can discuss both content, practice, and co-reflect on teaching. PSTs are benefiting from participating in and viewing an inquiry lesson in class and alongside their MT in learning more about how to translate practices that support SMP develop into classrooms.

MODULE 2: LESSON IMPLEMENTATION IN THE FIELD

The second module focuses on lesson plan implementation in their field experience. Part 1 asks PSTs to develop a lesson plan in class and then evaluate the lesson plan using the Mathematics Observation Protocol for Practices (MCOP2) (Gleason, Livers, & Zelkowski, 2015; Gleason, Livers, & Zelkowski, 2017). MCOP2 is an observation tool developed to measure the alignment of classroom practices with teaching reform documents such as the Standards for Mathematical Practice (National Governors Association Center for Best Practices & Council of Chief State School Officers, 2010), which was one main foci in Module 1 above. The MCOP2 tool focuses specifically on student engagement and teacher facilitation indicators. After a class discussion about the PST's self-rating, PSTs evaluate their lesson plans with a partner using the MCOP2 lesson planning rubric to further determine what is missing and still needs to be included to help address MCOP2 indicators. The MCOP2 lesson planning rubric is directly aligned with the MCOP2 observation rubric and examines for evidence of the following items; 1) exploration/investigation/problem solving; 2) multiple representation; 3) engagement in mathematical activity; 4) opportunities to critically assess mathematical strategies; 5) perseverance in problem solving; 6) concepts that promote relational/conceptual understanding; 7) modeling with mathematics; 8) mathematical structure; 9) tasks that have multiple paths to a solution or multiple solutions; 10) precision of mathematical language; 11) encourage student thinking, and; 12) provides opportunity for think/wait time.

Next, PSTs submit their lesson plan to the methods course instructor so he/she can evaluate the lesson plan using the MCOP2 lesson planning rubric. During initial implementation of the module, PSTs assessments of their lesson plans were inflated and warrant much discussion of the indicators listed above. Students needed to better understand the Standards for Mathematical Practices and have unpacked much of the vocabulary to have provided themselves with more accurate ratings.

Following the teacher evaluation of the PSTs' lesson plans, the instructors are encouraged to provide additional support to their students on lesson planning as they see fit. This is also a great time to further discuss the MCOP2 rubric indicators and provide video examples of each. However, much of this aspect of the module is left to the instructor's discretion but helps to prepare candidates for part 3 of module 2.

Module 2 culminates during Part 3 as PSTs fully implements their lesson plans in the field. PSTs and MTs co-plan a lesson together using the MCOP2 lesson planning rubric as a guide. The rubric helps the PST and the MT keep track of the indicators that are evident in the planned lesson and take note of those that are missing. There is a high emphasis on student engagement throughout the lesson and ensuring that the classroom is very student centered. The PST then implements the lesson while their MT observes the lesson using the MCOP2 observation instrument. After the lesson, the PST and MT post-conference to discuss how well the MCOP2 indicators were addressed during the lesson, followed with the PST's written reflection on the overall experience. Reflections from the PST post lesson indicate that this experience was very valuable for both PST and MT. One student stated:

Working with my Master Teacher to plan and implement this lesson was really great. I think using the MCOP2 planning tools were even more helpful. It allows both of us to plan through a common lens and have a similar idea of what we wanted for student outcomes. The immediate feedback I received right after teaching the lesson helped me to be more reflective and to see what improvements and changes I can make in my teaching.

After the implementation of this lesson, several PSTs reported wanting to make some changes in their styles and philosophy of teaching. They recognized that the way they envisioned the lesson playing out did not always happen and thus changes needed to be made overall.

I still want to strive to be better for my students: create engaging lessons and environment for the students to learn. I want to, however, have more planning in my questions. I wrote out some of the questions in the handouts, but perhaps they were too vague such that the conversations were not as rich in mathematical discussions. Additionally, I rely too heavily on the idea that there will be adaptations throughout the lesson and it will not always go according to plan. Something about writing it down on a lesson plan and scripting the questioning process seems unnatural to me. Therefore, I often opt to leave the minute questions not be written down. However, until I practice the lessons a couple more times, I believe I will begin to write them.

I have learned a lot from this mini lesson. I have learned to be flexible and understand that it is ok that students do not remember things right away. Something that the instructional coach, Kenny, told me is, it isn't important to get through the lesson, it is important that the students understand and comprehend the lesson. He advised me not to rush through tasks, lessons, or questions or else the students will miss the value of the lesson. His advice really stuck with me, and I would like to remember and work on that moving forward in my teaching practice.

Once all PSTs have completed Part 3, a whole group discussion occurs in the methods course to further unpack common successes and challenges across all PST lessons with the goal of enabling PSTs to create future lessons with the MCOP2 frameworks as a lesson planning mindset.

LESSONS LEARNED

As work is still in progress, the Lessons Learned List continues to grow. Working as part of a national initiative provides a unique opportunity to learn from colleagues who work in different states with varying programmatic parameters. Thus far, the authors have noted five lessons learned.

Lesson One: Module Implementation Varies

Methods courses are vastly different across campuses and states. Furthermore, field experiences connected to methods courses are as diverse. As expected, Module implementation varies with instructors. Part of the NIC model is offering ideas, Modules in this case, for sites to try and learn from in short time frames. Methods course instructors already have courses that consist of information and tasks they find valuable, so adding in an additional task can be challenging. Each Module takes at least two to three class meetings and that can be an enormous amount of time in a limited methods course. Therefore, the group has found that some programs implement a module at different stages in their program, rather than solely in the methods course. For example, one site implements Parts 1 and 2 of Module 1 during their initial PST orientation, and then completes Part 3 during the methods course when PSTs are in their field experiences. Another site implements Parts 1 and 2 during the first two class meetings of the methods course. PSTs at this site complete two different placements during an internship so complete Part 3 later in the semester and twice with two different mentor teachers. PSTs at other sites only complete Part 3 once with one mentor teacher.

Lesson Two: Instructor Reflections Needed

Another Lesson Learned is the need to capture methods course instructors' reflections once they have implemented the Modules. This piece of valuable information was not gathered when during initial iterations. However, as a result of the first Lesson Learned, there was a need to capture how and when methods instructors were implementing the Modules so as to better refine the Modules and improve understanding of the data being collected. When the RAC was smaller, the sub-RAC was more intimately familiar with group member contexts. As the RAC has grown and more instructors implement the modules, an even greater need has developed to better understand Module implementation. The Instructor Reflection Survey includes the following questions:

1. Describe the number of, sequence, and focus of methods courses your secondary mathematics PSTs are required to complete.
2. Describe the field experience component associated with each methods course. Include the number of hours and expectations of PSTs in the field.
3. In which methods course did you implement the module?
4. How many PSTs were enrolled in these courses?
5. What grade bands will PSTs be certified to teach (e.g. 5-8, 7-12)? How many PSTs will be certified at each level?
6. To what extent have PSTs been exposed to the SMPs before you implemented the module activities?
7. When (which week) in the semester did the PSTs complete Part 1 and how much class time did you devote to the activity?

8. What adjustments, if any, did you make when implementing Part 1? Please explain why you chose to make this change.

9. When (which week) in the semester did the PSTs complete Part 2 and how much class time did you devote to the activity?

10. What adjustments, if any, did you make when implementing Part 2? Please explain why you chose to make this change.

11. When (which week) in the semester did the PSTs complete Part 3 and how much class time did you devote to the activity?

12. What adjustments, if any, did you make when implementing Part 3? Please explain why you chose to make this change.

13. Do you have any suggestions for improving this module?

These questions help the sub-RAC gather information and context from each instructor. This growing database of information is becoming more valuable as Modules 1 and 2 are refined and the group determines what types of future Modules would be helpful.

Lesson Three: Versatile Data Collection

When Module implementation began, Module data was collected using an online fee-based survey collection platform. As the RAC membership and Module implementation grew, the need for a more accessible and versatile method for data collection so that the larger group could access the data across all programs, if desired, but was also able to access their own individual methods course or institutional data. By being able to access multiple levels of data, Module designers would be able to use larger data sets to refine and evaluate the Module across programs while individual instructors would also be able to access their pre- and post-assessments and exit slips so as to evaluate their own PST progress, growth, and remaining areas of need.

Lesson Four: Inclusive Field Based Work

The fourth lesson learned was that even more inclusion of field experiences into the Modules would be beneficial. Increased inclusion of both the MTs and Supervisors in the Modules will better align the work of the methods course with the field experience. The data on MT growth from the MT perspective, at this point, is only quantitative so involving more qualitative ways to learn further from the MTs regarding there experiences would be beneficial. The challenge remains that the group wants to include field experiences and MTs in the Modules without it serving as an "add-on" or additional burden to their work as MTs. Module 1 asked MTs to spend time watching a video alongside the PSTs and then engage in a conversation around the CCSS-M highlighted in that lesson. In working to improve inclusion of MTs into the methods course, Module 2 increases the field based section of the work. PSTs and MTs will work to co-plan a lesson and then evaluate the implemented lesson plan using the MCOP2. At one site, supervisors will join the PSTs and MTs in the planning and review of the lesson to further embed the field experience so that methods instructors, PSTs, MTs, and Supervisors are engaged in the same task.

Lesson Five: Data Informing Practice

Lesson five somewhat encompasses the previous four lessons learned as it attends to the ways in which our data has informed our practice of collaborating and developing Modules. For example, data from our Instructor Feedback Reflections (Lesson Three) indicated that implementation varied across campuses (Lesson One). Therefore, Module 1 was modified to allow for more time in between each of the three parts, if necessary. Finding 3 has informed modifications in Module 1 in terms of the number of times PSTs watch the same video. PSTs noted that too many times of watching the same video may be counterproductive so options were added to allow for different but related video segments. In addition, development of Module 1 indicated that MT feedback was important and informative so MT participation was increased in Module 2 (Lesson Four). Lesson Three speaks to more versatile data collection methods, which also continues to be a challenge in providing individual instructors with data as well as the collective group.

NEXT STEPS

The sub-RAC is currently working to develop a third module with the idea that these Modules will become part of an online MTE-Partnership library of resources available to all secondary mathematics methods course instructors such that they can select Modules to complement work they are already doing. These Modules focus on how to improve the integration of field experiences into the methods course such that when PSTs progress to full-time internships, they have had even more field experiences to bolster their preparation. The group continues to look for ways to involve MTs and internship supervisors into the methods course. Some ideas for future Modules include inviting MTs and Supervisors to attend method course meetings more regularly so that some of the work that now happens in Parts 3 of each Module is better integrated and happens collectively as a group of mathematics educators work collaboratively to improve mathematics teaching and learning for all students.

An additional component of the fourth lesson learned was the need to ensure data collection from field experience partners. Increased participation from the supervisors, as they are the liaisons between the university and the MTs, is becoming an additional component of the Modules. For example, embedding the pre- and post-survey completions as well as the upcoming Part 3 of each Module within the initial meetings with MTs is one way to work to better prepare MTs for the upcoming experiences. Including those expectations along with other work they are doing as mentor teachers helps not only increase the probability of MTs completing the data collection components but also emphasizes this work as important and part of the field experience. Furthermore, just this year at one site, supervisors participated in Module 1's Part 3 as part of their supervisor orientation so they were more informed about that activity. The modification also helped begin to develop more common language and expectations across all involved parties – the methods instructor, PSTs, MTs, and supervisors. Future ideas for increasing the value of the Modules are to invite MTs and supervisors to the methods courses during the implementation of these Modules so all parties can co-create and co-participate in these tasks.

CONCLUSION

The work continues to support the importance of a national effort to improve secondary mathematics teacher preparation and more specifically for this sub-RAC, field-based experiences in methods coursework. The luxury of having a multi-state partnership of a group of talented, dedicated mathematics teacher educators with whom to work has produced stronger, more comprehensive, and farther reaching tools that can be implemented in methods courses and used to better align this work with school partners. The group continues to refine Modules and grow from more Lessons Learned. The hope as membership continues to grow is that this work brings consistency and rigor to secondary mathematics methods courses while simultaneously better utilizing school partners in that work. As one PST said just this year at the end of the semester to one of the authors, "I thoroughly enjoyed this course, but please don't be offended when I say the most valuable experience was my work in the schools. I learned more from that than anything we did in class." The instructor assured her there was no offense taken as that same fact has been true since the instructor, herself, was a PST, and has been proven repeatedly in research (e.g., Evertson, Hawley, & Zlotnick, 1985; Forzani, 2014; Sleep, Boerst, & Ball, 2007; Wildo, Floden, and Ferrini-Mundy, 2001; Youngs & Qiang, 2013; Zeichner, 2010). Given that the education community knows this to be true anecdotally and by empirical research, there must be better utilization of the wealth of school partners within methods courses.

ACKNOWLEDGMENT

Special thanks to Drs. Michele Iiams, Gregory Chamblee, Rebekah Elliot, Mark Ellis, and Jeremy Zelkowski for their early work in the RAC and Module development.

REFERENCES

Arbaugh, F., & Taylor, M. (2008). Inquiring into mathematics teacher education. In F. Arbaugh & M. Taylor (Eds.), *Inquiry into mathematics teacher education* (Vol. 5, pp. 1–10). San Diego, CA: Association of Mathematics Teacher Educators.

Ball, D. L., Sleep, L., Boerst, T. A., & Bass, H. (2009). Combining the development of practice and the practice of development in teacher education. *The Elementary School Journal, 109*(5), 458–474. doi:10.1086/596996

Bogdan, R. C., & Biklen, S. K. (1998). *Qualitative research for education* (3rd ed.). Boston: Allyn and Bacon.

Bryk, A., Gomez, L. M., & Grunow, A. (2011). Getting ideas into action: Building networked improvement communities in education. In M. T. Hallinan (Ed.), *Frontiers in sociology of education* (pp. 1–42). Dordrecht, The Netherlands: Springer. doi:10.1007/978-94-007-1576-9_7

Cavey, L., & Berenson, S. (2005). Learning to teach high school mathematics: Patterns of growth in understanding right triangle trigonometry during plan study. *The Journal of Mathematical Behavior, 24*(2), 171–190. doi:10.1016/j.jmathb.2005.03.001

Clift, R. T., & Brady, P. (2005). Research on methods courses and field experiences. In M. Cochran-Smith & K. Zeichner (Eds.), *Studying teacher education: The report of the AERA panel on research and teacher education* (pp. 309–424). New York: Routledge.

Darling-Hammond, L. (2014). Strengthening clinical preparation: The holy grail of teacher education. *Peabody Journal of Education*, *89*(4), 547–561. doi:10.1080/0161956X.2014.939009

Downey, J. A., & Cobbs, G. A. (2007). "I actually learned a lot from this": A field assignment to prepare future preservice math teachers for culturally diverse classrooms. *School Science and Mathematics*, *107*(1), 391–403. doi:10.1111/j.1949-8594.2007.tb17762.x

Elementary Mathematics Specialists & Teacher Leader Project. (2012). *Engaging in the mathematical practices (Look Fors)*. Retrieved from http://www.nctm.org/Conferences-and-Professional-Development/Principles-to-Actions-Toolkit/Resources/5-SMPLookFors/

Evertson, C., Hawley, W., & Zlotnik, M. (1985). Making a difference in educational quality through teacher education. *Journal of Teacher Education*, *36*(3), 2–12. doi:10.1177/002248718503600302

Forzani, F. (2014). Understanding "core practices" and "practice-based" teacher education: Learning from the past. *Journal of Teacher Education*, *65*(4), 357–368. doi:10.1177/0022487114533800

Gareis, C. R., & Grant, L. W. (2014). The efficacy of training cooperating teachers. *Teaching and Teacher Education*, *39*, 77–88. doi:10.1016/j.tate.2013.12.007

Gleason, J., Livers, S. D., & Zelkowski, J. (2015). *Mathematics classroom observation protocol for practices: Descriptors manual*. Retrieved from jgleason.people.ua.edu/mcop2.html

Gleason, J. A., Livers, S. D., & Zelkowski, J. (2017). Mathematics Classroom Observation Protocol for Practices (MCOP2): A validation study. *Investigations in Mathematics Learning*, *9*(3), 111–129. doi:10.1080/19477503.2017.1308697

Goodwin, A. L., Roegman, R., & Reagan, E. M. (2016). Is experience the best teacher? Extensive clinical practice and mentor teachers' perspectives on effective teaching. *Urban Education*, *51*(10), 1198–1225. doi:10.1177/0042085915618720

Goos, M., Vale, C., & Stillman, G. (2017). *Teaching secondary school mathematics: Research and practice for the 21st century*. Allen & Unwin.

Grossman, P., Hammerness, K., & McDonald, M. (2009). Redefining teaching: Re-imagining teacher education. *Teachers and Teaching*, *15*(2), 273–290. doi:10.1080/13540600902875340

Gunckel, K. L., & Wood, M. B. (2016). The principle–practical discourse edge: Elementary preservice and mentor teachers working together on colearning tasks. *Science Education*, *100*(1), 96–121. doi:10.1002ce.21187

Hoffman, J. V., Wetzel, M. M., Maloch, B., Greeter, E., Taylor, L., DeJulio, S., & Vlach, S. K. (2015). What can we learn from studying the coaching interactions between cooperating teachers and preservice teachers? A literature review. *Teaching and Teacher Education*, *52*, 99–112. doi:10.1016/j.tate.2015.09.004

Inside Mathematics. (2017). *9ᵗʰ & 10ᵗʰ grade math – properties of quadrilaterals*. Retrieved from http://www.insidemathematics.org/classroom-videos/public-lessons/9th-10th-grade-math-properties-of-quadrilaterals

Izadinia, M. (2015). A closer look at the role of mentor teachers in shaping preservice teachers' professional identity. *Teaching and Teacher Education, 52*, 1–10. doi:10.1016/j.tate.2015.08.003

Kidd, M. (2008). A comparison of secondary mathematics methods courses in California. In P. M. Lutz (Ed.), *Secondary mathematics methods courses in California.* California Association of Mathematics Teacher Educators.

Lawley, J. J., Moore, J., & Smajic, A. (2014). Effective communication between preservice and cooperating teachers. *New Educator, 10*(2), 153–162. doi:10.1080/1547688X.2014.898495

Loughran, J. J. (2002). Effective reflective practice: In search of meaning in learning about teaching. *Journal of Teacher Education, 53*(1), 33–43. doi:10.1177/0022487102053001004

Martin, W. G., & Gobstein, H. (2015). Generating a networked improvement community to improve secondary mathematics teacher preparation: Network leadership, organization, and operation. *Journal of Teacher Education, 66*(5), 482–493. doi:10.1177/0022487115602312

National Governors Association Center for Best Practices & Council of Chief State School Officers. (2010). *Common Core State Standards for Mathematics.* Washington, DC: Authors. Retrieved from www.corestandards.org/Math

National Research Council. (2010). *Preparing Teachers: Building Evidence for Sound Policy.* Washington, DC: The National Academies Press; doi:10.17226/12882

Nguyen, T., Dekker, R., & Goedhart, M. (2008). Preparing Vietnamese student teachers for teaching with a student-centered approach. *Journal of Mathematics Teacher Education, 11*(1), 61–81. doi:10.100710857-007-9058-4

O'Donoghue, T., & Punch, K. (2003). *Qualitative Educational Research in Action: Doing and Reflecting.* New York: Routledge.

Otten, S., Yee, S., & Taylor, M. (2015) Secondary Mathematics Methods Course: What do we value? *Proceeding from the 37th annual meeting of the North American Chapter of the International Group for the Psychology of Mathematics Education.* East Lansing, MI: Michigan State University.

Posamentier, A. S., Smith, B. S., & Stepelman, J. (2009). *Teaching secondary school mathematics: Techniques and teaching units.* Academic Press.

Strutchens, M. (2017). Current research on prospective secondary mathematics teachers' field experiences. In The Mathematics Education of Prospective Secondary Teachers Around the World (pp. 33-44). ICME-13 Topical Surveys. Springer. DOI: doi:10.1007/978-3-319-38965-3_5

Taylor, M., & Ronau, R. (2006). Syllabus study: A structured look at mathematics methods courses. *AMTE Connections, 16*(1), 12–15.

Wilson, S., Floden, R., & Ferrini-Mundy, J. (2001). *Teacher preparation research: current knowledge, gaps, and recommendations.* Center for the Study of Teaching and Policy, University of Washington. Retrieved on December 28, 2017, from http://depts.washington.edu/ctpmail/PDFs/TeacherPrep-WFFM-02-2001.pdf

Wood, M. B., & Turner, E. E. (2015). Bringing the teacher into teacher preparation: Learning from mentor teachers in joint methods activities. *Journal of Mathematics Teacher Education, 18*(1), 27–51. doi:10.100710857-014-9269-4

Yee, S., Otten, S., & Taylor, M. (2017). What do we value in secondary mathematics teaching methods?. *Investigations in Mathematics Learning*, 1-15.

Youngs, P., & Hong, Q. (2013). The influence of university courses and field experiences on Chinese candidates' elementary mathematics knowledge for teaching. *Journal of Teacher Education, 64*(3), 244–261. doi:10.1177/0022487112473836

Zeichner, K. (2010). Rethinking the connections between campus courses and field experiences in college-and university-based teacher education. *Journal of Teacher Education, 61*(1-2), 89–99. doi:10.1177/0022487109347671

KEY TERMS AND DEFINITIONS

Common Core State Standards for Mathematics (CCSS-M): A set of standards for school mathematics released in 2010 developed by the Council of Chief State School Officers (CCSSO) and the National Governors Association Center for Best Practices (NGA Center).

Inquiry: A strategy of instruction that encourages activities where students investigate and study phenomena in order to develop knowledge and understanding of ideas based on systematic and empirical observation.

Methods Course: A university-based course that discusses the pedagogical aspects of teaching.

Secondary Mathematics: Mathematics that covers Grade 5 to Grade 12, typically including both middle and high school.

ENDNOTE

[1]   NCATE is now CAEP, Council for the Accreditation of Educator Preparation.

Chapter 18
Integrating Mathematics and Science Methods Classes With an Afterschool STEM Club

Rachael Eriksen Brown
Pennsylvania State University – Abington, USA

ABSTRACT

This chapter describes a model of integrating an elementary mathematics methods course with an afterschool club in order to support pre-service teachers' development of a teaching practice. The goal of the model was to help pre-service teachers integrate theory and practice as well as begin to notice particular elements of a classroom and lesson. Details of the model, the course, and how the partnership with the elementary school was formed are shared. In addition, results from analyzing pre-service teachers' journal responses indicate most teachers focused on classroom management initially; however, writing shifted to focus on students' mathematical ideas and the purpose of play. Learnings with respect to teacher education as well as ideas for future research are discussed.

INTRODUCTION

As pre-service teachers (PSTs) train for their careers, especially in the fields of mathematics and science, they have often not experienced learning mathematics and science in the ways that are promoted in their education program. In addition, PSTs often experience a mismatch between their field experience classrooms and the pedagogies encouraged in university courses (Grossman, Compton, Igra, Ronfeldt, Shahan, & Williamson, 2009; Shulman, 1986; Sowder, 2007). This mismatch can create a distinct separation of action and theory that Feiman-Nemser and Buchmann (1985) argue PSTs need help in making connections between action and theory. Ebby (2000) shared an example of how this dissonance has potential to be a learning experience. This, combined with typical teacher development trajectories, where beginning teachers tend to focus on themselves and concerns over their abilities to maintain control in the classroom, to meet the expectations of the school community, and to adequately master the content and shift to be more focused on students (Mewborn, 1999; Star, Lynch & Perova; 2011; Star & Strickland, 2008; van

DOI: 10.4018/978-1-5225-6249-8.ch018

Es & Sherin, 2002), supports the need for teacher education programs to create more opportunities for PSTs to experience the teaching and learning of mathematics and science, especially.

This chapter will share one type of informal field experience model for addressing the marriage of theory (from methods classes) and practice (from work with elementary students in an afterschool STEM club) in a way that supports undergraduate, elementary PST development. This chapter uses the construct of teacher noticing to examine the development of elementary PSTs over the course of a semester who were enrolled in both a mathematics and science methods course utilizing this model. In addition, details about the semester, including the methods course and afterschool STEM club, will be shared. The objective of this chapter is for other teacher educators to learn ways in which they can modify their programs to better merge theoretical and practical experiences for PSTs, support PST noticing, as well as pose ideas for further research.

BACKGROUND

The idea of using an after school venue for supporting field experiences is not entirely unique. Particularly in science education, researchers have explored informal settings and how they support PST development (e.g. Anderson, Lawson, Mayer-Smith, 2006; Chesebrough, 1994; Ferry, 1995; Jung & Tonso, 2006). Literature on these types of informal experiences merged with teacher education programs will be discussed followed by two ways to consider teacher development. These two ways are grounded in the premise of the informal field experience model shared here: merging theory and practice as well as teacher noticing. Thus, approaching teacher development through considering what PSTs experience through university coursework in terms of how closely and authentically the activities mimic actual teacher practice connects with the merge of theory and practice. Teacher development can also be approached through the construct of teacher noticing. The definition of noticing and the connection between noticing and development, particularly in the mathematics education field, is addressed.

Informal Field Experiences

Science, and to a lesser extent mathematics, teacher educators have studied the use of informal field experiences with PSTs (e.g. Katz, Randy McGinnis, Riedinger, Marbach-Ad, & Dai, 2013; Cartwright, 2012), particularly family science nights (e.g. Harlow, 2012; McCollough & Ramirez, 2010; McDonald, 1997). Through participation in family science nights PSTs tend to shift thinking to be more positive about science and the prospect of teaching science. Additional benefits vary based on the structure but most PSTs realize the power of assessing student's prior knowledge and recognize the intelligence of students and parents, particularly from diverse backgrounds (Harlow, 2012; McCollough & Ramirez, 2010; McDonald, 1997). In McDonald's study, the PSTs helped facilitate activities by working with children and parents in small groups where the directions and whole group discussions were led by faculty and paid undergraduate student workers. The results demonstrated PSTs held positive attitudes towards science and teaching science after the experience, even without the planning and leading of the activities. Harlow's and McCollough and Ramierz's studies reported family science nights that were planned and led by PSTs. The results of these two studies show the positive impact of these experiences on the PSTs' efficacies as teachers. The PSTs were successful in engaging elementary students in science and were able to see the students as sophisticated thinkers (Harlow, 2012). PSTs also saw students scientific thinking as developing over time and recognizing learning progressions students experience in science. With McCollough and Ramierz, PSTs engaged in family science or math nights and PSTs were able to interact with parents (an important skill for a teacher) as well as design culturally responsive activities.

Using other informal settings, Wallace (2013) shares how graduate PSTs used informal settings to not only teach science but to also engage in action research. All of the participants "gained enhanced understandings of *children as diverse learners* and the *importance of prior knowledge* in science learning" (p. 827). Of the three case studies reported, two experienced shifts in understanding of science learning and had powerful results from their action research. One participant's learning, however, was not changed. Disposition towards and beliefs about teaching and learning influences PSTs' learning. Using informal experiences does not guarantee learning or shifts in PSTs but these experiences have some success and there is no reported evidence of harm.

Cartwright (2012) shares a qualitative study on the use of "science talk" in an afterschool enrichment setting and how PSTs' learning from that context transferred into student teaching. PSTs collaboratively worked on lesson plans and implemented them and results showed the power of science talk, "student-centered discussions where students speak to one another and address one 'essential' question that may come from the student or the teacher" (p. 387). PSTs learned the value of encouraging student ideas and saw the science talk as a type of formative assessment. This focus on listening to students and giving up control as the instructor in order to allow more student voice translated into the student teaching classroom. Cartwright argues that without opportunity to practice ideas from theory, PSTs' "lack of experience magnifies the barriers for effective science teaching when they reach student teaching" (p. 389). Interestingly, the PSTs saw some connections between the after school program and their teaching practice during student teaching; however, their mentor teacher saw much skill and growth from these PSTs' practices, specifically around giving space for student voice.

In the model described in this chapter, the informal field experience was not a family night (or series of family nights) but was more similar to the setting in Cartwright's (2012) study. Faculty and PSTs worked together to run an afterschool STEM club for second and third graders (more details to follow). The STEM club has many parallels to the informal field experiences reported here: there was not curricular or state testing pressure, for example. As Harlow (2012) argues:

Informal science learning opportunities may allow pre-service teachers to apply what they are learning in their methods courses in authentic teaching contexts without the constraints associated with formal school environments. (p. 201)

Based on the results of these studies, I anticipated PSTs would enjoy the STEM club and evidence of shifts in their learning would be seen. In this case the shifts would be evident in what they noticed about their experiences in the methods class and STEM club.

Theory and Practice

One way to investigate teacher development is to critically look at representation, decompositions, and approximations of practice (Grossman, Compton, Igra, Ronfeldt, Shahan, & Williamson, 2009; Grossman & McDonald, 2008) in methods courses in order to ensure a variety of experiences and practices are well-represented. Representations are the different ways practice is represented in educational experiences like coursework and what is made visible to beginners. Decomposition is breaking a practice down in order to highlight pieces to better support novice learning. Approximations are opportunities for beginners to try practices on a continuum of similarity to those of a practicing teacher. Grossman and colleagues argue there are advantages to using less authentic tasks because novice teachers are able to focus on a single component of practice in order to take risks and learn from attempts to support student learning. Although in the real practice of teaching, one cannot ignore multiple students or slow down time, by allowing novices to engage in a variety of approximations and representations of practice, novices are able to build knowledge and skills that can be re-integrated into an authentic classroom. Thus, although activities like lesson planning may not mimic what expert teachers do exactly, the activity does highlight what expert teachers attend to and consider when planning and enacting a lesson. Lesson planning allows for a methods instructor to understand the thinking and reasoning behind a novice teacher's plans and provide feedback to highlight areas the teacher may have neglected in planning.

Forzani (2014) wrote about how teacher education has changed over the years and how there have been a variety of efforts for infusing practice, particularly recently. Forzani writes the current "notion that inquiry and experimentation are a part of both good teaching and learning to teach" (p. 365) is one way there is a connection between theory and practice. Forzani notes that the current view of teaching, built on ideas of Dewey (1965/1904), is as an improvisational practice (p. 365). Thus, uses of representations, decompositions, and approximations of practice support the novice development of this improvisational practice. Janset, Klette and Hammerness (2018) also write about the importance of connecting of theory and practice as it has a significant positive impact on students learning, can increase teacher retention as well as support PSTs' competence in the classroom (p. 184). In their work they propose an eight dimension framework grounded in literature and then operationalized across methods courses in teacher education programs in three countries. Their analysis revealed that PSTs had the fewest opportunities to connect theory and practice through practice having the teacher role as well as observing an explicit model of a particular pedagogy or teaching move (p. 192). This suggests the need for experiences like informal fieldwork to support PSTs connecting theory learned in coursework with the practice of teaching. Janset et. al's framework provides some explicit ideas on how to use Grossman and colleague's (2008; 2009) constructs of representation, decomposition and approximation in methods coursework.

Others have further investigated these ideas and considered how to scaffold PSTs' development in a methods course, particularly the TeachMath project (e.g. Aguirre, Turner, Bartell, Kalinec-Craig, Foote, Roth McDuffie, & Drake, 2012; Roth McDuffie, Foote, Bolson, Turner, Aguirre, Bartell, Drake, & Land, 2014; Turner, Drake, Roth McDuffie, Aguirre, Bartell, & Foote, 2012). For example, one module, the Community Exploration module (Turner, Aguirre, Drake, Bartell, Roth McDuffie, & Foote, 2015), asked students to engage in a community walk to learn about where and how mathematics occurs in the community by children and adults in the various establishments in the community. Thus, supporting PSTs' understanding of children's multiple mathematical knowledge bases. PSTs were then asked to create a problem-solving lesson plan that relied on these mathematical practices identified in the community. Analysis of the lesson plans resulted in three categories of connection type: emergent, transitional and meaningful (Aguirre, Turner, Bartell, Kalinec-Craig, Foote, Roth McDuffie, & Drake, 2012). Although these plans were not enacted, they approximate practice and provide instructors insight into how PSTs' are considering the connection between children's mathematical thinking and funds of knowledge from the community. Aguirre et al.'s work demonstrates that although recognizing and authentically incorporating funds of knowledge into a lesson plan is challenging for teachers at all experience levels, some PSTs were able to successfully create lesson plans that meaningfully connected the community to mathematical goals.

Lampert and colleagues (2013) created and studied a pedagogy for learning to teach called rehearsals. Rehearsals provide a way to not only approximate practice authentically but also to deliberately practice instruction. This deliberate practice allowed various interactions among and between PSTs and instructors. Across three teacher education programs embedded in mathematics methods courses, rehearsals allowed teacher educators to provide specialized coaching and focus PSTs attention on specific practices. Their work shows the potential of this pedagogical tool to support PSTs to focus on important principles such as "attending to students as individuals and learners" or "treating students as sense-makers" (p. 228).

Additionally, research has been done as methods instructors begin to situate methods classes in school settings in order to eliminate the false dichotomy of acquiring and applying knowledge (e.g. Bahr, Monroe, Balzotti, & Eggett, 2009; Bahr, Monroe & Eggett, 2014; Bahr, Monroe & Shaha, 2013; Darling-Hammond, 2000; Zeichner, 2010). These studies and recommendations suggest the importance of situating methods courses at school sites in ways that value practitioner knowledge as well as more academic knowledge. However, Bahr and colleagues (2014) have found "the effectiveness of this practice may not depend on being located at a school site as much as on the opportunity for immediate methods application the school site affords" (p. 274). The success of methods classes incorporating both structural interweaving (ex. gradual increase in responsibility, methods instructor as supervisor, and pairing PSTs in a clinical placement) and conceptual interweaving (ex. mentor teachers' practices align with those being discussed in methods classes) has been demonstrated to have a great influence on engaging in reform-based practices (Bahr, Monroe, & Eggett, 2014). Thus, there is a need to successfully support PSTs through merging methods coursework with field placement. Ziechner (2010) also wrote of hybrid spaces that blend university coursework and field experiences. He shares a variety of ways these hybrid spaces exist such as representing practice in various ways in coursework. This could be observing a teacher whose practice aligns with the ideas in the methods course or having a teacher facilitate course meetings with respect to content she has learned through her practice.

For teacher educators, critically evaluating our methods courses to ensure adequate support for PSTs through varied opportunities and activities that represent, decompose and approximate practice is essential. If possible, integrating methods classes with field experiences positively influences PSTs (Bahr, Monroe, & Eggett, 2014; Ziechner, 2010). Thus, in this chapter, I share details and my learnings as the mathematics methods instructor on one way to incorporate an authentic approximation of practice through the model of integrating theory and practice through planning and running a STEM club as part of a methods course while still maintaining the support of a methods instructor in a lower risk environment.

Noticing

Early career teachers tend to focus on the static elements of the classroom, such as classroom management (Berliner, 1988). This focus has also been seen throughout studies on teacher noticing (e.g. Roller, 2015; Star & Strickland, 2008; van Es & Sherin, 2008). Although a few versions of definitions of noticing are in the literature, for this chapter, I use Van Es and Sherin's (2008) definition of noticing as three parts: (a) identify core events in a lesson; (b) reason about these events through knowledge of the context, and; (c) connect these events to more theoretical principles in teaching and learning. All three components are important to the act of noticing; however, as other's have argued (e.g. Roller, 2015; Star, Lynch & Perova; 2011; Star & Strickland, 2008), PSTs need to first learn what to focus on before learning how to reason about and connect theory to these noticings. Similar to Star and Strickland, in this chapter I wanted to learn "what catches their [the PSTs'] attention, and what they miss" when viewing teaching (p. 111). PSTs are often distracted by other actions in the classroom and do not focus on salient features of teaching and learning, like more experienced teachers do (Carter, Cushing, Sabers, Stein, & Berliner, 1988; Star, Lynch & Perova; 2011). Thus, learning what PSTs do focus on and how to support any shifts in their attention is extremely important to teacher education.

The noticing of preservice or less experienced teachers is different than that of experienced teachers (e.g., Jacobs, Lamb & Philipp, 2010; Jacobs, Lamb, Philipp & Schappelle, 2011). For example, Jacobs and colleagues (2010) looked across professional experience levels (not years of teaching) to see differences in attending to and interpreting student thinking as well as determining next steps for the students. Across their participants, there were significant differences based on teaching and professional development experience. More professional development, including leadership experience helping other teachers learn to notice student thinking, led to improvement across attending to and interpreting student thinking as well as determining next steps. Jacobs et. al's study supports the teacher development literature showing detailed noticing of student's mathematical thinking is based on experience (both teaching and professional development activities).

Studies focused on PSTs indicate the potential for shifts in ability to notice (e.g. Roller, 2015; Roth McDuffie, Foote, Bolson, Turner, Aguirre, Bartell, Drake, & Land, 2014; Star & Strickland, 2008; Star, Lynch & Perova, 2011). The focus in these studies was on what PSTs were noticing (the first part of Van Es and Sherin's (2008) definition). For example, in both studies from Star and colleagues, a framework detailing observation categories was provided to PSTs and used as part of the coursework. Their studies demonstrated that for some categories PSTs were able to shift to notice various features of a classroom and lesson; although these categories were not 100% consistent across the two studies. Despite the differences, in both studies PSTs made large gains on classroom environment and communication. Thus, supporting the premise that "teachers may need explicit training in how to observe mathematics lessons" (Star, Lynch & Perova, 2011, p. 130) and that these skills can be improved in a single semester. Similar shifts in what PSTs notice and how the noticing is described has been examined in various studies (Barnhart & van Es, 2015; Fernández, Llinares & Valls, 2013; Roller, 2015; van Es & Sherin, 2002). For example, Roth McDuffie et. al (2014) shared successful results with supporting PSTs to learn to notice over the course of the semester by watching select video clips with a four lenses framework to focus PSTs attention. PSTs were able to notice and engage in more sophisticated ways over the semester. Repeated use of the lenses when analyzing video supported PSTs in more focused attention on important components of teaching. The common learning is PSTs can learn to notice student thinking and lessen their focus on issues like behavior if they are provided some sort of scaffolding and support (like a framework or video discussions). This support has also been shown necessary for in-service teacher development as well (e.g. Santagata, 2011; Sherin & Han, 2004; van Es & Sherin, 2008).

In the next sections of the chapter, I describe the model used to integrate an afterschool STEM club at a local elementary school with the mathematics and science methods courses. Details about how the STEM club came about and the context of the methods course are provided. Then a pilot study investigating the following two questions is described: what, if any, changes in noticing are in PSTs' writing? And what, if any, connections between theory and practice were written about by PSTs?

STEM CLUB MODEL

Despite these PSTs being in the field two days a week as part of a pre-student teaching field experience, I had noticed in past offerings of the methods course that some PSTs completed methods without having a good sense of what these pedagogical ideas looked like in action, how they could fit into a school-district's curriculum or pacing guide, or having the opportunity to try and lead a lesson with either a task or a number talk as a central feature (the big focus of the math methods course). Some PSTs in the past had reported not being able to even interview elementary students to learn more about them in this pre-student teaching field experience. This is consistent with what we know about field experiences disconnect with university coursework due to numerous factors (Ziechner, 2010). Another faculty member observes the PSTs in their pre-student teaching field experience and PSTs are each placed in a different classroom. The mentor teachers have various beliefs about the teaching and learning of mathematics. The prospect of trying to influence all mentor teachers and observe each PST was daunting. Thus, I wanted to provide an additional field experience where PSTs were free to experiment, observe and explore these mathematics pedagogical ideas with elementary students where I also could interact with the PSTs.

I shared my concerns with the science methods professor (referred to as science educator through rest of chapter) who also noticed similar challenges faced by our PSTs with respect to science instruction. In fact, some of our PSTs never saw a science lesson taught during their pre-student teaching field experience because the elementary school where they were placed taught Social Studies during the semester of methods and pre-student teaching fieldwork. Given that both mathematics and science methods courses were typically offered two days a week in the afternoon, I was interested in finding a way to situate the courses in an elementary school somehow. Fortunately, a member of a local elementary school's parent teacher organization (PTO) reached out to the education department.

The afterschool STEM club was initiated by one of the PTO's leaders who reached out to the science educator (who was the education program chair) looking for students to run some after school programs. This initial email request led to the program described in this chapter. The school had few afterschool offerings (Zumba and a garden club) and the PTO was open to anything we might be able to offer. Initially, the principal and curriculum coordinator were interested in coding at the elementary level, supporting the curriculum for math and science already in place at the school, offering engineering design challenges or focusing on problem solving skill development. In order to meet the needs of the elementary school and the needs of the methods courses (both mathematics and science), the idea of a STEM club with a focus on mathematics, science, and computational literacy formed. The STEM club met for eight consecutive weeks. The principal requested two offerings: one for second grade and one for third grade. The PTO took care of all paperwork and permits for the district and town, advertising the class and providing snacks for elementary students.

The STEM club was limited to 40 elementary students – 20 in each offering. (For clarity, students will be used for the rest of the chapter to indicate elementary students. PSTs will be used to indicate the undergraduate students who were preservice teachers.) The PTO ended up using a lottery system because the interest in the club by the school community was high. At every club meeting, there was a PTO member present who handled attendance and dismissal of students. We were able to meet in the classroom where the STEM club took place about 15-20 minutes before school let out to set up the room and materials. Initially, the idea was to go over the plans for the day, but this was challenging with the limited time. Additionally, we were able to debrief after the STEM club meeting in the classroom for

30-60 minutes. Some elementary students were picked up late or other events prevented a full debrief after some club meetings. Thus, the mathematics and science methods courses essentially halted except for running and debriefing the STEM club for these eight weeks.

Through conversations between myself and the science educator, a general plan was generated for the eight weeks of STEM club. For science content, the decision was made to focus on astronomy. Astronomy was not emphasized in either the second or third grade at the elementary school and the PSTs did not have strong content knowledge around astronomy. For mathematics content, the decision was made to focus primarily on number through number talks in the second grade group and through involving a high cognitive demand task for the third grade group. However, one PST created a lesson focused on gathering and representing data. These plans guided our decision making and only required small modifications as we implemented our plans. Table 1 shows the basic plans of the 8 weeks. This was our first attempt at offering the STEM club and integrating our two courses.

The thinking behind our design was to give these PSTs opportunities to experiment with key ideas with a small group of students (either two or four students). Each PST was partnered with a pair of elementary students. Based on challenges with student behavior, there was some mixing of pairs to form a variety of groups of 4 students. The original trio of PST and pair of elementary students remained together all 8 weeks, partnering with another trio for many lessons or activities.

As the general plan was put into action, the PSTs planned more detailed activities and lessons with our support. Before the club began, I assigned a PST or two to various activities described in the eight-week plan (Table 1), such as Beebots, a science lesson, or plans for my number talk and mini lesson. The idea was the assigned PSTs would generate the more detailed plan and communicate it with others. The other PSTs would provide feedback, suggest modifications, ask clarifying questions, etc. Then a decision about who would facilitate various parts would be determined. In actuality, the PSTs appeared to do little communicating online and a subset of the class would come to campus the hour or two before STEM club to plan, gather manipulatives, etc.

In order to address computational literacy, the STEM club used Beebots (https://www.bee-bot.us/), small basic robots that look like bees. The Beebot has 6 basic buttons for programming: forward, backward, right, left, clear, and go. The Beebot requires nothing besides itself so was a great tool for use in STEM club as a way to think about the mathematical and scientific practices alongside beginning coding ideas for a low cost.

Unfortunately, because the final agreement for running the club came through after the schedule for the semester was set, the science educator could not attend the full STEM club meeting. She taught on campus and joined the STEM club halfway through the hour and participated in, often leading, the debrief based on our conversations. My role was to make sure we were ready for the day's activities and then either lead or observe how the plans went. I often took notes on what I was observing and shared those with the science educator to discuss the debrief plan and make decisions about feedback to give PSTs and what activities should be included in our courses later in the semester or in future offerings.

At the conclusion of the STEM club, the PTO leaders, principal, elementary students and parents all seemed pleased with our work. Both the PTO and principal requested us to return and offer more clubs for their students. We plan to continue to strengthen our partnership with the school through offering the STEM club with methods classes in the future.

Table 1. STEM club plan for the eight weeks

Week	Monday (2nd grade)	Wednesday (3rd grade)
1	-Introductions -Get to Know Interview Students - each PSU student has 1-2 2nd graders -Beebot exploration	-Introductions -Get to Know Interview Students - each PSU student has 1-2 3rd graders -Beebot exploration
2	-Math/Science Interview -Beebot maze	-Math/Science Interview -Beebot maze
3	Science Lesson	Science Lesson
4	-Rachael leds number talk -Beebot drawing	-Rachael leds problem solving experience (based on community walk) -Beebot drawing
5	-Number Talk (2 PSU PSTs work together w/4 2nd graders, 1 PSU leads number talk, 1 observes) -Beebot number line	-Problem Solving mini lesson by PSU PSTs (2 PSU students work together w/4 3rd graders, 1 PSU leads, 1 observes) -Beebot number line
6	-Number Talk -Beebot number line	-Problem Solving mini lesson -Beebot number line
7	Science Lesson	Science Lesson
8	STEM Activity	STEM Activity

THEORETICAL FRAMEWORK

In order to investigate the two research questions: what, if any, changes in noticing are in PSTs' writing? And what, if any, connections between theory and practice were written about by PSTs?, the operational definitions of noticing and connections between theory and practice needs to be elaborated. As previously described, teacher development typically begins with PSTs focused on mechanics of the classroom and less on the students (e.g. Mewborn, 1999; Star, Lynch & Perova; 2011). The goal of the STEM club combined with the methods courses was to challenge this typical development and encourage PSTs to see more than just the mechanics of the classroom by focusing on listening to and learning from students as well as supporting PSTs to examine lessons and activities through various lenses. The assumption is that changes in what PSTs write about would indicate a positive shift in development.

Learning from and with students is inherent for a mathematics teacher. Mathematical knowledge needed for teaching (Ball, Thames, & Phelps, 2008) as well as various definitions of play in mathematics (e.g. Burke, 2017) indicate teachers must not only know mathematics for herself but also respect and understand student thinking and mathematical ideas. Mathematics involves a playfulness, a willingness to exchange and consider ideas to make sense of mathematics. Play involves "both experimentation and creativity to generate ideas, and using the formal rules of mathematics to follow any ideas to some sort of a conclusion" (De Holton, Ahmed, Williams, & Hill, 2001, p. 403). The idea of playfulness is represented in the Common Core mathematical practices (National Governors Association Center for Best Practices, & Council of Chief State School Officers, 2010) as well as in the Science and Engineering Practices in the New Framework (National Research Council, 2012). The idea of playfulness and being responsive to student ideas was emphasized in both the methods courses as well as the STEM club. Details on the methods course and more on the STEM club is below.

CONTEXT

The mathematics and science methods courses are offered the fall semester of senior year in a four-year, undergraduate, elementary education program. Upon completion of the program, PSTs receive a bachelor's degree and a state teacher certification in grades pre-Kindergarten through fourth. In the first two years of the program, PSTs take a course focused on observation in a pre-kindergarten classroom. While taking nine credits of language arts methods and six credits of early childhood courses during their junior year, PSTs lead about eight mini-lessons they planned in area elementary schools. During their final year, PSTs are enrolled in the mathematics, science, and social studies methods courses as well as in a seminar supporting a pre-student teaching experience that requires them to be in an assigned elementary school classroom two days a week. These methods courses are offered in a 15-week semester with one of the weeks dedicated to PSTs being at their fieldwork classroom full-time. In the iteration of the mathematics and science methods courses being shared in this chapter, PSTs participated in four weeks of class meetings followed by eight consecutive weeks exclusively dedicated to planning and running the STEM club. After STEM club, PSTs had a week in their pre-student teaching field experience classrooms followed by two weeks of methods class meetings to conclude the semester.

MATHEMATICS METHODS CLASS

The goal of the integration of theory and practice in the mathematics methods course was to support PSTs in listening to students, in planning and executing lessons that encouraged student mathematical talk, as well as learning to notice various dynamics in a mathematics classroom. Because PSTs were located in different schools with mentor teachers who had varying beliefs about the teaching and learning of mathematics, the STEM club provided a venue for PSTs to see theory put into practice by the course instructors and the preservice teachers themselves. This allowed for representations, decompositions, and approximations of practice in multiple ways (Grossman, Compton, Igra, Ronfeldt, Shahan, & Williamson, 2009). I could represent and decompose practice with elementary students by leading the afterschool club with the PSTs observing. The PSTs were able to plan and enact lessons themselves as an approximation of practice. The club was a proxy for a school setting and did not entirely mimic a classroom. Through debriefs and observing each other's teaching and debriefs of the club (Bahr, Monroe, & Eggett, 2014), we could decompose practice to support PST learning.

Listening to Students

Similar to Lampert et. al's (2013) and the TeachMath's focus (e.g. Roth McDuffie, Foote, Bolson, Turner, Aguirre, Bartell, Drake, & Land, 2014), the mathematics methods course aimed to support PSTs in getting to know students holistically and mathematically; to listen to and respect students' mathematical ideas; as well as to gain experience in supporting student talk through number talks (Kazemi & Hintz; 2014) and use of high cognitive demand tasks (Stein & Smith; 1998). These goals were accomplished through various activities, assignments, readings, and class discussions. For example, to support PSTs getting to know students we engaged in a modified version of the Community Exploration module (Turner, Aguirre, Drake, Bartell, Roth McDuffie, & Foote, 2015) and the Case Study module (Foote, Roth McDuffie,

Aguirre, Turner, Drake, & Bartell, 2015) from the TeachMath project. The modified activity included a community walk, two student interviews, and the creation of a mini-lesson plan. One interview focused on getting to know the student mathematically and the other focused on learning about the student's interests and family. This activity also supported the goal of listening and respecting student ideas. PSTs were encouraged to not teach during the interview but be curious about understanding the world through the student's perspective. When discussing student ideas or looking at sample student work, the instructor always began with asking the PSTs to talk about what strengths and mathematical ideas are demonstrated in the student work followed by what areas could be improved and how. Upon completion of these interviews and the community walk, PSTs created mini-lesson plans where the context of the mathematical concepts connected to the student. For example, one PST learned her student helped with grocery shopping and cooking at home. She planned a lesson around flyers from local grocery stores giving the students a budget and asking them to buy groceries for two meals. This allowed her to learn how students estimated and did basic addition and subtraction.

Planning Lessons Around Student Mathematical Talk

In order to learn how to support student talk, talk moves (such as revoicing and connecting) were embedded in number talks and discussions about high cognitive demand tasks. PSTs were asked to read various articles and chapters as well as discuss these readings in class. PSTs learned about these pedagogical constructs not only through reading but through experiencing themselves in methods class and watching video of elementary classrooms where teachers implemented these constructs. For example, PSTs watched a number talk in a Kindergarten classroom (https://www.teachingchannel.org/videos/visualizing-number-combinations) where the teacher used a quick image structure to have students see the number eight in various ways on a ten frame. After reading, experiencing, and watching these ideas and discussing them as a whole class, PSTs observed me model a number talk at STEM club and were asked to create a number talk plan for use during the club using the lesson plan format from Kazemi and Hintz (2014).

Learning to Notice

An additional goal of the course was to promote the development of noticing. Knowing the importance of providing scaffolding and support from the literature (e.g. Star & Strickland, 2008), the four lenses framework from Roth McDuffie et al. (2014) was used throughout the course on a variety of activities, like the viewing and discussion of classroom video and the Noticing Journal prompts (see Appendix for a list of all the prompts). This framework supported PSTs noticing important components of a lesson, not related to student behaviors. The four lenses were teaching, learning, task, and power and participation. The intent for Roth McDuffie et al. was to focus PSTs on "noticing of equitable instructional practices and children's MMKB [multiple mathematical knowledge bases]" (p. 266). In the methods class, I hoped to support PSTs to be less teacher-focused and begin to see and listen to students.

Throughout the mathematics methods course, PSTs engaged in a variety of assignments and experiences, such as a community walk to learn more about the community around the school or critiquing textbook lessons. The two assigned texts were *Principles to Actions: Ensuring Mathematical Success for All* (NCTM, 2014) and *Reimagining the Mathematics Classroom* (Yeh, Ellis & Hurtado, 2017). The majority of the *Reimagining* book was read prior to the start of STEM club and addressed talk moves, number talks and high cognitive demand tasks as well as other components of teaching and classrooms. The introduction and Effective Teaching and Learning sections of the *Principles to Action* was read and discussed after the STEM club.

STEM CLUB

The STEM club allowed the PSTs to consider how theory is expressed in practice. The benefits of the STEM club model were PSTs completed core methods assignments with faculty support; PSTs observed faculty and other PSTs modeling various pedagogical ideas; PSTs used various pedagogical ideas with a small group of students; and PSTs worked together to create and facilitate an integrated mathematics and science lesson. Details about these benefits are provided followed by more description on the use of the Beebots.

Because both the science and mathematics methods courses had a variety of core assignments, PSTs were expected to complete (as part of an agreed upon syllabus university-wide), the STEM club became a site for some of these assignments. Although this limited integration of mathematical and scientific concepts in a single lesson, the STEM club allowed us to observe our PSTs implementing ideas from the methods courses through these core assignments. For example, the importance of getting to know students holistically and mathematically was reinforced through dedicating the first two weeks of STEM club to PSTs interviewing pairs of students.

Through our STEM club plan, PSTs were able to see pedagogical techniques modeled by myself and the science educator and then try these same techniques themselves with a small group of elementary students (3-4 students). For example, PSTs observed me lead a number talk with the whole group of 2nd graders (Week 4). Then the following weeks (Week 5 and 6), they either led a number talk to a group of 4 elementary students or observed their partner lead a number talk to that same group of elementary students. A similar format was used for a mini-lesson for a small group of 3rd graders using a high cognitive demand task based on a community walk experience prior to STEM club starting and/or the student interviews (in Weeks 1 and 2). This allowed for PSTs to not only learn to listen to students but to also consider planning lessons that were responsive to student interests and needs as well as build a repertoire of talk moves. There were also two weeks dedicated exclusively to whole group science lessons lead by the PSTs. Prior to the start of the STEM club, the PSTs worked in pairs to plan a lesson on an astronomy concept. They then taught these lessons to each other. Through this experience, lessons were modified; and the PSTs with consultation of the science educator determined which lessons would be used during the STEM club.

For the final week of STEM club, one PST, based on observing students flipping water bottles during snack each week of club, designed a lesson where students experimented to learn the ideal water amount in a bottle to more frequently "land" the bottle. This lesson represented the culmination of the work the PSTs had done on planning, listening and respecting student ideas, and encouraging student talk as well as integrating the mathematical and scientific practices (in CCSM and Next Generation Science Standards, respectively). The whole group of PSTs facilitated the lesson to the whole group of students on both days of club.

Beebots were used for part of five of the eight week STEM club. The elementary students were very motivated and interested in exploring the Beebots. Because Beebots were new to PSTs and faculty, in mathematics methods we explored the potential uses of Beebots and PSTs were given time to explore and then program a Beebot to pass through a maze. In STEM club, I provided whole group directions and discussion during Beebot activities while PSTs worked with their students in small groups. Initially, the elementary students engaged in open play with the Beebots and shared what was learned to the whole group. Next, students were provided mazes and challenged to program their Beebot to get through the maze. Students were then challenged to recreate drawings by taping a pencil, pen or marker onto the back of the Beebot and programming the Beebot to create the drawing on a big sheet of paper. These initial activities focused more on computational literacy; however in the debriefs PSTs and faculty discussed the mathematical and scientific practices engaged in by the students. For two STEM club meetings, the Beebots were used with an explicit mathematical purpose. Students created and labelled number lines for the Beebots to travel on. Discussions around measurement and characteristics of number lines were explored. In the following club meeting, the students programmed the Beebot to "do math" by coding it to move along a number line to solve basic expressions, such as 3 + 4 or 8 − 2. This lead to discussions around direction on a number line and how a number line could be used to represent addition and subtraction.

PARTICIPANTS

All PSTs (10) enrolled in our mathematics and science methods courses participated in the STEM club experience. Eight PSTs agreed to participate in the study. All 8 were undergraduates and female. Six identified as Caucasian. Two PSTs would graduate after at least two more semesters, and 7 PSTs were planning to full-time student teach the semester following this course. All 8 were enrolled in science methods, mathematics methods and social studies methods courses during this semester. Seven of the eight PSTs were also enrolled in the pre-student teaching seminar as well as the pre-student teaching field experience two days a week. The design of the program is for PSTs to complete the final four semesters as a cohort; however only 6 of the PSTs participating in the study were planning on graduating after student teaching the following semester. One undergraduate changed her major so needed to complete some general education courses after student teaching. Another PST did not complete all of her entrance to major requirements in time to complete the recommended sequence of courses. Thus, the faculty agreed to allow her to complete her degree in a slightly different path than was traditional (by completing the Language Arts methods courses and pre-student teaching experience in the semester following the mathematics and science methods classes).

DATA SOURCES

In order to investigate if the PSTs saw connections between the theoretical ideas of the mathematics methods course and the STEM club experience as well as if there were changes in what the PSTs noticed, the Noticing Journal assignment from the mathematics methods course was analyzed as well as our planning document and an instructor journal that myself and the science educator kept of our observations, wonderings, etc. throughout the 8 weeks of the STEM club.

Noticing Journals

Over the course of the semester, the Noticing Journals contained 16 prompts. There was one prompt each for the first four weeks of class. The STEM club started Week 5 of the semester and typically there were two prompts (one after the Monday club meeting and one after the Wednesday club meeting). These prompts were responsive to observations the science educator and I were making about our PSTs. The primary purpose of the journal was to support the PSTs in learning and growing as educators in the methods courses. In general, Roth McDuffie et. al's (2014) framework using the four lenses was used to craft journal prompts. At times one or more lenses were highlighted in the journal prompt. The final prompt was at the conclusion of STEM club asking for a more thorough reflection on their own teaching practices across four domains used to evaluate their teaching in the fieldwork: planning, teaching, analyzing learning, and fulfilling responsibilities. Initially, the journal assignment requested the use of academic language and writing in the journals; however, upon reflection of the mathematics methods assignments there was too much emphasis on academic writing. PSTs need to learn to write in a variety of modes. Teachers write notes to parents, emails to administrators and colleagues and lesson plans. Some of these require more formal, academic writing but not all of them. Thus, the Noticing Journal assignment changed to be a place where academic language was not expected. Instead PSTs were expected to write clearly and the use of "I" was appropriate.

Each PST completed all 16 journal entries. A grade was assigned based on responding to all parts of the prompt on time (essentially a completion grade). If a PST was late in writing a journal reflection (which happened 19 times), the grade was lowered slightly for the late submission. All of the responses to the final prompt were 8 paragraphs long due to the structure of the prompt. The average number of paragraphs in a single prompt response, not including the final prompt, was 3.45 paragraphs. See the Appendix for the list of all prompts used.

Planning Document

In order to communicate the plans for each week, given PSTs did not have formal class meeting time outside of the STEM club, a Google document was used. The document had a calendar with the key components of each week (similar to Table 1) with links to more detailed lesson plans for each of the key components. The PSTs, for the most part, generated the more detailed lesson plans. Directions were provided for the two student interviews and lesson planning formats for the small group number talk and mini-lessons were provided to PSTs. The lesson plan for the number line activity with the Beebots was given to the PSTs.

Instructor Journal

The science educator and I kept a journal through a shared Google document. We used the document to reflect on the STEM club meeting including the debrief, our PSTs, things to consider for future assignments or prompts, etc. This reflection was not regularly written; however, there were 12 dated entries. Entries were typically written the evening or day after a club meeting.

METHODS FOR DATA ANALYSIS

In order to answer the two research questions (what, if any, changes in noticing are in PSTs' writing? And what, if any, connections between theory and practice were written about by PSTs?), twelve of the 16 Noticing Journal prompts were selected for analysis (see Appendix for all prompts). Prompts 2, 3, and 4 were analyzed to establish a baseline for what these PSTs were noticing in their writing. These are referred to as pre-club journals. Eleven prompts (from 5-15) all occurred during the STEM club. Eight of these prompts (excluding 9, 14 and 15) were focused on the teaching and learning of mathematics or noticing of students. The selected STEM club prompts were analyzed to see what the PSTs were noticing and any connections they wrote about with respect to the theory we had been learning and our practice in the STEM club. The final prompt was also analyzed and used as an ending point for the PSTs noticing and connection making between theory and practice.

Data were analyzed qualitatively focusing on what PSTs were noticing as well as writing specific to theory and practice connecting. Research memos were created for every journal prompt response for all 8 participants (excluding responses to journal prompts 1, 9, 14 and 15). These memos were then used to write summary memos of the baseline, STEM club and final prompts for each participant. These memos were analyzed for what PSTs noticed with respect to the STEM club, methods class, and their field work. Memos were created considering the Roth McDuffie et. al's (2014) framework that was used in the methods course in addition to van Es and Sherin's (2008) definition of noticing. In addition, the development literature that suggests beginning teachers focus more on themselves and management of students (Mewborn, 1999; Roller, 2015) was used. Because journal prompts varied (see Appendix), no a priori codes were used. Themes emerged across participants with respect to student behavior and play as well as ways students think mathematically. The Instructor Journal entries and Planning Document were used to look for confirming and disconfirming evidence of the results of the Noticing Journal analysis.

RESULTS

In this section, the first result discussed is how PST writing shifted from controlling student behavior to play, followed by the noticing of student ideas. Finally, a more detailed analysis of written responses to Prompt 11, after the club meeting with a modelled whole group number talk, will be shared highlighting what PSTs writing focused on towards the end of the experience. The whole group number talk was particularly interesting because there were student behavior issues and it was the first explicit modeling of a pedagogical idea during STEM club.

Shifts From Student Behavior to Play

Consistent with teacher development and noticing literature (e.g. Berliner, 1988; Star, Lynch & Perova; 2011; Star & Strickland, 2008), the PSTs initially focused on behavior management of students in the club. For example, many of the PSTs wrote about how chaotic the first day of club was for the second graders, particularly with respect to snack and dismissal. Although we had generated plans for the day together and we requested as much detail as possible, the PSTs were hesitant to document more than the big ideas of the plan. The norms for how we handle snack and dismissal became a large part of the discussion in the beginning few weeks of STEM club.

This focus on managing student behavior, particularly in the beginning of STEM club, is also reflected in the instructor journal. The PSTs limited elementary students use of manipulatives despite the high teacher to student ratio in the STEM club. For example, during the first day, one PST organized the crayons in a rainbow in the middle of the table and would not let students touch them until she said they could. This type of behavior across all PSTs was most evident in Week 3 (see Table 1) when the PSTs planned a crashing landing on the moon activity. This required the PSTs to assemble backpacks with the items that survived the crash. Despite assembling the backpacks as manipulatives for students to use in the lesson, most PSTs emptied the backpacks for their group of second grade students instead of allowing the students to see what was in the backpack themselves. During the second time teaching this same lesson, the PSTs allowed the students to unpack the backpack and made lots of intentional changes to their lesson plan to make it more interactive and engaging. These changes are evident in the instructor journal and planning document around this activity as well. Five PSTs wrote about this experience of teaching the crash landing activity with third graders indicating that the there was more student voice and participation. Two PSTs talked about the changes in the lesson plan representing risk-taking by the PSTs themselves and realizing the importance of "stepping back" as the instructor and giving students more freedom and play time. This lesson planning and enacting experience indicated a shift in experimentation with how lessons can involve play with manipulatives without sacrificing management.

As the club continued, the PSTs writing focused less on student behavior and more on how to put ideas of "play" into practice while maintaining some sort of structure. Thus, their focus began to shift from controlling student behavior to balancing freedom and structure in activities for students. As instructors of the methods courses, we encouraged the PSTs to take risks and allow students to play informally before giving too much structure to an activity. Many PSTs (5 of 8) wrote about the importance of play and the balance of that with structure when writing about the STEM club. Many saw connections to the idea of play from previous education coursework. One PST wrote, in response to Prompt 6:

As [our instructors] have stressed, allowing students time to explore and "play" with the manipulatives is extremely beneficial. Prior to working with the second graders, I was unaware of the importance of experimenting with materials. Although we learned a lot about the importance of play in [a previous] class, I was unaware that play is important when doing experiments and structured activities as well. Last week, we allowed the second grade students time to play and explore with the bee-bots before moving on to more structured activities. I feel that this really helped the students become engaged in the activity.

We can see earlier coursework and current instructors' suggestions were connecting to the STEM club. Through seeing second graders engaged in play in order to support our ultimate goals of developing beginning practices that support coding, this PST realized the power of play in engaging learners.

The idea of play was a tension for some as they made sense of play and structure in a classroom setting. Did play invite management issues? How do you (or can you) have a managed classroom and still allow students some freedom to play? Some dismissed the tension by suggesting this behavior of play was acceptable in an afterschool club setting but there would need to be more structure in a classroom setting (meaning less play). Others appeared to contemplate the tension and how it connects to their future classrooms. One PST suggested, in her final journal entry, she could aim for "organized chaos" in her classroom, a place "where students can still be themselves in the classroom, yet we all have a plan and purpose, thus managed". For some of the PSTs the concept of management and student behavior appeared to shift over time as the PST saw benefits to students when given time and space to play.

Over the course of the semester, as the PSTs gained confidence and were encouraged by the instructors to take risks in their teaching, the PSTs were able to see the benefits of play and began to see what elementary students do in a given situation instead of preventing what the PSTs assumed students would do. Through debriefing and writing about observations from the STEM club meetings, PSTs expanded their noticing of their role as teacher to not just be about controlling student behavior but focus on engagement with the planned activity. Despite this shift, there was still a tension with balancing play and structure and PSTs varied on how they managed that tension.

Student Ideas

In the pre-club journal writing, PSTs often wrote about the value they saw in tasks, connecting to the community, and encouraging student talk in math lessons. These were all ideas from readings and coursework. The writing tended to be more academic despite the directions indicating it did not need to be. The writing during STEM club, however, became more focused on the surprise and excitement of student ideas about mathematics. This is similar to the results of the science nights literature where PSTs realized students had scientific ideas (Harlow, 2012; McCollough & Ramirez, 2010). This shift, although about observations of students, also reflects how the PSTs did not expect students to have mathematical ideas to share at club.

Initially, during the weeks focused on interviewing students (Weeks 1 and 2, see Table 1), the PSTs wrote about listening to students and getting to know students more generically. As PSTs gained experience in the STEM club, the PSTs wrote more details about the student ideas that were being generated. For example, one PST wrote about seeing the students using addition and subtraction to figure out how to navigate the Beebots through a maze:

I also noticed that my students started to use math while doing this. If they needed it to go a little further they made an addition problem and if it needed to go back a little, they did subtraction. I was very happy to see this because it meant that they were really connecting this to math and not just considering it as a toy to play with. (Prompt 6)

Her writing indicates that she was "very happy" to see students using mathematics with the Beebots and described how the math was being used by students. This same PST, when describing her excitement about leading a number talk in a small group later in club wrote how she is "fascinated" by how different students think and felt the number talk would elicit various ideas. Similarly, another PST frequently wrote "cool" or "fascinating" when writing about seeing how students engaged in math problems and activities. For example, she wrote when reflecting on how her number talk went:

all of the students in my group approached 14 and 3 as an addition question FIRST. However, [student] was the only student out of the 3 to do addition AND subtraction and find multiple ways for both--quite fascinating! (Prompt 13)

The PST considered her prompting of the number talk and wondered if she influenced students approach because using addition was what she had anticipated.

Not surprisingly, when PSTs began working with students, as opposed to reading cases or watching video, their reflections became slightly more detailed and expressed more emotion about the mathematical ideas students were expressing. These approximations were more authentic to teaching and revealed how surprised PSTs were to see the mathematical creativity in the students. Although there were some writings guessing at why these things were happening and making connections to ideas from coursework, this was not true for all PSTs. These differences in making connections can best be seen through analysis of the journal entries about the number talk that was modelled for PSTs during the STEM club.

Whole Group Number Talk

During the Week 4 club meeting, the students engaged in a whole group number talk followed by an activity programming the Beebot to make a specific drawing. One PST was absent during this club meeting. During the whole group number talk, a few students were misbehaving and their behavior was distracting to the rest of the student group. One student in particular, Connor (all names are pseudonyms), was very disruptive by laying on the floor. During the debrief, the PSTs talked about my decisions about handling Connor's behavior. While facilitating the debrief, I also encouraged the PSTs to discuss the mathematics from the students who were participating in the number talk. As reported earlier, the PSTs were inclined to focus on management issues but were willing to discuss mathematical ideas surfaced in the number talk as well as the talk moves implemented (or not). PSTs did have observations on all of these topics to contribute to the debrief. In their journal (Prompt 11), the PSTs were asked to reflect on something that stuck out in their mind from this STEM club meeting.

Of the seven PSTs present, five wrote about the number talk and/or the misbehaving students. The other two PSTs wrote about the Beebot work that was completed that day. Further analysis of the five journal entries focused on the number talk show two categories of focus: one on Connor and the other on the mathematics and talk moves in the number talk.

Three PSTs wrote explicitly about Connor; however, their foci were slightly different. One PST described differences in Connor's behavior from the number talk to small group work after the number talk. Another PST wrote about Connor's misbehavior during the number talk and generated several other possible options I could have taken and wondered about my decisions. The third PST wrote about Connor's behavior compared to the other students commenting, "the students were chatty; however, many of them were participating." This PST wondered what math lessons look like in the second grade graders' classrooms. This third writing was still focused on noticing behavior but not with the end result of fixing the behavior. Instead this PST wondered about the continuity of what we were doing in club and what the students were experiencing during the school day. In these journal entries, the beginning shift for some PSTs to focus less on managing student behavior and to make sense of a student's experience is evident.

Of the five PSTs who wrote about the number talk, two PSTs' writing focused primarily on the mathematics and the talk moves implemented. The problem posed was 11 + 14. One student, Holly, shared her solution, which I wrote on chart paper, indicating she added the ones place and the tens place together. When I asked her where the "2" came from in 25, she was hesitant. After some wait time, another student, Max, offered to explain where he thought the 2 came from (adding the two tens together). One PST, in her journal, was surprised by Holly's inability to explain where the 2 came from and wondered if the students had ever experienced a number talk before. Another PST was impressed how Max helped Holly explain her thinking. She wondered if number talks were done regularly, if there would be an increase in the number of ways students had to solve problems like this. Both of these PSTs focused their reflection on what mathematically was happening during the number talk and wondered about the regular use of number talks in the classroom.

Because number talks and talk moves were a large part of the course readings, video watching and discussion prior to STEM club as well as the work during STEM club, these five PSTs writing reveals what the PSTs were focusing on during the number talk and any connections they were making between theory and practice. The two connections were about student behavior and management of the behavior as well as the mathematical ideas and talk moves during the number talk. This suggests these PSTs were beginning to make connections between their work in methods/STEM club and their regular classroom practice. There was also evidence indicating a wondering about the students' experiences in STEM club and if it was similar or different to their second-grade math lesson experiences.

The overall analysis of the writing shows the PSTs initially focused on classroom management but slowly shifted to considering the idea of play along with management. Many PSTs also wrote about what they were noticing in terms of students' mathematical ideas. These were not fully detailed or robust but indicated a shift towards student thinking. The students' experience in STEM club and their elementary classrooms became a wondering for some PSTs. This indicates some small success in supporting PST noticing as well as connecting the work in the informal field experience, the STEM club, with university coursework.

DISCUSSION

For teacher education practitioners, there are successes and limitations of this model as well as practical considerations for implementing something similar in a different setting. Upon completion of the first implementation of this model, the PSTs appreciated seeing their methods instructors in action with elementary students. This came up in verbal debriefs as well as in their noticing journals. The PSTs also appreciated seeing theory come to life and have the opportunity to try some of these ideas out. PST writing began to show shifts in ideas around student management and freedom to play in a lesson. Additionally, PST writing showed some PSTs surprised by student mathematical ideas and documenting those ideas in their journals. Similar to the informal field experience literature (e.g. Harlow, 2012; McCollough & Ramirez, 2010; McDonald, 1997), PSTs appeared to be surprised by student excitement about mathematics and science and began to see their own potential as instructors of mathematics and science.

Although there is no way to conclude what exactly about the model supported these beginning shifts, as the instructor, there are some aspects of the model to highlight that appeared to support these shifts. First, by repeating lessons each week, PSTs were able to reflect on their planning (Was there enough detail? Did they anticipate how students would react? Were they prepared to talk about the mathematical and scientific ideas? How did the discussion go?) as well as consider how students reacted to the planned lesson (Was it engaging? Were the mathematical and scientific ideas clearly the focus?). This allowed for immediate application of ideas discussed in the course as Bahr et. al (2014) suggested to be important. Second, having the time to debrief after the STEM club was important in supporting PSTs to focus on various elements that the teacher educators observed and felt needed to be highlighted. In general, we opened up the debrief broadly asking PSTs what went well and what did not go well. Then we would typically focus the conversation on a topic that we felt was important to highlight. Lastly, as Janset et. al (2018) highlighted, PSTs were able to see a model of number talks and implementing a high cognitive demand task as well as practice these same pedagogical techniques themselves. These experiences were absent in previous versions of the methods class and PSTs highlighted these as helpful components of the coursework.

Unfortunately, some of the PSTs felt they learned how to implement number talks, talk moves and gained some experiences with tasks but only for small groups and only in an afterschool club setting. These PSTs potentially left methods class without a solid understanding of how these ideas would scale to a whole class setting. Some also felt what they learned was only appropriate for an afterschool setting. Some of these ideas were certainly beliefs about the teaching and learning of mathematics. Others were a result of the limits they saw in their field work classroom. Despite knowing this might be a possibility and trying to counter these ideas by repeatedly suggesting how STEM club was run the same way the methods instructors would run a regular classroom, these beliefs were still present in some of our PSTs. Although we were able to provide an informal field experience space for PSTs to experiment, more work needs to be done to support PSTs in seeing the ways in which the STEM club is an authentic approximation of practice and how to support PSTs in extending their learning to a larger group of students and in other settings. This might be accomplished simply by giving PSTs the opportunity to share how the club is similar and different to their more formal two day a week field work (similar to one of the dimensions of Janset and colleagues' (2018) framework).

This leads to some ideas for future implementation. Although our program is small, it is still challenging to coordinate with other faculty members in the program. Some members of the faculty are part-time and others have conflicting schedules. This is similar to the challenges Zeichner (2010) detailed of other programs. Ideally the field experience supervisor and seminar leader would work closely with methods instructors in order to help PSTs see the applicability of their learnings from STEM club to the classrooms they student teach in. Further work needs to be done on how to logistically make this component of the program stronger. Additionally, the focus for the STEM club was on astronomy, number and computational literacy through the use of Beebots. This focus may not have been as clear to PSTs as they navigate five undergraduate courses as well as two days a week in a pre-student teaching field experience. Additionally, there may be other foci that are more important depending on the context of the coursework and the partnership school. In the future, we plan to have a more cohesive, explicit focus on these to more clearly communicate to PSTs the goals of the methods courses as well as the goals of the STEM club.

Other ways to address these beliefs some PSTs held on to about the value of what they were learning are to cut back on the number of club offerings per week. The methods course came to a halt and solely operated to run the STEM club for 8 weeks of a 15-week semester. Although being able to re-teach a lesson was beneficial to our PSTs, we think there is more to gain in having stronger preparation and debrief time by only offering the club one day a week. This would allow more questions to surface and more connections to their field work to be discussed. In the future we plan to run the STEM club for the first few weeks with third graders followed by similar plans for second graders. This way PSTs would still be re-teaching lessons with more time to debrief and plan.

There is also the possibility of engaging in rehearsals (Lampert, Franke, Kazemi, Ghousseini, Turrou, Beasley, ... & Crowe, 2013) to better support the development of practices. In addition, we assigned topics/weeks of the club to a PST or two in order to spread the planning out with the rest of the PSTs providing feedback. This was not successful as PSTs were not used to collaborating electronically and had varying views of what collaboration meant. This led myself and the science educator, as seen in the instructor journal, to believe PSTs often came to STEM club unprepared to teach the second graders (the first group of the week) and then significantly improved their lesson plan for the third graders.

Thus, work on what collaboration means and how to divide the work deserves attention and time. By giving more time to theory while we are also practicing in the STEM club, the hope is to better establish what it means to collaborate professionally and not just be encouraging of a classmate. Additionally, PSTs were asked to generate many of the plans for club meetings. In the future, we plan to experiment with providing lessons or the majority of a lesson plan and better scaffold PSTs learning how to create detailed lesson plans (similar to Billings, Ball, & Benincasa, 2018).

The benefit of using an afterschool setting is the PSTs are still able to practice components of ambitious teaching in a school setting with students from that school without the pressures of a prescribed curriculum or state testing (Grossman, Compton, Igra, Ronfeldt, Shahan, & Williamson, 2009; Harlow, 2012). The downfalls are PSTs may see the practices that are being developed to only be useful in an afterschool setting. Those PSTs who saw their mentor teachers in their field experiences implementing number talks or encouraging student talk were likely to see the club as a place to grow. More needs to be done to better support PSTs in seeing the value of what they were learning.

For teacher education researchers, a more detailed study on what the PSTs learned through the experience needs to be conducted. Ideally this could be done contrasting a traditional methods course with a course using this model, similar to Bahr et. al (2013). The journal prompts varied from week to week based on the perceived needs of the PSTs and the goals of the methods courses; however, varying the prompts may have influenced PSTs writing and may not reflect changes in noticing but instead suggest the flexibility of PSTs to notice when requested. In addition, seeing if the shifts in what PSTs write about in STEM club translates to their field experience during the same semester or when PSTs full-time student teach the following semester would help the field understand how methods coursework influences PSTs' teaching practice. Although the PSTs in this study tended to focus on student behavior as suspected from the literature (Berliner, 1998; Star & Strickland, 2008), they did begin to focus on students' mathematical ideas. Particularly when observing the whole group number talk, some PSTs let go of the behavior issues and focused in on the mathematical ideas and pedagogical ideas. This suggests the potential for a model like this to support teacher development of beginning PSTs. Future research could use frameworks like those of Aguirre et. al (2012), Santagata (2011), or van Es (2011), for example, to explore these shifts in more detail. Questions about the benefits and limitations to the elementary students and school community were not addressed but would be interesting to investigate.

Overall, this was a successful experience for the school, PTO, instructors and PSTs. By holding the club after school, we met the needs of the school community while also providing our PSTs an opportunity to experiment with pedagogical ideas with our supervision. Although there were some limitations to the model as executed, the science educator and I plan to continue to experiment to refine the model to strike a balance with time for planning and debriefing with PSTs as well as enacting plans through STEM club.

ACKNOWLEDGMENT

The author wishes to thank her colleagues that supported this work, particularly Dr. Kathy Fadigan. The author would also like to thank the PSTs, the PTO members, and the principal of our partnering elementary school for their willingness to explore and learn from this model.

REFERENCES

Aguirre, J. M., Turner, E. E., Bartell, T. G., Kalinec-Craig, C., Foote, M. Q., Roth McDuffie, A., & Drake, C. (2012). Making connections in practice: How prospective elementary teachers connect to children's mathematical thinking and community funds of knowledge in mathematics instruction. *Journal of Teacher Education, 64*(2), 178–192. doi:10.1177/0022487112466900

Anderson, D., Lawson, B., & Mayer-Smith, J. (2006). Investigating the impact of a practicum experience in an aquarium on pre-service teachers. *Teaching Education, 17*(4), 341–353. doi:10.1080/10476210601017527

Bahr, D., Monroe, E. E., Balzotti, M., & Eggett, D. (2009). Crossing the barriers between preservice and inservice mathematics teacher education: An evaluation of the Grant School professional development program. *School Science and Mathematics, 109*(4), 223–236. doi:10.1111/j.1949-8594.2009.tb18260.x

Bahr, D., Monroe, E. E., & Shaha, S. H. (2013). Examining preservice teacher belief changes in the context of coordinated mathematics methods coursework and classroom experiences. *School Science and Mathematics, 113*(3), 144–155. doi:10.1111sm.12010

Bahr, D. L., Monroe, E. E., & Eggett, D. (2014). Structural and conceptual interweaving of mathematics methods coursework and field practica. *Journal of Mathematics Teacher Education, 17*(3), 271–297. doi:10.100710857-013-9258-z

Ball, D. L., Thames, M. H., & Phelps, G. (2008). Content knowledge for teaching: What makes it special? *Journal of Teacher Education, 59*(5), 389–407. doi:10.1177/0022487108324554

Barnhart, T., & van Es, E. (2015). Studying teacher noticing: Examining the relationship among preservice science teachers' ability to attend, analyze and respond to student thinking. *Teaching and Teacher Education, 45*, 83–93. doi:10.1016/j.tate.2014.09.005

Berliner, D. C. (1988). Implications of studies on expertise in pedagogy for teacher education and evaluation. In *New Directions for Teacher Assessment* (Vol. 49, pp. 39–68). Princeton, NJ: Educational Testing Services.

Billings, E. M. H., Ball, D., & Benincasa, O. (2018) *Early school-based learning field experiences: Embedding and enacting core teaching practices in authentic classroom settings.* Paper presented at the meeting of the Association of Mathematics Teacher Educators, Houston, TX.

Burke, J. P. (2017). *Case study of mathematical playfulness in an adult mathematics classroom setting* (Unpublished doctoral dissertation). University of Massachusetts, Dartmouth, MA.

Carter, K., Cushing, K., Sabers, D., Stein, P., & Berliner, D. (1988). Expert-novice differences in perceiving and processing visual classroom information. *Journal of Teacher Education, 39*(3), 25–31. doi:10.1177/002248718803900306

Cartwright, T. J. (2012). Science talk: Preservice teachers facilitating science learning in diverse afterschool environments. *School Science and Mathematics, 112*(6), 384–391. doi:10.1111/j.1949-8594.2012.00147.x

Chesebrough, D. (1994). Informal science teacher preparation. *Science Education International, 5*(2), 28–33.

Darling-Hammond, L. (2000). How teacher education matters. *Journal of Teacher Education, 51*(3), 166–173. doi:10.1177/0022487100051003002

De Holton, D., Ahmed, A., Williams, H., & Hill, C. (2001). On the importance of mathematical play. *International Journal of Mathematical Education in Science and Technology, 32*(3), 401–415. doi:10.1080/00207390118654

Dewey, J. (1904). The relation of theory to practice in education. In M. L. Borrowman (Ed.), *Teacher education in America: A documentary history* (pp. 140–171). New York, NY: Teachers College Press. (Original work published 1965)

Ebby, C. B. (2000). Learning to teach mathematics differently: The interaction between coursework and fieldwork for preservice teachers. *Journal of Mathematics Teacher Education, 3*(1), 69–97. doi:10.1023/A:1009969527157

Feiman-Nemser, S., & Buchmann, M. (1985, April). *On what is learned in student teaching: Appraising the experience.* Paper presented at the annual meeting of the American Association of Colleges of Teacher Education, Chicago, IL.

Fernández, C., Llinares, S., & Valls, J. (2013). Primary school teacher's noticing of students' mathematical thinking in problem solving. *The Mathematics Enthusiast, 10*(1/2), 441.

Ferry, B. (1995). Science centers in Australia provide valuable training for preservice teachers. *Journal of Science Education and Technology, 4*(3), 255–260. doi:10.1007/BF02211840

Foote, M. Q., Roth McDuffie, A., Aguirre, J., Turner, E. E., Drake, C., & Bartell, T. G. (2015). Mathematics Learning Case Study Module. In *TeachMath learning modules for K-8 mathematics methods courses.* Teachers Empowered to Advance Change in Mathematics Project. Retrieved from: www.teachmath.info

Forzani, F. M. (2014). Understanding "core practices" and "practice-based" teacher education: Learning from the past. *Journal of Teacher Education, 65*(4), 357–368. doi:10.1177/0022487114533800

Grossman, P., Compton, C., Igra, D., Ronfeldt, M., Shahan, E., & Williamson, P. (2009). Teaching practice: A cross-professional perspective. *Teachers College Record, 111*(9), 2055–2100.

Grossman, P., & McDonald, M. (2008). Back to the future: Directions for research in teaching and teacher education. *American Educational Research Journal, 45*(1), 184–205. doi:10.3102/0002831207312906

Harlow, D. B. (2012). The excitement and wonder of teaching science: What pre-service teachers learn from facilitating family science night centers. *Journal of Science Teacher Education, 23*(2), 199–220. doi:10.100710972-012-9264-5

Jacobs, V. R., Lamb, L. L., & Philipp, R. A. (2010). Professional noticing of children's mathematical thinking. *Journal for Research in Mathematics Education, 41*(2), 169–202.

Jacobs, V. R., Lamb, L. L., Philipp, R. A., & Schappelle, B. P. (2011). Deciding how to respond on the basis of children's understandings. In M. G. Sherin, V. R. Jacobs & R. A. Philipp (Eds.), Mathematics teacher noticing: Seeing through teachers' eyes (pp. 97-116). New York: Routledge.

Jenset, I. S., Klette, K., & Hammerness, K. (2018). Grounding teacher education in practice around the world: An examination of teacher education coursework in teacher education programs in Finland, Norway, and the United States. *Journal of Teacher Education*, *69*(2), 184–197. doi:10.1177/0022487117728248

Jung, M. L., & Tonso, K. L. (2006). Elementary preservice teachers learning to teach science in science museums and nature centers: A novel program's impact on science knowledge, science pedagogy, and confidence teaching. *Journal of Elementary Science Education*, *18*(1), 15–31. doi:10.1007/BF03170651

Katz, P., Randy McGinnis, J., Riedinger, K., Marbach-Ad, G., & Dai, A. (2013). The influence of informal science education experiences on the development of two beginning teachers' science classroom teaching identity. *Journal of Science Teacher Education*, *24*(8), 1357–1379. doi:10.100710972-012-9330-z

Kazemi, E., & Hintz, A. (2014). *Intentional talk: How to structure and lead productive mathematical discussions*. Portland, ME: Stenhouse.

Lampert, M., Franke, M. L., Kazemi, E., Ghousseini, H., Turrou, A. C., Beasley, H., ... Crowe, K. (2013). Keeping it complex: Using rehearsals to support novice teacher learning of ambitious teaching. *Journal of Teacher Education*, *64*(3), 226–243. doi:10.1177/0022487112473837

McCollough, C., & Ramirez, O. (2010). Connecting math and science to home, school and community through preservice teacher education. *Academic Leadership: The Online Journal*, *8*(2), 15.

McCulloch, A. W., Marshall, P. L., & DeCuir-Gunby, J. T. (2009). Cultural capital in children's number representations. *Teaching Children Mathematics*, *16*(3), 184–189.

McDonald, R. B. (1997). Using participation in public school "family science night" programs as a component in the preparation of preservice elementary teachers. *Science Education*, *81*(5), 577–595. doi:10.1002/(SICI)1098-237X(199709)81:5<577::AID-SCE5>3.0.CO;2-7

Mewborn, D. S. (1999). Reflective thinking among preservice elementary mathematics teachers. *Journal for Research in Mathematics Education*, *30*(3), 316–341. doi:10.2307/749838

National Governors Association Center for Best Practices & Council of Chief State School Officers. (2010). *Common core state standards for mathematics*. Washington, DC: National Governors Association Center for Best Practices and Council of Chief State School Officers.

National Research Council. (2012). *A framework for K-12 science education: Practices, crosscutting concepts, and core ideas*. Washington, DC: The National Academies Press.

NCTM. (2014). *Principles to actions: Ensuring mathematical success for all*. Reston, VA: National Council of Teachers of Mathematics.

Roller, S. A. (2015). What they notice in video: A study of prospective secondary mathematics teachers learning to teach. *Journal of Mathematics Teacher Education*, *19*(5), 477–498. doi:10.100710857-015-9307-x

Roth McDuffie, A., Foote, M. Q., Bolson, C., Turner, E. E., Aguirre, J. M., Bartell, T. G., ... Land, T. (2014). Using video analysis to support prospective K-8 teachers' noticing of students' multiple mathematical knowledge bases. *Journal of Mathematics Teacher Education, 17*(3), 245–258. doi:10.100710857-013-9257-0

Santagata, R. (2011). From teacher noticing to a framework for analyzing and improving classroom lessons. In M. G. Sherin, V. R. Jacobs & R. A. Philipp (Eds.), Mathematics teacher noticing: Seeing through teachers' eyes (pp. 152-168). New York: Routledge.

Sherin, M. G., & Han, S. Y. (2004). Teacher learning in the context of a video club. *Teaching and Teacher Education, 20*(2), 163–183. doi:10.1016/j.tate.2003.08.001

Shulman, L. S. (1986). Those who understand: Knowledge growth in teaching. *Educational Researcher, 15*(2), 4–14. doi:10.3102/0013189X015002004

Sowder, J. T. (2007). The mathematical education and development of teachers. In F. K. Lester (Ed.), *Second handbook of research on mathematics teaching and learning* (pp. 157–223). Charlotte, NC: Information Age Pub.

Star, J. R., Lynch, K., & Perova, N. (2011). Using video to improve preservice mathematics teachers' abilities to attend to classroom features. In M. G. Sherin, V. R. Jacobs & R. A. Philipp (Eds.), Mathematics teacher noticing: Seeing through teachers' eyes (pp. 117-133). New York: Routledge.

Star, J. R., & Strickland, S. K. (2008). Learning to observe: Using video to improve preservice mathematics teachers' ability to notice. *Journal of Mathematics Teacher Education, 11*(2), 107–125. doi:10.100710857-007-9063-7

Stein, M. K., & Smith, M. S. (1998). Mathematical tasks as a framework for reflection: From research to practice. *Mathematics Teaching in the Middle School, 3*(4), 268–275.

Turner, E., Aguirre, J., Drake, C., Bartell, T. G., Roth McDuffie, A., & Foote, M. Q. (2015). Community Mathematics Exploration Module. In *TeachMath learning modules for K-8 mathematics methods courses*. Teachers Empowered to Advance Change in Mathematics Project. Retrieved from: www.teachmath.info

Turner, E. E., Drake, C., Roth McDuffie, A., Aguirre, J., Bartell, T. G., & Foote, M. Q. (2012). Promoting equity in mathematics teacher preparation: A framework for advancing teacher learning of children's multiple mathematics knowledge bases. *Journal of Mathematics Teacher Education, 15*(1), 67–82. doi:10.100710857-011-9196-6

Van Es, E. A. (2011). A framework for learning to notice student thinking. In M. G. Sherin, V. R. Jacobs & R. A. Philipp (Eds.), Mathematics teacher noticing: Seeing through teachers' eyes (pp. 134-151). New York: Routledge.

Van Es, E. A., & Sherin, M. G. (2002). Learning to notice: Scaffolding new teachers' interpretations of classroom interactions. *Journal of Technology and Teacher Education, 10*(4), 571–596.

Van Es, E. A., & Sherin, M. G. (2008). Mathematics teachers' "learning to notice" in the context of video club. *Teaching and Teacher Education, 24*(2), 244–276. doi:10.1016/j.tate.2006.11.005

Wallace, C. S. (2013). Promoting shifts in preservice science teachers' thinking through teaching and action research in informal science settings. *Journal of Science Teacher Education, 24*(5), 811–832. doi:10.100710972-013-9337-0

Yeh, C., Ellis, M. W., & Hurtado, C. K. (2017). *Reimagining the mathematics classroom*. Reston, VA: National Council of Teachers of Mathematics.

Zeichner, K. (2010). Rethinking the connections between campus courses and field experiences in college-and university-based teacher education. *Journal of Teacher Education, 61*(1-2), 89–99. doi:10.1177/0022487109347671

ADDITIONAL READING

Chapin, S. H., O'Connor, C., O'Connor, M. C., & Anderson, N. C. (2009). *Classroom discussions: Using math talk to help students learn, Grades K-6*. Math Solutions.

Drake, C., Aguirre, J. M., Bartell, T. G., Foote, M. Q., Roth McDuffie, A., & Turner, E. E. (2015). *TeachMath Learning Modules for K-8 Mathematics Methods Courses*. Teachers Empowered to Advance Change in Mathematics Project. Retrieved from www.teachmath.info

Hufferd-Ackles, K., Fuson, K. C., & Sherin, M. G. (2004). Describing levels and components of a math-talk learning community. *Journal for Research in Mathematics Education, 35*(2), 81–116. doi:10.2307/30034933

Kagan, D. M. (1990). Professional growth among preservice and beginning teachers. *Review of Educational Research, 62*(2), 129–169. doi:10.3102/00346543062002129

Sherin, M. G., Jacobs, V. R., & Philipp, R. A. (2011). *Mathematics teacher noticing: Seeing through teachers' eyes*. New York: Rutledge.

Smith, M. S., & Stein, M. K. (2011). *Five practices for orchestrating productive mathematics discussions*. Reston, VA: National Council of Teachers of Mathematics.

Trocki, A., Taylor, C., Starling, T., Sztajn, P., & Heck, D. (2015). Launching a discourse-rich mathematics lesson. *Teaching Children Mathematics, 21*(5), 276–281. doi:10.5951/teacchilmath.21.5.0276

Vick, M. (2017). Integrating science methods with professional development. *Science and Children, 55*(1), 42. doi:10.2505/4c17_055_01_42

KEY TERMS AND DEFINITIONS

Beebot: A robot designed to look like a bee with basic function buttons. See more at https://www.bee-bot.us/.

Cognitive Demand of a Task: The amount of thought needed to engage in a mathematical task.

Informal Field Experience: An experience for pre-service teachers that takes place in an alternative setting rather than a standard school day.

Number Talk: A short activity designed to elicit a variety of student strategies while solving a mental math problem.

Play: The creativity and flexibility within mathematics. Often useful when initially engaging with a manipulative.

STEM: Integrating multiple ideas in mathematics, science and/or computational literacy in a single activity.

Student Talk: The pedagogical phenomenon of listening to student ideas, arguments, and reasoning.

APPENDIX

Noticing Journal Prompts

Prompt 1

We will be using what I call the "4 lenses" to critically view the teaching and learning of mathematics. The 4 lenses are the following:

- Task
- Teaching
- Learning
- Power & Participation

For your first prompt, *define and share how you think about each category/lens including questions you have (what do you wonder?).*

Prompt 2

Now that we've used the 4 lenses framework in class.

1. Reflect on your own classroom experiences and how you engaged in mathematics, how would you describe how your teachers addressed (or did not address) each of the lenses?
2. What are your thoughts on the 4 lenses as a framework? Are they similar to anything you've used in previous education courses?

Prompt 3

1. Reflecting on the reading you have done in Reimagining Math Classroom (Intro, Ch 1-5) and the Number Talk chapters (Kazemi & Hintz, 2014), respond to the following questions:

   a. What is resonating with you?
   b. What questions do you have? What do you wonder about?

Please clearly reference which reading you are referring to as you write. This is not formal writing but knowing which chapter or pages you are talking about makes it clear to your reader. If you quote anything directly please use quotations and cite appropriately.

2. Consider the Reimaging Math Classroom chapters you have read (almost the whole book!), in what ways do you think the authors addressed the 4 lenses (task, teaching, learning, power & participation)? What have you learned about each lens through the reading? Describe some specific things you might try in the classroom to address each lens?

I imagine for #2 you will have 4 headings - task, teaching, learning, power & participation - and respond to each question for each heading.

Prompt 4

Thinking about the community walk, what ideas do you have about each of the 4 lenses? What has our exploration of the STEM Club school community have you thinking about tasks, teaching, learning, and power & participation? Consider this article (McCulloch, Marshall & DeCuir-Gunby, 2009) in addition to Ch. 5 in the Reimagining Math Classroom book as you consider community and the 4 lenses.

Prompt 5

1.   What did you learn today about:
     a.   The students in our club,
     b.   Our group as instructors/facilitators, and
     c.   Using Beebots with students?
2.   What other observations do you have about today?

Prompt 6

1.   What did you learn today about:
     a.   The students in our club,
     b.   Our group as instructors/facilitators, and
     c.   Using Beebots with students?
2.   What other observations do you have about today?

Prompt 7

1.   What are you learning about teaching and learning math?
2.   What are you learning about teaching and learning science?
3.   What are you noticing about our work with the 2nd graders?

Prompt 8

Although this prompt may seem more formal and academic, my expectation is <u>not</u> academic writing. Just give me your thoughts, ideas, etc.

In seminar, you recently talked about foundational theories about student behavior (Skinner, Glasser, and Kohn) and your instructor shared this link (https://online.husson.edu/classroom-management-theories/) summarizing the big ideas in each.

1.   What theories do you think we are relying on in the STEM club?
2.   How is this similar and different to how you hope to manage your own classroom?

Prompt 9

1. Name one person in our class that you would like to teach with at least once during the STEM club and explain why.
2. Which of the 5Es did you feel the best about today? Explain.

Prompt 10

Using the student lens, what did you notice about students during the lesson Wednesday compared to Monday? Provide evidence (describe examples of specifics from the lesson) to support your thinking.

Prompt 11

Think of an interaction or situation that you observed today in STEM club that sticks out in your mind. It could be a conversation you had or something you observed someone else doing.

Describe the interaction/situation. Why does it stick out for you? What does it make you wonder about?

Prompt 12

Thinking ahead to next week and you leading a number talk and a small task lesson, consider these questions:

*   What are you most looking forward to in facilitating these two discussions?
*   What are you feeling a little anxious about?
*   What talk move would you like to try and get more familiar with using?

Prompt 13

1. **For everyone:** Reflect (in writing) on how you like to collaborate. How would you prefer to communicate? work together? etc.
2. **If you facilitated the number talk today:**
    a. What were you most surprised by?
    b. What did you anticipate happening that happened? (Or if nothing you anticipated happened, why do you think that happened?)
3. **If you observed a number talk today:**
    a. What were you most surprised by?
    b. What is one thing you learned from observing that you would like to implement in your own practice?

Prompt 14

Based upon the learning process for the phases of the moon that you personally experienced during science methods, discuss why you think that the explore part of the 5e is critical to learning science? Why in this case is the 5e method better than direct instruction or some other instructional strategy?

Prompt 15

Today you taught your science lesson. Taking the lesson an "e" at a time, what went well and what could be improved?

Your reflection should result in at least 5 sections (1 per "e" in the 5e model) responding to the questions of what went well and what could be improved.

Prompt 16

Take time to reflect on your work individually over the course of the 8-week STEM club. As you know, reflecting on your practice (across the 4 domains below) is important. For each domain, write 2 paragraphs. In one paragraph write about your strengths within the domain and in the other paragraph write about areas of growth.

Chapter 19
Practice–Based Approaches to Mathematics Education:
Vignettes and Experiences

Drew Polly
University of North Carolina at Charlotte, USA

Holly Pinter
Western Carolina University, USA

Amanda R. Casto
University of North Carolina at Charlotte, USA

ABSTRACT

This chapter provides a description of three efforts to integrate practice-based approaches to preparing pre-service teachers to teach mathematics to elementary and middle grades learners. The vignettes include a university laboratory school focused on middle grades students, a tutoring program for elementary school students, and a small group teaching experience with elementary school learners. Within each vignette, the authors describe findings from examining how these experiences influenced pre-service teachers. Lastly, they close the chapter with implications and directions for future research.

INTRODUCTION

Need to Reconsider Approaches to Teacher Education

The American Association of Colleges for Teacher Education (2018) recently called for teacher education programs to reconsider what entails clinical work and clinical practice for pre-service teachers. They put forth a number of recommendations, including carefully structured and extended work in schools for pre-service teachers. These recommendations come at a time when teacher education programs are still trying to make revisions based on the Blue Ribbon Panel Report from the National Council for the Accreditation of Teacher Education (NCATE, 2010).

DOI: 10.4018/978-1-5225-6249-8.ch019

A "sink or swim" metaphor is commonly used to describe the induction into teaching for beginning educators (Wood, Jilk, & Paine, 2012). There are a few problems with this metaphor, however. First, it oversimplifies the varying struggles of new teachers and ignores the common areas of greatest need, including content knowledge and pedagogy (Sleep & Boerst, 2012). Furthermore, it insinuates the message that teaching is a static practice devoid of experimentation and improvisation (Forzani, 2014). Finally, and most importantly, it negates the experiences pre-service teachers gain during their student teaching experience. Teaching is a unique and difficult profession to learn; it cannot be learned from reading a book or passively observing another teacher in a classroom. Instead, it is a constructivist practice requiring exploration, trial and error, and reflection of practice (Wood, Jilk, & Paine, 2012). Student teaching, as part of teacher education programs, is intentionally designed to prepare novice teachers with these necessary opportunities.

Student teaching experience, or school-based clinical experience, is a critical component of teacher preparation and is increasingly emphasized as such in research (Darden, Scott, Darden, & Westfall, 2001; Gut, Beam, Henning, Cochran, & Knight, 2014). Student teaching provides preservice teachers with routine practice of essential aspects of teaching, which allows them to build a repertoire of successful instructional habits (Peercy & Troyan, 2017). Preservice experiences allow novice teachers to construct their pedagogical views, gain insight into the spoken and unspoken school norms, and practice classroom management (Darden, Scott, Darden, & Westfall, 2001). According to Darden and colleagues (2001), the multitude of tasks and rules learned during student teaching can be overwhelming and disconcerting for some preservice teachers, especially if they have had limited exposure to the classroom setting as a professional educator.

Practice-Based Teacher Education

Many variations of teacher education have been researched and attempted at preparing novice teachers for the complexities of the U.S. classroom. Teacher education researchers (e.g., Ball & Forzani, 2009; Zeichner, 2010) have called for a practice-based curriculum to prepare novice teachers with the necessary teaching skills in addition to the knowledge required to carry out teaching tasks. Instead of reading about and theorizing the teaching practice outside of the educational setting, practice-based teacher education emphasizes the need for preservice teachers to have routine exposure to classroom settings as well as multiple opportunities to practice the multi-layered tasks of teaching (Ball & Forzani, 2009). Immersing preservice teachers into the field as a method of teacher education is sometimes referred as "teacher training," "teacher residencies," or "field experience" (Forzani, 2014).

Practice-based teacher education is highly beneficial for novice student teachers in numerous ways. First, it equips student teachers with the practical tools necessary to facilitate learning (Ball & Forzani, 2009). Secondly, it deepens their theoretical understanding of educational best practices (Peercy & Troyan, 2017). Third, it offers "significantly more—and more deliberate— opportunities for novices to practice the interactive work of instruction" (Ball & Forzani, 2009, p. 503). Finally, it provides vast opportunities to experience the ambitious teaching conditions held as the norm expectancy in today's schools (Forzani, 2014). While practice-based teacher education has many benefits, it has not been widely adopted by teacher education programs across the U.S.(Forzani, 2014). According to Peercy and Troyan (2017), widespread adoption of practice-based curriculums would require "massive epistemological and practical shifts" in teacher education (p. 27).

Core Practices

Successful implementation of practice-based teacher education has relied on teaching the core, or "high-leverage," practices of teaching (Forzani, 2014). According to McDonald, Kazemi, and Kavanagh (2013), core practices are:

specific, routine aspects of teaching that demand the exercise of professional judgment and the creation of meaningful intellectual and social community for teachers, teacher educators, and students. (p. 378)

Three goals in teacher education have emerged as a product of recent research on core practices: (1) instruction should increase students' high-level thinking, reasoning, and problem-solving skills; (2) teaching is an improvisational practice and novice teachers should be prepared for the uncertainties that may result in the teaching and learning process, and; (3) content should be a critical component of curricular goals and activities (Forzani, 2014). Although the core practices are deemed a significant component of teacher education across the literature, they have not been unanimously identified (Peercy & Troyan, 2017). Similarly, a lack of consensus regarding best practices for teaching and assessing novice teachers has existed since formal teacher education began nearly 200 years ago (Forzani, 2014).

Preparing Preservice Teachers for Mathematics Education

Today, teaching is viewed as "work that teachers do to help students learn for themselves, using the curriculum and their peers as resources." (Forzani, 2014, p. 359). This statement is regarded just as true in mathematics education as in any other discipline. The "sink or swim" metaphor described earlier can be, and often is, used to describe novice teachers in mathematics education (Wood, Jilk, & Paine, 2012). Novice mathematics teachers are faced with several challenges, including developing a deep conceptual understanding of the content they teach and learning how to assess students' mathematical thinking (Sleep & Boerst, 2012). Biza, Nardi, and Joel (2015) found that preservice teachers' desires to establish sociomathematical norms in their classrooms are commonly overpowered by their attention to classroom management, which is another new skill novice teachers are trying to master.

Recent studies found that intensive, ongoing experiences for pre-service teachers led to gains in efficacy towards teaching mathematics, high rates of transfer of course content related to teaching and assessment into candidates' teaching, and gains in student learning outcomes compared to students who did not have candidates intensively working in those classrooms (Aydin, Tunç-Pekkan, Taylan, Birgili, & Özcan, 2018).

In 2014, the National Council for Teachers of Mathematics (NCTM) published *Principles to Actions: Ensuring Mathematical Success for All* in an effort to increase the quality of mathematics instruction across the U.S. In *Principles to Actions*, NCTM lists eight research-based mathematics teaching practices, which are regarded by many as the new standard of essential and effective teaching. NCTM's call for teachers to be skilled in these mathematics teaching practices have placed a greater emphasis on the need for strong mathematics teacher education. Therefore, while it is important for novice math teachers to have strong content knowledge, they unequivocally need support during their preservice and early professional teaching experiences to effectively teach mathematics in the classroom (Wood, Jilk, & Paine, 2012).

Recently state senate bills and state board of education policies have been passed to promote more of a focus on the settings that pre-service teachers are placed in for clinical experiences (*State blinded* Senate, 2017; *State blinded* Board of Education, 2017). Notably, pre-service teachers must complete a portion of their clinicals in high-need schools determined by socioeconomic status and the number of students who come from impoverished backgrounds. Further, they must complete a series of clinical activities across their teacher education program that increases in duration, complexity, and depth. These policies have caused educator preparation programs in our state to be more thoughtful about the establishment of clinical experiences. In this chapter we provide 3 vignettes from 2 universities that are exploring some of the ideas behind practice-based teacher education.

Contexts of Clinical Experiences

University One is a rural university that graduates approximately 20 middle grades majors each year. The university partners with 18 school districts for clinical field experience placements. The middle grades program begin field experiences as early as freshman year with approximately 10 hours of observations in multiple grade levels. In the sophomore year, middle grades majors take three professional education courses that require 14-16 hours each. Pre-service teachers then participate in an additional 15 hours of tutoring with english language learners in their added culturally responsive course. The junior year, explored in the case below, requires another 10-15 hour field experience in the fall and approximately 70 hours in the spring of their junior year.

University two graduates approximately 175 undergraduate in elementary education each year. Pre-service teachers complete 10 hours of courses in each introduction to education course as freshmen or sophomores in local schools. The university partners with 8 nearby school districts for student teaching, but focuses their clinical field experiences for their first semester of junior year in a large, urban district in schools that qualify for Title I funding due to the low socioeconomic status of students. During that semester they spend 40 hours in clinicals: 10 for a reading pedagogy/methods course, 10 for a mathematics pedagogy course, 10 for a child development and culturally relevant pedagogy course and 10 for an instructional planning course. In this chapter we share pre-service teachers' experiences in the first semester of junior year with a specific focus on the 10 hour clinical for the instructional planning course where pre-service teachers tutor students, and the 10 hour mathematics pedagogy course and its related activities.

VIGNETTES OF PRACTICE-BASED TEACHER EDUCATION

Vignette 1: State Legislated Laboratory School

The first vignette focuses on teacher candidates completing intensive clinical experiences in a middle school laboratory school (Grades 6-8) that is run and managed by the university of the lead author. Due to state legislation that mandated the opening of laboratory (lab) schools across the state, these lab schools are aimed at partnering local public schools with public universities. According to the legislation the mission of the lab school is:

to improve student performance in local school administrative units with low-performing schools by providing an enhanced education program for students residing in those units and to provide exposure and training for teachers and principals to successfully address challenges existing in high-needs school settings.

An important part of the planning process for the implementation of the lab school is the collaboration with university programs to offer the best opportunities for both the students in grades 6-9 and the pre-service teachers. The lab school is a school within a school that serves grades 6, 7, and 8. The school is placed in three classrooms on the district's high school campus. Serving just fewer than 60 students, the school is operated by the local university. The clinical experiences designed for the lab school collaboration focus primarily on the junior and senior level experiences described below.

Junior Year Clinical Experience

The junior clinical experiences are associated with six primary courses. Juniors in the middle grades program take methods for all core content areas in addition to an introductory course of the middle school child and curriculum with an associated seminar. In this first year of lab school implementation, we found ourselves in a unique situation where the methods course for mathematics could be truly integrated with the middle school classroom. This opportunity arose as the professor for the middle grades methods course was also serving as the full-time mathematics teacher for the lab school. This afforded an opportunity for very intentional planning of experiences and collaboration with both middle school and college students. The pre-service teachers spent approximately 10 contact hours doing direct and structured observations of mathematics teaching. Later in the week after school, those same pre-service teachers spent class time debriefing and learning the methodology that was presented in lessons. This model gave a more comprehensive lens to the practice of teaching and allowed for direct connections of theory to practice. These observations were organized in a way to highlight specific instructional moves and also give teacher educators the opportunity to have some informal practice. More specifically, in one observation, the teacher educators were directed to listen for and document specific styles of talk moves. In their readings for that week teacher educators read articles that supported their understanding of different talk moves and their role in promoting student understanding. The following week in their observation time they were to select at least one talk move that they wanted to utilize in their interactions with students that day. The teacher educators sat at the table with Math 1 students as they engaged in a discovery based task, "the cube problem," where students were analyzing patterns to create an equation for a sequence of growing "buildings." Teacher educators then reflected on their use of these talk moves and what they learned from the experience. In their reflections, over half of the students reported challenges in implementing something they had seen in a live setting and read about. Simultaneously, almost all students also reported it being a powerful experience to try to dig deeper in what a student understands by asking questions rather than just explaining a practiced procedure to them. The teacher educators who are not math concentrations found this to be most powerful as they realized that they were increasing their own mathematical understanding by exploring open ended questions with the middle school students.

For the second semester of the junior year, teacher educators take two additional courses in content are methods as well as course and aligned seminar in differentiated instruction. For the science methods course, much like the previous mathematics methods course, one of the full time teachers at the school serves as the methods instructor. This offers the pre-service teachers some continuity in their opportunities to engage with middle school students who they have already built initial relationships with. In this semester however, they also have a placement at another school in the area for one full day a week. Faculty members in the middle grades department have found it to be important for pre-service teachers to have a variety of experiences in addition to continued opportunities with the lab school.

Evaluating the Junior Year Experience

Overall, pre-service teachers responded very positively to the integrated experience. In order to evaluate the inaugural integrated course experience, the juniors participated in a survey to give feedback for the program. One student shared,

I really enjoyed being able to see my professor not only as a teacher to me but to middle school students as well. This is a unique opportunity that few are able to experience. I have learned a lot and even though I am not a math concentration so much of what I learned in this course will help me as a future educator.

Teacher educators were asked list the attributes of good teaching that were most prevalent in the teaching they saw at the laboratory school. We then sorted these contributions according to themes and summarized them into the general categories: discourse, problem-based learning, growth mindsets, and student engagement. In their qualitative comments, the majority of teacher educators (8 out of 10) related the importance of seeing these teaching practices rather than simply reading about them. One statement read:

I hated math before this math class. It always felt like it was something I could never get the hang of until I was put back in that middle school setting and had to think like a middle school student. I was able to see all of the things that we have talked about in the education program like differentiation, planning, reflection, group work, and heterogeneous grouping. All of the abstract ideas had a concrete example to go along with them. It really felt like the program was , 'practicing what they preach,' which allowed me to respect and learn from the experience. It was almost just being at the school helped me understand middle schoolers and what they need, like learning from osmosis.

As previously mentioned, we found a unique power in having all students observing in the same classroom. While this is a logistical challenge in terms of navigating large numbers of people in a small setting, teacher educators found having a common lesson to discuss to be helpful in discussing pedagogical and mathematical elements of a lesson. Of particular notice is the "realness" of this experience. Rather than watching videos that highlight strengths in particular teaching practices, this experience gave the comprehensive real-life view where teacher educators could see a high leverage practice and three minutes later see the handling of a classroom disruption. Nine of the ten teacher educators expressed appreciation of the raw and transparence of teaching. Several statements included,

Being able to talk to an experienced teacher who was completely real about things that she thought she did well and things that she thought did not go well was amazing. It opened my mind to the idea that not everything is going to go perfect all the time and mistakes or instances that we do not see coming happen, and another student reported,

I think that debriefing was the best thing to come out of this experience. Not only did we get to share our feelings and observations, but we also were able to see what the teacher thought about the class and how they thought the process went.

Despite all of the positives, teacher educators had several critiques of this experience as well. With a course only having 45 contact hours in the experience and 10-15 of those hours being spent in the classroom with direct observations, 3 of the 10 teacher educators felt that the course needed more lecture or traditional class time to help them understand the pedagogical aspects. This is perhaps something that could be re-framed into more of a hybrid experience with higher out of class expectations in terms of reading and reflections.

Senior Year Clinical Experience

For the senior experience one clinical educator was chosen from each content area to spend their one-year internship working at the laboratory school. Unlike many internship placements, these clinical educators had more than the usual opportunities to collaborate with their cooperating teachers. They were included in summer planning events, marketing and recruiting events, and any other associated activities for the school. While it was clearly stated to them that they were not required to participate outside the parameters of their student teaching handbook, each clinical educator took each and every opportunity they were given to be a part of the school staff. In the planning stages of the lab school, it was clear to faculty that the involvement of senior pre-service teachers needed to be a choice rather than something that was assigned. Because the context of the school is somewhat different than a "normal" middle school setting, and because the population of the lab school is somewhat different than a "nor-mal" middle school setting, we knew that we needed to recruit the best and strongest in our program to be a part of the journey. After being approached by program leaders and after agreeing to be a part of the team, the clinical educators began their first internship, spending two full days a week at the school. Additionally, three of the clinical educators were hired as part time research assistants to help in the data collection and analysis related to the lab school. This increased their presence in the school and gave them a more continuous experience than a typical first internship would. In their second semester at the school clinical educators began full time student teaching and took on all of the associated duties of teachers including the teaching of electives (such as team sports, entrepreneurship, STEM, etc). Ulti-mately these pre-service teachers are getting a full-time internship experience with the added benefits of serving as research assistants. We believe that these candidates will then be better prepared for pursuing a graduate education program.

Evaluating the Senior Experience

To evaluate the three senior internship experiences at the school we took more of a longitudinal view at their comprehensive development as responsive teachers. Before entering the senior year, middle grades faculty collected the work samples from junior level courses, particularly those with reflections, and identified each teacher educators self-identified strengths and areas of needed development. For the purpose of this article we are focusing on the teacher educator placed as the mathematics intern for her senior year. Ashley has always been a strong student academically and reported a strong desire to teach early on in her program. There were no clear themes in her early coursework to indicate particular strengths or anxieties entering her senior year. For her senior year work samples and reflections, we utilized open coding to find themes of particular areas that repeatedly appear in her work. From this we identified the following themes: classroom management, differentiation, engagement, and relationships. We then went back to earlier work samples from her junior year and coded for these themes that had emerged. We found that Ashley had consistently referred to these attributes of teaching as being important, but in her development as a senior intern they had divided into two strands: her strengths, and her continued areas of development. Ashley, her cooperating teacher, and supervisor all consistently recognized strengths in her ability to build relationships and differentiate instruction for individuals in her classroom which was evident in her planning of sophisticated tiered tasks for students to engage with. Her observations and self-reflections indicated that she is still developing in her ability to manage behavior and consistently engage students. The case below documents Ashley's own self-reflection of her experience at the laboratory school.

ASHLEY'S JOURNEY

An Aspiring Teacher

As an aspiring middle school teacher, I often think about my future classroom. I imagine how it will be decorated and wonder about all of the unique students that will fill the desks on a daily basis. While there is great excitement regarding these imaginations, there is also some anxiousness. In all honesty, the one thing that tends to bring the most anxiety is classroom management. The fact of the matter is that classroom management cannot be taught, at least not specifically or entirely. Ultimately, classroom management is a facet of teaching that has great variability; therefore, it demands extensive consideration and exploration.

One of the most exciting parts of being Dr. Anderson's intern is the fact that I get to observe and experience the same teaching and classroom management methods that we have discussed in the courses she taught at the university. In the seminar course last semester, we would often ask Dr. Anderson how she might handle a specific encounter or situation with a student, and her answers often challenged me with considerable thought and reflection. This semester, I have the incredible opportunity of witnessing the way that Dr. Anderson implements those methods, techniques, and strategies in her own middle school classroom. Based on my observations, I feel that Dr. Anderson's first approach to classroom management hinges on the relationship that she builds with each student individually and every class as a whole. In my classroom climate report, I made this statement: "I feel strongly that her passion for the Lab School students sets the stage for the learning that will take place in every class that she teaches." I am reiterating this point because it is so vital, not only to the climate of the classroom, but also to the management of the classroom. If we, as educators, do not have the respect of our students, we will not have their focus and attention either. While I have nothing but positive things to say about Dr. Anderson and her approach to teaching and classroom management, I feel strongly that there is room for improvement in regards to The Lab School as a whole, and in turn, Dr. Anderson's classroom. The number one thing that I feel needs to be improved at The Lab School is in regards to consistency. I will say that I believe the main reason that consistency has been a challenge is due to the fact that this is a first year school, and that is understood. Even so, I feel strongly that the climate, rapport, and most importantly learning would improve tremendously with greater consistency.

Reflecting on an Early Lesson

In this first lesson I was faced with two specific challenges: pacing and engagement. While many students were ready to move on, others needed me to take a step back. With that, some students were very engaged in the lesson and focused on instruction, while others were either zoned out or engaging in conversations with the person next to them. While engagement is always a challenge, this specific lesson was more difficult than any that I have experienced. This lesson is one that I will remember for a number of reasons. While there were strides made in mathematical thinking, there were also numerous challenges that hindered the lesson. I believe that these challenges with help me moving forward, but the lesson certainly did not go as I had intended or hoped. On a positive note, I feel that I have developed a very strong rapport with the students, and despite a few power struggles and engagement issues, I feel that there is mutual respect. As far as the students and mathematical concepts go, I feel very confident in front of the class.

A Mid-Year Self-Reflection

I feel confident in my ability to create and organize lesson plans, scaffold activities, and present mathematics content. I take pride in these things, as well as in the way that I am able to build relationships with the students that I teach. There is, of course, room for improvement in each of these areas, and I take that need quite seriously. As long as I am in the classroom, there will be room for improvement, and I will consistently work to better myself in such ways. One major area of concern is with classroom management. In pondering this struggle, I have realized that extensive improvement in classroom management demands time and experience. In other words, the more I do it, the better I will become at it. Another area that I would emphasize as needs improvement involves engagement in the classroom. While my lessons are created with every intention of being engaging to all, I feel that engagement varies greatly from class to class and from student to student. Therefore, I want to do whatever I can to make myself and my lessons more engaging for every student in every class.

The Evolution of an Intern

This past week was really great. In all honesty, I have never felt better about my identity as a middle grades teacher. That is not to say that I have it all figured out by any means, but I do feel confident in my ability to grow as a teacher. I just realized that I forgot to take up the w squared for eighth grade this week, so I clearly have a lot to work on, but I am excited to do so. I think that my biggest takeaway from this week is that teaching is mentally draining, and I don't mean academically. That math is the easy part. I know that this is not a surprising realization because we have been told in every class that teaching takes a lot of thinking, but it was not until my first ever full week that I realized how true that is. I often lay awake at night thinking about how I can manage the classroom better and wake up thinking about how I can manage the classroom better. I am realizing that there is no clear answer, as each day is completely different from the day before. There are so many factors involved in the classroom atmosphere. Each day, students come in with a different load, and that often impacts their mood, actions, and behaviors. Although I wish I had a solution to every problem, I recognize and accept the fact that I do not. What I do have however, is a knowledge of and love for mathematics. Therefore, all I can do is come in each day with a solid lesson plan, and the more engaging the better. With that being said, I also recognize that having a Teach Like a Pirate lesson every day is just not feasible. There has to be balance. But how can I expect students to engage and behave if my lessons bore them to tears? I think the key for me with this now and in the future is that balance.

Summary

In looking at Ashley's year long experience, there are many attributes of a typical evolution of a novice teacher. There is significant growth in particular aspects of teaching (planning, differentiation, etc), and continued challenges such as engagement and classroom management. What is seemingly unique to Ashley's context is the integration of a faculty member from her program being her cooperating teacher. As with the juniors, this experience seemed to connect theory to practice in a more meaningful way, particularly at the beginning of the year. The context of the Lab School also gave some particular challenges for Ashley in regard to classroom management and engagement. This is likely explained by the population served at the Lab School as our students are primarily students who have not found academic success in traditional settings. Moving forward this will be something to consider for placement of interns in what many may consider a challenging environment.

Vignette 2: Practice-Based Teaching in a Mathematics Tutoring Project

In order to create clinical experiences that progress in complexity throughout a pre-service teachers' program, elementary education pre-service teachers at *University 2* participate in a tutoring program. This work occurs when they are first semester juniors, their first semester in the program. The second author has led the implementation of this project in two different ways detailed below.

Development and Evolution of a Mathematics Tutoring Program

Through a partnership between the first author and local schools, the second author placed teacher with teachers in urban schools in which over 90% of the students were impoverished and qualified for the federal free and/or reduced lunch program. The goal of the program was to provide candidates with opportunities to tutor one or two students weekly in classrooms for 10 consecutive weeks (10 hours of work). Candidates and clinical educators were given autonomy to determine what time of day and what day of the week tutoring would occur. Candidates were also given the flexibility to complete their other 30 hours of clinicals for their reading, mathematics, and child development courses in that same classroom. In most cases these classrooms were in Kindergarten, Grade 1, or Grade 2 classrooms, which aligned to the grades they were focused on in their reading and mathematics methods courses.

Based on feedback from pre-service teachers and clinical educators that it was difficult to guarantee time each week to pull students away from instruction to tutor, the first author looked for alternative tutoring placements. The author approached Heart Tutoring, a non-profit organization which has adapted research-based mathematics resources to create a tutoring curriculum for students in the urban district that University 2 typically places all pre-service teachers during their junior years. As part of the Heart program, pre-service teachers tutored two students for 30 minutes per week across 10 weeks of the semester for a total of 10 hours of tutoring. We organize the vignette below by the feedback provided by the pre-service teachers who provided feedback during course meetings, reflections on tutoring, and course evaluations. This feedback was thematically coded using an inductive analytic approach (Patton, 2014).

Learning How to Plan and Teach

Most pre-service teachers were positive about both approaches to tutoring related to learning how to teach. However, comments varied in terms of the amount of support that the pre-service teachers received; tutoring in classrooms with the materials from their Clinical Educator varied greatly in terms of the types of materials and support provided.

Pre-service teachers who tutored in classrooms reported that they spent most of the time in the classroom tutoring and working with either individual or small groups of students on worksheets provided by the Clinical Educator. Since they were in the classroom with the teacher they reported noticing how the teacher taught content, organized students in groups, and how the classroom ran. One student wrote, "It was nice working in the classroom with the student I tutored. There were ample times to see what the teacher was doing and how she taught different topics."

Some students, however, were given only an activity sheet or a textbook without further instructions, which left them to figure out what to do and how to support students. In these cases, candidates reported that they learned how to teach by figuring out the content that students were working with, appropriate mathematics strategies that students may be able to make sense of, and ways to support them without telling them explicitly how to do the work. One candidate wrote:

I received no support from the teacher, just worksheets to do. As a result, I learned how to teach by doing all of the background work on my own and coming up with my own activities based on what the teacher told me to teach and do with the student.

Pre-service teachers who participated in Heart Tutoring reported that their experiences were beneficial in learning how to teach despite being in a cafeteria or media center instead of a classroom. Candidates were given the lesson plans from the tutoring program with activities and suggested questions, as well as directions on what to do next based on students' performance. Candidates felt very supported with these materials. One student commented, "I felt like I was in a low-risk environment since I was one-on-one and had a set of questions and activities given to me."

Another student wrote,

There were moments in which I was so caught up with working with the student that I lost track of what question or activity to pose next. Luckily, having the materials provided a lot of support to help me keep track of what I needed to do as a teacher.

Learning About Children

Both the classroom-based tutoring and Heart tutoring programs provided candidates with ample opportunities to learn about children. Pre-service teachers reported a lot of satisfaction and favorable comments about how the experience provided opportunities to learn about and work with children. Most of these comments focused on the one-on-one nature of tutoring and how that helped them get to know and build strong relationships with the children they were tutoring during the 10-week period.

One of the pre-service teachers who tutored in a classroom reported, "This was by far the most powerful experience of my time in college. I spent time with just one student at a time and learned a lot about their interests, background, and how to help them learn.

Understanding What Students Know and How They Learn Mathematics

Another theme that pre-service teacher reported was how tutoring supported their understanding of how students learn mathematics. In both classroom-based tutoring and Heart tutoring, candidates reported a benefit in working one-on-one with a student. They reported comments about how working one-on-one enabled them to go deeper into what students know and how they learn mathematics. They also reported that it was easier to do in a tutoring setting than in a classroom when they pulled small groups for their mathematics pedagogy course.

A pre-service teacher who participated in classroom-based tutoring said, "I learned so much about what my students knew in math, what concepts they were working on, and as I tried different strategies I learned what worked and what didn't."

Another pre-service teacher who tutored in classrooms wrote:

Since my clinical educator did not give me anything except a worksheet, I benefited from having to go online or to my math book from my course and pull strategies and ideas from there. It was hard but definitely worth it.

With the pre-service teachers who participated in Heart Tutoring their comments focused on attending to students' thinking rather than pulling instructional materials, since the lessons and materials were already provided for them.

One pre-service teacher wrote,

Heart Tutoring was a great experience because I was able to focus on working with the student, noticing what they were and were not doing well, and give them my full attention. I learned a lot about my students' understanding of math and saw a lot of growth.

In some cases the Heart Tutoring experience was the only experience pre-service teachers had to teach mathematics through the use of hands-on activities and manipulatives. One pre-service teacher wrote:

Even though we heard in our math course the benefit of using manipulatives and teaching through activities and tasks, my math classroom placement did not look like that at all. Heart Tutoring was the only place I was able to do that and see students' growth. So without Heart I would not have gotten to teach that way and see how students benefit from the use of manipulatives and math activities.

Classroom Management

Pre-service teachers from both the classroom-based tutoring and the Heart tutoring program reported that tutoring students supported their development of classroom management. A pre-service teacher who participated in Heart tutoring reported, "It was challenging at times to redirect and keep my one student on task. I am glad I had this experience before having to manage an entire classroom of students."

Pre-service teachers who tutored with the Heart program were in classrooms for other clinicals and wrote about the combination of their experiences. One wrote, "Being able to observe and teach small groups in math and also

Pre-service teachers who tutored in classrooms were able to tutor and also see how their teacher interacted with others. These observations were both positive and negative. In some cases, pre-service teachers who tutored in classrooms reported they learned by observing teacher behaviors that did not align to what they were learning in their courses, and in some cases observed unprofessional behaviors. One pre-service teacher who tutored in classrooms wrote,

It was hard to tutor in the classroom when the teacher was constantly yelling and insulting the children. The classroom management was not strong and it seemed that the teacher and students did not respect one another. Still it was a learning experience!

Summary

As indicated above both tutoring in classrooms and participating in Heart tutoring outside of classrooms supported pre-service teachers' development of knowledge and skills related to learning how to plan and teach, learning about children, understanding what students know and how they learn about mathematics, and classroom management. Table 1 summarizes the comparison between the two tutoring programs.

In both the classroom-based tutoring and the pull out Heart tutoring program pre-service teachers were able to get intensive time in one-on-one settings working with students. This tutoring clinical experience sets a foundation for their program, which gets extended and built upon as pre-service teachers teach both small groups and the whole class throughout the remainder of their program.

Vignette 3: Practice-Based Teaching in Mathematics Focusing on a Small Group of Students Structure of Clinical

During the same semester that pre-service teachers at *University 2* complete the mathematics tutoring, they also take a course on mathematics pedagogy for primary grade children (Kindergarten through

Table 1. Summary of Findings about Mathematics Tutoring

	Classroom-Based Tutoring	Heart Tutoring
Learning how to plan and teach	Teachers provided tutoring materials for most pre-service teachers. Some pre-service teachers had to select and prepare materials.	Research-based materials based on student data. Pre-service teachers were given all materials.
Learning about children	Pre-service teachers in both programs talked about value of working with individual students. Some classroom based tutors reported that at times their clinical educator did not let them tutor and they observed the whole class.	
Understanding what students know and how they learn mathematics	Occasional link between data and activities used	Clear link between data and the activities used, use of hands-on activities
Classroom management	Practice working with one student. Observing clinical educator's management, which in some cases was positive and negative.	Practice with working with one student and redirecting behavior occasionally.

Grade 2). During their time in classrooms, pre-service teachers complete targeted observations where they examine the mathematical tasks and level of questions that clinical educators ask, and they teach 3 mathematics lessons to a small group of students.

All of these clinical experiences take place in a school that classifies for federal Title I funding due to the large percentage of students who qualify for free and/or reduced lunch. The first author personally placed all of the pre-service teachers in this placement based on his knowledge that mathematics is typically taught using standards-based approaches such as worthwhile mathematical tasks, mathematical conversations, differentiation, and small group teaching. During the semester, pre-service teachers build relationships with the clinical educator and the students since they are in this classroom for 30 hours; 10 hours each for their child development course, a reading pedagogy course, and this mathematics pedagogy course.

Preparing Pre-Service Teachers to Teach

Leading up to the clinical experience, pre-service teachers completed a series of course activities focused on how children develop number sense and problem solving skills. Activities also include work on learning about materials, such as manipulatives, and strategies to support students' understanding of mathematics. Prior to teaching their three lessons, pre-service teachers work with their clinical educator to identify which students they are going to teach, and what the focus of the lessons will be. The only guideline is that pre-service teachers need to include word problems in their lesson.

Based on the word problem emphasis, most pre-service teachers complete their lessons on addition and/or subtraction word problems. In class, the research base from Cognitively Guided Instruction (CGI) is covered and heavily emphasized. Hence, pre-service teachers prepare their lessons to include opportunities for the direct modeling of word problems with manipulatives, opportunities to draw pictures to represent problems and represent problems with number sentences or equations.

The three pre-service teachers' lessons were planned with feedback from the course instructor and the clinical educator. The lessons were supposed to be based off of data that they clinical educator had on students' performance in their mathematics class. Their lessons were a practice for their edTPA student teaching project, where they teach lessons, assess students, and then teach a follow-up lesson based on the data collected from a previous lesson.

Analysis of Clinical Project

Over the course of the four semesters when the first author taught this course pre-service teachers reported the following themes in their project reflections: planning engaging mathematics lessons, building relationships, and using data to inform teaching,

Planning Engaging Mathematics Lessons

Pre-service teachers reported that they felt motivated to plan engaging lessons since they had a small group of students to work with for the lessons they were writing. One pre-service teacher wrote, "I put a lot of effort in to make sure the lessons would be engaging and fun since I had to teach every lesson."

Another pre-service teacher wrote:

I learned about the amount of effort and time it takes to actually create a strong lesson plan. Even with resources to pull from, it took a lot of work to modify them to meet the needs of my students.

Relationships With Clinical Educator and Students

Nearly every pre-service teacher reported the benefit of working with only one clinical educator and one class for 30 hours during the semester. A pre-service teacher wrote,

By the time I had to teach my mathematics lessons I felt comfortable in the class with the teacher [clinical educator] and the students. Going to only one classroom for all of my clinicals definitely helped build those relationships.

The extended time with one clinical educator and one class of students helped pre-service teachers feel comfortable and supported when they were teaching their lessons.

Using Data to Inform Teaching

As part of their edTPA practice project, pre-service teachers had to use data to modify and adjust their third and final lesson plan. Many pre-service teachers reflected about that process. One pre-service teacher commented:

The idea of planning and adjusting lessons based on data and how students are doing makes a lot of sense. I felt like a pre-test or knowing more about my students before even the first lesson would have made that lesson better. It is a time-consuming process to analyze data then plan, but it ensures that I am meeting the needs of my students.

Another pre-service teacher reported how beneficial it was to know her students and have data from her clinical educator prior to teaching:

Since I had been in the classroom all semester and my teacher had helped me to identify the students in my small group, I knew what strengths my students had and where they needed to grow the most. There was definitely a benefit in having my teacher help me determine what activities were and were not okay based on the group that I was teaching.

In summary, there was benefit in the practice-based approach of having pre-service teachers work for 30 hours in one classroom for multiple courses, and deepening their participation over the semester from targeted observations up to teaching small group lessons based on data. Pre-service teachers reported benefits related to planning engaging mathematics lessons, building relationships, and using data to inform teaching.

DISCUSSION AND FUTURE DIRECTIONS

The three vignettes and examples we have provided earlier in this chapter all included the following characteristics: focusing on students' thinking, giving pre-service teachers structure and flexibility, and giving ownership to clinical educators.

Focusing on Students' Thinking

The focus on students' thinking was central to all three vignettes in this chapter, which is consistent with recommendations for practice-based teaching (Forzani, 2014). In the case of the middle school laboratory school, the clinical experiences all included opportunities for pre-service teachers to observe the faculty member (second author) teach middle school students, and then work with students themselves. With the tutoring clinical, pre-service teachers focused on students' mathematical thinking in a one-on-one setting allowing them to focus solely on one student prior to working with small groups and entire classrooms of students later in the program. The small group teaching clinical, vignette three, also focused on students' thinking, as pre-service teachers planned and modified lessons based on their knowledge of students and student performance on previous lessons. By focusing on students' thinking and learning, the emphasis is on how to support students and not on being the perfect teacher. Recommendations from researchers have documented the benefit of adopting student-centered pedagogies when focusing on student learning (e.g. Hawley & Valli, 2000).

Clinical Activities That Are Structured Yet Flexible

All three clinical activities above provide pre-service teachers with structure and scaffolding to help support their development as a mathematics teacher, yet they are flexible enough to allow for teacher decision making and collaboration with the clinical educator in the classroom or tutoring supervisor. In the case of tutoring, while the Heart program provides research-based materials to pre-service teachers, the candidates make decisions about questions to ask and which tasks or activities to do next based on the elementary school student's performance. During the small group clinical work in Vignette 3, the course instructor provided support with a detailed template and lengthy feedback on the lessons from the instructor before they were taught. However, the pre-service teacher has been told to be ready to modify their lesson based on student performance and their observations of students during the lesson.

The idea of supporting candidates during their time in schools is common during their full-time student teaching internships, but not prior to that.

Practice-based approaches to teacher education require structure from a combination of course instructors, clinical educators, and curriculum materials (Kilic, & Tunc Pekkan, 2017; McDonald, Kazemi, & Kavanagh, 2013). The focus on preparing pre-service teachers through intensive, extended clinical experiences in classrooms does not mean that teacher education programs can just set up a clinical placement and let them go. Rather, as described in the vignettes in this chapter, scaffolding and support must be ongoing and refined to meet the needs of pre-service teachers (Ball & Forzani, 2009).

Giving Ownership to Clinical Educators

Another noteworthy point is the need to allow clinical educators to have ownership to support teacher candidates in ways that work in their classroom. Historically, pre-service teachers are guests in clinical educators' classrooms and clinical educators have complete reign over the amount of teaching time pre-service teachers complete, the content taught, and to some extent who preservice teachers work with. In the case of the mathematics tutoring clinical, vignette two in this chapter, during the classroom-based tutoring pre-service teachers reported that at times their clinical educator kept them from tutoring and working with students, so pre-service teachers just logged more observation hours. In the case of Heart tutoring, schools and teachers had previously agreed and committed to allowing their students to be tutored during the school day.

With the small group mathematics clinical, vignette three, the course instructor gave clinical educators ownership of providing feedback to the pre-service teachers, working with them to identify a small group of students to teach, and making sure that pre-service teachers had access to materials to teach their lesson. Pre-service teachers reported that they had established a strong relationship with their teachers since they spent the entire semester in that class for all 30 hours of their clinical work. In order for practice-based teacher approaches to be effective for pre-service teachers, clinical educators must be open to working with pre-service teachers, and support and mentor them with guidance, feedback and opportunities to learn (Ball & Forzani, 2009; Kilic, & Tunc Pekkan, 2017).

These dispositions of clinical educators only comes from trusting and working with clinical educators, while giving them freedom and latitude to work with pre-service teachers in ways that they find beneficial. The elephant in the room in most teacher education programs is the alignment (or lack thereof) between research-based strategies covered in coursework and the daily reality of teaching. Practice-based approaches to teacher education give a lot of credence and authority to pedagogies in schools, which means that university faculty must make sure they are aware of and able to help pre-service teachers make sense of what they are seeing in their clinical experiences, especially if it conflicts with research-based pedagogies covered in courses.

CONCLUSION

This chapter provided three vignettes and examples of practice-based teacher education efforts related to teaching mathematics: a middle school laboratory school where pre-service teachers completed clinical experiences, an elementary school tutoring program that occurred either in classrooms or in a pull-out setting, and an elementary school small group teaching project in classrooms that they spent extended time in over the course of the semester. These practice-based approaches provided candidates with authentic opportunities to work with students and clinical educators to develop their knowledge and skills related to teaching mathematics.

The American Association of Colleges for Teacher Education (AACTE) recently published a white paper on clinical practice (AACTE, 2018). In its white paper multiple recommendations were made, including the establishment and maintenance of school-university partnerships, often referred to as Professional Development School partnerships (NAPDS, 2008), and teacher residency programs (Papay, West, Fullerton, & Kane, 2011), which involve pre-service teachers spending considerable enormous amounts of time in schools in a mentorship relationship learning how to teach. Residency programs have

Table 2. Possible research approaches for practice-based teacher education

Level	Project Specific
Level 1: Participants' reactions	Reactions of pre-service teachers, clinical educators, faculty, and P-12 school administrators Collected via surveys, focus groups, interviews
Level 2: Participants' knowledge and skills	Knowledge and skills acquired through practice-based experiences Collected via reflective journals, assessments (edTPA, licensure tests)
Level 3: Participants' use of knowledge and skills	Demonstration of knowledge and skills Collected via portfolios, lesson plans, videos of classrooms, documentation of collaborations and mentorships, student work samples
Level 4: Impact on the organization	Evidence of how practice-based efforts have influenced and changed the organization Collected via interviews, surveys, documents about organizational change
Level 5: Impact on P-12 student learning	Influence of efforts on P-12 student learning Curriculum-based assessments, high stakes tests, diagnostic assessments

produced teachers who have a strong sense of the content, communities, and students they have worked with; residency programs historically have been used to develop career changers or those pre-service teachers who are able to work full-time in a school setting.

Meanwhile, school-university and Professional Development School (PDS) partnerships include formal partnerships between universities and PK-12 schools, which often includes agreements to host and mentor large numbers of pre-service teachers, for faculty to support and work with clinical educators and administrators on topics related to professional development and school improvement. PDS partnerships are more open than residency programs and can support the development of career changes and traditional undergraduate pre-service teachers earning their first bachelor's degree and teaching license simultaneously.

While these ideas have potential to continue to transform teacher education efforts, there is a need to further develop and conduct research on the specific influences of these approaches to developing pre-service teachers. The research agenda for practice-based teacher education could take on multiple approaches. Table 2 is an adaptation of Guskey's (2000) framework for examining teacher professional development efforts.

Within each level there is potential to examine the influence of one-shot projects such as clinicals in the laboratory school, the tutoring project or the small group teaching project within the span of one semester, as detailed in this chapter. However, there is also potential for long-range or longitudinal examinations of these efforts from a few different approaches. Researchers could study the modification and refinement of these programs, such as how the tutoring program morphed and changed over the past three years.

Researchers could also look at pre-service teachers across time, such as their four semesters in the teacher education program completing a variety of clinical experiences in their schools. There is a need for a wide range and variety of studies in order to more reliably and validly claim the extent and manner that clinical experiences influence pre-service teachers' development. Further, these studies must be well designed with consideration of how the findings can be generalized in order to maximize the impact of these efforts.

REFERENCES

American Association of Colleges for Teacher Education. (2018). *A pivot toward clinical practice, its lexicon, and the renewal of educator preparation.* Washington, DC: Author. Retrieved from: https://aacte.org/professional-development-and-events/clinical-practice-commission-press-conference

Aydin, U., Tunç-Pekkan, Z., Taylan, D., Birgili, B., & Özcan, M. (2018). Impacts of a university–school partnership on middle school students' fractional knowledge: A quasiexperimental study. *The Journal of Educational Research, 111*(2), 151–162. doi:10.1080/00220671.2016.1220358

Ball, D., & Forzani, F. (2009). The work of teaching and the challenge for teacher education. *Journal of Teacher Education, 60*(5), 497–511. doi:10.1177/0022487109348479

Biza, I., Nardi, E., & Joel, G. (2015). Balancing classroom management with mathematical learning: Using practice-based task design in mathematics teacher education. *Mathematics Teacher Education and Development, 17*(2), 182–198.

Darden, G., Scott, K., Darden, A., & Westfall, S. (2001). The student-teaching experience. *Journal of Physical Education, Recreation & Dance, 72*(4), 50–53. doi:10.1080/07303084.2001.10605740

Forzani, F. (2014). Understanding "core practices" and "practice-based" teacher education: Learning from the past. *Journal of Teacher Education, 65*(4), 357–368. doi:10.1177/0022487114533800

Guskey, T. R. (2000). *Evaluating professional development.* Thousand Oaks, CA: Corwin.

Gut, D. M., Beam, P. C., Henning, J. E., Cochran, D. C., & Knight, R. T. (2014). Teachers' perceptions of their mentoring role in three different clinical settings: Student teaching, early field experiences, and entry year teaching, mentoring & tutoring. *Partnership in Learning, 22*(3), 240–263. doi:10.1080/13611267.2014.926664

Kilic, H., & Tunc Pekkan, Z. (2017). University-school collaboration as a tool for promoting pre-service mathematics teachers' professional skills. *International Journal of Research in Education and Science, 3*(2), 383–394. doi:10.21890/ijres.327897

Levin, D., Hammer, D., & Coffey, J. (2009). Novice Teachers' Attention to Student Thinking. *Journal of Teacher Education, 60*(2), 142–154. doi:10.1177/0022487108330245

McDonald, M., Kazemi, E., & Kavanagh, S. S. (2013). Core practices and pedagogies of teacher education: A call for a common language and collective activity. *Journal of Teacher Education, 64*(5), 378–386. doi:10.1177/0022487113493807

National Association for Professional Development Schools. (2008). *What it means to be a Professional Development School.* Retrieved from: https://napds.org/wp-content/uploads/2014/10/Nine-Essentials.pdf

National Council for the Accreditation of Teacher Education. (2010). *Transforming teacher education through clinical practice: A national strategy to prepare effective teachers. A report of the Blue Ribbon Panel on Clinical Preparation and Partnership for Improved Student Learning.* Washington, DC: NCATE.

National Council of Teachers of Mathematics. (2014). *Principles to actions: Ensuring mathematical success for all.* Reston, VA: NCTM.

Papay, J., West, M., Fullerton, J., & Kane, T. (2011). *Does Practice-Based Teacher Preparation Increase Student Achievement? Early Evidence from the Boston Teacher Residency*. Retrieved from: https://cepr.harvard.edu/project-name/boston-teacher-residency-evaluation

Peercy, M., & Troyan, F. (2017). Making transparent the challenges of developing a practice-based pedagogy of teacher education. *Teaching and Teacher Education*, *61*, 26–36. doi:10.1016/j.tate.2016.10.005

Sleep, L., & Boerst, T. (2012). Preparing beginning teachers to elicit and interpret students' mathematical thinking. *Teaching and Teacher Education: An International Journal of Research and Studies, 28*(7), 1038-1048. doi:10.1016/j.tate.2012.04.005

Wood, M., Jilk, L., & Paine, L. (2012). Moving beyond sinking or swimming: Reconceptualizing the needs of beginning mathematics teachers. *Teachers College Record*, *114*(8), 1–44. PMID:24013958

Zeichner, K. (2010). Rethinking the connections between campus courses and field experiences in college and university-based teacher education. *Journal of Teacher Education*, *89*(11), 89–99. doi:10.1177/0022487109347671

Chapter 20
Four Perspectives on the Benefits of an Early Field Experience for High School Teacher Candidates:
Connecting Theory and Practice

Christine Lotter
University of South Carolina, USA

Kimberly Smoak
Dutch Fork High School, USA

William Roy Blakeney
Dreher High School, USA

Stacey Plotner
University of South Carolina, USA

ABSTRACT

This chapter describes an innovative early field experience course for secondary teacher candidates that is held onsite at two local high schools. The chapter presents the course experience from the perspective of three stakeholders involved in the teaching and planning of the experiences: the university faculty instructor, a school administrator, and a practicum high school teacher. University candidate voices are also included through an analysis of survey data collected at the end of the most recent course offering. Each stakeholder describes both the tensions and benefits of the partnership and course experiences. By connecting theory and practice through interactions with all stakeholders during the course, the experience honors the expertise of all involved and builds a community of educators working together to improve secondary teacher education.

DOI: 10.4018/978-1-5225-6249-8.ch020

INTRODUCTION

Teacher education programs often strive to provide a balance of practical education experiences with theoretical knowledge. Early field experiences which place university students in P-12 schools to observe and gain teaching experience before student teaching are an important part of the transition of teacher candidates (individuals enrolled in a teacher preparation program) to full time teachers. However, these field experiences often remain disconnected from academic coursework and lead to even greater disconnects or a continuation of the status quo (Bullough, Burrell, Young, Clark, Erickson, & Earle, 1999; Darling-Hammond, 2009). The National Council for Accreditation of Teacher Education (NCATE) 2010 report of the Blue Ribbon Panel on Clinical Preparation and Partnerships for Improved Student Learning outlines a vision for teacher education that puts "practice at the center of teaching preparation" and calls for Universities and school district partners to work together to transform education through ten design principles (p. 2). These design principles emphasize P-12 student learning and clinical practice that provides teacher candidates with opportunities for mentorship and feedback using student learning data. The NCATE report also calls for an integration of content, pedagogy and field experiences. Some urban school districts have moved teacher preparation under their control, working with University programs through teacher residency programs that integrate teacher preparation with on the job training through paid yearlong residencies that are showing some positive influence on student achievement (Papay, West, Fullerton, & Kane, 2011) as well as teacher retention (Berry, Montgomery, Curtis, Hernandez, Wurtzel, & Snyder, 2008; Solomon, 2009).

Without current funding for teacher residency programs, our University teacher preparation programs have instead worked to move teacher preparation coursework into local schools. This chapter describes an early field experience course that works to connect the academic and field components of the teacher education experience through a school-based course that was designed through a partnership between University-based teacher educators, school administration, and classroom mentor teachers (AACTE, 2017). Onsite school-based experiences such as the one described in this chapter are often referred to as "hybrid" or "third spaces" that create stronger connections between academia, P-12 schools, and local communities to improve teacher education (AACTE, 2017; Bhabba, 1990; Lee, 2018; Zeichner, 2010; Zeichner, Payne, & Brayko, 2015). Zeichner (2010) states, "Creating third spaces in teacher education involves an equal and more dialectical relationship between academic and practitioner knowledge in support of student teacher learning" (p. 92). Building partnerships that value and learn from the expertise of all stakeholders engaged in these spaces is often difficult due to University and school constraints (Bullough, Draper, Smith & Burrell, 2004; Labaree, 2004) but necessary to prepare the next generation of teachers to successfully teach all students in diverse settings (Intrator & Kunzman, 2009; Zeichner, 2010).

Welsh and Schaffer (2017) describe how early field experiences can improve candidates instructional strategies and classroom management skills and deepen their focus on student learning through interactions with P-12 students and practicing teachers. Field experiences also serve as an introduction for University teacher candidates into the community of practice of teaching (Wenger, 1998). Teacher candidates learn the language and practices of teaching through these apprenticeships that continue with full time student teaching before earning certification. Wenger (1998) describes three dimensions that characterize communities of practice: mutual engagement, joint enterprise and a shared repertoire. According to Wenger, mutual engagement involves a diverse group of people working together to negotiate meaning with each other. Central to this negotiation of meaning is the members effort towards a joint enterprise which involves members working together to develop mutual accountability, shared goals and rhythms. Eventually this mutual engagement and work towards a joint enterprise creates a shared repertoire of meaning, resources, and tools that are common to the community of practice and help to sustain it (Wenger, 1998). Community participation can limit or expand teachers' learning opportunities and often requires novice teachers to be apprenticed through practice (Lave & Wenger, 1991). The more closely aligned the community of practice and shared knowledge is across all facets of a teacher candidates' training, the more likely reform-based practices will be enacted and P-12 student learning enhanced (Grossman, Ronfeldt, & Cohen, 2011; Ronfeldt, 2015).

Building this community of practice may be more difficult for education programs that have limited time with their candidates. This is often the case with high school certification programs that require candidates to earn an undergraduate degree in their content area before beginning a certification program. The course and practicum experience described in this chapter aims to immerse secondary teacher candidates in a high school environment to provide them with a practical learning environment in which to apply the theoretical knowledge they have received throughout their education. The course also maintains a focus on theory through an emphasis on current educational topics and reform-based instructional strategies. The course is described from the perspective of four different stakeholders: University-based teacher educator and course instructor, high school administrator, and high school mentor teachers. In each section, University teacher candidate voices will also be heard through a compilation of their responses to a survey given to them in the most recent semester. We hope that in sharing our perspectives, our expected and unexpected gains and our struggles, more innovative teacher education experiences can be created.

BACKGROUND

This innovative course is part of a 12-hour education cognate that our University secondary education teacher candidates must take in order to enter a Master's level high school certification program. The teacher candidates range from sophomores to seniors enrolled at a large Southeastern United States University. The 12-hour cognate includes four education courses that focus on human growth and development, equity in education, educational foundations, and a methods course. The methods course is the focus of this chapter. This course is held at two local high schools, each of which has partnered with the University as a professional development school (PDS). As a PDS school, the University enters into a mutually beneficial partnership with the school in which the school provides a welcome environment to place our teacher candidates and the University provides professional development support to the school's teachers (Goodlad, 1984). The University also supplies a faculty liaison that works at the school for at least 10 hours a week providing a link between the university and the school and offering support to both the teachers and the candidates through professional development and coaching.

Of the two schools used each semester, the one closest to the University has been used since the course moved off campus in 2010. This high school, a midsize city school with 1,130 students and approximately 75 teachers, is located about two miles from the education building at the partner University. This school is an ideal location for the course due to proximity to the University, availability of parking, and classroom meeting space with flexible furnishings and current technology including Wi-Fi. The school's demographics are especially appropriate for student candidates with 55% Black, 38% Caucasian, 5% Hispanic, and 2% Other designated students. The school's zone places it in the limits of a midsize city with 134,000 people, and the attendance zone provides students who represent all socio-economic, racial, and religious groups in the city. The school has students who live in homes where there is extreme wealth and those who are homeless. The school's special needs population is about 10% of the total school population and contains both itinerant and self-contained classrooms. This diversity provides an excellent opportunity for the University students to have authentic classroom experiences which should easily transfer to later internships and teaching. This school is home to the school administrator who has provided his perspective in this chapter. The second school location has varied over time based on PDS school partnerships and clinical faculty contacts with the most recent school location added this school year. This new school is located in a rural fringe locale about 30 minutes from the University. This school has approximately 1,800 students with 57% Caucasian, 34% Black, 3% Asian, 2% Hispanic, and 4% Other designated students and 117 teachers. This school is home to the mentor teacher giving her perspective in this chapter; however, she has worked in both school course locations. The University-based teacher educator who is first author on this chapter has taught the course at both current school locations.

The course described in this chapter is a general education course with teacher candidates enrolled from multiple content majors including social studies, English, math, and science. Each course enrollment is capped at 25; with typical enrollment in both sections between 30-45 teacher candidates. The focus of the course is on providing students with their first instructional experience in a regular classroom setting. The students have previous experience working in an informal education setting (one-on-one tutoring) through the equity course, but most have never taught a full lesson in a classroom. The course meets four hours each week, with two hours a week for a more typical class session and two hours for practicum. During the practicum time, the candidates observe and participate in their mentor teacher's class one day each week for a total of 20 hours. We typically place one student in a mentor teacher's classroom, however, we have had to double up candidates in some circumstances. Thus, the practicum requires 10-25 teachers at each school location to accept a teacher candidate into their classroom once a week during the semester. Candidates move from observation to engaging with everyday classroom tasks such as grading and taking role to teaching a full lesson in the mentor teacher's classroom. As they become more comfortable with the high school students, they begin to take on additional responsibilities that include leading small groups of students and teaching segments of daily lessons. The teacher candidates work with the course instructor and their mentor teacher to plan and teach a 90-minute lesson in their content area. Both the instructor and mentor teacher provide written and oral feedback on their teaching using a professionalism rubric and a state-level teaching performance rubric.

In the sections that follow, the course will be described from the perspective of the three main stakeholders involved in the partnership: a University teacher educator, one of the school administrators that works closely with the course, and mentor teachers. Teacher candidates from the most recent semester of the course were asked to provide their comments on the value of the course, their interaction with their mentor teacher, high school students and the school administrators. A total of 21 of the 34 candidates (62%) provided feedback through the online survey. At the end of each of the stakeholder sections, the course instructor (a University-based teacher educator) provides the common themes from the teacher candidate survey. We also sent out an online survey to each mentor teacher (n= 38) that had a candidate in their classroom this current school year asking them to provide additional feedback on what they felt was their own and their teacher candidate's greatest gains from the practicum experience and any feedback they had to improve the course. Feedback from 20 participating mentor teachers (53%) across both school locations has been incorporated into the administrator and mentor teacher sections.

FOUR PERSPECTIVES

Instructor Focus: Balance of Theory and Practice

As the University-based teacher educator and course instructor, my goals for the course are to prepare the teacher candidates to successfully teach within their mentor teacher's classroom (lesson planning tools, classroom management), introduce them to innovative student-centered instructional practices (inquiry, project-based instruction) and provide them with the tools to critically analyze different teaching environments in an effort to improve student learning (reflection tools). This course and my own instruction have benefited from co-planning the course with a variety of faculty at all levels (adjunct, clinical, and tenure track) that bring different expertise and ways of viewing teacher education. All faculty involved with the course share their ideas during planning sessions that occur before and after each semester the course is offered. The blending of ideas from instructors who have taught high school in different content areas in different contexts adds depth to the course. I have also benefited from learning how to think like a social studies or English teacher, as I am a science educator, who may sometimes think narrowly around my own area of practice if not pushed by a larger community interested in enhancing teacher education. After teaching the course for several years, I have found that the following themes are important for providing a successful balance of theory and practice: a) building a community of practice (Wenner, 1998) that includes the school mentor teachers, school administrators, and the teacher candidates; b) supporting students in using innovative teaching practices, and; c) building in time for students to reflect on the instructional practices they are learning about and observing in their mentor teacher's classroom.

Community of Practice

Building a community of practice starts from day one when the University candidates are welcomed into the school with a tour given by an administrator or student body representative. Students often receive a school identification name tag and are introduced to key office and administrative staff so that they feel like they are immediately a part of the school culture. Students are assigned a mentor teacher whom they work with starting in the third week of the class. As described above, candidates spend two hours each week in the classwork portion of the course. This time is spent in a room in the high school that is not occupied by a classroom teacher. Having a dedicated space at the school is important for building the community of practice that without it can lead to feelings that the program is separate and not valued by the school.

During this course time, I invite teachers and administrators to come speak to the candidates about how they effectively run their classroom and the school. In addition to guest speakers, our candidates observe in rounds (spend 15-20 minutes in several teachers' classrooms) teachers who have been nominated based on their effective instructional practices and positive classroom culture by the school administrator or their teacher peers. During these rounds of observations, candidates are asked to focus their observations on classroom elements connected to course topics. For example, candidates read and learn about developing classroom procedures and classroom management techniques, so that during the rounds for that week, candidates' observations followed by classroom discussions are focused on how the teachers' demonstrated these elements. To help candidates analyze different teaching environments, candidates engage in a number of different activities from reading about different classroom environments, listening to teacher or administrator presentations about how they establish their classroom cultures or maintain school discipline structures, and visiting and analyzing two teachers' classrooms using the Environment section of our state teacher evaluation rubric. Typically about an hour of each two hour class is spent interacting directly with high school students and/or teachers in the school.

Thus, to be a successful field-based course, the students must value their time in the school and not feel as though they could have the same experience in a University setting. Through surveys given to students, a majority of the students report that by midterm they feel a part of the school culture with a focus on the positive relationships they have built with the teacher and the students in their practicum class.

Innovative Teaching

Throughout the course, I introduce multiple instructional practices and ask candidates to question and critique the teaching practices they are both learning about in theory through various course assignments as well as the practices they are observing in the high school classroom through the lens of student learning. The course culminates with the candidates each producing a 5-day project-based learning unit in their content area, bringing together the instructional strategies and lesson planning skills they have learned throughout the semester. Project-based learning curriculum engages K-12 students in creating a product to solve an authentic real-world problem or answer a challenging question through research, collaborative discussion, and investigations (Larmer, Mergendoller, & Boss, 2015). Three guiding principles are used to develop project-based learning units that lead to meaningful student learning. Effective project-based unit components: a) create a need for students to acquire content knowledge; b) engage students in actively constructing their own content understandings, and; c) help students organize their content knowledge so that it connects with past learning and makes application of the new knowledge possible (Kanter, 2010; Krajcik & Czerniak, 2007). During a project-based unit, students often work in collaborative teams developing communication and problem solving skills and utilize technology to investigate the unit question (Colley, 2008).

Our candidates work up to this unit through two peer teaching opportunities that take place within the regular class time. Candidates progress from teaching a 20-minute lesson with a partner on a "hot topic" of their choice in education (e.g., teacher pay, meeting the needs of diverse learners, influence of poverty on student learning, etc.) to teaching a 15-minute content-standard focused lesson alone. For each lesson, candidates develop a lesson plan and receive feedback from their peers and the instructor before and after teaching the lesson. The candidates then prepare their 90-minute lesson plan with their mentor teacher to teach within the practicum classroom. By the end of the semester, the candidates have taught at least three formal lessons (often many more within their practicum classroom) and are prepared to design a longer project-based learning unit. The candidates develop a 5-day project-based unit that is aligned to state content standards in their concentration area (e.g., Algebra, Biology, American History) and this unit plan serves as the final summative assessment for the course. This project-based unit plan pushes the candidates to develop innovative instruction that places high school students in the center of the learning. I support the development of this unit through teaching the candidates about lesson planning design, unit planning using the theory in *Understanding by Design* (Wiggins & McTighe, 2005) that has candidates plan their assessments first using their unit objectives and then design the instructional activities and daily lessons that will support students' successful learning of those objectives. We also use some of our classroom time to observe teachers at the high school that engage students in project-based instruction—including less traditional courses such as computer design and engineering to help candidates develop a stronger vision of this instruction in action. Toward the end of the semester, students participate in a gallery walk to share their unit plan ideas on large post-it posters and receive critical feedback from their peers. These posters outline how the candidate's unit aligns to key project-based learning elements such as inclusion of opportunities for students to engage in critique and revision, student's voice and choice, in-depth inquiry and other elements that are introduced to candidates earlier in the semester (Larmer, Mergendoller, & Boss, 2015). Some recent candidate units focused on driving questions such as: a) "How do we interpret what is relevant history?"; b) "How can we sustain the life of beaches in our state?"; c) "Are markets fair or rational?", and; d) "How can I use a variety of triangles to create 'beautiful' artwork?".

Reflection

Throughout the semester, I ask the candidates to connect theory to practice through five practicum-based written reflections that ask students to connect what they are observing in the classroom to course readings, assignments and presentations. After teaching the course for several years, I have found that candidates must have time to be active participants during the practicum time, therefore candidates attend two practicum sessions before writing up a short reflection paper that focuses on student learning strategies, classroom management, their contribution to the classes, and an explicit reflection on what they see as the connection between their observations and class readings or presentations. These reflections also allow for me to communicate with the candidates providing answers to questions they have about events they observe during practicum. I then bring common candidate concerns to the next whole class session so that all candidates can benefit from the discussion of solutions or next directions.

Through these reflections, I also ask candidates to specifically reflect on student learning issues in an effort to push them to focus on student learning in addition to classroom management and other procedural issues that are the most common focus of new teachers (Danielowich, 2007; Grossman, 1992). The candidates' final reflection is a written self-reflection on their own 90-minute classroom lesson. In preparing this final written reflection, candidates use feedback they have received from the high school students and their mentor teacher to reflect on their preparation, lesson planning, presentation, and quality of student learning.

Candidate Value

In the survey given to this past year's cohort of University candidates, candidates described how they most valued the time during the course spent interacting with high school teachers (n=9) and students in the school (n=11) . For example, one candidate described that "doing rounds and observing different teachers" was the most valued component. Candidates also valued lesson and unit planning (n= 9), learning a variety of instructional practices (n=6), and being able to practice these strategies and their instruction during the two peer teaching experiences (n=6). For example, a candidate stated:

The biggest thing that I value from the course portion is being taught how to teach a lesson, as well as building a lesson plan. This was my first experience with doing either of these things and I really appreciated being given that experience before I get to the Master's program.

Similarly, another candidate stated:

Our content lesson plans. They were extremely useful in allowing us to prepare and practice before doing our practicum lesson plan in the classroom. It was also helpful to see other future educator's different teaching methods.

The candidates also valued working collaboratively with their peers and the instructor (n=6). This quote is representative of several candidates' comments, "I loved having a space to connect with and learn alongside other people who want to teach in high schools."

Administrator Focus: Unexpected Benefits

When our University partners and I first discussed the possibility of housing a University course at the high school, I believed that the experience for candidates and the early opportunity for them to be a part of a real school environment would easily offset any logistical frustrations for the school setting. I did not expect that there would be many, or any, benefits to our school other than strengthening the long established partnership with the University. After eight years of implementation the faculty and I have realized many more benefits than expected. These benefits include building empathy between administrators and teachers, improvement of mentor teachers' instructional strategies, the positive aspects of having another adult in the classroom to tutor and support high school students, and positive administration and candidate relationships that provide the school with a pool of eager recruits after they earn their certification.

Building the Community of Practice to Support Student Learning

For me, as an administrator, student learning is one of our significant priorities. Thus, University candidates must collaborate with our mentor teachers to determine how they can best support learning for our high school students within the scope of the internship. Mentor teachers need to feel as though they are a part of the decision making regarding whether or not they receive a candidate as well as how that candidate will be involved in their class. Mentor teachers are accountable for the grades earned by their students so allowing someone with whom they are not familiar to influence those grades is not comfortable. I have found that student learning is enhanced and anxieties lowered through finding ways for mentor teachers and candidates to meet ahead of time to collaborate, having the university provide some measure of candidate capability ahead of class meetings, or having a stepped approach which allows the mentor teacher an opportunity to observe the candidates' capability for student interaction before releasing the candidate to teach on their own in the mentor teacher's classroom.

At the beginning of the University class, I have an opportunity to greet and address the class. During this greeting I describe the student demographics, professional expectations, and give candidates a tour of the school. I also discuss the school's emphasis on individual student success, faculty collaboration, and sense of community. I encourage honest communication within the class setting regarding experiences while at the school and emphasize the expectation that absolute confidentially be maintained. Throughout the semester, administration and faculty are invited to speak to the class on various relevant topics. Classroom management is one topic we are asked to address which has led to the development of a class activity involving our high school drama students. This activity places candidates in front of a mock class that has been prepared to either escalate negative behavior or to respond in a positive manner depending on the candidate's approach. The reflection afterward is open to all and the feedback is always productive. Not only do candidates have the opportunity to share their feelings about the experience but they also receive feedback on their classroom management attempts from the high school drama students, who comprised the mock class, the university instructor, and myself, the school's PDS administrator.

Benefits to the School

Our school has reaped several benefits from the teacher-candidate interactions. University professors and candidates bring new, innovative strategies and cutting-edge pedagogy to an open and capable faculty of practitioners. The candidates have an opportunity to put theoretical strategies into practice and measure the results in a safe and supportive environment while under the tutelage of an experienced classroom teacher. Further, having another set of hands in the classroom, assisting students individually and in small groups, augments our ability to provide a safe and supportive environment for students. Ultimately, our students profit from the presence of the University candidate who can explain concepts in different ways, incorporate the latest technological advances into lessons, and increase student engagement. Students are also provided with an authentic model of collaboration and cooperation provided by the working relationship between the mentor teacher and the candidate.

Another unexpected benefit of interacting with the class is that I, who have been out of the classroom for a number of years, appreciate the time to become a teacher again. Administrators like myself often do not have many opportunities to prepare lessons and deliver material in this type of setting and the experience has led to refreshed empathy for those who do it daily. This time also allows me to model different approaches to dealing with students and parents which gives the candidates more material for consideration and refreshes my communication skills.

In addition, new insights have been gained through the collaboration with university faculty. Over the years, the course has been taught by several different University faculty members and each of their perspectives have increased the quality of professional development for the school. I also hope that the sharing of experiences has helped university faculty, who are further removed from the high school environment, gain a better perspective of the experiences necessary to prepare a teacher for today's classroom.

Student Learning Gains

Although I have not done research to quantify any achievement gains by the students populating classrooms where University candidates are practicing, I do believe that gains exist. University candidates are encouraged to collaborate with their mentor teachers to find the most efficient way to assist in the classroom. Students who have University candidates are able to gain assistance through one-on-one, small group, and team teaching situations. I have to believe that this added assistance is a benefit to our students and that having another motivated adult available positively affects the classroom climate. Preliminary data from the mentor teacher survey supports that the teachers believe that their students are benefiting from having more than one instructor in the classroom ($n=10$) and that they are reflecting more on their own teaching through their preparation and interaction with the teacher candidates ($n=14$). For example, one teacher described the benefits of "being able to provide more one-on-one help for students" with the candidate in the room. Another stated that the candidate "was great at helping monitor both independent and group work and brought some fresh new ideas to the table." Teachers also described how they benefitted from reflecting on their own teaching. A mentor teacher stated, "I was reflecting more on my teaching practices having a student teacher in the room with me. I wanted to make sure that I was demonstrating a variety of strategies (e.g., direct instruction, discussions, wet/dry labs)."

Although, as the school administrator, I strive to minimize the overall time requirements associated with hosting an intern, I feel strongly that more specific data on the impact of the course is necessary. One of the PDS goals for the next school year is to meet with the participating teachers and design a process that would yield research friendly data. Research opportunities exist in actual gains in student achievement, possible impacts to normal pedagogy, and the culture of the classrooms and school.

Candidate Value

Through the interaction of the school administrators with the University candidates during the course, the candidates described learning more about the hiring process (n=7), school personnel roles and responsibilities (n=8), and classroom and school management policies (n=7). Candidates also learned to see administrators as real people who are invested in student learning and teacher growth (n=5). For example, a candidate wrote about the value of the administration in the survey:

I learned a lot more about how hard [administrators] work to make the school a safe and healthy environment to learn. They really think a lot about every aspect of a student's experience and truly care about every student.

The involvement of the administrator in the course also helped to make the candidates feel welcome (n=7) and a part of the school community. A candidate described how interacting with the administrator, "made me feel more comfortable going out and observing in their school because it felt as if they are fully supporting us in our endeavors there and are wanting us to succeed." Similarly, another candidate wrote:

Everybody who I spoke to individually or who spoke to us as a class were friendly, encouraging, and gave great advice. I felt so welcomed every day, and I think that says a lot about the success of this program and the school in general.

In reference to gaining a better understanding of school roles, a candidate described how "…it seems important to recognize how much the administration does behind the scenes that teachers might not see."

The candidates also described learning about the importance of professionalism and valuable lessons about the hiring process from the administrators. A candidate stated, "I liked that I was able to get into the heads of school administration--to know what they are looking for in their teachers." Thus, candidates felt a part of the school community and learned valuable lessons about the school and their future profession from the inclusion of an administrator in the class lessons.

Mentor Teacher Focus: Reality for the Classroom

It is no secret that the teacher shortage crisis is no longer just looming; it is, indeed, here. According to a 2016 report from Learning Policy Institute, there was a 35% reduction in enrollment in teacher education programs between 2009 and 2014 (Sutcher, Darling-Hammond, & Carver-Thomas, 2016). With this comes not only a shortage of prospective teacher candidates but the real danger of candidates who are not the best additions to the profession becoming certified teachers as schools race to fill vacant positions and states lower the requirements for a teacher to be placed in a classroom. It has never been more important to ensure that teacher preparation programs are producing well-qualified, committed candidates who can do more than just fill a teaching vacancy. A key player in identifying such candidates is the classroom mentor teacher who plays a vital role in recognizing qualities in pre-service candidates that make that candidate a high caliber one or, perhaps, one that should be counseled to consider other professional possibilities. However, the current climate of high-stakes testing and accountability makes it a daunting prospect to bring an inexperienced teacher candidate into your classroom and allow them to influence student learning while there.

With data-teams, benchmarks, end-of-course testing, AP exams and other such markers hanging over their head, teachers feel the pressure of pacing, content standards and ensuring rigorous instruction in such a way that will help students be academically successful. District pacing guides often leave little room for error in how quickly material must be covered by the teacher and mastered by the students. Each school year, it takes time to find your teaching "groove". This is the groove that allows you to meet that pacing and to get to know your students well enough to know how to make that pacing work while ensuring they are mastering the material, and doing so at a level that also provides rigorous learning opportunities. Then comes the request from administration to host a preservice teaching candidate in your classroom and panic tends to set in. How can I possibly host this candidate in my classroom, help them learn the ins and outs of the job, give them time to interact with my students, explain why I do what I do, the way I do and still maintain my tenuous grasp on the groove I have finally found to move my classes forward? The knee-jerk reaction is to decline the administrator's request to be a mentor teacher. However, if we always decline, we cannot expect to influence the caliber of teachers entering our profession and then, we cannot complain when the quality of our colleagues begins to decline.

In the book *Cultivating Communities of Practice*, Wenger, McDermott and Snyder (2002) define communities of practice as "groups of people who share a concern, a set of problems, or a passion about a topic, and who deepen their knowledge and expertise in this area by interacting on an ongoing basis" (p. 4). Creating such a community would go a long way in ensuring that preservice candidates are well-prepared for entering a classroom. Classroom teachers are a vital part of such a community. They must be willing to engage in a relationship with university faculty and their preservice candidates in order to ensure that quality teachers are entering the field of teaching and that they have experiences prior to that which enable them to be successful teachers. The practicum experience is an important introduction to teaching for those who may not have been inside a high school classroom since they were a student themselves.

The reality of the classroom is that there are more demands than ever being placed on teachers. Rather than using that as an excuse not to coach those who wish to become teachers, we must recognize the importance of our role in helping identify and nurture those who are up to that challenge. We must also realize how coaching a teacher candidate contributes to our own professional growth, how it benefits our students and how it can actually help us manage some of the challenges mentioned above. Instead of seeing this coaching opportunity as just one more thing added to the plate, it is time to recognize the benefits of having these teacher candidates in our classroom and taking advantage of having fresh eyes and ears examining our practice, ready to assist in many ways if we will simply let them.

Classroom Teacher Growth

The mentor teacher has opportunities for tremendous professional growth when hosting a university teacher candidate in the classroom. It requires a great deal of reflection on one's professional practice and having the teacher candidate actively engaging in dialog about that practice puts the mentor teacher in a position of having to be able explain why things are done in a specific way. Often, in such times of self-reflection, it is revealed that the teacher's practice can be improved upon, while also providing an opportunity to celebrate those practices that have proven successful. Even the best veteran teachers can fall into the trap of doing things in their classroom because it is the way things have always been done, particularly if those methods have shown past success. However, that is not best practice and coaching a teacher candidate forces the mentor teacher to take a closer look at not only what is being taught, but the how and why of the process.

One example of how dialog with a teacher candidate benefitted me occurred when I was asked about how I handle note-taking in my class. Through our conversation, I was able to explain my use of scaffolding with students in teaching them note-taking skills. I realized that I had not really taken my honors students to the next level in that process and was not adequately preparing them for the types of note-taking they would likely need to be able to do beyond high school. In the course of this one conversation with my teacher candidate, we were able to examine the necessity of incorporating skills instruction with content instruction, differentiation between honors level and lower level students, and the importance of knowing where our students are, as well as where we need to help them go based on their likely future experiences. I was also able to re-focus my efforts with my honors students in order to move them forward. The conversation was eye-opening for the teacher candidate because he saw how much more there is to teaching than just covering the content, and it was eye opening for me because I realized the effectiveness of the scaffolding in their skill development and the need to take it further.

In helping the University candidate see what goes on behind the teaching curtain, the mentor teacher has to be willing to candidly share the day-to-day process of working with diverse groups of students while managing such things as pacing guidelines, multiple preparations, behavior and procedure routines, and state-mandated testing, as well as analysis of student performance data to ensure student success. In the process of explaining these things to a teacher candidate, the mentor teacher is reminded of why it is important to continually reflect on their practice and the needs of their students. This reflection has helped me, as a mentor teacher, be much more thoughtful about not just what I do, as dictated by standards, but how and why I act as I do.

Teacher Candidate Growth

One of the first things many teacher candidates say is, "This is my first time in a high school since I was a high school student myself." That statement alone conveys so much about the importance of the practicum experience in providing the teacher candidates the opportunity to see the classroom from the other side of the desk and to gain some experience in interacting with teenagers from the perspective of being the adult in the room, responsible for engaging those students and helping them be successful. By having the teacher candidate consistently present in a class, they begin to build a rapport with students and gain some understanding of their varying ability levels. Then when they develop a lesson that they must teach to those students in the role of a teacher candidate rather than a peer, they must consider what they have learned about those students and teach their lesson in such a way as to engage those students, while also keeping them accountable for mastery of the content. This is vital in enabling the teacher candidate to see the real-world application of the theories they have learned in their university coursework and gain a better understanding of what it takes to put those theories into practice. Being required to teach a lesson provides opportunities for both the teacher candidate and mentor teacher to see where the university program and real-world classroom come together. At times gaps are revealed when it comes to such things as the teacher candidate having an idea for an innovative approach to a lesson while the classroom teacher has to remind them of time constraints in pacing which may limit how much time can be allowed to carry out their model lesson. This gap often results in teacher candidates being given little opportunity to shape curriculum (Passe, 1994) and can be another stumbling block in creating a meaningful field experience for teacher candidates. However, it is important to realize that the reality of the classroom and the innovations of the teacher preparation program do not need to contradict each other.

As already discussed, the reality of the classroom is one of state- or district-mandated pacing often driven by high-stakes tests and accountability. It can feel like this leaves little time for some of the innovative strategies and lessons teacher candidates have learned about, and are encouraged to use, in their university courses. Indeed, time is limited but that does not mean there is no room for innovation and fresh ideas. In my most recent experience hosting a teacher candidate, it became clear that there is some disconnect in their understanding of how certain strategies might happen in the ideal classroom versus the real-world classroom. The teacher candidate created a lesson plan that included a segment of direct instruction around the content being covered at the time but that content was much too in-depth and was not focused on what is outlined in the standards for the course. It was an excellent example of a teacher candidate's love for the material, and enthusiasm, taking a hit when faced with such factors as standards and pacing, as well as the high school students' abilities and potential lack of background knowledge. We do not want that enthusiasm to constantly be taking a hit or it will be lost and that is unthinkable for our future educators. So, the key is to find out how to bridge that gap between the ideal classroom, with space for innovation and creativity, and the realities of time constraints and limitations among high school students that might hinder such lessons. The truth is, there is plenty of space for both.

The key is to recognize that we have to guide the teacher candidate and hold firm, due to accountability, in what is to be taught and how much time can be given to teaching it but we can be flexible when it comes to how the teacher candidate goes about that teaching. Another advantage of hosting a teacher candidate, in addition to the reflection on our own teaching it demands, is the opportunity to hear fresh ideas from students who are learning the most current approaches and theories in education while in their teacher preparation programs, and to work with them helping put that theory into practice. We all have our favorite strategies and our go to methods, which we can excitedly share with our teacher candidates but these preservice candidates may have ideas that can freshen up a lesson in ways we have not considered.

When my teacher candidate presented his lesson plan to me, with the too-detailed section for direct instruction, I had to re-focus him in that area but ultimately, we were able to tweak his lesson in such a way that it met the standards, would be completed in the allotted time and would allow him to use some strategies and resources he was excited about. Furthermore, I gained some great new resources that I saw work with my students when he taught the class. It was a win-win for me and him, as well as being a good lesson for my students. For example, he used various quotes from Booker T. Washington and W.E.B. DuBois, after providing direct instruction on what each believed in the post-Reconstruction era. He simply listed the quote, without revealing the author, and students had to apply their knowledge of each man's teachings to predict who said which quote. The activity was brief, engaging and showed students' mastery of the content. I proceeded to ask the teacher candidate if I could have extra copies of his resources so that I could use them in future lessons. This proved that, despite time constraints, with guidance the teacher candidate was able to be innovative and engaging while adhering to the requisite pacing. Furthermore, he realized that, despite being a novice, he brings valuable ideas to the classroom that even a veteran teacher can learn from. That is where we must go in our thinking, as mentor teachers, in order to realize we can welcome a teacher candidate's ideas and innovation while still meeting the very real demands in our classrooms. I realized that I may have to tell the teacher candidate what material needs to be taught, and how much time can be spent on that material, but I can be flexible by allowing the teacher candidate to decide how that material will be taught. Such an approach can help the teacher candidates find their own teaching style and identity within the constraints of the real-world classroom.

Hosting a teacher candidate in our classrooms also has benefits for our high school students. I recently told one of my classes that I would be hosting a university student in my classroom and I was asked why I would do that. It was a perfect opportunity for me to talk with my students about the importance of always being willing to grow and learn from others, as well as the importance of paying it forward professionally. My students were essentially asking what was in it for me. I explained how I felt that I needed to do for someone what another teacher had done for me by allowing me into their classroom when I was learning to be a teacher. This part of the conversation actually had two benefits. The first was the clear realization by my students that I had to learn how to do my job, I had to learn from those who were more experienced than I was, and that that was okay. The second was that, through this realization, it made me more human to them. Our students do not really think about what our lives were like before we became their teacher but our students may appreciate seeing that we have been through many of the same experiences they are having, or are facing, in order to reach where we are. I also explained that, every time I have had a preservice teacher in my classroom, I learn something new that has helped me become a better teacher. This provided me an excellent opportunity to model being a life-long learner which is something we want to foster in our own students. We want students to see models of lifelong learning and having college students in the classroom provides them opportunities to see that, as well as to learn more about life beyond high school from someone closer to their own age, under the supervision of the classroom teacher. Also, it is important that I show a positive attitude regarding having a teacher candidate in my classroom so that my own students will be more positive in their reception of the teacher candidate (Beebe & Margerison, 1995). By hosting a teacher candidate, the classroom teacher is able to demonstrate the desire to help others and prepare future teachers out of a commitment to education and the future of the profession. Ideally, the high school students recognize this spirit of service is a result of the teacher's care for their education, as well as that of future generations.

Additional Mentor Teacher Feedback

As seen in the survey results, feedback from mentor teachers consistently reiterates the benefits of hosting a teacher candidate such as an extra set of hands and eyes in the room, the thoughtful reflection on one's own practice, and fresh instructional ideas that the candidates bring to the classroom. However, mentor teachers also shared various challenges that come with the experience. Based on this feedback, these challenges appear to be related to a variety of things from block scheduling, state standards and strict pacing for the teacher, to the limited knowledge of the teacher candidates about what it takes to run a classroom, their own transition from candidate to professional and some lack of confidence in their own ability to engage with students. If a high school is operating on a block schedule, it severely limits the amount of time the teacher candidate spends with a particular class of students. With a course requirement of being in the classroom only one morning per week, their time is already limited. On an A/B schedule, this is further limited by the fact they would likely only see the same group of students every other week. This makes it difficult for the practicum student to get to know the high school class, as well as it being hard for the high school students to recognize any authority of the teacher candidate. An additional challenge for the mentor teacher is finding space within their district pacing guide to give teaching time to the teacher candidate. Multiple mentor teachers surveyed reported the aforementioned disconnect between what the teacher candidate wants to do when they begin thinking about the lesson they need to teach and where the teacher may actually be in the course curriculum. Although the candidates bring enthusiasm and passion about a topic, they may be unfamiliar with how the content fits within the content standards for the course. Feedback from the mentor teachers also emphasized the need for more communication and planning time between the teacher candidates and the teachers. This additional planning time could help teacher candidates align content standards to their planned lessons. In order to build the confidence of the teacher candidate and make them more aware of where the classroom teacher may be in the curriculum, the mentor teachers suggested that teacher candidates be given more structured tasks to complete within their practicum to gradually build up their instructional skills until they are ready to teach their full lesson. For example, one teacher stated on the survey:

I also think it would be beneficial to incorporate additional teaching requirements. I encouraged the teacher candidate multiple times to do a bell ringer or exit activity, but I think she was a little intimidated by the Advanced Placement (AP) students, resulting in her only doing her one teaching requirement. They would benefit from being required to do some sort of 5 minute mini-lesson (bell ringer, exit slip) and 15-20 minute lesson/activity to ease them into their full lesson. I would benefit from seeing the student more. I really only saw her the 5-10 minutes before/after class and during class itself, which made planning with her a little difficult.

These additional experiences would provide appropriate scaffolding for teacher candidates to improve their knowledge and confidence level. Such an approach would engage them more with students, give them opportunities to develop their own self-efficacy, and help them see where their full lesson fits into the bigger picture of the course. Time for more communication among all stakeholders is also needed but is not always manageable since the mentor teacher is likely to have another class coming in right after the class in which the practicum student is serving, leaving little time to conference with one another. These circumstances make this challenge a difficult one to overcome.

In joining the high school classroom, the teacher candidate finds themselves in the role of a pre-professional adult, rather than a student, and this can lead to issues in professional etiquette. From proper attire, to promptness, and cell phone usage, teacher candidates are having to make a shift that they may have not given a great deal of consideration to. Do they have professional clothing to wear? What type of reflection is it on them when they are late to class, and what type of example are they setting for the high school students who are closely watching them? These are all questions that may be addressed in the course but may not hit home until they are actually in the high school classroom, in an adult role. It is a valuable opportunity for the mentor teacher and the university instructor to start discussing the soft skills that are necessary in any workplace, and to point out those that are relevant to the classroom. Such conversations would require communication between the practicum teacher and the university faculty member, which some mentor teachers (n=2) reported as being limited.

Early field experience opportunities can be an excellent first-look for the teacher candidate at what it is like on the other side of the desk, and enables them to decide whether pursuing a career in teaching really is for them. This early experience can serve to either encourage the teacher candidate in their pursuits or be an important stop-gap in which they themselves may recognize the job is not for them or where others may be able to broach conversations counseling those who may be ill-suited for the field to consider other options. In a time when schools are desperate for teachers, teacher preparation programs must be sure they are producing quality candidates and early practicum experiences are excellent opportunities for identifying such candidates. Practicum experiences provide opportunities for learning and growth for the teacher candidate, the classroom teacher and the high school students in the classrooms in which the teacher candidate is placed while fostering the relationship between universities and P-12 classrooms in order to bridge the gap between theory and practice.

Candidate Value

Candidates when asked to describe what they valued most from their interactions with their mentor teacher and high school students focused on how their mentors provided them with honest feedback on how they could improve as an educator (n=9). Often they described how their teaching experiences and teacher's guidance helped them to understand how to teach a group of diverse students with different learning abilities (n=15). Candidates also described how they gained confidence from student and teacher feedback (n= 7). For example, a candidate wrote about how his teacher supported his teaching of her Advanced Placement class:

I am a strong believer in the fact that people learn more when they are in uncomfortable situations, which is kind of what I was in to an extent when I taught my lesson to the Advanced Placement class, but it was done in a way that I was able to learn and grow from the experience, which I really appreciated.

Candidates also valued observing how their teacher planned lessons and their daily routines and classroom management (n =10). A candidate described how his teacher "challenged me while simultaneously supporting and encouraging me". Another candidate described how the interactions with his teacher:

...opens up new perspectives. We read a lot in education classes, but seeing things actually executed is very beneficial. I like hearing why he chooses to do specific things. It's also very helpful to receive advice and encouragement for my future career from someone who has gone through this same program.

Candidates also valued their practicum experience more if they had a high level of collaboration and interaction with the teacher and students. A candidate described how the high level of collaboration led to a successful experience:

During every single class I was allowed to teach in front of the class, work one-on-one with students who were having trouble, grade papers, take attendance, reply to emails, and meet other teachers on the hall. From the beginning, he aimed to make me feel like a real teacher every time I came into the classroom and I learned invaluable lessons from that mindset.

Candidates also appreciated the time to build relationships and work with the high school students (n= 11). Often these experiences help to solidify candidates' commitment to pursuing an education career. A candidate described how he was uncertain about "interacting with students" and did not know "if I'd be helpful or good at interacting with students, but I felt I really connected with some of them and helped them figure out things they didn't understand." Similarly, another candidate stated, "Honestly, [working with students] reaffirmed my desire to teach and be a positive influence in education."

Candidates also described learning new instructional strategies (questioning skills) and classroom management techniques that they could not completely understand from a textbook or class lecture. A candidate described how he got to practice being responsive to students' questions. He wrote: "I can work on my lesson plan for a week and even have a script to say and everything, but the moment someone asks a question somewhat off-task I had to switch it up. I felt like being with the students helped this a lot". With expert mentors, our candidates also observed that all students can learn with properly scaffolded experiences. A candidate wrote, "I learned that every student has the capacity to learn the material, even when they seem uninterested or struggling. I really loved helping students grasp concepts." Another described having greater clarity about the type of students he would be teaching in the future:

I gained a clearer picture of what students will look like outside of my memories of who I was as a student. It's easy to forget, during college, that we'll be working with real live humans. We talk so much about students, but it's always hypothetical. Being in a classroom with students took away the hypothetical and made it into a real thing.

Similarly another stated, "I became aware of how to handle students from different backgrounds and at different academic levels." Having this understanding of students, content, and instructional strategies during an early field experience can enrich their future interactions with students during their student teaching practicums. However, as is true of any course that involves complex human interaction, not all candidate-teacher relationships were true collaborations. For example one of our candidates described that, "My teachers did not have me work with the students as much as I would have hoped, while they had a set schedule they had laid out before I was in the class." Although these comments were among the minority, they show that better alignment of course expectations to mentor teacher goals will enhance the partnership for all involved.

In the teacher survey, the mentor teachers shared most often that they believed that the candidates gained practice applying content and teaching practices in a real world setting (n=11), gained classroom management skills (n=10) and new instructional strategies (n=8). Teachers also described gains in candidates' content knowledge, lesson planning skills, information about student learning needs, and time management to a lesser degree.

CONCLUSION

This onsite course experience provides an example of how teacher education programs can work collaboratively with school administrators and teachers to provide learning experiences that blend together theory and practice for teacher candidates. Through sharing the perspectives of the different stakeholders involved in our partnership, we hope that additional teacher education programs can work with school personnel to build similar programs with mutual benefits for the school teachers, students, and community. This course aligns with Zeichner's (2010) call for:

a shift in the epistemology of teacher education from a situation where academic knowledge is seen as the authoritative source of knowledge about teaching to one where different aspects of expertise that exist in schools and communities are brought into teacher education and coexist on a more equal plane with academic knowledge. (p. 95)

Sharing knowledge across a wider school-based community can lead to gains across all parties and a stronger educational community of practice.

Analyzing our course experience using Wenger's (1998) three community of practice components (mutual engagement, joint enterprise and a shared repertoire) allows us to determine the strengths and needed areas for improvement of our early field experience. All stakeholder are mutually engaged in improving high school student learning; however communication between stakeholders could be strengthened to better align course assignments and practicum activities with school and mentor teacher goals and time constraints. Critical feedback from mentor teachers focused on a need for more communication between mentor teachers and the course instructors and teacher candidates to improve the practicum experience. Setting up meetings with mentor teachers at each school setting both prior to placement of candidates as well as mid-semester to align course goals and requirements with school and teacher needs would improve the candidate experience and student learning. The addition of the new PDS school hosting this course may have added to the need for more communication as teachers and administrators were unfamiliar with the course expectations. Mentor teachers also described a need for more planning time during the practicum experience so that mentor teachers and candidates can plan instruction together and spend more time reflecting on the outcomes of that practice. This increased communication can help create a shared repertoire of meaning, resources, and tools that are common to the community of practice and help to sustain it (Wenger, 1998). These shared conversations should not just maintain the status quo but push all parties involved to find new ways to improve student learning, whether through project-based instruction or other reform-based instructional strategies that are being emphasized within the school districts. The more closely aligned the community of practice and shared knowledge is across all facets of the teacher candidates' training, the more likely reform-based practices will be enacted and P-12 student learning enhanced (Grossman, Ronfeldt, & Cohen, 2011; Ronfeldt, 2015; Solomon, 2009). Relaxing the time constraints of the field placements to allow candidates to observe their mentor teachers' classrooms throughout the day (instead of only during first period) may allow for more planning, reflection, and instructional time with the high school students. As this program grows in numbers, or programs of larger sizes attempt to replicate this model, more school sites and flexible schedules will need to be arranged to limit the impact of the course on the school and mentor teachers' time. In one recent semester, we had to place four of our social studies candidates (often our largest group) at another local high school due to a larger number of candidates than mentor teachers in that content area at the course school location. Larger programs will have to find ways to balance not only the number of candidates, but also the number of candidates in each subject area based on the size and teacher composition of the host schools. As our program caters to Masters level students who are typically older and have cars, our program does not provide our teacher candidates transportation to the school locations. Programs that work with younger teacher candidates may need to invest in transportation to local schools.

As described above, not all mentor teachers are equally willing or qualified to serve as mentor teachers. Mentor teachers that do not want to share their classroom with a teacher candidate or feel too much stress from district guidelines or end of course assessments can decide to contribute in other ways to the practicum experience through short presentations during class time or volunteering for students to observe their class once during the semester observation rounds. Thus, providing candidates with mentor teachers that value and even celebrate learning alongside a teacher candidate. The placement of candidates with flexible and supportive mentor teachers is supported by Schmidt (2010) who reported that preservice teachers found field experiences of least value to them when "they had limited autonomy, contextual knowledge, or sense of community" (p. 141).

Unlike paid residency programs (Solomon, 2009), this school-university partnership also shows that innovative course experiences can occur without additional funding if faculty are willing to move their coursework out into the P-12 environment and build course experiences alongside teachers and administrators in the field.

ACKNOWLEDGMENT

This research received no specific grant from any funding agency in the public, commercial, or not-for-profit sectors. We would like to thank Dreher High School and Dutch Fork High School administrators, teachers, and staff for hosting our courses and mentoring our teacher candidates.

REFERENCES

Beck, C., & Kosnik, C. (2002). Professors and the practicum: Involvement of university Faculty in preservice practicum supervision. *Journal of Teacher Education, 53*(1), 6–19. doi:10.1177/0022487102053001002

Beebe, S., & Margerison, P. (1995). Teaching the Newest Members of the Family to Teach: Whose Responsibility? *English Journal, 84*(2), 33–37. doi:10.2307/821029

Berry, B., Montgomery, D., Curtis, R., Hernandez, M., Wurtzel, J., & Snyder, J. (2008). *Creating and sustaining urban teacher residencies: A new way to recruit, prepare and retain effective teachers in high-needs districts*. Retrieved from https://www.aspeninstitute.org/publications/creating-sustaining-urban-teacher-residencies-new-way-recruit-prepare-retain-effective/

Bhabba, H. (1990). The third space. In J. Rutherford (Ed.), *Identity, community, culture and difference* (pp. 207–221). London: Lawrence and Wishart.

Bullough, R., Burrell, J., Young, J., Clark, D., Erickson, L., & Earle, R. (1999). Paradise unrealized: Teacher education and the costs and benefits of school-university partnerships. *Journal of Teacher Education, 50*(5), 381–390. doi:10.1177/002248719905000511

Bullough, R. V., Draper, M. J., Smith, L., & Burrell, J. (2004). Moving beyond collusion: Clinical faculty and university/public school partnership. *Teaching and Teacher Education, 20*(5), 505–521. doi:10.1016/j.tate.2004.04.007

Danielowich, R. (2007). Negotiating the conflicts: Reexamining the structure and function of reflection in science teacher learning. *Science Education, 91*(4), 629–663. doi:10.1002ce.20207

Darling-Hammond, L. (2006). Constructing 21st-century teacher education. *Journal of Teacher Education, 57*(3), 300–314. doi:10.1177/0022487105285962

Darling-Hammond, L. (2010). Teacher education and the American future. *Journal of Teacher Education, 61*(1–2), 35–47. doi:10.1177/0022487109348024

Feldman, P., & Moore Kent, A. (2006). A collaborative effort: Bridging theory and practice in pre-service preparation. *New Educator, 2*(4), 277–288. doi:10.1080/15476880600820193

Goodlad, J. I. (1984). *A place called school.* New York: McGraw-Hill.

Grossman, P., Ronfeldt, M., & Cohen, J. (2011). The power of setting: The role of field experience in learning to teach. In K. Harris, S. Graham, T. Urdan, A. Bus, S. Major, & H. L. Swanson (Eds.), American Psychological Association (APA) educational psychology handbook, Vol. 3: Applications to teaching and learning (pp. 311-334). Washington, DC: American Psychological Association.

Grossman, P. L. (1992). Why models matter: An alternative view on professional growth in teaching. *Review of Educational Research, 62*(2), 171–179. doi:10.3102/00346543062002171

Intrator, S., & Kunzman, R. (2009). Grounded: Practicing what we preach. *Journal of Teacher Education, 60*(5), 512–519. doi:10.1177/0022487109348598

Labaree, D. (2004). The trouble with ed schools. New Haven, CT: Yale University Press.

Lave, J., & Wenger, E. (1991). *Situated learning: Legitimate peripheral participation.* Cambridge, UK: Cambridge University Press. doi:10.1017/CBO9780511815355

Lee, R. (2018). Breaking down barriers and building bridges: Transformative practices in community- and school-based urban teacher preparation. *Journal of Teacher Education*, 1–19. doi:10.1177/0022487117751127

Marzano, R. J. (2003). *What works in schools: Translating Research into Action.* Alexandria, VA: Association for Supervision and Curriculum Development.

Papay, J., West, M., Fullerton, J., & Kane, T. (2011). *Does Practice-based teacher preparation increase student achievement? Early evidence form the Boston teacher residency.* National Bureau of Economic Research. Retrieved from http://www.nber.org/papers/w17646

Passe, J. (1994). Early field experience in elementary and secondary social studies methods courses. *Social Studies, 85*(3), 130–133. doi:10.1080/00377996.1994.9956291

Ronfeldt, M. (2015). Field placement schools and instructional effectiveness. *Journal of Teacher Education, 66*(4), 304–320. doi:10.1177/0022487115592463

Scherff, L., & Singer, N. R. (2012). The preservice teachers are watching: Framing and re-framing the field experience. *Teaching and Teacher Education, 28*(2), 263–272. doi:10.1016/j.tate.2011.10.003

Schmidt, M. (2010). Learning from teaching experience: Dewey's theory and preservice teachers' learning. *Journal of Research in Music Education*, *58*(2), 131–146. doi:10.1177/0022429410368723

Solomon, J. (2009). The Boston teacher residency: District-based teacher education. *Journal of Teacher Education*, *60*(5), 478–488. doi:10.1177/0022487109349915

Sutcher, L., Darling-Hammond, L., & Carver-Thomas, D. (2016). *A coming crisis in teaching? Teacher supply, demand, and shortages in the U.S.* Palo Alto, CA: Learning Policy Institute.

The National Council for Accreditation of Teacher Education (NCATE). (2010). *Transforming Teacher Education through clinical practice: A national strategy to prepare effective teachers.* Report of the Blue Ribbon Panel on Clinical Preparation and Partnerships for Improved Student Learning.

Welsh, K. A., & Schaffer, C. (2017). Developing the Effective Teaching Skills of Teacher Candidates During Early Field Experiences. *The Educational Forum*, *81*(3), 301–321. doi:10.1080/00131725.2017.1314574

Wenger, E. (1998). *Communities of practice: learning, meaning, and identity.* Cambridge, UK: Cambridge University Press. doi:10.1017/CBO9780511803932

Wenger, E., McDermott, R., & Snyder, W. (2002). *Cultivating communities of practice: A guide to managing knowledge.* Boston: Harvard Business School Publishing.

Wiggins, G., & McTighe, J. (2005). *Understanding by Design.* Alexandria, VA: Association for Supervision and Curriculum Development.

Zeichner, K. (2010). Rethinking the connections between campus courses and field experiences in college- and university-based teacher education. *Journal of Teacher Education*, *61*(1–2), 89–99. doi:10.1177/0022487109347671

Zeichner, K., Payne, K., & Brayko, K. (2015). Democratizing teacher education. *Journal of Teacher Education*, *66*(2), 122–135. doi:10.1177/0022487114560908

ADDITIONAL READING

Ball, D. (2000). Bridging practices: Intertwining content and pedagogy in teaching and learning to teach. *Journal of Teacher Education*, *51*(3), 241–247. doi:10.1177/0022487100051003013

Ball, D., & Forzani, F. (2009). The work of teaching and the challenge for teacher education. *Journal of Teacher Education*, *60*(5), 497–510. doi:10.1177/0022487109348479

Cooper, J. E., & He, Y. (2012). Journey of "becoming": Secondary teacher candidates' concerns and struggles. *Issues in Teacher Education*, *21*(1), 89–108.

Darling-Hammond, L. (Ed.). (1994). *Professional Development Schools.* New York: Teachers College Press.

Darling-Hammond, L. (2006). *Powerful Teacher Education: Lessons from Exemplary Programs*. San Francisco: Jossey-Bass.

Lotter, C., Singer, J., & Godley, J. (2009). The influence of repeated teaching and reflection on preservice teachers' views of inquiry and nature of science. *Journal of Science Teacher Education*, *20*(6), 553–582. doi:10.100710972-009-9144-9

Lotter, C., Yow, J., & Peters, T. (2014). Building a Community of Practice around Inquiry Instruction through a Professional Development Program. *International Journal of Science and Mathematics Education*, *12*(1), 1–23. doi:10.100710763-012-9391-7

Marzano, R. J. (2003). *What works in schools: Translating research into action*. Alexandria, VA: Association for Supervision and Curriculum Development.

Zeichner, K. (2009). *Teacher education and the struggle for social justice*. New York, NY: Routledge.

KEY TERMS AND DEFINITIONS

Administrator: High school-based instructional or school facility leader with managerial oversight over classroom teachers.

Early Field Experience: Time spent by a university pre-service teacher in a P-12 environment learning to teach before full time student teaching.

Mentor Teacher: High school teacher who supports a university teacher candidate in their high school classroom.

Professional Development School: P-12 school that enters into a partnership with a university teacher preparation program for the mutual benefit of current and future educators.

University Teacher Candidate: University student who is enrolled in a teacher certification degree program.

University Teacher Educator: Teacher education professor whose main employer is a university teacher preparation program.

APPENDIX

Mentor Teacher Survey Questions

1. What do you think was your greatest gain from having a teacher candidate in your classroom (for example, extra help with students, learning new teaching ideas, reflection on your own practices, etc.)? Please provide some specific examples.
2. What do you think your teacher candidate gained from spending time in your classroom (new strategies, content knowledge, understanding of teaching logistics, etc.)? Please provide some specific examples.
3. What do you think would improve the practicum experience for you, your high school students, and the teacher candidates (more time in class, specific teaching requirements, more planning time, etc.)?

Teacher Candidate Survey Questions

1. What do you most value from working with your mentor teacher?
2. What did you gain from working with students in your practicum class?
3. What did you gain from your interactions with the school administration?
4. What do value most from the course portion of this experience?
5. What do you value least from the course portion of this experience?
6. What suggestions do you have to improve the course?

Section 4
Systems of Feedback

Chapter 21

Pivoting From Evaluative to Educative Feedback During Post–Observation Conferencing:
Supporting the Development of Preservice Teachers

Amy B. Palmeri
Vanderbilt University, USA

Jeanne A. Peter
Vanderbilt University, USA

ABSTRACT

In disentangling the, often conflated, evaluative and educative functions of preservice teacher supervision, the authors reimagine supervisory practice within the specific context of the post-observation conference. Claiming the post-observation conference as a teaching space provided the impetus leading to the design of a theoretically grounded post-observation conference protocol foregrounding the educative function of supervision, leveraging the mediating role of the university supervisor in supporting preservice teacher learning, and reflecting the principles of effective feedback. A critical feature of the protocol is the intentional focusing of feedback on one of four superordinate elements of teaching that provides continuity and consistency across post-observation conferences allowing preservice teachers to connect knowledge and skill related to the development of complex practice.

INTRODUCTION

It is well understood that one cannot perfect a practice-oriented activity solely from reading about it in a book. However, it does not follow that book learning has no place when one is initially learning, continuously refining, and over the course of a career, perfecting a practice-oriented activity such as teaching. The long-standing schism between learning to teach in the context of the college classroom

DOI: 10.4018/978-1-5225-6249-8.ch021

versus learning to teach in the context of field experiences serves to establish a dichotomy familiar to teacher educators across the globe: the theory-practice divide. Too often, preparation programs design curricula as though theory and practice are opposite ends of the same continuum with the goal of striking what they perceive to be the right balance between the two. This approach seems to simplify the process of learning to teach and the role of teacher education and teacher educators, by framing it as a linear space where the inferred challenge is to bring the dichotomy between theory and practice into balance.

In contrast, the authors envision learning to teach, and the relationship between theory and practice, not in this linear fashion but within an orthogonal space where theory and practice are independent entities each with their own unique and independent learning trajectories. Others have referred to this orthogonal space as hybrid or third spaces, where dichotomous thinking is reimagined bringing knowledge and skill together in new ways serving to create new teaching and learning opportunities for the teacher educators and preservice teachers in that space (Bhabba, 1990; Gutiérrez, 2008; Zeichner, 2010). One can imagine that within this orthogonal, or third space there are times when the preservice teacher (PST) might first be introduced to a pedagogical practice along with opportunities to enact the practice (the how) and then is introduced to and learns the theoretical and research base that informs the practice (the why) or vice versa. Regardless of the sequence, the authors, like others, contend it is the iterative back and forth between theory, research, and practice that makes what teachers do both visible to and learnable for the novice (Ball & Forzani, 2009, 2010: Grossman, Compton, Shahan, Ronfeldt, Igra, & Shiang, 2007; Kazemi, Lampert, & Franke, 2009). It is within this iterative space that the PST most needs the assistance of a more experienced teacher. This third space, therefore deserves greater attention by teacher educators as they consider, develop, and enact particular teacher educational pedagogies that are well suited to supporting PST learning.

Finally, in the context of teacher education, this orthogonal space, focused on the iterative interaction between theory, research, and practice is challenging because the teacher educator and the PST must engage in productive and educative conversation about a practice they are both simultaneously engaged in, albeit with quite different levels of experience, knowledge, skill, and ways of talking and thinking about teaching. The challenge is pervasive and difficult to overcome because to the novice, teaching *looks* simple (Bransford, Darling-Hammond, & LePage, 2005). Much of what and how a teacher thinks about content and students, the wide array of factors teachers take into account prior to making a pedagogical decision, and the enactment of those decisions through specifically chosen and intentional instructional moves are inaccessible to a novice through mere observation and thus require the instructional support provided by the teacher educator (Hundley, Palmeri, Hostetler, Johnson, Dunleavy, & Self, 2018). The authors contend that the long-standing problem typically framed as the theory-practice divide can only be solved when theory and practice are no longer positioned as being at odds with one another, but rather are recognized as being iteratively related. Consistent with this perspective, the authors further suggest that theory and practice are both essential and integral to the initial learning, on-going refinement, and never-ending striving toward effective practice necessary for and characteristic of teaching that supports student learning. Applying these ideas, the authors draw upon their experience as university-based teacher educators who teach content methods coursework and supervise preservice teachers in early fieldwork and student teaching. The authors' work focuses on a particular teacher educational context warranting closer attention, particularly when reframing theory and practice not as a divide to be bridged but rather as an iterative third space where theory, research, and practice continually and repeatedly come into intersection with one another in support of PST learning.

Specifically, a critical element of teacher preparation is the teacher educators' use of educative feedback within the context of the post-observation conference (POC) and the pedagogies that inform and shape both the delivery and content of that feedback. Such feedback enhances novice teachers' reflection, learning, and growth, in order to inform future teaching practice. In line with Cambourne's theory of learning, feedback (termed *response* in his work) is one of 7 conditions necessary for learning to occur (Cambourne, 1995, 2001). As a teacher educator responds to a novice learner, Cambourne describes a kind of feedback that serves as a "learning scaffold" supporting growth toward a desired target level (Cambourne, 2001 p. 785). The purpose of this type of feedback, referred to in this current work as educative feedback, is ultimately to support PST's critical thinking about the impact of their teaching on student learning and how this shapes future teaching. The use of educative feedback by teacher educators and the uptake of that feedback by PSTs provides additional teaching opportunities for the teacher educator and learning opportunities for the novice teacher. Over the course of a number of academic years, the authors have reconceptualized their supervisory practices and designed a POC protocol that provides PSTs with substantive, focused, and developmental feedback that primarily serves an educative rather than an evaluative purpose. This innovative shift from an evaluative to an educative focus has the potential to address prevailing problems of practice in ways that benefit novice teacher development.

THE NATURE OF SUPERVISION

Given increased attention on learning through clinical experience there is a need for more systematic and higher quality PST supervision (AACTE, 2010; Darling-Hammond, 2014). Historically, the labor-intensive work of supervision is delegated to adjunct faculty, and/or retired teachers or principals (NCATE, 2010; Zeichner, 2005). Many have argued that supervision within clinical experience in teacher education has been undervalued and underconceptualized (Beck & Kosnik, 2002; Feiman-Nemser, 2001).

In this section the authors articulate a theoretically grounded conceptualization of the work of PST supervision firmly establishing the critical role of the teacher educator in this process. First, the authors tease apart the multiple and often conflicting roles taken on by a university supervisor during PST supervision. They make the argument that the evaluative function of PST supervision should be explicitly disentangled from the educative function. Next the authors examine teacher educational pedagogies designed to help the PST learn in and from the complex practice of teaching (Lampert, 2010). The authors situate their work in the context of the POC focusing on a particular teacher educational pedagogy that is a cornerstone of the POC: The provision of feedback. Drawing upon this research-base the authors articulate design criteria used to inform the development of a supervisory tool foregrounding the educative function of PST supervision situated in the context of the post-observation conference.

The Educative Function of Preservice Teacher Supervision

Like Burns, Jacobs and Yendol-Hoppey (2016), the authors believe a primary intention of PST supervision is the cultivation of PST learning. However it is also well established that the university supervisor fulfills a variety of roles that range from serving as a liaison between the university and the school contexts to evaluating student teacher performance at the end of the experience (Burns, Jacobs, & Yendol-Hoppey, 2016; Dangel & Tanguary, 2014; Range, Duncan, & Hvidston, 2013). Rather than addressing the vast array of these roles, the authors focus their work on a particular supervisory role: Providing the PST with targeted support to enhance the development of their practice.

Even though supervision and evaluation are fundamentally different processes (Nolan & Hoover, 2010) it is well documented that PST supervision is often conflated with evaluation (Burns & Badiali, 2015; Glickman, Gordon, & Ross-Gordon, 2014). Supervisors frequently take an evaluative stance in the context of the POC, either explicitly as they employ a programmatic observational tool designed for evaluation, or implicitly when, during a conference, they elaborate on strengths and weaknesses of the lesson or provide examples of what they would have done differently were they the one teaching the lesson. When university supervisors fail to disentangle supervision from evaluation, the PST is left wondering if they are making satisfactory progress toward the benchmark. This uncertainty has the potential to undermine the PST's learner stance that is so critical in the context of supervision. Because the purpose of supervision is to foster PST learning (Nolan & Hoover, 2010) it is important to design supervisory tools and pedagogies that clearly and consistently establish supervision as an educative process.

Those who supervise must be able to teach *about* teaching while working with PSTs in the field (Burns & Badiali, 2016). The work of supervision has been shown to be complex and challenging even for experienced teacher educators (Cuenca, Schmeichel, Butler, Dinkelman, & Nichols, 2011; Martin, Snow, & Franklin-Torrez, 2011). As teacher preparation increasingly places clinical experiences at the core of the curriculum, understanding more about the knowledge and skills needed to teach about teaching in field contexts is essential (Burns & Badiali, 2016). Additionally, it is imperative that teacher educators engaged in this work create effective tools that focus supervision and provide support and professional development for teacher educators who take on the supervisory role (Williams, 2014).

From the authors' extensive work, both as and with supervisors, they know that supervisors have developed a set of intuitive practices grounded in personal theories about the nature of supervision (Palmeri & Peter, 2014, 2015, 2017). As teacher educators design professional development and other supports for university supervisors they seek to challenge existing practices as well as establish new practices.

Teacher Educators Explicitly Mediate the Learning of Complex Practice

Teaching is a complex endeavor and learning to teach through practice is equally complex (Lampert, 2010; Wideen, Mayer-Smith, & Moon, 1998). Teacher educators think about, plan for, talk about, and teach with much greater nuance than the novice (Borko & Livingston, 1989; Hogan, Rabinowitz, & Craven, 2003). However, beyond this greater experience from which to draw upon, teacher educators possess additional and unique pedagogical skills, knowledge, and expertise essential to supporting PST learning (Korthagen, Loughran, & Lunenberg, 2005). For example, teacher educators must know how *students of teaching* learn and develop and they must make use of teacher educational pedagogies that align with this PST developmental trajectory (Hundley, Palmeri, Hostetler, Johnson, Dunleavy, & Self, 2018; Swennen, Volman, & vanEssen, 2008). Without the unique and specific supports that teacher educators provide, PSTs have difficulty connecting their nascent understandings of teaching to their emerging pedagogical skills (Berry, 2009; Loughran & Berry, 2005).

Emerging teacher educational pedagogies, consistent with the framework for conceptualizing effective clinical preparation articulated by Grossman and colleagues (Grossman et al., 2009) have been developed to support PST learning and development. For example, the University of Michigan has identified a set of core practices to be taught and mastered during preservice teacher education (Teaching Works, 2015). These 19 core practices are considered to be high-leverage because the skills are pervasive in teaching, can be learned and practiced in isolation, and can be incorporated into more complex teaching structures as the PST gains facility with the isolated practice.

By design, these high-leverage practices are often learned in isolation and outside of the context of real-time teaching. The practices are typically approximated in highly controlled contexts where the practice is slowed down to the point that the approximation of practice is incongruent with the nature and demands of real-time practice (Ball & Forzani, 2010; Boerst, Sleep, Bass, & Ball, 2011; Kucan, Palincsar, Busse, Heisey, Klingelhofer, Rimbey, & Schutz, 2011; Windschitl, Thompson, Braaten, & Stroupe, 2012). In an effort to move toward approximations reflecting the pace of real-time teaching, teachers educators have begun developing teacher educational pedagogies involving rehearsals that often occur in the context of the university classroom (McDonald, Kazemi, & Kavanagh, 2013). Rehearsals themselves have a developmental trajectory where the scaffolding provided by the teacher educator changes over the course of teacher preparation (Lampert, Franke, Kazemi, Ghousseini, Turrou, Beasley,... & Crowe, 2013; McDonald, Kazemi, & Kavanagh, 2013; Scheeler, McKinnon, & Stout, 2012).

The teacher educator, therefore plays a critical role in helping PSTs make sense of the complex practice they see and are learning to enact (Burns & Badiali, 2016). While the intensity of the scaffolding provided by the teacher educator to the PST is being reduced over time, it is important to note that even in the case of bug-in-ear technology used in real-time teaching, the voice of the teacher educator quite literally continues to play a mediating role (Hollett, Brock, & Hinton, 2017). The authors' work, situated in the context of the POC, seeks to remove the last explicit scaffold where the PST must begin to make real-time instructional decisions by drawing upon their own internal teaching voice. Although the voice of the teacher educator is removed from real-time teaching, it continues to mediate PST learning in the context of the POC. The provision of educative feedback is key in mediating this process.

Principles of Educative Feedback

Feedback has the potential to affect learning, but modes of feedback commonly provided as generic comments ("good job!"), advice ("include more details"), or assigned grades (B+), have little impact (Hattie & Timperley, 2007). Effective feedback provides information about how the learner is doing in their effort to reach a goal (Wiggins, 2012); it is timely and is targeted toward specific ideas or skills that focus on the gap between what a learner understands and the goal that is being sought (Hattie & Timperley, 2007); and it emphasizes the elements of performance most critical to the attainment of the articulated goal (Bronkhorst, Meijer, Koster, & Vermunt, 2011). Such feedback is informed by conceptions of quality, making it both deliberate and explicit (Moss, 2011). However, even the most effective feedback does not become educative unless the learner accepts the feedback, clarifies how to utilize the feedback, and then has the opportunity to act on that feedback in the future (Bronkhorst, Meijer, Koster, & Vermunt, 2011; Cambourne, 1999; Lampert, 2010). When effective feedback is actionable, ongoing, and consistent, it is more likely to become immediately useful. When it is provided during continuing learning opportunities, and where standards of quality remain consistent, feedback has the potential to become generative, and thus educative.

In the context of preservice teacher education, educative feedback is used to enhance PST learning and to inform future teaching practice. The challenge faced by teacher educators is that the effectiveness of feedback tends to decrease as task complexity increases (Hattie & Timperley, 2007). Because teaching is a highly complex practice (Hammerness, Darling-Hammond, & Bransford, 2005), it is imperative that feedback given to PSTs as part of the supervision process be attentive to the complexity of the task, focused on critical elements of teaching practice, and sensitive to the developmental trajectories of the PST receiving the feedback. Thus, supervisory tools should be designed to support the teacher educator in providing feedback. Further, the broader context of post-observation conferencing should explicitly provide opportunities for the novice to both internalize and utilize that feedback in future planning and teaching to ensure that the feedback becomes educative.

Design Criteria Emerging From This Theoretical Grounding

Emerging from this theoretical grounding, the authors articulate criteria that can be used to evaluate and/or create effective supervisory tools. In short, these criteria indicate that effective supervisory tools should: (1) intentionally foreground the educative function of PST supervision; (2) explicitly leverage the active role the teacher educator plays as the PST makes sense of complex practice, and; (3) comprehensively align with the features of effective feedback.

EXAMINING EXISTING POST-OBSERVATION CONFERENCE PROTOCOLS

After clarifying the design criteria, the authors searched for existing tools developed to support PST learning in the context of supervision. Given space limitations the authors examine two specific tools, chosen because they are representative of broader types of supervisory tools. First, the authors chose to examine The Danielson Framework for Teaching because this model articulates a broad framework for teaching and was designed to serve as a professional roadmap for use with a variety of audiences and for a variety of purposes (Danielson, 2007). Second, the authors examine a tool that was designed with a more specific intent: Supporting PST learning in the context of student teacher supervision (Soslau, 2012, 2015). Soslau (2015) developed a theoretically grounded POC protocol intended to help PSTs develop adaptive teaching expertise. This tool shares many features of other contemporary protocols in that it engages the PST in a reflective process aimed at helping the novice understand and improve their practice. The authors initially undertook this analysis in order to determine if they might simply adopt, or perhaps modify an existing tool. However neither of these types of tools were found to satisfactorily meet all three of their design criteria.

The Danielson Framework for Teaching

The Danielson Framework for Teaching, first published in 1996 and revised in 2007, is designed to describe the complex practice of teaching. The framework seeks to articulate and describe what teachers should know and be able to do in service of their profession. Specifically the framework identifies "those aspects of a teacher's responsibility that have been documented through empirical studies and theoretical research as promoting improved student learning" (Danielson, 2007, p. 1). Because the Danielson Framework has been widely adopted across the United States for use with practicing teachers and with PST in teacher preparation programs (Danielson, 2007), the authors determined it would be a useful framework to consider in relation to their design criteria.

In order to decompose the complexity of teaching, the framework articulates 22 components which are clustered into 4 domains: Planning and preparation, the classroom environment, instruction, and professional responsibilities. Further, each of the 22 components of teaching are broken down into a total of 76 smaller elements. The Framework for Teaching consists of 22 rubrics and across these rubrics, criteria for measuring the performance related to each of the 76 smaller elements is articulated. Performance can be characterized as: Unsatisfactory, basic, proficient, and distinguished.

In reviewing the Danielson Framework for Teaching against their three design principles, the authors conclude that the model is illustrative of an observation tool that foregrounds the evaluative rather than the educative function of supervision and thus is inconsistent with their first design principle. The Danielson Group webpage (2018) states that the framework can be used to link together the various activities related to school or district level mentoring, coaching, professional development, and teacher evaluation. Rather than explicitly teasing apart the educative and the evaluative functions of using such a tool, it intentionally conflates the two. Second, the authors conclude that the Danielson Framework is sensitive to the active and essential role the teacher educator plays as the PST makes sense of complex practice. For example, Danielson (2007) advocates for the use of the framework as an organizing structure to direct the feedback given to the PST by the teacher educator in the context of student teaching supervision. The authors acknowledge the utility of the rubrics and the articulated levels of performance in helping them envision a developmental trajectory of how skills develop over time. Thus, the authors conclude that the Danielson Framework is supportive of their second design principle. Finally, the authors conclude that the Danielson Framework for Teaching is inconsistent with their third design criteria which focuses on providing effective feedback. Effective feedback is timely, is targeted on specific ideas or skills, and emphasizes the elements of performance most critical to the attainment of the articulated goal - in this case effective teaching (Hattie & Timperley, 2007). The authors agree that the Framework for Teaching emphasizes, in its 76 elements, those practices essential for effective teaching. Further, the authors agree that the feedback given to the novice using the Danielson Framework for Teaching would be timely as it is recommended that the framework can best be used to structure a conversation about teaching directly following an observation (Danielson, 2007). However, by focusing on 76 distinct elements of teaching, the Danielson Framework for Teaching fails to focus the PST's attention toward a specific idea or skill, which is a critical feature of effective feedback. Charlotte Danielson (2016) seems to share the authors' concern when she states, "I'm deeply troubled by the transformation of teaching from a complex profession requiring nuanced judgment to the performance of certain behaviors that can be ticked off on a checklist".

In short, the authors conclude that Danielson's Framework for Teaching (Danielson, 2007) is a useful tool that articulates a vision for the on-going professional learning of teachers across a career. However, the authors determine that the Danielson Framework would not, as is, be a useful tool for PST supervision because it does not sufficiently address or support the specific learning needs of novice teachers.

Soslau's Model to Support the Development of Adaptive Expertise

A different type of tool utilized in the supervision of novice teachers is grounded in the assumption that reflective practices are key in learning to teach. Learning to teach is viewed as the development of reflective thinking where PSTs learn by doing and develop the abilities of critical thinking, continued learning, and problem solving (Orland-Barak & Yinon, 2007; Schön, 1983, 1987). Reflective practices are seen as having the potential to provide the link between the gap that separates the theory and practice of professional preparation (Leavy, McSorley, & Bote, 2007) with self-directed reflection incorporating characteristics of intentionality, thoughtfulness, systematicity, and interrogation which would then serve to form a bridge from reflection to action (Cochran-Smith & Lytle, 1999). In this type of tool, open-ended questions posed to the novice teacher invite and support the important work of reflection. These tools emphasize reflection in practice as a means for a novice teacher to think critically about their teaching.

A supervisory tool developed by Soslau (2015) exemplifies this second type of protocol. The authors have chosen this tool as representative of those grounded in reflection because Soslau (2012) provides insight into her thinking as a supervisor who used an evaluative tool early in her career but transitioned to what she characterizes as a more reflective tool. The body of her protocol consists of 15 open ended questions, each followed by several probes designed to elicit critical self-assessment and reflection by the PST. Many of these probes ask the novice teacher to provide evidence for a claim being made and encourages them to articulate the influences on their planning and teaching decisions. Eight of the first 10 questions posed to the student teacher focus on pupil learning and how decisions made during planning and teaching affect that learning. One question provides a specific opportunity for the student teacher to pose their own questions. The final four questions (and additional probes) direct the student teacher's attention inwardly toward their own developing identity as a professional and also prompt the student teacher's thinking toward how they may self-direct their own reflection and learning in the future.

In reviewing Soslau's (21015) protocol against their three design principles, the authors conclude that her protocol achieved their first principle as it foregrounds the educative function of the post-observation conference. For example, she states:

My ongoing engagement in research about my and other field instructors' practices made me increasingly committed to the idea that solely providing feedback based on a checklist of observed behaviors does not create a sufficient learning environment for novice teacher growth. (Soslau, 2015, p. 25)

Soslau determined that, given her focus and goals, she needed a different tool for supporting student teacher growth, one that was consistent with her beliefs about the key role that reflection plays in developing novice teacher expertise as well as preparing PSTs to be reflective practitioners in the future. Second, the authors conclude that Soslau's (2015) protocol has the potential to meet their second design principle. However the scope of Soslau's protocol suggests that her intent is to address a wide range of teaching issues, concerns, and practices rather than focus in-depth on a key element of practice. For example, Soslau's protocol launches with a series of questions focused on engaging the preservice teacher in reflecting on pupil learning. This framing is immediately followed by the supervisor asking the student teacher, "Is there anything you would like to discuss first?" This question, asked early in the conference, opens the door for the student teacher to shift the focus of the conversation from being educative to being evaluative. Thus, the authors conclude that it is difficult to determine if Soslau's protocol fully leverages the active role the university supervisor plays in mediating the PST's thinking and learning as they make sense of complex practice. Finally, the authors conclude that Soslau's protocol does not fully meet their third design criteria which attends to the features of effective feedback. Soslau (2015) recognizes the importance of feedback, stating,

The fact that I had no idea what my students made of my feedback pointed to the evaluative, as opposed to the instructional, nature of my early post-lesson observation conversations. Additionally, how could I have possibly been conducting instructive conferences, when I never engaged my students in the type of discourse (producing rationales and justifications) that would help me uncover their internal thinking? (p. 25).

In response, Soslau designed her protocol to provide feedback to the PST, to invite PST reflection to uncover their thinking, and to establish patterns that would enable self-directed reflection in the future. In using her protocol, Soslau establishes trust to ensure that her PSTs hear her feedback and through the process of reflection ensures that novices are able to make meaning of the feedback. However, in the absence of closure that includes a specific actionable plan for the novice teacher, the authors conclude that the Soslau protocol fails to provide the educative feedback that will inform preservice teachers' future teaching practice.

In short, the authors conclude that Soslau's (2015) protocol is an example of a tool that foregrounds the educative function of supervision. Soslau's protocol doesn't fully leverage the mediating role of the university supervisor or provide actionable feedback and consequently is not fully consistent with their other two design criteria. Through a careful examination of these two common types of protocols the authors found that neither type was fully consistent with all three of their design criteria. Therefore in order to achieve their goal of pivoting from evaluative to educative feedback during the POC the authors designed a new protocol consistent with the theoretically grounded design principles outlined above.

DESIGNING THE NEW POST-OBSERVATION CONFERENCE PROTOCOL

In this section the authors describe the new POC protocol presented in Table 1 and make explicit how the structure of the protocol presented and described is consistent with their three design principles.

This protocol provides an intentional structure as articulated in the purpose column as well as a set of sentence stems for the university supervisor to choose from in order to accomplish each of the purposes articulated. The PST is invited to *reflect* on the lesson, then the PST and the university supervisor together *elaborate* on specific instances from the lesson. Next the university supervisor supports the PST in making *productive connections*, and finally the PST is invited to articulate an *action plan*. The authors intend for the POC to be a brief, but highly focused and deliberate activity with a distinct structure therefore a running time column is included. This new protocol provides an explicit and directed structure prompting the PST to reflect with focus and intention on their developing practice in substantive and generative ways.

Launching the Post-Observation Conference

When using the protocol, the supervisor chooses a focus for the conference that is specifically informed by the teaching episode just observed. This serves to ensure that there are opportunities to: 1) critically examine multifaceted and nuanced practice; 2) build toward the generation of an action plan for continued growth and development, and; 3) cycle back to and incorporate previous action plans as appropriate. Notice the four potential foci listed in bold under the instructional prompts (see Table 1). The authors consider these foci to be superordinate elements of teaching because they are elements of teaching that are a part of any lesson regardless of subject matter, level (e.g. elementary, secondary, etc.), or lesson structure (e.g. direct instruction, whole or small group, inquiry-oriented, etc.). In sum, the new protocol focuses on a limited set of core ideas essential to teaching consisting of four superordinate elements: 1) something is being taught, *subject matter*; 2) the teacher is communicating this subject matter to the learner, *teacher language*; 3) in order for learning to occur, the learner needs to be engaged with the

Table 1. The Post-Observation Conference Protocol

Instructional Purpose	Running Time	Potential Instructional Prompts
Invite the PST to **reflect** on his/her teaching as related to the specific lesson observed	0-3 min.	In light this lesson (*reflect on; talk to me about; or tell me what you think about*) the (choose one) • **flow of** • **subject matter** (*introduced, explored, covered, applied, assessed etc.*) during • **teacher language** you made use of during • **students' engagement** during the lesson and how this influenced student learning.
To **elaborate** on instances that increase the variation and provide contrast for analysis that supports productive connections	3-8 min.	Build on the PSTs opening response: • Thinking about what you had planned for this lesson what are you noticing about your planning and enactment? • Let's consider ways in which [summarize what the PST said] impacted opportunities for student learning. • Let's generate additional instances or examples from the lesson where [summarize what the PST said] came into play in ways that did or didn't move your lesson forward Another instance that I noticed related to [restate chosen focus] was … • How do you think this impacted opportunities for student learning? • How do you think this did or didn't move your lesson forward? • What was similar or different about the instances that seemed more effective than other instances?
Leverage the analysis across instances to help the PST make **productive connections** between theory, research, and practice	8-11 min.	Some stems to help the PST begin to make connections: • Why is this (name the element of practice) important? • Why is it helpful to remember that (name the focus) is multifaceted? • What are the elements of good/effective…? • What happens when you…? • Do you remember in… when we… how might that help us think about this? • Is there a resource you might revisit, seek out, or tap into that would be helpful? Now try to articulate a generalization or general principle from what you are learning here that will help keep you focused as you plan future lessons.
Based on the analysis of practice, the PST articulates an **action plan** for future planning and/or instruction	11- 15 min.	Ways to encourage teacher candidate to begin to generate an action plan: • So what might you try tomorrow or within the next week that you think will help your practice and improve upon …? • What are you thinking about right now in terms of improving or refining your practice? • How might we see evidence of your attention to … in your future plans? Teaching?

subject matter, *student engagement*, and; 4) the intentional learning experience is designed to unfold in a particular way, *lesson flow*.

Naming the four superordinate elements of teaching in this way might give the false impression that these elements of teaching stand alone or that they are unidimensional, but neither is the case. These superordinate elements of teaching are multifaceted in nature. Further, the authors intentionally blur the lines between superordinate elements to highlight ways in which focusing intently on one element of practice provides natural points of entry to make productive connections within, between, and among the various superordinate elements during and/or across POCs as the preservice teachers' thinking about and enactment of practice becomes more sophisticated.

Defining *subject matter* might be the most straightforward, as teachers at the elementary level, usually trained as generalists, easily parse the curriculum into subject matter areas. One might intuitively move to naming topics of study within each discipline, articulating factual information, or listing key skills involved when one is reading, writing, doing math, etc.. However, such framing continues to mask what teachers are doing (and therefore must learn to do) if they are to effectively engage their students in learning the subject matter. The authors therefore define subject matter as the factual content knowledge, disciplinary specific practices, or conceptual ideas as reflected and explored instructionally through definitions, conceptual explanations, the use of essential questions to frame instruction or build connections across subject matter ideas, the kinds of questions posed and how these change over the course of instruction, and the choice of instructional materials (e.g. visuals, manipulatives, texts, primary source materials, etc.) among other facets of teaching practice. In addition, subject matter has a developmental dimension that requires a teacher to transform accurate subject matter information so that it is accessible to students (Ball, Thames, & Phelps, 2008; Shulman, 1987). For example, what we expect a first grader to know and understand about living things is clearly different from what we expect a fourth grader to know and understand. While we expect one group to have more sophisticated, complex, and nuanced understanding, both groups are expected to be presented with sound and accurate subject matter. Therefore, a teacher's subject matter explanations, definitions, choice of instructional questions and instructional materials, must be consistent with articulated grade level expectations or theoretically acknowledged developmental understandings. The clarity of teacher language and the ability of the teacher to frame and articulate subject matter learning at the right developmental level impacts students' engagement, and thus learning (Skinner & Pitzer, 2012).

Teacher language is nearly impossible to separate from subject matter, as one of the primary ways teachers use language in the classroom is instructional. In addition to the definitions, explanations, questions, etc. that teachers communicate related to the subject matter, instructional language includes attention to other academic language demands which extend beyond academic vocabulary to include academic task vocabulary and disciplinary specific symbolic or representational language (Bauman & Graves, 2010). Instructional language also incorporates a repertoire of teacher talk moves such as revoicing, restating, summarizing, connecting, etc. (Hufferd-Ackles, Fuson, & Sherin, 2004). However teachers also make use of procedural language which includes the ways in which teachers gain students attention, provide directions, set and articulate expectations, and establish routines among other things. It would include the ways in which these procedures are initially taught to the students as well as the short-hand cues that alert the students to a particular routine or a set of expectations/norms for a particular activity structure. For example in some activities the teacher may want students to raise their hands to be called on but in other activities the teacher may allow students to share without waiting to be called upon. Teacher language may also serve to establish and support a sense of community in the classroom by using inclusive language that helps establish norms, builds rapport, and establishes trust within the classroom all of which are related to student engagement (Parsons, Nuland, & Parsons, 2014). In short, teacher language would be all the ways in which the teacher communicates with students through verbal communication or non-verbally through facial expressions, body language, choice of visual materials, and use of auditory cues (e.g. use of a chime or clapping patterns).

Student engagement is a multifaceted construct that has been shown to be "a robust predictor of student learning" (Skinner & Pitzer, 2012 p.21). Generally there are three types of engagement teachers attend to: affective, behavioral and cognitive. Affective engagement is nurtured when students feel a sense of belonging and it is evident when students express curiosity, excitement, or interest in specific topics or tasks (Parsons, Nuland, & Parsons, 2014). Behavioral engagement is characterized by positive conduct where students follow classroom rules, adhere to classroom norms and routines, and complete work in a timely manner (Fredricks, Blumenfeld, & Paris, 2004). Cognitive engagement is characterized as an investment in learning and is related to self-regulation, the use of metacognitive strategies, flexible problem-solving, perseverance, and what many refer to as 'having grit' (Dweck, 2007; Hichanadel,

& Finamore, 2015; Parsons, Nuland, & Parsons, 2014). While it might be easy to think that student engagement is a disposition within the learner themselves, there is much a teacher can do to foster and support student engagement (Malloy, Parsons, & Parsons, 2013). For example, engaging classrooms tend to be cooperative and efficient. Building and maintaining affective engagement is related to teachers' community building language which can be used to establish and reinforce a cooperative, rather than a competitive, classroom context. While there are many reasons that a student may or may not be behaviorally engaged, such engagement may often be related to the clarity of a teacher's procedural language - students need to have a clear sense of what they should be doing in order to abide by classroom rules, follow the norms and routines for the classroom, and to settle into completing group and independent work. Additionally both behavioral engagement and cognitive engagement can be undermined or enhanced when the subject matter being conveyed falls within the zone of proximal development. When students are adequately challenged by the subject matter and the tasks they are asked to do, cognitive engagement may be enhanced. In contrast, when the subject matter and related tasks are too easy or too challenging both cognitive and behavioral engagement may be hindered. Finally, affective and cognitive engagement can be supported when instructional tasks are authentic, collaborative, and when students are given choices about how to approach instructional tasks or which tasks to engage in (Perry, Turner, & Meyer, 2006). When identifying a strength or weakness in pedagogical practice linked to student engagement, the root cause is often linked to the subject matter framing and/or characteristics of the teacher's language.

Finally, the idea of *lesson flow* is used as a general term to encompass the structures, routines, organization around lessons, transitions within and between lessons, how activities within a lesson are sequenced, and how each of these individually and collectively contribute to seamless implementation and effective teaching practice. While some of these "things" might be perceived as issues of management, attending to them effectively necessitates attention to subject matter content, teacher language, and student engagement. Moving toward effective and seamless instruction that supports student learning is challenging for the novice along both the conceptual/theoretical dimension and the practice dimension. When the other three superordinate elements come together and are accomplished efficiently and effectively the results are what the authors refer to as simultaneous and integrated practice that supports student learning. Being able to engage in simultaneous and integrated practice requires that the novice demonstrates not only knowledge and skill related to the wide array of pedagogical practices that are often learned in isolation (as a way of simplifying the complex task of learning how to teach - see Wideen, Mayer-Smith, & Moon, 1998) but that they can also put all of these pieces back together in a comprehensive manner and at the pace required of real-time teaching. The authors view such simultaneous and integrated practice as a hallmark of accomplished teaching and is therefore viewed as the benchmark to be attained by the PST by the end of their preparation program.

The Structure of the Post-Observation Conference Protocol

By framing the POC as a teaching space, the protocol is viewed as the teacher educators lesson plan for the conference. The protocol therefore appropriates features of effective planning. The provision of instructional prompts in the form of statement or question stems provides guidance for the university supervisor. This allows the supervisor to select specific prompts for the POC that best fit the specific lesson observed, aligns well with what the supervisor knows about the PST, and is consistent with the supervisors own teaching/supervisory style.

With these details in mind, the authors turn their focus on making explicit how their POC protocol reflects the theoretically grounded design principles that informed their work. The POC should: (1) intentionally foreground the educative function of PST supervision; (2) explicitly provide support to aid the PST in making sense of complex practice, and; (3) comprehensively align with the features of effective feedback.

COHERENCE BETWEEN THE DESIGN CRITERIA AND THE NEW PROTOCOL

The authors make the case that their newly designed POC protocol comprehensively accomplishes each of the design criteria articulated. The authors explain how their protocol is similar to yet different from two other types of POC protocols. While each design criteria is addressed individually, the authors also make connections that highlight how considerations and insights from one criteria feed into and shape consideration regarding other criteria.

Establishing the Post-Observation Conference as an Educative Space

First, the protocol establishes the POC as an intentional space for learning and teaching and this is reflected in the structure of the protocol itself. As elaborated upon above, the column headings (see Table 1) of instructional purposes and instructional prompts serve as an explicit reminder to the supervisor that the POC is a time of teaching and learning. The authors utilize the protocol as their lesson plan for the post-observation conference.

From an educative standpoint, the intentional launch immediately focusing the POC on one of the four superordinate elements of teaching is important. We know that how one launches a lesson has consequences for how the lesson unfolds and therefore shapes opportunities for student learning (Jackson, Shahan, Gibbons, & Cobb, 2012). Further, from a pedagogical perspective, this intentional and focused launch is significantly different from the more generic launch of "how did it go?" that many supervisors (including, prior this this work, the authors) report using. When launching a POC with the question "how did it go?" the university supervisor is left to react to any number of issues raised by the student teacher that may or may not be the most critical or productive points of entry. In contrast, a focused and direct launch allows the supervisor to use their expertise to immediately and deeply engage the PST in a critical element of practice. By launching the conference with a clear focus on a substantive element of practice, the teacher educator immediately directs the PST's attention and reflection. This sets the stage for the rest of the conference to unfold as a generative and formative conversation establishing and reinforcing the educative purpose of the post-observation conference.

In hindsight, this seemingly simple pivot from evaluative to educative may not seem significant. However, for the authors, claiming the POC as a teaching space sparked the ah-ha moment that served as the initial impetus for their work. This reframing has also been shown to be powerful for other supervisors. For example, after being introduced to the new protocol, one university supervisor said, "If you could see the lightbulbs—of course this shouldn't be a conference, but it should be a lesson plan." In other comments by this supervisor it was clear that in her mind a conference meant *telling* and a lesson plan meant *teaching*. Further, by referencing "lightbulbs" this supervisor reconceptualized supervision as a teaching opportunity that required intentional planning by the teacher educator. This supervisor was then able to activate and apply sound instructional pedagogies to her supervisory practice.

Leveraging the Role of the Teacher Educator in the Post-Observation Conference

Second, the design of the protocol provides a pedagogical structure that shapes the instructional conversation between the PST and the university supervisor. This conversation begins by inviting the PST to reflect on a critical element of teaching. Then together the PST and the university supervisor elaborate on examples of practice emerging from this reflection. Following this elaboration, the university supervisor supports the PST in making connections between theory, research, and practice. Finally, the university supervisor invites the PST to craft a specific action plan for future planning and teaching.

Achieving each of these instructional purposes not only supports PST learning but relies on the mediation and pedagogical expertise of the teacher educator (Gardiner, 2012, 2017). The university supervisor draws on their nuanced understanding of each of the superordinate elements of teaching to select a focus for the conference that will ground a robust conversation about complex teaching practice. The university supervisor plays an important role as the PST elaborates on examples of practice related to the superordinate element of teaching that grounds the instructional conversation. Specifically the university supervisor does two key things during this part of the POC to ensure that the preservice teacher: (1) considers the multifaceted nature of the given superordinate element of teaching and; (2) engages in nuanced analysis to identify how and why different facets of a given superordinate element of teaching played out over the course of the lesson. Because learning in and from practice emerges from the iterative back and forth between theory, research and practice, the university supervisor plays a critical role. They must point the PST toward the theory and research their practice might be implicitly informed by or point them toward theory and research that informs how they approach solving a pervasive problem of practice. By always seeking to make connections between theory, research, and practice the supervisor plays a critical role in helping the PST situate a particular teaching episode in relation to other teaching episodes. The importance of the supervisor's mediation of this space cannot be underestimated as it has been shown that when the supervisor does not foster theory and practice connections, many PSTs disregard the professional knowledge shared in their coursework in favor of the practices they witness and engage in during their daily practice (Moore, 2003; Ward, Nolen, & Horn, 2011). Finally, by closing each POC with an action plan the supervisor and PST are no longer speaking of one teaching moment - the lesson just observed - but of teaching more broadly. Taken together, these elements individually and collectively leverage the unique teacher educational and pedagogical expertise of the university supervisor to scaffold the PST in becoming an active and critical participant in the POC rather than a passive recipient of the knowledge and expertise of someone else.

Utilizing this new protocol requires that supervisors change their long standing and familiar supervisory practices. One supervisor articulated her struggle with making a shift from the supervisor doing most of the talking to following a protocol which guides the novice to take the lead in critically reflecting on teaching. Expressing surprise, one supervisor noted: "I am the one making the recommendations. The first thing I got out of [the protocol], is that I am working harder than my students." This supervisor noted that the structure of the new protocol helped her step back from primarily giving advice to the PST to providing space for the novice to be actively engaged in constructing an understanding of key elements of teaching.

Consistent With Features of Effective Feedback

Finally, the protocol leverages the role feedback plays in supporting PSTs in developing competent teaching practices. Given what we know about the complexity of learning to teach (Wideen, Mayer-Smith, & Moon, 1998) it makes little sense to expect the PST to make sense of feedback regarding a wide range of pedagogical knowledge and skill. Therefore, the careful attention to the features of effective and educative feedback is the most salient difference between this new POC protocol and the two types critically examined by the authors.

First, by intentionally focusing a POC on one of four superordinate elements of teaching the new protocol ensures that feedback provided to the PST is both focused and specific (Bronkhorst, Meijer, Koster, & Vermunt, 2011). The small number of foci allows for consistency across POCs by providing a conceptual framework for building the preservice teachers' understandings of the multifaceted and nuanced nature of teaching. The limited number of superordinate elements therefore provides a set of four "hooks" upon which the PST can hang specific points of feedback enabling them to make meaning of that feedback in relation to other things they know. Consistent with the second design principle, the supervisor explicitly supports this process by articulating the connections between the facets within a superordinate element (e.g. feedback related to teacher questioning, providing procedural directions, giving and elaborating on definitions, etc. are all explicitly examined as different facets of teacher language) as well as across superordinate elements (e.g. feedback related to student engagement may identify cognitive engagement as an area for growth and the action plan may require action in relation to a different superordinate element such as calling for increasing the rigor of the subject matter). By closing the POC with an action plan, not only does the feedback become actionable, but by asking the PST to articulate the action plan, it provides further evidence to the supervisor that the novice is making appropriate meaning of and internalizing the feedback. The action plan can also serve to connect one POC to the next by intentionally revisiting the preservice teacher's progress in relation to the prior action plan at the beginning of the next conference. Further the repeated focus on one of four essential elements of teaching over a series of POCs ensures that the feedback is on-going. The standard sequence of the POC provides another layer of consistency that emerges from familiarity with the procedure itself. Together these features enhance the preservice teachers' ability to build interconnected understandings about practice that more accurately mirror the complexity of teaching.

Supervisors new to the protocol initially express concern that the four superordinate elements of teaching are too narrow. One supervisor stated, "But as I observe I see hundreds of things the novice needs to work on, how can I only choose one thing to focus on?" This skepticism immediately creates a barrier to accomplishing a key tenet of effective feedback that a supervisor has to confront in their supervisory practice - focus on one thing so as not to overwhelm the novice with a laundry list of elements of practice to master. Following a semester of using the protocol, this same supervisor described her evolving supervisory practice this way:

I now realize my past practice consisted of providing the novice with a list of grows and glows and I freely offered suggestions of what the novice should do. Now I provide feedback so the novice can learn what to do.

This shift is important as it seems to reveal that supervisors carry with them an expert blindspot that impacts their supervisory practice. In short, the expert blindspot emerges when one is teaching or talking about elements of practice or skill without making explicit the broader context within which that practice or skill is situated (Nathan & Petrosino, 2003). This new awareness provides a context for supervisors to examine the simple ways they talk about complex practice and to recognize how, when talking with other experienced teachers, their meaning is transparent but when talking with a novice their meaning is often opaque.

FUTURE DIRECTIONS

The authors recognize how situating their work outside of the traditional dichotomy of theory or practice has had far-reaching implications for their work beyond using the POC protocol with student teachers. For example: 1) utilizing the protocol across the pre-service experience from initial field work through student teaching; 2) considering the program-wide implications of a educative structure for post-observation conferencing, and; 3) providing initial training and ongoing professional development for university supervisors using the protocol.

The design of the POC protocol leverages the authors understanding of what novice teachers know and can do at the beginning of student teaching. Realizing that a single POC captures a particular moment in time, the protocol is intentionally structured to create opportunities for connected and grounded conversations that generate teachable moments. These teachable moments are situated within a broader set of opportunities within a teacher education program that, over time, hold the potential to be educative and generative. Future work might address how a POC protocol designed for use with student teachers could move both forward and backward along a trajectory of novice teacher development. Moving forward along the trajectory, such work might consider how the protocol needs to change to support student teachers as they move beyond reflecting on practice to reflecting in practice. This more nuanced focus during the POC could illuminate the conscious and recognizable "in the moment" decisions made by the student teacher while teaching. In contrast, moving backward along the trajectory, future work could explore ways to adapt the protocol to better target the developmental needs and constraints of novices during early field experiences. The goal of this work would be to ensure the type of feedback given at particular points in the program are informed by one's current understanding of novice teacher development and firmly rooted in learning theory. Formalizing this knowledge in the form of a theoretically grounded developmental trajectory articulating what PSTs know and what they are able to demonstrate in practice would be invaluable when used to inform future teacher educational practice designed to prepare school-ready and learner-ready teachers.

To the extent that the POC is educative and viewed as a teaching space, the role of supervisor needs to be reconceptualized as that of teacher educator who brings to the work specific knowledge regarding the development of PSTs and the pedagogies that support this development. This acknowledgement has critical implications for both who is employed to do the work of supervision and the kind of professional development provided for those typically engaged in this role who might have limited knowledge of PST development or the pedagogical skills best suited to helping a novice learn complex practice.

CONCLUSION

The design of this new protocol was undertaken in response to many who have called attention to the complexity of supervision within the context of preservice teacher education (Burns & Badiali, 2016; Williams, 2014). Predicated on the assumption that the work of teacher educators, teaching in the third space between universities and schools, is anything but straightforward and unproblematic (Cuenca, Schmeichel, Butler, Dinkelman, & Nichols, 2011) the authors identified specific theoretically grounded criteria to inform the design of a new supervisory tool.

The utility of the new POC protocol as an educative tool has emerged and was solidified through an iterative design process. By limiting the focus of a POC to one of four superordinate elements of teaching, the authors' protocol brings continuity and consistency across POCs thereby supporting PSTs as they connect knowledge and skill related to complex practice. Consistent with effective feedback, the POC ends with an actionable plan, scaffolding the novice in articulating a specific intention informing their next planning and teaching opportunity.

The use of the POC protocol during student teaching has transformed the authors' supervisory practices. As the authors have gained proficiency at implementing their protocol and student teachers have demonstrated an ability to identify and critically reflect upon compelling elements of their teaching the outcome has been fertile ground supporting the growth of the student teacher as well as the teacher educator.

It is widely accepted that good teaching appears easy to the inexperienced teacher (Lortie, 1975), therefore it should not be surprising that the authors, like Burns and Badiali (2016), found that supervision as a teaching endeavor often appears easy to an experienced teacher or teacher educator. However, when PST supervision is viewed as a unique teacher educational context that calls for its own knowledge and pedagogical skill, it is imperative that educative tools are available to support this work (Burns, Jacobs, & Yendol-Hoppey, 2016). Thus, the use of the new protocol has the potential to integrate dichotomous worlds: evaluative and educative stances; theory and practice; field-based supervisor and teacher educator.

ACKNOWLEDGMENT

This research received no specific grant from any funding agency in the public, commercial, or not-for-profit sectors.

REFERENCES

American Association of Colleges of Teacher Education. (2010). *The clinical preparation of teachers: A policy brief.* Retrieved from http://oacte.org/pdf/ClinicalPrepPaper_03-11-2010.pdf

Ball, D. L., & Forzani, F. M. (2009). The work of teaching and the challenge for teacher education. *Journal of Teacher Education*, 60(5), 497–511. doi:10.1177/0022487109348479

Ball, D. L., & Forzani, F. M. (2010). Teaching skillful teaching. *Educational Leadership*, 68(4), 40–45.

Ball, D. L., Thames, M. H., & Phelps, G. (2008). Content knowledge for teaching: What makes it special? *Journal of Teacher Education, 59*(5), 389–407. doi:10.1177/0022487108324554

Baumann, J. F., & Graves, M. F. (2010). What is academic vocabulary? *Journal of Adolescent & Adult Literacy, 54*(1), 4–12. doi:10.1598/JAAL.54.1.1

Beck, C., & Kosnik, C. (2002). Professors and the practicum: Involvement of university faculty in preservice practicum supervision. *Journal of Teacher Education, 53*(1), 6–19. doi:10.1177/0022487102053001002

Berry, A. (2009). Professional self-understanding as expertise in teaching about teaching. *Teachers and Teaching, 15*(2), 305–318. doi:10.1080/13540600902875365

Bhabba, H. (1990). The third space. In J. Rutherford (Ed.), *Identity, community, culture, and difference* (pp. 207–221). London: Lawrence & Wishart.

Boerst, T. A., Sleep, L., Ball, D. L., & Bass, H. (2011). Preparing teachers to lead mathematics discussions. *Teachers College Record, 113*(12), 2844–2877.

Borko, H., & Livingston, C. (1989). Cognition and improvisation: Differences in mathematics instruction by expert and novice teachers. *American Educational Research Journal, 26*(4), 473–498. doi:10.3102/00028312026004473

Bransford, J., Darling-Hammond, L., & LePage, P. (2005). Introduction. In L. Darling-Hammond & J. Bransford (Eds.), *Preparing teachers for a changing world: What teachers should learn and be able to do* (pp. 1–39). San Francisco, CA: Jossey-Bass.

Bronkhorst, L. H., Meijer, P. C., Koster, B., & Vermunt, J. D. (2011). Fostering meaning-oriented learning and deliberate practice in teacher education. *Teaching and Teacher Education, 27*(7), 1120–1130. doi:10.1016/j.tate.2011.05.008

Burns, R. W., & Badiali, B. (2015). When supervision is conflated with evaluation: Teacher candidates' perceptions of their novice supervisor. *Action in Teacher Education, 37*(4), 418–437. doi:10.1080/01626620.2015.1078757

Burns, R. W., & Badiali, B. (2016). Unearthing the complexities of clinical pedagogy in supervision: Identifying the pedagogical skills of supervisors. *Action in Teacher Education, 38*(2), 156–174. doi:10.1080/01626620.2016.1155097

Burns, R. W., Jacobs, J., & Yendol-Hoppey, D. (2016). The changing nature of the role of the university supervisor and function of preservice teacher supervision in an era of clinically-rich practice. *Action in Teacher Education, 38*(4), 410–425. doi:10.1080/01626620.2016.1226203

Cambourne, B. (1995). Toward an educationally relevant theory of literacy learning: Twenty years of inquiry. *The Reading Teacher, 49*(3), 182–190. doi:10.1598/RT.49.3.1

Cambourne, B. (2001). Conditions for literacy learning: Why do some students fail to learn to read? Ockham's razor and the conditions of learning. *The Reading Teacher, 54*(8), 784–786.

Cochran-Smith, M., & Lytle, S. L. (1999). Relationships of knowledge and practice: Teacher learning communities. *Review of Research in Education, 24*, 249–305.

Cuenca, A., Schmeichel, M., Butler, B. M., Dinkelman, T., & Nichols, J. R. Jr. (2011). Creating a "third space" in student teaching: Implications for the university supervisor's status as outsider. *Teaching and Teacher Education*, *27*(7), 1068–1077. doi:10.1016/j.tate.2011.05.003

Dangel, J. R., & Tanguay, C. (2014). "Don't leave us out there alone": A framework for supporting supervisors. *Action in Teacher Education*, *36*(3), 3–19. doi:10.1080/01626620.2013.864574

Danielson, C. (2007). *Enhancing professional practice: A framework for teaching* (2nd ed.). Alexandria, VA: ASCD.

Danielson, C. (2016). Charlotte Danielson on rethinking teacher evaluation. *Education Week*. Retrieved from https://www.edweek.org/ew/articles/2016/04/20/charlotte-danielson-on-rethinking-teacher-evaluation.html

Danielson Group. (2018). *The Framework*. Retrieved from http://www.danielsongroup.org/framework/

Darling-Hammond, L. (2014). Strengthening clinical preparation: The holy grail of teacher education. *Peabody Journal of Education*, *89*(4), 547–561. doi:10.1080/0161956X.2014.939009

Dweck, C. S. (2007). *Mindset: The new psychology of success*. New York: Random House.

Feiman-Nemser, S. (2001). From perspective to practice: Designing a continuum to strengthen and sustain teaching. *Teachers College Record*, *103*(6), 1013–1055. doi:10.1111/0161-4681.00141

Fredricks, J. A., Blumenfeld, P. C., & Paris, A. H. (2004). School engagement: Potential of the concept, state of the evidence. *Review of Educational Research*, *74*(1), 59–109. doi:10.3102/00346543074001059

Gardiner, W. (2012). Coaches' and new urban teachers' perceptions of induction coaching: TIme, trust, and accelerated learning curves. *Teacher Educator*, *47*(3), 195–215. doi:10.1080/08878730.2012.685797

Gardiner, W. (2017). Mentoring "inside" and "outside" the action of teaching: A professional framework for mentoring. *New Educator*, *13*(1), 53–71. doi:10.1080/1547688X.2016.1258849

Glickman, C., Gordon, S. P., & Ross-Gordon, J. M. (2014). *Supervision and instructional leadership: A developmental approach* (9th ed.). Boston, MA: Allyn & Bacon.

Grossman, P., Compton, C., Shahan, E., Ronfeldt, M., Igra, D., & Shiang, J. (2007). Preparing practitioners to respond to resistance: A cross-professional view. *Teachers and Teaching*, *13*(2), 109–123. doi:10.1080/13540600601152371

Gutiérrez, K. D. (2008). Developing a sociocritical literacy in the third space. *Reading Research Quarterly*, *43*(2), 148–164. doi:10.1598/RRQ.43.2.3

Hammerness, K., Darling-Hammond, L., & Bransford, J. (2005). How teachers learn and develop. In L. Darling-Hammond & J. Bransford (Eds.), *Preparing teachers for a changing world: What teachers should learn and be able to do* (pp. 358–389). San Francisco: Jossey-Bass.

Hattie, J., & Timperley, H. (2007). The power of feedback. *Review of Educational Research*, *77*(1), 81–112. doi:10.3102/003465430298487

Hichanadel, A., & Finamore, D. (2015). Fixed and growth mindset in education and how grit helps students persist in the face of adversity. *Journal of International Education Research, 11*(1), 47–50.

Hogan, T., Rabinowitz, M., & Craven, J. A. III. (2003). Representation in teaching: Inferences from research of expert and novice teachers. *Educational Psychologist, 38*(4), 235–247. doi:10.1207/S15326985EP3804_3

Hollett, N. L., Brock, S. J., & Hinton, V. (2017). Bug-in-ear technology to enhance preservice teacher training: Peer versus instructor feedback. *International Journal of Learning, Teaching, and Educational Research, 16*(2), 1–10.

Hufferd-Ackles, K., Fuson, K., & Sherin, M. (2004). Describing levels of components of a mathematics talk learning community. *Journal for Research in Mathematics Education, 35*(2), 81–116. doi:10.2307/30034933

Hundley, M., Palmeri, A., Hostetler, A., Johnson, H., Dunleavy, T. K., & Self, E. A. (2018). Developmental trajectories, disciplinary practices, and sites of practice in novice teacher learning: A thing to be learned. In D. Polly, M. Putman, T. M. Petty, & A. J. Good (Eds.), *Innovative practices in teacher preparation and graduate-level teacher education programs* (pp. 153–180). Hershey, PA: IGI Global. doi:10.4018/978-1-5225-3068-8.ch010

Jackson, K. J., Shahan, E. C., Gibbons, L. K., & Cobb, P. A. (2012). Launching complex tasks. *Mathematics Teaching in the Middle School, 18*(1), 24–29. doi:10.5951/mathteacmiddscho.18.1.0024

Kazemi, E., Franke, M., & Lampert, M. (2009, July). Developing pedagogies in teacher education to support novice teachers' ability to enact ambitious instruction. In *Crossing divides: Proceedings of the 32nd annual conference of the Mathematics Education Research Group of Australasia* (Vol. 1, pp. 12-30). Adelaide, SA: MERGA.

Korthagen, F., Loughran, J., & Lunenberg, M. (2005). Teaching teachers – studies into the expertise of teacher educators: An introduction to this theme issue. *Teaching and Teacher Education, 21*(2), 107–115. doi:10.1016/j.tate.2004.12.007

Kucan, L., Palincsar, A. S., Busse, T., Heisey, N., Klingelhofer, R., Rimbey, M., & Schutz, K. (2011). Applying the Grossman et al. theoretical framework: The case of reading. *Teachers College Record, 113*(12), 2897-2921.

Lampert, M. (2010). Learning teaching in, from, and for practice: What do we mean? *Journal of Teacher Education, 61*(1-2), 21–34. doi:10.1177/0022487109347321

Lampert, M., Franke, M. L., Kazemi, E., Ghousseini, H., Turrou, A. C., Beasley, H., ... Crowe, K. (2013). Keeping it complex: Using rehearsals to support novice teacher learning of ambitious teaching. *Journal of Teacher Education, 64*(3), 226–243. doi:10.1177/0022487112473837

Leavy, A. M., McSorley, F. A., & Boté, L. A. (2007). An examination of what metaphor construction reveals about the evolution of preservice teachers' beliefs about teaching and learning. *Teaching and Teacher Education, 23*(7), 1217–1233. doi:10.1016/j.tate.2006.07.016

Lortie, D. C. (1975). *Schoolteacher: A sociological study*. Chicago: University of Chicago Press.

Loughran, J., & Berry, A. (2005). Modelling by teacher educators. *Teaching and Teacher Education*, *21*(2), 193–203. doi:10.1016/j.tate.2004.12.005

Malloy, J. A., Parsons, S. A., & Parsons, A. W. (2013). Methods for evaluating literacy engagement as a fluid construct. *62nd Yearbook of the Literacy Research Association*, 124-139.

Martin, S. D., Snow, J. L., & Franklin Torrez, C. A. (2011). Navigating the terrain of third space: Tensions with/in relationships in school-university partnerships. *Journal of Teacher Education*, *62*(3), 299–311. doi:10.1177/0022487110396096

McDonald, M., Kazemi, E., & Kavanagh, S. S. (2013). Core practices and pedagogies of teacher education: A call for a common language and collective activity. *Journal of Teacher Education*, *64*(5), 378–386. doi:10.1177/0022487113493807

Moore, R. (2003). Reexamining the field experience of preservice teachers. *Journal of Teacher Education*, *54*(1), 31–42. doi:10.1177/0022487102238656

Moss, P. A. (2011). Analyzing the teaching of professional practice. *Teachers College Record*, *113*(12), 2878–2896.

Nathan, M. J., & Petrosino, A. (2003). Expert blind spot among preservice teachers. *American Educational Research Journal*, *40*(4), 905–928. doi:10.3102/00028312040004905

National Council for Accreditation of Teacher Education. (2010). *Transforming teacher education through clinical practice: A national strategy to prepare effective teachers. Blue Ribbon Panel on Clinical Preparation and Partnerships for Improved Student Learning*. Washington, DC: Author.

Nolan, J., & Hoover, L. A. (2010). *Teacher supervision and evaluation: Theory into practice* (3rd ed.). Hoboken, NJ: John Wiley & Sons.

Orland-Barak, L., & Yinon, H. (2007). When theory meets practice: What student teachers learn from guided reflection on their own classroom discourse. *Teaching and Teacher Education*, *23*(6), 957–969. doi:10.1016/j.tate.2006.06.005

Palmeri, A., & Peter, J. (2014). *Moving beyond: "How did it go?": A systematic and developmental approach to mentoring teacher candidates*. Paper presented at the NAECTE conference, Dallas, TX.

Palmeri, A., & Peter, J. (2015). *All that glitters is not gold: Scaffolding student teachers' reflections on practice*. Paper presented at the AACTE conference, Atlanta, GA.

Palmeri, A., & Peter, J. (2017). *Revisiting traditional supervisory practices: Innovations to enhance preservice teachers' practice through developmental feedback*. Paper presented at the ATE conference, Orlando, FL.

Parsons, S. A., Nuland, L. R., & Parsons, A. W. (2014). The ABCs of student engagement. *Phi Delta Kappan*, *95*(8), 23–27. doi:10.1177/003172171409500806

Perry, N. E., Turner, J. C., & Meyer, D. K. (2006). Classrooms as contexts for motivating learning. In P. A. Alexander & P. H. Winne (Eds.), *Handbook of educational psychology* (2nd ed.; pp. 327–348). Mahwah, NJ: Lawrence Erlbaum.

Range, B., Duncan, H., & Hvidston, D. (2013). How faculty supervise and mentor pre-service teachers: Implications for principal supervision of novice teachers. *The International Journal of Educational Leadership Preparation, 8*(2), 43–58.

Scheeler, M. C., McKinnon, K., & Stout, J. (2012). Effects of immediate feedback delivered via webcam and bug-in-ear technology on preservice teacher performance. *Teacher Education and Special Education, 35*(1), 77–90. doi:10.1177/0888406411401919

Schön, D. A. (1983). *The reflective practitioner: How professionals think in action.* New York: Basic Books.

Schön, D. A. (1987). *Educating the reflective practitioner: Toward a new design for teaching and learning in the professions.* San Francisco: Jossey-Bass.

Shulman, L. (1987). Knowledge and teaching: Foundations of the new reform. *Harvard Educational Review, 57*(1), 1–23. doi:10.17763/haer.57.1.j463w79r56455411

Skinner, E. A., & Pitzer, J. R. (2012). Developmental dynamics of student engagement, coping, and everyday resilience. In S. L. Christenson, A. L. Reschly, & C. Wylie (Eds.), *Handbook of research on student engagement* (pp. 21–44). New York: Springer. doi:10.1007/978-1-4614-2018-7_2

Soslau, E. (2012). Opportunities to develop adaptive teaching expertise during supervisory conferences. *Teaching and Teacher Education, 28*(5), 768–779. doi:10.1016/j.tate.2012.02.009

Soslau, E. (2015). Development of a post-lesson observation conferencing protocol: Situated in theory, research, and practice. *Teaching and Teacher Education, 49*, 22–35. doi:10.1016/j.tate.2015.02.012

Swennen, A., Volman, M., & van Essen, M. (2008). The development of the professional identity of two teacher educators in the context of Dutch teacher education. *European Journal of Teacher Education, 31*(2), 169–184. doi:10.1080/02619760802000180

Teaching Works. (2015). *High-leverage practices.* University of Michigan. Retrieved from http://www.teachingworks.org/work-of-teaching/high-leverage-practices

Ward, C. J., Nolen, S. B., & Horn, I. S. (2011). Productive friction: How conflict in student teaching creates opportunities for learning at the boundary. *International Journal of Educational Research, 50*(1), 14–20. doi:10.1016/j.ijer.2011.04.004

Wideen, M., Mayer-Smith, J., & Moon, B. (1998). A critical analysis of the research on learning to teach: Making the case for an ecological perspective on inquiry. *Review of Educational Research, 68*(2), 130–178. doi:10.3102/00346543068002130

Wiggins, G. (2012). Seven keys to effective feedback. *Feedback, 70*(1), 10–16.

Williams, J. (2014). Teacher educator professional learning in the third space: Implications for identity and practice. *Journal of Teacher Education, 65*(4), 315–326. doi:10.1177/0022487114533128

Windschitl, M., Thompson, J., Braaten, M., & Stroupe, D. (2012). Proposing a core set of instructional practices and tools for teachers of science. *Science Education, 96*(5), 878–903. doi:10.1002ce.21027

Zeichner, K. (2005). Becoming a teacher educator: A personal perspective. *Teaching and Teacher Education*, *21*(2), 117–124. doi:10.1016/j.tate.2004.12.001

Zeichner, K. (2010). Rethinking the connections between campus courses and field experiences in college-and university-based teacher education. *Journal of Teacher Education*, *61*(1-2), 89–99. doi:10.1177/0022487109347671

Chapter 22
University Supervisors' and Mentor Teachers' Evaluations of Teaching Episodes

Melissa M. Goldsmith
University of Utah, USA

Janice A. Dole
University of Utah, USA

Mary D. Burbank
University of Utah, USA

ABSTRACT

Teacher candidates receive mentorship and evaluations from university supervisors and cooperating teachers, qualified educational professionals and stakeholders performing two different roles. The study examined to what extent university supervisors and cooperating teachers agreed and disagreed on effective teaching. University supervisors and cooperating teachers were asked to watch three videos of teaching episodes and rate them using a 20-question observation instrument. Follow-up focus groups were held to discuss reasons for the ratings. Results indicated that these groups generally agreed on many aspects of quality teaching, but substantive differences existed as well. Raters varied by role when rating facets of language development for language learners, instructional strategies and assessment. Differences in ratings between these groups were explained by the way they view their roles and responsibilities in the classroom as well as the way they interpreted the components of the observation instrument.

INTRODUCTION

The respective roles of university supervisors and cooperating teachers in the student teaching triad with student teachers are complex and informed by the contexts of members' roles and responsibilities in teacher preparation (Bullough & Draper, 2004; Clarke, Triggs, & Nielsen, 2014; Tillema, 2009; Wolff, van den Bogert, Jarodzka, & Boshuizen, 2015). The primary role and responsibility of university supervisors is

DOI: 10.4018/978-1-5225-6249-8.ch022

to mentor, supervise, and evaluate the student teachers in their charge to become effective teachers. As well, they have an obligation to espouse and promote the goals and missions of the university teacher education program. On the other hand, cooperating teachers answer first to their young charges as well as parents, the principal, and the larger community within and outside of the school. While they are concerned about the student teachers with whom they work, their main role is to help their students academically, socially and emotionally. Despite these differences in roles and responsibilities, university supervisors and cooperating teachers are a critical component of the sustained partnerships in teacher preparation and essential for reciprocal teaching, learning, and bridge-building from theory and research to practice.

Past research on stakeholder roles in supervision reveal not only variance in how classrooms are viewed by these individuals, but differences in the priorities and expectations of university supervisors and cooperating teachers who mentor preservice teachers (Slick, 1998; Thompson, Hagenah, Lohwasser, & Laxton, 2015; Veal & Rickard, 1998). For example, university supervisors may look for student teachers' application of what they have learned in methods classes, whereas cooperating teachers may look for instruction that is consistent with what they already do within the context of daily teaching. Additional research has further defined the diverse roles of various classroom observers in ways that reveal their individual stances on evaluating beginning teachers' competencies (Bullough & Draper, 2004; Clarke, Triggs, & Nielsen, 2014; Feiman-Nemser, 2000, 2001; Tillema, 2009: Valencia, Martin, Place, & Grossman, 2009; Wolff, van den Bogert, Jarodzka, & Boshuizen, 2015).

The current study furthers past work linked to student teaching triads by investigating the sources of agreement and variability between university supervisors and cooperating teachers. To this end, the research questions were: To what extent do university supervisors and cooperating teachers agree or disagree on quality ratings of teachers' lessons? More importantly, what are the sources of variability in their agreements and disagreements?

BACKGROUND

Teaching is complex and multifaceted. Students, teachers, curriculum, leadership, and assessment are among the many variables that contribute to the tapestry of teaching. These variables mediate what is taught in classrooms and how it is taught. Importantly, teaching is also mediated by school and community cultures as well as by the past histories of each.

Activity theory serves as a useful framework for understanding the complex relationships and interactions involved in schools and classrooms and the university supervisors, cooperating teachers, and student teachers who work in them (Grossman, Smagorinsky, & Valencia, 1999; Valencia, Martin, Place, & Grossman, 2009). Activity theory has its roots in the cultural and historical school of psychology (Vygotsky, 1978; Leont'ev, 1978), as well as constructs in anthropology and sociology, which foreground cultural and historical pasts in understanding current behavior (Engeström, 1993). It is the social context that is the unit of analysis in activity theory, a fact that makes it appropriate for analyzing and understanding pre-service teaching in classrooms (Grossman, Smagorinsky, & Valencia, 1999).

According to activity theory, systems such as classrooms are "dynamic, open, and semiotic" places where people make meaning (Lemke, 1990, pp. 191). In classrooms, teachers are involved in the meaning-making process, as are students. As well, actions by teachers and students contribute to the ongoing culture of the classroom (Cobb, Gresalfi, & Hodge, 2008; Gresalfi, Martin, Hand, & Greeno, 2009) and give additional meaning to events and episodes that occur within it. According to Engeström (1993), actions in classrooms represent "successive momentary instantiations of a wider, more stable system of collective activity" (pp. 961).

Activity theory considers these "successive momentary instantiations" as short-term actions and events and the "wider, more stable system of collective activity" as the long-term cultural and historical background that influences these momentary instantiations. For example, a university supervisor notices that one-third of the students in one student teacher's classroom are Language Learners, but the student teacher makes no effort to adjust her instruction for these students. This isolated event can be understood within the cultural and historical past of the student teacher, the cooperating teacher, the classroom, school, and the community. Maybe the student teacher is modeling her instruction after the cooperating teacher who does not change her instruction for her Language Learners. Perhaps the student teacher is failing to transfer skills she learned in class into her student teaching. These many and varied past experiences all carry meanings that mediate the student teacher's present-day understandings, actions, and behaviors in her student teaching experience.

Activity theorists would call the triad of university supervisors, cooperating teachers and student teachers a "collective activity system" (Engeström, 1993). The activity system shares the common goal of preparing student teachers to become effective classroom teachers. This system of educator preparation often unites university supervisors and cooperating teachers in that it is likely to contain shared knowledge across both groups. At the same time, basic differences between these groups exist as well.

Similarities Between University Supervisors and Cooperating Teachers

University supervisors and cooperating teachers share a common goal in preparing student teachers to become effective classroom teachers. This is the primary goal shared by both groups as part of a teacher education licensure program. Toward this end, university supervisors and cooperating teachers share general understandings about maintaining classroom management throughout a lesson, motivating, engaging, and maintaining students' interests in the content, meeting learning objectives, and so forth. Both groups are also likely to possess the typical expectations for classroom-based supervision and mentoring (e.g., providing information on the logistics of teaching, mentoring, evaluating, etc.) (Darling-Hammond, 2010; Feiman-Nemser, 2001; Goodwin, Smith, Souto-Manning, Cheruvu, Tan, Reed, & Taveras, 2014).

University supervisors can relate to cooperating teachers because many university supervisors were at one time themselves practicing teachers and perhaps even cooperating teachers (Bullough & Draper, 2004; Jacobs, Hogarty, & Burns, 2017). Both groups were trained as classroom teachers and are familiar with teaching standards, regulations, and anticipated outcomes. These common understandings are based on shared cultural and historical background and pasts as experienced teachers, as well as commonly agreed upon conventions of effective performance standards in classrooms.

Differences Between University Supervisors and Cooperating Teachers

While there are similarities, university supervisors and cooperating teachers also have different motivations and expectations of their student teachers based on their respective roles and responsibilities and different cultural and historical backgrounds. Their beliefs about teaching are rooted in their backgrounds, and they shape and mediate their understanding of what they observe in classrooms.

University supervisors hold dual roles in the student teaching process. Almost all of them have extensive experience in schools and classrooms, and they understand the culture of schools (Bullough & Draper, 2004; Jacobs, Hogarty, & Burns, 2017). At the same time, many university supervisors—especially doctoral students and clinical faculty—are embedded within colleges and universities and ensconced within a culture that values theory and research. Many of them have taken classes related to theory and research in content area disciplines and/or teacher education. Because of their backgrounds and work within a university context, university supervisors are likely to focus on theory and research as the foundation for teaching a subject area. In addition, they often espouse the mission of the teacher education program within the university toward social justice and equality of access.

Past research helps elucidate the unique roles of university supervisors (Slick, 1998). For example, Borko and Mayfield (1995) found that university supervisors engaged in behaviors designed to assist student teachers in feeling confident and comfortable in their student teaching experience. As practitioners, many of them have had first-hand experience on the overwhelming nature of teaching (Slick, 1997). Perhaps because of their own experiences student teaching, many university supervisors may be hesitant to challenge or question the student teachers in their study, remaining positive throughout the student teaching experience (see also Valencia, Martin, Place, & Grossman, 2009).

Historically, university supervisors have assumed varied roles including coach, negotiator, or evaluator (Borko & Mayfield, 1995; Clarke, Triggs, & Nielsen, 2014; Slick, 1997). Recent research highlights university supervisors and their roles as negotiators between the cooperating teacher and the student teacher, particularly when information sharing is required to inform practice within the context of increasingly diverse communities (Bates & Rosaen, 2010; Clarke, Triggs, & Nielsen, 2014; Clara, 2014).

Beck and Kosnick (2000) reported a school-university partnership in which they changed the roles and responsibilities of the university supervisors. In this study, they did not conduct the evaluation of student teachers. Instead, they served as bridges between the school and the university, built trust and goodwill among all members of the team, communicated the general approach of the university, and supported the cooperating teachers and the student teachers in their work. Further, all faculty took part in the supervision process.

While results of the study were positive for the school-university partnership and for student teachers, Beck and Kosnick (2000) found that there were negative consequences for the university supervisors. They reported more time-consuming and challenging roles, a widening gap between themselves and other faculty, and difficulty having their work recognized by the university. Thus, the partnership worked well for cooperating teachers and the student teachers, but not for the university supervisors. These results demonstrate the influence of a university culture that can constrain and mediate how university supervisors conduct their work.

Cooperating teachers on the other hand, are embedded in a classroom culture within a given school and often have different concerns related to their student teachers (Valencia, Martin, Place, & Grossman, 2009). Cooperating teachers are typically veteran classroom teachers who agree to supervise a student teacher (Clarke, Triggs, & Nielsen, 2014). They are focused on the craft of teaching with specific attention to the context of their own classroom school, community, and related responsibilities for quality and outcomes (Ronfeldt, 2015). As a rule, they lack an intentional focus on theoretical factors that influence their daily work. Cooperating teachers' individual experiences often inform their perceptions of teaching quality (Bullough & Draper, 2004; Clarke, Triggs, & Nielsen, 2014). The repertoires of cooperating teachers often include experiences teaching subject areas with different groups of students in vastly different school settings or at different grade levels. Overall, they are more likely to see practice as more important than theory and research.

In addition, for those serving as cooperating teachers, expectations for effective supervision and mentoring are not clearly defined in terms of what constitutes quality and success. Most cooperating teachers lack special training to assist student teachers in becoming effective (Bullough, 2012; McIntyre, Byrd, & Foxx, 1996). In addition, most cooperating teachers are not matched to university supervisors in terms of philosophy, expertise, and teaching style, thereby creating a potential incompatibility with each other and with student teachers (Bullough & Draper, 2004; Valencia, Martin, Place, & Grossman, 2009). When cooperating teachers observe student teachers, they may ask questions such as: "Is everyone paying attention?"; "Is the objective part of a state standard?"; "Will there be enough time left in the lesson for students to complete the assignment?".

Activity theory explains the sometimes-conflicting messages university supervisors and cooperating teachers give to student teachers and why these differences occur. Because of differing roles and responsibilities of universities and schools, the outcomes can lead to the disparate advice and evaluations of quality sent to beginning teachers (Valencia, Martin, Place, & Grossman, 2009). Cooperating teachers may attend to the more immediate needs of classroom management while university supervisors encourage beginners to consider more broad-based issues related to social justice, access, and equity (Valencia, Martin, Place, & Grossman, 2009). These differences emerge in the ways in which feedback is shared with student teachers.

Tillema (2009) examined the student teaching triad by asking 17 different triads to evaluate a given lesson taught by each of the 17 student teachers. Following the ratings of the individual lessons, each member of the triad team wrote a narrative review of the lesson and problems they identified in the lesson. Tillema (2009) then compared the ratings and the problems identified by the 17 triads. Results of the study indicated large variability in ratings within each triad, indicating that university supervisors, cooperating teachers, and student teachers did not agree on their appraisals of the lessons on a number of different dimensions. Tillema (2009) argued that some of the disagreement lies in different perceptions of teaching as well as a lack of clear guidelines for assessing student teachers. In terms of activity theory, differences in perceptions can be explained through the differing social, historical, and cultural pasts of the participants in the triad.

While research on university supervisors and cooperating teachers highlights similar goals for their student teachers—preparation to teach effectively—differences in individuals' social, historical, and cultural pasts as well as differences in current roles and responsibilities help explain unique and differing perspectives within the supervisory triad (Clarke, Triggs, & Nielsen, 2014; Bullough & Draper, 2004; Tillema, 2009). Further investigation is necessary into the nuances between and within groups when evaluating teaching episodes. Efforts to strengthen both consistency in the types of feedback provided within the context of pre-service teaching requires dedicated attention to the degree to which feedback is reliable across observers.

Despite what may be viewed as an incongruity between university supervisors and cooperating teachers in terms of their roles and responsibilities, both are expected to provide guidance to student teachers as well as appraisals of their teaching performance. While research on guiding and coaching student teachers is plentiful, research on evaluating student teachers' lessons lacks specificity in terms of the differences in evaluators' perspectives. Further, the research base is limited in attempts to discern viewpoints that examine and assess student teaching lessons by both university supervisors and cooperating teachers (Burbank, Bates, & Gupta, 2016; Tillema, 2009).

METHOD

The purpose of this study was to identify similarities and differences in observers' perspectives on classroom teaching and to determine the sources of those similarities and differences. This mixed method study included quantitative data and qualitative data, where the qualitative data explains the results of the quantitative findings (Creswell, 2002; Tashakkori & Teddlie, 1998). This study consisted of a 20-item observation instrument and five focus group discussions designed to examine the consistency between university supervisors and cooperating teachers' evaluations of three, 12-minute video teaching episodes. The observation instrument was programmed using the on-line survey tool Qualtrics, so that quantitative data could be collected electronically. Qualitative data from the focus groups, as well as the open-ended comment sections on the observation instrument, clarified the reasoning behind agreements and disagreements between university supervisors' and cooperating teachers' ratings.

Participants

Participants included eight elementary and eight secondary university supervisors from the University of Utah and five elementary cooperating teachers who taught in the community student teaching sites. Table 1 indicates the grade level assignments, gender, ethnicity, and years of teaching experience of both groups.

University supervisors were asked to participate in this study as part of the teacher education program's efforts to ensure consistency in feedback provided during supervisory observations of their student teachers. The participating university supervisors included three clinical faculty and five doctoral students working with elementary licensure students, and two clinical faculty and six doctoral students working in the secondary licensure program.

The cooperating teachers in this study had been regularly asked to work with the university's student teachers as part of the teacher licensure program. Elementary cooperating teachers were identified by the university supervisors and sent an email invitation to participate in the study, with follow-up reminders. Secondary cooperating teachers were not used for the study due to difficulties in time commitments.

As Table 1 indicates, there was a difference between university supervisors and cooperating teachers in grade level assignment, with the lack of cooperating teachers in secondary. There was slightly more ethnic diversity among university supervisors than among cooperating teachers. There was also a difference between these groups in teaching experience with the university supervisors having more years of experience than the cooperating teachers in the study. The differences between these groups in terms of their grade level assignment, years of experience, and ethnicity indicate a difference between the backgrounds of the raters. As activity theory would suggest, this may lead the rating groups to have differing perspectives in coaching and mentorship of preservice student teachers.

Table 1. Participant counts for key demographics

Demographic Characteristic	Role of Raters	
	University Supervisor	Cooperating Teacher
Grade Level Assignment		
Elementary	8	5
Secondary	8	0
Gender		
Female	9	3
Male	4	2
Did not identify	3	0
Ethnicity		
Caucasian	11	5
Non-Caucasian	2	0
Did not identify	3	0
Years of Teaching Experience in Schools		
Less than 10	0	2
10 to less than 20	5	1
20 to less than 30	5	0
30 or more	3	1
Did not identify	3	1

Video Episodes

Three videos of teaching episodes were identified using publicly available videos and video scenarios from a project researcher's individual research. These particular video episodes were selected because of their diverse student populations, a specific focal area of the university's urban teacher preparation program, and because the video episodes presented different teaching styles and instructional strategies. The three videos included a 5th grade elementary social studies lesson, an 8th grade secondary science lesson, and a 5th grade elementary language arts lesson—all of which were approximately 12 minutes in length.

Participating university supervisors and cooperating teachers were each given the videos, via a CD or sent through a link in an email, by a project researcher. This procedure was chosen for the convenience of the raters. Instructions on how to access the video and a due date accompanied the CD or email. Communications also included a description of the time and place for when the follow up focus group would take place. Raters in this study were also provided with a rubric and encouraged to use it as they scored the teaching video episodes.

As Table 2 indicates, many raters watched multiple videos regardless of the elementary or secondary assignment of the university supervisors (i.e., raters from the elementary education program rated

Table 2. Number of raters by grade level assignment and role for each video lesson

Video Lesson	Grade Level Assignment of Raters		Role of Raters	
	Elementary	Secondary	University Supervisor	Cooperating Teacher
Elementary Social Studies	10	2	7	5
Secondary Science	7	4	7	4
Elementary Language Arts	5	10	15	0

a secondary lesson and raters from the secondary education program rated an elementary lesson). This method created a more robust sample size. Cooperating teachers also watched the selected video lessons and used the instrument to rate the teaching episodes. Cooperating teachers observed the elementary 5th grade social studies lesson and the secondary 8th grade science lesson. In an effort to avoid burdening the cooperating teachers, the researchers asked them to watch two, and not all three, of the video episode lessons.

Observation Instrument

The observation instrument used for this study was adapted from The Teacher Candidate Observation Form (TCOF) informed by the State Department of Education's teaching standards. The State Department of Education based the TCOF on 10 teaching domains identified by the Interstate Teacher Assessment and Support Consortium (INTASC), a national set of core teaching standards that describe teaching competencies. Additionally, informed by the State Department of Education's teaching standards, the teacher education program developed 49 individual items for the 10 teaching domains. The domains are: 1) learner development; 2) accommodations for learner differences; 3) learning environments; 4) demonstrations of content knowledge; 5) assessment; 6) instructional planning; 7) instructional strategies; 8) reflection and continuous growth; 9) leadership and collaboration, and; 10) professional and ethical behavior.

Study researchers wanted an observation instrument that retained as many of the TCOF items as possible. Items were state-identified and developed by local education experts, ensuring content validity, and were also being used extensively to evaluate student teachers at universities across the state as well as the researchers' university. However, the TCOF had to be adapted, as three of the 10 INTASC domains were not directly observable in a single video lesson. Also, the TCOF was exceedingly long at 49 items. Therefore, researchers adapted the TCOF for this study by eliminating three domains: 1) reflection and continuous growth; 2) leadership and collaboration, and; 3) professional and ethical behavior. These items were only observable through extensive and sustained contact with teachers and were inappropriate for studying single video lessons from the Internet. An example of such an item was, "The teacher candidate works with other school professionals to plan and jointly facilitate learning to meet the diverse needs of learners." This item would have to be determined through long-term knowledge of the student teacher. The elimination of these domains resulted in a paring down of the 49 items to 20 items.

When the State Department of Education developed the TCOF, they included a rubric that detailed evidence of the specific teacher competencies, or lack thereof, for each of the teaching competencies within the domains. Figure 1 presents an example of the rubric for one of the teacher competencies.

Figure 1. Example rubric for a teaching competency (Source: State Office of Education, 2011)

Standard 7: Instructional Strategies: The teacher uses various instructional strategies to ensure that all learners develop a deep understanding of content areas and their connections, and build skills to apply and extend knowledge in meaningful ways.			
The Teacher:	**Practicing**	**Effective**	**Highly Effective**
uses a variety of instructional strategies to support and expand learners' communication skills.	Provides opportunities for students to articulate thoughts and ideas.	Uses a variety of strategies to support and expand learners' communication skills.	Encourages and supports students in learning and using multiple forms of communication to convey ideas.

The final study instrument, the Teacher Candidate Evaluation Study Tool (TCEST) consisted of seven "broad-based domains" and 20 items or "teaching competencies." Hereafter, the individual items are referenced as "teaching competencies," because they address the degree to which the student teacher demonstrates an ability to accomplish individual teaching skills identified on the TCOF.

The TCEST, consistent with State Department of Education's standards, directed observers, university supervisors or cooperating teachers, to rate teachers on the teaching competencies using a 5-point scale, with an additional non-applicable option. The scale categories 1 and 2 represented "unsatisfactory" performance, 3 represented performance expected of a "practicing teacher," 4 represented "effective" performance, and 5 represented a "highly effective" performance. The non-applicable option, or the "n/a" option, was used when raters determined that it was not possible to observe a particular competency within the context of that particular teaching lesson. After each numerical rating, raters were provided with a space to comment on the reasoning behind their rating. Internal reliability of the TCEST was established at a high level ($\alpha = .95$).

Focus Groups

To provide qualitative data that would explain the quantitative data, five focus groups were initiated after all raters had scored their video episodes. The purpose of the focus groups was to understand more clearly the rationale for the chosen ratings of video episodes. These focus groups were convened immediately following the submission of their quantitative scores while their rationales for ratings were fresh in their minds. Each focus group discussion lasted 45 minutes. Table 3 includes the characteristics of each of the focus groups including the role of the raters, the grade level assignments of the raters (i.e., Elementary (EL) or Secondary (SC)), the lesson observed (i.e., Elementary (EL) social studies, Secondary (SC) science, and Elementary (EL) language arts), as well as the number of individuals participating in each focus group.

A project researcher moderated the focus groups. The researcher was assisted by another project researcher who had analyzed the quantitative data and identified the TCEST items with the greatest variability in the ratings through the use of descriptive statistics. Focus group questions were designed to probe reasons for the individual ratings that had been provided by the university supervisors and the cooperating teachers. For example, for one of the focus groups, quantitative data revealed variability among

Table 3. Characteristics of Each Focus Group

Group Discussion	Role of Raters	Assigned Grades of Raters	Lesson(s) Observed	Number of Discussants
1	University Supervisor	Elementary & Secondary	5th grade social studies & 8th grade science	11
2	University Supervisor	Elementary & Secondary	5th grade language arts	6
3	University Supervisor	Secondary	5th grade language arts	9
4	University Supervisor	Elementary	5th grade language arts	3
5	Cooperating Teacher	Elementary	5th grade social studies & 8th grade science	3

the ratings for three items, each of which addressed meeting the needs of diverse learners. Therefore, a set of focus group questions revolved around what raters were looking for when observing whether or not teachers in the video episodes were meeting the needs of diverse learners in the classroom.

DATA ANALYSIS

Quantitative data from the 1-5 scale presented on the TCEST were analyzed through descriptive statistics where sample sizes, means, and standard deviations were calculated for each broad-based domain and teaching competency found on the observation instrument (Neuman, 2003). Raters were asked to use the 1-5 scale, but at the times when raters felt like they could not offer a score, they chose the "n/a" option. Ratings for the broad-based domains and teaching competencies were evaluated to identify areas where the two groups of raters agreed or disagreed.

Qualitative data to be analyzed were generated from the observational notes taken during the five focus groups and the open comments offered on the TCEST. Observational notes captured the participants' rationales for ratings of video episodes and identified the reasons for similarities and differences in item ratings. Qualitative data were also garnered from open-ended comments available after each rating on the instrument. For these qualitative data, university supervisors tended to comment disproportionately more than the cooperating teachers.

The qualitative data were coded into themes organized according to the broad-based domains and the individual teaching competencies of the TCEST (Miles & Huberman, 1994). Specifically, qualitative data were analyzed first through a coding of the comments and notes on the teaching competencies, and then by combining those teaching competencies into the broad-based domains. Thus, results are presented by agreements and disagreements on the domains and teaching competencies, offering a multiple layered thematic analysis (Creswell, 2002).

RESULTS

One of the most important responsibilities of university supervisors and cooperating teachers is to make judgments about the quality of their student teachers' teaching and assess its effectiveness. Video analyses of teaching episodes afforded a window on how these two groups of educators evaluate effective teaching, despite different orientations, roles, and responsibilities. The researchers sought to determine the extent of agreement or disagreement between university supervisors and cooperating teachers after they viewed videos of teachers teaching a lesson. Quantitative and qualitative data were combined in the next sections to give a fuller picture of agreement and disagreement.

To identify university supervisors' and cooperating teachers' similarities and differences in the evaluation of domains and competencies more specifically, the quantitative and qualitative data were first organized according to the broad-based domains present on the TCEST. Looking at these ratings is important because university supervisors and cooperating teachers use these domains when they evaluate the student teachers in our university program. The broad-based domains help both groups focus their observations and evaluations within a specific context. When discussing broad-based domains, generally, university supervisors said that noting this "question category can sometimes help" them to rate a student teacher's teaching performance.

Rater Agreement in the Broad-Based Domains

Table 4 presents each broad-based domain, the State Department of Education's description of the meaning of each domain, and university supervisors and cooperating teachers' overall rating of each domain

Table 4. Average ratings by rater role for the broad-based domains

Broad-Based Domain	University Supervisor			Cooperating Teacher		
	N	Mean (1-5 scale)	SD	N	Mean (1-5 scale)	SD
1. Learner Development: *The teacher understands cognitive, linguistic, social, emotional and physical areas of student development.*	28	3.93	0.98	9	3.67	1.22
2. Learning Differences: *The teacher understands individual learner differences and cultural and linguistic diversity.*	29	3.53	0.98	9	3.22	1.18
3. Learning Environments: *The teacher works with learners to create environments that support individual and collaborative learning, social interactions, active engagement in learning, and self-motivation.*	29	3.98	0.78	9	3.44	1.03
4. Content Knowledge: *The teacher understands the central concepts, tools of inquiry, and structures of the discipline.*	29	4.10	0.79	9	3.78	1.15
5. Assessment: *The teacher uses multiple methods of assessment to engage learners in their own growth, monitors learner progress, guides planning and instruction, and determines whether the outcomes described in content standards have been met.*	21	3.69	0.94	7	2.93	1.10
6. Instructional Planning: *The teacher plans instruction to support students in meeting rigorous learning goals by drawing upon knowledge of content areas, core curriculum standards, instructional best practices, and the community context.*	28	3.88	0.72	9	3.41	1.08
7. Instructional Strategies: *The teacher uses various instructional strategies to ensure that all learners develop a deep understanding of content areas and their connections, and build skills to apply and extend knowledge in meaningful ways.*	29	3.64	0.85	9	2.94	1.13

across all the video episodes. Both quantitative and qualitative analyses of the video lessons revealed that, in general, university supervisors and cooperating teachers agreed on what constitutes a high-quality teaching lesson, broadly defined.

University supervisors and cooperating teachers rated the broad-based domain of Content Knowledge the highest, indicating agreement about the scoring of this broad-based domain. Both groups agreed that the teachers in the videos appeared to understand their disciplines and the content related to their respective disciplines. In common, university supervisors and cooperating teachers evaluated content knowledge based on the teacher's range of knowledge and representativeness of the content.

There were levels of agreement between both groups across other broad-based domains. For the elementary social studies lesson, both groups commented that one teacher made very little adjustment for cultural relevance, offering no "differentiation on diversity," making the lesson uncomfortable and confusing to watch given the lesson topic of the Civil War. They also reported that the teacher failed to check in with students to make sure they understood the new words and concepts presented in the lesson. Both groups agreed that another teacher's lesson (i.e., the secondary science lesson) was "engaging," and incorporated hands-on learning—another culturally appropriate tool seen as beneficial by both university supervisors and cooperating teachers. Both groups viewed one teacher's encouragement of student participation through questioning and activities as positive. Raters agreed that the teacher was continually using formative assessment to check for student comprehension, most evident through the teacher's questioning strategies.

Only university supervisors observed the elementary language arts lesson. They indicated that the lesson was generally successful, but they were hesitant to offer ratings based on the video lesson, specifically in the areas of language development, planning, and instruction. University supervisors revealed they had to make inferences about the diversity of the classroom because students were not captured in the video. This conundrum was notable given the University's programmatic emphasis in diversity areas, as well as university supervisors' beliefs about the importance of language development and differentiation within language arts lessons.

Shared understandings among and between university supervisors and cooperating teachers can be explained through activity theory in that both groups had common experiences of classrooms in the past that enabled them to agree on certain foundational elements of effective teaching, including the use of "culturally mediated tools" (Levine, 2010) to engage students—like hands-on learning and effective questioning strategies—as well as sensitivity to issues related to social justice and the Civil War.

Rater Disagreement in the Broad-Based Domains

Both quantitative and qualitative analyses shed light on university supervisors' and cooperating teachers' differences in thinking and evaluating quality teaching in the broad-based domains, likely based on their respective roles and responsibilities as teacher educators. Qualitative data revealed that university supervisors made the argument that the way they rated content knowledge was by giving a rating of "4" if the student teacher was continually showing development and a "5" if higher order thinking and questioning was involved. Cooperating teachers made no such comments.

Thus, university supervisors seemed to be using somewhat different criteria on which to base their judgments. Their rationale for rating is based on a student teacher's continuous development toward becoming a professional. This difference in part revolved around the dual role of the university supervisors, where some of their evaluation was tied to university standards and performance. These criteria were not evident in comments by cooperating teachers.

Learner Differences and Instructional Strategies

The broad-based domain with the lowest score for university supervisors was Learning Differences. Here, university supervisors reported that they looked for a "variety of strategies in a lesson." They reported giving a low rating if the lesson was too teacher-centered. They also noted that there was not a consensus about whether diverse learning pertains to Language Learners or whether this term references different learning abilities. They were thus unclear about how to evaluate this domain.

Related to Learner Differences was the issue of language development. University supervisors mentioned that they looked at the extent to which visuals were used, ostensibly to determine whether there were sufficient supports for Language Learners. Cooperating teachers reported that they looked for complex vocabulary in the lesson. The cooperating teachers also noted they "know the class, so they know whether there needs to be special instruction" when addressing Language Learners. These different comments likely reflected their different emphases on language learning and development based on their roles as university supervisors or classroom teachers. However, these differences also could reflect the multiple issues surrounding how to teach Language Learners. On the one hand, employing multiple and varied visuals is critical to helping students learning English. However, using complex vocabulary is as well—so long as that vocabulary is thoroughly discussed and taught.

Even though focus group comments indicated that both groups considered Instructional Strategies important for enhancing student learning, university supervisors were more pointed and specific than cooperating teachers in their comments about employing instructional strategies to create a successful and inclusive lesson with respect to learner differences. University supervisors noted that practicing a range of developmentally, culturally, and linguistically appropriate instructional strategies "should be there," and all lessons should be "developmentally spanning." One university supervisor noted that, "if there is a Language Learner in the room, it is always possible to incorporate language development." Conversely, cooperating teachers reported that they "just do what is appropriate for students," although some reported that creating culturally sensitive instructional strategies was sometimes a "confusing point." These comments reflect in part the ethos of the university with its mission of inclusive, diverse classrooms, and university supervisors' attention to this particular component of effective teaching.

Assessment and Teaching Competencies

For cooperating teachers, the broad-based domain of Assessment was scored low for the video lessons. Cooperating teachers noted that their student teachers were with the students constantly, each day, and so they "know students" and therefore might not need to do assessments continually. On the other hand, university supervisors felt they needed more evidence that their student teachers were incorporating assessment as part of their instruction. Since assessment is a critical component of methods courses and the objectives of the teacher education program, it makes sense that university supervisors focused more on this component of teaching.

Rater Agreement in the Individual Teaching Competencies

As shown in Table 5, university supervisors and cooperating teachers scored similarly for most of the teaching competencies, indicating a general level of agreement on the TCEST. Again, similarities in how these two groups scored teaching competencies can be explained through activity theory, since both university supervisors and cooperating teachers share the common goal of preparing effective classroom teachers and shared teaching experiences of the past for both university supervisors and cooperating teachers.

Similar to what was found in evaluating the broad-based domains, the teaching competency with the highest mean for university supervisors and cooperating teachers was Teaching Competency 9, which is a component of the content knowledge broad-based domain. Teaching Competency 9 states:

The Teacher Candidate knows the content of discipline and conveys accurate information and concepts.

Both groups agreed that the foundation of the lesson must present accurate discipline-specific concepts.

University supervisors and cooperating teachers also scored Teacher Competency 5 about language development similarly. Teacher Competency 5 states:

The Teacher Candidate incorporates tools of language development in planning and instruction for English Language Learners, and supports development in English proficiency.

Both noted in focus group comments that they appreciated one teacher's writing of words on the board and introducing those new words to students. Similarly, both groups found complexity in rating this teaching competency, and they preferred to give student teachers leeway in their evaluations. Specifically, university supervisors reported that they would rather give a student teacher a score of an "n/a" than a low score when tools of language development were not incorporated in the lesson – although they would give a low score when necessary. This result reinforces research demonstrating that university supervisors tend to be supportive of their student teachers and provide positive feedback (Borko & Mayfield, 1995; Slick, 1997). Cooperating teachers in this study also reported they typically give the student teacher "the benefit of the doubt at the start," though they commented they would become "harder on the teacher" as time passed or if the teaching performance "becomes clearly bad."

Rater Disagreement in the Individual Teaching Competencies

Pre-assessment is a competency on which university supervisors and cooperating teachers disagreed. University supervisors reported they were interested in whether or not students could "access knowledge from previous lessons." This difference within assessment can be traced to comments about rating Teaching Competency 11:

The Teacher Candidate designs, and/or selects pre-assessments, formative, and summative assessments in a variety of formats that match learning objectives and engages learners in demonstrating knowledge and skills.

Table 5. Similarities and differences in average rating by rater role for each teaching competency

Teaching Competency	University Supervisor			Cooperating Teacher		
	N	Mean (1-5 scale)	SD	N	Mean (1-5 scale)	SD
1. The Teacher Candidate creates developmentally appropriate and challenging learning experiences based on individual students' strengths, interests and needs.	28	3.93	0.98	9	3.67	1.22
2. The Teacher Candidate encourages students to use speaking, listening, reading, writing, analysis, synthesis and decision-making skills in various real-world contexts.	28	3.86	0.93	9	3.56	1.24
3. The Teacher Candidate designs, adapts, and delivers instruction to address students' diverse learning strengths and needs.	28	3.57	1.07	9	3.00	1.32
4. The Teacher Candidate allows students different ways to demonstrate learning sensitive to their multiple experiences and diversity.	29	3.66	1.23	9	3.22	1.48
5. The Teacher Candidate incorporates tools of language development into planning and instruction for English Language Learners, and supports development of English proficiency.	19	3.05	0.85	9	3.44	1.01
6. The Teacher Candidate provides multiple opportunities for students to develop higher order and meta-cognitive skills.	29	4.00	0.87	9	3.44	1.24
7. The Teacher Candidate uses a variety of classroom management strategies to effectively maintain a positive learning environment.	29	4.07	0.84	9	3.44	1.24
8. The Teacher Candidate equitably engages students in learning by organizing, allocating, and managing the resources of time, space, and attention.	28	4.00	0.94	9	3.33	1.12
9. The Teacher Candidate knows the content of discipline and conveys accurate information and concepts.	29	4.17	0.76	9	4.33	0.87
10. The Teacher Candidate uses multiple representations and explanations of concepts that capture key ideas.	29	4.03	1.02	9	3.22	1.48
11. The Teacher Candidate designs, and/or selects pre-assessments, formative, and summative assessments in variety of formats that match learning objectives and engages learners in demonstrating knowledge and skills.	20	3.85	0.88	7	2.86	1.07
12. The Teacher Candidate understands and practices a range of developmentally, culturally, and linguistically appropriate instructional strategies.	25	3.08	1.15	9	2.89	1.27
13. The Teacher Candidate uses data to assess the effectiveness of instruction and to make adjustments in planning and instruction.	8	3.25	1.16	5	2.80	1.30
14. The Teacher Candidate plans instruction based on the approved state curriculum.	17	3.88	0.70	8	4.13	0.64
15. The Teacher Candidate individually and collaboratively selects and creates learning experiences that are appropriate for reaching content standards, relevant to learners, based on principles of effective instruction.	28	3.96	1.00	8	3.62	1.19
16. The Teacher Candidate differentiates instruction for individuals and groups of students by choosing appropriate strategies and accommodations, resources, materials, sequencing, technical tools, and demonstrations of learning.	21	3.71	0.96	9	2.89	1.62
17. The Teacher Candidate uses appropriate strategies and resources to adapt instruction and vary his or her role to meet the needs of individual and group learners.	26	3.61	1.10	9	2.78	1.30
18. The Teacher Candidate uses a variety of instructional strategies to support and expand learners' communication skills.	29	3.55	0.99	9	2.78	1.30
19. The Teacher Candidate supports content and skill development by using multiple media and technology resources and knows how to evaluate these resources for quality, accuracy, and effectiveness.	24	3.33	1.10	9	2.11	1.05
20. The Teacher Candidate uses a variety of questioning strategies to promote engagement and learning.	29	4.10	0.90	9	3.67	1.32

For this item, university supervisors were more likely to offer an "n/a" rating than cooperating teachers, but when the former did offer a rating, it was, on average, higher than that of cooperating teachers. Further, university supervisors included questioning, assignments, scaffolding, and checks for understanding as part of the assessment construct, while cooperating teachers focused only on assignments and questioning.

Specific differences also emerged when university supervisors and cooperating teachers rated Teaching Competency 17:

The Teacher Candidate uses appropriate strategies and resources to adapt instruction and vary his or her role to meet the needs of individual and group learners.

University supervisors reported they were looking for differentiated instruction in order to meet the needs of diverse learners. On the other hand, cooperating teachers reported being more focused on varied instructional strategies including media and questioning.

A key difference between the two groups was that each group focused on a different aspect of the teaching competency. Cooperating teachers were more focused on "appropriate strategies and resources"; university supervisors were more focused on "meeting the needs of individual and group learners." This difference could arise from differences in their respective roles and responsibilities, with university supervisors more focused on one of the critical missions of the teacher education program—meeting the needs of diverse learners.

When rating and discussing the instructional strategies within Teaching Competency 18, "The Teacher Candidate uses a variety of instructional strategies to support and expand learners' communication skills," university supervisors seemed to value this competency more than cooperating teachers, and they looked for lessons to be "student-centered." They noted that instructional strategies needed to include "appropriate student communication" through students talking to each other, using strategies such as "think, pair, share," getting students to "reflect and describe," and involving more than just a few students in the lesson. On the other hand, cooperating teachers tended to focus more on the importance of teacher-student communication rather than student-to-student communication. One cooperating teacher said:

In order to expand communication, there must be communication. [In the lesson observed], there was no discussion of topics—only a few students answering manipulative questions.

For cooperating teachers, the teaching competency rated the lowest was Teaching Competency 19:

The Teacher Candidate supports content and skill development by using multiple media and technology resources and knows how to evaluate these resources for quality, accuracy, and effectiveness.

For this competency, university supervisors reported that they observed teachers' use of "visuals" such as "maps," and they considered this evidence of multiple media. On the other hand, the cooperating teachers reported that they were looking for more modern applications of multimedia in the classroom, implying the use of technology, such as the Internet.

ACTIVITY THEORY AND SOURCES OF VARIABILITY

Consistent with activity theory, university supervisors' and cooperating teachers' different roles in the activity system likely played a significant part in their approach, method and focus as they evaluated the broad-based domains and individual teaching competencies of the three teaching episodes. Qualitative evidence indicated both domains and competencies were interpreted differently by raters based on multiple interpretations of: 1) the vocabulary, concepts and competencies measured in individual items; 2) the rating scale itself, and; 3) the use of the rubric to interpret the competencies.

Raters' responses included strong evidence of different interpretations of the teaching episodes based on the university supervisors' emphasis on diversity issues within a classroom. These differences were most clearly seen in all the competencies related to learner and language differences and instructional strategies related to Language Learners. Teacher Competency 5 stated:

The Teacher Candidate incorporates tools of language development into planning and instruction for English Language Learners, and supports development of English proficiency.

Focus groups questions specifically asked raters to explain what they were looking for in a lesson to see if teachers were meeting the needs of diverse learners. University supervisors wanted to parse the definition of "diverse learners," questioning whether raters were applying "diverse learners" solely to Language Learners or also to students with learning disabilities or different learning aptitudes. University supervisors noted that every elementary education student lesson has language built into it, so it was harder for them to make differentiations between "language-rich instruction" versus "Language Learner instruction."

Concerns about diversity issues were also evident in raters' responses to Teacher Competency 12:

The Teacher Candidate understands and practices a range of developmentally, culturally, and linguistically appropriate instructional strategies.

University supervisors based their rating on the phrase "culturally appropriate instructional strategies," and this is what they looked for. Meanwhile, cooperating teachers focused on the "developmentally appropriate instructional strategies," and their responses were based on the extent to which these strategies were utilized in the lessons they observed.

A second source of the variability among raters revolved around the rating scale itself. While university supervisors and cooperating teachers thought that the 5-point scale was a good scale for raters because it had enough variability and range to accommodate rating a myriad of lessons and teaching styles, they differed in how they interpreted the scale itself. Raters discussed the appropriate time to use an "n/a" as there were discrepancies among raters in this area. University supervisors said they used an "n/a" when there is no opportunity within the context of a particular lesson to observe that item. Cooperating teachers expressed that they were not always certain when the use of an "n/a" was appropriate.

Although ratings of a "1" or a "2" are both considered to communicate that a student teacher has performed in an unsatisfactory manner, raters reported that the difference between a "1" and a "2" was that a "1" was a "detrimental" rating. Some of the university supervisors did not rate any teaching competency as a "1" because they felt it was a "demoralizing" rating. Across all groups, raters only gave a "1" if they observed the teacher doing something "damaging" to a student or if they observed that student learning became more difficult as a result of a student teachers' actions. The university supervisors indicated that they would rather rate a teaching competency as an "n/a" rather than a "1" or "2", since giving a "1" or a "2" might make the student teacher feel defeated. Again, a theme arising from the university supervisors' comments is that they wanted to provide support, assistance to and confidence in their student teachers.

In general, university supervisors and cooperating teachers noted that the difference between a lower score and a higher score on the rating scale might be that the student teacher missed the opportunity to perform better in a certain area. University supervisors discussed this difference in the areas of meeting the diverse needs of students. They also noted that the difference between a rating of a "4" and a "5" was whether or not higher order thinking is required ("5"). Cooperating teachers indicated that it was hard to give a rating of a "4" or "5" when the instructor did not use visual aids, tried to do too much in a lesson, and/or if the lesson was not engaging.

A final source of variability again reflected the different roles of university supervisors and cooperating teachers. University supervisors reported that they used the rubric when they assessed the teaching episodes; cooperating teachers reported that they did not. An understanding of university supervisors' more careful adherence to the scale and its accompanying rubric confirms their primary responsibility as supervisors of student teachers and the accompanying time spent on evaluation—their primary responsibilities in the student teaching triad. Cooperating teachers likely did not attend to the accompanying rubric due to time constraints as well as competing demands of the classroom on their time—mediating the time spent on the evaluation.

SOLUTIONS AND RECOMMENDATIONS

Because of the university's commitment to high-quality teacher preparation, supervisory and mentoring support of their student teachers in field experiences is central to its mission. In addition to complying with accreditation, quality supervision and mentoring lend themselves to sustained partnerships with K-12 educators and the growth of effective classroom teachers.

Despite different educator preparation roles and their accompanying responsibilities and the various kinds of relationships they develop as part of the student teaching triad, university supervisors and cooperating teachers must judge the quality of their student teachers' teaching, assess its effectiveness and provide quality feedback to them. Study data revealed overall general agreement among university supervisors likely arising from similar past histories in schools and classrooms. However, there were also varied perspectives on what counts as quality teaching. Many of the inconsistencies in scoring and judging effectiveness can be explained through activity theory, the differing roles, responsibilities, and past cultural and historical backgrounds of university supervisors and cooperating teachers.

Findings from this study can be used to form more effective partnerships between schools and universities. Universities need to improve their mentoring of their cooperating teachers so that the mission of the teacher education programs can be a joint mission shared by university supervisors and cooperating teachers. Such mentoring includes meetings with cooperating teachers in which the mission and broad goals of the teacher preparation program are explained and discussed. At the University of Utah, a cooperating teacher tutorial has been developed online so that cooperating teachers can learn more about the mission and purposes of the teacher education program. Cooperating teachers have found this tutorial helpful in better understanding the teacher education program.

Findings from the study indicate that users of the TCEST can have multiple interpretations of many of the items on the test. Unless a test is written unambiguously, varied perspectives will always mediate raters' interpretations of items. Because the TCEST and accompanying state-adopted TCOF are state approved and more or less mandated, the university will need to partner more with school districts to include professional development and focused trainings on the use of these tests to ensure agreement of quality teaching and pre-service teacher feedback. More focused sessions on the interpretation of the items on the test should help university supervisors and cooperating teachers understand the scoring system better and be more consistent in their ratings.

FUTURE RESEARCH DIRECTIONS

Research has established differences in university supervisors' and cooperating teachers' perspectives in the student teaching experience (Burbank, Bates, & Gupta, 2016; Bullough & Draper, 2004; Slick, 1998, Valencia, Martin, Place, & Grossman, 2009). These different perspectives arising from shared and varied cultural and historical pasts can and do result in different evaluations of student teachers and sometimes inconsistent feedback to them (Bullough & Draper, 2004). However, consistency in evaluations and accompanying feedback is critical for maintaining high-quality programs and effective university-district partnerships.

Future research should examine other universities and districts in different areas of the country and use larger sample sizes. In addition, future research needs to incorporate different video lessons as well as live observations with several observers. While the videos used in this study secured similar evaluations, other perhaps more complex videos would result in more differences than was found in this study.

In addition, an important area for future research involves comparing and contrasting video observations under different conditions. While most supervision still takes place in real time, the use of videos for observing and evaluating student teachers has become more common. As well, researchers are experimenting with robotic observations in which a robot allows university supervisors to observe real-time lessons through the Internet. These ideas are compelling, as they would interrupt the necessity of university supervisors' trips to multiple schools on multiple occasions. How do these different formats for observation result in similar and different evaluations of student teaching lessons? This is an empirical question that should be addressed in the future.

Research might also examine professional development interventions that lead to consistency among university supervisors as well as between university supervisors and cooperating teachers. The University of Utah's Teacher Licensure Program developed an online tutorial for cooperating teachers, but the next step should be to evaluate the effectiveness of the tutorial as a professional development intervention. To what extent does such a tutorial lead to better agreement between university supervisors and cooperating teachers?

In particular, professional development among university supervisors, cooperating teachers, and principals would do well to focus on the question: "What does high-quality teaching look like in a classroom?" Such a study might shed additional light on similarities and differences among and between these groups of people who all evaluate student teachers.

In addition to discussions of the factors that embody quality teaching, researchers should examine more closely the instruments designed and used to measure quality teaching. The development of reliable and valid instruments needs to continue, and the best instruments need to be more widely known and distributed. This study used an instrument informed by state standards for teaching proficiencies and established a high level of internal consistency. Yet, the study uncovered several areas where observers made different decisions based on how individual teaching competencies, individual vocabulary words, and rating scales were interpreted and understood. Different observation instruments are likely to yield different results.

Evaluating student teachers is somewhat different from evaluating practicing teachers because university supervisors and cooperating teachers examine growth over time in ways that differ from the evaluations of practicing teachers. What would be regarded as a sufficient lesson at the beginning of student teaching is likely very different from what would be regarded as sufficient at the end of student teaching. More widely used instruments based upon validated performance standards across time and settings may be more effective than tools that are state and/or university-developed. Efforts to capture effectiveness across practicing teachers may result in instruments that lack the necessary reliability and validity for work with student teachers.

CONCLUSION

The purpose of this study was to determine the extent to which university supervisors and cooperating teachers agreed on quality teaching by examining agreement and disagreement across rating scores on three teaching video lessons. Study data revealed that, in general, the two groups agreed on many aspects of quality teaching in the broad-based domains and teaching competencies within the video lessons they observed. Combined quantitative and qualitative data revealed similarities in rating content knowledge as well as many aspects of the lessons themselves, including instructional strategies such as encouraging engagement in the lessons through hands on learning, questioning and using visuals. They also agreed on some components of the language development domain and teaching competency, and they also generally agreed to "give the student teacher the benefit of the doubt."

Where university supervisors and cooperating teachers disagreed had to do with specific components of instruction university supervisors were looking for, "higher-order thinking," as well as specific instructional strategies designed to meet the needs of Language Learners as well as other forms of diversity. In addition, university supervisors seemed to view assessment differently than cooperating teachers, with the former looking for more specific evidence that pre-assessments were utilized by the student teachers. Cooperating teachers, on the other hand, seemed to trust student teachers more, based on their everyday experiences in the classroom.

Results from the study can be interpreted through activity theory where university supervisors and cooperating teachers act within the activity system of classrooms and teaching episodes. Even though these two groups may not share all the same motivations and objectives as they view student teachers in classrooms, they share enough common historical and cultural backgrounds in terms of understanding students, teachers and classrooms so that they are able to view teaching episodes in generally similar ways. The collective activity system of a classroom is likely to be similar in terms of understanding and interpreting teachers' actions, student behavior and norms, expectations and routines. This collective activity system explains university supervisors and cooperating teachers' general agreement on many aspects of effective teaching.

At the same time, activity theory can also help explain some of the differences observed between university supervisors' and cooperating teachers' evaluations of teaching episodes. For example, one important source of variability in scoring revolved around diverse learners. These differences manifested themselves in both groups' scores on instructional strategies and were discussed in the focus groups. Disagreement on this issue likely arose from different motivations and performance standards within each collective activity system. The mission of the university supervisors' teacher preparation program specifically focused on the use of instructional strategies appropriate for a range of culturally and linguistically different students. The particularities of accomplishing this mission did not seem to be equally shared by the cooperating teachers who may have had other particulars with which to contend.

Differences in activity systems also likely contributed to variation on university supervisors' and cooperating teachers' understanding of the TCEST. Important differences arose in the interpretation of the test, likely based on different objectives, motivations and goals of the two groups. In fact, many TCEST items contained multiple concepts, abilities, and behaviors. Items also contained ambiguous vocabulary terms as well as incomplete instructions on how to interpret the rating scale. These complexities likely contributed to different interpretations based on cultural and historical backgrounds and different motivations and goals for learning and teaching.

Results from this study have to be interpreted with caution for a number of reasons. First, the sample size was small. Second, the teacher preparation program at the university in the study was fairly small and cohesive, likely resulting in more agreement than would be found in larger, more complex universities involving more university supervisors. Third, only three videos were used in the study, and not all of the observers rated all of the videos.

Despite these limitations, findings from the study suggest that, at least for some teaching episodes, university supervisors and cooperating teachers can essentially agree on many aspects of quality teaching. At the same time, it is clear that university-district partnerships and observation instruments can be improved to foster more consistency and provide more uniform feedback to student teachers. Such a move would improve the quality of the mentorship student teachers receive when they student teach.

ACKNOWLEDGMENT

Thank you to Brooke Barrigar and Don Kauchak for their work in project development and data collection.

REFERENCES

Bates, A., & Rosaen, C. (2010). Making sense of classroom diversity: How can field instruction practices support interns' learning? *Studying Teacher Education*, *1*(6), 45–61. doi:10.1080/17425961003669151

Beck, C., & Kosnik, C. (2000). Associate teachers in preservice education: Clarifying and enhancing their role. *Journal of Education for Teaching*, *26*(3), 207–224. doi:10.1080/713676888

Borko, H., & Mayfield, V. (1995). The roles of the cooperating teacher and university supervisor in learning to teach. *Teaching and Teacher Education*, *11*(5), 501–518. doi:10.1016/0742-051X(95)00008-8

Bullough, R. V. Jr. (2012). Mentoring and new teacher induction in the United States: A review and analysis of current practices. *Mentoring & Tutoring*, *20*(1), 57–74. doi:10.1080/13611267.2012.645600

Bullough, R. V. Jr, & Draper, R. J. (2004). Making sense of a failed triad: Mentors, university supervisors, and positioning theory. *Journal of Teacher Education*, *5*(55), 407–420. doi:10.1177/0022487104269804

Burbank, M. D., Bates, A., & Gupta, U. (2016). The influence of teacher development on preservice supervision: A case study across content areas. *Teacher Educator*, *51*, 5–69. doi:10.1080/08878730.2015.1107441

Clara, M. (2014). What is reflection? Looking for clarity in an ambiguous notion. *Journal of Teacher Education*, *66*(3), 261–271. doi:10.1177/0022487114552028

Clarke, A., Triggs, V., & Nielsen, W. (2014). Cooperating teacher participation in teacher education: A review of the literature. *Review of Educational Research*, *84*(2), 163–202. doi:10.3102/0034654313499618

Cobb, P., Gresalfi, M. S., & Hodge, L. (2008). An interpretive scheme for analyzing the identities that students develop in mathematics classrooms. *Journal for Research in Mathematics Education*, *39*(0), 1–29.

Creswell, J. W. (2002). *Educational research: Planning, conducting, and evaluating quantitative and qualitative research*. Upper Saddle River, NJ: Merrill.

Darling-Hammond, L. (2010). Teacher education and the American future. *Journal of Teacher Education*, *61*(1-2), 35–47. doi:10.1177/0022487109348024

Engeström, Y. (1993). Developmental studies of work as a testbench of activity theory: The case of primary care medical practice. In S. Chaiklin & J. Lave (Eds.), *Understanding practice: Perspectives on activity and context* (pp. 64–103). Cambridge, UK: Cambridge University Press. doi:10.1017/CBO9780511625510.004

Feiman-Nemser, S. (2000). *From preparation to practice: Designing a continuum to strengthen and sustain teaching*. New York: Bank Street College of Education.

Feiman-Nemser, S. (2001). Helping novices learn to teach: Lessons from an exemplary support teacher. *Journal of Teacher Education*, *52*(1), 17–30. doi:10.1177/0022487101052001003

Goodwin, A. L., Smith, L., Souto-Manning, M., Cheruvu, R., Tan, M. Y., Reed, R., & Taveras, L. (2014). What should teacher educators know and be able to do? Perspectives from practicing teacher educators. *Journal of Teacher Education*, *65*(4), 284–302. doi:10.1177/0022487114535266

Gresalfi, M., Martin, T., Hand, V., & Greeno, J. (2009). Constructing competence: An analysis of student participation in the activity systems of mathematics classrooms. *Educational Studies in Mathematics*, *70*(1), 49–70. doi:10.100710649-008-9141-5

Grossman, P. L., Smagorinsky, P., & Valencia, S. (1999). Appropriating tools for teaching English: A theoretical framework for research on learning to teach. *American Journal of Education*, *108*(1), 1–29. doi:10.1086/444230

Jacobs, J., Hogarty, K., & Burns, R. (2017). Elementary preservice teacher field supervision: A survey of teacher education programs. *Action in Teacher Education*, *39*(2), 172–186. doi:10.1080/01626620.2016.1248300

Lemke, J. L. (1990). *Talking science*. Norwood, NJ: Ablex.

Leont'ev, A. N. (1978). *Activity, consciousness, and personality.* Englewood Cliffs, NJ: Prentice-Hall.

Levine, T. H. (2010). Tools for study and design of collaborative teacher learning: The affordances of different conceptions of teacher community and activity theory. *Teacher Education Quarterly*, *37*(1), 109–130.

McIntyre, D. J., Byrd, D. M., & Foxx, S. M. (1996). Field and laboratory experiences. In J. Sikula, T. J. Buttery, & E. Guyton (Eds.), *Handbook of Research on Teacher Education* (2nd ed.; pp. 171–193). New York: Macmillan.

Miles, M. B., & Huberman, A. M. (1994). *Qualitative data analysis: An expanded source book.* Thousand Oaks, CA: Sage.

Neuman, W. L. (2003). *Social research methods: Qualitative and quantitative approaches* (5th ed.). Boston, MA: Pearson Education, Inc.

Ronfeldt, M. (2015). Field placement schools and instructional effectiveness. *Journal of Teacher Education*, *66*(4), 304–320. doi:10.1177/0022487115592463

Slick, S. K. (1997). Assessing versus assisting: The supervisor's role in the complex dynamics of the student teaching triad. *Teaching and Teacher Education*, *13*(7), 713–726. doi:10.1016/S0742-051X(97)00016-4

Slick, S. K. (1998). The university supervisor: A disenfranchised outsider. *Teaching and Teacher Education*, *14*(8), 821–834. doi:10.1016/S0742-051X(98)00028-6

Tashakkori, A., & Teddlie, C. (1998). *Mixed methodology: Combining qualitative and quantitative approaches.* Thousand Oaks, CA: Sage Publications.

Thompson, J., Hagenah, S., Lohwasser, K., & Laxton, K. (2015). Problems with ceilings and problems without: How mentoring communities frame and solve problems around ambitious and equitable teaching and learning. *Journal of Teacher Education*, *66*(4), 363–381. doi:10.1177/0022487115592462

Tillema, H. (2009). Assessment for learning to teach appraisal of practice teaching lessons by mentors, supervisors, and student teachers. *Journal of Teacher Education*, *60*(2), 155–167. doi:10.1177/0022487108330551

Utah State Office of Education. (2011). *Utah effective teaching standards.* Salt Lake City, UT: Utah State Office of Education.

Valencia, S. W., Martin, S. D., Place, N. A., & Grossman, P. (2009). Complex interactions in student teaching: Lost opportunities for learning. *Journal of Teacher Education*, *60*(3), 304–322. doi:10.1177/0022487109336543

Veal, M. L., & Rickard, L. (1998). Cooperating teachers' perspectives on the student teaching triad. *Journal of Teacher Education*, *49*(2), 108–119. doi:10.1177/0022487198049002004

Vygotsky, L. (1978). *Mind in society: The development of higher mental process.* Cambridge, MA: Harvard University Press.

Wolff, C. E., van den Bogert, N., Jarodzka, H., & Boshuizen, H. P. (2015). Keeping an eye on learning: Differences between expert and novice teachers' representations of classroom management events. *Journal of Teacher Education*, *66*(1), 68–85. doi:10.1177/0022487114549810

ADDITIONAL READING

Allen, J., Gregory, A., Mikami, A., Lun, J., Hamre, B., & Pianta, R. (2013). Observations of effective teacher-student interactions in secondary school classrooms: Predicting student achievement with the Classroom Assessment Scoring System-Secondary. *School Psychology Review, 42*(1), 76–98. PMID:28931966

Fives, H., & Buehl, M. M. (2014). Exploring differences in practicing teachers' valuing of pedagogical knowledge based on teaching ability beliefs. *Journal of Teacher Education, 65*(5), 435–448. doi:10.1177/0022487114541813

Halpin, P. F., & Kieffer, M. J. (2015). Describing profiles of instructional practice: A new approach to analyzing classroom observation data. *Educational Researcher, 44*(5), 263–277. doi:10.3102/0013189X15590804

Hawkey, K. (1997). Roles, responsibilities, and relationships in mentoring: A literature review and agenda for research. *Journal of Teacher Education, 48*(5), 325–335. doi:10.1177/0022487197048005002

Ho, A. D., & Kane, T. J. (2013). *The reliability of classroom observations by school personnel.* Seattle, WA: The Bill and Linda Gates Foundation.

Kraft, M. A., & Gilmour, A. F. (2017). Revisiting the widget effect: Teacher evaluation reforms and the distribution of teacher effectiveness. *Educational Researcher, 46*(5), 234–249. doi:10.3102/0013189X17718797

Ledwell, K., & Oyler, C. (2016). Unstandardized responses to a "standardized" test: The edTPA as gatekeeper and curriculum change agent. *Journal of Teacher Education, 67*(2), 120–134. doi:10.1177/0022487115624739

Sato, M. (2014). What is the underlying conception of teaching of the edTPA? *Journal of Teacher Education, 65*(5), 421–434. doi:10.1177/0022487114542518

Steinberg, M. P., & Kraft, M. E. (2017). The sensitivity of teacher performance ratings to the design of teacher evaluation systems. *Educational Researcher, 46*(7), 378–396. doi:10.3102/0013189X17726752

Wilson, E. K. (2006). The impact of an alternative model of student teacher supervision: Views of the participants. *Teaching and Teacher Education, 22*(1), 22–31. doi:10.1016/j.tate.2005.07.007

Chapter 23
Digitally Mediated Supervision:
Redefining Feedback Systems in Field–Based Courses

David S. Allen
Kansas State University, USA

A. Jill Wood
Kansas State University, USA

Erica Sponberg
Kansas State University, USA

Täna M. Arnold
Kansas State University, USA

ABSTRACT

This chapter focuses on the praxis behind the development of digitally mediated supervision and distance-based field experiences. The theoretical framework combines past principles of supervision with present technological models. The practical application lies in both a hybrid digitally mediated program at the undergraduate level and a fully functional model at the graduate level. The concerns addressed represent those facing higher education institutions across the United States, and the solutions presented are those initiated at a Mid-Western land-grant institution. The authors examine the hardware, firmware, and cloud technology used to deliver the program, and the reflective feedback model developed for online teacher preparation. Four types of feedback are defined: (1) self-reflection, (2) 10-minute walk-though, (3) focused feedback, and (4) formal evaluation.

INTRODUCTION

Kansas State University developed a comprehensive digitally-mediated supervision system forming the foundation of an online program. The culmination of five years of field-based research, this system is currently used as the sole supervision model in the M.A.T. program and in a hybrid format for supervision in the undergraduate campus-based program. The program development was bound by a theoretical

DOI: 10.4018/978-1-5225-6249-8.ch023

framework incorporating the ideals of Schwille (2008); He (2007); Cogan (1972) and Dussault (1970). Additionally, the development of the program focused on the characteristics of Millennials, the largest demographic in the current teacher pool (Ingersoll, Merrill, & Stuckey, 2014) and used contemporary innovative technologies in a manner consistent with the SAMR model (Hamilton, Rosenberg, & Akcaoglu, 2016; Puentedura, 2014) as a means of creating a common language to reimagine the roles of reflection, feedback, and collegial relationship.

National Context

The quality of the classroom teacher is the single most predictive school-related variable of student academic achievement. Teacher quality is representative of the unique blend of knowledge, skills, and values that individuals bring to the profession. These assertions are supported by decades of educational research and by the policies and expenditures of local, state, and national governments (American Association of Colleges for Teacher Education, 2013; Aud, Wilkinson-Flicker, Kristapovich, Rathbun, Wang & Zhang, 2013; Darling-Hammond, Holtzman, Gatlin, & Heilig 2005; United States Department of Labor, 2016). Foundationally, the ways in which teachers are educated, developed, and mentored matters. Unfortunately, politically volatile trends exist within the world of education. The national shortage of teachers in high needs areas is currently one issue demanding attention. While many individuals and organizations weigh in on causes and explanations for this phenomenon, others engage in a rhetoric of denial. In Kansas, stakeholders are keenly aware that long-term substitute teachers with little training in classroom management, assessment, or pedagogy currently staff elementary classrooms.

Teacher shortages have caused a growing number of U.S. Americans to turn to teaching as a second or third career. Although the vast majority of initial teaching licenses are issued through traditional four-year programs, the number of students pursuing non-traditional pathways to teaching has grown dramatically in the United States over the last decade (Aud, Wilkinson-Flicker, Kristapovich, Rathbun, Wang, & Zhang, 2013). The number of initial teaching licenses issued through alternative routes has more than doubled, and more than one-third (39% or 45,444 students) of those awarded an initial teaching license in 2011 did so through post-baccalaureate or graduate programs (Aud, Wilkinson-Flicker, Kristapovich, Rathbun, Wang, & Zhang, 2013).

A few of the large, exclusively online universities (e.g., Western Governors University, Liberty Online University, University of Phoenix, and American College of Education) and a handful of traditional universities (e.g., University of Southern California, Drexel University, Grand Canyon University, and Southern New Hampshire University) offer a graduate degree (M.A.T. or M.S.) in education and initial elementary licensure. Two major online universities recently reported graduating 18,000 students in education over a three-year period. These universities utilized a traditional supervision model of hiring local supervisors for observation and evaluation purposes. This process is fraught with inconsistencies in the preparation and process of evaluating student teachers. Local stakeholders have reported a definite distinction between the preparation of students in on-campus programs and that of students who have taken courses from online institutions other than Kansas State University.

Nationally, alternative pathways to teacher licensure most often focus on secondary teachers and/or teaching in urban areas. High quality teachers are important at every level but especially in elementary school as children build foundational ideas, skills, and attitudes that persist into future schooling and adult life. The Bureau of Labor Statistics (2017) lists "elementary school teachers" among the "occupations with the most job growth" and projects that elementary teaching jobs will increase 168,000 (12.3%) by

2022. Ingersoll (2012) stated that, "After two decades of flat growth, since the mid-1980s, the teaching force in the U.S. has dramatically increased in size" (p. 48). Nevertheless, traditional pathways to elementary teaching present a host of practical obstacles—financial, educational, and geographic, especially for those individuals who are coming to the profession for a career change.

Kansas Context

The College of Education at Kansas State University has a long-standing partnership with local schools rooted in a collaborative relationship focused specifically on the concept of simultaneous renewal (Shroyer, Yahnke, Mercer, & Allen, 2014). This partnership evolved through the collaborative vision of local educational agencies and their higher education counterparts. This work helped define the direction for teacher education at KSU (Allen, Perl, Goodson, & Sprouse, 2014). However, dwindling local resources, increasing demand for teachers in high-need, inaccessible areas, and the widening economic gap for new or returning students, were the impetus for the university to consider methods for delivering high quality programing to placed-bound students within the extended geographic footprint identified by the Kansas Board of Regents. In other words, the university was moved to address the needs of stakeholders from across the State of Kansas by developing a program accessible anywhere within the state's confines. By thinking creatively about existing and emerging technology, the college bridged the boundaries of space and time and created a formula for redesigning the equation for effective classroom supervision (Allen, Goodson, Rothwell, & Sprouse, 2017).

Kansas State University (KSU) responded to its stakeholders by focusing efforts in two key areas; the development and delivery of high-quality online programing and by creating an innovative Master of Arts in Teaching (M.A.T.) program based upon an exclusively online delivery model. KSU celebrates a long-standing tradition of a fully integrated network of Professional Development Schools, which have produced an award-winning program, due in no small part to the field-based experiences of students. When considering an M.A.T. program the College of Education focused on specific district needs, student demographics, and reaching potential students in inaccessible areas of the state. Perhaps the most significant issue for many potential M.A.T. teacher candidates in the state of Kansas is geography.

Place-bound students often are not financially situated to attend the traditional on-campus teacher education track nor afford to abandon current employment and/or geographic location to attend courses. Therefore, they seek online education as a vehicle for developing their potential as educators. Although online coursework has been, and continues to be, offered by multiple institutions, one component of every teacher education program that has received little attention is that of the field experience. For many years, field supervisors have come from the ranks of the retired professional educators who are looking to give back to the profession as they assist in the development of future teachers. At KSU these supervisors historically have been hired on a part time basis to supervise 8-12 student interns during a semester. Identifying and training these individuals in contemporary practice, research, and technology, to such a level necessary to ensure quality supervision is not always feasible especially when the supervisors themselves are located a great distances from the campus. Therefore, this traditional supervision model has not demonstrated itself to be the most effective model for students in the KSU program. Given the educational budget issues faced by the state of Kansas during the last few years resulting in financial reductions to the college budget, travel budgets were cut extensively for field-based supervisors. This created a reduction in the number of face to face opportunities within the classroom context. The college sought to maintain the high standard for supervision while attempting to operate within a depleted budget.

During the past five years, KSU has developed a video-based supervision system, which has become the basis for the M.A.T. program. This system was developed in conjunction with KSU's undergraduate program and is currently being utilized by 350 students in local placements as well as 140 M.A.T. graduate students located across Kansas, 17 other states, and 3 international locations. A summary of this journey is found in Table 1.

This video-based feedback system functions as the core supervision model in both the graduate and undergraduate programs regardless of the location of the placement. To date, students have generated over 371,000 minutes of recorded video in classrooms during the past three years. Through the use of tablet technology in conjunction with the Swivl™ Robot, faculty are supervising students in early field experience courses, methods practicums, and student internships in a solely digitally-mediated environment. KSU currently has over 200 Swivl™ Robots deployed in multiple schools across the state and a one-to-one requirement for the students enrolled in the M.A.T. program. With the use of Swivl™ and their web-based platform, supervision offers time-stamped, video-embedded feedback allowing for greater potential in the reflection process. This video enhancement led to the development of four specific observation protocols. Developed by the university faculty to provide feedback in a manner consistent with a growth mindset, KSU's current feedback protocols are focused around the following four practices:

Table 1. Timeline of Distance Supervision at Kansas State University

AY 13-14	AY 14-15	AY 15-16	AY 16-17	AY 17-18	AY 18-19
Identified the need for some form of distance supervision model which would allow: • **Students to return to their home communities for student teaching** • **Supervision of students without burdening the department budget** • **Collaboration with university personnel, school-based staff, and students**	Purchased three Swivl™ robots and deployed the robots into three classrooms in two districts Implemented the use of video communication Attempted to identify a documentation process for feedback and assessment	Purchased additional Swivl™ robots and deployed them to 13 classrooms in four different schools across Kansas Implemented CANVAS as the learning management system Began focusing on Swivl™ Cloud accounts for giving feedback to students on video recordings Developed the online Master of Arts in Teaching Program	Purchased 50 additional Swivl™ robots for the undergraduate program and placed them in PDS schools for checkout by field-based students Required a Swivl™ robot for each person in the MAT program Developed a new evaluation form aligned to KSDE and INTASC standards Launched first cohort of MAT program with 53 students Total number of Swivl™ Cloud accounts: 360	Integrated Power BI-CANVAS-Swivl™- Qualtrics Developed 16-week module approach for a successful student internship Improved efficiency of time-delayed feedback system Tagged comments made on video to correspond to evaluation document Researched essential components of feedback and reflection and developed protocols Launched second cohort of MAT program with 84 students Currently manage over 450 preservice teacher accounts Pre-service teachers have uploaded over 371,000 minutes of video	Develop training modules for supervisors and cooperating teachers Develop protocols for timely and purposeful communication Develop protocols to enhance relationships among stakeholders in an online environment Compile short videos of "teachable moments" and solid instructional strategies from the Swivl™ videos for use in undergraduate and MAT courses Launched third cohort of MAT program with 140 students

1.   Self-Reflection
2.   10-minute Walkthrough
3.   Focused Feedback
4.   Formal Evaluation

In developing these feedback protocols, video best practices over the past 40 years were investigated. Recognizing that technological advancement has been occurring at an exponential rate, interactions with classroom teachers and school district administrators indicated their difficulty in keeping pace with rapidly changing trends. These trends include the intersection of funding formula, policy makers, evolving communities, and technological advances (U.S. Department of Education, 2010); all of which pre-service teachers and supervisors must navigate.

MILLENNIALS: A NEW GENERATION OF TEACHERS

Ingersoll, Merrill, and Stuckey (2014) identified seven trends impacting the teaching force in the United States. Despite teacher shortages, the data indicate the teaching force is increasing (Ingersoll, 2012). The field is attracting more individuals with diverse backgrounds and with higher academic achievements. The researchers consider the field to be less stable than in the past, and, most significantly, propose that the field lies within a grayer and greener demographic (Ingersoll, Merrill, & May, 2014). Ingersoll, Merrill, and Stuckey (2014) present the bimodal nature of the teaching force; a larger population of experienced teachers nearing retirement (grayer) and a large population of new inexperienced teachers, which included older beginning teachers (greener). In 2011-12, almost one-third of the new hires were age 29 or older and one-tenth were 40 (Ingersoll, 2014).

Many of these new teachers come from a generation vastly different from previous ones. When comparing the current Millennial generation to Baby Boomers and GenX populations, Twenge et al. (2010) reported that Millennials seek employment offering work-life balance, are less likely to work overtime, and value extrinsic rewards. They place less value on intrinsic motivation and social interaction at work than previous generations (Twenge, Campbell, Hoffman, & Lance, 2010). Millennials are also less likely to see value in working for free, particularly in unpaid internships (Twenge, Campbell, Hoffman, & Lance, 2010). Some argue this is indicative of the entitlement attached to the Millennial generation, while others point out economic factors inhibiting Millennials from engaging in unpaid work (Manuti & de Palma, 2018; Mazer & Hess, 2016; Twenge, Campbell, Hoffman, & Lance, 2010; Vohs, Baumeister, Schmeichel, Twenge, Nelson, & Tice, 2008). Given that educational practica and internships are typically unpaid work experiences, this affects the value placed upon those experiences by the Millennial generation and how universities should approach the student teaching field experience.

Manuti and de Palma (2018) identified both the pros and cons of Millennials from the existing research. The authors found positive traits of Millennials, e.g., ambitious, assertive, autonomous, and adaptable. They characterized Millennials as entrepreneurial thinkers who are partial to meaningful work. In addition, Millennials are found to be extremely familiar with technology and desire immediate feedback and support. Conversely, Manuti and de Palma claimed Millennials to be narcissistic, impatient, extremely self-confident, and self-important. These diametrically opposing personas exemplified by a generation pose challenges to the standard academic community. Some older faculty members struggle to bridge the generational gap and this widens the divide between them and their students. Manuti and de Palma accentuate this divide by stating:

Millennials do not view managers as content experts (like their predecessors) because they know where to find multiple versions of the information, they are continuous learners. Instead, they view managers more as coaches and mentors. (2018, pp. 26-27)

One of the ways in which an institution, course, or single class evolves is by providing a defined structure and minimizing choice. Vohs et al. (2008) investigated decision fatigue in university students and found a decrease in self-control to stay on task when presented with a high number of choice-making tasks. They asserted cognitive abilities used to make decisions or solve difficult problems are a limited resource. When depleted, performance on challenging and unsolvable problems decreases. Vohs et al. (2008) stated self-regulation is necessary for persisting through difficult tasks.

When considering the multiple planning, teaching, assessing, and reflection cycles teachers undergo each day, Millennial students must be provided a structure that provides enough guidance while additionally allowing for creativity and flexibility within a defined space. This concept also applies to feedback protocols during field experiences. As noted previously, Millennials tend to care more about creative expression than leadership roles in organizations (Manuti & de Palma, 2018), which may make them more successful in classrooms that provide opportunities for deep thinking and learner-centered engagement (McGlynn, 2007; Reeves, 2013). While Millennial students are more likely to find abstract assignments with too much freedom overwhelming, they may perform better when teachers provide a flexible structure that allows for guided creativity (Head & Eisenberg, 2010; Mazer & Hess, 2016).

Current literature recommends student interns be exposed to learning experiences that involve creative expression through narrative pedagogy (Reeves, 2013; Moll, Amanti, Neff, & Gonzalez, 1992). Garcia & Rossiter (2010) define narrative pedagogy as promoting the "natural tendency to create stories, to give coherence to the whole of the lived experience" (p. 1093). Reeves (2013) grounds the pedagogical approach in the understanding of self, greater society, and culture (p. 55). He further asserts "narrative pedagogy is authentically learner-centered and therefore, highly engaging" (2013, p. 55). It allows students to become consumers and owners of the ideas and approaches in the classroom. Students express ideas in a reflective narrative manner by focusing on their lived experiences, which leads to greater growth within a structured framework (Mazer & Hess, 2016).

SUPERVISION: RELATIONSHIPS, ROLES, AND APPLICATIONS

Field experiences are a critical component of the professional development of pre-service teachers (Bailey, 2006; Darling-Hammond, 2006; Darling-Hammond & Snyder, 2000; Henry & Weber, 2010; LePage, Darling-Hammond, Akar, Guiterrez, Jenkins-Gunn, & Rosebrock, 2005). Not only is this one of the few times future teachers will receive individualized instruction (Henry & Weber, 2010), but it is also the time where they enact and test learned theory (Jacobs, Hogarty, Burns, 2017; He, 2009; Siwatu, 2011; Schwille, 2008). University supervisors, whose roles and responsibilities are varied and complex, guide future teachers throughout these fundamental experiences (He, 2009; Schwille, 2008; Henry & Weber, 2010). However, no matter what role the supervisor plays, frequent and purposeful feedback provided by supervisors encourages teacher behavior and classroom habits that have the potential to stay with novice teachers throughout their career (Bailey, 2006; Henry & Weber, 2010).

Unfortunately, the reality of supervising within a traditional model can become clouded by logistics (e.g., lengthy travel time to and from schools) and number of supervisees (Capizzi, Wehby, & Sandmel, 2010). Additionally, research has shown that supervisor feedback is often delayed (e.g., 3 days after observation) and anecdotal (Scheeler & Lee, 2002). Bailey (2006) diminished the emphasis of administrative duties for supervising, stating the role has evolved and describes a shift towards relationship building, so that pre-service teachers (PST) are open to change. The author underscores the importance of reflective practices and learner autonomy for PST because constant supervision is nearly impossible and not indicative of real-world teaching experiences (p. 193).

In this section, the interpersonal dimensions of supervision as it relates to the development of our distance supervision model and feedback cycles will be discussed; after which its application within a digital space will be presented.

Supervision as Relationship Building

As previously stated, supervision and mentorship for PSTs is critical to their professional development. Within the digital-mediated supervision space, supervisory duties shift towards the establishment of presence within a distance model; therefore making change the desired skill set for a distance supervisor. Presented in this section are four approaches of mentorship that establish a foundation for a digitally-mediated feedback model.

Because of the US's complex role they need to possess the skills of both an administer, yet also a mentor. Henry and Weber (2010) discuss nine roles for the supervisor; of those nine, eight arguably remain within a managerial space. The US oversees classroom placements, upholds both university and school policies, evaluates performance, develops assessment, and liaises with school personal, university faculty and students to preempt and resolve conflict (Henry & Weber, 2010). There is acknowledgement of mentorship and relationship building within the authors work, however it is couched within logistical duties that have slightly shifted with the development of digital-mediated supervision.

This shift in roles closely align with the concept of educative mentoring, where the PST and US are in active conversation about praxis to reach the PST's learning threshold (Freiman-Nemser, 1998, 2001; Schwille, 2008; Vygotsky, 1978). Schwille's (2008) work on educative mentoring sought out to discover how mentors access this developmental space through their forms of mentoring. Although Schwille (2008) focused on an apprenticeship or induction type model, the findings are relevant to the development of the feedback model discussed in the proceeding sections. Schwille (2008) investigated the mentor-mentee relationship during classroom teaching, or *inside the action*, and the relationship while the mentor and mentee were not leading a class, or *outside the action*. For example, an *inside the action* might be co-teaching, or stepping in when the mentee struggles, and an *outside the action* would include debriefing sessions or videotape analysis (p. 156). Within the digital-medium, the interactions are clearly *outside the action*; however the mentoring framework developed from Schwille's research team reflects a professional skill set necessary for effective digital-mediated supervision. These include: a) a deep understanding of the learner; b) an accurate, individualized, and continual professional assessment of mentee performance, and; c) attend to immediate development with long term goals in mind, or *bifocal vision*. The culmination of the aforementioned skills ultimately results in teacher change; and at their very core is in an aptitude for vulnerable and empathic communication, which stems from theoretical work developed by Giles Dussault.

Dussault (1970) developed his theory of teacher supervision by drawing from psychologist, Carl Rogers', Theory of Therapy and Personality Change (Rogers, 1961). Dussault applies Rogers's theory of therapeutic and personality change to student teacher development. Thus, if the supervisor creates a space that accepts students for who they are, they, in turn, become comfortable in accepting themselves, open to experience (or critique), and make lasting behavioral changes. Dussault (1970) postulates that the greater this atmosphere, the more likely the PST will become less defensive and have a more realistic and accurate perception of the classroom experience. With a clear picture of the experience, the student maintains a positive self-regard, which affords better decision-making; "the supervisee . . . will be more creative, more flexible, and more uniquely adaptive to each new situation and each new problem" (Dussault, 1970, p. 189). Dussault asserts student teacher behavioral change shifts from imitation to idiosyncratic style. The supervisee "will not readily adopt his supervisor's teaching practices but will rather tend to develop an own personal teaching style" (Dussault, 1970, p. 189). Although Dussault (1970) remains in theory, it serves as a lens through which to view digitally-mediated supervision and the intention of the feedback models. For a more pragmatic approach in ways to develop the professional and personal skills of the PST, Dussaults' contemporary, Cogan (1972) is discussed.

Cogan (1972) defines clinical supervision as the interaction of peers and colleagues, where the PST takes on traditional supervision roles:

[The PST] initiates action, proposes hypotheses, analyzes his [sic] own performance, shares responsi-bilities for devising supervisory strategies, and is equally responsible for the maintenance of morale in the supervisory processes. (Cogan, 1972, p. xi)

The relationship between the supervisor and supervisee is fluid, blended, and collaborative. Cogan states that through these negotiations and interactions, positive and colleague relationships are estab-lished and maintained. Clinical supervision as colleagueship reflects elements of Dussault (1970) and Schwille (2008) in not wanting to diminish the autonomy and independence of the PST. Cogan (1972) does this by breaking down the process of supervision into eight phases. Table 2 provides a description of the phases. At each phase, there is an element of collaboration, and/or teacher autonomy in deciding the direction they want to go, and/or problem they want to solve.

During conferencing, analysis, and observation, Cogan (1972) recommends focusing on pattern analysis. Instead of focusing on isolated classroom events, the teacher and supervisor are asked to look for classroom behavioral patterns. Students found this process rewarding because the data provided a commonality upon which both the supervisor and supervisee could draw and the process inducted students into supervision practices. These phases have been updated and adapted in the creation of the feedback cycles.

Another model worth mentioning for its adaptability to a digital mediated space is He (2009) strengths-based mentoring model. Rooted in educative mentoring (Freiman-Nemser, 1998, 2001; Schwille, 2008), it asks of the mentor, or in this case the supervisor, to take an asset mind-set with the PST. As the relationship is established, the supervisor actively uses the strengths of the PST to the PST reach their desired goals and work through challenges. Similar to Dussault (1970) and Cogan (1972), the model

Table 2. Phases of student intern supervision

Phase	Title	Description
1	Establishing the Intern-Supervisor relationship	• Supervisor establishes relationship with Intern • Helps Intern understand what supervision is
2	Lesson, unit, or course co-planning	• Supervisor and Intern collaborate in lesson planning • Supervisor gains a better understanding of Intern's thought process, developing skill set
3	Co-planning an observation strategy	Helps to familiarize Intern with the process of clinical supervision
4	Observing instruction	Supervisor observes Intern during classroom practice
5	Analyzing the teaching-learning process	Supervisor and Intern work separately in reflecting on classroom experience
6	Planning the strategy of the conference	Supervisor might develop this alone at first, however, over time, as the Intern's skills strengthen, can be carried out by the Intern
7	The conference	• Supervisor and Intern discuss observations from phase 5 • Supervisor shifts between supervisor roles depending on the needs of the Intern
8	Renewed planning	Revisit phase 2, however, supervisor can determine how much co-planning to do depending on the level of the Intern

Source: (Adapted from Cogan, 1972, pp. 10 -12)

sees development as co-constructed and relies on social interaction between the supervisor and PST. The strengths-based model also seeks to enact change within the PST through the establishment of a positive mind set. A portion of He's (2009) model can be seen in Table 3.

MEDIATING SUPERVISION WITH TECHNOLOGY

In an age of innovation in the K-12 setting and at the university level, the SAMR model (Hamilton, Rosenberg & Akcaoglu, 2016; Puentedura, 2014) is used to develop a common language with which to reimagine the roles of reflection, feedback, and collegial relationships (Cogan, 1972; Dussault, 1970). The Substitution, Augmentation, Modification and Redefinition (SAMR) Model created by Dr. Ruben

Table 3. Strengths-based model for supervision

Strength-Based Mentoring Model		
		DESCRIPTION
PHASE	Disarm	Establishment of an open relationship.
	Discover	Identifying assets and strengths of both the supervisor and and PST
	Dream	Goal setting, establishment of expectations and roles throughout the semester.
	Design	Co-development of the methods used within the mentoring/supervision process - finding a path and developing agency when facing challenges.
	Deliver	Reflection that seeks alternative actions to classroom experiences
	Don't settle	Collaborative progress monitoring that connects strengths, goals, and reflection throughout the semester.

Source: (Adapted from He, 2009, pp. 271-272)

Puentedura in 2006 provides a common language in which to evaluate the use of technology in educational tasks (Puentedura, 2006). The four levels of the SAMR model are broken into two categories, enhancement and transformative (Puentedura, 2009). When at the *substitution* level, one is simply trading one task without technology for a task utilizing technology. *Augmentation* incorporates technology into a task to augment the product. A *modification* level task changes the educational task completely with the use of technology and *redefinition* creates an entirely new educational task based on the technology available (Puentedura, 2006). This model gives educators a means to evaluate the effectiveness of the integration of technology. Koehler and Mishra suggested that all efforts to integrate technology:

should be creatively designed or structured for particular subject matter ideas in specific classroom contexts....understanding approaches to successful technology integration requires educators to develop new ways of comprehending and accommodating this complexity. (2009, p. 62)

Video-analysis of teacher performance and corresponding feedback have been effective methods to overcome the challenges of supervision and teacher training (Capizzi, Wehby, & Sandmel, 2010; Etscheidt, Curran, & Sawyer, 2012). One advantage of using video analysis in teacher preparation is awareness raising; quickly moving from the focus on self to the focus on students (Darling-Hammond & Snyder, 2000; Etscheidt, Curran, & Sawyer, 2012). Etscheidt, Curran, and Sawyer (2012) reported on successful video-feedback models that promoted teacher reflection. Rosaen, Lundeberg, Cooper, Fritzen, and Terpstra (2008) found that using video to promote reflective feedback produced more specific comments than writing from memory. The ability to offer more specific feedback or facilitate timely and productive conversations with pre-service teachers through video performative analysis unfetters the supervisor from hindrances such as travel time and number of supervisees.

Shifting away from absolute assessment toward progressive feedback, digitally-mediated supervision acted as a catalyst for students and teachers to adopt a growth mindset (Blackwell, Trzesniewski, & Dweck, 2007) throughout all phases of field experiences in the KSU M.A.T. program. Simply providing feedback on video recordings does not meet the threshold for high-quality distance supervision models. Therefore, feedback protocols are used in conjunction with several modes of communication technologies to achieve the level of supervision effectiveness desired. These communication technologies include, an online Learning Management System (LMS), Canvas; an online video conference support system, Zoom; a Swivl™ robot; and iPad for video creation. Students are required to engage in the completion of weekly modules of instructional materials within Canvas and meet with their virtual supervisors on a weekly basis during their 16-week internship. Additionally, virtual supervisors are in contact with the cooperating teachers via traditional electronic communication and Zoom video-based conferences on a regular basis. The supervisor, student teacher, and cooperating teacher form a professional learning community that evaluates the instructional methods and skills based on results, rather than intentions or artificial behavior. "Using distance learning for supervision and learning forges a connection between colleges and schools that may be separated by miles, but not in thinking" (Bolton, 2010, p. 67). Bolton (2010) also found that PST reported that the technology was less intrusive than having a supervisor present, collaborations were more beneficial, and feedback was more timely. Integrating these pieces seamlessly together creates the overall system.

Technology Tools for Distance Supervision

Canvas LMS operates at the modification level. Canvas modules allow for differentiated learning opportunities and discussion boards offer asynchronous communication. It also updates students in real time about their course. Zoom is a teleconferencing software, which alone operates at the modification level. Supervisors and student interns talk face-to-face without travel and share information on their computer in real time. The Swivl™ robot is a device that holds an iPad while using Bluetooth technology to track a marker hanging from a lanyard around the teacher's neck. The iPad records teachers teaching and uploads the videos to a secure cloud-based server. The use of the robot is a modification of an educational task when viewed in isolation. Teacher preparation programs have required supervisors to watch the interns teach since the invention of portable video recording devices. Now, students have multiple modalities and opportunities for viewing their work and choice in what best represents them as an educator. While all of these systems individually are considered a modification, their use within the pedagogical context and intent redefine the way field experiences are conducted.

The combination and effective use of multiple digital innovations enhances the opportunities for student growth in the area of teaching and learning. Using time-delayed classroom activity, focused reflection, and collegial dialogue, the complex variables that constitute a high-quality supervision model have begun to take shape. This, however, is not static but by definition must be dynamic. Within the first year of the fully functional distance-mediated field component, data analyses engendered significant changes to the current system, ensuring smooth systematic flow in both the undergraduate and graduate programs. In-house feedback loops ensure ongoing improvements in delivery, communication, and supervision. Most notable was the development and refinement of the feedback system.

FOUR FEEDBACK MODELS

Kansas State University uses a video-based supervision system with a majority of its field experiences for undergraduates and the M.A.T. graduate program. The two semester-long undergraduate methods blocks that utilize digital supervision both carry a practicum component of 45 hours in the local school districts. For their capstone semester, students who choose to complete their internship outside of the local area will do so in a digitally-mediated format. The M.A.T. program requires a 70-90 hour practicum in the fall semester to apply theory learned from the concurrent methods courses. Students then remain in that same classroom in the spring to complete their internship. Because so much of the supervision is done via video, it has become imperative that an effective model be created. With the evolution of this system, best practices have emerged for utilizing video in a responsible, professional, and effective manner. The model strays from the term evaluation in lieu of the more accurate term, feedback. While evaluation implies a rating given to a performance at a specific moment in time, feedback is based more on a growth model and focuses on growing a teacher.

The process begins with the pre-service teacher (PST) co-planning a lesson with the cooperating teacher (CT), then sharing the lesson plan with the university supervisor (US). The US gives feedback on the lesson plan, then returns it to the PST to be taught. After teaching the lesson, the PST uploads a 20-minute portion of the video to a cloud-based system and watches the video, reflecting in a prescribed manner on the teaching sequence within the video itself. Early on in the distance supervision program, a PST would upload and comment on an entire lesson, but it has been found that identifying a 20-minute portion focused on the PST's goals is more manageable and time-efficient. After this has been completed, the PST shares the video with the observer (i.e. US and/or CT) who then views the teaching sequence and gives specific, targeted feedback to the PST. This feedback, in turn, is viewed by the PST and applied to future teaching sessions. After the initial lesson is viewed and feedback is given, the PST, with guidance from the cooperating teacher and/or university supervisor, identifies one to two areas of focus and improvement then composes goals that meet these areas. These goals will then drive the focus of the observations for the remainder of the semester. By consistently utilizing this process of reflecting on their practice and receiving feedback from peers and experienced observers, PSTs improve their practice in a focused and goal-oriented manner. Having an agreed-upon timetable of feedback has been shown to greatly reduce student anxiety (Chilton & McCracken, 2017); therefore, this process is duplicated every two weeks through the course of the semester to ensure timely feedback and implementation. Two weeks is an adequate time frame for stakeholders to complete their part of the cycle as thoroughly as is needed and is an essential component to the success of the model.

Self-Reflection

Self-reflection is one of the best methods available to produce growth in a PST. Initially, when watching themselves teach, PSTs will focus on minutiae such as how they look, their mannerisms, voice inflection and volume, as well as other inconsequential details. However, after the initial shock of seeing themselves teach on video has subsided, PSTs begin focusing more on their teaching and the students. It is difficult initially to know how to properly reflect when it is not a familiar practice. In the beginning, many students simply report what is happening or react to situations in the video. These are *components* of a reflection but are not true reflective statements. True reflection will be comprised of a combination of the following: a statement of observation, response to the observed lesson element, reasoning for why it went well/did not go well, the connection to assessment, and a proposition for future lessons. These guidelines and an example are depicted in Table 4.

Figure 1. Feedback cycle

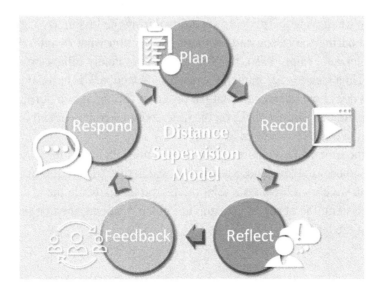

Table 4. Construction of a Reflective Response

Construction of a Reflective Response
Sentence #1: A statement of observation
Sentence #2: Response to the observed lesson element
Sentence #3: Reasoning for why it went well/did not go well
Sentence #4: The connection to assessment
Sentence #5: A proposition for future lessons
Example Response:
"I had students work in groups of 6 for this project. I noticed that in most groups, there were about 3-4 people who took on the majority of the work while 1-2 were always off task. If students are off task, they are not learning. This is probably why some students did not fully participate in the project presentations the next day. If I were to teach this lesson again, I would make groups of 3-4. By making the groups smaller, it would give each member more of a chance to participate and improve overall engagement."

Source: (Adapted from Porath, 2017

Providing question stems and look-fors to the PSTs will further assist them in reflection that focuses on video evidence as depicted in Table 5. These questions and topics follow guidelines or categories found on the evaluation document used at the beginning and end of the PST's time in the classroom. It will help them focus their comments within the areas that will be used to measure their progress and help them better understand the expectations set forth for them.

Ultimately, the goal of this practice is for the PST to grow as a teacher and professional and to improve instruction through purposeful, targeted reflection. The quality of the reflection will most likely be in direct correlation with the PST's growth as a teacher, so they should be encouraged to do their best to make it meaningful by devoting adequate time to the process.

After the PST has completed the self-reflection, it is shared with the observer for that particular lesson. The observer then reviews the PST's time-stamped comments and joins the conversation, creating comments from their own list of guidelines and prompts as shown in Table 6. The observer gives targeted, time-stamped feedback that the PST then accesses and reviews. The PST then responds to the observer's feedback, thereby engaging in dialogue about the lesson in a time-shifted manner. This practice also helps the observer understand the PST's thinking and to assess professional growth.

There are two main benefits to this type of self-reflection model. The first is that PSTs see the lesson not as they think it was but as it *actually* was. Oftentimes, PSTs are more focused on lesson delivery and be relatively unaware of what the students are doing during the lesson. By viewing the video, PSTs see what they missed during the lesson and accurately reflect on what *actually* happened rather than on what they *remember* happening. Also, the PST is not completely reliant on an outside observer's account of the lesson. In a face-to-face model, the observer's feedback is based on what he/she saw, but the PST is sometimes does not understand what the observer is referring to during the conversation. In a video-based system, the PST simply clicks on the time-stamped comment and is taken directly to that point in time to view the observer's reference.

Also, because of the time-shifted nature of the observation, PSTs and the observer have more time to reflect on the lesson because they choose when they watch the video. Oftentimes, when an observer sits in a classroom and watches a lesson, some of the lesson is lost while the observer makes notes. In a cloud-based video system, the observer can stop the video, respond, then begin the video again and not miss any aspect of the lesson.

Table 5. Reflection prompts and look-fors

Learner Development	Identify and describe an activity within the lesson that gives evidence of planning developmentally appropriate activities for students. Describe your thought process in designing the activities. • Look for: Scaffolding within the lesson to meet diverse student needs
Learning Differences	Identify and describe an activity within the lesson that shows your understanding of differences in the learners in your classroom. • Look for: Scaffolding within the lesson to meet diverse student needs
Learning Environments	How did the classroom environment contribute to a positive, respectful culture for learning? • Look for: Transitions, time spent with individual students or small groups, time spent getting lesson/class started, evidence of routines and procedures, student movement and behavior, arrangement of furniture, quality of visuals on walls, organization/distribution of materials, quality of student handouts, pacing of lesson, adequate time is spent in each lesson component
Content Knowledge	Identify an instance in the lesson where you clearly understood the central concepts and/or structure of the discipline you are teaching. How have you made the content relevant to your students? • Look for: Concepts and content of the subject taught in the lesson are accurate, relevance of the subject matter has been established with students (connection to their lives)
Application of Content	How did you make the content engaging to the learners? Was critical and/or creative thinking used? What did you do to actively engage students in the learning process? Did your activities effectively engage the students? How do you know the students were or were not engaged? • Look for: Strategic questions connect to lesson objective, assess understanding, and/or stretch student thinking (HOTS), use of "cold call" to ensure a variety of student responses, use of established discussion protocols, use of adequate wait time, students volunteer answers, are on task, interact appropriately with other students, and listen to instruction
Assessment	What did you want students to learn or know how to do? Did you meet your goals? What assessment did you use to measure your goals? Provide evidence of the effectiveness of this lesson based on student work, and/or evidence of student misunderstanding. Based on your assessment of the student work, what needs to be done next? • Look for: Use of strategic questioning to assess understanding, monitoring student progress during independent work time and frequently checking for understanding, use of modeling and guided practice, provides clear directions
Planning for Instruction	How did you decide what instructional strategies to use for this lesson? Were they successful? Were there others you considered? • Look for: Success of instructional strategies used, student engagement
Instructional Strategies	Which teaching strategies, materials, and activities did you find most effective? What is your evidence that this was effective? How did the instruction help your students meet rigorous learning goals? • Look for: Use of cooperative learning, different types of groupings, use of technology, project-based learning, use of questions and discussion, student participation, pacing of lesson, adequate time is spent in each lesson component

Source: (Adapted from Houser, 2017; Kansas State University, 2018)

10-Minute Walkthrough

The 10-minute walkthrough is a method by which an observer gives targeted feedback on a 10-minute portion of a lesson. The feedback focuses on a wide range of topics, such as questioning strategies, classroom management, or transitions. The observer provides feedback on all lesson elements that are present in the lesson during that snapshot in time. The PST identifies a segment they want feedback on or the segment is chosen at random by the observer. The walkthrough is a way to do a quick check-in with the student and give informal feedback without spending time watching an entire lesson. It is also a way for the PST to share a portion of a lesson from which they desire specific feedback.

After the video is recorded, it is first shared with the observer, unlike in the self-reflection model. Because the purpose is to receive feedback first, the PST becomes the second viewer of the video. The

Table 6. Feedback prompts

Context	I noticed that you... ...could you talk to me about how that fits within this lesson or unit?
Perception	Here's what I saw... ...what were you thinking was happening at that time?
Interpretation	At one point in the lesson, it seemed like... ...what was your take?
Decision	Tell me about when you... ...what went into that choice?
Comparison	I noticed that students... ...how did that compare with what you had expected to happen when you planned the lesson?
Antecedent	I noticed that... ...could you tell me about what led up to that, perhaps in an earlier lesson?
Adjustment	I saw that... ...what did you think of that, and what do you plan to do tomorrow?
Intuition	I noticed that... ...how did you feel about how that went?
Alignment	I noticed that... ...what links do you see to our instructional framework (state standards, district curriculum, etc.)?
Impact	What effect did you think it had when you... ?

Source: (Adapted from Baeder, n.d.)

observer views the segment and gives holistic feedback on every aspect of the lesson. There are several lenses with which to view the lesson, and it is possible the observer will watch a portion several times in order to give feedback from different perspectives. After comments are made, the student then accesses the video, reads the comments, and responds to the feedback.

The 10-minute walkthrough provides one main benefit—immediate feedback. Because the shared segment is short, the observer easily accesses the video, scrolls to the specified time, and starts commenting. Even if the observer watches the segment multiple times, the time frame is shorter than watching a full lesson. Much like a coach does with a player who is learning a new skill, the observer coaches the PST to make adjustments in instruction based on the observation of the segment.

Focused Feedback

Oftentimes, observers feel the need to critique everything they see in the lesson and offer suggestions for improvement. This is, in part, because they want the PST to be a good teacher, and it is relatively easy to give feedback for obvious areas of improvement. As such, observers inadvertently bombard the PST with too much feedback about parts of the lesson that may or may not be the most important. By using the focused feedback method, the observer targets only two to three areas for the PST's focus for improvement in future lessons. These areas may include, for example, classroom management, transitions, questioning strategies, and verbal directions. Most often, these areas will correlate with the goals the PST has identified in conjunction with the cooperating teacher and university supervisor early in the semester. These goals should be ever-evolving—when one is deemed consistent, it can be shelved and another area is identified for improvement. The main goal is providing feedback to the PST in manageable increments so as to implement it in instruction immediately in the days that follow.

The kind of feedback the observer gives is just as important as what is targeted. According to Wiggins (2012), feedback should be formative, actionable, clear, timely, and supportive. Many well-meaning observers write phrases such as "Good job!" and "Way to go!" when providing feedback to PSTs, but this has been shown to have a relatively low effect on their achievement (Hattie & Timperley, 2007).

Pre-service teachers need to know *what* specifically was good and *why* it was a good instructional choice at that time. Ending a specific comment with a supportive statement such as the example above would be an appropriate use of one of these phrases; however, on their own, they lack the specificity needed to provide adequate and useful feedback to the PST.

A second mistake that observers make is giving too many suggestions. According to Cheliotes and Reilly (2010), when those in a position of power give advice, it sends the message that only they have the right answers and discourages independent thinking. As seasoned educators, many observers have a wealth of experience to draw upon with which to provide suggestions about a wide variety of topics. However, much like a teacher who is attempting to lead her students to understand a concept through a series of questions, observers should be helping PSTs reflect on their instruction and grow as teachers through a series of statements and questions. In this way, students must think critically about their instruction and come to their own conclusions about how to make improvements. The following is a hypothetical example of a common comment observers make:

I noticed that when you told the students to go back to their seats after calendar time that they all stood up and ran to their desks, bumping into each other and falling down. One girl even ran a victory lap after she "won" the race to her seat. That happened to me when I taught Kindergarten, too. I had a really unique way of dismissing students individually or in small groups to go to their seats from the carpet that the kids responded well to. Let me share it with you...

This comment is meant to be helpful, but it takes any ownership or critical thinking away from the PST. The observer has just stated that the PST needs a transition strategy and here it is. To encourage critical thinking and creativity from the PST, the observer would be encouraged to comment like this:

In this part of the video, I saw that when you told the students to go back to their seats after calendar time that they all stood up and ran to their desks, bumping into each other and falling down. One girl even ran a victory lap after she "won" the race to her seat. That happened to me once when I taught Kindergarten, too. What did you think of that, and what do you plan to do tomorrow?

Good feedback begins with noticing specific aspects of the lesson, then sharing those observations with the PST as the starting point for the discussion. It is like a teacher asking a well-crafted, thought-provoking question in the classroom, then spending the majority of the time listening to the student responses and asking follow-up questions. By encouraging PSTs to critically think about particular aspects of the instruction through evidenced-based feedback and powerful questions, it will have a larger impact on his or her learning and self-confidence than if the observer is quick to offer a suggestion.

Formal Evaluation

Though not the main focus of the feedback cycle, formal evaluation has its place. At the beginning of the semester, the PST teaches a lesson that is evaluated by the cooperating teacher, university supervisor, and self-evaluated by the PST. By performing an evaluation at this point, it creates a baseline with which to measure growth throughout the semester. This evaluation also helps identify some potential areas of emphasis for the PST to create short-term and long-term goals.

The cycle begins with the PST writing a lesson plan to be taught the next week. After the plan is complete, it is sent to the cooperating teacher and the university supervisor for approval and suggested changes. This step is important because it gives context for the university supervisor who is not in the classroom every day. By viewing the lesson plan ahead of time, the supervisor sees all the aspects of the planning such as modifications or accommodations for all students as well as certain types of assessments that may not be evident in the video. Once approved, the lesson is ready to be taught.

After teaching and recording the lesson, the video is uploaded. The university supervisor and the cooperating teacher view the lesson and document evidence for the evaluation within the video itself using the cloud-based system. These comments become the basis for the ratings given in the evaluation. In some online video systems, comments are tagged by category to further facilitate this process and provide a direct correlation between the comments and the categories of the evaluation document. Unlike a face-to-face evaluation, the evidence collected here is based upon actual footage of the lesson and provides a sound, factual basis for the evaluation. All three stakeholders—the university supervisor, cooperating teacher, and the pre-service teacher—will participate in this process to provide a triangulation of evidence and give each stakeholder a voice. It also provides a broader perspective of the lesson based upon the unique experiences and knowledge of each person. From this base evaluation, goals are established for future instruction and a baseline is provided to assess future growth.

Near the end of the PST's time in the classroom, a post-evaluation will be performed using the same process as the pre-evaluation. By this point, multiple reflections and interactions have occurred among the three stakeholders adding ease to the process due to the familiarity they each have with the others' expectations and teaching styles. At the end of the evaluation process, data can be obtained by comparing the pre- and post-evaluations for the purposes of program evaluation and data analysis. It also provides concrete evidence of growth in a PST for cooperating teachers and university supervisors to reference when recommending a PST for teaching positions or honors. In conclusion, while evaluation is not the focus of the feedback cycle, it serves an essential role in the overall process.

ADDITIONAL CONSIDERATIONS

Given the exponential growth of online delivery systems, the future of the educational landscape is bound only by the level of creativity and determination of the individuals who create the program. However, online education is not a panacea and can create as many hurdles as it does opportunities. Feedback systems designed to meet the needs of a newer generation are only a beginning step in the future of teacher education. The use of technology, which relies heavily on the implementation of a video management system such as that used at Kansas State University, provides challenges in the elementary classroom.

As stated previously, supervision in an online environment must be distinctly different than that provided in a traditional student teaching experience. The lack of a physically present supervisor in the classroom may be daunting to many experienced teachers. In the KSU system, the traditional supervision triad relied heavily on developing a personal level of trust among the cooperating teacher, university supervisor, and student intern (Allen, Perl, Goodson, & Sprouse, 2014). When implementing a video-based supervision system, the university supervisor rarely, if ever, physically enters the classroom. The physical absence sometimes creates instances of distrust and must be addressed early in the field experience through the use of synchronous communication technologies.

Video conferencing using applications like Facetime or Zoom are critical to establishing a connection that facilitates open lines of communication and established expectations for the field experience. However, this form of communication only works as long as all stakeholders buy into the communication method. Not all supervisors and cooperating teachers are supportive of distance supervision techniques. The authors have often encountered reluctance on the part of cooperating teachers, and even university supervisors, to abandon the traditional, paper/pencil classroom observation and work within a distance-mediated environment. This reluctance is in part due to a lack of familiarity with the technology, but more often is associated with a strong adherence to "doing things the way they have always done it." Simply stated, classroom teachers desire face-to-face communication with a university representative. Often, even the more seasoned mentors, who are strong advocates for students, are reluctant to enter into agreements to host students within a distance mediated program. The authors work diligently to meet physically with as many teachers as possible to share the vision for the future of video-based supervision with the college's program. By offering professional development and technology support, the program has seen a great deal of growth in terms of teacher buy-in to the program, but much work remains.

Professional development focused on new technologies must be ongoing and sustained. Tyack and Cuban (1995) reported the struggle of reform efforts through the 20th century in American schools. This struggle is not only related to curriculum changes but also to systemic changes. A traditional triad model of supervision (Allen, Perl, Goodson, & Sprouse, 2014) not only relies on trust and collegiality but also on a system of observations, evaluations, and schedules. The use of video-based observation focused on feedback rather than evaluation disrupts the traditional system. For example, under the traditional system, observations are scheduled and follow a rigid framework involving lesson plan development and approval, pre-conferencing, observation, reflection, and evaluation. These components still exist in the new observation system but they are not bounded by time. No longer does the evaluation cycle have to be dependent upon the time a lesson is taught or when a supervisor is available for the observation. With the video system in place, lessons can be recorded at any time, viewed at any time, and feedback provided at any time. In fact, the use of time-shifted observation creates opportunity for deeper, more meaningful, and relevant feedback. No longer is this model bounded by space and time. Teachers who are acclimated to structured supervision systems find it difficult to adjust their approach to supervision. With a video-based supervision model, student interns can prepare lessons in advance, record those lessons, and reflect on the videos without the observer's presence. In some instances, when the lesson does not go well for the student intern, they have chosen to reteach the lesson, record the second teaching episode, and submit that video for feedback rather than the initial lesson. This freedom aligns well with the characteristics of the Millennial but not so well with the practices of the experienced traditional mentor.

Systems that rely heavily on new technologies do not adhere to traditional time schedules, and a different theoretical supposition must be implemented into the school system methodically. University administrators must work closely with school-based partnerships to develop systematic professional development for teachers that address technology usage and contain clearly articulated systems and guidelines. Additionally, the university must communicate the dynamic nature of the fluid supervision model and allow cooperating teachers to provide input to make the system work within their individual classrooms. Teachers must feel as though they have the opportunity to be a part of the creative process. Additionally, feedback should be sought at the end of each semester from the university supervisors, cooperating teachers, and student interns. This feedback is essential to validate the involvement of all stakeholders and for continuous improvement.

A final consideration worthy of note is that of the legal issues surrounding the video recording of students in classrooms. During the university's implementation of the technology-mediated supervision process, teachers, parents, and administrators have voiced concern regarding the privacy and rights of the elementary students. These concerns are valid and each stakeholder has the right and obligation to voice concern over the use of video recording devices in classrooms. Given that the university currently utilizes video recording in over 100 school districts, there is little consistency in the policies that govern access to classrooms. Therefore, KSU developed a Memorandum of Agreement that outlines both the school district and university's role in the video recording process. First, since there are so many school district policies, the authors felt that the responsibility for seeking permission for the use of the video recorders should be placed upon the school district. In this way, the district ensures that proper procedure is followed, appropriate forms are signed, and the necessary documentation for each district is in place prior to the use of the recording device. The university's responsibility is to work with the Swivl™ Cloud system to ensure proper security is in place to protect the recordings and to monitor the appropriate use of videos by the student interns. Additionally, the university is responsible for deleting the videos at the conclusion of the student internship. The university addresses parent and teacher concerns about video recording devices within the classroom only by working in partnership with school districts.

CONCLUSION

The role of the mentor and feedback systems form a critical component of any online supervision system. The authors are currently implementing and collecting data on four feedback systems designed to work within an environment unbounded by time and space. The concept of time-shifted feedback is relatively new—one that enhances opportunities for more targeted feedback and fosters ongoing dialogue long after the teaching episode. Capturing the teaching episode on video and housing the recording in an unlimited cloud-based storage facility allows for sustained, ongoing dialogue in an environment that facilitates the growth process of pre-service teachers.

The authors' future efforts will involve an in-depth analysis of each feedback system to assess both the fidelity of the system and the quality of the feedback provided by the cooperating teachers and the university supervisors. Additionally, this analysis will examine the role of the student intern within the feedback systems.

REFERENCES

Allen, D. S., Goodson, L., Rothwell, A., & Sprouse, T. (2017). Miles of progress: Our journey into distance supervision. *PDS Partners, 12*(1), 20–22.

Allen, D. S., Perl, M., Goodson, L., & Sprouse, T. K. (2014). Changing traditions: Supervision, co-teaching, and lessons learned in a professional development school partnership. *Educational Considerations, 42*(1), 19–29. doi:10.4148/0146-9282.1041

American Association of Colleges for Teacher Education. (2013). *The changing teacher preparation profession.* Washington, DC: Author. Retrieved from https://secure.aacte.org/apps/rl/resource.php?resid=118&ref=rl

Aud, S., Wilkinson-Flicker, S., Kristapovich, P., Rathbun, A., Wang, X., & Zhang, J. (2013). *The condition of education 2013 (NCES 2013-037)*. Washington, DC: U.S. Department of Education, National Center for Education Statistics. Retrieved from http://nces.ed.gov/pubsearch

Baeder, J. (n.d.). *10 questions for better feedback on teaching*. The Principal Center. Retrieved from https://www.principalcenter.com/wp-content/uploads/10-questions-better-feedback.pdf

Bailey, K. (2006). *Language teacher supervision*. New York, NY: Cambridge University Press. doi:10.1017/CBO9780511667329

Blackwell, L. S., Trzesniewski, K. H., & Dweck, C. S. (2007). Implicit theories of intelligence predict achievement across an adolescent transition: A longitudinal study and an intervention. *Child Development*, *78*(1), 246–263. doi:10.1111/j.1467-8624.2007.00995.x PMID:17328703

Bolton, M. (2010). Fly on the wall: Using teleconferencing to supervise student teacher performance. *Journal of Open. Flexible and Distance Learning*, *14*(1), 62.

Capizzi, A. M., Wehby, J. H., & Sandmel, K. N. (2010). Enhancing mentoring of teacher candidates through consultative feedback and self-evaluation of instructional delivery. *Teacher Education and Special Education*, *33*(3), 191–212. doi:10.1177/0888406409360012

Chamberlin, C. R. (2000). Nonverbal behaviors and initial impressions of trustworthiness in teacher-supervisor relationships. *Communication Education*, *49*(4), 352–364. doi:10.1080/03634520009379223

Cheliotes, L. G., & Reilly, M. F. (2010). *Coaching conversations: Transforming your school one conversation at a time*. Thousand Oaks, CA: Corwin.

Chilton, H., & McCracken, W. (2017). New technology, changing pedagogies? Exploring the concept of remote teaching placement supervision. *Higher Education Pedagogies*, *2*(1), 116–130. doi:10.1080/23752696.2017.1366276

Cogan, M. L. (1972). *Clinical supervision*. Boston, MA: Houghton Mifflin Company.

Darling-Hammond, L. (2006). *Powerful teacher education: Lessons from exemplary programs*. San Francisco, CA: Jossey-Bass.

Darling-Hammond, L., Holtzman, D. J., Gatlin, S. J., & Heilig, J. V. (2005). Does teacher preparation matter? Evidence about teacher certification, teach for America, and teacher effectiveness. *Education Policy Analysis Archives*, *13*(42). Retrieved from http://epaa.asu.edu/epaa/v13n42/

Darling-Hammond, L., & Snyder, J. (2000). Authentic assessment of teaching in context. *Teaching and Teacher Education*, *16*(5-6), 523–545. doi:10.1016/S0742-051X(00)00015-9

Dussault, G. (1970). *A theory of supervision in teacher education*. New York, NY: Teachers College Press.

Etscheidt, S., Curran, C. M., & Sawyer, C. M. (2012). Promoting reflection in teacher preparation programs: A multilevel model. *Teacher Education and Special Education: The Journal of the Teacher Education Division of the Council for Exceptional Children*, *35*(1), 7–26. doi:10.1177/0888406411420887

Feiman-Nemser, S. (1998). Teachers as teacher educators. *European Journal of Teacher Education*, *21*(1), 63–74. doi:10.1080/0261976980210107

Feiman-Nemser, S. (2001). Helping novices learn to teach: Lessons from an experienced support teacher. *Journal of Teacher Education, 52*(1), 17–30. doi:10.1177/0022487101052001003

Garcia, P., & Rossitier, M. (2010). Digital storytelling as narrative pedagogy. In D. Gibson & B. Dodge (Eds.), *Proceedings of Society for Information Technology & Teacher Education International Conference*. Chesapeake, VA: AACE.

Hamilton, E. R., Rosenberg, J. M., & Akcaoglu, M. (2016). The substitution augmentation modification redefinition (SAMR) model: A critical review and suggestion for its use. *TechTrends, 60*(5), 433–441. doi:10.100711528-016-0091-y

Hattie, J., & Timperley, H. (2007). The power of feedback. *Review of Educational Research, 77*(1), 81–112. doi:10.3102/003465430298487

He, Y. (2009). Strength-based mentoring in pre-service teacher education: A literature review. *Mentoring & Tutoring, 17*(3), 263–275. doi:10.1080/13611260903050205

Head, A. J., & Eisenberg, M. B. (2010). *Truth be told: How college students evaluate and use information in the digital age*. Project Information Literacy. Retrieved from http://projectinfolit.org/ images/ pdfs/pil_fall2010_survey_fullreport1.pdf

Henry, M. A., & Weber, A. (2010). *Supervising student teachers: The professional way* (7th ed.). Lanham, MD: Roman & Littlefield Education.

Houser, K. (2017, February 7). 11 things coaches should look for in classroom observations [Web log post]. Retrieved from https://www.mshouser.com/instructional-coaching/11-things-coaches-should-look-for-in-classroom-observations

Ingersoll, R., Merrill, L., & May, H. (2014). What are the effects of teacher education and preparation on beginning Teacher Attrition? *CPRE Research Reports*. Retrieved from https://repository.upenn.edu/ cpre_researchreports/78

Ingersoll, R. M. (2012). Beginning teacher induction what the data tell us. *Phi Delta Kappan, 93*(8), 47–51. doi:10.1177/003172171209300811

Ingersoll, R., Merrill, L., Stuckey, D., & Consortium for Policy Research in Education. (2014). *Seven trends: The transformation of the teaching force. Updated April 2014. CPRE report. #RR-80*. Consortium for Policy Research in Education. Retrieved from http://search.ebscohost.com.er.lib.k-state.edu/login.as px?direct=true&db=eric&AN=ED566879&site=ehost-live

Jacobs, J., Hogarty, K., & Burns, R. W. (2017). Elementary preservice teacher field supervision: A survey of teacher education programs. *Action in Teacher Education, 39*(2), 172–186. doi:10.1080/016 26620.2016.1248300

Kansas State University. (2018). *Kansas state university student teacher handbook: Reflections on a single lesson*. Retrieved from https://www.coe.ksu.edu/field-experiences/docs/UG-ST-Handbook-2018.pdf

Koehler, M. J., & Mishra, P. (2009). What is technological pedagogical content knowledge? *Contemporary Issues in Technology & Teacher Education, 9*(1), 60–70.

LePage, P., Darling-Hammond, L., Akar, H., Guiterrez, C., Jenkins-Gunn, E., & Rosebrock, K. (2005). Classroom management. In L. Darling-Hammond, J. Bransford, P. LePage, K. Hammerness, & H. Duffy (Eds.), *Preparing teachers for a changing world: What teachers should learn and be able to do* (pp. 327–357). San Francisco, CA: Jossey-Bass.

Manuti, A., & de Palma, P. D. (2018). The cognitive technology revolution: A new identity for workers. In A. Manuti & P. D. de Palma (Eds.), Digital hr: A critical management approach to the digitalization of organizations (pp. 21-27). Cham: Palgrave Macmillan. doi:10.1007/978-3-319-60210-3_2

Mazer, J. P., & Hess, J. A. (2016). Editor's Introduction. *Communication Education, 65*(3), 356–376. doi:10.1080/03634523.2016.1173715

McGlynn, A. P. (2007). *Teaching today's college students: Widening the circle of success*. Madison, WI: Atwood Publishing.

Moll, L., Amanti, C., Neff, D., & Gonzalez, N. (1992). Funds of knowledge for teaching: Using a qualitative approach to connect homes and classrooms. *Theory into Practice, 31*(2), 132–140. doi:10.1080/00405849209543534

Porath, S. (2017). *Student reflection on Swivl video*. Manhattan, KS: Author.

Puentedura, R. (2006, November 26). *Transformation, technology, and education in the state of Maine*. Retrieved from http://www.hippasus.com/rrpweblog/archives/2006_11.html

Puentedura, R. (2009, February 4). *As we may teach: Educational technology, from theory into practice*. Retrieved from http://www.hippasus.com/rrpweblog/archives/2014/06/29/ LearningTechnologySAMRModel.pdf

Puentedura, R. (2014). Building transformation: An introduction to the SAMR model [Web log comment]. Retrieved from http://www.hippasus.com/rrpweblog/archives/2014/08/22/ BuildingTransformation_AnIntroductionToSAMR.pdf

Reeves, A. G. (2013). Selves, Lives, and videotape: Leveraging self-revelation through narrative pedagogy. In D. S. Knowlton & K. J. Hagopian (Eds.), New Directions for Teaching and Learning: 135(3). From entitlement to engagement: Affirming millennial students' egos in the higher education classroom (pp. 55–60). Academic Press. doi:10.1002/tl.20065

Rogers, C. R. (1961). *On becoming a person: A therapist's view of psychotherapy*. Boston, MA: Houghton Mifflin.

Rosaen, C., Lundeberg, M., Cooper, M., Fritzen, A., & Terpstra, M. (2008). Noticing noticing: How does investigation of video records change how teachers reflect on their experiences? *Journal of Teacher Education, 59*(4), 347–360. doi:10.1177/0022487108322128

Scheeler, M., & Lee, D. (2002). Using technology to deliver immediate corrective feedback to preservice teachers. *Journal of Behavioral Education, 11*(4), 231–241. doi:10.1023/A:1021158805714

Schwille, S. A. (2008). The professional practice of mentoring. *American Journal of Education, 115*(1), 139–167. doi:10.1086/590678

Shroyer, M. G., Yahnke, S. J., Mercer, D. K., & Allen, D. S. (2014). Foreword. *Educational Considerations*, *42*(1), 1–2. doi:10.4148/0146-9282.1038

Siwatu, K. O. (2011). Preservice teachers' sense of preparedness and self-efficacy to teach in America's urban and suburban schools: Does context matter? *Teaching and Teacher Education*, *27*(2), 357–365. doi:10.1016/j.tate.2010.09.004

Twenge, J., Campbell, S., Hoffman, B., & Lance, C. (2010). Generational differences in work values: Leisure and extrinsic values increasing, social and intrinsic values decreasing. *Journal of Management*, *5*(36), 1117–1142. doi:10.1177/0149206309352246

Tyack, D., & Cuban, L. (1995). *Tinkering toward utopia: A century of public school reform*. Cambridge, MA: Harvard University Press.

United States Department of Labor, Bureau of Labor Statistics. (2017). *Occupations with the most job growth*. Retrieved from http://www.bls.gov/emp/ep_table_104.htm

U.S. Department of Education, Office of Planning, Evaluation, and Policy Development. (2010). *Evaluation of evidence-based practices in online learning: A meta-analysis and review of online learning studies*. Washington, DC: Author. Retrieved from https://www2.ed.gov/rschstat/eval/tech/evidence-based-practices/finalreport.pdf

U.S. Department of Labor, Bureau of Labor Statistics. (2016). *Occupational outlook handbook*. Washington, DC: Author. Retrieved from https://www.bls.gov/ooh/education-training-and-library/kindergarten-andelementary-school-teachers.htm

Vohs, K. D., Baumeister, R. F., Schmeichel, B. J., Twenge, J. M., Nelson, N. M., & Tice, D. M. (2008). Making choices impairs subsequent self-control: A limited-resource account of decision making, self-regulation, and active initiative. *Journal of Personality and Social Psychology*, *94*(5), 883–898. doi:10.1037/0022-3514.94.5.883 PMID:18444745

Wiggins, G. (2012). Seven keys to effective feedback. *Educational Leadership*, *70*(1), 10–16. Retrieved from http://www.ascd.org/publications/educational-leadership/sept12/vol70/ num01/Seven-Keys-to-Effective-Feedback.aspx

Chapter 24
Reflection Activities Within Clinical Experiences:
An Important Component of Field–Based Teacher Education

Sarah A. Nagro
George Mason University, USA

Laurie U. deBettencourt
Johns Hopkins University, USA

ABSTRACT

The purpose of this chapter is to explore the importance of reflection activities within clinical experiences that often are prescribed components of field-based teacher education. This chapter will include a review of documented attempts to understand the impact reflection activities have on teacher candidate growth. More specifically, this chapter will review what we know about the emphasis on reflective practice within teacher education and professional practice, what typical reflection activities within a field-based teacher education context are, and how reflective ability is measured within field-based clinical experiences. The chapter finishes with implications and recommendations for research and practice within teacher education.

INTRODUCTION

A universal goal of teacher preparation is to produce profession-ready individuals with the knowledge, skills, and dispositions of a reflective practitioner able to respond to students' needs in dynamic classroom environments. Teacher preparation programs have moved beyond emphasizing only theory of effective teaching without exposure to real-world contexts. The current movement towards field-based teacher education integrates coursework and clinical experiences. The clinical experiences are considered by many teacher educators to be the most important aspect of authentic learning and the key to profession-readiness (Nagro & deBettencourt, 2017; Blanton, Pugach, Florian, 2011; Connelly & Graham, 2009;

DOI: 10.4018/978-1-5225-6249-8.ch024

Gelfuso, Dennis, & Parker, 2015; Maheady, Smith, & Jabot, 2014; Recchia & Puig, 2011; Sayeski & Paulsen, 2012). Therefore, it is not surprising that clinical experiences are considered to be a critical component of all preparation programs by education accreditation organizations (e.g., Allen, Coble, & Crowe, 2014; National Council for Accreditation of Teacher Education's [NCATE], 2010). Many teacher educators have identified best practices for implementing clinical experiences (e.g., Leko, Brownell, Sindelar, & Murphy, 2012). Most agree that clinical experiences should be strategically developed to allow teacher candidates to complete the following: use theory in practice, have opportunities for self-reflection, and have multiple opportunities for meaningful feedback and guidance (see Brownell, Ross, Colon, & McCallum, 2005; Darling-Hammond & Bransford, 2005). Clinical experiences within teacher preparation programs often include a number of required activities such as lesson planning, teaching observations, and portfolios, but one of the most common across emperically documented field-based experiences is reflection activities (see Nagro & deBettencourt, 2017).

Most teacher education programs create clinical experiences that allow teacher candidates opportunities to apply their knowledge in real classroom situations and then think about their choices in a meaningful way through reflection. In fact, Roth (1989) indicated that reflection cannot be taught in isolation of clinical experiences. One possible reason for the common pairing is that teacher candidates' reflective practices are more likely to translate to professional routines if taught directly during teacher preparation field-experiences (Etscheidt, Curran, & Sawyer, 2012; Moore, 2003). Additionally, professional teaching standards place emphasis on reflective practice and view it as a professional practice needing attention during teacher preparation. For example, both the Council of Chief State School Officers (CCSSO), through its Interstate Teacher Assessment and Support Consortium (InTASC), and the Council for Exceptional Children (CEC) include professional teaching standards that focus on reflection on one's own teaching practices (CCSSO, 2011; CEC, 2012). For example the InTASC Model Core Teaching Standards and Learning Progressions for Teachers (CCSSO, 2017) state teachers should reflect to:

- *Examine practice to see how well it addresses individual learner needs;*
- *Share practice with others (e.g., invite peers to observe in class, share video of self) and use feedback to better meet learner needs; and*
- *Work with a [mentor] to better understand current practice and make adjustments (p. 18).*

Similarly, CEC's (2015) What Every Special Educator Must Know: Ethics, Standards and Guidelines explain that an emhasis on reflection is important so that special educators:

- *Are aware of how their own and others' attitudes, behaviors, and ways of communicating can influence their practice;*
- *Understand that culture and language can interact with exceptionalities, and are sensitive to the many aspects of diversity of individuals with exceptional learning needs and their families;*
- *Actively plan and engage in activities that foster their professional growth and keep them current with evidence-based best practices, and;*
- *Know their own limits of practice and practice within them (p. 50).*

The purpose of this chapter is to explore the importance of reflective practice, one of the most common clinical experience activities. This chapter provides a review of the research to date on the use of reflection activities within teacher preparation. In addition, the chapter defines key terms including reflective practice and reflective ability, provides a description of typical reflection activities within a field-based teacher education context, and synthesizes how teacher candidates' reflective abilities have been measured across the body of literature. The chapter concludes with recommendations for both embedding reflective practices within teacher education as well as emperically studying the impacts of reflective practice on teacher candidates' reflective ability.

BACKGROUND: DEFINING KEY TERMS

Reflective Practice

Dewey (1910), most often credited for his role in defining reflection, contrasted reflective thought with stream of consciousness. Dewey (1933) suggested that reflecting on experiences is necessary for learning, meaning-making, and new knowledge that informs future action. Schon (1983) advanced the work of Dewey (1933) by identifying two categories of reflection, reflecting-in-action and reflecting-on-action. Reflecting-in-action is akin to making decisions about an event as it unfolds in order to take next steps (Finley, 2008; Laverick, 2017; Schon, 1983). This may require real-time problem solving, responsivity, or resourcefulness but the key is that the individual reflecting is doing so at a time when they can still influence the outcome. In contrast, reflecting-on-action includes revisiting past events in some capacity, after an outcome has already happened, and therefore the individual reflecting cannot influence the outcome. The key distinction is that revisiting the past allows for connection-making and may influence future outcomes but cannot influence past outcomes (Laverick, 2017; Schon, 1987). For the purpose of this chapter, we will focus exclusively on reflecting-on-action in its various forms within a teacher preparation context.

Reflecting-on-action, or *reflective practice*, is defined broadly as reviewing past experiences with intentionality for the purpose of gaining new insights. These insights can be derived from refection through the lens of taking perspectives, confronting beliefs, questioning causation, or comparing expectations to reality. Reflective practices can take place at the individual level, with peers, or even in professional communities of learning. Reflective practices can occur during purposeful discussions, in written form (e.g., journals or after action reviews), or can leverage technology such as a video post or webcast. Because the uses for and types of reflective practice are wide ranging, the specific definitions of reflective practice vary as well. For example, Rodgers (2002) defined reflective practice as activities that meet four criteria including meaning making, scientific inquiry, community, and growth of self and others. Specifically, Rogers (2002) explained:

1. *Reflection is a meaning-making process that moves a learner from one experience into the next with deeper understanding of its relationships with- and connections to- other experiences and ideas. It is the thread that makes continuity of learning possible and ensures the progress of the individual and, ultimately, of society. It is a means to essentially moral ends.*
2. *Reflection is a systematic, rigorous, disciplined way of thinking, with its roots in scientific inquiry.*
3. *Reflection needs to happen in community, in interaction with others.*
4. *Reflection requires attitudes that value the personal and intellectual growth of oneself and of others. (p. 845)*

This definition of reflective practice is one example of the complexities associated with understanding this professional practice. Specific to teaching, Beck, King, and Marshall (2002) took a more concrete approach to defining reflective practice by focusing on four actions taken by a teacher during reflective practice, which include:

1. Identifying a teaching objective or goal;
2. Examining the selected teaching strategy given the identified goal;
3. Providing a rationale or justification for employing the strategy, and;
4. Comparing anticipated outcomes to actual student outcomes.

Taken together, through reflective practice, teacher candidates can make sense of past events to systematically examine experiences and when similar events happen, teacher candidates can recognize the experience and apply new knowledge based on past insights. Therefore, past experiences give meaning to present events.

Reflective Ability

The ability to engage in reflective practice in a meaningful way is known as reflective ability. *Reflective ability* is defined as the quantifiable ability to critically review, analyze, and evaluate a teaching situation in order to learn from the experience and apply such insights to future situations. Reflective ability, within the context of teaching, is essential for teachers to improve their practice and optimize their instructional performance. The ability to critically reflect goes beyond recalling a lesson or sharing feelings about perceived student learning. Through reflective practice, teachers can recognize their own strengths and weaknesses, explore new ways of improving, and further develop their own instructional decision-making aptitude (Calandra, Brantley-Dias, & Dias, 2006; Calandra, Brantley-Dias, Lee, & Fox, 2009; Crawford, O'Reilly, & Luttrell, 2012). While past research has used slight variations of levels or dimensions to define reflective ability ranging from recalling the past to planning for the future based on analysis of the lesson, few research investigations have used the same definition. The list in Table 1, adapted from Etscheidt and colleagues (2012), demonstrates differences in how researchers define reflective ability, which results in differences in measurement.

REFLECTIVE PRACTICES WITHIN A FIELD-BASED TEACHER EDUCATION CONTEXT

This section will describe several reflection activities documented within teacher education research, as well as efforts to support reflective practice, particularly the practice of pairing video evidence with written reflections.

Examples of Reflection Activities

Similar to the ranging purposes for and definitions of reflective practice, reflection activities as documented in the literature also vary. The many approaches to facilitating reflective practice can include reflecting on artifacts (e.g., assigned readings, salient quotes, or discussion board posts), reflecting on

Table 1. Defining Reflective Ability

Source by Date	Defining Reflective Ability through Reflective Practices
Van Manen (1977)	Level 1 Technical: • Addressing the application of specific skills and pedagogy in the classroom and considering alternative actions and strategies Level 2 Practical: • Interpreting the value of specific teaching practices for independent, individual teaching decisions Level 3 Critical: • Examining the influence of structural and societal constraints and how personal values may conflict with those constraints
Schon (1983, 1987)	Reflection-in-Action: • Developing an awareness of decisions in practices Reflection-on-Action: • Developing an interpretive critique of practice
Gibbs (1988)	• Describing what happened • Expressing what was felt and thought • Evaluating positives and negatives about the experience • Analyzing to make sense of the situation • Drawing conclusions about what else could have been done • Developing an action plan in case something similar happens again
Pfeiffer and Ballew (1988)	The Experiential Process: • Experiencing • Publishing • Processing • Generalizing • Applying
Grimmet, MacKinnon, Erickson, and Riecken (1990)	Technical Mode: • Enabling teachers to determine how to meet professional standards Deliberative Mode: • Guiding teachers' consideration of competing or diverse views of teaching Dialectical Mode: • Transforming personal belief and practice
Valli (1990)	Technical Reflection: • Applying reflection to specific teaching practices Reflection on Action: • Evaluating a teaching performance Deliberative Reflection: • Considering alternative perspectives and actions Personalistic Reflection: • Appraising individual development Critical Reflection: • Considering social and political influences on teaching practices
Gore and Zeicher (1991)	Academic: • Focusing on subject matter knowledge to promote student understanding Social Efficiency: • Emphasizing application of evidence-based teaching strategies Developmental: • Prioritizing teaching practices sensitive to individual student preferences and interests Social Reconstructionist: • Stressing the social and political context of schooling
Sparks-Langer and Colton (1991)	Cognitive Element: • Constructing knowledge to make effective decisions about classroom situations Critical Element: • Addressing personal experiences, beliefs, sociopolitical values, and goals Teacher Narratives: • Interpreting contexts and developing rationale for professional decision making
Van Manen (1991)	Anticipatory Reflection: • Examining teaching actions through an organized and deliberate selection of a teaching action Active or Interactive Reflection: • Using reflection to support an informed on-the-spot decision Recollective Reflection: • Using past experiences to gain insight into teaching Mindfulness: • Engaging in continuous sensitivity to the dynamic aspects of teaching

continued on following page

Table 1. Continued

Source by Date	Defining Reflective Ability through Reflective Practices
Pultorak (1996)	Technical Rationality: • Focusing on teacher competency and effectiveness Subjective Reflection: • Revealing personal bias and values based on personal perceptions Critical Reflection: • Considering the value of knowledge and moral or ethical dimensions of schooling
Wellington and Austin (1996)	Immediate Orientation: • Addressing the immediate, situational demands related to teaching and learning Technical Orientation: • Developing and refining instructional methodologies. Deliberative Orientation: • Emphasizing discovery, assignment, and personal meaning of educational practices Dialectic Orientation: • Questioning, revising, and validating educational practices and beliefs Transpersonal Orientation: • Sustaining self-development, personal responsibility, experience, and decision making
Zeichner and Liston (1996)	Rapid Reflection: • Instantaneous and automatic action Repair: • Make adjustments and decisions in response to cues from the students Review: • Think about, discuss, or write about aspects of teaching through the lens of justice and equity Research: • Engage in systematic and sustained thinking over time, typically supplemented by data collection and analysis Retheorizing and Reformulating: • Critically examine personal theories and practice compared to academic theories
Stanley (1998)	Engaging with Reflection: • Engaging in a committed process of reflection with consideration of the personal and contextual factors influencing the process Thinking Reflectively: • Learning to think reflectively through guided scaffolds or questions Using Reflection: • Using reflection as a tool to examine actions and beliefs which benefit professional and personal practices Sustaining Reflection: • Maintaining committed reflective practice in workable formats for improved understanding Practicing Reflection: • Using reflection as an integral part of practice and developing an analytic personal framework of multiple lenses to examine classroom, school and societal practices, and influences
Jay and Johnson (2002)	Descriptive: • Examining personal classroom actions Comparative: • Inviting alternative views, perspectives, and research Critical: • Posing questions pertaining to the public democratic purposes of schooling and the moral and political dimensions of schooling
Ward and McCotter (2004)	Routine Reflection: • Investigating the impact of the practice or experience on the preservice teacher with little inquiry or personal response Technical Reflection: • Examining specific teaching tasks. Inquiry guided by questions about specific classroom situations Dialogic Reflection: • Reflecting on student outcome with considerations of divergent perspectives Transformative Reflection: • Revealing fundamental pedagogical, ethical, moral, cultural, or historical concerns leading to changes in practice
Robinson and Kelley (2007)	Technical Rationality • Description of observed event with terminology Descriptive Rationality • Description of an observed event with associated terminology and personal perspective; looks at impact on others. Dialogic Reflection • Description of an observed event with associated terminology/concepts; Uses multiple perspectives Critical Reflection • Considers entire context; discourse with self and explores possible reasons for actions; steps out of self and observes from a distance Reflect-on-Action • Ethical and moral issues; considers a holistic picture and considers implications for future practice (outside of a role-play)

continued on following page

Table 1. Continued

Source by Date	Defining Reflective Ability through Reflective Practices
Stockero (2008)	Describing • Reports a classroom event with no interpretation Explaining • Discusses possible causes of classroom events or student thinking Theorizing • Refers to research, course readings, or other evidence to provide support for analysis Confronting • Considers alternate explanations for events and/or considers others' points of view; beginning to question fundamental assumptions about teaching Restructuring • Focuses on how an experience could be redesigned to avoid potential problems or better support student learning; must show evidence of theorizing and confronting
Calandra, Brantley-Dias, Lee, and Fox (2009)	1A: In Action, 1B: For Action, 1C: On Action 2A: Technical, 2B: Contextual, 2C: Critical 3A: Knowledge, 3B: Skills, 3C: Dispositions
Crawford, O'Reilly, & Luttrell (2012)	Technical Situational Sensitising Description Description and justification Description and critique Description, justification, and critique
Nagro, deBettencourt, Rosenberg, Carran, and Weiss (2017)	Describe • Concrete statements of what happened that can include basic mention of individual elements or a detailed retelling of the lesson Analyze • Rationale, reasoning, or justification for teaching decisions that may tie back to coursework or knowledge of evidence-based practices Judge • Assessing (positive, negative, or neutral) a teaching decision during the lesson by noting the specific effect that decision had on the outcome of a portion of the lesson or the lesson overall Apply • Use insight from the lesson to create a plan for extending effective practices or changing of ineffective practices in future lessons

the actions of others (e.g., veteran teacher observations, peer observations, or teaching videos), or reflecting on self (e.g., coursework performance or teaching experiences). Following are some examples of reflection activities as described in teacher education literature:

1. Horvits and Vellom (2012) directed teacher candidates to reflect with their peers during web-based online threaded discussions as a way to supplement classroom discussions and promote reflective practice.

2. In an effort to help students "see" critical classroom events, McFadden, Ellis, Anwar and Reohrig (2014) required teacher candidates to use video annotation software to review video evidence of teaching and write reflective statements throughout the teaching video;

3. As a process for targeting teacher candidates' communication competence, Bower, Cavanagh, Moloney and Dao (2011) instructed candidates to post video reflections in which they discussed their teaching experiences;

4. Crawford and colleagues (2012) asked teacher candidates to maintain reflection logs paired with video commentary to promote both written and spoken reflective thought.

5. In an effort to focus their reflective practice, Santagat and Angelici (2010) required teacher candidates to answer specific probing questions while watching video evidence of a lesson, and;

6. To allow teacher candidates to articulate their thinking in writing, Nagro and colleagues (2017) directed teacher candidates to compose topical written entries using video evidence of their teaching with a checklist of topics for and types of reflection, providing a concrete approach to an otherwise conceptual learning experience.

While the types of reflection activities can include one or more modalities, the most common approach to reflective practice during field-based clinical experiences is written reflection (Conderman, Morin, & Stephens, 2005; Etscheidt, Curran, & Sawyer, 2012), which also varies widely. For example,

-   Griffin, Jones, and Kilgore (2006) required teacher candidates to write a collaborative reflection journal with their co-teacher about their shared experiences;
-   Knapczyk, Hew, Frey, and Wall-Marencik (2005) required teacher candidates to align reflection journal entries to field experience assignments such as data collection or evaluating student interventions; and
-   In an effort to promote creativity and reflective thinking, Bain and Hasio (2011) directed teacher candidates to create visual reflection journals that paired images with reflective statements.

Written reflections also offer a method for tracking reflective practice over time while maintaining flexibility such as changing the goals of and purposes for reflecting. Through written reflection, teacher candidates can learn to recognize diverse and challenging teaching situations. Without guidance during the reflective process, however, teacher candidates have not demonstrated improvement, maintaining low level reflective abilities (see Calandra, Gurvitch, & Lund, 2008). Additionally, repeated exposure to reflective practice alone does not necessarily lead to improved reflective ability (see deBettencourt & Nagro, 2018). Without the necessary tools and structured guidance on how to reflect, teacher candidates' reflective ability does not improve, but instead their reflective practices remain superficial (Calandra, Gurvitch, & Lund, 2008; Kalk, Luik, Taimalu, & That, 2014; Nagro, deBettencourt, Rosenberg, Carran, & Weiss, 2017).

Supporting Reflective Practice

Constructing reflective ability does not happen spontaneously. In order to support candidates' developing reflective ability, teacher education researchers are investigating the use of additional supports such as teaching artifacts (i.e., lesson plans, student work, and video evidence) during field-based reflection activities. Supporting reflection activities using video evidence seems to be one of the most popular options and is now common practice in more than 100 teacher preparation programs across the United States (Pearson Education, 2014). Reviewing video-recorded lessons of teaching is particularly important for teacher candidates just beginning to form their professional identities because the classroom is a dynamic work environment that calls for teachers who can demonstrate awareness, flexibility, and responsiveness in order to meet the ever changing needs of all students (see Domain 3, Instruction, of the Danielson Framework for Teaching, 2017). Through such teacher preparation activities, candidates can think about the success of their teaching choices without having to simultaneously teach.

The growing popularity of reflection activities combined with video evidence is justified by literature stating that this combination is more effective for developing reflective abilities when compared to the sole use of memory-based reflection activities (Borko, Jacobs, Eiteljorg, & Pittman, 2008; Robinson &

Kelley, 2007; Seidel, Stürmer, Blomberg, Kobarg, & Schwindt, 2011). For example, Rosaen and colleagues (2008) found that the reflection statements of three teacher candidates were more specific and detailed when using video evidence than when they relied on memory alone. In addition, Robinson and Kelley (2007) directed teacher candidates who were teaching simulated lessons to their peers to complete either memory-based written reflections or written reflections using video evidence. The authors found that candidates who reflected from memory wrote about feelings and focused on retelling events whereas the candidates who used video evidence to support the reflection process demonstrated deeper levels of reflective thought. Further, reflection activities that integrate video supports help candidates develop the ability to identify critical classroom events during authentic classroom situations by allowing opportunities to re-watch a single clinical experience multiple times, through different lenses, while pausing, rewinding, and re-watching at will (Martin & Ertzberger, 2013; McDuffie, Foote, Bolson, Turner, Aguirre, Bartell, & ... Land, 2014; Nagro, deBettencourt, Rosenberg, Carran, & Weiss, 2017).

Video evidence can supplement the reflective process in a variety of ways. For example, teacher candidates can:

1. Edit video evidence of clinical experiences to make meaning of critical teaching events (e.g., identifying classroom management in action or verbal instruction, Calandra, Gurvitch, & Lund, 2008);
2. Work collaboratively to review video evidence and provide peer-to-peer feedback in a group setting (e.g., *video club*, Sherin & van Es, 2005; 2009; van Es, 2010);
3. Receive feedback from a university supervisor or mentor teacher about their video-recorded instruction to prompt topics for written reflection (e.g., Hefner-Berg & Smith, 1996); or
4. Watch video evidence of their own teaching to then write a reflection (e.g., *video analysis,* Tripp & Rich, 2012).

Video analysis is fundamentally different than other types of reflection activities using video evidence. During video analysis, teacher candidates watch video evidence of their own teaching rather than reviewing the recorded instruction of peers or in-service teachers. This technique optimizes the learning experience while minimizing the pressures associated with real-time decision making (reflecting-in-action) that will be present upon entering the workforce. Reflecting on video evidence of self (i.e., video analysis) has resulted in higher levels of immersion in and motivation for genuine teaching reflection when compared to reflecting on video evidence of others (see Seidel, Stürmer, Blomberg, Kobarg, & Schwindt, 2011). Video analysis has been shown as a more effective method for developing reflective abilities when compared to memory-based self-reflection as well as when compared to alternative forms of reflection including watching videos of other teachers (see Borko, Jacobs, Eiteljorg, & Pittman, 2008; Robinson & Kelley, 2007; Seidel, Stürmer, Blomberg, Kobarg, & Schwindt, 2011). The flexibility of video technology, combined with familiarity of watching one's own video, supports both a means for reflection and a method for assessing evolving teaching abilities during field-based experience.

Building Prerequisite Skills

Teacher candidates need to build prerequisite skills, such as the ability to identify critical classroom events and specific teaching elements before they are able to use video evidence to reflect in a meaningful way (Kalk, Luik, Taimalu, & Täht, 2014). In one research study, teacher candidates watched videos of in-service teachers and were asked to identify effective teaching characteristics. Most of these teacher candidates, however, were unable to identify examples of good instruction (see Wiens, Hessberg, LoCasale-Crouch, & DeCoster, 2013). Additionally, in an effort to understand what teacher candidates looked for and focused on during video review, Calandra and colleagues (2006; 2008) conducted two case studies in which candidates wrote reflections, without additional guidance, using video-recorded materials. The authors described these candidates' reflections as being written at a low level demonstrating little reflective ability. Their findings were not surprising given that many teacher candidates lack prior experience reviewing videos of teaching situations and are uncertain of how to identify critical classroom events (van Es & Sherin, 2010). Moreover, the overabundance of information captured on a video can add complications for teacher candidates who are attempting to identify specifics of a lesson (DeCuir-Gunby, Marshall, & McCulloch, 2012). Given the previously described benefits of pairing reflection activities with video evidence, teacher candidates must be taught how to how to watch and analyze video evidence, including video of their own teaching (Deniz, 2012; Seidel, Stürmer, Blomberg, Kobarg, & Schwindt, 2011).

Teacher candidates who have not been taught how to critically observe their own teaching tend to focus their written reflections on student behaviors, rather than reflecting on the classroom "through the eyes of the teacher" (Jenkins, 2014 p. 304). If the ultimate goal of reflection is to help teacher candidates generalize lessons learned while self-reflecting to their own teaching actions, candidates need to recognize themselves, the teacher, as the change agent in the classroom. This requires that candidates develop the ability to view classroom events through a professional, rather than personal, lens (Sherin & Linsenmeier, 2011). Teacher educators can take intentional steps to support teacher candidates as they develop this perspective. For example, providing teacher candidates with a specific evaluation framework or checklist to use during self-reflection activities may help them understand how to better use video evidence of their own teaching to improve their instructional performance. In fact, teacher educators may already employ an evaluation or assessment tool within their clinical experiences that teacher candidates can use to reflect on their own teaching characteristics and practices.

The degree to which reflection activities are prescriptive can also vary. For example, while some reflection activities include free writing, (e.g., Rosaen, Lundeberg, Cooper, Fritzen, & Terpstra, 2008), other activities require teacher candidates to respond to specific guided questions (e.g., Ajayi, 2016) or prompt candidates to reflect on specific components of their teaching or a particular content area (e.g., Stockero, 2008). The most prescriptive reflection activities use a sequential framework for reflective practice (see Table 1). Some authors suggest that when teacher candidates self-reflect on their instruction through a predetermined framework, the quality of their written reflections is enhanced (see Fox, Brantley-Dias, & Calandra, 2007; Tripp & Rich, 2012). Adopting a multi-step evaluation framework, however, can overwhelm teacher candidates who are just learning to notice effective teaching (Sherin & van Es, 2005; 2009). As an example, the *Framework for Teaching*, created by Danielson (2017)

is a research-based set of components of instruction, aligned to the INTASC standards, and grounded in a constructivist view of learning and teaching. The complex activity of teaching is divided into 22 components (and 76 smaller elements) clustered into four domains of teaching responsibility. (para. 1)

It may be more effective to concentrate on just one or two teaching components (including the smaller corresponding elements) within the framework to help candidates focus as they are developing their reflective abilities. Table 2 illustrates an example of a prescriptive framework for written reflection focused on just one component, *Communicating with Students,* of the Framework for Teaching (the

Table 2. Example of Structuring Reflective Practice

Focus Items	Describe what happened or detail specific elements of the lesson	Analyze and explain the reasons why you made a teaching decision	Judge the success of specific decision by noticing the effect that decision had on a portion of or the lesson overall	Apply insight from this review to create a plan for extending effective or changing ineffective practices in future lessons
Expectations for Learning Goals for learning are communicated clearly to students. Even if the goals are not conveyed at the outset of a lesson, students are clear about what they have been learning by the end of the lesson.				
Directions for Activities Students understand what they are expected to do during a lesson, particularly during independent or small group work, without direct supervision. Directions are provided orally, in writing, or in some combination of the two, with modeling when appropriate.				
Explaining Content Teacher makes no errors when explaining content and connects content to students' interests and lives beyond school. The explanations are clear, with appropriate scaffolding, and, the teacher anticipates possible student misconceptions.				
Using Oral and Written Language Teacher models both precise language and rich vocabulary when communicating with students. When appropriate, the teacher inserts quick vocabulary lessons to deepen student understanding.				

Note: Focus items within this table were adapted from the Framework for Teaching (The Danielson Group, 2017).

Danielson Group, 2017). This example also demonstrates how a model for reflective practice can be paired with such a narrowed framework to provide structure for candidates new to reflection activities.

MEASURING REFLECTIVE ABILITY WITHIN A FIELD-BASED TEACHER EDUCATION CONTEXT

Understanding previous research and how investigators measure teacher candidate growth in reflective ability can inform future practice. Much of the literature on reflection is descriptive in nature, used exploratory methods, was a case study or pilot, or reported changes in reflective practice as a proxy for changes in reflective ability. Early methods for measuring reflective ability using written reflections started with counting the number of words and number of topics teacher candidates wrote (e.g., Calandra, Brantley-Dias, Lee, & Fox, 2009). In such cases, longer journal entries and a greater number of topics (*multifaceted*) mentioned by candidates were seen as a sign of improvement in reflective ability. Currently, the belief is that although word count is useful, other methods need to be used. If teacher candidates simply summarize events demonstrating low levels of reflective ability rather than engage in critical reflection across dimensions or levels of reflection; solely counting the number of words written or topics included may not provide valuable information. Similar to the information presented in Table 2, more recent methods of measuring reflective ability have combined elements of teaching from frameworks with levels or dimension of reflective practice to create a reflection checklist (e.g., Crawford, O'Reilly, & Luttrell, 2012).

A checklist can serve as both a framework for defining reflection activities and a method for teacher educators to systematically measure candidates' reflective abilities. For example, Robinson and Kelley (2007) measured reflective ability through the use of a rubric that categorized reflective statements as one of seven types of reflective practice ranging from a 'statement of fact' to 'technical reflection' to 'critical reflection'. Each statement received a score from 0-7 with the more critical or advanced levels of reflective practice weighted more heavily. The numerical scale was then used to calculate a mean reflective ability score. While the researchers demonstrated a systematic approach to quantifying reflective ability, this study was not without limitation. For example, the teacher candidates in this study only wrote three reflections. In addition, their reflections were completed on role-playing activities within their teacher preparation coursework rather than during actual clinical experiences. In the end, the results of this study demonstrated no change in candidates' ($n = 23$) reflective ability over time (Robinson & Kelley, 2007). While this study moved the field forward in terms of quantifying reflective ability, it is possible that the lack of authentic clinical experience paired with limited exposure to reflective practice was not sufficient to prompt change in teacher candidates. More recent research on measuring reflective ability is illustrated in a study in which teacher candidates were guided to include four dimensions of reflective practice in their written self-reflections (Nagro, deBettencourt, Rosenberg, Carran, & Weiss, 2017). This method of measuring reflective ability was based on the concept that teacher candidates should know about and be able to reflect across a continuum of reflective practices. Thus, candidates should understand how to:

1.   Describe their teaching choices,
2.   Analyze why such choices were made,
3.   Judge the success of those choices based on student outcomes, and
4.   Apply insights to plans for future lessons (see Table 2).

Other methods used to measure reflective ability have focused either on changes in reflective practice or shifts in reflective focus. Rosaen and colleagues (2008) conducted a case study using qualitative methods to measure changes in three teacher candidates' written reflections. The researchers reported the total frequency and percentage of reflection segments according to four categories:

1.   General versus specific observations,
2.   Focus on teacher management of the classroom versus student behaviors or attitudes,
3.   Focus on teacher instructional decisions versus student responses to instruction, and

4.   Teacher listening versus teacher probing (Rosaen, Lundeberg, Cooper, Fritzen, & Terpstra, 2008).

This coding schema highlights another possible method for measuring change in written reflection. The authors (2008) recognized, however, that their measure of reflective practice was limited and unlikely to capture change in teacher candidates' reflective ability.

Teacher candidates' reflective ability is a nuanced construct and requires a sensitive, multi-faceted methodological approach (i.e., mixed methods) when measuring growth (deBettencourt & Nagro, 2018). In a recent study, deBettencourt and Nagro (2018) employed a mixed methods approach to determine if teacher candidates' reflective abilities changed as a result of repeated exposure to reflection activities during clinical field-based experiences. Reflective ability was measured by tracking both qualitative analyses of changes in topics for and focus of written self-reflections. In addition, changes in a reflective ability score were calculated by assigning each sentence of the written self-reflection a specified point value where deeper dimensions of reflective practice corresponded to higher points. Conclusions suggest that candidates demonstrated subtle changes made evident by implementing this nuanced approach to measuring growth (deBettencourt & Nagro, 2018).

The Realities of Reflection Activities Research Within Field-Based Experiences

Previous methods for measuring changes in teacher candidates' reflective ability have resulted in multiple ways to understand and report on the usefulness of reflection activities within teacher preparation. Agreed upon "best" practices regarding the ways in which to embed reflection activities in field experiences or employ empirical methods to conduct research on this important practice have yet to be identified. There are several challenges present when conducting research on reflective practices within clinical field-based experiences, including:

1.   The difficulty of employing certain empirical research methodologies, particularly related to random sampling, random assignment, and generalizability across clinical experience settings.
2.   The difficulty of isolating the effect of one specific reflection activity within the context of the entire clinical teacher preparation experience.
3.   Ensuring candidates can participate in sufficient authentic clinical experiences in which to conduct research, and
4.   The complexities of introducing video-recording equipment into classrooms.

Random sampling and even random assignment to group, the hallmark of experimental research, is a common challenge when researching the effects of reflection activities because teacher candidates are completing clinical experiences in specific classrooms, nested in specific teacher preparation programs within universities. Often these classroom placements cannot be randomly chosen. When you add in the specificity of different teacher preparation programs, it becomes very difficult to find large groups of teacher candidates with common teacher preparation experiences that can serve as a sample pool. Randomly selecting participants is often not feasible and random assignment to group can be disrupted by scheduling conflicts (Andrews, Bobo, & Spurlock, 2010) or varied other issues such as policies that restrict video-recording during field experiences (e.g., Pianta, Mashburn, Downer, Hamre, & Justice, 2008). These issues with sampling and group assignment not only threaten internal validity, but as groups of teacher candidates become more homogeneous within a study, the findings become less generalizable across heterogeneous teacher candidate populations. This is a challenge with which researchers have been grappling for quite some time. For example, in an effort to transform the existing beliefs and practices of teacher candidates from three different colleges, Borg, et al. (1969) required candidates to engage in reflection activities with video evidence (video analysis). When discussing the generalizability of their findings, the researchers expressed the need for greater control over the methods for measuring teacher candidate improvements.

The authors also recognized the need to track teacher candidate clinical experience activities, such as seminar discussion, outside of the video analysis process because it was difficult to determine the role one specific teacher preparation activity played among the many other preparation activities. Research within clinical experiences makes controlling for mediating variables, such as mentor teacher feedback, difficult to disentangle. Additionally, the diverse nature of clinical experiences results in varied exposure to meaningful classroom events.

A second challenge for researchers investigating the effects of reflection activities during clinical experiences is the ability to collect data in actual classroom settings where teacher candidates are instructing children. For example, Andrews and colleagues (2010), conducted a study on reflective practices, however the teacher candidates were reflecting on role-playing classroom experiences where they taught their peers. The authors concluded this approach was not an effective stand-alone teacher preparation technique (Andrews, Bobo, & Spurlock, 2010). Additionally, Chuanjun and Chunmei (2011) investigated the authenticity of changes that resulted from reflection activities where teacher candidates taught in controlled settings with small numbers of children. The authors concluded this approach was artificial and limited, stressing the need for authentic classroom experiences and practice in conjunction with reflection activities.

A final challenge of reflection activity research is how to control for unintended consequences associated with introducing video-recording equipment (e.g., camera, smartphone, laptop, or tablet) into authentic classroom contexts. Teacher candidates have reported anxiety about being recorded while teaching and to control for the potential moderating effect of being video-recorded, researchers have opted to include video-recording equipment across both treatment and comparison conditions (e.g., Andrews, Bobo, & Spurlock, 2010; Nagro, deBettencourt, Rosenberg, Carran, & Weiss, 2017). Pianta and colleagues (2008) noted several other challenges when introducing video-recording equipment into a classroom including: (a) inconsistent availability of video-recording resources; (b) technological limitations of sharing video evidence with teacher educators; (c) varied comfort levels with computer-based and mobile technology as well as internet use, and; (d) differing parent consent requirements for including children in the teaching videos. These challenges highlight the limitations of conducting large-scale randomized control trials to investigate the effects of video analysis on teacher candidates' reflective abilities. As computer-based and mobile technologies continue to improve, however, capturing video evidence for reflection activities may become more feasible during teacher preparation clinical experiences.

SOLUTIONS, RECOMMENDATIONS, AND FUTURE DIRECTIONS

In closing, this section summarizes recommendations for teacher educators looking for ways to include reflection activities in field-based teacher preparation experiences. In addition, the authors provide recommendations for teacher education researchers searching for effective ways to study reflection activities and measure reflective ability.

Recommendations for Teacher Educators

1. Provide specific and direct guidance to teacher candidates engaging in reflection activities. This guidance will support the development of a professional lens by which candidates can view themselves as change agents and more broadly improve their understanding of the profession.
2. Define the construct of reflective ability. The definition will add clarity for teacher candidates who are developing their professional skills in this area.
3. Introduce a rubric or checklist including clearly defined elements for reflection such as those provided in an evaluation framework. This should include levels or dimensions of reflective practice to strive for when writing about teaching experiences. This rubric will help teacher candidates develop an orderly, focused approach to their reflective practice.
4. Include video evidence as a necessary part of the reflection process. The video will provide teacher candidates with concrete data by which to become deeply immersed in self-confrontation and self-evaluation.
5. Facilitate reflection activities in authentic clinical experiences. This facilitation will optimize genuine learning experiences for teacher candidates who likely lack a depth of prior teaching experiences from which to reflect.
6. Use a systematic approach to scheduling, documenting, and analyzing reflection activities, while recognizing reflection activities are one of many clinical experience activities in which teacher candidates engage. This approach will help clarify how such activities impact candidate growth.

Recommendations for Teacher Education Researchers

1. As recommended above, clearly define the construct of reflective ability to provide the foundation for high quality research and measurement.
2. Set a reflection activity schedule a priori that is frequent enough to improve candidates' comfort level with the process, prompt and then capture changes, and maintain feasibility for candidates who likely have additional assignments during clinical experiences (e.g., once or twice a week).
3. Consider any unintended consequences of technical decisions such as introducing video-recording equipment into a classroom, the length of video clips, and who and what is captured on video.
4. Provide candidates with a timeline of reflection activities before beginning their field experiences so they are aware of the procedures including standard processes for collecting, storing, and sharing video data.
5. Require candidates to log their process to track alignment between the intended and actual reflection activities.
6. Recognize and address the implications of selected settings (i.e., college classroom with peers, controlled small group environment, authentic classroom settings) from which reflection activities stem.
7. Use a multi-faceted approach that may require both qualitative and quantitative analyses to understand changes in both reflective practice and reflective ability.
8. Develop methods to account for the fact that reflection activities are one part of a larger teacher preparation curriculum. Consider ways to systematically document other clinical activities, such as seminar discussions, to better understand the impact of individual reflection activities.

CONCLUSION

Teacher educators agree that clinical field experiences and reflective practices, in particular, are integral components of teacher preparation programs. Given the rising popularity of using reflective practice as a measure of teacher candidates' development, continued efforts to understand how to guide reflective practices that lead to genuine teacher growth remain important. Teacher candidates first need to be taught what reflective practice is, why it matters, and how to engage in reflection activities. After these foundational steps, candidates can be expected to demonstrate growth in their ability to reflect across deeper dimensions of reflective practice. Teacher educators need to continue to study methods for measuring the impacts of reflection activities on teacher candidates' professional development during field-based experiences. This chapter serves as both a summary of what we currently know and a call to action to move this body of work forward.

REFERENCES

Ajayi, L. L. (2016). How intern teachers use classroom video for self-reflection on teaching. *The Educational Forum*, *80*(1), 79–94. doi:10.1080/00131725.2015.1102365

Allen, M., Coble, C., & Crowe, D. (2014, September). *Building an evidence-based system for teacher preparation*. Teacher Preparation Analytics. Retrieved from http://caepnet.org/accreditation/caep-accreditation/caep-accreditation-resources

Andrews, A., Bobo, L., & Spurlock, A. (2010). Use of video feedback in the training of pre-service teachers. *Journal of Instructional Pedagogies*, *2*, 1–11.

Bain, C., & Hasio, C. (2011). Authentic learning experience prepares preservice students to teach art to children with special needs. *Art Education*, *64*(2), 33–39. doi:10.1080/00043125.2011.11519118

Beck, R. J., King, A., & Marshall, S. K. (2002). Effects of videocase construction on teacher candidates' observations of teaching. *Journal of Experimental Education*, *70*(4), 345–361. doi:10.1080/00220970209599512

Blanton, L. P., Pugach, M. C., & Florian, L. (2011). *Preparing general education teachers to improve outcomes for students with disabilities*. Washington, DC: American Association of Colleges for Teacher Education (AACTE) and National Center for Learning Disabilities (NCLD). Retrieved from https://secure.aacte.org/apps/rl/resource.php

Borg, W. R., Kallenbach, W., Morris, M., & Friebel, A. (1969). Videotape feedback and microteaching in a teacher training model. *Journal of Experimental Education*, *37*(4), 9–16. doi:10.1080/00220973.1969.11011141

Borko, H., Jacobs, J., Eiteljorg, E., & Pittman, M. E. (2008). Video as a tool for fostering productive discussions in mathematics professional development. *Teaching and Teacher Education*, *24*(2), 417–436. doi:10.1016/j.tate.2006.11.012

Bower, M., Cavanagh, M., Moloney, R., & Dao, M. (2011). Developing communication competence using an online video reflection system: Pre-service teachers' experiences. *Asia-Pacific Journal of Teacher Education*, *39*(4), 311–326. doi:10.1080/1359866X.2011.614685

Brownell, M. T., Ross, D. D., Colon, E. P., & McCallum, C. L. (2005). Critical features of special education teacher preparation: A comparison with general teacher education. *The Journal of Special Education, 38*(4), 242–252. doi:10.1177/00224669050380040601

Calandra, B., Brantley-Dias, L., & Dias, M. (2006). Using digital video for professional development in urban schools: A teacher candidates experience with reflection. *Journal of Computing in Teacher Education, 22,* 137–145.

Calandra, B., Brantley-Dias, L., Lee, J. K., & Fox, D. L. (2009). Using video editing to cultivate novice teachers' practice. *Journal of Research on Technology in Education, 42*(1), 73–94. doi:10.1080/15391 523.2009.10782542

Calandra, B., Gurvitch, R., & Lund, J. (2008). An exploratory study of digital video editing as a tool for teacher preparation. *Technology and Teacher Education, 16*(2), 137–153.

Chuanjun, H., & Chunmei, Y. (2011). Exploring authenticity of microteaching in pre-service teacher education programmes. *Teaching Education, 22*(3), 291–302. doi:10.1080/10476210.2011.590588

Conderman, G., Morin, J., & Stephens, J. (2005). Special education student teaching practices. *Preventing School Failure, 49*(3), 5–10. doi:10.3200/PSFL.49.3.5-10

Connelly, V., & Graham, S. (2009). Student teaching and teacher attrition in special education. *Teacher Education and Special Education, 32*(3), 257–269. doi:10.1177/0888406409339472

Council for Exceptional Children. (2012). *Initial preparation standards with elaborations.* Retrieved from http://www.cec.sped.org/Standards/Special-Educator-Professional-Preparation

Council for Exceptional Children. (2015). *What every special educator must know: Ethics, standards and guidelines.* Retrieved from http://pubs.cec.sped.org/p6166/

Council of Chief State School Officers. (2011, April). *Interstate teacher assessment and support consortium (Intasc) model core teaching standards: A resource for state dialogue.* Washington, DC: Author.

Council of Chief State School Officers. (2017). *InTASC model core teaching standards and learning progressions for teachers 1.0.* Retrieved from https://www.ccsso.org/resource-library/intasc-model-core-teaching-standards-and-learning-progressions-teachers-10

Crawford, S., O'Reilly, R., & Luttrell, S. (2012). Assessing the effects of integrating the reflective framework for teaching in physical education (RFTPE) on the teaching and learning of undergraduate sport studies and physical education students. *Reflective Practice, 13*(1), 115–129. doi:10.1080/14623 943.2011.626025

Darling-Hammond, L., & Bransford, J. (Eds.). (2005). *Preparing teachers for a changing world: what teachers should learn and be able to do. National Academy of Education, Committee on Teacher Education.* San Francisco: Jossey Bass.

deBettencourt, L. U., & Nagro, S. A. (2018). Tracking special education teacher candidates' reflective practices over time to understand the role of theory in clinically-based teacher preparation. *Remedial and Special Education.* doi:10.1177/0741932518762573

DeCuir-Gunby, J. T., Marshall, P. L., & McCulloch, A. W. (2012). Using mixed methods to analyze video data: A mathematics teacher professional development example. *Journal of Mixed Methods Research*, *6*(3), 199–216. doi:10.1177/1558689811421174

Deniz, J. (2012). Video recorded feedback for self-regulation of prospective music teachers in piano lessons. *Journal of Instructional Psychology*, *39*, 17–25.

Dewey, J. (1933). *How we think*. Buffalo, NY: Prometheus Books.

Etscheidt, S., Curran, C. M., & Sawyer, C. M. (2012). Promoting reflection in teacher preparation programs: A multilevel model. *Teacher Education and Special Education*, *35*(1), 7–26. doi:10.1177/0888406411420887

Finley, L. (2008). Reflecting on 'reflective practice. *Practice-based Professional Learning Centre*, *52*, 1–27.

Fox, D. L., Brantley-Dias, L., & Calandra, B. (2007, November). *Promoting preservice teachers' reflective practice through digital video and critical incident analysis in secondary English education*. Paper presented at the 57th National Reading Conference, Austin, TX.

Gelfuso, A., Dennis, D. V., & Parker, A. (2015). Turning teacher education upside down: Enacting the inversion of teacher preparation through the symbiotic relationship of theory and practice. *Professional Educator*, *39*(2), 1–16.

Gibbs, G. (1988). *Learning by doing: A guide to teaching and learning methods. Further Education Unit*. Oxford, UK: Oxford Brookes University.

Gore, J., & Zeichner, K. (1991). Action research and reflective teaching in preservice teacher education: A case study from the United States. *Teaching and Teacher Education*, *7*(2), 119–136. doi:10.1016/0742-051X(91)90022-H

Griffin, C. C., Winn, J. A., Otis-Wilborn, A., & Kilgore, K. L. (2003). New teacher induction in special education. [Executive Summary]. Center on Personnel Studies in Special Education, University of Florida.

Grimmet, P. P., MacKinnon, A. M., Erickson, G., & Riecken, T. J. (1990). Reflective practice in teacher education. In R. Clift, W. R. Houston, & M. C. Pugach (Eds.), *Encouraging reflective practice in education* (pp. 20–38). New York, NY: Teachers College Press.

Haefner-Berg, M., & Smith, J. P. (1996). Using videotapes to improve teaching. *Music Educators Journal*, *82*(4), 31–37. doi:10.2307/3398914

Harford, J., & MacRuairc, G. (2008). Engaging student teachers in meaningful reflective practice. *Teaching and Teacher Education*, *24*(7), 1884–1892. doi:10.1016/j.tate.2008.02.010

Horvitz, B. S., & Paul Vellom, R. (2012). Using blended learning to enhance reflective practice among science teacher candidates. *National Teacher Education Journal*, *5*(3), 77–83.

Jay, J. K., & Johnson, K. L. (2002). Capturing complexity: A typology of reflective practice for teacher education. *Teaching and Teacher Education*, *18*(1), 73–85. doi:10.1016/S0742-051X(01)00051-8

Jenkins, J. J. (2014). Pre-service teachers' observations of experienced teachers. *Physical Educator*, *71*, 303–319.

Kalk, K., Luik, P., Taimalu, M., & Täht, K. (2014). Validity and reliability of two instruments to measure reflection: A confirmatory study. *Journal of the Humanities and Social Sciences, 18*, 121–134. doi:10.3176/tr.2014.2.02

Laverick, V. T. (2017). Secondary teachers' understanding and use of reflection: An exploratory study. *American Secondary Education, 45*(2), 56–68.

Leko, M. M., Brownell, M. T., Sindelar, P. T., & Murphy, K. (2012). Promoting special education preservice teacher expertise. *Focus on Exceptional Children, 44*(7), 1–16. doi:10.17161/fec.v44i7.6684 PMID:23997274

Maheady, L., Smith, C., & Jabot, M. (2014). Field experiences and instructional pedagogies in teacher education: What we know, don't know, and must learn soon. In P. T. Sindelar, E. D. McCray, M. T. Brownell, & B. Lignugaris-Kraft (Eds.), *Handbook of research on special education teacher preparation* (pp. 161–177). New York, NY: Routledge.

Martin, F., & Ertzberger, J. (2013). Here and now mobile learning: An experimental study on the use of mobile technology. *Computers & Education, 68*, 76–85. doi:10.1016/j.compedu.2013.04.021

McDuffie, A. R., Foote, M. Q., Bolson, C., Turner, E. E., Aguirre, J. M., Bartell, T. G., ... Land, T. (2014). Using video analysis to support prospective K-8 teachers' noticing of students' multiple mathematical knowledge bases. *Journal of Mathematics Teacher Education, 17*(3), 245–270. doi:10.100710857-013-9257-0

McFadden, J., Ellis, J., Anwar, T., & Roehrig, G. (2014). Beginning science teachers' use of a digital video annotation tool to promote reflective practices. *Journal of Science Education and Technology, 23*(3), 458–470. doi:10.100710956-013-9476-2

Moore, R. (2003). Reexamining the field experiences of teacher candidate. *Journal of Teacher Education, 54*(1), 31–42. doi:10.1177/0022487102238656

Nagro, S. A., & deBettencourt, L. U. (2017). Reviewing special education teacher preparation field experience placements, activities, and research: Do we know the difference maker? *Teacher Education Quarterly, 44*(3), 7–33.

Nagro, S. A., deBettencourt, L. U., Rosenberg, M. S., Carran, D. T., & Weiss, M. P. (2017). The effects of guided video analysis on teacher candidates' reflective ability and instructional skills. *Teacher Education and Special Education, 40*(1), 7–25. doi:10.1177/0888406416680469

National Council for Accreditation of Teacher Education. (2010, November). *Transforming teacher education through clinical practice: A national strategy to prepare effective teachers.* Washington, DC: Author. Retrieved from http://www.ncate.org/Public/researchreports/NCAtEinitiatives/BlueribbonPanel/tabid/715/Default.aspx

Pearson Education. (2014). *edTPA fact sheet.* Retrieved from http://edtpa.aacte.org/about-edtpa

Pfeiffer, J. W., & Ballow, A. C. (1988). *Using structured experiences in human resource development.* San Diego, CA: University Associates.

Pianta, R. C., Mashburn, A. J., Downer, J. T., Hamre, B. K., & Justice, L. (2008). Effects of web-mediated professional development resources on teacher-child interactions in pre-kindergarten classrooms. *Early Childhood Research Quarterly*, *23*(4), 431–451. doi:10.1016/j.ecresq.2008.02.001 PMID:25717217

Pultorak, E. G. (1996). Following the developmental process of reflection in novice teachers: Three years of investigation. *Journal of Teacher Education*, *47*(4), 283–291. doi:10.1177/0022487196474006

Recchia, S. L., & Puig, V. I. (2011). Challenges and inspirations: Student teachers' experiences in early childhood special education classrooms. *Teacher Education and Special Education*, *34*(2), 133–151. doi:10.1177/0888406410387444

Robinson, L., & Kelley, B. (2007). Developing reflective thought in preservice educators: Utilizing role-plays and digital video. *Journal of Special Education Technology*, *22*(2), 31–43. doi:10.1177/016264340702200203

Rodgers, C. (2002). Defining reflection: Another look at john dewey and reflective thinking. *Teachers College Record*, *104*(4), 842–866. doi:10.1111/1467-9620.00181

Rosaen, C. L., Lundeberg, M., Cooper, M., Fritzen, A., & Terpstra, M. (2008). Noticing noticing: How does investigation of video records change how teachers reflect on their experiences? *Journal of Teacher Education*, *59*(4), 347–360. doi:10.1177/0022487108322128

Santagata, R., & Angelici, G. (2010). Studying the impact of the lesson analysis framework on preservice teachers' abilities to reflect on videos of classroom teaching. *Journal of Teacher Education*, *61*(4), 339–349. doi:10.1177/0022487110369555

Sayeski, K., & Paulsen, K. (2012). Student teacher evaluations of cooperating teachers as indices of effective mentoring. *Teacher Education Quarterly*, *39*, 117–130.

Schon, D. A. (1983). *The reflective practitioner*. New York, NY: Basic Books.

Schon, D. A. (1987). *Educating the reflective practitioner: Toward a new design for teaching and learning in the professions*. San Francisco, CA: Jossey-Bass.

Seidel, T., Stürmer, K., Blomberg, G., Kobarg, M., & Schwindt, K. (2011). Teachers learning from analysis of videotaped classroom situations: Does it make a difference whether teachers observe their own teaching or that of others? *Teaching and Teacher Education*, *27*(2), 259–267. doi:10.1016/j.tate.2010.08.009

Sherin, M., & Linsenmeier, K. (2011). Pause, rewind, reflect. *Journal of Staff Development*, *32*(5), 38–41.

Sherin, M. G., & van Es, E. A. (2005). Using video to support teachers' ability to notice classroom interactions. *Technology and Teacher Education*, *13*, 475–491.

Sherin, M. G., & van Es, E. A. (2009). Effects of video club participation on teachers' professional vision. *Journal of Teacher Education*, *60*(1), 20–37. doi:10.1177/0022487108328155

Sindelar, P. T., Brownell, M. T., & Billingsley, B. (2010). Special education teacher education research: Current status and future directions. *Teacher Education and Special Education*, *33*(1), 8–24. doi:10.1177/0888406409358593

Sparks-Langer, G. M., & Colton, A. B. (1991). Synthesis of research on teachers' reflective thinking. *Educational Leadership, 48*(6), 37–44.

Stanley, C. (1998). A framework for teacher reflectivity. *TESOL Quarterly, 32*(3), 584–591. doi:10.2307/3588129

Stockero, S. (2008). Differences in preservice mathematics teachers' reflective abilities attributable to use of a video case curriculum. *Journal of Technology and Teacher Education, 16*, 483–509.

The Danielson Group. (2017). *The framework*. Retrieved from https://www.danielsongroup.org/framework/

Tripp, T. R., & Rich, P. J. (2012). The influence of video analysis on the process of teacher change. *Teaching and Teacher Education, 28*(5), 728–739. doi:10.1016/j.tate.2012.01.011

Valli, L. (Ed.). (1990). *Reflective teacher education: Cases and critiques*. Albany, NY: State University of New York Press.

van Es, E. A. (2010). Viewer discussion is advised: Video clubs focus teacher discussion on student learning. *Journal of Staff Development, 31*, 54–58.

van Es, E. A., & Sherin, M. G. (2010). The influence of video clubs on teachers' thinking and practice. *Math Teacher Education, 13*(2), 155–176. doi:10.100710857-009-9130-3

Van Manen, M. (1977). Linking ways of knowing with ways of being practical. *Curriculum Inquiry, 6*(3), 205–228. doi:10.1080/03626784.1977.11075533

Van Manen, M. (1991). Reflectivity and the pedagogical movement: The normativity of pedagogical thinking and acting. *Journal of Curriculum Studies, 23*(6), 507–536. doi:10.1080/0022027910230602

Ward, J. R., & McCotter, S. S. (2004). Reflection as a visible outcome for preservice teachers. *Teaching and Teacher Education, 20*(3), 243–257. doi:10.1016/j.tate.2004.02.004

Wellington, B., & Austin, P. (1996). Orientations to reflective practice. *Educational Research, 38*(3), 307–316. doi:10.1080/0013188960380304

Wiens, P. D., Hessberg, K., LoCasale-Crouch, J., & DeCoster, J. (2013). Using a standardized video-based assessment in a university teacher education program to examine preservice teachers' knowledge related to effective teaching. *Teaching and Teacher Education, 33*, 24–33. doi:10.1016/j.tate.2013.01.010

Zeichner, K., & Liston, D. (1987). Teaching student teachers to reflect. *Harvard Educational Review, 57*(1), 23–48. doi:10.17763/haer.57.1.j18v7162275t1w3w

ADDITIONAL READING

Admiraal, W., Hoeksma, M., van de Kamp, M.-T., & van Duin, G. (2011). Assessment of teacher competence using video portfolios: Reliability, construct validity, and consequential validity. *Teaching and Teacher Education, 27*(6), 1019–1028. doi:10.1016/j.tate.2011.04.002

Cantrell, S., & Kane, T. J. (2013). *Ensuring fair and reliable measures of effective teaching culminating findings from the met project's three-year study* [Research Brief]. Retrieved from http://metproject.org/downloads/MET_Ensuring_Fair_and_Reliable_Measures_Practitioner_Brief.pdf

Dieker, L. A., & Monda-Amaya, L. E. (1997). Using problem solving and effective teaching frameworks to promote reflective thinking in preservice special educators. *Teacher Education and Special Education, 20*(1), 22–36. doi:10.1177/088840649702000104

Gun, B. (2011). Quality self-reflection through reflection training. *ELT Journal English Language Teachers Journal, 65*, 126–135.

O'Brian, M., Stoner, J., Appel, K., & House, J. J. (2007). The first field experience: Perspectives of preservice and cooperating teachers. *Teacher Education and Special Education, 30*(4), 264–275. doi:10.1177/088840640703000406

Osipova, A., Prichard, B., Boardman, A. G., Kiely, M. T., & Carroll, P. E. (2011). Refocusing the lens: Enhancing elementary special education reading instruction through video self-reflection. *Learning Disabilities Research & Practice, 26*(3), 158–171. doi:10.1111/j.1540-5826.2011.00335.x

Rock, M. L., Spooner, F., Nagro, S. A., Vasquez, E., Dunn, C., Leko, M., ... Jones, J. L. (2016). 21st century change drivers: Considerations for constructing transformative models of special education teacher development. *Teacher Education and Special Education, 39*(2), 98–120. doi:10.1177/0888406416640634

Snoeyink, R. (2010). Using video self-analysis to improve the withitness of student teachers. *Journal of Digital Learning in Teacher Education, 26*(3), 101–110.

van Es, E. A., Tunney, J., Goldsmith, L. T., & Seago, N. (2014). A framework for the facilitation of teachers' analysis of video. *Journal of Teacher Education, 65*(4), 340–356. doi:10.1177/0022487114534266

Ward, J. R., & McCotter, S. S. (2004). Reflection as a visible outcome for preservice teachers. *Teaching and Teacher Education, 20*(3), 243–257. doi:10.1016/j.tate.2004.02.004

KEY TERMS AND DEFINITIONS

Reflection Rubric: Combines clearly defined elements for reflection such as those in an evaluation framework with levels or dimensions of reflective practice to strive for when writing about teaching experiences serving as both a guide for reflection activities and a method for systematically measuring reflective abilities.

Reflective Ability: The quantifiable ability to critically review, analyze, and evaluate a situation in order to learn from the experience and apply such insights to future situations.

Reflective Practice: Reflecting-on-action, or *reflective practice*, is defined broadly as reviewing past experiences with intentionality for the purpose of gaining new insights.

Video Analysis: Teacher candidates watch video evidence of their own teaching to critically examine their actions as part of a reflective process.

Chapter 25
Learning to Teach:
Cultivating Practice in a Mentor–Candidate Relationship

Gabrièle Abowd Damico
Indiana University, USA

Lawrence J. Ruich
Indiana University – Purdue University Columbus, USA

John M. Andrésen
Indiana University, USA

Gretchen Butera
Indiana University, USA

ABSTRACT

This chapter describes an approach to field experience that provides the opportunity for a long-term relationship between a teacher candidate and their supervising teacher in a teacher preparation program called Community of Teachers (CoT). CoT emphasizes the importance of this relationship in several ways. The program empowers teacher candidates and their mentors to choose one another. In addition, the length of the field experience provides an opportunity for teacher candidates to more deeply engage in the process of becoming a teacher within the context of a classroom and a school that they come to know well. A triadic relationship between the teacher candidate, supervising teacher, and university supervisor provides the opportunity for support as well as evaluative feedback for the teacher candidate. Benefits also accrue to the supervising teacher.

INTRODUCTION

Field experience is touted as one of the most important components of successful teacher preparation. During field experiences, teacher candidates identify and develop lessons and materials for classroom activities as they facilitate classroom routines and address classroom management. They work with students from culturally diverse backgrounds and those who have specific learning differences (Hanline, 2010;

DOI: 10.4018/978-1-5225-6249-8.ch025

Villegas, 2007). While participating in field experience, teacher candidates are given the opportunity to apply what they have learned in coursework in an authentic context (Glazer & Hannafin, 2006). Field experiences are often the first opportunity teacher candidates have to learn about their own teaching propensities. They are provided the opportunity to try out who they may become as teachers. They ask themselves if they like the duties and responsibilities the role entails.

Teacher candidates best learn how to be teachers when university teacher preparation is complemented by extensive experience in a field setting under a master teacher (Zeichner, 2012).

Learning to teach is a complex, emotional, and demanding undertaking. Simply providing teacher candidates with access to a classroom during field experience does not guarantee that they will emerge from the experience with skills needed to successfully teach in their own classroom. Furthermore, field experience alone does not provide the opportunity for teacher candidates to reflect about themselves in the midst of their professional development. Zeichner's (2012) emphasis on the importance of the master teacher in a field setting is well noted, several other strategies to ensure that teacher candidates derive benefit from field experience are also critical to note.

The purpose of this chapter is to describe an approach to teacher preparation that encourages teacher candidates to reflect about their professional growth as they strive to become teachers and includes a rather unique approach to field experience. At our university there are three secondary teacher preparation programs. Our approach is called Community of Teachers (CoT). Students participate in long-term engagement in the field with a teacher who mentors them about teaching, and this is considered a cornerstone of the program. CoT emphasizes the importance of this relationship by empowering teacher candidates and their mentors to choose one another rather than placing teacher candidates in classrooms. This approach to field experience also differs from field experiences in many teacher education programs in that it requires teacher candidates to attend their mentor's classroom one day a week throughout their preparation. Finally, the approach also includes two other aspects of teacher preparation that are viewed as essential: 1.) a weekly seminar that provides the opportunity that socializes teacher candidates into the professions and allows them to practice teaching skills and; 2.) a professional performance portfolio that documents teacher candidates' developmental processes in becoming teachers. It is important to note that teacher candidates are guided throughout their preparation by a CoT faculty member who also serves as their seminar facilitator and supervises field experience and student teaching.

COMMUNITY OF TEACHERS

Community of Teachers was designed to address some of the shortcomings of traditional teacher preparation. According to the founders of CoT, Drs. Tom Gregory and Susan Klein, limitations of typical teacher preparation included the relatively short duration of field experiences and the limited time spent deeply engaging with the work of a teacher (T. Gregory, personal communication, September 14, 2016). In addition, too often teacher candidates spent time in their field experience simply observing instead of taking the opportunity to enact some of the skills they were learning in university coursework. Finally, the seemingly random assignment of mentor teachers and candidates to each other, and the lack of preparation for mentor teachers to work effectively with teacher candidates was also considered problematic. Importantly, the founders of CoT, influenced by the work of Frances F. Fuller (1969), noted that too often teacher education does not address the personal concerns of teacher candidates until rather late in the process.

CoT responds to these limitations by providing candidates with a communal format that puts candidates and their concerns about teaching at the forefront of the program. In order to support students' agency in the process of becoming a teacher, CoT emphasizes self-directed learning, shared responsibility for the community, learning through experience, and performance-based assessment. The mission of the program, as outlined in the CoT Handbook (2015), is to develop teachers who will advocate for change as needed, both within their classrooms, in the community, and in the educational system as a whole (see Appendix A).

Important in this process is the early opportunity for teacher candidates to be in classrooms where they work closely with practicing teachers. A key feature of CoT is for teacher candidates to find a practicing teacher who will mentor them through the entirety of their program. These mentor-candidate partnerships may last several years. Through this relationship, prospective teachers are immersed into a classroom and a school community in which they complete their student teaching at the end of their program.

At its core, the Community of Teachers' aim is to cultivate a community of practice where teacher candidates gain teaching competencies and work toward a teaching license. In CoT, we concur with E. & B. Wenger-Trayner's (2015) description as follows: "Communities of practice are groups of people who share a concern or passion for something they do and learn how to do it better as they interact regularly." Teacher candidates and their mentors are encouraged to set their own goals and solve teaching problems in the field, rather than performing a series of activities that relate to teaching competencies as envisioned by others. Key aspects of this democratically run program are two student-led program wide committees: Lead and Recruitment. Lead's focus centers on student government and gives students decision-making power in how the program runs. This includes organizing two community-wide meetings each semester, which focus on current interests in education, often including local education professionals. In an ongoing effort to fortify numbers of students in the program, Recruitment works to attract new members to the community. The recruitment committee also plans a mentor appreciation dinner which occurs each spring.

Seminar

Weekly seminars in CoT are comprised of teacher candidates who represent all stages of preparation including both undergraduate and graduate students who may be beginners in the program, about to complete it, or somewhere in between. The seminar includes teacher candidates focusing on secondary content areas licensed in the state of Indiana (social studies, science, language arts and mathematics) and several K-12 licensing areas (art, music, world languages, physical and special education). During seminar, teacher candidates take turns leading planned lessons. In this way, seminar activities provide the opportunity for teacher candidates to practice their teaching. More experienced seminar leaders are paired with seminar "newbies" to plan and implement their activities, and the faculty facilitator provides guidance both before and during the session. They also encourage session leaders to seek peer feedback from the seminar to inform the development of their teaching practice. Activities examine various educational themes, pedagogical theories, and instructional strategies focusing on a topic selected by the students in the seminar each semester.

There are also consistent weekly activities within a three-hour seminar session. Many of these were originally adapted from protocols of the Critical Friends Group, a registered trademark of the National School Reform Faculty (2014). "Connections" and "Notes from the Field" are opening activities during which individuals reflect, within the context of seminar, upon a thought, a story, an insight, a question, or a feeling that they are carrying with them when arriving to seminar and connect it to their teaching (NSRF, 2014).

Routine activities in seminar also include "Nuts and Bolts" during which information about assignments and events, program requirements, and other logistical information are provided. Finally, session leaders demonstrate a teaching resource or present a current event occurring in the field of education, which is then discussed. This may include a list of suggestions for how, when, and why a teacher might use a particular resource or why a current event is especially relevant to them and to the group.

A bulk of the seminar's time following the routine events involves candidate-created lessons related to the week's readings. The idea is to deepen understanding of the readings, present and practice various instructional strategies, and contribute to building community within the group. A typical activity includes learning objectives in order to focus the group on what is to be learned or understood from the session. Seminar concludes with an evaluation in which the leaders ask their seminar to provide feedback on the activities by responding to questions. These include how the activities relate to one's practice as a teacher, particularly in terms of how their readings and the activities relate to what they are experiencing in the field.

A recent seminar session illustrates how this process works. Millie, an art education student in CoT, partnered with Anna who is majoring in special education. The readings for the week dealt with student resistance. Prior to seminar, Millie and Anna met with their seminar facilitator to discuss learning objectives and the lesson plan for class, brainstorming ideas, and making use of the content area knowledge each student possessed. In this lesson, Millie explained artistic critique of a picture that depicted student resistance to help deepen her fellow students' understanding of the reading for the week. Anna arranged the students into small groups to discuss how they might teach this activity to high school students emphasizing the ways in which the activity might be differentiated for learners with disabilities. Afterwards, each small group reported out to the whole seminar. Many of the suggestions were innovative and one of the students explained the principles of Universal Design for Learning to the seminar as a method of ensuring that lessons were more accessible. At the end of the seminar, both Millie and Anna collected brief evaluations from their peers about the activities they had planned.

In addition to learning about teaching in seminar, CoT candidates demonstrate teaching competencies by collecting evidence of it in a portfolio. Millie and Anna added the lesson plans they developed and their peers' evaluation in their respective portfolios; several other students also used this lesson as evidence for their portfolio.

Portfolio

Teacher candidates earn their respective licenses by presenting accumulated evidence in a performance-based professional portfolio that faculty judge to demonstrate that a candidate is prepared to teach. In the portfolio, teacher competencies are identified as individualized "expectations" based on those outlined by the Interstate New Teacher Assessment and Support Consortium (INTASC). Originating in 1987 and sponsored by the Council of Chief State School Officers (CCSSO), INTASC is a consortium of state and national education agencies and organizations focused on the preparation, licensure, and professional development of teachers (CCSSO, 2016; Darling-Hammond & Berry, 2006). Descriptions of each portfolio expectation were developed by a CoT committee comprised of students and faculty and are based on INTASC principles. CoT portfolio expectations have evolved over the course of the program's history. Currently, the CoT portfolio consists of sixteen expectations, which are outlined in the CoT Handbook (2015) (see Appendix B). The portfolio evidence for each teacher candidate for each expectation includes an explanation of why the various pieces of evidence are included in the candidate's portfolio. In addition, the expectation includes a personal narrative (called a reflection or commentary) about the candidates' professional development. Candidates describe their evidence, tell why it is significant, and discuss how they will utilize this information in the future.

For the purposes of supporting the CoT teacher candidates in their reflective process, the CoT handbook outlines a framework labeled "What, So What, Now What" (CoT Handbook, 2015). Within each expectation, CoT expects teacher-candidates to be able to explain what the specific piece of evidence is and the source of the evidence. After a thorough explanation, the teacher-candidates then explain why the evidence is a worthwhile example of their teaching competence. Finally, CoT teacher candidates describe how they will utilize this knowledge in their future practice. For example, Millie and Anna inserted the lesson plans and evaluation from the seminar session they led, explained what the evidence was, why it was significant evidence, and how they would use what they had learned in the future.

In another example of how the portfolio is used in CoT, Marvin, a special education teacher with a temporary emergency license, developed a lesson for his special education classroom to teach reading and writing. He used artifacts from this activity to demonstrate his competence for the expectation Teaching Reading and Writing. Marvin attached his lesson plan to the portfolio and wrote a description of the various instructional strategies he used to teach students a specific writing task. After his description, Marvin wrote about how his lesson plan illustrated his ability to employ a variety of instructional strategies. Finally, Marvin wrote about different ways he could implement this instructional strategy, including how he might alter the strategy based on the academic needs of the students in the classroom. Through this "What, So What, Now What" process, Marvin explained the decisions he made as a teacher and demonstrated his ability to be reflective. Each expectation is evaluated with regard to three criteria: 1) the source of the evidence; 2) the context in which the evidence was collected, and; 3) the coherence and reflection of the expectation overall (see Appendix C).

Sources of evidence in a portfolio expectation include personal experiences that may be captured in compiled artifacts, statements from others (i.e., observation notes from the seminar facilitator or letters of recommendation from the mentor), or journal entries. Teacher candidates collect evidence through a variety of sources, including university coursework, school settings, extracurricular activities, church youth group settings, summer camps, or employment in a variety of fields. Students are able to use any source they deem appropriate as long as they make a clear connection to the expectation and explain how this experience or event influenced their development as a teacher.

Contexts in a portfolio expectation refer to the places where the teacher candidate experienced events that relate to evidence. In general, actual experiences teaching in a middle or high school provide more compelling evidence and are required for most expectations to be judged as ready to teach. However, teaching in non-school settings, mentoring another person, formal presentations or participation at a meeting, and class assignments or presentations within a university course are also viewed as important opportunities for professional growth and are often included as evidence.

Coherence and reflection relate to other aspects of a teacher candidate's portfolio. Coherence is the sense of connection within an expectation and across the portfolio. Reflection relates to the thoughtfulness about teaching that is apparent in the portfolio.

The CoT portfolio evolves over time and is personalized. Chip, who is preparing to become an English teacher, had considerable teaching experience prior to entrance into the program, having worked as a cadet teacher assisting a junior high school special education teacher. At the beginning of his CoT experience, Chip used evidence from his experience as a cadet teacher to create an early portfolio expectation. However, as he progressed through the program, Chip began deleting old pieces of evidence based on his high school experiences and replaced them with evidence of the teaching proficiencies he had gained in his CoT mentor's classroom. In his mentor's classroom, Chip was involved in planning and instructing, and this helped provide evidence for his expectations. Chip transitioned his portfolio expectations into more recent examples of his competency by utilizing the experiences he had through university courses and his mentor teacher's classroom.

Throughout the program, faculty review candidate's expectations. Submitted expectations are evaluated on a three-point scale: formative (F), substantial progress (SP), and ready to teach (RtT). Chip's early work was judged as substantial progress. As he added evidence from his field setting, especially during his student teaching, his portfolio was enriched, and this expectation was judged as ready to teach. To support the development of teacher candidates and ensure that they are at a proficient level in all expectations by the end of their student teaching experience, CoT faculty members evaluate portfolio expectations on an ongoing basis using a recursive process. Each semester, teacher candidates submit a minimum of two portfolio expectations, faculty members provide feedback, and students resubmit with revised evidence as needed.

Portfolio work serves to mark the progress of teacher candidates as they move through the program. Satisfactory progress in the portfolio also marks milestones in the School of Education. Ten of the sixteen expectations must be rated at substantial progress before a teacher candidate begins student teaching. Upon successful completion of student teaching, teacher candidates earn a teaching license by completing their portfolio. Two CoT faculty members review all sixteen expectations and judge that the portfolio demonstrates a candidate's preparedness to enter the teaching profession.

CoT places inherent value on learning in the field in collaboration with more experienced professionals who agree to mentor teacher candidates. This is emphasized both in seminar and throughout the portfolio process. A critical task for all CoT teacher candidates is to seek and find a mentor in their content area(s) by the end of their second semester in the program. Depending on when in their university career a teacher candidate enters the program, they may complete up to six semesters of weekly (six hours) fieldwork with their mentor; the program requires at least two semesters of this field experience prior to student teaching.

Figure 1 represents the three overlapping components of the program: the weekly seminar, a portfolio that details the competencies of teacher candidates as they relate to teaching, and a long-term field experience with a mentor who is chosen by the teacher candidate (Chapman & Flinders, 2006; CoT Handbook, 2015).

Field Experience and Mentors

Mentors have substantial influence on the teacher candidate and their future practice. It is widely accepted that a mentor impacts pre-service teaching behaviors –intentionally or unintentionally (Rozelle & Wilson, 2012; Sykes, Bird, & Kennedy, 2010). Kemmis, et al. (2014) suggest that the efforts of a mentor may serve various purposes including supervision and support for the teacher candidate and collaborative self-development for both in the relationship. The researchers assert that all three purposes may occur within a relationship and may sometimes conflict with one another. However, the authors also emphasize the reciprocal nature of the relationship by describing that, "members participate as equals

Figure 1. How candidates progress through three components of CoT

	Beginning	During	Completing
Seminar	• Learn How to Lead a Seminar Class • Deliver Lessons	• Deliver Lessons • Assume Leadership Role	• Vocal Leader of Seminar Experience • Visit Once a Month During Student Teaching • Discuss Experience with Seminar Group
Portfolio	• Finish At Least 2 Expectations to SP Each Semester	• Finish At Least 2 Expectations to SP each Semester	• Finish 10 Expectations to SP Level Before Student Teaching • Finish All Expectations to RtT Level
Field Experience	• Mentor Search and Selection • Begin Teaching Small Groups	• Instruct At Least 5 Whole Group Lessons	• Begin Instructing Whole Group 1x Per Week • Student Teach

in professional dialogue aimed at their individual and collective self-development" (p. 162). The mentor identifies as the experienced professional in the relationship, while the teacher candidate provides know-how derived from theoretical frameworks provided in the university setting.

Extended time with an experienced teacher is at the heart of the CoT program. Unlike many traditional teacher preparation models where teacher candidates are placed with the supervising teachers who will mentor them, the CoT program requires prospective teachers to find a mentor in their content area they feel is the kind of teacher they want to become, as described previously. Once a prospective mentor has been identified by a teacher candidate, the CoT faculty member from their seminar (who serves as the university supervisor of the field experience) meets with the selected mentor and the candidate to discuss the expectations of all parties. This is a critical juncture at which point questions and concerns are attended to before a formal mentor-candidate relationship is established.

The process of finding a mentor is considered an important part of the teacher preparation process and teacher candidates are encouraged to be thoughtful about it. Visiting classrooms to observe teachers with a variety of teaching styles and in diverse classroom and school settings before making a decision is important. The program maintains a list of mentors who have previously worked with the program, but teacher candidates are encouraged to observe others as well. Once the teacher candidate and mentor teacher have decided to partner, a meeting with the CoT faculty member is called to discuss and formalize the relationship and ensure that the school is in agreement with the placement. Subsequently, CoT faculty members visit teacher candidates and mentors in the classroom at least once each semester, observing classroom activities, making suggestions and discussing what they see, as well as noting any issues of concern. Faculty members who observe teacher candidates often encourage greater involvement in the classroom activities over time. However, the choice of when and how to do this is left to the teacher candidate and their mentor.

LESSONS LEARNED FROM COT

Since the program's beginnings in the early 1990s, Community of Teachers has continued to prepare secondary teachers across content areas and in special education, maintaining a close connection between the university and the field of practice. For purposes of program improvement, we conduct program evaluation research on an ongoing basis by engaging in dialogue with key stakeholders including practicing teachers who have graduated from CoT and the mentors who have worked with us. Last year, CoT faculty conducted an evaluation study seeking to understand the perspective of mentor teachers who had worked in the program. We sought to understand their view about their own personal professional development and also what they thought about their experiences as a CoT mentor. For the purposes of this chapter, interpretation of this data provides an understanding of a field-based experience and the perspectives of the central participants (e.g., mentors and teacher candidates) within the CoT program (Maxwell, 2008).

We employed a qualitative design that is exploratory and discovery-oriented in nature (Creswell, 1994). As a means to generate an understanding of the CoT program specific to the field experience, a variety of source data was compiled and analyzed. Semi-structured interviews of mentors and teacher candidates who participated in CoT, direct observation of field practicums, journal correspondence and a collection of teacher candidate artifacts including, lessons, portfolio entries and journals were examined. Such a design allows the researchers to gain a new perspective on things about which much is already known or gain more in-depth information that may be difficult to convey quantitatively (Creswell, 1994).

Participant mentors were randomly chosen from a list of teachers currently active in the CoT program and we sought teacher candidates currently in the field with a mentor. All participants provided informed consent to partake in the study. The complete investigation and gathering of data, including all procedures, gained approval by the Institutional Review Board's Human Subjects Committee.

Semi-structured interviews framed the guiding questions of mentor and teacher candidate conversations. Open-ended interview questions provided interpretive, naturalistic approaches that describe participant experience (Denzin & Lincoln, 1994; Seidman, 2006). Original participant interviews varied in length from twenty minutes to an hour and a half. Running field notes were collected and expanded upon shortly after each interview. An interview protocol included questions about background, history, and experiences in teaching and in CoT (see Appendix D). Mentors described their reasons for becoming a mentor and their initiation into the program. They reflected upon the teacher candidates in their field placement and how the mentors themselves provided opportunities for teacher candidates to learn to teach. We also asked them how they learned to teach themselves, as well as how they participated in various opportunities for professional development. Questions for teacher candidates followed a similar format and sequence, but they specifically accounted for their role in their mentor's classroom.

Guided field observations provided a rich description of actions within the mentor's classroom while teacher candidates conducted their field practicum. Scheduled observations based on program protocols to visit during field experience and student teaching involved at least a one to two hours within the mentor's classroom. The classroom deliberations and activities specific to lesson delivery and interaction with learners in the setting served as a focus of analysis and informed the faculty supervisor regarding teacher candidate performance. Descriptive note taking includes a chronological description of classroom events, performance evaluation, and post lesson delivery discussion.

As an approach to expand data collection and to further understand the scope of a field-based experience specific to the teacher candidate's role in the program, targeted materials (e.g., journal entries, portfolio submissions, lesson delivered) were gleaned to authenticate to serve as an anchor to ideas understood from the interview and focus group discussion data.

As a means to substantiate and to build a deeper understanding of our findings, we conducted group discussions that included CoT faculty after the initial interviews and gathering of assorted materials (e.g., field notes, journal entries, portfolio reflections). The faculty correspondence data verified our findings and built a coherent justification for the lessons learned in our study. This provided an opportunity to examine and validate the data (Creswell, 1994; Seidman, 2006).

In this study, the data collection and data analysis were a simultaneous and recursive process. We compiled the data into one data set and analyzed it by reading and rereading the data in order to identify common themes across the mentor and teacher candidate field experience. We came to consensus about several themes using a reiterative process of discussion across researchers. A list of major ideas that surfaced were chronicled as hypothesized relationships among themes that provided insight into the individual lessons learned (Creswell, 1994).

We anticipate that mentor teacher perspectives and our own will serve to inform other teacher preparation programs as well as our current approach. Three specific questions guided our investigation: 1.) Overtime, how do mentors and teacher candidates describe their relationship?; 2.) How does an extended field engagement effect and shape the relationship? And; 3.) What are the benefits and challenges of a long-term field experience?

In this section of the chapter we reflect about the lessons learned about field experience in teacher preparation from the perspective of CoT. Although the lessons have direct implications for Community of Teachers as a program, there are implications for field experience across other teacher preparation programs as well. Learning to be a teacher builds on the personal and professional development of the individual in question. Each teacher candidate proceeds in their professional development in an idiosyncratic fashion. Even as we ask teacher candidates to plan and adapt instruction with an understanding that student learners differ in development from one another, teacher preparation programs would do well to acknowledge that the individuals they are preparing to be teachers also differ from one another and preparation should be planned and adapted acknowledging those differences. This is difficult undertaking. CoT provides some illustrations of how this might occur.

A Cross-Disciplinary Preparation Prepares Teacher Candidates to Work in Diverse Secondary Schools

CoT seminars are purposefully comprised of a variety of teacher candidates who universally share only the goal of becoming a teacher. "Newbies," "old-hands," and those who are somewhere in between come together to share their experiences as they strive to become teachers. Routine activities that occur within each seminar session are designed to encourage teacher candidates to describe what they are learning in the field with one another in an effort to identify good teaching practices as well as those that are less then successful. Instead of having methods courses solely with all of the other English education majors, for example, teacher candidates learn about pedagogy with a diverse peer group that may include those studying to become special educators as well as teachers of physical education, music, science, mathematics or social studies. In this environment teacher candidates openly express their opinions and insights contributing to a variety of expressed ideas.

The make-up of CoT seminars is purposefully planned to resemble the diversity of a secondary school faculty. Some teacher candidates may have considerable previous teaching experience when they enter CoT. They may work in a public-school setting where they are employed with a temporary teaching license or as a para-educator. Other candidates have taught in a private school setting or with organizations such as the Peace Corps, VISTA or AmeriCorps, as well as other community or religious institutions. Seminar members also bring a variety of life experiences to the task of becoming a teacher and the seminar membership varies in terms of gender, age, and life style characteristics. The diversity in each seminar serves to emphasize the importance of collaboration across these differences and interdisciplinary thinking about curriculum development and instructional strategies. In this way teacher candidates are socialized to acknowledge the importance of professional expertise that comes from a variety of sources including and especially from experiences in the field.

Teacher candidates in CoT remain with their seminar group throughout their time in the program. For many, seminar becomes their professional home base where they are comfortable expressing issues of concern as well as celebrating professional success. For example, Rose, a mentor and former CoT student herself, told the story of how she gradually became more comfortable in the classroom. She explained that when she first began in her mentor's classroom, "a lot of the students would ignore me." Yet she continued to attend once a week and gradually students began to see her "more as a teacher." After a while she realized that a change had occurred, and she noted that even "a student's request to use the restroom increased my level or position of authority" in the eyes of the students. Once Rose and her mentor realized that students in the classroom viewed her in this way, Rose began to take over instructing small groups. Rose often discussed her teaching ideas in seminar and she gathered feedback from her peers. After trying out her ideas in the field, she reported back to her seminar that she was "actually becoming a teacher."

In the portfolio, CoT emphasizes personal individual development by insisting that each teacher candidate's evidence is unique. Although several students used artifacts from Millie and Anna's activities, their descriptions of the significance of this evidence varied based on the student. Certainly, all evidence must reflect the teacher competencies as identified in the portfolio expectation, but they also must reflect the individual in question. By asking teacher candidates to include evidence from their own lives, the program acknowledges the unique experiences that led to their decision to become a teacher. Requiring that portfolio evidence include description of the context in which the evidence was collected also emphasizes each individual's unique developmental trajectory within the field.

In essence the CoT portfolio reflects each teacher candidate's life history, their choices in life, and how they present themselves in their professional development process. Some teacher candidates relate that they always wanted to be a teacher, or they explain that they were influenced by others. An interviewed mentor who was a CoT graduate in our study explained that, "many of my teachers when I was in school said I would be a good at teaching." Others in the study reported that experiences influenced them. It is important to note that these influential experiences most often included their own experiences in school. Interviewed mentors remembered teachers and they wanted to become one either to be like one they admired or unlike one they despised.

Reflection About Field Experience Plays a Valuable Role in Supporting the Professional Development of Teacher Candidates

CoT teacher candidates reflect on their work in several ways. As described previously, in the CoT portfolio, teacher candidates include a reflective essay about the expectation evidence and about their own professional development related to each expectation. In these portfolio reflection essays, teacher candidates describe, explain the significance of, and consider the future implications of the evidence they provide for review. The reflection process continues recursively as the facilitator reviews the expectation, provides feedback, and the teacher candidate revises it, over the course of two or more years.

CoT teacher candidates keep a field journal throughout their field experience and continue with this practice on a daily basis during their student teaching. They submit their journal weekly to their faculty seminar leader who reviews it and provides feedback to them. The idea is that the practice of regularly writing down what one has observed on a given day in the classroom is an exercise that will lead to the long-term habit of and the skills needed to mediate one's work in order to improve it. In addition, because the journal is shared on a weekly basis with the seminar facilitator, it serves to keep the lines of communication open regarding the field experience. When needed, seminar facilitators can intervene to support teacher candidates.

When teacher candidates have a long-term field experience and a strong mentor relationship, they are better able to manage the concerns that many beginning teachers encounter by reflecting on the events that troubled them. CoT teacher candidates debrief with their mentors frequently and in a variety of ways (i.e., in person, via email, on the phone or by text). Because the field experience is long-term, CoT benefits students in their career choice as they can find out early on through reflection if they are on the correct professional path and make changes accordingly if necessary. Difficulties certainly arise. Teacher candidates question themselves, and it is within the framework of an established relationship that candidates can explore the tensions, work through them, and resolve issues. This proves to be a benefit of the arrangement.

Kallie's experience illustrates this circumstance. Kallie joined CoT as a first-year college student and had been in the program for the greatest length of time possible, working with the same mentor weekly for five semesters. Student teaching in her mentor's classroom, Kallie had the breadth of experience with the mentor, her students, and the school environment so she was comfortable praising her mentor, acknowledging all she's learned from her, as well as critiquing what she observed the mentor doing on occasion. Further, because Kallie's mentor was well-acquainted with Kallie and realized that her observations were offered as a way be helpful, it was easier for her to accept suggestions than she might have otherwise ignored. This critical view of teaching develops through reflection when the sheen of apprenticing with a "master teacher" wears down to the patina of the daily grind of teaching. It is at this moment of reality that many teacher candidates become aware that teaching is not what they dreamed it would be. In most circumstances, teacher candidates choose to continue. Perhaps their resolve is reinforced by having both space and time to acknowledge the tough realities they experience in the field and having many opportunities to work through them.

For the CoT teacher candidates we interviewed, developing an awareness of the need to advocate for students in particular and for education in general emerges in part as an outcome of their participation in the field. Teacher candidates are often idealistic and usually enthusiastic. Teacher candidates in CoT often describe teaching as "a calling more than a job," and they describe "sacrificing oneself for the greater good." As Rose summarized it in a focus group, "I have a passion for making the world a better place and that this is one job that really lets you, I guess, envision that, and really help people." No doubt field experiences may act to temper Rose's enthusiasm, but hopefully it will not destroy it. Ideally field experience will help show Rose a way to act on her passion.

Long-Term Partnerships Between Teacher Candidates and Their Mentors Facilitate Communication About Teaching

Given the length of their time together most teacher candidates and their mentors come to know each other well as is evident in Kallie's relationship with her mentor described above. The relationship mentors and teacher candidates develop serves a variety of purposes. Most importantly, a long-term relationship allows more opportunity for discussion about teaching. Adam, a CoT mentor in our study, explained that, "the personal friction that can interfere with communication when you're mentoring smooths out because of the long-term contact." Adam also realized that, "the time together provides an opportunity to learn how much to say to a teacher candidate about their performance" and he noted that as time in the classroom accumulates, teacher candidates become comfortable asking questions, no longer "worrying so much about what the mentor is thinking."

For teacher candidates, the act of selecting a mentor serves as a first step in defining the teacher they may become. Cathy, a graduate student in CoT, felt that becoming a special educator emerged from her experience as a social worker. In her social worker role, she had "worked with teachers all the time" and felt she understood the importance of children's school experiences. What was missing, she reported, was the fact that she "wasn't licensed" to teach in special education. Cathy's story emphasized that she needed to "go forward and become a special education teacher."

Cathy chose Steven, a mentor with whom she could identify. Steven also had a background in social work and saw the need for more cross-disciplinary collaboration between schools and communities. Cathy appreciated how Steven identified her "strengths and weaknesses" and realized that he felt responsible for Cathy's growth as a teacher to be. She recognized that her mentor assumed a role that was similar to the role Steven had with his students. It was different, Cathy acknowledged but all in all, teaching is teaching. Cathy and her mentor were well-able to partner in working to serve students with disabilities. As Cathy acquired knowledge and skills related to teaching children with disabilities she and Steven also partnered to improve collaboration between the school and the community on behalf of the children they taught.

As Cathy's story illustrates, the length of time teacher candidates spend with their mentors provides the opportunity for them to have field experiences in the school at large and the community in addition to the classroom. One CoT mentor in our study, Charles, noted that his "school has been a very hospitable environment" and that the faculty "have been very open to having" teacher candidates work beyond the classroom. He pointed out that, "since the faculty work as a team, it's logical and quite natural that a CoT teacher candidate usually has significant relationships with other teachers and related personnel in the school building and beyond. The length of time of the field experience provides the opportunity for mentors and teacher candidates to know one another and develop as Steven described it "the human part, the interactive part" of becoming a teacher.

As a special educator, Bill, another mentor interviewed, especially valued the length of time a teacher candidate spent in his classroom because his students with disabilities required special understanding. Bill described that the length of the placement allowed the teacher candidate to "get to know me, know my class." Field experiences that are long-term may be especially important in preparing special educators because of the many mandated procedures associated with special education practice. Over time teacher candidates have the opportunity to become familiar with individualized assessment and planning that is needed to effectively address the individual needs of students with disabilities.

Asked about their experience in CoT, graduates interviewed in our ongoing evaluation study frequently credit length of time with their mentor as the best part. Martin, a recent graduate in mathematics education recollected what he had learned in part because of the time he spent in his mentor's classroom in the field. Martin knew his content area algebra well, yet during one of his lessons, he realized that he "didn't know how to relate it well" to his students. This "was a pretty tough experience," he remembered. He described thinking about how his mentor taught the particular topic of that algebra lesson and he resolved to take the time to discuss it with her. He realized that if he had done that sooner, he would not "have led [students] the wrong way." By coming to terms with this mishap and knowing he could turn to his mentor for guidance when he made a mistake, he learned a valuable lesson about collaborating with others in his teaching.

It is important to note that discussing teaching with mentor teachers does not mean that teacher candidates should become replicas of the teachers that provide them with guidance. Most teachers explain that their own teaching styles emerges as they work to become the teachers they want to be. In Martin's case, his mentor told him how she might handle the algebra lesson, but she also urged Martin to "make the lesson his own." Martin admired his mentor but he "just doesn't teach the way she does." As he succinctly put it, "I can't be her."

Long Term Field Experience Provides the Opportunity for Professional Development of Practicing Teachers

A high-quality field placement has been identified in the literature as essential for preparing effective teachers (Scott, Gentry, & Phillips, 2014; Torrez & Krebs, 2012.) When this time is extended over several semesters, mentors and teacher candidates learn about each other and they gain trust. Trust enables them to be forthcoming in their communication with one another as they learn to discuss complex and potentially volatile issues such as the inevitable uncertainties of teaching. Under these circumstances, their relationship becomes closer and they are more likely to trust one another. This was evident in Cathy's relationship with her mentor in the story above. It is important to note that Cathy's mentor learned from his relationship with Cathy even as he also helped Cathy to learn.

Another example of how practicing teachers benefit from participating in field experiences with teacher candidates emerges in the story of Larry, an English teacher who was a CoT mentor we interviewed. He explained that as much as possible he tried to treat the teacher candidate in his room "as an equal" and was proud to report that they often collaborated in planning and teaching. He acknowledged that sometimes he wasn't sure if a lesson would work when he was told about it. Larry explained that he made it a point to discuss his concerns and suggested, "well, what if we were clearer with this objective?" Even if he suggested an alternative objective, he felt that the teacher candidate was comfortable enough to counter his ideas. He thought she would say something like, "I am a little worried about how I would handle that. Could you help me during that part of the lesson, like a co-teacher? Or if changes are needed during the lesson, could we change it then?" Like many CoT mentors in our study, Larry welcomed the opportunity to have a teacher candidate in his classroom. He thought the students benefitted from having the extra help that was provided but he also acknowledged that he learned from the teacher candidate, remarking that the teacher candidate came with "all the new ideas that she has learned from the university." He went on to say, "some of those ideas won't work, but some will, and I am always willing to try them out. We all learn here."

Faculty in CoT who also serve as university supervisors during the field experience and student teaching support the relationship between the teacher candidate and the mentor by trying to facilitate the relationship and interfering as little as possible. A recent incident in CoT shows how this may happen. In her field journal, Karen, a CoT undergraduate student in English education, questioned her mentor teacher's use of a film in class starring an actor recently accused of sexual harassment. Karen used her journal to think through how to approach this topic in a discussion with her mentor. Responding to the journal entry digitally, the CoT faculty member working with Karen was able to "discuss" the matter and offer clarifying questions for her to consider as she moved through her thinking on the issue. In Karen's journal she was free to question the actions of her mentor whom she admires greatly. While it would be difficult for her to wonder aloud to her mentor about issues that may have more to do with generational differences and cultural touch points, in her journal Karen has done exactly that. The journal served as a safe space in which to work out some of the more personal or seemingly controversial issues that arise for a teacher candidate. Because a mentor teacher would be hard pressed to, and is not expected to, fill every role and meet every instructional need for the teacher candidate, the field journal serves as the conduit for processing what candidates are experiencing in their mentor's classroom and bringing to light new questions. The journal gives the CoT faculty a window into the day-to-day happenings in the field experience and allows for continuing the conversation from another perspective.

Being chosen by a teacher candidate serves to validate mentors' sense of themselves as good teachers. Both mentors and teacher candidates describe their relationship as a sort of partnership. The ability to choose one another helps them form this sort of relationship, which serves to foster mentor self-confidence, professionalism, and the opportunity to discover who you are as a teacher. It enables mentors to actualize their desire to leave a legacy as they pick teacher candidates who seems likely to appreciate who they are as a teacher instead of having a student teacher assigned to them. The selection by a teacher candidate not only becomes an endorsement of mentor's teaching ability but also encourages mentors to reflect on effective practice in their own teaching by sponsoring the teacher candidates with whom they collaborate.

For mentors, an important outcome of their relationship with teacher candidates is the opportunity to leave a legacy to the field. As a special educator, Steven espoused an "innate to the core sense that every kid deserves an education. You can't tell me that God wants one kid to have a higher education and the other kid no education!" Also expressing a similar sentiment, Ellen insisted that every student "could learn and everybody was capable." She wanted to make sure teacher candidates adopted that belief. She explained, "[most] mentors really would much prefer to be part of turning out a good teacher into the world and not an ill-prepared one." Steven stated that he had a "responsibility…to take the work seriously" and "to contribute to the preparation of the people who will take our places."

It is critical that university teacher preparation programs acknowledge the important role practicing teachers (mentors) play in making field experiences effective. Mentors are well-aware of their importance and this should be acknowledged. Mentors, like Ellen, explained there was a "need for good teachers" and thought as mentors, they "have a lot to give" and had "a lot to offer." They remembered those who had helped them become teachers. Steven spoke of his mentors who had shared "a lot of stuff with" him. Ellen said that being a mentor gave her the opportunity "to help guide other people or give them guidance that I've gotten, you know, kind of pay back and give back some of the same thing[s] I got."

Situated Learning and Communities of Practice Are Needed for Effective Professional Development of Teacher Candidates

In the CoT program, situated learning provides an opportunity for the development of the professional identity of the teacher candidate (Lave & Wenger, 1991). Mentors and teacher candidates negotiate their relationship within the classroom. Tensions may emerge from internal beliefs (e.g., how I think things should go) versus the coercive power of structures coming from the outside. (e.g., how administrators want things to go). Britzman's (2003) ethnographic study of two student teachers illuminates this struggle of maintaining a sense of self within the demands of an institutional setting. The student teachers in her study were deeply invested in being humanistic teachers although they were discouraged by the conditions within field experiences in a school setting where they were placed. Each student teacher thought there was an identity to possess and to represent through their teaching; yet, they viewed the context of the institutional setting as a site that demanded they hold their real selves in check. Other research also demonstrates that societal expectations may conflict with what teachers personally desire and what they would describe as good teaching (Beijaard, Meijer, & Verloop, 2004; Geerts, Steenbeek, & Geert Paul, 2017; Korthagen, 2004).

What appears to be lacking in the saga of Britzman's student teachers is what Lave and Wenger (1991) describe as a learning experience in which members participate in practice with other involved members. In CoT, this situated learning experience is available within seminar and the relationships the teacher candidate has with their mentor and others in their field experience. Within the community, a shared interpretation of meanings regarding the work of teacher candidates and their mentors emerges. Both improved classroom practice and teacher development are supported by interactions in the school environment. By working together and developing a shared discourse, participants contribute to the development of sustainable educational practice. In this way, participation in a community of learners contributes to the personal and professional teacher development of both the teacher candidate and the mentor. In this way, the teacher candidate takes on the responsibility for their role in relation to that of others and to the school.

The relationship between mentors and teacher candidates could be described as what Lave and Wenger (1991) define as legitimate peripheral acts of participation. The teacher candidates in CoT are not gaining a discrete body of abstract knowledge from the mentors that is intended to be reapplied in a later context, but instead are acquiring the knowledge and skills to perform as a teacher by engaging in the process of teaching.

Choice Strengthens the Relationship Between the Teacher Candidate and the Mentor

In CoT the relationship between a teacher candidate and their mentor is benefitted by the fact that they chose one another. Because both individuals have the opportunity to choose, they are more likely to have a relationship that is compatible and facilitates open communication about teaching and learning.

For the teacher candidates, the task initially seems overwhelming. Jasmine told us she actively sought to consider a variety of teachers by compiling a list and outlining "qualities in a potential mentor…so [she] could wrap her head around" what to look for in her selection process. Other candidates in a focus group explained that they were not as deliberate as Jasmine and felt unable to move forward initially. They wondered how to make contacts, worried about the procedures, and questioned if they would be able to identify their mentor when they met them.

In a focus group, teacher candidates told us they sought advice from other candidates in the program. One student, Margaret reported that she went to visit someone that she had heard was a strong teacher near the university, hoping to make her choice easy. She found this did not work for her and remarked that she "just didn't bond with him at all. I was like, 'this guy is just out there!'"

Some teacher candidates reported thinking about their own experiences as students in school to help them think about finding a mentor. Under these circumstances, they increasingly thought about how potential mentors varied in their teaching styles and personal qualities. Over time, the teacher candidates explained that they came to realize the importance of "fit." In most cases, how the potential mentor interacted with their students became an important consideration. As a former teacher candidate in CoT who is now a mentor, Mary recalled her own mentor recognizing that, "she prides herself on her relationships with students in the classroom and expects them to do well." Other teacher candidates echoed this sentiment. They appreciated witnessing potential mentors developing positive relationships with the students they taught and the warm relationships they seem to develop in their classroom community.

Teacher candidates also valued a potential mentors' ability to make them feel comfortable. This quality was not always easy for them to describe. After acknowledging, "you can learn from somebody who's different from you, and they'll teach you things that maybe you don't know," Alan, another CoT student went on to explain that it's probably better to "be with someone you like" because it "creates a better experience." Alan explained that after observing two potential mentors who were "very nice," he selected the mentor he felt was friendlier to him. Alan deliberated and finally chose one because he "just had a better feeling."

During the process of selection, some mentors reported feeling a bit uncomfortable. Joel who was a very experienced CoT mentor in English explained, "I'm not sure how the first person found me, maybe by word of mouth." He reflected that this "shopping" rankled some and that "not all teachers like that." Yet over time, mentors in our study realized that their stature as a teacher increased within their school and at the university when students chose them. Joel explained that the selection "becomes more of a privilege or a badge" and that such procedures "shouldn't hurt your sense of dignity or anything."

As Joel described it over time, the process of selection became a form of validation for many of the CoT mentors. The mentors in our study described feeling invested in the development of teachers and feeling empowered to have a say in which candidate to work with instead of having them placed in their classroom. Samuel, another mentor explained, "I agreed to it and was pleased that Katie asked me and that I was allowed to say yes or no." For Karen, "a whole host of problems [were] eliminated" when a student observed her class and found "something inspiring." To Karen, the process became "a validation of [me]," especially when a student stated that they observed the classroom and "want[ed] to continue being around" her.

Mentors reported looking for certain qualities in the teacher candidates they choose to mentor. As Joel thought about working with a CoT teacher candidate, he commented:

If she had been a different personality type I don't know if I would have been willing to make this commitment. She's very enthusiastic and very sincere. She's interested in kids and subjects. She's helpful to me and almost able to anticipate, like forward thinking. She's innovative and can give good feedback. She's much further along in the process, not sure if that's because of the program or her as an individual.

Mentors in our study explained that they were well aware that they had the ability to choose and that they could refuse to mentor a teacher candidate. Joel explained that he needed to be careful in his selection for several reasons. He pointed out that his "department head will reject certain candidates for student teaching for one reason or another." Sometimes the school does not "want the students, your product out there, to be damaged." The interviewed mentors wanted to choose well and described how they come to a decision to mentor a teacher candidate. Karen, like many of the other mentors in CoT noted that she was successful in making good choices, commenting that the teacher candidates she works with "have been so responsible." To Karen, her teacher candidates "knew how to talk to an adult," and personified a "professionalism and personality" in both manner and dress.

The mentor selection process does not always proceed smoothly. Elise, a CoT teacher candidate in a focus group recalled her first mentor selection in this way, "[over time as] the mentor relationship unfolded, the interests, the common interests" she and her mentor initially appeared to have, were not evident. What she began to realize was that her mentor "didn't want [her] to be involved at all" and the anticipation of building a relationship "was continually discouraged" and Elise "didn't feel that was productive." As a result, she "decided not to be her [mentor's] secretary anymore and instead put [her] frustration into action and [found] a new mentor." However, Elise's situation was unusual. Most CoT students select a mentor and continue with them throughout the program.

CONCLUSION

In the Community of Teachers program, field experience is central to the mission, and the implications for teacher preparation are profound. For teacher candidates, the value of choice of a mentor with whom to work and the length of the experience they have in the field leads to deeper understanding of the day-to-day life of a teacher. Field experience provides an opportunity for teacher candidates to understand the context in which they will work in addition to the instructional practices they will use in their teaching. They come to view the school as a system revolving around the people who make up the school community. This understanding assists in the transition from student to teacher as their student teaching semester begins. The advantages associated with already knowing the way schools work, knowing both the students in the classroom and the colleagues in the building are enormous, and having already developed these relationships leads to a more meaningful and productive student teaching experience for all involved.

Students in the classroom benefit when teacher candidates are already acclimated to the job, and as a result there can be more confidence in the teacher candidate, which may lead to better classroom behavior and more learning taking place. With a competent and well-integrated student teacher, there is a better chance of improving learner outcomes. For teachers, being a mentor has benefits as well. The opportunity to critically reflect on one's practice, while simultaneously teaching what they know to a student teacher reinforces their own professional knowledge and provides many opportunities for their own continued development as an educator.

The long-term field experience, as implemented in the Community of Teachers program, could also be viewed as effective in promoting teacher longevity in the field because of the meaningful way in which the teacher candidates are integrated into the profession. Our research suggests that CoT candidates are likely to stay in classrooms and schools after they graduate, and they often return to the program serving as mentors themselves. We are heartened by this finding and think that given the rapidly changing landscape of the twenty-first century, the Community of Teachers' emphasis on lifelong learning prepares teachers well for the decades ahead.

REFERENCES

A Community of Teachers Handbook (10th ed.) (2015). Bloomington, IN: Community of Teachers.

Beijaard, D., Meijer, P. C., & Verloop, N. (2004). Reconsidering research on teachers' professional identity. *Teaching and Teacher Education*, *20*(2), 107–128. doi:10.1016/j.tate.2003.07.001

Britzman, D. (2003). Practice makes practice (Rev. ed.). Academic Press.

Carver, C. L., & Feiman-Nemser, S. (2009). Using policy to improve teacher induction: Critical elements and missing pieces. *Educational Policy, 23*(2), 295–328. doi:10.1177/0895904807310036

Chapman, C., & Flinders, D. (2006). Systemic Change in Teacher Education. *TechTrends, 50*(2), 54–55.

Council of Chief School State Officers. (2016). *InTASC model core teaching standards and learning progressions for teachers 1.0.* Retrieved from https://www.ccsso.org/resource-library/intasc-model-core-teaching-standards-and-learning-progressions-teachers-10

Creswell, J. W. (1994). *Research design: Qualitative & quantitative approaches.* Sage Publications, Inc.

Darling-Hammond, L., & Berry, B. (2006). Highly qualified teachers for all. *Educational Leadership, 64*(3), 14.

Davis, E., Sinclair, S., & Gschwend, L. (2015). A mentoring program drills down on the Common Core. *Phi Delta Kappan, 96*(6), 59–64. doi:10.1177/0031721715575302

Denzin, N., & Lincoln, Y. (1994). Introduction: Entering the field of qualitative research. In N. Denzin & Y. Lincoln (Eds.), *Handbook of Qualitative Research* (pp. 1–17). Thousand Oaks, CA: Sage Publications.

Fuller, F. F. (1969). Concerns of teachers: A developmental conceptualization. *American Educational Research Journal, 6*(2), 207–226. doi:10.3102/00028312006002207

Geerts, W. M., Steenbeek, H. W., & van Geert, P. L. (2017). Effect of video-cases on the acquisition of situated knowledge of teachers. *International Education Studies, 11*(1), 64. doi:10.5539/ies.v11n1p64

Glazer, E. M., & Hannafin, M. J. (2006). The collaborative apprenticeship model: Situated professional development within school settings. *Teaching and Teacher Education, 22*(2), 179–193. doi:10.1016/j.tate.2005.09.004

Hanline, M. F. (2010). Preservice teachers' perceptions of field experiences in inclusive preschool settings: Implications for personnel preparation. *Teacher Education and Special Education, 33*(4), 335–351. doi:10.1177/0888406409360144

Kemmis, S., Heikkinen, H. L. T., Fransson, G., Aspfors, J., & Edwards-Groves, C. (2014). Mentoring of new teachers as a contested practice: Supervision, support and collaborative self-development. *Teaching and Teacher Education, 43*, 154–164. doi:10.1016/j.tate.2014.07.001

Korthagen, F. A. (2004). In search of the essence of a good teacher: Towards a more holistic approach in teacher education. *Teaching and Teacher Education, 20*(1), 77–97. doi:10.1016/j.tate.2003.10.002

Lave, J., & Wenger, E. (1991). *Situated learning: Legitimate peripheral participation.* Cambridge University Press. doi:10.1017/CBO9780511815355

Maxwell, J. A. (2008). Designing a qualitative study. The SAGE handbook of applied social research methods, 2, 214-253.

National School Reform Faculty. (2014). *NSRF protocols and activities ... from a to z.* Retrieved from https://www.nsrfharmony.org/free-resources/protocols/a-z

Rozelle, J. J., & Wilson, S. M. (2012). Opening the black box of field experiences: How cooperating teachers' beliefs and practices shape student teachers' beliefs and practices. *Teaching and Teacher Education*, *28*(8), 1196–1205. doi:10.1016/j.tate.2012.07.008

Scott, L. A., Gentry, R., & Phillips, M. (2014). Making preservice teachers better: Examining the impact of a practicum in a teacher preparation program. *Educational Research Review*, *9*(10), 294–301. doi:10.5897/ERR2014.1748

Seidman, I. (2006). *Interviewing as qualitative research: A guide for researchers in education and the social sciences* (3rd ed.). New York, NY: Teachers College Press.

Sykes, G., Bird, T., & Kennedy, M. (2010). Teacher education: Its problems and some prospects. *Journal of Teacher Education*, *61*(5), 464–476. doi:10.1177/0022487110375804

Torrez, C. A. F., & Krebs, M. M. (2012). Expert voices: What cooperating teachers and teacher candidates say about quality student teaching placements and experiences. *Action in Teacher Education*, *34*(5-6), 485–499. doi:10.1080/01626620.2012.729477

Villegas, A. M. (2007). Dispositions in teacher education: A look at social justice. *Journal of Teacher Education*, *58*(5), 370–380. doi:10.1177/0022487107308419

Wenger-Trayner, E., & Wenger-Trayner, B. (2015). *Introduction to communities of practice*. Retrieved from http://wenger-trayner.com/introduction

Zeichner, K. (2012). The turn once again toward practice-based teacher education. *Journal of Teacher Education*, *63*(5), 376–382. doi:10.1177/0022487112445789

ADDITIONAL READING

Barab, S., Barnett, M., & Squire, K. (2002). Developing an empirical account of a community of practice: Characterizing the essential tensions. *Journal of the Learning Sciences*, *11*(4), 489–542. doi:10.1207/S15327809JLS1104_3

Beck, C., & Kosnik, C. (2006). *Innovations in teacher education: A social constructivist approach.* Albany, NY: SUNY Press.

Bennett, S. V. (2013). Effective facets of a field experience that contributed to eight preservice teachers' developing understandings about culturally responsive teaching. *Urban Education*, *48*(3), 380–419. doi:10.1177/0042085912452155

Caprano, R. M., Capraro, M. M., Capraro, R. M., & Helfeldt, J. (2010). Do different types of field experiences make a difference in teacher candidates' perceived level of competence? *Teacher Education Quarterly*, *37*(1), 131–154.

Cochran-Smith, M., Villegas, A. M., Abrams, L., Chavez-Moreno, L., Mills, T., & Stern, R. (2015). Critiquing teacher preparation research: An overview of the field, part II. *Journal of Teacher Education*, *66*(2), 109–121. doi:10.1177/0022487114558268

Kolb, D. A. (2015). *Experiential learning: Experience as the source of learning and development.* Upper Saddle River, NJ: Pearson.

Rozelle, J. J., & Wilson, S. M. (2012). Opening the black box of field experiences: How cooperating teachers' beliefs and practices shape student teachers' beliefs and practices. *Teaching and Teacher Education*, *28*(8), 1196–1205. doi:10.1016/j.tate.2012.07.008

Spooner, M., Flowers, C., Lambert, R., & Algozzine, B. (2008). Is more really better? Examining perceived benefits of an extended student teaching experience. *The Clearing House: A Journal of Educational Strategies, Issues and Ideas*, *81*(6), 263–270. doi:10.3200/TCHS.81.6.263-270

Torrez, C. A. F., & Krebs, M. M. (2012). Expert voices: What cooperating teachers and teacher candidates say about quality student teaching placements and experiences. *Action in Teacher Education*, *34*(5-6), 485–499. doi:10.1080/01626620.2012.729477

Woodgate-Jones, A. (2012). The student teacher and the school community of practice: An exploration of the contribution of the legitimate peripheral participant. *Educational Review*, *64*(2), 145–160. doi:10.1080/00131911.2011.590180

KEY TERMS AND DEFINITIONS

Field Experience: In CoT, this time is extended over several semesters as both the mentor and teacher candidate identify beliefs and understandings, which allow them to implement practice from a mutually informed perspective.

Mentor: An experienced teacher acting as a host to a teacher candidate in their classroom, guiding them toward licensure.

Portfolio: Teacher candidates earn a license by presenting accumulated evidence in a performance-based professional portfolio that faculty judge to demonstrate that a candidate is prepared to teach.

Seminar: A required course comprised of teacher candidates who represent all stages of preparation from beginners to student teachers and all content areas, whereby a seminar leader guides the activities that focus on educational theories, practice, and effective instructional strategies.

Teacher Candidate: A student accepted in CoT who attends seminar, finds a mentor, and completes a portfolio for the duration of the program including student teaching.

APPENDIX A: WORDS TO LIVE BY

A Community of Teachers

Why this Document? Even in the closest, most affectionate of families, problems arise which are unavoidable. Miscommunication occurs or the dedication of some members of the group flags. It is in such predicaments where relationships, personal identities, and communities can be strengthened or injured. In order to maintain a healthy community, we must be able to overcome such obstacles. And in order to do this, it is vital that we lay down a strong foundation of the things we value for ourselves and expect of each other. What these things essentially boil down to are: our commitment to each other, both personally and professionally, and our commitment to becoming successful educators. If each of us learns to value and honor these commitments, our effectiveness as students, teachers, and members of a community is greatly strengthened.

Our Commitment to Each Other

By opting to join **A Community of Teachers**, we are saying that we want the process of becoming a teacher to be more than a solitary pursuit. As teachers, we need to learn how to help each other to become effective. Teaching also occurs in a social context; that, too, demands that together we learn how to enhance our social skills as we learn how to help each other.

- **Communication:** Community is an empty concept without communication. Access to email enables us to build and maintain this communication with ease. Unless all of us regularly use that system, its power to build community is diminished; communication with some of us is closed off and some of us may become fringe members of the community. We each need to acquire the habit of checking our email every day or two. If we can't, we need to stay in contact with people through other means. We need to be mindful of the importance of helping those who care about us know our current state of well-being. Let someone know.
- **Support:** One of the advantages that we have in this program is its support system. In this community, we may be more aware of the needs of others in our program, and when we sense that another member needs some help, we can offer it. When we need the help of others, we need to learn how to ask for it. We should be able to trust others in the community and, in turn, offer them our understanding and support. We all become resources to each other through the acts of sharing, collaborating, and mentoring.
- **Reaching Out:** Mentor Teachers are important members of our community. We need to make them feel a welcome part of the community, occasionally attending our Seminars, for example. All members of the community can learn from each other.
- **Improving the Community and the Program: CoT** operates on the philosophy of one person-one vote. Being an active member of **CoT** means being responsible for the creation and development of a community not only within a Seminar but also within the whole program. Governance, **CoT**'s self-correcting mechanism, places the responsibility on each member and the community as a whole to determine how the program should evolve to meet new circumstances. Any **CoT** member can propose a change in the program's operation and every member has an obligation to

exercise his or her role of considering, shaping, and voting on these proposals for change. The dialogue that occurs across Seminars as we deliberate about changes becomes an important vehicle for building a program-wide sense of community.

Our Commitment to the Profession

We take much from the settings in which we work and the people with whom we work. We need to find ways also to "give back." Professional development needs to be an ongoing process. Our commitment to improving ourselves and our colleagues should be clear.

APPENDIX B: PORTFOLIO EXPECTATIONS

1.   Subject Matter

Our teacher candidates will demonstrate their knowledge of and commitment to subject matter through their teaching.

2.   Teaching Reading and Writing (1.4)

Secondary: Our teacher candidates will demonstrate that they can effectively incorporate reading, writing, and thinking activities into their day-to-day instruction.
Elementary: Our teacher candidates will demonstrate that they can effectively incorporate reading, writing, and thinking activities into their day-to-day instruction.

3.   Individual Development (2.1)

Our teacher candidates will demonstrate that they understand the cultural, physical, cognitive, psychological, and social-emotional dimensions of their students' development.

4.   Curriculum Development (1.2, 7.1)

Our teacher candidates will demonstrate that they can critically review learning materials and develop curricula appropriate for their students.

5.   Instructional Strategies (4.1, 4.2, 4.3)

Our teacher candidates will demonstrate that they can employ a variety of instructional approaches in developing their students' critical thinking, problem-solving, and inquiry abilities and that they understand how to integrate technology effectively into their instruction.

6.   Self-Directed Learning (2.2, 6.3)

Our teacher candidates will demonstrate that they can help students take responsibility for their own learning and develop a sense of influence in the world around them.

7.   Diverse Learners (3.3, 7.4)

Our teacher candidates will demonstrate an ability to work effectively with students who have diverse abilities and/or special needs, and to personalize their students' learning by working with them and their families to develop individually meaningful learning programs.

8.   Classroom Management & Community (5.1, 5.2)

Our teacher candidates will demonstrate that they can effectively employ a variety of approaches in designing and managing daily classroom routines and fostering a sense of community among their students.

9.   Learning From Others (6.2, 6.3)

Our teacher candidates will demonstrate that they can facilitate their students' learning in a variety of group situations.

10.   Multicultural Understanding (3.2)

Our teacher candidates will demonstrate that they can function effectively in multicultural settings.

11.   Evaluating Students' Learning (8.1, 8.2)

Our teacher candidates will demonstrate that they can systematically and intelligently gather and analyze information regarding their students' performance in school and that they can employ a variety of assessment tools and strategies to evaluate their students' work.

12.   School and Community Specialists (3.1, 7.2)

Our teacher candidates will demonstrate responsiveness to their students' specific needs by seeking the help of school specialists and community resources when appropriate.

13.   Collaboration (10.1, 10.2, 10.3)

Our teacher candidates will demonstrate that they have interpersonal skills related to working with other key stakeholders (e.g. parents, colleagues, and members of the larger community) in the education of their students.

14. Professional Growth (1.2, 9.3, 9.4)

Our teacher candidates will demonstrate that they are committed to ongoing professional growth, asking questions about their teaching and their students' learning and finding ways to answer those questions.

15. Expressing Convictions (7.3, 9.1, 9.2) Our teacher candidates will demonstrate that they support human rights, can participate in salient debates on major social issues and can respond thoughtfully and appropriately when controversial issues arise in the classroom. They will also demonstrate that they are able to create a classroom climate that encourages similar behavior in their students.
16. (a) Extracurricular Activities (9.6). Our teacher candidates will demonstrate their dedication to roles and responsibilities outside the instructional school day. (b) Equity and School Law (10.4) Our teacher candidates will demonstrate that they can provide their students with a fair and equitable education based upon their knowledge of school policies as well as state and federal legislation that affects their students' well-being as individuals within the school system.

*For #16, students will choose either (a) or (b). Any newly created expectations will be designated as additional options for #16.

APPENDIX C: EVALUATING EVIDENCE FOR THE PORTFOLIO

Figure 2.

A Community of Teachers
Evaluating Evidence for the Portfolio

Source of Information	Context of the Evidence	Coherence and Reflection
Self-evident products such as videotapes, term papers (for verbal communication).	Real experience in actual school settings with real kids where you are in charge.	Reflecting in substantive essays that present your views on each of the Expectations.
Spontaneous events that are captured in some credible manner that connotes a successful response.	College teaching where you are in charge.	Providing a narrative of your development as a teacher.
Curricula or materials that you develop and use in a school, including an evaluation of how it worked.	Other teaching-related settings with adolescents in groups (coaching, church work, camp work, etc.).	Providing some sort of overview of yourself as a teacher, something similar to a professional profile.
Curricula or materials that you develop but never try out in a school.	Helping experiences with one child or adolescent.	Providing a clear summary of the major activities and projects which you have developed or participated in as a part of your teaching.
Unsolicited comments (notes, letters, email messages) from teachers and school administrators.	Other teaching-related settings with children in groups (camp counseling, day care, etc.).	Providing an effective, consistently-formatted introduction to each Expectation that goes beyond a simple list of the contents of the folder; it explains why this information fits this Expectation.
Solicited Mentor Teacher's testimonials.	Helping experiences with one younger child (but probably not babysitting).	
Unsolicited comments (notes, letters, email messages) from professors and instructors.	Long term participation in a professional association.	Incorporating an effective system for cross-referencing evidence that supports more than one Expectation.
Your Seminar leader's comments about your work.	Formal presentations at professional meetings (conferences, workshops, etc.)	Organizing all of your evidence into a consistent, easy to use (from the reader's perspective) format.
Unsolicited comments (notes, letters, email messages) from other CoTers.		
Your narrative of an activity, accompanied by someone else's evaluation of how well it worked.	Formal presentations at non-professional meetings.	Developing a clear, consistent organization of evidence throughout the Portfolio that clearly delineates each Expectation, and perhaps each of the ten categories of Expectations.
A reflective essay on a topic		
Your narrative of an activity, accompanied by evidence that it actually happened (e.g., photos, materials).	Products of on-campus assignments (except for Subject Matter).	
Your narrative of an activity, accompanied (only) by your evaluation of how well it worked.		
Materials developed by others that you have adapted.	Attendance only at professional meetings, workshops, lectures, etc.	

(vertical axis, left margin: More Compelling — Moderately Compelling — Less Compelling)

APPENDIX D: INTERVIEW PROTOCOLS

Mentor Interview Outline

1. How long have you been a mentor for COT? How were you recruited to be a mentor? Have you mentored for other programs at the SoE?
2. What were your own experiences like with a mentor when you were a student teacher?
3. How did you learn to teach?
4. What makes you want to be a mentor?
5. How prepared did you feel becoming a mentor for the first time?
6. How would you describe your mentor experience, so far? How would you describe the COT program and the students you work with?
7. What questions did you have as a mentor? To whom could you direct your questions?
8. What seems to help student teachers when you are working with them?
9. Do you have any other comments or suggestions about the program or mentoring in general?

Teacher Candidate Interview Outline

10. How long have you been or were a student in IU Bloomington's Teacher Preparation Program (CoT)?
11. How did you discover CoT?
    a. Were you in any teacher preparation programs before CoT?
12. What were your influences in becoming a teacher?
13. Why teaching?
    a. What is your concept of a quality teacher? Any examples? Examples of a poor-quality teacher?
14. Explain your CoT seminar experience?
15. How did you discover your mentor(s)?
16. How would you describe this stage in your development as a teacher?
17. What is your relationship with other staff at your mentor's school?
18. What questions do/did you have as a teacher candidate?
19. What are/were your biggest challenges or successes as a teacher candidate?
20. When are/were you scheduled to student-teach?
21. How can CoT support your role further as a teacher candidate?
22. What characteristics within your role that assist/ed your mentor in the classroom, in the school, with parents?

Chapter 26
Investigating How Rehearsals and Teacher Educator Feedback Influences Preservice Teacher Development

Rajeev K. Virmani
Sonoma State University, USA

ABSTRACT

This chapter examines how three secondary mathematics preservice teachers and two teacher educators rehearse and enact the core teaching practice of leading a whole-class discussion in a math methods course and in student teaching placements. Findings indicate that there was substantial variation in the three preservice teachers' opportunities to practice key aspects of leading a whole-class discussion, the type of feedback they received from the teacher educators, and the authenticity of the rehearsal. The opportunity to approximate practice and receive feedback played a significant role in the generative nature of the preservice teachers' enactments of a whole-class discussion in their student teaching placements.

INTRODUCTION

As many teacher education programs shift towards practice-based preparation models, much emphasis has been placed on the development of pedagogies that provide preservice teachers (PSTs) with rich experiences to support their professional knowledge for teaching (Grossman & McDonald, 2008; McDonald, Kazemi, Kavanaugh, 2013). In particular, one approach that has garnered much interest in teacher preparation is the use of learning cycles for PSTs to investigate and enact core or high leverage teaching practices in university and fieldwork settings (McDonald, Kazemi, & Kavanagh, 2013; Lampert, Franke, Kazemi, Ghousseini, Turrou, Beasley, Cunard, & Crowe, 2013). The underlying goal for the learning cycle is for PSTs to learn to enact principled practices and to develop knowledge for ambitious teaching (Kazemi, Franke, & Lampert, 2009). The teacher educator (TE) and PSTs collectively engage with core teaching practices embedded in an instructional activity (IA) and then the PST enacts the IA

DOI: 10.4018/978-1-5225-6249-8.ch026

in the field (Ball & Forzani, 2009; Grossman, Hammerness, & McDonald, 2009; Kazemi, Ghousseini, Cunard, & Turrou, 2016; Lampert, Franke, Kazemi, Ghousseini, Turrou, Beasley, Cunard, & Crowe, 2013; McDonald, Kazemi, & Kavanaugh, 2013) (see Figure 1).

Within one stage of the learning cycle, the PST will rehearse core teaching practices embedded in an IA. Core teaching practices have been characterized by a cadre of education researchers as those teaching practices that: support student understanding; occur frequently in teaching; are accessible to preservice teachers, and are practices that preservice teachers can enact in the field (Core Practices Consortium, 2013; Grossman & McDonald, 2008). The TE provides coaching by either interrupting the PST to revise their actions or by responding with what a typical student response might be, pressing the PST to think deeply about his or her role in attending to student thinking. Through the rehearsal process, the goal is for PSTs to become more adept at specific core teaching practices such as eliciting and responding to student thinking, and to continue to build their teaching skills and professional knowledge of teaching.

Instructional activities act as containers in which PSTs engage in the teacher education setting through rehearsal with TEs and peers in authentic interactions about content, student thinking, and pedagogy within the learning cycle (Kazemi, Franke, & Lampert, 2009; Lampert, Franke, Kazemi, Ghousseini, Turrou, Beasley, Cunard, & Crowe, 2013; Lampert & Graziani, 2009). The IAs can then be enacted in the fieldwork setting where PSTs use their experiences from the rehearsal to inform their interactions

Figure 1. Cycle for collectively learning to engage in authentic and ambitious instructional activity
Source: "Core practices and pedagogies of teacher education: A call for a common language and collective activity," by M. A. McDonald, E. Kazemi, S. S. Kavanagh, 2013, Journal of Teacher Education, 64, 5, p. 382. Copyright 2013 by SAGE Publications.

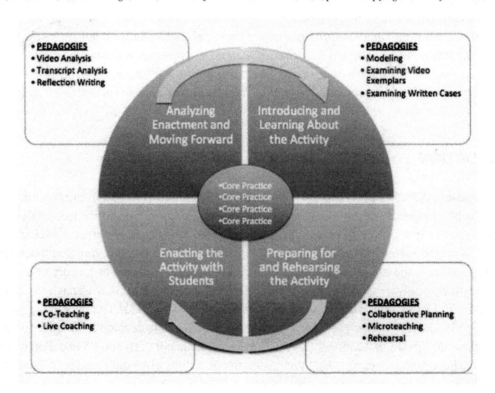

with students. IAs are used to lessen the cognitive load as PSTs routinize certain aspects, allowing them to have the capacity to respond to student ideas and adapt content and methods based on student thinking (Kazemi, Lampert, & Ghousseini, 2007; Lampert, Beasley, Ghousseini, Kazemi, & Franke, 2010; Leinhardt & Greeno, 1986).

The major components of learning cycles draw upon the Grossman et al. (2009) "pedagogies of practice in professional education" framework. This framework underpins the learning process in the mathematics methods course in which the PSTs observe and make sense of the ways core teaching practices are represented and made visible (representation), examine the practice broken into smaller parts for the purposes of teaching and learning (decomposition), and rehearse core teaching practices (approximations). By approximating key practices within university coursework, TEs can design a variety of pedagogical activities that contain core teaching practices, tools, and principles of effective teaching to provide support and guidance to PSTs before they enact the practices in the field (Lampert & Graziani, 2009; Kazemi, Franke, & Lampert, 2009). Approximating teaching practices within the less complex university setting allows for the PST to be free from the constraints of the classroom as they develop a greater control of the actions of teaching (Rogoff, 2003). The social interactions and negotiation with other members in the university setting initiates the process of modifying the PSTs' initial perceptions of teaching and sets the stage for PSTs to apply their understanding of principled teaching practices to the classroom setting (Kennedy, 1999).

Throughout the cycle, PSTs need support to develop pedagogical content knowledge as they learn how to re-contextualize the discourse from the methods course into student teaching (Borko, Eisenhart, Brown, Underhill, Jones, & Agard, 1992; Ensor, 2001). While the IA allows for a bounded activity that is rehearsed and then enacted, the social contexts of the two settings are different with regard to relationships, knowledge bases, and pedagogic practices (Ensor, 2001). The learning cycle aims to bridge the two settings, by supporting PSTs as they learn how to approximate core teaching practices in the teacher education context and then enact the rehearsed IA in the student teaching context.

Purpose of Study

As teacher education programs begin to incorporate learning cycles into university courses, at present, we are limited in our understanding of what TEs do and what PSTs learn from this type of preparation, especially at the secondary level (Baldinger, Selling, & Virmani, 2016; Ghousseini & Herbst, 2016; Kazemi, Ghousseini, Cunard, & Turrou, 2016; Lampert, Franke, Kazemi, Ghousseini, Turrou, Beasley, Cunard, & Crowe, 2013). Emerging research has been focused on the initial stages of the learning cycle as the PSTs and TEs investigate and rehearse, while even fewer studies have examined PSTs in the field enacting the instructional activities. In this study, I first investigate how three secondary PSTs and two TEs rehearse the core teaching practice of leading a whole-class discussion bounded by a sorting task IA in the math methods course. Through a sorting task IA, the PSTs are to steer the discussion to a specific mathematical point, by eliciting and responding to student ideas and orienting students to each other ideas and the content, to ultimately develop a definition of a mathematical idea (Sleep, 2012). I then examine how the three PSTs enact the sorting task IA in each of their student teaching placements. Finally, I draw connections between the two settings to understand how the preparation influenced the PSTs' practice, primarily examining the role of rehearsal on PST learning.

This research study investigates these two research questions:

1. How do PSTs and TEs rehearse the core teaching practice of leading a whole-class discussion in the math methods course?
2. How do PSTs enact the core teaching practice of leading a whole-class discussion in their student teaching placements?

Leading a Whole-Class Discussion

The field of mathematics education has placed increased emphasis on discussions as a substantial part of classroom instruction and teacher preparation (Boerst, Sleep, Ball, & Bass 2011; Chapin, O'Connor, & Anderson, 2013; Sleep & Boerst, 2012). Reform efforts in mathematics education have begun to examine effective teaching practices that support students to communicate their thinking and construct and evaluate their own as well as other students' mathematical ideas during productive whole-class discussions (Stein, Engle, Smith, & Hughes, 2008). While there is no consensus on what constitutes a strong discussion in classroom instruction, the main underlying feature of effective discussion is the verbal exchange between the teacher and students bounded by a certain focus. The focus of the mathematical discussion may be about a mathematical concept, definition, procedure, or problem where both the students and teachers are collectively engaged and participating (Boerst, Sleep, Ball, & Bass, 2011; Chapin, O'Connor, & Anderson, 2013). The teacher pays close attention to student thinking, supporting student ideas and steering the direction of the discussion. While the teacher's role is essential to the success of the discussion, other key factors include the content, the norms and routines of the classroom, the student ideas, and the objectives of the discussion (Boerst, Sleep, Ball, & Bass, 2011; Sleep 2012).

Discussions to Facilitate Student Learning

Past research on discussions in mathematics classrooms have suggested that discussions promote increased student learning, motivation, and agency (Boaler, 2008; Chapin, O'Connor, & Anderson, 2013; Obrycki, Herbel-Eisenmann, & Cirillo, 2009). Cengiz, Kline, and Grant (2011) found that specific instructional (or talk moves) during whole-class discussions extended student thinking. Classroom discussions provide opportunities for students to share a diverse set of approaches, and allow for students to build upon and learn from other students' ideas (NCTM, 2000). Although past research has identified strategies for effectively conducting a discussion, designing learning activities and preparing PSTs for leading a discussion remains a challenging task (Kazemi & Hintz, 2014; Ghousseni & Herbst, 2016; Stein, Engle, Smith, & Hughes, 2008; Williamson, 2013). PSTs may not have a strong knowledge base to respond to student thinking, nor may not have the pedagogical content knowledge needed to improvise during facilitating a discussion (Stein, Engle, Smith, & Hughes, 2008). Furthermore, PSTs may tend to follow a less complex "show and tell" method of discussion that may focus solely on procedural understanding in which the teacher is solely looking for correct answers (Chazan & Ball, 1999).

While discussions can have different purposes (e.g. compare and connect strategies, generate justifications of strategies) and can be structured in varying formats, in this study, I focus on the development of an IA that aims to define and clarify a mathematical idea (Kazemi & Hintz, 2014, Sleep, 2012). The IA was designed for students to sort cards into example and non-example piles. The teacher facilitates a discussion with students about how they sorted the cards asking students to provide reasoning for their categorization. As students provide reasoning, they develop ideas about the defining characteristics of the mathematical object. Throughout the discussion, the teacher surfaces ambiguities in the cards that were difficult for students to sort. The ambiguity drives the discussion in which students defend their reasoning and in turn the teacher uses facilitation moves to guide the discussion towards the mathematical point, to collectively construct the definition of the mathematical object (Baldinger, Selling, & Virmani, 2016). Within this IA, PSTs are faced with multiple tasks including having a clear mathematical goal that they hope to steer the conversation to, understanding how student ideas relate to the mathematical point, and responding to and building upon student ideas (Leatham, Peterson, Stockero, & Van Zoest, 2015; Sleep, 2012).

METHODS

Participants and Setting

I purposefully selected a specific teacher preparation program for this study because the TEs employed the use of rehearsals in the math methods course as an integral component in preparing the PSTs for learning core teaching practices. The participants in this case study were three secondary mathematics PSTs enrolled in a two-semester mathematics methods course. There were a total of 6 PSTs (1 additional PST in Spring) in the course co-taught by two TEs who at the time were graduate students pursuing their doctorate in mathematics education. The TEs typically took a team teaching approach (Buckley, 2000; Davis, 1975) with a mutual understanding of their general and specific objectives as they worked interactively to reach the common goals set for the class. Together, the TEs were able to play different roles in class (and during the rehearsals) as they brought in their areas of strength and expertise.

I aimed to reduce confounding variables by focusing the study on the three PSTs - Victor, Kaya, and Julia (pseudonyms) who shared common characteristics (e.g. they all came into the program with no teaching experience, they had the same coursework and fieldwork schedule, and they had similar supports throughout the program). In addition to student teaching during the day, the PSTs in this study took classes in the evening, had weekly meetings with university supervisors, and participated in instructional rounds to learn about other teaching settings.

The TEs were committed to providing the PSTs a training experience that integrated investigation, practice, and reflection on core teaching practices for mathematics. Throughout the course, the PSTs were given opportunities to rehearse core teaching practices through a variety of IAs. During the first semester, the PSTs and TEs rehearsed a "number talk" (Parrish, 2010) IA aimed for PSTs to learn how to elicit and interpret student thinking, make content explicit through representations and examples, lead a whole-class discussion, and recognize common patterns of student-thinking. During the second semester, the PSTs rehearsed leading a whole-discussion by using a sorting task IA and were given an assignment to enact the IA in their student teaching placements (see Baldinger, Selling, & Virmani, 2016). Additionally, throughout the course, the PSTs had many readings related to leading whole-class discussions (Smith & Stein, 2011) and the use of talk moves (Chapin, O'Connor, & Anderson, 2013) as well as watched video to analyze and decompose practice.

In this study, I focused primarily on the three PSTs as they rehearsed and enacted the sorting task IA as they led a whole-class discussion. The rehearsal and enactment of this IA was selected since it was the only time during the two-semester course in which the PSTs were given the assignment to enact the rehearsed IA in their student teaching placements. It is important to note that Kaya was absent for one of the planning sessions leading up to the rehearsal and both Kaya and Julia were absent on the rehearsal day. They both rehearsed their IAs the following week after class with four out of six of their peers present and only one TE.

Data Collection

The data collection methodologies for this study primarily consisted of video documentation and observation field notes in the mathematics methods course and in student teaching placements, and interviews with PSTs. Data collection in the mathematics methods class included videotaping PSTs and TEs as they investigated, planned, and rehearsed the sorting task IA focused on leading a whole-class discussion. I observed and videotaped the three PSTs in their student teaching placements during second semester, particularly interested in how they enacted the sorting task IA. I interviewed the PSTs immediately after the enactment of the sorting task IA in their student teaching placements to better understand how they viewed the rehearsals preparing them to lead the whole-class discussion using the sorting task IA with students and the impact on their teaching practice. Additionally, I collected a variety of artifacts from the math methods class that included: assignment protocols and rubrics created by the TEs, PSTs' assignment write-ups, and the PSTs' reflections.

Data Analyses

To answer the research questions for this study, I examined the video data using StudioCode® video coding software (Studio Code Business Group, 2012). I identified who was speaking in each of the settings with the participant's statement considered the unit of analysis. I coded the rehearsal statements as: 1) the PST making a statement (PST Statement); 2) the "student" making a statement (Student Statement) or; 3) an exchange between the TE and rehearsing PST (TE/PST Exchange). Student statements in the math methods class were statements made by the non-rehearsing PSTs during the rehearsal to simulate actual student responses in the classroom setting. In analyzing the student teaching placements, I used the same initial coding scheme to code for who was talking, however the code TE/PST Exchange was not relevant and thus not utilized. I then attached labels to each of the participant's statements and focused primarily on PST Statements and TE/PST Exchanges. Multiple studies in analyses of rehearsals (Lampert, Franke, Kazemi, Ghousseini, Turrou, Beasley, Cunard, & Crowe, 2013), facilitation practices (Borko, Virmani, Khachatryan, & Mangram, 2014; van Es, 2012), and classroom discussions (Chapin, O'Connor, & Anderson, 2013; Kazemi & Hintz, 2014; Marshall, Smagorinsky, & Smith, 1995) were drawn upon to guide the development of labels for coding the participants' statements (See Table 1).

Analyses of Rehearsals

In order to examine the first research question, how the PSTs and TEs rehearsed core teaching practices within the sorting task IA in the math methods course, I attached labels to the statements made by the PSTs and TEs. The labels attached to the PSTs identified to whom the PSTs directed their statement towards (student or class), how the PSTs facilitated the discussion (e.g. elicit, press, inform, evaluate),

Table 1. Coding Scheme for Participant Statements

Preservice Teacher Statement	TE/PST Exchange
Directed statement to - student or class	Type of feedback – directive, evaluative, scaffolds enactment, or facilitates discussion
Type of facilitation move (e.g. elicit, press, inform, evaluate)	Feedback on type of facilitation move (e.g. elicit, press, inform, evaluate)
Substantive focus of statement (e.g. student reasoning/thinking, representation)	Substantive focus of statement (e.g. student reasoning/thinking, representation)

and the substantive focus of statement (e.g. student thinking, representation, procedure). I drew upon multiple studies to help characterize the substantive focus of the PST statements (Lampert, Franke, Kazemi, Ghousseini, Turrou, Beasley, Cunard, & Crowe, 2013; Stein & Smith, 2011). I took a similar approach to code the TEs' feedback and their exchanges with the PSTs. I used the Lampert et al. (2013) study's coding scheme to characterize the four types of feedback provided by the TEs during the rehearsal (directive feedback, evaluative feedback, scaffolds enactment, facilitates discussion). For example, in an exchange during a rehearsal the TE may call a time-out and give the PST directive feedback to ask the student for mathematical reasoning for a particular representation before moving on to another example. This statement would be labeled as directive feedback (type of feedback), press (type of facilitation move), and student thinking/reasoning (substantive focus). The aim for coding and labeling the interactions during rehearsals was to analyze the frequency and the types of opportunities that PSTs had to practice and receive feedback in leading a whole-class discussion

Analyses of Enactments

In order to answer the second research question, how PSTs enact the sorting task IA, I analyzed the PSTs' video data of them leading the whole-class discussion in their student teaching placements. The initial phase of coding consisted of segmenting the PST facilitating the discussion based on who was making a statement (PST or student). To examine how PSTs enacted the rehearsed core teaching practices during the sorting task in their student teaching placements, I took the same approach as used to code the discussion rehearsals. For example, during the enactment the PST may press a student about a misconception they had when providing reasoning for their categorization of a card. This statement would be labeled as student (to whom the question is directed), press (type of facilitation move), and student error, student thinking/reasoning (substantive focus). The aim for coding and labeling the interactions during enactments was to examine the frequency of the types facilitation moves the PSTs used as they led the whole-class discussion.

After coding and labeling the PST and TE statements for each unit of analysis in both settings, I examined the frequency of facilitation moves and substantive labels for each of the PSTs. Next, I used an iterative process in which I alternated between video and coding analysis to develop the description for each of the PST's case study. For each of the PSTs' case studies, I used examples, descriptions, and quotations to explain the events that occurred while the PSTs rehearsed the discussion activity, received feedback from the TEs, and enacted the discussion activity in the field. Certain common themes emerged from the video analyses, observations, interviews, and reflections as I was able to draw conclusions based on trends in the data and then confirmed results by triangulating data sources.

RESULTS AND DISCUSSION

Research Question 1

Leading up to the rehearsal, one of the TEs modeled how to lead a whole-class discussion using the sorting task instructional activity about equations and non-equations. The PSTs were given the option to choose the mathematical content and develop cards for the discussion of their IA on their own or to pick from a set of already developed cards. Each of the PSTs chose their own content areas and developed their own cards that fit into the curriculum of their student teaching classroom.

The PSTs analyzed their set of cards, identifying for each card the features of the mathematical object and provided rationale for how the card would be categorized (Baldinger, Selling, & Virmani, 2016). One major goal of the sorting task IA was for the PST to facilitate a discussion that moved towards a specific mathematical point (Sleep, 2012) (Table 2). The mathematical point for Victor's IA was to develop a definition of a polygon and quadrilateral. The mathematical point for Julia's IA was to develop a definition of the arithmetic mean and for students to develop a conceptual understanding of the measures of central tendency. The mathematical point for Kaya's IA was to determine if two expressions are always, sometimes, or never true and connecting this mathematical idea to graphing linear systems of equations. The initial idea for Kaya's sort came from the Shell Center's identities and non/identities sorting activity (See: http://map.mathshell.org/lessons.php?unit=9210&collection=8).

Opportunities to Rehearse the IA

I first recorded the total time the PSTs spent either rehearsing the IA, receiving feedback from TEs, or planning of the enactment and calculated the PSTs' respective percentage for each category (Table 3). The time that counted as PST *rehearsing IA* was when the PSTs made facilitation moves as they led the discussion and also included the time the PSTs spent sorting the cards. The time that counted as *feedback on the rehearsal* was when a timeout was called in which the PSTs and TEs discussed in the moment moves focused on student thinking, pedagogy, and/or content. The time counted as *planning for enactment* included TE and PST discussions in preparation for the enactment in the student teaching placement and were not related to the rehearsal. Table 3 shows the variation between PSTs, and in particular highlights Kaya's limited rehearsal time with the focus primarily on planning. Victor and Julia spent much of the rehearsal practicing facilitation moves and receiving feedback related to leading a whole-class discussion. Looking at Table 3, Victor spent nearly 70% of his overall time rehearsing the sorting task IA while Kaya spent nearly 65% planning for the enactment.

Table 2. PSTs' Grade/course, Content for Sorting Task, and Mathematical Point

PST	Grade/Course	Content Area
Victor	6th	Polygons; quadrilaterals
Julia	6th	Arithmetic mean (average)
Kaya	Algebra 1 (10th grade)	Linear systems of equations (always, sometimes, never true)

Table 3. PST Percentages of Time Spent During Rehearsal

PST	Rehearsing IA	Feedback on Rehearsal	Planning for Enactment
Victor	69.3%	28.7%	2%
Julia	56.8%	20.6%	22.6%
Kaya	26.4%	8.9%	64.7%

Next, I examined the frequency of facilitation moves made during the rehearsal, detailing the type of move made by each of three PSTs (Table 4). To better understand the nature of the PST facilitation moves during the rehearsal, I examined the frequencies of their substantive foci label drawing upon the Lampert et al. (2013) codes (Table 5). During this analysis, I examined the PSTs facilitation moves as they rehearsed the sorting task IA.

Victor and Julia had a similar number of facilitation moves during their rehearsals while Kaya had much fewer. Victor's rehearsal had a consistent pattern of facilitation throughout where he elicited a card, pressed the student or class for reasoning, and then restated their ideas about the quadrilateral. Victor continued to press "students" until he had multiple student ideas and then would move onto another card representation. During the rehearsal, the TEs provided student ideas that Victor had to interpret and

Table 4. PST Frequencies of Types of Facilitation Moves in Rehearsal

	Victor	Julia	Kaya
Type of move			
Restate/acknowledge	22	17	12
Press	20	18	18
Elicit	6	8	2
Hold thought	4	0	0
Evaluate	2	5	2
Inform/Tell	2	10	2
Total	56	58	36

Table 5. PST Frequencies of Substantive Foci in Rehearsal

	Victor	Julia	Kaya
Substantive Focus of Move			
Representation	32	24	6
Student thinking/reasoning	20	15	20
Student error	7	15	3
Orienting students	6	3	3
Other	5	4	1
Total	70	62	33

respond to and coached him with specific feedback on his interactions. Julia also made many facilitation moves in her rehearsal, but had a less consistent facilitation pattern. Julia's rehearsal was stopped multiple times by either the TE or herself to discuss the ambiguity in the cards and how to guide students to correctly categorize the cards. The conversation was primarily around how to best navigate student ideas in relation to the content and the IA. Kaya made the fewest number of facilitation moves during the rehearsal as it could have been characterized as a planning session rather than an interactional rehearsal. The majority of her rehearsal was spent discussing how to align the sorting task with the many learning objectives and about ways to display student ideas and cards.

The frequency of Victor and Julia's moves were again similar in regards to frequency of substantive foci labels and mostly aligned with objectives of the sorting task assignment - elicit card (representation), press for student thinking/reasoning, and orient students thinking toward each other. Julia spent a large majority of time during the rehearsal pressing the students for their reasoning and errors on the card representations. The large number of facilitation moves made by Julia that addressed errors during the rehearsal seemed to have surfaced due to the ambiguity in the cards and her peers unsure how to correctly categorize them. Kaya had a fewer number of substantive foci labels attached to her facilitation moves because the majority of time was not in rehearsal, but planning for the enactment. As a result, Kaya had limited interactions to work on key relational aspects of leading a whole-class discussion.

TE Feedback

One of the stark differences between rehearsals is how the TEs engaged with the PSTs. Table 3 highlights the differences between PSTs in the percentage of total time the TEs provided feedback during the rehearsal and Table 6 compares the frequency of the types of feedback the TEs provided. Both tables indicate that Victor received the most feedback from the TEs. Victor may have benefited by having two TEs (Julia and Kaya had only one TE present). Additionally, Kaya and Julia's rehearsal took place after class with fewer other PSTs participating.

TE Exchanges With Victor

Both TEs during Victor's rehearsal provided feedback often, as well as responded with student ideas and misconceptions. The TEs took on distinct roles (e.g. coach, student) and forced Victor to work on his adaptive teaching skills in steering the class towards the mathematical point. As coaches, the TEs provided

Table 6. Types of Feedback from TEs in Rehearsal

	Victor	Julia	Kaya
Type of Feedback			
Directive feedback	5	3	3
Facilitates discussion	4	5	4
Scaffolds enactment	8	0	0
Evaluative feedback	2	0	1
Total	19	8	8

directive feedback and facilitated discussions where they posed questions to make Victor think deeply about his facilitation moves. As students, the TEs provided possible student ideas and misconceptions for Victor to make sense of and respond appropriately. One potential impactful interaction that occurred during the rehearsal was when the TEs acted as students as they led their respective table groups in developing an understanding of the defining characteristic of a quadrilateral (see Figure 2). One TE-led group made the case that a quadrilateral has to have four right angle symbols (student error), while the other TE-led group stated that a quadrilateral must have four sides (correct definition).

Victor first surfaced this ambiguity through eliciting and then pressing each group for their understanding of the right-angle symbols. When the two groups were at an impasse, he asked for another example of a quadrilateral, presumably, to clear up the confusion. The TE quickly interrupted saying that since the difference between the two groups' understanding is clear, eliciting another quadrilateral example may not help in moving the discussion toward the mathematical point. The TE remarked, *I am going to stop you there. You have reached a point where you have seen where the disagreement is in the room... it would be a good place to get in some non-examples.* The TEs followed up with feedback about certain actions that Victor could use to deal with the ambiguous cards such as moving the card to the "unsure" column or drawing a question mark around the card. The TEs' feedback was important for the IA to help Victor understand when it might be the right time to elicit cards for the next category. The TEs created a complex situation with their student ideas and misconceptions for Victor to try to navigate. With feedback from the TEs as coaches, Victor oriented the two groups' thinking towards each other to allow for a rich conversation about the characteristics of quadrilaterals.

Throughout the IA, Victor had a clear mathematical point - to develop a precise definition of a quadrilateral. The well-defined mathematical point may have helped the TEs as they provided specific and complex feedback and scaffolded the enactment with authentic student responses. Victor was receptive to the TEs' feedback, as he would immediately "redo" his facilitation move following their advice. The discussions that the TEs initiated allowed Victor to examine concrete classroom situations and allowed for him to enact the reflected upon practice.

Figure 2. Shape 7

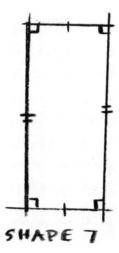

SHAPE 7

TE Exchanges With Julia

Throughout the rehearsal, the TE engaged with Julia as a coach, but not as a student. Specifically, there were no exchanges where the TE provided a student idea or misconception that Julia had to interpret and respond to. By having only one TE instead of two may have also contributed to the type of feedback. The majority of the exchanges between the TE and Julia were about instructional decision-making and more specifically, about how to categorize the ambiguous cards to help the students make sense of the cards. In particular, one interaction that Julia had with the TE was around a "bell-curved" graph (see Figure 3).

Julia said that she heard students in small-groups discussing ideas such as "bell-curve", "symmetrical", and that the card could be both, the mean and the median. Without asking for students to discuss their thinking, Julia moved the card representation to the "not sure" column. The TE paused the rehearsal and wondered why Julia moved the card to "not sure" column without students sharing out their small-group discussions. The TE remarked, *You heard an argument for the mean...you then heard an argument for the median...does that mean it's not the mean?* The TE advised Julia that she could press the class for an argument about why the card representation could also be the median or for an argument about why the card is not the mean. After the exchange, Julia agreed with the TE and put the card back into the "mean" column. Using the TE's guidance, Julia took up the suggestion by circling the card, drawing a question mark on top of it, and pressed the class further about their ideas of the mean and median.

Julia's less clear mathematical point and the ambiguity in the cards that she developed may have made it difficult for the TE to provide authentic student responses during the rehearsal. However, the TE seemed to have identified Julia's major need and worked with her to understand the ambiguities in her cards to effectively navigate potential student ideas and help them correctly categorize of the cards. The TE feedback integrated student ideas, content of the activity, and pedagogical moves – all three important to the success of leading a whole class discussion. The rehearsal gave Julia multiple opportunities to think deeply with others about how to best respond and guide students toward a definition of the mean and to develop a conceptual understanding of the three measures of central tendency.

Figure 3. Bell-Curved Graph

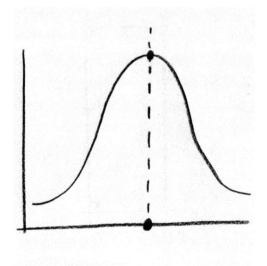

TE Exchanges With Kaya

Throughout Kaya's rehearsal Kaya and the TEs engaged in lengthy discussions about the non-performance aspects of leading a whole class discussion. The conversations included how to best display the cards, the content of the handouts that accompanied the cards, and the tension that Kaya felt between the demands of the math methods class assignment and her cooperating teacher. Kaya did not have many opportunities to rehearse and receive feedback on interactional aspects of leading a whole-class discussion as evidenced in Table 3. This could be because she was not yet ready to enact the IA. The majority of the exchanges during Kaya's rehearsal related to planning and defining the lesson objectives that could have been addressed prior to the rehearsal. Kaya only had a few opportunities to receive feedback from TEs about the core practices associated with leading a whole-class discussion.

Kaya did have one interaction during the rehearsal that allowed her to navigate student ideas and receive TE feedback. The discussion centered on the equation $x/6 = 6/x$ when Kaya asked for values that may or may not make the equation true. A PST acting as a student responded with *x equals zero*. Kaya did not expect that response as she paused and responded to her peers and TE about how they (referring to her actual students) had not previously discussed the mathematical idea of dividing by zero. Kaya decided not to use the PST's value for *x* and asked the class for another value that would make the equations always true. The TE called a timeout and asked Kaya, *Do you think your students are going to suggest zero? And what are you going to do if they do?* Kaya was unsure what to do in this situation. The TE further elaborated, *It's okay of you are going to table that one, but you need to think carefully how you are going to table it.* The TE offered ideas to Kaya how she may want to respond in that situation. In particular, the TE said, *You can say we are going to put that one to the side, I am going to make a note, and we will come back to talk about that one.* The TE further elaborated that at times during the IA, it may be necessary to ask the student to hold their thought, especially if the student's response was not moving the discussion toward the mathematical point. Kaya listened to the TE's feedback but did not rehearse the suggested facilitation move.

Having only one TE present may have limited the frequency and the type of feedback that Kaya received during the rehearsal. The TE did not scaffold the rehearsal enactment with student ideas or misconceptions, but rather acted as a coach providing directive feedback and facilitating discussions. While some of the exchanges with the TE were about the interaction between student ideas, pedagogy, and content, the majority of Kaya's rehearsal was spent trying to make sense of how the multiple learning objectives fit with the IA and to plan for the enactment. Unlike Julia's rehearsal, Kaya did not receive much feedback from the TE (other than the one interaction) on relational aspects of teaching. This may be in large part due to Kaya not being ready for the rehearsal, but also the balancing act that Kaya had to navigate between her cooperating teacher's expectations and the course assignment. Moreover, Kaya's cooperating teacher did not support the use of the sorting task activity as whole-class discussions were not generally used in the classroom. Unlike the other PSTs, Kaya had to find a way to modify the sorting task activity that better aligned with the cooperating teacher's expectations.

The rehearsals for Victor and Julia provided multiple opportunities for practice and feedback on facilitation moves that may have helped them succeed in enacting the sorting task IA and leading the whole-class discussion in their respective student teaching placements. The frequency and the type of feedback that they received on instructional decisions may have been a key difference between Victor's and Julia's rehearsals and Kaya's rehearsal. While Kaya's rehearsal feedback focused on planning and finding ways to clarify the mathematical point, Victor and Julia worked on core teaching practices and had productive discussions about student thinking, pedagogy, and content in relation to the mathematical point.

Research Question 2

The three PSTs in this study enacted the IA in their student teaching placements within two days following their rehearsals. In this section, I discuss how the PSTs facilitated the rehearsed IA with their students and describe some of the influences that may have supported or constrained the PSTs in leading the whole-class discussion. For each PST, I provide examples from their enactment that highlight the nature of discussion.

Victor's Enactment

In Victor's enactment, he conducted two sorting task activities in which students collectively developed a definition of a polygon and a quadrilateral respectively. During Victor's student teaching enactment, he elicited, discussed, and guided students to categorize multiple cards and reach a mathematical point. Victor's approach to facilitating the discussion was similar in both sorting activities. He first elicited a card that students were sure could be categorized as an example. Victor then followed up by pressing the class or the student on reasoning for the categorization. After he had a few ideas that supported the categorization, he elicited one to two more examples. Victor's methods of facilitation allowed for many students to share their ideas as they formed their definitions.

An example that represents Victor's facilitation style takes place at the beginning of the sort when Victor asked the class for a card categorized as a polygon. Shana replied with shape #10, a regular hexagon (see Figure 4).

Victor pressed the class for their reasoning on this card categorization. Gary responded that the card looked like a *stop sign*. Victor restated the students' reasoning and continued to press the class for another explanation, *What else makes this a polygon?* Miguel argued that since the shape closed, it must

Figure 4. Shape 10

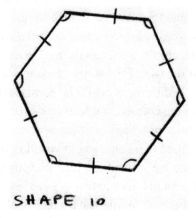

SHAPE 10

be a polygon. Victor repeated Miguel's reasoning in English and Spanish and wrote, *closed,* next to the card. Victor then elicited the class for another card that they categorized as a polygon. Miguel offered shape #5 (see Figure 5), a square with markings of right angles and congruent sides.

Victor pressed Miguel for his reasoning and he responded by saying the shape *is closed and has parallel lines.* Victor taped the card to the whiteboard and wrote Miguel's reasoning next to the card. Gary then raised his hand and argued that, *there are no polygons in the sixteen shapes.* Victor acknowledged Gary but directed him to hold his idea until they discussed non-example cards. *Interesting. I am glad you brought that up, Gary. Before we move onto what we are sure are not polygons, can anyone say why shape #5 is a polygon?* Victor pressed the class for more reasoning on card #5. Sarah responded by saying that *if the shape is closed, then it is a polygon.* Victor restated her comment and pressed the class for cards that they categorized as not polygons.

When student ideas did not move the conversation towards the mathematical point, Victor asked students to hold their thoughts and elicited more ideas. He restated, acknowledged, and pressed students while guiding them towards the mathematical point. Victor ended each of the sorting tasks by explicitly stating the definition of the object, the mathematical point, of the discussion. Throughout the discussion, Victor's students were fully engaged in the task and were excited to share their ideas with the class.

Julia's Enactment

Julia had a fluid approach to how she led the whole-class discussion. Although the mathematical point for her IA was less clear, she was able to lead a discussion filled with rich conversations about the different measures of central tendency. During the discussion, students were able to communicate their ideas showing both conceptual and procedural understanding and able to clearly justify and provide reasoning for their ideas. Julia was able to navigate her students' ideas and the ambiguities that surfaced with her cards.

An example from Julia's discussion is when she asked the class for a card that could be categorized as *mean.* Nicolas provided card #10 (see Figure 6), the data set containing the numbers {2, 6, 7, 12, 7, 3} with the number 7 in a box below them.

Figure 5. Shape 5

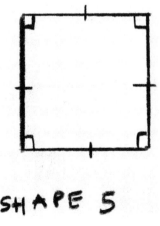

SHAPE 5

Figure 6. Data Set

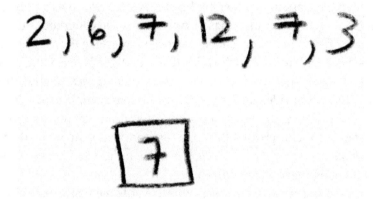

Julia placed the card in the *mean* column and then pressed Nicolas on how he found the average of these numbers. After a few seconds of silence, Julia asked the class for a strategy to calculate the average of the data set. Andrew proposed that the numbers should be added together and divided by the number of values in the data set. Julia wrote this method on the board, but decided not to calculate the mean. Sienna said, *That's not mean. I disagree with Andrew. It's mode.* Julia then wrote *not mean* on the board and moved this card underneath this new heading. Sienna continued with her explanation, *Mode is the number that appears most. That's why seven is in the box, since it repeats more than the other numbers.* During her explanation Nicolas noticed his error and agreed with Sienna by saying, *Oh yeah.* Julia restated Sienna's explanation and then asked the class, *Is it ever possible for the mode and mean to be the same?* Julia pointed to the method that Andrew had proposed earlier and said that by adding up all of the numbers in this data set and dividing by 6 does not result in a mean of seven. Julia continued to explain that if the mean calculation resulted in 7, the mean and the mode would be the same value.

As Julia facilitated the discussion by pressing, restating, and informing students when necessary, the students were able to develop complex ideas about the multiple representations of central tendency and eventually developed an understanding of the arithmetic mean, the mathematical point of the IA. Even though the cards surfaced much ambiguity throughout the discussion, Julia was able to provide scaffolding to guide her students to correctly categorize the cards. Julia took up the feedback and discussions during the rehearsal and adjusted accordingly. Julia responded to student thinking and connected student ideas to ultimately facilitate a generative discussion.

Kaya's Enactment

To launch the sorting task, Kaya gave each group of 3-4 students a sheet of paper with three columns: always, sometimes, and never true. She also distributed the sorting cards and instructed students to sort the cards into these three categories within their groups. After a few minutes, Kaya asked, *Can someone give me one that is always true?* Daniel (pseudonym) responded from the back of the classroom that he had a card. He offered card #6, *$2(x+3) = 2x+6$*. Kaya taped the card to the front board and then pressed Daniel on why this card was always true. Daniel said, *Because the lines are infinite.* Kaya pressed Daniel about his understanding of infinite solutions, *How do you know the lines are infinite?* Daniel explained, *It's the same line. If you switch them around, the lines will be the same.* Kaya continued to press Daniel on how to distribute the expression on the left side of the equal sign to have equivalent expressions, *How do you change them around?* Daniel was not sure, so Kaya drew two arrows on the board to indicate that the "2" could be distributed. The majority of the enactment consisted of interactions between Kaya and one student (Daniel). Kaya attempted to involve other students in the class, but was unsuccessful. Kaya's seemed frustrated with the lack of engagement from her students and how the discussion was progressing.

Another example from Kaya's enactment that highlights her discussion was when she pressed Jimmy on why he categorized the card $x/6 = 6/x$ as *never true*. Jimmy said that he did not know and requested that Kaya call on a different student. Daniel explained, *They are parallel and they never touch.* Since the initial categorization (by Jimmy) was said to be never true, Daniel connected "never true" categorization to parallel lines, an idea they developed in the warm-up before the discussion. Kaya proposed an example that disproved Daniel's reasoning, *What about if x equals 6?* She said that if *6* were substituted for *x*, the equation would be true. To press students on their understanding of categorizing cards, Kaya asked students for values that would show that the equation was equivalent or not equivalent. After a few incorrect responses, Kaya provided the values that would make true and untrue statements. Kaya showed that substituting the value of *3* for *x* would result in an equation that is not true. Kaya summarized by saying that if one value works and the other did not, the card should be categorized as *sometimes true* instead of *never true*. During this exchange, students seemed to struggle to connect that non-equivalent equations do not necessarily mean that they are parallel and overall with evaluating values for equations to determine their truth.

Kaya decided to end the activity after eliciting and discussing three cards, perhaps, because the activity was not progressing towards the mathematical point and students were not engaging with the IA. There were some key factors that may have contributed to the non-generative nature of the discussion. The tension between the assignment objectives from the math methods course and the expectations from the cooperating teacher seemed to have Kaya trying to fit multiple learning objectives in the IA. With an unclear mathematical point for the IA, the students did not have a clear picture of what they were to learn. Additionally, the whole-class discussion format was new for her students as they had mostly worked in small-groups throughout the year. Finally, with the format being new for Kaya and her students and the limited opportunities to practice and receive feedback during the rehearsal, she may have been unprepared for enacting the IA.

Victor and Julia seemed to be more equipped to use their experience from the rehearsal as they re-contextualized the IA from the math methods course and implemented it in their respective student teaching placements. In particular, Victor and Julia were able to take up the feedback and practice from the rehearsals to facilitate generative discussions. However, it is not clear if the success for these two PSTs could be attributed to the rehearsal, preparation, or other factors. Having the mathematical goals and content aligned with the IA before the rehearsal may be essential to open up opportunities for PSTs to learn. It may be that certain mathematical content is better suited than others for facilitating the sorting task IA to reach a mathematical point. Sleep (2012) argues that a set of cohesive mathematical ideas is essential in moving the discussion towards a mathematical point. The lack of a consistent storyline may have contributed to Kaya's rehearsal or lack of rehearsal. It seems as if the TE and the other PSTs were unaware of the direction that Kaya intended to move the discussion. The unclear mathematical point as well as her absence from class in the previous week may have influenced the opportunities for practice and feedback as the rehearsal did not allow for an organized process for Kaya to have authentic interactions with peers and TEs within the math methods class.

CONCLUSION

The three case studies presented in this chapter highlight the complexity of TE feedback and the importance of affording PSTs opportunities to practice interactional aspects of teaching during rehearsals. Further investigation is needed to examine the roles the TEs play during rehearsals and the decisions they make to scaffold the enactment with student ideas. In this study, the TEs were novices and were still developing their practice as they engaged in this new and complex practice-based teacher education work. As TEs are often provided limited formal training for preparing PSTs, this study highlights the need for further training for TEs on the pedagogies and mathematics used in rehearsals. For example, training programs might address how to effectively design pedagogies to decompose core teaching practices, provide scaffolding prior to the rehearsals, and effective ways to provide feedback during rehearsals. The feedback that the TE provides is a key aspect of the PST learning and contributes to the authenticity and complexity of the rehearsal. Feedback can come in different forms and seems to be most effective during the rehearsals when the content and learning objectives are in alignment with the instructional activity. Having two TEs present may also add to the authenticity and complexity of a rehearsal and better prepare the PST for their student teaching enactment. In particular, the two TEs can switch off roles during the rehearsal – one acting as a student and the other acting like a coach. Additionally, this study brings up this issue of how content is developed for the IAs – should TEs design all materials (e.g. sorting activity cards) to ensure alignment, even if it may impact the authenticity of the approximation? The fieldwork norms and demands (e.g. cooperating teacher, instructional format, curriculum) placed on the PST may also need to be in accordance with the teacher education program for a successful rehearsal and student teaching enactment. Further IA development that aligns fieldwork experiences with coursework is needed in teacher preparation.

Learning cycles provide a tangible method for schools and universities to collaborate in preparing PSTs. However, for rehearsals to effectively approximate the teaching practice and prepare PSTs for the complexities of teaching, certain structures must be in place. In particular, TEs and cooperating teachers may need to collaborate to find content that can be investigated, analyzed, and rehearsed in the university setting and then enacted in the school setting. Collaboration between the TE and cooperating teachers may allow for the development of a more comprehensive IA and an authentic rehearsal that closely approximates the classroom setting, and supports PST fieldwork experiences. Further, to better prepare for the different school contexts in which they teach, teacher education programs may want to look at holding rehearsals in school settings. In particular, some teacher education programs have begun to partner with schools, conducting rehearsals with actual students in classrooms (Kazemi & Wæge, 2015; Virmani, Taylor, Rumsey, Box, Kazemi, Knapp, ... Woods, 2017; Weston & Henderson, 2015). This might allow for more authentic interactions with students within a setting that nearly resembles the actual classroom and allow for more natural opportunities for collaboration between TEs and cooperating teachers.

Facilitating a whole-class discussion with the aim of moving the discussion towards a mathematical point is a cognitively demanding task as PSTs often struggle with enacting complex teaching practices (Borko, Eisenhart, Brown, Underhill, Jones, & Agard, 1992; Inoue, 2009; Thanheiser, 2009). As the Inoue (2009) study suggested, opportunities to investigate and reflect on core teaching practices are critical to the success of the rehearsal process. Extensive research still needs to be conducted on the multiple stages associated with learning cycles, especially the pedagogical approaches that TEs use to prepare PSTs before the rehearsal. Further, this study raised the issue if a PST is not ready for rehearsal, how should the TE adjust the design and timing of rehearsal activities to meet the immediate learning needs of the PST. For instance, should the TE redirect a PST to engage in the rehearsal if it shifts to planning? Or does a shift toward planning simply indicate that the PST is not yet prepared for the rehearsal and that planning is precisely what the PST needs at this stage in developing his/her practice? How does the TE adjust to the individual needs of PSTs in a way that best prepares the PST for the demands of teaching? PSTs seem to need ample opportunities to investigate and make sense of the teaching practices as TEs pay close attention to the scaffolding that they provide and how the teaching practice is decomposed.

Learning cycles within practice-based teacher education models may provide PSTs the opportunities they need to engage in and think deeply about core teaching practices and potentially strengthen the connection between university and fieldwork experiences. TEs play an essential role in learning cycles as they develop pedagogies for PSTs to make sense of the teaching practice. As PSTs engage in rehearsals of IAs with specific TE feedback, they begin to understand the interaction between student thinking, pedagogy, and content, and their role in facilitating student learning. Rehearsals may be considered an integral component for preparing PSTs as they enact core teaching practices in their field-based experiences. By engaging PSTs in the cycle of investigation, planning, rehearsal, and enactment with robust and frequent opportunities for analysis and reflection on their practice, PSTs will be well positioned to teach.

REFERENCES

Baldinger, E., Selling, S. K., & Virmani, R. (2016). Supporting novice teachers to lead discussions that reach a mathematical point. *Mathematics Teacher Educator*, *5*(1), 8–28. doi:10.5951/mathteaceduc.5.1.0008

Ball, D. L., & Forzani, F. M. (2009). The work of teaching and the challenge for teacher education. *Journal of Teacher Education*, *60*(5), 497–511. doi:10.1177/0022487109348479

Boaler, J. (2008). Promoting 'relational equity' and high mathematics achievement through an innovative mixed-ability approach. *British Educational Research Journal*, *34*(2), 167–194. doi:10.1080/01411920701532145

Boerst, T. A., Sleep, L., Ball, D. L., & Bass, H. (2011). Preparing teachers to lead mathematics discussions. *Teachers College Record*, *113*(12), 2844–2877.

Borko, H., Eisenhart, M., Brown, C., Underhill, R., Jones, D., & Agard, P. (1992). Learning to teach hard mathematics: Do novice teachers and their instructors give up too easily? *Journal for Research in Mathematics Education*, *23*(3), 194–222. doi:10.2307/749118

Borko, H., Virmani, R., Khachatryan, E., & Mangram, C. (2014). The role of video-based discussions in professional development and the preparation of professional development leaders. In B. D. Calandra & P. Rich (Eds.), *Digital video for teacher education: Research and practice* (pp. 89–108). Philadelphia, PA: Routledge.

Buckley, F. J. (2000). *Team teaching: What, why and how?* Thousand Oaks, CA: Sage Publications, Inc.

Cengiz, N., Kline, K., & Grant, T. J. (2011). Extending students' mathematical thinking during whole-group discussions. *Journal of Mathematics Teacher Education*, *14*(5), 355–374. doi:10.100710857-011-9179-7

Chapin, S. H., O'Connor, C., & Anderson, N. C. (2013). *Classroom discussions in math: A teacher's guide for using talk moves to support the Common Core and more, Grades K-6* (3rd ed.). Sausalito, CA: Math Solutions Publications.

Chazan, D., & Ball, D. L. (1999). Beyond being told not to tell. *For the Learning of Mathematics, 19*(2), 2–10.

Core Practices Consortium. (2013). Building a shared understanding for designing and studying practice-based teacher education. In *Symposium presented at the annual meeting of the American Educational Research Association*, San Francisco, CA.

Davis, J. E. (1975). *Team teaching. What research says to the teacher*. Washington, DC: National Education Association.

Dewey, J. (1904). The relation of theory to practice in education. In *The Third yearbook of the National Society for the Scientific Study of Education: Part 1: The Relation of theory to practice in the education of teachers* (pp. 9–30). Chicago: University of Chicago Press.

Dewey, J. (1925). Logic: The Theory of Inquiry (1938). *The later works, 1953*, 1-549.

Ensor, P. (2001). From preservice mathematics teacher education to beginning teaching: A study in re-contextualizing. *Journal for Research in Mathematics Education, 32*(3), 296–320. doi:10.2307/749829

Ghousseini, H., & Herbst, P. (2016). Pedagogies of practice and opportunities to learn about classroom mathematics discussions. *Journal of Mathematics Teacher Education, 19*(1), 79–103. doi:10.100710857-014-9296-1

Grossman, P., Compton, C., Igra, D., Rondfelt, M., Shahan, E., & Williamson, P. (2009). Teaching practice: A cross-professional perspective. *Teachers College Record, 111*(9), 2055–2100.

Grossman, P., Hammerness, K., & McDonald, M. (2009). Redefining teaching, re-imagining teacher education. *Teachers and Teaching, 15*(2), 273–289. doi:10.1080/13540600902875340

Grossman, P., & McDonald, M. (2008). Back to the future: Directions for research in teaching and teacher education. *American Educational Research Journal, 45*(1), 184–205. doi:10.3102/0002831207312906

Inoue, N. (2009). Rehearsing to teach: Content-specific deconstruction of instructional explanations in pre-service teacher training. *Journal of Education for Teaching, 35*(1), 47–60. doi:10.1080/02607470802587137

Kazemi, E., Franke, M., & Lampert, M. (2009). Developing pedagogies in teacher education to support novice teachers' ability to enact ambitious instruction. In *Crossing Divides, Proceedings of the 32nd Annual Conference of The Mathematics Education Research Group of Australasia* (Vol. 1, pp. 11-29). Academic Press.

Kazemi, E., Ghousseini, H., Cunard, A., & Turrou, A. C. (2016). Getting inside rehearsals: Insights from teacher educators support work on complex practice. *Journal of Teacher Education, 67*(1), 18–31. doi:10.1177/0022487115615191

Kazemi, E., & Hintz, A. (2014). *Intentional talk: How to structure and lead productive mathematical discussions*. Portland, ME: Stenhouse Publishers.

Kazemi, E., Lampert, M., & Ghousseini, H. (2007). Conceptualizing and using routines of practice in mathematics teaching to advance professional education. Report to the Spencer Foundation.

Kazemi, E., & Wæge, K. (2015). Learning to teach within practice-based methods courses. *Mathematics Teacher Education and Development*, *17*(2), 125–145.

Kennedy, M. M. (1999). The role of preservice teacher education. In L. Darling-Hammond & G. Sykes (Eds.), *Teaching as the learning profession: Handbook of policy and practice* (pp. 54–86). San Francisco, CA: Josey-Bass.

Lampert, M., Beasley, H., Ghousseini, H., Kazemi, E., & Franke, M. (2010). Using designed instructional activities to enable novices to manage ambitious mathematics teaching. In M. K. Stein & L. Kucan (Eds.), *Instructional explanations in the disciplines* (pp. 129–141). Springer, US. doi:10.1007/978-1-4419-0594-9_9

Lampert, M., Franke, M. L., Kazemi, E., Ghousseini, H., Turrou, A. C., Beasley, H., ... Crowe, K. (2013). Keeping it complex using rehearsals to support novice teacher learning of ambitious teaching. *Journal of Teacher Education*, *64*(3), 226–243. doi:10.1177/0022487112473837

Lampert, M., & Graziani, F. (2009). Instructional activities as a tool for teachers' and teacher educators' learning. *The Elementary School Journal*, *109*(5), 491–509. doi:10.1086/596998

Lave, J., & Wenger, E. (1991). *Situated learning: Legitimate peripheral participation*. Cambridge University Press. doi:10.1017/CBO9780511815355

Leatham, K. R., Peterson, B. E., Stockero, S. L., & Van Zoest, L. R. (2015). Conceptualizing mathematically significant pedagogical opportunities to build on student thinking. *Journal for Research in Mathematics Education*, *46*(1), 88–124. doi:10.5951/jresematheduc.46.1.0088

Leinhardt, G. (2001). Instructional explanations: A commonplace for teaching and a location for contrast. In V. Richardson (Ed.), *Handbook of research on teaching* (4th ed.; pp. 333–357). Washington, DC: American Educational Research Association.

Leinhardt, G., & Greeno, J. G. (1986). The cognitive skill of teaching. *Journal of Educational Psychology*, *78*(2), 75–95. doi:10.1037/0022-0663.78.2.75

Marshall, J. D., Smagorinsky, & Smith, M. (1995). *The language of interpretation: Patterns of discourse in discussions of literature*. Academic Press.

McDonald, M. A., Kazemi, E., & Kavanagh, S. S. (2013). Core practices and pedagogies of teacher education: A call for a common language and collective activity. *Journal of Teacher Education*, *64*(5), 378–386. doi:10.1177/0022487113493807

National Council of Teachers of Mathematics (NCTM). (2000). *Principles and standards for school mathematics*. Reston, VA: Author.

Obrycki, J., Herbel-Eisenmann, B. & Cirillo, M. (2009) Listening to my students' thoughts on mathematics education. *Promoting purposeful discourse: Teacher research in mathematics classrooms*, 187-202.

Parrish, S. (2010). *Number talks: Helping children build mental math and computation strategies, grades K–5*. Sausalito, CA: Math Solutions.

Rogoff, B. (2003). *The cultural nature of human development*. Oxford University Press.

Sleep, L. (2012). The work of steering instruction toward the mathematical point: A decomposition of teaching practice. *American Educational Research Journal, 49*(5), 935–970. doi:10.3102/0002831212448095

Sleep, L., & Boerst, T. A. (2012). Preparing beginning teachers to elicit and interpret students' mathematical thinking. *Teaching and Teacher Education, 28*(7), 1038–1048. doi:10.1016/j.tate.2012.04.005

Smith, M. S., & Stein, M. K. (2011). *5 practices for orchestrating productive mathematical discussions*. Reston, VA: National Council of Teachers of Mathematics.

Stein, M. K., Engle, R. A., Smith, M. S., & Hughes, E. K. (2008). Orchestrating productive mathematical discussions: Five practices for helping teachers move beyond show and tell. *Mathematical Thinking and Learning, 10*(4), 313–340. doi:10.1080/10986060802229675

Studio Code Business Group. (2012). *Studiocode*. Warriewood, NSW: Sportstec.

Thanheiser, E. (2009). Preservice elementary school teachers' conceptions of multidigit whole numbers. *Journal for Research in Mathematics Education, 40*, 251–281.

van Es, E. A. (2012). Examining the development of a teacher learning community: The case of a video club. *Teaching and Teacher Education, 28*(2), 182–192. doi:10.1016/j.tate.2011.09.005

Virmani, R., Taylor, M., Rumsey, C., Box, T., Kazemi, E., & Knapp, M. … Woods, D. (2017). Bringing methods into schools. In S. Kastberg, A. Tyminski, A. Lischka, & W. Sanchez (Eds.), Building support for scholarly practices in mathematics methods. Charlotte, NC: IAP.

Weston, T. L., & Henderson, S. C. (2015). Coherent experiences: The new missing paradigm in teacher education. *The Educational Forum, 79*(3), 321–335. doi:10.1080/00131725.2015.1037514

Williamson, P. (2013). Enacting high leverage practices in English methods: The case of discussion. *English Education, 46*(1), 34–67.

Chapter 27
Developing Teacher Leaders Through Self-Study:
A Mathematics Education Field Experience

Courtney K. Baker
George Mason University, USA

Laura E. Bitto
George Mason University, USA

Theresa Wills
George Mason University, USA

Terrie McLaughlin Galanti
George Mason University, USA

Cassandra Cook Eatmon
George Mason University, USA

ABSTRACT

Effective mathematics specialists require opportunities to apply knowledge from their advanced preparation programs to their practice. Just as pre-service teachers engage in field experiences to practice instructional strategies, in-service educators should engage in field experiences to apply leadership knowledge and skills while under the supervision of an experienced and highly-qualified teacher educator. This chapter describes the culminating self-study field experiences in a masters-level advanced certification program which prepares in-service teachers to be K-8 mathematics specialists. Through collaboration with critical friends, the mathematics specialist candidates connected research to practice in the design and implementation of a self-study project. Their work chronicled an important transformation from teachers to teacher leaders. The candidates also described their interest and their new capacity to conduct research beyond their certification programs for the purposes of impacting teacher and student learning within their organizations.

DOI: 10.4018/978-1-5225-6249-8.ch027

INTRODUCTION

Teaching mathematics requires specialized pedagogical content knowledge (Ball, Hill, & Bass, 2005; Ball, Thames, & Phelps, 2008), yet many elementary educators are generalists (Wu, 2009). As a result, individuals are entering the teaching profession with the need to further develop the specialized pedagogical content knowledge required for mathematics in order to possess strong understanding of mathematics content at all levels (Spangler & Ovrick, 2017). Mathematics specialists, at times referred to as mathematics coaches, are a viable solution to improving practicing teachers' mathematics instruction (Campbell & Malkus, 2011). Across the nation, there is little agreement regarding both the titles (McGatha & Rigelman, 2017) and roles (Fennell, 2017) of mathematics specialists. McGatha and Rigelman (2017) define a mathematics specialist as "a professional with an advanced certification as a mathematics instructional leader or who works in such a leadership role" (p. xiv). In their definition, McGatha and Rigelman describe three primary roles that a mathematics specialist might take on: 1) a mathematics teacher who is situated in a K-12 classroom; 2) a mathematics intervention specialist whose work centers on K-12 "push in" or "pull out" intervention programs and students, and; 3) a mathematics coach that works primarily with teachers. No matter how situated, a mathematics specialist synthesizes content, pedagogical, and leadership knowledge to connect research to practice in schools.

According to the 2011 National Assessment of Educational Progress (NAEP) survey, 3,010 out of 7,940 elementary schools (38%) reported the use of either a full- or part-time elementary mathematics specialist (Harbour, 2015). Currently, 20 states have either a state certification or endorsement pathway to become a mathematics specialist (Rigelman & Wray, 2017; Fennell, 2017; Spangler & Ovrick, 2017). These advanced certificate programs prepare practicing teachers to further develop expertise in mathematics content, pedagogy, and leadership (Association of Mathematics Teacher Educators [AMTE], 2013) and mathematics specialists to flexibly work with any student or teacher at any level (Spangler & Ovrick, 2017). "An interest in leadership does not necessarily indicate strong content knowledge on the part of participants" (Whitenack & Ellington, 2013). Specialized leadership coursework is required to provide specific experiences not found in content and pedagogy courses such as: developing and implementing high-quality professional development; providing constructive feedback; understanding how teachers' beliefs are sustained and changed; and advocating for high-quality mathematics instruction for all (Spangler & Ovrick, 2017).

The certification and licensure of mathematics specialists are handled differently by different states (Spangler & Ovrick, 2017) and universities (Burton & Beaver, 2017; Goodman, McCoy & Campbell, 2017; Rigelman, 2017; Schwartz, Morge, Rachlin, & Hargrove, 2017). Throughout the United States, university programs utilize not only traditional face-to-face instruction but also various types of online instruction such as synchronous, asynchronous and blended learning models (Bezuk & Becker, 2017; Burton & Beaver, 2017; Spangler & Ovrick, 2017). Both the AMTE (2013) and National Council of Teachers of Mathematics (NCTM) Council for the Accreditation of Educator Preparation (CAEP) Standards (2012) recommend a supervised teaching practicum in which mathematics specialist candidates acquire experience working with both student and adult learners in a variety of professional settings. Upon examination of the state endorsement program documents, Bitto (2015) found that ten states did not specify such practicum requirements. However, several universities implementing the mathematics specialist advanced certification included additional components, such as practicum or field experiences, within their programs. Similar to pre-service teachers, mathematics specialist candidates need opportunities to apply new knowledge through a field experience under the supervision of a highly-qualified teacher educator (Spangler & Ovrick, 2017).

Although AMTE (2013) suggests a practicum or field experience as a part of the certification for mathematics specialists, there are no articles to date on field experiences of mathematics specialist candidates (Baker, Bailey, Larsen, & Galanti, 2017). While few models exist to guide the evaluation of advanced licensure programs (Rigelman, 2017), a culminating field experience could potentially serve as an assessment of a particular program. Field experiences as part of mathematics specialist advanced licensure programs are worthy of consideration. Because of the variety of anticipated or actual roles and responsibilities for mathematics specialist candidates, "it is important for program developers to consider a wide range of both what counts as a field experience and how such a field experience can be documented and assessed" (Spangler & Ovrick, 2017, p. 50).

The purpose of this chapter is to share how one advanced certification program prepares in-service teachers to be K-8 mathematics specialists through a culminating field experience centered on self-study. A unique challenge to developing a field experience for mathematics specialist candidates is that, in most cases, these advanced candidates are already in a full-time teaching or coaching position. Self-study research is a practical and meaningful way for in-service teachers and coaches to apply theory to practice while simultaneously enacting their current role. Different than action research, self-study places an emphasis on change of the self (Samaras, 2011), making it an ideal process for mathematics specialists to engage in to not only promote growth in their pedagogical, content, and leadership knowledge, but also to demonstrate professional application of this specialized knowledge.

Designing Field Experiences for Teacher Leaders

Preservice teacher preparation programs include culminating field experiences or internships in which students apply their knowledge from coursework to classroom settings. During these experiences, prospective teachers align their emerging beliefs and their new knowledge with the culture of the assigned classrooms or schools. They may struggle with the incongruence of the "advocated practice" of their coursework and the "situated practice" of the teachers and schools in which they are working (Clift & Brady, 2005, p. 332). In contrast, in-service teachers who are studying in master's level leadership development programs have teaching beliefs that have been informed by their current roles and responsibilities in K-12 settings. The field experiences for these in-service teachers must allow them to apply their new leadership knowledge within their current contexts, to build expertise in teaching colleagues (Reys, Webel, & de Araujo, 2017), and to reflect on their experiences (Rigelman, 2017). They need opportunities to exercise their emerging skills in connecting research to practice as they purposefully integrate content knowledge and pedagogical content knowledge (Shulman, 1986) along with specialized leadership skills and knowledge (Spangler & Ovrick, 2017). These in-service teachers can achieve these goals through a carefully designed culminating self-study project.

Preparing Mathematics Specialists

Advanced preparation programs for mathematics teacher leaders should provide experiences where candidates learn to balance the responsibilities of "building relationships with community stakeholders and fostering the growth of mathematical and pedagogical content knowledge in classrooms" (Baker, Bailey, Hjalmarson, & King, 2017, p. 184). The joint position statement of the AMTE, the Association of State Supervisors of Mathematics (ASSM), the National Council of Supervisors of Mathematics (NCSM), and the NCTM describes "teacher leaders who are responsible for supporting effective PK–6 mathematics instruction and student learning" (2013, p. 1) as elementary *mathematics specialists*. The Virginia Mathematics and Science Coalition (2016) further describes mathematics specialists as individuals in elementary and middle schools who "are released from full-time classroom responsibilities so that they can support the professional growth of their colleagues" (para. 1).

The call to support mathematics teaching and learning through the use of mathematics specialists began in the early 1970s but has rapidly progressed over the past decade. Mathematics specialists, also called mathematics teacher leaders or mathematics coaches, can act as "transition agents" to implement policy initiatives related to standards, curriculum, assessment, and professional development (Fennell, 2017, p. 4). The specific roles and responsibilities of mathematics specialists may include mentoring, coaching, planning and providing professional development, assisting with curriculum and instruction, coordinating and monitoring intervention, and supporting professional learning communities (Fennell, 2017).

The preparation of mathematics specialists should connect research to practice and facilitate the construction of content knowledge, pedagogical content knowledge, expertise in working with adult learners, and leadership skills (de Araujo, Webel, & Reys, 2017). NCTM *Principles to Actions* (2014) acknowledges the critical role of mathematics specialists in enhancing teacher capacity to enact research-based teaching practices. Teacher educators and researchers are working toward identifying accompanying high-leverage practices to support mathematics specialists as they balance the responsibilities of "building relationships with community stakeholders and fostering the growth of mathematical and pedagogical content knowledge in classrooms" (Baker, Bailey, Hjalmarson, & King, 2017, p. 184).

Following the National Mathematics Advisory Panel (2008) endorsement of the use of mathematics specialists, AMTE (2013) published the *Standards for Elementary Mathematics Specialists: A Reference for Teacher Credentialing and Degree Programs* as a guiding framework for states creating mathematics specialist endorsements or certifications. The AMTE Standards (2013) suggest content for programs which includes: content knowledge for teaching mathematics, pedagogical knowledge for teaching mathematics, and leadership knowledge and skills. Also recommended is a minimum number of credit hours and a supervised practicum, or field experience, in which mathematics specialist candidates experience work with both students and adult learners (e.g. teachers, administrators, parents) in one or more of a variety of professional settings. Self-study, as a research methodology, provided the necessary structure for these field experiences.

Developing Leadership Through Self-Study

Teachers who engage in self-study seek to understand their practice in order to revise it and better understand themselves in relation to others (Pinnegar & Hamilton, 2009). Samaras (2011) outlines five foci for teachers who engage in self-study research methodology. First, they must understand themselves and the context in which they work. They select a *personal situated inquiry* with immediate utility in the pursuit of educational reform (Samaras, 2011, p. 74). Teachers can draw upon research-based understandings to *generate and present knowledge* which changes not only their own practice but that of others within and beyond their contextual realm. Next, self-study researchers engage in *critical collaborative inquiry* to generate this new knowledge. They must seek the support of critical friends to "enhance learning and to better inform the subsequent claims derived from such learning" (Bullough & Pinnegar, 2004, p. 313).

Personal situated inquiry and critical collaborative inquiry work in concert, resulting in *improved learning* not only for themselves but for their students and the educational field (Samaras, 2011, p. 72). Finally, self-study is more than action and reflection; it is defined by *a transparent and systematic research process* with a rigorous review of literature, data collection, and a data analysis trail (Samaras, 2011, p. 81).

Self-study "urges teachers to find their own voices, to improve their practices, to extend their relationships, and to discover and document their potential as leaders of change" (Austin & Senese, 2004, p. 1231), yet there is a limited base of literature on the use of self-study within educational master's programs. Freese (2005) described her use of self-study for pre-service teachers enrolled in a two-year master's preparation program. As her students engaged in critical analysis and systematic written reflection based upon their field observations and practicum experiences, they described a transformation of their thinking and teaching. The products of their self-study could be used to influence teaching and learning beyond individual experiences. Koster and van den Berg (2011) studied the written work of 30 in-service teachers enrolled in a master's program in teaching and learning. These teachers explored their professional identities and defined critical moments using three research methodologies: biography, core reflection, and Socratic dialogue. They shared pedagogical dilemmas in order to understand their core values as teachers and to build perspectives. Both of these master's level self-study projects emphasized reflection on a personal experience; the students did not articulate a research question that framed their actions and reflections.

A research-based design of a field experience, with reliance on critical friends for ongoing support, strengthens the opportunities for teacher leaders to impact not only their own practice but the educational field.

Self-study research transcends the individual through collaborative, questioning, dialogic and action-oriented processes... and interaction with others is deeply bound to constituent elements of self-study research – learning, action and knowledge creation. (Bodone, Gudjo´nsdo´ttir, & Dalmau, 2004, pp. 746-747).

These elements of self-study research are especially relevant for teacher leaders enrolled in a master's program as they identify a problem which transcends their individual practice and work toward a stronger alignment of practices and beliefs (Loughran, 2004).

Methods

The following question guided this study: How does a self-study field experience in an advanced program for mathematics specialists prepare candidates to become effective leaders? By analyzing candidates' self-study projects, the researchers identified evidence supporting and documenting the growth in the candidates as they worked toward certification as mathematics teacher leaders.

The Mathematics Specialist Leader Preparation Program

The Mathematics Specialist Leader (K-8) program at George Mason University, established in 2005, provides opportunities for candidates to simultaneously deepen and apply their mathematical content, pedagogy, and leadership knowledge. The program is designed to encapsulate both the expectation of constructed expertise and the range of roles in which the graduates will engage as they improve the overall mathematics teaching and learning within their contexts. The 30-credit program meets requirements for Virginia licensure and is aligned with both the AMTE (2013) *Standards for Elementary Mathematics Specialists* and the NCTM (2012) CAEP *Standards for Elementary Mathematics Specialists*. The program includes all coursework required for Virginia licensure as a K-8 mathematics specialist in addition to a master's degree in Education Leadership with a concentration in Mathematics Specialist Leadership (K-8). Candidates study mathematics content, pedagogy, research, curriculum, and leadership. Each course in the program allows mathematics specialist candidates to apply learning as they promote instructional shifts in practice and advocate for rigorous and coherent learning opportunities within their schools.

The mathematics specialist candidates in the advanced program at George Mason University are experienced educators in a variety of K-12 school positions. As a result, their field experiences must be flexibly constructed to demonstrate the development of their mathematics leadership skills in authentic and relevant practical experiences. To meet this need, the capstone course of the program, Internship in Mathematics Education, requires candidates to complete a self-study field experience in which they learn to use knowledge of mathematics content, pedagogy, and leadership *simultaneously* while acting in their roles and fulfilling their responsibilities (Bitto, 2015).

The Participants: Mathematics Specialist Candidates

This study analyzed the work of 21 mathematics specialist candidates enrolled in either the fall or spring semester of the 2016-2017 academic year. All participants were female, ranging in age from mid-20's to late 40s. Participants included 13 teachers, six mathematics specialists, a special education teacher, and an English as a Second Language teacher. They represented 15 elementary schools, four middle schools, and two high schools in a mid-Atlantic metropolitan area.

The Mathematics Specialist Field Experience: A Self-Study Research Project

The culminating self-study project was incorporated into the 15-week hybrid class Internship in Mathematics Education. Approximately 50% of the class sessions met synchronously online in the web-based platform Blackboard Collaborate Ultra. Five classes were held asynchronously, and two classes occurred face-to-face at weeks 10 and 15.

The self-study assignment in the mathematics specialist advanced certification program required candidates to identify a problem of practice and design a research project around that topic. The flexibility of topic choice allowed candidates to meet the diverse expectations of their positions and communities. Throughout the semester, candidates collaborated with critical friends to catalog their research and reflect on practice. The five foci for self-study reflective inquiry (Samaras, 2011) guided shared critical reflections that were incorporated into all components of the self-study research project.

The primary textbook for the course was *Self-Study Teacher Research: Improving Your Practice through Collaborative Inquiry* (Samaras, 2011). During the first class the candidates received an overview of self-study, briefly explored their situational wonderings, and identified their critical friends. Once candidates identified their topics, several weeks were spent gathering literature that served as a research-based foundation and conceptual framework. The problems of practice that candidates identified for their self-study research projects centered on current issues in mathematics education (Table 1).

During online discussions and activities, candidates were expected to demonstrate positive and collaborative professional dispositions towards their peers along with a willingness to accept constructive

Table 1. Mathematics Specialist Candidates' Self-Study Research Projects

Self-Study Themes	Titles of Projects
Developing Effective Student Interventions	1. Building Number Sense: Effective, Targeted Intervention onStructuring Numbers 2. Teacher-Created Math Intervention Programs 3. Fact Fluency: Using Strategies to Become Fluent with Addition 4. Understanding Fractions by Having Students Explore in a Small Group Intervention Time
Equity and Access	5. Incorporating Language into Secondary Math Classrooms: Increasing Math Literacy and Critical Thinking Skills through Math Discourse 6. Flipping Out in the Math Classroom: A Study in How the Flipped Classroom Model Impacts Learning and Engagement for Students with Learning Disabilities 7. Math Vocabulary: How to Teach Students for Better Understanding and Retention 8. Numberless Word Problems: Building Mathematical Reasoning in Problem Solving 9. Effective Practices in Math Vocabulary Instruction of ELLs 10. Supporting English Language Learners in Understanding Grade-Level Mathematics Vocabulary 11. Raising Engagement Levels of Students in Poverty Through the Use of Rich Mathematical Tasks 12. Teaching Math to English Language Learners
Ambitious Teaching	13. The Effects of Math Journals on Student Achievement 14. Math Workshop: Increasing Student Motivation, Engagement, and Accountability 15. The Impact of Math Workshop on Engaging Algebra 2 Students in Learning Math 16. Exploring the Role of Technology in Differentiated Math Lessons 17. Math Stations 18. Impact of Implementing Number Talks in a 4th Grade Classroom 19. Rich Tasks in the Mathematics Classroom: A Study in How Rich Tasks Impact Academic Performance
Becoming A Leader	20. From Teacher to Leader: A Novice Coach's Journey
Co-Teaching	21. Co-teaching in Mathematics

criticism. They worked with their critical friends to catalogue their research by sharing weekly updates in class, exchanging research memos (Samaras, 2011), brainstorming ideas about their problems of practice, researching ideas for strategies and lessons, sharing how they had integrated standards in meaningful ways, and participating in ongoing peer review of their research reports. Critical friends supported one another's research and provided alternative perspectives on interpretations. All critical friend memos and responses were maintained on the course Blackboard space in blogs with access restricted to partnerships.

Role of the Instructor

During the self-study field experience, candidates were supervised and mentored by a mathematics education instructor who also served as the instructor of the field experience course. This instructor did not visit the mathematics specialist candidates in the field as a pre-service field supervisor might, but rather guided the advanced candidates' research and inquiry via online collaborations synchronously and asynchronously throughout the field experience. The overall role of the instructor was to pace and guide the mathematics specialist candidates during their self-study projects, while simultaneously transitioning authority. Candidates thus become leaders not only within their self-studies but within their professional contexts as well.

In the first few weeks of the course, the instructor utilized online synchronous course sessions to introduce candidates to the self-study process. She guided the students to examine problems of practice in their personally-situated contexts and explore research-based instructional practices. The instructor facilitated conversations about such practices and urged candidates to reflect upon how they may be put into practice in the candidates' contextual settings. Mathematics specialist candidates reflected on roadblocks or challenges they currently faced as well as the questions they pondered.

The online synchronous sessions during the first weeks of the course were purposefully planned to build relationships between the critical friend peers and to provide feedback to the candidates about their possible research wonderings. During these synchronous sessions the instructor also set and communicated deadlines for segments of the self-study projects. For example, separate deadlines were set for identifying a topic, gathering literature, identifying problems of practice, collecting and analyzing data. Peer partnerships engaged in reflective practice each week as they responded to critical friend inquiries (Samaras, 2011) and one another's responses.

The instructor also facilitated opportunities for feedback during asynchronous components of the course. Within the online platform, group blogs were created for each critical friend pairing to confidentially reflect and respond to one another. This space was utilized to complete critical friend inquiry assignments as well as to provide one another feedback on various aspects of the self-study process. Additionally, individual phone consults were held between the instructor and each candidate several times throughout the 15-week course to discuss specific problems of practice.

Data Analysis

The research team, comprised of three faculty members and two doctoral students, used qualitative data analysis with a set of first-cycle descriptive codes (Saldãna, 2016) to examine the 21 candidate projects from two semesters. A within-case study approach was first utilized to understand the complexity of each case in its own situation (Stake, 2006). Initial open-coding by researchers began individually and was later discussed collaboratively to achieve both coherence and a shared understanding of the codes (Maxwell, 2005). Agreed-upon codes and their corresponding definitions were recorded in a synchronous electronic organizer that all team members accessed. The team of researchers then met virtually to collectively code a second candidate's self-study project. Researchers took turns offering codes for data segments and providing feedback until all team members reached agreement. Initial analysis treated each candidate's self-study project as an individual case. Analysis continued with each of the three faculty researchers coding a candidate's self-study project individually prior to collaboratively discussing each case and any emerging codes. Doctoral students documented each of the virtual conversations to create analytic memos of the discussions.

A second cycle of pattern coding (Miles, Huberman, & Saldãna, 2014) occurred concurrently throughout the data analysis as codes were elaborated on to create hierarchies. For example, as additional projects were coded, the code "impact on student" became more specific and a string of sub codes emerged such as "impact on student: increased mathematics content knowledge" and "impact on student: confidence." Analysis of the code categorization yielded an emerging set of themes which focused upon how the self-study projects impacted the both the mathematics specialist candidates and the teachers and students with whom they worked.

After the initial within-case analysis, a cross-case analysis was conducted to better understand the similarities and differences of the phenomenon that existed between cases (Stake, 2006). Researchers copied and pasted evidence from the candidates' self-study projects into an electronic graphic organizer. This process resulted in evidence organized by theme across all 21 of the candidates. The results of this combined case analysis yielded five themes that occurred across the majority of the mathematics candidates' self-study projects. These findings along with evidence to support the demonstrated growth are presented in the following sections.

Findings

In their self-study projects, the mathematics specialist candidates were required to plan and implement a research-based, transformative initiative to improve the mathematics programs at their schools. Findings indicate that the participants developed mathematics-specific teacher leader skills (AMTE, 2013; NCTM, 2012; Teacher Leader Exploratory Consortium, 2011) as a result of participation in a self-study field experience embedded into the program's capstone course. Specifically, the candidates have demonstrated evidence of growth in: 1) effecting instructional change: connecting theory to school settings; 2) recognizing the value and impact of a critical friend; 3) enriching the mathematics in school settings; 4) developing a broader view of mathematics education leadership through self-study, and; 5) transitioning from teacher to teacher leader.

Effecting Instructional Change: Connecting Theory to School Settings

Mathematics specialists are lifelong learners who "draw upon mathematics education research to inform their practice and the practice of colleagues" (NCTM, 2012, p. 5). The mathematics specialist candidates in this field experience researched an area of interest within mathematics education, applied their research to their practice, collected data on the impact of their actions, and reflected to theorize further implications for their work. In their reflections, it was evident that the candidates' beliefs and practices continued to be informed by the knowledge gained and theories learned from literature.

Candidates directly referenced the effect that the literature had on their instruction. They discussed how reading the literature provided them with the required tools and strategies to implement their identified instructional practice.

Through my review of literature I became much more thoughtful when differentiating instruction and gained a lot of tools and strategies that help support student's development of number sense understanding. (Laney, K-6 teacher)

Laney continued to discuss the impact the literature had on her instruction. She had confidence in the implemented instructional practice because it was situated in research. As a result, she felt comfortable extending these proven practices to her own students.

By utilizing a variety of strategies directly from research to develop facile non-counting strategies such as using tens frames, arithmetic racks, and dot cards, I was able to plan instruction that is research based and proven to be effective in other situations similar to my classroom needs. (Laney, K-6 teacher)

Similarly, Danielle (K-6 ESOL teacher) shared that while the literature provided her with a generation of ideas that she could select from, it was not necessary for her to attempt implementing all. Specifically, candidates shared that deeply engaging with and reflecting on the literature encouraged instructional shifts in their practice.

This self-study positively impacted my teaching because it gave me the correct tools [through reading literature] to adequately teach children in small groups (Mary, K-6 teacher).

The enactment of applying research-based knowledge and theories empowered the mathematics specialist candidates and positively impacted their beliefs about teaching and learning mathematics. Candidates discussed how the evidence gained from both the literature and study implementation increased their positionality as a knowledgeable other. Not only did candidates want to continue the application of these instructional practices to advance their own practice; they also expressed that others *should* be teaching mathematics in these specific research-based ways. Hannah identified that basing her implementation on existing research and theories helped her to guide her vision of ideal mathematics instruction and increased her confidence by providing her with first-hand evidence of its impact to share with others.

My research helped to validate my personal beliefs of what math instruction should look like in the classroom...I feel empowered having done this research as now I can use it as proof and avenues to show teachers the impact that the use of tasks can have. (Hannah, K-6 mathematics coach)

Naomi (K-6 teacher), became more optimistic about teaching mathematics because of the knowledge gained from reading literature and applying it in action.

My work gives me optimism about facing the challenges of a weaker student-teacher ratio, because it provides me with yet another option to promote differentiation within my classroom.

Additionally, Lara (K-6 teacher) noted how reading research and then immediately applying it to her own practice gave her evidence of a strategy that positively impacted a specific student population she was targeting.

One important implication from my study is that mathematics intervention programs can truly make a difference for low-performing students, and with the proper support, teachers can learn to create programs specific to their students.

Through the immersion in research, the mathematics specialist candidates were able to connect theory directly to their own school setting. Unlike previous professional development opportunities, the self-study process engaged the candidates directly in the literature rather than asking them to apply knowledge without understanding the reasoning behind it. This personal synthesis afforded opportunities for candidates to differentiate implementation to meet the needs of their unique K-12 school setting. The immediate impact on the implementation of their newly-gained research understandings supported the candidates' transition from being consumers of knowledge to producers of knowledge and ultimately influenced their beliefs of teaching mathematics. However, while engaging with the literature was one aspect of self-study methodology that led to an increase in knowledge and skills, a candidate's critical friend was a second component that proved just as essential.

Recognizing the Value and Impact of a Critical Friend

Collaboration with a critical friend was both one of the five foci and an essential aspect of self-study methodology (Samaras, 2011). In the self-study field experience, critical friends served multiple roles, supporting all aspects of the research project from design to data analysis. Many candidates attributed the success of the practices implemented to the specific support and feedback provided by the critical friend. Laney shared how she valued having this specific feedback during her self-study.

Throughout this entire process I had opportunities to bring my data and questions in front of my peers and they played a big role in helping me to shape and refine my work. Their feedback, particularly my critical friends, throughout the process helped me progress towards making this study one that can be useful to my own teaching, other teachers at my school, my district, and education in general. (Laney, K-6 teacher)

This success was primarily due to the way in which the critical friend provided valuable feedback. Critical friends assisted their peers by asking questions that prompted candidates to think through their goals and desired outcomes. Suggestions and feedback increased the transparency of the research and allowed candidates to reflect on perspectives different from their own to benefit all stakeholders, but specifically students. Lynn described how her critical friend challenged and progressed her thinking.

She readily offered advice or questioned me when she thought I should have made a different choice. I strongly respect and value her input and expertise and therefore took her ideas to heart during self-reflection and allowed it to impact how I approached the subsequent number talks. Her line of thinking always revolved around what would be most beneficial to students learning. As such, she also gave her perspective on what students' comments revealed about their level of understanding. (Lynn, 6-8 teacher)

The knowledge gained from the content and leadership courses was applied in these partnerships. Gaining perspective from an individual who was intimate with a candidate's study, yet situated in a different context, positioned each candidate as a knowledgeable other. "We would question certain ideas and perspectives within our study and offer feedback, suggestions, and validation to help each other along the way" (Laney, K-6 teacher). Having a knowledgeable other as an outside source was helpful in gaining perspective on the research process.

Seeing first-hand how valuable it is to have a partner in research made me appreciate the collaboration of my critical friend. For future research, it will be vital for me to find someone to support my study and bounce ideas off of. (Debbie, 9-12 teacher)

Additionally, critical friends provided motivation and encouragement along the way. Many candidates reflected that the critical friend motivated and encouraged them in moments of concern or frustration. Penny (6-8 teacher) described how her critical friend helped her to "sift through my results to find all of the positive aspects of this study" when her data did not directly indicate positive results. Penny attributes her completion of the self-study to her critical friend collaboration.

Critical friends allowed participants to grow as mathematics coaches and teacher leaders. It also provided practice and insight into the role and responsibilities of a mathematics teacher leader.

I have had an experience with a critical friend that brings a new perspective to the role a coach may have at a school; coaching can be more than for novice teachers, and for more experienced teachers, it can take on a role like this. I feel like the experience with a critical friend throughout this self-study has allowed the idea of what a math coach is to come full circle. (Naomi, K-6 teacher)

Candidates recognized the importance self-reflection played in developing coaching skills. "What I would like for novice coaches to gain from this experience is that reflection is a critical component toward developing one's abilities as an effective coach" (Carmen, K-6 mathematics coach). Overall, critical friends provided a systematic research methodology (Samaras, 2011), support, and motivation. They valued collaboration in their projects and having a knowledgeable peer with whom to reflect.

Enriching the Mathematics in School Settings

Through the enactment of the self-study field experience, the mathematics specialist candidates positively impacted the mathematics teaching and learning in their educational contexts. Enrichments occurred at multiple levels within schools as the candidates applied research-based teaching strategies within their K-12 organizations. Candidates reported both an increase in student knowledge and positive behaviors, as well as an alignment of teachers' beliefs towards research-based mathematics teaching and learning.

Impact on Students

Student academic growth in specific mathematics content areas was visible for many candidates. "In comparing pre- and post-assessment data, students demonstrated significant progress in knowledge of multiplication and division" (Lara, K-6 teacher). During the implementation of their self-studies, candidates became aware of the beneficial student impact from exposure to an instructional strategy that the candidates may not have otherwise implemented. In addition to senoticeable student growth in understanding mathematics content, many candidates saw increases in student confidence.

A common theme among many candidates was that they noticed their students feeling more confident about the mathematics as the candidates implemented the instructional strategies during their self-studies.

Resulting from the interventions, my students became more and more confident in their mathematical ability and displayed a greater willingness to think through problems and justify their thinking. (Danielle, K-6 ESOL teacher)

Similarly, students were engaged and became more willing to participate in these research-based lessons. "Reviewing my data from students and my field experience journal I can determine a noticeable shift in engagement" (Hannah, K-6 mathematics coach). Julie (6-8 teacher) shared that, "As student participation increased because of more understanding, students also became more open and willing to try new methods of learning." Carmen (K-6 mathematics coach) also noticed these shifts in the students of the teachers' classrooms with whom she was coaching.

The classroom teachers noticed students who are not normally comfortable sharing their thinking aloud, eager to participate more in conversations around math as they accepted the beauty of mistakes.

Candidates also noticed positive shifts in other student behaviors connected to mathematics learning. Many of the teaching practices that candidates applied during their self- studies included student collaboration and communication to develop rich mathematical discourse. As a result of these implemented practices, students found themselves having a voice in the mathematics classroom and were able to increase their knowledge construction through peer learning.

In addition to their achievement, students also showed growth in their motivation, independence, and attitudes towards mathematics. As my self-study progressed, I noticed that students were more willing to share and describe their strategies to others. They gradually relied less on my prompting, and had group discussions on the problems we were solving. Students also communicated that they had more confidence in solving multiplication and division problems on the surveys given to them. (Lara, K-6 teacher)

Lynn described her own observations of students engaging with their peers.

Students were truly co-learning from each other, sharing and respecting other ideas, promoting sense-making, and encouraging and expecting active participation from their peers. (Lynn, 9-12 teacher)

Similarly, Patti (K-6 teacher) noticed positive changes in her students during group work. "I found that the small group learning helped students understand the concepts as it built a sense of unity." In general, the candidates had many positive reflections about the behavioral growth their students underwent as a result of enacting the self-study. "Students showed growth in their independence, and progress towards greater resilience" (Naomi, K-6 teacher).

Impact on Teachers

Many of the mathematics specialist candidates who were teachers themselves discussed the impact of the self-study on their own teaching practices. They highlighted the enrichment that resulted from implementing research-based instructional practices and how they were able to experience and see first-hand growth in students' knowledge and learning behaviors. Because of this experiential research, the candidates gained insight into the value of their chosen self-study topic. Many described how the experience of self-study research provided understandings unlike any other professional development or trainings previously attended

This study has provided me with a new understanding of how important it is for students to communicate their knowledge and understanding, whether in writing or in a discussion with others. I have been to multiple professional developments and teacher trainings, which stress the importance of language development in all content areas for English Language Learners, but I have always felt the strategies discussed at these trainings and in this paper are useful for all students. I feel that this study has provided evidence of that. (Debbie, 9-12 teacher)

Due to the understandings gained, candidates expressed a desire and eagerness to share the successes of their newly-implemented practices with other teachers. "I have found trends and ways to remediate fractions that I cannot wait to share with anyone interested in the topic matter" (Patti, K-6 teacher).

In addition to enhancing their own teaching practices, enacting the self-study also enriched classroom teachers in each of the candidate's school settings. Candidates in coaching roles noticed a positive impact on the teachers with whom they worked; their cooperating teachers described changes in their own instructional practices and indicated they would likely continue such practices even after the work of the self-study had ended. These teachers also changed their own beliefs about mathematics teaching and learning to reflect a mindset consistent with the theory and research that the mathematics specialist candidate had shared. "The fifth-grade teachers displayed a shift in thinking, by moving away from knowledge-level tasks to rich, open-ended ones through their work around rich tasks" (Carmen, K-6 mathematics coach). Jessica (K-6 mathematics coach) explained that the teachers with whom she worked planned to continue implementing the new instructional practices. "Both of the cooperating teachers from my study indicated that they would likely continue using the numberless word problems to support student problem solving."

The self-study field experience afforded each mathematics specialist candidate a unique experience in regards to the identification and implementation of research-based instructional practices. Tailoring the self-study experience provided differentiation that allowed each candidate to meet the needs of their context and observe an overall enrichment of school stakeholders.

Developing A Broader View of Mathematics Education Leadership Through Self-Study

A defining characteristic of mathematics teacher leaders is having a broader view of mathematics and understanding how mathematics is situated in a global context (AMTE, 2013; NCTM, 2012; Teacher Leader Exploratory Consortium, 2011). More specifically, AMTE's (2013) standards require a mathematics specialist to "have a broad view of the many aspects and resources needed to support and facilitate effective instruction and professional growth" (p. 8). These resources may include (but are not limited to) using professional organization journals, networks, and/or discussion groups to stay informed about critical mathematical issues; engaging and facilitating continuous collaborative learning that involves various professional colleagues and stakeholders within and outside of their organizations; evaluating and ensuring students' access to high quality mathematics instruction; collaborating to develop action plans for school improvement; and establishing and maintaining learning communities (AMTE, 2013).

The structure of the field experience connected the candidates' classroom learning about the broad array of mathematics education leadership resources to work in their own school settings. Over the course of the semester, the self-study field experience provided opportunities for the candidates to engage in conversations that critically analyzed specific actions and supported implementing interventions. Specifically, many candidates discussed how the observed impacts of their self-study led to a desire to continue their research for the betterment of their practice and ultimately promote student success. For example, Jessica (K-6 mathematics coach) discussed a desire to implement an additional study to extend investigations of her self-study, while Debbie (9-12 mathematics teacher) noted that she would like to continue her data collection to further analyze its trend. Through ongoing reflection, candidates engaged in continual questioning of their own practice and that of their peers. However, even at the end of the field experience, the candidates were left with many unanswered questions and wonderings that they expressed interest in exploring.

The drop in the scores on the second-grade post assessment make me wonder if the students would apply their use of situational models to problems that are more grade level appropriate. (Jessica, K-6 mathematics coach)

The specialist candidates presented broad views of how content, pedagogy, and their own leadership fit into their surrounding contexts. Specifically, they expressed an increased awareness of the content and pedagogical knowledge required of effective mathematics teaching and the limitations of teacher preparation programs. Ingrid (K-6 teacher) reflected on this topic and said:

One large realization was the lack of preparedness that teachers have coming into their profession. Four years of undergraduate work is simply not enough time to teach all of the content necessary and the teaching skills.

Similarly, Paula (K-6 teacher) discussed the importance of professional development (PD) experiences for teachers. She said:

If teachers were also to go through more PD experiences and get the opportunities for support, their students would be impacted positively as a result of the changes to the teachers' instruction.

They recognized that it would be their responsibility, as mathematics teacher leaders, to facilitate collaborative learning experiences that are relevant, ongoing, and at a teacher's developmental readiness, to ultimately support mathematical learning for all students.

Now that many schools in the country have moved toward team-based and data-based meetings, teachers have time built into their day to talk deeply about content and what is expected of children (Ingrid, K-6 teacher).

Furthermore, the candidates also recognized the power of connecting the practices to learning standards and engaging teachers with this knowledge. Several candidates discussed the need for additional resources, such as rich tasks that are directly linked to state standards.

Candidates provided additional evidence of developing a broader view of mathematics when they discussed how their self-study research could potentially impact their larger mathematical communities, rather than narrowly viewing it from their own context and perspective. "The more I researched the more I was confirming my beliefs that students in poverty is not just an issue in [my school], but a national concern" (Hannah, K-6 mathematics coach). Candidates also made connections to the relevance of their topics to the broader educational community as a whole.

Although this study applies to primary students developing number sense, in reality this is important to the entire educational community as it sets the foundation for learning through high school. (Laney, K-6 teacher)

As a result of viewing the mathematics in a broader context, the candidates communicated a desire to apply and continue their research-based practice.

I intend to continue a process of reflection beyond this study and in my years to come as a coach. Thinking about next school year, I would also like to continue the professional development work that I started with the second and fifth grade teachers. (Carmen, K-6 mathematics coach)

Many shared how they disseminated what they had learned with others outside of their immediate school settings. Several candidates expressed plans to share their knowledge at state-level mathematics teaching conferences and with others in their school and division. They saw the value in sharing their knowledge gained with the greater teaching community to benefit educators at all levels. With the understanding of the importance of disseminating research-based knowledge and practices came an acceptance of the responsibility that belonged to a mathematics teacher leader. One candidate specifically spoke to how she felt empowered to share her successful instructional strategies.

Now that I have developed a structure that works for me, I believe that I can easily adapt it to include other content areas. My work has also made me feel empowered, and I am hopeful that I can share my success with my colleagues. (Lara, K-6 teacher)

The self-study field experience developed teacher leaders who had a broader view of mathematics, demonstrated that they were lifelong learners, possessed knowledge on research-based practices, expressed a desire to learn more, and recognized the importance of advocacy within contexts as well as in broader state and national contexts.

Transitioning From Teacher to Teacher Leader

Specialist candidates in this program reported a transformation in their identity from a teacher to a teacher leader as a result of the self-study field experience. Candidates reflected on this transition and referenced examples of personal growth through the application of leadership skills required of mathematics specialists. Specifically, the candidates shared a newfound motivation and enthusiasm to expand their self-study and disseminate the results to inspire the other stakeholders at their schools. In Catherine's case, by conducting her self-study, her findings were already spread throughout the school. "I have shared my findings with the two teachers participating in my research. Both of them have already shared this information with their team members" (Catherine, 9-12 mathematics teacher). Other candidates identified the need to share their self-study findings to support practitioners who share similar challenges.

I have also worked hard to share the experiences from my own classroom so that others can apply this information...I know others in my school struggle with how to help English Language Learners who are not performing at grade level standards. (Danielle, K-6 ESOL teacher)

However, classroom teachers were not the only stakeholders with whom that candidates shared their results. Many candidates discussed disseminating their findings to school leadership. "I have shared my research and goals with my administration and members of the school leadership team. My hope is to inspire teachers" (Jessica, K-6 mathematics coach).

While disseminating knowledge is an entry way into a leadership role, two specialist candidates explained a personal transformation in terms of empowerment and advocating for best practices. Specifically, Lara (K-6 teacher) discussed how completing her self-study made her feel empowered to share her success with others and Hannah (K-6 mathematics coach) felt confident to advocate for the use of rich tasks, the topic of her self-study, within her school even though she knew there would be hurdles to others accepting the methodology.

Specialist candidates also expressed an interest in expanding their study. These future aspirations often revolved around continued research and motivation to change their classroom or school setting. Danielle was one of several candidates who recognized the immediate impact of the field experience. "The information I discovered has motivated me to find out more as I know how instantly this information will be applicable to the students in my classroom." (Danielle, K-6 ESOL teacher). Other candidates, such as Lynn, considered a more in-depth continuation of her study.

I am encouraged to extend my self-study through the full school year with some modifications to data collection. Moreover, I have started to put in writing a plan for incorporating more thinking structures, critical reflection, self-assessments and growth-mindsets practices in order to improve the Math Workshop activities in my classroom for deeper student learning. (Lynn, 9-12 teacher)

Danielle's analysis provided insight into the gains she experienced as a result of the personal reflection practice embedded within self-study. "I think this process engaged me the most through the nature of personal situated inquiry" (Danielle, K-6 ESOL teacher). This reflection allowed many candidates to recognize that the transition from teacher to teacher leader was similar to that they experienced as a novice educator.

As someone who considers myself relatively comfortable with technology, this study pushed me out of my comfort zone and required me to learn along with my students. It was a humbling experience to feel like a first- year teacher again, but I think that kind of cognitive dissonance is needed if I am going to continue to grow as a professional in the field of education and to have the most positive impact on student learning in my classroom. (Penny, 6-8 teacher)

Through the self-study field experience, candidates' reflective practices began to transition from those of practitioners who only analyzed their individual actions towards those of a leader with a broader perspective. "Engaging in deep reflection almost daily was a critical component to developing my abilities as a leader" (Carmen, K-6 mathematics coach). Overall, the self-study field experience guided the mathematics specialist candidates to adapt their reflective practice and transition towards becoming reflective leaders. As a result, they better understood the complexity and importance of their work.

Discussion and Implications

The mathematics specialist candidates who participated in the self-study field experience communicated growth in teacher leadership in the areas of: 1) effecting instructional change: connecting theory to school settings; 2) recognizing the value and impact of a critical friend; 3) enriching the mathematics in school settings; 4) developing a broader view of mathematics education leadership through self-study, and; 5) transitioning from teacher to teacher leader. The overarching goal of the Mathematics Specialist program at George Mason University is to cultivate leaders who are advocates of researched-based mathematics instruction and learning. The hope is that these specialist candidates become agents of change in their chosen "spheres of teacher leadership" (Fairman & Mackenzie, 2015, p. 63), whether within their own classrooms, schools, or within the broader mathematics community. Merely studying research-based mathematics practices is not enough; this program is designed with the belief that the candidates should experience and immerse themselves in these high-leverage practices during the implementation of the field experience.

Complexities of Advanced Program Field Experiences

Recognizing the often apparent disconnect between research and practice, the mathematics specialists in the Internship in Mathematics Education course were asked to reflect and share the limitations they encountered during their self-study field experience. Several of the limitations were foreseeable, such as time, sample size, and the complexities that arose due to the variety of school stakeholder relationships. While these limitations were expected and even warranted, further implications for candidates' growth can be found in one unforeseeable limitation and the acknowledgement many candidates identified: there were often too many factors to discern if student or teacher outcomes were directly related to only one specific action or intervention. By identifying this limitation, the mathematics specialist candidates demonstrated a better understanding of the complexity of mathematics education. "There is not a one size fits all model" for teaching and learning mathematics (Carmen, K-6 mathematics coach). This take-away is also affirmed by national researchers and speaks to the fields of both teaching and mathematics education. "There are no quick fixes or magic pills by which mathematics teaching and learning can be instantly improved" (Lappan, 1999, p.1). Specifically, the variety of contexts and roles in which a mathematics specialist might be placed highlights the constant adjustment of positionality faced by the mathematics specialist with each administrator, teacher or student interaction. This complexity is something each course in the George Mason University Mathematics Specialist Program strives to address to better prepare candidates for the variety of leadership positions they might one day possess. As a result of the self-study field experience, candidates' awareness of these complexities increased due to the visible connections between their practical experiences and the comprehensive research in mathematics education.

Historically, teachers have been continuously provided ineffective, one-stop workshops to improve their practice (Ball & Cohen, 1999). As school districts begin to supplement or replace the individual workshop models with instructional or content-specific coaching models (Campbell & Malkus, 2011), it is essential for advanced program candidates, in this case mathematics specialist candidates, to consider a multitude of factors whenever implementing and reporting on the effectiveness of a new mathematics practice. In order to discern the value of a mathematics teaching practice, consideration of the implementation limitations must be done with fidelity. Through reflection on their own self-study limitations, the mathematics specialist candidates demonstrated the ability to thoughtfully analyze and situate their findings within various K-12 contexts.

Boundaries of the Research

During the implementation of the self-study field experience, neither the instructor nor the research team gathered observations regarding the implementation within the participants' school settings to identify outsider evidence of what actually occurred. It may be that the candidates' behaviors and actions within their own K-12 classrooms differed from their reported perceptions and beliefs. Throughout each of the final projects, the teachers' perceptions appeared honest and reflective. They openly admitted their flaws and faults as teachers and leaders and came to some moments of deeper understanding of their own practices and understanding of mathematics education. However, as self-selected candidates in a master's level program, they were already looking to reflect on their practice.

This research was focused on analyzing 21 candidates' self-study written research experiences. While a sample of 21 individuals from one university is not likely to represent an entire population of advanced candidates in mathematics education, certain commonalities existed between the participants that potentially will hold true and relate to the lives of others (Merriam, 2009). Whether it is the implementation of research-based mathematics teaching practices, an individual's transition into leadership, or the process of developing and evaluating a field experience for an advanced program, mathematics teacher educators will make connections with various aspects of this study.

There is a challenge to faculty analyzing the impact of a program with which they are intimately involved. As researchers and teachers, we recognize that researching our own students has boundaries. Candidates in our program are likely to write about the aspects of teaching and learning mathematics that they anticipate we want to hear. There is a tendency for faculty to think candidates have made measured growth when there is also a candidate-teacher relationship that must be addressed. Prior research has described that the likelihood of pre-service teachers connecting theory to practice was often dependent on the beliefs of cooperating teachers and the cultures of schools in which they were placed (Clift & Brady, 2005). While it is nearly impossible to eliminate researcher positionality, better understanding the impact of these relationships is essential. Clift and Brady (2005) also asserted that additional professional development could bridge these disconnects. The faculty in the Mathematics Education Leadership program have sought ways to support their candidates and other regional mathematics teacher leaders once they graduate through statewide coaching institutes and professional learning communities specifically targeting mathematics teacher leaders (Baker, Bailey, Hjalmarson, & King, 2017).

Learning From Advanced Program Field Experiences

The AMTE (2013) and NCTM CAEP Standards (NCTM, 2012) indicate the importance of including a supervised practicum, or field experience, for licensure of mathematics specialists. The organizations advocate for mathematics specialist candidates to acquire experiences working with both student and adult learners in a variety of professional settings. However, of the states that currently have mathematics specialist state licensure endorsements or certificates, approximately half of these states require a practicum field experience (Bitto, 2015). Furthermore, there is currently no discussion or evidence within extant literature that describes or researches such field experiences for mathematics specialists (Baker, Bailey, Hjalmarson, & King, 2017). It is imperative that researchers discuss and document the successes of such field experiences so that university programs can learn from one another and ultimately refine their own implementation of these field experiences.

Pre-service teacher preparation programs use field-based experiences to provide opportunities for teacher candidates to apply theories of teaching and practice in their instruction. Practicum opportunities may be limited for specialist candidates as they are usually practicing in a school setting as a classroom teacher or as a mathematics specialist. Having a full-time position may also limit a candidate's availability to practice a formal mathematics specialist role via a practicum experience. The mathematics specialist program at George Mason University requires the candidates to investigate a mathematics topic of their choice in the context of their own school setting, working with both students and other teachers as advised by AMTE (2013) and NCTM (2012). Participation in this self-study field experience allowed the mathematics specialist candidates to become mathematics teacher leaders enacting and advocating for research-based practices in their school settings. These teachers and mathematics coaches refined their instructional skills as they intentionally applied theory and critically reflected to increase their knowledge of effective instructional practices. The field experience elicited analysis of these instructional practices, and as a result the candidates became reflective teacher leaders.

Developing Teacher Leadership

Teacher leadership is about teachers "influencing each other to improve their own learning and ultimately student learning" (Fairman & MacKenzie, 2015, p. 81). Overall, the mathematics specialist candidates described in this study demonstrated growth towards teacher leadership as they influenced and mentored one another throughout their self-studies. One role of teacher leaders is to serve as mentors, usually to novice teachers (Harrison & Killion, 2007). Each of the 21 mathematics specialist candidates in this study demonstrated teacher leadership as they served as *peer* mentors to one another during their self-studies. As demonstrated in the findings discussion, critical friends played a crucial role in the success of the candidate's growth during the self-study. However, while acting as a critical friend in this field experience, the candidates also engaged in the role of peer mentor in addition to that of mentee. Requiring the mathematics specialist candidates to switch their positionality between mentor and mentee allowed each to experience multiple ways and roles in which they could advocate for research-based mathematics teaching practices. The critical-friend role was crucial to the methods of their self-study projects (Samaras, 2011) but also allowed these specialist candidates to practice and develop a coaching lens as they provided constructive feedback to their peers.

The systematic field experiences in pre-service teacher preparation programs promote the development of reflective teacher practitioners focused upon their own practice (Adams, 2016). More specifically, through pre-service field experiences, teachers were prepared "with a sense of efficacy and success as reflective practitioners, collaborative learners, and early-career teacher researchers" (Adams, 2016, p. 32). Preparation for teacher leadership must offer structured opportunities to build upon informal leadership moves in teacher experiences with the purposefulness of research-based formal leadership actions. A culminating self-study field experience designed by the teacher leader creates a unique opportunity to move within and among the spheres of teacher leadership action (Fairman & MacKenzie, 2015) and prepares graduates to navigate both informal and formal leadership roles. This systematic, advanced-program field experience for in-service teachers preparing to be mathematics specialists promoted reflective practitioners to develop into reflective leaders of teachers, with an emphasis on providing critical feedback within collaborations.

Future Research and Impact

Currently, there is no research on the field experiences of mathematics specialist candidates (Baker, Bailey, Hjalmarson, & King, 2017) and few opportunities exist for practicing teachers to connect new knowledge in their practice under supervision. Sharing the results of the leadership growth of these mathematics specialist candidates may encourage other universities to implement, and then share, field experiences for practicing teachers who seek further certificates and endorsements.

Additional research is required to better understand the impact of including a self-study research project as a culminating field experience for mathematics specialist candidates. The candidates should be observed in the field by researchers. As previously mentioned, a boundary of this field experience is that the advanced candidates are already practicing teachers with classroom responsibilities. Further research is required to explore and measure the impact of enacting the mathematics specialist candidates' self-study projects on their colleagues, students and selves. Specifically, looking at the influence of the mathematics specialist candidate on other school stakeholders will provide insight into the leadership development of the advanced candidates.

Teacher leadership within a school has the power to positively influence instruction and learning (Campbell & Malkus, 2011). While this aspect of internship was specific to mathematics specialist candidates, the overall field experience design may prove valuable to university programs seeking to develop practicing teachers into teacher leaders through other advanced programs or continuing professional development. Because teacher leadership positions are often subject to budget constraints, researchers and policy-makers should explore viable models that increase availability of these positions to K-12 schools.

It is important that advanced certification programs for practicing teachers, such as the mathematics specialist certification program, offer opportunities for teachers to connect learning to practice while reflecting deeply on such practices. Using self-study as a field experience has the potential to support the acquisition of the necessary content, pedagogy, and leadership skills required for content-specific teacher leaders. Advanced learning experiences that target development of teacher leaders situated within schools have the potential to influence not only individual knowledge and understanding, but the collective knowledge and overall quality of the teaching force within the school community.

REFERENCES

Adams, P. (2016). Preparing learning teachers: The role of collaborative inquiry. *Canadian Journal of Action Research*, *17*(1), 20–35.

Association of Mathematics Teacher Educators. (2013). *Standards for elementary mathematics specialists: A reference for teacher credentialing and degree programs*. San Diego, CA: Author.

Association of Mathematics Teacher Educators, Association of State Supervisors of Mathematics, National Council of Supervisors of Mathematics, & National Council of Teachers of Mathematics. (2013). *The role of elementary mathematics specialists in the teaching and learning of mathematics*. Retrieved from https://www.mathedleadership.org/docs/ccss/JointStatementOnMathSpecialists.pdf

Austin, T., & Senese, J. C. (2004). Self-study in school teaching: Teachers' perspectives. In J. J. Loughran, M. L. Hamilton, V. K. LaBoskey, & T. Russell (Eds.), *International handbook of self-study of teaching and teacher education practices* (pp. 1231–1258). Dordrecht: Kluwer. doi:10.1007/978-1-4020-6545-3_32

Baker, C., Bailey, P., Larsen, S., & Galanti, T. (2017). A critical analysis of emerging high-leverage practices for mathematics specialists. In M. McGatha & N. Riegelman (Eds.), *Elementary mathematics specialists* (pp. 183–192). Charlotte, NC: Association of Mathematics Teacher Educators.

Baker, C. K., Bailey, P., Hjalmarson, M. A., & King, L. (2017). Mentoring mathematics teacher leaders: Guiding the transition from classroom teacher to agent of change. In A. M. Kent & A. M. Green (Eds.), *Across the Domains: Examining Best Practices in Mentoring Public School Educators* (pp. 189–202). Charlotte, NC: Information Age Publishing.

Ball, D. L., & Cohen, D. K. (1999). *Developing practice, developing practitioners: Toward a practice-based theory of professional education. Teaching as the learning profession: Handbook of policy and practice.* San Francisco, CA: Jossey-Bass.

Ball, D. L., Hill, H. C., & Bass, H. (2005). Knowing mathematics for teaching. *American Educator*, *29*(3), 14–46.

Ball, D. L., Thames, M. H., & Phelps, G. (2008). Content knowledge for teaching: What makes it special? *Journal of Teacher Education*, *59*(5), 389–407. doi:10.1177/0022487108324554

Bitto, L. E. (2015). *Roles, responsibilities, and background experiences of elementary mathematics specialists* (Doctoral dissertation). Available from ProQuest Dissertations and Theses database. (UMI No. 3663010)

Bodone, F., Gudjo'nsdo'ttir, H., & Dalmau, M. C. (2004). Revisioning and recreating practice: Collaboration in self-study. In J. J. Loughran, M. L. Hamilton, V. K. LaBoskey, & T. Russell (Eds.), *International handbook of self-study of teaching and teacher education practices* (pp. 743–784). Dordrecht: Kluwer. doi:10.1007/978-1-4020-6545-3_19

Bullough, R. V. Jr, & Pinnegar, S. E. (2004). Thinking about the thinking about self-study: An analysis of eight chapters. In J. J. Loughran, M. L. Hamilton, V. K. LaBoskey, & T. Russell (Eds.), *International handbook of self-study of teaching and teacher education practices* (pp. 313–342). Dordrecht: Kluwer. doi:10.1007/978-1-4020-6545-3_9

Campbell, P. F., & Malkus, N. N. (2011). The impact of elementary mathematics coaches on student achievement. *The Elementary School Journal*, *111*(30), 430–454. doi:10.1086/657654

Clift, R. T., & Brady, P. (2005). Research on methods courses and field experiences. In M. Cochran-Smith & K. Zeichner (Eds.), *Studying teacher education: The report of the AERA panel on research and teacher education* (pp. 309–424). Mahwah, NJ: Lawrence Erlbaum Associates.

de Araujo, Z., Webel, C., & Reys, B. (2017). Preparing elementary mathematics specialists: Essential knowledge, skills, and experiences. In M. McGatha & N. Riegelman (Eds.), *Elementary mathematics specialists* (pp. 19–32). Charlotte, NC: Association of Mathematics Teacher Educators.

Fairman, J. C., & Mackenzie, S. V. (2015). How teacher leaders influence others and understand their leadership. *International Journal of Leadership in Education*, *18*(1), 61–87. doi:10.1080/13603124.2014.904002

Fennell, F. (2017). We need mathematics specialists now: A historical perspective and next steps. In M. McGatha & N. Riegelman (Eds.), *Elementary mathematics specialists* (pp. 3–18). Charlotte, NC: Association of Mathematics Teacher Educators.

Freese, A. R. (2005). Transformation Through Self-Study. In C. Kosnik, C. Beck, A. R. Freese, & A. P. Samaras (Eds.), *Making a Difference in Teacher Education Through Self-Study. Self-Study of Teaching and Teacher Education Practices* (Vol. 2). Dordrecht: Springer. doi:10.1007/1-4020-3528-4_5

Harbour, K. (2015). *A multi-level analysis using NAEP data: Examining the relationships among mathematics coaches and specialists, student achievement, and disability status* (Doctoral dissertation). Retrieved from Electronic Theses and Dissertations (Paper 2088). doi:10.18297/etd/2088

Harrison, C., & Killion, J. (2007). Ten Roles for Teacher Leaders. *Educational Leadership*, *65*(1), 74–77.

Koster, B., & van den Berg, B. (2014). Increasing professional self-understanding: Self-study research by teachers with the help of biography, core reflection and dialogue. *Studying Teacher Education*, *10*(1), 86–100. doi:10.1080/17425964.2013.866083

Lappan, G. (1999). Revitalizing and refocusing our efforts. *Teaching Children Mathematics*, *6*(2), 104. Retrieved from https://search.proquest.com/docview/214140114?accountid=14541

Loughran, J. J. (2004). A history and context of self-study of teaching and teacher education practices. In J. J. Loughran, M. L. Hamilton, V. K. LaBoskey, & T. Russell (Eds.), *International handbook of self-study of teaching and teacher education practices* (pp. 7–39). Dordrecht: Kluwer. doi:10.1007/978-1-4020-6545-3_1

Maxwell, J. A. (2005). *Qualitative research design: An interactive approach* (2nd ed.). Thousand Oaks, CA: Sage.

Merriam, S. B. (2009). *Qualitative research: A guide to design and implementation*. San Francisco, CA: Jossey-Bass.

Miles, M. B., Huberman, A. M., & Saldãna, J. (2014). *Qualitative data analysis: A methods sourcebook* (3rd ed.). Thousand Oaks, CA: Sage.

National Council of Teachers of Mathematics. (1999). *High-quality teachers or high-quality teaching?* Retrieved from http://www.nctm.org/News-and-Calendar/Messages-from-the-President/Archive/Glenda-Lappan/High-Quality-Teachers-or-High-Quality-Teaching_/

National Council of Teachers of Mathematics. (2012). *NCTM CAEP standards – elementary mathematics specialist*. Retrieved from http://www.nctm.org/Standards-and-Positions/CAEP-Standards/

National Council of Teachers of Mathematics. (2014). *Principles to actions: ensuring mathematical success for all*. Reston, VA: NCTM.

National Mathematics Advisory Panel. (2008). *Foundations for success: The final report of the national mathematics advisory panel*. Washington, DC: US Department of Education.

Pinnegar, S., & Hamilton, M. L. (2009). *Self-study of practice as a genre of qualitative research: Theory, methodology and practice*. Dordrecht: Springer.

Reys, B., Webel, C., & de Araujo, Z. (2017). Elementary mathematics specialist preparation: What's next? What's needed? In M. McGatha & N. Riegelman (Eds.), *Elementary mathematics specialists* (pp. 221–234). Charlotte, NC: Association of Mathematics Teacher Educators.

Rigelman, N. R. (2017). Evaluation of elementary mathematics specialist programs. In M. McGatha & N. Riegelman (Eds.), *Elementary mathematics specialists* (pp. 211–220). Charlotte, NC: Association of Mathematics Teacher Educators.

Rigelman, N. R., & Wray, J. A. (2017). Current state of mathematics specialist state certification and standards. In M. McGatha & N. Riegelman (Eds.), *Elementary mathematics specialists* (pp. 33–40). Charlotte, NC: Association of Mathematics Teacher Educators.

Saldãna, J. (2016). *The coding manual for qualitative researchers*. Thousand Oaks, CA: Sage.

Samaras, A. P. (2011). *Self-study teacher research. Improving your practice through collaborative inquiry*. Thousand Oaks, CA: Sage Publications, Inc.

Shulman, L. S. (1986). Those who understand: Knowledge growth in teaching. *Educational Researcher*, *15*(2), 4–14. doi:10.3102/0013189X015002004

Spangler, D. A., & Orvick, R. L. B. (2017). Models for mathematics specialist program development and delivery. In M. McGatha & N. Riegelman (Eds.), *Elementary mathematics specialists* (pp. 41–52). Charlotte, NC: Association of Mathematics Teacher Educators.

Stake, R. E. (2006). *Multiple case study analysis*. New York, NY: Guilford Press.

Teacher Leadership Exploratory Consortium. (2011). *Teacher leader model standards*. Retrieved from http://teacherleaderstandards.org/downloads/TLS_Brochure.pdf

Virginia Mathematics and Science Coalition. (2016). *Mathematics specialists*. Retrieved from http://www.vamsc.org/index.php/mathematics-specialists/

Whitenack, J. W., & Ellington, A. J. (2013). Supporting middle school mathematics specialists' work: A case for learning and changing teachers' perspectives. *The Mathematics Enthusiast, 10*(3), 647-677. Retrieved from https://search.proquest.com/docview/1434424733?accountid=14541

Wu, H. H. (2009). What's sophisticated about elementary mathematics? Plenty—that's why elementary schools need math teachers. *American Educator, 33*(3), 4–14.

Compilation of References

A Community of Teachers Handbook (10th ed.) (2015). Bloomington, IN: Community of Teachers.

Adams, P. (2016). Preparing learning teachers: The role of collaborative inquiry. *Canadian Journal of Action Research*, *17*(1), 20–35.

Affolter, T., Cooper, C., Miller-Lane, J., & Weston, T. (2015). *Education Studies Program mission statement*. Retrieved from http://www.middlebury.edu/academics/edst/about

Aguirre, J. M., Turner, E. E., Bartell, T. G., Kalinec-Craig, C., Foote, M. Q., Roth McDuffie, A., & Drake, C. (2012). Making connections in practice: How prospective elementary teachers connect to children's mathematical thinking and community funds of knowledge in mathematics instruction. *Journal of Teacher Education*, *64*(2), 178–192. doi:10.1177/0022487112466900

Ajayi, L. L. (2016). How intern teachers use classroom video for self-reflection on teaching. *The Educational Forum*, *80*(1), 79–94. doi:10.1080/00131725.2015.1102365

Akiba, M., & Reichardt, R. (2004). What predicts the mobility of elementary school leaders? An analysis of longitudinal data in Colorado. *Education Policy Analysis Archives*, *12*(18), n18. doi:10.14507/epaa.v12n18.2004

Allen, M., Coble, C., & Crowe, D. (2014, September). *Building an evidence-based system for teacher preparation*. Teacher Preparation Analytics. Retrieved from http://caepnet.org/accreditation/caep-accreditation/caep-accreditation-resources

Allen, D. S., Goodson, L., Rothwell, A., & Sprouse, T. (2017). Miles of progress: Our journey into distance supervision. *PDS Partners*, *12*(1), 20–22.

Allen, D. S., Perl, M., Goodson, L., & Sprouse, T. K. (2014). Changing traditions: Supervision, co-teaching, and lessons learned in a professional development school partnership. *Educational Considerations*, *42*(1), 19–29. doi:10.4148/0146-9282.1041

Almasi, J. F., & Fullerton, S. K. (2012). *Teaching strategic processes in reading*. New York: The Guilford Press.

Alsup, J. (2006). *Teacher identity discourses: Negotiating personal and professional discourses*. Mahwah, NJ: Lawrence Erlbaum.

Alternative Teacher Certification Guide. (2018). Retrieved from http://www.teachercertificationdegrees.com/become/#alt

American Association for Colleges of Teacher Education. (2016). *The renewal of the teaching profession: A pivot toward clinical practice*. Unpublished manuscript.

American Association of Colleges for Teacher Education (AACTE). (2010). *The clinical preparation of teachers: A policy brief*. Washington, DC: Author.

American Association of Colleges for Teacher Education (AACTE). (2018). *A Pivot Toward Clinical Practice, Its Lexicon, and the Renewal of Educator Preparation.* Washington, DC: Author.

American Association of Colleges for Teacher Education (AACTE). (2018). *A pivot toward clinical practice, its lexicon, and the renewal of educator preparation: A report of the AACTE Clinical Practice Commission.* Retrieved from https://aacte.org/professional-development-and-events/clinical-practice-commission-press-conference

American Association of Colleges for Teacher Education. (2011). *Transformations in educator preparation: Effectiveness and accountability.* Washington, DC: Author.

American Association of Colleges for Teacher Education. (2012). *Where We Stand: Clinical Preparation of Teachers.* Washington, DC: Author.

American Association of Colleges for Teacher Education. (2013). *The changing teacher preparation profession.* Washington, DC: Author. Retrieved from https://secure.aacte.org/apps/rl/resource.php?resid=118&ref=rl

American Association of Colleges for Teacher Education. (2018). *A pivot toward clinical practice, its lexicon, and the renewal of educator preparation. A Report of the AACTE Clinical Practice Commission.* Washington, DC: AACTE.

American Association of Colleges for Teacher Education. (2018). *A pivot toward clinical practice, its lexicon, and the renewal of educator preparation.* Washington, DC: Author. Retrieved from: https://aacte.org/professional-development-and-events/clinical-practice-commission-press-conference

American Association of Colleges for Teacher Education. (2018). *A pivot toward clinical practice, its lexicon, and the renewal of educator preparation: A report of the AACTE clinical practice commission.* Washington, DC: AACTE.

American Association of Colleges of Teacher Education. (2010). *The clinical preparation of teachers: A policy brief.* Retrieved from http://oacte.org/pdf/ClinicalPrepPaper_03-11-2010.pdf

American Association of Colleges of Teacher Education. (2018). *A pivot towards clinical practice, its lexicon, and the renewal of educator preparation: A report of the AACTE Clinical Practice Commission.* Washington, DC: Author.

American Mathematical Society. (2012). *The mathematical education of teachers II.* Retrieved from http://www.cbmsweb.org/archive/MET2/met2.pdf

Anderson, C. R. (Ed.). (1993). *Voices of change: A report of clinical schools project.* Washington, DC: American Association of Colleges for Teacher Education.

Anderson, D., Lawson, B., & Mayer-Smith, J. (2006). Investigating the impact of a practicum experience in an aquarium on pre-service teachers. *Teaching Education, 17*(4), 341–353. doi:10.1080/10476210601017527

Anderson, L. M., & Stillman, J. A. (2013). Student teaching's contribution to preservice teacher development: A review of research focused on the preparation of teachers for urban and high-needs contexts. *Review of Educational Research, 83*(1), 3–69. doi:10.3102/0034654312468619

Andrews, A., Bobo, L., & Spurlock, A. (2010). Use of video feedback in the training of pre-service teachers. *Journal of Instructional Pedagogies, 2,* 1–11.

Aragon, S. (2016). *Teacher shortages: What we know.* Denver, CO: Education Commission of the States. Retrieved from http://www.ecs.org/ec-content/uploads/Teacher-Shortages-What-We-Know.pdf

Arbaugh, F., & Taylor, M. (2008). Inquiring into mathematics teacher education. In F. Arbaugh & M. Taylor (Eds.), *Inquiry into mathematics teacher education* (Vol. 5, pp. 1–10). San Diego, CA: Association of Mathematics Teacher Educators.

Argyris, C., & Schon, D. (1974). *Theory in practice: Increasing professional effectiveness.* San Francisco: Jossey-Bass.

Armor, D., Conroy-Oseguera, P., Cox, M., King, N., McDonnell, L., Pascal, A., . . . Zellman, G. (1976). Analysis of the school preferred reading programs in selected Los Angeles minority schools (Rep. No. R-2007-LAUSD). Santa Monica, CA: RAND. (ERIC Document Reproduction Service No. 130 243)

Asante, M. K. (1992, December). Afrocentric curriculum. *Educational Leadership*, 28-31.

Asante, M. K. (2017). *Revolutionary pedagogy: Primer for teachers of Black children*. New York, NY: Universal Write Publications.

Assaf, L. C., & López, M. M. (2015). Generative Learning in a Service-Learning Project and Field-Base Teacher Education Program: Learning to Become Culturally Responsive Teachers. *Literacy Research: Theory, Method, and Practice*, *64*(1), 323–338.

Association of Mathematics Teacher Educators, Association of State Supervisors of Mathematics, National Council of Supervisors of Mathematics, & National Council of Teachers of Mathematics. (2013). *The role of elementary mathematics specialists in the teaching and learning of mathematics*. Retrieved from https://www.mathedleadership.org/docs/ccss/JointStatementOnMathSpecialists.pdf

Association of Mathematics Teacher Educators. (2013). *Standards for elementary mathematics specialists: A reference for teacher credentialing and degree programs*. San Diego, CA: Author.

Association of Mathematics Teacher Educators. (2017). *Standards for Preparing Teachers of Mathematics*. Available online at amte.net/standards

Association of Mathematics Teacher Educators. (2017). *Standards for preparing teachers of mathematics: Executive summary*. Retrieved from https://amte.net/sites/default/files/SPTM_ExecSummary.pdf

Association of Teacher Educators (2015). *Revised standards for field experience*. Author.

Aud, S., Wilkinson-Flicker, S., Kristapovich, P., Rathbun, A., Wang, X., & Zhang, J. (2013). *The condition of education 2013 (NCES 2013-037)*. Washington, DC: U.S. Department of Education, National Center for Education Statistics. Retrieved from http://nces.ed.gov/pubsearch

Austin, T., & Senese, J. C. (2004). Self-study in school teaching: Teachers' perspectives. In J. J. Loughran, M. L. Hamilton, V. K. LaBoskey, & T. Russell (Eds.), *International handbook of self-study of teaching and teacher education practices* (pp. 1231–1258). Dordrecht: Kluwer. doi:10.1007/978-1-4020-6545-3_32

Au, W., Brown, A. L., & Calderón, D. (2016). *Reclaiming the multicultural roots of U.S. curriculum: Communities of color and official knowledge in education*. New York, NY: Teachers College press.

Aydin, U., Tunç-Pekkan, Z., Taylan, D., Birgili, B., & Özcan, M. (2018). Impacts of a university–school partnership on middle school students' fractional knowledge: A quasiexperimental study. *The Journal of Educational Research*, *111*(2), 151–162. doi:10.1080/00220671.2016.1220358

Azano, A. P., & Stewart, T. T. (2015). Exploring place and practicing justice: Preparing Pre-service teachers for success in rural schools. *Journal of Research in Rural Education*, *30*(9), 1–12.

Bacharach, N., & Heck, T. W. (2012). Voices from the field: Multiple perspectives on a co-teaching in student teaching model. *Educational Renaissance, 1*(1).

Bacharach, N., & Heck, T. W. (2012). Voices from the field: Multiple perspectives on a co-teaching in student teaching model. *Educational Renaissance, 1*(1), 49–69.

Bacharach, N., Heck, T. W., & Dahlberg, K. (2010). Changing the face of student teaching through co-teaching. *Action in Teacher Education*, *32*(1), 3–14. doi:10.1080/01626620.2010.10463538

Bacharach, N., Heck, T. W., & Dahlberg, K. (2011). What makes co-teaching work? Identifying the essential elements. *College Teaching Methods & Styles Journal*, *4*(3), 43. doi:10.19030/ctms.v4i3.5534

Bacon, J., Martinez, K., Mitchell, R., & Shaler, L. (2015). *Teaching in Colorado: Who wants the job? Who stays? Who leaves?* Education Policy Networking Series: CU Boulder.

Baeder, J. (n.d.). *10 questions for better feedback on teaching*. The Principal Center. Retrieved from https://www.principalcenter.com/wp-content/uploads/10-questions-better-feedback.pdf

Baeton, M., & Simons, M. (2016). Innovative Field Experiences in Teacher Education: Student-Teachers and Mentors as Partners in Teaching. *International Journal on Teaching and Learning in Higher Education*, *28*(1), 38–51.

Bahr, D. L., Monroe, E. E., & Eggett, D. (2014). Structural and conceptual interweaving of mathematics methods coursework and field practica. *Journal of Mathematics Teacher Education*, *17*(3), 271–297. doi:10.100710857-013-9258-z

Bahr, D., Monroe, E. E., Balzotti, M., & Eggett, D. (2009). Crossing the barriers between preservice and inservice mathematics teacher education: An evaluation of the Grant School professional development program. *School Science and Mathematics*, *109*(4), 223–236. doi:10.1111/j.1949-8594.2009.tb18260.x

Bahr, D., Monroe, E. E., & Shaha, S. H. (2013). Examining preservice teacher belief changes in the context of coordinated mathematics methods coursework and classroom experiences. *School Science and Mathematics*, *113*(3), 144–155. doi:10.1111sm.12010

Bailey, K. (2006). *Language teacher supervision*. New York, NY: Cambridge University Press. doi:10.1017/CBO9780511667329

Bain, C., & Hasio, C. (2011). Authentic learning experience prepares preservice students to teach art to children with special needs. *Art Education*, *64*(2), 33–39. doi:10.1080/00043125.2011.11519118

Baines, J., Tisdale, C., & Long, S. (2018). *"We've been doing it your way long enough": Choosing the culturally relevant classroom*. New York, NY: Teachers College Press.

Bain, R. B., & Moje, E. B. (2012). Mapping the teacher education terrain for novices. *Phi Delta Kappan*, *93*(5), 62–65. doi:10.1177/003172171209300514

Baker, B. D., Punswick, E., & Belt, C. (2010). School leadership stability, principal moves, and departures: Evidence from Missouri. *Educational Administration Quarterly*, *46*(4), 523–557. doi:10.1177/0013161X10383832

Baker, C. K., Bailey, P., Hjalmarson, M. A., & King, L. (2017). Mentoring mathematics teacher leaders: Guiding the transition from classroom teacher to agent of change. In A. M. Kent & A. M. Green (Eds.), *Across the Domains: Examining Best Practices in Mentoring Public School Educators* (pp. 189–202). Charlotte, NC: Information Age Publishing.

Baker, C., Bailey, P., Larsen, S., & Galanti, T. (2017). A critical analysis of emerging high-leverage practices for mathematics specialists. In M. McGatha & N. Riegelman (Eds.), *Elementary mathematics specialists* (pp. 183–192). Charlotte, NC: Association of Mathematics Teacher Educators.

Baldinger, E., Selling, S. K., & Virmani, R. (2016). Supporting novice teachers to lead discussions that reach a mathematical point. *Mathematics Teacher Educator*, *5*(1), 8–28. doi:10.5951/mathteaceduc.5.1.0008

Ball, D., & Forzani, F. (2010). Teaching skillful teaching. *Educational Leadership: The Effective Educator, 68*(4), 40-45. Retrieved from http://www.highered.nysed.gov/Ballteaching.pdf

Ball, D. L. (2000). Bridging practices: Intertwining content and pedagogy in teaching and learning to teach. *Journal of Teacher Education*, *51*(3), 241–247. doi:10.1177/0022487100051003013

Ball, D. L., & Cohen, D. K. (1999). Developing practice, developing practitioners: Toward a practice-based theory of professional education. In G. Sykes & L. Darling-Hammond (Eds.), *Teaching as the learning profession: Handbook of policy and practice* (pp. 3–32). San Francisco: Jossey Bass.

Ball, D. L., & Cohen, D. K. (1999). *Developing practice, developing practitioners: Toward a practice-based theory of professional education. Teaching as the learning profession: Handbook of policy and practice.* San Francisco, CA: Jossey-Bass.

Ball, D. L., & Forzani, F. M. (2010). Teaching skillful teaching. *Educational Leadership*, *68*(4), 40–45.

Ball, D. L., & Forzani, F. M. (2011). Building a common core for learning to teach, and connecting professional learning to practice. *American Educator*, *35*(2), 17–21, 38–39.

Ball, D. L., & Forzani, F. M. (2011). Building a common core for learning to teach: And connecting professional learning to practice. *American Educator*, *35*(2), 17.

Ball, D. L., Hill, H. C., & Bass, H. (2005). Knowing mathematics for teaching. *American Educator*, *29*(3), 14–46.

Ball, D. L., Sleep, L., Boerst, T., & Bass, H. (2009). Combining the development of practice and the practice of development in teacher education. *The Elementary School Journal*, *109*(5), 458–476. doi:10.1086/596996

Ball, D., & Cohen, D. (1999). Developing practitioners: Toward a practice-based theory of professional development. In G. Sykes & L. Darling-Hammond (Eds.), *Teaching as the learning profession: Handbook of policy and practice* (pp. 3–32). San Francisco, CA: Jossey-Bass.

Ball, D., & Forzani, F. (2009). The work of teaching and the challenge for teacher education. *Journal of Teacher Education*, *60*(5), 497–511. doi:10.1177/0022487109348479

Ball, D., & Forzani, M. (2010). What does it take to make a teacher? *Teaching Education*, *92*(2), 8–12.

Ball, D., Themes, M., & Phelps, G. (2008). Content knowledge for teaching: What makes it special? *Journal of Teacher Education*, *59*(5), 389–407. doi:10.1177/0022487108324554

Bamfield, L. (Ed.). (2014). *The role of research in teacher education: Reviewing the evidence: Interim report of the BERA-RSA inquiry.* London: British Educational Research.

Bandura, A. (1997). *Self-efficacy: The exercise of control.* New York, NY: W.H. Freeman and Company.

Barnett, E., & Friedrichsen, P. J. (2015). Educative Mentoring: How a mentor supported a preservice biology teacher's pedagogical content knowledge development. *Journal of Science Teacher Education*, *26*(7), 647–668. doi:10.100710972-015-9442-3

Barnhart, T., & van Es, E. (2015). Studying teacher noticing: Examining the relationship among pre-service science teachers' ability to attend, analyze and respond to student thinking. *Teaching and Teacher Education*, *45*, 83–93. doi:10.1016/j.tate.2014.09.005

Bateman, D., Taylor, S., Janik, E., & Logan, A. (2008). *Curriculum coherence and student access.* Saint-Lambert, Quebec, Canada: Champlain Saint Lambery Cegep.

Bates, A., & Rosaen, C. (2010). Making sense of classroom diversity: How can field instruction practices support interns' learning? *Studying Teacher Education*, *1*(6), 45–61. doi:10.1080/17425961003669151

Battiste, M. (2013). *Decolonizing education: Nourishing the learning spirit*. Saskatoom, Canada: Purich Publishing Limited.

Baum, A. C., & Korth, B. B. (2013). Preparing classroom teachers to be cooperating teachers: A report of current efforts, beliefs, challenges, and associated recommendations. *Journal of Early Childhood Teacher Education, 34*(2), 171–190. doi:10.1080/10901027.2013.787478

Baum, A. C., Powers-Costello, B., VanScoy, I., Miller, E., & James, U. (2011). We're all in this together: Collaborative professional development with student teaching supervisors. *Action in Teacher Education, 33*(1), 38–46. doi:10.1080/01626620.2011.559429

Baumann, J. F., & Graves, M. F. (2010). What is academic vocabulary? *Journal of Adolescent & Adult Literacy, 54*(1), 4–12. doi:10.1598/JAAL.54.1.1

Beck, C., & Kosnik, C. (2000). Associate teachers in preservice education: Clarifying and enhancing their role. *Journal of Education for Teaching, 26*(3), 207–224. doi:10.1080/713676888

Beck, C., & Kosnik, C. (2002). Professors in the practicum: Involvement of university faculty in preservice practicum supervision. *Journal of Teacher Education, 5*(1), 6–19. doi:10.1177/0022487102053001002

Beck, R. J., King, A., & Marshall, S. K. (2002). Effects of videocase construction on teacher candidates' observations of teaching. *Journal of Experimental Education, 70*(4), 345–361. doi:10.1080/00220970209599512

Beebe, S., & Margerison, P. (1995). Teaching the Newest Members of the Family to Teach: Whose Responsibility? *English Journal, 84*(2), 33–37. doi:10.2307/821029

Beesley, A., & Clark, T. (2015). How rural and nonrural principals differ in high plains U.S. states. *Peabody Journal of Education, 90*(2), 242–249. doi:10.1080/0161956X.2015.1022114

Beijaard, D., Meijer, P. C., & Verloop, N. (2004). Reconsidering research on teachers' professional identity. *Teaching and Teacher Education, 20*(2), 107–128. doi:10.1016/j.tate.2003.07.001

Bell, L. A. (2007). Theoretical Foundations for social justice education. In M. Adams, L. A. Bell, & P. Griffin (Eds.), *Teachings for diversity and social justice* (2nd ed.; pp. 1–14). New York: Routledge.

Berliner, D. C. (1988). Implications of studies on expertise in pedagogy for teacher education and evaluation. In *New Directions for Teacher Assessment* (Vol. 49, pp. 39–68). Princeton, NJ: Educational Testing Services.

Berliner, D. C. (1994). Expertise, The wonder of exemplary performances. In J. N. Mangieri & C. C. Block (Eds.), *Creating powerful thinking in teachers and students: Diverse perspectives* (pp. 161–186). Fort Worth, TX: Harcourt Brace.

Berrong, D. A. (2012). *The relationship between principal turnover and student achievement un reading/English language arts and math grades six through eight*. Lynchburg, VA: Liberty University.

Berry, B., Montgomery, D., Curtis, R., Hernandez, M., Wurtzel, J., & Snyder, J. (2008). *Creating and sustaining urban teacher residencies: A new way to recruit, prepare and retain effective teachers in high-needs districts*. Retrieved from https://www.aspeninstitute.org/publications/creating-sustaining-urban-teacher-residencies-new-way-recruit-prepare-retain-effective/

Berry, A. (2009). Professional self-understanding as expertise in teaching about teaching. *Teachers and Teaching, 15*(2), 305–318. doi:10.1080/13540600902875365

Berry, B., Montgomery, D., & Snyder, J. (2008). *Urban teacher residency models and institutes of higher education: Implications for teacher preparation*. Center for Teacher Quality Report.

Berry, B., Montgomery, D., & Snyder, J. (2008). *Urban teacher residency models and institutes of higher education: Implications for Teacher Preparation*. Chapel Hill, NC: Center for Teaching Quality.

Bhabba, H. (1990). The third space. In J. Rutherford (Ed.), *Identity, community, culture and difference* (pp. 207–221). London: Lawrence and Wishart.

Bhabba, H. (1990). The third space. In J. Rutherford (Ed.), *Identity, community, culture, and difference* (pp. 207–221). London: Lawrence & Wishart.

Biddle, C., & Azano, A. P. (2016). Constructing and reconstructing the "rural school problem": A century of rural education research. *Review of Research in Education*, *40*(1), 298–325. doi:10.3102/0091732X16667700

Bieda, K. N., Cavanna, J., & Ji, X. (2015). Mentor-guided lesson study as a tool to support learning in field experiences. *Mathematics Teacher Educator*, *4*(1), 20–31. doi:10.5951/mathteaceduc.4.1.0020

Billings, E. M. H., Ball, D., & Benincasa, O. (2018) *Early school-based learning field experiences: Embedding and enacting core teaching practices in authentic classroom settings.* Paper presented at the meeting of the Association of Mathematics Teacher Educators, Houston, TX.

Bitto, L. E. (2015). *Roles, responsibilities, and background experiences of elementary mathematics specialists* (Doctoral dissertation). Available from ProQuest Dissertations and Theses database. (UMI No. 3663010)

Biza, I., Nardi, E., & Joel, G. (2015). Balancing classroom management with mathematical learning: Using practice-based task design in mathematics teacher education. *Mathematics Teacher Education and Development*, *17*(2), 182–198.

Blackwell, L. S., Trzesniewski, K. H., & Dweck, C. S. (2007). Implicit theories of intelligence predict achievement across an adolescent transition: A longitudinal study and an intervention. *Child Development*, *78*(1), 246–263. doi:10.1111/j.1467-8624.2007.00995.x PMID:17328703

Blanton, L. P., Pugach, M. C., & Florian, L. (2011). *Preparing general education teachers to improve outcomes for students with disabilities.* Washington, DC: American Association of Colleges for Teacher Education (AACTE) and National Center for Learning Disabilities (NCLD). Retrieved from https://secure.aacte.org/apps/rl/resource.php

Boaler, J. (2008). Promoting 'relational equity' and high mathematics achievement through an innovative mixed-ability approach. *British Educational Research Journal*, *34*(2), 167–194. doi:10.1080/01411920701532145

Boaler, J., & Brodie, K. (2004, October). The importance, nature and impact of teacher questions. *Proceedings of the twenty-sixth annual meeting of the North American Chapter of the International Group for the Psychology of Mathematics Education, 2,* 774-782.

Bodone, F., Gudjo'nsdo'ttir, H., & Dalmau, M. C. (2004). Revisioning and recreating practice: Collaboration in self-study. In J. J. Loughran, M. L. Hamilton, V. K. LaBoskey, & T. Russell (Eds.), *International handbook of self-study of teaching and teacher education practices* (pp. 743–784). Dordrecht: Kluwer. doi:10.1007/978-1-4020-6545-3_19

Boerst, T. A., Sleep, L., Ball, D. L., & Bass, H. (2011). Preparing teachers to lead mathematics discussions. *Teachers College Record*, *113*(12), 2844–2877.

Bogdan, R. C., & Biklen, S. K. (1998). *Qualitative research for education* (3rd ed.). Boston: Allyn and Bacon.

Bogdan, R., & Biklen, S. (2007). *Qualitative research for education: An introduction to theory and practice* (5th ed.). New York: Pearson Education, Inc.

Bolton, M. (2010). Fly on the wall: Using teleconferencing to supervise student teacher performance. *Journal of Open. Flexible and Distance Learning, 14*(1), 62.

Bonilla-Silva, E. (2006). *Racism without racists. Color-blind racism and the persistence of racial inequality in the United States*. Lanham, MD: Rowman and Littlefield.

Borg, W. R., Kallenbach, W., Morris, M., & Friebel, A. (1969). Videotape feedback and microteaching in a teacher training model. *Journal of Experimental Education*, *37*(4), 9–16. doi:10.1080/00220973.1969.11011141

Borko, H., Eisenhart, M., Brown, C., Underhill, R., Jones, D., & Agard, P. (1992). Learning to teach hard mathematics: Do novice teachers and their instructors give up too easily? *Journal for Research in Mathematics Education*, *23*(3), 194–222. doi:10.2307/749118

Borko, H., Jacobs, J., Eiteljorg, E., & Pittman, M. E. (2008). Video as a tool for fostering productive discussions in mathematics professional development. *Teaching and Teacher Education*, *24*(2), 417–436. doi:10.1016/j.tate.2006.11.012

Borko, H., & Livingston, C. (1989). Cognition and improvisation: Differences in mathematics instruction by expert and novice teachers. *American Educational Research Journal*, *26*(4), 473–498. doi:10.3102/00028312026004473

Borko, H., & Mayfield, V. (1995). The roles of the cooperating teacher and university supervisor in learning to teach. *Teaching and Teacher Education*, *11*(5), 501–518. doi:10.1016/0742-051X(95)00008-8

Borko, H., Virmani, R., Khachatryan, E., & Mangram, C. (2014). The role of video-based discussions in professional development and the preparation of professional development leaders. In B. D. Calandra & P. Rich (Eds.), *Digital video for teacher education: Research and practice* (pp. 89–108). Philadelphia, PA: Routledge.

Bostic, J., Matney, G., & Sondergeld, T. (in press). A lens on teachers' promotion of the Standards for Mathematical Practice. *Investigations in Mathematics Learning*. doi:10.1080/19477503.2017.1379894

Boutte, G. (2016). *Educating African American students: And how are the children?* New York, NY: Routledge.

Boutte, G. S. (2008). Beyond the illusion of diversity: How Early Childhood teachers can promote social justice. *Social Studies*, *99*(4), 165–173. doi:10.3200/TSSS.99.4.165-173

Boutte, G. S. (2012). Urban Schools: Challenges and Possibilities for Early Childhood and Elementary Education. *Urban Education*, *47*(2), 515–550. doi:10.1177/0042085911429583

Boutte, G. S. (2017). Teaching About Racial Equity Issues in Teacher Education. In T. Durden, S. Curenton, & I. Iruka (Eds.), *African American children in Early Childhood Education: Making the case for policy investments in families, schools, and communities* (pp. 247–266). Emerald. doi:10.1108/S2051-231720170000005011

Boutte, G. S., Lopez-Robertson, J., & Costello, E. (2011). Moving beyond colorblindness in early childhood classrooms. *Early Childhood Education Journal*, *39*(5), 335–342. doi:10.100710643-011-0457-x

Boutte, G. S., & Strickland, J. (2008). Making African American culture and history central to teaching and learning of young children. *The Journal of Negro Education*, *77*(2), 131–142.

Bower, M., Cavanagh, M., Moloney, R., & Dao, M. (2011). Developing communication competence using an online video reflection system: Pre-service teachers' experiences. *Asia-Pacific Journal of Teacher Education*, *39*(4), 311–326. doi:10.1080/1359866X.2011.614685

Boyd, D., Goldhaber, D., Lankford, H., & Wyckoff, J. (2007). The effect of certification and preparation on teacher quality. *The Future of Children*, *17*(1), 45–68. doi:10.1353/foc.2007.0000 PMID:17407922

Boyd, D., Grossman, P., Lankford, H., Loeb, S., & Wyckoff, J. (2006). How changes in entry requirements alter the teacher workforce and affect student achievement. *Education Finance and Policy*, *1*(2), 176–216. doi:10.1162/edfp.2006.1.2.176

Boyd, D., Grossman, P., Lankford, H., Loeb, S., & Wyckoff, J. (2009). Teacher preparation and student achievement. *Educational Evaluation and Policy Analysis*, *31*(4), 416–440. doi:10.3102/0162373709353129

Boyd, D., Lankford, H., Loeb, S., & Wyckoff, J. (2005). The draw of home: How teachers' preferences for proximity disadvantage urban schools. *Journal of Policy Analysis and Management*, *24*(1), 113–132. doi:10.1002/pam.20072

Boyle-Baise, M., & McIntyre, D. J. (2008). What kind of experience? Preparing teachers in PDS or community settings. In M. Cochran-Smith, S. Feiman-Nemser, D. J. McIntyre, & K. E. Demers (Eds.), Handbook of research on teacher education: Enduring questions in changing contexts (3rd ed.; pp. 307–329). New York, NY: Routledge.

Bradbury, L. U. (2010). Educative mentoring: Promoting reform-based science teaching through mentoring relationships. *Science Teacher Education*, *94*, 1049–1071.

Bradbury, L. U., & Koballa, T. R. (2007). Mentor advice giving in an alternate certification program for secondary science teaching: Opportunities and roadblocks in developing a knowledge base for teaching. *Journal of Science Teacher Education*, *18*(6), 817–840. doi:10.100710972-007-9076-1

Bradley, B. A., & Emerson, A. M. (2017). Learning about culture and teaching during an immersion study abroad program. In H. An (Ed.), *Efficacy and implementation of study abroad programs for P-12 teachers* (pp. 174–191). Hershey, PA: IGI Global Publications. doi:10.4018/978-1-5225-1057-4.ch010

Bradshaw, D. (2015). Short tenure of deans signals a leadership void. *Financial Times*. Retrieved from https://www.ft.com/content/8af77ab4-e442-11e4-9039-00144feab7de

Bransford, J., Brown, A., & Cocking, R. (Eds.). (2000). Effective teaching: Examples in history, mathematics, and science. In How people learn: Brain, mind, experience, and school (pp. 155-189). Washington, DC: National Academy Press.

Bransford, J., Darling-Hammond, L., & LePage, P. (2005). Introduction. In L. Darling-Hammond & J. Bransford (Eds.), *Preparing teachers for a changing world: What teachers should learn and be able to do* (pp. 1–39). San Francisco, CA: Jossey-Bass.

Britzman, D. (2003). Practice makes practice (Rev. ed.). Academic Press.

Britzman, D. (2000). Teacher education in the confusion of our times. *Journal of Teacher Education*, *51*(3), 200–205. doi:10.1177/0022487100051003007

Britzman, D. P. (2003). *Practice makes practice: A critical study of teaming to teach* (Rev. ed.). Albany, NY: SUNY Press.

Broad, K., Stewart Rose, L., Lopez, A. E., & Baxan, V. (2013). Coherence as a verb: Reconceptualizing coherence in teacher education. In L. Thomas (Ed.), *What is Canadian about teacher education in Canada?* (pp. 234–258). San Fransisco, CA: Jossey Bass.

Bronkhorst, L. H., Meijer, P. C., Koster, B., & Vermunt, J. D. (2011). Fostering meaning-oriented learning and deliberate practice in teacher education. *Teaching and Teacher Education*, *27*(7), 1120–1130. doi:10.1016/j.tate.2011.05.008

Brosnan, P. (2014) *Co-Planning/Co-Teaching Professional Development Module 1: Focus on Learning*. MTEP Meeting, Milwaukee, WI.

Browne-Ferrigno, T., & Allen, L. W. (2006). Preparing principals for high-need rural schools: A central office perspective about collaborative efforts to transform school leadership. *Journal of Research in Rural Education*, *21*(1), 1–16.

Brownell, M. T., Ross, D. D., Colon, E. P., & McCallum, C. L. (2005). Critical features of special education teacher preparation: A comparison with general teacher education. *The Journal of Special Education*, *38*(4), 242–252. doi:10.1177/00224669050380040601

Brown, R. (2011). The rediscovery of the North Country. In J. R. Harris, K. Morgan, & M. Dickerman (Eds.), *Beyond the notches: Stories of place in New Hampshire's North Country* (pp. 367–374). Littleton, NH: Bondcliff Books.

Bruner, J. (1966). *Toward a theory of instruction.* Cambridge, MA: Harvard University Press.

Bryan, N. (2017). White teachers' role in sustaining the school-to-prison pipeline: Recommendations for Teacher Education. *The Urban Review, 49*(2), 326–345. doi:10.100711256-017-0403-3

Bryant Davis, K. E., Dieker, L., Pearl, C., & Kirkpatrick, R. M. (2012). Planning in the middle: Co-planning between general and special education. *Journal of Educational & Psychological Consultation, 22*(3), 208–226. doi:10.1080/10 474412.2012.706561

Bryk, A. S., Gomez, L. M., Grunow, A., & LeMahieu, P. G. (2015). *Learning to improve: How America's schools can get better at getting better.* Cambridge, MA: Harvard Education Press.

Bryk, A. S., Gomez, L. M., Grunow, A., & LeMahieu, P. G. (2015). *Learning to Improve: How America's Schools Can Get Better at Getting Better.* Cambridge, MA: Harvard Education Press.

Bryk, A., Gomez, L. M., & Grunow, A. (2011). Getting ideas into action: Building networked improvement communities in education. In M. T. Hallinan (Ed.), *Frontiers in sociology of education* (pp. 1–42). Dordrecht, The Netherlands: Springer. doi:10.1007/978-94-007-1576-9_7

Buchmann, M., & Floden, R. E. (1991). Programme coherence in teacher education: A view from the USA. *Oxford Review of Education, 17*(1), 65–72. doi:10.1080/0305498910170105

Buckley, F. J. (2000). *Team teaching: What, why and how?* Thousand Oaks, CA: Sage Publications, Inc.

Budge, K. (2006). Rural leaders, rural places: Problem, privilege, and possibility. *Journal of Research in Rural Education, 21*(13), 1–10.

Bullough, R. V., Draper, M. J., Smith, L., & Burrell, J. (2004). Moving beyond collusion: Clinical faculty and university/ public school partnership. *Teaching and Teacher Education, 20*(5), 505–521. doi:10.1016/j.tate.2004.04.007

Bullough, R. V. Jr. (2012). Mentoring and new teacher induction in the United States: A review and analysis of current practices. *Mentoring & Tutoring, 20*(1), 57–74. doi:10.1080/13611267.2012.645600

Bullough, R. V. Jr, & Draper, R. J. (2004). Making sense of a failed triad: Mentors, university supervisors, and positioning theory. *Journal of Teacher Education, 5*(55), 407–420. doi:10.1177/0022487104269804

Bullough, R. V. Jr, & Pinnegar, S. E. (2004). Thinking about the thinking about self-study: An analysis of eight chapters. In J. J. Loughran, M. L. Hamilton, V. K. LaBoskey, & T. Russell (Eds.), *International handbook of self-study of teaching and teacher education practices* (pp. 313–342). Dordrecht: Kluwer. doi:10.1007/978-1-4020-6545-3_9

Bullough, R., Burrell, J., Young, J., Clark, D., Erickson, L., & Earle, R. (1999). Paradise unrealized: Teacher education and the costs and benefits of school-university partnerships. *Journal of Teacher Education, 50*(5), 381–390. doi:10.1177/002248719905000511

Burbank, M. D., Bates, A., & Gupta, U. (2016). The influence of teacher development on preservice supervision: A case study across content areas. *Teacher Educator, 51*, 5–69. doi:10.1080/08878730.2015.1107441

Burbank, M. D., Ramirez, L., & Bates, A. (2016). The impact of critical reflective teaching: A rhetoric continuum. *Action in Teacher Education, 38*(2), 104–119. doi:10.1080/01626620.2016.1155095

Burke, J. P. (2017). *Case study of mathematical playfulness in an adult mathematics classroom setting* (Unpublished doctoral dissertation). University of Massachusetts, Dartmouth, MA.

Burke, J. (2007). *The English teacher's companion* (3rd ed.). Portsmouth, NH: Heinemann.

Burn, K., & Mutton, T. (2015). A review of 'research-informed clinical practice' in Initial Teacher Education. *Oxford Review of Education*, *41*(2), 217–233. doi:10.1080/03054985.2015.1020104

Burns, M. (2005). Looking at how students reason. *Educational Leadership*, *63*(3).

Burns, R. W., & Badiali, B. (2015). When supervision is conflated with evaluation: Teacher candidates' perceptions of their novice supervisor. *Action in Teacher Education*, *37*(4), 418–437. doi:10.1080/01626620.2015.1078757

Burns, R. W., & Badiali, B. (2016). Unearthing the complexities of clinical pedagogy in supervision: Identifying the pedagogical skills of supervisors. *Action in Teacher Education*, *38*(2), 156–174. doi:10.1080/01626620.2016.1155097

Burns, R. W., Jacobs, J., & Yendol-Hoppey, D. (2016). The changing nature of the role of the university supervisor and the function of preservice teacher supervision in an era of clinically-rich practice. *Action in Teacher Education*, *38*(4), 410–425. doi:10.1080/01626620.2016.1226203

Business Dictionary. (n.d.). Policy. In *Business Dictionary*. Retrieved from http://www.businessdictionary.com/definition/policies-and-procedures.html

Butler, B. M., & Cuenca, A. (2012). Conceptualizing the role of mentor teachers during student teaching. *Action in Teacher Education*, *34*(4), 296–308. doi:10.1080/01626620.2012.717012

Cajkler, W., & Wood, P. (2016). Mentors and student-teachers' 'lesson studying' in initial teacher education. *International Journal of Lesson and Learning Studies*, *5*(2), 1–18. doi:10.1108/IJLLS-04-2015-0015

Calandra, B., Brantley-Dias, L., & Dias, M. (2006). Using digital video for professional development in urban schools: A teacher candidates experience with reflection. *Journal of Computing in Teacher Education*, *22*, 137–145.

Calandra, B., Brantley-Dias, L., Lee, J. K., & Fox, D. L. (2009). Using video editing to cultivate novice teachers' practice. *Journal of Research on Technology in Education*, *42*(1), 73–94. doi:10.1080/15391523.2009.10782542

Calandra, B., Gurvitch, R., & Lund, J. (2008). An exploratory study of digital video editing as a tool for teacher preparation. *Technology and Teacher Education*, *16*(2), 137–153.

Cambourne, B. (1984). *Towards a Reading-Writing Classroom*. Portsmouth, NH: Heinemann.

Cambourne, B. (1995). Toward an educationally relevant theory of literacy learning: Twenty years of inquiry. *The Reading Teacher*, *49*(3), 182–190. doi:10.1598/RT.49.3.1

Cambourne, B. (2001). Conditions for literacy learning: Why do some students fail to learn to read? Ockham's razor and the conditions of learning. *The Reading Teacher*, *54*(8), 784–786.

Campbell, P. F., & Malkus, N. N. (2011). The impact of elementary mathematics coaches on student achievement. *The Elementary School Journal*, *111*(30), 430–454. doi:10.1086/657654

Canrinus, E. T., Klette, K., & Hammerness, K. (2017). Diversity in coherence: Strengths and opportunities of three programs. *Journal of Teacher Education*, 1–14.

Capizzi, A. M., Wehby, J. H., & Sandmel, K. N. (2010). Enhancing mentoring of teacher candidates through consultative feedback and self-evaluation of instructional delivery. *Teacher Education and Special Education*, *33*(3), 191–212. doi:10.1177/0888406409360012

Capraro, M. M., Capraro, R. M., & Helfeldt, J. (2010). Do differing types of field experiences make a difference in teacher candidates' perceived level of competence? *Teacher Education Quarterly*, *37*(1), 131–154.

Cardullo, V. M., & Forsythe, L. (2013). Co-teaching a new pedagogical practice for pre-service teachers. *School-University Partnerships, 6*(2), 90–96.

Carmichael, S., & Hamilton, C. V. (1967). *Black Power: The Politics of Liberation in America.* New York: Vintage Books.

Carnegie Corporation of New York. (2001). *Teachers for a new era: A national initiative to improve the quality of teaching.* New York, NY: Author.

Carnegie Forum on Education and the Economy. (1986). *A nation prepared: Teachers for the 21st century: The report of the task force on teaching as a profession.* New York, NY: Author.

Caro-Bruce, C. & Zeichner, K. (1998). *The nature and impact of an action research professional development program in one urban school district.* Final report to the Spencer Foundation.

Carroll, D., Featherstone, H., Featherstone, J., Feiman-Nemser, S., & Roosevelt, D. (2007). *Transforming teacher education: Reflections from the field.* Cambridge, MA: Harvard University Press.

Carter, K., Cushing, K., Sabers, D., Stein, P., & Berliner, D. (1988). Expert-novice differences in perceiving and processing visual classroom information. *Journal of Teacher Education, 39*(3), 25–31. doi:10.1177/002248718803900306

Cartwright, T. J. (2012). Science talk: Preservice teachers facilitating science learning in diverse afterschool environments. *School Science and Mathematics, 112*(6), 384–391. doi:10.1111/j.1949-8594.2012.00147.x

Carver, C. L., & Feiman-Nemser, S. (2009). Using policy to improve teacher induction: Critical elements and missing pieces. *Educational Policy, 23*(2), 295–328. doi:10.1177/0895904807310036

Castle, S., Fox, R. K., & Fuhrman, C. (2009). Does professional development school preparation make a difference? A comparison of three teacher candidate studies. *School-University Partnerships, 3*(2), 58-68. Retrieved from https://eric.ed.gov/?id=EJ915871

Castle, S., Arends, R., & Rockwood, K. (2008). Student learning in a professional development school and a control school. *Professional Educator, 32*(1), 1–16.

Castle, S., Fox, R. K., & Souder, K. O. (2006). Do professional development schools (PDSs) make a difference? A comparative study of PDS and non-PDS teacher candidates. *Journal of Teacher Education, 58*(1), 65–80. doi:10.1177/0022487105284211

Castle, S., Rockwood, K. D., & Tortorra, M. (2008). Tracking professional development and student learning in a professional development school partnership. *School-University Partnerships, 2*(1), 47–60.

Cavey, L., & Berenson, S. (2005). Learning to teach high school mathematics: Patterns of growth in understanding right triangle trigonometry during plan study. *The Journal of Mathematical Behavior, 24*(2), 171–190. doi:10.1016/j.jmathb.2005.03.001

CCSSI (Common Core State Standards Initiative). (2010). *Common Core State Standards for Mathematics.* Retrieved from http://www.corestandards.org/the-standards/mathematics

Cengiz, N., Kline, K., & Grant, T. J. (2011). Extending students' mathematical thinking during whole-group discussions. *Journal of Mathematics Teacher Education, 14*(5), 355–374. doi:10.100710857-011-9179-7

Center for Youth Wellness. (2013, June). *A hidden crisis: Findings on adverse childhood experiences in California.* San Francisco, CA: Author. Retrieved from https://centerforyouthwellness.org/wp-content/themes/cyw/build/img/building-a-movement/hidden-crisis.pdf

Cervetti, G., Damico, J., & Pearson, P. (2006). Multiple literacies, New Literacies, and teacher education. *Theory into Practice, 45*(4), 378–386. doi:10.120715430421tip4504_12

Chamberlin, C. R. (2000). Nonverbal behaviors and initial impressions of trustworthiness in teacher-supervisor relationships. *Communication Education*, *49*(4), 352–364. doi:10.1080/03634520009379223

Chapin, S. H., O'Connor, C., & Anderson, N. C. (2013). *Classroom discussions in math: A teacher's guide for using talk moves to support the Common Core and more, Grades K-6* (3rd ed.). Sausalito, CA: Math Solutions Publications.

Chapin, S. H., O'Connor, M. C., & Anderson, N. C. (2009). *Classroom discussions: Using math talk to help students learn* (2nd ed.). Sausalito, CA: Math Solutions Publications.

Chapman, C., & Flinders, D. (2006). Systemic Change in Teacher Education. *TechTrends*, *50*(2), 54–55.

Charmaz, K. (2006). *Constructing grounded theory: A practical guide through qualitative analysis*. London: Sage.

Chazan, D., & Ball, D. L. (1999). Beyond being told not to tell. *For the Learning of Mathematics*, *19*(2), 2–10.

Cheliotes, L. G., & Reilly, M. F. (2010). *Coaching conversations: Transforming your school one conversation at a time*. Thousand Oaks, CA: Corwin.

Chesebrough, D. (1994). Informal science teacher preparation. *Science Education International*, *5*(2), 28–33.

Chilton, H., & McCracken, W. (2017). New technology, changing pedagogies? Exploring the concept of remote teaching placement supervision. *Higher Education Pedagogies*, *2*(1), 116–130. doi:10.1080/23752696.2017.1366276

Chingos, M., Whitehurst, G., & Lindquist, K. (2014). *School superintendents: Vital or irrelevant*. Retrieved from https://www.brookings.edu/wp-content/uploads/2016/06/SuperintendentsBrown-Center9314.pdf

Chuanjun, H., & Chunmei, Y. (2011). Exploring authenticity of microteaching in pre-service teacher education programmes. *Teaching Education*, *22*(3), 291–302. doi:10.1080/10476210.2011.590588

City, E. A., Elmore, R. F., Fiarman, S. E., & Teitel, L. (2009). *Instructional rounds in education: A network approach to improving teaching and learning*. Cambridge, MA: Harvard Education Press.

Clara, M. (2014). What is reflection? Looking for clarity in an ambiguous notion. *Journal of Teacher Education*, *66*(3), 261–271. doi:10.1177/0022487114552028

Clarke, A., Triggs, V., & Nielsen, W. (2014). Cooperating teacher participation in teacher education: A review of the literature. *Review of Educational Research*, *84*(2), 163–202. doi:10.3102/0034654313499618

Clift, R., & Brady, P. (Eds.). (2005). Research on methods courses and field experiences. In M. Cochran-Smith & K. Zeichner (Eds.), Studying teacher education (pp. 309-424). New York, NY: Routledge.

Clift, R. (1991). Learning to teach English-maybe: A study of knowledge development. *Journal of Teacher Education*, *42*(5), 357–372. doi:10.1177/002248719104200505

Clift, R. T., & Brady, P. (2005). Research on methods courses and field experiences. In M. Cochran-Smith & K. M. Zeichner (Eds.), *Studying teacher education: The report of the AERA panel on research and teacher education* (pp. 309–424). Mahwah, NJ: Erlbaum.

Clotfelter, C., Ladd, H., & Vigdor, J. (2010). Teacher-student matching and the assessment of teacher effectiveness. *The Journal of Human Resources*, *41*(4), 778–782. doi:10.3368/jhr.XLI.4.778

Cobb, P., Gresalfi, M. S., & Hodge, L. (2008). An interpretive scheme for analyzing the identities that students develop in mathematics classrooms. *Journal for Research in Mathematics Education*, *39*(0), 1–29.

Coburn, C., Penuel, W., & Geil, K. (2013). *Research-practice partnerships: A strategy for leveraging research for educational improvement in school districts* (A white paper prepared for the William T. Grant Foundation). Retrieved from http://rpp.wtgrantfoundation.org/library/uploads/2016/01/R-P-Partnerships-White-Paper-Jan-2013-Coburn-Penuel-Geil.pdf

Coburn, C.E., Penuel, W.R., & Geil, K.E. (2013). *Research-practice partnerships: A strategy for leveraging research for educational improvement in school districts.* William T. Grant Foundation.

Cochran-Smith, M. (2010). Toward a theory of teacher education for social justice. In M. Fullan, A. Hargreaves, D. Hopkins, & A. Lieberman (Eds.), The International Handbook of Educational Change. Academic Press. doi:10.1007/978-90-481-2660-6_27

Cochran-Smith, M., Barnatt, J., Friedman, A., & Pine, G. (2009). Inquiry on inquiry: Practitioner research and student learning. *Action in Teacher Education, 31*(2), 17–32. doi:10.1080/01626620.2009.10463515

Cochran-Smith, M., Ell, F., Grudnoff, L., Haigh, M., Hill, M., & Ludlow, L. (2016). Initial teacher education: What does it take to put equity at the center? *Teaching and Teacher Education, 57,* 67–78. doi:10.1016/j.tate.2016.03.006

Cochran-Smith, M., & Lytle, S. (2009). *Inquiry as Stance: Practitioner research in the next generation.* New York: Teachers College Press.

Cochran-Smith, M., & Lytle, S. L. (1999). Relationships of knowledge and practice: Teacher learning communities. *Review of Research in Education, 24,* 249–305.

Cochran-Smith, M., & Lytle, S. L. (1999). Relationships of knowledge and practice: Teacher learning in communities. *Review of Research in Education, 24,* 249–305.

Cochran-Smith, M., Villegas, A. M., Abrams, L., Chavez-Moreno, L., Mills, T., & Stern, R. (2015). Critiquing Teacher Preparation Research: An Overview of the Field, Part II. *Journal of Teacher Education, 66*(2), 109–121. doi:10.1177/0022487114558268

Cochran-Smith, M., & Zeichner, K. (Eds.). (2005). *Studying teacher education: The Report of the AERA Panel on Research and Teacher Education.* Washington, DC: American Educational Research Association.

Codrington, J., & Fairchild, H. H. (2013). *Special education and the mis-education of African American children: A call to action.* Washington, DC: The Association of Black Psychologists.

Coffey, H. (2010). *"They* taught *me"*: The benefits of early community-based field experiences in teacher education. *Teaching and Teacher Education, 26*(2), 335–342. doi:10.1016/j.tate.2009.09.014

Cogan, M. L. (1972). *Clinical supervision.* Boston, MA: Houghton Mifflin Company.

Coggshall, J. G., Rasmussen, C., Colton, A., Milton, J., & Jacques, C. (2012). *Generating teaching effectiveness: The role of job-embedded professional learning in teacher evaluation.* Washington, DC: National Comprehensive Center for Teacher Quality. Retrieved from https://www.gtlcenter.org/sites/default/files/docs/GeneratingTeachingEffectiveness.pdf

Colburn, A. (1993). *Creating professional development schools.* Bloomington, IN: Phi Delta Kappa.

Cole, K. N., Mills, P. E., Jenkins, J. R., & Dale, P. S. (2005). Getting to the second generation questions. *Journal of Early Intervention, 27*(2), 92–93. doi:10.1177/105381510502700204

Colorado Association of School Personnel Administrators. (2015). *CASPA monthly meeting–Adams 12 five star schools.* Retrieved from https://co-case.site-ym.com/events/EventDetails.aspx?id=671493&hhSearchTerms=%22caspa%22

Colorado Department of Education. (2017). *Senate Bill 10-191.* Retrieved from https://www.cde.state.co.us/educatoreffectiveness/overviewofsb191

Colorado Department of Higher Education. (2016). *2016 legislative report: Educator preparation report AY2014-2015*. Retrieved from http://highered.colorado.gov/Publications/Reports/Legislative/TED/201602_TED_toGGA.pdf

Colwell, J., Nielsen, D. C., Bradley, B. A., & Spearman, M. (2016). Preservice teacher reflections about a short-term summer study abroad experience. In J. A. Rhodes & T. M. Milby (Eds.), *Advancing Teacher Education and Curriculum Development through Study Abroad Programs* (pp. 90–110). Hershey, PA: IGI Global Publications. doi:10.4018/978-1-4666-9672-3.ch006

Comber, B., Reid, J., & Nixon, H. (2007). Environmental communications: Pedagogies of responsibility and place. In B. Comber, H. Nixon, & J. A. Reid (Eds.), *Literacies in place: Teaching environmental communications* (pp. 11–23). Newton, NSW: PETA.

Conderman, G., Morin, J., & Stephens, J. (2005). Special education student teaching practices. *Preventing School Failure*, *49*(3), 5–10. doi:10.3200/PSFL.49.3.5-10

Connelly, V., & Graham, S. (2009). Student teaching and teacher attrition in special education. *Teacher Education and Special Education*, *32*(3), 257–269. doi:10.1177/0888406409339472

Conway, P. F., & Munthe, E. (2015). The practice turn: Research-informed clinical teacher education in two countries. In J.-K. Smedby & M. Stephen (Eds.), *From vocational to professional education: Educating for social welfare* (pp. 146–163). London: Routledge.

Cook, L., & Friend, M. (2010). The state of the art of collaboration on behalf of students with disabilities. *Journal of Educational & Psychological Consultation*, *20*(1), 1–8. doi:10.1080/10474410903535398

Cook-Sather, A. (2009). *Learning from the student's perspective: A methods sourcebook for effective teaching*. Boulder, CO: Paradigm.

Corbett, M. (2007). *Learning to leave: The irony of schooling in a coastal community*. Black Point, NS: Fernwood.

Corbett, M. (2016). Rural futures: Development, aspirations, mobilities, place, and education. *Peabody Journal of Education*, *91*(2), 270–282. doi:10.1080/0161956X.2016.1151750

Core Practices Consortium. (2013). Building a shared understanding for designing and studying practice-based teacher education. In *Symposium presented at the annual meeting of the American Educational Research Association*, San Francisco, CA.

Council for Exceptional Children. (2012). *Initial preparation standards with elaborations*. Retrieved from http://www.cec.sped.org/Standards/Special-Educator-Professional-Preparation

Council for Exceptional Children. (2015). *What every special educator must know: Ethics, standards and guidelines*. Retrieved from http://pubs.cec.sped.org/p6166/

Council for the Accreditation of Education Programs, Council for the Accreditation of Education Programs Commission on Standards and Performance Reporting to the Council for the Accreditation of Education Programs Board of Directors. (2013). *CAEP accreditation standards and evidence: Aspirations for educator preparation*. Retrieved from http://docplayer.net/11050566-Caep-accreditation-standards-and-evidence-aspirations-for-educator-preparation.html

Council for the Accreditation of Educator Preparation (CAEP). (2015). *Standard 2: Clinical partnerships and practice*. Retrieved from http://caepnet.org/standards/standard-2

Council for the Accreditation of Educator Preparation. (2013, June). *The CAEP Standards*. Retrieved from http://caepnet.org/standards/

Council of Chief School State Officers. (2016). *InTASC model core teaching standards and learning progressions for teachers 1.0.* Retrieved from https://www.ccsso.org/resource-library/intasc-model-core-teaching-standards-and-learning-progressions-teachers-10

Council of Chief State School Officers. (2010). *Common Core State Standards English Language Arts.* Washington, DC: National Governors Association Center for Best Practices, Council of Chief State School Officers.

Council of Chief State School Officers. (2010). *Common core state standards initiative: Common core state standards for mathematics.* Washington, DC: National Governors Association Center for Best Practices and Council of Chief State School Officers. Retrieved from http://www.corestandards.org

Council of Chief State School Officers. (2011). *Interstate Teacher Assessment and Support Consortium (InTASC) Model Core Teaching Standards: A Resource for State Dialogue.* Washington, DC: Author.

Council of Chief State School Officers. (2011, April). *Interstate teacher assessment and support consortium (Intasc) model core teaching standards: A resource for state dialogue.* Washington, DC: Author.

Council of Chief State School Officers. (2017). *InTASC model core teaching standards and learning progressions for teachers 1.0.* Retrieved from https://www.ccsso.org/resource-library/intasc-model-core-teaching-standards-and-learning-progressions-teachers-10

Cowhey, M. (2006). *Black ants and Buddhists: Thinking critically and teaching differently in the primary grades.* Portland, ME: Sternhouse.

Cozza, B. (2010). Transforming teaching into a collaborative culture: An attempt to create a professional development school-university partnership. *The Educational Forum, 74*(3), 227–241. doi:10.1080/00131725.2010.483906

Crawford, S., O'Reilly, R., & Luttrell, S. (2012). Assessing the effects of integrating the reflective framework for teaching in physical education (RFTPE) on the teaching and learning of undergraduate sport studies and physical education students. *Reflective Practice, 13*(1), 115–129. doi:10.1080/14623943.2011.626025

Creswell, J. (2008). *Educational research: Planning, conducting, and evaluating quantitative and qualitative research* (3rd ed.). Upper Saddle River, NJ: Pearson.

Creswell, J. W. (1994). *Research design: Qualitative & quantitative approaches.* Sage Publications, Inc.

Cuenca, A., Schmeichel, M., Butler, B. M., Dinkelman, T., & Nichols, J. R. Jr. (2011). Creating a "third space" in student teaching: Implications for the university supervisor's status as outsider. *Teaching and Teacher Education, 27*(7), 1068–1077. doi:10.1016/j.tate.2011.05.003

Dangel, J. R., & Tanguay, C. (2014). "Don't leave us out there alone": A framework for supporting supervisors. *Action in Teacher Education, 36*(3), 3–19. doi:10.1080/01626620.2013.864574

Danielowich, R. (2007). Negotiating the conflicts: Reexamining the structure and function of reflection in science teacher learning. *Science Education, 91*(4), 629–663. doi:10.1002ce.20207

Daniels, H., Edwards, A., Engeström, Y., Gallagher, T., & Ludvigsen, S. (Eds.). (2010). *Activity theory in practice: Promoting learning across boundaries and agencies.* London: Routledge.

Danielson Group. (2018). *The Framework.* Retrieved from http://www.danielsongroup.org/framework/

Danielson, C. (2016). Charlotte Danielson on rethinking teacher evaluation. *Education Week.* Retrieved from https://www.edweek.org/ew/articles/2016/04/20/charlotte-danielson-on-rethinking-teacher-evaluation.html

Danielson, C. (2007). *Enhancing professional practice: A framework for teaching* (2nd ed.). Alexandria, VA: ASCD.

Danielson, C. (2013). *The framework for teaching evaluation instrument*. The Danielson Group.

Darden, G., Scott, K., Darden, A., & Westfall, S. (2001). The student-teaching experience. *Journal of Physical Education, Recreation & Dance, 72*(4), 50–53. doi:10.1080/07303084.2001.10605740

Darling-Hammond, D. (2009, February). *Teacher education and the American future*. Charles W. Hunt Lecture Presented at the annual meeting of the American Association of Colleges for Teacher Education, Chicago, IL.

Darling-Hammond, L. (2009, February). *Teacher education and the American future*. Charles W. Hunt Lecture presented at the annual meeting of the American Association of Colleges for Teacher Education, Chicago, IL.

Darling-Hammond, L. (1989). Accountability for professional practice. *Teachers College Record, 91*(1), 59–80.

Darling-Hammond, L. (2000). How teacher education matters. *Journal of Teacher Education, 51*(3), 166–173. doi:10.1177/0022487100051003002

Darling-Hammond, L. (2003). Access to quality teaching: An analysis of inequality in California's public schools. *Santa Clara Law Review, 43*(4), 101–239. Retrieved from http://digitalcommons.law.scu.edu

Darling-Hammond, L. (2006). Constructing 21st-century teacher education. *Journal of Teacher Education, 57*(3), 300–314. doi:10.1177/0022487105285962

Darling-Hammond, L. (2006). *Powerful teacher education*. San Francisco: Jossey-Bass.

Darling-Hammond, L. (2006). *Powerful teacher education: Lessons from exemplary programs*. San Francisco, CA: Jossey-Bass.

Darling-Hammond, L. (2006). Securing the right to learn: Policy and practice for powerful teaching and learning. *Educational Researcher, 35*(7), 13–24. doi:10.3102/0013189X035007013

Darling-Hammond, L. (2007). The story of Gloria is a future vision of the new teacher. *Journal of Staff Development, 28*(3), 25–26. Retrieved from http://eric.ed.gov

Darling-Hammond, L. (2010). Teacher education and the American future. *Journal of Teacher Education, 12*(1-2), 35–47. doi:10.1177/0022487109348024

Darling-Hammond, L. (2014). Strengthening clinical preparation: The holy grail of teacher education. *Peabody Journal of Education, 89*(4), 547–561. doi:10.1080/0161956X.2014.939009

Darling-Hammond, L. (2015). Want to close the achievement gap? Close the teaching gap. *American Educator, 38*(4), 14–18.

Darling-Hammond, L., & Baratz-Snowden, J. (2007). A good teacher in every classroom: Preparing the highly qualified teachers our children deserve. *Educational Horizons*, 111–132.

Darling-Hammond, L., & Berry, B. (2006). Highly qualified teachers for all. *Educational Leadership, 64*(3), 14.

Darling-Hammond, L., & Bransford, J. (Eds.). (2005). *Preparing teachers for a changing world: what teachers should learn and be able to do. National Academy of Education, Committee on Teacher Education*. San Francisco: Jossey Bass.

Darling-Hammond, L., & Bransford, J. (Eds.). (2005). *Preparing teachers for a changing world: What teachers should learn and be able to do*. San Francisco: Jossey-Bass.

Darling-Hammond, L., Burns, D., Campbell, C., Goodwin, A. L., Hammerness, K., Low, E. L., & Zeichner, K. (2017). *Empowered educators: How high-performing systems shape teaching quality around the world*. San Francisco, CA: Jossey-Bass.

Darling-Hammond, L., Chung, R., & Frelow, F. (2002). Variation in teacher preparation: How well do different pathways prepare teachers to teach? *Journal of Teacher Education, 53*(4), 286–302. doi:10.1177/0022487102053004002

Darling-Hammond, L., Holtzman, D. J., Gatlin, S. J., & Heilig, J. V. (2005). Does teacher preparation matter? Evidence about teacher certification, teach for America, and teacher effectiveness. *Education Policy Analysis Archives, 13*(42). Retrieved from http://epaa.asu.edu/epaa/v13n42/

Darling-Hammond, L., Holtzman, D., Gatlin, S., & Heilig, J. (2010). Does teacher preparation matter? Evidence about teacher certification, Teach for America, and teacher effectiveness. *Education Policy Analysis Archives, 13*(42), 1–28.

Darling-Hammond, L., & Snyder, J. (2000). Authentic assessment of teaching in context. *Teaching and Teacher Education, 16*(5-6), 523–545. doi:10.1016/S0742-051X(00)00015-9

Davis, E., Sinclair, S., & Gschwend, L. (2015). A mentoring program drills down on the Common Core. *Phi Delta Kappan, 96*(6), 59–64. doi:10.1177/0031721715575302

Davis, J. E. (1975). *Team teaching. What research says to the teacher.* Washington, DC: National Education Association.

de Araujo, Z., Webel, C., & Reys, B. (2017). Preparing elementary mathematics specialists: Essential knowledge, skills, and experiences. In M. McGatha & N. Riegelman (Eds.), *Elementary mathematics specialists* (pp. 19–32). Charlotte, NC: Association of Mathematics Teacher Educators.

De Holton, D., Ahmed, A., Williams, H., & Hill, C. (2001). On the importance of mathematical play. *International Journal of Mathematical Education in Science and Technology, 32*(3), 401–415. doi:10.1080/00207390118654

deBettencourt, L. U., & Nagro, S. A. (2018). Tracking special education teacher candidates' reflective practices over time to understand the role of theory in clinically-based teacher preparation. *Remedial and Special Education.* doi:10.1177/0741932518762573

DeCuir-Gunby, J. T., Marshall, P. L., & McCulloch, A. W. (2012). Using mixed methods to analyze video data: A mathematics teacher professional development example. *Journal of Mixed Methods Research, 6*(3), 199–216. doi:10.1177/1558689811421174

Del Prete, T. (2013). *Teacher rounds: A guide to collaborative learning in and from practice.* Thousand Oaks, CA: Corwin Press. doi:10.4135/9781452268200

Delpit, L. (2007). Seeing color. In W. Au, B. Bigelow, & S. Karp (Eds.), *Rethinking our classrooms: Teaching for equity and justice* (2nd ed.; Vol. 1, pp. 158–160). Milwaukee, WI: Rethinking Schools.

Deniz, J. (2012). Video recorded feedback for self-regulation of prospective music teachers in piano lessons. *Journal of Instructional Psychology, 39*, 17–25.

Dennis, D., Burns, R. W., Tricarico, K., Van Ingen, S., Jacobs, J., & Davis, J. (2017). Problematizing clinical education: What is our future? In. R. Flessner & D. Lecklider (Eds.), The Power of Clinical Preparation in Teacher Education. Lanham, MD: Rowman & Littlefield Education in association with the Association of Teacher Educators.

Denzin, N. K., & Lincoln, Y. S. (Eds.). (2000). *Handbook of qualitative research* (2nd ed.). Thousand Oaks, CA: Sage Publications.

Denzin, N., & Lincoln, Y. (1994). Introduction: Entering the field of qualitative research. In N. Denzin & Y. Lincoln (Eds.), *Handbook of Qualitative Research* (pp. 1–17). Thousand Oaks, CA: Sage Publications.

Derman-Sparks, L., & Edwards, J. (2010). *Anti-Bias education for young children and ourselves.* Washington, DC: National Association for the Education of Young Children.

Desimone, L. M. (2009). Improving impact studies of teachers' professional development: Toward better conceptualizations and measures. *Educational Researcher, 38*(3), 181–200. doi:10.3102/0013189X08331140

Desimone, L., & Long, D. (2010). Teacher effects and the achievement gap: Do teacher and teaching quality influence the achievement gap between Black and White and high-and low-SES students in the early grades? *Teachers College Record, 112*(12), 3024–3073.

Dewey, J. (1925). Logic: The Theory of Inquiry (1938). *The later works, 1953*, 1-549.

Dewey, J. (1904). The relation of theory to practice in education. In M. L. Borrowman (Ed.), *Teacher education in America: A documentary history* (pp. 140–171). New York, NY: Teachers College Press. (Original work published 1965)

Dewey, J. (1904). The relation of theory to practice in education. In *The Third yearbook of the National Society for the Scientific Study of Education: Part 1: The Relation of theory to practice in the education of teachers* (pp. 9–30). Chicago: University of Chicago Press.

Dewey, J. (1916). *Democracy and education.* New York, NY: MacMillan Press.

Dewey, J. (1933). *How we think.* Buffalo, NY: Prometheus Books.

Dewey, J. (1938). *Experience and education.* New York, NY: Macmillan Press.

Dewey, J. (1964). The relation of theory to practice in education. In R. D. Archambault (Ed.), *John Dewey on education: Selected writings* (pp. 313–338). Chicago, IL: University of Chicago Press. (Original work published 1904)

Diana, T. J. Jr. (2011). Becoming a teacher leader through action research. *Kappa Delta Pi Record, 47*(4), 170–173. doi:10.1080/00228958.2011.10516586

Dieker, L. A. (1998). Rationale for co-teaching. *Social Studies Review, 37*(2), 62–65.

Dillon, E., & Silva, E. (2011). Grading the teachers' teachers: Higher education comes under scrutiny. *Phi Delta Kappan, 93*(1), 54–58. doi:10.1177/003172171109300109

Downey, J. A., & Cobbs, G. A. (2007). "I actually learned a lot from this": A field assignment to prepare future preservice math teachers for culturally diverse classrooms. *School Science and Mathematics, 107*(1), 391–403. doi:10.1111/j.1949-8594.2007.tb17762.x

Drago-Severson, E. (2012). The need for principal renewal: The promise of sustaining principals through principal-to-principal reflective practice. *Teachers College Record, 114*(12), 1–56. Retrieved from http://www.tcrecord.org/ PMID:24013958

DuFour, R. (2004). What is a "Professional Learning Community?" *Educational Leadership, 61*(8), 6–11.

DuFour, R. (2011). Work together, but only if you want to. *Kappan, 92*(5), 57–61. doi:10.1177/003172171109200513

Duncan, C. M. (2014). *Worlds apart: Poverty and politics in rural America.* New Haven, CT: Yale University Press.

Duncan-Howell, J. A. (2010). Teachers making connections: Online communities as a source of professional learning. *British Journal of Educational Technology, 41*(2), 324–340. doi:10.1111/j.1467-8535.2009.00953.x

Dussault, G. (1970). *A theory of supervision in teacher education.* New York, NY: Teachers College Press.

Dweck, C. S. (2006). *Mindset: The new psychology of success.* New York, NY: Ballantine Books.

Eargle, J. C. (2013). "I'm Not a Bystander": Developing Teacher Leadership in a Rural School-University Collaboration. *Rural Educator, 35*(1).

Earick, M. (2009). *Racially Equitable Teaching: Beyond the Whiteness of Professional Development For Early Childhood Teachers*. New York, NY: Peter Lang.

Easton, L., & Condon, D. (2009). A school-wide model for student voice in curriculum development and teacher preparation. In A. Cook-Sather (Ed.), *Learning from the student's perspective: A secondary methods sourcebook for effective teaching* (pp. 176–193). Boulder, CO: Paradigm Press.

Eaton, C. (2011). Education Department's reform plan for teacher training gets mixed reviews. *The Chronicle of Higher Education*. Retrieved from https://www.chronicle.com/article/Education-Depts-Reform-Plan/129258

Ebby, C. B. (2000). Learning to teach mathematics differently: The interaction between coursework and fieldwork for preservice teachers. *Journal of Mathematics Teacher Education*, *3*(1), 69–97. doi:10.1023/A:1009969527157

Edwards, C., Gandini, L., & Forman, G. (Eds.). (1998). *The hundred languages of children: The Reggio Emilia experience in transformation* (3rd ed.). Santa Barbra, CA: Praeger.

Eisenhart, M., Behm, L., & Romagnano, L. (1991). Learning to teach: Developing expertise or rite of passage? *Journal of Education for Teaching*, *17*(1), 51–71. doi:10.1080/0260747910170106

Elementary Mathematics Specialists & Teacher Leader Project. (2012). *Engaging in the mathematical practices (Look Fors)*. Retrieved from http://www.nctm.org/Conferences-and-Professional-Development/Principles-to-Actions-Toolkit/Resources/5-SMPLookFors/

Ellis, V., Gower, C., Frederick, K., & Childs, A. (2015). Formative interventions and practice-development: A methodological perspective on teacher rounds. *International Journal of Educational Research*, *73*, 44–52. doi:10.1016/j.ijer.2015.06.002

Engeström, Y. (1993). Developmental studies of work as a testbench of activity theory: The case of primary care medical practice. In S. Chaiklin & J. Lave (Eds.), *Understanding practice: Perspectives on activity and context* (pp. 64–103). Cambridge, UK: Cambridge University Press. doi:10.1017/CBO9780511625510.004

English Oxford Living Dictionaries. (2016). Logistics. In *English Oxford Living Dictionaries*. Retrieved from https://en.oxforddictionaries.com/definition/logistics

Ensor, P. (2001). From preservice mathematics teacher education to beginning teaching: A study in recontextualizing. *Journal for Research in Mathematics Education*, *32*(3), 296–320. doi:10.2307/749829

Epstein, S. (2010). Activists and Writers: Student expression in a social action literacy project. *Language Arts*, *87*(5), 363–372.

Erdrich, L. (2002). *Birchbark House*. New York: First Hyperion.

Erickson, H. L. (2002). *Concept-based curriculum: Teaching beyond the facts*. Thousand Oaks, CA: Corwin Press.

Erickson, H. L., Lanning, L. A., & French, R. (2017). *Concept-based Curriculum and Instruction for the Thinking Classroom*. Thousand Oaks, CA: Corwin.

Etscheidt, S., Curran, C. M., & Sawyer, C. M. (2012). Promoting reflection in teacher preparation programs: A multilevel model. *Teacher Education and Special Education: The Journal of the Teacher Education Division of the Council for Exceptional Children*, *35*(1), 7–26. doi:10.1177/0888406411420887

Evans-Andris, M., Kyle, D. W., Larson, A. E., Buecker, H., Haselton, W. B., Howell, P., ... Weiland, I. (2014). Clinical preparation of teachers in the context of a university-wide community engagement emphasis. *Peabody Journal of Education*, *89*(4), 466–481. doi:10.1080/0161956X.2014.942106

Evertson, C., Hawley, W., & Zlotnik, M. (1985). Making a difference in educational quality through teacher education. *Journal of Teacher Education, 36*(3), 2–12. doi:10.1177/002248718503600302

Fairman, J. C., & Mackenzie, S. V. (2015). How teacher leaders influence others and understand their leadership. *International Journal of Leadership in Education, 18*(1), 61–87. doi:10.1080/13603124.2014.904002

Feiman-Nemser, S., & Buchmann, M. (1985, April). *On what is learned in student teaching: Appraising the experience.* Paper presented at the annual meeting of the American Association of Colleges of Teacher Education, Chicago, IL.

Feiman-Nemser, S., Parker, M. B., & Zeichner, K. (1990, April). *Are mentor teachers teacher educators?* Paper presented at the annual meeting of the American Educational Research Association, Boston, MA.

Feiman-Nemser, S. (1990). Teacher preparation: Structural and conceptual analysis. In W. R. Houston, M. Haberman, & J. Sikula (Eds.), *Handbook of research on teacher education* (pp. 212–233). New York, NY: Macmillan.

Feiman-Nemser, S. (1998). Teachers as teacher educators. *European Journal of Teacher Education, 21*(1), 63–74. doi:10.1080/0261976980210107

Feiman-Nemser, S. (2000). *From preparation to practice: Designing a continuum to strengthen and sustain teaching.* New York: Bank Street College of Education.

Feiman-Nemser, S. (2001). From preparation to practice: Designing a continuum to strengthen and sustain teaching. *Teachers College Record, 103*(6), 1013–1055. doi:10.1111/0161-4681.00141

Feiman-Nemser, S. (2001). Helping novices learn to teach: Lessons from an exemplary support teacher. *Journal of Teacher Education, 52*(1), 17–30. doi:10.1177/0022487101052001003

Feiman-Nemser, S., & Buchman, M. (1987). When is student teaching teacher education? *Teaching and Teacher Education, 3*(4), 255–273. doi:10.1016/0742-051X(87)90019-9

Feiman-Nemser, S., & Buchmann, M. (1985). Pitfalls of experience in teacher preparation. *Teachers College Record, 87*, 53–65.

Feimen-Nemser, S. (2012). Beyond solo teaching. *Educational Leadership, 69*(8), 10–16.

Feldman, P., & Moore Kent, A. (2006). A collaborative effort: Bridging theory and practice in pre-service preparation. *New Educator, 2*(4), 277–288. doi:10.1080/15476880600820193

Fennell, F. (2015, February). *Mathematics teacher education: Normal schools to now.* Paper presented at the meeting of the Association of Mathematics Teacher Educators conference, Orlando, FL.

Fennell, F. (2017). We need mathematics specialists now: A historical perspective and next steps. In M. McGatha & N. Riegelman (Eds.), *Elementary mathematics specialists* (pp. 3–18). Charlotte, NC: Association of Mathematics Teacher Educators.

Fernandez, C., Cannon, J., & Chokshi, S. (2003). A U.S.-Japan lesson study collaboration reveals critical lenses for examining practice. *Teaching and Teacher Education, 19*(2), 171–185. doi:10.1016/S0742-051X(02)00102-6

Fernández, C., Llinares, S., & Valls, J. (2013). Primary school teacher's noticing of students' mathematical thinking in problem solving. *The Mathematics Enthusiast, 10*(1/2), 441.

Fernandez, C., & Yoshida, M. (2004). *Improving mathematics teaching and learning: The Japanese lesson study approach (Studies in Mathematical Thinking and Learning Series).* Mahwah, NJ: Lawrence Erlbaum Associates.

Fernandez, M. L. (2010). Investigating how and what prospective teachers learn through microteaching Lesson Study. *Teaching and Teacher Education*, *26*(2), 351–362. doi:10.1016/j.tate.2009.09.012

Ferry, B. (1995). Science centers in Australia provide valuable training for preservice teachers. *Journal of Science Education and Technology*, *4*(3), 255–260. doi:10.1007/BF02211840

Feuer, M., Floden, R., Chudowsky, N., & Ahn, J. (2013). *Evaluation of teacher preparation programs: Purposes, methods, and policy options*. Washington, DC: National Academy of Education. Retrieved from http://naeducation.org/NAED_080456.htm

Fey, J. T. (1978). Mathematics teaching today: Perspectives from three national surveys. *Mathematics Teacher*, *72*(7), 490–504.

Fine, M., Torre, M. E., Burns, A., & Payne, Y. (2007). Youth research/participatory methods for reform. In D. Thiessen & A. Cook-Sather (Eds.), *International handbook of student experience in elementary and secondary school* (pp. 805–828). Dordrecht, The Netherlands: Springer. doi:10.1007/1-4020-3367-2_32

Finley, L. (2008). Reflecting on 'reflective practice. *Practice-based Professional Learning Centre*, *52*, 1–27.

Fleener, C., & Dahm, P. F. (2007). Elementary teacher attrition: A comparison of the effects of professional development schools and traditional campus-based programs. *Teacher Education and Practice*, *20*(3), 263–283.

Flessner, R., & Lecklider, D. R. (Eds.). (2017). The power of clinical preparation in teacher education. Rowman & Littlefield Education in association with the Association of Teacher Education.

Flores, A. (2007). Examining disparities in mathematics education: Achievement gap or opportunity gap? *High School Journal*, *91*(1), 29–42. doi:10.1353/hsj.2007.0022

Florio Ruane, S., & Lensmire, T. (1990). Transforming future teachers' ideas about writing instruction. *Journal of Curriculum Studies*, *22*(3), 277–289. doi:10.1080/0022027900220305

Flower, L. (1997). Partners in inquiry: A logic for community outreach. In L. Adler-Kassner, R. Crooks, & A. Watters (Eds.), *Writing the community: Concepts and models for service learning in composition* (pp. 95–117). Washington, DC: American Association for Higher Education Press.

Flower, L. (2002). Intercultural inquiry and the transformation of service. *College English*, *65*(2), 181–201. doi:10.2307/3250762

Flower, L. (2008). *Community literacy and the rhetoric of public engagement*. Carbondale, IL: Southern Illinois Press.

Flower, L., Long, E., & Higgins, L. (2000). *Learning to rival: A literate practice for intercultural inquiry*. Mayhew, NJ: Lawrence Erlbaum.

Flynn, J., Kemp, A. T., & Callejo-Perez, D. (2010). You can't teach where you don't know: Fusing place-based education and Whiteness studies for social justice. *Curriculum and Teaching Dialogue*, *12*(1-2), 137–151.

Fong, A., Makkonen, R., & Jaquet, K. (2016). *Projection of California teaching retirements: A county and regional perspective*. Regional Educational Laboratory West. Retrieved from http://ies.ed.gov/ncee/edlabs/projects/project.asp?projectID=4551

Foote, M. Q., Roth McDuffie, A., Aguirre, J., Turner, E. E., Drake, C., & Bartell, T. G. (2015). Mathematics Learning Case Study Module. In *TeachMath learning modules for K-8 mathematics methods courses*. Teachers Empowered to Advance Change in Mathematics Project. Retrieved from: www.teachmath.info

Foote, M., Brantlinger, A., Haydar, H., Smith, B., & Gonzalez, L. (2011). Are we supporting teacher success?: Insights from an alternative route mathematics teacher certification program for urban public schools. *Education and Urban Society, 43*(3), 396–425. doi:10.1177/0013124510380420

Ford, D. (2013). *Recruiting and retaining culturally different students in gifted education.* Waco, TX: Prufock Press, Inc.

Forzani, F. M. (2014). Understanding "core practices" and "practice-based" teacher education: Learning from the past. *Journal of Teacher Education, 65*(4), 357–368. doi:10.1177/0022487114533800

Fountas, I., & Pinnell, G. S. (2006). *Teaching for comprehending and fluency: Thinking, talking, and writing about reading, K-8.* Portsmouth, NH: Heinemann.

Fox, D. L., Brantley-Dias, L., & Calandra, B. (2007, November). *Promoting preservice teachers' reflective practice through digital video and critical incident analysis in secondary English education.* Paper presented at the 57th National Reading Conference, Austin, TX.

Frankenburg, E., Taylor, A., & Merseth, K. (2009). Walking the walk: Teacher candidates' professed commitment to urban teaching and their subsequent career decisions. *Urban Education,* 1–35.

Fraser, J. (2007). *Preparing America's teachers: A history.* New York, NY: Teachers College Press.

Fredricks, J. A., Blumenfeld, P. C., & Paris, A. H. (2004). School engagement: Potential of the concept, state of the evidence. *Review of Educational Research, 74*(1), 59–109. doi:10.3102/00346543074001059

Freese, A. R. (2005). Transformation Through Self-Study. In C. Kosnik, C. Beck, A. R. Freese, & A. P. Samaras (Eds.), *Making a Difference in Teacher Education Through Self-Study. Self-Study of Teaching and Teacher Education Practices* (Vol. 2). Dordrecht: Springer. doi:10.1007/1-4020-3528-4_5

Freire, P. (1986). *Pedagogy of the oppressed.* New York: Continuum.

Friend, M. (2007). *Co-Teach! A handbook for creating and sustaining effective classroom partnerships in inclusive schools.* Marilyn Friend.

Friend, M., & Cook, L. (2007). *Co-teaching. In Interactions: Collaboration skills for professionals* (5th ed.). Boston, MA: Pearson.

Friend, M., Cook, L., Hurely-Chamberlin, D., & Shamberger, C. (2010). Co-teaching: An illustration of the complexity of collaboration in special education. *Journal of Educational & Psychological Consultation, 20*(1), 9–27. doi:10.1080/10474410903535380

Fry, E. (1977). Fry's readability graph: Clarifications, validity, and extensions to level 17. *Journal of Reading, 21*(3), 242–252.

Fullan, M. G., & Stiegelbauer, S. (1991). *The new meaning of educational change.* New York, NY: Teachers College Press.

Fuller, F. F. (1969). Concerns of teachers: A developmental conceptualization. *American Educational Research Journal, 6*(2), 207–226. doi:10.3102/00028312006002207

Gadsden, V. L., & Dixon-Roman, E. J. (2017). "Urban" schooling and "urban" families: The role of context and place. *Urban Education, 52*(4), 431–459. doi:10.1177/0042085916652189

Garcia, P., & Rossitier, M. (2010). Digital storytelling as narrative pedagogy. In D. Gibson & B. Dodge (Eds.), *Proceedings of Society for Information Technology & Teacher Education International Conference.* Chesapeake, VA: AACE.

Gardiner, W. (2012). Coaches' and new urban teachers' perceptions of induction coaching: TIme, trust, and accelerated learning curves. *Teacher Educator*, *47*(3), 195–215. doi:10.1080/08878730.2012.685797

Gardiner, W. (2017). Mentoring "inside" and "outside" the action of teaching: A professional framework for mentoring. *New Educator*, *13*(1), 53–71. doi:10.1080/1547688X.2016.1258849

Gardner, D. P. (1983). A nation at risk. Washington, DC: The National Commission on Excellence in Education, US Department of Education.

Gareis, C. R., & Grant, L. W. (2014). The efficacy of training cooperating teachers. *Teaching and Teacher Education*, *39*, 77–88. doi:10.1016/j.tate.2013.12.007

Gatti, L. (2016). *Toward a framework of resources for learning to teach: Rethinking US teacher preparation*. New York: Palgrave Macmillan. doi:10.1057/978-1-137-50145-5

Gee, J. P. (1999). *An introduction to discourse analysis: theory and method*. New York: Routledge.

Gee, J. P. (2001). Literacy, discourse, and linguistics: Introduction. In E. Cushman, M. Rose, B. Kroll, & E. R. Kintgen (Eds.), *Literacy: A critical sourcebook* (pp. 525–544). Boston: Bedford/ St. Martin's.

Geerts, W. M., Steenbeek, H. W., & van Geert, P. L. (2017). Effect of video-cases on the acquisition of situated knowledge of teachers. *International Education Studies*, *11*(1), 64. doi:10.5539/ies.v11n1p64

Geertz, C. (1973). *Toward an interpretive theory of culture*. New York: Basic Books.

Gelfuso, A., Dennis, D. V., & Parker, A. K. (2015). Turning teacher education upside down: Enacting the inversion of teacher preparation through the symbiotic relationship of theory and practice. *Professional Educator*, *39*(2).

George, M. (2010). Chapter seven: Resisting mandated literacy curricula in urban middle schools. *Counterpoints*, *376*, 105–124.

Gershenson, S., Hold, S. B., & Papageorge, N. W. (2016). Who believes me? The effect of student-teacher demographic match on teacher expectations. *Economics of Education Review*, *52*, 209–224. doi:10.1016/j.econedurev.2016.03.002

Ghousseini, H. (2009). Designing opportunities to learn to lead classroom mathematical discussions in pre-service teacher education: Focusing on enactment. In D. Mewborn & H. S. Lee (Eds.), Association of mathematics teacher educators monograph vi: Scholarly practices and inquiry in the preparation of mathematics teachers (pp. 137-152). San Diego, CA: Association of Mathematics Teacher Educators.

Ghousseini, H., & Herbst, P. (2016). Pedagogies of practice and opportunities to learn about classroom mathematics discussions. *Journal of Mathematics Teacher Education*, *19*(1), 79–103. doi:10.100710857-014-9296-1

Gibbs, G. (1988). *Learning by doing: A guide to teaching and learning methods. Further Education Unit*. Oxford, UK: Oxford Brookes University.

Gibbs, G. (2007). *Analyzing qualitative data*. Los Angeles: Sage. doi:10.4135/9781849208574

Gibbs, G. K. (2008). Tooting your own horn? *Management in Education*, *22*(1), 14–17. doi:10.1177/0892020607085625

Gibson, C. B., & Gibbs, J. L. (2006). Unpacking the concept of virtuality: The effects of geographic dispersion, electronic dependence, dynamic structure, and national diversity on team innovation. *Administrative Science Quarterly*, *51*(3), 451–495. doi:10.2189/asqu.51.3.451

Gieryn, T. F. (2000). A space for place in sociology. *Annual Review of Sociology*, *26*(1), 463–496. doi:10.1146/annurev.soc.26.1.463

Glaser, B. G., & Strauss, A. L. (1967). *The discovery of grounded theory: Strategies for qualitative research*. Hawthorne, NY: Aldine.

Glazer, E. M., & Hannafin, M. J. (2006). The collaborative apprenticeship model: Situated professional development within school settings. *Teaching and Teacher Education*, *22*(2), 179–193. doi:10.1016/j.tate.2005.09.004

Gleason, J., & Cofer, L. D. (2014). Mathematics classroom observation protocol for practices results in undergraduate mathematics classrooms. *Proceedings of the Conference on Research on Undergraduate Mathematics Education*, *17*(1).

Gleason, J., Livers, S. D., & Zelkowski, J. (2015). *Mathematics classroom observation protocol for practices: Descriptors manual*. Retrieved from jgleason.people.ua.edu/mcop2.html

Gleason, J. A., Livers, S. D., & Zelkowski, J. (2017). Mathematics Classroom Observation Protocol for Practices (MCOP2): A validation study. *Investigations in Mathematics Learning*, *9*(3), 111–129. doi:10.1080/19477503.2017.1308697

Glenn, W. J. (2006). Model versus mentor: Defining the necessary qualities of the effective cooperating teacher. *Teacher Education Quarterly*, *33*(1), 85–95.

Glickman, C., Gordon, S. P., & Ross-Gordon, J. M. (2014). *Supervision and instructional leadership: A developmental approach* (9th ed.). Boston, MA: Allyn & Bacon.

Goddard, Y. L., Goddard, R. D., & Tschannen-Moran, M. (2007). A theoretical and empirical investigation of teacher collaboration for school improvement and student achievement in public elementary schools. *Teachers College Record*, *109*(4), 877–896.

Goe, L., Bell, C., & Little, O. (2008). *Approaches to evaluating teacher effectiveness: A research synthesis*. Washington, DC: National Comprehensive Center for Teacher Quality.

Goldhaber, D., & Brewer, D. J. (1999). Teacher licensing and student achievement. In M. Kanstoroom & C. E. Finn, Jr. (Eds.), Better teacher, better schools (pp. 83-102). Washington, DC: The Thomas B. Fordham Foundation.

Goldhaber, D., Lavery, L., & Theobald, R. (2016). Inconvenient truth? Do collective bargaining agreements help explain the mobility of teachers within school districts? *Journal of Policy Analysis and Management*, *35*(4), 848–880. doi:10.1002/pam.21914

Goldrick, L., Osta, D., Barlin, D., & Burn, J. (2012). *Review of state policies on teacher induction*. Santa Cruz, CA: New Teacher Center. Retrieved from https://newteachercenter.org/wp-content/uploads/brf-ntc-policy-state-teacher-induction.pdf

Goldring, R., Taie, S., & Riddles, M. (2014). *Teacher attrition and mobility: Results from the 2012-2013 teacher follow-up survey* (NCES 2014-077). U.S. Department of Education. Washington, DC: National Center for Education Statistics. Retrieved September 19, 2014 from http://nces.ed.gov/pubs2014/2014077.pdf

Goldring, R., Gray, L., & Bitterman, A. (2013). *Characteristics of Public and Private Elementary and Secondary School Teachers in the United States: Results from the 2011-12 Schools and Staffing Survey. First Look. NCES 2013-314*. National Center for Education Statistics.

Goldstein, D. (2014). *The teacher wars*. New York, NY: Doubleday.

Gomez, M. L., Black, R. W., & Allen, A. (2007). "Becoming" a teacher. *Teachers College Record*, *109*(9), 2107–2135.

Gonzalez, N., Moll, L., & Amanti, A. (2005). *Funds of Knowledge: Theorizing Practices in Households, Communities, and Classrooms*. New York, NY: Routledge.

González, N., Moll, L., & Amanti, C. (2005). *Funds of knowledge: Theorizing practices in households, communities, and classrooms*. Lawrence Erlbaum Associates, Publishers.

Goodlad, J. (1984). *A place called school: Prospects for the future*. New York, NY: McGraw-Hill.

Goodlad, J. (1990). *Teachers for our nation's schools*. San Francisco, CA: Jossey-Bass.

Goodlad, J. (1994). *Educational renewal: Better teachers, better schools*. San Francisco, CA: Jossey-Bass.

Goodlad, J. I. (1984). *A place called school*. New York: McGraw-Hill.

Goodlad, J. I., Mantle-Bromley, C., & Goodlad, S. J. (2004). *Education for everyone: Agenda for education in a democracy*. San Francisco, CA: Jossey-Bass.

Goodlad, J. I., Soder, R., & McDaniel, B. L. (2008). *Education and the making of a democratic people*. Boulder, CO: Paradigm Publishers.

Goodlad, J., Soder, R., & Sirotnik, K. A. (1990). *The moral dimensions of teaching*. San Francisco, CA: Jossey-Bass.

Goodman, J. (1985). What students learn from early field experiences: A case study and critical analysis. *Journal of Teacher Education*, *38*(6), 42–48. doi:10.1177/002248718503600607

Goodnough, K., Osmond, P., Dibbon, D., Glassman, M., & Stevens, K. (2009). Exploring a tri model of student teaching: Teacher candidate and mentor teacher perceptions. *Teaching and Teacher Education*, *25*(2), 285–296. doi:10.1016/j.tate.2008.10.003

Goodwin, A. L., Roegman, R., & Reagan, E. M. (2016). Is experience the best teacher? Extensive clinical practice and mentor teachers' perspectives on effective teaching. *Urban Education*, *51*(10), 1198–1225. doi:10.1177/0042085915618720

Goodwin, A. L., Smith, L., Souto-Manning, M., Cheruvu, R., Tan, M. Y., Reed, R., & Taveras, L. (2014). What should teacher educators know and be able to do? Perspectives from practicing teacher educators. *Journal of Teacher Education*, *65*(4), 284–302. doi:10.1177/0022487114535266

Goos, M., Vale, C., & Stillman, G. (2017). *Teaching secondary school mathematics: Research and practice for the 21st century*. Allen & Unwin.

Gore, J., & Zeichner, K. (1991). Action research and reflective teaching in preservice teacher education: A case study from the United States. *Teaching and Teacher Education*, *7*(2), 119–136. doi:10.1016/0742-051X(91)90022-H

Grady, G., & Cayton, C. (2014). *Co-Planning/Co-Teaching Professional Development Module 2: Co-Teaching*. MTEP Meeting, Milwaukee, WI.

Grady, G., & Cayton, C. (2016). *Co-Planning/Co-Teaching Professional Development Module 3: Co-Planning*. MTEP Meeting, Atlanta, GA.

Graham, B. (2006). Conditions for successful field experiences: Perceptions of cooperating teachers. *Teaching and Teacher Education*, *22*(8), 1118–1129. doi:10.1016/j.tate.2006.07.007

Greenwood, D. A. (2013). A critical theory of place-conscious education. New York: Routledge. doi:10.4324/9780203813331.ch9

Gregory, E., Long, S., & Volk, D. (2004). *Many pathways to literacy*. London, UK: Routledge Falmer.

Gresalfi, M., Martin, T., Hand, V., & Greeno, J. (2009). Constructing competence: An analysis of student participation in the activity systems of mathematics classrooms. *Educational Studies in Mathematics*, *70*(1), 49–70. doi:10.100710649-008-9141-5

Greunewald, D. A. (2003). Foundations of place: A multidisciplinary framework for place-conscious education. *American Educational Research Journal*, *40*(3), 619–654. doi:10.3102/00028312040003619

Griffin, C. C., Winn, J. A., Otis-Wilborn, A., & Kilgore, K. L. (2003). New teacher induction in special education. [Executive Summary]. Center on Personnel Studies in Special Education, University of Florida.

Griffin, G. A. (1989). A descriptive study of student teaching. *The Elementary School Journal*, *89*(3), 343–364. doi:10.1086/461579

Grimes, W. (2015). *Where New Yorkers worship: Finding God in a city of bustle*. Retrieved from: https://www.nytimes.com/2015/12/25/arts/where-new-yorkers-worship-finding-god-in-a-city-of-bustle.html

Grimmet, P. P., MacKinnon, A. M., Erickson, G., & Riecken, T. J. (1990). Reflective practice in teacher education. In R. Clift, W. R. Houston, & M. C. Pugach (Eds.), *Encouraging reflective practice in education* (pp. 20–38). New York, NY: Teachers College Press.

Grisham, D. L., Laguardia, A., & Brink, B. (2000). Partners in professionalism: Creating a quality field experience for preservice teachers. *Action in Teacher Education*, *21*(4), 27–40. doi:10.1080/01626620.2000.10462978

Grose, K., & Strachan, J. (2011). In demonstration classrooms, it's show-and-tell every day. *Journal of Staff Development*, *32*(5), 24–29.

Grossman, P., Ronfeldt, M., & Cohen, J. (2011). The power of setting: The role of field experience in learning to teach. In K. Harris, S. Graham, T. Urdan, A. Bus, S. Major, & H. L. Swanson (Eds.), American Psychological Association (APA) educational psychology handbook, Vol. 3: Applications to teaching and learning (pp. 311-334). Washington, DC: American Psychological Association.

Grossman, P. (2010). *Learning to practice: The design of clinical experience in teacher preparation*. Washington, DC: American Association of Colleges for Teacher Education.

Grossman, P. L. (1992). Why models matter: An alternative view on professional growth in teaching. *Review of Educational Research*, *62*(2), 171–179. doi:10.3102/00346543062002171

Grossman, P. L., Smagorinsky, P., & Valencia, S. (1999). Appropriating tools for teaching English: A theoretical framework for research on learning to teach. *American Journal of Education*, *108*(1), 1–29. doi:10.1086/444230

Grossman, P. L., Valencia, S., Evans, K., Thompson, C., Martin, S., & Place, N. (2000). Transitions into teaching: Learning to teach writing in teacher education and beyond. *Journal of Literacy Research*, *32*(4), 631–662. doi:10.1080/10862960009548098

Grossman, P., Compton, C., Igra, D., Rongeldt, M., Shahan, E., & Williamson, P. (2009). Teaching practice: A cross-professional perspective. *Teachers College Record*, *111*(9), 2055–2100. Retrieved from http://www.tcrecord.org/

Grossman, P., Compton, C., Shahan, E., Ronfeldt, M., Igra, D., & Shiang, J. (2007). Preparing practitioners to respond to resistance: A cross-professional view. *Teachers and Teaching*, *13*(2), 109–123. doi:10.1080/13540600601152371

Grossman, P., Hammerness, K. M., McDonald, M., & Ronfeldt, M. (2008). Constructing coherence: Structural predictors of perceptions of coherence in NYC teacher education programs. *Journal of Teacher Education*, *59*(4), 273–287. doi:10.1177/0022487108322127

Grossman, P., Hammerness, K., & McDonald, M. (2009). Redefining teaching, reimagining teacher education. *Teachers and Teaching*, *15*(2), 273–289. doi:10.1080/13540600902875340

Grossman, P., & McDonald, M. (2008). Back to the future: Directions for research in teaching and teacher education. *American Educational Research Journal*, *45*(1), 184–205. doi:10.3102/0002831207312906

Guha, R., Hyler, M. E., & Darling-Hammond, L. (2017, Spring). The teacher residency: A practical path to recruitment and retention. *American Educator*, 31–44.

Gunckel, K. L., & Wood, M. B. (2016). The principle–practical discourse edge: Elementary preservice and mentor teachers working together on colearning tasks. *Science Education*, *100*(1), 96–121. doi:10.1002ce.21187

Gurl, T. (2011). A model for incorporating lesson study into the student teaching placement: What worked and what did not? *Educational Studies*, *37*(5), 523–528. doi:10.1080/03055698.2010.539777

Guskey, T. R. (2000). *Evaluating professional development*. Thousand Oaks, CA: Corwin.

Guskey, T. R., & Passaro, P. D. (1994). Teacher efficacy: A study of construct dimensions. *American Educational Research Journal*, *31*(3), 627–643. doi:10.3102/00028312031003627

Gut, D. M., Beam, P. C., Henning, J. E., Cochran, D. C., & Knight, R. T. (2014). Teachers' perceptions of their mentoring role in three different clinical settings: Student teaching, early field experiences, and entry year teaching, mentoring & tutoring. *Partnership in Learning*, *22*(3), 240–263. doi:10.1080/13611267.2014.926664

Gutiérrez, K. D. (2008). Developing a sociocritical literacy in the third space. *Reading Research Quarterly*, *43*(2), 148–164. doi:10.1598/RRQ.43.2.3

Guyton, E., & McIntyre, D. (1990). Student teaching and school experiences. In W. Houston (Ed.), *Handbook of research on teacher education* (pp. 514–534). New York: Macmillan.

Haddix, M., & Sealey-Ruiz, Y. (2012). Cultivating digital and popular literacies as empowering and emancipatory acts upon urban youth. *Journal of Adolescent & Adult Literacy*, *56*(3), 192–198. doi:10.1002/JAAL.00126

Haefner-Berg, M., & Smith, J. P. (1996). Using videotapes to improve teaching. *Music Educators Journal*, *82*(4), 31–37. doi:10.2307/3398914

Haj-Broussard, M., Husbands, J. L., Karge, B. D., McAalister, K. W., McCabe, M., Omelan, J. A., ... Stephens, C. (2015). Clinical prototypes: Nontraditional teacher preparation programs. In E. R. Hollins (Ed.), *Rethinking field experiences in preservice teacher preparation: Meeting new challenges for accountability* (pp. 135–150). New York, NY: Routledge.

Hallman, H. L. (2012). Community-based field experiences in teacher education: Possibilities for a pedagogical third space. *Teaching Education*, *23*(3), 241–263. doi:10.1080/10476210.2011.641528

Hallman, H. L., & Burdick, M. N. (2011). Service learning and the preparation of English teachers. *English Education*, *43*(4), 341–368.

Hallman, H. L., & Burdick, M. N. (2015). *Community Fieldwork in Teacher Education: Theory and Practice*. New York: Routledge.

Hall, S. (2000). Foreword. In D. A. Yon (Ed.), *Elusive culture: Schooling, race, and identity in Global times* (pp. ix–xii). Albany, NY: SUNY Press.

Hamilton, E. R., Rosenberg, J. M., & Akcaoglu, M. (2016). The substitution augmentation modification redefinition (SAMR) model: A critical review and suggestion for its use. *TechTrends*, *60*(5), 433–441. doi:10.100711528-016-0091-y

Hamilton, L. C., Fogg, L. M., & Grimm, C. (2017). *Challenge and hope in the North Country. (Issue Brief No. 130)*. Durham, NH: Carsey School of Public Policy.

Hammer, P. Hughes, G., McClure, C., Reeves, C., & Salgado, D. (2005, December). *Rural teacher recruitment and retention practices: A review of the research literature, national survey of rural superintendents, and case studies of programs in Virginia*. Nashville, TN: Edvantia.

Hammerness, K. (2003). Learning to hope, or hoping to learn? The role of vision in the early professional lives of teachers. *Journal of Teacher Education*, *54*(1), 43–56. doi:10.1177/0022487102238657

Hammerness, K. (2006). From coherence in theory to coherence in practice. *Teachers College Record*, *108*(7), 1241–1265. doi:10.1111/j.1467-9620.2006.00692.x

Hammerness, K. (2013). Examining features of teacher education in Norway. *Scandinavian Journal of Educational Research*, *54*(4), 400–419. doi:10.1080/00313831.2012.656285

Hammerness, K., & Craig, E. (2016). "Context-specific" teacher preparation for New York City: An exploration of the content of context in Bard College's urban teacher residency program. *Urban Education*, *51*(10), 1226–1258. doi:10.1177/0042085915618722

Hammerness, K., Darling-Hammond, L., & Bransford, J. (2005). How teachers learn and develop. In L. Darling-Hammond & J. Bransford (Eds.), *Preparing teachers for a changing world: What teachers should learn and be able to do* (pp. 358–389). San Francisco: Jossey-Bass.

Hammerness, K., Darling-Hammond, L., Grossman, P., Rust, F., & Shulman, L. (2005). The design of teacher education programs. In L. Darling-Hammond & J. Bransford (Eds.), *Preparing teachers for a changing world: What teachers should learn and be able to do* (pp. 390–441). San Francisco: Jossey-Bass.

Hammerness, K., Williamson, P., & Kosnick, C. (2016). Introduction to the special issue on urban teacher residencies: The trouble with "generic" teacher education. *Urban Education*, *51*(10), 1155–1169. doi:10.1177/0042085915618723

Hanline, M. F. (2010). Preservice teachers' perceptions of field experiences in inclusive preschool settings: Implications for personnel preparation. *Teacher Education and Special Education*, *33*(4), 335–351. doi:10.1177/0888406409360144

Hansman, C. A. (2001). Context-based adult learning. In S. B. Merriam (Ed.), *New directions in adult and continuing education* (pp. 43–51). San Francisco, CA: Jossey-Bass.

Harbour, K. (2015). *A multi-level analysis using NAEP data: Examining the relationships among mathematics coaches and specialists, student achievement, and disability status* (Doctoral dissertation). Retrieved from Electronic Theses and Dissertations (Paper 2088). doi:10.18297/etd/2088

Harford, J., & MacRuairc, G. (2008). Engaging student teachers in meaningful reflective practice. *Teaching and Teacher Education*, *24*(7), 1884–1892. doi:10.1016/j.tate.2008.02.010

Hargreaves, A., & Fullan, M. (2012). *Professional capital: Transforming teaching in every school*. New York, NY: Teachers College Press.

Harkavy, I., & Hartley, M. (2009). University-school-community partnerships for youth development and democratic renewal. *New Directions for Youth Development*, *122*(122), 7–18. doi:10.1002/yd.303 PMID:19593810

Harlow, D. B. (2012). The excitement and wonder of teaching science: What pre-service teachers learn from facilitating family science night centers. *Journal of Science Teacher Education*, *23*(2), 199–220. doi:10.100710972-012-9264-5

Harris, D., & Sass, T. (2011). Teacher training, teacher quality and student achievement. *Journal of Public Economics*, *95*(7-8), 798–812. doi:10.1016/j.jpubeco.2010.11.009

Harris, J. H. (2011). Introduction. In J. R. Harris, K. Morgan, & M. Dickerman (Eds.), *Beyond the notches: Stories of place in New Hampshire's North Country* (pp. 74–78). Littleton, NH: Bondcliff Books.

Harrison, C., & Killion, J. (2007). Ten Roles for Teacher Leaders. *Educational Leadership*, *65*(1), 74–77.

Harro, B. (2000). The cycle of socialization. *Readings for Diversity and Social Justice, 15,* 21.

Hashweh, M. Z. (2005). Teacher pedagogical constructions: A reconfiguration of pedagogical content knowledge. *Teachers and Teaching*, *11*(3), 273–292. doi:10.1080/13450600500105502

Hatch, A. (2002). *Doing qualitative research in education settings*. Albany, NY: State University of New York Press.

Hattie, J., & Timperley, H. (2007). The power of feedback. *Review of Educational Research*, *77*(1), 81–112. doi:10.3102/003465430298487

Head, A. J., & Eisenberg, M. B. (2010). *Truth be told: How college students evaluate and use information in the digital age*. Project Information Literacy. Retrieved from http://projectinfolit.org/images/pdfs/pil_fall2010_survey_fullreport1.pdf

Heck, T. W. (2013, Nov. 1). *A new student teaching model for pairing interns with clinical teachers*. Retrieved from https://www.edutopia.org/blog/co-teaching-internship-model-teresa-heck

Heck, T., & Bacharach, N. (2015). A better model for student teaching. *Educational Leadership*, *73*(4), 24–28.

Heilig, J. V., & Jez, S. J. (2010). *Teach For America: A Review of the Evidence*. Education and the Public Interest Center & Education Policy Research Unit. Retrieved from http://epicpolicy.org/publication/teach-for-america

Henderson, S. C. (2013). *Iterative development of a literacy methods course inside a failing school*. Paper presented at the meeting of the American Educational Research Association, San Francisco, CA.

Henderson, S. C., & Weston, T. L. (2014). *Uncovering a problem of practice: Supervisors' field observations of preservice teachers' approximations of practice*. Paper presented at the meeting of the American Educational Research Association, Philadelphia, PA.

Henning, J. E., Erb, D. J., Randles, H. S., Fults, N., & Webb, K. (2016). Designing a curriculum for clinical experiences. *Issues in Teacher Education*, *25*, 23–38.

Henning, J. E., Gut, D., & Beam, P. (2015). Designing and implementing a mentoring program to support clinically-based teacher education. *Teacher Educator*, *50*(2), 145–162. doi:10.1080/08878730.2015.1011046

Henry, G. T., Purtell, K. M., Bastian, K. C., Fortner, C. K., Thompson, C. L., Campbell, S. L., & Patterson, K. M. (2013). The effects of teacher entry portals on student achievement. *Journal of Teacher Education*, *65*(1), 7–23. doi:10.1177/0022487113503871

Henry, J. J., Tryjankowski, A. M., Dicamillo, L., & Bailey, N. (2010). How professional development schools can help to create friendly environments for teachers to integrate theory, research, and practice. *Childhood Education*, *86*(5), 327–331. doi:10.1080/00094056.2010.10521419

Henry, M. A., & Weber, A. (2010). *Supervising student teachers: The professional way* (7th ed.). Lanham, MD: Roman & Littlefield Education.

He, Y. (2009). Strength-based mentoring in pre-service teacher education: A literature review. *Mentoring & Tutoring*, *17*(3), 263–275. doi:10.1080/13611260903050205

Hichanadel, A., & Finamore, D. (2015). Fixed and growth mindset in education and how grit helps students persist in the face of adversity. *Journal of International Education Research*, *11*(1), 47–50.

Hiebert, J., Carpenter, T. P., Fennema, E., Fuson, K. C., Wearne, D., Murray, H., & Human, P. (1997). *Making sense: Teaching and learning mathematics with understanding*. Portsmouth, NH: Heinemann.

Hiebert, J., Gallimore, R., & Stigler, J. W. (2002). A knowledge base for the teaching profession: What would it look like and how can we get one? *Educational Researcher*, *31*(5), 3–15. doi:10.3102/0013189X031005003

Hiebert, J., & Grouws, D. A. (2007). The effects of classroom mathematics teaching on students' learning. In F. K. Lester (Ed.), *Second handbook of research on mathematics teaching and learning*. Charlotte, NC: Information Age Publishing.

Hiebert, J., Morris, A. K., Berk, B., & Jansen, A. (2007). Preparing teachers to learn from teaching. *Journal of Teacher Education*, *58*(1), 47–61. doi:10.1177/0022487106295726

Hiebert, J., Morris, A. K., & Glass, B. (2003). Learning to learn to teach: An "experiment" model for teaching and teacher preparation in mathematics. *Journal of Mathematics Teacher Education*, *6*, 201–222. doi:10.1023/A:1025162108648

Hiebert, J., Stigler, J. W., Jacobs, J. K., Givvin, K. B., Garnier, H., Smith, M., ... Gallimore, R. (2005). Mathematics teaching in the United States today (and tomorrow): Results from the TIMSS 1999 video study. *Educational Evaluation and Policy Analysis*, *27*(2), 111–132. doi:10.3102/01623737027002111

Hill, H. C., Blunk, M. L., Charalambous, C. Y., Lewis, J. M., Phelps, G. C., Sleep, L., & Ball, D. L. (2008). Mathematical knowledge for teaching and the mathematical quality of instruction: An exploratory study. *Cognition and Instruction*, *26*(4), 430–511. doi:10.1080/07370000802177235

Hoban, G. F. (Ed.). (2005). *The missing links in teacher education design. Developing a multi-linked conceptual framework*. Dordrecht, The Netherlands: Springer. doi:10.1007/1-4020-3346-X

Hodges, T. E., & Hodge, L. L. (2017). Unpacking personal identities for teaching mathematics within the context of prospective teacher education. *Journal of Mathematics Teacher Education*, *20*(2), 101–118. doi:10.100710857-015-9339-2

Hodges, T. E., & Mills, H. (2014). Embedded field experiences as professional apprenticeships. In K. Karp (Ed.), *Annual Perspectives in Mathematics Education* (pp. 249–260). Reston, VA: National Council of Teachers of Mathematics.

Hodges, T. E., Mills, H. A., Blackwell, B., Scott, J., & Somerall, S. (2017). Learning to theorize from practice: The power of embedded field experiences. In D. Polly & C. Martin (Eds.), *Handbook of Research on Teacher Education and Professional Development*. Hershey, PA: IGI Global. doi:10.4018/978-1-5225-1067-3.ch002

Hoffman, J. V., Wetzel, M. M., Maloch, B., Greeter, E., Taylor, L., DeJulio, S., & Vlach, S. K. (2015). What can we learn from studying the coaching interactions between cooperating teachers and preservice teachers? A literature review. *Teaching and Teacher Education*, *52*, 99–112. doi:10.1016/j.tate.2015.09.004

Hogan, T., Rabinowitz, M., & Craven, J. A. III. (2003). Representation in teaching: Inferences from research of expert and novice teachers. *Educational Psychologist*, *38*(4), 235–247. doi:10.1207/S15326985EP3804_3

Hollett, N. L., Brock, S. J., & Hinton, V. (2017). Bug-in-ear technology to enhance preservice teacher training: Peer versus instructor feedback. *International Journal of Learning, Teaching, and Educational Research*, *16*(2), 1–10.

Hollins, E. (2012). *Learning to teach in urban schools: The transition from preparation to practice*. New York: Teachers College Press.

Hollins, E. (Ed.). (2015). *Rethinking field experiences in preservice teacher preparation: Meeting the challenges for accountability*. New York: Routledge.

Hollins, E. R. (Ed.). (2015). *Rethinking field experiences in preservice teacher preparation: Meeting new challenges for accountability*. New York: Routledge.

Holmes Group. (1986). *Tomorrow's teachers: A report of the Holmes Group*. East Lansing, MI: Author.

Holmes Group. (1990). *Tomorrow's schools: Principles for the design of professional development schools*. East Lansing, MI: Author.

Holmes, P., Bavieri, L., & Ganassin, S. (2015). Developing intercultural understanding for study abroad: Students' and teachers' perspectives on pre-departure intercultural learning. *Intercultural Education*, *26*(1), 16–30. doi:10.1080/146 75986.2015.993250

Holzberger, D., Phillipp, A., & Kunter, M. (2013). How teachers' self-efficacy is related to instructional quality: A longitudinal analysis. *Journal of Educational Psychology*, *105*(3), 774–786. doi:10.1037/a0032198

Honig, M. I., & Hatch, T. C. (2004). Crafting coherence: How schools strategically manage multiple, external demands. *Educational Researcher*, *33*(8), 16–30. doi:10.3102/0013189X033008016

Horvitz, B. S., & Paul Vellom, R. (2012). Using blended learning to enhance reflective practice among science teacher candidates. *National Teacher Education Journal*, *5*(3), 77–83.

Houser, K. (2017, February 7). 11 things coaches should look for in classroom observations [Web log post]. Retrieved from https://www.mshouser.com/instructional-coaching/11-things-coaches-should-look-for-in-classroom-observations

Howell, J., & Saye, W. J. (2015). Using lesson study to develop a shared professional teaching knowledge culture among 4th grade social studies teachers. *Journal of Social Studies Research*, *40*(1), 25–37. doi:10.1016/j.jssr.2015.03.001

Howey, K., & Zimpher, N. (1989). *Profiles of preservice teacher education*. Albany, NY: State University of New York.

Hoy, A. W. (2000). *Changes in teacher efficacy during the early years of teaching*. Paper presented at the Annual Meeting of the American Educational Research Association, New Orleans, LA.

Hoy, A. W., & Spero, R. B. (2005). Changes in teacher efficacy during the early years of teaching: A comparison of four measures. *Teaching and Teacher Education: An International Journal of Research and Studies*, *21*(4), 343–356. doi:10.1016/j.tate.2005.01.007

Huang, R., Gong, Z., & Han, X. (2015). Implementing mathematics teaching that promotes students' understanding through theory-driven lesson study. *ZDM*, 1-15.

Hubbard, R. S., & Power, B. M. (2012). *Living the questions: A guide for teacher-researchers*. Portland, ME: Stenhouse Publishers.

Hufford-Ackles, K., Fuson, K., & Sherin, M. (2004). Describing levels of components of a mathematics talk learning community. *Journal for Research in Mathematics Education*, *35*(2), 81–116. doi:10.2307/30034933

Hughes, C. E., & Murawski, W. A. (2001). Lessons from another field: Applying coteaching strategies to gifted education. *Gifted Child Quarterly*, *45*(3), 195–204. doi:10.1177/001698620104500304

Huling, L. (1998). *Early field experiences in Teacher Education*. Washington, DC: ERIC Clearinghouse on Teacher Education.

Hull, G., & Schultz, K. (2002). *School's Out! Bridging out-of-school literacies with classroom practice*. New York: Teachers College Press.

Hundley, M., Palmeri, A., Hostetler, A., Johnson, H., Dunleavy, T. K., & Self, E. A. (2018). Developmental trajectories, disciplinary practices, and sites of practice in novice teacher learning: A thing to be learned. In D. Polly, M. Putman, T. M. Petty, & A. J. Good (Eds.), *Innovative practices in teacher preparation and graduate-level teacher education programs* (pp. 153–180). Hershey, PA: IGI Global. doi:10.4018/978-1-5225-3068-8.ch010

Idol, L. (2006). Toward inclusion of special education students in general education: A program evaluation of eight schools. *Remedial and Special Education*, *27*(2), 77–94. doi:10.1177/07419325060270020601

Ingersoll, R. M., & May, H. (2011). *Recruitment, retention and the minority teacher shortage* (CPRE Research Report # RR-69). Retrieved from Consortium for Policy Research in Education University of Pennsylvania and The Center for Educational Research in the Interest of Underserved Students, University of California, Santa Cruz website: http://www.cpre.org/sites/default/files/researchreport/1221_minorityteachershortagereportrr69septfinal.pdf

Ingersoll, R., Merrill, L., & May, H. (2014). *What are the effects of teacher education and preparation on beginning teacher attrition?* CPRE Research Reports. Retrieved from https://repository.upenn.edu/cgi/viewcontent.cgi?article=1002&context=cpre_researchrep

Ingersoll, R., Merrill, L., & May, H. (2014). What are the effects of teacher education and preparation on beginning Teacher Attrition? *CPRE Research Reports.* Retrieved from https://repository.upenn.edu/cpre_researchreports/78

Ingersoll, R., Merrill, L., Stuckey, D., & Consortium for Policy Research in Education. (2014). *Seven trends: The transformation of the teaching force. Updated April 2014. CPRE report. #RR-80.* Consortium for Policy Research in Education. Retrieved from http://search.ebscohost.com.er.lib.k-state.edu/login.aspx?direct=true&db=eric&AN=ED566879&site=ehost-live

Ingersoll, R. (2011). Do we produce enough mathematics and science teachers? *Phi Delta Kappan, 92*(6), 37–41. doi:10.1177/003172171109200608

Ingersoll, R. M. (2012). Beginning teacher induction what the data tell us. *Phi Delta Kappan, 93*(8), 47–51. doi:10.1177/003172171209300811

Ingersoll, R. M., & Perda, D. (2010). Is the supply of mathematics and science teachers sufficient? *American Educational Research Journal, 47*(3), 563–594. doi:10.3102/0002831210370711

Ingersoll, R. M., & Strong, M. (2011). The impact of induction and mentoring programs for beginning teachers: A critical review of the research. *Review of Educational Research, 81*(2), 201–233. doi:10.3102/0034654311403323

Inoue, N. (2009). Rehearsing to teach: Content-specific deconstruction of instructional explanations in pre-service teacher training. *Journal of Education for Teaching, 35*(1), 47–60. doi:10.1080/02607470802587137

Inside Mathematics. (2017). *9ᵗʰ & 10ᵗʰ grade math – properties of quadrilaterals.* Retrieved from http://www.insidemathematics.org/classroom-videos/public-lessons/9th-10th-grade-math-properties-of-quadrilaterals

Intrator, S., & Kunzman, R. (2009). Grounded: Practicing what we preach. *Journal of Teacher Education, 60*(5), 512–519. doi:10.1177/0022487109348598

Ipkeze, C. H., Broikou, K. A., Hildenbrand, S., & Gladstone-Brown, W. (2012). PDS collaboration as Third Space: An analysis of the quality of learning experiences in a PDS partnership. *Studying Teacher Education, 8*(3), 275–288. doi:10.1080/17425964.2012.719125

Izadinia, M. (2015). A closer look at the role of mentor teachers in shaping preservice teachers' professional identity. *Teaching and Teacher Education, 52,* 1–10. doi:10.1016/j.tate.2015.08.003

Jackson, K. J., Shahan, E. C., Gibbons, L. K., & Cobb, P. A. (2012). Launching complex tasks. *Mathematics Teaching in the Middle School, 18*(1), 24–29. doi:10.5951/mathteacmiddscho.18.1.0024

Jackson, K., Garrison, A., Wilson, J., Gibbons, L., & Shahan, E. (2013). Exploring relationships between setting up complex tasks and opportunities to learn in concluding while-class discussions in middle-grades mathematics instruction. *Journal for Research in Mathematics Education, 44*(4), 646–682. doi:10.5951/jresematheduc.44.4.0646

Jackson, P. (1986). *The practice of teaching.* New York, NY: Teachers College Press.

Jacobs, V. R., Lamb, L. L., Philipp, R. A., & Schappelle, B. P. (2011). Deciding how to respond on the basis of children's understandings. In M. G. Sherin, V. R. Jacobs & R. A. Philipp (Eds.), Mathematics teacher noticing: Seeing through teachers' eyes (pp. 97-116). New York: Routledge.

Jacobs, J. (1992). *The death and life of great American cities*. New York: Vintage Books.

Jacobs, J., Hogarty, K., & Burns, R. (2017). Elementary preservice teacher field supervision: A survey of teacher education programs. *Action in Teacher Education, 39*(2), 172–186. doi:10.1080/01626620.2016.1248300

Jacobs, V. R., Lamb, L. L. C., & Philipp, R. A. (2010). Professional noticing of children's mathematical thinking. *Journal for Research in Mathematics Education, 41*(2), 169–202.

Jay, J. K., & Johnson, K. L. (2002). Capturing complexity: A typology of reflective practice for teacher education. *Teaching and Teacher Education, 18*(1), 73–85. doi:10.1016/S0742-051X(01)00051-8

Jenkins, J. J. (2014). Pre-service teachers' observations of experienced teachers. *Physical Educator, 71*, 303–319.

Jenkins, L. (1997). *Improving student learning: Applying Deming's quality principles in classrooms*. Milwaukee, WI: ASQC Quality Press.

Jensen, J. W., & Winitzky, N. (1999, Feb.) *What works in teacher education?* Paper presented at the Annual meeting of the American Association of Colleges for Teacher Education, Washington, DC.

Jensen, S. B. (2012). Special education & school choice: The complex effects of small schools, school choice and public high school policy in New York City. *Educational Policy, 27*(3), 427–466. doi:10.1177/0895904812453997

Jenset, I. S., Klette, K., & Hammerness, K. (2018). Grounding teacher education in practice around the world: An examination of teacher education coursework in teacher education programs in Finland, Norway, and the United States. *Journal of Teacher Education, 69*(2), 184–197. doi:10.1177/0022487117728248

Johnson, S. M., Kraft, M. A., & Papay, J. P. (2012). How context matters in high-need schools: The effects of teachers' working conditions on their professional satisfaction and their students' achievement. *Teachers College Record, 114*(10), 1–39. PMID:24013958

Johnston, P. H. (2004). *Choice words: How our language affects children's learning*. Stenhouse Publishers.

Jones, M., Hobbs, L., Kenny, J., Campbell, C., Chittleborough, G., Gilbert, A., ... Redman, C. (2016). Successful university-school partnerships: An interpretive framework to inform partnership practice. *Teaching and Teacher Education, 60*, 108–120. doi:10.1016/j.tate.2016.08.006

Jorgensen, K. (2008). Second Language Development Stages: Sample Behaviors in the Classroom [Class handout]. Lawrence, KS: University of Kansas, C&T 649.

Jung, M. L., & Tonso, K. L. (2006). Elementary preservice teachers learning to teach science in science museums and nature centers: A novel program's impact on science knowledge, science pedagogy, and confidence teaching. *Journal of Elementary Science Education, 18*(1), 15–31. doi:10.1007/BF03170651

Kalk, K., Luik, P., Taimalu, M., & Täht, K. (2014). Validity and reliability of two instruments to measure reflection: A confirmatory study. *Journal of the Humanities and Social Sciences, 18*, 121–134. doi:10.3176/tr.2014.2.02

Kanold, T., & Larson, M. (2012). *Common Core Mathematics in a PLC at work™: Leader's guide*. Bloomington, IN: Solution Tree Press.

Kansas State University. (2018). *Kansas state university student teacher handbook: Reflections on a single lesson*. Retrieved from https://www.coe.ksu.edu/field-experiences/docs/UG-ST-Handbook-2018.pdf

Compilation of References

Katz, P., Randy McGinnis, J., Riedinger, K., Marbach-Ad, G., & Dai, A. (2013). The influence of informal science education experiences on the development of two beginning teachers' science classroom teaching identity. *Journal of Science Teacher Education*, *24*(8), 1357–1379. doi:10.100710972-012-9330-z

Kazemi, E., Franke, M., & Lampert, M. (2009). Developing pedagogies in teacher education to support novice teachers' ability to enact ambitious instruction. In *Crossing Divides, Proceedings of the 32nd Annual Conference of The Mathematics Education Research Group of Australasia (Vol. 1*, pp. 11-29). Academic Press.

Kazemi, E., Franke, M., & Lampert, M. (2009). Developing pedagogies in teacher education to support novice teachers' ability to enact ambitious instruction. In R. Hunter & T. Burgess (Eds.), *Crossing divides: Proceedings of the 32nd annual conference of the Mathematics Research Group of Australia*, 1.

Kazemi, E., Franke, M., & Lampert, M. (2009). Developing pedagogies in teacher education to support teachers' ability to enact ambitious instruction. In R. Hunter, B. Bicknell & T. Burgess (Eds.), *Crossing divides: Proceedings of the 32nd annual conference of the Math Education Research Group of Australasia*. Palmerston North, NZ: MERGA.

Kazemi, E., Franke, M., & Lampert, M. (2009, July). Developing pedagogies in teacher education to support novice teachers' ability to enact ambitious instruction. In *Crossing divides: Proceedings of the 32nd annual conference of the Mathematics Education Research Group of Australasia (Vol. 1*, pp. 12-30). Adelaide, SA: MERGA.

Kazemi, E., Lampert, M., & Ghousseini, H. (2007). Conceptualizing and using routines of practice in mathematics teaching to advance professional education. Report to the Spencer Foundation.

Kazemi, E., Ghousseini, H., Cunard, A., & Turrou, A. C. (2016). Getting inside rehearsals: Insights from teacher educators support work on complex practice. *Journal of Teacher Education*, *67*(1), 18–31. doi:10.1177/0022487115615191

Kazemi, E., & Hintz, A. (2014). *Intentional talk: How to structure and lead productive mathematical discussions*. Portland, ME: Stenhouse.

Kazemi, E., & Wæge, K. (2015). Learning to teach within practice-based methods courses. *Mathematics Teacher Education and Development*, *17*(2), 125–145.

Kee, A. N. (2012). Feelings of preparedness among alternatively certified teachers: What is the role of program features? *Journal of Teacher Education*, *63*(1), 23–38. doi:10.1177/0022487111421933

Kehl, K., & Morris, J. (2007). Differences in global-mindedness between short-term and semester-long study abroad participants at selected private universities. *Frontiers: The Interdisciplinary Journal of Study Abroad*, *15*, 67–79.

Kelchtermans, G. (2006). Teacher collaboration and collegiality as workplace conditions. A review. *Zeitschrift fur Padagogik*, *52*(2), 220.

Kellogg Foundation. (2004). *W.K. Kellogg Foundation logic model development guide*. Retrieved from https://www.wkkf.org/resource-directory/resource/2006/02/wk-kellogg-foundation-logic-model-development-guide

Kemmis, S., Heikkinen, H. L. T., Fransson, G., Aspfors, J., & Edwards-Groves, C. (2014). Mentoring of new teachers as a contested practice: Supervision, support and collaborative self-development. *Teaching and Teacher Education*, *43*, 154–164. doi:10.1016/j.tate.2014.07.001

Kennedy, M. M. (1999). Ed schools and the problem of knowledge. In J. D. Raths & A. C. McAninch (Eds.), What counts as knowledge in teacher education. Stamford, CT: Ablex.

Kennedy, M. M. (1999). The role of preservice teacher education. In L. Darling-Hammond & G. Sykes (Eds.), *Teaching as the learning profession: Handbook of policy and practice* (pp. 54–86). San Francisco, CA: Josey-Bass.

Kidd, M. (2008). A comparison of secondary mathematics methods courses in California. In P. M. Lutz (Ed.), *Secondary mathematics methods courses in California*. California Association of Mathematics Teacher Educators.

Kilic, H., & Tunc Pekkan, Z. (2017). University-school collaboration as a tool for promoting pre-service mathematics teachers' professional skills. *International Journal of Research in Education and Science*, *3*(2), 383–394. doi:10.21890/ijres.327897

Killian, J. E., & Wilkins, E. A. (2009). Characteristics of highly effective cooperating teachers: A study of their backgrounds and preparation. *Action in Teacher Education*, *30*(4), 67–83. doi:10.1080/01626620.2009.10734453

King, J. E. (2005). *Black Education: A Transformative Research & Action Agenda for the New Century*. Lawrence Erlbaum.

King, J. E., & Swartz, E. (2014). *"Re-membering" history in student and teacher learning: An Afrocentric culturally informed praxis*. New York, NY: Routledge.

King, J. E., & Swartz, E. E. (2016). *The Afrocentric praxis of teaching for freedom: Connecting culture to learning*. New York: Routledge.

King, S. (2006). Promoting paired placements in initial teacher education. *International Research in Geographical and Environmental Education*, *15*(4), 370–386. doi:10.2167/irg201.0

Kinloch, V., & Dixon, K. (2017). Equity and justice for all: The politics of cultivating anti-racist practices in urban teacher education. *English Teaching*, *16*(3), 331–346. doi:10.1108/ETPC-05-2017-0074

Klassen, R. M., Tze, V. M., Betts, S. M., & Gordon, K. A. (2011). Teacher efficacy research 1998-2009: Signs of progress or unfulfilled promise? *Educational Psychology Review*, *23*(1), 21–43. doi:10.100710648-010-9141-8

Klehm, M. (2014). The effects of teacher beliefs on teaching practices and achievement of students with disabilities. *Teacher Education and Special Education*, *37*(3), 216–240. doi:10.1177/0888406414525050

Klein, E. J., Taylor, M., Onore, C., Strom, K., & Abrams, L. (2013). Finding a third space in teacher education: Creating an urban teacher residency. *Teaching Education*, *24*(1), 27–57. doi:10.1080/10476210.2012.711305

Kline, J., & Walker-Gibbs, B. (2015). Graduate teacher preparation for rural schools in Victoria and Queensland. *Australian Journal of Teacher Education*, *40*(3), 68–88.

Kline, J., White, S., & Lock, G. (2013). The rural practicum: Preparing a quality teacher workforce for rural and regional Australia. *Journal of Research in Rural Education*, *28*(3), 1–13.

Knowlton, L., & Phillips, C. (2013). *The logic model guidebook: Better strategies for great results*. Thousand Oaks, CA: Sage Publication.

Kochan, F. K., & Trimble, S. B. (2000). From mentoring to co-mentoring: Establishing collaborative relationships. *Theory into Practice*, *39*(1), 20–28. doi:10.120715430421tip3901_4

Koehler, M. J., & Mishra, P. (2009). What is technological pedagogical content knowledge? *Contemporary Issues in Technology & Teacher Education*, *9*(1), 60–70.

Koemer, M., Rust, F., & Baumgartner, F. (2002). Exploring roles in student teaching placements. *Teacher Education Quarterly*, *29*, 35–58.

Kohler-Evans, P. A. (2006). Co-teaching: How to make this marriage work in front of the kids. *Education*, *127*(2), 260–264.

Korthagen, F. A. (2004). In search of the essence of a good teacher: Towards a more holistic approach in teacher education. *Teaching and Teacher Education*, *20*(1), 77–97. doi:10.1016/j.tate.2003.10.002

Korthagen, F. A. J. (2010). Situated learning theory and the pedagogy of teacher education: Towards an integrated view of teacher behavior and teacher learning. *Teaching and Teacher Education*, *26*(1), 98–106. doi:10.1016/j.tate.2009.05.001

Korthagen, F., & Kessels, J. (1999). Linking theory and practice: Changing the pedagogy of teacher education. *Educational Researcher*, *28*(4), 4–17. doi:10.3102/0013189X028004004

Korthagen, F., Loughran, J., & Lunenberg, M. (2005). Teaching teachers – studies into the expertise of teacher educators: An introduction to this theme issue. *Teaching and Teacher Education*, *21*(2), 107–115. doi:10.1016/j.tate.2004.12.007

Kosnik, C., & Beck, B. (2008). In the shadows: Non-tenure line instructors in preservice teacher education. *European Journal of Teacher Education*, *31*(2), 185–202. doi:10.1080/02619760802000214

Kosnik, C., & Beck, C. (2000). The action research process as a means of helping student teachers understand and fulfill the complex role of the teacher. *Educational Action Research*, *8*(1), 115–136. doi:10.1080/09650790000200107

Koster, B., & van den Berg, B. (2014). Increasing professional self-understanding: Self-study research by teachers with the help of biography, core reflection and dialogue. *Studying Teacher Education*, *10*(1), 86–100. doi:10.1080/17425964.2013.866083

Kotelawala, U. (2012). Lesson study in a methods course: Connecting teacher education to the field. *Teacher Educator*, *47*(1), 67–89. doi:10.1080/08878730.2012.633840

Kozol, J. (1991). *Savage inequalities*. New York: Crown Publishers.

Kozol, J. (2005). *Shame of a nation*. New York: Crown Publishers.

Kucan, L., Palincsar, A. S., Busse, T., Heisey, N., Klingelhofer, R., Rimbey, M., & Schutz, K. (2011). Applying the Grossman et al. theoretical framework: The case of reading. *Teachers College Record*, *113*(12), 2897-2921.

Labaree, D. (2004). The trouble with ed schools. New Haven, CT: Yale University Press.

Laczko-Kerr, I., & Berliner, D. (2002). The effectiveness of "Teach for America" and other under-certified teachers on student academic achievement: A case of harmful public policy. *Education Policy Analysis Archives*, *37*(10). Retrieved from https://epaa.asu.edu/ojs/article/view/316

Ladson-Billings, G. (2017). The (r)evolution will not be standardized: Teacher education, hip hop pedagogy, and culturally relevant pedagogy 2.0. In D. Paris & S. Alim (Eds.), Culturally Sustaining Pedagogies: Teaching and Learning for Justice in a Changing World. Academic Press.

Ladson-Billings, G. (1994). *The dreamkeepers: Successful teachers of African-American children*. San Francisco: Jossey-Bass.

Ladson-Billings, G. (1995). But that's just good teaching! The case for culturally relevant pedagogy. *Theory into Practice*, *34*(3), 159–165. doi:10.1080/00405849509543675

Ladson-Billings, G. (1995). Toward a theory of culturally relevant pedagogy. *American Educational Research Journal*, *32*(3), 465–491. doi:10.3102/00028312032003465

Ladson-Billings, G. (2001). *Crossing over to Canaan: The journey of new teachers in diverse classrooms*. San Francisco: Jossey-Bass.

Ladson-Billings, G. (2006). It's not the culture of poverty, it's the poverty of culture: The problem with teacher education. *Anthropology & Education Quarterly*, *37*(2), 104–109. doi:10.1525/aeq.2006.37.2.104

Ladson-Billings, G. (2008). I ain't writin' nuttin': Permissions to fail and demands to succeed. In L. Delpit & J. K. Dowdy (Eds.), *The Skin that We Speak: Thought on Language Culture in the Classroom* (pp. 109–120). New York: The New Press.

Ladson-Billings, G. (2014). Culturally relevant pedagogy 2.0: A.k.a. the remix. *Harvard Educational Review*, *84*(1), 74–84. doi:10.17763/haer.84.1.p2rj131485484751

Lampert, M. (2001). *Teaching problems and the problems of teaching*. New Haven, CT: Yale University Press.

Lampert, M. L. (2010). Learning teaching in, from and for practice: What do we mean? *Journal of Teacher Education*, *61*(1-2), 21–34. doi:10.1177/0022487109347321

Lampert, M., Beasley, H., Ghousseini, H., Kazemi, E., & Franke, M. (2010). Using designed instructional activities to enable novices to manage ambitious mathematics teaching. In M. K. Stein & L. Kucan (Eds.), *Instructional explanations in the disciplines* (pp. 129–141). New York: Springer. doi:10.1007/978-1-4419-0594-9_9

Lampert, M., Franke, M. L., Kazemi, E., Ghousseini, H., Turrou, A. C., Beasley, H., ... Crowe, K. (2013). Keeping it complex: Using rehearsals to support novice teacher learning of ambitious teaching. *Journal of Teacher Education*, *64*(3), 226–243. doi:10.1177/0022487112473837

Lampert, M., & Graziani, F. (2009). Instructional activities as a tool for teachers' and teacher educators' learning in and for practice. *The Elementary School Journal*, *109*(5), 491–509. doi:10.1086/596998

Lang, C., Neal, D., Karvouni, M., & Chandler, D. (2015). An embedded professional paired placement model: "I know I am not an expert, but I am at a point now where I could step into a classroom and be responsible for learning. *Asia-Pacific Journal of Teacher Education*, *43*(4), 338–354. doi:10.1080/1359866X.2015.1060296

Lanier, J., & Little, J. (1986). Research on teacher education. In M. Wittrock (Ed.), *Handbook of research on teaching* (pp. 527–569). New York, NY: Macmillan.

Lappan, G. (1999). Revitalizing and refocusing our efforts. *Teaching Children Mathematics*, *6*(2), 104. Retrieved from https://search.proquest.com/docview/214140114?accountid=14541

Lappan, G., Fey, J. T., Fitzgerald, W. M., Friel, S. N., & Phillips, E. D. (2006). *Stretching and shrinking: Understanding similarity (Connected Mathematics 2, Grade 7)*. Boston: Pearson/Prentice Hall.

Latham, N. I., & Vogt, W. P. (2007, March). Do professional development schools reduce teacher attrition? Evidence from a longitudinal study of 1,000 graduates. *Journal of Teacher Education*, *58*(2), 153–167. doi:10.1177/0022487106297840

Lavadenz, M., & Hollins, E. (2015). Urban schools as settings for learning teaching. In E. Hollins (Ed.), *Rethinking field experiences in preservice teacher education* (pp. 1–14). New York, NY: Routledge.

Lave, J. (1988). *Cognition in practice*. Cambridge, UK: Cambridge University Press. doi:10.1017/CBO9780511609268

Lave, J., & Wenger, E. (1991). *Situated learning: Legitimate peripheral participation*. Cambridge, UK: Cambridge University Press. doi:10.1017/CBO9780511815355

Laverick, V. T. (2017). Secondary teachers' understanding and use of reflection: An exploratory study. *American Secondary Education*, *45*(2), 56–68.

Lawley, J. J., Moore, J., & Smajic, A. (2014). Effective communication between preservice and cooperating teachers. *New Educator*, *10*(2), 153–162. doi:10.1080/1547688X.2014.898495

Lazar, A. M. (1998). Helping preservice teachers inquire about caregivers: A critical experience for field-based courses. *Action in Teacher Education*, *19*(4), 14–28. doi:10.1080/01626620.1998.10462888

Leana, C. (2011). *The missing link in school reform.* Retrieved from https://www2.ed.gov/programs/slcp/2011progdirmtg/mislinkinrfm.pdf

Learning Policy Institute. (2016). *Understanding shortages: A state-by-state analysis of the factors influencing teacher supply, demand and equity.* Retrieved from https://learningpolicyinstitute.org/product/understanding-teacher-shortages-interactive

Leatham, K. R., & Peterson, B. E. (2010a). Purposefully designing student teaching to focus on students' mathematical thinking. In J. W. Lott & J. Luebeck (Eds.), *Mathematics teaching: Putting research into practice at all levels* (pp. 225–239). San Diego, CA: Association of Mathematics Teacher Education.

Leatham, K. R., & Peterson, B. E. (2010b). Secondary mathematics mentor teachers' perceptions of the purpose of student teaching. *Journal of Mathematics Teacher Education, 13*(2), 99–119. doi:10.100710857-009-9125-0

Leatham, K. R., Peterson, B. E., Stockero, S. L., & Van Zoest, L. R. (2015). Conceptualizing mathematically significant pedagogical opportunities to build on student thinking. *Journal for Research in Mathematics Education, 46*(1), 88–124. doi:10.5951/jresematheduc.46.1.0088

Leavy, A. M., McSorley, F. A., & Boté, L. A. (2007). An examination of what metaphor construction reveals about the evolution of preservice teachers' beliefs about teaching and learning. *Teaching and Teacher Education, 23*(7), 1217–1233. doi:10.1016/j.tate.2006.07.016

Lee, J. C., & Feng, S. (2007). Mentoring support and the professional development of beginning teachers: A Chinese perspective. *Mentoring & Tutoring, 15*(3), 243–263. doi:10.1080/13611260701201760

Lee, R. (2018). Breaking down barriers and building bridges: Transformative practices in community- and school-based urban teacher preparation. *Journal of Teacher Education*, 1–19. doi:10.1177/0022487117751127

Leinhardt, G. (2001). Instructional explanations: A commonplace for teaching and a location for contrast. In V. Richardson (Ed.), *Handbook of research on teaching* (4th ed.; pp. 333–357). Washington, DC: American Educational Research Association.

Leinhardt, G., & Greeno, J. G. (1986). The cognitive skill of teaching. *Journal of Educational Psychology, 78*(2), 75–95. doi:10.1037/0022-0663.78.2.75

Leko, M. M., Brownell, M. T., Sindelar, P. T., & Murphy, K. (2012). Promoting special education preservice teacher expertise. *Focus on Exceptional Children, 44*(7), 1–16. doi:10.17161/fec.v44i7.6684 PMID:23997274

Lemke, J. L. (1990). *Talking science.* Norwood, NJ: Ablex.

Leont'ev, A. N. (1978). *Activity, consciousness, and personality.* Englewood Cliffs, NJ: Prentice-Hall.

LePage, P., Darling-Hammond, L., Akar, H., Guiterrez, C., Jenkins-Gunn, E., & Rosebrock, K. (2005). Classroom management. In L. Darling-Hammond, J. Bransford, P. LePage, K. Hammerness, & H. Duffy (Eds.), *Preparing teachers for a changing world: What teachers should learn and be able to do* (pp. 327–357). San Francisco, CA: Jossey-Bass.

Levin, B. B., & Rock, T. C. (2003). The effects of collaborative action research on preservice and experienced teacher partners in professional development schools. *Journal of Teacher Education, 54*(2), 135–149. doi:10.1177/0022487102250287

Levin, D., Hammer, D., & Coffey, J. (2009). Novice Teachers' Attention to Student Thinking. *Journal of Teacher Education, 60*(2), 142–154. doi:10.1177/0022487108330245

Levine, A. (2006). *Educating school teachers.* Washington, DC: Education Schools Project.

Levine, A. (2006). Will universities maintain control of teacher education? *Change, 38*(4), 36–43. doi:10.3200/CHNG.38.4.36-43

Levine, H. (2011). Features and strategies of supervisor professional community as a means of improving the supervision of preservice teachers. *Teaching and Teacher Education, 27*(5), 930–941. doi:10.1016/j.tate.2011.03.004

Levine, M. (2002). Why invest in professional development schools? *Educational Leadership, 59*(6), 65–70. Retrieved from https://eric.ed.gov

Levine, M., & Trachtman, R. (Eds.). (1997). *Making professional development schools work: Politics, practice and policy.* New York, NY: Teachers College Press.

Levine, T. H. (2010). Tools for study and design of collaborative teacher learning: The affordances of different conceptions of teacher community and activity theory. *Teacher Education Quarterly, 37*(1), 109–130.

Lewis, C. (2002). *Lesson study: A handbook of teacher-led instructional change.* Philadelphia: Research for Better Schools.

Lewis, C. (2002). What are the essential elements of lesson study? *The California Science Project Connection, 2*(6), 1–4.

Lewis, C. (2015). What is improvement science? Do we need it in education? *Educational Researcher, 44*(1), 54–61. doi:10.3102/0013189X15570388

Lewis, C. (2016). How does lesson study improve mathematics instruction? *ZDM, 48*(4), 571–580. doi:10.100711858-016-0792-x

Lewis, C., & Hurd, J. (2011). *Lesson study step by step: How teacher learning communities improve instruction.* Portsmouth: Heinemann.

Lewis, C., Perry, R., & Hurd, J. (2004). A deeper look at lesson study. *Educational Leadership, 61*(5), 18–22.

Lewis, C., Perry, R., Hurd, J., & O'Connell, M. P. (2006). Lesson study comes of age in North America. *Phi Delta Kappan, 88*(4), 273–281. doi:10.1177/003172170608800406

Lewis, C., Perry, R., & Murata, A. (2006). What is the role of the research in an emerging innovation? The case of lesson study. *Educational Researcher, 35*(3), 3–14. doi:10.3102/0013189X035003003

Lipman, P. (2004, April). *Regionalization of urban education: The political economy and racial politics of Chicago-metro region schools.* Paper presented at the Annual Meeting of the American Educational Research Association, San Diego, CA.

Little, J. W. (2003). Inside teacher community: Representations of classroom practice. *Teachers College Record, 105*(6), 913–945. doi:10.1111/1467-9620.00273

Liu, M. (2013). Disrupting teacher education. *Education Next, 13*(3). Retrieved from http://educationnext.org/disrupting-teacher-education

Long, S. (2011). Supporting students in the time of Common Core Standards, 4K Through Grade 2. Urbana, IL: National Council of Teachers of English.

Longo, N. V. (2007). *Why community matters: Connecting education with civic life.* Albany, NY: SUNY Press.

Longo, N. V. (2013). Deliberative pedagogy in the community: Connecting deliberative dialogue, community engagement, and democratic education. *Journal of Public Deliberation, 9*(2), 1–18. Retrieved from http://publicdeliberation.net/jpd/vol9/iss2/art16

Lortie, D. (1975). *Schoolteacher: A sociological analysis.* Chicago, IL: University of Chicago Press.

Lortie, D. (1975). *Schoolteacher: A sociological study.* Chicago: University of Chicago Press.

Loughran, J. J. (2002). Effective reflective practice: In search of meaning in learning about teaching. *Journal of Teacher Education, 53*(1), 33–43. doi:10.1177/0022487102053001004

Loughran, J. J. (2004). A history and context of self-study of teaching and teacher education practices. In J. J. Loughran, M. L. Hamilton, V. K. LaBoskey, & T. Russell (Eds.), *International handbook of self-study of teaching and teacher education practices* (pp. 7–39). Dordrecht: Kluwer. doi:10.1007/978-1-4020-6545-3_1

Loughran, J., & Berry, A. (2005). Modelling by teacher educators. *Teaching and Teacher Education, 21*(2), 193–203. doi:10.1016/j.tate.2004.12.005

Louis, K. S., & Marks, H. (1998). Does professional community affect the classroom? Teachers' work and student experiences in restructuring schools. *American Journal of Education, 106*(8), 532–575. doi:10.1086/444197

Luft, J. A., Roehrig, G. H., & Patterson, N. C. (2003). Contrasting landscapes: A comparison of the impact of different induction programs on beginning secondary science teachers' practices, beliefs and experiences. *Journal of Research in Science Teaching, 40*(1), 77–97. doi:10.1002/tea.10061

Lytle, S. L., & Cochran-Smith, M. (1993). *Inside/Outside: Teacher research and knowledge.* New York: Teachers College Press.

Maheady, L., Smith, C., & Jabot, M. (2014). Field experiences and instructional pedagogies in teacher education: What we know, don't know, and must learn soon. In P. T. Sindelar, E. D. McCray, M. T. Brownell, & B. Lignugaris-Kraft (Eds.), *Handbook of research on special education teacher preparation* (pp. 161–177). New York, NY: Routledge.

Ma, L. (1999). *Knowing and teaching elementary mathematics.* Mahwah, NJ: Lawrence Earlbaum Associates.

Malloy, J. A., Parsons, S. A., & Parsons, A. W. (2013). Methods for evaluating literacy engagement as a fluid construct. *62nd Yearbook of the Literacy Research Association,* 124-139.

Malsbary, C. B. (2016). Youth and schools' practices in hyper-diverse contexts. *American Educational Research Journal, 53*(6), 1491–1521. doi:10.3102/0002831216676569

Manuti, A., & de Palma, P. D. (2018). The cognitive technology revolution: A new identity for workers. In A. Manuti & P. D. de Palma (Eds.), Digital hr: A critical management approach to the digitalization of organizations (pp. 21-27). Cham: Palgrave Macmillan. doi:10.1007/978-3-319-60210-3_2

Many, J. E., Fisher, T. R., Ogletree, S., & Taylor, D. (2012). Crisscrossing the university and public school contexts as professional development school boundary spanners. *Issues in Teacher Education, 21*(2), 83–102.

Marshall, J. D., Smagorinsky, & Smith, M. (1995). *The language of interpretation: Patterns of discourse in discussions of literature.* Academic Press.

Marshall, C., & Rossman, G. (2016). *Designing Qualitative Research, 6th Education.* Thousand Oaks, CA: Sage.

Martin, F., & Ertzberger, J. (2013). Here and now mobile learning: An experimental study on the use of mobile technology. *Computers & Education, 68,* 76–85. doi:10.1016/j.compedu.2013.04.021

Martin, S. D., Snow, J. L., & Franklin Torrez, C. A. (2011). Navigating the terrain of Third Space: Tensions with/in relationships in school-university partnerships. *Journal of Teacher Education, 62*(3), 299–311. doi:10.1177/0022487110396096

Martin, W. G., & Gobstein, H. (2015). Generating a networked improvement community to improve secondary mathematics teacher preparation: Network leadership, organization, and operation. *Journal of Teacher Education, 66*(5), 482–493. doi:10.1177/0022487115602312

Marzano, R. J. (2003). *What works in schools: Translating Research into Action.* Alexandria, VA: Association for Supervision and Curriculum Development.

Marzano, R. J. (2011). Making the most of instructional rounds. *Educational Leadership, 68*(5), 80–81.

Massey, D. D., & Lewis, J. (2011). Learning from the "Little Guys": What do middle and high school preservice teachers learn from tutoring elementary students? *Literacy Research and Instruction, 50*(2), 120–132. doi:10.1080/19388071003725705

Mathematics Teacher Education- Partnership (MTE-P). (2014). *Guiding Principles.* Retrieved on May 10, 2018 from http://www.aplu.org/projects-and-initiatives/stem-education/SMTI_Library/mte-partnership-guiding-principles-for-secondary-mathematics-teacher-preparation-programs/File

Matsko, K. K., & Hammerness, K. (2014). Unpacking the "urban" in urban teacher education: Making a case for context-specific preparation. *Journal of Teacher Education, 65*(2), 128–144. doi:10.1177/0022487113511645

Mau, S. (2013). Letter from the editor: Better together? Considering paired-placements for student teaching. School Science and Mathematics, 113(2), 53–55.

Maxwell, J. A. (2008). Designing a qualitative study. The SAGE handbook of applied social research methods, 2, 214-253.

Maxwell, J. A. (2005). *Qualitative research design: An interactive approach* (2nd ed.). Thousand Oaks, CA: Sage.

Mazer, J. P., & Hess, J. A. (2016). Editor's Introduction. *Communication Education, 65*(3), 356–376. doi:10.1080/03634523.2016.1173715

McAdams, R. P. (1997). A systems approach to school reform. *Phi Delta Kappan, 79*(2), 138–142.

McAllister, G., & Irvine, J. J. (2002). The role of empathy in teaching culturally diverse students: A qualitative study of teachers' beliefs. *Journal of Teacher Education, 53*(5), 433–443. doi:10.1177/002248702237397

McCaffrey, J. R., Lockwood, D. F., Koretz, D. M., & Hamilton, L. S. (2003). *Evaluating value added models for teacher accountability.* Retrieved from http://www.rand.org/pubs/monographs/2004/RAND_MG158.pdf

McClay, W. M. (2014). Introduction: Why place matters. In W.M. McClay & T.V. McAllister (Eds.), Why place matters: Geography, identity, and civic life in modern America (pp. 1-3). New York: Encounter Books.

McCollough, C., & Ramirez, O. (2010). Connecting math and science to home, school and community through preservice teacher education. *Academic Leadership: The Online Journal, 8*(2), 15.

McCulloch, A. W., Marshall, P. L., & DeCuir-Gunby, J. T. (2009). Cultural capital in children's number representations. *Teaching Children Mathematics, 16*(3), 184–189.

McDonald, M. A., Bowman, M., & Brayko, K. (2013). Learning to see students: Opportunities to develop relational practices of teaching through community-based placements in teacher education. *Teachers College Record, 115*(4). Retrieved from https://www.tcrecord.org/content.asp?contentid=16916

McDonald, M., Kazemi, E., & Kavanagh, S. S. (2013). Core practices and pedagogies of teacher education: A call for a common language and collective activity. *Journal of Teacher Education, 64*(5), 378–386. doi:10.1177/0022487113493807

McDonald, R. B. (1997). Using participation in public school "family science night" programs as a component in the preparation of preservice elementary teachers. *Science Education, 81*(5), 577–595. doi:10.1002/(SICI)1098-237X(199709)81:5<577::AID-SCE5>3.0.CO;2-7

McDuffie, K. A., Mastropieri, M. A., & Scruggs, T. E. (2009). Differential effects of peer tutoring in co-taught and non-co-taught classes: Results for content learning and student-teacher interactions. *Exceptional Children*, *75*(4), 493–510. doi:10.1177/001440290907500406

McFadden, J., Ellis, J., Anwar, T., & Roehrig, G. (2014). Beginning science teachers' use of a digital video annotation tool to promote reflective practices. *Journal of Science Education and Technology*, *23*(3), 458–470. doi:10.100710956-013-9476-2

McGaha, J. M., & Linder, S. M. (2014). Determining candidates' attitudes toward global-mindedness. *Action in Teacher Education*, *36*(4), 305–321. doi:10.1080/01626620.2014.948225

McGlynn, A. P. (2007). *Teaching today's college students: Widening the circle of success*. Madison, WI: Atwood Publishing.

McIntyre, D. J., Byrd, D. M., & Foxx, S. M. (1996). Field and laboratory experiences. In J. Sikula, T. J. Buttery, & E. Guyton (Eds.), *Handbook of Research on Teacher Education* (2nd ed.; pp. 171–193). New York: Macmillan.

McNally, J. C. (2016). Learning from one's own teaching: New science teachers analyzing their practice through classroom observation cycles. *Journal of Research in Science Teaching*, *53*(3), 473–501. doi:10.1002/tea.21253

McNamara, D. (1995). The influence of student teachers' tutors and mentors upon their classroom practice: An exploratory study. *Teaching and Teacher Education*, *11*(1), 51–61. doi:10.1016/0742-051X(94)00014-W

McNaughton, S. (2002). *Meeting of the minds*. Wellington, NZ: Learning Media.

Medina, M. (2015). *Mango, Abuela, and me*. New York: Candlewick Press.

Meijer, P. C., Korthagen, F. A. J., & Vasalos, A. (2009). Supporting presence in teacher education: The connection between the personal and professional aspects of teaching. *Teaching and Teacher Education*, *21*(2), 297–308. doi:10.1016/j.tate.2008.09.013

Merriam, S. B. (2009). *Qualitative research: A guide to design and implementation*. San Francisco, CA: Jossey-Bass.

Metropolitan Transportation Authority. (2018). *Facts and figures: Subways*. Retrieved from: http://web.mta.info/nyct/facts/ffsubway.htm

Mewborn, D. S. (1999). Reflective thinking among preservice elementary mathematics teachers. *Journal for Research in Mathematics Education*, *30*(3), 316–341. doi:10.2307/749838

Meyer, S. J. (2016). *Understanding field experiences in traditional teacher preparation programs in Missouri (REL 2016–145)*. Washington, DC: U.S. Department of Education, Institute of Education Sciences, National Center for Education Evaluation and Regional Assistance, Regional Educational Laboratory Central. Retrieved from http://ies.ed.gov/ncee/edlabs

Mikolchak, M. (2014). Service-learning in English comp. In V. Kinloch & P. Smagorinsky (Eds.), *Service-learning in literacy education: Possibilities for teaching and learning* (pp. 211–224). Charlotte, NC: Information Age Publishing.

Miles, M. B., & Huberman, A. M. (1994). *Qualitative data analysis: An expanded source book*. Thousand Oaks, CA: Sage.

Miles, M. B., Huberman, A. M., & Saldãna, J. (2014). *Qualitative data analysis: A methods sourcebook* (3rd ed.). Thousand Oaks, CA: Sage.

Miller, A. (2013). Principal turnover and student achievement. *Economics of Education Review*, *36*, 60–72. doi:10.1016/j.econedurev.2013.05.004

Mills Teacher Scholars. (2017, June 13). The impact of teacher-led collaborative inquiry [Blog post]. Retrieved from http://millsscholars.org/the-impact-of-teacher-led-collaborative-inquiry/

Mills, G. E. (2017). *Action research: A guide for the teacher researcher* (6th ed.). Boston, MA: Pearson.

Milner, H. R. IV. (2012). But what is urban education? *Urban Education, 47*(3), 556–561. doi:10.1177/0042085912447516

Mintz, S. & Hesser, G. (1996). Principles of good practice in service-learning. *Service-learning in higher education*, 26-52.

Mishler, E. (1999). *Storylines: Craftartists' narratives of identity*. Cambridge, MA: Harvard University Press.

Moll, L. C., Amanti, C., Neff, D., & Gonzalez, N. (1992). Funds of knowledge for teaching: Using a qualitative approach to connect homes and classrooms. *Theory into Practice, 31*(1), 132–141. doi:10.1080/00405849209543534

Moon, B. (Ed.). (2016). *Do universities have a role in the education and training of teachers? An international analysis of policy and practice*. Cambridge, UK: Cambridge University Press.

Moore, M. (2014). Service-learning and the fields-based literacy methods course. In V. Kinloch & P. Smagorinsky (Eds.), *Service-learning in literacy education: Possibilities for teaching and learning* (pp. 105–115). Charlotte, NC: Information Age Publishing.

Moore, R. (2003). Reexamining the field experiences of preservice teachers. *Journal of Teacher Education, 54*(1), 31–42. doi:10.1177/0022487102238656

Moss, P. A. (2011). Analyzing the teaching of professional practice. *Teachers College Record, 113*(12), 2878–2896.

Murawski, W. W., & Dieker, L. (2013). *Leading the co-teaching dance: Leadership strategies to enhance team outcomes*. Arlington, VA: Council for Exceptional Children.

Murray, F. (1989). Explanations in education. In M. Reynolds (Ed.), *Knowledge base for the beginning teacher* (pp. 1–12)., doi:10.1080/1047621910040129

Nagro, S. A., & deBettencourt, L. U. (2017). Reviewing special education teacher preparation field experience placements, activities, and research: Do we know the difference maker? *Teacher Education Quarterly, 44*(3), 7–33.

Nagro, S. A., deBettencourt, L. U., Rosenberg, M. S., Carran, D. T., & Weiss, M. P. (2017). The effects of guided video analysis on teacher candidates' reflective ability and instructional skills. *Teacher Education and Special Education, 40*(1), 7–25. doi:10.1177/0888406416680469

Nathan, M. J., & Petrosino, A. (2003). Expert blind spot among preservice teachers. *American Educational Research Journal, 40*(4), 905–928. doi:10.3102/00028312040004905

National Alliance to End Homelessness. (2017). Retrieved December 1, 2017 from http://www.endhomelessness.org/

National Association for Professional Development Schools. (2008). *What it means to be a professional development school*. Retrieved from http://napds.org/wp- content/uploads/2014/10/Nine-Essentials.pdf

National Association for Professional Development Schools. (2008). *What it means to be a Professional Development School*. Retrieved from: https://napds.org/wp-content/uploads/2014/10/Nine-Essentials.pdf

National Association of Professional Development Schools (NAPDS). (2008). *What it means to be a professional development school?* Retrieved from http://www.napds.org/9%20Essentials/statement.pdf

National Commission on Mathematics and Science Teaching for the 21st Century (US), & Chair Glenn. (2000). *Before it's too late: A report to the nation from the National Commission on Mathematics and Science Teaching for the 21st Century*. United States. Department of Education.

National Council for Accreditation for Teacher Education (NCATE), Report of the Blue Ribbon Panel on Clinical Preparation and Partnerships for Improved Student Learning. (2010). *Transforming teacher education through clinical practice: A national strategy to prepare effective teachers.* Retrieved from http://www.ncate.org/LinkClick.aspx?filetic ket=zzeiB1OoqPk%3D&tabid=7

National Council for Accreditation for Teacher Education (NCATE). (2014). Professional development schools. Retrieved from http://www.ncate.org/ProfessionalDevelopmentSchools/tabid/497/Default.aspx

National Council for Accreditation for Teacher Education, Report of the Blue Ribbon Panel on Clinical Preparation and Partnerships for Improved Student Learning. (2010). *Transforming teacher education through clinical practice: A national strategy to prepare effective teachers.* Retrieved from http://www.ncate.org/LinkClick.aspx?fileticket=zzeiB1 OoqPk%3D&tabid=7

National Council for Accreditation of Teacher Education (NCATE). (2001). *Standards for professional development schools.* Washington, DC: Author.

National Council for Accreditation of Teacher Education (NCATE). (2008). *Professional standards for the accreditation of teacher preparation institutions.* Washington, DC: Author.

National Council for Accreditation of Teacher Education (NCATE). (2010). *Transforming teacher education through clinical practice: A national strategy to prepare effective teachers.* Washington, DC: Author.

National Council for Accreditation of Teacher Education. (2010). *Transforming teacher education through clinical practice: A national strategy to prepare effective teachers. Blue Ribbon Panel on Clinical Preparation and Partnerships for Improved Student Learning.* Washington, DC: Author.

National Council for Accreditation of Teacher Education. (2010). *Transforming teacher education through clinical practice: A national strategy to prepare effective teachers. Report of Blue Ribbon Panel on clinical preparation and partnerships for improved student landing.* Washington, DC: NCATE.

National Council for Accreditation of Teacher Education. (2010). *Transforming teacher education through clinical practice: A national strategy to prepare effective teachers. Report of the blue ribbon panel on clinical preparation and partnerships for improved student learning.* Washington, DC: National Council for Accreditation of Teacher Education.

National Council for Accreditation of Teacher Education. (2010, November). *Transforming teacher education through clinical practice: A national strategy to prepare effective teachers.* Washington, DC: Author. Retrieved from http://www. ncate.org/Public/researchreports/NCAtEinitiatives/BlueribbonPanel/tabid/715/Default.aspx

National Council for the Accreditation of Teacher Education. (2010). *Transforming teacher education through clinical practice: A national strategy to prepare effective teachers. A report of the Blue Ribbon Panel on Clinical Preparation and Partnership for Improved Student Learning.* Washington, DC: NCATE.

National Council for the Social Studies (NCSS), The College, Career, and Civic Life (C3). (2013). *Framework for Social Studies State Standards: Guidance for Enhancing the Rigor of K-12 Civics, Economics, Geography, and History.* Silver Spring, MD: Author.

National Council for the Social Studies (NCSS). (2013). *The College, Career, and Civic Life (C3) Framework for Social Studies State Standards: Guidance for Enhancing the Rigor of K-12 Civics, Economics, Geography, and History.* Silver Spring, MD: NCSS.

National Council of Teachers of English. (2016). *Professional knowledge for the teaching of writing.* Retrieved from: http://www2.ncte.org/statement/teaching-writing/

National Council of Teachers of Mathematics (NCTM). (2014). *Principles to actions: Ensuring mathematical success for all*. Reston, VA: Author.

National Council of Teachers of Mathematics. (1989). *Curriculum and evaluation standards for school mathematics*. Reston, VA: Author.

National Council of Teachers of Mathematics. (1991). *Professional standards for teaching mathematics*. Reston, VA: Author.

National Council of Teachers of Mathematics. (1995). *Assessment standards for school mathematics*. Reston, VA: Author.

National Council of Teachers of Mathematics. (1999). *High-quality teachers or high-quality teaching?* Retrieved from http://www.nctm.org/News-and-Calendar/Messages-from-the-President/Archive/Glenda-Lappan/High-Quality-Teachers-or-High-Quality-Teaching_/

National Council of Teachers of Mathematics. (2000). *Principles and standards for school mathematics*. Reston, VA: Author.

National Council of Teachers of Mathematics. (2007). Mathematics teaching today: Improving practice. In T. Martin (Ed.), *Improving student learning* (2nd ed.). Reston, VA: National Council of Teachers of Mathematics.

National Council of Teachers of Mathematics. (2012). *NCTM CAEP standards – elementary mathematics specialist*. Retrieved from http://www.nctm.org/Standards-and-Positions/CAEP-Standards/

National Council of Teachers of Mathematics. (2014). *Principles to action: Ensuring mathematical success for all*. Reston, VA: Author.

National Council of Teachers of Mathematics. (2014). *Principles to actions: ensuring mathematical success for all*. Reston, VA: NCTM.

National Council on Teacher Quality. (2014). *State Teacher Policy Yearbook: National Summary*. Retrieved from https://files.eric.ed.gov/fulltext/ED556317.pdf

National Council on Teacher Quality. (2017). *2017 State Teacher Policy Yearbook*. Retrieved https://www.nctq.org/publications/2017-State-Teacher-Policy-Yearbook

National Governors Association Center for Best Practices & Council of Chief State School Officers. (2010). *Common core state standards for mathematics*. Author.

National Governors Association Center for Best Practices & Council of Chief State School Officers. (2010). *Common Core State Standards for Mathematics*. Washington, DC: Authors. Retrieved from www.corestandards.org/Math

National Governors Association Center for Best Practices & Council of Chief State School Officers. (2010). *Common core state standards for mathematics*. Washington, DC: National Governors Association Center for Best Practices and Council of Chief State School Officers.

National Mathematics Advisory Panel. (2008). *Foundations for success: The final report of the National Mathematics Advisory Panel*. Retrieved from https://www2.ed.gov/about/bdscomm/list/mathpanel/report/final-report.pdf

National Mathematics Advisory Panel. (2008). *Foundations for success: The final report of the national mathematics advisory panel*. Washington, DC: US Department of Education.

National Network for Educational Renewal. (2018). *Four pillars and twenty postulates*. Retrieved from https://nnerpartnerships.org/about-nner/four-pillars-twenty-postulates/

National Research Council. (2010). *Preparing teachers: Building evidence for sound policy*. Washington, DC: Author.

National Research Council. (2010). *Preparing Teachers: Building Evidence for Sound Policy*. Washington, DC: The National Academies Press; doi:10.17226/12882

National Research Council. (2012). *A framework for K-12 science education: Practices, crosscutting concepts, and core ideas*. Washington, DC: The National Academies Press.

National School Reform Faculty. (2014). *NSRF protocols and activities ... from a to z*. Retrieved from https://www.nsrfharmony.org/free-resources/protocols/a-z

NCATE. (2010). *Transforming teacher education through clinical practice: A national strategy to prepare effective teachers. Report of the Blue Ribbon Panel on Clinical Preparation and Partnerships for Improved Student Learning*. Washington, DC: Author.

Ness, M. K. (2008). Supporting secondary readers: When teachers provide the "What," not the "How.". *American Secondary Education, 37*(1), 80–95.

Neuman, W. L. (2003). *Social research methods: Qualitative and quantitative approaches* (5th ed.). Boston, MA: Pearson Education, Inc.

New York City Department of City Planning. (2010). *Population density by census tract New York City, 1950-2010*. Retrieved from: https://www1.nyc.gov/assets/planning/download/pdf/data-maps/nyc-population/historical-population/pop_density_1950_2010.pdf

New York City Department of City Planning. (2018). *New York City Population*. Retrieved from: https://www1.nyc.gov/site/planning/data-maps/nyc-population/population-facts.page)

New York City Department of Education. (2009). *Children First: A bold, common-sense plan to create great schools for all New York City children*. Retrieved from: http://schools.nyc.gov/NR/rdonlyres/51C61E8F-1AE9-4D37-8881-4D688D4F843A/0/cf_corenarrative.pdf

New York City Department of Education. (2018). *2017-2018 Anticipated bilingual education programs*. Retrieved from: http://schools.nyc.gov/NR/rdonlyres/9B8CC63A-85BD-4884-AB52-5A35CF72DC48/0/201718BilingualProgramListAugust2017.pdf

New York City Economic Development Corporation. (2012). *New Yorkers and cars*. Retrieved from: https://www.nycedc.com/blog-entry/new-yorkers-and-cars

New York City Independent Budget Office. (2014a). *How long is the commute for New York City high school students from their homes to their schools?* Retrieved from: https://ibo.nyc.ny.us/cgi-park2/2014/05/how-long-is-the-commute-for-new-york-city-high-school-students-from-their-homes-to-their-schools/

New York City Independent Budget Office. (2014b). *How many students attend nonpublic K-12 schools in New York City?* Retrieved from: https://ibo.nyc.ny.us/cgi-park2/2014/04/how-many-students-attend-nonpublic-k-12-schools-in-new-york-city/

New York City Independent Budget Office. (2015). *How much do public school budgets vary across the city's school districts and boroughs?* Retrieved from: https://ibo.nyc.ny.us/cgi-park2/2015/09/how-much-do-public-school-budgets-vary-across-the-citys-school-districts-and-boroughs/

New York City Office of the Mayor. (2006). *Mayor Bloomberg announces tentative agreement with the United Federation Of Teachers nearly one year before expiration of current contract*. Retrieved from: http://www1.nyc.gov/office-of-the-mayor/news/388-06/mayor-bloomberg-tentative-agreement-the-united-federation-teachers-nearly-one#/1

New York City Teaching Fellows. (2018). *Our history.* Retrieved from: https://nycteachingfellows.org/our-history

Newsday. (2014). *School spending data.* Retrieved from: http://data.newsday.com/long-island/data/education/school-spending/#o:c=;l

Nguyen, T., Dekker, R., & Goedhart, M. (2008). Preparing Vietnamese student teachers for teaching with a student-centered approach. *Journal of Mathematics Teacher Education, 11*(1), 61–81. doi:10.100710857-007-9058-4

Nieto, S. (2000). Placing equity front and center: Some thoughts on transforming teacher education for a new century. *Journal of Teacher Education, 51*(3), 180–187. doi:10.1177/0022487100051003004

Nieto, S. (2009). *The light in their eyes: Creating multicultural learning communities.* New York: Teachers College Press.

Nixon, J. (1991). Reclaiming coherence: Cross-curriculum provision and the National Curriculum. *Journal of Curriculum Studies, 23*(2), 187–192. doi:10.1080/0022027910230209

No Child Left Behind Act of 2001, P.L. 107-110, 20 U.S.C. § 6319 (2002).

Noguera, P. (2003). *City schools and the American dream.* New York: Teachers College Press.

Nokes, J. D., Bullough, R. V. Jr, Egan, W. M., Birrell, J. R., & Hansen, J. M. (2008). The paired-placement of student teachers: An alternative to traditional placements in secondary schools. *Teaching and Teacher Education, 24*(8), 2168–2177. doi:10.1016/j.tate.2008.05.001

Nolan, J. (2015) *Clinical Experiences as the Centerpiece of Excellent Teacher Preparation.* Invited Keynote Presentation at the Annual Spring Conference of the Pennsylvania Association of Colleges and Teacher Educators, State College, PA.

Nolan, J., & Hoover, L. A. (2010). *Teacher supervision and evaluation: Theory into practice* (3rd ed.). Hoboken, NJ: John Wiley & Sons.

North Country Listens. (2018). *About us.* Retrieved from: https://www.northcountrylistens.org/about

Norton, S., & Bird, G. (2017). *Education finance in New Hampshire: Headed to a rural crisis?* Concord, NH: New Hampshire Center for Public policy. *Studies.*

O'Donoghue, T., & Punch, K. (2003). *Qualitative Educational Research in Action: Doing and Reflecting.* New York: Routledge.

Oakes, J., Franke, M. L., Quartz, K. H., & Rogers, J. (2002). Research for high-quality urban teaching: Defining it, developing it, assessing it. *Journal of Teacher Education, 53*(3), 228–234. doi:10.1177/0022487102053003006

Obara, S. (2010). Mathematics coaching: A new kind of professional development. *Teacher Development, 14*(2), 241–251. doi:10.1080/13664530.2010.494504

Obrycki, J., Herbel-Eisenmann, B. & Cirillo, M. (2009) Listening to my students' thoughts on mathematics education. *Promoting purposeful discourse: Teacher research in mathematics classrooms,* 187-202.

Oloff-Lewis, J., Biagetti, S., Cayton, C., Grady, M., Stone, J., McCulloch, A., Edgington, C., Sears, R. (2014a). *Mentor Teacher Pre-Survey* [Survey instrument].

Oloff-Lewis, J., Biagetti, S., Cayton, C., Grady, M., Stone, J., McCulloch, A., Edgington, C., Sears, R. (2014b). *Mentee Exit Survey* [Survey instrument].

Onwuegbuzie, A. J., Dickinson, W. B., Leech, N. L., & Zoran, A. G. (2009). A qualitative framework for collecting and analyzing data in focus group research. *International Journal of Qualitative Methods, 8*(3), 1–21. doi:10.1177/160940690900800301

Orland-Barak, L., & Yinon, H. (2007). When theory meets practice: What student teachers learn from guided reflection on their own classroom discourse. *Teaching and Teacher Education, 23*(6), 957–969. doi:10.1016/j.tate.2006.06.005

Otten, S., Yee, S., & Taylor, M. (2015) Secondary Mathematics Methods Course: What do we value? *Proceeding from the 37th annual meeting of the North American Chapter of the International Group for the Psychology of Mathematics Education.* East Lansing, MI: Michigan State University.

Palacio, R. J. (2012). *Wonder.* New York: Random House.

Palmeri, A., & Peter, J. (2014). *Moving beyond: "How did it go?": A systematic and developmental approach to mentoring teacher candidates.* Paper presented at the NAECTE conference, Dallas, TX.

Palmeri, A., & Peter, J. (2015). *All that glitters is not gold: Scaffolding student teachers' reflections on practice.* Paper presented at the AACTE conference, Atlanta, GA.

Palmeri, A., & Peter, J. (2017). *Revisiting traditional supervisory practices: Innovations to enhance preservice teachers' practice through developmental feedback.* Paper presented at the ATE conference, Orlando, FL.

Papay, J., West, M., Fullerton, J., & Kane, T. (2011). *Does Practice-based teacher preparation increase student achievement? Early evidence form the Boston teacher residency.* National Bureau of Economic Research. Retrieved from http://www.nber.org/papers/w17646

Papay, J., West, M., Fullerton, J., & Kane, T. (2011). *Does Practice-Based Teacher Preparation Increase Student Achievement? Early Evidence from the Boston Teacher Residency.* Retrieved from: https://cepr.harvard.edu/project-name/boston-teacher-residency-evaluation

Papay, J., Bacher-Hicks, A., Page, L., & Marinell, W. (2017). The challenge of teacher retention in urban schools: Evidence of variation from a cross-site analysis. *Educational Researcher, 46*(8), 434–448. doi:10.3102/0013189X17735812

Papay, J., & Kraft, M. (2015). Productivity returns to experience in the teacher labor market: Methodological challenges and new evidence on long-term career improvement. *Journal of Public Economics, 130*, 105–119. doi:10.1016/j.jpubeco.2015.02.008

Pardini, P. (2006). In one voice: Mainstream and ELL teachers work side-by-side in the classroom teaching language through content. *Journal of Staff Development, 27*(4), 20–25.

Paris, D. (2012). Culturally sustaining pedagogy: A needed change in stance, terminology, and practice. *Educational Researcher, 41*(3), 93–97. doi:10.3102/0013189X12441244

Paris, D., & Alim, S. (2017). *Culturally sustaining pedagogies: Teaching and learning for justice in a changing world.* New York, NY: Teachers College Press.

Parker, A. K., Parsons, S. A., Groth, L., & Levine-Brown, E. (2016). Pathways to partnership: A developmental framework for building PDS relationships. *School University Partnerships, 9*(3), 34-48.

Parrish, S. (2010). *Number talks: Helping children build mental math and computation strategies, grades K–5.* Sausalito, CA: Math Solutions.

Parsons, S. A., Parker, A. K., Brunying, A., & Daoud, N. (2016). Striving to enact the Professional Development School philosophy: George Mason University's Elementary Education program. *The Teacher Educators' Journal, 9.*

Parsons, S. A., Groth, L. A., Parker, A. K., Brown, E. L., Sell, C., & Sprague, D. (2017). Elementary teacher preparation at George Mason University: Evolution of our program. In R. Flessner & D. Lecklider (Eds.), *Case studies of clinical preparation in teacher education.* Lanham, MD: Rowman & Littlefield.

Parsons, S. A., Nuland, L. R., & Parsons, A. W. (2014). The ABCs of student engagement. *Phi Delta Kappan*, *95*(8), 23–27. doi:10.1177/003172171409500806

Partnership for 21st Century Learning (P21). (2016). *Framework for 21st century learning*. Retrieved from http://www.p21.org/our-work/p21-framework

Passe, J. (1994). Early field experience in elementary and secondary social studies methods courses. *Social Studies*, *85*(3), 130–133. doi:10.1080/00377996.1994.9956291

Pearson Education. (2014). *edTPA fact sheet*. Retrieved from http://edtpa.aacte.org/about-edtpa

Peercy, M., & Troyan, F. (2017). Making transparent the challenges of developing a practice-based pedagogy of teacher education. *Teaching and Teacher Education*, *61*, 26–36. doi:10.1016/j.tate.2016.10.005

Pellegrino, A., Zenkov, K., & Calamito, N. (2013). "I just want to be heard": Developing civic identity through performance poetry. *Social Studies Research & Practice*, *8*(1).

Pellegrino, A., Zenkov, K., & Calamito, N. (2013). "Pay attention and take some notes": Middle school youth, multimodal instruction, and notions of citizenship. *Journal of Social Studies Research*, *37*(4), 221–238. doi:10.1016/j.jssr.2013.04.007

Pellegrino, A., Zenkov, K., Calamito, N., & Sells, C. (2014). Lifting as we climb: A citizenship project in a Professional Development School setting. *School-University Partnerships*, *7*(1), 64–84.

Pelo, A. (2008). *Rethinking Early Childhood Education*. Milwaukee, WS. *Rethinking Schools*.

Perry, N. E., Turner, J. C., & Meyer, D. K. (2006). Classrooms as contexts for motivating learning. In P. A. Alexander & P. II. Winne (Eds.), *Handbook of educational psychology* (2nd ed.; pp. 327–348). Mahwah, NJ: Lawrence Erlbaum.

Perry, R. K. (2016, Summer). Influences of co-teaching in student teaching on pre-service teachers' teacher efficacy. *Newsletter of the California Council on Teacher Education*, *27*(2), 29–33.

Pfeiffer, J. W., & Ballow, A. C. (1988). *Using structured experiences in human resource development*. San Diego, CA: University Associates.

Piaget, J. (1954). *The construction of reality in the child*. Basic Books. doi:10.1037/11168-000

Pianta, R. C., Mashburn, A. J., Downer, J. T., Hamre, B. K., & Justice, L. (2008). Effects of web-mediated professional development resources on teacher-child interactions in pre-kindergarten classrooms. *Early Childhood Research Quarterly*, *23*(4), 431–451. doi:10.1016/j.ecresq.2008.02.001 PMID:25717217

Picower, B. (2009). The unexamined Whiteness of teaching: How White teachers maintain and enact dominant racial ideologies. *Race, Ethnicity and Education*, *12*(2), 197–215. doi:10.1080/13613320902995475

Pinnegar, S., & Hamilton, M. L. (2009). *Self-study of practice as a genre of qualitative research: Theory, methodology and practice*. Dordrecht: Springer.

Plucker, J. M. (2010). Baiting the reading hook. *Educational Leadership*, *68*(2), 58–63.

Pole, C. (Ed.). (2004). *Seeing is believing? Approaches to visual research* (Vol. 7). New York, NY: Elsevier. doi:10.1016/S1042-3192(04)07001-6

Pollock, K. (2016). Principals' work in Ontario, Canada: Changing demographics, advancements in information communication technology and health and wellbeing. *International Studies in Educational Administration*, *44*(3), 55–73.

Polzer, J. T., Crisp, C. B., Jarvenpaa, S. L., & Kim, J. W. (2006). Extending the faultline model to geographically dispersed teams: How colocated subgroups can impair group functioning. *Academy of Management Journal*, *49*(4), 679–692. doi:10.5465/amj.2006.22083024

Porath, S. (2017). *Student reflection on Swivl video*. Manhattan, KS: Author.

Portes & Smagorinsky, P. (2010). Static structures, changing demographics: Educating teachers for shifting populations in stable schools. *English Education*, *42*(3), 236–247.

Posamentier, A. S., Smith, B. S., & Stepelman, J. (2009). *Teaching secondary school mathematics: Techniques and teaching units*. Academic Press.

Powers-Costello, B., Lopez-Robertson, Boutte, G., Miller, E., Long, S., & Collins, S. (2012). Teaching for transformation: Responsive program planning and professional development aimed at justice and equity in urban settings. In A. Cohan & A. Honigsfeld (Eds.), Breaking the mold of education for culturally and linguistically diverse learners: Innovative and successful practices for the twenty-first century (Vol. 2, pp. 2330). Lanham, MD: Rowman & Littlefield Education.

Preparing and Credentialing the Nation's Teachers: The Secretary's 10th Report on Teacher Quality. (2016). Retrieved from https://title2.ed.gov/Public/TitleIIReport16.pdf

Puchner, L. P., & Taylor, A. R. (2006). Lesson study, collaboration and teacher efficacy: Stories from two school-based math lesson study groups. *Teaching and Teacher Education*, *22*(7), 922–934. doi:10.1016/j.tate.2006.04.011

Puentedura, R. (2006, November 26). *Transformation, technology, and education in the state of Maine*. Retrieved from http://www.hippasus.com/rrpweblog/archives/2006_11.html

Puentedura, R. (2009, February 4). *As we may teach: Educational technology, from theory into practice*. Retrieved from http://www.hippasus.com/rrpweblog/archives/2014/06/29/ LearningTechnologySAMRModel.pdf

Puentedura, R. (2014). Building transformation: An introduction to the SAMR model [Web log comment]. Retrieved from http://www.hippasus.com/rrpweblog/archives/2014/08/22/ BuildingTransformation_AnIntroductionToSAMR.pdf

Pultorak, E. G. (1996). Following the developmental process of reflection in novice teachers: Three years of investigation. *Journal of Teacher Education*, *47*(4), 283–291. doi:10.1177/0022487196474006

Putnam, R., & Borko, H. (2000). What do new views of knowledge and thinking have to say about research on teacher learning? *Educational Researcher*, *29*(1), 4–15. doi:10.3102/0013189X029001004

Pytash, K. E. (2017). Preservice teachers' experiences facilitating writing instruction in a juvenile detention facility. *High School Journal*, *100*(2), 109–129. doi:10.1353/hsj.2017.0002

Pytash, K. E., & Zenkov, K. (2018). Introduction to the guest-edited issue. *New Educator*, *14*(3), 1–7. doi:10.1080/15 47688X.2018.1486564

Qu, Y., & Becker, B. J. (2003). *Does traditional teacher certification imply quality? A meta-analysis*. Paper presented at the Annual Meeting of the American Educational Research Association, Chicago, IL.

Queens Library. (2014). *Queens library facts*. Retrieved from: http://www.queenslibrary.org/sites/default/files/about-us/Facts%20Sheet.pdf

Range, B., Duncan, H., & Hvidston, D. (2013). How faculty supervise and mentor pre-service teachers: Implications for principal supervision of novice teachers. *The International Journal of Educational Leadership Preparation*, *8*(2), 43–58.

Reagan, E. M., Coppens, A., Couse, L., Hambacher, E., Lord, D., McCurdy, K., & Silva Pimentel, D. (2018). Toward a framework for the design and implementation of the Teacher Residency for Rural Education. In M. Reardon & J. Leanord (Eds.), Innovation and Implementation: School-University-Community Partnerships in Rural Communities (pp. 81–106). Academic Press.

Reagan, E. M., Roegman, R., & Goodwin, A. L. (2017). Inquiry in the round? Education rounds in a teacher residency program. *Action in Teacher Education*, *39*(3), 239–254. doi:10.1080/01626620.2017.1317299

Rea, P. J., McLaughlin, V. L., & Walther-Thomas, C. (2002). Outcomes for students with learning disabilities in inclusive and pullout programs. *Exceptional Children*, *68*(2), 203–222. doi:10.1177/001440290206800204

Recchia, S. L., & Puig, V. I. (2011). Challenges and inspirations: Student teachers' experiences in early childhood special education classrooms. *Teacher Education and Special Education*, *34*(2), 133–151. doi:10.1177/0888406410387444

Reeves, A. G. (2013). Selves, Lives, and videotape: Leveraging self-revelation through narrative pedagogy. In D. S. Knowlton & K. J. Hagopian (Eds.), New Directions for Teaching and Learning: 135(3). From entitlement to engagement: Affirming millennial students' egos in the higher education classroom (pp. 55–60). Academic Press. doi:10.1002/tl.20065

Reid, J.-A., Green, B., Cooper, M., Hastings, W., Lock, G., & White, S. (2010, November). Rural Social Space? Teacher Education for Rural—Regional Sustainability. *Australian Journal of Education*, *54*(3), 262–276. doi:10.1177/000494411005400304

Reininger, M. (2012). Hometown disadvantage? It depends on where you're from: Teachers' location preferences and the implications for staffing schools. *Educational Evaluation and Policy Analysis*, *34*(2), 127–145. doi:10.3102/0162373711420864

Reischl, C., Khasnabis, D., & Karr, K. (2017, May). Cultivating a school-university partnership for teacher learning. *Phi Delta Kappan*, 48-53.

Reynolds, A., Ross, S. M., & Rakow, J. H. (2002). Teacher retention, teaching effectiveness, and professional preparation: A comparison of professional development school and non-professional development school graduates. *Teaching and Teacher Education*, *18*(3), 289–303. doi:10.1016/S0742-051X(01)00070-1

Reys, B., Webel, C., & de Araujo, Z. (2017). Elementary mathematics specialist preparation: What's next? What's needed? In M. McGatha & N. Riegelman (Eds.), *Elementary mathematics specialists* (pp. 221–234). Charlotte, NC: Association of Mathematics Teacher Educators.

Rice, D., & Zigmond, N. (2000). Co-teaching in secondary schools: Teacher reports of developments in Australian and American classrooms. *Learning Disabilities Research & Practice*, *15*(4), 190–197. doi:10.1207/SLDRP1504_3

Rice, J. K. (2003). *Teacher quality: Understanding the effectiveness of teacher attributes*. Washington, DC: Economic Policy Institute.

Rich, M. (2015). Teacher shortages spur a nationwide hiring scramble (Credentials Optional). *New York Times*. Retrieved from http://www.nytimes.com/2015/08/10/us/teacher-shortages-spur-a-nationwide-hiring-scramble-credentials-optional.html

Richardson, V., & Kile, R. S. (1999). The use of videocases in teacher education. In M.L. Lundberg, B. Levin, & H. Herrington (Eds.), Who Learns from Cases and How? The Research Base for Teaching With Cases. Jossey Bass.

Richards, S. (2012). Coast to country: An initiative aimed at changing pre-service teachers' perceptions of teaching in rural and remote locations. *Australian and International Journal of Rural Education*, *22*(2), 53.

Rigelman, N. M. (2017). Learning in and from practice with others. In L. West & M. Boston (Eds.), *Annual perspectives in mathematics education: Reflective and collaborative processes to improve mathematics teaching* (pp. 65–76). Reston, VA: National Council of Teachers of Mathematics.

Rigelman, N. M., & Ruben, B. (2012). Creating foundations for collaboration in schools: Utilizing professional learning communities to support teacher candidate learning and visions of teaching. *Teaching and Teacher Education, 28*(7), 979–989. doi:10.1016/j.tate.2012.05.004

Rigelman, N. R. (2017). Evaluation of elementary mathematics specialist programs. In M. McGatha & N. Riegelman (Eds.), *Elementary mathematics specialists* (pp. 211–220). Charlotte, NC: Association of Mathematics Teacher Educators.

Rigelman, N. R., & Wray, J. A. (2017). Current state of mathematics specialist state certification and standards. In M. McGatha & N. Riegelman (Eds.), *Elementary mathematics specialists* (pp. 33–40). Charlotte, NC: Association of Mathematics Teacher Educators.

Risko, V. J., Roller, C. M., Cummins, C., Bean, R. M., Block, C. C., Anders, P. L., & Flood, J. (2008). A critical analysis of research on reading teacher education. *Reading Research Quarterly, 43*(3), 252–288. doi:10.1598/RRQ.43.3.3

Ritchhart, R. (2015). *Creating Cultures of Thinking.* San Francisco, CA: Jossey-Bass.

Rivkin, S. G., Hanushek, E. A., & Kain, J. F. (2005). Teachers, schools, and academic achievement. *Econometrics, 73*, 417-458. Retrieved from http://econ.ucsb.edu/~jon/Econ230C/HanushekRivkin.pdf

Robelen, E. (2011). Fellowship program works to beef up math teaching. *Education Week, 9*(February). Retrieved from https://www.edweek.org/ew/articles/2011/02/09/20math_ep.h30.html

Robinson, L., & Kelley, B. (2007). Developing reflective thought in preservice educators: Utilizing role-plays and digital video. *Journal of Special Education Technology, 22*(2), 31–43. doi:10.1177/016264340702200203

Robinson, V. M., Lloyd, C. A., & Rowe, K. J. (2008). The impact of leadership on student outcomes: An analysis of the differential effects of leadership types. *Educational Administration Quarterly, 44*(5), 635–674. doi:10.1177/0013161X08321509

Rodgers, C. (2002). Defining reflection: Another look at john dewey and reflective thinking. *Teachers College Record, 104*(4), 842–866. doi:10.1111/1467-9620.00181

Roe, B., & Burns, P. (2011). *Informal Reading Inventory: Preprimer to twelfth grade* (8th ed.). Belmont, CA: Wadsworth.

Rogers, C. R. (1961). *On becoming a person: A therapist's view of psychotherapy.* Boston, MA: Houghton Mifflin.

Rogers, R. R. (2001). Reflection in higher education: A concept analysis. *Innovative Higher Education, 26*(1), 37–57. doi:10.1023/A:1010986404527

Rogoff, B. (2003). *The cultural nature of human development.* Oxford University Press.

Roller, S. A. (2015). What they notice in video: A study of prospective secondary mathematics teachers learning to teach. *Journal of Mathematics Teacher Education, 19*(5), 477–498. doi:10.100710857-015-9307-x

Ronfeldt, M. (2012). Where should student teachers learn to teach? Effects of field placement school characteristics on teacher retention and effectiveness. *Educational Evaluation and Policy Analysis, 34*(1), 3–26. doi:10.3102/0162373711420865

Ronfeldt, M. (2015). Field placement schools and instructional effectiveness. *Journal of Teacher Education, 66*(4), 304–320. doi:10.1177/0022487115592463

Ronfeldt, M., Farmer, S., McQueen, K., & Grissom, J. (2015). Teacher collaboration in instructional teams and student achievement. *American Educational Research Journal, 3*(52), 475–514. doi:10.3102/0002831215585562

Ronfeldt, M., Loeb, S., & Wyckoff, J. (2013). How teacher turnover harms student achievement. *American Educational Research Journal, 1*(50), 4–36. doi:10.3102/0002831212463813

Rosaen, C., Lundeberg, M., Cooper, M., Fritzen, A., & Terpstra, M. (2008). Noticing noticing: How does investigation of video records change how teachers reflect on their experiences? *Journal of Teacher Education, 59*(4), 347–360. doi:10.1177/0022487108322128

Rosenblatt, L. M. (1994). *The reader, the text, the poem: The transactional theory of the literary work.* Southern Illinois University Press.

Rosner, J. (2002). The SAT: Quantifying the unfairness behind the bubbles. In SAT Wars. 2012. Academic Press.

Roth McDuffie, A., Foote, M. Q., Bolson, C., Turner, E. E., Aguirre, J. M., Bartell, T. G., ... Land, T. (2014). Using video analysis to support prospective K-8 teachers' noticing of students' multiple mathematical knowledge bases. *Journal of Mathematics Teacher Education, 17*(3), 245–258. doi:10.100710857-013-9257-0

Roth, J. (2017). *Clinical partnerships in action: Renewal and innovation in educator preparation and research* (Doctoral dissertation). Retrieved from ProQuest Dissertations and Theses database.

Routman, R. (2004). *Writing essentials: Raising expectations and results while simplifying teaching.* Portsmouth, NH: Heinemann.

Rowan, B., Correnti, R., & Miller, R. (2002). What large-scale survey research tells us about teacher effects on student achievement: Insights from the prospects study of elementary schools. *Teachers College Record, 104*(8), 1525–1567. doi:10.1111/1467-9620.00212

Rozelle, J. J., & Wilson, S. M. (2012). Opening the black box of field experiences: How cooperating teachers' beliefs and practices shape student teachers' beliefs and practices. *Teaching and Teacher Education, 28*(8), 1196–1205. doi:10.1016/j. tate.2012.07.008

Russell, J. L., Bryk, A. S., Dolle, J. R., Gomez, L. M., Lemahieu, P. G., & Grunow, A. (2017). A Framework for the Initiation of Networked Improvement Communities. Teachers College Record, 119(5).

Rust, F. O., & Clift, R. T. (2015). Moving from recommendations to action in preparing professional educators. In E. R. Hollins (Ed.), *Rethinking field experiences in preservice teacher preparation: Meeting new challenges for accountability* (pp. 47–69). New York, NY: Routledge.

Rychly, L., & Graves, E. (2012). Teacher characteristics for culturally responsive pedagogy. *Multicultural Perspectives, 14*(1), 44–49. doi:10.1080/15210960.2012.646853

Sachar, L. (1989). *Sideways arithmetic from the Wayside School.* New York: Scholastic.

Saldãna, J. (2016). *The coding manual for qualitative researchers.* Thousand Oaks, CA: Sage.

Salisbury, M., An, B., & Pascarella, E. (2013). The effect of study abroad on intercultural competence among undergraduate college students. *Journal of Student Affairs Research and Practice, 50*(1), 1–20. doi:10.1515/jsarp-2013-0001

Samaras, A. P. (2011). *Self-study teacher research. Improving your practice through collaborative inquiry.* Thousand Oaks, CA: Sage Publications, Inc.

Samaras, A. P., Frank, T. J., Williams, M. A., Christopher, E., & Rodick, W. H. III. (2016). A collective self-study to improve program coherence of clinical experiences. *Studying Teacher Education, 12*(2), 170–187. doi:10.1080/17425 964.2016.1192033

Sandholtz, J., & Wasserman, K. (2001). Student and cooperating teachers: Contrasting experiences in teacher preparation programs. *Action in Teacher Education, 23*(3), 54–65. doi:10.1080/01626620.2001.10463075

Santagata, R. (2011). From teacher noticing to a framework for analyzing and improving classroom lessons. In M. G. Sherin, V. R. Jacobs & R. A. Philipp (Eds.), Mathematics teacher noticing: Seeing through teachers' eyes (pp. 152-168). New York: Routledge.

Santagata, R., & Angelici, G. (2010). Studying the impact of the lesson analysis framework on preservice teachers' abilities to reflect on videos of classroom teaching. *Journal of Teacher Education, 61*(4), 339–349. doi:10.1177/0022487110369555

Santagata, R., Zannoni, C., & Stigler, J. W. (2007). The role of lesson analysis in pre-service teacher education: An empirical investigation of teacher learning from a virtual video-based field experience. *Journal of Mathematics Teacher Education, 10*(2), 123–140. doi:10.100710857-007-9029-9

Sass, T. (2013). *Licensure and worker quality: A comparison of alternative routes to teaching.* Department of Economics W. J. Usery Workplace Research Group. Retrieved from http://aysps.gsu.edu/files/2016/01/13-09-Sass-Licensureand-workerquality.pdf

Sayeski, K., & Paulsen, K. (2012). Student teacher evaluations of cooperating teachers as indices of effective mentoring. *Teacher Education Quarterly, 39*, 117–130.

Schafft, K. (2016). Rural education as rural development: Understanding the rural school-community well-being linkage in a 21st-century policy context. *Peabody Journal of Education, 91*(2), 137–154. doi:10.1080/0161956X.2016.1151734

Schafft, K. A. (2010). Economics, community, and rural education: Rethinking the nature of accountability in the twenty-first century. In K. A. Schafft & A. Y. Jackson (Eds.), *Rural education for the twenty-first century: Identity, place, and community in a globalizing world* (pp. 275–290). University Park, PA: Penn State Press.

Scheeler, M. C., McKinnon, K., & Stout, J. (2012). Effects of immediate feedback delivered via webcam and bug-in-ear technology on preservice teacher performance. *Teacher Education and Special Education, 35*(1), 77–90. doi:10.1177/0888406411401919

Scheeler, M., & Lee, D. (2002). Using technology to deliver immediate corrective feedback to preservice teachers. *Journal of Behavioral Education, 11*(4), 231–241. doi:10.1023/A:1021158805714

Scherer, M. (2012). The challenge of supporting new teachers: A conversation with Linda Darling Hammond. *Educational Leadership, 69*(8). Retrieved from http://www.ascd.org/publications/educational-leadership/may12/vol69/num08/The-Challenges-of-Supporting-New-Teachers.aspx

Scherff, L., & Singer, N. R. (2012). The preservice teachers are watching: Framing and re-framing the field experience. *Teaching and Teacher Education, 28*(2), 263–272. doi:10.1016/j.tate.2011.10.003

Schmidt, M. (2010). Learning from teaching experience: Dewey's theory and preservice teachers' learning. *Journal of Research in Music Education, 58*(2), 131–146. doi:10.1177/0022429410368723

Schon, D. (1983). *The reflective practitioner.* New York: Basic Books.

Schön, D. A. (1983). *The reflective practitioner: How professionals think in action.* New York: Basic Books.

Schön, D. A. (1987). *Educating the reflective practitioner: Toward a new design for teaching and learning in the professions.* San Francisco: Jossey-Bass.

Schön, D. A. (1995). Knowing-in-action: The new scholarship requires a new epistemology. *Change: The Magazine of Higher Learning, 27*(6), 27–34. doi:10.1080/00091383.1995.10544673

Schram, T. (2006). *Conceptualizing and Proposing Qualitative Research*. Upper Saddle River, NJ: Merrill/Prentice Hall.

Schulte, A. K. (2014). The preparation of mentors who support novice teacher researchers. *Networks: An Online Journal for Teacher Research, 16*(1), 1–11.

Schutz, A., & Gere, A. R. (1998). Service learning and English studies: Rethinking "public" service. *College English, 60*(2), 129–149. doi:10.2307/378323

Schwab, J. (1978). Education and the structure of the disciplines. In J. Westbury & N. Wilkof (Eds.), *Science, curriculum, and liberal education*. Chicago: University of Chicago Press.

Schwille, S. A. (2008). The professional practice of mentoring. *American Journal of Education, 115*(1), 139–167. doi:10.1086/590678

Scott, L. A., Gentry, R., & Phillips, M. (2014). Making preservice teachers better: Examining the impact of a practicum in a teacher preparation program. *Educational Research Review, 9*(10), 294–301. doi:10.5897/ERR2014.1748

Scruggs, T. E., Mastropieri, M. A., & McDuffie, K. A. (2007). Co-teaching in inclusive classrooms: A metasynthesis of qualitative research. *Exceptional Children, 73*(4), 392–416. doi:10.1177/001440290707300401

Sears, R., Brosnan, P., Gainsburg, J., Oloff-Lewis, J., Stone, J., Spencer, C., . . . Andreason, J. (2017). Using improvement science to transform clinical experiences with co-teaching strategies. In L. West and M. Boston (Eds.), Annual Perspectives of Mathematics Education (APME) (pp. 265–274). Reston, VA: National Council of Teachers of Mathematics.

Sears, R., Brosnan, P., Oloff-Lewis, J., Gainsburg, J., Stone, J., Biagetti, S., . . . Junor Clarke, P. (2017, January 3-7). *Co-Teaching Mathematics: A Shift in Paradigm to Promote Student Success*. Research report presentation at the Hawaii International Conference on Education, Honolulu, HI.

Sears, R., Maynor, J., Cayton, C., Grady, M., Stone, J., McCulloch, A., Edgington, C. & Oloff-Lewis, J. (2014). *Mentee Just in Time Survey* [Survey instrument].

Sebald, A., & Frederiksen, H. (2017). Leading through logic modeling: Capturing the complexity. *Journal of Educational Leadership in Action, 4*(3). Retrieved from http://www.lindenwood.edu/academics/beyond-the-classroom/publications/journal-of-educational-leadership-in-action/all-issues/volume-5-issue-1/faculty-articles/sebald-frederiksen/

Sebald, A., Myers, A., Frederiksen, H., & Pike, E. (in review). Collaborative co-teaching during student teaching pilot project: What difference does context make? *Journal of Education*.

Seidel, T., Stürmer, K., Blomberg, G., Kobarg, M., & Schwindt, K. (2011). Teachers learning from analysis of videotaped classroom situations: Does it make a difference whether teachers observe their own teaching or that of others? *Teaching and Teacher Education, 27*(2), 259–267. doi:10.1016/j.tate.2010.08.009

Seidman, I. (2006). *Interviewing as qualitative research: A guide for researchers in education and the social sciences* (3rd ed.). New York, NY: Teachers College Press.

Shamah, D., & MacTavish, K. A. (2009). Purpose and perceptions of family social location among rural youth. *Youth & Society, 50*(1), 26–48. doi:10.1177/0044118X15583655

Sharplin, E. (2002). Rural retreat or outback hell: Expectations of rural and remote teaching. *Issues in Educational Research, 12*. Retrieved from http://www.iier.org.au/iier12/sharplin.html

Sharp, S., & Turner, W. (2008). Sustaining relationships in teacher education partnerships: The possibilities, practices and challenges of a school-university partnership, preparing teachers for the future. *International Journal of Learning, 15*(5), 9–14. doi:10.18848/1447-9494/CGP/v15i05/45772

714

Sherin, M. G., & Han, S. Y. (2004). Teacher learning in the context of a video club. *Teaching and Teacher Education, 20*(2), 163–183. doi:10.1016/j.tate.2003.08.001

Sherin, M. G., & van Es, E. A. (2005). Using video to support teachers' ability to notice classroom interactions. *Technology and Teacher Education, 13*, 475–491.

Sherin, M. G., & van Es, E. A. (2009). Effects of video club participation on teachers' professional vision. *Journal of Teacher Education, 60*(1), 20–37. doi:10.1177/0022487108328155

Sherin, M., & Linsenmeier, K. (2011). Pause, rewind, reflect. *Journal of Staff Development, 32*(5), 38–41.

Shroyer, G., Yahnke, S., Bennett, A., & Dunn, C. (2007). Simultaneous renewal through professional development school partnerships. *The Journal of Educational Research, 100*(4), 211–225. doi:10.3200/JOER.100.4.211-225

Shroyer, M. G., Yahnke, S. J., Mercer, D. K., & Allen, D. S. (2014). Foreword. *Educational Considerations, 42*(1), 1–2. doi:10.4148/0146-9282.1038

Shulman, L. (2005). Pedagogies. *Liberal Education, 91*(2), 18–25.

Shulman, L. S. (1986). Those who understand: Knowledge growth in teaching. *Educational Researcher, 15*(2), 4–14. doi:10.3102/0013189X015002004

Shulman, L. S. (1987). Knowledge and teaching: Foundations of a new reform. *Harvard Educational Review, 57*(1), 1–21. doi:10.17763/haer.57.1.j463w79r56455411

Siegel, M. (1995). More than words: The generative power of transmediation for learning. *Canadian Journal of Education/Revue canadienne de l'éducation,* 455-475.

Sileo, J. M., & van Garderen, D. (2010). Creating optimal opportunities to learn mathematics: Blending co-teaching structures with research-based practices. *Teaching Exceptional Children, 42*(3), 14–21. doi:10.1177/004005991004200302

Sims, L., & Walsh, D. (2009). Lesson study with pre-service teachers: Lessons from lessons. *Teaching and Teacher Education, 25*(5), 724–733. doi:10.1016/j.tate.2008.10.005

Sindelar, P. T., Brownell, M. T., & Billingsley, B. (2010). Special education teacher education research: Current status and future directions. *Teacher Education and Special Education, 33*(1), 8–24. doi:10.1177/0888406409358593

Singer, S. (2016). *Standardized tests have always been keeping people in their place.* Retrieved from: https://gadfly-onthewallblog.wordpress.com/2016/04/05/standardized-tests-have-always-been-about-keeping-people-in-their-place/

Siwatu, K. O. (2011). Preservice teachers' sense of preparedness and self-efficacy to teach in America's urban and sub-urban schools: Does context matter? *Teaching and Teacher Education, 27*(2), 357–365. doi:10.1016/j.tate.2010.09.004

Skinner, E. A., & Pitzer, J. R. (2012). Developmental dynamics of student engagement, coping, and everyday resilience. In S. L. Christenson, A. L. Reschly, & C. Wylie (Eds.), *Handbook of research on student engagement* (pp. 21–44). New York: Springer. doi:10.1007/978-1-4614-2018-7_2

Skott, J. (2005). The role of the practice of theorising practice. In M. Bosch, & ... (Eds.), *Proceedings of the 4th Conference of the European Society for Research in Mathematics Education* (pp. 1598-1608). Barcelona: FunEmi.

Sleep, L., & Boerst, T. (2012). Preparing beginning teachers to elicit and interpret students' mathematical thinking. *Teaching and Teacher Education: An International Journal of Research and Studies, 28*(7), 1038-1048. doi:10.1016/j.tate.2012.04.005

Sleep, L. (2012). The work of steering instruction toward the mathematical point: A decomposition of teaching practice. *American Educational Research Journal, 49*(5), 935–970. doi:10.3102/0002831212448095

Sleep, L., Boerst, T., & Ball, D. (2007). *Learning to do the work of teaching in a practice-based methods course.* Atlanta, GA: NCTM Research Pre-session.

Sleeter, C. (2008). Equity, democracy, and neoliberal assaults on teacher education. *Teaching and Teacher Education, 24*(8), 1947–1957. doi:10.1016/j.tate.2008.04.003

Sleeter, C. E. (1995). An analysis of the critiques of multicultural education. In J. A. Banks & C. A. McGee Banks (Eds.), *Handbook of research on multicultural education* (pp. 81–94). New York: Simon & Schuster Macmillan.

Sleeter, C. E. (2001). Preparing teachers for culturally diverse schools: Research and the overwhelming presence of whiteness. *Journal of Teacher Education, 52*(2), 94–106. doi:10.1177/0022487101052002002

Sleeter, C., Neal, L. V., & Kumashiro, K. (2014). *Addressing the demographic imperative: Recruiting, preparing, and retaining a diverse and highly effective teaching force.* New York: Routledge.

Slick, S. K. (1997). Assessing versus assisting: The supervisor's role in the complex dynamics of the student teaching triad. *Teaching and Teacher Education, 13*(7), 713–726. doi:10.1016/S0742-051X(97)00016-4

Slick, S. K. (1998). The university supervisor: A disenfranchised outsider. *Teaching and Teacher Education, 14*(8), 821–834. doi:10.1016/S0742-051X(98)00028-6

Smagorinsky, P., Rhym, D., & Moore, C. P. (2013, January). Competing centers of gravity: A beginning English teacher's socialization process within conflictual settings. *English Education, 45*(2), 147–183.

Smagorinsky, P., Shelton, S. A., & Moore, C. (2015). The role of reflection in developing eupraxis in learning to teach English. *Pedagogies, 10*(4), 285–308. doi:10.1080/1554480X.2015.1067146

Smith, J. B., Lee, V. E., & Newmann, F. M. (2001). *Instruction and achievement in Chicago elementary schools.* Chicago, IL: Consortium on Chicago School Research.

Smith, M. S. (2001). *Practice-based professional development for teachers of mathematics.* Reston, VA: National Council of Teachers of Mathematics.

Smith, M. S., & Stein, M. K. (2011). *5 practices for orchestrating productive mathematical discussions.* Reston, VA: National Council of Teachers of Mathematics.

Snyder, J. (1999). Professional development schools: Why? So what? Now what? *Peabody Journal of Education, 74*(3), 136–143. doi:10.120715327930pje7403&4_11

Sobel, D. (2004). *Place-based education: Connecting classrooms and communities* (2nd ed.). Great Barrington, MA: The Orion Society.

Sobel, D. (2005). *Place-based education: Reclaiming the heart in nature education.* Great Barrington, MA: The Orion Society and the Myrin Institute.

Solomon, J. (2009). The Boston teacher residency: District-based teacher education. *Journal of Teacher Education, 60*(5), 478–488. doi:10.1177/0022487109349915

Soslau, E. (2012). Opportunities to develop adaptive teaching expertise during supervisory conferences. *Teaching and Teacher Education, 28*(5), 768–779. doi:10.1016/j.tate.2012.02.009

Soslau, E. (2015). Development of a post-lesson observation conferencing protocol: Situated in theory, research, and practice. *Teaching and Teacher Education, 49*, 22–35. doi:10.1016/j.tate.2015.02.012

Souto-Manning, M. (2013). *Multicultural teaching in the early childhood classroom: Approaches, strategies, and tools preschool-2*nd *grade*. New York: Teachers College Press.

Sowder, J. T. (2007). The mathematical education and development of teachers. In F. K. Lester (Ed.), *Second handbook of research on mathematics teaching and learning* (pp. 157–223). Charlotte, NC: Information Age Pub.

Spangler, D. A., & Orvick, R. L. B. (2017). Models for mathematics specialist program development and delivery. In M. McGatha & N. Riegelman (Eds.), *Elementary mathematics specialists* (pp. 41–52). Charlotte, NC: Association of Mathematics Teacher Educators.

Sparks-Langer, G. M., & Colton, A. B. (1991). Synthesis of research on teachers' reflective thinking. *Educational Leadership, 48*(6), 37–44.

Spector, J. (2005). How reliable are informal reading inventories? *Psychology in the Schools, 42*(6), 593–603. doi:10.1002/pits.20104

St. Cloud State University, Teacher Quality Enhancement Center. (2011). *Co-teaching in student teaching*. Retrieved from http://www.cehd.umn.edu/assets/docs/teaching/co-teaching-modules/SCSU-Facts-Sheet.pdf

Stake, R. E. (2006). *Multiple case study analysis*. New York, NY: Guilford Press.

Stanford History Education Group (SHEG). (2015). *Reading like a historian*. Retrieved from https://sheg.stanford.edu/

Stanley, C. (1998). A framework for teacher reflectivity. *TESOL Quarterly, 32*(3), 584–591. doi:10.2307/3588129

Star, J. R., Lynch, K., & Perova, N. (2011). Using video to improve preservice mathematics teachers' abilities to attend to classroom features. In M. G. Sherin, V. R. Jacobs & R. A. Philipp (Eds.), Mathematics teacher noticing: Seeing through teachers' eyes (pp. 117-133). New York: Routledge.

Star, J. R., Herbel-Eisenmann, B., & Smith, J. P. (2000). Algebraic concepts: What's really new in new curricula? *Mathematics Teaching in the Middle School, 5*(7), 446–451.

Star, J. R., & Strickland, S. K. (2008). Learning to observe: Using video to improve preservice mathematics teachers' ability to notice. *Journal of Mathematics Teacher Education, 11*(2), 107–125. doi:10.100710857-007-9063-7

Staunton, M. S., & Jaffee, E. M. (2014). *Key findings and recommendations from the Coos youth study: Research from the first half of the study (Issue Brief No. 41)*. Durham, NH: Carsey School of Public Policy.

Stein, M. K., Engle, R. A., Smith, M. S., & Hughes, E. K. (2008). Orchestrating productive mathematical discussions: Five practices for helping teachers move beyond show and tell. *Mathematical Thinking and Learning, 10*(4), 313–340. doi:10.1080/10986060802229675

Stein, M. K., Grover, B. W., & Henningsen, M. (1996). Building student capacity for mathematical thinking and reasoning: An analysis of mathematical tasks used in reform classrooms. *American Educational Research Journal, 33*(2), 455–488. doi:10.3102/00028312033002455

Stein, M. K., & Lane, S. (1996). Instructional tasks and the development of student capacity to think and reason: An analysis of the relationship between teaching and learning in a reform mathematics project. *Educational Research and Evaluation, 2*(1), 50–80. doi:10.1080/1380361960020103

Stein, M. K., & Smith, M. S. (1998). Mathematical tasks as a framework for reflection: From research to practice. *Mathematics Teaching in the Middle School, 3*(4), 268–275.

Stephens, D., Cox, R., Downs, A., Goforth, J., Jaeger, L., Matheny, A., ... Thompson, T. (2012). "I Know There Ain't no Pigs with Wigs": Challenges of Tier 2 Intervention. *The Reading Teacher, 66*(2), 93–103. doi:10.1002/TRTR.01094

Stigler, J. W., & Hiebert, J. (1999). *The teaching gap: Best ideas from the world's teachers for improving education in the classroom.* New York: The Free Press.

Stipek, D. (2002). *Motivation to learn* (4th ed.). Upper Saddle River, NJ: Pearson.

Stockero, S. (2008). Differences in preservice mathematics teachers' reflective abilities attributable to use of a video case curriculum. *Journal of Technology and Teacher Education, 16*, 483–509.

Strauss, A., & Corbin, J. (1998). *Basics of qualitative research: Techniques and procedures for developing grounded theory.* Thousand Oaks, CA: Sage.

Streng, J. M., Rhodes, S. D., Ayala, G. X., Eng, E., Arceo, R., & Phipps, S. (2004). Realidad Latina: Latino adolescents, their school, and a university use photo voice to examine and address the influence of immigration. *Journal of Interprofessional Care, 18*(4), 403–415. doi:10.1080/13561820400011701 PMID:15801555

Strutchens, M. (2017). Current research on prospective secondary mathematics teachers' field experiences. In The Mathematics Education of Prospective Secondary Teachers Around the World (pp. 33-44). ICME-13 Topical Surveys. Springer. Doi:10.1007/978-3-319-38965-3_5

Strutchens, M. E., Quander, J. R., & Gutierréz, R. (2011). Mathematics learning communities that foster reasoning and sense making for all high school students. In M. E. Strutchens & J. R. Quander (Eds.), *Focus in high school mathematics: Fostering reasoning and sense making for all students* (pp. 101–114). Reston, VA: National Council of Teachers of Mathematics.

Studio Code Business Group. (2012). *Studiocode.* Warriewood, NSW: Sportstec.

Stufflebeam, D. L. (2003). The CIPP Model for Evaluation. In T. Kellaghan & D. Stufflebeam (Eds.), *International Handbook of Educational Evaluation.* Dordrecht, Netherlands: Springer. doi:10.1007/978-94-010-0309-4_4

Suárez-Orozco, M., & Sattin, C. (2007). Wanted: Global citizens. *Educational Leadership, 64*(7), 58–62.

Success Academy. (2018). *Who we are.* Retrieved from: https://www.successacademies.org/about/#history

Suh, J. M., King, L. A., & Weiss, A. (2014). Co-development of professional practice at a professional development school through instructional rounds and lesson study. In D. Polly, T. Heafner, M. Chapman, & M. Spooner (Eds.), *Professional Development Schools and Transformative Partnerships* (pp. 176–182). Hershey, PA: IGI Global.

Sutcher, L., Darling-Hammond, L., & Carver-Thomas, D. (2016). *A coming crisis in teaching? Teacher supply, demand, and shortages in the U.S.* Learning Policy Institute. Retrieved from https://learningpolicyinstitute.org/product/coming-crisis-teaching

Sutcher, L., Darling-Hammond, L., & Carver-Thomas, D. (2016). *A coming crisis in teaching? Teacher supply, demand, and shortages in the U.S.* Palo Alto, CA: Learning Policy Institute.

Sutton, J. (2018). *Professional development survey* [Survey instrument].

Swartz, P. C. (2005). It's elementary in Appalachia: Helping prospective teachers and their students understand sexuality and gender. In J. T. Sears (Ed.), *Gay, lesbian, and transgender issues in education: Programs, policies, and practices* (pp. 125–146). New York, NY: Harrington Park Press.

Swennen, A., Volman, M., & van Essen, M. (2008). The development of the professional identity of two teacher educators in the context of Dutch teacher education. *European Journal of Teacher Education*, *31*(2), 169–184. doi:10.1080/02619760802000180

Sykes, G., Bird, T., & Kennedy, M. (2010). Teacher education: Its problems and some prospects. *Journal of Teacher Education*, *61*(5), 464–476. doi:10.1177/0022487110375804

Tabachnick, B. R., & Zeichner, K. M. (1984). The impact of student teaching experience on the development of teachers' perspectives. *Journal of Teacher Education*, *35*(6), 28–36. doi:10.1177/002248718403500608

Tashakkori, A., & Teddlie, C. (1998). *Mixed methodology: Combining qualitative and quantitative approaches*. Thousand Oaks, CA: Sage Publications.

Tatto, M. (1996). Examining values and beliefs about teaching diverse students: Understanding the challenges for teacher education. *Educational Evaluation and Policy Analysis*, *18*(2), 155–180. doi:10.3102/01623737018002155

Taylor, M., & Ronau, R. (2006). Syllabus study: A structured look at mathematics methods courses. *AMTE Connections*, *16*(1), 12–15.

Teacher Leadership Exploratory Consortium. (2011). *Teacher leader model standards*. Retrieved from http://teacher-leaderstandards.org/downloads/TLS_Brochure.pdf

Teaching Works. (2015). *High-leverage practices*. University of Michigan. Retrieved from http://www.teachingworks.org/work-of-teaching/high-leverage-practices

Tenorio, R. (2007). Race and respect among young children. In W. Au, B. Bigelow, & S. Karp (Eds.), *Rethinking our classrooms: Teaching for equity and justice* (2nd ed.; Vol. 1, pp. 20–24). Milwaukee, WI: Rethinking Schools.

Thanheiser, E. (2009). Preservice elementary school teachers' conceptions of multidigit whole numbers. *Journal for Research in Mathematics Education*, *40*, 251–281.

The Danielson Group. (2017). *The framework*. Retrieved from https://www.danielsongroup.org/framework/

The National Council for Accreditation of Teacher Education (NCATE). (2010). *Transforming Teacher Education through clinical practice: A national strategy to prepare effective teachers*. Report of the Blue Ribbon Panel on Clinical Preparation and Partnerships for Improved Student Learning.

The New Teacher Project. (2014, February 18). *TNTP core teaching rubric: A tool for conducting common core-aligned classroom observations*. Brooklyn, NY: Author. Retrieved from https://tntp.org/publications/view/tntp-core-teaching-rubric-a-tool-for-conducting-classroom-observations

Thompson, J., Hagenah, S., Lohwasser, K., & Laxton, K. (2015). Problems without ceilings: How mentors and novices frame and work on problems-of-practice. *Journal of Teacher Education*, *66*(4), 364–381. doi:10.1177/0022487115592462

Thonus, T. (2001). Triangulation in the writing center: Tutor, tutee, and instructor's perception of the tutor's role. *Writing Center Journal*, *22*(1), 59–82.

Tieken, M. C. (2014). *Why rural schools matter*. Chapel Hill, NC: University of North Carolina Press. doi:10.5149/northcarolina/9781469618487.001.0001

Tillema, H. (2009). Assessment for learning to teach appraisal of practice teaching lessons by mentors, supervisors, and student teachers. *Journal of Teacher Education*, *60*(2), 155–167. doi:10.1177/0022487108330551

Tindle, K., Freund, M., Belknap, B., Green, C., & Shotel, J. (2011). The urban teacher residency program: A recursive process to develop professional dispositions, knowledge, and skills of candidates to teach diverse students. *Educational Considerations, 38*(2), 28–35. doi:10.4148/0146-9282.1132

Tomanek, D. (2005). Building successful partnerships between k–12 and universities. *Cell Biology Education, 4*(1), 28–29. doi:10.1187/cbe.04-11-0051 PMID:15746977

Torrez, C. A. F., & Krebs, M. M. (2012). Expert voices: What cooperating teachers and teacher candidates say about quality student teaching placements and experiences. *Action in Teacher Education, 34*(5-6), 485–499. doi:10.1080/01 626620.2012.729477

Trinidad, S., Sharplin, E., Lock, G., Ledger, S., Boyd, D., & Terry, E. (2011). Developing strategies at the pre-service level to address critical teacher attraction and retention issues. *Australian and International Journal of Rural Education, 23*(2), 43-52.

Tripp, T. R., & Rich, P. J. (2012). The influence of video analysis on the process of teacher change. *Teaching and Teacher Education, 28*(5), 728–739. doi:10.1016/j.tate.2012.01.011

Troen, V., & Boles, K. C. (2014). Rounds process puts teachers in charge of learning. *Journal of Staff Development, 35*(2), 20–28.

Tschannen-Moran, Hoy, & Hoy (1998). Teacher efficacy: its meaning and measure. *Review of Educational Research, 68*(2), 202-248. Retrieved from http://www.jstor.org/stable/1170754

Tschannen-Moran, M., & Hoy, A. W. (2001). Teacher efficacy: Capturing an elusive construct. *Teaching and Teacher Education, 17*(7), 783–805. doi:10.1016/S0742-051X(01)00036-1

Tschida, C., Smith, J., & Fogarty, E. (2015). "It just works better": Introducing the 2:1 model of co-teaching in teacher preparation. *Rural Educator, 36*(1), 11–26.

Tseng, V. (2012). *Partnerships: Shifting the dynamics between research and practice.* New York, NY: William T. Grant Foundation.

Turner, E., Aguirre, J., Drake, C., Bartell, T. G., Roth McDuffie, A., & Foote, M. Q. (2015). Community Mathematics Exploration Module. In *TeachMath learning modules for K-8 mathematics methods courses.* Teachers Empowered to Advance Change in Mathematics Project. Retrieved from: www.teachmath.info

Turner, E. E., Drake, C., Roth McDuffie, A., Aguirre, J., Bartell, T. G., & Foote, M. Q. (2012). Promoting equity in mathematics teacher preparation: A framework for advancing teacher learning of children's multiple mathematics knowledge bases. *Journal of Mathematics Teacher Education, 15*(1), 67–82. doi:10.100710857-011-9196-6

Tuss, P., & Wang, Y. (2016, February 5). *Evaluation of the Co-STARS Rural Teacher Residency Program at California State University, Chico: First-Year Extended Evaluation Report on Baseline Student Achievement Results.* California State University Center for Teacher Quality.

Twenge, J., Campbell, S., Hoffman, B., & Lance, C. (2010). Generational differences in work values: Leisure and extrinsic values increasing, social and intrinsic values decreasing. *Journal of Management, 5*(36), 1117–1142. doi:10.1177/0149206309352246

Tyack, D., & Cuban, L. (1995). *Tinkering toward utopia: A century of public school reform.* Cambridge, MA: Harvard University Press.

U.S. Department of Education Office for Civil Rights. (2014). Retrieved from https://www2.ed.gov/policy/gen/guid/school-discipline/index.html

U.S. Department of Education, Institute of Education Sciences, National Center for Education Statistics. (2017). *Racial/ Ethnic Enrollment in Public Schools*. Retrieved from https://nces.ed.gov/programs/coe/indicator_cge.asp

U.S. Department of Education, Office of Planning, Evaluation, and Policy Development. (2010). *Evaluation of evidence-based practices in online learning: A meta-analysis and review of online learning studies*. Washington, DC: Author. Retrieved from https://www2.ed.gov/rschstat/eval/tech/evidence-based-practices/finalreport.pdf

U.S. Department of Education, Office of Postsecondary Education (2015). *Higher Education Act Title II Reporting System*. Author.

U.S. Department of Labor, Bureau of Labor Statistics. (2016). *Occupational outlook handbook*. Washington, DC: Author. Retrieved from https://www.bls.gov/ooh/education-training-and-library/kindergarten-andelementary-school-teachers.htm

Ukpokodu, N. O. (2007). Preparing socially conscious teachers: A social justice-oriented teacher education. *Multicultural Education*, *15*(1), 8–22.

United States Department of Labor, Bureau of Labor Statistics. (2017). *Occupations with the most job growth*. Retrieved from http://www.bls.gov/emp/ep_table_104.htm

Urzúa, A., & Vásquez, C. (2008). Reflection and professional identity in teachers' future-oriented discourse. *Teaching and Teacher Education*, *24*(7), 1935–1946. doi:10.1016/j.tate.2008.04.008

US Department of Education. (n.d.). *Teacher Quality Partnership Grants*. Retrieved from https://www2.ed.gov/programs/tqpartnership/index.html

Utah State Board of Education. (2017). *Academic Pathway to Teaching*. Retrieved from https://www.schools.utah.gov/curr/licensing/earning

Utah State Office of Education. (2011). *Utah effective teaching standards*. Salt Lake City, UT: Utah State Office of Education.

Valencia, S., Martin, S., Place, N., & Grossman, P. (2009). Complex interactions in student teaching: Lost opportunities for learning. *Journal of Teacher Education*, *60*(3), 304–322. doi:10.1177/0022487109336543

Valli, L. (Ed.). (1990). *Reflective teacher education: Cases and critiques*. Albany, NY: State University of New York Press.

Van Es, E. A. (2011). A framework for learning to notice student thinking. In M. G. Sherin, V. R. Jacobs & R. A. Philipp (Eds.), Mathematics teacher noticing: Seeing through teachers' eyes (pp. 134-151). New York: Routledge.

van Es, E. A. (2010). Viewer discussion is advised: Video clubs focus teacher discussion on student learning. *Journal of Staff Development*, *31*, 54–58.

van Es, E. A. (2012). Examining the development of a teacher learning community: The case of a video club. *Teaching and Teacher Education*, *28*(2), 182–192. doi:10.1016/j.tate.2011.09.005

Van Es, E. A., & Sherin, M. G. (2002). Learning to notice: Scaffolding new teachers' interpretations of classroom interactions. *Journal of Technology and Teacher Education*, *10*(4), 571–596.

Van Es, E. A., & Sherin, M. G. (2008). Mathematics teachers' "learning to notice" in the context of video club. *Teaching and Teacher Education*, *24*(2), 244–276. doi:10.1016/j.tate.2006.11.005

van Es, E. A., & Sherin, M. G. (2010). The influence of video clubs on teachers' thinking and practice. *Math Teacher Education*, *13*(2), 155–176. doi:10.100710857-009-9130-3

Van Manen, M. (1977). Linking ways of knowing with ways of being practical. *Curriculum Inquiry, 6*(3), 205–228. do i:10.1080/03626784.1977.11075533

Van Manen, M. (1991). Reflectivity and the pedagogical movement: The normativity of pedagogical thinking and acting. *Journal of Curriculum Studies, 23*(6), 507–536. doi:10.1080/0022027910230602

Vanderhaar, J. E., Munoz, M. A., & Rodosky, R. J. (2006). Leadership as accountability for learning: The effects of school poverty, teacher experience, previous achievement, and principal preparation programs on student achievement. *Journal of Personnel Evaluation in Education, 19*(1-2), 17–33. doi:10.100711092-007-9033-8

Veal, M. L., & Rickard, L. (1998). Cooperating teachers' perspectives on the student teaching triad. *Journal of Teacher Education, 49*(2), 108–119. doi:10.1177/0022487198049002004

Venugopal, A. (2011). *Census pinpoints city's wealthiest, poorest neighborhoods.* Retrieved from: https://www.wnyc.org/story/174508-blog-census-locates-citys-wealthiest-and-poorest-neighborhoods/

Vernikoff, L., Goodwin, A. L., Horn, C., & Akin, S. (in press). Urban residents' place-based funds of knowledge: An untapped resource in urban teacher residencies. *Urban Education.*

Vescio, V., Ross, D., & Adams, A. (2007). A review of research on the impact of professional learning communities on teaching practice and student learning. *Teaching and Teacher Education, 24*(1), 80–91. doi:10.1016/j.tate.2007.01.004

Viadero, D. (2009). *Turnover in principalship focus of research.* Retrieved from http://www.edweek.org/ew/articles/2009/10/28/09principal_ep.h29.html

Villegas, A. M. (2007). Dispositions in teacher education: A look at social justice. *Journal of Teacher Education, 58*(5), 370–380. doi:10.1177/0022487107308419

Villegas, A. M., & Lucas, T. (2002). *Educating culturally responsive teachers: A coherent approach.* Albany, NY: State University of New York Press.

Virginia Mathematics and Science Coalition. (2016). *Mathematics specialists.* Retrieved from http://www.vamsc.org/index.php/mathematics-specialists/

Virmani, R., Taylor, M., Rumsey, C., Box, T., Kazemi, E., & Knapp, M. … Woods, D. (2017). Bringing methods into schools. In S. Kastberg, A. Tyminski, A. Lischka, & W. Sanchez (Eds.), Building support for scholarly practices in mathematics methods. Charlotte, NC: IAP.

Vohs, K. D., Baumeister, R. F., Schmeichel, B. J., Twenge, J. M., Nelson, N. M., & Tice, D. M. (2008). Making choices impairs subsequent self-control: A limited-resource account of decision making, self-regulation, and active initiative. *Journal of Personality and Social Psychology, 94*(5), 883–898. doi:10.1037/0022-3514.94.5.883 PMID:18444745

Vygotsky, L. (1978). *Mind in society.* Boston, MA: Harvard University Press.

Vygotsky, L. (1978). *Mind in society: The development of higher mental process.* Cambridge, MA: Harvard University Press.

Vygotsky, L. (1978). *Mind in society: The development of higher psychological processes.* Cambridge, MA: Harvard University Press.

Vygotsky, L. V. (1986). *Thought and language* (A. Kozulin, Ed.). Cambridge, MA: The MIT Press.

Wade, R. C. (2000). Beyond Charity: Service learning for social justice. *Social Studies and the Young Learner, 12*(4), 6–9.

Wade, R. C. (2001). Social Action in the Social Studies: From the ideal to the real. *Theory into Practice, 40*(1), 23–28. doi:10.120715430421tip4001_4

Walker-Gibbs, B., Ludecke, M., & Kline, J. (2015). Pedagogy of the rural: Implications of size on conceptualisations of rural. *International Journal of Pedagogies and Learning, 10*(1), 81–89. doi:10.1080/22040552.2015.1086292

Walkington, J. (2007). Improving partnerships between schools and universities: Professional learning with benefits beyond preservice teacher education. *Teacher Development, 11*(3), 277–294. doi:10.1080/13664530701644581

Wallace Foundation. (2016). *Improving university principal preparation programs: Five themes from the field.* Retrieved from http://www.wallacefoundation.org/knowledge-center/Documents/Improving-University-Principal-Preparation-Programs.pdf

Wallace, C. S. (2013). Promoting shifts in preservice science teachers' thinking through teaching and action research in informal science settings. *Journal of Science Teacher Education, 24*(5), 811–832. doi:10.100710972-013-9337-0

Waller, W. (1932/1961). *The sociology of teaching.* Hoboken, NJ: John Wiley & Sons. doi:10.1037/11443-000

Walsh, K., & Jacobs, S. (2007). *Alternative certification isn't alternative.* Washington, DC: National Council on Teacher Quality. Retrieved from https://files.eric.ed.gov/fulltext/ED498382.pdf

Wang, J., Lin, E., Spalding, E., Odell, S., & Klecka, C. (2011). Understanding Teacher Education in an Era of Globalization. *Journal of Teacher Education, 62*(2), 115–120. doi:10.1177/0022487110394334

Wang, J., Odell, S., & Schwille, S. (2008). Effects of teacher induction on beginning teachers' teaching: A critical review of the literature. *Journal of Teacher Education, 59*(2), 132–152. doi:10.1177/0022487107314002

Wang, J., Spalding, E., Odell, S. J., Klecka, C. L., & Lin, E. (2010). Bold ideas for improving teacher education and teaching. *Journal of Teacher Education, 61*(4), 2–15.

Ward, C. J., Nolen, S. B., & Horn, I. S. (2011). Productive friction: How conflict in student teaching creates opportunities for learning at the boundary. *International Journal of Educational Research, 50*(1), 14–20. doi:10.1016/j.ijer.2011.04.004

Ward, J. R., & McCotter, S. S. (2004). Reflection as a visible outcome for preservice teachers. *Teaching and Teacher Education, 20*(3), 243–257. doi:10.1016/j.tate.2004.02.004

Warshauer, H. K. (2015). Productive struggle in middle school mathematics classrooms. *Journal of Mathematics Teacher Education, 18*(4), 375–400. doi:10.100710857-014-9286-3

Watson, D. (2011). What do you mean when you say "urban"? Speaking honestly about race and students. *Rethinking Schools, 26*(1), 48–50.

Watson, D. (2012). Norming suburban: How teachers talk about race without using race words. *Urban Education, 47*(5), 983–1004. doi:10.1177/0042085912445642

Wayman, J. C., Foster, A. M., Mantle-Bromley, C., & Wilson, C. A. (2003). A comparison of the professional concerns of traditionally prepared and alternatively licensed new teachers. *High School Journal, 3*(86), 35–40. doi:10.1353/hsj.2003.0005

Wayne, A., & Young, P. (2002). Teacher characteristics and student achievement gains: A review. *Review of Educational Research, 73*(1), 89–122. doi:10.3102/00346543073001089

Weaver, D., Dick, T., Higgins, K., Marrongelle, K., Foreman, L., & Rigelman, N. M. (2005). *OMLI classroom observation protocol.* Portland, OR: RMC Research Corporation. Available at http://goo.gl/doQJ2p

Weiner, L. (2006). *Urban teaching: The essentials.* New York: Teachers College Press.

Weinstein, C. S. (1990). Prospective elementary teachers' beliefs about teaching: Implications for teacher education. *Teaching and Teacher Education, 6*(3), 279–290. doi:10.1016/0742-051X(90)90019-2

Weiss, M. P., & Brigham, F. J. (2000). Co-teaching and the model of shared responsibility: What does the research support? *Advances in Learning and Behavioral Disabilities, 14,* 217–246.

Weiss, M., Pellegrino, A., & Brigham, F. (2017). Practicing collaboration in teacher preparation: Effects of learning by doing together. *Teacher Education and Special Education, 40*(1), 65–76. doi:10.1177/0888406416655457

Wellington, B., & Austin, P. (1996). Orientations to reflective practice. *Educational Research, 38*(3), 307–316. doi:10.1080/0013188960380304

Welsh, K. A., & Schaffer, C. (2017). Developing the Effective Teaching Skills of Teacher Candidates During Early Field Experiences. *The Educational Forum, 81*(3), 301–321. doi:10.1080/00131725.2017.1314574

Wenger, E. (2011). *Communities of practice: A brief introduction.* Retrieved from https://scholarsbank.uoregon.edu/xmlui/handle/1794/11736?show=full

Wenger, E. (1998). *Communities of practice: Learning, meaning and Identity.* Cambridge, UK: Cambridge University Press. doi:10.1017/CBO9780511803932

Wenger, E., McDermott, R., & Snyder, W. (2002). *Cultivating communities of practice: A guide to managing knowledge.* Boston: Harvard Business School Publishing.

Wenger-Trayner, E., & Wenger-Trayner, B. (2015). *Introduction to communities of practice.* Retrieved from http://wenger-trayner.com/introduction

Wertsch, J. (1991). *Voices of the mind: A Sociocultural approach to mediated action.* Cambridge, MA: Harvard University Press.

West, L., & Staub, F. C. (2003). *Content-focused coaching: Transforming mathematics lessons.* Portsmouth, NH: Heinemann.

Weston, T. L. (2011). *Elementary preservice teachers' mathematical knowledge for teaching: Using situated case studies and educative experiences to examine and improve the development of MKT in teacher education* (Doctoral dissertation). Available from ProQuest Dissertations and Theses database. (UMI No. 3477561)

Weston, T. L. (2018). Using the Knowledge Quartet to support prospective teacher development during methods coursework. In S. E. Kastberg, A. M. Tyminski, A. E. Lischka, & W. B. Sanchez (Eds.), *Building Scholarly Practices in Mathematics Methods* (pp. 69–83). Charlotte, NC: Information Age Publishing.

Weston, T. L., & Henderson, S. C. (2015). Coherent experiences: The new missing paradigm in teacher education. *The Educational Forum, 79*(3), 321–335. doi:10.1080/00131725.2015.1037514

Whitenack, J. W., & Ellington, A. J. (2013). Supporting middle school mathematics specialists' work: A case for learning and changing teachers' perspectives. *The Mathematics Enthusiast, 10*(3), 647-677. Retrieved from https://search.proquest.com/docview/1434424733?accountid=14541

White, S., & Reid, J. (2008). Placing teachers? Sustaining rural teaching through place-consciousness in teacher education. *Journal of Research in Rural Education, 23*(7), 1–11.

Wideen, M., Mayer-Smith, J., & Moon, B. (1998). A critical analysis of the research on learning to teach: Making the case for an ecological perspective on inquiry. *Review of Educational Research, 68*(2), 130–178. doi:10.3102/00346543068002130

Wieman, R. (2018). Data do not drive themselves. *Mathematics Teacher*, *111*(7), 535–539. doi:10.5951/mathteacher.111.7.0535

Wiens, P. D., Hessberg, K., LoCasale-Crouch, J., & DeCoster, J. (2013). Using a standardized video-based assessment in a university teacher education program to examine preservice teachers' knowledge related to effective teaching. *Teaching and Teacher Education*, *33*, 24–33. doi:10.1016/j.tate.2013.01.010

Wiggins, G. (2012). Seven keys to effective feedback. *Educational Leadership*, *70*(1), 10–16. Retrieved from http://www.ascd.org/publications/educational-leadership/sept12/vol70/ num01/Seven-Keys-to-Effective-Feedback.aspx

Wiggins, G. (2012). Seven keys to effective feedback. *Feedback*, *70*(1), 10–16.

Wiggins, G., & McTighe, J. (2005). *Understanding by Design*. Alexandria, VA: Association for Supervision and Curriculum Development.

Wilhelm, I. (2016). Owning the k-12 challenge. *The Chronicle of Higher Education*. Retrieved from http://chronicle.com/article/Video-Owning-the-K-12/236400

Will, M. (2014). Average urban school superintendent tenure decreases, survey shows [blog]. Retrieved from http://blogs.edweek.org/edweek/District_Dossier/2014/11/urban_school_superintendent_te.html

Williams, J. (2014). Teacher educator professional learning in the third space: Implications for identity and practice. *Journal of Teacher Education*, *65*(4), 315–326. doi:10.1177/0022487114533128

Williamson, P. (2013). Enacting high leverage practices in English methods: The case of discussion. *English Education*, *46*(1), 34–67.

Williamson, P., Apedoe, X., & Thomas, C. (2016). Context as Content in Urban Teacher Education: Learning to Teach in and for San Francisco. *Urban Education*, *51*(10), 1170–1197. doi:10.1177/0042085915623342

Wilson, S., Floden, R., & Ferrini-Mundy, J. (2001). *Teacher preparation research: current knowledge, gaps, and recommendations*. Center for the Study of Teaching and Policy, University of Washington. Retrieved on December 28, 2017, from http://depts.washington.edu/ctpmail/PDFs/TeacherPrep-WFFM-02-2001.pdf

Wilson, J. D. (1996). An evaluation of the field experiences of the innovative model for the preparation of elementary teachers for science, mathematics, and technology. *Journal of Teacher Education*, *47*(1), 53–59. doi:10.1177/0022487196047001009

Wilson, S. M. (1990). The secret garden of teacher education. *Phi Delta Kappan*, *72*(3), 204–209.

Wilson, S. R., Floden, R. E., & Ferrini-Mundy, J. (2001). *Teacher preparation research: Current knowledge, gaps, and recommendations*. Center for the Study of Teaching and Policy, University of Washington.

Wimmer, R. (2008). A multi-disciplinary study of field experiences: Possibilities for teacher education. *The Journal of Educational Thought (JET)*. *Revue De La Pensée Éducative*, *42*(3), 339–351. Retrieved from http://www.jstor.org/stable/23758502

Windschitl, M., Thompson, J., Braaten, M., & Stroupe, D. (2012). Proposing a core set of instructional practices and tools for teachers of science. *Science Education*, *96*(5), 878–903. doi:10.1002ce.21027

Wingeier, D. E. (1980). Generative words in six cultures. *Religious Education (Chicago, Ill.)*, *75*(5), 563–576. doi:10.1080/0034408800750508

Wiswall, M. (2013). The dynamics of teacher quality. *Journal of Public Economics*, *100*, 61–78. doi:10.1016/j.jpubeco.2013.01.006

Wolcott, H. F. (2005). *The art of fieldwork* (2nd ed.). Walnut Creek, CA: Sage.

Wolff, C. E., van den Bogert, N., Jarodzka, H., & Boshuizen, H. P. (2015). Keeping an eye on learning: Differences between expert and novice teachers' representations of classroom management events. *Journal of Teacher Education*, *66*(1), 68–85. doi:10.1177/0022487114549810

Wong, P. L., & Glass, R. D. (2005). Assessing a professional development school approach to preparing teachers for urban schools serving low-income, culturally and linguistically diverse communities. *Teacher Education Quarterly*, *32*(3), 63–77. Retrieved from http://files.eric.ed.gov/fulltext/EJ795321.pdf

Wong, P. L., & Glass, R. D. (Eds.). (2009). *Prioritizing urban children, teachers, and schools through professional development schools*. Albany, NY: State University of New York Press.

Wood, M. B., & Turner, E. E. (2015). Bringing the teacher into teacher preparation: Learning from mentor teachers in joint methods activities. *Journal of Mathematics Teacher Education*, *18*(1), 27–51. doi:10.100710857-014-9269-4

Wood, M., Jilk, L., & Paine, L. (2012). Moving beyond sinking or swimming: Reconceptualizing the needs of beginning mathematics teachers. *Teachers College Record*, *114*(8), 1–44. PMID:24013958

Woodson, C. G. (1933). *The mis-education of the Negro*. Trenton, NJ: Africa World Press.

Woodson, J. (2016). *Brown Girl Dreaming*. New York: Puffin Books.

Wright, S., Horn, S., & Sanders, W. (1997). Teachers and classroom context effects on student achievement: Implications for teacher evaluation. *Journal of Personnel Evaluation in Education*, *11*(1), 57–67. doi:10.1023/A:1007999204543

Wu, H. H. (2009). What's sophisticated about elementary mathematics? Plenty—that's why elementary schools need math teachers. *American Educator*, *33*(3), 4–14.

Wuthnow, R. (2013). *Small-town America: Finding community, shaping the future*. Princeton, NJ: Princeton University Press. doi:10.1515/9781400846498

Wynter–Hoyte, K., Braden, E., Rodriguez, S., & Thornton, N. (2017). Disrupting the status quo: Exploring Culturally Relevant and Sustaining Pedagogies for Young Diverse Learners. *Race, Ethnicity and Education*, 1–20. doi:10.1080/13613324.2017.1382465

Yee, S., Otten, S., & Taylor, M. (2017). What do we value in secondary mathematics teaching methods?. *Investigations in Mathematics Learning*, 1-15.

Yeh, C., Ellis, M. W., & Hurtado, C. K. (2017). *Reimagining the mathematics classroom*. Reston, VA: National Council of Teachers of Mathematics.

Yohalem, N., & Tseng, V. (2015). Commentary: Moving from practice to research, and back. *Applied Developmental Science*, *19*(2), 117–120. doi:10.1080/10888691.2014.983033

Yonezawa, S., & Jones, M. (2009). Student voices: Generating reform from the inside out. *Theory into Practice*, *48*(3), 205–212. doi:10.1080/00405840902997386

Yopp, D., Burroughs, E., Luebeck, J., Heldema, C., Mitchell, A., & Sutton, J. (2011). How to be a Wise Consumer of Coaching. *Journal of Staff Development*, *32*(1), 50–53.

Youngs, P., & Hong, Q. (2013). The influence of university courses and field experiences on Chinese candidates' elementary mathematics knowledge for teaching. *Journal of Teacher Education*, *64*(3), 244–261. doi:10.1177/0022487112473836

Yousafzai, M. (2015). I am Malala: How one girl stood up for education and changed the world (Young reader's edition). New York: Little, Brown and Company.

Zeichner, K., & Conklin, H. G. (2008). Teacher education programs as sites for teacher preparation. In M. Cochran-Smith, S. Feiman-Nemser, & D. J. McIntyre (Eds.), Handbook on teacher education: Enduring questions in changing contexts (3rd ed.; pp. 269–289). Academic Press.

Zeichner, K. (1996). Designing education practicum experiences for prospective teachers. In K. Zeichner, S. Melnick, & M. L. Gomez (Eds.), *Currents of reform in preservice teacher education* (pp. 215–234). New York: Teachers College Press.

Zeichner, K. (2002). Beyond traditional structures of student teaching. *Teacher Education Quarterly, 29*(2), 59–64. Retrieved from http://teqjournal.org/backvols/2002/29_2/sp02zeichner.pdf

Zeichner, K. (2006). Reflections of a university-based teacher educator on the future of college-and university-based teacher education. *Journal of Teacher Education, 57*(3), 326–340. doi:10.1177/0022487105285893

Zeichner, K. (2010). Rethinking the connections between campus courses and field based experience in college- and university- based teacher education. *Journal of Teacher Education, 61*(1-2), 89–99. doi:10.1177/0022487109347671

Zeichner, K. (2012). The turn once again toward practice-based teacher education. *Journal of Teacher Education, 63*(5), 376–382. doi:10.1177/0022487112445789

Zeichner, K. M. (2005). Becoming a teacher educator: A personal perspective. *Teaching and Teacher Education, 21*(2), 117–124. doi:10.1016/j.tate.2004.12.001

Zeichner, K. M., & Conklin, H. (2005). Teacher education programs. In M. Cochran Smith & K. M. Zeichner (Eds.), *Studying teacher education: The report of the AERA panel on research and teacher education* (pp. 645–735). Mahwah, NJ: Lawrence Erlbaum Associates.

Zeichner, K., & Bier, M. (2015). Opportunities and pitfalls in the turn toward clinical experience in U.S. teacher education. In E. R. Hollins (Ed.), *Rethinking field experiences in preservice teacher preparation: Meeting new challenges for accountability*. New York, NY: Routledge.

Zeichner, K., & Bier, M. (2015). Opportunities and pitfalls in the turn toward clinical experience in US teacher education. In E. R. Hollins (Ed.), *Rethinking clinical experience in teacher candidate education* (pp. 20–46). New York, NY: Routledge.

Zeichner, K., Bowman, M., Guillen, L., & Napolitan, K. (2016). Engaging and working in solidarity with local communities in preparing the teachers of their children. *Journal of Teacher Education, 67*(4), 277–290. doi:10.1177/0022487116660623

Zeichner, K., & Liston, D. (1987). Teaching student teachers to reflect. *Harvard Educational Review, 57*(1), 23–48. doi:10.17763/haer.57.1.j18v7162275t1w3w

Zeichner, K., & McDonald, M. (2011). Practice-based teaching and community field experiences for prospective teachers. In A. Cohan & A. Honigsfeld (Eds.), *Breaking the mold of preservice and inservice teacher education: Innovative and successful practices for the 21st century* (pp. 45–54). Lanham, MD: Rowman & Littlefield Education.

Zeichner, K., Payne, K., & Brayko, K. (2014). Democratizing teacher education. *Journal of Teacher Education, 66*(2), 122–135. doi:10.1177/0022487114560908

Zeichner, K., & Tabachnik, B. R. (1981). Are the effects of university teacher education "washed out" by school experience? *Journal of Teacher Education, 32*(3), 7–11. doi:10.1177/002248718103200302

Zembylas, M. (2008). Interrogating 'Teacher identity': Emotion, resistance, and self- formation. *Educational Theory, 58*(1), 107–127. doi:10.1111/j.1741-5446.2003.00107.x

Zenkov, K. (2009, Summer). The teachers and schools they deserve: *Seeing* the pedagogies, practices, and programs urban students want. *Theory into Practice, 48*(3), 168–175. doi:10.1080/00405840902997253

Zenkov, K., Bell, A., Lynch, M., Ewaida, M., Harmon, J., & Pellegrino, A. (2012). Youth as sources of educational equity: Using photographs to help adolescents make sense of school, injustice, and their lives. *Education in a Democracy, 4*, 79–98.

Zenkov, K., & Harmon, J. (2009). Picturing a writing process: Using photovoice to learn how to teach writing to urban youth. *Journal of Adolescent & Adult Literacy, 52*(7), 575–584. doi:10.1598/JAAL.52.7.3

Zenkov, K., Parker, A. K., Parsons, S., Pellegrino, A., & Pytash, K. (2017). From project-based clinical experiences to collaborative inquiries: Pathways to Professional Development Schools. In J. Ferrara, J. Nath, I. Guadarrama, & R. Beebe (Eds.), *Expanding opportunities to link research and clinical practice: A volume in Research in Professional Development Schools* (pp. 9–33). Charlotte, NC: Information Age Publishing.

Zenkov, K., Pellegrino, A. M., Sell, C., Ewaida, M., Bell, A., Fell, M., ... McManis, M. (2014). Picturing kids and "kids" as researchers: English language learners, preservice teachers and effective writing instruction. *New Educator, 10*, 306–330. doi:10.1080/1547688X.2014.965107

Zenkov, K., & Pytash, K. E. (in press). Critical, project-based clinical experiences: Their origins and their elements. In K. Zenkov & K. E. Pytash (Eds.), *Clinical experiences in teacher education: Critical, project-based interventions in diverse classrooms* (pp. 1–18). New York: Routledge.

Zimpher, N. L., & Howey, K. R. (1992). *Policy and practice toward the improvement of teacher education: An analysis of issues from recruitment to continuing professional development with recommendations.* Oak Brook, IL: North Central Regional Educational Laboratory.

Zimpher, N. L., & Howey, K. R. (2013). Creating 21st century centers of pedagogy: Explicating key laboratory and clinical elements of teacher preparation. *Education, 133*(4), 409–421. Retrieved from https://eric.ed.gov/?id=EJ1032005

Zlotkowski, E. (1996). A new voice at the table? Linking service-learning and the academy. *Change, 28*(1), 21-27. doi:10.1080/00091383.1996.1054425

Zygmunt, E., & Clark, P. (2016). *Transforming teacher education for social justice.* New York: Teachers College Press.

About the Contributors

Thomas E. Hodges is Associate Dean for Academic Affairs and a mathematics education faculty member in the College of Education at the University of South Carolina. He conducts research on the development of teachers of mathematics using the constructs of identity, beliefs, attitudes and dispositions. As Director for the Center for Research on Teacher Education, he leads research efforts on innovative designs within teacher preparation program recruitment, preparation, and induction support.

Angela C. Baum is Associate Chair and an early childhood education faculty member in the Department of Instruction and Teacher Education at the University of South Carolina. Her research focuses on early childhood teacher preparation and professional development, specifically issues of policy and practice in the care of infants and toddlers. Angela directs multiple research and service projects in affiliation with the South Carolina Department of Social Services, and currently serves as President of the National Association of Early Childhood Teacher Educators.

***

Gabrièle Abowd Damico is a Clinical Assistant Professor of Arts Education in the Department of Curriculum & Instruction at Indiana University, Bloomington. She teaches visual art education courses and has a special interest in oral history, material culture, and museums as pedagogical resources. Dr. Abowd Damico serves as a faculty member and the current director of the Community of Teachers program. She is interested in experiential learning and apprenticeship as a model for teacher education. Prior to entering higher education, she was a middle school and high school French teacher.

David S. Allen is an Associate Professor in the Department of Curriculum and Instruction at Kansas State University. A mathematics educator, and former Director of the Office of Field Experiences, he has recently been appointed as the new Director of the STEM Center in the College of Education. His research originated in professional development models for inservice teachers of elementary mathematics and has evolved into working with digitally-mediated supervision models for pre-service teachers. His current research focuses on cloud-based management and storage of large video-based feedback systems and the interplay of the supervision triad as a factor of teacher development.

John Andrésen is a doctoral student in Special Education at Indiana University. He works as an associate instructor in the Community of Teachers. Prior to IU, John Andrésen was a middle school special education teacher in rural Indiana. John's research focuses primarily on the transition to adulthood for individuals with intellectual disabilities. John has also been involved in research regarding teacher preparation and federal educational policy.

Täna Arnold is a doctoral candidate in the Department of Special Education, Counseling and Student Affairs. Additionally, she is the Early Field Experience Placement Coordinator in the Office of Field Experiences for the College of Education. Täna currently supervises students in the Block C field experience using the distance-mediated supervision process.

Courtney Baker is an assistant professor in the Mathematics Education Leadership program at George Mason University. She holds a PhD in education with specializations in mathematics education leadership and teaching and teacher education. Prior to working in higher education, Baker worked as a teacher, mathematics specialist and professional development facilitator for Fairfax County Public Schools. Baker's research agenda is centered in mathematics education and teacher development. She is interested in advancing the role of mathematics specialists to develop effective mathematics teacher leaders that both impact student achievement and increase interest in mathematics. Additionally, she works with in-service teachers and mathematics coaches to examine how they might integrate STEM via Model-Eliciting Activities into K-12 classrooms.

Laura E. Bitto is a mathematics teacher educator and researcher who works with pre-and-in-service mathematics teachers to refine their mathematical content, pedagogical, and leadership knowledge and skills. Laura believes that mathematics is fundamental to understanding our universe and teachers of mathematics play the critical role of unlocking that knowledge to our future generations. Laura holds a Ph.D. in Educational Policy, Planning, and Leadership with a focus on Mathematics Education from the College of William and Mary. She also has a Masters degree as a K-8 Mathematics Specialist from the College of William and Mary and a B.A. in mathematics from McDaniel College. Her research focuses on mathematics specialists and developing mathematics teacher leaders. Prior to working in higher education, Laura was a mathematics specialist for K-12 teachers and an elementary teacher.

William Blakeney is an Assistant Principal at Dreher High School in Richland School District One and the administrative representative to the University Professional Development Schools Network.

Jonathan Bostic is an Associate Professor of Mathematics Education in the School of Teaching & Learning at Bowling Green State University. His research explores instructional contexts where teachers and students become active problem solvers.

Gloria Boutte holds the academic rank of professor at the University of South Carolina. For more than three decades, Dr. Boutte's scholarship, teaching, and service have focused on equity pedagogies and teaching for social justice in Early Childhood Education. She has served as Department Chair and held a distinguished endowed chair for four years. Dr. Boutte is the author of three books: (1) Educating African American Students: And how are the children; (2) Multicultural Education: Raising Consciousness and (3) Resounding Voices: School Experiences of People From Diverse Ethnic Backgrounds. She has received nearly $2 million in grants and has more than 90 publications. Additionally, she has presented nationally and internationally on equity, community, curriculum, instruction, and diversity issues. She has received presitigous awards such as the Fulbright Scholar and Fulbright Specialist. Dr. Boutte is the founder of the statewide Center of Excellence for the Education and Equity of African American Students (CEEEAAS). She has presented her work internationally in Cameroon, Colombia, China, Sierra Leone, Ghana, England, Zambia, Botswana, South Africa, Australia, South America, Jamaica, Mexico, New Zealand, Nigeria, and Canada.

Eliza Braden is an Assistant Professor in Elementary Education in the Department of Instruction and Teacher Education at the University of South Carolina. She currently teaches literacy methods courses in the Elementary Education program. Her research interests include critical language and literacy practices of culturally and linguistically diverse young children (i.e., African American and Latinx children), family literacy, social justice education, and digital literacy. Eliza's work has been published in Race Ethnicity and Education, English Journal, Language Arts Journal of Michigan, Journal of Language and Literacy Education, and other venues.

Barbara A. Bradley, PhD, is as Professor in Reading Education in the Department of Curriculum & Teaching at the University of Kansas. Dr. Bradley's research focuses on early literacy and book sharing, and she teaches courses related to literacy in the elementary grades, reading comprehension, and the evaluation of reading research. She has been co-directing a study abroad for education majors in Italy since its inception in 2000.

Elizabeth Levine Brown (PhD, University of Pittsburgh; MA, Washington College; MAT, American University & BA, Colgate University) is an Associate Professor in the College of Education and Human Development at George Mason University within the Elementary Education and Human Development and Family Science programs. Her research focuses on developmental and psychosocial influences on learning for marginalized children across PreK-12 schooling. Dr. Brown is a certified K-6 educator and taught for five years in the Washington DC and rural Maryland areas.

Rachael Eriksen Brown received her PhD in Mathematics Education from University of Georgia in 2009. She worked at the Knowles Teaching Initiative until 2014. In 2014 she was hired as an assistant professor by Penn State Abington to teach in the elementary education program as well as teach undergraduate general education mathematics courses. She writes and presents on mathematical knowledge for teaching, particularly around proportional reasoning, as well as professional development and community development with pre-service and in-service teachers of mathematics. Rachael is passionate about supporting teachers in engaging students in activities that encourage mathematical creativity and discussion.

Mary D. Burbank is the Assistant Dean for Teacher Education and Director of the Urban Institute for Teacher Education in the College of Education at the University of Utah. As a faculty member since 1994 she holds the rank of Clinical Professor, is a 2014 recipient of a University of Utah Diversity Award, a 2005 Distinguished Teaching Award, a 2002 College of Education Teaching Award, and service awards from the College of Education, University Alumni Association, and the community. Her teaching, research, and service interests examine pathways to higher education for under-represented students and families. She is the author/co-author of two books and has written multiple book chapters and peer reviewed research articles. She oversees accreditation for the university's teacher education programs.

Gretchen Butera is a Professor of Special Education in the Department of Curriculum and Instruction at Indiana University, Bloomington where she serves as the director of graduate licensure and masters program in Special Education. Dr. Butera conducts research in teacher preparation and curriculum in special education and is especially interested in schools in rural communities. She worked as a special educator for ten years before entering higher education.

Amanda R. Casto is a doctoral student at the University of North Carolina at Charlotte. She is a former elementary and middle school teacher. Her primary research interests include multicultural mathematics pedagogy and increasing underrepresented female students' interests and achievement in STEM.

Jennifer Castor, M.Ed., has been in education for 14 years. She taught for 13 years at the elementary level, grades ranging from second to fourth as well as literacy intervention. In 2010, she received her M.Ed. from University of Colorado, Boulder in Equity and Equality in Education with an emphasis in Linguistically Diverse Education. It was through this program that she discovered a passion for teaching the whole child and for cultivating community, specifically with family relationships. As a classroom teacher, Jennifer was able to mentor over 20 pre-service teachers which developed another passion. It was then that her transition into higher education began as she started teaching for the Early Childhood Education Master's Program at Colorado State University. She is now a Professional Development Collaborator and Instructor for the Center for Educator Preparation at Colorado State University. Currently, her professional development workshops include co-teaching for student teachers and licensed teachers as well as facilitating workshops for coaches of pre-service teachers.

Catherine Compton-Lilly is the John C. Hungerpiller Professor in the Department of Instruction and Teacher Education at the University of South Carolina. Dr. Compton-Lilly teaches courses in literacy studies and literacy education. She has a passion for helping teachers to support children in learning to read and write. Her interests include early reading and writing, student diversity, and working with families. Throughout her career, Dr. Compton-Lilly is a strong advocate for developing knowledgeable teachers that are committed to continual learning and improved practice. Dr. Compton-Lilly is the author/editor of several books and has published widely in educational journals. Dr. Compton-Lilly has authored articles in the Reading Research Quarterly, Research in the Teaching of English, The Reading Teacher, Journal of Early Childhood Literacy, Written Communication, and Language Arts. She engages in longitudinal research projects that last over long periods of time. Her interests include examining how time operates as a contextual factor in children's lives as they progress through school and construct their identities as students and readers. In an ongoing study, Dr. Compton-Lilly is following children from immigrant families from primary school through high school.

Basil Conway IV is a teacher educator at Columbus State University. He has taught middle and high school mathematics for ten years and received his MS in Statistical Science from Colorado State University and his BS, MS, and PhD from Auburn University in mathematics education. During his professional career he has presented at numerous local, regional, and national conferences on topics ranging from statistics, technology in statistics, differentiated mathematics instruction, and access to rigorous mathematics courses. His research interests are in statistics education, mathematical empowerment through effective teaching practices, and student opportunity-access to rich mathematics.

Donna Cooner, a former teacher and school administrator, currently serves as a professor of education at Colorado State University. She teaches and advises in the principal preparation Master of Education program and supervises doctoral students in educational leadership. Prior to her full time return to School of Education faculty in 2015, Dr. Cooner was the director of the teacher preparation program at Colorado State University for nine years. During her administrative career in educator preparation, Dr. Cooner served as a national Commissioner for the Council for the Accreditation of Educator Preparation (CAEP) and as an invited panelist for the Teacher Education Accreditation Council (TEAC). Her research agenda is focused on teacher and principal preparation for PK-12 schools. In addition to her research, Dr. Cooner is also the author of over twenty picture books and has also written children's television shows for PBS. Donna's debut novel, SKINNY, was named an ALA's Best Young Adult Fiction Award, BEA's Young Adult Buzz Book, and a Bankstreet College's Best Children's Book of the Year. Her book, CAN'T LOOK AWAY, was a Teen Choice Nominee and an ALA Top Pick for Reluctant Readers. The Texas Library Association selected Donna as a 2017 Spirit of Texas High School Featured Author (CAN'T LOOK AWAY) and as a 2014 Spirit of Texas High School Featured Author (SKINNY). Her books have been translated into Norwegian, Swedish, Russian and Finnish.

Leslie J. Couse (Ph.D., Syracuse University) is Executive Director of Engagement and Faculty Development, and Professor of Education at the University of New Hampshire. Her interest lies in preparing teachers to support the learning of all students through interdisciplinary collaboration with parents, teachers, service providers, and the community. Through community partnerships she researches preservice and in-service teacher education, technology supports in early education, leadership development, and faculty development in higher education. She is Principal Investigator for two U.S. Department of Education grant funded projects: the Teacher Residency for Rural Education Program out of the Office of Innovation and Improvement, and the Early Childhood Special Education Assistive Technology Project out of the Office of Special Education. Dr. Couse is co-editor of The Handbook of Early Childhood Teacher Education (Routledge, 2016), has served as guest editor for a special issue and as a member of the editorial board for the Journal of Early Childhood Teacher Education (JECTE).

Danielle Dani is an associate professor in the Department of Teacher Education at Ohio University, where she teaches courses in science education and curriculum and instruction. Her research investigates strategies for developing teacher knowledge, skills, and dispositions for teaching science.

Laurie U. deBettencourt, Ph.D., Professor, serves as the Program Lead for Special Education at Johns Hopkins School of Education. She oversees all masters' programs and certificates within the special education programs. Her recent research concentrates on the special education labor market and its implications for policymakers and educators. She has studied how Institutions of Higher Education partner with school districts to prepare, develop, and retain high quality special education teachers. In particular, she has focused most of her recent research efforts on improving the induction of beginning special education teachers into the classroom.

Derek Decker, Ph.D., is an assistant professor in the Center for Educator Preparation in the School of Education at Colorado State University. He is a coordinator in the master's plus teaching licensure program, instructs within the master's program, and supervises teacher candidates. Coming directly from the public school classroom as a teacher, Dr. Decker understands the importance of high quality teachers, teaching, and leadership. His scholarly interests center on the benefits of clinical practice where strong partnerships between PK-12 schools and teacher preparation programs flourish.

Janice A. Dole received her BA from the University of Massachusetts, Boston, and her MA and PhD from the University of Colorado. A former elementary and middle school teacher, she has held positions at the University of Denver, the Center for the Study of Reading at the University of Illinois, Champaign-Urbana, Michigan State University and is currently Professor at the University of Utah. She is a current member of the Reading Hall of Fame and was an Appointed Panel Member of the National Academy of Sciences, Committee on the Study of Teacher Preparation Programs, 2005-2010 and the RAND Reading Study Group, Office of Educational Research and Improvement, 2000-2002. Her current research interests include comprehension instruction, school reform in reading in urban low-income schools, and teacher preparation and professional development in literacy.

Jody Drager, M.Ed., has been in education for 23 years. She taught at the elementary level for 16 years in Poudre School District in Fort Collins, Colorado. She is passionate about children and supporting their growth and learning both academically and socially. Jody was hired at Colorado State University (CSU) in 2011 as the Student Teaching Coordinator. She enjoyed supporting teacher candidates and mentor teachers as well as building relationships with district leaders in that role for 5 years. She completed her M.Ed. in Education Sciences in addition to Principal Licensure in 2017. The skills she gained through those programs, in addition to her entire career, prepared her for her current role. She is an instructor in the Early Childhood Program as well as the Career Development Coordinator and School District Liaison for the Center for Educator Preparation at CSU. Jody's focus is on co-teaching as an effective method of preparing teacher candidates for the ever-changing field, providing ongoing authentic professional development for mentor teachers and best meeting the needs of all PK-12 students. She believes relationships are at the core of all work in education.

Jodi Dunham is an assistant professor in the School of Education at Shawnee State University. Having been a high school mathematics teacher for 18 years, her doctoral work focused on educational leadership and mathematics education. She teaches introductory education courses, elementary mathematics courses, and mathematics methods courses in the undergraduate program, as well as data analysis courses in the graduate program. She is a former District Director of the Ohio Council of Teachers of Mathematics (2014-2017), a former National Board Certified Teacher (2001-2011), and a facilitator for Ohio's RESA program. Her educational interests include the clinical model of supervision, cooperative learning, creative instructional strategies, and technology implementation in the classroom.

Cassie Cook Eatmon is a doctoral student in mathematics education leadership at George Mason University. Her experience in elementary and secondary education as a mathematics teacher with a specialization in working with bilingual students inspires her research interests in professional development for pre-service and in-service teachers to support English learners in the mathematics classroom.

Belinda Edwards is an associate professor at Kennesaw State University where she teaches mathematics and mathematics education courses at the graduate and undergraduate levels. Her research focuses on issues of access and equity in mathematics education.

Ruby Ellis is a doctoral candidate in Secondary Mathematics Education and a Holmes Scholar at Auburn University. Prior to coming to Auburn, Mrs. Ellis had a variety of teaching experiences, ranging from middle and high school mathematics to an adjunct instructor in the Department of Science and Mathematics at Talladega College. Currently, she serves as a Graduate Teaching and Research assistant in the Department of Curriculum and Teaching at Auburn University. This position allows her to teach undergraduate pre-service teaching methods courses, supervise interns, and assist with the data collection and analysis for several research projects. Her research interests include mathematical action technology integration, teacher pedagogical beliefs and practices, and professional development.

Andrea M. Emerson, PhD, graduated from Clemson University in May 2018 with a degree in Curriculum and Instruction. Dr. Emerson's research focuses on play and family engagement in early childhood education. She has been co-directing a study abroad for education majors in Italy since 2017. She will begin an Assistant Professor position in the Fall of 2018 at Western Oregon University.

David R. Erickson is Professor and mathematics education faculty member in the Phyllis J. Washington College of Education and Human Sciences at the University of Montana. His research focuses on teacher change and the preparation of teachers of secondary mathematics including investigations into Mathematics Teachers' Circles, NSF Noyce Learning Assistants Become Teachers (DUE 1136412), and Mathematics and Science Partnership Leadership in Montana mathematics and science. For 24 years, he has placed future secondary teachers of mathematics in paired placements during the semester before student teaching, and now for the past five years, also pairing student teachers in their final clinical internship when possible.

Mathew Felton-Koestler is an associate professor in the Department of Teacher Education at Ohio University, where he teaches courses in mathematics education and curriculum and instruction. His scholarship focuses on teachers' beliefs and practices with respect to addressing issues of equity, diversity, and social justice in the mathematics classroom.

Nancy Fordham is an Associate Professor in the School of Teaching & Learning at Bowling Green State University. As assistant school director, she oversees edTPA and other assessment components of teacher education. Her research focuses on literacy, teacher education, and middle childhood education.

Wendy Fothergill, Ph.D., has been an educator for 21 years. She has taught and led at all levels within the PK-12 system. She taught high school language arts, was a middle school media specialist, was an elementary principal, and was a district-level administrator. While serving as an elementary principal, she began instructing as an adjunct at Colorado State University and earned her Ph. D. In 2013, she was hired on full-time to be an advisor, instructor and program coordinator for the Center for Educator Preparation. Her research is focused on mentorship for and retention of principal licensure students in their first years as instructional leaders.

Heidi Frederiksen, Ph.D., has been in education for 27 years. She taught secondary mathematics and science for 16 years before becoming an administrator, which she did for 5 years as a summer school principal for 800+ students. Her passion is educating all children and knows that it takes great teachers to do so. In her doctoral studies in educational leadership, starting in 2003, she focused on teacher dispositions and how they develop in pre-service teachers and how setting (urban/suburban) affects dispositional development. In 2008, she was hired at Colorado State University as an Instructor and Key Advisor in the School for Teacher Education and Principal Preparation, and then as an Assistant Professor in 2010, taking on leadership roles as Interim Associate Director, and most recently, the Co-Director of the Center for Educator Preparation at Colorado State University. Her current research areas of interest include dispositional development of pre-service teachers, how dispositions affect preparation and persistence in education, and school district induction and mentoring programs that support educators new to the field.

Terrie McLaughlin Galanti is a doctoral student in mathematics education leadership at George Mason University. Her experiences as a systems engineer and high school mathematics teacher have converged to inspire her research interest in preparing teacher leaders and fostering mathematical readiness for STEM undergraduate study.

Melissa M. Goldsmith is a research analyst at the Urban Institute for Teacher Education in the College of Education at the University of Utah. She has a Ph.D. in Political Science from the University of Utah and a master's degree in survey research from the University of Connecticut. She applies her knowledge of survey methods and data analysis for the purposes of measuring program outcomes and meeting accreditation standards for the Teacher Education Licensure Program at the University of Utah. She has published in the area of local political involvement, immigration, and educator preparation.

A. Lin Goodwin is Professor and Dean of the Faculty of Education at the University of Hong Kong. She holds the Evenden Foundation Chair Professor of Education at Teachers College, Columbia University, New York, and is immediate past Vice President of the American Educational Research Association—Division K: Teaching and Teacher Education. Her latest book, co-authored Ee-Ling Low (National Institute of Education, Singapore) and Linda Darling-Hammond (Learning Policy Institute, Washington, DC), is titled, Empowered educators in Singapore: How high-performing systems shape teaching quality.

Lois A. Groth is an Associate Professor in the Graduate School of Education at George Mason University in Fairfax, VA. Her teaching and research interests include literacy methods, action research in PDS settings, critical reflection and teacher language. She facilitates in Mason's Professional Development Schools Network.

Heidi L. Hallman is a Professor of English education at the University of Kansas. Her research interests include studying "at risk" students' literacy learning as well as how prospective English teachers are prepared to teach in diverse school contexts. Dr. Hallman is co-author of the books Secondary English Teacher Education in the United States (Bloomsbury, 2018), Millennial Teachers: Learning to Teach in Uncertain Times (Routledge, 2017), and Community Fieldwork in Teacher Education: Theory and Practice (Routledge, 2015). Her work has been published in English Education, Teacher Education Quarterly, Equity & Excellence in Education, Journal of Adolescent & Adult Literacy, English Journal, and Teaching Education, among others. In 2010, Hallman received the Conference on English Education's (CEE) Research Initiative Grant for her research on prospective teachers' work with homeless youth.

Allyson Hallman-Thrasher is an associate professor of mathematics education jointly appointed in the departments of Teacher Education and Mathematics at Ohio University in Athens, Ohio. She teaches methods and content courses for preservice elementary and secondary teachers. Her research analyzes ways to support preservice teachers in learning to engage their K-12 students in rich mathematical discussions and cognitively demand mathematical tasks.

Lisa Harrison is an associate professor of Middle Childhood Education (MCE) at Ohio University where she also serves as the MCE program coordinator. She teaches general methods courses in middle childhood education and teacher action research. Her research interest focuses on issues of equity and social justice in middle level education and teacher preparation. She also explores racial identity construction and the lived experiences of African American young adolescent girls.

Loretta W. Harvey holds the B.S. in Natural Science from Shawnee State University in Portsmouth, Ohio. She holds a M.S. in Biology/Botany from Marshall University in Huntington, WV. Loretta will receive her Ph.D. in Science Education in 2018 from Ohio University in Athens, Ohio. Currently she is a visiting faculty member in the School of Education at Shawnee State University, where she teaches undergraduate courses in secondary, middle childhood, and early childhood education, as well as courses in technology and science. Her research investigates strategies for developing university- school clinical partnerships. Loretta is additionally interested in promoting pre-service teacher development through a focus on reflection, discourse, and clinical practice.

Colleen Horn is the Partnership Coordinator for TR@TC2. She taught in classrooms for more than twelve years, working with students with disabilities and newcomer students. She also worked as a staff developer and graduate level instructor. Colleen received her MA from Roehampton University, London and her Ed. D from Trinity College, Dublin.

Pier A. Junor Clarke, a graduate from OISE of University of Toronto, is a Clinical Associate Professor of Mathematics Education at Georgia State University (GSU), Atlanta, Georgia. Currently, she is the coordinator of the Initial Teacher Preparation Program for secondary mathematics education and the mathematics education concentration of the Doctor of Education – Curriculum & Instruction degree. Dr. Junor Clarke is also the Team Leader for the GSU - Mathematics Teacher Education Partnership of a national reform for secondary mathematics teacher preparation programs. As co-principal investigator on several awarded National Science Foundation grants that supported her work, many secondary mathematics teachers received support from preparation to induction. Her research interests include the development and sustainability of effective professional learning communities that support secondary mathematics teachers in urban and other settings.

Rebecca Justeson is a professor and director of the School of Education at California State University, Chico. She previously served for many years as the director of the Rural Teacher Residency program, as well as serving an interim term as director of the Residency in Secondary Education (RiSE) program, both blended credential and master's degree programs within the School of Education. In addition to her experience with field-based models of teacher preparation, she teaches and provides professional development in the areas of both literacy and resilience development. Prior to arriving at CSU, Chico, Justeson served as both a reading specialist and a bilingual elementary teacher. Her research interests include field-based approaches to teacher preparation, as well as understanding/developing resilience in all populations. Rebecca studied positive psychology in the MAPP Program at the University of Pennsylvania, and has also earned degrees in Educational Psychology and Bilingual/Multicultural Education. In addition, she has experience as a lead trainer, serving in that role as a co-teaching trainer in her region, and as a master resilience trainer with both the United States Army and the University of Texas system.

Michael Kopish is an Assistant Professor of Teacher Education at Ohio University where he teaches graduate and undergraduate courses in social studies education and global education. His research interests include service learning, civic engagement, global citizenship education, and social studies education.

Susi Long is a Professor in the Department of Instruction and Teacher Education at the University of South Carolina. Her research focuses on culturally relevant, decolonizing, and equity pedagogies in early childhood literacy and teacher education. Her books include Tensions and Triumphs in the Early Years of Teaching, Supporting Students in a Time of Core Standards, Many Pathways to Literacy, and Courageous Leadership in Early Childhood Education, and "We've been doing it your way long enough": Choosing the Culturally Relevant Classroom. Susi teaches courses in literacy methods, culturally relevant pedagogies, linguistic pluralism, language acquisition in diverse communities, and critical qualitative methodologies. She is the past Chair of the Board of Trustees of the National Council of Teachers of English Research Foundation, and the 2013 Early Childhood Education Assembly's Early Literacy Educator of the Year. She is a mentor in NCTE's Cultivating New Voices Among Scholars of Color initiative and co-founded the NCTE Early Childhood Assembly's Professional Dyads and Culturally Relevant Teaching project.

Christine Lotter is an Associate Professor of Science Education at The University of South Carolina. Her research involves investigating science teacher professional development and teacher beliefs as well as research into improving secondary teacher education.

Meir Muller has earned rabbinical ordination as well as a doctorate in the area of early childhood education. Dr. Muller serves as an assistant professor in the College of Education at the University of South Carolina. In 2016 Dr. Muller was awarded the Early Childhood Teacher Educator Award by National Association for Early Childhood Teacher Education. His research interests include cultural relevant pedagogy, anti-racist pedagogy, constructivist theory, Jewish education, and pre-service teacher education. Dr. Muller is also in his 26th year as head of the Cutler Jewish Day School, a NAEYC accredited school for children birth through the fifth grade. Dr. Muller has lectured across America and delivered a paper in Israel for the International Research Group on Jewish Education in the Early Years.

Tim Murnen is an associate professor in the School of Teaching & Learning at Bowling Green State University. He is engaged in literacy research and outreach in the Martha Gesling Weber Reading Center, where he is director of Literacy in the Park. His research focuses on pre-service and in-service teachers' professional development in reading and writing assessment and intervention.

Michele Myers is a Clinical Associate Professor and the Coordinator for the Elementary Education Master of Arts in Teaching Program at the University of South Carolina (USC) where she has been a faculty member since 2014. Michele earned a BA in early childhood education from Clemson University, a Master's degree in Administration and Supervision from Charleston Southern University, an Education Specialist degree in Teaching from USC, and a doctorate in Language and Literacy from USC in 2013. Michele is a member of the National Council of Teachers of English, Center for the Expansion of Language and Thinking (CELT) member, the Professional Dyad for Culturally Relevant Teaching member, board member of the Whole Language Umbrella (WLU) and the chair for the Early Childhood Education Assembly. She has several academic publications. In addition, Dr. Myers works as a consultant, providing professional development for teachers and parents on a variety of topics.

Sarah Nagro is an assistant professor at George Mason University in the Graduate School of Education where her research focuses on determining best practices for teacher education. Specifically, she focuses on understanding effective approaches to preparing profession-ready teachers through meaningful field-based experiences that emphasize reflection, self-evaluation, and professional buy-in.

Jennifer Oloff-Lewis is associate professor of curriculum and instruction in the School of Education. She was awarded a Ph.D. in curriculum and instruction with an emphasis in mathematics education at the Mary Lou Fulton Institute and Graduate School of Education at Arizona State University in 2009. Dr. Oloff-Lewis has worked in the K-12 setting for over 10 years, with an emphasis on middle school mathematics and gifted education. At Chico State, she teaches courses on mathematics methods for credential candidates and master's degree courses.

Amy B. Palmeri is an Assistant Professor of the Practice of Early Childhood and Elementary Education. Her teaching and research interests focus on the development of scientific and historical disciplinary practices and related pedagogical knowledge and skills in pre-service teachers. The mentoring of pre-service teachers in both subject specific practicum and student teaching is central to her curricular/program design work, teaching, and research. She views the mentoring of pre-service teachers in their fieldwork as the most authentic context where theory, research, and practice intersect.

Audra Parker, PhD, is an Associate Professor and Academic Program Coordinator in Elementary Education at George Mason University. She teaches courses in elementary methods and management and supervises interns at a Professional Development School. Her areas of research center on clinical teacher education and young adolescents' school experiences.

Christopher Parrish received his Ph.D. in mathematics education from Auburn University and is currently an assistant professor of mathematics education at the University of South Alabama.

Seth A. Parsons, PhD, is an associate professor in the College of Education and Human Development at George Mason University. He teaches courses in the Elementary Education, Literacy, and Research Methods program areas. His research focuses on teachers' instructional adaptations, teacher education and development, and students' motivation and engagement.

Anthony Pellegrino is assistant professor of secondary, social science education at the University of Tennessee, Knoxville. His research interests include cognition in history education, youth civic engagement, and clinical experiences in educator preparation.

Jeanne A. Peter is a Lecturer in the Department of Teaching and Learning at Peabody College of Vanderbilt University. She teaches literacy methods courses and supervises preservice teachers in the early field experiences and student teaching. Her scholarly interests focus on the developmental trajectories of preservice teachers, supervision of field experiences, and the intersection of theory, research and practice in teaching.

Stacey Plotner is a former high school teacher and current University of South Carolina graduate student in the PhD in Teaching and Learning Program. She has been an instructor for the University course described in the chapter as well as a Professional Development School liaison at Dreher High School.

Drew Polly is a professor in the Department of Reading and Elementary Education at the University of North Carolina at Charlotte. His research agenda focuses on examining how to support the implementation of technology and standards-based pedagogies. More information can be found at: http://drewpolly.org/me.

Kristine E. Pytash is an Associate Professor in Teaching, Learning and Curriculum Studies at Kent State University's College of Education, Health, and Human Services where she co-directs the secondary Integrated Language Arts teacher preparation program. Her research focuses on the literacy practices of youth in alternative schools and juvenile detention facilities. In addition, she studies disciplinary writing and how to prepare teachers to teach writing. An underlying theme across all her lines of inquiry is how technology significantly influences young adults' literacy practices and their literacy instruction.

Emilie Mitescu Reagan is an assistant professor of Assessment and Policy in the University of New Hampshire Department of Education. Emilie began her career in education as a fifth grade teacher in Philadelphia, PA. Her research focuses on teacher education policy and practice, with an emphasis on teacher education for social justice. Emilie is currently the Principal Investigator on a Spencer Foundation grant and Co-Principal Investigator on the U.S. Department of Education Teacher Quality Partnership grant, Teacher Residency for Rural Education.

Nicole Miller Rigelman, EdD, is a professor of mathematics education in the Department of Curriculum and Instruction at Portland State University. Her current research interests lie in mathematics teacher preparation and professional development, influence of curriculum materials on student and teacher learning, mathematical reasoning and problem solving as it relates to standards implementation and assessment.

Andrea K. Rorrer is a Professor in the Department of Educational Leadership and Policy Studies, Director of the Utah Education Policy Center, and Associate Dean in the College of Education. She has over 29 years of experience in education, including a policy analyst and research associate in Texas and a school administrator and a classroom teacher in Virginia. Her research focuses on leadership, organizational, and policy change at the school, district, and state. Her scholarship includes publications in Educational Administration Quarterly, Theory into Practice, Educational Policy, the Journal of Educational Policy, Journal of Special Education Leadership, Journal of Cases in Educational Leadership, Peabody Journal of Education, Journal of Research on Educational Leadership and Economics of Education Review, and the UCEA Review, among other publications. She is the 2006 recipient of the Jack A. Culbertson Award and the 2008 Research Award in the College of Education at the University of Utah.

Jennifer Roth, Ph.D., is an assistant principal at Fort Collins High School in Colorado. She is deeply invested in the long-standing partnership between her school district and Colorado State University to support their successful teacher preparation program. Her 30-year career includes experiences as a teacher, university instructor, and school administrator. Roth has presented nationally about the professional development school model and effective clinical partnerships.

Angela Roybal Lewis, Ph.D., is an Assistant Professor at Colorado State University in the School of Education, Center for Educator Preparation. She has dedicated her career to the preschool years as an early childhood special education teacher and as a general education preschool teacher. She earned her social sciences degree from the University of Northern Colorado in 2000 and her doctorate degree in curriculum and instruction from the University of Wyoming in 2017. She teaches undergraduate and graduate early childhood professional education courses and research methods. She collaborates with a network of infant through third grade professional development school settings to provide early childhood education teacher candidate's opportunities to explore and develop: (1) evidence-based curricula and instructional strategies, (2) inquiry-oriented learning and assessments, and (3) reflective teaching practices. She is interested in researching early childhood Praxis and teacher preparation.

Lawrence J. Ruich is a Clinical Assistant Professor at Indiana University Purdue University in Columbus, Indiana. He serves as the Director of Special Education and is a former junior high school special education teacher. He supports teacher candidates in the development of pedagogical knowledge and skill that promotes social justice in the classroom.

Tom Schram is Associate Professor and Director of the Division of Educator Preparation in the Department of Education at the University of New Hampshire. He began his career as an elementary school teacher in rural Wyoming, and has over thirty years of experience in education ranging from K-6 teaching to higher education teaching, research, and administration. His scholarly interests encompass teacher education program development and policies, rural teacher education and community engagement, school-university partnerships, educational anthropology, and field-based qualitative research design and methods.

Ann Schulte is the graduate coordinator in the School of Education and a Faculty Fellow for Rural Partnerships in the office of Civic Engagement. She has taught a variety of teacher education courses, with an emphasis on social justice, place-conscious education and rural contexts. Professor Schulte has advised and supervised students in the Multiple Subject, Rural Teacher Residency, and in the MA in Education programs. She also served on the Statewide CSU Academic Senate. Schulte is an advocate and consultant for Rural Schools Collaborative, an organization that works to strengthen the bonds between rural schools and communities. Schulte is a self-study scholar and has co-edited a text with Dr. Bernadette Walker-Gibbs titled Self-studies in Rural Teacher Education (Springer, 2015). In addition, Schulte has authored a chapter in the 2004 The International Handbook of Self-Study of Teaching and Teacher Education Practices and is the author of Seeking Integrity in Teacher Education (Springer, 2009). In 2011, Dr. Schulte was awarded the Taking it to the Classroom Award and the Outstanding Teacher Award in 2011-12.

Juliana Searle received her M.Ed. in Education and Human Resource Studies, Counseling and Career Development, from Colorado State University in 2013. She has served in various roles related to advising and instructing pre-service teachers in the Center for Educator Preparation (CEP) at Colorado State University (CSU) since 2011, and was hired full-time in 2013. She is currently the Student Teaching Coordinator and Key Advisor for the M.Ed. and Teacher Licensure program at CSU. Her interests center on recruiting diverse teachers into the profession and supporting the next generation of educators entering the profession. She was involved in initial efforts of CSU's implementation of co-teaching during student teaching, and she continues to be involved in CEP's work to support pre-service and in-service teachers implement effective co-teaching strategies.

Ruthmae Sears is an associate professor for mathematics education, in the Department of Teaching and Learning, at the University of South Florida. Currently, she coordinates the Beginning and Intermediate Algebra Mathematics courses, and the Masters program for mathematics education. Her research interests include technology, curriculum issues, and reasoning and proof. She is currently the principal investigator for the NSF-IUSE collaborative grant entitled, Attaining Excellence in Secondary Mathematics Clinical Experiences with a Lens on Equity. Dr. Sears is also a co-principal investigator for the Robert Noyce Teacher Scholarship Program.

Ann Sebald, Ed.D., has been in education for 22 years. She co-taught at the elementary level working as both a general education and deaf education teacher. In 2002 she went back for her terminal degree to explore self-determination and language development among children who are deaf. She worked for the National Center for Low-Incidence Disabilities as a project manager, was hired as Assistant Professor for the University of Northern Colorado working at the Denver campus employing an apprenticeship model to prepare educators for urban settings, and has most recently held the position of Co-Director of the Center for Educator Preparation at Colorado State University. Her current research areas of interest include the Cognitive Apprenticeship Model through the continuum of teacher preparation: reviewing the effectiveness of apprenticeship and mentoring for the preparation of teacher candidates through co-teaching, and school district induction and mentoring programs that support educators new to the field.

Wynn Shooter is an Assistant Director for the Utah Education Policy Center where he works primarily on education program evaluations. Much of his work involves serving out-school-time programs and community partners. Wynn has over 18 years of experience designing, implementing, and studying educational experiences. Prior to joining the Utah Education Policy Center team, his research and field work focused on implementing principles of experiential education to achieve a variety of learning and developmental outcomes.

Arsenio F. Silva is a doctoral student in Literacy, Language, & Culture in the Department of Education and Human Development at Clemson University. Mr. Silva is a former secondary English educator with experience teaching secondary students in Italy and Kenya as well as experience designing and implementing professional development for in-service teachers in Tanzania.

Kimberly Smoak is a social studies teacher at Dutch Fork High School in Irmo, South Carolina. Before returning to the classroom in 2016, she held a Clinical Faculty position at the University of South Carolina in the Department of Instruction & Teacher Education.

Erica Sponberg is a doctoral candidate in the Department of Curriculum and Instruction at Kansas State University. She is also the Elementary Placement Coordinator in the Office of Field Experience and supervises Block C students using the digitally-mediated supervision system.

Cerissa Stevenson, Ph.D., has been in education for 18 years. She taught early elementary and literacy intervention for nearly a decade. After completed her Ph.D. in Education and Human Resource Studies with a concentration in School Leadership, she was hired at Colorado State University. Currently she serves at the Early Childhood Education, Teacher Licensure graduate and undergraduate program coordinator. Her current research areas of interest include clinical practice in teacher education, professional development school models, and teacher preparation.

Jamalee (Jami) Stone is an associate professor of mathematics education in the College of Education and Behavioral Sciences at Black Hills State University (BHSU) in Spearfish, SD. Her research interests include equity and mathematics education, and pre-service students' co-planning and co-teaching during their clinical experiences. Prior to earning her Ed.D. in Educational Studies from the University of Nebraska-Lincoln, Jami taught 8-12 mathematics in Nebraska for 21 years.

Marilyn E. Strutchens is an Emily R. and Gerald S. Leischuck Endowed Professor, Mildred Cheshire Fraley Distinguished Professor, and coordinator of secondary mathematics education at Auburn University, Auburn, AL. Her research focuses on equity issues, clinical experiences for secondary teacher candidates, and teacher change in mathematics education. She is an editor and author of several mathematics educational publications. In fact, she served on the writing group for AMTE's Standards for Preparing Teachers of Mathematics. Currently, she is a member of the National Council of Teachers of Mathematics Board of Directors, an Advisory Committee Member of the National Science Foundation's Directorate for Education and Human Resources, and an Advisory Board-Member for the AAAS initiative --Stimulating Research and Innovation in STEM Teacher Preservice Education, funded by the NSF Robert Noyce Teacher Scholarships Program. Dr. Strutchens served as president of the Association of Mathematics Teacher Educators (2011 -2013) and a member of the Executive Board of Directors for the Conference Board of Mathematical Sciences (2012 -2014). Recently, she received the 2017 Judith Jacobs Lectureship from the Association of Mathematics Teacher Educators.

Laura Vernikoff is a doctoral candidate in Curriculum and Teaching at Teachers College, Columbia University. She has also been a special education teacher in New York City. Her research interests include urban education, inclusive education, and teacher education.

Rajeev Virmani is an Assistant Professor of Mathematics Education in the Department of Curriculum Studies and Secondary Education at Sonoma State University. Virmani has focused on providing rich learning experiences for preservice and inservice teachers to improve their skills and knowledge for teaching mathematics and ultimately support student learning. His research and teaching centers on eliciting and attending to student thinking. Virmani collaborates with teacher educators and practitioners to develop learning environments that provide opportunities to learn about teaching practices through pedagogies that approximate practice. In particular, he uses rehearsals of instructional activities with teachers to engage in and reflect upon equitable pedagogical practices, student thinking, and mathematics content. He has extended this work to embed mathematics methods courses in school classrooms in which teachers have authentic interactions with students and build upon student mathematical, cultural, and linguistic strengths.

Patrice Waller, PhD, is an assistant professor at California State University, Fullerton. Dr. Waller's research interests include improving the teaching and learning of mathematics in grades K-12 and in undergraduate mathematics, as well as teaching and learning mathematics abroad.

Joanna Weaver is an Assistant Professor in the School of Teaching & Learning at Bowling Green State University. Her research focuses on pre-service and in-service teachers' professional development in reading and writing assessment and intervention.

Andrea Weinberg, Ph.D., a former special education teacher, is an assistant professor in the Mary Lou Fulton Teachers College. Her scholarship and teaching are grounded in her commitment to enhancing teacher quality, improving teacher retention and satisfaction, and elevating teaching as a profession within universities, across society, and among educators themselves. Using collaborative and interdisciplinary approaches, Weinberg examines practices that have the potential to increase the effectiveness and retention of early-career teachers, and critically analyzes systems or practices that do not. She strives to harness the power of intellectual curiosity to ignite passion in teacher candidates—a passion that will enable them to not only excel and persevere in the profession, but become fervent advocates for their students and communities as well as for the profession of teaching.

Tracy Weston, Ph.D., is an assistant professor of Education Studies at Middlebury College. She leads the elementary licensure program, teaches the elementary methods courses, and works with student teachers. Dr. Weston is a mathematics teacher educator who studies mathematical knowledge in teaching, teacher noticing, and coherence in pre-service teacher education. She began her career in education by learning to teach in a professional development school setting, and since then has been interested in field-based approaches to teacher education. Currently, she is working to establish the recently announced professional development school between Addison Central School District and Middlebury College.

Beth Lucas White, Ed.S., is a clinical instructor in elementary education at the University of South Carolina. She teaches a literacy methods course and a reading assessment course, coordinates the undergraduate program for elementary education, and serves as the faculty liaison for an elementary school as part of the Professional Development Schools Network. Before joining the university, Beth served as a literacy coach in elementary schools and taught middle school.

Jennifer Whitfield is an Instructional Assistant Professor and Assistant Head in the Department of Mathematics and is the Director for the aggieTEACH Program at Texas A&M University. Her research interests include math teacher preparation, secondary teacher induction and retention, and student success in post-secondary mathematics courses.

Rob Wieman is an associate professor in the STEAM Education department at Rowan University in Glassboro, New Jersey. His research interests include professional collaboration, instructional improvement in secondary mathematics, and practice-based teacher education. Before entering academia, Rob worked for many years as a math teacher and instructional coach in public high schools in New York

City. Rob is the author, with Fran Arbaugh, of Success from the Start: Your First Years Teaching Secondary Mathematics, and is the principal investigator (with Jill Perry and Karen Heinz, co-PIs) of the South Jersey Mathematics Ambassador Project, a collaborative effort between Rowan and six districts in Southern New Jersey to develop lasting capacity for instructional improvement in mathematics.

Theresa Wills is an Assistant Professor of Mathematics Education at George Mason University. She teaches and mentors students in the art of coaching and mathematics leadership. She is a former mathematics coach in elementary and secondary schools, and a formal general technology coach in the middle schools. Her research focuses on mathematical discourse, online synchronous instruction, and implementation of rich tasks in the math class.

A. Jill Wood is an Instructor in the Department of Curriculum and Instruction within the College of Education at Kansas State University. She teaches social studies methods courses at both the elementary and secondary level and serves as the Block C Coordinator for the department. Additionally, Ms. Wood coordinates the use of video for the supervision of graduate student interns in the MAT program who are placed outside of the local network of school partners.

Maika J. Yeigh is an Assistant Professor in the Graduate School of Education at Portland State University where she works with teacher candidates at the secondary level. Her research interests include clinical practice and teacher induction.

Jan A. Yow, PhD, is an associate professor at the University of South Carolina. Before joining the university, Dr. Yow taught high school mathematics and earned National Board Certification. Her research focuses on developing mathematics teacher leaders to strengthen mathematics teaching and learning for all students.

Kristien Zenkov, PhD, is Professor of Education and the Academic Program Coordinator for the Secondary Education (SEED) program at George Mason University (GMU). He is the author and editor of more than one hundred fifty articles and book chapters and seven books, focusing on teacher education, literacy pedagogy and curricula, social justice education, school-university partnerships, and Professional Development Schools. Dr. Zenkov is a long-time boundary-spanning educator and school-university partnership facilitator, currently collaborating as a co-teacher at TC Williams High School in Alexandria, Virginia and conducting numerous project-based clinical experiences with youths and preservice and in-service teachers at TC Williams and schools throughout Northern Virginia. He co-directs "Through Students' Eyes," a Youth Participatory Action Research and photovice project through which youths document with photographs and writings what they believe about citizenship, justice, school, and literacy.

Index

A

action research 70, 100-101, 213, 216-217, 220, 222-224, 229, 233, 422, 637

administration 5, 33, 155, 224, 472, 478, 480-481, 650

administrator 77, 97, 99, 196-197, 218, 224, 471, 473-476, 478-481, 492, 652

ambitious instruction 322-324, 326, 335, 338, 340-342, 344

B

Beebot 427, 432, 437, 445

C

CAEP Standards 155, 640, 653

classroom observation 559

clinical educator 122-135, 141, 148, 153, 457, 461-462, 464-467

clinical model of teacher education 118, 141

clinical partnerships 3-5, 24, 92, 142, 146-148, 150-151, 153-154, 156-158, 368, 375

clinical practice 1-3, 5, 7, 9-13, 18-21, 23-24, 31, 33, 90-94, 97-100, 107-108, 118-119, 123, 134, 141, 146, 152, 154, 157-159, 170-171, 192, 199-200, 207, 257, 369, 372, 398, 451, 467, 472

Cognitive Demand of a Task 445

cohort model 15, 19, 79, 224, 233, 310

collaborative mentoring 117-118, 120-121, 133-135, 141

Common Core 175, 227, 323, 395, 398-399, 419, 428

Common Core State Standards for Mathematics (CCSS-M) 395, 419

community-based field experiences 348-354, 356, 359, 363-364

community of practice 119-120, 134-135, 141, 158, 207, 472-473, 475, 478, 488, 589

Community of Teachers 587-589, 593, 595, 603, 607

community partnerships 349

competencies 7, 33, 66, 73, 81, 242, 305, 519, 525-528, 530-531, 534, 537, 589-590, 592, 596

contexts 4, 32, 34, 48, 50, 56-57, 70, 77, 79-80, 82-83, 89-95, 103-104, 106, 116, 133, 154, 170, 213-215, 225-228, 256, 261, 269, 273, 293, 301, 317, 323, 325, 343, 350, 370, 372, 375-376, 396, 413, 422, 454, 475, 497-499, 518, 551, 565, 578, 591, 615, 630, 637, 640-641, 646, 649-650, 652

co-planning and co-teaching 33, 38, 40-43, 47, 52, 57, 62, 136, 220-221

co-teaching 13, 17-19, 31-33, 38, 40-47, 51-52, 57, 62, 98, 121-122, 133-134, 136, 193-194, 196-197, 204, 207, 213, 216, 220-221, 223-224, 229, 233, 264, 368, 373, 383, 548

co-teaching during student teaching 17, 19, 31

critical friend 641-646, 651, 654

cultural competence 236-243, 248-249, 251-253

Culturally and Linguistically Diverse Learners 298

culturally relevant pedagogy 241, 264, 309, 316, 348, 454

D

democratic 21, 40, 102

E

early field experience 471-472, 486-488, 492, 545

Education Preparation Program (EPP) 163

Education Specialist 217, 234

educative feedback 495, 497, 499, 503, 509

Millennials 543, 546-547

mutually beneficial 3, 18, 88-90, 94, 101, 116, 118, 141, 150, 152, 154, 156-157, 192-194, 196-197, 205-208, 473

N

network improvement community 34, 62

number talk 426-427, 430-431, 433-434, 436-438, 440, 446, 449, 617

O

online 45-46, 48, 95, 252, 304, 381, 414-415, 427, 448, 462, 474, 535-536, 542-544, 551, 558, 560, 636, 640-642

P

paired placement 32, 38, 40, 48-50, 52-57, 62

pedagogical content knowledge 33, 120, 132-133, 135, 141, 397, 615-616, 636-638

pedagogies of teacher education 614

performance standards 88, 520, 537-538

place-based education 265

play 15, 21, 57, 98, 106, 128, 143, 153, 181, 201, 259, 262, 265-266, 289, 330, 333, 336, 360, 420, 428, 432, 434-436, 438, 446, 499, 600, 617, 630-631

portfolio 171, 588, 590-592, 594, 596, 606, 608, 611

post-observation conference 495, 497, 500, 502-503, 506-508

practice-based teacher education 120, 122, 452-454, 467-468, 630-631

practicum 44, 65, 192-193, 198, 240, 322, 324-326, 333, 341-343, 471, 473-474, 476-478, 481-482, 485-486, 488-489, 552, 594, 636-639, 653

practicum experiences 65, 240, 486, 639

praxis 19, 21-22, 24, 68, 313-314, 542, 548

preservice teacher 45-46, 71, 80, 90-91, 97, 103-104, 116, 151, 153, 168, 187, 203, 240-243, 247-248, 250, 280, 286-287, 291, 295, 298-299, 303, 307, 314, 317, 484, 495-499, 502, 508-509, 511, 613, 637

Preservice teacher education 91, 151, 168, 187, 317, 498-499, 511

pre-service teachers 11, 13, 31, 33, 182, 215-216, 281, 296, 302, 304, 308, 322, 325, 342, 349, 352, 359, 376, 420, 422, 445, 451-457, 460-468, 546-548, 551, 557, 560, 635-636, 639, 653

Preservice Teacher Supervision 495, 497

principal preparation 12-13, 15-17

Professional Development School Model 14, 18, 31, 146

Professional Development Schools (PDS) 1, 3, 6, 14, 18, 31, 49, 89-90, 92, 116, 118, 142, 146, 467-468, 473, 492, 544

program coherence 171, 177

Q

quality teaching 19, 88, 144, 518, 529, 535-538

R

reflection activities 565-568, 571-578, 580, 586

Reflection Rubric 586

reflective ability 565, 567-568, 572, 574-578, 586

reflective practice 101, 120, 193, 195, 199, 205-206, 565-568, 572, 574-577, 580, 586, 642, 651

rehearsals 424, 439, 499, 613, 617-619, 621-622, 625-626, 629-631

Research Action Cluster 34, 62

residency 149-150, 213-214, 216-220, 224, 228-229, 234, 256-261, 265-267, 270-271, 467-468, 472, 489

rural 6, 14, 121, 135, 172, 213-217, 219, 224-230, 234, 256-260, 266-272, 307, 351, 380, 454, 474

rural education 215, 226, 257-258, 260, 266

S

SAMR 543, 550-551

School-Based Teacher Educator (SBTE) 163

school placement 227, 257, 299

school-university partnerships 89-94, 101, 106, 108, 116, 118, 134-136, 141, 193, 467

secondary education 90, 94, 101, 108, 228, 281, 372, 473, 525

secondary mathematics 34-35, 37, 39-43, 47-48, 50, 53, 55, 57, 63, 67, 71, 80, 127, 258, 322, 326, 371-374, 376, 395-399, 405, 415-416, 419, 613, 617

secondary mathematics teacher candidates 34, 41, 47, 57, 63, 376

seminar 123, 264, 429, 432, 439, 448, 455, 458, 578, 588-593, 595-597, 601, 606

service-learning 349-350, 352

simultaneous renewal 1-2, 7, 11-12, 16, 18, 133, 544

situated learning 120, 600-601

social justice 21, 55, 102, 236, 242, 263-264, 302, 306, 311, 318, 521-522, 529

Standards of Mathematics Practice 37, 52-53, 62, 323-324, 328, 374, 397-398, 411

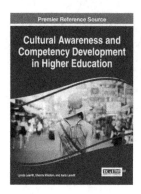

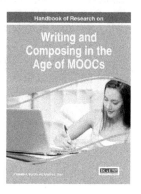

Ensure Quality Research is Introduced to the Academic Community

Become an IGI Global Reviewer for Authored Book Projects

Premier Reference Source

Emerging GIS Applications for Emergency and Disaster Management

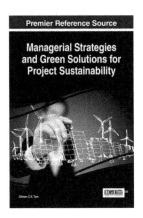

Premier Reference Source

Managerial Strategies and Green Solutions for Project Sustainability

Premier Reference Source

Comparative Approaches to Using R and Python for Statistical Data Analysis

Premier Reference Source

Solutions for High-Touch Communications in a High-Tech World

The overall success of an authored book project is dependent on quality and timely reviews.

In this competitive age of scholarly publishing, constructive and timely feedback significantly expedites the turnaround time of manuscripts from submission to acceptance, allowing the publication and discovery of forward-thinking research at a much more expeditious rate. Several IGI Global authored book projects are currently seeking highly qualified experts in the field to fill vacancies on their respective editorial review boards:

Applications may be sent to:
development@igi-global.com

Applicants must have a doctorate (or an equivalent degree) as well as publishing and reviewing experience. Reviewers are asked to write reviews in a timely, collegial, and constructive manner. All reviewers will begin their role on an ad-hoc basis for a period of one year, and upon successful completion of this term can be considered for full editorial review board status, with the potential for a subsequent promotion to Associate Editor.

If you have a colleague that may be interested in this opportunity, we encourage you to share this information with them.

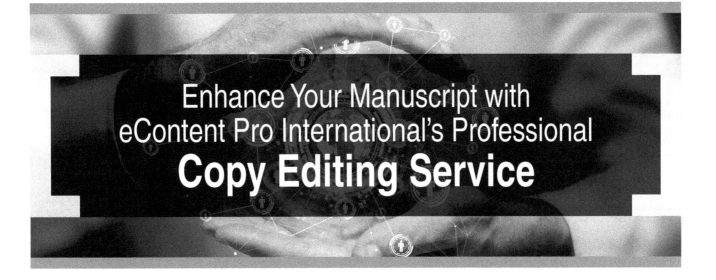

CPSIA information can be obtained
at www.ICGtesting.com
Printed in the USA
BVHW011209231219
566423BV00014B/70/P